CONSTITUTIONAL CRIMINAL PROCEDURE

FOURTH EDITION

by

ANDREW E. TASLITZ
Professor of Law
Howard University School of Law

MARGARET L. PARIS
Dean
University of Oregon School of Law

LENESE C. HERBERT
Professor of Law
Albany Law School

FOUNDATION PRESS
2010

THOMSON REUTERS™

© 1997, 2003 FOUNDATION PRESS
© 2007 THOMSON REUTERS/FOUNDATION PRESS
© 2010 By THOMSON REUTERS/FOUNDATION PRESS

 195 Broadway, 9th Floor
 New York, NY 10007
 Phone Toll Free 1–877–888–1330
 Fax (212) 367–6799
 foundation–press.com

Printed in the United States of America

ISBN 978–1–59941–738–7

Mat #40879909

PREFACE

This fourth edition of Constitutional Criminal Procedure continues what we hope have been the particular strengths of our book: a heavy use of problems, the availability of role-plays and review exercises for those who are interested, a significant use of explanatory text, a practical concern with the real-world problems of the practicing lawyer, an emphasis on various theoretical approaches to constitutional interpretation, and the use of a wide variety of sources and topics, thus allowing for flexibility based upon users' differing needs and teaching styles. The book also tries to point out connections between the various issues studied and the concerns of the rising innocence movement and to place technical legal issues into their broader social and historical context.

Additionally, this edition makes several important changes from the last one. First, of course, the law and scholarship have been updated through February 2010 (cases after that date will be discussed in a brief letter update or a supplement, depending upon the need). This time around, however, the updating also involves some of the most critical conceptual changes in the field in several decades, including new or amended tests for the attenuation doctrine, the good faith exception to the exclusionary rule, and the nature of the Sixth Amendment right to counsel in the context of interrogations. Second, we have tightened and revised the chapters on the effective assistance of counsel and the good faith exception to the exclusionary rule to make them more accessible to students and more consistent with the style in other chapters of the book.

Third, at the same time, we have retained two important changes made in the third edition that have met with the approval of many of our users: (a) the retention of a completely revised (from the first two editions), tighter, and we hope more interesting and teachable chapter on terrorism and electronic surveillance, a subject of growing importance, even in the basic course; and (b) the addition of substantial new (again, in comparison to the first two editions) textual material, questions, and problems on alternatives to the exclusionary rule, including civil, criminal, and administrative options. This latter new material can be selectively taught in one class but can also occupy two or even three days of class for those who want to explore the subject in great depth. Given the narrowing scope of the protections of the exclusionary rule, which has accelerated dramatically since the third edition, we thought it important to address the strengths and weaknesses of existing and proposed alternative options. We also wanted to point out the relevance of the course to those many students who intend to be entirely civil practitioners. Fourth, we have added a variety of new or expanded issue checklists and problems and tinkered with the organization in ways that we hope will make the book more accessible yet more challenging. Finally, adopters and users of the third edition will notice that we have moved Chapter 11 from the casebook to the course website, http://www.constitutionalcriminalprocedure.com/index.asp., where we continue to keep you up-to-date with significant new cases, interesting articles, links, primary documents, state-law developments, film suggestions, Power Points, annual supplements or updates, our extensive Teachers' Manual, and a host of other materials for either the adopter's use in class preparation or for direct access by students. That website material will eventually be transferred to Foundation Press's new electronic platform for casebooks. The current website address is http://www.constitution alcriminalprocedure.com/index.asp.

The two original authors of this casebook (Taslitz and Paris) also want to thank the newest addition to our authorial ranks, Professor Lenese Herbert, who first joined us on the third edition. Professor Herbert has written primarily (though not solely) on criminal procedure issues involving race. She has done so with a particularly novel, unique, and fresh perspective, for example, writing about free speech and other expressive concerns in policing, the impact of race-based search practices on racial minorities' fundamental right to parent, and the nature of the obligations of African–American prosecutors to the African–American community, the larger legal system, and justice. Her work combines history, social science, doctrine, and philosophy. We hope that readers saw her fresh perspective further enlivening the pages of the text of the third edition and that readers will see more of her supportive hand in the pages of this newest edition.

Users new to the book should be reminded (as briefly noted above) that there is a very substantial revised teachers' manual containing answers to all the problems, summaries of cases and other materials, and teaching hints. The first chapter of that Manual should probably be read before using the book as its heavy use of problems and textual material is a different experience for many teachers, particularly in the area of constitutional criminal procedure. That teachers' manual chapter suggests alternative ways to use these materials effectively. Finally, although our primary concern has been the classroom needs of students, the use of explanatory text and citations is also intended to make the book a first stop for students and faculty researching topics in selected areas, and we encourage you so to use the book.

Please feel free to contact any of us with suggestions for the website or the Fourth Edition at ataslitz@law.howard.edu, mparis@law.uoregon.edu, or lherb@albanylaw.edu.

Professor Andrew E. Taslitz
Howard University School of Law

Dean and Professor, Margaret L. Paris
University of Oregon School of Law

Professor Lenese C. Herbert
Albany Law School

ACKNOWLEDGMENTS

I thank my wife, Patricia V. Sun, Esquire, for her input on several chapters, as well as for her guidance, inspiration, and moral support; my research assistants, Jeanne Laurenceau, Natasha Williams, Jasmine Modoor, and Sandi Pessin–Boyd (for assistance on the Fourth Edition); Keri Fiore, Stacy Chaffin, William Jacobs, and Adrienne Moran (for assistance on the Third Edition); Leander Altifois, Monya Bunch, Stephanie Stevens, Eli Mazur, Amy Pope, and Nicole Crawford (for assistance on the Second Edition); Mikee Gildea–Beatty, Dalhi Myers, Crystal Collier, Vernita Fairley, and Burnette Williams (for assistance on the First Edition). Thanks also to Professors Robert Mosteller, Douglas Colbert, Anne Poulin, and Adam Kurland for their reviews of earlier drafts of these materials. Thanks also to Rhea Ballard–Thrower, Library Director extraordinaire, and her entire professional staff for their outstanding research help; Adrian White, former Electronic Services Librarian at the Allen Mercer Daniel Law Library of the Howard University School of Law, whose computer wizardry brought the police of Exum, Culdeva to life; Deans Kurt L. Schmoke and Alice Gresham–Bullock and Interim Dean Patricia Worthy for financial and moral support for this project; and the many scholars and judges whose insights make their way into these pages. I am especially grateful as well to the members of the Editorial Board of the American Bar Association Criminal Justice Section's periodical, *Criminal Justice*, who constantly teach me and keep me grounded in reality; and to my friend and colleague, Andrew I. Gavil, whose endless willingness to debate and contribute ideas has been an invaluable contribution to the Second Edition, as well as his feedback and input upon portions of the Third and Fourth Editions. Additionally, I thank the two newest and most sharp-toothed members of my family, B'lanna and Odo Sun–Taslitz, for woofing good moral support. Finally, special thanks to my co-author, Margie Paris, whose patience, creativity, sheer brilliance, friendship, good humor and good heart have made for an outstanding professional partnership for well over a decade, and to my new co-author, Lenese Herbert, whose diligence, kindness, fresh perspectives, brilliant scholarship, personal warmth, and hearty smile promise to expand Margie and my professional duo into a trio for many years to come.

ANDREW E. TASLITZ
("TAZ")

Many students helped me with this book. Most recently, Robert Kaiser has been invaluable; in previous editions, Carla Rhoden, now a published author herself but once a lowly research assistant, was instrumental in developing new materials and problems for the standing, government action, and computer search sections; Kari Hathorn and Van Quan took the laboring oar on many clean-up details. My loving family has always cheered me on—thanks, guys. And thanks most of all to Taz, my wonderful friend and co-author, and to our newest partner in criminal procedure, Lenese, whose intelligence, hard work, and good humor have contributed so much to this edition.

MARGIE PARIS

I remain grateful to and thank my co-authors, Dean Paris and Professor Taslitz, for bringing me aboard such an amazing project; it has been and remains both an absolute blast and a labor of love. I am also grateful to and thank my former legal assistant, Lisa Potter, whose hard work was essential to the Third Edition and my current legal assistant, Sherri Anne Meyer, whose hard work was essential to the Fourth Edition. Thanks also to my research assistant, Ms. Tracy Q. Guo. My former colleague and current friend, Kimberly N. Tarver, Esq., remains as instrumental to my intellectual development today as she was during our time as Civil AUSAs. Toussaint Tyson, Esq., keeps me on my toes and consistently forces me to answer hard questions. My nieces (Lacey and Bria), nephews (Christopher and Brandon), godchildren (Glenn and Jackie), and former mentee (Ronzelle) stoke my passion for a just America. As my foray into co-authorship involved drafting and editing in her hospital room shortly before she passed, I know that the spirit of my mother, Josephine Frances Herbert, continues to inspire my life. Finally, thanks also to the wonderful scholarship of those whose articles infuse the study of constitutional criminal procedure with nuance, brilliance, accuracy, history, and hope.

LENESE HERBERT

The authors would like to acknowledge the permission of the authors, publishers, and copyright holders of the following publications for permission to reproduce the portions cited:

Amar, Akhil Reed, Fourth Amendment, First Principles, 107 Harvard Law Review, 757 (1994). Copyright © Harvard Law Review and Akhil Reed Amar.

The Bill of Rights as a Constitution, 100 Yale L. J. 1131 (1991); The Bill of Rights and the Fourteenth Amendment, 101 Yale L. J. 1193 (1991) Copyright © The Yale Law Journal Company, Inc., and Akhil Reed Amar c/o Writers Representatives LLC. All rights reserved.

Amann, Diane Marie, Guantanamo, 42 Colum. J. Transnat'l L. 263 (2004).

Excerpted from Bryonn Bain, "Walking While Black: The Bill of Rights for Black Men," The Village Voice (April 26–May 2, 2000), Copyright © 2000, The Village Voice Media. Reprinted with the permission of the Village Voice.

Binder, David A., and Price, Susan C., Legal Interviewing and Counseling: A Client–Centered Approach (1977). Copyright © 1977 West Publishing Company, David A. Binder, and Susan C. Price. Reprinted by permission.

Broder, John M., California Ending Use of Minor Traffic Stops as Search Pretext, New York Times, February 28, 2003; Copyright © 2003 New York Times and John M. Broder.

Bok, Sissela, Lying: Moral Choice in Public and Private Life (1978).

Brown, Michael K., Working the Street (1981). Copyright © 1981 Russell Sage Foundation. Reprinted by permission.

Caldwell, H. Mitchell, Fixing the Constable's Blunder: Can One Trial Judge in One Country in One State Nudge a Nation Beyond the Exclusionary Rule?, 2006 B.Y.U.L. Rev. 1 (2006).

Carbado, Devon, [E]racing the Fourth Amendment, 100 Mich. L. Rev. 946 (2002). Copyright © 2002 Michigan Law Review Association and Devon Carbado. Reprinted by permission.

Casey, Lee A., David Rivkin, Jr., and Bartram, David R., The Supreme Court's 2004 "War on Terror" Cases, The Federalist Society for Law and Policy Studies (July 2004).

Chin, Gabriel J. and Wells, Scott C., The "Blue Wall of Silence" as Evidence of Bias and Motive to Lie: A New Approach to Police Perjury, 59 U. Pitt. L. Rev. 233 (1998).

Connell, James G., III & Valladares, Rene L., Cultural Factors in Motions to Suppress, 25 The Champion 18 (March 2001). Copyright © 2001 National Association of Criminal Defense Lawyers, Inc., James G. Connell III, and Rene L. Valladares. Reprinted by permission.

Covington, James S., Jr., The Structure of Legal Argument and Proof: Cases, Materials, and Analyses (1993). Copyright © 1993 John Marshall Publishing Co. and James S. Covington. Reprinted by permission.

Davies, Sharon L., The Reality of False Confessions–Lessons of the Central Park Jogger Case, 30 N.Y.U. L. & Soc. Change 209 (2006).

Drizin, Steven A. and Leo, Richard A., The Problem of False Confessions in the Post–DNA World, 82 N.C. L. Rev. 891 (2004).

Drizin, Steven A. and Reich, Marissa J., Heeding the Lessons of History: The Need for Mandatory Recording of Police Interrogations to Accurately Assess the Reliability and Voluntariness of Confessions, 52 Drake L. Rev. 619 (2004).

Philip M. Feldman, THE PSYCHOLOGY OF CRIME: A SOCIAL SCIENCE TEXTBOOK 87 (1993).

Foner, Eric, Reconstruction: America's Unfinished Revolution, 1863–1877 (1988).

Frederick, Jeffrey T., The Psychology of the American Jury (1987).

Gilles, Myriam E., Reinventing Structural Reform Litigation: Deputizing Private Citizens in the Enforcement of Civil Rights, 100 Colum. L. Rev. 1384 (2000).

Godsey, Mark A., Rethinking the Involuntary Confession Rule: Toward a Workable Test for Identifying Compelled Self–Incrimination, 93 Cal. L. Rev. 465 (2005).

Grano, Joseph D., "Confessions, Truth and the Law," (Ann Arbor: The University of Michigan Press, 1993).

Greenawalt, R. Kent, The Right to Silence and Human Dignity, in The Constitution of Rights: Human Dignity and American Values (Meyer & Parent, eds., 1992). Copyright © 1992 Cornell University Press and R. Kent Greenawalt. Reprinted by permission.

Greenawalt, R. Kent, Silence as a Moral and Constitutional Right, 23 Wm. & Mary L. Rev. 15 (1981).

Greenhouse, Linda, Justices, 5–3, Broadly Reject Bush Plan to Try Detainees, (June 39, 2006).

Hans, Valerie P. and Neil Vidmar, Judging the Jury (1986).

Hansen, Mark, Second Look at the Lineup, 87 ABA Journal 20 (December 2001). Copyright © 2001 American Bar Association and Mark Hansen. Reprinted by permission.

Harris, Angela P., Equality Trouble: Sameness and Difference in Twentieth Century Race Law, 88 Cal. L. Rev. 1923 (2000).

Harris, David A., Racial Profiling Revisited: "Just Common Sense" in the Fight Against Terror?, 17 Crim. Just. 36 (Summer 2002). Copyright © 2002 American Bar Association and David A. Harris. Reprinted by permission.

Herbert, Lenese C., Can't You See What I'm Saying? Making Expressive Conduct a Crime in High–Crime Areas, 9 Georgetown J. Pov. Law & Pol'y 135 (2002).

Herbert, Lenese, Et in Arcadia Ego: A Perspective On Black Prosecutors' Loyalty Within the American Criminal Justice System, 49 Howard L.J. 495 (2006).

Herbert, Lenese, Plantation Lullabies: How Fourth Amendment Policing Violates the Fourteenth Amendment Right of African Americans to Parent, 19 St. John's J. of Legal Comm'tary 197 (2005).

Hess, Matthew V., Good Cop–Bad Cop: Reassessing the Legal Remedies for Police Misconduct, 1993 Utah L. Rev. 149 (1993).

Jeffries, John C., Civil Rights Actions: 2006 Supplement to Civil Rights Actions: Enforcing the Constitution (2006).

Jeffries, John C., Civil Rights Actions: Enforcing the Constitution (2000).

Johnson, Robert L., Dr., and Simring, Steven, Dr., ("The Race Trap:") Smart Strategies for Effective Racial Communication in Business and Life (Diane Publishing Co. 2000); Copyright © 2000 Diane Publishing Co. and Dr. Robert L. Johnson and Dr. Steven Simring.

Johnson, Sheri Lynn, Race and the Decision to Detain a Suspect, 93 Yale L.J. 214 (1983). Copyright © 1983 The Yale Law Journal Company, Inc. and Sheri Lynn Johnson. Reprinted by permission.

Kerr, Orin S., Search Warrants in an Era of Digital Evidence, 75 Miss. L.J. 85 (2005).

Kobylak, Wesley, Annotation, Civil Action for Damages under 18 U.S.C.A. 1964© of the Racketeer Influenced and Corrupt Organizations Act for Injuries Sustained by Reason of Racketeering Activity, 70 A.L.R. Fed. 538 (1984).

Kurland, Adam H., Prosecuting Ol' Man River: The Fifth Amendment, the Good Faith Defense, and the Non–Testifying Defendant, 51 U. Pitt. L. Rev. 841 (1990).

Kurland, Adam H., Successive Criminal Prosecutions: The Dual Sovereignty Exception to Double Jeopardy in State and Federal Courts (2001).

LaFave, Wayne R., A Treatise on the Fourth Amendment (3d ed. 1996). Copyright © 1996 West Publishing Company and Wayne R. LaFave. Reprinted by permission.

LaFave, Wayne R., & Israel, Jerold H., Criminal Procedure (2d ed. 1992). Copyright © 1992 West Publishing Company, Wayne R. LaFave, and Jerold H. Israel. Reprinted by permission.

Larabee, Mark, Portland Case Fuels Rights Debate, The Oregonian (May 31, 2004).

Lewis, Detainees May Test Reach of Guantanamo Ruling, New York Times (July 1, 2006).

Leo, Richard A., Inside the Interrogation Room, 86 J. Crim. Law & Criminol. 266 (1996).

Louisell, David W. and Christopher Mueller, Federal Evidence (1977).

Lynch, Timothy, In Defense of the Exclusionary Rule, Cato Policy Analysis No. 319 (October 1, 1998). Copyright © 1998 Cato Institute. Reprinted by permission.

Lynch, Timothy, No Blank Check, The Federalist Society for Law and Policy Studies (July 2004).

MacDougall, Donald V., Criminal Law: The Exclusionary Rule and Its Alternatives–Remedies for Constitutional Violations in Canada and the United States, 76 J. Crim. L. & Criminology 608 (1985).

Maclin, Tracey, Is Obtaining an Arrestee's DNA a Valid Special Needs Search Under the Fourth Amendment? What Should (and Will) the Supreme Court Do?, 33 J.L. Med. & Ethics 102 (2005).

Maclin, Tracey, Book Review: Seeing the Constitution From the Backseat of a Police Squad Car, 70 B.U. L. Rev. 543 (1990). Copyright © 1990 Trustees of Boston University and Tracey Maclin. Reprinted by permission.

Maclin, Tracey, Black and Blue Encounters: Some Preliminary Thoughts About Fourth Amendment Seizures: Should Race Matter?, 26

Perrin, Timothy, Caldwell, Mitchell H., Chase, Carol A., and Fagan, Ronald W., If It's Broken, Fix It: Moving Beyond the Exclusionary Rule, 83 Iowa L. Rev. 669 (1988).

Ragland, Steven P., Using the Master's Tools: Fighting Persistent Police Misconduct with Civil RICO, 51 Am. U.L. Rev. 139 (2001).

Rhoden, Carla, Challenging Searches & Seizures of Computers at Home or in the Office: From a Reasonable Expectation of Privacy to Fruit of the Poisonous Tree and Beyond, 30 Am. J. Crim. L. 101 (2002). Copyright © 2002 University of Texas School of Law and Carla Rhoden. Reprinted by permission.

Richards, David A., Originalism Without Foundations, 65 New York University Law Review 1373 (1990). Copyright © New York University Law Review and David A. Richards.

Sanchez, Rene, L.A. Police Misconduct Likened to Racketeering: Judge's Order Could Widen City's Liability, The Washington Post (Aug. 31, 2004).

Saltzburg, Stephen A., Capra, Daniel J., American Criminal Procedure Cases and Commentary (6th ed. 2000).

Schulhofer, Stephen, The Constitution and the Police: Individual Rights and Law Enforcement, 66 Wash. U. L.Q. 11 (1988). Copyright © Washington University Law Quarterly and Stephen Schulhofer. Reprinted by permission.

Shapiro, Barbara, Beyond "Reasonable Doubt" and "Probable Cause": Historical Perspectives on the Anglo–American Law of Evidence (1991). Copyright © University of California Press and Barbara Shapiro. Reprinted by permission.

Skolnick, Jerome H., and Fyfe, James J., Above the Law: Police and the Excessive Use of Force (1993). Copyright © 1993 Simon & Schuster, Jerome H. Skolnick, and James J. Fyfe. Reprinted by permission.

Slobogin, Christopher, Criminal Procedure: Regulation of Police Investigation (2nd ed. 1998).

Slobogin, Christopher, and Schumacher, Joseph, Reasonable Expectations of Privacy and Autonomy in Fourth Amendment Cases, 42 Duke L.J. 727 (1993). Copyright © 1993 Duke University Law Journal, Christopher Slobogin, and Joseph Schumacher. Reprinted by permission.

Steinberg, David E., The Drive Toward Warrantless Auto Searches: Suggestions from a Back–Seat Driver, 80 Boston University Law Review 545 (2002). Copyright © 2002 Boston University Law Review and David E. Steinberg.

Taslitz, Andrew E., Terrorism and the Citizenry's Safety, 17 Crim. Just. 4 (Summer 2002). Copyright © 2002 American Bar Association and Andrew E. Taslitz. Reprinted by permission.

Taslitz, Andrew E., Wrongful Rights, 18 Crim. Just. 4 (Spring 2003). Copyright © 2003 American Bar Association and Andrew E. Taslitz. Reprinted by permission.

Taslitz, Andrew E., and Styles–Anderson, Sharon, Still Officers of the Court: Why the First Amendment is No Bar to Challenging Racism, Sexism, and Ethnic Bias in the Legal Profession, 9 Georgetown Journal of Legal Ethics 781 (1996).

Trende, Sean P., Why Modest Proposals Offer the Best Solution for Combating Racial Profiling, 50 Duke L.J. 331 (2000).

Van Natta, Don, Jr., Questioning Terror Suspects in a Dark and Surreal World, New York Times (March 9, 2003). Copyright © 2003 New York Times Company. Reprinted by permission.

Wallis, Jim, The Soul of Politics (1994). Copyright © 1994 The New Press. Reprinted by permission.

Walker, Samuel, Taming the System: The Control of Discretion in Criminal Justice (1993).

Wasserstrom, Silas J. and Seidman, Louis Michael, The Fourth Amendment as Constitutional Theory, 77 Geo. L.J. 19 (1988).

White, Peter H., Let's make a Deal: Negotiating and Defending Immunity for "Targets and Subjects," 29 Litigation 44 (2002). Copyright © 2002 American Bar Association and Peter H. White. Reprinted by permission.

Whitebread, Charles H., Slobogin, Christopher, Criminal Procedure: An Analysis of Cases and Concepts (4th ed. 2000).

Williams, Mark, Pleading the Fifth in Civil Cases, 20 Litigation 31 (1994). Copyright © 1994 American Bar Association and Mark Williams. Reprinted by permission.

Witt, April, Allegations of Abuses Mar Murder Cases, Wash. Post (June 3, 2001). Copyright © 2001 The Washington Post Co. Reprinted by permission.

Witt, April, No Rest for the Suspects, Wash. Post (June 4, 2001). Copyright © 2001 The Washington Post Co. Reprinted by permission.

Wolfram, Charles W., Modern Legal Ethics (1986).

SUMMARY OF CONTENTS

TABLE OF CONTENTS

CHAPTER 9. Self–Incrimination Outside the Interrogation Room 815

TABLE OF CASES

Principal cases are in bold type. Non-principal cases are in roman type. References are to Pages.

CONSTITUTIONAL CRIMINAL PROCEDURE

CHAPTER 1

OVERVIEW

- PHILOSOPHY OF CONSTITUTIONAL CRIMINAL PROCEDURE

- METHOD OF CONSTITUTIONAL INTERPRETATION

- DEDUCTIVE BRIEFING

- STEPS IN THE CRIMINAL PROCESS

I. WHAT THIS BOOK IS ABOUT

This book offers a lawyering perspective on basic constitutional criminal procedure—the constitutional rules governing pre-trial criminal investigation by police officers and prosecutors. It covers the full range of police investigative techniques, including arrest, search and seizure, wiretapping, interrogation, lineups, and photospreads. It also considers the primary prosecutorial investigative techniques of interviewing, negotiation, informal discovery, grand jury subpoenas, and grand jury testimony. The only pre-trial investigative technique not covered, for reasons of limited space and tradition, is formal discovery. While the book emphasizes the constitutional restrictions on these techniques, it also discusses selected statutes, rules of court, and ethical rules, because no competent practitioner can function without a basic knowledge of these matters.

The constitutional rules governing pre-trial criminal investigation are defined by both federal and state constitutions and interpreted by their respective courts. However, our primary emphasis is on the federal constitution. The federal constitution sets constitutional minima that apply to every state, although states may, and often do, provide greater constitutional protections to their own citizens. Moreover, United States Supreme Court cases, including the views of the differing justices, serve as a paradigm for state constitutional analysis. Many states interpret their constitutions to move in "lock-step" with the federal constitution. Even states that provide greater protection than the federal constitution employ principles and arguments similar to those considered by the Supreme Court, often differing only in the weight to be accorded certain values or other data. We make occasional reference to state constitutional decisions that differ from the Court's in order to highlight debates about the proper modes of analysis.

Our concern is primarily with how practicing lawyers think about these issues. But the best practicing lawyers recognize that the theory/practice dichotomy is a false one. Only lawyers well-versed in constitutional interpretive theory can intelligently address a case of first impression, effectively distinguish a case, or successfully argue that a contrary precedent should be overruled. Only lawyers skilled at logical reasoning can spot the flaws in an opponent's arguments or avoid such pitfalls in their own arguments. And only lawyers aware of the policies and values underlying the law, and the empirical data regarding police, judicial, and prosecutorial behavior, can craft a rhetorically satisfying case theory.

Thus theory must interact with practice, guiding it and learning from it. Theory must play a role in every lawyer's strategic and tactical judgments and preparations for interviews, negotiating sessions, and suppression hearings. Studying practical lawyering tasks helps students to develop legal artistry, but doing these tasks helps students to understand both constitutional theory and doctrine.

The purpose of this chapter is to give students the tools to take an activist attitude toward these materials. More specifically, this chapter has three functions: first, to introduce the philosophy of constitutional criminal procedure; second, to introduce the logical, interpretive, and rhetorical structure of decisions interpreting constitutional criminal procedure; and third, to introduce the steps in the criminal process.

II.   The "Philosophy" of Constitutional Criminal Procedure

By "philosophy" we mean something quite simple: those overarching themes that we find implicit in constitutional criminal procedure cases and that offer one effective way to organize your approach to these materials.

A.   The Central Constitutional Provisions

In order to understand the fundamental themes of criminal procedure, you must be familiar with the provisions of the federal Bill of Rights that are the primary focus of this course:

1.   SEARCH AND SEIZURE

Searches and seizures are governed by the Fourth Amendment:

"The right of the people to be secure in their persons, houses, papers, and effects against unreasonable searches and seizure, shall not be violated, and no warrants shall issue, but upon probable cause, supported by oath or affirmation and particularly describing the place to be searched, and the persons or things to be seized."

2. COMPELLED OR INVOLUNTARY CONFESSIONS AND OTHER FUNDAMENTALLY UNFAIR PROCEDURES

These matters are governed by portions of the Fifth Amendment:

"No person ... shall be compelled in any criminal case to be a witness against himself, nor be deprived of life, liberty, or property without due process of law."

3. RIGHT TO COUNSEL

The right to counsel is recited in the relevant portion of the Sixth Amendment:

"[T]he accused shall ... have the Assistance of Counsel for his defense."

4. APPLICATION OF THE BILL OF RIGHTS AND OF PRINCIPLES OF FUNDAMENTAL FAIRNESS TO THE STATES

These matters are governed by portions of Section 1 of the Fourteenth Amendment:

"No State shall make or enforce any law which shall abridge the privileges or immunities of citizens of the United States; nor shall any state deprive any person of life, liberty or property without due process of law; nor deny to any person within its jurisdiction the equal protection of the laws."

PROBLEM 1–1

Police Officer Osborn received a phone call from Diaz, who was worried about his 72–year–old aunt, Belle, because he had not heard from her in several weeks. "She's meticulous about everything," Diaz explained to Osborn. "There's never a thing out of place in her house or in her life, but she hasn't returned my phone calls." Osborn told Diaz to wait a day and call back if his aunt did not respond to further inquiries. Diaz went to Belle's house the next day. When no one answered his knock, he left a note on the door saying, "Please call me—Diaz." When he went home that night he found a voicemail message saying, "Belle's gone away for the weekend and will call you when she gets back." The message was from Juan, Belle's 36–year–old handyman, who had been renting a room in her house for the past year. The next morning, Diaz returned to Belle's house, finding a posted note saying, "I'm gone for the weekend. Back on Monday—Belle." But the note was not in his aunt's handwriting.

Officer Osborn, upon hearing this report, accompanied Diaz to Belle's house. Osborn knocked on the door, calling out "This is the police. We're checking on your whereabouts." Receiving no response, Osborn climbed through the front window into the living room. He noticed that beer cans and food were strewn about the floor. While Diaz waited outside, Osborn moved from the living room into a hallway that appeared to lead to the bedrooms. He was struck immediately by a powerful garbage-like odor. He tried to enter a room from which the odor seemed to be emanating, but the door was locked. He forced open the door with his shoulder, peered in, and saw what looked like dried blood on the floor. He immediately called for a backup officer, who secured the house while Osborn went to get a search warrant. Osborn returned an hour later with the warrant, re-entered the bedroom, and in one of its closets found Belle's decomposing body.

The police department put out a bulletin directing officers to look for Juan, and several hours later he was arrested in a nearby motel. Further investigation revealed that a number of Belle's checks had been forged, and Juan was charged with forgery and theft in addition to the murder of Belle.

Immediately after these charges were filed, Osborn visited Juan in jail. He asked Juan for a sample of his handwriting and for a saliva swab. After Juan professed his innocence and refused to cooperate, Osborn said, "If you're innocent, then what do you have to hide? Do you want me to tell the jury about how you refused to give me things that could clear your name?" Juan hesitated for a moment and then provided the handwriting and the swab, saying, "Look, I wouldn't hurt the old lady. She loved me. After all, she told me she put me in her will." Experts later stated that Juan's handwriting matched that on the forged checks and that his DNA matched that of skin found under Belle's fingernails.

Question: Based upon the text of the four amendments above, as well as your common sense, what potential constitutional violations, if any, do you see in the above scenario? How can Juan raise these violations, and what relief can he ask for?

B.   THEMES IN CONSTITUTIONAL CRIMINAL PROCEDURE

The leading opinions and scholarly writings address several basic themes in constitutional criminal procedure. Although these themes are often explicit, sometimes they are most notable in their absence from judicial opinions—by the courts' unwillingness to recognize the pervasive nature and importance of these themes in constitutional analysis of criminal procedure questions.

1.   CONTROLLING DISCRETION

The police make many discretionary decisions, including whom to investigate and where to direct their limited resources. Some of these discretionary judgments may be made by officials in the police hierarchy, but most are made by the individual detective or the cop on the beat. Should I stop this person and question him? Should I arrest him or let him go, search his apartment or not, use a wiretap, plant an informant, send in an undercover officer, use force, and, if so, how much? If I arrest him, should I question him, place him in a lineup, show his photograph to the victims, take blood or urine samples? Each of these decisions has obvious importance for a person charged with a crime, but they also matter for those never charged and those who experience wrongful arrests, unjustified searches that uncover no evidence of crime, and excessive force.

Prosecutors too have discretion in deciding whom to charge with what, how much bail to seek, whether to agree to separate trials for co-defendants, whether to agree to the exclusion of certain evidence, and whether and how much evidence to share with the defense before trial.

Finally, defense counsel have discretion in making certain decisions that may affect the quality of justice, such as whether to talk to a witness before trial, what to tell a client in preparing him to testify, and what to share with the prosecution when negotiating a plea.

In each instance, the question is how much discretion to permit, how to guide and control it, and how to prevent its abuse.

2. CRIMINAL PROCEDURE AS EVIDENCE LAW

In at least two ways, basic constitutional criminal procedure can be viewed as a branch of the law of evidence. First, the remedy for many constitutional violations is exclusion of the evidence at trial. In criminal procedure, as in evidence law, the primary justifications for exclusion are: (1) it serves some overriding public policy unconnected with trial, such as discouraging the police from conducting illegal searches; or (2) it protects the jury from unreliable information, such as coerced confessions, planted evidence, and suggestive lineups and photospreads.

Second, in deciding whether the legal requirements for exclusion of evidence have been met, the trial court must often find certain preliminary facts, facts that usually go to the trustworthiness of the evidence, as is true under evidence law. Thus, before a judge can find probable cause for a search, she must first decide on what evidence to base that judgment, how reliable that evidence is, and whether the amount of reliable evidence is adequate. With regard to a pretrial identification, the judge must decide whether the procedure was unfairly suggestive. If it was, she then decides whether it was necessary and whether it created a very substantial likelihood of misidentification by the witness.

By recognizing the similarity between criminal procedure and evidence questions, we focus more clearly on the underlying notions of probative value, prejudice, and credibility, and we can clarify our analysis by analogizing to evidence cases and doctrine. Even where we do not do so explicitly, those familiar with evidence law and theory will recognize its significance in our commentary and in the reasoning of leading cases.

3. RACE AND ETHNICITY OF SUSPECTS

Both anecdotal and empirical data suggest that members of minority groups often perceive that police treat them with greater suspicion and force than is directed toward whites, and that police do in fact sometimes treat members of minority groups differently. We argue in a later chapter that the Fourteenth Amendment—the driving force behind which was attaining greater protection for the rights of newly freed slaves and which ultimately "incorporated" most of the Bill of Rights against the states—altered the nature of those rights, requiring, at a minimum, that race be taken into account in interpreting the Fourth, Fifth, and Sixth Amendments to achieve true equality in the treatment of criminal suspects.[1] This argument suggests that race and ethnicity frequently offer a *sub silentio* explanation for judicial decisions, and it criticizes decisions that do not expressly address underlying questions of race and ethnicity.

4.   ROLE OF THE LAWYER

In our adversarial system, both prosecutors and defense counsel are expected to play a crucial role in achieving justice. However, they have somewhat different obligations: the prosecutor's being to "do justice," and defense counsel's being to represent her client "zealously" while also meeting her obligations to the court and to the justice system. Questions arise at each stage of the proceedings regarding what role counsel on each side should play, how that role might help to achieve a just system, and what is a "just system," as well as what defines the boundaries of ethical conduct by the lawyers playing these roles. Thus, to understand fully the constraints on pre-trial investigation, we must examine constitutional, statutory, and ethical requirements concerning appropriate lawyering conduct.

5.   SOCIAL SCIENCE AND OTHER DISCIPLINES

Many rules of constitutional criminal procedure are based upon assumptions about how people or institutions have behaved or will behave. For example, the "exclusionary rule," which excludes from trial evidence obtained in violation of constitutional provisions, is based largely upon the belief that it will deter wrongful police behavior. To date, social scientists have produced inadequate empirical data confirming or undercutting this rationale. Nevertheless, the astute lawyer should examine the Court's empirical assumptions carefully in order to determine whether those assumptions are sound. Similarly, in interpreting constitutional language and structure, lawyers may find that both the social sciences and the humanities help in critiquing the Court's decisions.

PROBLEM 1–2

Consider the role of each of these themes in Problem 1–1. Did Officer Osborn exercise discretion? Where? Did he abuse his discretion? If so, what could be done to prevent such abuses? Will evidence-type questions arise regarding what data to rely upon and how trustworthy that data is? If so,

---

1.   This argument is developed in ANDREW E. TASLITZ, RECONSTRUCTING THE FOURTH AMENDMENT: A HISTORY OF SEARCH AND SEIZURE (2006); *see also* Andrew E. Taslitz, *Stories of Fourth Amendment Disrespect: From Elian to the Internment*, 70 FORDHAM L. REV. 2257 (2002) (illustrative applications). This view, which we call the "mutation" of the Fourth Amendment by the Fourteenth, is not yet "mainstream." However, it has important implications for all of the law of criminal procedure. We will address it in a later chapter.

how should they be resolved? Did race or ethnicity play a role, and, if so, how could that role be minimized? What role, if any, should prosecutor or defense counsel play at each stage, and why? What constitutional or ethical rules should be crafted to ensure that the lawyers play their proper roles in the future? Would social science or other disciplines help? How and why? What disciplines?

III. DEDUCTIVE BRIEFING

"Deductive briefing" is a technique for analyzing the logical, interpretive, and rhetorical structure of constitutional criminal procedure cases. The approach in this chapter involves four steps: first, a review of the current debates over proper interpretive method; second, a description of the basics of deductive and inductive reasoning; third, application of the first two lessons to create a deductive brief; and, fourth, practice in deductive briefing of selected leading opinions.

A. INTERPRETIVE METHOD

Every constitutional opinion has a logical structure that can be broken down into a series of premises that, taken together, support a conclusion with varying levels of confidence. Every premise must, however, have a proof—that is, evidence that demonstrates the truth of the premise. According to Professor van Geel, a court can rely on seven broad types of evidence to support the premises of its constitutional arguments:

1. The text of the constitution;

2. Evidence of the intent of the framers and drafters of the constitution;

3. Implicit premises or "tacit postulates" of the constitution which order the relationship among the branches of the federal government and the states, between governments at all levels and the individual;

4. Precedent—prior opinions of the Supreme Court;

5. Evidence of American traditions, customs, and practices;

6. Evidence of contemporary morality and attitudes; and

7. Considerations of practicality and prudence.[2]

The debates over the proper way to interpret the constitution can generally be viewed as disagreements over which of these seven (or other) types of evidence can or should be relied upon by a court in support of its constitutional premises. For example, a "strict textualist" (if such a person really existed) would rely solely on the words of the text to support a premise. A more moderate textualist might turn to other sources where the text is ambiguous, but questions would remain. To which other sources

---

2. T.R. van Geel, Understanding Supreme Court Opinions 44 (1991).

should we turn? How much weight should each source be given? Even where we agree on which of the seven types of evidence should be relied upon, we might disagree over which preliminary facts are necessary to using one of the seven categories. For example, if we agree that framers' intent alone should control, we must decide who the framers were and how to determine their intent. Do we rely on The Federalist Papers, James Madison's Notes on the Constitutional Convention, newspaper articles, general knowledge of social, political, and economic history, the text itself, or all of these? These kinds of questions pervade most interpretive debates.

The discussion that follows elaborates upon, expands, and modifies van Geel's broad categories of evidence as a way to understand some of the leading interpretive debates. The discussion also addresses in greater detail how to prove the preliminary fact that one of these seven types of data exists—for example, that the framers had a certain "intent," or that "contemporary attitudes" favor a particular result. These interpretive debates guide much of the analysis of constitutional doctrine in succeeding chapters and provide the tools for better examining the interpretive structure of the Court's decisions.[3] Courts, commentators, and criminal procedure casebooks too often forget, as you should not, that criminal procedure cannot be divorced from constitutional interpretation.[4]

1.   THE ROLE OF TEXT

Cass Sunstein has said that "[a]ny system of interpretation that disregards the constitutional text cannot deserve support."[5] However, not all scholars and judges agree. "Non-interpretivists" argue for results that are not confined to the text and that sometimes are even in conflict with the text. In doing so, they draw on such extra-textual sources as moral philosophy, social desirability, and perceived need to fit fundamental law to evolving social patterns, sources that are nevertheless deemed part of the authoritative "constitution."[6] According to non-interpretivists, the "constitution" is more than text—it is a set of fundamental understandings of the basic rules of the game for our society, a largely "unwritten" constitution.

---

3.   While a wide variety of sources were drawn upon to draft this discussion of interpretive method, we owe particular debts to MICHAEL J. GERHARDT AND THOMAS D. ROWE, JR., CONSTITUTIONAL THEORY: ARGUMENTS AND PERSPECTIVES (1993), and the sources cited or excerpted therein, and to van Geel, *supra*. The first of these sources has recently been expanded and updated as MICHAEL J. GERHARDT, THOMAS D. ROWE, JR., REBECCA L. BROWN & GIRARDEAU SPANN, CONSTITUTIONAL THEORY: ARGUMENTS AND PERSPECTIVES (2d ed. 2002). Other helpful sources include LESLIE FRIEDMAN GOLDSTEIN, IN DEFENSE OF THE TEXT: DEMOCRACY AND CONSTITUTIONAL THEORY (1991); RONALD KAHN, THE SUPREME COURT AND CONSTITUTIONAL THEORY 1953–1993 (1994); EARL M. MALTZ, RETHINKING CONSTITUTIONAL LAW (1994); MICHAEL J. PERRY, THE CONSTITUTION IN THE COURTS: LAW OR POLITICS (1994); LAURENCE H. TRIBE & MICHAEL J. DORF, ON READING THE CONSTITUTION (1991).

4.   *See, e.g.*, Donald Dripps, *Akhil Amar on Criminal Procedure and Constitutional Law: "Here I Go Down That Wrong Road Again,"* 74 U.N.C. L. REV. 1559 (1996) (making similar point). Thus text and history too often take a back bench, with precedent and prudential reasons dominating. Yet no justifications are offered for limiting criminal procedure analyses to just two out of the seven relevant data sources.

5.   CASS SUNSTEIN, THE PARTIAL CONSTITUTION 119 (1993).

6.   *See* Gerhardt & Rowe, THEORY, *supra* note 3, at 40.

The courts generally do not accept this most extreme form of non-interpretivism. Instead, they assume that the text must always be the starting point for constitutional analysis and the question is mainly how to give meaning to that text.

Some theorists stress the literal meaning of text whenever possible. A portion of the Fourth Amendment illustrates this approach. The Fourth Amendment declares that:

> The right of the people to be secure in their persons, houses, papers, and effects, against unreasonable searches and seizures, shall not be violated, and no warrants shall issue, but upon probable cause, supported by oath or affirmation and particularly describing the place to be searched and the persons or things to be seized.

A literal reading of the text would suggest that every search warrant must be supported by probable cause. Yet the Court has in fact approved some warrants on less than probable cause, although that may mean only that the Court has unjustifiably departed from the literal text. Moreover, the literal text does not tell us whether warrants are always required. We might infer that the amendment would not have mentioned warrants unless warrants generally should be issued. Indeed, we might also infer that because the warrant and probable cause clauses follow the general proscription against unreasonable searches and seizures, the later clauses modify the earlier; that is, a search without a warrant or without probable cause is at least presumptively, if not always, unreasonable. But the text does not explicitly state any such presumption. The presumption relies on assumed interpretive principles that are nowhere stated in the text—for example, that the intent of the framers should control, or that a later clause must be assumed to give meaning to an earlier clause. With one exception not relevant to our purpose, the constitutional text nowhere recites interpretive principles. These principles must be divined from other sources and defended on bases other than text.[7]

What the text does say is that there shall be no unreasonable searches and seizures and, arguably, that a warrant not based upon probable cause is unreasonable. But the text says nothing specifically about when, if ever, warrantless searches are "unreasonable," nor does the text define either that term or "probable cause." A literalist might argue that "probable" sounds like "more probable than not," but, again, that is not precisely what the text says. "Probable" cause might mean "more probable than the cause we would have with no evidence of guilt" (similar to the definition of "relevant evidence" in the Federal Rules of Evidence), or more than a possibility, or substantially more than a possibility. Indeed, the Court appears to have adopted this last definition. Broad, sweeping constitutional terminology, therefore, simply does not have a literal meaning or a "plain," inherent meaning. The words must be given meaning from some other source.

---

7. *See* Sunstein, Partial, *supra* note 5, at 101–19.

However, the generally agreed-upon dictionary sense of words does play a role. The requirement that warrants be supported by "oath or affirmation" is plain enough, and the point of requiring a "particular," as opposed to a general, description of the persons, places, and things to be searched and seized is clear, even if in applying these rules we may disagree over whether a particular description is "particular" enough. Similarly, the textual arguments regarding a presumptive requirement of a warrant and probable cause certainly deserve some weight, although how much weight remains subject to debate, especially where plausible competing interpretations of the text are possible. Nonetheless, giving the text great weight limits judicial discretion, so the constitution acquires a meaning that is at least moderately determinate, not subject to mere judicial whim.

Some theorists, while recognizing that text often serves only a limiting role, argue that in a relevant "interpretive community," there may be agreement about the meaning of text. But this requires us to define and justify a particular interpretive community as the relevant one. Is it the understanding of most modern-day constitutional lawyers? Judges? Scholars? Or is it the meaning given by the drafters?

Still other theorists find certain broad, natural law principles embodied in the constitutional text. But, once again, the text does not recite those principles in a way that they can be divined from a dictionary. We must look beyond dictionaries and common sense understandings, and one place to look is the intention of the framers.

2. CONSTITUTIONAL HISTORY AND ORIGINAL INTENT

The theory that we should look solely to the intention of the framers is often called "originalism." Some originalists would follow original intent even if it contradicts apparently clear meaning. Others would look to original intent only to give meaning to otherwise ambiguous words. Still others recognize that the Constitution's framers simply did not think about certain matters and would, therefore, insist on original intent only where a reasonably clear intent can be discerned with some significant level of certainty.

The most important distinction among originalists is the level of generality of intent that they consider relevant. One form of originalism looks to highly specific intentions, understanding the meaning of a constitutional provision

> in terms of the things in the world to which the relevant founders would have applied the term at the time the constitutional provision was adopted authoritatively. A provision should be interpreted to include certain things only if those things would have been included within the meaning of the clause by the founders.[8]

---

8. David A. J. Richards, *Originalism Without Foundations*, 65 N.Y.U. L. Rev. 1373, 1380 (1990).

This approach can be problematic in application, however, even if we have relatively clear evidence of the founders' specific intentions.

For example, we might inquire whether it is "reasonable" under the Fourth Amendment for the police to arrest a felon on a public street without a warrant. When the Fourth Amendment was adopted, under a well-accepted common law rule a peace officer could make a warrantless arrest any time a misdemeanor or felony was committed in his presence and, moreover, could make a warrantless felony arrest even if the felony was not committed in his presence so long as there was reasonable ground for the arrest.[9] One reason for the "felony arrest" part of the common law rule may have been to dispense with warrant protections for serious crimes in which society had a strong interest in apprehending the perpetrator. A second reason may have been that felons posed a greater risk of flight given the higher penalties for felonies relative to misdemeanors. Because nothing in the Fourth Amendment's text or history indicates a specific intention to change the common law rule, it seems likely that the founders assumed that warrantless arrests of felons were reasonable.

But in the two centuries since the amendment was adopted, the conceptions of felonies and misdemeanors have changed. Common law felonies were extremely serious (most were punished by death), and "many crimes now classified as felonies under federal or state law were treated as misdemeanors." Yet warrants were required at common law for misdemeanors not committed in the officer's presence. What, then, is the warrant requirement for a modern felony, committed outside the officer's presence, if the felony was a misdemeanor at common law? An originalist interested in following the framers' specific intentions might argue that the framers meant to relieve police of the warrant requirement only for those crimes that were felonies at the time the Fourth Amendment was enacted. On the other hand, given the reasons for the common law rule, the framers may have assumed the warrantless arrest rule would change over time to govern any crime society deemed serious enough to classify as a felony. This suggests that honoring the framers' general intent would better serve their goals than attempting to fathom a specific intent from the language of the Fourth Amendment.

What about matters about which the framers simply did not and could not form a specific intention? For example, they could not have considered whether electronic surveillance is a "search" under the Fourth Amendment. An originalist committed to the framers' specific intentions could argue that the framers never expected the Fourth Amendment to protect against such intrusions, so they are not now prohibited. Or that originalist could argue that the closest analogy considered by the framers, eavesdropping, was not mentioned in the Fourth Amendment, so again electronic intrusions are not prohibited. One of the justifications for originalism is that it respects majority rule—the courts merely implement the will of the majority as expressed in the founding document[10]—so many originalists

---

9. United States v. Watson, 423 U.S. 411, 418 (1976).

10. The "founding document" is the federal Constitution. That document is thought to embody the desires of a majority of the American people at the time the document was

believe that clear evidence of intent is needed to block present majority will. Eavesdropping was for the framers' generation an ancient practice condemned as a nuisance, yet nowhere does the text or the history of the Fourth Amendment evidence an intention to regulate eavesdropping. Accordingly, an adherent of this brand of specific intentionalism would find that electronic eavesdropping does not constitute a "search" within the meaning of the amendment.[11] Less "specific" originalists might look for more general intent, perhaps concluding that the framers meant for the amendment to protect against invasions of "reasonable" privacy expectations. The question of how to determine what privacy expectations are "reasonable" is discussed in greater detail in Chapter 2, but at this general level of intent, it is obvious that a court might conclude that people have a reasonable expectation that what is said in the privacy of the home or in private telephone conversations will not be invaded by electronic means.

Choosing the appropriate level of generality is often a value-laden exercise. Some, like defeated Supreme Court nominee Robert Bork, deny this, maintaining that the most specific intent that the text, structure, and history of the constitution fairly support should be chosen because higher levels of generality give too much discretion to interpreting judges.[12] But whether this is a bad thing is another value choice, not a historical one, especially since it is unlikely, albeit still debatable, that the framers had an intention about the proper level of generality.

Originalism can be attacked as imposing other difficult and value-laden tasks on lawyers and judges. Originalism demands that we decide who the framers were. Because the state ratifying conventions made the constitution law, arguably the intentions of those conventions are controlling, yet there is sparse evidence of what happened at those conventions and it is likely that the various conventions' intentions differed. Instead, we could view the federal convention that proposed the constitution as the relevant body. Yet again, the documentation is sparse and tends to show that delegates had different, perhaps conflicting, intentions on many matters. Our primary source is the work of one man, James Madison. Although Madison's views are important, they provide us with a very limited sample from which to judge the collective intentions of the convention. Moreover, Madison took notes on only a small portion of the debates that took place in the federal convention, so that even if his notes are accurate, we cannot presume them to provide a complete picture of the intentions expressed there. We might be able to engage in a broader inquiry about social and political history, but such an inquiry would require us to decide how those broader social currents affected delegate decisionmaking. It would also

---

ratified. The "people" are like a general giving orders to the government on how to behave. If the government ignores the will of the "people," that is, of the majority, the government undermines majority rule and thus undermines the legitimacy of our democracy, according to many originalists.

11. *See* Katz v. United States, 389 U.S. 347, 366 (1967) (Black, J., dissenting).

12. *See* Robert Bork, *The Constitution, Original Intent, and Economic Rights*, 23 San Diego L. Rev. 823, 828 (1986); Gerhardt & Rowe, Theory, *supra* note 3, at 107.

require sophisticated historical training, which few lawyers and judges possess.

Originalism can also be attacked as a doctrine that ties modern hands with ropes fashioned by generations long departed. Critics of originalism argue that the republic is more likely to survive and prosper amid modern challenges if the constitution is interpreted in light of changing attitudes and circumstances. For some of these critics history remains relevant, but only to understand the problems facing the framers and thus the values underlying the document. These critics also point out that originalists focus solely on the original constitution, as amended by the Bill of Rights, while ignoring the fact that the constitution has been subsequently amended, most significantly by the Fourteenth Amendment. That amendment has been construed to apply most of the Bill of Rights, which formerly applied only to the federal government, to the states. In "incorporating" portions of the Bill of Rights against the states, therefore, the Fourteenth Amendment may have altered those rights, arguably requiring today a race-conscious constitutional criminal procedure jurisprudence to protect African–Americans and other minority groups from racial and ethnic stereotyping by police and prosecutors.

3. CONSTITUTIONAL STRUCTURE

Structural reasoning may rely on both constitutional text and constitutional history, but can be differentiated in two ways: first, structural reasoning entails reading the document holistically, looking for the interconnections among and patterns revealed by relevant clauses read as part of a greater whole; second, it involves looking to the interrelations among the institutions created by the document, the goals of their interactions, and the individual interests affected. Structural reasoning looks, in short, for the general themes revealed by the text and the structures it creates, the "fundamental principles expressed by the larger constitutional whole."[13]

Professor Akhil Reed Amar is a leading modern scholar who focuses on structural reasoning. Amar uses structural reasoning to argue, for example, that the original, pre-Reconstruction Bill of Rights focuses on empowering the people collectively against federal government agents. In his view, the original Bill of Rights limited only the federal government because state governments were perceived to be more responsive to the people. Moreover, Amar contends that the emphasis on rights connected with jury trials allowed the people to monitor governmental abuses. Amar summarizes his reasoning as follows:

> [T]he Bill of Rights protected the ability of local governments to monitor and deter federal abuse, ensured that ordinary citizens would participate in the federal administration of justice through various jury-trial provisions, and preserved the transcendent sovereign right of a majority of the people themselves to alter or abolish government and

---

13. *Id.* at 158.

thereby pronounce the last word on constitutional questions. The essence of the Bill of Rights was more structural than not, and more majoritarian than counter.[14]

Amar concludes that the Fourth Amendment's reasonableness and warrant clauses were designed to enable civil juries to find warrantless searches unreasonable, thereby exposing abusive government officials to strict liability for damages in a civil trespass action. Before the amendment was enacted, a search with a warrant insulated government agents from such suits. "Judges and warrants are the heavies, not the heroes, of our story," says Amar. In his view the Fourth Amendment sought to restrict warrants by requiring them to be predicated on probable cause and does not require warrants for all searches and seizures. In order to safeguard the people against police abuses, Amar would rely on civil juries exercising damages remedies, rather than unelected judges using the exclusionary rule.[15]

Other scholars have come to very different conclusions using structural reasoning. Chief among these is the conclusion that the Bill of Rights sought not so much to protect majorities from the federal government, but to protect minorities from majority tyranny.

4. PRECEDENT

Because the constitution cannot be amended as easily as statutes can be rewritten, scholars have argued that the Court should be readier to correct constitutional than statutory precedents.[16] In other words, the doctrine of stare decisis should not operate as forcefully in constitutional law as in other areas. Nevertheless, the Court clearly gives its constitutional precedents considerable weight. The reasons for this have been summarized as follows:

> Several justifications are commonly offered for the doctrine of precedent. First, we do not have unlimited judicial resources. If every issue in every case is a question of first impression, our judicial system would simply be overwhelmed with endless litigation. Second, we need a degree of predictability in our affairs. Interests of fairness, efficiency, and the enhancement of social interaction require that governments and citizens have a reasonably settled sense of what they may and may not do. Third, the doctrine of precedent raises the stakes. The Justice who knows that each decision governs not only the litigants to the particular case, but the rights of millions of individuals in the present and future, will approach the issue with less concern with the merits of the litigants as individuals and more concern with the merits of the

---

14. Akhil Reed Amar, *The Bill of Rights as a Constitution*, 100 YALE L. J. 1131, 1133 (1991).

15. *The Crime Bill and the Exclusionary Rule: Testimony Before Senate Judiciary Comm.*, 104th Cong., 1st Sess. (1995), available in WESTLAW, U.S. TESTIMONY (testimony of Akhil Reed Amar, Southmayd Professor of Law, Yale Law School).

16. Gerhardt & Rowe, THEORY, *supra* note 3, at 177.

underlying legal question to be decided. Fourth, the doctrine of precedent reflects a generally cautious approach to the resolution of legal issues. It reflects the view that change poses unknown risks, and that we generally should prefer the risks we know to those we cannot foresee.... Fifth, the doctrine of precedent reduces the potential politicization of the Court. It moderates ideological swings and thus preserves both the appearance and the reality of the Court as a legal rather than a purely political institution. And finally, from the perspective of the Justices themselves, the doctrine of precedent enhances the potential of the Justices to make lasting contributions. If a Justice disregards the judgments of those who preceded him, he invites the very same treatment from those who succeed him. A Justice who wants to preserve the value of his own coin must not devalue the coin of his predecessors.[17]

Disputes about precedent arise primarily over whether to read a precedent broadly or narrowly. The reading given a precedent can affect police and other governmental power quite differently where the precedent strikes down a government policy rather than upholding a government policy. These differential impacts are summarized in the following chart:[18]

	precedent striking down government policy	precedent upholding government policy
narrow interpretation of precedent	I **narrows the area of impermissible actions**	II **narrows the area of permissible actions**
broad interpretation of precedent	III **broadens the area of impermissible actions**	IV **broadens the area of permissible actions**

The impact of a precedent will vary. Factors affecting that impact may include (1) a particular Justice's interpretation of the policies and values that the precedent sought to serve, (2) the similarity between the precedent's facts and that of the case before the Court, and (3) the congruence between the precedent and the problem now facing the Court. Because precedent continues to play an important role, however, the sole proof for many rules will be that they were stated in case "X," freeing the Court from engaging in an examination of constitutional text, structure, or history. The new rule will be applied deductively or will call for the balancing of interests, two reasoning modes explained shortly in our discussion of the logic of constitutional adjudication.

---

17. Geoffrey R. Stone, *Precedent, the Amendment Process, and Evolution in Constitutional Doctrine*, 11 Harv. J.L. & Pub. Pol'y 67, 70 (1988).

18. This chart is adapted from J. R. van Geel, Opinions, *supra* note 2, at 106.

5. EVIDENCE OF AMERICAN TRADITIONS, CUSTOMS, AND PRACTICES

The often ambiguous language of the constitution seems to call for an examination of values to give the terms meaning.[19] The terms "due process of law," "unreasonable searches and seizures," and "assistance" of counsel are not self-defining. "Due Process," for example, has been defined as "fundamental fairness"—those procedures required by a scheme of "ordered liberty" in an "Anglo–American system of justice." The nature of "ordered liberty" can be revealed only in our people's traditions, customs, and practices. The problem is determining whose traditions count. Is it the majority's? If so, that may be problematic, for majorities have a history of oppressing minorities, and some scholars view the historical purpose of the Bill of Rights to be antimajoritarian, intended to prevent such oppression. Moreover, majorities shift and change, as do traditions, customs, and practices.

An alternative vision might look to defining "constitutional moments," periods of major historical change in which super-majorities craft new, enduring values, as setting the outer boundaries of what counts as a tradition, custom, or practice. Bruce Ackerman has suggested such a view, distinguishing such moments of constitutional politics from "normal politics," which is limited to the regular interplay of interest groups. Constitutional politics rises above group interests to articulate an enduring public interest that survives until modified by the next constitutional moment.[20] This view demands that we understand the historical forces leading to the pertinent constitutional moment. For example, if we are attempting to interpret the meaning of "due process," we must understand the historical forces present when the Fourteenth Amendment was adopted so that we can divine the enduring values embodied in that amendment. In theory, these enduring values provide the central interpretation, which can then be informed by changing traditions.

6. CONTEMPORARY MORALITY AND ATTITUDES

In defining constitutional terms, the Court may look to evidence of contemporary morality and attitudes, raising many of the same issues raised by considering traditions, customs, and practices. Here the emphasis is on contemporary, rather than historical or continuing, morality and attitudes. For example, when determining when there is a "reasonable expectation of privacy" and thus a search under the Fourth Amendment, the Court may focus on current majority attitudes about privacy to define what expectations are "reasonable." Under such an approach, a survey of

---

19. For examples of a "moral constitutionalism," *see* RONALD DWORKIN, FREEDOM'S LAW: THE MORAL READING OF THE AMERICAN CONSTITUTION (1996); Michael J. Perry, THE CONSTITUTION IN THE COURTS: LAW OR POLITICS? 70–82 (1994); MICHAEL J. PERRY, MORALITY, POLITICS, AND LAW: A BICENTENNIAL ESSAY (1988).

20. *See generally* BRUCE ACKERMAN, WE THE PEOPLE: TRANSFORMATIONS (1998); BRUCE ACKERMAN, WE THE PEOPLE: FOUNDATIONS (1991).

those practices Americans currently consider "private" would be relevant to defining a particular government invasion as search or non-search.

The attitudes of smaller groups than majorities might also matter. For example, the Court currently defines the Fourth Amendment term "seizure" in terms of what a "reasonable person" would perceive given the circumstances. Under this objective view, a person has been seized if the reasonable person would not feel free to leave. The Court has so far not acknowledged that the reasonable white person's perceptions might differ from those of the reasonable African–American, the reasonable Asian–American, the reasonable Mexican–American, and so on. It is not inconceivable, though, that the Court might in the future define "seizure" by taking into account the historic distrust of police experienced by racial and ethnic minorities.

7. CONSIDERATIONS OF PRACTICALITY AND PRUDENCE

Courts often consider the real-world impact of rules. For example, a rule requiring proof of wrongful police intent might create an insuperable burden on the individual seeking to redress police abuses. Courts also consider the efficacy of the remedies they create. For example, the exclusion of evidence is thought to deter police misconduct more effectively than the imposition of civil liability. "Practicality and prudence" remind courts to consider the actual effect of their decisions on people and institutions. When courts do this seriously, they turn to empirical data, and perhaps to anecdotal evidence and personal narratives, before creating legal rules. The success of their efforts to tailor their rules to desired effects depends on the quality of empirical studies, the representativeness of anecdotal evidence, and the degree of insight offered by personal narratives. Lawyers play an important role in educating courts about the effects of legal rules, and they must therefore be sensitive to both social science and literary method and steeped broadly in life experience, common sense, and American culture.[21]

B. THE LOGIC OF CONSTITUTIONAL CRIMINAL PROCEDURE

1. INTRODUCTION

The Court's opinions either implicitly or explicitly use the principles of basic logic. Attention to logic will thus lead to more effective analysis of the

---

21. One data source not on Professor van Geel's list is "natural law," basic principles either ordained by a Supreme Being or part of unchanging human nature. *See, e.g.*, RAYMOND A. BELLIOTTI, JUSTIFYING LAW: THE DEBATE OVER FOUNDATIONS, GOALS, AND METHODS 17–43 (1992). To the extent that natural law plays a significant role in the area of criminal procedure in modern constitutional jurisprudence, we see that role as generally treating natural law as part of another data source. For example, it may be argued that the framers intended certain natural law principles to govern a particular clause's meaning. The relevant data source is thus constitutional history and original intent. While this view may upset some natural law theorists, we think our understanding of natural law's role in constitutional criminal procedure is both fair and the most effective way to organize the teaching of interpretive method. Accordingly, we do not treat natural law in a separate section of this chapter, although we return to natural law later in the context of particular interpretive problems.

Court's reasoning. In this section, we will cover three forms of logical reasoning: deduction, induction, and balancing. We will also introduce you to a form of case-briefing called "deductive briefing," which will enable you to understand and critique the logical structure of the Court's decisions.

2.   OVERVIEW OF THE FORMS OF ARGUMENT

a.   *Covington's Explanation*

Professor Covington gives a concise and effective summary of the forms of logical reasoning used in law.[22] We provide an excerpt of his summary below and then explain how it applies to the Supreme Court's constitutional criminal procedure cases:

> There are two forms of reasoning and therefore two forms of argument—inductive and deductive.... The two forms ... have different ways of reaching conclusions. Valid (sound) deductive argument begins with propositions which, if accepted, *mandate* (make inescapable) certain conclusions. The conclusion is "pulled from" the propositions, which are called "premises." The conclusion of sound deductive arguments is called *necessary*.

> Inductive argument begins with data (evidence) which are accumulated to support or refute a conclusion. The data in a successful inductive argument "converges on" a conclusion to make the conclusion probable. The inductive argument conclusion is not inescapable, as it may be in deductive argument. Sound inductive argument yields a conclusion which is *probable*.

The two forms of argument each have a set of kinds:

1.   The deductive argument form has two kinds:

    a.   The syllogism

    b.   The theorem

2.   The inductive argument form has three kinds:

    a.   The hypothesis

    b.   The analogy

    c.   The generalization

* * *

The syllogism is one of two kinds of deductive argument. The theorem, rarely identified and defended in legal argument, is the second kind of deductive argument. The argument by syllogism claims that its conclusion is *necessary*. The hypothesis, generalization and analogy claim only *probable* conclusions.

> The claims of the four most active kinds of legal argument may be expressed in sentences:

---

22.   J. S. Covington, Jr., The Structure of Legal Argument and Proof: Cases, Materials, and Analyses 2–6 (1993).

The *syllogism* claims that its valid conclusion is *necessary*, or inescapable if its premises are accepted.

The *hypothesis* claims that its conclusion is *more likely than not* (probable), based on the data that converge on the conclusion.

The *analogy* claims that its conclusion is *more likely than not* (probable), based on its close resemblance to an accepted model of circumstances or transactions.

The *generalization* claims that its conclusion is *more likely than not* (probable), based on observations which invariably yield the same result.

Virtually all legal argument and proof is constructed from these four kinds of argument. Symbolized, the four main kinds of reasoning are:

Type of reasoning	Data or Premises	Explanation
1. *The Generalization*		
Observations:	black black black black cow cow cow cow	(all data are the same)
Conclusion:	All cows are black	(*probable*, inductive)
2. *The Hypothesis*		
Conclusion:	Able ran the red light	(*probable*, inductive)
Evidence:	fact fact fact fact a b c d	(all data converge)
3. *The Analogy*		
Assertion:	if A has characteristics 1, 2, 3, and 4 and if B has characteristics 1, 3, and 4	
Conclusion:	therefore B has characteristic 2	(*probable*, inductive)
4. *The Syllogism*		
Premise:	if A then B [proven by data]	
Premise:	A [proven by data]	
Conclusion:	B	(*necessary*, deductive)

b.   *Deductive Reasoning in Legal Analysis*

A deductive syllogism is a necessary argument, that is, its conclusion is logically inescapable if its premises are admitted. It is, therefore, crucial to ask for every premise, "What data support this premise?" For constitutional reasoning, the relevant data will be one or more of the sources reviewed earlier in this chapter: text, intent of the framers, and so on. Opinions using deductive reasoning often do not expressly adopt this form of argument, so you must "dig out" the deductive form where it is implicit in the Court's analysis. In doing so, however, you must identify what data the Court has relied on for its premises. At times the data is unconvincing or even nonexistent. When the supporting data is simply absent, ask yourself what data could support or refute the premises and whether the Court simply assumed certain data to be true. You will also discover that premises and supporting data do not always follow in order of the logical syllogism. By writing them down and putting them into a logical order, you can better understand the Court's analysis and its holding. We call this record a "deductive brief."[23]

To illustrate, assume that the Court is asked for the first time whether electronic eavesdropping via a "bug" placed on a public telephone booth is governed by the Fourth Amendment. If the Court held that the Fourth Amendment did govern, an outline of the premises in a deductive argument supporting that conclusion might look like this:

Premise 1: The Fourth Amendment prohibits unreasonable governmental "searches."

Premise 2: A "search" is an invasion of a reasonable expectation of privacy.

Premise 3: A caller from a public telephone booth, where the door to the booth is closed and the booth's occupant sees no one else within listening distance, has a reasonable expectation of privacy in his phone call.

Conclusion: Therefore, an invasion of such a call by electronic or any other means of eavesdropping is a search, governed by the Fourth Amendment.

The conclusion logically follows from the premises, but is it clear that the premises are correct? What data support them? Premise 1 is obviously correct, as shown by the text of the Fourth Amendment itself. But that text does not define a "search," so what data support premise 2? Precedent might do so, where all previous cases finding a "search" involved reasonable expectations of privacy, while those finding no search involved unreasonable or no expectations of privacy. Such review of precedent may also involve inductive reasoning, which is discussed below. Another source of data might be the intent of the framers. While they did not expressly define a "search," we might consider why they would limit the amendment to "searches" and "seizures," what kinds of interests they were trying to protect, and what historical forces made them believe protection was needed. This kind of "imaginative reconstruction" of what the framers

---

23. Although we have coined the term "deductive brief," the concept is a modified form of a method first suggested by van Geel, OPINIONS, *supra* note 2, at 47–65.

wanted or would have wanted if they had thought about the matter is a variant of a framers' intent-based argument.

What data support premise 3? One source might be customs, practices, and traditions. For example, a social science survey, historical review, or common experience might tell us that most people assume their telephone calls, even from public booths, are private. Using customs, practices, and traditions may complicate the syllogism, for these data raise questions of when an expectation of privacy is "reasonable" and whether reasonableness is determined by the majority or by the values of the Fourth Amendment. We will return to this critical question later, but for now, we will assume for simplicity in our example that "reasonableness" is determined by the majority.

A revised deductive brief might thus look like this:

Premise 1: The Fourth Amendment prohibits unreasonable governmental "searches."

Proof: The text of the Fourth Amendment, which says . . . [explain].

Premise 2: A "search" is an invasion of a reasonable expectation of privacy.

Proof (a): Precedent [explain how it supports the premise].

Proof (b): Intent of the Framers [explain how it supports the premise].

Premise 3: A caller from a public telephone booth, where the door to the booth is closed and the booth's occupant sees no one else within listening distance, has a reasonable expectation of privacy in his phone call.

Proof: American customs, practices and traditions, as revealed by social science, history, and common experience [explain how these support the premise].

Conclusion: Therefore, an invasion of such a telephone call by electronic or other means of eavesdropping is a search, governed by the Fourth Amendment.

When you engage in deductive briefing, remember that: (1) premises should move from general to specific as you approach the conclusion; and (2) there may be multiple deductions in a single opinion, each supporting different conclusions.

c. *Inductive Reasoning in Legal Analysis*

Although deductive reasoning is the most common type of legal argumentation, inductive analysis is often used in the law as well, especially where it supports premises that comprise pieces of deductive syllogisms. As a result, you need to become familiar with inductive reasoning.

(1) INDUCTIVE GENERALIZATION

If deductive reasoning moves from the general to the specific, then one useful definition of induction is moving from either the specific to the general or the specific to the specific.[24] A simple example of the former type of induction, also called "inductive generalization," is this:

Observation: A's oral conveyance of real estate is invalid.

Observation: B's oral conveyance of real estate is invalid.

Observation: C's oral conveyance of real estate is invalid.

Observation: Z's oral conveyance of real estate is invalid.

Conclusion: Therefore, all oral conveyances of real estate are invalid.

The example proceeds from a number of specific examples to reach a general conclusion. The conclusion depends on the assumption that all new specific instances will resemble the old. But there is no way to prove unequivocally that this assumption is correct, for there are an infinite number of specific examples that can be amassed. Therefore, the conclusion is not necessarily dictated by the specific instances, but is thought *probably* to follow from them. In short, the conclusion is more probable than not. Another example of reasoning by inductive generalization is suggested by our earlier illustration of deduction. One way to prove the premise that all searches involve invasions of reasonable expectations of privacy was by induction. We accumulated all prior search cases and found a pattern: in every case found to involve a "search," a reasonable expectation of privacy was invaded. Therefore, we assumed all searches must involve such invasions, supporting the general rule that all searches are by definition invasions of reasonable expectations of privacy.

Because the conclusion rests on an assumption, it is only probable and might later be disproved. Thus if we found a search where there was no invasion of privacy, or an invasion only of an unreasonable privacy expectation, we would disprove (or at least need to modify) the hypothesis that all searches involve invasions of reasonable privacy expectations. Indeed, one way to challenge the conclusion in inductive generalization is by challenging the validity of the necessary, albeit often silent, assumptions.

A brief that lays out each premise in an inductive generalization, the proof for each premise, and all assumptions and conclusions should properly be called an "inductive generalization brief." However, as a shorthand, we will use the term "deductive brief" to refer to any brief that organizes a court's rationale in terms of the logical forms studied here.

(2) ANALOGY

Analogy depends not upon the quantity of instances but upon the quality of resemblances between things. In legal analogies, two cases

---

24. RUGGERO J. ALDISERT, LOGIC FOR LAWYERS: A GUIDE TO CLEAR LEGAL THINKING 87 (1989).

resemble each other in some significant ways, and we infer that they therefore must resemble each other in some additional critical respect.[25]

The structure of analogy may be summarized as follows:

Assertion: If thing A (the model) has properties 1, 2, and 3;

Assertion: And if thing B (the analogue) has properties 1 and 2;

Observation: And if property 3 is not inconsistent with B;

Conclusion: Then B has property 3

In other words, A and B are almost the same by examination of their properties, and characteristics of A may be imputed to B, even though it is not known for sure that B has those characteristics.[26]

Suppose we now want to determine whether a person has a reasonable expectation of privacy in the garbage can that he placed on the public sidewalk for sanitation pickup and that was searched by the police. Assume that in a previous case no reasonable privacy expectation was found in an open container in an open field, and that the previous case had these properties: (1) the contents of the container were visible to the public walking by; (2) no efforts, such as fences, were made to prevent people from looking inside the container; and (3) the owners of the open field knew that people had looked inside the container in the past but took no action to stop others from doing so in the future. The garbage can case differs in one respect: the contents of the closed can were not visible to the public except for the brief period when the sanitation men opened the can and its enclosed plastic bag to dump the garbage in the truck. But if properties 2 and 3 are present in the garbage case, we might conclude those are the more important similarities and that the garbage case thus shares another quality with the open field case: the absence of a reasonable expectation of privacy.

There are many ways to challenge the analogy. The conclusion is only probable and may be flawed. For example, if a "reasonable" expectation of privacy is one shared by the majority, a social science survey might reveal sharp differences in majority privacy expectations in open fields versus residential garbage cans. Moreover, each premise must be proved. What evidence is there that the homeowners knew that people sometimes went through the homeowners' garbage? If there is evidence only that they should have known, does that weaken the analogy? What if the only evidence is that they should have known easy inspection by unknown third parties was possible; would that be enough to maintain the analogy? Even if the premises are adequately proved, analogy requires us to decide which properties matter and which do not. We disregarded the fact that garbage was not instantly observable by casual passersby but the contents of the container in the open field were easily observable. Why? Determining which analogies matter and whether premises have been proved depends on the

---

25. Id. at 91.

26. *See* Covington, STRUCTURE, *supra* note 22, at 239.

kinds of data to which we have repeatedly returned (practicality and prudence, values, etc.) above.

d. Balancing

With "balancing," the Court employs the metaphor of a scale, placing state interests on one side and individual interests on the other. Then the Court simply weighs the interests on one side against those on the other. The weightier interests tip the balance. A balancing opinion will include these steps:

1. Identify the individual's interests;
2. Determine the impact on those interests of the policy being challenged;
3. Identify the state's interests that the challenged policy seeks to realize;
4. Determine the extent to which the challenged policy actually realizes the state's interests; and
5. Determine whether the state's or the individual's interests are weightier.[27]

One major problem with balancing is that interests do not have numerical weights. Judges must assign weights, opening the process to the influence of subjectivity and the imposition of personal values. Sometimes judges try to prove that certain interests exist and that those interests deserve a certain weight. They use both deduction and induction to do this, and inductive analogy tends to be a favorite tool for identifying and weighing interests. All the data forms we have looked at may be used in this process.

Two uses may be made of balancing. First, balancing may be used simply to decide the case before the Court. Thus the "reasonableness" of a search might depend on state interests outweighing individual interests. If, for example, a strip search were conducted to locate a single suspected marijuana cigarette, a court may conclude that the search was unreasonable because the state's interests did not outweigh the intrusion on the individual.

Second, balancing can be used to create rules that relieve courts from engaging in balancing in future cases.[28] For example, in *Terry v. Ohio*[29] the

---

27. *See* van Geel, Opinions, *supra* note 2, at 49–50.

28. In Ohio v. Robinette, 519 U.S. 33 (1996), the Court declared that it has "consistently eschewed bright-line rules, instead emphasizing the fact-specific nature of the reasonableness inquiry." This statement suggests that the Court has concluded that bright-line rules are unwise under the Fourth Amendment, although such rules exist under the Fifth Amendment. (For example, the famous bright-line rule in Miranda v. Arizona requires certain warnings for *all* "custodial interrogations.") Nevertheless, the Court in *Robinette* did not reject the general approach of "categorical balancing," in which the Court crafts a rule to govern an entire future category of cases. Indeed, categorical balancing has dominated the Court's Fourth Amendment analysis. Moreover, as we will see, in Fourth Amendment cases other than *Robinette* the Court has continued to search for supposedly bright-line rules.

29. 392 U.S. 1 (1968).

Court held that a "stop," a brief intrusion on a person's freedom of movement to investigate possible criminal activity, serves such a great state interest that it requires only "reasonable suspicion" and not probable cause. Because of the rule in *Terry*, courts do not have to engage in further balancing in cases involving this sort of police activity. If a case is classified as a "stop," then the reasonableness of the search will turn only on whether there was "reasonable suspicion." The Court's primary approach to search and seizure issues involves this method.

3. PRACTICE IN DEDUCTIVE BRIEFING

Following are excerpts from two cases: *Atwater v. City of Lago Vista*[30] and *Mapp v. Ohio*.[31] We have provided several opinions from each case. Your instructor may ask you to prepare deductive briefs for one or both of these cases. If so, prepare a deductive brief for each justice's opinion. In preparing your deductive briefs, consider when deductive syllogisms, inductive generalization, inductive analogy, and balancing are used and in what combination. For each premise, identify what proof, if any, supports it and critique the persuasiveness of that proof. Finally, think about which justice crafted the most persuasive argument and why.

a.   The Atwater Case

Atwater v. City of Lago Vista

532 U.S. 318 (2001).

■ SOUTER, J. The question is whether the Fourth Amendment forbids a warrantless arrest for a minor criminal offense, such as a misdemeanor seatbelt violation punishable only by a fine. We hold that it does not.

I

A

In Texas, if a car is equipped with safety belts, a front-seat passenger must wear one, and the driver must secure any small child riding in front. Violation of either provision is "a misdemeanor punishable by a fine not less than $25 or more than $50." Texas law expressly authorizes "[a]ny peace officer [to] arrest without warrant a person found committing a violation" of these seatbelt laws, although it permits police to issue citations in lieu of arrest.

In March 1997, petitioner Gail Atwater was driving her pickup truck in Lago Vista, Texas, with her 3–year–old son and 5–year–old daughter in the

---

30.   532 U.S. 318 (2001).

31.   367 U.S. 643 (1961).

front seat. None of them was wearing a seatbelt. Respondent Bart Turek, a Lago Vista police officer at the time, observed the seatbelt violations and pulled Atwater over. According to Atwater's complaint (the allegations of which we assume to be true for present purposes), Turek approached the truck and "yell[ed]" something to the effect of "[w]e've met before" and "[y]ou're going to jail." He then called for backup and asked to see Atwater's driver's license and insurance documentation, which state law required her to carry. When Atwater told Turek that she did not have the papers because her purse had been stolen the day before, Turek said that he had "heard that story two-hundred times."

Atwater asked to take her "frightened, upset, and crying" children to a friend's house nearby, but Turek told her, "[y]ou're not going anywhere." As it turned out, Atwater's friend learned what was going on and soon arrived to take charge of the children. Turek then handcuffed Atwater, placed her in his squad car, and drove her to the local police station, where booking officers had her remove her shoes, jewelry, and eyeglasses, and empty her pockets. Officers took Atwater's "mug shot" and placed her, alone, in a jail cell for about one hour, after which she was taken before a magistrate and released on $310 bond.

Atwater was charged with driving without her seatbelt fastened, failing to secure her children in seatbelts, driving without a license, and failing to provide proof of insurance. She ultimately pleaded no contest to the misdemeanor seatbelt offenses and paid a $50 fine; the other charges were dismissed.

B

Atwater ... filed suit ... under 42 U.S.C. § 1983 against Turek and respondents City of Lago Vista and Chief of Police Frank Miller. [P]etitioner[] alleged that respondents ... had violated Atwater's Fourth Amendment "right to be free from unreasonable seizure," and sought compensatory and punitive damages.

... Given Atwater's admission that she had "violated the law" and the absence of any allegation "that she was harmed or detained in any way inconsistent with the law," the District Court ruled the Fourth Amendment claim "meritless" and granted the City's summary judgment motion. A panel of the United States Court of Appeals for the Fifth Circuit reversed. It concluded that "an arrest for a first-time seat belt offense" was an unreasonable seizure within the meaning of the Fourth Amendment, and held that Turek was not entitled to qualified immunity.

Sitting en banc, the Court of Appeals vacated the panel's decision and affirmed the District Court's summary judgment for the City. Relying on *Whren v. United States,* 517 U.S. 806 (1996), the *en banc* court observed that, although the Fourth Amendment generally requires a balancing of individual and governmental interests, where "an arrest is based on probable cause then 'with rare exceptions' ... the result of that balancing is not in doubt." Because "[n]either party dispute[d] that Officer Turek had probable cause to arrest Atwater," and because "there [was] no evidence in the record that Officer Turek conducted the arrest in an 'extraordinary manner, unusually harmful' to Atwater's privacy interests," the en banc court held that the arrest was not unreasonable for Fourth Amendment purposes.

Three judges issued dissenting opinions. On the understanding that citation is the "usual procedure" in a traffic stop situation, Judge Reynaldo Garza thought Atwater's arrest unreasonable, since there was no particular reason for taking her into custody. Judge Weiner likewise believed that "even with probable cause, [an] officer must have a plausible, articulable reason" for making a custodial arrest. Judge Dennis understood the Fourth Amendment to have incorporated an earlier, common-law prohibition on warrantless arrests for misdemeanors that do not amount to or involve a "breach of the peace."

We granted certiorari to consider whether the Fourth Amendment, either by incorporating common-law restrictions on misdemeanor arrests or otherwise, limits police officers' authority to arrest without warrant for minor criminal offenses. We now affirm.

II

The Fourth Amendment safeguards "[t]he right of the people to be secure in their persons, houses, papers, and effects, against unreasonable searches and seizures." In reading the Amendment, we are guided by the traditional protections against unreasonable searches and seizures afforded by the common law at the time of the framing, since an examination of the common-law understanding of an officer's authority to arrest sheds light on the obviously relevant, if not entirely dispositive, consideration of what the Framers of the Amendment might have thought to be reasonable. Thus, the first step here is to assess Atwater's claim that peace officers' authority to make warrantless arrests for misdemeanors was restricted at common law (whether "common law" is understood strictly as law judicially derived or, instead, as the whole body of law extant at the time of the framing). Atwater's specific contention is that "founding-era common-law rules" forbade peace officers to make warrantless misdemeanor arrests except in cases of "breach of the peace," a category she claims was then understood narrowly as covering only those nonfelony offenses "involving or tending toward violence." Although her historical argument is by no means insubstantial, it ultimately fails.

A

We begin with the state of pre-founding English common law and find that, even after making some allowance for variations in the common-law usage of the term "breach of the peace," the "founding-era common-law rules" were not nearly as clear as Atwater claims; on the contrary, the common-law commentators (as well as the sparsely reported cases) reached divergent conclusions with respect to officers' warrantless misdemeanor arrest power. Moreover, in the years leading up to American independence, Parliament repeatedly extended express warrantless arrest authority to cover misdemeanor-level offenses not amounting to or involving any violent breach of the peace. . . .

B

An examination of specifically American evidence is to the same effect. Neither the history of the framing era nor subsequent legal development indicates that the Fourth Amendment was originally understood, or has traditionally been read, to embrace Atwater's position.

1

To begin with, Atwater has cited no particular evidence that those who framed and ratified the Fourth Amendment sought to limit peace officers' warrantless misdemeanor arrest authority to instances of actual breach of the peace, and our own review of the recent and respected compilations of framing-era documentary history has likewise failed to reveal any such design. Nor have we found in any of the modern historical accounts of the Fourth Amendment's adoption any substantial indication that the Framers intended such a restriction. . . .

The evidence of actual practice also counsels against Atwater's position. During the period leading up to and surrounding the framing of the Bill of Rights, colonial and state legislatures, like Parliament before them, regularly authorized local peace officers to make warrantless misdemeanor arrests without conditioning statutory authority on breach of the peace.

. . . Of course, the Fourth Amendment did not originally apply to the States, but that does not make state practice irrelevant in unearthing the Amendment's original meaning. A number of state constitutional search-and-seizure provisions served as models for the Fourth Amendment, and the fact that many of the original States with such constitutional limitations continued to grant their own peace officers broad warrantless misdemeanor arrest authority undermines Atwater's contention that the founding generation meant to bar federal law enforcement officers from exercising the same authority. Given the early state practice, it is likewise troublesome for Atwater's view that just one year after the ratification of the Fourth Amendment, Congress vested federal marshals with "the same powers in executing the laws of the United States, as sheriffs and their deputies in the several states have by law, in executing the laws of their respective states." Act of May 2, 1792, ch. 28, § 9, 1 Stat. 265. Thus, as we have said before in only slightly different circumstances, the Second Congress apparently "saw no inconsistency between the Fourth Amendment and legislation giving United States marshals the same power as local peace officers" to make warrantless arrests. *United States v. Watson,* 423 U.S. 411 (1976).

. . . We simply cannot conclude that the Fourth Amendment, as originally understood, forbade peace officers to arrest without a warrant for misdemeanors not amounting to or involving breach of the peace.

2

Nor does Atwater's argument from tradition pick up any steam from the historical record as it has unfolded since the framing, there being no indication that her claimed rule has ever become woven into the fabric of American law. The story, on the contrary, is of two centuries of uninterrupted (and largely unchallenged) state and federal practice permitting warrantless arrests for misdemeanors not amounting to or involving breach of the peace.

First, there is no support for Atwater's position in this Court's cases.... Although the Court has not had much to say about warrantless misdemeanor arrest authority, what little we have said tends to cut against Atwater's argument. In discussing this authority, we have focused on the circumstance that an offense was committed in an officer's presence, to the omission of any reference to a breach-of-the-peace limitation.

Second, . . . it is not the case here that early American courts embraced an accepted common-law rule with anything approaching unanimity. To be sure, Atwater has cited several 19th-century decisions that, at least at first glance, might seem to support her contention that "warrantless misdemeanor arrest was unlawful when not [for] a breach of the peace." Brief for Petitioners 17 (citing *Pow v. Beckner,* 3 Ind. 475 (1852), *Commonwealth v. Carey,* 66 Mass. 246 (1853), and *Robison v. Miner,* 68 Mich. 549 (1888)). But none is ultimately availing. *Pow* is fundamentally a "presence" case; it stands only for the proposition, not at issue here, that a nonfelony arrest should be made while the offense is "in [the officer's] view and . . . still continuing" and not subsequently "upon vague information communicated to him." 3 Ind., at 478. The language Atwater attributes to *Carey* ("[E]ven if he were a constable, he had no power to arrest for any misdemeanor without a warrant, except to stay a breach of the peace, or to prevent the commission of such an offense") is taken from the reporter's summary of one of the party's arguments, not from the opinion of the court. While the court in *Carey* (through Chief Justice Shaw) said that "the old established rule of the common law" was that "a constable or other peace officer could not arrest one without a warrant . . . if such crime were not an offence amounting in law to felony," it said just as clearly that the common-law rule could be "altered by the legislature" (notwithstanding Massachusetts's own Fourth Amendment equivalent in its State Constitution). *Miner,* the third and final case upon which Atwater relies, was expressly overruled just six years after it was decided.

The reports may well contain early American cases more favorable to Atwater's position than the ones she has herself invoked. But more to the point, we think, are the numerous early-and mid–19th-century decisions expressly sustaining (often against constitutional challenge) state and local laws authorizing peace officers to make warrantless arrests for misdemeanors not involving any breach of the peace. *See, e.g., Mayo v. Wilson,* 1 N.H. 53 (1817) (upholding statute authorizing warrantless arrests of those unnecessarily traveling on Sunday against challenge based on state due process and search-and-seizure provisions); *Holcomb v. Cornish,* 8 Conn.

375 (1831) (upholding statute permitting warrantless arrests for "drunken-ness, profane swearing, cursing or sabbath-breaking," against argument that "[t]he power of a justice of the peace to arrest and detain a citizen without complaint or warrant against him, is surely not given by the common law"); *Jones v. Root,* 72 Mass. 435 (1856) (rebuffing constitutional challenge to statute authorizing officers "without a warrant [to] arrest any person or persons whom they may find in the act of illegally selling, transporting, or distributing intoxicating liquors"); *Main v. McCarty,* 15 Ill. 441 (1854) (concluding that a law expressly authorizing arrests for city-ordinance violations was "not repugnant to the constitution or the general provisions of law"); *White v. Kent,* 11 Ohio St. 550 (1860) (upholding municipal ordinance permitting warrantless arrest of any person found violating any city ordinance or state law); *Davis v. American Soc. for Prevention of Cruelty to Animals,* 75 N.Y. 362 (1878) (upholding statute permitting warrantless arrest for misdemeanor violation of cruelty-to-animals prohibition).

Finally, both the legislative tradition of granting warrantless misde-meanor arrest authority and the judicial tradition of sustaining such statutes against constitutional attack are buttressed by legal commentary that, for more than a century now, has almost uniformly recognized the constitutionality of extending warrantless arrest power to misdemeanors without limitation to breaches of the peace. *See, e.g.,* E. Fisher, LAWS OF ARREST § 59, p. 130 (1967) ("[I]t is generally recognized today that the common law authority to arrest without a warrant in misdemeanor cases may be enlarged by statute, and this has been done in many of the states"); ... J. Beale, CRIMINAL PLEADING AND PRACTICE § 21, p. 20, and n. 7 (1899) ("By statute the power of peace officers to arrest without a warrant is often extended to all misdemeanors committed in their presence." "Such a statute is constitutional"); ... J. Bassett, CRIMINAL PLEADING AND PRACTICE § 89, p. 104 (2d ed. 1885) ("[A]s to the lesser misdemeanors, except breaches of the peace, the power extends only so far as some statute gives it"). *But cf.* H. Vorhees, LAW OF ARREST § 131, pp. 78–79 (1904) (acknowl-edging that "by authority of statute, city charter, or ordinance, [an officer] may arrest without a warrant, one who ... commits a misdemeanor other than a breach of the peace," but suggesting that courts look with "disfa-vor" on such legislative enactments "as interfering with the constitutional liberties of the subject").

Small wonder, then, that today statutes in all 50 States and the District of Columbia permit warrantless misdemeanor arrests by at least some (if not all) peace officers without requiring any breach of the peace, as do a host of congressional enactments. The American Law Institute has long endorsed the validity of such legislation, and the consensus, as stated in the current literature, is that statutes "remov[ing] the breach of the peace limitation and thereby permit[ting] arrest without warrant for any misdemeanor committed in the arresting officer's presence" have "never been successfully challenged and stan[d] as the law of the land." 3 W. LaFave, SEARCH AND SEIZURE § 5.1(b), pp. 13–14, and n. 76 (1996). This, therefore, simply is not a case in which the claimant can point to a clear answer that existed in 1791 and has been generally adhered to by the traditions of our society ever since.

III

While it is true here that history, if not unequivocal, has expressed a decided, majority view that the police need not obtain an arrest warrant merely because a misdemeanor stopped short of violence or a threat of it, Atwater does not wager all on history. Instead, she asks us to mint a new rule of constitutional law on the understanding that when historical practice fails to speak conclusively to a claim grounded on the Fourth Amendment, courts are left to strike a current balance between individual and societal interests by subjecting particular contemporary circumstances to traditional standards of reasonableness. Atwater accordingly argues for a modern arrest rule, one not necessarily requiring violent breach of the peace, but nonetheless forbidding custodial arrest, even upon probable cause, when conviction could not ultimately carry any jail time and when the government shows no compelling need for immediate detention.

If we were to derive a rule exclusively to address the uncontested facts of this case, Atwater might well prevail. She was a known and established resident of Lago Vista with no place to hide and no incentive to flee, and common sense says she would almost certainly have buckled up as a condition of driving off with a citation. In her case, the physical incidents of arrest were merely gratuitous humiliations imposed by a police officer who was (at best) exercising extremely poor judgment. Atwater's claim to live free of pointless indignity and confinement clearly outweighs anything the City can raise against it specific to her case.

But we have traditionally recognized that a responsible Fourth Amendment balance is not well served by standards requiring sensitive, case-by-case determinations of government need, lest every discretionary judgment in the field be converted into an occasion for constitutional review. Often enough, the Fourth Amendment has to be applied on the spur (and in the heat) of the moment, and the object in implementing its command of reasonableness is to draw standards sufficiently clear and simple to be applied with a fair prospect of surviving judicial second-guessing months and years after an arrest or search is made. Courts attempting to strike a reasonable Fourth Amendment balance thus credit the government's side with an essential interest in readily administrable rules.

At first glance, Atwater's argument may seem to respect the values of clarity and simplicity, so far as she claims that the Fourth Amendment generally forbids warrantless arrests for minor crimes not accompanied by violence or some demonstrable threat of it whether "minor crime" be defined as a fine-only traffic offense, a fine-only offense more generally, or a misdemeanor. But the claim is not ultimately so simple, nor could it be, for complications arise the moment we begin to think about the possible applications of the several criteria Atwater proposes for drawing a line between minor crimes with limited arrest authority and others not so restricted.

One line, she suggests, might be between "jailable" and "fine-only" offenses, between those for which conviction could result in commitment and those for which it could not. The trouble with this distinction, of course, is that an officer on the street might not be able to tell. It is not merely that we cannot expect every police officer to know the details of frequently complex penalty schemes, but that penalties for ostensibly identical conduct can vary on account of facts difficult (if not impossible) to know at the scene of an arrest. Is this the first offense or is the suspect a repeat offender? Is the weight of the marijuana a gram above or a gram below the fine-only line? Where conduct could implicate more than one criminal prohibition, which one will the district attorney ultimately decide to charge? And so on.

But Atwater's refinements would not end there. She represents that if the line were drawn at nonjailable traffic offenses, her proposed limitation should be qualified by a proviso authorizing warrantless arrests where "necessary for enforcement of the traffic laws or when [an] offense would otherwise continue and pose a danger to others on the road." (Were the line drawn at misdemeanors generally, a comparable qualification would presumably apply.) The proviso only compounds the difficulties. Would, for instance, either exception apply to speeding? At oral argument, Atwater's counsel said that "it would not be reasonable to arrest a driver for speeding unless the speeding rose to the level of reckless driving." But is it not fair to expect that the chronic speeder will speed again despite a citation in his pocket, and should that not qualify as showing that the "offense would . . . continue" under Atwater's rule? And why, as a constitutional matter, should we assume that only reckless driving will "pose a danger to others on the road" while speeding will not?

There is no need for more examples to show that Atwater's general rule and limiting proviso promise very little in the way of administrability. It is no answer that the police routinely make judgments on grounds like risk of immediate repetition; they surely do and should. But there is a world of difference between making that judgment in choosing between the discretionary leniency of a summons in place of a clearly lawful arrest, and making the same judgment when the question is the lawfulness of the warrantless arrest itself. It is the difference between no basis for legal action challenging the discretionary judgment, on the one hand, and the prospect of evidentiary exclusion or (as here) personal § 1983 liability for the misapplication of a constitutional standard, on the other. Atwater's rule therefore would not only place police in an almost impossible spot but would guarantee increased litigation over many of the arrests that would occur. For all these reasons, Atwater's various distinctions between permissible and impermissible arrests for minor crimes strike us as very unsatisfactory lines to require police officers to draw on a moment's notice. . . .

Accordingly, we confirm today what our prior cases have intimated: the standard of probable cause applies to all arrests, without the need to 'balance' the interests and circumstances involved in particular situations. If an officer has probable cause to believe that an individual has committed even a very minor criminal offense in his presence, he may, without violating the Fourth Amendment, arrest the offender.

IV

Atwater's arrest satisfied constitutional requirements. There is no dispute that Officer Turek had probable cause to believe that Atwater had committed a crime in his presence. She admits that neither she nor her children were wearing seatbelts. Turek was accordingly authorized (not required, but authorized) to make a custodial arrest without balancing costs and benefits or determining whether or not Atwater's arrest was in some sense necessary.

■ O'Connor, J., dissenting (joined by Stevens, Ginsburg, and Breyer, JJ.). The Fourth Amendment guarantees the right to be free from "unreasonable searches and seizures." The Court recognizes that the arrest of Gail Atwater was a "pointless indignity" that served no discernible state interest and yet holds that her arrest was constitutionally permissible. Because the Court's position is inconsistent with the explicit guarantee of the Fourth Amendment, I dissent.

I

A full custodial arrest, such as the one to which Ms. Atwater was subjected, is the quintessential seizure. When a full custodial arrest is effected without a warrant, the plain language of the Fourth Amendment requires that the arrest be reasonable. It is beyond cavil that "[t]he touchstone of our analysis under the Fourth Amendment is always the reasonableness in all the circumstances of the particular governmental invasion of a citizen's personal security." *Pennsylvania v. Mimms,* 434 U.S. 106 (1977) (per curiam).

We have often looked to the common law in evaluating the reasonableness, for Fourth Amendment purposes, of police activity. But history is just one of the tools we use in conducting the reasonableness inquiry. And when history is inconclusive, as the majority amply demonstrates it is in this case, we will evaluate the search or seizure under traditional standards of reasonableness by assessing, on the one hand, the degree to which it intrudes upon an individual's privacy and, on the other, the degree to which it is needed for the promotion of legitimate governmental interests.

The majority gives a brief nod to this bedrock principle of our Fourth Amendment jurisprudence, and even acknowledges that "Atwater's claim to live free of pointless indignity and confinement clearly outweighs anything the City can raise against it specific to her case." But instead of remedying this imbalance, the majority allows itself to be swayed by the worry that "every discretionary judgment in the field [will] be converted into an occasion for constitutional review." It therefore mints a new rule that "[i]f an officer has probable cause to believe that an individual has committed even a very minor criminal offense in his presence, he may, without violating the Fourth Amendment, arrest the offender." This rule is not only unsupported by our precedent, but runs contrary to the principles that lie at the core of the Fourth Amendment.

As the majority tacitly acknowledges, we have never considered the precise question presented here, namely, the constitutionality of a warrantless arrest for an offense punishable only by fine. Indeed, on the rare occasions that Members of this Court have contemplated such an arrest, they have indicated disapproval. *See, e.g., Gustafson v. Florida,* 414 U.S. 260 (1973) (Stewart, J., concurring) ("[A] persuasive claim might have been made . . . that the custodial arrest of the petitioner for a minor traffic offense violated his rights under the Fourth and Fourteenth Amendments. But no such claim has been made"); *United States v. Robinson,* 414 U.S. 218 (1973) (Powell, J., concurring) (the validity of a custodial arrest for a minor traffic offense is not "self-evident").

To be sure, we have held that the existence of probable cause is a necessary condition for an arrest. *See Dunaway v. New York,* 442 U.S. 200 (1979). And in the case of felonies punishable by a term of imprisonment, we have held that the existence of probable cause is also a sufficient condition for an arrest. *See United States v. Watson,* 423 U.S. 411 (1976). In *Watson,* however, there was a clear and consistently applied common law rule permitting warrantless felony arrests. Accordingly, our inquiry ended there and we had no need to assess the reasonableness of such arrests by weighing individual liberty interests against state interests.

Here, however, we have no such luxury. The Court's thorough exegesis makes it abundantly clear that warrantless misdemeanor arrests were not the subject of a clear and consistently applied rule at common law. We therefore must engage in the balancing test required by the Fourth Amendment. While probable cause is surely a necessary condition for warrantless arrests for fine-only offenses, any realistic assessment of the interests implicated by such arrests demonstrates that probable cause alone is not a sufficient condition. . . .

A custodial arrest exacts an obvious toll on an individual's liberty and privacy, even when the period of custody is relatively brief. The arrestee is subject to a full search of her person and confiscation of her possessions. If the arrestee is the occupant of a car, the entire passenger compartment of the car, including packages therein, is subject to search as well. The arrestee may be detained for up to 48 hours without having a magistrate determine whether there in fact was probable cause for the arrest. Because people arrested for all types of violent and nonviolent offenses may be housed together awaiting such review, this detention period is potentially dangerous. And once the period of custody is over, the fact of the arrest is a permanent part of the public record.

We have said that the penalty that may attach to any particular offense seems to provide the clearest and most consistent indication of the State's interest in arresting individuals suspected of committing that offense. If the State has decided that a fine, and not imprisonment, is the appropriate punishment for an offense, the State's interest in taking a person suspected of committing that offense into custody is surely limited, at best. This is not to say that the State will never have such an interest. A full custodial arrest may on occasion vindicate legitimate state interests, even if the crime is punishable only by fine. Arrest is the surest way to abate criminal conduct. It may also allow the police to verify the offender's identity and, if the offender poses a flight risk, to ensure her appearance at trial. But when such considerations are not present, a citation or summons may serve the State's remaining law enforcement interests every bit as effectively as an arrest.

Because a full custodial arrest is such a severe intrusion on an individual's liberty, its reasonableness hinges on the degree to which it is needed for the promotion of legitimate governmental interests. In light of the availability of citations to promote a State's interests when a fine-only offense has been committed, I cannot concur in a rule which deems a full custodial arrest to be reasonable in every circumstance. Giving police officers constitutional carte blanche to effect an arrest whenever there is probable cause to believe a fine-only misdemeanor has been committed is irreconcilable with the Fourth Amendment's command that seizures be reasonable. Instead, I would require that when there is probable cause to believe that a fine-only offense has been committed, the police officer should issue a citation unless the officer is able to point to specific and articulable facts which, taken together with rational inferences from those facts, reasonably warrant the additional intrusion of a full custodial arrest.

The majority insists that a bright-line rule focused on probable cause is necessary to vindicate the State's interest in easily administrable law enforcement rules. Probable cause itself, however, is not a model of precision. "The quantum of information which constitutes probable cause—evidence which would 'warrant a man of reasonable caution in the belief' that a [crime] has been committed—must be measured by the facts of the particular case." *Wong Sun v. United States,* 371 U.S. 471 (1963). The rule I propose—which merely requires a legitimate reason for the decision to escalate the seizure into a full custodial arrest—thus does not undermine an otherwise "clear and simple" rule. While clarity is certainly a value worthy of consideration in our Fourth Amendment jurisprudence, it by no means trumps the values of liberty and privacy at the heart of the Amendment's protections. . . .

At bottom, the majority offers two related reasons why a bright-line rule is necessary: the fear that officers who arrest for fine-only offenses will be subject to personal 42 U.S.C. § 1983 liability for the misapplication of a constitutional standard, and the resulting systematic disincentive to arrest where arresting would serve an important societal interest. These concerns are certainly valid, but they are more than adequately resolved by the doctrine of qualified immunity.

Qualified immunity was created to shield government officials from civil liability for the performance of discretionary functions so long as their conduct does not violate clearly established statutory or constitutional rights of which a reasonable person would have known. This doctrine is the best attainable accommodation of competing values, namely, the obligation to enforce constitutional guarantees and the need to protect officials who are required to exercise their discretion.

In *Anderson v. Creighton,* 483 U.S. 635 (1987), we made clear that the standard of reasonableness for a search or seizure under the Fourth Amendment is distinct from the standard of reasonableness for qualified immunity purposes. If a law enforcement officer "reasonably but mistakenly conclude[s]" that the constitutional predicate for a search or seizure is present, he "should not be held personally liable."

This doctrine thus allays any concerns about liability or disincentives to arrest. If, for example, an officer reasonably thinks that a suspect poses a flight risk or might be a danger to the community if released, he may arrest without fear of the legal consequences. Similarly, if an officer reasonably concludes that a suspect may possess more than four ounces of marijuana and thus might be guilty of a felony, the officer will be insulated from liability for arresting the suspect even if the initial assessment turns out to be factually incorrect. . . . [O]fficials will not be liable for mere mistakes in judgment. Of course, even the specter of liability can entail substantial social costs, such as inhibiting public officials in the discharge of their duties. We may not ignore the central command of the Fourth Amendment, however, to avoid these costs.

II

The record in this case makes it abundantly clear that Ms. Atwater's arrest was constitutionally unreasonable. Atwater readily admits—as she did when Officer Turek pulled her over—that she violated Texas' seatbelt law. While Turek was justified in stopping Atwater, neither law nor reason supports his decision to arrest her instead of simply giving her a citation. The officer's actions cannot sensibly be viewed as a permissible means of balancing Atwater's Fourth Amendment interests with the State's own legitimate interests.

There is no question that Officer Turek's actions severely infringed Atwater's liberty and privacy. Turek was loud and accusatory from the moment he approached Atwater's car. Atwater's young children were terrified and hysterical. Yet when Atwater asked Turek to lower his voice because he was scaring the children, he responded by jabbing his finger in Atwater's face and saying, "You're going to jail." Having made the decision to arrest, Turek did not inform Atwater of her right to remain silent. He instead asked for her license and insurance information.

Atwater asked if she could at least take her children to a friend's house down the street before going to the police station. But Turek—who had just castigated Atwater for not caring for her children—refused and said he would take the children into custody as well. Only the intervention of neighborhood children who had witnessed the scene and summoned one of Atwater's friends saved the children from being hauled to jail with their mother.

With the children gone, Officer Turek handcuffed Ms. Atwater with her hands behind her back, placed her in the police car, and drove her to the police station. Ironically, Turek did not secure Atwater in a seatbelt for the drive. At the station, Atwater was forced to remove her shoes, relinquish her possessions, and wait in a holding cell for about an hour. A judge finally informed Atwater of her rights and the charges against her, and released her when she posted bond. Atwater returned to the scene of the arrest, only to find that her car had been towed.

Ms. Atwater ultimately pleaded no contest to violating the seatbelt law and was fined $50. Even though that fine was the maximum penalty for her crime, and even though Officer Turek has never articulated any justification for his actions, the city contends that arresting Atwater was constitutionally reasonable because it advanced two legitimate interests: "the enforcement of child safety laws and encouraging [Atwater] to appear for trial."

It is difficult to see how arresting Atwater served either of these goals any more effectively than the issuance of a citation. With respect to the goal of law enforcement generally, Atwater did not pose a great danger to the community. She had been driving very slowly—approximately 15 miles per hour—in broad daylight on a residential street that had no other traffic. Nor was she a repeat offender; until that day, she had received one traffic citation in her life—a ticket, more than 10 years earlier, for failure to signal a lane change. ... Moreover, Atwater immediately accepted responsibility and apologized for her conduct. Thus, there was every indication that Atwater would have buckled herself and her children in had she been cited and allowed to leave.

With respect to the related goal of child welfare, the decision to arrest Atwater was nothing short of counterproductive. Atwater's children witnessed Officer Turek yell at their mother and threaten to take them all into custody. Ultimately, they were forced to leave her behind with Turek, knowing that she was being taken to jail. Understandably, the 3–year-old boy was "very, very, very traumatized." After the incident, he had to see a child psychologist regularly, who reported that the boy "felt very guilty that he couldn't stop this horrible thing ... he was powerless to help his mother or sister." Both of Atwater's children are now terrified at the sight of any police car. According to Atwater, the arrest "just never leaves us. It's a conversation we have every other day, once a week, and it's—it raises its head constantly in our lives."

Citing Atwater surely would have served the children's interests well. It would have taught Atwater to ensure that her children were buckled up in the future. It also would have taught the children an important lesson in accepting responsibility and obeying the law. Arresting Atwater, though, taught the children an entirely different lesson: that "the bad person could just as easily be the policeman as it could be the most horrible person they could imagine."

Respondents also contend that the arrest was necessary to ensure Atwater's appearance in court. Atwater, however, was far from a flight risk.

A 16–year resident of Lago Vista, population 2,486, Atwater was not likely to abscond. Although she was unable to produce her driver's license because it had been stolen, she gave Officer Turek her license number and address. In addition, Officer Turek knew ... that Atwater was a local resident.

The city's justifications fall far short of rationalizing the extraordinary intrusion on Gail Atwater and her children. Measuring the degree to which Atwater's custodial arrest was needed for the promotion of legitimate governmental interests, against the degree to which it intruded upon her privacy, it can hardly be doubted that Turek's actions were disproportionate to Atwater's crime. The majority's assessment that "Atwater's claim to live free of pointless indignity and confinement clearly outweighs anything the City can raise against it specific to her case," is quite correct. In my view, the Fourth Amendment inquiry ends there.

III

The Court's error, however, does not merely affect the disposition of this case. The per se rule that the Court creates has potentially serious consequences for the everyday lives of Americans. A broad range of conduct falls into the category of fine-only misdemeanors. In Texas alone, for example, disobeying any sort of traffic warning sign is a misdemeanor punishable only by fine, as is failing to pay a highway toll, and driving with expired license plates. Nor are fine-only crimes limited to the traffic context. In several States, for example, littering is a criminal offense punishable only by fine.

To be sure, such laws are valid and wise exercises of the States' power to protect the public health and welfare. My concern lies not with the decision to enact or enforce these laws, but rather with the manner in which they may be enforced. Under today's holding, when a police officer has probable cause to believe that a fine-only misdemeanor offense has occurred, that officer may stop the suspect, issue a citation, and let the person continue on her way. Or, if a traffic violation, the officer may stop the car, arrest the driver, search the driver, search the entire passenger compartment of the car including any purse or package inside, and impound the car and inventory all of its contents. Although the Fourth Amendment expressly requires that the latter course be a reasonable and proportional response to the circumstances of the offense, the majority gives officers unfettered discretion to choose that course without articulating a single reason why such action is appropriate.

Such unbounded discretion carries with it grave potential for abuse. The majority takes comfort in the lack of evidence of "an epidemic of unnecessary minor-offense arrests." But the relatively small number of published cases dealing with such arrests proves little and should provide little solace. Indeed, as the recent debate over racial profiling demonstrates all too clearly, a relatively minor traffic infraction may often serve as an excuse for stopping and harassing an individual. After today, the arsenal available to any officer extends to a full arrest and the searches permissible concomitant to that arrest. An officer's subjective motivations for making a traffic stop are not relevant considerations in determining the reasonableness of the stop. But it is precisely because these motivations are beyond our purview that we must vigilantly ensure that officers' poststop actions—which are properly within our reach—comport with the Fourth Amendment's guarantee of reasonableness.

The Court neglects the Fourth Amendment's express command in the name of administrative ease. In so doing, it cloaks the pointless indignity that Gail Atwater suffered with the mantle of reasonableness. I respectfully dissent.

b. *The Mapp Case*

The Court and constitutional scholars have long debated whether the exclusion of evidence is the appropriate remedy for Fourth Amendment violations. Prior to the Court's opinion in *Mapp*, the Court had applied the exclusionary remedy to trials in federal court but not to trials in state court. *Mapp* represented a turning point for the Court, and the rule it created in that case remains the law of the land today.

In order to understand *Mapp*, some background is necessary on what is known as the "incorporation debate," which was on-going at the time the Court issued the *Mapp* decision. The debate concerned which of the limitations on governmental power found in the Bill of Rights (which originally applied only to the federal government) should be "incorporated against"—i.e., applied to—the states through the post-Civil War Fourteenth Amendment, which changed profoundly the relationship between the people, the federal government, and the states. For example, did the 14th Amendment mean that the states had to begin observing the restrictions of the 4th Amendment, which permits the federal government to conduct only reasonable searches and seizures?[32] Many in the country believed that the Fourteenth Amendment automatically imposed on state actors the same restrictions that federal government actors had to observe. Others disagreed. In the Supreme Court, the incorporation debate consumed judicial energy for almost a century. At issue in the Court's piece of the debate was whether the "due process" clause of the Fourteenth Amendment (which was interpreted to guaranty "fundamental fairness") should be read to incorporate all or part of the Bill of Rights against the states. These are the four positions taken by various justices during the incorporation debate:

(1) TOTAL INCORPORATION. According to some justices, the Fourteenth Amendment required the application of the entire Bill of Rights against the states. The total incorporation approach would limit judicial discretion because judges need not determine the issue of incorporation on a case-by-case basis.

---

32. Many states limit their agents' search and seizure authority through state constitutional provisions that mirror the Fourth Amendment. We will discuss some of these in a later chapter.

(2) SELECTIVE INCORPORATION. Some justices believed that the due process clause of the Fourteenth Amendment did not require incorporating against the states every provision of the Bill of Rights, because some rights were not necessary to fundamental fairness. The selective incorporation approach would limit judicial discretion once the Court decided which parts of the Bill of Rights were required by fundamental fairness and which were not.

(3) FUNDAMENTAL FAIRNESS. Justices who subscribed to this position argued that fundamental fairness might mean one thing in one case and another thing in another case. Thus, judges would have to decide on a case-by-case basis whether a certain procedure was required by fundamental fairness. This approach would allow courts to adapt to changing circumstances and arguably is most consistent with the term "due process." It also would increase judicial discretion.

(4) INCORPORATION PLUS. Some justices believed that fundamental fairness required incorporating all of the Bill of Rights against the states, and more. The "more" would consist of additional procedures that, on a case-by-case basis, courts determined were mandated by fundamental fairness. This approach would result in a great amount of judicial discretion.

As you will discern from the opinions in *Mapp*, by the time the Court decided the case, it was becoming clear that the doctrine of selective incorporation was winning the debate.

Mapp v. Ohio
367 U.S. 643 (1961).

■ CLARK, J. Appellant stands convicted of knowingly having had in her possession and under her control certain lewd and lascivious books, pictures, and photographs in violation of . . . Ohio's Revised Code. . . . [T]he Supreme Court of Ohio found that her conviction was valid though "based primarily upon the introduction in evidence of lewd and lascivious books and pictures unlawfully seized during an unlawful search of defendant's home. . . ."

On May 23, 1957, three Cleveland police officers arrived at appellant's residence in that city pursuant to information that "a person [was] hiding out in the home, who was wanted for questioning in connection with a recent bombing, and that there was a large amount of policy paraphernalia being hidden in the home." Miss Mapp and her daughter by a former marriage lived on the top floor of the two-family dwelling. Upon their arrival at that house, the officers knocked on the door and demanded entrance but appellant, after telephoning her attorney, refused to admit them without a search warrant. They advised their headquarters of the situation and undertook a surveillance of the house.

The officers again sought entrance some three hours later when four or more additional officers arrived on the scene. When Miss Mapp did not come to the door immediately, at least one of the several doors to the house was forcibly opened and the policemen gained admittance. Meanwhile Miss Mapp's attorney arrived, but the officers, having secured their own entry, and continuing in their defiance of the law, would permit him neither to see Miss Mapp nor to enter the house. It appears that Miss Mapp was halfway down the stairs from the upper floor to the front door when the officers, in this highhanded manner, broke into the hall. She demanded to see the search warrant. A paper, claimed to be a warrant, was held up by one of the officers. She grabbed the "warrant" and placed it in her bosom. A struggle ensued in which the officers recovered the piece of paper and as a result of which they handcuffed appellant because she had been "belligerent" in resisting their official rescue of the "warrant" from her person. Running roughshod over appellant, a policeman "grabbed" her, "twisted [her] hand," and she "yelled [and] pleaded with him" because "it was hurting." Appellant, in handcuffs, was then forcibly taken upstairs to her bedroom where the officers searched a dresser, a chest of drawers, a closet and some suitcases. They also looked into a photo album and through personal papers belonging to the appellant. The search spread to the rest of the second floor including the child's bedroom, the living room, the kitchen and a dinette. The basement of the building and a trunk found therein were also searched. The obscene materials for possession of which she was ultimately convicted were discovered in the course of that widespread search.

At the trial no search warrant was produced by the prosecution, nor was the failure to produce one explained or accounted for. At best, "There is, in the record, considerable doubt as to whether there ever was any warrant for the search of defendant's home." . . .

The State says that even if the search were made without authority, or otherwise unreasonably, it is not prevented from using the unconstitutionally seized evidence at trial, citing *Wolf v. Colorado*, 338 U.S. 25 (1949), in which this Court did indeed hold "that in a prosecution in a State court for a State crime the Fourteenth Amendment does not forbid the admission of evidence obtained by an unreasonable search and seizure."

I

Seventy-five years ago, in *Boyd v. United States*, 116 U.S. 616 (1886), . . . this Court held that . . . "It is the duty of courts to be watchful for the constitutional rights of the citizen, and against any stealthy encroachments thereon." In this jealous regard for maintaining the integrity of individual rights, the Court gave life to Madison's prediction that "independent tribunals of justice . . . will be naturally led to resist every encroachment upon rights expressly stipulated for in the Constitution by the declaration of rights." I Annals of Cong. 439 (1789). Concluding, the Court specifically referred to the use of the evidence there seized as "unconstitutional."

Less than 30 years after *Boyd*, this Court, in *Weeks v. United States*, 232 U.S. 383 (1914), stated that "the 4th Amendment . . . put the courts of the United States and Federal officials, in the exercise of their power and authority, under limitations and restraints [and] . . . forever secure[d] the people, their persons, houses, papers, and effects, against all unreasonable searches and seizures under the guise of law . . . and the duty of giving to it force and effect is obligatory upon all entrusted under our Federal system with the enforcement of the laws." Specifically dealing with the use of the evidence unconstitutionally seized, the Court concluded: "If letters and private documents can thus be seized and held and used in evidence against a citizen accused of an offense, the protection of the Fourth Amendment declaring his right to be secure against such searches and seizures is of no value, and, so far as those thus placed are concerned, might as well be stricken from the Constitution. The efforts of the courts and their officials to bring the guilty to punishment, praiseworthy as they are, are not to be aided by the sacrifice of those great principles established by years of endeavor and suffering which have resulted in their embodiment in the fundamental law of the land."

. . . [T]he Court in that case clearly stated that use of the seized evidence involved "a denial of the constitutional rights of the accused." Thus, in the year 1914, in the *Weeks* case, this Court "for the first time" held that "in a federal prosecution the Fourth Amendment barred the use of evidence secured through an illegal search and seizure." This Court has ever since required of federal law officers a strict adherence to that command which this Court has held to be a clear, specific, and constitutionally required—even if judicially implied—deterrent safeguard without insistence upon which the Fourth Amendment would have been reduced to "a form of words." Holmes J., *Silverthorne Lumber Co. v. United States*, 251 U.S. 385 (1920). It meant, quite simply, that "conviction by means of unlawful seizures and enforced confessions should find no sanction in the judgments of the courts," and that such evidence "shall not be used at all." . . . .

II

In 1949, 35 years after *Weeks* was announced, this Court, in *Wolf v. Colorado* . . . discussed the effect of the Fourth Amendment upon the States through the operation of the Due Process Clause of the Fourteenth Amendment. . . . [A]fter declaring that the "security of one's privacy against arbitrary intrusion by the police" is "implicit in 'the concept of ordered liberty' and as such enforceable against the States through the Due Process Clause," and announcing that it "stoutly adhere[d]" to the *Weeks* decision, the Court decided that the *Weeks* exclusionary rule would not then be imposed upon the States as "an essential ingredient of the right." The Court's reasons for not considering essential to the right to privacy, as a curb imposed upon the States by the Due Process Clause, that which decades before had been posited as part and parcel of the Fourth Amendment's limitations upon federal encroachment of individual privacy, were bottomed on factual considerations.

While they are not basically relevant to a decision that the exclusionary rule is an essential ingredient of the Fourth Amendment as the right it embodies is vouchsafed against the States by the Due Process Clause, we will consider the current validity of the factual grounds upon which *Wolf* was based.

The Court in *Wolf* ... stated that "[t]he contrariety of views of the States" on the adoption of the exclusionary rule of *Weeks* was "particularly impressive"; and, in this connection that it could not "brush aside the experience of States which deem the incidence of such conduct by the police too slight to call for a deterrent remedy ... by overriding the [States'] relevant rules of evidence." While in 1949, prior to the *Wolf* case, almost two-thirds of the States were opposed to the use of the exclusionary rule, now, despite the *Wolf* case, more than half of those since passing upon it, by their own legislative or judicial decision, have wholly or partly adopted or adhered to the *Weeks* rule....

It, therefore, plainly appears that the factual considerations supporting the failure of the *Wolf* Court to include the *Weeks* exclusionary rule when it recognized the enforceability of the right to privacy against the States in 1949, while not basically relevant to the constitutional consideration, could not, in any analysis, now be deemed controlling.

III

Today we ... examine *Wolf's* constitutional documentation of the right to privacy free from unreasonable state intrusion, and, after its dozen years on our books, are led by it to close the only courtroom door remaining open to evidence secured by official lawlessness in flagrant abuse of that basic right, reserved to all persons as a specific guarantee against that very same unlawful conduct. We hold that all evidence obtained by searches and seizures in violation of the Constitution is, by that same authority, inadmissible in a state court.

IV

Since the Fourth Amendment's right of privacy has been declared enforceable against the States through the Due Process Clause of the Fourteenth, it is enforceable against them by the same sanction of exclusion as is used against the Federal Government.... To hold otherwise is to grant the right but in reality to withhold its privilege and enjoyment. Only last year the Court itself recognized that the purpose of the exclusionary rule "is to deter—to compel respect for the constitutional guaranty in the only effectively available way—by removing the incentive to disregard it." *Elkins v. United States*, 364 U.S. 206 (1960)....

V

Moreover, our holding that the exclusionary rule is an essential part of both the Fourth and Fourteenth Amendments is not only the logical dictate of prior cases, but it also makes very good sense. There is no war between the Constitution and common sense. Presently, a federal prosecutor may make no use of evidence illegally seized, but a State's attorney across the street may, although he supposedly is operating under the enforceable prohibitions of the same Amendment. Thus the State, by admitting evidence unlawfully seized, serves to encourage disobedience to the Federal Constitution which it is bound to uphold. . . .

Federal-state cooperation in the solution of crime under constitutional standards will be promoted, if only by recognition of their now mutual obligation to respect the same fundamental criteria in their approaches. "However much in a particular case insistence upon such rules may appear as a technicality that inures to the benefit of a guilty person, the history of the criminal law proves that tolerance of shortcut methods in law enforcement impairs its enduring effectiveness." Denying shortcuts to only one of two cooperating law enforcement agencies tends naturally to breed legitimate suspicion of "working arrangements" whose results are equally tainted.

There are those who say, as did Justice (then Judge) Cardozo, that under our constitutional exclusionary doctrine "[t]he criminal is to go free because the constable has blundered." In some cases this will undoubtedly be the result. But . . . "there is another consideration—the imperative of judicial integrity." The criminal goes free, if he must, but it is the law that sets him free. Nothing can destroy a government more quickly than its failure to observe its own laws, or worse, its disregard of the charter of its own existence. As Mr. Justice Brandeis, dissenting, said in *Olmstead v. United States*, 277 U.S. 438 (1928): "Our government is the potent, the omnipresent teacher. For good or for ill, it teaches the whole people by its example. . . . If the government becomes a lawbreaker, it breeds contempt for law; it invites every man to become a law unto himself; it invites anarchy." . . .

The ignoble shortcut to conviction left open to the State tends to destroy the entire system of constitutional restraints on which the liberties of the people rest. Having once recognized that the right to privacy embodied in the Fourth Amendment is enforceable against the States, and that the right to be secure against rude invasions of privacy by state officers is, therefore, constitutional in origin, we can no longer permit that right to remain an empty promise. Because it is enforceable in the same manner and to like effect as other basic rights secured by the Due Process Clause, we can no longer permit it to be revocable at the whim of any police officer who, in the name of law enforcement itself, chooses to suspend its enjoyment. Our decision, founded on reason and truth, gives to the individual no more than that which the Constitution guarantees him, to the police officer no less than that to which honest law enforcement is entitled, and, to the courts, that judicial integrity so necessary in the true administration of justice.

■ BLACK, J., concurring. . . . I am still not persuaded that the Fourth Amendment, standing alone, would be enough to bar the introduction into evidence against an accused of papers and effects seized from him in violation of its commands. For the Fourth Amendment does not itself contain any provision expressly precluding the use of such evidence, and I am extremely doubtful that such a provision could properly be inferred from nothing more than the basic command against unreasonable searches and seizures. Reflection on the problem, however, in the light of cases coming before the Court since Wolf, has led me to conclude that when the Fourth Amendment's ban against unreasonable searches and seizures is considered together with the Fifth Amendment's ban against compelled self-incrimination, a constitutional basis emerges which not only justifies but actually requires the exclusionary rule.

The close interrelationship between the Fourth and Fifth Amendments, as they apply to this problem, has long been recognized and, indeed, was expressly made the ground for this Court's holding in *Boyd v. United States*. There the Court fully discussed this relationship and declared itself "unable to perceive that the seizure of a man's private books and papers to be used in evidence against him is substantially different from compelling him to be a witness against himself." It was upon this ground that Mr. Justice Rutledge largely relied in his dissenting opinion in the *Wolf* case. And, although I rejected the argument at that time, its force has, for me at least, become compelling with the more thorough understanding of the problem brought on by recent cases. In the final analysis, it seems to me that the *Boyd* doctrine, though perhaps not required by the express language of the Constitution strictly construed, is amply justified from an historical standpoint, soundly based in reason, and entirely consistent with what I regard to be the proper approach to interpretation of our Bill of Rights—an approach well set out by Mr. Justice Bradley in the *Boyd* case:

> [C]onstitutional provisions for the security of person and property should be liberally construed. A close and literal construction deprives them of half their efficacy, and leads to gradual depreciation of the right, as if it consisted more in sound than in substance. It is the duty of (the) courts to be watchful for the constitutional rights of the citizen, and against any stealthy encroachments thereon.[a]

■ HARLAN, J. (joined by FRANKFURTER and WHITTAKER, JJ.), dissenting. In overruling the Wolf case the Court, in my opinion, has forgotten the sense of judicial restraint which, with due regard for stare decisis, is one element that should enter into deciding whether a past decision of this Court should be overruled. Apart from that I also believe that the Wolf rule represents sounder Constitutional doctrine than the new rule which now replaces it.

I

From the Court's statement of the case one would gather that the central, if not controlling, issue on this appeal is whether illegally state-seized evidence is Constitutionally admissible in a state prosecution, an

---

a.   As the Court points out, Mr. Justice Bradley's approach to interpretation of the Bill of Rights stemmed directly from the spirit in which that great charter of liberty was offered for adoption on the floor of the House of Representatives by its framer, James Madison: "If they [the first ten Amendments] are incorporated into the Constitution, independent tribunals of justice will consider themselves in a peculiar manner the guardians of those rights; they will be an impenetrable bulwark against every assumption of power in the Legislative or Executive; they will be naturally led to resist every encroachment upon rights expressly stipulated for in the Constitution by the declaration of rights." I ANNALS OF CONGRESS 439 (1789).

issue which would of course face us with the need for re-examining *Wolf*. However, such is not the situation. For, although that question was indeed raised here and below among appellant's subordinate points, the new and pivotal issue brought to the Court by this appeal is whether section 2905.34 of the Ohio Revised Code making criminal the mere knowing possession or control of obscene material, and under which appellant has been convicted, is consistent with the rights of free thought and expression assured against state action by the Fourteenth Amendment. That was the principal issue which was decided by the Ohio Supreme Court, which was tendered by appellant's Jurisdictional Statement, and which was briefed and argued in this Court.

In this posture of things, I think it fair to say that five members of this Court have simply "reached out" to overrule *Wolf*. With all respect for the views of the majority, and recognizing that stare decisis carries different weight in Constitutional adjudication than it does in nonconstitutional decision, I can perceive no justification for regarding this case as an appropriate occasion for re-examining *Wolf*. . . .

I am bound to say that what has been done is not likely to promote respect either for the Court's adjudicatory process or for the stability of its decisions. Having been unable, however, to persuade any of the majority to a different procedural course, I now turn to the merits of the present decision.

II

Essential to the majority's argument against *Wolf* is the proposition that the rule of *Weeks v. United States*, excluding in federal criminal trials the use of evidence obtained in violation of the Fourth Amendment, derives not from the "supervisory power" of this Court over the federal judicial system, but from Constitutional requirement. This is so because no one, I suppose, would suggest that this Court possesses any general supervisory power over the state courts. Although I entertain considerable doubt as to the soundness of this foundational proposition of the majority, I shall assume, for present purposes, that the *Weeks* rule "is of constitutional origin."

At the heart of the majority's opinion in this case is the following syllogism: (1) the rule excluding in federal criminal trials evidence which is the product of all illegal search and seizure is a "part and parcel" of the Fourth Amendment; (2) *Wolf* held that the "privacy" assured against federal action by the Fourth Amendment is also protected against state action by the Fourteenth Amendment; and (3) it is therefore "logically and constitutionally necessary" that the *Weeks* exclusionary rule should also be enforced against the States.

This reasoning ultimately rests on the unsound premise that because *Wolf* carried into the States, as part of "the concept of ordered liberty" embodied in the Fourteenth Amendment, the principle of "privacy" under-lying the Fourth Amendment, it must follow that whatever configurations of the Fourth Amendment have been developed in the particularizing federal precedents are likewise to be deemed a part of "ordered liberty," and as such are enforceable against the States. For me, this does not follow at all.

It cannot be too much emphasized that what was recognized in *Wolf* was not that the Fourth Amendment as such is enforceable against the States as a facet of due process, a view of the Fourteenth Amendment which, as *Wolf* itself pointed out, has long since been discredited, but the principle of privacy "which is at the core of the Fourth Amendment." It would not be proper to expect or impose any precise equivalence, either as regards the scope of the right or the means of its implementation, between the requirements of the Fourth and Fourteenth Amendments. For the Fourth, unlike what was said in *Wolf* of the Fourteenth, does not state a general principle only; it is a particular command, having its setting in a pre-existing legal context on which both interpreting decisions and enabling statutes must at least build.

Thus, even in a case which presented simply the question of whether a particular search and seizure was constitutionally "unreasonable"—say in a tort action against state officers—we would not be true to the Fourteenth Amendment were we merely to stretch the general principle of individual privacy on a Procrustean bed of federal precedents under the Fourth Amendment. But in this instance more than that is involved, for here we are reviewing not a determination that what the state police did was Constitutionally permissible (since the state court quite evidently assumed that it was not), but a determination that appellant was properly found guilty of conduct which, for present purposes, it is to be assumed the State could Constitutionally punish. Since there is not the slightest suggestion that Ohio's policy is "affirmatively to sanction ... police incursion into privacy," what the Court is now doing is to impose upon the States not only federal substantive standards of "search and seizure" but also the basic federal remedy for violation of those standards. For I think it entirely clear that the *Weeks* exclusionary rule is but a remedy which, by penalizing past official misconduct, is aimed at deterring such conduct in the future.

I would not impose upon the States this federal exclusionary remedy. The reasons given by the majority for now suddenly turning its back on *Wolf* seem to me notably unconvincing.

First, it is said that "the factual grounds upon which *Wolf* was based" have since changed, in that more States now follow the *Weeks* exclusionary rule than was so at the time *Wolf* was decided. While that is true, a recent survey indicates that at present one-half of the States still adhere to the common-law non-exclusionary rule, and one, Maryland, retains the rule as to felonies. But in any case surely all this is beside the point, as the majority itself indeed seems to recognize. Our concern here, as it was in *Wolf*, is not with the desirability of that rule but only with the question whether the States are Constitutionally free to follow it or not as they may themselves determine, and the relevance of the disparity of views among the States on this point lies simply in the fact that the judgment involved is a debatable one. Moreover, the very fact on which the majority relies, instead of lending support to what is now being done, points away from the need of replacing voluntary state action with federal compulsion.

The preservation of a proper balance between state and federal responsibility in the administration of criminal justice demands patience on the part of those who might like to see things move faster among the States in this respect. Problems of criminal law enforcement vary widely from State to State. One State, in considering the totality of its legal picture, may conclude that the need for embracing the *Weeks* rule is pressing because other remedies are unavailable or inadequate to secure compliance with the substantive Constitutional principle involved. Another, though equally solicitous of Constitutional rights, may choose to pursue one purpose at a time, allowing all evidence relevant to guilt to be brought into a criminal trial, and dealing with Constitutional infractions by other means. Still another may consider the exclusionary rule too rough-and-ready a remedy, in that it reaches only unconstitutional intrusions which eventuate in criminal prosecution of the victims. Further, a State after experimenting with the *Weeks* rule for a time may, because of unsatisfactory experience with it, decide to revert to a non-exclusionary rule. And so on.... For us the question remains, as it has always been, one of state power, not one of passing judgment on the wisdom of one state course or another. In my view this Court should continue to forbear from fettering the States with an adamant rule which may embarrass them in coping with their own peculiar problems in criminal law enforcement....

IV.   THE STEPS IN THE CRIMINAL PROCESS

Understanding criminal procedure cases requires a brief review of the steps in the criminal process, which are presented in rough chronological order below. We say "rough" because the order may vary based upon a number of factors. We will review these steps by following Juan, the defendant from Problem 1–1, from arrest through appeal.

A.   REPORT OF CRIME

For street crimes, the criminal process usually begins with an after-the-fact crime report by a victim or eyewitness or by a police officer who observes a crime in progress. The police then investigate the events observed. In white-collar cases, and some others, the prosecutor may merely suspect that a crime has taken place, and the process begins when the prosecutor brings the matter to the attention of a grand jury. By exercising its subpoena power, the grand jury can hear testimony from witnesses and review documents and physical evidence to determine whether a crime took place. The grand jury may issue an indictment if it finds probable cause to believe that a crime has taken place.

In Juan's case, Officer Osborn merely suspected that a crime had been committed and therefore began an investigation to confirm or allay his suspicions. Consequently, unlike the more usual case, much police officer investigation took place before anyone knew there was a crime.

B. PRE-ARREST INVESTIGATION

Most pre-arrest investigation by the police is quick and inexpert, not because of bad motives but because the police are overwhelmed. For minor crimes, there may be little investigation, because the defendant is either caught in the act or fortuitously falls into police hands. Complex investigation is generally done only in serious cases. Pre-arrest investigation has two purposes: first, to determine whether a crime was committed, and second, if a crime was committed, to determine who did it.

Officer Osborn's initial investigation was done to confirm that there was a crime. He began with a search of Belle' home, a search without a warrant or the consent of the home's residents. His search revealed a pool of blood, suggesting either a serious accident or foul play. He then obtained a warrant, conducting a second search that revealed a dead body whose condition confirmed that there had been a murder. Earlier reports from the citizen-informant, Diaz, had revealed a message from Juan lying about the decedent's whereabouts, followed by the sudden appearance of a note purportedly from the decedent but, according to the citizen-informant, in Juan's handwriting. Juan therefore became the natural suspect and was arrested.

C. ARREST

Arrests may be with or without a warrant, depending upon the circumstances. A warrant, whether for an arrest or a search, must be supported by an affidavit (a document made under oath), establishing probable cause. Upon arrest, a defendant's entire person is searched and any weapons or contraband confiscated. Other, perfectly legal, items may be taken as well, inventoried, and kept for safekeeping. The defendant is also "Mirandized"—given the now-famous warnings of the right to remain silent and to have an attorney before and during questioning—and taken to the station-house for "booking."

D. BOOKING

During "booking," a suspect is fingerprinted, his photo is taken, and background information helpful to later police investigation may be obtained. In some jurisdictions, immediately after booking a suspect is interviewed by persons who serve as assistants to the court in making later bail decisions. During these interviews, defendants are questioned about matters relevant to bail, such as residence, job history, location of family and friends, income, education, and criminal record. Defendants are then preliminarily "arraigned." Preliminary arraignments are also often called "first appearances", or (as is the case in the federal system) "initial appearances."

E. PRELIMINARY ARRAIGNMENT

Before the defendant is preliminarily arraigned, either police superiors or the prosecutor's office will likely have reviewed the decision whether and how to charge the defendant. Prosecutors' offices in large cities often have a charging unit, staffed with assistant district attorneys whose primary job is to review incoming cases and draft complaints. In appropriate cases such as non-violent first offenders, a prosecutor may recommend diversion, a kind of pre-trial probation. A defendant will be told that he must comply with certain conditions, such as successfully completing a drug treatment program over a specified period of time, and stay out of further trouble with the law for that time. If he does so, the charges against him will be dismissed, but, if he fails to do so, the case proceeds to trial. Busy prosecutors facing overcrowded jails and large numbers of violent criminals often have a strong incentive to recommend diversion. Where diversion is recommended, however, the defendant usually still proceeds to preliminary arraignment, where he is also told the conditions of diversion and asked on the record whether he agrees to and understands them. Because Juan is charged with a serious, violent crime, murder, he would not be recommended for diversion at his preliminary arraignment.

At preliminary arraignment, the defendant is informed of the charges against him and receives a copy of the initial charging document, generally called the "complaint." For misdemeanors, the complaint will usually serve as the charging document throughout the proceedings. For felonies, an information (issued after a preliminary hearing) or indictment (issued by a grand jury) will eventually replace the complaint. The information or indictment procedure will be followed in Juan's case because murder is a felony.

At the preliminary arraignment, which is usually quite brief, the defendant is normally informed that throughout the criminal process he will enjoy certain important rights, such as the right to counsel. If the defendant is indigent, either a public defender or private appointed counsel will be assigned to represent him. For a misdemeanor, a trial date or status date will also be set. For a felony, a preliminary hearing date will be scheduled. Finally, bail will be set, including any conditions for release on bail or preventive detention. Preventive detention protects the public, while bail ensures that the defendant will appear at trial. In Juan's case, high bail is likely, given the high penalties for murder and thus the strong incentive to flee, although Juan's community ties, criminal record, and other factors will also be considered. Many felony defendants in urban areas are indigent, so the setting of bail (which they cannot pay) accomplishes de facto preventive detention.

F. CONTINUING INVESTIGATION

Post-arrest investigation may happen at any stage of the proceedings but is most likely after preliminary arraignment. The full range of investigative techniques—lineups, photospreads, witness interviews, DNA and other laboratory analysis, subpoenas, searches and seizures—may be relied upon. Note that some investigation will likely take place only after arrest, such as placing the defendant in a lineup, questioning him, or taking hair or blood samples. Direct contact with the defendant after arraignment and at any "critical stage" (a term to be defined later) is more difficult, however, because the Sixth Amendment right to counsel will have attached by then. What post-arrest investigation would be helpful in Juan's case?

G. PRELIMINARY HEARING

There are two predominant models for criminal prosecution in the United States. Under the federal model, a defendant's charges usually are contained in an indictment, which has been approved by a grand jury upon a finding of probable cause. Under the other model, prevailing in many states, the defendant attends a preliminary hearing (sometimes called a "preliminary examination") held before a judge, and the charges are then embodied in an information, which is filed by the prosecutor. State courts use numerous variations on these two models. States are free to vary from the federal model because the Court has held that the Fourteenth Amendment does not incorporate against the states the Fifth Amendment requirement of a grand jury indictment in felony cases.

The preliminary hearing may sometimes be waived where a defendant plans to plead guilty. Also, there is no preliminary hearing if a defendant is first indicted. Where a hearing is held, the judge must decide whether there is probable cause to "bind the case over for trial" or whether the case should be dismissed due to insufficient evidence. Evidentiary rules vary widely among jurisdictions, but many require at least some live witnesses, although hearsay rules as to documents are often relaxed.

Although the sole purpose of a preliminary hearing is to determine whether probable cause has been established, many defense lawyers see their role as asking relatively wide-ranging questions, viewing the hearing as an opportunity for discovery. Most judges will permit some such inquiry, but, at some point, they will rein in defense counsel, reminding her that the hearing's purpose is probable cause determination, not discovery.

If you are the prosecutor at Juan's preliminary hearing, whom would you call to the stand, what questions would you ask, and why? If you are defense counsel at Juan's preliminary hearing, what questions will you ask each likely witness, and why? Is it ethical for you to treat the hearing as a discovery opportunity? For you not to do so? How far do you think you could go before the judge would rein you in?

H. GRAND JURY REVIEW

The states vary widely in their use of grand juries. In some states, grand jury review and indictment are required for felonies. In others, the prosecutor may proceed either by information or grand jury indictment. Some states require grand jury indictment only in the most serious cases. The federal system requires indictment for all felonies, unless waived by the defendant. If a preliminary hearing has been held, the grand jury is not bound by the decision of the hearing judge in deciding whether to indict.

Where a prosecutor has the option, she may prefer the greater speed, efficiency, and routine of a preliminary hearing followed by an information. However, where the prosecutor needs further evidence, she may prefer to initiate grand jury proceedings so that she can subpoena witnesses and documents or objects (via a subpoena duces tecum). Moreover, grand jury proceedings are conducted ex parte, so the prosecutor can investigate the case without revealing too much to the defendant. Not even the judge is present when the prosecutor presents a case to the grand jury. Some argue that the secretive nature of grand jury proceedings gives prosecutors inordinate power over them and renders them a mere rubber stamp. This is not always true, as the "Rocky Flats" case demonstrated. In that case, a grand jury investigated alleged violations of environmental laws. When the prosecution told the grand jury that it would not be asked to return an indictment because of a plea bargain, the grand jury held a press conference to protest what it perceived to be overly-lenient treatment of the defendants.

Would Juan's prosecutor prefer a preliminary hearing or a grand jury hearing? Why? How would defense counsel prepare herself and her client for testifying before the grand jury?

I.   FILING THE INFORMATION OR INDICTMENT

If a defendant is bound over after a preliminary hearing, an information (which replaces the complaint) is filed against him. If a grand jury has reviewed the case, the indictment becomes the charging document. The prosecutor drafts both the information and indictment. The information must conform to the hearing judge's ruling; the indictment must be signed by the grand jury foreperson as well as the prosecutor.

A sample information and a sample indictment appear later in this chapter. In a complex case, an indictment may be much lengthier than the one in the sample. In a simple case, an indictment may only be a page or two long.

J.   ARRAIGNMENT ON THE INFORMATION OR INDICTMENT

Before trial and after the final charging documents have been filed, the defendant is again arraigned. At this time, he is told what charges he will face at trial and is asked to enter a plea. Many, in fact most, cases are disposed of by guilty plea, either at this stage or a later stage.

K.   PRETRIAL MOTIONS

Hearings on pretrial motions will then be held, often immediately before trial. Such motions are held before trial because the Double Jeopardy Clause prevents the prosecutor from appealing what she believes to be an erroneous ruling unless the ruling is made before jeopardy attaches.

Jeopardy attaches when the trial jury has been empaneled and sworn, or, in a bench trial, after the first witness has been sworn. Pretrial motions might include motions to dismiss for lack of speedy trial, motions to compel discovery, or motions to suppress evidence. Most suppression motions require the taking of testimony, often of police officers who did the arrest, search, or seizure; took the confession; or conducted the lineup or photo-spread.

As the prosecutor in the Juan case, what witnesses would you call to the stand on each of the suppression motions you identified earlier? What questions would you ask? What questions would you expect the defense to ask on cross-examination, and why?

L. TRIAL

The steps at trial are discussed in detail in evidence and trial practice courses. For your purposes, you need simply to remember that all your planning must be geared toward discovery and trial. Even if the defendant pleads guilty, his likelihood of doing so turns on his expected outcome at trial. That outcome is often in turn strongly affected by the result of suppression motions. If key evidence is suppressed, a defendant's chances of prevailing at trial will rise dramatically, thus reducing the likelihood of a guilty plea.

If the defendant is convicted, whether after a plea or a trial, post-trial motions to set aside the verdict or for a new trial will be heard. Motions for a new trial can be based on improperly admitted evidence or other errors at trial. The defendant may also move to "arrest judgment"—in other words, to set aside the verdict because no reasonable jury could have found the elements of the crime beyond a reasonable doubt on the evidence present-ed. If those motions are denied, the case moves to sentencing.

M. SENTENCING

In many jurisdictions, sentencing guidelines based on prior record and offense severity scores limit trial judge discretion. For example, a prior record score (perhaps for a prior unarmed robbery) and an offense severity score (perhaps for an armed robbery) would intersect on a grid, requiring a sentence of between 60 and 80 months. Various factors can, however, alter these scores. An offense severity score might be lowered if a relatively minor offender helped the police capture the criminal mastermind. There may be a dispute over what the proper score should be so that testimony or other fact-finding is required. Similarly, fact-finding might be necessary to determine the defendant's sentence in the narrow band of discretion afforded the judge. Judges are also free to depart from the guidelines where there are unusual circumstances not contemplated or adequately consid-ered by the state commissions that drafted the guidelines.

In states without guidelines, the judge has wide discretion within statutory limits to choose a sentence that best serves the goals of the criminal law: deterrence, rehabilitation, retribution, isolation, and education. Again, testimony will often be needed, for example, to show that a defendant has enrolled in a drug treatment program, is completing his G.E.D., or is receiving psychological counseling.

In all states, there will usually be court psychologist and probation officer reports as well, and, in guidelines states, a report tentatively computing proposed sentencing scores.

A criminal practitioner must be familiar with guidelines, sentencing case law, and the relevant psychological and probation officer reports. The practitioner must also investigate and consider calling witnesses relevant to the purposes of sentencing, and before sentencing help to arrange counseling, drug treatment, and other programs that will improve the client's position before the court. Moreover, the likely result at sentencing must be kept in mind throughout the proceedings in counseling the client on whether to plead guilty, so investigation into matters relevant to sentencing should start early, simultaneously with pre-trial and trial preparation.

A defendant, after sentence, usually must file post-sentencing motions to modify the sentence, or he will lose the right to challenge the sentence on appeal.

N.   APPEALS

If post-sentencing motions are denied, a notice of appeal must be filed within a specified time limit, usually 30 days. Untimely notice forfeits the right to appeal.

O.   POSTCONVICTION REMEDIES

Many states have Postconviction Hearing Acts, specifying grounds that may be raised to challenge a conviction even after exhausting state appeals. One common ground (though not usually a successful one, as a later chapter explains) is the ineffectiveness of prior counsel that prevented the defendant from earlier raising an important issue. A hearing might be held on the ineffectiveness claim and the defendant can appeal an adverse finding. Exhaustion of state remedies, where available, is often a prerequisite to seeking habeas corpus relief in the federal courts for ineffective assistance of counsel or other constitutional claims.

V.   CRIMINAL PROCEDURE AND THE PROBLEM OF WRONGFUL CONVICTIONS

The rights you will learn about in this text have far-reaching implications to the successful functioning of the criminal justice system. The article[33] below explores some of these implications.

---

33.   .Andrew E. Taslitz, *Wrongful Rights*, 18 CRIM. JUS. 1 (2003).

Wrongful Rights

Andrew E. Taslitz.

Americans' confidence in the fairness of their criminal justice system has lately suffered some serious blows. The popular media once fed the public primarily on images of brutal criminals freed by soft-on-crime judges. But competing images of men convicted of crimes they did not commit also now fill television shows, novels, and news magazines. . . . National news magazines, such as Time and Newsweek, recently ran extensive stories about the causes of wrongful convictions, stories prompted by new evidence calling into question the reliability of the convictions of several young men—some of whom spent more than a decade in prison— for the brutal rape of a woman in New York City in the infamous "Central Park Jogger" case. . . .

I am a former prosecutor, and, as I am sure is true of most prosecutors, not once did I help to convict someone whose guilt I doubted. I was, therefore, initially skeptical about the media's coverage of the wrongful convictions issue. I still believe that the vast majority of those convicted because of my efforts were guilty as charged. But the accumulating evidence examined by the media suggests that my confidence in my near-infallibility was misplaced. There is a significant chance that at least a few of those suspects whom I prosecuted were entirely innocent. Furthermore, if they were innocent, then some guilty, occasionally violent, offenders remained unpunished and free to prey upon the community. I have found these plausible observations deeply disturbing. Therefore, I have begun to join the many other practicing lawyers, academics, victims' advocates, and social scientists who are energetically seeking ways to further improve our criminal justice system's accuracy. . . .

. . . If death penalty litigation is what has brought this issue onto the national radar screen, the results of inquiries into the causes of capital case error suggest that similar causes are likely at work in noncapital cases, at least for serious crimes for which the police face intense political pressure for a resolution. The causes of error are many but can roughly be divided, from perusing the many commentaries on the question, into three broad groups: intentional police officer or laboratory fraud, sloppy investigations, and systemic causes at work even when all parties are both honest and careful. Intentional frame-ups are in some ways the least interesting, and I will have little to say about them. Intentional wrongdoing certainly requires greater watchfulness, greater certainty of capture and punishment, and better ethical training of both officers and lab technicians. But if fraud and perjury were the only problems at work, mistakes could be seen as isolated wrongs done by a few bad apples. What research is available suggests that the causes of error are more widespread and arise even in the daily struggle of the many honest people involved in the criminal justice process. . . .

Even careful, concerned police and prosecutors can . . . unknowingly contribute to error. New empirical evidence is accumulating that suggests that tried-and-true methods for police lineup administration raise an unacceptable risk of misidentification; that standard police interrogation methods can lead the innocent to confess; and that long-accepted "scientific" forensic methods for identifying the guilty—such as by fingerprint identification or handwriting analysis—are seriously flawed. Moreover, a mistake at one point of an investigation can compound errors at later points. For example, an officer inadvertently obtaining a false confession may convey subconscious minimal clues to witnesses that lead them wrongly to identify the confessor as the evildoer. Well-trained, hardworking, but misguided police, forensic technicians, and prosecutors can do just as much damage as their colleagues who are fraudulent or incompetent.

The size of the problem of convicting the innocent is hard to estimate and is subject to great debate. But in a system as large as ours, even a very small error rate can mean the conviction of many thousands of innocent persons each year. . . . The problems are significant and call for serious and sustained efforts to do better. . . .

Why, however, have we reached this stage? Why have these sources of error been ignored for so long? These questions are puzzling because our Constitution's Bill of Rights is replete with procedural protections meant in part to avoid just these sorts of mistakes. Thus the Constitution, as interpreted by the courts, guarantees rights to the effective assistance of counsel, to freedom from coerced or compelled incrimination, to the opportunity for effective cross-examination and to produce witnesses in your favor, and to the potentially sweeping guarantee of due process, that is, of fundamental fairness in criminal trials. These rights are widely understood as partly serving to reveal police and prosecutorial fraud and negligence, to promote judicial reliance on trustworthy evidence, and to keep fact-finders fully informed of the risks of error. Yet these rights have failed to achieve these lofty goals in too many cases. Why?

The answer, I will suggest, though I do not claim to prove, is that American criminal procedural rights in action inevitably promote wrongs. What I mean by "rights in action" is the way in which rights are often practiced and understood by our courts, our police, and our prosecutors. This conception of rights is only occasionally made express and is not consistently followed by criminal justice system participants. But this conception is sufficiently widespread to spell trouble. These wrongful rights, I suggest here, have at least four characteristics that, when combined, too often lead courts to undervalue truth as a primary goal of the criminal justice system.

Obsession with "wrongful" police action

Truth discovery—who did what to whom with what state of mind—is not the only goal of a criminal trial. For example, the Fourth Amendment exclusionary rule deprives jurors of truthful, probative evidence of a suspect's guilt when the evidence is wrongly seized. That exclusion is meant to deter further unreasonable search and seizures by the police. Some commentators decry precisely this state of affairs, bemoaning the exclusionary rule's undermining of the trial's truth-discovery function. Yet these same commentators raise little, if any, objection to legal doctrines that undermine the truth-quest in a way that works against the plausibly innocent suspect. These doctrines can operate subtly and in contradiction to the United States Supreme Court's purported paens to embracing truth-discovery as essential to a fair criminal trial.

One source of the under-valuing of truth when factual innocence is in question is those doctrines that exclude untrustworthy evidence only if its unreliability stems from police action. But evidence can be unreliable even when it is created independently of police coercion or carelessness.

Thus, the High Court rejected the defendant's argument in *Colorado v. Connelly*, that due process required exclusion of his confession because it was compelled by "command hallucinations" and the "voice of God." Connelly, a chronic schizophrenic, had approached the police, saying he wanted to confess to a murder. The officer promptly Mirandized Connelly, who waived his rights, then confessed to a detective. The detective did not then suspect that Connelly was mentally ill. State courts, relying on psychiatric testimony offered by Connelly about his mental condition, found his confession to be involuntary and therefore suppressed it.

The Supreme Court reversed, relying on the absence of police exploitation of a known suspect vulnerability and police reticence to use any coercive interrogation techniques. The Court explained that Connelly's statement:

> might be proved to be quite unreliable, but this is a matter to be governed by the evidentiary laws of the forum, and not by the Due Process Clause of the Fourteenth Amendment. "The aim of the requirement of due process is not to exclude presumptively unreliable evidence, but to prevent fundamental unfairness in the use of evidence, whether true or false." . . .

. . . [T]he Court is thoroughly unconcerned with evidence's "presumptively unreliable" nature, a presumption fairly at work where a confession stems from hallucinations and longstanding mental illness. The *Connelly* result may seem to be dictated by the Fourteenth Amendment's state action requirement, but that appearance is false. The Court could easily treat the trial judge's act of admitting an unreliable confession into evidence as ample state action, a conclusion consistent with some of the Court's precedent outside the criminal procedure context.

Even where flawed evidence is indeed the product of state action, the courts still implicitly insist that such action must in some sense be "wrongful," or the evidence will not be suppressed despite its untrustworthiness.

Perhaps the most salient example of this wrongfulness requirement is the Court's doctrine concerning the due process regulation of lineups. An out-of-court identification will be suppressed as fundamentally unfair if, and only if, the process was so unnecessarily suggestive as to create a very substantial likelihood of misidentification. That means that untrustworthy lineup or photo identifications may be admitted despite the risks of error if the suggestive procedure was "necessary." Yet, by "necessary," the Court means something like "urgent" or even "helpful in minimizing expense and time-consumption" rather than meaning "unavoidable."

The state's need for swift action to protect the public from imminent danger should sensibly be recognized as often overriding competing concerns in any sound system of justice. But when the need is less pressing, and when the sort of police action involved raises a risk of convicting the innocent, too flexible notions of "necessity," such as the police's needing to confirm that they are "on the right track," can be dangerous, especially given recent empirical data showing the unreliability of eyewitness identifications and the significant distorting effects of even the smallest of flaws in an identification procedure.

Diminished concern for pretrial accuracy

The Court also undervalues truth when it limits its most enthusiastic search for accuracy to procedures used at trial. The Court has, of course, recognized that flawed pretrial procedures, such as unnecessarily suggestive lineups, can infect later identifications made by the witness at trial. Nevertheless, the Court often pays too little attention to the adequacy of the pretrial fact-finding processes used to determine whether, for example, a lineup was too suggestive or a confession coerced in the first place.

Hearings to suppress confessions inevitably involve credibility disputes between the suspect and the police, yet judges invariably believe the police, even though empirical data offers strong evidence that these credibility determinations are often wrong. Moreover, even where there is no credibility conflict, it is hard to re-create in a courtroom subtleties in the interrogator's conduct ... or in the suspect's reaction ... Requiring the videotaping of all interrogations, subject to only a few exceptions in cases of extreme need, would help to improve suppression judges' abilities to make accurate credibility assessments and correct determinations of the coercive impact of interrogations. However, all interrogation efforts in a case must be taped, not merely the ultimate confession, as the *New York Times* recently [January 20, 2003] explained:

> By the time five teenage suspects gave the videotaped confessions that helped convict them in the 1989 rape of the Central Park jogger, they had been through hours of unrecorded interrogation.... [T]he exoneration of the young men begs for reforming the way suspects are led to rehearsed statements of guilt.

> According to the Innocence Project at the Cardozo School of Law at Yeshiva University, 23 percent of the people who are exonerated after conviction turn out to have falsely confessed to the crime. Many of these confessions were taped and played as compelling evidence to a jury. As the jogger case and other reversals demonstrate, innocent people can be led into confessions. Their questioners—wittingly or not—also often provide them with details that would seem to be known only to the real criminal.

Errors in the suppression hearing can, the Times continued, not merely ruin innocent suspects' lives but endanger the public's safety:

> Beyond the injustice of punishing the wrong people, false admissions of guilt allow the real culprits to remain free to commit more crimes; as did Matias Reyes, who raped four other women, killing one of them, after he attacked the jogger in Central Park....

> [T]here is no real excuse for not acting. By videotaping every minute of interrogations, the police would help protect themselves against charges of coercion, improve the integrity of confessions, and plug a gaping hole in the system.

Similar laxity about the quality of suppression hearing fact-finding processes plagues other aspects of the system as well. Most notably, much criticism has been directed at police and prosecutorial reliance on informants. The problems with informants can be many: They can literally be manufactured by the police, who tell them what to say; they can testify falsely because of some undisclosed but real or simply hoped-for benefit from the prosecution; or they can be mentally deranged. Informants' testimony may lead police and prosecutors to ignore other leads or to play down or ignore contradictory evidence. Triers of fact tend to believe in informants, whose stories are difficult to undermine unless they recant. Proving lies by informants or their police handlers, or the more frequent incompetence of such handlers in inadvertently molding informant testimony, is centrally important if pretrial screening devices for such testimony. Commentators have suggested a wide range of solutions, including a duty imposed on police and prosecutors to investigate informant background and to disclose the results to the defense. Such disclosure would extend to the informant's criminal record, prior testimony as an informant, handler interview notes about the informant, how he or she came to the handler's attention, and whether he or she received any monetary benefits or express or implied promises of leniency. Other analysts have recommended videotaping informant conversations with the police, or rejected any use of informants absent significant corroboration of their stories. Still other thinkers would go beyond improving pretrial fact-finding processes to reducing the incentives for informant or police officer lies or sloppiness, such as by eliminating all rewards for informants' tips and treating informants as government agents. Further protections of fact-finding accuracy at trial as a backup for the possible failure of pretrial screening mechanisms have also been recommended, for example, cautionary jury instructions and expert testimony concerning the causes of informant unreliability.

Minimizing systemic thinking

The Court further undervalues truth by too often adopting an atomistic rather than a systemic constitutional analysis. By this I mean that the Court tends to explore evidentiary reliability questions on a case-by-case basis, treating each case as unique and in isolation from arguably similar cases. The Court's frequent preference for multi-factor balancing tests also expands trial judges' discretion to treat facially similar cases as if they are different. The result is a failure to see patterns that systematically operate to raise the average risk of mistaken convictions.

Confessions once again offer a fruitful example. Empirical research demonstrates that the risk of false confessions is significantly heightened in five circumstances. Professor Welsh White has therefore recommended five *per se* or nearly *per se* rules: (1) be reluctant to admit confessions by the mentally handicapped, even where the police were unaware of the suspect's vulnerability; (2) automatically deem involuntary any confession resulting from more than six hours of questioning; (3) automatically exclude any confession where the interrogator should be aware that either the suspect or a reasonable person in the suspect's position would perceive the officer's statement as expressing the likelihood that the suspect will receive leniency or avoid adverse consequences if only he or she will confess; (4) prohibit confessions stemming from threats of adverse consequences to a friend or loved one; and (5) flatly bar tactics likely to suggest to the suspect that the evidence against him or her is so overwhelming that continued resistance would be futile. Under White's approach, the risk of mistaken acquittals might rise, for a confession obtained after seven (rather than six) hours of interrogation or from a mentally ill suspect or one bribed or threatened might nevertheless be true in an individual case. But the risk of mistaken convictions based upon false confessions, that is, the average error rate for guilty verdicts generated by the entire justice system based upon current systemic practices, should fall significantly.

Miranda v. Arizona, of course, did take a systemic view of confessions and use per se rules—required warnings and a right to counsel during interrogation—to control police tactics. As Professor White has explained, however, *Miranda* was designed more to prevent even subtle compulsion to confess, undermining human dignity, than to protect against the risk of false convictions. In any event, argue many commentators, *Miranda* has become a mere piece of "stationhouse furniture," a rote set of warnings that police have learned to circumvent or to present to suspects in a fashion that minimizes their impact. Furthermore, *Miranda* has been watered down by later precedent. Even more importantly, once suspects are warned and their *Miranda* rights waived, *Miranda* says nothing about how police must conduct suspect interrogations. That "how" question is governed by due process, and due process in this area, as in many others, remains an individualized assessment based upon vague and flexible multi-factor balancing tests.

The Court also fails to think systemically when it bases its decisions upon assumed (rather than proven) systemic realities that are, in fact, false. Much as early twentieth-century economists assumed a world of perfect competition, zero transaction costs, and perfect information that made markets efficient and recessions impossible, so does the Court assume that the battle of equals in the adversary system will yield perfect justice. Yet neither the Court's rulings nor political realities have created the sort of equal playing field that the adversary system assumes. . . .

. . . Energetic efforts to right this state-individual power imbalance are afoot in some quarters, but only a judiciary more actively involved in acknowledging and correcting the flawed assumption of equality underlying the adversary system can improve justice in the short term and help to foster the political will for long-term reform.

Treating social science as window dressing

Finally, the Court undervalues truth by its inadequate use of social science. Many decisions in the area of constitutional criminal procedure turn in part on empirical judgments about the nature of the real world. The constitutional rule ultimately to be crafted by the Court turns, however, on normative judgments. . . . But that normative judgment merits respect only if it is fully informed by the best data available, enabling a thoughtful balancing of interests and the articulation of a persuasive rationale for the doctrinal rule chosen. For example, a rule of law that freely permitted showups rather than lineups as means of eyewitness identification would, the social science arguably suggests, dramatically raise the chances of innocents being convicted. The Court might decide that, despite this social science, the needs of law enforcement are more important than the risk of error. But examining the empirical data requires the Court either to explain why those needs prevail or to alter its rule to reduce the chances of mistakes.

The Court does, indeed, occasionally use social science well, but more often it ignores it, examines only one-sided views of the data, or outright misinterprets it to support a decision reached on other grounds. . . .

Several examples of how more careful use of social science could have altered doctrine for the better have been touched upon in this essay. Thus *per se* rules flatly excluding confessions obtained by risky methods seem well supported by the empirical data. . . . Perhaps among the Court's most glaring faults has been its insufficient attention to how subconscious mental processes affect witness perceptions and fact-finder decision making, especially in the area of race. Recent studies emphasize the heightened dangers of error in cross-racial eyewitness identifications, the effect of racial bias in jury deliberations, prosecutors' occasional use of covert racial appeals in closing arguments, and the pervasive effects on jury assessments of credibility of subconscious racial stereotyping of black men as dangerous, less intelligent, less hardworking, and less polite than whites. Real and perceived racial basis in the criminal justice system breeds minority group distrust of the police, reducing their willingness to cooperate in police investigations. That decreased willingness may, in turn, however, reduce the quality and quantity of information available to the police, foreclosing alternative investigatory options that might have revealed a suspect's innocence, thus amplifying the chance of being prosecuted mistakenly.

All the blame cannot, of course, be placed on the courts. Other institutions—such as legislatures, the executive, and an aroused citizenry—may jointly have better access to social science data, to the political resources needed for real change, and to the speed of action needed to cope with rapidly changing social conditions and scientific insights. Indeed, the other branches of government and the citizenry also have constitutional obligations to deliberate and to act to make the criminal justice system function well. Yet where these branches fail, the judiciary's burden to act is especially powerful. At the least, it should create incentives—such as exclusion of shoddy evidence—to promote right conduct by other criminal justice actors.... Some police departments have voluntarily adopted sounder procedures, but others have done so only as a result of the specter of lawsuits. The courts need to do better to ensure that all criminal justice system participants act to maximize the likelihood that the guilty are punished and the innocent set free.

Taking stock

The Court, and the judiciary more generally, do not consistently operate in the ways that I have outlined here. That inconsistency, however, is precisely what offers the practicing lawyer the opportunity to challenge truth-defeating judicial practices. The advocate can point out to a court the instances where judicial decisions have appropriately given truth primacy over solely regulating state misconduct, created sound pretrial fact-finding processes, taken a systemic view of the sources of error, been attentive to power imbalances, or carefully used relevant social science. Next, the advocate can provide courts with the data and policy arguments for achieving consistency by bringing bad precedent into line with the good. No court, for example, consciously or openly commits itself to using bad social science or to ignoring it completely. A court educated by an informed advocate about the empirical data on why the innocent sometimes confess, why witnesses are often wrong, and how informants can mislead police handlers has ample freedom to consider that data in crafting and applying rules embraced by the idea of "due process of law." ...

Implications for state legal practice and law reform

... I [am not] suggesting that the High Court has acted in bad faith. Rather, the Court has crafted a jurisprudence from some assumptions—assumptions that I myself once saw as "self-evident"—that have simply turned out to be wrong. The first assumption was that the sheer number of procedural protections for the accused in the due process clauses and in the Bill of Rights—including especially the rights to a jury trial and to proof beyond a reasonable doubt—offer ample protection against error. ... The second assumption was that law enforcement and prosecutors always act in good faith and that good faith is enough to ensure accurate results. ... The third assumption was that hard decisions turn on credibility, and credibility judgments cannot be verified as true or false in some objective sense, so courts need to protect jury verdict finality as the very definition of "truth."

... [E]ach of these assumptions were mistaken. Constitutional guarantees as currently understood have not been adequate to avoid a significant number of mistaken convictions. The vast majority of criminal justice system actors *do* act in good faith, but the numbers that do not are more than minimal. More importantly, absent better procedures, police and prosecutor good faith have not proven up to the task of adequately minimizing error. Finally, DNA and other technological developments have created an objective benchmark that sometimes enables us to label a jury verdict as accurate or not. In short, there is now ample empirical data to justify the High Court's revisiting its constitutional criminal procedure jurisprudence. Until that happens, however, most advocates must look elsewhere for relief.

... Many readers ... may come away with the impression that the system is in frightening disrepair. That, at least, is not my position. Large numbers of guilty offenders are convicted every day after the energetic, professional efforts of honest police officers, careful prosecutors, zealous defense lawyers, and admirable judges. The mounting evidence that there are nevertheless a significant number of mistakes made requires all persons of good will to take action, not only to acquit the innocent, but to protect public safety (by convicting the guilty) and safeguard the public trust in the system, a trust that is essential to the health of America's democracy.

QUESTIONS

1. Are procedures that promote the truth at trial more important when they lead to conviction of the guilty or to acquittal of the innocent? Are there values that compete with the truth? Are these various goals inconsistent with the truth and/or with each other?

2. When does the exclusionary rule promote truth and when does it undermine truth? Consider its application to (a) wrongfully seized evidence, (b) coerced confessions, and (c) uncounseled or suggestive lineups.

3. Why should promotion of the truth be a concern of constitutional law rather than state evidentiary law?

4. Assume evidence is obtained as the result of a search and seizure. Whether that evidence was rightly seized may turn on whether there was probable cause to conduct the search or seizure. But witnesses tell different stories about the facts—some stories establishing probable cause, others not. So the factfinder must decide whom to believe. Also, even when witnesses are truthful, the adequacy of the bases of their information affects whether probable cause exists. If probable cause does not exist, truthful evidence may be suppressed at trial. But if probable cause does exist, then truthful evidence will not be suppressed at trial. It is therefore critical that we accurately determine the "truth" of the facts that do or do not establish probable cause. What sorts of factors and procedures would help to promote accurate truth-determination at a pretrial suppression hearing concerning whether or not there was probable cause?

5. Review the Boson case file below. What facts, if any, raise concerns about the accuracy and reliability of the evidence that might be offered at trial? About the truth or falsity of the evidence establishing probable cause or exigent circumstances? In answering these questions, make sure that you consider lineups, photospreads, confessions, any physical evidence seized, and any evidence observed during the course of the search.

6.   Does appellate court deference to trial court factfinding promote accurate truth-determination?

7.   The United States Constitution sets substantive constitutional standards such as requiring that searches and seizures be justified by probable cause. Why should we not defer, however, to state court choices of procedures for determining the existence of probable cause for crimes within the jurisdiction of a particular state?

PROBLEM 1–3

On the following pages are excerpts from two case files that will be the basis for many of the problems to come. Those files are State v. Daniel Boson, a murder case, and United States v. Arthur Brunell, a white-collar crime case involving tax evasion.[34] Please review those files now. In reviewing them, ask yourself these questions:

1.   What suppression motions will you file and on what grounds? What witnesses will the prosecutor call on those motions, and what questions will he ask those witnesses, and why? What questions will you as defense counsel ask on cross-examination, and why?

2.   What investigation will the prosecution and the defense conduct? What methods will be used and what persons will be involved?

VI.   CASE FILES

In the following pages you will find two case files: a street crime file and a white collar crime file. These will provide helpful information about the documents that accompany a case, as well as serve as foundational material for some of the problems in later chapters.

---

34.   These two cases are based on an amalgam of the facts of several reported cases and of cases that we handled personally in our respective practices.

Street Crime File

State v. Boson

County of Exum
CULDEVA

☐ Juvenile Arrest

OFFENSE/INCIDENT REPORT

POLICE DEPARTMENT				☒ Original ☐ Supplement	Case No. 427328	

Offense/Incident Homicide	No. 1	UCR Code	Date Occurred 4/11/0_	Time Occurred Approx. 04:00

Date/Time Reported 4/11/0_ 04:00	Location of Offense/Incident 2003 West Ox Road	Apt. No. 11G	Domestic ☒ Yes ☐ No	Property No.

Name	I-Code	Address		Apt. No.
City	State	Zip	Home Phone	DOB	Age
SSN (Optional)	Sex	Race	Ethnic	Occupation	Place of Work	Work Phone

Name	I-Code			Apt. No.
City	State	Zip	Home Phone	DOB	Age
SSN (Optional)	Sex	Race	Ethnic	Occupation	Place of Work	Work Phone

Veh ☐ Victim ☐ Stolen ☐ Accident ☐ Suspect ☐ Recov'd ☐ Impound	V Yr	Make	Model	Style	Color(s)
Lic. No.	Lic. Type	State	Lic Yr	Vin	Value	Recvd Code ☐1 ☐2 ☐3
Additional Description		Mo Code	NIC	VIC	

Veh ☐ Victim ☐ Stolen ☐ Accident ☐ Suspect ☐ Recov'd ☐ Impound	V Yr	Make	Model	Style	Color(s)
Lic. No.	Lic. Type	State	Lic Yr	Vin	Value	Recvd Code ☐1 ☐2 ☐3
Additional Description		Mo Code	NIC	VIC	

Item ☐ Add ☐ Delete ☐ Stolen ☐ Change ☐ Recv'd	Type of Item	Brand Name	Model	Desc Code
Serial No.	Owner Applied No.	Additional Description	Value	I Code

Susp #	Suspect Name	Address (Street, City, State, Zip)	Home Phone
DOB	SSN	Age	Sex	Race	Ethnic	Hair	Eyes	Hgt	Wgt	Clothing

Narrative

Arrived at 2003 West Ox Road, Apt. 11G, approx. 05:15, 4/11/0_.

Scene had been secured by Off. Centile, and I consulted forensics. At 07:00, I interviewed victim, Susan Oldham's parents, John and Mary Oldham.

Other Agency Notified (Who)	IMU Notified (Date/Time/Who) ☐ Stolen Vehicle/Recovery		ID Requested ☐ Yes ☐ No
Officer Det. Mandelevoy	Ser. No. 0825	Div. 2d	Follow-Up By	Status... ☐ Open ☐ Pending ☐ Terminated ☐ Unchanged	☐ Arrest ☐ Unfounded ☐ Exceptional ☐ Referral	Dist 2 / Rev 2 / Page 1 of 3
Ref. Case No. 427328-1	Damage Amt.	Supv. Approval				

F-EPD-0007-ASW (6/96)

County of Exum
CULDEVA

SUPPLEMENT

POLICE DEPARTMENT		☐ Original ☒ Supplement	Case No.
Original Offense	Original Complainant's Name		Date This Rpt.

Narrative

They said Susan had just recently broken up, at their request, with a 28

year old male named "Ace." The parents throught "Ace" spoke "roughly" and

looked "like he was on drugs." Susan came home crying the night she broke

up with Ace and said Ace had threatened her, saying something like, "If

you're not my girl, you're no one's. I'll fix it that way." Those

threats were made about two days ago.

 The next day (4/12/0_), I received an anonymous phone phone tip.

Informant said he'd heard a guy named "Ace" did the killing and heard a

neighbor say "Goodbye, Ace" to one Daniel Boson, whom informant knew since

high school. Boson lives at 263 S. 20th St., Apt. 15E. Informant said he

was at a party last week where Boson bragged about a girlfriend named

Susan and threatened to kill her if she ever left him. Boson then showed

informant a hunting knife, which Boson wore in a scabbard about his waist.

Informant remembered the knife because it was unusual, having a picture of

a zebra overfaced with a skull and crossbones on the handle. Also the

knife had a 3-sided blade, about 6" long, 3" wide at the base. Informant

asked Boson what knife was for, and Boson said, "For people who get out of

line" and laughed. Informant then said, "Check him out. The son-of-a-

bitch needs checking. If I could, I'd do it myself."

 Record check showed Boson with prior gunpoint robbery arrest, charge

dropped when victim FTA. Showed 8 photo spread to E/W (Abernathy), who

Corrected Offense			Corrected Compl Name		Status... ☐ Open ☐ Pending ☐ Terminated ☐ Unchanged	☐ Arrest ☐ Unfounded ☐ Exceptional ☐ Referral	Dist 2	Rev 2
Officer Det. Mandelevoy	Ser. No. 0825	Div. 2d	Supv. Approval				Page 2 of 3	

F-EPD-1271-ASW (8/96)

County of Exum
CULDEVA

SUPPLEMENT

POLICE DEPARTMENT	☐ Original ☒ Supplement	Case No.
Original Offense	Original Complainant's Name	Date This Rpt.

Narrative
positively identified Boson. Based on I.D., obtained S/W, executed 4/13/0_

at Boson's apt., 263 S. 20th St., Apt. 15E. Found 3-sided, blood-spattered

knife. DNA tests showed to match to victim's blood.

    Off. Glemp arrested Boson 4/14/97. Boson's statement taken by Off.

Johann 4/14/0_. Det. Rimbaud did lineup 4/14/0_, again resulting in a

positive I.D.

Corrected Offense	Corrected Compl Name		Status... ☐ Open ☐ Pending ☐ Terminated ☐ Unchanged	☐ Arrest ☐ Unfounded ☐ Exceptional ☐ Referral	Dist 2	Rev 2
Officer Det. Mandelevoy	Ser. No. 0825	Div. 2d	Supv. Approval		Page 3 of 3	

F-EPD-1271-ASW (8/96)

County of Exum
CULDEVA

☐ Juvenile Arrest

OFFENSE/INCIDENT REPORT

POLICE DEPARTMENT			☑ Original ☐ Supplement	Case No. 427328

Offense/Incident Homicide	No. 1	UCR Code	Date Occurred 4/11/0_	Time Occurred Approx. 04:00

Date/Time Reported 4/11/0_ 04:00	Location of Offense/Incident 2003 West Ox Road		Apt. No. 11G	Domestic ☑ Yes ☐ No	Property No.

Name Carolyn Abernathy	I-Code J	Address 2003 West Ox Road		Apt. No. 11A

City Exum	State Culdeva	Zip 00000	Home Phone 555-5555	DOB 1/1/47	Age 50

SSN (Optional)	Sex F	Race W	Ethnic	Occupation Sales	Place of Work Ridge Clothing	Work Phone 444-4444

Name	I-Code			Apt. No.

City	State	Zip	Home Phone	DOB	Age

SSN (Optional)	Sex	Race	Ethnic	Occupation	Place of Work	Work Phone

Veh ☐ Victim ☐ Stolen ☐ Accident ☐ Suspect ☐ Recov'd ☐ Impound	V Yr	Make	Model	Style	Color(s)
Lic. No.	Lic. Type	State	Lic Yr	Vin	Value	Recvd Code ☐1 ☐2 ☐3

Additional Description	Mo Code	NIC	VIC

Veh ☐ Victim ☐ Stolen ☐ Accident ☐ Suspect ☐ Recov'd ☐ Impound	V Yr	Make	Model	Style	Color(s)
Lic. No.	Lic. Type	State	Lic Yr	Vin	Value	Recvd Code ☐1 ☐2 ☐3

Additional Description	Mo Code	NIC	VIC

Item ☐ Add ☐ Delete ☐ Stolen ☐ Change ☐ Recv'd	Type of Item	Brand Name	Model	Desc Code
Serial No.	Owner Applied No.	Additional Description	Value	I Code

Susp #	Suspect Name	Address (Street, City, State, Zip)	Home Phone
DOB	SSN	Age	Sex	Race	Ethnic	Hair	Eyes	Hgt	Wgt	Clothing

Narrative

04:15 received radio call, possible assault Apt 11G, 2003 W. Ox Road,

Carolyn Abernathy, Apt. 11A being a possible witness. No answer when we

knocked and announced, so I broke the lock and entered, along with Off.

Other Agency Notified (Who)	IMU Notified (Date/Time/Who) ☐ Stolen Vehicle/Recovery		ID Requested ☐ Yes ☐ No

Officer Centile	Ser. No. 0457	Div. 2d	Follow-Up By Mandeleve	Status... ☑ Open ☐ Pending ☐ Terminated ☐ Unchanged	☐ Arrest ☐ Unfounded ☐ Exceptional ☐ Referral	Dist 2	Rev 2
Ref. Case No. 427328-1	Damage Amt.	Supv. Approval J. Smith				Page 1 of 2	

F-EPD-0007-ASW (6/96)

County of Exum
CULDEVA

SUPPLEMENT

POLICE DEPARTMENT	☐ Original ☒ Supplement	Case No. 427328
Original Offense Homicide	Original Complainant's Name Susan Oldham	Date This Rpt. 4//12/0_

Narrative
O'Herlihy, Bdg. # 224. We found dead body of a 15 year old girl, later

identified as Susan Oldham. Secured the apartment and called Homicide,

then turning over to Det. Mandelevoy, who arrived about 05:15.

No suspect yet identified.

Corrected Offense	Corrected Compl Name		Status... ☒ Open ☐ Pending ☐ Terminated ☐ Unchanged	☒ Arrest ☐ Unfounded ☐ Exceptional ☐ Referral	Dist 2	Rev 2
Officer Centile	Ser. No. 0457	Div. 2d	Supv. Approval J. Smith		Page 2 of 2	

F-EPD-1271-ASW (8/96)

County of Exum
CULDEVA

☐ Juvenile Arrest

SUSPECT/ARREST REPORT

POLICE DEPARTMENT		☒ Original ☐ Supplement	Case No. 427328

Offense/Incident Homicide	Complainant's Name Susan Oldham		Date/Time 4/11/0_

Address		Home Phone	Work Phone/Ext

Susp # 1	Suspect Name Daniel Boson		Alias/Nickname Ace

Address 263 S. 20th St.	Apt No. 15E	City Exum		State CVA	Zip 00000	Home Phone 666-6666

DOB 2/2/69	Age 28	SSN 000-00-0000	Sex M	Race W	Ethnic	Hair Br	Eyes Br	Hgt 5'10	Wgt 170	Other ID Type Ble. Jeans , lt. T-shirt		

Scars/Marks/Tattoo(2 Max) None	SMT Code 2	SMT Code 2

School/Employer	Work Phone/Ext	Clothing

Place of Birth Exum, CVA	Location of Arrest I-95, just N. of Exum	Date/Time of Arrest 4/14/0_

Location of Offense/Contact I95, just N. of Exum	Charge Code 486,271	Arrested ☒ Yes ☐ No	Arrest Type	Caution Code

HAIR TYPE	HAIR STYLE	FACIAL HAIR	COMPLEXION	DRESS	DEMEANOR	SPEECH
1 ☐ Unknown	1 ☐ Unknown	1 ☒ Shaven	1 ☐ Unknown	1 ☐ Unknown	1 ☐ Unknown	1 ☐ Abusive
2 ☐ Bald	2 ☐ Afro	2 ☐ Low/Lip	2 ☐ Light	2 ☐ Dirty	2 ☐ Angry	2 ☐ Accent
3 ☐ Receding	3 ☐ Braided	3 ☐ Unshaven	3 ☒ Medium	3 ☐ Disguise	3 ☐ Apologetic	3 ☒ Clear
4 ☐ Short	4 ☐ Bushy	4 ☐ Sideburn	4 ☐ Dark	4 ☐ Flashy	4 ☐ Calm	4 ☐ Foreign
5 ☒ Neck	5 ☐ Crewcut	5 ☐ Mustache	5 ☐ Freckls	5 ☐ Military	5 ☐ Confused	5 ☐ Lisp
6 ☒ Collar	6 ☐ Curly	6 ☐ Fumanchu	6 ☐ Tanned	6 ☐ Unkempt	6 ☐ Irrational	6 ☐ Mumbles
7 ☐ Shoulder	7 ☐ Greasy	7 ☐ Goatee	7 ☐ Yellow	7 ☐ Odor	7 ☒ Nervous	7 ☐ Obscene
8 ☐ Long	8 ☐ Recruit			8 ☒ Groomed	8 ☐ Polite	8 ☐ Rapid
	9 ☐ Ponytail	Beard	8 ☐ Acne		9 ☐ Violent	9 ☐ Slow
9 ☐ Coarse	10 ☐ Prcess		9 ☐ Pocked	9 ☐ Cap/Hat	10 ☐ Intox/High	10 ☐ Slurred
10 ☐ Fine	11 ☐ Straight	8 ☐ Thin	10 ☐ Ruddy	10 ☐ Glasses		11 ☐ Stutter
11 ☐ Thinning	12 ☒ Wavy	9 ☐ Full	11 ☒ Clean	11 ☐ Gloves		12 ☐ Talky
12 ☐ Wiry	13 ☐ Wig			12 ☐ Mask		

Father's Name George Boson	Address 423 Rosebud Lane	Home Phone 718-999-9999	Work Phone/Ext. Retired
Mother's Name Mitzi Boson	Address 423 Rosebud Lane	Home Phone 718-999-9999	Work Phone/Ext. Retired
Father's Name	Address	Home Phone	Work Phone/Ext.

Lic. No.	State NY	Lic Yr 96	VIN Missing	Vyr	Make	Model	Color

Narrative

Patrolling I-95, just N. Exum, when spotted '97 yellow Mustang heading N., NY plates, 03:00, doing 50mph and fitting aspects drug cover profile, so stopped. Had broken tail light. Had driver and passenger exit and found marijuana rolling paper in glove compartment. Did conset search

Follow-Up By	IMU Notified (Date/Time Who)	Status... ☒ Open ☐ Pending ☐ Terminated ☐ Unchanged	☒ Arrest ☐ Unfounded ☐ Exceptional ☐ Referral	Dist 4	Rev 4
Officer J. Glemp	Ser. No. 467	Div. 3d	Supv. Approval R. Jones	Page 1 of 1	

F-EPD-0971-ASW (8/96)

JUVENILE ARREST INFORMATION			Case No.	
Witness 1	Address		Home Phone	Work Phone/Ext
Witness 2	Address		Home Phone	Work Phone/Ext
Juvenile Detained ☐ Yes ☐ No	Where	Authorized By		Date/Time
Parents Nofied By	Date/Time	Released To		Date/Time

CODES

TATTOO	ARREST TYPE	CAUTION CODES
1 Insignia 2 Picture 3 Design 4 Name 5 Words 6 Initials 7 Numbers 8 Other	W - Warrant S - Summons C - Capias D - Detention Order I - In Field P - Probation/Parole Violation B - Bench Warrant	AR - Hazardous; Armed ER - Escape Risk FT - Fighter MA - Medical Alert

RACE CODES	ETHNIC CODES
I - American Indian, Alaskan A - Asian or Pacific Islander B - Black W - White	A - African G - Afghan H - Hispanic I - Indochinese (Vietnamese, Laotian, Cambodian) J - Jamaican K - Korean

Additional
of trunk and found about 1 kilo cocaine. Arrested driver (Boson) and
passenger (Patsy O'Donnell) and called backup. Mirandized both but no
response. Handed over to backup, Off. M. Johann, Badge # 250.

F-EPD-0971-ASW (PAGE 2)

County of Exum
CULDEVA

☐ Juvenile Arrest

OFFENSE/INCIDENT REPORT

POLICE DEPARTMENT			☒ Original ☐ Supplement	Case No. 427328

Offense/Incident Homicide	No. 1	UCR Code 0_	Date Occurred 4/11/0_	Time Occurred Approx. 04:00

Date/Time Reported 4/11/0_ 04:00	Location of Offense/Incident 2003 West Ox Road	Apt. No. 11G	Domestic ☒ Yes ☐ No	Property No.

Name	I-Code	Address		Apt. No.
City	State	Zip	Home Phone	DOB	Age
SSN (Optional)	Sex	Race	Ethnic	Occupation	Place of Work	Work Phone

Name	I-Code			Apt. No.
City	State	Zip	Home Phone	DOB	Age
SSN (Optional)	Sex	Race	Ethnic	Occupation	Place of Work	Work Phone

Veh ☐ Victim ☐ Stolen ☐ Accident ☐ Suspect ☐ Recov'd ☐ Impound	V Yr	Make	Model	Style	Color(s)
Lic. No.	Lic. Type	State	Lic Yr	Vin	Value	Recvd Code ☐1 ☐2 ☐3
Additional Description			Mo Code	NIC	VIC

Veh ☐ Victim ☐ Stolen ☐ Accident ☐ Suspect ☐ Recov'd ☐ Impound	V Yr	Make	Model	Style	Color(s)
Lic. No.	Lic. Type	State	Lic Yr	Vin	Value	Recvd Code ☐1 ☐2 ☐3
Additional Description			Mo Code	NIC	VIC

Item ☐ Add ☐ Delete ☐ Stolen ☐ Change ☐ Recv'd	Type of Item	Brand Name	Model	Desc Code
Serial No.	Owner Applied No.	Additional Description	Value	I Code

Susp #	Suspect Name	Address (Street, City, State, Zip)	Home Phone
DOB	SSN	Age	Sex	Race	Ethnic	Hair	Eyes	Hgt	Wgt	Clothing

Narrative
Transported D. Bosom from arrest scene in veh. #24, along with Officers
Mercedeh and Francis. Boson protested car he was driving was not his, but
Patsy (passenger's) sister's who had loaned the car to Patsy.

Other Agency Notified (Who)	IMU Notified (Date/Time/Who) ☐ Stolen Vehicle/Recovery		ID Requested ☐ Yes ☐ No
Officer Johann	Ser. No. 877	Div. 2d	Follow-Up By	Status... ☒ Open ☐ Pending	☐ Arrest ☐ Unfounded ☐ Exceptional	Dist 2	Rev 2
Ref. Case No. 427328-1	Damage Amt.	Supv. Approval	☐ Terminated ☐ Unchanged	☐ Referral	Page 1 of 2

F-EPD-0007-ASW (6/96)

County of Exum
CULDEVA

SUPPLEMENT

POLICE DEPARTMENT	☐ Original ☒ Supplement	Case No. 427328

Original Offense Homicide	Original Complainant's Name Susan Oldham	Date This Rpt.

Narrative

Off. Mercedeh Mirandized Boron, but no statement taken then. Boson's arrest was for drug possession, but I expressed concern to Officers

Mercedeh and Francis about Oldham's murder, a case on all our minds. Boson

must have heard and said, "Alright, I did it, but I won't say any more."

A few minutes later, however, he said, "I stabbed her in the chest with a

triangle knife, the kind that makes sure cuts don't heal. I was dripping in it." Boson subsequently refused to sign rights waiver form or a written

statement.

Corrected Offense	Corrected Compl Name			Status... ☐ Open ☐ Pending ☐ Terminated ☐ Unchanged	☐ Arrest ☐ Unfounded ☐ Exceptional ☐ Referral	Dist 2	Rev 2
Officer Johann	Ser. No. 877	Div 2d	Supv. Approval			Page 2 of 2	

F-EPD-1271-ASW (8/96)

County of Exum
CULDEVA

POLICE DEPARTMENT COUNTY OF EXUM, CULDEVA
LINE-UP IDENTIFICATION

CASE NO.: 427328

OFFENSE: Homicide

LOCATION: 2d Div.

DATE: 4/14/0   TIME: 06:00

SUBJECTS	1	2	3	4	5	6
NAME	Elbert Fudd	Marvin Jones	Daniel Boson	John Rivera	Justin Gold	Howard Cate
ADDRESS						
AGE-HT.-WT.	32, 5'11" 180lbs	44, 5'9" 170lbs	28, 5'10" 170lbs	21, 5'9" 160lbs	30, 6'0" 190lbs	27, 5'10" 170lbs
COLOR - SEX	W/M	W/M	W/M	W/M	W/M	W/M
DESCRIPTION OF CLOTHING	blue jeans, white t-shirt	black jeans, white t-shirt	blue jeans, white t-shirt	dockers, blue t-shirt	dark jeans, dockers, khaki button light t-down shirt	

POSITION No.	TIME	RESULTS
3	06:00	Positive

OFFICERS PARTICIPATING

Detective Assigned - Det .Mandelevqy

Conducted By -   Det. Denise

Farhquar, #355

WITNESSES

No.	NAME	ADDRESS
1	Carolyn Abernathy	2003 W. Ox. Rd.. Apt 11A
2		
3		
4		
5		

AFFIDAVIT FOR SEARCH WARRANT

CVA CODE §19.2.54
RULE 3A.27

The undersigned Applicant states under oath:

1. A search is requested in relation to an offense substantially described as follows:

Murder by stabbing of Susan Oldham about 4a.m., 4/11/0_, at 2003

West Ox Road, Apt. 11G, Exum, Culdeva.

. . . .

□ CONTINUED ON
ATTACHED SHEET.

2. The place, person, or thing to be searched is described as follows:

Apt. 15E, 263 South 20th St., Exum, Culdeva, where Daniel Boson

resides, and Daniel Boson.

. . . .

□ CONTINUED ON
ATTACHED SHEET.

3. The things or persons to be searched for are described as follows:

Knife or other sharp weapons or implements; bloodstains, hair, skin,

clothing, or personal belongings of Susan Oldham; and clothes,

sheets, or other items stained with Daniel Boson's blood.

. . . .

□ CONTINUED ON
ATTACHED SHEET.

FORM CVA 338 11/88/114-3-021 9/96 (OVER)

CASE NO.

AFFIDAVIT FOR
SEARCH WARRANT

. . . .

. . . .

APPLICANT:

Howard Mandelevoy
NAME

Detective
TITLE (IF ANY)

. . . .
ADDRESS

. . . .

Certified to Clerk of

Exum, Culdeva _____ Circuit Court on

April 12, 200_

□ CONTINUED ON
ATTACHED SHEET

Delivered to Clerk of

Exum, Culdeva _____ Circuit Court on

April 12, 200_ by the undersigned

_____
TITLE   SIGNATURE

Det. Mandelevoy _____
TITLE   SIGNATURE

4. The material facts constituting probable cause that the search should be made are:

See Supplemental Affidavit

....

(☐ CONTINUED ON ATTACHED SHEET)

5. The object, thing or person searched for constitutes evidence of the commison of such offense.

6. ☐ I have personal knowledge of the facts set forth in this affidavit OR

☒ I was advised of the facts set forth in this affidavit, in whole or in part, by an informer. This informer's credibility or the reliability of the information may be determined from the following facts:

See Supplemental Affidavit

....

The statements above are true and accurate to the best of my knowledge and belief.

Howard Mandelevoy
APPLICANT

Detective
TITLE OF APPLICANT (IF ANY)

Suscribed and sworn to before me this day.

April 12, 200_
DATE AND TIME

George Johnson

☐ CLERK   ☐ MAGISTRATE   ☐ JUDGE

SUPPLEMENTAL AFFIDAVIT FOR SEARCH WARRANT

I, Detective Howard Mandelevoy, being duly sworn, depose and say:

1. On April 11, Mrs. Martin Abernathy, hearing screams about 0400, looked through her apartment window and saw in nearby apartment 11G a man struggling with a young woman Abernathy recognized as a neighbor, Susan Oldham. Abernathy called the police, and Officer Centile and her partner, arriving about 0415 found Oldham dead in her apartment, having been stabbed in the chest twice. This detective was assigned by Homicide and that morning, a search of the crime scene revealed no weapons.

2. At 0700, I interviewed Oldham's parents, who told me Oldham had just broken up with her boyfriend, "Ace," and Oldham was frightened, telling the parents that Ace had threatened to harm Oldham just two days before the murder, saying, "If you're not my girl, you're no one's. I'll 'fix it' that way."

3. I received an anonymous phone tip 4/12 saying the informant had heard that "Ace" did the killing and heard a neighbor once say to Daniel Boson, informant's acquaintance for many years, "Goodbye, Ace." At a party last week attended by informant, informant heard Boson brag about his girlfriend Susan, threatening to kill her if she ever left him. Boson then showed informant a hunting knife Boson wore in a scabbard about his waist. Informant remembered the knife because it was unusual, with a skull and crossbones on the handle. The knife also had a 3–sided blade, about 6′ long, 3″ wide at the base. Informant asked Boson what the knife was for, and Boson said, "For people who get out of line" and laughed. Informant then said, "Check him out. The son-of-a-bitch needs checking. If I could, I'd do it myself."

4. Record check showed Boson with prior gunpoint robbery arrest, charges dropped when the victim failed to appear.

5. Showed 8 photo-spread to eyewitness Abernathy, who positively identified Boson.

6. Based on the facts set forth above, his training and experience, your affiant is of the opinion that there is probable cause to believe the items set forth in the attachment will be found on the listed premises and will constitute fruits or instrumentalities or evidence of the crime listed.

_____/S/

Signature of Affiant

Duly sworn and subscribed to before me this ___ of April

_____/S/

Circuit Court Judge

SEARCH WARRANT

CVA CODE ANN §19-234
RULE 3A-27

FILE NO. 222

SEARCH WARRANT
STATE OF CULDEVA

In re/V.

Daniel Boson

☐ To any policeman of a county, city or town:

☒ To Detective Howard Mandelevoy

You are hereby commanded in the name of the State to forthwith search either in day or night

Apt. 15E, 263 South 20th St., Exum, Culdeva, and the person of
LOCATION / DESCRIPTION OF PLACE, PERSON, OR THING TO BE SEARCHED

Daniel Boson

for the following property, objects and / or persons:

Knives or other sharp weapons or implements including, but not lim
LIST PROPERTY, OBJECTS, AND / OR PERSONS SOUGHT IN SEARCH

ited to, a knife with a skull and crossbones handle; various types

of trace evidence transfer, including but not limited to hair, sa

liva, blood, fibers, fingerprints, and other trace evidence.

You are further commanded to seize said property, persons, and / or objects if they be found and to produce before the Court an inventory of all property, persons, and / or objects seized.

This search warrant is issued in relation to an offense substantially described as follows:

Murder of Susan Oldham, 4/11/0_, about 04:00, 4/11/0_, at 2003 West

Ox Road, Apt. 11G, Exum, Culdeva

I, the undersigned, have found probable cause to believe that the property or person constitutes evidence of the crime identified herein or tends to show that the person(s) named or described herein has committed or is committing a crime, and further that the search should be made, based on the statements in the attached affidavit sworn to by

Detective Howard Mandelevoy
NAME OF AFFIANT

George Johnson

☒ CLERK   ☐ MAGISTRATE   ☐ JUDGE

April 12, 200_
DATE AND TIME

FORM CVA 338 01/09/71-4-3-027 9/96

SEARCH INVENTORY AND RETURN

The following items, and no others, were seized under authority of this warrant:

1. .... Blood-spattered, three-sided knife ....

2. ....

3. ....

4. ....

5. ....

6. ....

7. ....

8. ....

9. ....

10. ....

11. ....

12. ....

13. ....

14. ....

15. ....

The statement above is true and accurate to the best of my knowledge and belief.

Det. Howard Mandelevoy
EXECUTING OFFICER

Subscribed and sworn to before me this day

4/13/0_
DATE

4/13/0_
DATE

George Johnson

☑ CLERK   ☐ MAGISTRATE   ☐ JUDGE

NOTARY PUBLIC: My commission expires .... 4/15/0_

FORM CVA 338 01/RW71-4-1-027 9/96

EXECUTION

Executed by searching the within described place, person or thing.

4/12/97
DATE AND TIME EXECUTED

Det. Howard Mandelevoy
EXECUTING OFFICER

Certified to ...... Hon. John Jacobs

Circuit Court on ...... 4/13/0_
(DATE)

Det. Howard Mandelevoy
EXECUTING OFFICER

Received on ...... 4/13/0_
(DATE)

by ...... George Johnson
(CLERK, CIRCUIT COURT)

IN THE CIRCUIT COURT OF THE STATE OF CULDEVA
IN AND FOR THE COUNTY OF EXUM

STATE OF CULDEVA,	)	
	)	
Plaintiff	)	
	)	
vs.	)	NO. 333
	)	INFORMATION
DANIEL BOSON,	)	
	)	
Defendant	)	

COUNT I

I, Jorge Landis, Prosecuting Attorney for the County of Exum, in the name and authority of the State of Culdeva, do accuse that on or about 4/11, Daniel Boson did violate 210.2, Murder, in that he purposely or knowingly killed Susan Oldham, without justification or excuse.

COUNT II

I, Jorge Landis, Prosecuting Attorney for the County of Exum, in the name and authority of the State of Culdeva, do accuse that on 4/11, Daniel Boson did violate 211, Aggravated Assault, in that he purposely inflicted bodily injury on Susan Oldham, without justification or excuse.

COUNT III

I, Jorge Landis, Prosecuting Attorney for the County of Exum, in the name and authority of the State of Culdeva, do accuse that on 4/11, Daniel Boson did violate 233, Abuse of Corpse, in that he mutilated by knife or other sharp implement the dead body of Susan Oldham.

DATED this 8th day of May.

_____

JORGE LANDIS
Prosecuting Attorney in and for
said County and State

———

MEMORANDUM

TO: File
FROM: Jonathan Switt, Assistant District Attorney
DATE: May 12
RE: *Boson Case Summary*

This memorandum will summarize the case facts for the ADA who will replace me when I leave the office at the end of this month.

On April 11, Police Officer Marguerite Centile found a 15 year old girl's body in apartment 11G, 2003 West Ox Road, Exum, Culdeva. The girl had been stabbed in the chest, piercing the heart, once. The police had been called by a neighbor, Mrs. Martha Abernathy, whose window faces the apartment. She had heard screams at about 4 a.m., looked through her apartment window, and saw the girl struggling with a much larger male. Abernathy knew the girl, Susan Oldham, well from the building (the two often met in the building's basement laundry) and caught sight of her and her assailant's face from the lights on in the apartment. Abernathy had never seen the male before and promptly called the police, who arrived about 4:15 a.m.

When Officer Centile and her partner arrived, they knocked and, when there was no answer, broke the door lock and entered. The assailant was gone by then. Centile promptly called in the Homicide detectives, the lead detective assigned being Howard Mandelevoy. Neither Mandelevoy nor his team found a knife or similar sharp object anywhere. Detective Mandelevoy interviewed Oldham's parents. They explained that Susan had a wild older boyfriend, about 28 years old, whom the parents did not like. They had only met him once, over a year ago, and did not think they would recognize him if they saw him. He spoke "roughly," they said, and then had a full beard, had glazed eyes, "like he was on drugs." They did not know the boyfriend's real name (Susan would not tell them), but Susan called him "Ace." One day, however, about two days before the killing, Susan finally took her parents' advice, dumping "Ace." Susan was scared, however, telling her parents that Ace had gotten very angry when Susan declared their relationship over. Ace said that "If you're not my girl, you're no one's. I'll 'fix it' that way."

The day after the murder, Mandelevoy got a phone call from an anonymous tipster. The informant said that he had heard in the area that a guy named "Ace" did the crime. The tipster also had heard the very morning of making his call to Mandelevoy a neighbor saying "Goodbye, Ace" to a guy named Daniel Boson, with whom the informant had gone to high school. Boson, said the informant, lived at 263 South 20th Street, Apartment 15E. The informant said that he had been at a party at Boson's house a week earlier. Boson had bragged about his new girlfriend, Susan, and how beautiful Susan was and how she adored Boson. He swore to kill her, however, if he ever saw her with another man or she ever tried to leave him.

The informant said as well that Boson showed off a hunting knife that he kept in a small scabbard about his waist. The knife had unusual markings, a Zebra overfaced with a skull and crossbones. The informant asked Boson what the knife was for. Boson replied, "For people who get out of line," and laughed loudly. The knife blade was unusual too, about 6' long, 3" wide at the base of a 3–sided blade. The informant hung up, but, before doing so said, "Check him out. The son-of-a-bitch needs checking. If I could, I'd do it myself." Mandelevoy has refused to share with me the identity of the informant.

Mandelevoy tried to locate Boson, but he was never home when Mandelevoy checked, nor could Mandelevoy (despite repeated tries) reach

Boson by phone. Mandelevoy then checked for priors and discovered that Boson had been arrested once before for a gunpoint robbery, but the charges were dropped when the victim failed to appear at trial. Mandelevoy took Boson's photo from that arrest, covered up any identifying marks or information, and put the photo in a spread of 8 total color photos, asking Mrs. Abernathy whether she recognized anyone. She picked out two photos, one of which was Boson's, and said: "Both look like the guy, but I'm not sure. The one on the right [Boson's photo] might look a little more like the guy than the one on the left, but it's real close."[a]

Mandelevoy, on the basis of this identification, then sought and obtained a search warrant for Boson's apartment. The search uncovered a blood-spattered, three-sided knife under the bedroom mattress. DNA blood tests revealed that the blood was the victim's.

Two days later, Patrol Officer Joseph Glemp spotted a 1997 yellow Mustang heading North on I–95, out of Exum. The Mustang had New York license plates. It was 3 a.m., and the car was traveling 5 miles per hour under the speed limit in the middle lane, doing so over a long stretch of road. The car fit 3 out of 7 elements of a drug courier profile, so Glemp stopped the car, although he had also noticed a broken tail light. He asked the driver (Boson) and front-seat passenger to get out immediately. The officer checked the glove compartment and found rolling paper for marijuana cigarettes. The officer then said, "Let's have the keys. I'd like to check out your trunk, if that's O.K. with you." Boson did not respond but handed the keys over to the officer. The officer searched the trunk and found one kilo of cocaine. The officer immediately thereafter placed Boson and his passenger, Patsy O'Donnell, under arrest, Mirandized them, and handcuffed them both. Boson at that time gave no response to questions. Three officers rode with Boson (the passenger traveled in a separate squad car) toward the police station, two officers in the back seat with Boson, one officer in the front seat, driving. Boson then said, "The car is Patsy's sister's. She loaned the car to Patsy, and Patsy let me drive. How can you arrest me for possessing drugs?" One officer re-Mirandized Boson, asked Boson the Miranda questions, and Boson responded, "Yeah, I think I'll keep quiet now."[b]

One officer, Michael Johann, then started chatting with the other officers, saying, "You know, it's a shame about that girl, what's her name, Susan Oldham, who got cut last week at the old Bell Ridge apartments. The joke on the sucker who cut her is that she had a particularly virulent strain of hepatitis, according to the lab guys, and I hear the killer must have gotten soaked in blood. If he gets treatment, there might be hope, but it may take us too long to track him down."

---

a.   Abernathy recounted this version when I interviewed her by phone. Detective Mandelevoy's report simply says "positive i.d."

b.   The details regarding Officer Johann's conversations with Boson are from my interview with Johann. His report is less complete.

Johann, defense counsel has maintained, had heard from his sources that Boson was a fairly extreme hypochondriac. Indeed, defense counsel has, in plea negotiations, stressed this hypochondria. Johann denies, however, being then aware of Boson's hypochondria or of Boson's suspected connection to Oldham's murder. Johann says he was just making small talk. Defense counsel, Fran Freed, usually does not tip her hand, but she insists Johann is a habitual liar, and, if I check him out, I will be ethically obligated either not to call him to the stand or to call him but impeach him on his knowledge of Boson's hypochondria. My replacement should investigate these assertions. Boson apparently loved violence but was terrified of disease.

Boson then stammered, "All right, I did it, but I won't say any more until I see a lawyer and you guys get me the cure." Johann, according to Boson's counsel, then said, "We'll get you your lawyer immediately, but if we knew more about how you did it, we'd know what to tell the doctor about your exposure." Boson, again according to his defense counsel, then said, "I stabbed her in the chest with a triangle knife, the kind that makes sure cuts don't heal. I was dripping in it." Johann says, on the other hand, that Boson just blurted out this last statement, without ever first being urged to describe how he did the killing.

At the police station, Boson was placed in a lineup with five other white males, each of whom had dark hair. None were represented by attorneys. As the lineup was proceeding, a complaint was being drafted, which was filed immediately after the lineup, charging Boson with murder and with possession of narcotics.

Ms. Abernathy again identified two men, one of whom was Boson (the other was position #6 at the lineup), saying, "It might be either, but I think he's the killer. I'm pretty sure it's him."[c]

---

c. These lineup details come from my phone interview with Detective Farhquar.

White Collar Crime File

United States v. Brunell

AO 110 (Rev. 5/85) Subpoena to Testify Before Grand Jury   ⊛

United States District Court

Northern _____ DISTRICT OF _Culdeva_ _____

TO:

Arthur Graham Brunell
5983 Irving Park Road
Exum, Culdeva 00000

**SUBPOENA TO TESTIFY
BEFORE GRAND JURY**

SUBPOENA FOR:
☒ PERSON   ☒ DOCUMENT(S) OR OBJECT(S)

YOU ARE HEREBY COMMANDED to appear and testify before the Grand Jury of the United States District Court at the place, date, and time specified below.

PLACE	COURTROOM Grand Jury Room B
United States Courthouse 9892 Torrence Boulevard Exum, Culdeva 00000	DATE AND TIME May 29, 200_

YOU ARE ALSO COMMANDED to bring with you the following document(s) or object(s):*

All records reflecting income and expenses of Arthur Graham Brunell, including pay stubs, W-2s, bank statements, cancelled checks, income tax returns, materials used in the preparation of tax returns, receipts, bills of lading, accounts payable, and personal calendars or diaries containing notes or records of income and expenditures; and all records reflecting income and expenses of Brunell's Natural Foods, Inc., including corporate books and records, minutes of shareholder meetings, balance sheets, bank statements, cancelled checks, tax returns, materials used in the preparation of tax returns, receipts, bills of lading, accounts receivable and payable, personnel records, and computer databases reflecting income and expenses.

☐ *Please see additional information on reverse*

This subpoena shall remain in effect until you are granted leave to depart by the court or by an officer acting on behalf of the court.

CLERK Wright Nudelman	DATE May 14, 200_
(BY) DEPUTY CLERK	

This subpoena is issued on application of the United States of America	NAME, ADDRESS AND PHONE NUMBER OF ASSISTANT U.S. ATTORNEY Darrell Monson Room 323, United States Courthouse

*If not applicable, enter "none"

AO 110 (Rev. 5/85) Subpoena to Testify Before Grand Jury

RETURN OF SERVICE [1]

	DATE	PLACE
RECEIVED BY SERVER		
SERVED	DATE	PLACE

SERVED ON (NAME)

SERVED BY	TITLE

STATEMENT OF SERVICE FEES

TRAVEL	SERVICES	TOTAL

DECLARATION OF SERVER [2]

I declare under penalty of perjury under the laws of the United States of America that the foregoing information contained in the Return of Service and Statement of Service Fees is true and correct.

Executed on_____   _____
                Date   *Signature of Server*

                            _____
                                   Address of Server

ADDITIONAL INFORMATION

(1) As to who may serve a subpoena and the manner of its service see Rule 17(d), Federal Rules of Criminal Procedure, or Rule 45(c), Federal Rules of Civil Procedure.

(2) "Fees and mileage need not be tendered to the witness upon service of a subpoena issued on behalf of the United States or an officer or agency thereof (Rule 45(c), Federal Rules of Civil Procedure; Rule 17(d), Federal Rules of Criminal Procedure) or on behalf of certain indigent parties and criminal defendants who are unable to pay such costs (28 USC 1825, Rule 17(b) Federal Rules of Criminal Procedure)".

AO 110 (Rev. 5/85) Subpoena to Testify Before Grand Jury

United States District Court

Northern _____ DISTRICT OF _____ Culdeva _____

TO:

Boyd Gregory
3198 Thayer Street
Exum, Culdeva 00000

**SUBPOENA TO TESTIFY
BEFORE GRAND JURY**

SUBPOENA FOR:
☐ PERSON   ☒ DOCUMENT(S) OR OBJECT(S)

YOU ARE HEREBY COMMANDED to appear and testify before the Grand Jury of the United States District Court at the place, date, and time specified below.

PLACE	COURTROOM
United States Courthouse 9892 Torrence Boulevard Exum, Culdeva 00000	Grand Jury Room B
	DATE AND TIME May 29, 200_

YOU ARE ALSO COMMANDED to bring with you the following document(s) or object(s):*

All records reflecting income and expenses of Brunell's Natural Foods, Inc. including corporate books and records, minutes of shareholder meetings, balance sheets, bank statements, cancelled checks, tax returns, materials used by you in the preparation of tax returns, receipts, bills of lading, accounts receivable and payable, personnel records, and computer databases reflecting income and expenses.

☐ *Please see additional information on reverse*

This subpoena shall remain in effect until you are granted leave to depart by the court or by an officer acting on behalf of the court.

CLERK Wright Nudelman	DATE May 14, 200_
(BY) DEPUTY CLERK	

This subpoena is issued on application of the United States of America	NAME, ADDRESS AND PHONE NUMBER OF ASSISTANT U.S. ATTORNEY Darrell Monson Room 323, United States Courthouse

*If not applicable, enter "none"

AO 110 (Rev. 5/85) Subpoena to Testify Before Grand Jury

	RETURN OF SERVICE [1]	
RECEIVED BY SERVER	DATE	PLACE
SERVED	DATE	PLACE

SERVED ON (NAME)

SERVED BY	TITLE

STATEMENT OF SERVICE FEES

TRAVEL	SERVICES	TOTAL

DECLARATION OF SERVER [2]

I declare under penalty of perjury under the laws of the United States of America that the foregoing information contained in the Return of Service and Statement of Service Fees is true and correct.

Executed on _____   _____
              Date   *Signature of Server*

                          _____
                              Address of Server

ADDITIONAL INFORMATION

(1) As to who may serve a subpoena and the manner of its service see Rule 17(d), Federal Rules of Criminal Procedure, or Rule 45(c), Federal Rules of Civil Procedure.

(2) "Fees and mileage need not be tendered to the witness upon service of a subpoena issued on behalf of the United States or an officer or agency thereof (Rule 45(c), Federal Rules of Civil Procedure; Rule 17(d), Federal Rules of Criminal Procedure) or on behalf of certain indigent parties and criminal defendants who are unable to pay such costs (28 USC 1825, Rule 17(b) Federal Rules of Criminal Procedure)".

IN THE UNITED STATES DISTRICT COURT FOR
THE NORTHERN DISTRICT OF CULDEVA

United States of America	)	
	)	
vs.	)	
	)	No. CR 903
Arthur Graham Brunell,	)	
Terri Lynn Marvoal, and	)	
Brunell's Natural Foods, Inc.	)	

The February Grand Jury charges:

COUNT ONE

(Conspiracy to Commit Tax Evasion)

1. Beginning in January 200_ and continuing thereafter until on or about February 200_, in Exum, in the Northern District of Culdeva, and elsewhere,

ARTHUR GRAHAM BRUNELL,
TERRI LYNN MARVOAL,
and BRUNELL'S NATURAL FOODS, INC.

defendants herein, did knowingly, intentionally, willfully and maliciously conspire, combine and agree together and with others unknown to the Grand Jury to evade or defeat federal income taxes imposed by the Internal Revenue Code and due and owing by Arthur Graham Brunell, individually, and by Brunell's Natural Foods, Inc., a Culdeva corporation.

2. It was the object of the conspiracy that defendants Arthur Graham Brunell and Brunell's Natural Foods, Inc., would avoid paying taxes on income earned by them but not reported as income on their federal income tax returns.

3. At all times pertinent to this Indictment, defendant Arthur Graham Brunell is and was the president and chief financial officer of Brunell's Natural Foods, Inc., a corporation that purchases health food products from manufacturers and distributes them throughout a three state region encompassing Culdeva and two other states.

4. At all times pertinent to this Indictment, defendant Terri Lynn Marvoal is and was employed as a bookkeeper by Brunell's Natural Foods, Inc. Defendant Marvoal received a salary and other compensation in the form of a year-end bonus.

5. At all times pertinent to this Indictment, the books and records of Brunell's Natural Foods, Inc. are and were maintained at its business premises at 5983 Irving Park Road, Exum, Culdeva, 00000.

OVERT ACTS

6. Beginning in 200_, and continuing thereafter until June 200_, the federal income tax returns filed on behalf of defendant Brunell's Natural

Foods, Inc., reported that its gross receipts were largely used to purchase the health food products and to pay defendant Arthur Graham Brunell's business-related travel and entertainment expenses, when in fact, defendant Brunell's Natural Foods, Inc. also paid for the personal expenses of defendant Arthur Graham Brunell. These payments of personal expenses were unlawful and were concealed by the actions of defendants Arthur Graham Brunell and Terri Lynn Marvoal.

7. Beginning in 200_, and continuing thereafter until June 200_, defendants Arthur Graham Brunell and Terri Lynn Marvoal manipulated the books and records of defendant Brunell's Natural Foods, Inc., in order to inflate its expenses and to conceal that monies belonging to the corporation were used to pay the personal expenses of defendant Arthur Graham Brunell.

a. As a result of the manipulation of its books and records, the expenses of defendant Brunell's Natural Foods, Inc. were unlawfully inflated.

b. As a result of the manipulation of its books and records, the net income reported on the federal income tax returns filed on behalf of defendant Brunell's Natural Foods, Inc., was unlawfully underreported, and its tax liability was falsely understated.

c. As a result of the manipulation of its books and records, defendant Brunell's Natural Foods, Inc., unlawfully paid for the personal expenses of defendant Arthur Graham Brunell. These expenses were falsely reported as business expenses and included costs incurred as a result of the installation of a Olympic-sized swimming pool at the personal residence of defendant Arthur Graham Brunell, other repairs and remodeling to that residence, domestic and overseas travel of defendant Arthur Graham Brunell and his family that was personal in nature, and the purchase and maintenance by defendant Arthur Graham Brunell of a 60–foot yacht that he christened "The Nature Boy" and used for personal pleasure. The personal expenses of Arthur Graham Brunell constituted income to him, which he failed to report on his personal income tax returns. As a result, his income was unlawfully underreported, and his tax liability was falsely understated.

d. As a direct result of and reward for her involvement in the manipulation of the books and records of defendant Brunell's Natural Foods, Inc., defendant Terri Lynn Marvoal was paid a substantial bonus in addition to her annual salary.

8. Beginning in 200_, and continuing thereafter until February 200_, defendants Arthur Graham Brunell and Terri Lynn Marvoal conspired and agreed to conceal their manipulation of the books and records of defendant Brunell's Natural Foods, Inc., and the resulting tax evasion, by falsifying expense reports, falsifying invoices from vendors, falsifying reports that were given accountants, and making false statements to agents of the Internal Revenue Service.

All in violation of Title 18, United States Code, Section 371.

COUNT TWO

(Tax Evasion)

1.–8. Paragraphs 1 through 8 of Count One are incorporated as paragraphs 1 through 8 of Count Two.

9. Beginning in 200_ and continuing thereafter until June 200_, in Exum, in the Northern District of Culdeva, and elsewhere,

ARTHUR GRAHAM BRUNELL,
TERRI LYNN MARVOAL,
and BRUNELL'S NATURAL FOODS, INC.

defendants herein, did knowingly and willfully attempt to and did evade and defeat federal income taxes imposed by the Internal Revenue Code and due and owing by Arthur Graham Brunell, individually, and by Brunell's Natural Foods, Inc., a Culdeva corporation.

All in violation of 26 United States Code, section 7201, and Title 18, United States Code, Section 2.

COUNT THREE

(False Statement)

1.–8. Paragraphs 1 through 8 of Count One are incorporated as paragraphs 1 through 8 of Count Three.

9. On April 15, 200_, in Exum, in the Northern District of Culdeva, and elsewhere,

ARTHUR GRAHAM BRUNELL,
TERRI LYNN MARVOAL,
and BRUNELL'S NATURAL FOODS, INC.

defendants herein, did knowingly and willfully make and subscribe to a false return which contained a written declaration that it was made under penalties of perjury, and which they did not believe to be true and correct, to wit: 200_ corporate income tax return of Brunell's Natural Foods, Inc.

All in violation of Title 26, United States Code, Section 7206 and Title 18, United States Code, Section 2.

COUNT FOUR

(False Statement)

1.–8. Paragraphs 1 through 8 of Count One are incorporated as paragraphs 1 through 8 of Count Four.

9. On April 15, 200_, in Exum, in the Northern District of Culdeva, and elsewhere,

ARTHUR GRAHAM BRUNELL and TERRI LYNN MARVOAL

defendants herein, did knowingly and willfully make and subscribe to a false return which contained a written declaration that it was made under penalties of perjury, and which they did not believe to be true and correct, to wit: 200_ individual income tax return of Arthur Graham Brunell.

All in violation of Title 26, United States Code, Section 7206 and Title 18, United States Code, Section 2.

A TRUE BILL:

_____/s/
Foreperson of the Grand Jury

_____/s/
United States Attorney

MEMORANDUM

To: First Assistant United States Attorney Jones
From: Assistant United States Attorney Monson
Date: August 23

This memorandum will report on the status of our investigation of Arthur Graham Brunell for tax evasion and related crimes. In addition, it seeks authorization to offer informal immunity to one witness and to engage in plea negotiations with an indicted co-conspirator.

Arthur G. Brunell is the president and chief financial officer of Brunell's Natural Foods, Inc., a health food distributing company. The company purchases health food products from manufacturers and distributes them throughout a three state region. The company's books, which are maintained by bookkeeper Terri L. Marvoal, reflect that the company's gross receipts are largely used to purchase the health food products and to pay Brunell's business-related travel and entertainment expenses. The company has reported very little net income.

Brunell apparently began using the company to pay his personal expenses in 200_. Between 200_ and 200_, Brunell took his family on several trips to Disney World in Orlando, Florida, and to Paris. We have solid evidence that the company paid for these trips. We can also prove that Brunell used company money to remodel his house, adding 3000 square feet of living space and an Olympic-sized swimming pool. In 200_, the company purchased a 60–foot yacht, "The Nature Boy," ostensibly for business purposes. There is substantial evidence demonstrating that the yacht was used for Brunell's personal pleasure. As an aside, we have gotten information from attorney Sarah Cunningham, who is representing Mrs. Brunell in a divorce action against Brunell, that Brunell may have stashed large amounts of cash in a safety deposit box. We believe that Brunell skimmed this cash from the company and failed to pay income taxes on it.

In early November of 200_, IRS Agent Rita Kurlan contacted Brunell concerning an audit of his company's tax returns for the years 200_ through 200_. Kurlan informed Brunell that she suspected the company of having underreported its net income for those years by paying for Brunell's personal expenses, thus vastly inflating its expenses. In addition, she advised Brunell that the personal expenses paid by the company should have been included as income on his individual income tax return, and that his failure to declare that income resulted in underpayment of his personal income taxes. Kurlan told Brunell to file amended returns for the company and himself for each of the pertinent years, reflecting the correct amounts of expenses, net income, and income taxes due and owing. Kurlan also warned Brunell that the IRS was considering referring the matter to this office for criminal investigation.

It appears that Brunell hired a lawyer, Anne Classen, to represent him in the investigation, because shortly after his conversation with Kurlan, Classen contacted Kurlan and asked that Kurlan address all questions to her. Kurlan disregarded this request because she felt the lawyer was "overreaching." She continued to call Brunell, or drop in at his office, to ask questions relevant to the investigation. She asked Brunell to provide him with documentation of certain expenses, which he did. Kurlan doesn't know whether Classen knew that Brunell was providing Kurlan with documentation. In any event, Kurlan's investigation revealed that the documentation had been falsified. In December 200_, Brunell told Kurlan that he had decided not to file amended returns for himself or his company. That statement, combined with the falsified documents, prompted her to refer the matter to this office.

I opened a file and brought the matter to the grand jury's attention. Subpoenas were issued to Brunell and the tax attorney who had prepared the company's returns. The grand jury's investigation culminated last month in an indictment charging Brunell with tax evasion, false statement, and conspiracy to commit tax evasion.

In addition to Brunell himself, the grand jury investigation uncovered complicity by two of Brunell's agents or employees: Brunell's personal tax accountant, Randi Spaari, and the company's bookkeeper, Marvoal. Spaari prepared Brunell's personal income tax returns and was a close friend of Brunell's. From what we can gather, she knew or at least should have known that Brunell was using company money to pay for his lavish lifestyle. Nevertheless, Spaari's level of culpability is relatively low, and she has offered to cooperate in exchange for informal immunity. Her testimony would be very helpful, and I recommend that we take her offer.

With respect to Marvoal, on my recommendation, this office obtained an indictment against her, but I am concerned with one aspect of our investigation. Several months ago, three FBI agents and Assistant United States Attorney Leston Parker, one of the newest AUSAs in this office, visited her at her home late at night. I was not informed about this visit until the next day and would not have authorized it. According to Parker, he and the agents felt Marvoal would cooperate with them if they ap-proached her away from Brunell and her job at the company. They rang her doorbell after they figured her children were in bed—Parker doesn't remember the exact time but believes it was shortly after 10 p.m. Marvoal agreed to speak with them and provided detailed information about Brunell after Parker explained her potential criminal exposure. Parker told me he was careful to advise her of her rights and felt she understood her options.

I recommend that this office negotiate a plea agreement with Marvoal. Her testimony would be very helpful in our case against Brunell, and her culpability is relatively low, since she was his employee. Moreover, I am concerned that Parker's night-time escapade might jeopardize the admissibility of the statements she made.

United States Attorney for the Northern District of Culdeva
United States Courthouse
9892 Torrence Boulevard
Exum, Culdeva 00000

Milt Ralston

2093 Barry Avenue

Exum, Culdeva 00000

Re: Plea Agreement—Terri Lynn Marvoal

Dear Mr. Ralston:

The following is the plea agreement between the United States Attorney for the Northern District of Culdeva and your client, Terri Lynn Marvoal.

1. Marvoal agrees to provide to the government complete, truthful, and accurate disclosure of all information she has concerning tax fraud, tax evasion, and other offenses involving Arthur Graham Brunell and Brunell's Natural Foods, Inc. She further agrees that she will neither attempt to protect any person or entity through false information or omissions nor falsely implicate any person or entity.

2. Marvoal's cooperation will include debriefing concerning her knowledge of tax fraud, tax evasion, and other offenses involving Arthur Graham Brunell and Brunell's Natural Foods, Inc. Marvoal will provide all documents in her possession relating to tax fraud, tax evasion, and other offenses involving Arthur Graham Brunell and Brunell's Natural Foods, Inc.

3. Marvoal will testify as a witness before any grand jury or trial jury as this Office may require, concerning tax fraud, tax evasion, and other offenses involving Arthur Graham Brunell and Brunell's Natural Foods, Inc.

4. Marvoal agrees to enter a plea of guilt to Count One of the Indictment in the Northern District of Culdeva.

5. In return for Marvoal's complete, truthful, and accurate information, the government agrees to recommend to the court that it accept her plea of guilty to Count One of the Indictment.

6. The government further agrees that the plea of guilty to Count One will end Terri Lynn Marvoal's criminal exposure for conduct over which the United States Attorney for the Northern District of Culdeva has

jurisdiction and of which she is aware, as that conduct relates to tax fraud, tax evasion, and other offenses involving Arthur Graham Brunell and Brunell's Natural Foods, Inc. This agreement does not extend to a prosecution for perjury, false statement, or obstruction of justice.

7.   The government further agrees to seek dismissal of Counts Two, Three, and Four of the Indictment.

8.   The government agrees to advise the Court and the Probation Department about the nature and full extent of Terri Lynn Marvoal's cooperation in the government's investigation of Arthur Graham Brunell and Brunell's Natural Foods, Inc.

9.   The disposition of this case is governed by the Federal Sentencing Guidelines and is not premised on agreement about a Guidelines sentence or on the government's sentencing recommendation, because the government wants to review the presentence report before deciding upon its recommendation.

10.   The government acknowledges that Marvoal reserves the right to make her own sentencing recommendations to the Court.

11.   Marvoal acknowledges that the sentence imposed on her will be determined in the sole discretion of the Court, within the limits provided by law. Marvoal also acknowledges that she may not withdraw the plea of guilty solely as a result of the sentence imposed.

12.   No additional promises, agreements, or conditions have been entered into other than those set forth herein. This agreement may be modified only in writing signed by the government and Marvoal.

If the above accurately reflects our agreement, please have your client execute this letter as set forth below.

Very truly yours,
United States Attorney

I have read this letter in its entirety and have discussed it with my attorney. I acknowledge that it sets forth my entire agreement with the United States Attorney for the Northern District of Culdeva. I enter into this agreement freely, voluntarily, and knowingly and with full understanding of my constitutional rights as explained to me by my attorney. No additional promises, inducements, or representations have been made to me by any representative of the United States Attorney's Office.

Executed: Witnesses:
Terri Lynn Marvoal   Milt Ralston

United States Attorney for the Northern District of Culdeva
United States Courthouse
9892 Torrence Boulevard
Exum, Culdeva 00000

Gwen Volence, Esq.
Volence & Berber

2394 Pratt Avenue
Exum, Culdeva 00000

Re: Immunity Agreement—Randi Spaari

Dear Ms. Volence:

This letter confirms the agreement entered into between this Office and your client, Randi Spaari. It is agreed, in exchange for a promise of use and derivative use immunity, that Randi Spaari will cooperate fully with this Office, agents of the Federal Bureau of Investigation, the Internal Revenue Service, and any other law enforcement agency that the circumstances require.

It is agreed that Randi Spaari's cooperation will include debriefing concerning her knowledge of tax fraud, tax evasion, and other offenses involving Arthur Graham Brunell and Brunell's Natural Foods, Inc. Randi Spaari agrees to provide truthful, accurate, and complete information.

It is further agreed that Randi Spaari will provide all documents in her possession relating to tax fraud, tax evasion, and other offenses involving Arthur Graham Brunell and Brunell's Natural Foods, Inc.

It is further agreed that Randi Spaari will testify as a witness before any grand jury or trial jury as this Office may require, concerning tax fraud, tax evasion, and other offenses involving Arthur Graham Brunell and Brunell's Natural Foods, Inc.

In exchange for the agreements set forth above, this Office agrees not to use against Randi Spaari in a criminal case any information that is a direct or indirect product of her debriefing, document production, or testimony, except in a prosecution for perjury, false statement, or obstruction of justice. The immunity accorded under this agreement shall be identical to the immunity accorded under 18 U.S.C. section 6002. It does not bar this Office from using information to prosecute her for crimes or acts occurring after the date of this agreement.

It is further agreed that if this Office demonstrates that Randi Spaari has given intentionally false, misleading, or incomplete information or testimony, or has otherwise failed to honor this agreement, the Office will consider the agreement null and void and may prosecute Randi Spaari based on any information directly or indirectly provided by her.

If this letter encompasses your understanding of the agreement between this Office and your client, please sign the duplicate original and return it to the Office.

_____

United States Attorney

_____

Attorney for Randi Spaari

CHAPTER 2

Searches and Seizures: Basic Concepts

- Searches   • Seizures   • Government Action

- Standing   • Extraterritorial Searches and Seizures

- Reasonableness Balancing   • Probable Cause

I. Introduction to the Fourth Amendment

A. Overview

Modern courts view the Fourth Amendment as serving one primary function: limiting the discretion of police and government agents to violate liberty, privacy, and possessory rights. The Fourth Amendment limits discretion by requiring a significant degree of justification before police can intrude on one of those rights. For example, before a police officer can conduct a search or seizure, the officer ordinarily must have probable cause to believe that a suspect has committed a crime or that fruits, contraband, instrumentalities, or evidence of crime will be found in a particular location at a particular time. Moreover, the officer ordinarily must establish probable cause to the satisfaction of a "neutral and detached magistrate" before the search or seizure. Neutral, *ex ante* review ensures an unbiased decision and creates a record that will be useful if the individual affected by the search or seizure later claims that it was unlawful. It also limits police discretion by requiring in advance "particularity" in terms of the persons, places, and things being sought.

Although *per se* rules prohibiting certain types of police conduct might advance the amendment's discretion-limiting goal, the Court has followed a surprisingly flexible approach to police activity[1] One source of this flexibility is the text of the amendment itself. Remember that the Fourth Amendment reads as follows:

> The right of the people to be secure in their persons, houses, papers, and effects against unreasonable searches and seizures, shall not be violated, and no warrants shall issue, but upon probable cause, sup-

---

[1]. *See* Scott Sundby, *A Return to Fourth Amendment Basics: Undoing the Mischief of Camara and Terry*, 72 Minn. L. Rev. 383 (1988).

ported by oath or affirmation, and particularly describing the place to be searched and the persons or things to be seized.

The amendment requires probable cause, oath, and a particular description whenever a warrant is issued, but it says nothing about whether a warrant is always required. The only limitation that appears to apply across the board is the prohibition against "unreasonable" searches and seizures. Consistent with the amendment's text, the Court's modern approach views "reasonableness" as the touchstone of Fourth Amendment jurisprudence.

"Reasonableness" is a product of balancing. The Court weighs the state's interests against the individual's interest to determine whether a warrant is necessary, what level of suspicion is necessary, and whether the police have otherwise behaved properly. The Court does not usually balance these interests on a case-by-case basis. Rather, it engages in balancing to craft a new rule for future cases fitting into a certain category. In subsequent cases of that category, it applies the rule to the facts in order to determine whether police acted reasonably.

Some scholars believe that the predominance of the reasonableness balancing test over *per se* rules undermines the purposes of the Fourth Amendment. These scholars point out, for example, that ideologically-driven judges may overvalue state interests and undervalue individual ones, or vice versa. Moreover, public pressure to stop crime may erode judicial willingness to insist upon probable cause and warrants. In addition, these scholars point out that the balancing approach has encouraged the Court to approve some warrants as "reasonable" that involved neither probable cause nor particularity, in apparent direct violation of the Fourth Amendment's text. Whether this critique is valid is a matter we will address in more detail later, together with historical factors that may shed light on whether the Court's approach is the correct one.

A preliminary overview of three other matters will facilitate your understanding of the Fourth Amendment. First is the issue of remedy. Even if a court finds a Fourth Amendment violation, a remedy is not necessarily available. The usual remedy for a Fourth Amendment violation is application of the exclusionary rule, which requires that any evidence obtained as a result of the violation cannot be used against the defendant at a criminal trial. But a later chapter will reveal, the Court does not apply the exclusionary rule if certain factors are present. Where the exclusionary rule does not apply, the aggrieved individual's only remedy is a civil rights suit, but this is a rarely used and frequently ineffective option.

The second matter for preliminary overview is the importance of the Fourteenth Amendment to Fourth Amendment analysis. The Court engaged in a lengthy process of wrestling with the issue of whether the Fourteenth Amendment "incorporated," or applied, the provisions in the Bill of Rights to the states. Once the Court found that the Fourteenth Amendment due process clause incorporated the Fourth Amendment against the states, it ignored the role of due process in Fourth Amendment analysis. Yet a strong interpretive argument can be made that the Fourteenth Amendment fundamentally altered the meaning of the Fourth

Amendment. That argument was summarized briefly in Chapter 1 and will be discussed further in a later part of this book. The most important implication of this argument is that the Fourth Amendment is not colorblind—an argument that, as you will see, the Court has not yet accepted.

The third matter for preliminary overview involves the steps that a lawyer must follow in analyzing a Fourth Amendment problem. These steps are outlined in the checklist below.

B.   HOW TO APPROACH FOURTH AMENDMENT PROBLEMS

In the checklist below, we set forth the structure of a Fourth Amendment analysis. The items listed in points 1 and 2 of the checklist are covered in this chapter. For the matters listed in points 3 and 4, see later chapters.

Checklist 1: Is There a Fourth Amendment Claim?

1. Does the Fourth Amendment Apply?
   a. Was there government action?
      (i) Did the government know of and acquiesce in the intrusive conduct?
      (ii) If so, was the private actor's purpose to assist law enforcement efforts rather than to further his or her own ends?
   b. Was there a search or seizure?
      (i) Was there a search—an invasion of a reasonable expectation of privacy?
      (ii) Was there a seizure of the person—government action that a reasonable person would believe limited his or her freedom of movement?
      (iii) Was there a seizure of a thing—an interference with a person's possessory interests in property?

2. If the Fourth Amendment applies, does the defendant have standing to object to admitting the evidence?
   a. Did the search affect *this defendant's* reasonable expectation of privacy, freedom of movement, or possessory interests?
   b. Did *this defendant* have sufficient connections with the American community to be considered a member of "the people" protected by the Fourth Amendment?

3. If the Fourth Amendment applies and the defendant has standing, was the search or seizure reasonable?
   a. What level of justification—probable cause, reasonable suspicion, or something else—did the Fourth Amendment require?
   b. Was the level of justification met?
   c. Was a warrant required, or was there an applicable warrant exception?
   d. If a warrant was required, was the warrant supported on oath by probable cause, issued by a neutral and detached magistrate, and sufficiently particular?

e. If the search or seizure was accompanied by a warrant, did the police execute the warrant reasonably?

4. If the Fourth Amendment was violated, is the appropriate remedy exclusion of evidence?
   a. Does an exclusionary rule limitation apply?
       (i) Was the evidence discovered through an independent source?
       (ii) If not, was the evidence likely to have been inevitably discovered through an independent source?
       (iii) If not, was the taint of the constitutional violation attenuated?
   b. Does the good faith exception apply—did the police reasonably rely on a warrant?

II. What Is a "Search"?

The Fourth Amendment applies only to searches and seizures conducted by government actors. We begin with the definition of "search."

A. The *Katz* Test Articulated

The modern definition of "search" was first articulated in *Katz v. United States*[2] an excerpt of which is reproduced below. The *Katz* test is generally referred to as the "reasonable expectation of privacy" test. As you read the *Katz* opinion, ask yourself what interpretive theory or theories the Court used to derive the test. Does the test make sense? How would you determine whether the test is met in a particular case?

Katz v. United States

389 U.S. 347 (1967).

■ STEWART, J. The petitioner was convicted in the District Court for the Southern District of California under an eight-count indictment charging him with transmitting wagering information by telephone from Los Angeles to Miami and Boston in violation of a federal statute. At trial the Government was permitted, over the petitioner's objection, to introduce evidence of the petitioner's end of telephone conversations, overheard by FBI agents who had attached an electronic listening and recording device to the outside of the public telephone booth from which he had placed his calls. In affirming his conviction, the Court of Appeals rejected the contention that the recordings had been obtained in violation of the Fourth Amendment, because "[t]here was no physical entrance into the area occupied by [the petitioner]." We granted certiorari in order to consider the constitutional questions thus presented.

The petitioner had phrased those questions as follows:

---

2. 389 U.S. 347, 353 (1967).

A.   Whether a public telephone booth is a constitutionally protected area so that evidence obtained by attaching an electronic listening recording device to the top of such a booth is obtained in violation of the right to privacy of the user of the booth.

B.   Whether physical penetration of a constitutionally protected area is necessary before a search and seizure can be said to be violative of the Fourth Amendment to the United States Constitution.

We decline to adopt this formulation of the issues. In the first place the correct solution of Fourth Amendment problems is not necessarily promoted by incantation of the phrase "constitutionally protected area." Secondly, the Fourth Amendment cannot be translated into a general constitutional "right to privacy." That Amendment protects individual privacy against certain kinds of governmental intrusion, but its protections go further, and often have nothing to do with privacy at all. Other provisions of the Constitution protect personal privacy from other forms of governmental invasion. But the protection of a person's general right to privacy—his right to be let alone by other people—is, like the protection of his property and of his very life, left largely to the law of the individual States.

Because of the misleading way the issues have been formulated, the parties have attached great significance to the characterization of the telephone booth from which the petitioner placed his calls. The petitioner has strenuously argued that the booth was a "constitutionally protected area." The Government has maintained with equal vigor that it was not. But this effort to decide whether or not a given "area," viewed in the abstract, is "constitutionally protected" deflects attention from the problem presented by this case. For the Fourth Amendment protects people, not places. What a person knowingly exposes to the public, even in his own home or office, is not a subject of Fourth Amendment protection. *See Lewis v. United States*, 385 U.S. 206 [1966]; *United States v. Lee*, 274 U.S. 559 [1927]. But what he seeks to preserve as private, even in an area accessible to the public, may be constitutionally protected. *See Rios v. United States*, 364 U.S. 253; *Ex parte Jackson*, 96 U.S. 727, 733 [1877].

The Government stresses the fact that the telephone booth from which the petitioner made his calls was constructed partly of glass, so that he was as visible after he entered it as he would have been if he had remained outside. But what he sought to exclude when he entered the booth was not the intruding eye—it was the uninvited ear. He did not shed his right to do so simply because he made his calls from a place where he might be seen. No less than an individual in a business office, in a friend's apartment, or in a taxicab, a person in a telephone booth may rely upon the protection of the Fourth Amendment. One who occupies it, shuts the door behind him, and pays the toll that permits him to place a call is surely entitled to assume that the words he utters into the mouthpiece will not be broadcast to the world. To read the Constitution more narrowly is to ignore the vital role that the public telephone has come to play in private communication.

The Government contends, however, that the activities of its agents in this case should not be tested by Fourth Amendment requirements, for the surveillance technique they employed involved no physical penetration of the telephone booth from which the petitioner placed his calls. It is true that the absence of such penetration was at one time thought to foreclose further Fourth Amendment inquiry, *Olmstead v. United States*, 277 U.S. 438 [1928], for that Amendment was thought to limit only searches and seizures of tangible property. But "[t]he premise that property interests control the right of the Government to search and seize has been discredited." *Warden v. Hayden*, 387 U.S. 294 [1967]. Thus, although a closely divided Court supposed in *Olmstead* that surveillance without any trespass and without the seizure of any material object fell outside the ambit of the Constitution, we have since departed from the narrow view on which that decision rested. Indeed, we have expressly held that the Fourth Amendment governs not only the seizure of tangible items, but extends as well to the recording of oral statements overheard without any "technical trespass under ... local property law." *Silverman v. United States*, 365 U.S. 505 [1961]. Once this much is acknowledged, and once it is recognized that the Fourth Amendment protects people—and not simply "areas"—against unreasonable searches and seizures it becomes clear that the reach of that Amendment cannot turn upon the presence or absence of a physical intrusion into any given enclosure.

We conclude that the underpinnings of *Olmstead* ... have been so eroded by our subsequent decisions that the "trespass" doctrine there enunciated can no longer be regarded as controlling. The Government's activities in electronically listening to and recording the petitioner's words violated the privacy upon which he justifiably relied while using the telephone booth and thus constituted a "search and seizure" within the meaning of the Fourth Amendment. The fact that the electronic device employed to achieve that end did not happen to penetrate the wall of the booth can have no constitutional significance.

The question remaining for decision, then, is whether the search and seizure conducted in this case complied with constitutional standards. In that regard, the Government's position is that its agents acted in an entirely defensible manner: They did not begin their electronic surveillance until investigation of the petitioner's activities had established a strong probability that he was using the telephone in question to transmit gambling information to persons in other States, in violation of federal law. Moreover, the surveillance was limited, both in scope and in duration, to the specific purpose of establishing the contents of the petitioner's unlawful telephonic communications. The agents confined their surveillance to the brief periods during which he used the telephone booth, and they took great care to overhear only the conversations of the petitioner himself.

Accepting this account of the Government's actions as accurate, it is clear that this surveillance was so narrowly circumscribed that a duly authorized magistrate, properly notified of the need for such investigation, specifically informed of the basis on which it was to proceed, and clearly apprised of the precise intrusion it would entail, could constitutionally have authorized, with appropriate safeguards, the very limited search and seizure that the Government asserts in fact took place. Only last Term we sustained the validity of such an authorization, holding that, under sufficiently "precise and discriminate circumstances," a federal court may empower government agents to employ a concealed electronic device "for the narrow and particularized purpose of ascertaining the truth of the . . . allegations" of a "detailed factual affidavit alleging the commission of a specific criminal offense." *Osborn v. United States*, 385 U.S. 323 [1966]. Discussing that holding, the Court in *Berger v. New York*, 388 U.S. 41 [1935], said that "the order authorizing the use of the electronic device" in *Osborn* "afforded similar protections to those . . . of conventional warrants authorizing the seizure of tangible evidence." Through those protections, "no greater invasion of privacy was permitted than was necessary under the circumstances." *Id.* Here, too, a similar judicial order could have accommodated "the legitimate needs of law enforcement" by authorizing the carefully limited use of electronic surveillance.

The Government urges that, because its agents relied upon the decision[] in *Olmstead*, and because they did no more here than they might properly have done with prior judicial sanction, we should retroactively validate their conduct. That we cannot do. It is apparent that the agents in this case acted with restraint. Yet the inescapable fact is that this restraint was imposed by the agents themselves, not by a judicial officer. They were not required, before commencing the search, to present their estimate of probable cause for detached scrutiny by a neutral magistrate. They were not compelled, during the conduct of the search itself, to observe precise limits established in advance by a specific court order. Nor were they directed, after the search had been completed, to notify the authorizing magistrate in detail of all that had been seized. In the absence of such safeguards, this Court has never sustained a search upon the sole ground that officers reasonably expected to find evidence of a particular crime and voluntarily confined their activities to the least intrusive means consistent with that end. Searches conducted without warrants have been held unlawful "notwithstanding facts unquestionably showing probable cause," *Agnello v. United States*, 269 U.S. 20 [1925], for the Constitution requires "that the deliberate, impartial judgment of a judicial officer . . . be interposed between the citizen and the police. . . ." *Wong Sun v. United States*, 371 U.S. 471 [1963]. "Over and again this Court has emphasized that the mandate of the (Fourth) Amendment requires adherence to judicial processes," *United States v. Jeffers*, 342 U.S. 48 [1951], and that searches conducted outside the judicial process, without prior approval by judge or magistrate, are per se unreasonable under the Fourth Amendment—subject only to a few specifically established and well-delineated exceptions. . . .

The Government does not question these basic principles. Rather, it urges the creation of a new exception to cover this case. It argues that surveillance of a telephone booth should be exempted from the usual requirement of advance authorization by a magistrate upon a showing of probable cause. We cannot agree. Omission of such authorization "bypasses the safeguards provided by an objective predetermination of probable cause, and substitutes instead the far less reliable procedure of an after-the-event justification for the ... search, too likely to be subtly influenced by the familiar shortcomings of hindsight judgment." *Beck v. State of Ohio*, 379 U.S. 89 [1964]. And bypassing a neutral predetermination of the scope of a search leaves individuals secure from Fourth Amendment violations only in the discretion of the police.

These considerations do not vanish when the search in question is transferred from the setting of a home, an office, or a hotel room to that of a telephone booth. Wherever a man may be, he is entitled to know that he will remain free from unreasonable searches and seizures. The government agents here ignored the procedure of antecedent justification ... that is central to the Fourth Amendment, a procedure that we hold to be a constitutional precondition of the kind of electronic surveillance involved in this case. Because the surveillance here failed to meet that condition, and because it led to the petitioner's conviction, the judgment must be reversed.

■ HARLAN, J., concurring. I join the opinion of the Court, which I read to hold only (a) that an enclosed telephone booth is an area where, like a home, *Weeks v. United States*, 232 U.S. 383 [1914], and unlike a field, *Hester v. United States*, 265 U.S. 57 [1924], a person has a constitutionally protected reasonable expectation of privacy; (b) that electronic as well as physical intrusion into a place that is in this sense private may constitute a violation of the Fourth Amendment; and (c) that the invasion of a constitutionally protected area by federal authorities is, as the Court has long held, presumptively unreasonable in the absence of a search warrant.

As the Court's opinion states, "the Fourth Amendment protects people, not places." The question, however, is what protection it affords to those people. Generally, as here, the answer to that question requires reference to a "place." My understanding of the rule that has emerged from prior decisions is that there is a twofold requirement, first that a person have exhibited an actual (subjective) expectation of privacy and, second, that the expectation be one that society is prepared to recognize as "reasonable." Thus a man's home is, for most purposes, a place where he expects privacy, but objects, activities, or statements that he exposes to the "plain view" of outsiders are not "protected" because no intention to keep them to himself has been exhibited. On the other hand, conversations in the open would not be protected against being overheard, for the expectation of privacy under the circumstances would be unreasonable. *Cf. Hester v. United States, supra.*

The critical fact in this case is that "[o]ne who occupies it [a telephone booth] shuts the door behind him, and pays the toll that permits him to place a call is surely entitled to assume" that his conversation is not being intercepted. The point is not that the booth is "accessible to the public" at other times, but that it is a temporarily private place whose momentary occupants' expectations of freedom from intrusion are recognized as reasonable.

In *Silverman v. United States*, 365 U.S. 505 [1961], we held that eavesdropping accomplished by means of an electronic device that penetrated the premises occupied by petitioner was a violation of the Fourth

Amendment. That case established that interception of conversations reasonably intended to be private could constitute a "search and seizure," and that the examination or taking of physical property was not required. . . . In *Silverman* we found it unnecessary to re-examine *Goldman v. United States*, 316 U.S. 129 [1942], which had held that electronic surveillance accomplished without the physical penetration of petitioner's premises by a tangible object did not violate the Fourth Amendment. This case requires us to reconsider *Goldman*, and I agree that it should now be overruled. Its limitation on Fourth Amendment protection is, in the present day, bad physics as well as bad law, for reasonable expectations of privacy may be defeated by electronic as well as physical invasion.

Finally, I do not read the Court's opinion to declare that no interception of a conversation one-half of which occurs in a public telephone can be reasonable in the absence of a warrant. As elsewhere under the Fourth Amendment, warrants are the general rule, to which the legitimate needs of law enforcement may demand specific exceptions. It will be time enough to consider any such exceptions when an appropriate occasion presents itself, and I agree with the Court that this is not one.

■ BLACK, J., dissenting. . . . My basic objection is twofold: (1) I do not believe that the words of the Amendment will bear the meaning given them by today's decision, and (2) I do not believe that it is the proper role of this Court to rewrite the Amendment in order "to bring it into harmony with the times" and thus reach a result that many people believe to be desirable.

While I realize that an argument based on the meaning of words lacks the scope, and no doubt the appeal, of broad policy discussions and philosophical discourses on such nebulous subjects as privacy, for me the language of the Amendment is the crucial place to look in construing a written document such as our Constitution. The Fourth Amendment says that "The right of the people to be secure in their persons, houses, papers, and effects, against unreasonable searches and seizures, shall not be violated, and no Warrants shall issue, but upon probable cause, supported by Oath or affirmation, and particularly describing the place to be searched, and the persons or things to be seized." The first clause protects "persons, houses, papers, and effects, against unreasonable searches and seizures. . . ." These words connote the idea of tangible things with size, form, and weight, things capable of being searched, seized, or both. The second clause of the Amendment still further establishes its Framers' purpose to limit its protection to tangible things by providing that no warrants shall issue but those "particularly describing the place to be searched, and the persons or things to be seized." A conversation overheard by eavesdropping, whether by plain snooping or wiretapping, is not tangible and, under the normally accepted meanings of the words, can neither be searched nor seized. In addition the language of the second clause indicates that the Amendment refers not only to something tangible so it can be seized but to something already in existence so it can be described. Yet the Court's interpretation would have the Amendment apply to overhearing future conversations which by their very nature are nonexistent until they take place. How can one "describe" a future conversation, and, if one cannot, how can a magistrate issue a warrant to eavesdrop one in the future? It is argued that information showing what is expected to be said is sufficient to limit the boundaries of what later can be admitted into evidence; but does such general information really meet the specific language of the Amendment which says "particularly describing"? Rather than using language in a completely artificial way, I must conclude that the Fourth Amendment simply does not apply to eavesdropping.

Tapping telephone wires, of course, was an unknown possibility at the time the Fourth Amendment was adopted. But eavesdropping (and wiretapping is nothing more than eavesdropping by telephone) was recognized, an ancient practice which at common law was condemned as a nuisance. IV Blackstone, Commentaries § 168. In those days the eavesdropper listened by naked ear under the eaves of houses or their windows, or beyond their walls seeking out private discourse. There can be no doubt that the Framers were aware of this practice, and if they had desired to outlaw or restrict the use of evidence obtained by eavesdropping, I believe that they would have used the appropriate language to do so in the Fourth Amendment. They certainly would not have left such a task to the ingenuity of language-stretching judges. No one, it seems to me, can read the debates on the Bill of Rights without reaching the conclusion that its Framers and critics well knew the meaning of the words they used, what they would be understood to mean by others, their scope and their limitations. Under these circumstances it strikes me as a charge against their scholarship, their common sense and their candor to give to the Fourth Amendment's language the eavesdropping meaning the Court imputes to it today.

Since I see no way in which the words of the Fourth Amendment can be construed to apply to eavesdropping, that closes the matter for me. In interpreting the Bill of Rights, I willingly go as far as a liberal construction of the language takes me, but I simply cannot in good conscience give a meaning to words which they have never before been thought to have and which they certainly do not have in common ordinary usage. I will not distort the words of the Amendment in order to "keep the Constitution up to date" or "to bring it into harmony with the times." It was never meant that this Court have such power, which in effect would make us a continuously functioning constitutional convention.

With this decision the Court has completed, I hope, its rewriting of the Fourth Amendment, which started only recently when the Court began referring incessantly to the Fourth Amendment not so much as a law against unreasonable searches and seizures as one to protect an individual's privacy. By clever word juggling the Court finds it plausible to argue that language aimed specifically at searches and seizures of things that can be searched and seized may, to protect privacy, be applied to eavesdropped evidence of conversations that can neither be searched nor seized. Few things happen to an individual that do not affect his privacy in one way or another. Thus, by arbitrarily substituting the Court's language, designed to protect privacy, for the Constitution's language, designed to protect against unreasonable searches and seizures, the Court has made the Fourth Amendment its vehicle for holding all laws violative of the Constitution which offend the Court's broadest concept of privacy. As I said in *Griswold v. State of Connecticut*, 381 U.S. 479 [1965], "The Court talks about a constitutional 'right of privacy' as though there is some constitutional provision or provisions forbidding any law ever to be passed which might abridge the 'privacy' of individuals. But there is not." I made clear in that dissent my fear of the dangers involved when this Court uses the "broad, abstract and ambiguous concept" of "privacy" as a "comprehensive substitute for the Fourth Amendment's guarantee against unreasonable searches and seizures."

The Fourth Amendment protects privacy only to the extent that it prohibits unreasonable searches and seizures of "persons, houses, papers, and effects." No general right is created by the Amendment so as to give this Court the unlimited power to hold unconstitutional everything which affects privacy. Certainly the Framers, well acquainted as they were with the excesses of governmental power, did not intend to grant this Court such omnipotent lawmaking authority as that. The history of governments proves that it is dangerous to freedom to repose such powers in courts.

QUESTIONS

1. In his concurrence, Justice Harlan articulated a two-fold test: first, a person must exhibit a subjective expectation of privacy; second, the expectation must be one that society is prepared to recognize as "reasonable." This two-part test has become what judges and lawyers call "the *Katz* test." Consider Justice Harlan's test in light of the following hypothetical: at the request of a majority of the residents of a public housing project (and over the objections of a minority), the government agency running the project announced in letters to every resident that the agency planned to engage in random, unannounced searches of apartments for illegal drugs. Would the first prong of Justice Harlan's test be met? Would your answer change if the notice had been given to new tenants prior to signing their leases and to old tenants prior to renewing their leases? Is Justice Harlan's test consistent with the values underlying the Fourth Amendment?

2. Which of the seven sources of interpretive data discussed in Chapter 1 did each opinion rely upon in reaching its conclusions? How did Justice Black's interpretive method differ from that of Justices Stewart and Harlan? In the context of defining a search, which interpretive method makes the most sense? Which sources would you have relied upon had you been a member of the Court?

3. Was the majority correct in concluding that Katz's expectation of privacy was "reasonable"?

B.   MAJORITY VIEW VERSUS NORMATIVE JUDGMENT

The *Katz* test demands that courts define privacy and determine when it can reasonably be expected. Nevertheless, the Court has never clearly defined privacy or even provided a workable set of guidelines[3] Instead, it uses an array of conclusory phrases that fall into two categories:

> . . . The privacy at stake covers both being in private—doing what one chooses to do, with whom one chooses, without intrusion—and having in private—preserving what one treasures, or merely possesses, unexposed to the world. Both kinds of privacy enable the individual to constitute himself as the unique person he is. Both are aspects of the fully realized life. And both importantly provide conditions for the realization of the common good as well.[4]

Similarly, the Court has never clearly defined reasonableness, or stated clearly whether the definition depends on majority views or normative decisions. If the definition of reasonableness depended on majority views, the Court would examine American views about privacy and tailor its definition to fit the attitudes of the majority or even of a sizeable minority. This approach invites empirical analyses of majority views in the form of polls, interviews, and surveys, or, where empirical data is unavailable, a review of history, legislative actions, jury verdicts, and other indicia of popular will that the Court has sometimes relied upon in its constitutional jurisprudence.[5]

Christopher Slobogin and Joseph Schumacher have attempted an empirical analysis of this kind. They asked over two hundred subjects to rate the intrusiveness of 50 different types of law enforcement investigative techniques, most of which have been addressed in Supreme Court cases[6] They then ranked the types of techniques according to the subjects' responses from least intrusive (R=1) to most intrusive. These researchers found marked contrasts between the Court's and the public's views of reasonable privacy expectations:

> For instance, the Court has held that police use of undercover agents to obtain information does not violate "justifiable expectations of privacy," because one assumes the risk that one's acquaintances will reveal confidences. The survey participants, in contrast, found various types of undercover activity, including covert use of a chauffeur (R=31) and a secretary (R=34), to be very intrusive, at least as invasive as, for instance, searches of cars (R=29, 30). Along the same lines, whereas *United States v. Miller* held that a bank depositor "takes the risk, in revealing his affairs to another, that the information will be

---

3. *See* Daniel B. Yeager, *Search, Seizure and the Positive Law: Expectations of Privacy Outside the Fourth Amendment*, 84 J. Crim. L. & Criminology 249, 280 (1993).

4. Lloyd Weinreb, *The Fourth Amendment Today*, in The Bill of Rights: Original Meaning and Current Understanding 185–86 (Eugene W. Hickok, Jr., ed. 1991).

5. *See, e.g.*, Gregg v. Georgia, 428 U.S. 153 (1976) (considering several of these data sources in determining what "evolving standards of decency" tell us about the constitutional validity of the death penalty).

6. Christopher Slobogin & Joseph E. Schumacher, *Reasonable Expectations of Privacy and Autonomy in Fourth Amendment Cases: An Empirical Look at "Understandings Recognized and Permitted by Society,"* 42 Duke L. J. 727, 733–39, 759–61 (1993).

conveyed by that person to the Government," the scenario involving government perusal of bank records received a high ranking (R=38).

The Court has also held that police entry onto fenced-in private property outside the curtilage of the home is not a search, and has strongly suggested that a "dog sniff" of a person does not implicate the Fourth Amendment. Yet both of these actions received fairly high rankings (R=21 and R=23, respectively).... Indeed, both are ranked at the same general level as a "frisk" (R=19 ...), which, according to the Court, is a search for Fourth Amendment purposes....

If this empirical data is confirmed by other studies, is the Court likely to revise its case law on when privacy expectations are reasonable? We suspect the answer is "no," because we believe that the Court implicitly emphasizes a normative approach over a majority one. Recall the hypothetical posed in Question Number 1 following the *Katz* case. That hypothetical asked whether an individual's subjective expectation of privacy is a necessary prerequisite for finding a search under *Katz*. If it is, then government actions would condition majority expectations and could prevent individuals from having any subjective expectations of privacy. For example, the majority in *Smith v. Maryland* [7] noted:

> [I]f the Government were suddenly to announce on nationwide television that all homes henceforth would be subject to warrantless entry, individuals thereafter might not in fact entertain any actual expectation of privacy regarding their homes, papers, and effects. Similarly, if a refugee from a totalitarian country, unaware of this nation's traditions, erroneously assumed that police were continuously monitoring his telephone conversations, a subjective expectation of privacy regarding the contents of his calls might be lacking as well.

In response to this problem, the Court has suggested that it must adopt a normative inquiry. In *Smith v. Maryland*, it explained that "where an individual's subjective expectations had been 'conditioned' by influences alien to well-recognized Fourth Amendment freedoms, those subjective expectations obviously could play no meaningful role in ascertaining what the scope of Fourth Amendment protection was. In determining whether a 'legitimate expectation of privacy' existed in such cases, a normative inquiry would be proper." Later in this book (especially in the discussion of "special needs" searches) it will become clear that some government conditioning of freedoms—for example, government regulation of automobiles and businesses—affects the reasonableness and importance of privacy interests. Apparently the Court finds some government conditioning normatively acceptable and some not.

Using a normative approach, the Court determines whether expectations of privacy are reasonable by referring to the values underlying the Fourth Amendment. Under such an approach, the Court's assumptions about majority expectations are still relevant, though not controlling. In other words, the second part of the *Katz* test, which requires the Court to

---

7.   442 U.S. 735, 741 n.5 (1979).

examine whether society is prepared to recognize privacy expectations as reasonable, is determined by the Court as society's representative in the realm of constitutional values.

This normative approach presents the Court with several difficult issues. For example, the Court may recognize values in the Fourth Amendment that conflict with each other or with other constitutional rights. Moreover, the degree to which a Fourth Amendment value is implicated may depend on the effect of a particular police action on various parties. Under a normative approach, therefore, "finding out where privacy lies requires resort to one of the Court's many 'balancing' tests."[8] This implicit or explicit balancing test to determine whether a privacy interest is worthy of protection requires cataloging what Professor Yeager calls the Court's "highly factualized holdings" to assess both the factors entering the weighing process and the relative weights given them.

C.   FACTORS IN A *KATZ* ANALYSIS

If the search inquiry is at least sometimes normative, we must identify the factors that enter into the Court's weighing process. Several factors are probably at work. Seven of them are identified here, but bear in mind that this list is not exhaustive—the Court may identify others at any time, and you may find others in the case law.

1.   LOCATION, LOCATION, LOCATION

Although the Court stated in *Katz* that the Fourth Amendment protects persons, not places, the setting in which government action takes place is nevertheless the most important factor in determining the existence of a "search." Thus "open fields"—"unoccupied and undeveloped open areas (even if enclosed and posted with 'no trespassing' signs)"[9] have no Fourth Amendment protection. Such fields do not involve those "intimate activities" that the Court believes the amendment is meant to protect. By contrast, activities outside the home but on the "curtilage," an area adjacent to and intimately connected with the home, are protected. The terms "open fields" and "curtilage" are conclusory labels that reflect the Court's efforts to create a bright-line rule concerning where expectations of privacy will be found reasonable. The distinction is so important that it is worth reviewing its history in the Court's opinions.

In the pre-*Katz* case of *Hester v. United States*[10] the Court held that "[t]he special protection accorded by the Fourth Amendment to the people in their 'persons, houses, papers and effects' is not extended to the open fields. The distinction between the latter and the house is as old as the common law." In *Oliver v. United States*[11] the Court held that *Hester's*

---

8.   Yeager, *Positive Law, supra* note 3, at 281.

9.   ROBERT M. BLOOM & MARK S. BRODIN, CRIMINAL PROCEDURE: EXAMPLES & EXPLANATIONS 27 (4th ed. 2004).

10.   265 U.S. 57 (1924).

11.   466 U.S. 170 (1984).

"open fields doctrine" survived *Katz*. The facts of *Oliver* are these: two narcotics agents, acting on reports that Oliver was growing marijuana, arrived on his farm to investigate. They drove past Oliver's house to a locked gate with a "No Trespassing" sign. A footpath led around one side of the gate. The agents skirted the gate and continued to walk through Oliver's property for several hundred yards, passing a barn and a parked camper. Eventually, about a mile from Oliver's house, the officers came across a crop of marijuana. Oliver was arrested and indicted for manufacturing a controlled substance. The district court suppressed the discovery of the marijuana, emphasizing Oliver's efforts to keep his property private. The Sixth Circuit Court of Appeals reversed, concluding that the police merely entered an open field.

The Supreme Court agreed. The Court relied heavily on the Fourth Amendment's text, pointing out that the phrase "persons, houses, papers, and effects" does not include open fields. The Court also noted that the framers had rejected Madison's original draft of the amendment, which included the term "property." The framers replaced that broad term with the narrower term "effects." In light of the fact that the common law at the time the amendment was enacted recognized open fields as a distinct concept, the framers' choice of words indicates that they did not intend the Fourth Amendment to extend to open fields.

Secondly, the Court emphasized that the open fields doctrine is fully consistent with *Katz*, because an individual may not legitimately demand privacy for activities conducted out of doors, except in the area immediately surrounding the home. As a practical matter, signs and fences are unlikely to keep the public out of large spaces, and open fields can be surveyed from the air. Oliver's efforts to keep his property private were irrelevant, because the Court noted that "[c]ertainly the Framers did not intend that the Fourth Amendment should shelter criminal activity whenever persons with criminal intent choose to erect barriers and post 'No Trespassing' signs." Moreover, the kinds of activities that occur in open fields are not intimate, home-like ones. Instead, they involve such things as crop cultivation, the privacy of which society has no interest in protecting.[12]

Finally, the Court explained that property rights were unimportant to its open fields analysis. The officers clearly had committed common law trespass when they entered Oliver's property. However, the Court observed that the common law of trespass is broader than the privacy rights protected by the Fourth Amendment.

The dissent by Justice Marshall, joined by Justices Brennan and Stevens, disagreed on every point. First, the dissent argued that the majority's textual analysis of the amendment was inconsistent with precedent. For example, the protected phone booth in *Katz* cannot fairly be described as a "person, house, paper, or effect." Similarly, the dissent

---

12. In reaching this conclusion, the Court noted that the intention of the framers, the uses to which an individual puts a location, and our societal understandings about what areas deserve the most scrupulous protection from government invasion are all factors relevant to whether there is a "reasonable" privacy expectation. *Id.* at 178.

argued that *Katz* shifted the analysis from the idea of protected places to protected persons. Second, according to the dissent many of the factors ignored or minimized by the majority had in other precedent been given great weight in determining the "reasonableness" of privacy expectations, notably: (a) whether the expectation is rooted in positive law, (b) the nature and uses to which the property can be put, and (c) whether the person claiming a privacy interest manifested that interest in a way that most persons would understand and respect, such as posting no trespassing signs. Third, the dissent proposed an alternative rule, which it argued would be easily administrable: the Fourth Amendment would protect private land marked in a fashion sufficient to render entry thereon a criminal trespass under state law. Finally, the dissent noted that property rights, while not determinative, should ordinarily entitle one to a reasonable expectation of privacy precisely because such rights include excluding others. These views, emphasizing property rights and social convention, are very similar to those of Professor Yeager, noted earlier.

The Court's decision in *Oliver* is especially significant because it created a bright-line rule: open fields are not protected by the Fourth Amendment. The Court rejected a case-by-case inquiry into whether a particular open field might reflect reasonable privacy expectations because such an approach would provide police with little guidance. The Court expressed confidence that in most cases it would be relatively easy to distinguish "open fields" from the curtilage of a home, and that courts would face only occasional difficulties in identifying the two.

In *United States v. Dunn*[13] the Court had an opportunity to address one of those "occasional difficulties," and it used the opportunity to define the term "curtilage." Ronald Dale Dunn owned a 198–acre ranch, which was completely encircled by a perimeter fence and which contained several interior fences constructed mainly of posts and barbed wire. The ranch residence was some distance from a public road, and a fence encircled the residence and a nearby greenhouse. Outside of that fence, and some 50 yards from it, were two barns. The barns were encircled by fencing. Moreover, the front of the larger of the two barns was enclosed by a wooden fence and had an open overhang. Locked, waist-high gates barred entry into the barn proper, and netting stretched from the ceiling to the top of the wooden gates.

Acting without a warrant, DEA agents crossed over the ranch's perimeter fence and one interior fence. From the direction of the barns, one of the agents smelled what he believed to be phenylacetic acid, a substance used to manufacture illegal drugs. The officers approached the smaller of the barns, crossing over barbed-wire fencing. They looked into the barn and, after observing only empty boxes, proceeded to the larger barn, crossing over another barbed-wire fence as well as the wooden fence that enclosed the front portion of the barn. The officers walked under the barn's overhang to the locked wooden gates and, shining a flashlight through the

---

13.   480 U.S. 294 (1987).

netting on top of the gates, peered into the barn. There, one officer saw what he thought was a phenyl acetone laboratory. The officers left and returned with a search warrant on a later date. Their search revealed chemicals, equipment, and amphetamines. Dunn was convicted after the trial court denied his suppression motion. The Court of Appeals reversed the conviction, concluding that the barn was within the ranch house curtilage and thus enjoyed Fourth Amendment protection.

The Supreme Court disagreed, relying on four factors to demonstrate that the barn was situated in an open field as opposed to the ranch house curtilage:

- First, the barn was not proximate to the house, being 50 yards from the fence surrounding the house and 60 yards from the house itself.

- Second, the barn was outside the fenced-in area surrounding the house. It was clear from the layout of the ranch that the fence served to demark a specific area connected with the house. Similarly, the barn stood out as a distinct portion of the ranch, quite separate from the home.

- Third, the use to which the barn was put (it was a drug laboratory) "could not fairly be characterized as so associated with the activities and privacies of domestic life that the officers should have deemed the barn as part of respondent's home."

- Fourth, the steps taken by Dunn to protect the barn from observation by those standing in the open fields were minimal. Nothing in the record suggested that the interior fences were made to prevent persons from observing what lay inside the enclosed areas.

Aside from establishing a four-factor curtilage test, the Court's opinion in *Dunn* is important for its focus on vantage point. Dunn had asserted that he possessed a reasonable privacy expectation in the barn's contents because the barn was an essential part of his ranch business. For all practical purposes, the barn was his office. The Court declined to address that argument directly, but it pointed out the agents had not entered the barn. Rather, they made their observations of the barn's contents from an open field in which Dunn had no legitimate privacy interest. It made no difference that the agents crossed fences on the open field to get close enough to see into the barn.

Comment on State Constitutions: Using their own constitutions, some states reject the open fields doctrine. Mississippi's constitution, for example, protects "persons, houses, and possessions" rather than "persons, houses, papers, and effects."[14] The Mississippi Supreme Court interpreted "possessions" as "a very comprehensive term, [which] includes practically everything which may be owned, and over which a person may exercise control," including open fields.

---

14.   *See* Falkner v. State, 98 So. 691 (Miss. 1924).

New York courts have stated that the open fields doctrine is inconsistent with the *Katz* notion that the Fourth Amendment protects people, not places[15] Rejecting the reasoning in *Oliver*, a New York court stated:

> The reasoning of the *Oliver* majority seems to be this, in effect: that law-abiding persons should have nothing to hide on their property and, thus, there can be no reasonable objection to the State's unpermitted entry on posted or fenced land to conduct a general search for contraband. But this presupposes the ideal of a conforming society, a concept which seems foreign to New York's tradition of tolerance of the unconventional and of what may appear bizarre or even offensive. So also does this reasoning ignore the truism that even law-abiding citizens may have good reasons for keeping their activities private and the general notion that the only legitimate purpose for governmental infringement on the rights of the individual is to prevent harm to others.

New York protects the privacy of landowners who post "No Trespassing" signs and engage in other efforts to indicate that entry on their land is prohibited.

Vermont takes a different approach. Vermont's constitution, like Mississippi's, uses the word "possessions" rather than effects[16] Beyond that, Vermont's highest court rejected the *Katz* test because it is too dependent upon majoritarian views and is subject to "political winds and the perceived exigencies of the day." According to the Vermont court, fundamental constitutional values require it to protect privacy, not to acquiesce in its erosion. Moreover,

> [e]ven assuming that society's perception of what is reasonable is the relevant standard for measuring constitutional rights, *Oliver's* conclusion is an *ipse dixit*. The Court sought to rationalize the *Katz* test with Oliver Holmes' declaration in 1924 that "open fields" are not among the places protected by the Fourth Amendment. *Hester v. United States*, 265 U.S. 57, 59 (1924). But there is no empirical evidence on whether society is willing to recognize an expectation of privacy in "open fields" as reasonable or unreasonable. Certainly, it was a bold and unsupported pronouncement in *Oliver* that society is not prepared under any circumstances to recognize as reasonable an expectation of privacy in all lands outside the curtilage. Indeed, the fact that society may adjudge one who trespasses on such lands a criminal belies the claim.

QUESTIONS

1. What are the differences in interpretive approach among the United States Supreme Court and the three state courts examined above?

---

15. People v. Scott, 593 N.E.2d 1328 (N.Y. 1992).
16. State v. Kirchoff, 587 A.2d 988 (Vt. 1991).

2. Do these differences stem from textual or historical differences between state and federal constitutions, or do some of the differences reflect a different interpretive attitude?

3. Vermont uses burdens of proof to help it decide whether to recognize expectations of privacy in a particular case. Is that analysis sound? Would a similar analysis have altered the U.S. Supreme Court's *Oliver* decision, or was such an analysis implicit in that decision but supporting contrary conclusions? Which approach is most consistent with *Katz*?

PROBLEM 2–1

Frank Brazen owned a 1,800–acre cattle ranch containing an airstrip. The airstrip is some 2,000 feet from the house trailer where Brazen resided, in the middle of the ranch property. Police participating in a drug task force received a tip that a plane with a load of marijuana would be landing on the airstrip at 2 p.m. They crossed a dike, rammed through a gate blocking the entrance to the airfield, cut the chain lock on a second such gate, cut a fence posted "No Trespassing," and then walked several hundred yards to hide behind a clump of bushes to conduct surveillance. When the plane landed, the officers saw bales of marijuana being unloaded from the plane. The officers arrested all doing the unloading, including Brazen.

Question: Brazen filed a suppression motion, which the trial court denied on the ground that the airstrip was in an open field; thus there was no "search," and the Fourth Amendment does not apply. The defense has appealed, and you are the defense lawyer making the argument to the appellate court on Brazen's behalf. What will you argue, and will you succeed?

PROBLEM 2–2

In response to complaints about John Rusco's dogs running free and chasing deer, Police Officer Ronald Wood drove to Rusco's house, located on 120 acres of mountainous and heavily wooded terrain. A long driveway led from the main road to Rusco's house, but the officer was unable to drive up to the house, as a cable blocked the driveway at one point. A sign on the cable read:

> This is the front door to our home. Please honk your horn; if we're home and available for visitors, we'll come to the door within five minutes. If we don't come, we're not home or not available. Please leave your name and message and we'll contact you.

Officer Wood honked his horn repeatedly, but no one answered. Finally, he got out of his car, walked around the cable about one-eighth of a mile to defendant's house, crossed a wooded walkway to the front door, and there observed 385 marijuana plants growing approximately 40 yards beyond the house.

Question: You and a colleague are defense counsel engaging in a debate about the likelihood of succeeding on a motion to suppress the marijuana at Rusco's trial on charges of possessing marijuana with intent to distribute. Your colleague believes that a motion to suppress will lose and cannot therefore be a controlling consideration in planning case strategy. What arguments would you make to convince him otherwise, and how is he likely to respond? Be ready to engage in such a debate.

PROBLEM 2–3

Assume that in the Boson case in Chapter 1 the murder victim there had a sister, Stefni. Stefni had been missing for five days at the time of Boson's confession. Neither her parents nor her friends had heard from her, getting no response when they called her home. Assume that Stefni lived on a farm, and that Boson had acknowledged during his confession that he had visited this farm. The police went to the farm looking for Stefni, investigating whether she too had been harmed.

The farm was on about 40 acres of unfenced land, a portion of which was heavily wooded. The house was set back from the road about 150 feet. Several dog houses were located just north of the house. Two hundred feet north was another structure known as a pigeon building. The horse barn was 30 to 40 feet northeast of the pigeon building. Two hundred feet further north, approximately 450 feet from the house, was a pile of rocks. Stefni's body was found buried in the earth three feet under the ground beneath this pile of rocks. The rock pile was located in a clearing about 100 yards from the road and was not visible from the road.

The state crime lab's examination revealed that Stefni had been killed with the same type of three-sided knife stab to the heart as had her sister.

Question: What arguments will each side make at a motion to suppress the body at Boson's trial for murdering Stefni, particularly concerning whether the Fourth Amendment even applies?

PROBLEM 2–4

In January the Drug Enforcement Administration ("DEA") and State Police investigated and prosecuted an organization involved in manufacturing large quantities of methamphetamines. Some members of the organization cooperated with law enforcement by identifying other members that had not yet been prosecuted, including Mr. Pibb. Mr. Pibb's involvement was confirmed using phone records and establishing that he communicated with other confirmed members of the organization.

On March 23, sheriff deputies found 2,000 empty pseudoephedrine bottles with the bottoms cut open. From his extensive training in DEA seminars and twelve years experience in the narcotics division of the State Police, Detective Carbon knew that pseudoephedrine was an ingredient for manufacturing methamphetamines and that cutting out the bottoms of bottles was common practice in the manufacture of methamphetamines.

The bottles were found near a fence on the corner of Soda Pop Farm, which was subsequently determined to belong to Mr. Pibb.

DEA agents and Detective Carbon began investigating Mr. Pibb and observed him purchasing Methyl–Sulfonyl–Methane (''MSM''), a cutting agent for methamphetamine, on several occasions and in large quantities. They also learned that Mr. Pibb was part owner of Soda Pop Farm, although his place of residence was across town. After conducting surveillance of the farm over a dozen times, agents determined that no one resided at the property, as trucks arrived in the morning and left after dark. Also, there was no movement or activity after the trucks left the property at night. Neighbors told the agents that they did not know if anyone lived on the property.

In September, Special Agent Mann and Detective Carbon entered Soda Pop Farm without a warrant or consent from the owners. On the property, they found a travel trailer, a metal-framed structure with a vinyl covering that was popped open, and an old pickup truck with a canopy. Detective Carbon peered inside the canopy and saw large pails labeled MSM, a propane burner, blenders, plastic gloves, and pots. Inside the metal structure, agents found a long stick with a red stain on one end. Detective Carbon knew from his experience that red phosphorus was an ingredient used to make methamphetamines and that materials seen in the canopy window are commonly used to make the drug. Agents also found glass lids similar to those seized from the Organization. The agents did not enter the travel trailer, but did shine a flashlight into the window. The interior was dirty and contained four propane tanks. The countertops were empty and there was an old foam pad but no bedding or personal effects. There were no electrical power lines leading to the trailer.

A week later, the surveillance team observed Mr. Pibb's truck at Soda Pop Farm and heard noises coming from the metal structure that sounded like movement of pots and pans. Mr. Pibb left the farm after dark and arrived at his house across town shortly thereafter. The next day, Detective Carbon submitted an affidavit of his findings to a judge and obtained a warrant to search Mr. Pibb's residence across town, his truck, and Soda Pop Farm. Subsequently, Mr. Pibb was arrested and charged with manufacturing methamphetamine.

Question: First determine whether the doctrines of curtilage and/or open fields apply. Second, assume that you are Mr. Pibb's attorney. What arguments would you make to suppress the evidence seized pursuant to the warrant? Third, how would prosecutors argue that law enforcement established probable cause to obtain a warrant? Finally, what facts, if any (besides a confession), would help to ensure that the motion to suppress would be denied?

2.   ASSUMPTION OF RISK

The second major factor in the ''search'' analysis is whether an individual ''assumed the risk'' that certain information will not be kept private. The Court has rejected several times privacy claims regarding information conveyed to third parties, on the ground that the speaker assumed the risk of the recipient's disloyalty. This rationale explains in part the "secret agent" cases, discussed below, in which the Court held that there was no reasonable expectation of privacy when an informant reported his conversation with a defendant to government agents, or when government agents overheard such a conversation transmitted by a radio device worn by the informant. Other cases have extended this analysis to institutional third parties. For example, where an individual gave information to a bank in the ordinary course of business[17] he was viewed as running the risk that the bank would divulge the information to the Government.[18]

This "assumption of risk" factor can be overcome by other weighty factors. To illustrate, one might argue that the defendant in *Katz* assumed the risk that the recipient of his phone call would reveal his criminal overtures to the police, yet the Court held that Katz did have a reasonable expectation against an electronic bug. Why did the Court decide differently where the recipients of communications were government informants? There are two possible reasons. The first is simply that Katz got lucky—he assumed the risk that the recipient of the telephone call would become an informant, but that risk never materialized. The second reason rests on the consent of the recipient. When the recipient chooses to become a government informant, or to permit the government to listen in on the conversation as an "invited ear," that factor combines with assumption of risk to render an expectation no longer normatively "reasonable."[19]

"Assumption of risk" usually requires a decision to engage in conduct despite conscious awareness of the risk. In the Fourth Amendment arena, however, the Court appears willing to apply that doctrine even in situations in which the person may not have been consciously aware of the risk. For example, the Slobogin and Schumacher study suggests that individuals are not aware of the risk that banks will reveal their account records to government agents (the study found that individuals viewed "perusing bank records" as more intrusive than a patdown or even an arrest for 48 hours)[20] Nevertheless the Court applies the "assumption of risk" doctrine across the board to bank account records, stating that a "depositor takes the risk, in revealing his affairs to another, that the information will be conveyed by that person to the Government." Given the apparent rejection of majority views in this area, and given the frequent absence of inquiry into whether a particular suspect was aware of a risk, the Court's notion of assumption of risk must extend beyond actual awareness. Rather, the

---

17. United States v. Miller, 425 U.S. 435 (1976).

18. *See* Bloom & Brodin, Examples & Explanations, *supra* note 9, at 25 (making this point).

19. Slobogin & Schumacher, *Reasonable Expectations*, *supra* note 6, at 737.

20. United States v. Miller, 425 U.S. 435, 442 (1976); *see also* California Bankers Ass'n v. Shultz, 416 U.S. 21 (1974) (rejecting argument certain bank record-keeping and reporting requirements are searches or seizures).

doctrine includes as well those risks of which the Court concludes the suspect should have been aware—an objective (and probably normative) inquiry.

The Court has dealt with assumption of risk in several special situations:

a. Agents and Informants

Before *Katz*, the validity of using undercover agents and wiretaps often was judged by whether there had been a trespass[21] or an unauthorized physical penetration into premises occupied by the defendant.[22] However, some "secret agent" cases used a reasonable expectation of privacy analysis. For example, in *Hoffa v. United States*[23] the Court based its Fourth Amendment holding on such an analysis. The case arose in the context of what was known as the "Test Fleet trial," in which James Hoffa (who was then president of the Teamsters Union), was being tried for violations of the Taft–Hartley Act. During the trial, a local Teamsters Union official, Edward Partin, met repeatedly with Hoffa in his hotel suite. In Partin's presence, Hoffa discussed bribing Test Fleet jury members. Partin reported these conversations to a federal agent, and Hoffa was arrested, charged, and convicted for endeavoring to bribe the Test Fleet jurors. Hoffa appealed that conviction to the Supreme Court, arguing that his conversations with Partin should have been suppressed because Partin was a government informer. Although Partin's entry into Hoffa's room was consensual, Hoffa contended that Partin's failure to disclose his role as a government informer vitiated Hoffa's consent and turned the interactions into an illegal search for verbal evidence. The Supreme Court disagreed:

> In the present case, however, it is evident that no interest legitimately protected by the Fourth Amendment is involved. It is obvious that the petitioner was not relying on the security of his hotel suite when he made the incriminating statements to Partin or in Partin's presence. Partin did not enter the suite by force or by stealth. He was not a surreptitious eavesdropper. Partin was in the suite by invitation, and every conversation which he heard was either directed to him or knowingly carried on in his presence. The petitioner, in a word, was not relying on the security of the hotel room; he was relying upon his misplaced confidence that Partin would not reveal his wrongdoing. . . .
>
> Neither this Court nor any member of it has ever expressed the view that the Fourth Amendment protects a wrongdoer's misplaced

---

21. *See* Olmstead v. United States, 277 U.S. 438 (1928); Goldman v. United States, 316 U.S. 129 (1942); On Lee v. United States, 343 U.S. 747 (1952); United States v. White, 401 U.S. 745, 748 (1971).

22. *See* Silverman v. United States, 365 U.S. 505 (1961) (constitutional violation in placing a spike microphone into contact with a heating duct that ran to the suspect's location; the Court's decision did "not turn upon the technicality of a trespass upon a party wall as a matter of local law. It is based upon the reality of an intrusion upon a constitutionally protected area.").

23. 385 U.S. 293 (1966).

belief that a person to whom he voluntarily confides his wrongdoing will not reveal it.

The Court made its reasoning even clearer by approving both its earlier holding in *Lopez v. United States*[24] and reiterating this quote from the *Lopez* dissent: "The risk of being overheard by an eavesdropper or betrayed by an informer or deceived as to the identity of one with whom one deals is probably inherent in the condition of human society. It is the kind of risk we necessarily assume whenever we speak."

Lopez differed from *Hoffa* in that the government agent in *Lopez* had worn a pocket wire recorder, which recorded conversations between the agent and Lopez. This was not constitutionally relevant, however:

> Indeed this case involves no "eavesdropping" whatever in any proper sense of that term. The Government did not use an electronic device to listen in on conversations it could not otherwise have heard. Instead, the device was used only to obtain the most reliable evidence possible of a conversation in which the Government's own agent was a participant and which that agent was fully entitled to disclose. And the device was not planted by means of an unlawful physical invasion of petitioner's premises under circumstances which would violate the Fourth Amendment. It was carried in and out by an agent who was there with petitioner's assent, and it neither saw nor heard more than the agent himself.

In *Lewis v. United States,*[25] decided about the same time as the *Hoffa* case, the Court rejected the argument that an undercover drug purchase in the defendant's home violated the defendant's Fourth Amendment rights. Where the home was converted into a "commercial center" in which outsiders were invited in for business, it had no greater sanctity than a store, garage, or street. The Court emphasized the practical implications of its holding:

> Were we to hold the deceptions of the agent in this case constitutionally prohibited, we would come near to a rule that the use of undercover agents in any manner is virtually unconstitutional per se. Such a rule would, for example, severely hamper the Government in ferreting out those organized criminal activities that are characterized by covert dealings with victims who either cannot or do not protest. A prime example is provided by the narcotics traffic.

Finally, in its first post-*Katz* undercover agents decision, *United States v. White,*[26] the Court reaffirmed *Hoffa*, *Lopez*, and *Lewis* as consistent with the *Katz* analysis. In White, the government wired an informant with a radio transmitter. As White and the informant conversed, government agents listened in. White claimed that this situation was no different than *Katz*, but the Court distinguished *Katz* because neither party to the

---

24. 373 U.S. 427 (1963).

25. 385 U.S. 206 (1966).

26. 401 U.S. 745 (1971).

telephone conversation in that case had been a willing government informant. The Court conceded that individuals in White's situation subjectively expect privacy when they talk with informants, because they neither know nor suspect that their colleagues are "wired." But that expectation is not legitimate for these reasons:

Inescapably, one contemplating illegal activities must realize that his companions may be reporting to the police. If he sufficiently doubts their trustworthiness, the association will very probably end or never materialize. But if he has doubts, or allays them, or risks what doubt he has, the risk is his. In terms of what his course will be, what he will or will not do or say, we are unpersuaded that he would distinguish between probable informers on the one hand and probable informers with transmitters on the other. Given the possibility or probability that one of his colleagues is cooperating with the police, it is only speculation to assert that the defendant's utterances would be substantially different or his sense of security any less if he also thought it possible that the suspected colleague is wired for sound. At least there is no persuasive evidence that the difference in this respect between the electronically equipped and the unequipped agent is substantial enough to require discrete constitutional recognition, particularly under the Fourth Amendment which is ruled by fluid concepts of "reasonableness."

Nor should we be too ready to erect constitutional barriers to relevant and probative evidence which is also accurate and reliable. An electronic recording will many times produce a more reliable rendition of what a defendant has said than will the unaided memory of a police agent. It may also be that with the recording in existence it is less likely that the informant will change his mind, less chance that threat or injury will suppress unfavorable evidence and less chance that cross-examination will confound the testimony. Considerations like these obviously do not favor the defendant, but we are not prepared to hold that a defendant who has no constitutional right to exclude the informer's unaided testimony nevertheless has a Fourth Amendment privilege against a more accurate version of the events in question.

QUESTIONS

1. Did the Court in *White* apply a majority or a normative approach to the question whether the defendant had a reasonable expectation of privacy?

2. Would the outcome of *White* have been different if the Court had determined that the defendant did have a reasonable expectation of privacy, or would it have engaged in balancing to find the government conduct reasonable under the Fourth Amendment? Does the Court in *White* clearly draw a distinction between these two approaches? Can it be drawn?

3. Notice that the Court in *White* emphasized the need for relevant, probative, accurate, and reliable evidence at trial. This is a standard concern of evidence law as well. Should evidentiary needs affect Fourth Amendment analysis? Should they affect whether the amendment applies in the first place? What are the differences, if any, among evidence that is "relevant," "probative," "accurate," and "reliable"? Do tape recordings or video recordings necessarily result in more probative, accurate, and reliable evidence?

4. Cal meets Bart at a local gas station and invites Bart back to Cal's home specifically to purchase methamphetamine. Bart arrives at Cal's home to make the purchase. Unbeknownst to Cal, Bart is working with police, who are waiting outside of Cal's home for Bart's signal that the transaction has occurred. After Bart gives the signal, officers enter Cal's home, arrest Cal, and seize evidence of the illegal transaction. Does the *Katz* test help or hurt Cal's subsequent assertion of a legitimate privacy interest in his home? How might the Court's decisions in *Lewis* and *White* influence your answer? *See Pearson v. Callahan*[27] (noting underlying issue in lower courts was whether the Fourth Amendment is violated when police enter a suspect's home without a warrant after the suspect admits a non-police confidential informant to purchase illegal drugs and, upon completion of the purchase, the confidential informant signals waiting officers outside the suspect's home that the illegal purchase was made. The United States Supreme Court ultimately did not answer that question). Did Cal's giving permission to Bart to enter Cal's home constitute "consent," even though it is "once-removed" from the homeowner, for the police to enter as well? ("Once-removed" meaning that the homeowner, Cal, only gave *Bart* permission to enter the home, but Bart now uses his new status as someone lawfully on the premises to invite the police to enter the home— an invitation that homeowner Cal himself never extended).

PROBLEM 2–5

John Holme was caught by the police while selling cocaine. The police were more interested in John's brother Robert, who the police believed was the "Mr. Big" in a local drug ring. Accordingly, the police asked John (who was very close to Robert) to wear a wire transmitter and engage Robert in conversations about major drug shipments. When John refused, the police offered John immunity on the drug charge for which he had been arrested. When he still refused, the police said they would press for the maximum possible sentence in his case if he did not cooperate. This time, and after eight hours of questioning without food or rest that lasted until 3:00 a.m., and with the promise of immunity, he agreed.

The next day John, wearing a device designed to record and transmit conversations to police officers, went to Robert's home. The two discussed several scheduled incoming cocaine shipments, and Robert gave John instructions concerning how to handle those shipments. They also discussed lessons they had learned from mistakes in earlier shipments. Robert then brought out some cocaine, inviting John to share, which he did. John left, and the police used the tapes made from the transmitter to obtain a

---

27. *See* Pearson v. Callahan, 129 S.Ct. 808 (2009).

search warrant for Robert's home. The search revealed a large quantity of cocaine in his bedroom.

Question: You are a state court judge who has just gleaned these facts from the testimony presented at a motion to suppress both Robert's statements to John and the cocaine found in Robert's bedroom. What ruling and why? If you are in a state whose constitution has been interpreted as providing greater privacy protection than the U.S. Constitution, how would you argue there had been a search here?

PROBLEM 2–6

Wilson Burke and the Indiana Department of Natural Resources (DNR) entered into a license and concession agreement to allow Burke to operate a camp store at the Whitewater State Park. The store is located on land owned by the State of Indiana. The license allowed Burke to operate the store to provide those goods and services specified in his license, although the State retained some authority over the store's operations and management. In exchange for the license, Burke agreed to pay the DNR a monthly fee consisting of ten percent of all gross sales.

The State Chief of Inns, Gary Minor, upon visiting the store on several occasions, noticed questionable sales practices and so asked the conservation officers of the DNR to investigate. With Mr. Minor's permission, the officers, using a key obtained from the DNR property manager, Saul Merle (the key was needed because Burke locked the store every night), entered the store at 11 p.m. one night and installed video surveillance cameras in the attic. The cameras looked through two small holes that the officers drilled in the store ceiling, aiming the cameras at the cash register. The officers returned to the store every night over a four-week period to remove that day's videotape and insert a new one.

Based on these tapes, the officers concluded Burke had received significantly more revenue than he reported to the State. Accordingly, Burke was arrested for theft.

Question: You are Burke's defense counsel preparing to meet with the prosecutor tomorrow to discuss a plea bargain. You understand that your case likely rises or falls on the outcome of the suppression motion. Indeed, for that reason, you would prefer to postpone plea discussions until after your motion to suppress the videotapes is heard. But the prosecutor, probably for similar reasons, has said that plea bargaining takes place now or not at all. You must make a judgment about whether to bargain, and, if so, for what, and therefore must first decide how likely it is that your motion will be granted. What will you do and why?

PROBLEM 2–7

Police intercepted and recorded, without a warrant, the conversations transmitted by a Mr. George Neller from his cordless telephone, used in his residence. Those conversations concerned illegal arms sales.

Question: Was there a "search" under the Fourth Amendment?

PROBLEM 2–8

Assume in the Boson problem in Chapter 1 that the police, when arriving at the police station, had offered Patsy a deal: "Wear a wire and chat with Daniel, and we will press the prosecutor to treat you kindly." Patsy agrees and, after the police have finished their interrogation described in Chapter 1, they leave Patsy and Daniel in the interrogation room together, telling them they can chat briefly while awaiting preliminary arraignment. They did indeed chat, with Daniel revealing many details that he had not told the police.

Question: You are the judge at a hearing to suppress Daniel's statements to Patsy. How will you rule?

b.   *Pen Registers and Pagers*

A "pen register" records the numbers dialed from a telephone. In *Smith v. Maryland*,[28] the Court held that police use of a pen register is not a search, because individuals using their telephones voluntarily convey "numerical information" to the telephone company and thus assume the risk that the company will reveal that information to the police. Some telephone companies now have the capacity to record the telephone numbers of calls made to a telephone. Should those records be treated the same as pen registers? What about electronic pagers, which forward and store the telephone numbers of people calling the pager? Consider the following problems.

PROBLEM 2–9

Using a pen register, police obtained a series of phone numbers of calls dialed from the residence of Judy Thomas. Police interrogated the persons whose names were registered under those phone numbers, and many of those questioned implicated Thomas in an illegal gambling operation. Thomas concedes that no search was conducted under the U.S. Constitution but argues that one was made under the Idaho Constitution.

Question: What arguments would you raise in support of a different approach under the Idaho Constitution, which has a search and seizure provision whose text is substantially identical to that of the U.S. Constitution's Fourth Amendment? What additional information might you require, and where would you find it?

PROBLEM 2–10

On November 10, Snohomish County Police, Washington State, seized a pager pursuant to the arrest of Art Zunega, a suspected cocaine dealer.

---

28.   442 U.S. 735 (1979).

For the next six days, the pager was left on, and incoming calls were monitored. On November 16, the pager received an incoming call from Jeffrey Walley, who was known to be a large cocaine distributor. An undercover agent called Walley at the number left on the pager and, pretending to be Zunega, arranged to sell cocaine for him. During this telephone call, Walley made several statements implicating Zunega in prior cocaine deals. The prosecution intends to use Walley's statements against Zunega.

Question: Washington State has previously held under its state constitutional Fourth Amendment equivalent that use of pen registers is a "search." You represent Zunega and are preparing to advise him regarding the likely success of a motion to suppress Walley's statements as the fruit of an illegal search by means of the pager. What will you advise him? What sources of difference would you look to in arguing that a state constitution, like Washington's, offers more protection than the federal constitution?

c.   *Electronic Tracking Devices*

In *United States v. Knotts*[29] officers installed a battery-operated radio transmitter—a "beeper"—inside a five-gallon container of chloroform (which is often used to manufacture illegal drugs). The officers did so after receiving a tip that Tristan Armstrong, a former employee of 3M Company, had been stealing from 3M chemicals used to make illegal drugs but was now buying similar chemicals from Hawkins Chemical Company. The officers obtained Hawkins' consent before installing the beeper. When Armstrong purchased the beeper-implanted chloroform container, the officers followed him, using visual surveillance and monitoring the beeper, to Petschen's house. There, the container was transferred to Petschen's car, which drove away. When Petschen made evasive maneuvers, the officers lost him, but used the beeper to track him to a cabin. Relying on the beeper and additional information, the officers secured a search warrant, finding inside the cabin a clandestine drug laboratory and chemicals used to make amphetamine, including the chloroform container.

After his suppression motion was denied, the defendant was convicted of conspiracy to manufacture controlled substances. The Eighth Circuit reversed on appeal, finding that the beeper violated defendant's reasonable expectation of privacy. The United States Supreme Court disagreed, finding no invasion of a reasonable expectation of privacy. The Court held that a person traveling in an automobile on public thoroughfares has no reasonable expectation of privacy in his movements, because those movements are open to the public. While Knotts, the owner of the cabin, had a reasonable expectation of privacy in that cabin, no such expectation extended to the automobile's movements or to the movements of the chloroform container outside the cabin in the open fields. Moreover, the beeper did not alter the analysis: "Nothing in the Fourth Amendment prohibited the police from augmenting the sensory faculties bestowed upon them at birth with such

---

29.   460 U.S. 276 (1983).

enhancements as science and technology afforded them in this case." "We have never," concluded the Court, "equated police efficiency with unconstitutionality, and we decline to do so now."

One year later, in *United States v. Karo*[30] the Court struck down the government's use of a beeper as intruding too far into privacy interests. The facts were these: DEA agents learned that Karo and others had ordered 50 gallons of ether from a government informant. The ether was to be used to extract cocaine from the fabric in which it had been transported across national borders. The government obtained a court order authorizing installation and monitoring of a beeper in one of the cans of ether. With the informant's consent, the agents substituted their own can containing a beeper for one of the ten cans in the shipment and had all ten painted to give them a uniform appearance. Agents then watched Karo pick up the cans from the informant and used the beeper to track the ether's location. The agents eventually used the beeper to monitor the ether's presence in a house while they obtained a search warrant for the house. The fruits of the warrant search included cocaine and drug manufacturing equipment.

The Supreme Court agreed with the lower courts that the beeper use had gone too far. The beeper had been used to reveal activities inside a private residence, a location not open to visual surveillance. That use invaded reasonable expectations of privacy, because even though visual surveillance was possible up to entry into the house, the beeper enabled the police to determine what they otherwise could not have known: that the article remained in the house during the period in which the warrant was being obtained. Therefore, the monitoring constituted a search. However, unlike the lower courts, the Supreme Court found no violation of Fourth Amendment rights in the installation of the beeper, because the defendants had no reasonable expectation of privacy in the can while it belonged to the DEA. The informant owned and possessed the original ten cans, but the can substitution was done with his consent. Finally, no Fourth Amendment rights were implicated when the informant transferred the can to the defendants, because that transfer did not convey private information to the government.

Comment on State Constitutions: In *State v. Campbell*[31] the Oregon Supreme Court took a very different approach to electronic tracking. The Oregon court pointedly rejected the *Katz* analysis, adopting an expressly normative test: "[T]he privacy protected by . . . [the Oregon constitution] is not the privacy that one reasonably expects but the privacy to which one has a right." Moreover, the court rejected the notion that "information legitimately available through one means [for example, visual surveillance] may be obtained through any other means without engaging in a search." The court concluded that Oregon's constitution protects the people's "interest in freedom from particular forms of scrutiny." That interest extended to surveillance by radio transmitter:

---

30. 468 U.S. 705 (1984).

31. 759 P.2d 1040 (Or. 1988).

As we noted above, use of a radio transmitter to locate an object to which the transmitter is attached cannot be equated with visual tracking. Any device that enables the police quickly to locate a person or object anywhere within a 40–mile radius, day or night, over a period of several days, is a significant limitation on freedom from scrutiny, as the facts of this case demonstrate. The limitation is made more substantial by the fact that the radio transmitter is much more difficult to detect than would-be observers who must rely upon the sense of sight. Without an ongoing, meticulous examination of one's possessions, one can never be sure that one's location is not being monitored by means of a radio transmitter. Thus, individuals must more readily assume that they are the objects of government scrutiny.

But if the State's position in this case is correct, no movement, no location and no conversation in a "public place" would in any measure be secure from the prying of the Government. There would in addition be no ready means for individuals to ascertain when they were being scrutinized and when they were not. That is nothing short of a staggering limitation upon personal freedom.

QUESTIONS

1. Could the Oregon court's reasoning have applied under the federal constitution?

2. Which approach gives the clearest guidance to police?

3. Which approach, as a matter of both interpretive theory and good policy, is the "right" one?

PROBLEM 2–11

Police received an informant's tip that a major local supplier of various illegal drugs would be picking up a shipment of several barrels of chemicals at a warehouse in Greenwich, Connecticut. The police staked out the warehouse. At one point, a cargo bay door was opened by two men, who then lugged four barrels to the loading dock. When the men then re-entered the warehouse, an officer surreptitiously placed a tracking device on the barrel lid and left.

Shortly thereafter, a van pulled up to the loading dock and two men loaded the barrels into the back of the van. The police followed the van visually in an unmarked car, and when they lost sight of the van, continued tracking based solely on the signals from the tracking device. The police relocated the van and saw it enter a garage attached to a single-family residence. The tracking device signal told the police, who could not see inside the residence or the garage, that the barrel had been moved to the basement. An increase in the volume of the signal received further told the police that the barrel had been opened.

The police obtained a warrant, then searched the basement and found open barrels of chemicals used in the manufacture of illegal drugs.

Question: The homeowner, John Device, was tried and convicted of drug offenses, after the trial court denied his motion to suppress the police officers' observations in the basement. As a member of the appellate panel addressing the propriety of the trial court's decision, will you vote to affirm or reverse the conviction?

PROBLEM 2–12

Customs agents placed an electronic device on Judith Strayne's private plane. They approached the plane while parked at the Cimarron, Kansas, airport; removed a panel from the tail section of the exterior of the plane; inserted the tracking device; and replaced the panel. The plane took off from the airport, flying to a small airport north of San Francisco, California. The customs agents tracked the plane, using the tracking device, and notified customs agents in San Francisco, who watched two men unload a shipment of illegal arms.

Question: Should the customs agents' observation be suppressed?

d. *Aerial Surveillance*

In *California v. Ciraolo*[32] Santa Clara police, acting on an anonymous tip about marijuana growing in Ciraolo's back yard, found themselves unable to observe that yard because it was enclosed by a six-foot outer fence and ten-foot inner fence. Accordingly, two officers trained in marijuana detection secured a private plane and flew 1,000 feet over Ciraolo's home, in navigable air space, and identified the marijuana from that height. Based on their aerial observations, the officers obtained a search warrant, which revealed 73 marijuana plants. Even though the plants were growing within the curtilage of Ciraolo's home, the United States Supreme Court found that Ciraolo had no reasonable expectation of privacy against the airborne observations:

> The observations by Officers Shutz and Rodriguez in this case took place within public navigable airspace . . . in a physically non-intrusive manner; from this point they were able to observe plants readily discernible to the naked eye as marijuana. That the observation from aircraft was directed at identifying the plants and the officers were trained to recognize marijuana is irrelevant. Such observation is precisely what a judicial officer needs to provide a basis for a warrant. Any member of the public flying in this airspace who glanced down could have seen everything that these officers observed. On this record, we readily conclude that respondent's expectation that his garden was protected from such observation is unreasonable and is not an expectation that society is prepared to honor.

---

32. 476 U.S. 207 (1986).

In *Dow Chemical Company v. United States*[33] Dow Chemical Company denied the EPA a second on-site inspection of Dow's 2,000–acre chemical-manufacturing facility. Consequently, the EPA used a sophisticated aerial mapping camera to take photographs of the facilities from altitudes ranging from 1,200 to 12,000 feet but always within lawful navigable airspace. Dow successfully brought an action for injunctive relief against further aerial photography. The Court of Appeals reversed, and the U.S. Supreme Court agreed, finding no invasion of "industrial curtilage." The Court agreed that Dow had a reasonable expectation of privacy in the interior of the covered buildings on the facility. It also acknowledged that the outdoor areas were somewhere between open fields and curtilage, but it ultimately found those areas more akin to open fields than to curtilage. The Court emphasized that expectations of privacy are reduced when the property is commercial rather than residential. According to the Court, those expectations do not include the expectation of freedom from regulatory inspections. While there might be protection from highly sophisticated surveillance equipment penetrating walls and windows, there was no such protection from lawful surveys from the air that did not reveal intimate domestic affairs.

PROBLEM 2–13

Cheryl Anson lives on approximately 14 acres of rural property. The front portion of the rectangular-shaped property is pasture land. The house is behind the pasture land in the center of a two-acre lot. Other than the house, the lot is largely covered by a wood of 50–foot–high trees. The large number of dense trees forms a blanket of green leaves that cover the lot and the house. The entire lot, wood and all, is enclosed by a four-foot high animal fence topped with two strands of barbed wire. No-trespassing signs are placed 50 feet apart on the fence for its entire length around the lot.

Two officers, acting on a tip, chartered a helicopter with a pilot to scout the area. The helicopter hovered about 15 feet above the trees, tilting and circling four times to gain a line of sight through the trees. The officers saw what they recognized as marijuana plants, each about five feet high, growing in plastic buckets at the foot of several of the tall trees. Based on these observations, the officers obtained a search warrant and seized the marijuana plants.

Question: Did the officers' observations from the helicopter constitute a "search"?

e.   *Thermal Imaging Devices*

In *Kyllo v. United States*[34] the Supreme Court held that a Fourth Amendment search takes place when government agents employ a device "that is not in general public use" in order to "explore details of [a] home that would previously have been unknowable without physical intrusion."

---

33.   476 U.S. 227 (1986).

34.   533 U.S. 27 (2001).

Federal agents had received a tip that Kyllo was growing marijuana inside of his home, an operation that typically requires high-intensity lamps. A review of Kyllo's utility bills suggested that his electrical needs were unusually high. The agents then employed a "thermal imager" to scan Kyllo's home for infrared radiation emanating from the roof. The thermal imager suggested that certain parts of the home were generating more heat than others and more than surrounding homes. Based on that finding, as well as on the tips and utility bills, the agents obtained a search warrant and discovered a marijuana growing operation.

Kyllo moved to suppress the fruits of the search warrant, arguing that use of the thermal imager constituted a search. Because the agents did not have a warrant to use the thermal imager, he argued, the search was illegal. Although lower courts ultimately denied his claim, the Supreme Court agreed. Writing for the majority, Justice Scalia revisited the *Katz* test and its application to technological advances, concluding that the nature of the location under technological surveillance is critically important to the analysis. Specifically, the majority observed that "obtaining by sense-enhancing technology any information regarding the interior of [a] home that could not otherwise have been obtained without physical intrusion" constitutes a search, "at least where (as here) the technology in question is not in general public use." The majority explained that its rule "assures preservation of that degree of privacy against government that existed when the Fourth Amendment was adopted."

Justice Stevens dissented, joined by Chief Justice Rehnquist and Justices O'Connor and Kennedy. The dissenters would not characterize use of a thermal imager as a search because "all that the infrared camera did in this case was passively measure heat emitted from the exterior surfaces of petitioner's home . . . [and] no details regarding the interior of petitioner's home were revealed." The dissent observed that "[h]eat waves, like aromas that are generated in a kitchen, or in a laboratory or opium den, enter the public domain if and when they leave a building. A subjective expectation that they would remain private is not only implausible but also surely not 'one that society is prepared to recognize as reasonable.'" The dissent also stated that the thermal imager did nothing more than implicate the principle that "[w]hat a person knowingly exposes to the public, even in his own home or office, is not a subject of Fourth Amendment protection." Finally, the dissent contrasted the electronic listening device used in *Katz* and the thermal imager: "the thermal imager here disclosed only the relative amounts of heat radiating from the house; it would be as if, in *Katz*, the listening device disclosed only the relative volume of sound leaving the [phone] booth."

PROBLEM 2–14

Federal law enforcement agents have begun employing Quadropole Resonance technology ["QR"] to detect explosives. QR technology can be built into hand-held wands, which emit radiation to excite molecular nuclei and then measure the nucleic response. The devices can be calibrated to distinguish among nucleic responses and to recognize those coming from molecules of certain explosive materials. If the device detects a response from such materials, it registers a positive identification on an indicator light. There are virtually no false alarms. Similar technology is being developed to detect hidden guns. The gun-detection device registers nucleic response in such a way as to reveal the outline of a weapon. Both of these devices can be used at some distance from their targets. In several cases, law enforcement agents have used these devices to detect explosives or guns, and they have used the devices to justify stops and searches.[35]

Question: Under the Fourth Amendment, does the use of a QR device constitute a search? Does it matter whether the device is used to detect explosives or weapons inside of a home? Would your answer change if the devices were "passive"—that is, if they merely reacted to particles ordinarily emitted by explosives or guns, rather than creating (and then detecting) a nucleic response? Do you need any more information about either the QR device or the passive device, and if so, what?

Professor Taslitz, while approving of the result in *Kyllo*, has criticized the Court's reasoning because it continues to embrace a flawed concept of privacy that turns primarily on the risk of being observed:[36]

[The Court's] stingy definition of "private" information relies on a primarily cognitively-driven conception of privacy. If a person is or should be aware of a high probability that revelation of information to one person entails revelation to other persons, then the disclosing party no longer has a reasonable expectation of privacy in the data. However, probability-assessment is not the end-all of the analysis. The Court at times does consider the emotional impact of privacy invasion, but, absent special circumstances, emotions are almost always subordinated to risk. Part of the inquiry is normative as well, but the values stressed by the Court usually concern the state's need for the search rather than the individual's need for privacy. The Court provides for protection of activities in the home, but this too seems to depend significantly on risk analysis.

Moreover, the Court's precedent generally ignores or minimizes the impact of a search or seizure on broader social groups. That the absence of constitutional protection may *in practice* lead to more "searches" of racial minorities, for example, rarely appears on the Court's radar screen or shows up only as an evanescent blip.

The implications for growing state surveillance into our lives are unattractive. If the means electronically to monitor the inside of the

---

35. *Cf.* Alan L. Calnan & Andrew E. Taslitz, *An Analysis of the Legal Issues Attendant to the Marking, Inerting, or Regulation of Explosive Materials*, in NATIONAL RESEARCH COUNCIL, CONTAINING THE THREAT FROM ILLEGAL BOMBINGS: AN INTEGRATED NATIONAL STRATEGY FOR MARKING, TAGGING, RENDERING INERT, AND LICENSING EXPLOSIVES AND THEIR PRECURSORS 215, 218–37 (1998) (addressing search and seizure issues involved in using analogous anti-terrorism techniques).

36. Andrew E. Taslitz, *The Fourth Amendment in the Twenty–First Century: Technology, Privacy, and Human Emotions*, 65 L. & CONTEMP. PROB. 125, 151–56 (2002).

home become more widespread, then police viewing of our intimate activities may be possible without a warrant or reasonable suspicion. If tracking devices that monitor our movements on the street—in cars, on foot, in stores, or at ATMs—improve, so does the likelihood of secret police monitoring of our lives. Our growing use of e-mail, the Internet, and online banking might expand the risk of government access to personal information. To be sure, political forces may eventually curb the worst abuses, but too many insulting personal invasions may happen along the way, and those with reduced political power may never gain protection.

Professor Taslitz suggests an alternative conception of privacy as facilitating self-definition. Privacy, he says, "is the creation of boundaries that protect us against the risk of being misdefined and judged out of context:"

> Any sound conception of privacy must begin with a conception of personhood, of the "self." Both common experience and psychological research reveal that the "self" is a multiple, rather than unitary, concept. Psychologist Walter Mischel explains, albeit in somewhat different language, that different aspects of our character or personality—our propensities to think and act in certain ways—are called forth by different situations. We may be tardy when attending parties but punctual when attending church. We may be rude under time pressure, but otherwise civil and kind. We wear one mask at a ball game and another at work.

> No single one of these masks is inauthentic. Each reflects one aspect of our nature. The totality of who each of us believes we really are consists, however, not of any one of these masks but of all of them together. We often do not want to be judged, for example, as "cruel" by someone who has not seen us be kind. Since it takes time for another to achieve "true knowledge" of our nature, we are vulnerable to their misjudgments during the long period when only aspects of our selves are slowly being revealed. We therefore research such total revelation for a small circle of intimates, and, partly because of its rarity, this revelation in turn becomes a symbol of, and a process for, achieving personal closeness. Correspondingly, safety from the misjudgments of nonintimates requires protection from their gaze. Professor Jeffrey Rosen explains:

>> True knowledge of another person . . . requires the gradual setting aside of social masks, the incremental building of trust, which leads to the exchange of personal disclosure. It cannot be rushed. . . . True knowledge of another person, in all of his or her complexity, can be achieved only with a handful of friends, lovers, or family members. In order to flourish, the intimate relationships on which true knowledge of another person depends need space as well as time: sanctuaries from the gaze of the crowd in which slow mutual self-disclosure is possible.

>> . . . The individual's fear of misjudgment by "the unwanted gaze" of the crowd is fully justified. People generally employ a "halo effect"—

a tendency to judge another's entire nature based on one perceived good trait. Moreover, such judgments are readily based on little evidence, perhaps by observing a few isolated deeds, which are often taken entirely out of context. Once these judgments are made, they are hard to change, despite subsequent evidence to the contrary. A corollary effect, the "devil's horn effect," is even more powerful; that is, observers are more likely to generalize from past misdeeds that one is a bad person than to generalize from past good deeds that one is a good person. The part becomes the whole, and the bad drives out the good. Peter Lewis made this point well in the New York Times:

> Surveillance cameras followed the attractive young blond woman through the lobby of the midtown Manhattan hotel, kept a glassy eye on her as she rode the elevator up to the 23rd floor and peered discreetly down the hall as she knocked at the door to my room. I have not seen the videotapes, but I can imagine the digital readout superimposed on the scenes, noting the exact time of the encounter. That would come in handy if someone were to question later why this woman, who is not my wife, was visiting my hotel room during a recent business trip. The cameras later saw us heading off to dinner and to the theater—a middle-aged, married man from Texas with his arm around a pretty East Village woman young enough to be his daughter.
>
> As a matter of fact, she was my daughter.

This fear of being misjudged based upon others' observing isolated actions taken out of context may describe why we suppress certain aspects of ourselves in some settings. We may believe that wearing pyramid-shaped hats channels universal invisible energies into our soul, be sloppy in caring for our personal finances and leisure dress, and spend most of our time at home sleeping and watching television. Yet we may rightly fear that revealing these traits at our job as an investment banker will lead our boss and co-workers to suspect that we are weird, careless, and lazy when, at least on the job, we are none of these things. Similarly, we would not want word of one mistake that we made at work to be gossiped about at the water cooler, for we fear that the bad will drive out the good, that our previously justly-earned reputation as a meticulous employee—the employee we believe we still are, when judged in the totality of all our office actions—will vanish.

Being misdefined causes humiliation, indignity, and mental distress. "There are," Jeffrey Rosen explains, "few experiences more harrowing than being described: to be described is to be narrowed and simplified and judged out of context." Consequently, "there are few acts more aggressive than describing someone else."

. . . Privacy . . . is one way by which we express our need for individualized justice: for being judged for who we really are. Privacy enables us to define our sense of self so that we experience invasions of privacy as assaults on our identity. The freedom that privacy gives us to express parts of our identity to select others in certain situations, and all of our identity to a select few, promotes life-enhancing intimate relationships and human autonomy. We can pursue our own unique interests, learning and doing what we want within broad limits, without the fear of another's gaze. As one commentator has explained, the root of the right to read anonymously, that is, without others knowing and perhaps disapproving what we read, is not First Amendment free speech alone but Fourth Amendment privacy as well.

PROBLEM 2–15

Consider the following two scenarios. How would each be resolved under the Court's current privacy definition? How would you resolve each using Taslitz's alternative conception of privacy?

Scenario One: The Tampa (Florida) Police Department began using FaceIt, a video surveillance system based on face-recognition software, to monitor a popular downtown nightlife district. FaceIt uses complex mathematical formulas to represent facial features, searching for database matches to the faces of wanted criminals and suspected terrorists. FaceIt also uses voice-recognition technology to scan conversations, selecting and recording any discussions involving certain words and phrases that are considered "hallmarks" of criminal activity or terrorist planning. The monitoring is necessary, claim law enforcement experts, because criminals—especially terrorists—now are so fearful of wiretaps that they avoid engaging in incriminating conversations while in their homes or on telephones.

The police installed FaceIt in three dozen security cameras in the nightlife district. Shortly thereafter, during a monitoring period, the system alerted officers that it had identified a database match. As officers watched their computer screens, one of the cameras zeroed in on a couple standing in a large crowd outside of a nightclub. The couple appeared to be fondling each other. The system identified the male as an 18–year–old fugitive charged with selling marijuana in another state and the female as a 15–year–old wanted on similar charges by juvenile authorities in that state. The system recorded the couple's conversation, which included the male's offer to share "white powder" with his female companion.

Two of the officers rushed from their monitoring station, pulled the couple from the crowd, and arrested and searched them. The male, Adam Jones, was arrested on charges of lewd fondling and possession of cocaine. Jones's counsel filed a motion to suppress the videotape and audiotape, as well as the cocaine. The prosecutor argued in response that Jones's conduct did not even implicate the Fourth Amendment, because he had no expectation of privacy under the circumstances. Is the prosecutor correct?

Scenario Two: The Administrative Office of the United States Courts [the "AO"] has been secretly monitoring email communications and Internet searches engaged in by judges and staff of the United States Court of Appeals for the Ninth Circuit. The AO's goals are to discover weaknesses in its anti-hacking firewall and also to find out whether the judiciary and its staff are engaging in such personal activities as downloading music or surfing the web for pornography. As a result of the surveillance, the AO discovers that Judge Centrum has been downloading copyrighted music and burning it onto CDs on his office computer. After Judge Centrum is charged criminally with misuse of federal property, he seeks to suppress the results of the surveillance. Centrum anticipates that the prosecutor will contend that no Fourth Amendment search took place because no privacy rights were invaded. Will the judge be able to respond successfully to the prosecutor's argument?

f.   Container Searches

In *California v. Greenwood,*[37] police suspected Greenwood of narcotics trafficking, and they asked the neighborhood trash collector to pick up the plastic garbage bags that Greenwood left on the curb in front of his house and them over. An officer searched the bags, found items indicative of drug use, and then obtained a warrant, which, when executed, revealed cocaine and hashish inside Greenwood's home. The issue that ultimately worked its way to the Court was whether Greenwood (and his significant other) had a reasonable expectation of privacy in bagged garbage once outside the home and the curtilage. The Court said "no." It is common knowledge, said the Court, that plastic garbage bags on a public street are readily accessible to animals, children, scavengers, and snoops. Moreover, the garbage was left on the curb to be conveyed to a third party, who might have sorted through the trash. Furthermore, the police cannot reasonably be expected to "avert their eyes from criminal activity that could have been observed by any member of the public." Accordingly, the trash was analogous to pen registers (because they consist of information voluntarily conveyed to telephone companies when the telephone is dialed) and to items exposed by aerial surveillance (because any member of the public could observe them from navigable airspace). Finally, the Court found it irrelevant that the California constitution, as interpreted by that state's highest court, prohibited warrantless searches and seizures of garbage, stating that the Fourth Amendment does not turn on the varying law of the states.

On the other hand, in *Bond v. United States*[38] a border patrol agent did violate reasonable expectations of privacy when he squeezed soft luggage that passengers had placed in the overhead storage space of a bus. The agent had boarded the bus to check the immigration status of its passengers. He then walked toward the front of the bus, feeling and squeezing bags overhead. The agent felt a "brick-like" object in Bond's canvas bag and, after obtaining Bond's permission to open the bag, discovered methamphetamine. Bond was convicted in federal court on drug charges and appealed, arguing that the agent's actions constituted a search. The government argued that Bond had no reasonable expectation of privacy in the contours of the bag because any passenger on the bus could have squeezed

---

37.   486 U.S. 35 (1988).

38.   529 U.S. 334 (2000).

it. In support of its position, the government relied on *California v. Ciraolo* (referred to above) and a similar case, *Florida v. Riley*[39] both of which held that aerial surveillance does not violate reasonable expectations of privacy if members of the public could lawfully observe from that vantage point. The Supreme Court held that *Ciraolo* and *Riley* did not govern the situation in *Bond*, because they involved "only visual, as opposed to tactile, observation." Chief Justice Rehnquist, writing for the majority, stated, "[p]hysically invasive inspection is simply more intrusive than purely visual inspection." He went on to apply the two-part test:

> Our Fourth Amendment analysis embraces two questions. First, we ask whether the individual, by his conduct, has exhibited an actual expectation of privacy; that is, whether he has shown that he sought to preserve something as private. Here, petitioner sought to preserve privacy by using an opaque bag and placing that bag directly above his seat. Second, we inquire whether the individual's expectation of privacy is one that society is prepared to recognize as reasonable. When a bus passenger places a bag in an overhead bin, he expects that other passengers or bus employees may move it for one reason or another. Thus, a bus passenger clearly expects that his bag may be handled. He does not expect that other passengers or bus employees will, as a matter of course, feel the bag in an exploratory manner. But this is exactly what the agent did here. We therefore hold that the agent's physical manipulation of petitioner's bag violated the Fourth Amendment.

Comment on State Constitutions: In *State v. Hempele,*[40] the New Jersey State Supreme Court rejected Greenwood. "Clues to people's most private traits and affairs can be found in their garbage," said the court. Moreover, opaque bags conceal their contents from plain view, and what is concealed is presumed protected by a reasonable privacy expectation. The court remarked that the vulnerability of such concealment to prying eyes cannot be determinative or a lock and key would be needed to have any privacy interest. Furthermore, the risks of occasional intrusions by dogs and systematic intrusions by police are very different. Finally, extensive regulation of garbage does not eliminate all privacy interests, even if it may reduce them, and an "abandonment" analogy is meaningless, as that term is a conclusion regarding whether there is a reasonable privacy expectation, not an explanation of whether such an expectation exists in the first place.

3. OTHER FACTORS IN THE SEARCH ANALYSIS

While location and assumption of the risk are the two most important factors in the Court's "search" analysis, there are others that come into play as well.

---

39. 488 U.S. 445 (1989).

40. 576 A.2d 793 (N.J. 1990).

a. *Property Interests*

Property interests also are a relevant factor in the privacy analysis, but usually they are not dispositive. Before *Katz*, property interests were dispositive—a search meant a common law trespass of a constitutionally protected area (the Fourth Amendment protects only "persons, houses, papers and effects"). *Katz* rejected both the trespass and constitutionally-protected-areas limitations. Using the *Katz* test in a later case, Justice Rehnquist held that a passenger in an automobile ordinarily has no expectation of privacy therein, explaining that:

> Legitimation of expectations of privacy by law must have a source outside of the Fourth Amendment, either by reference to concepts of real or personal property law or to understandings that are recognized and permitted by society. One of the main rights attaching to property is the right to exclude others, . . . and one who owns or lawfully possesses or controls property will in all likelihood have a legitimate expectation of privacy by virtue of this right to exclude. Expectations of privacy . . . need not be based on a common-law interest in real or personal property, . . . [b]ut . . . the Court has not altogether abandoned use of property concepts in determining the presence or absence of the privacy interests protected by that Amendment.[41]

In another case, *Rawlings v. Kentucky*,[42] Justice Rehnquist's majority opinion made clear that property concepts mattered in determining whether the defendant's expectations of privacy were reasonable, but that those concepts did not control the issue. The Court acknowledged that ownership was "one fact to be considered" but "emphatically rejected the notion that 'arcane' concepts of property law ought to control . . . the Fourth Amendment." Having done so, the Court rejected the defendant's claim that his ownership of contraband in a friend's purse meant that a search of that purse violated his privacy rights.

It now appears that every member of the Court agrees that ownership or possession is relevant. Nevertheless confusion reigns over the weight that should be given interests defined by property law. The Court has described property interests as "marginally relevant," "weighty," "principal," or not altogether "snuffed out."[43] Professor Yeager sees those references as mere "verbiage," contributing nothing to the Court's opinions. He disagrees with the Court's approach, favoring instead an approach giving positive law, including property and contractual rights, a much greater role on the theory that it reflects societal feelings about privacy. For example, in *California v. Greenwood*,[44] the Court found no reasonable expectation of privacy in trash bags that the defendant placed on his curb for pickup by a sanitation company. Professor Yeager argues that the Fourth Amendment should have applied if a local ordinance prohibited the sanitation company

---

41. Rakas v. Illinois, 439 U.S. 128, 143 (1978).

42. 448 U.S. 98 (1980).

43. *See* Yeager, *Positive Law, supra* note 3, at 307 & n.357 (citing sources).

44. 486 U.S. 35 (1988).

from snooping in the defendant's garbage or if the defendant had contracted for such protection with the sanitation company. Because no such ordinance or contract existed in Greenwood, he thought the case properly decided.[45]

There is no question that property law is paramount where an individual can be said to have legally "abandoned" his or her property interest.[46] Courts have declared that there is no search where police examine previously protected property in which an owner has voluntarily relinquished his or her proprietary interest. The most common situation in which abandonment arises is a police chase of a suspect who, in the course of the chase, throws away a weapon, illegal drugs, or stolen money. If these items are examined by police, they often become the subjects of motions to suppress. Many courts hold that where items are abandoned voluntarily during a chase, they no longer belong to the individual and can be examined by police without any constitutional violation. Other courts view this kind of abandonment as having been "forced" by the police activity and will suppress the results of the police examination if the police chase cannot be justified.[47] The United States Supreme Court has refused to adopt the latter approach. In *California v. Hodari D*, it found that even if the police were not justified in chasing Hodari, the cocaine that he threw away could be admitted into evidence because he had not been captured at the time he disposed of it.[48]

b. Social Custom

Longstanding social custom is another factor that affects the reasonableness inquiry. In *Minnesota v. Olson*,[49] police arrested Olson after developing probable cause to believe that he was the getaway driver in a felony-murder of a gas-station attendant. Olson was arrested in the home of two women with whom he was staying and claimed that the police violated his expectations of privacy when they entered and searched that home. The Court agreed, holding that Olson had a privacy interest in the premises because of his status as an overnight guest. By "longstanding social custom," said the Court, we seek temporary shelter "when we are in between jobs or homes, or when we house-sit for a friend," as well as when "we travel to a strange city . . . [to] visit . . . relatives out-of-town." Moreover, because temporary guests are especially vulnerable to the loss of

---

45. Yeager, *Positive Law, supra,* note 3, at 301. Justice Brennan, in dissent, had argued that the Greenwood holding would erase our privacy interest in mail. 486 U.S. at 51. Professor Yeager rejects this, arguing that the positive law protects mail but not trash, and positive law matters because it reflects our feelings respectively about mail and trash.

46. This abandonment discussion is drawn in part from State v. Hempele, 576 A.2d 793 (N.J. 1990).

47. *See* Thomas K. Clancy, *The Future of Fourth Amendment Seizure Analysis After Hodari D. and Bostick*, 28 Am. Crim. L. Rev. 799, 826–30 (1991).

48. 499 U.S. 621 (1991).

49. 495 U.S. 91 (1990).

privacy, hosts customarily defer carefully to their privacy needs.[50] These social customs involving guests and hosts encouraged the Court to recognize the legitimacy of Olson's privacy expectations.

Social custom suggests that a more temporary visitor is not given privacy protection by his host. In *Minnesota v. Carter*, the Court held that a cocaine dealer who spent approximately two hours in the apartment of an acquaintance did not have a reasonable expectation of privacy there.[51] The Court acknowledged that, while the text of the Fourth Amendment suggests it extends only to people in their own houses, "in some circumstances a person may have a legitimate expectation of privacy in the house of someone else." But it clarified that a very temporary visitor may not have such an expectation. The facts in *Carter* involved a cocaine transaction observed by a police officer who peered through an apartment's window blinds. Carter was one of the men observed in the transaction, but he had no connection with the apartment and had been there just over two hours. Chief Justice Rehnquist denied that Carter had a legitimate expectation of privacy in the apartment, citing "the purely commercial nature of the transaction engaged in here, the relatively short period of time on the premises, and the lack of any previous connection between [Carter] and the householder." Justice Ginsburg, dissenting with three other justices, felt that the length of the guest's stay should not be determinative. Rather, the key fact is that the host invited the guest and therefore chose to share with the guest the privacy of the home. In these circumstances, both the host and guest have exhibited a subjective expectation of privacy and, according to common understandings, society is prepared to recognize that expectation as reasonable.

c.   Past Practices and Expectations

The Court pays attention to past practices and expectations in determining expectations of privacy. Notably, in *O'Connor v. Ortega*,[52] the Court found that a state hospital administrator had a reasonable expectation of privacy in his office, even though in government offices many others— fellow employees, supervisors, consensual visitors, and the general public— have access to the office. The Court reasoned that the expectation of privacy in one's place of work has "deep roots in the history of the Fourth Amendment."

d.   Legality and Intimacy of Activities

It makes a difference whether the individuals claiming a privacy expectation were engaging in illegal or legal activities, and whether they are intimate or completely commercial. The Court has suggested that individuals enjoy little or no privacy interests when they engage in purely

---

50.   *See* Yeager, *Positive Law, supra* note 3, at 289.

51.   525 U.S. 83 (1998).

52.   480 U.S. 709, 717 (1987).

illegal activities. For example, in *United States v. Place*,[53] the Court held that a canine sniff of luggage did not constitute a search, explaining that:

> [a] "canine sniff" by a well-trained narcotics detection dog ... does not require opening the luggage. It does not expose noncontraband items that otherwise would remain hidden from public view, as does, for example, an officer's rummaging through the contents of the luggage. Thus, the manner in which information is obtained is much less intrusive than a typical search. Moreover, the sniff discloses only the presence or absence of narcotics, a contraband item.

Similarly, in *United States v. Jacobsen*,[54] the Court noted that "[a] chemical test that merely discloses whether or not a particular substance is cocaine does not compromise any legitimate interest in privacy." And in *Minnesota v. Carter*, cited above, the Court suggested that illegal drug dealing, which was "purely commercial" in nature, contributed to its finding that the dealer had no reasonable expectation of privacy in the apartment in which he had been cutting up cocaine for distribution.[55] In her dissent, Justice Ginsburg stated that she believed that the illegality of the conduct in which Carter engaged was irrelevant: "if the illegality of the activity made constitutional an otherwise unconstitutional search, such Fourth Amendment protection, reserved for the innocent only, would have little force in regulating police behavior toward either the innocent or the guilty."

In *Illinois v. Caballes*,[56] the Court followed the reasoning of both *Jacobsen* and *Place* in holding that a drug dog sniff of a lawfully-seized car did not violate the Fourth Amendment. In the ten minutes it took one officer to effectuate the routine traffic stop, a second officer walked his drug dog around Caballes's car, searched the car after the dog alerted, and found marijuana. Caballes was arrested and convicted for narcotics offenses. The Court reasoned that the drug dog sniff did not prolong the length of the lawful stop beyond what was "justified by the traffic offense and the ordinary inquiries incident to such a stop." Therefore, the stop could only have violated the Fourth Amendment if the use of the dog unconstitutionally expanded the scope of the stop.

The Court found that the dog sniff was not a search, and therefore did not unconstitutionally expand the scope of the lawful traffic stop. In reaffirming the holding of *Place* that a drug dog sniff is treated as *"sui generis"* and not a search under the Fourth Amendment, the Court pointed to the teachings of *Jacobsen*: "governmental conduct that *only* reveals the possession of contraband 'compromises no legitimate privacy interest.' "[57]

Justice Souter argued in his dissent that a dog sniff should not be classified as *"sui generis"* and should be treated as a Fourth Amendment

---

53. 462 U.S. 696 (1983).

54. 466 U.S. 109 (1984).

55. 525 U.S. 83 (1998).

56. 543 U.S. 405 (2005).

57. *Id.* at 408.

search. According to Souter, "[t]he classification [of a dog sniff as '*sui generis*'] rests ... on a ... premise that experience has shown to be untenable, the assumption that trained sniffing dogs do not err."[58] Studies have shown that drug dogs have an error rate between seven and 60 percent. Souter went on to say that the dog sniff search of Caballes's car was not reasonable because the police did not have probable cause to believe that Caballes was violating a drug law.

Souter also argued that *Jacobsen* is distinct from *Caballes* in that the plaintiff in *Jacobsen* did not have a privacy interest in cocaine that was already lawfully in police possession. Dissimilarly, in *Caballes*, the dog alert merely "informe[ed] the police ... of a reasonable chance of finding contraband they have yet to put their hands on, so the certainty and limit on disclosure that may [have] follow[ed] [were] missing."[59]

Justice Ginsburg's dissent, which Justice Souter joined, argued that dog sniffs should be subject to the two-part *Terry* test. Ginsburg wrote that she "would apply *Terry*'s reasonable-relation test, as the Illinois Supreme Court did, to determine whether the canine sniff impermissibly expanded the scope of the initially valid seizure of Caballes."[60] Ginsburg concluded that because the "expansion of the seizure here from a routine traffic stop to a drug investigation broadened the scope of the investigation in a manner that ... runs afoul of the Fourth Amendment."[61] She also pointed out that injecting such an intimidating animal as a drug dog "change[d] the character of the encounter" in a way that deserves Fourth Amendment protection.

Finally, Ginsburg argued that the majority's decision has dealt a serious blow to Fourth Amendment protection from unreasonable searches. "Under today's decision," she wrote, "every traffic stop could become an occasion to call in the dogs, to the distress and embarrassment of the law-abiding population." Furthermore, the Court's decision "clears the way for suspicionless, dog-accompanied drug sweeps of parked cars along sidewalks and in parking lots."[62]

Using reasoning similar to that of the majority in *Caballes*, the United States Supreme Court held in *Muehler v. Mena*[63] that when police executing a search warrant questioned a resident about her immigration status, they did not expand the scope of the search. The *Muehler* petitioners were lead officers of a police detachment executing a warrant to search for gang-related contraband in a residence that respondent *Mena* shared with several others. Officers handcuffed her for the duration of the search, and while she was handcuffed, they questioned her about her immigration status. She sued the officers, alleging (among other things) that their

---

58. *Id.* at 410 (Souter, J., dissenting).

59. *Id.* at 416 (Souter, J., dissenting).

60. *Id.* at 422 (Ginsburg, J., dissenting).

61. *Id.* at 420 (Ginsburg, J., dissenting).

62. *Id.* at 422 (Ginsburg, J., dissenting).

63. 544 U.S. 93 (2005).

questioning violated her Fourth Amendment rights. The Court rejected her claim, emphasizing that the questioning did not extend the duration of the search. Furthermore, the Court observed that "mere police questioning does not constitute a seizure."

Several state courts have interpreted their states' constitutions so as to impose greater limitations on police actions. This is particularly true in the area of dog sniffs. For example, several years after the United States Supreme Court issued its opinion in *Place*, the Court of Appeals of New York held that dog sniffs are searches under New York's constitution.[64] Said that court, "[u]nlike the Supreme Court, we believe that the fact that a given investigative procedure can disclose only evidence of criminality should have little bearing on whether it constitutes a search." The New York court did hold, however, that a dog sniff was minimally intrusive and needed to be justified only by reasonable suspicion, as opposed to probable cause. In 2003, the Montana Supreme Court found a search where police led a dog around a suspected drug dealer's car, which was parked in a public parking lot.[65] The dog alerted to the trunk, which was searched and resulted in a prosecution. The Montana court reasoned that the dealer had put items into his trunk to keep them private. This expectation, said the court, had been interfered with and hence a search had occurred.

PROBLEM 2–16

Having received reliable information that Marsha was manufacturing methamphetamine in her kitchen, police obtained a warrant to search her house for drugs. At the same time, the IRS believed that Marsha had committed tax fraud, and it sent two of its agents to accompany police as they executed the warrant. Believing their safety to be at risk whenever they worked on drug cases, the police handcuffed Marsha as they entered her house. While she was handcuffed, the IRS agents questioned her about her taxes. She claimed that she had never done anything wrong but that she couldn't answer their questions completely, explaining that "it's all complicated, and I'd have to check the files over there." The agents opened the cabinet to which Marsha had inclined her head and located several files labeled "Tax Returns." A thorough analysis indicated that Marsha's returns were accurate. Did the IRS agents violate Marsha's Fourth Amendment rights when they questioned her? When they searched her cabinet and read her files?

e. *Vantage Point*

Recall the *Dunn* case, discussed above in the section on curtilage. There, the Court refused to find a search had taken place, in part because agents were standing in an open field (not protected under the Fourth Amendment) when they peered into a barn. As you can tell from that case,

---

64. State v. Dunn, 563 N.Y.S.2d 388 (1990).

65. State v. Tackitt, 67 P.3d 295 (2003).

the vantage point of government actors matters a great deal. Simply put, the Court has refused to recognize privacy in areas open to public observation. Moreover, as the discussion above about electronic devices suggests, it permits police to facilitate their observations from such public vantage points by using enhancement devices (flashlights, for example), so long as those devices simply enable police to see more clearly something that they could otherwise see without the devices. On the other hand, where the enhancement device reveals what would otherwise not be exposed to public view, a reasonable privacy expectation exists.[66] The "public vantage point" factor can remove protection from an individual's innermost thoughts and feelings, even though at one time the Court appeared to have special regard for repositories of private thoughts, such as "private papers."[67] Similarly, no reasonable expectation of privacy inheres in physical characteristics ordinarily observable by the public,[68] such as the sound of a voice,[69] physical appearance,[70] and the characteristics of handwriting[71] and fingerprints.[72] On the other hand, a reasonable expectation of privacy protects physical characteristics not ordinarily observable by the public, such as the content of blood.[73] Breath tests for alcohol,[74] urinalysis,[75] the scraping of fingernails,[76] forced surgical procedures,[77] and other intrusive scientific procedures invade reasonable privacy expectations.

f.   Reduced Expectations of Privacy

Under various circumstances, the Court concedes that a person has a reasonable expectation of privacy but finds that expectation "reduced" for

---

66. *See* Bloom & Brodin, EXAMPLES & EXPLANATIONS, *supra* note 9, at 30.

67. For instance, the Court's earlier holdings protected "private papers" from government scrutiny, but the Fourth Amendment apparently no longer provides such protection. *See* Anne Marie Demarco and Elisa Scott, *Confusion Among the Courts: Should the Contents of Personal Papers Be Privileged By the Fifth Amendment's Self–Incrimination Clause?*, 9 ST. JOHN'S J. LEGAL COMMENT. 219 (1993) (tracing Circuit split on whether special protection for private papers has survived recent Supreme Court decisions suggesting that the answer is "no"); Russell W. Galloway, Jr., *The Intruding Eye: A Status Report on the Constitutional Ban Against Paper Searches*, 25 HOW. L.J. 367 (1982) (tracing Fourth and Fifth Amendment roots of special protections for private papers and arguing that privacy concerns justify, contrary to the apparent trend of the law, retaining those special protections).

68. Paul C. Giannelli, *Forensic Science: Seizing Evidence From Suspects for Forensic Analysis*, 31 CR. L. BULL. 161,173 (1995) (citing cases finding searches in taking shoeprints, examining teeth, and inspecting hands under ultraviolet light).

69. United States v. Dionisio, 410 U.S. 1 (1973).

70. *Id.*

71. United States v. Mara, 410 U.S. 19 (1973).

72. Davis v. Mississippi, 394 U.S. 721 (1969).

73. Schmerber v. California, 384 U.S. 757, 767 (1966) (involving extraction of blood for purposes of forensic analysis).

74. Skinner v. Railway Labor Executives' Ass'n, 489 U.S. 602 (1989).

75. *Id.* at 617.

76. Cupp v. Murphy, 412 U.S. 291 (1973).

77. *See* Winston v. Lee, 470 U.S. 753 (1985).

purposes of Fourth Amendment balancing. This reasoning assumes that some baseline level exists for comparison, or that the privacy interests in various places are weighed relative to each other—against the high expectations persons enjoy in their homes, for example. However, the Court has never clearly defined a baseline expectation of privacy. Instead, it appears to speak of "reduced" expectations of privacy to signify situations in which privacy interests are relatively small compared to the State's interest in obtaining the evidence. It then uses that disparity to justify departures from the usual requirements of probable cause and a warrant.

We will address reduced expectations in greater detail when we examine the exceptions to the usual probable cause and warrant requirements. Here we catalogue some instances in which the Court has found reduced expectations to point out that the *Katz* test does not necessarily pose a dichotomy between a reasonable expectation of privacy and no reasonable expectation. Rather, there appears to be a spectrum of privacy expectations, ranging along a continuum from no expectation (for example, where police seize an unattended item on a public street), to intermediate expectations (to be discussed shortly), to very high ones (for example, where police search a home). The same methodological questions arise about how the Court determines relative degrees of privacy: by majority views, normative judgments, or both?

The Court has found privacy expectations to be reduced in vehicles, at least where they are parked in public places, partly because the interiors of passenger compartments can be easily observed from those outside the vehicle and partly because vehicles are heavily regulated. At some point regulation becomes so "pervasive" that the Court deems privacy expectations to be minimal, justifying even warrantless and suspicionless searches. The Court has also found privacy expectations to be reduced in school settings. For example, the Court upheld random urine testing of high school athletes in *Vernonia School District 47J v. Acton*.[78] The Court noted:

> Fourth Amendment rights ... are different in public schools than elsewhere. The "reasonableness" inquiry cannot disregard the schools' custodial and tutelary responsibility for children. For their own good and that of their classmates, public school children are routinely required to submit to various physical examinations, and to be vaccinated against various diseases ... Particularly with regard to medical examinations and procedures, therefore, students within the school environment have a lesser expectation of privacy than members of the population generally.
>
> Legitimate privacy expectations are even less with regard to student athletes. School sports are not for the bashful. They require "suiting up" before each practice or event, and showering and changing afterwards. Public school locker rooms, the usual sites for these activities, are not notable for the privacy they afford. The locker rooms in Vernonia are typical: no individual dressing rooms are provided;

---

78. 515 U.S. 646 (1995).

shower heads are lined up along a wall, unseparated by any sort of partition or curtain; not even all the toilet stalls have doors.

There is an additional respect in which school athletes have a reduced expectation of privacy. By choosing to "go out for the team," they voluntarily subject themselves to a degree of regulation even higher than imposed on students generally. In Vernonia's public schools, they must submit to a preseason physical exam, ... they must acquire adequate insurance coverage or sign an insurance waiver, maintain a minimum grade point average, and comply with any "rules of conduct, dress, training hours and related matters as may be established for each sport by the head coach and athletic director with the principal's approval." Somewhat like adults who choose to partici-pate in a "closely regulated industry," students who voluntarily partic-ipate in school athletics have reason to expect intrusions upon normal rights and privileges, including privacy.

This excerpt illustrates how the Court establishes relative degrees of legitimate privacy expectations. The gradations can be quite fine. For example, in *New Jersey v. T.L.O.*,[79] the Court also considered the privacy rights of high school students, but not in the context of student athletes and urinalysis. T.L.O., a high school student (she was subjected to juvenile court proceedings, hence the abbreviation of her name), had been reported to a school administrator after a teacher saw her smoking cigarettes in the school lavatory in violation of school rules. The administrator reached into T.L.O.'s purse for cigarettes, but in doing so noticed cigarette rolling papers that he associated with marijuana use. Based on the presence of the papers (which gave him reasonable suspicion to believe that T.L.O. was engaging in criminal activity and that the purse contained evidence of that activity), he engaged in a more thorough search of the purse and discovered marijua-na and indicia of drug-dealing. The Court upheld the search but expressly rejected the state's claim that school children have no legitimate expecta-tion of privacy in their effects. Nevertheless, the expectations they have are not so great, relative to the state's interests, as to require warrants and probable cause for school searches.[80]

There are other situations in which privacy expectations might be reduced. For example, in *Hudson v. Palmer*,[81] the Court held that a prisoner does not have a reasonable expectation of privacy in his prison cell. The Court did so by engaging in balancing the interests present in the jail setting: "The uncertainty that attends random searches of cells renders

---

79.   469 U.S. 325 (1985).

80.   Foreshadowing its later decision in *Vernonia*, the Court also noted, however, that it did not decide whether individualized suspicion would be necessary under other circum-stances. *T.L.O.*, 469 U.S. at 342 n.8. Exceptions to the individualized suspicion requirement, held the Court, would be appropriate where privacy interests are minimal and other safe-guards to limit official discretion are in place. *Id.* This analysis seemed to follow from the Court's conclusion that probable cause and warrants are not irreducible requirements of a valid search but merely bear on the fundamental question of reasonableness. *Id.* at 341.

81.   468 U.S. 517 (1984).

these searches perhaps the most effective weapon of the prison administrator in the constant fight against the proliferation of knives and guns, illicit drugs, and other contraband."

PROBLEM 2–17

Marlon McCaw was tipped off that the police were imminently arriving at his parents' home, where McCaw had been living for the last three months, with a warrant for his arrest. As the police were entering the front door, McCaw threw a briefcase out the window of his second-floor bedroom at the rear of the house. The briefcase landed in the rear yard between the house and a wrought iron fence that separated the yard from the adjacent sidewalk. The fence completely enclosed the rear yard, but the gate to the fence was wide open. The yard had tall grass and wild-growing plants and flowers. A sign on the open gate read, "Welcome all who wish to enter and enjoy the solitude of nature's bounty."

A Boston police officer stationed at the rear of the house to intercept any attempted flight by McCaw entered the rear yard to retrieve the briefcase. He noticed that the right side latch was unlocked, leaving that side of the briefcase slightly ajar. He pried open the right side of the case, looked inside, and saw a plastic glassine bag containing a white, powdery substance that he believed to be cocaine. Accordingly, he seized the briefcase and its contents, leading to McCaw's subsequent indictment for trafficking in cocaine.

Question: McCaw files a motion to suppress the briefcase and its contents in his cocaine-trafficking trial. What arguments might the prosecutor make to establish that the officer's conduct was no "search"? What responses might the defense make, and who should prevail?

Given the factors set out in section II(C) of this chapter, do you think the Supreme Court will (or should) treat states' taking individuals' DNA as a search? While "appellate courts in this country are virtually unanimous in upholding statutes [that require taking DNA from certain categories of convicted persons,]"[82] Professor Tracey Maclin argues that the Court will likely find that states' forcibly obtaining and testing DNA samples of arrestees constitutes a search under the Fourth Amendment for three reasons.[83]

According to Maclin, although an individual's DNA is exposed to the public, the Court will likely follow the holding of *Kyllo v. United States*—"a search occurs when government agents use sense-enhancing technology to collect any information ... that could not otherwise be obtained without a physical invasion." DNA sampling and analysis certainly uses sense-enhancing technology and is therefore a search. Also, "[a]ny physical intru-

---

82. Nason v. State, 102 P.3d 962 at 694 (Alaska App. 2004) (citing cases).

83. Tracey Maclin, *Is Obtaining an Arrestee's DNA a Valid Special Needs Search Under the Fourth Amendment? What Should (and Will) the Supreme Court Do?*, 33 J. L. Med. & Ethics 102 (2005).

sion into the body ... constitutes a search for Fourth Amendment proposes. ... Therefore, although DNA sampling can be accomplished in a minimally invasive manner by testing epithelial cells, the odds are very good that the court will conclude that the taking and analysis of the sample is a search under the Fourth Amendment." Furthermore, "[b]ecause DNA has the potential to reveal a host of private facts about an arrestee, the Court will probably find that forcibly taking and testing DNA is a search."

D. SUBPOENAS

A subpoena (a court order to produce a person, document, or object) is generally considered neither a search nor a seizure.[84] However, an unreasonably broad subpoena may implicate the Fourth Amendment. Furthermore, before subpoenas may be enforced by contempt proceedings, some courts invoke their supervisory powers to require the state to prove certain minimal facts. Illustrative is the court's opinion in *In re Schofield*[85] that required proof that each item sought by a grand jury subpoena was: (1) relevant to the grand jury's investigation, (2) properly within the grand jury's jurisdiction, and (3) not sought primarily for another purpose. Moreover, under both state and federal constitutions, some courts require individualized suspicion for highly invasive subpoenas, such as those requesting blood samples, pubic hair samples, or placement in a lineup.[86]

III. WHAT IS A "SEIZURE"?

The Fourth Amendment protects against more than just unreasonable searches: it also prohibits unreasonable "seizures." And just as a "search" does not occur for Fourth Amendment purposes unless the government has invaded a reasonable expectation of privacy, so too does a "seizure" require the deprivation of a constitutionally protected interest. In the case of the seizure of a *person*, the interest protected is in liberty: a seizure of a person occurs when a government actor significantly interferes with a person's freedom of movement.[87] The seizure of a person sometimes, but not always, amounts to an "arrest." We will discuss seizures of the person in more detail later in the next chapter.

In the case of a seizure of a *thing*, the interest protected is a possessory one: a seizure of a thing occurs when the government works "some meaningful interference with an individual's possessory interests in that property."[88] Possessory interests are defined according to principles of

---

84.   *See* United States v. Dionisio, 410 U.S. 1, 10.

85.   486 F.2d 85 (3d Cir. 1973) ("Schofield I"); *see also* In re Schofield, 507 F.2d 963 (3d Cir. 1975) ("Schofield II") (elaborating on these requirements).

86.   *See* Edward Imwinkelried, *Forensic Science: Seizing Evidence From Suspects for Forensic Analysis*, 31 CR. L. BULL. 161, 170–71 (1995) (summarizing case law).

87.   United States v. Jacobsen, 466 U.S. 109, 113 (1984).

88.   *See, e.g.,* United States v. Mendenhall, 446 U.S. 544 (1980).

property law. So, for example, if a police officer were to burn this book, a seizure would have occurred because your possessory interest in the book would have been affected in a significant way. The seizure might be reasonable, depending on whether the police officer had a warrant to seize and destroy the book or, if not, whether an exception to the warrant requirement was present. But the action would constitute a seizure nonetheless. On the other hand, some interference with possessory interests might be so insignificant as to be meaningless in Fourth Amendment terms. For example, if a police officer were to pick up this book, leaf through its pages, and set it down again, your possessory interest would have been affected in such a minor way that a seizure would not have occurred (but a "search" might have, if the book-leafing invaded reasonable privacy expectations).[89]

IV. "Standing," or, Who May Complain About Searches & Seizures?

A. The *Rakas* Test

One of the fundamental principles of the American legal system is that a litigant must have "standing" before asserting a claim for relief. The term "standing" connotes a host of issues concerning justiciability, including these: was there an injury? Is the injury redressable? Did this litigant sustain the injury? Is this litigant the appropriate party to bring the controversy to a court? Generally, courts encompass these issues within two broad inquiries: "first, whether the proponent of a particular legal right has alleged 'injury in fact,' and second, whether the proponent is asserting his own legal rights and interests rather than basing his claim for relief upon the rights of third parties.[90] The Supreme Court has explained that these standing inquiries ensure that litigants have 'a personal stake in the outcome of the controversy,' a stake that 'sharpens the presentation of issues upon which the court so largely depends for illumination of difficult constitutional questions.' "[91]

Claims about unlawful searches are no exception to the rule of standing: a person aggrieved by an allegedly unlawful search or seizure and seeking a remedy (including the exclusion of evidence in a criminal case) must establish standing before a court will find the claim to be justiciable. How does a litigant (typically a criminal defendant) establish standing in the context of an allegedly unlawful search or seizure? The remainder of this section will explore that question.

---

89. *Cf.* Jacobsen, 466 U.S. at 123–25 (when agents took minute quantity of cocaine in order to perform field test, no seizure occurred because the possessory interest in that quantity was de minimus).

90. Rakas v. Illinois, 439 U.S. 128, 139 (1978).

91. Baker v. Carr, 369 U.S. 186, 204 (1962).

The principal case on the issue of standing for Fourth Amendment purposes, *Rakas v. Illinois*,[92] remains good law today. There, the Court held that "Fourth Amendment rights are personal rights that may not be asserted vicariously"; that is, to use language from an earlier case, a Fourth Amendment violation "can be successfully urged only by those whose rights were violated by the search [or seizure] itself, not by those who are aggrieved solely by the introduction of damaging evidence." The tests for determining whether a person's rights were violated by a search or seizure are set forth above: in the case of an unlawful search, did the person "ha[ve] a legitimate expectation of privacy in the invaded place?" In the case of an unlawful seizure, did the person have a possessory interest in the items seized? If so, the person has standing to assert an unlawful search or seizure claim under the Fourth Amendment.

The rule set forth in *Rakas*, particularly as it applies to unlawful search claims, obviously has its roots in the *Katz* holding, because the rule emphasizes whose reasonable privacy expectations were invaded. Moreover, the *Rakas* rule marks a departure from the Court's previous, broader test. The earlier test had provided that "anyone legitimately on premises where a search occurs may challenge its legality."[93] The Court in *Rakas* held that the earlier test "creates too broad a gauge for measurement of Fourth Amendment rights."

In order to discern how the *Rakas* test differs from the earlier one, consider the facts in *Rakas* itself. The defendants in that case had been passengers in a car that was stopped and searched by police officers investigating an armed robbery. The search revealed a sawed-off rifle under the front passenger seat and a box of rifle shells in the glove compartment. When these items were introduced against the defendants at their trial for armed robbery, they objected on the ground that the search and seizure had violated their Fourth Amendment rights, although they conceded that they owned neither the automobile nor the items seized. According to the Court, the defendants had not made a sufficient showing that they had a legitimate expectation of privacy in the areas in which the items were found because they failed to demonstrate that they had exercised complete dominion and control over, and the right to exclude others from, those areas. The Court likened those areas to the trunk of a car, remarking that "a passenger qua passenger simply would not normally have a legitimate expectation of privacy" in such a space. Under the newly announced test, therefore, the defendants in *Rakas* could not move successfully for exclusion of the items.

Would the *Rakas* defendants have had standing to challenge the search under the old test articulated permitting anyone "legitimately on the premises" to complain? Probably so, for the Court acknowledged that they were legitimately on the premises "in the sense that they were in the car with the permission of its owner." It is important to recognize that some

---

92.   439 U.S. 128 (1978).

93.   Jones v. United States, 362 U.S. 257, 267 (1960).

states retain standing rules similar to or even broader than "legitimately on the premises" test for purposes of their own constitutional search and seizure provisions, and that state criminal defendants therefore may enjoy broader protection from unlawful police activity by asserting state constitutional claims rather than federal constitutional ones.[94]

Aside from its articulation of a narrower range of litigants who can raise Fourth Amendment claims, *Rakas* represents a departure from prior law in another sense. Under the old test, standing was considered a "threshold" issue that a court had to decide before addressing the merits of the claim. The Court in *Rakas* rephrased the standing inquiry, however, as one "more properly subsumed under substantive Fourth Amendment doctrine." The Court went on to concede that "[t]he inquiry under either approach is the same." "But," it continued, "we think the better analysis forthrightly focuses on the extent of a particular defendant's rights under the Fourth Amendment, rather than on any theoretically separate, but invariably intertwined concept of standing." Many courts continue to refer to the inquiry as one involving "standing," but in actuality they appear to use that term to refer to the first part of a two-part substantive Fourth Amendment inquiry: first, did the defendant have a reasonable expectation of privacy in the place searched, or a possessory interest in the item seized (the "standing" inquiry), and second, if so, was the search or seizure unlawful?

B.   AUTHORITY, LEGALITY, AND STANDING

Two issues arise with such frequency when a defendant's standing is challenged that the lawyer should have special familiarity with them. The first is whether the defendant was legally authorized to occupy the premises searched. Not atypically, courts deny standing where a defendant was not legally authorized to be present, presumably because the lack of legal authority precludes a reasonable expectation of privacy. This is the inverse of the old "legitimately on the premises" test. Recall that, prior to *Rakas*, a defendant who was legitimately on the premises searched could establish standing. *Rakas* disavowed this test, holding that the defendant would have to establish a reasonable expectation of privacy in order to gain standing. Extending *Rakas*, and turning the old test on its head, many courts now hold that defendants who cannot establish they were legitimately on the premises searched likewise cannot establish that they reasonably and legitimately expected privacy in those premises.

In the Fifth Circuit case of *United States v. Boruff*,[95] for example, the defendant contested the legality of a car search. He had been driving the

---

94. *See, e.g.*, State v. Rivas, 788 P.2d 464 (Or.App. 1990) (anyone who has a right to be on premises may contest search); State v. Welch, 160 Vt. 70, 77, 624 A.2d 1105, 1109 (1992) (defendant "need only assert a possessory, proprietary or participatory interest in the . . . area searched to establish standing"); State v. Mollica, 114 N.J. 329, 554 A.2d 1315 (1989) (same); *cf.* State v. Culotta, 343 So.2d 977, 981–82 (La. 1976) (any defendant adversely affected by illegal search can challenge admissibility of evidence).

95. 909 F.2d 111 (5th Cir. 1990), *cert. denied*, 499 U.S. 975 (1991).

car at the time it was searched, but he was not the owner. Instead, his girlfriend had rented the car from a leasing company and had permitted the defendant to drive it. The court denied standing to the defendant because the rental agreement between his girlfriend and the leasing company specified that she was the only legal operator of the vehicle. Since she "had no authority to give control of the car to Boruff," he was not legally authorized to drive it himself and legitimately could expect no privacy in it.

Boruff raises a second typical standing problem: the rental agreement expressly forbade any use of the car for illegal purposes. Since Boruff was using the car to transport drugs, his use was unauthorized and he could not claim standing. Not every jurisdiction has been as restrictive on these standing issues as the court in *Boruff*. A plurality of the Utah Supreme Court, for example, recently held that a car thief may establish standing in the stolen vehicle in order to challenge a search.[96] This view is a minority one, however.

As you work through the problems below, consider the privacy and possessory interests that the defendants might articulate, the legitimacy of those interests, and how those interests affect their ability to gain standing.

PROBLEM 2–18

You represent brothers Art and Bob Jones. On July 28, Bob signed a five-month lease agreement for a condominium apartment at the beautiful Gulf Sands Resort in Orange Beach, Alabama. The apartment that Bob leased is actually owned by a retired couple in Huntsville, but since they only use it for two months out of the year they allow it to be leased by the resort management during the other ten months of the year. The resort was happy to lease the apartment to Bob, but warned him that a vacationing couple from Vermont had leased the apartment for the month of November, and that he would have to spend the last two months of the lease in a different apartment.

Bob agreed to do this, and on November 1 he signed a new lease agreement for the replacement apartment that covered his stay until the following January 1. Each of the lease agreements specified that check-in was between 2:00 p.m. and 5:00 p.m., and that checkout time was 10:00 a.m. Bob was told that the second apartment had been leased to another person commencing on January 1. The second apartment, like the first, is owned by a private individual who allows the management to lease it when the owners are not using it.

Bob and Art lived in the condos without incident. On January 1 a cleaning service hired by the property manager knocked on the apartment door and discovered that Bob and Art were still in the apartment. The cleaners called their boss, who told them to go clean other apartments and come back around noon. When the cleaners returned at noon, Bob and Art were nowhere to be found. However, it was obvious that some of Bob's and

---

96.   *See* State v. Larocco, 794 P.2d 460 (Utah 1990) (plurality opinion).

Art's personal property was still in the apartment. The cleaners called their boss, who told them to pack it all up in plastic bags and prepare the room for the incoming tenants.

While packing up the items, the cleaners discovered that a locked closet containing property belonging to the apartment's owner had been broken into, apparently by Art or Bob. The cleaners then tried to figure out what property belonged at the apartment, and what belonged to Art and Bob. The cleaners found two twenty-dollar bills: one in the owner's closet and the other in the bathroom. Both bills were thinly covered with some sort of white, powdery substance. Under the bed in the master bedroom one of the cleaners found a briefcase without any identifying tags. One of the cleaners tried to open the briefcase, but the left side of the case was locked shut. By prying open the right side, the cleaner saw some napkins wrapped by rubber bands. The cleaner could not tell what was inside the napkins, nor could the cleaner discern any items that identified the briefcase's owner.

The cleaners called the property manager and told him that either drugs or money were in a briefcase they had just found under a bed in Art and Bob's second apartment. The cleaners also told the manager about the two twenty-dollar bills. The manager told the cleaners to leave everything as it was and get out of the apartment. The manager then called the state police and reported that he suspected that there was cocaine in a briefcase left behind by some former tenants. Trooper Stone soon arrived on the scene. The manager let him into the apartment. Stone located the briefcase and looked through its unlocked side. He saw some plastic baggies. He then forced the lock on the briefcase with a pocketknife. Stone found white powder in one of the baggies. He field-tested some of the powder and it tested positively for cocaine. Stone then went outside and called Agent Mason of the Federal Drug Enforcement Administration.

Stone and Mason went before a magistrate and obtained a search warrant to search the entire apartment. On their way to search the apartment, they received a phone call from the property manager. The manager told them that Bob had called a few minutes earlier and told the manager that he had left his briefcase behind and would return for it in a few days. After searching the apartment a second time, Stone and Mason arrested Art and Bob and charged them both with possession with the intent to distribute cocaine. Bob admitted that the briefcase was his, but Art chose not to talk without a lawyer present.

You hired a private investigator to interview the property manager and cleaning crew. Her report says that the manager recalls that Art and Bob failed to move out of their first apartment on time as well. In that instance, their belongings were moved to the replacement apartment by the cleaning crew. The cleaners remember doing this. One of the cleaners said that "people don't get out right at ten" very often. All of the cleaners agreed that standard procedure was to gather all the belongings left behind, place them in bags, and hold them until claimed by the departing lessee. The property manager admitted that the lease agreement is silent as to the effect that moving out late would have on the lessee's property.

Art and Bob are facing about ten years in prison if convicted. Early conversations with the prosecuting attorney suggest that a satisfactory plea agreement cannot be arranged.

Question: Assume that there is no conflict of interest in your representation of Art and Bob, and that you have decided to draft a motion to suppress on their behalf. In drafting the motion you run right into the threshold question: do Art and Bob have standing to challenge the search of the briefcase? Prepare an argument on this issue.

PROBLEM 2–19

Acting on an informant's tip, Detectives Garcia and Hutchinson set up surveillance at a house on Spruce Street. Soon they saw two men, later identified as Barker and Chavez, leave the house. The detectives followed and observed Barker and Chavez hand a package to Dahl. (This package later turned out to contain 35 kilograms of cocaine.) The detectives immediately arrested the three men. During booking, Barker stated that the house on Spruce Street belonged to his parents, but that he kept some of his things there.

The detectives returned to the house on Spruce Street, knocked on the door and asked if they could look around inside. The people who were there gave permission to do so. The detectives entered and found two kilograms of cocaine and $15,000 in a closet. Also in the home was an electric bill for an apartment on Cedar Lane in the name of Enid Emerson and money order receipts made out to the Cedar Lane apartment landlord. When asked about these things, Barker's sister, who lived at home, said that she had been given some money orders by Enid in order for her to pay rent on the apartment while Enid was on a trip to visit relatives upstate. When asked if she had keys to the apartment, the sister said she did not.

The detectives went to the Cedar Lane apartment. No one answered their knock, but neighbors said that a single woman usually lived there. However, one neighbor recalled that for the last couple of months a Hispanic male had come and gone from the apartment every now and then. On a hunch, Detective Hutchinson tried out a set of keys that he had taken from Chavez earlier. One of the keys opened the door to the apartment. Inside, the detectives noted that the apartment was very sparsely furnished. The front room contained only a television and a small table. There were no cooking utensils or food in the kitchen. In the sole bedroom they found a mattress on the floor. In the bedroom closet they found a nice suit with Chavez's Colombian passport in the coat pocket, a packed suitcase, nearly $500,000 in cash, and 12 kilograms of cocaine wrapped in the same manner as the other 35 kilograms previously seized. In a kitchen drawer, Detective Hutchinson found a lease for the apartment in Enid' s name. A few hours later, Detective Garcia asked Chavez if he lived at the Cedar Lane apartment. Chavez said he did not.

Chavez was charged with drug crimes for both the 35–kilogram and the 12–kilogram packages. Chavez's court-appointed counsel, Kathy Ferella, has started negotiations with the assistant district attorney assigned to the case. During negotiations the D.A. admitted the Cedar Lane search was illegal, but she told Ferella that none of the defendants had standing to challenge it. Ferella told the D.A. to rethink her stand, since Chavez obviously had some personal effects stored there. The D.A. quickly shot back, "Rakas says you have to have a legitimate expectation in privacy. A drug safehouse is not a legitimate place to have such an expectation."

Question: Ferella comes to you, her trusty law clerk, and asks you to research the case law and prepare a rough draft of a motion to suppress. She is especially worried about the D.A.'s claim. Does it matter whether the only reason Chavez sought privacy in the apartment was to conceal drugs? What other reasons might Chavez have for leaving his things at the apartment? What arguments should Ferella make in her motion to suppress, knowing that the government will concede the illegality of the search?

PROBLEM 2–20

All is not well in the quiet town of Buckland. The FBI learned that the long-time mayor of Buckland, Alphonse Amar, accepted nearly $5,000 from a group of building contractors in exchange for certificates indicating that some recently completed apartments had passed safety code inspections. (Assume that it is a federal crime to issue false safety certificates.) It seems that the Mayor had threatened the contractors, via local strongarm Buzz Batson, that the apartments would never pass a safety inspection unless they paid him the money. The contractors had decided to pay the money, and had met with Batson and given him the required sum in cash.

FBI agents Sculder and Mulley drove out to Buckland to serve grand jury subpoenas on the town's building inspector. The subpoenas called for the production of the allegedly illegal certificates by the following day. The building inspector told the agents that the certificates would be in the town archives, which happened to be in the town hall's attic. He offered to find the certificates for the agents and turn them over at that time. The inspector didn't have a key to the attic, but he was able to borrow one from a maintenance worker. "Only the maintenance workers and a few people who work for the Mayor have keys," the inspector explained. The inspector told Sculder and Mulley to come along and help him find the certificates.

When they got to the attic, it became clear that Buckland did not use any particular filing system to keep track of its old records. The inspector thought that the certificates would be in a box labeled "Building Department Records." The inspector and the agents looked around the attic without much success. Agent Sculder noticed a box labeled "Mayor's Appointment Books" in the corner. The box was not sealed shut, but the flaps were closed. Sculder opened the flaps and saw that the box did have the Mayor's appointment books in it. In fact, sitting right on top was an appointment book with "Appointments" on the cover. Sculder started to look through the book, but the inspector came over and said, "Sorry, but nobody is supposed to look in the mayor's box.'' Sculder put away the book and said, "I thought I might have found the certificates, but I guess I was wrong." At that moment, agent Mulley located the certificates. The inspector found the correct ones and handed them to Mulley.

A few weeks later the FBI applied for a warrant to search the attic and seize the appointment book. The warrant was approved and Sculder and Mulley retrieved the book. The contents of the book proved to be important to the case, since they showed that the Mayor had several appointments with Buzz Batson before and one appointment just after the payoff by the contractors.

Mayor Amar was indicted for violation of the federal statute prohibiting false issuance of certificates and extortion under color of official right. Prior to trial, Amar moved to suppress the appointment book on these grounds: (1) the initial discovery of the book was an illegal, warrantless search; and (2) the later search pursuant to a warrant was a fruit of the previous illegal search. Amar submitted an affidavit at the suppression hearing stating that he kept the appointment book as a personal, rather than public, document and had done so during the fifteen years he was mayor. Moreover, he had maintained a separate appointment book for official appointments. The affidavit revealed that he had directed his Chief of Staff to keep the personal appointment book in a closed box marked "Mayor's Appointment Books" inside a locked attic. The affidavit also stated that Amar at all times believed that the books were his private property and would be left alone. The Mayor's Chief of Staff submitted her own affidavit stating, among other things, that the Mayor had told her "no one was to have access to any of my boxes, especially the one with my appointment books," and that it was generally known among the people who had keys to the archive that they could only access the records from their own department.

The Government claims the appointment book is a public record. The Assistant U.S. Attorney points out that Amar's secretaries had access to it. The AUSA also pointed out that the names of town officials appear in the book, suggesting that not all the appointments noted within were strictly personal. Primarily, she claims that Amar lacks standing to challenge the search because the archive was a depository for public records for several departments of the town government.

Question: As a threshold issue, does Amar have standing to contest the search? Does it matter whether the appointment book is a public document or not? Can a public employee have an expectation of privacy in a public records archive? In a labeled box within such an archive?

PROBLEM 2–21

Review Problem 2–3. As the prosecution, can you argue that Boson has no standing to challenge the search of Stefni's farm? Next, review the prosecutor's file memorandum in Chapter 1. Can you argue that Boson has no standing to challenge the glove compartment and trunk searches of the automobile there described?

C. STANDING IN THE BUSINESS CONTEXT

It can be especially difficult to decide issues of standing in the business context, where individuals share work spaces and access to desks, computers, and files. The following excerpt from an article by Carla Rhoden,[97] one of Professor Paris's former students, explains how courts deal with these questions:

> ... The "expectation of privacy in commercial premises ... is different from, and indeed less than, a similar expectation in an individual's home." But "[t]here is no doubt that a corporate officer or employee may assert a reasonable or legitimate expectation of privacy in his corporate office." A defendant does not have standing, however, to challenge a search of corporate offices merely because he is a corporate officer or shareholder. And access or control over certain areas also does not in itself impart standing to an employee.

> Given the great variety of work environments, courts address the question of whether an employee has a reasonable expectation of privacy in business premises on a case-by-case basis. Significantly, expectations of privacy in offices, desks, computers, and file cabinets "may be reduced by virtue of actual office practices or procedures." Nevertheless, the Supreme Court has recognized that expectations of privacy in private business offices is not defeated by visits of coworkers, supervisors, and the public, unless the office is "so open to fellow employees or the public that no expectation of privacy is reasonable."

> Most lower courts addressing standing to challenge a search of commercial premises apply a "business nexus" test. Under this test, "the relationship or 'nexus' of the employee to the area searched is an important consideration in determining whether the employee has standing."[98] Where evidence is seized from an employee's work area, courts applying this test generally find that the employee has standing.[99] But where the area searched is not part of the employee's work space, such courts find no reasonable expectation of privacy.[100] Signifi-

---

97. *See* Carla Rhoden, *Challenging Searches & Seizures of Computers at Home or in the Office: From a Reasonable Expectation of Privacy to Fruit of the Poisonous Tree*, 30 AM. J. CRIM. L. 107 (2002).

98. United States v. Anderson, 154 F.3d 1225, 1230 (10th Cir. 1998).

99. *See, e.g.*, Henzel v. United States, 296 F.2d 650, 653 (5th Cir. 1961) (finding standing where the defendant was the organizer, sole stockholder and president of the corporation, "spent the greater part of every average working day there," and prepared much of the material seized); United States v. Lefkowitz, 464 F.Supp. 227 (C.D. Cal. 1979), *aff'd* 618 F.2d 1313, 1316 n.2 (9th Cir. 1980).

100. *See, e.g.*, United States v. Mohney, 949 F.2d 1397, 1403–04 (6th Cir. 1991) (en banc) (defendant who was head of corporations, which he ran as if they were sole proprietorships, was without standing to challenge seizure of corporate records, with which he was "completely uninvolved in preparing and which were kept in offices he claimed to rarely

cantly, a corporate employee's standing to challenge a search at corporate premises under this approach is not necessarily limited to his or her own desk or office. In *United States v. Lefkowitz*, for example, the corporation's president and secretary who worked at the corporate premises were found to have standing to challenge the search not only as to their own desks and offices, but as to the entire suite of offices.[101] The fact that they did not reserve exclusive use of the entire suite did not, in and of itself, vitiate a finding of a reasonable expectation of privacy. The court rejected standing, however, with respect to another co-defendant in that case who did not work anywhere at the suite searched. Similarly, a defendant in *United States v. Taketa* did not have standing to challenge a search of his co-worker's office, because that office had been "given over to [the co-worker's] exclusive use."[102] Conversely, the co-worker in *Taketa*, who was also a defendant, did have standing to challenge the search of that office, because he clearly had a reasonable expectation of privacy there.[103]

It should be noted that not all Circuits have adopted the "business nexus" test as a bright-line rule. The Tenth Circuit, for example, adopted this test only to a limited extent:

> We endorse the "business nexus" test to the extent that we share the belief than an employee enjoys a reasonable expectation of privacy in his work space. Certainly an employee should be able to establish standing by demonstrating he works in the searched area on a regular basis. However, we do not believe the fact that a defendant does or does not work in a particular area should categorically control his ability to challenge a warrantless search of that area. Instead the better approach is to consider all of the circumstances of the working environment and the relevant search. There are numerous circumstances which are highly relevant when considering whether an employee should have standing to contest the search and seizure of items from his workplace for which the "business nexus" test does not account.[104]

Thus, in determining whether a corporate employee has standing to challenge seizure of an item from corporate premises, the Tenth Circuit "will

---

visit."); United States v. Chuang, 897 F.2d 646, 649–52 (2d Cir. 1990) (chairman, president and CEO of bank, and who, with his family owned almost half of the outstanding stock, could not challenge seizure of evidence found in another employee's office); United States v. Judd, 889 F.2d 1410 (5th Cir. 1989) (defendant who was sole shareholder, president and CEO of corporation lacked standing to challenge seizure of records from corporate bookkeeping office in which he did not work); United States v. Britt, 508 F.2d 1052, 1056 (5th Cir. 1975) (corporate president did not have standing to challenge seizure of documents from an off-site warehouse because he failed to demonstrate a "nexus between the area searched and [his] workspace").

101.   Lefkowitz, 464 F.Supp. at 231, *aff'd* 618 F.2d 1313.

102.   923 F.2d 665, 670–71 (9th Cir. 1991).

103.   Rhoden, *Challenging Searches, supra,* note 97, at 110–11.

104.   United States v. Anderson, 154 F.3d 1225, 1230 (10th Cir. 1998) .

consider all the relevant circumstances, including (1) the employee's relationship to the items seized; (2) whether the item was in the immediate control of the employee when it was seized; and (3) whether the employee took actions to maintain his privacy in the item." In evaluating whether an item was in the immediate control of the employee when it is seized, it is useful to consider, though not controlling in the Tenth Circuit's analysis, whether the employee was present at the time of the search, and whether the employee had a right to exclude others from the area searched.

PROBLEM 2–22

As part of a wide-sweeping investigation of several medical practices for Medicare fraud, federal agents executed a search warrant at South Town Family Wellness, P.C. The warrant authorized seizure of all Medicare-related billing files, including those stored on computers. Dr. Wilson is a shareholder of South Town, and he is one of five doctors who, along with three nurses, work throughout the office. The doctors and nurses at South Town examine and treat patients in five examination rooms, which they use interchangeably. The nurses' station is frequented by both doctors and nurses. Behind the receptionist area is an office occupied by the bookkeeper, Susan Marker. Susan handles all of the billing for services performed by the doctors and nurses at South Town, and she works with them to clarify or correct the bills as needed. When this is necessary, a doctor or nurse will either speak to her in her office or she will bring a billing question to the doctors in their private offices. The doctors, nurses, and front office staff all have access to the billing files located in Susan's office, including those stored on computer. But they do not ordinarily access the computer files without Susan's assistance. Susan's desk is given over to her exclusive use and everyone in the office is under strict instruction not to go into her desk drawers, because those drawers are designated for her private belongings. Nowhere, besides the waiting room, is the office open to the public.

During their search pursuant to the warrant, the agents broke the lock on Susan's lower desk file drawer and discovered several Medicare billing files and specific handwritten billing instructions from Dr. Wilson, all of which were seized. And they took Susan's computer in order to search it at a later time. The agents also seized paper billing files from Susan's office, the reception area, the nursing stations, examination rooms, and the doctors' private offices. The government has indicted Dr. Wilson, Susan Marker, and Dr. Anderson (South Town's founder, primary shareholder, and a director who does not work out of South Town's offices, but who oversees its billing practices).

Question: Does Dr. Wilson have standing to challenge the search of Susan Marker's desk drawer? Of her computer? Of her office? Of his office? Of the other doctors' offices? What about the nurses' station and the examination rooms? Can Susan challenge the search of her desk drawer, her computer, and her office? Can she challenge the search of the doctors' private offices, examination rooms, or the nurses' station? Can Dr. Anderson challenge any of the evidence seized at South Town?

V.   THE GOVERNMENT ACTION REQUIREMENT

A person aggrieved because of an allegedly illegal search or seizure must establish more than standing before obtaining relief. Yet another threshold to be crossed is the "government action" requirement: the search or seizure must have been accomplished by a government actor, as opposed to a private party, in order to be considered illegal under the Fourth Amendment. The reason for this rule is obvious: the Bill of Rights generally does not limit the conduct of purely private actors. Indeed, as we saw in Chapter 1, its limitations originally affected only federal government actors. Since 1961, however, individuals who act on behalf of state and local governmental bodies must also abide by the limitations of the Fourth Amendment. But if a private individual conducts a search or seizure and subsequently reveals to law enforcement officials evidence obtained during such a search or seizure, that evidence is admissible if offered by the government.

The United States Supreme Court articulated this rule in *Burdeau v. McDowell*.[105] In that case, it was uncontested that McDowell's papers had been stolen from his office by private detectives and later turned over to a United States prosecutor. The conduct of the private detectives was egregious: they "drilled [McDowell's] private safes, broke the locks upon his private desk, and broke into and abstracted from the files in his offices his private papers." McDowell claimed that the government's use of the stolen papers violated his Fourth Amendment rights, but the Court disagreed:

> The Fourth Amendment gives protection against unlawful searches and seizures, and ... its protection applies to governmental action. Its origin and history clearly show that it was intended as a restraint upon the activities of sovereign authority, and was not intended to be a limitation upon other than governmental agencies; as against such authority it was the purpose of the Fourth Amendment to secure the citizen in the right of unmolested occupation of his dwelling and the possession of his property, subject to the right of seizure by process duly issued. [T]he record clearly shows that no official of the federal government had anything to do with the wrongful seizure of [McDowell's] property, or any knowledge thereof until several months after the property had been taken from him.... It is manifest that there was no invasion of the security afforded by the Fourth Amendment against unreasonable search and seizure, as whatever wrong was done was the act of individuals in taking the property of another. A portion of the property so taken and held was turned over to the prosecuting officers of the federal government. We assume that [McDowell] has an unquestionable right of redress against those who illegally

---

105.   256 U.S. 465 (1921).

and wrongfully took his private property under the circumstances herein disclosed, but with such remedies we are not now concerned.

McDowell complained in addition that the theft of his papers had violated his Fifth Amendment rights as well, and that the government was required to return the papers to him without using them.[106] The Court disposed of McDowell's Fifth Amendment claim quickly:

> We know of no constitutional principle which requires the government to surrender the papers under such circumstances. Had it learned that such incriminatory papers, tending to show a violation of federal law, were in the hands of a person other than the accused, it having had no part in wrongfully obtaining them, we know of no reason why a subpoena might not issue for the production of the papers as evidence. Such production would require no unreasonable search or seizure, nor would it amount to compelling the accused to testify against himself. The papers having come into the possession of the government without a violation of petitioner's rights by governmental authority, we see no reason why the fact that individuals, unconnected with the government, may have wrongfully taken them, should prevent them from being held for use in prosecuting an offense where the documents are of an incriminatory character.

Justice Brandeis, joined by Justice Holmes, dissented from the Court's decision. In his opinion, Brandeis conceded that no constitutional provision appeared directly to prohibit what had happened. Nevertheless, Brandeis argued, the result was unconscionable:

> I cannot believe that action of a public official is necessarily lawful, because it does not violate constitutional prohibitions and because the same result might have been attained by other and proper means. At the foundation of our civil liberty lies the principle which denies to government officials an exceptional position before the law and which subjects them to the same rules of conduct that are commands to the citizen. And in the development of our liberty insistence upon procedural regularity has been a large factor. Respect for law will not be advanced by resort, in its enforcement, to means which shock the common man's sense of decency and fair play.

We might perceive in Justice Brandeis's dissent a precursor to the Court's later holding in *Rochin v. California*[107] that government activity that "shocks the conscience" violates due process. This due-process-like argument has never been successful as a substitute for the requirement of government action before Fourth Amendment limitations can govern searches and seizures. As a result, the government action requirement now is so firmly entrenched that it is no longer questioned. But, like most constitutional rules, the government action requirement gives rise to prob-

---

106. The Fifth Amendment privilege against self-incrimination was once thought to prohibit the compelled disclosure of a person's "papers." More recently the Court has abandoned this view.

107. 342 U.S. 165 (1952).

lems of line-drawing: when does private action become government action? The Court was able to avoid that question in the *McDowell* case because the private detectives had waited until several months after the thefts to give McDowell's papers to the government. What if, instead, the private detectives had turned over the papers immediately? What if the government knew before the thefts of the private detectives' plans? Would these facts turn "private action" into "government action" for purposes of the Fourth Amendment?

The answer depends on the degree of government knowledge of, and participation in, the private person's action, as well as the purpose of the private person. Generally speaking, if the private person can be said to have been an intentional "instrument or agent" of the government at the time of the search or seizure, then the government action requirement will be satisfied. One court put it this way:[108]

> For a private person to be considered an agent of the government, we look to two critical factors: (1) whether the government knew of and acquiesced in the intrusive conduct, and (2) whether the private actor's purpose was to assist law enforcement efforts rather than to further his own ends.

Often the most difficult prong of the test is discerning what the government knew, and how much it "acquiesced in" the private actor's conduct. Generally, the courts have read this prong of the test broadly. A good example of this breadth can be found in *Skinner v. Railway Labor Executives' Ass'n.*[109] That case began when the Federal Railway Administration [FRA] promulgated regulations that authorized private railroads to take breath and urine samples from their employees for alcohol and drug testing purposes. In compliance with these regulations, private railroads implemented breath and urine testing programs, and a group of railroad employees sought a judgment declaring the testing unconstitutional. A threshold issue was whether the testing implicated the Fourth Amendment in the first instance. The Supreme Court held that it did, observing that "[a]lthough the Fourth Amendment does not apply to a search or seizure, even an arbitrary one, effected by a private party on his own initiative, the Amendment protects against such intrusions if the private party acted as an instrument or agent of the Government. A railroad that complies with [federal regulations] does so by compulsion of sovereign authority, and the lawfulness of its acts is controlled by the Fourth Amendment."

In response to the railroad's contention that the government action requirement was not satisfied because the federal regulations merely authorized the testing, and did not compel it, the Court held as follows:

> We are unwilling to conclude ... that breath and urine tests required by private railroads in reliance on Subpart D [of the regulations] will not implicate the Fourth Amendment. Whether a private party should be deemed an agent or instrument of the Government for

---

108.   United States v. Steiger, 318 F.3d 1039 (11th Cir. 2003)

109.   489 U.S. 602 (1989).

Fourth Amendment purposes necessarily turns on the degree of the Government's participation in the private party's activities, a question that can only be resolved "in light of all the circumstances." The fact that the Government has not compelled a private party to perform a search does not, by itself, establish that the search is a private one. Here, specific features of the regulations combine to convince us that the Government did more than adopt a passive position toward the underlying private conduct. The regulations, including those in Subpart D, pre-empt state laws, rules, or regulations covering the same subject matter, and are intended to supersede "any provision of a collective bargaining agreement, or arbitration award construing such an agreement." They also confer upon the FRA the right to receive certain biological samples and test results procured by railroads pursuant to Subpart D. In addition, a railroad may not divest itself of, or otherwise compromise by contract, the authority conferred by Subpart D. As the FRA explained, such "authority . . . is conferred for the purpose of promoting the public safety, and a railroad may not shackle itself in a way inconsistent with its duty to promote the public safety." . . . In light of these provisions, we are unwilling to accept [the railroad's] submission that tests conducted by private railroads in reliance on Subpart D will be primarily the result of private initiative. The Government has removed all legal barriers to the testing authorized by Subpart D and indeed has made plain not only its strong preference for testing, but also its desire to share the fruits of such intrusions. . . . These are clear indices of the Government's encouragement, endorsement, and participation, and suffice to implicate the Fourth Amendment.

Even where a private individual has acted without the "encouragement, endorsement, and participation" of the government, the Fourth Amendment still might be implicated if the later government conduct intrudes further on the aggrieved party's Fourth Amendment interests than did the private actor's conduct. In such a situation, the government's further intrusion constitutes a separate search or seizure that satisfies the government action requirement. The task for courts in these situations is to evaluate the extent of the private party's intrusion and compare that with the intrusion occasioned by the government.

For example, in *United States v. Jacobsen*,[110] an employee of Federal Express Company, a private mail carrier, opened a package that had been damaged in shipment. Inside the package, the employee found newspaper packing material surrounding a tube about ten inches long. The employee slit open the tube, discovered zip-lock plastic bags containing white powder, and notified the Drug Enforcement Administration [DEA]. Before an agent from the DEA arrived, however, the employee reinserted the plastic bags into the tube and put the tube and its packing material back into the box. The DEA agent, on arrival, observed the box with its top open and a hole punched in its side. He was able to see the tube in the box and a slit in one

---

110. 466 U.S. 109, 111–19 (1984).

of its ends, from which he removed the plastic bags of white powder. He opened each of the bags and removed a trace of the powder, which tested positive as cocaine. The persons involved in the cocaine transaction were indicted and moved to suppress the cocaine from their trial, arguing that the DEA agent's conduct constituted an unreasonable search and seizure.

The Court held that the agent's conduct did not violate a protected privacy interest. The Court first articulated that "[t]he additional invasions of respondents' privacy by the government agent must be tested by the degree to which they exceeded the scope of the private search." Applying this standard, the Court reasoned as follows:

> Respondents do not dispute that the Government could utilize the Federal Express employees' testimony concerning the contents of the package. If that is the case, it hardly infringed respondents' privacy for the agents to reexamine the contents of the open package by brushing aside a crumpled newspaper and picking up the tube. The advantage the Government gained thereby was merely avoiding the risk of a flaw in the employees' recollection, rather than in further infringing respondents' privacy. Protecting the risk of misdescription hardly enhances any legitimate privacy interest, and is not protected by the Fourth Amendment. Respondents could have no privacy interest in the contents of the package, since it remained unsealed and since the Federal Express employees had just examined the package and had, of their own accord, invited the federal agent to their offices for the express purpose of viewing its contents. The agent's viewing of what a private party had freely made available for his inspection did not violate the Fourth Amendment.

As to the seizure of the trace quantity of cocaine necessary for the field test, the Court held that the intrusion on the respondents' possessory interests was so minimal as to be non-cognizable under the Fourth Amendment.

Yet another question is raised in some cases by the government actor requirement: is every federal, state, and local public official, from FBI agent down to a local school board member, considered a government actor, or does the Fourth Amendment prohibit only unreasonable searches and seizures carried out by law enforcement officers? The Supreme Court chose the inclusive approach, holding in a case involving a search and seizure in a high school that the Constitution prohibits all unreasonable governmental intrusions: it "protects the citizen against the State itself and all of its creatures—Boards of Education not excepted."[111] The state had argued "that the history of the Fourth Amendment indicates that the Amendment was intended to regulate only searches and seizures carried out by law enforcement officers; accordingly, although public school officials are concededly state agents for purposes of the Fourteenth Amendment, the Fourth Amendment creates no rights enforceable against them." The Court responded to this argument by explaining:

---

111. New Jersey v. T.L.O., 469 U.S. 325, 334 (1985).

It may well be true that the evil toward which the Fourth Amendment was primarily directed was the resurrection of the pre-Revolutionary practice of using general warrants or "writs of assistance" to authorize searches for contraband by officers of the Crown. But this Court has never limited the Amendment's prohibition on unreasonable searches and seizures to operations conducted by the police. Rather, the Court has long spoken of the Fourth Amendment's strictures as restraints imposed upon "governmental action"—that is, "upon the activities of sovereign authority." Accordingly, we have held the Fourth Amendment applicable to the activities of civil as well as criminal authorities: building inspectors, Occupational Safety and Health Act inspectors, and even firemen entering privately owned premises to battle a fire, are all subject to the restraints imposed by the Fourth Amendment. As we [have] observed, "[t]he basic purpose of this Amendment . . . is to safeguard the privacy and security of individuals against arbitrary invasions by governmental officials." Because the individual's interest in privacy and personal security "suffers whether the government's motivation is to investigate violations of criminal laws or breaches of other statutory or regulatory standards," it would be "anomalous to say that the individual and his private property are fully protected by the Fourth Amendment only when the individual is suspected of criminal behavior."

More recently, the Court reaffirmed that school officials are government actors for purposes of the Fourth Amendment, subjecting a school drug testing policy to Fourth Amendment scrutiny, but ultimately upholding it.[112]

PROBLEM 2–23

Last September Steve Sandovar was on duty as a ticket agent for Swiftwing Air, an airline with destinations all over the globe. Around 10:30 p.m. two men approached the counter and asked for one-way tickets to Chicago. Each had a suitcase to be turned in as checked baggage. One of the men, later identified as Art Ackerman, paid for the two tickets in cash while his companion, Bob Brickhouse, filled out identification tags for the suitcases. Sandovar noticed that each of the men seemed nervous, and that Bob frequently looked back and forth between Sandovar and the suitcases. Sandovar realized that the two men met a Federal Aviation Agency [FAA] profile used to identify terrorists. Sandovar pretended to put the suitcases on a cart to be taken to the plane and told the men to have a safe flight.

Once the two men were gone, Sandovar took the two bags to a back room to be X-rayed. Sandovar was searching for bombs or weapons. The bags showed large black areas, which represent objects that the X-rays cannot pass through. Sandovar opened the first suitcase and discovered several packages wrapped in duct tape. There was a particularly strong odor coming from the package. Sandovar recognized the odor as that of

---

112. Vernonia School District 47J v. Acton, 515 U.S. 646 (1995).

marijuana. Sandovar then opened the second bag and discovered that the packages found within contained a white powder. This powder was later identified as cocaine. Sandovar contacted the airport police and gave complete descriptions of the two men and gave the authorities the names the two men used on the tickets. When Bob and Art got off the plane in Chicago, they were placed under arrest.

All of Sandovar's actions were according to Swiftwing Air's written policy for handling the baggage of suspected terrorists. Swiftwing's plan is identical to a model plan written by the FAA. Such plans are required by 14 C.F.R. § 108, a code section aimed at preventing explosive devices from being placed aboard commercial airlines.

Question: Has there been a "search" within the meaning of the Fourth Amendment? How many searches were there? Does it help to analyze each search separately?

PROBLEM 2–24

The Portland International Airport is wholly owned by the City of Portland, Oregon. The airport has its own police department. Some of the airport policemen are members of the Portland Airport Interagency Narcotics Team (PAINT). To crack down on the amount of drug traffic at the airport, PAINT distributed "drug trafficker profile" sheets to all of the airlines that flew out of Portland International. PAINT has given some airline employees cash rewards of $100 or $200 for tipping them to possible drug dealers.

Nick Chusad started working last month for Sunrise Air, a small freight airline that serves the Pacific Northwest and is based out of Portland. Nick was working at the customer service counter when Yasmine Jones approached with a package she wanted to send to her friend Zelda Welsey in Boise, Idaho. Yasmine told Nick that the box contained several cast iron napkin holders. They were a belated birthday present. Nick gave Yasmine a standard form for her to read. The form stated that Sunrise reserved the right to inspect the contents of any package entrusted to them. Yasmine paid the shipping cost and left without reading the form.

Nick was rather suspicious of Yasmine. Nick thought she was acting as if she had been taking drugs, and the package seemed too light to contain cast iron napkin holders. As soon as Yasmine left, Nick tore open the package and found a white powder later identified as methamphetamine. Unsure what to do with the powder, Nick suddenly recalled hearing about PAINT. He decided to give them a call. PAINT officers decided to send the package to Boise and arrest Zelda when she picked it up. Zelda now stands accused of possession of a controlled substance.

Question: If you were Zelda's attorney, would you challenge Nick's search of the package in Portland? What argument would you make in support of suppression? What arguments would you expect from the government against suppression?

PROBLEM 2–25

FBI Agent Maldeve received an email from an anonymous source located overseas. The email stated:

> I found a child molester on the net. I'm not sure if he is abusing his own child or a child he kidnapped. He is from LaSault, Louisiana. As you can see he is torturing the kid. She is 5–6 years old. His face is seen clearly on some of the pictures. I know his name, internet account, home address and I can see when he is online. What should I do? Can I send all the pics and info I have to you?

The anonymous source attached to the email a photo displaying a white male engaged in sexually explicit acts with a young girl. Agent Maldeve replied to the source, saying "Feel free to send any information that you have." The source then sent another email with more photographs attached. In the email the source identified the perpetrator as Cheney Coudreaux and provided Coudreaux's home address and the telephone number from which Coudreaux had connected to the internet. The source further stated that he had Coudreaux's Internet Protocol ["IP"] address— the unique number assigned to each computer that connects to the internet. The source explained that he had gotten all of this information by posting sexually explicit photos to an internet bulletin board site and attaching to them a "Trojan Horse"—a program that, once Coudreaux downloaded the photos to his computer, permitted the source to enter into Coudreaux's computer from the internet and find the information he sent to Maldeve.

After reviewing this email and the attached photographs, Agent Maldeve asked the source to send Coudreaux's IP address. The source did so, and using that IP address Maldeve obtained from Coudreaux's internet provider information confirming his identity and address. Maldeve used that confirmation, together with the information obtained by the source, to get a search warrant for Coudreaux's home and computer. When Maldeve executed the warrant, she discovered incriminating evidence that was used to prosecute Coudreaux on federal charges involving sexual exploitation of minors. Coudreaux filed a motion to suppress all of the evidence seized by Maldeve, alleging among other things that the anonymous source had acted as a government actor and had illegally hacked into his computer.

Question: As the prosecutor in the case, how would you respond to Coudreaux's government actor argument? If the court were to find that the source acted as an agent of the government, will it likely find that the source invaded Coudreaux's reasonable expectations of privacy?

VI.   Searches and Seizures Outside of United States Territory

A final set of questions arises when the government action complained of occurs outside of United States territory. Unquestionably, the constitution binds only United States actors: in other words, agents of the federal government or one of the states or territories. But United States government actors often perform their functions beyond the country's borders. Does the Fourth Amendment reach beyond those borders as well? The Court has not yet given a clear answer. Its most recent opinion suggests that the answer may depend on the identity of the person aggrieved by the government actors. The opinion came in a case involving a joint project between the DEA and the Mexican police [MFJP] to uncover the source of a Mexican marijuana smuggling ring.[113] Agents from both governments searched the Mexican residence of Mr. Verdugo–Urquidez, a Mexican citizen who had no ties to the United States. When the United States government attempted to use documents seized during that search in a criminal case against Verdugo–Urquidez, he moved to suppress them on Fourth Amendment grounds. The United States Court of Appeals for the Ninth Circuit sided with Verdugo–Urquidez, but the Supreme Court disagreed, holding that the search did not implicate the Fourth Amendment because Verdugo–Urquidez was not protected by the Fourth Amendment. According to a plurality of the Court, Fourth Amendment protections are extended only to the "people," a word that "refers to a class of persons who are part of a national community or who have otherwise developed sufficient connection with this country to be considered part of that community." Because Verdugo–Urquidez was a Mexican citizen without ties to the United States, and because the otherwise-illegal search and seizure had transpired on Mexican soil, the DEA agents did not violate the Fourth Amendment when they engaged in the activity.

The Court's opinion merits attention here because in reaching its holding it used several of the interpretive techniques that we discussed in Chapter 1. As you read the following excerpts, make a list of the techniques on which the Court relied.

United States v. Verdugo–Urquidez

494 U.S. 259 (1990).

■ REHNQUIST, C.J. Before analyzing the scope of the Fourth Amendment, we think it significant to note that it operates in a different manner than the Fifth Amendment, which is not at issue in this case. The privilege against self-incrimination guaranteed by the Fifth Amendment is a fundamental trial right of criminal defendants. Although conduct by law enforcement officials prior to trial may ultimately impair that right, a constitutional violation occurs only at trial. The Fourth Amendment functions differently. It prohibits "unreasonable searches and seizures" whether or not the evidence is sought to be used in a criminal trial, and a violation of the Amendment is "fully accomplished" at the time of an unreasonable governmental intrusion. For purposes of this case, therefore, if there were a constitutional violation, it occurred solely in Mexico. Whether evidence

---

113. United States v. Verdugo–Urquidez, 494 U.S. 259, 262 (1990).

obtained from respondent's Mexican residences should be excluded at trial in the United States is a remedial question separate from the existence *vel non* of the constitutional violation. . . .

. . . Th[e] text [of the Fourth Amendment], by contrast with the Fifth and Sixth Amendments, extends its reach only to "the people." [That phrase] seems to have been a term of art employed in select parts of the Constitution. The Preamble declares that the Constitution is ordained and established by "the People of the United States." The Second Amendment protects "the right of the people to keep and bear Arms," and the Ninth and Tenth Amendments provide that certain rights and powers are retained by and reserved to "the people." See also U.S. Constitution, Amendment 1 ("Congress shall make no law . . . abridging . . . the right of the people peaceably to assemble"); Article I, section 2, clause 1 ("The House of Representatives shall be composed of Members chosen every second Year by the People of the several States"). While this textual exegesis is by no means conclusive, it suggests that "the people" protected by the Fourth Amendment, and by the First and Second Amendments, and to whom rights and powers are reserved in the Ninth and Tenth Amendments, refers to a class of persons who are part of a national community or who have otherwise developed sufficient connection with this country to be considered part of that community. . . .

The available historical data show . . . that the purpose of the Fourth Amendment was to protect the people of the United States against arbitrary action by their own Government; it was never suggested that the provision was intended to restrain the actions of the Federal Government against aliens outside of the United States territory. There is likewise no indication that the Fourth Amendment was understood by contemporaries of the Framers to apply to activities of the United States directed against aliens in foreign territory or in international waters. . . .

The global view taken by the Court of Appeals of the application of the Constitution is . . . contrary to this Court's decisions in the *Insular Cases*, which held that not every constitutional provision applies to governmental activity even where the United States has sovereign power. *See, e.g., Balzac v. Porto Rico*, 258 U.S. 298 (1922) (Sixth Amendment right to jury trial inapplicable in Puerto Rico); *Ocampo v. United States*, 234 U.S. 91 (1914) (Fifth Amendment grand jury provision inapplicable in Philippines); *Dorr v. United States*, 195 U.S. 138 (1904) (jury trial provision inapplicable in Philippines); *Hawaii v. Mankichi*, 190 U.S. 197 (1903) (provisions on indictment by grand jury and jury trial inapplicable in Hawaii). . . . And certainly, it is not open to us in light of the *Insular Cases* to endorse the view that every constitutional provision applies wherever the United States Government exercises its power. . . .

[Respondent points to cases, such as *Yick Wo v. Hopkins*, in which Court applied constitutional protections to aliens.] These cases, however, establish only that aliens receive constitutional protections when they have come within the territory of the United States and developed substantial connections with this country. . . . Respondent is an alien who has had no previous significant voluntary connection with the United States, so these cases avail him not. . . .

Not only are history and case law against respondent, but . . . the result of accepting his claim would have significant and deleterious consequences for the United States in conducting activities beyond its boundaries. The rule adopted by the Court of Appeals would apply not only to law enforcement operations abroad, but also to other foreign policy operations which might result in "searches or seizures." The United States frequently employs Armed Forces outside this country—over 200 times in our history—for the protection of American citizens or national security. Application of the Fourth Amendment to those circumstances could significantly disrupt the ability of the political branches to respond to foreign situations involving our national interest. Were respondent to prevail, aliens with no attachment to this country might well bring actions for damages to remedy claimed violations of the Fourth Amendment in foreign countries or in international waters. *See Bivens v. Six Unknown Federal Narcotics Agents*, 403 U.S. 388 (1971); *cf. Tennessee v. Garner*, 471 U.S. 1 (1985). Perhaps a *Bivens* action might be unavailable in some or all of these situations due to "special factors counseling hesitation," but the Government would still be faced with case-by-case adjudications concerning the availability of such an action. And even were *Bivens* deemed wholly inapplicable in cases of foreign activity, that would not obviate the problems attending the application of the Fourth Amendment abroad to aliens. The Members of the Executive and Legislative Branches are sworn to uphold the Constitution, and they presumably desire to follow its commands. But the Court of Appeals' global view of its applicability would plunge them into a sea of uncertainty as to what might be reasonable in the way of searches and seizures conducted abroad. Indeed, the Court of Appeals held that absent exigent circumstances, United States agents could not effect a "search or seizure" for law enforcement purposes in a foreign country without first obtaining a warrant—which would be a dead letter outside the United States—from a magistrate in this country. Even if no warrant were required, American agents would have to articulate specific facts giving them probable cause to undertake a search or seizure if they wished to comply with the Fourth Amendment as conceived by the Court of Appeals.

We think that the text of the Fourth Amendment, its history, and our cases discussing the application of the Constitution to aliens and extraterritoriality require rejection of respondent's claim. At the time of the search, he was a citizen and resident of Mexico with no voluntary attachment to the United States, and the place searched was located in Mexico. Under these circumstances, the Fourth Amendment has no application.

Chief Justice Rehnquist's opinion was joined by four other justices, making it a majority opinion. Nevertheless, Justice Kennedy, one of the four who joined Rehnquist's opinion, wrote his own concurrence in which he appeared to disagree with Rehnquist's use of the term "people." Justice Kennedy stated:

I agree that no violation of the Fourth Amendment has occurred and that we must reverse the judgment of the Court of Appeals. Although some explanation of my views is appropriate given the difficulties of this case, I do not believe they depart in fundamental respects from the opinion of the Court, which I join.

In cases involving the extraterritorial application of the Constitution, we have taken care to state whether the person claiming its protection is a citizen, or an alien. The distinction between citizens and aliens follows from the undoubted proposition that the Constitution does not create, nor do general principles of law create, any juridical relation between our country and some undefined, limitless class of noncitizens who are beyond our territory. We should note, however, that the absence of this relation does not depend on the idea that only a limited class of persons ratified the instrument that formed our Government. Though it must be beyond dispute that persons outside the United States did not and could not assent to the Constitution, that is quite irrelevant to any construction of the powers conferred or the limitations imposed by it. As Justice Story explained in his Commentaries:

> A government may originate in the voluntary compact or assent of the people of several states, or of a people never before united, and yet when adopted and ratified by them, be no longer a matter resting in compact; but become an executed government or constitution, a fundamental law, and not a mere league. But the difficulty in asserting it to be a compact between the people of each state, and all the people of the other states is, that the constitution itself contains no such expression, and no such designation of parties.

The force of the Constitution is not confined because it was brought into being by certain persons who gave their immediate assent to its terms.

For somewhat similar reasons, I cannot place any weight on the reference to "the people" in the Fourth Amendment as a source of restricting its protections. With respect, I submit these words do not detract from its force or its reach. Given the history of our Nation's concern over warrantless and unreasonable searches, explicit recognition of "the right of the people" to Fourth Amendment protection may be interpreted to underscore the importance of the right, rather than to restrict the category of persons who may assert it. The restrictions that the United States must observe with reference to aliens beyond its territory or jurisdiction depend, as a consequence, on general principles of interpretation, not on an inquiry as to who formed the Constitution or a construction that some rights are mentioned as being those of "the people."

I take it to be correct . . . that the Government may act only as the Constitution authorizes, whether the actions in question are foreign or domestic. But this principle is only a first step in resolving this case. The question before us then becomes what constitutional standards apply when the Government acts, in reference to an alien, within its sphere of foreign operations. We have not overruled ... the so-called *Insular Cases*. These authorities stand for the proposition that we must interpret constitutional protections in light of the undoubted power of the United States to take actions to assert its legitimate power and authority abroad. Justice Harlan made this observation:

> I cannot agree with the suggestion that every provision of the Constitution must always be deemed automatically applicable to American citizens in every part of the world. For ... the *Insular Cases* do stand for an important proposition, one which seems to me a wise and necessary gloss on our Constitution. The proposition is, of course, not that the Constitution "does not apply" overseas, but that there are provisions in the Constitution which do not *necessarily* apply in all circumstances in every foreign place. In other words, it seems to me that the basic teaching of ... the *Insular Cases* is that there is no rigid and abstract rule that Congress, as a condition precedent to exercising power over Americans overseas, must exercise it subject to all the guarantees of the Constitution, no matter what the conditions and considerations are that would make adherence to a specific guarantee altogether impracticable and anomalous.

The conditions and considerations of this case would make adherence to the Fourth Amendment's warrant requirement impracticable and anomalous. Just as the Constitution in the *Insular Cases* did not require Congress to implement all constitutional guarantees in its territories because of their "wholly dissimilar traditions and institutions," the Constitution does not require United States agents to obtain a warrant when searching the foreign home of a nonresident alien. If the search had occurred in a residence within the United States, I have little doubt that the full protections of the Fourth Amendment would apply. But that is not this case. The absence of local judges or magistrates available to issue warrants, the differing and perhaps unascertainable conceptions of reasonableness and privacy that prevail abroad, and the need to cooperate with foreign officials all indicate that the Fourth Amendment's warrant requirement should not apply in Mexico as it does in this country. For this reason, in addition to the other persuasive justifications stated by the Court, I agree that no violation of the Fourth Amendment has occurred in the case before us. The rights of a citizen, as to whom the United States has continuing obligations, are not presented by this case.

Consider how the Court would decide the problems below using the interpretive techniques applied in *Verdugo–Urquidez*. Consider also how Justice Kennedy would decide these problems.

PROBLEM 2–26

In response to growing pressure to stop the flow of illegal drugs into the United States, the Drug Enforcement Administration initiated Operation Lariat, a program in which individual undercover agents were given a broad range of authority to work on their own and track down leads as they saw fit, thus eliminating the costly time delays caused by traditional DEA bureaucracy. One of the Lariat agents, Agent Peabody, flew to the Dominican Republic to check out a lead he had on a suspected multi-national cocaine importing operation. Peabody had a valid U.S. arrest warrant for a suspected dealer with ties to the organization, one Rosita Reyes. Upon arrival, Peabody informed Dominican police about the arrest warrant and asked them to arrest Reyes. They were reluctant to do so, but after fifteen minutes of heated conversation, Peabody persuaded them.

After the arrest, Dominican police searched Reyes's apartment. Peabody requested copies of any paperwork they found, and the next day, a Dominican police courier gave Peabody a large envelope containing photocopies of papers revealing names, dates, and quantities of drugs shipped from the Dominican Republic. Two of the names on the list were familiar to Peabody: Karl Kassel, a former East German who now lived in Costa Rica, and "El Tiburon," an elusive smuggler who operated out of Tampico, Mexico.

Peabody had long suspected Kassel was a drug smuggler, but he could never put together enough physical evidence to arrest him. Peabody telephoned an associate who worked for the Costa Rican police, Lt. Lorenzo, and told him about the lead between Reyes and Kassel. Peabody also telephoned the Mexican Federal Judicial Police (FJP) and asked for information on "El Tiburon."

While Peabody was on the phone with the FJP, Lt. Lorenzo ordered a wiretap on Kassel's phone. The Costa Rican police had suspected Kassel of wrongdoing for some time, and this tip was just what they needed to spur them into action. Two days later, Peabody arrived in Costa Rica and met with Lt. Lorenzo. Lorenzo handed him a box of cassette tapes. These tapes contained numerous incriminating conversations between Karl and "El Tiburon" in German. Because Peabody was fluent in German, he agreed to translate them into Spanish for the Costa Rican police. Peabody thanked Lt. Lorenzo for the evidence, explaining that he never could have done it so quickly in the United States.

Just then, a call came in on Peabody's cellular phone. It was the FJP, who told him that they had "El Tiburon" in custody. According to the FJP, the prisoner had confessed to taking nearly 250 kilograms of cocaine from Mexico to San Antonio, Texas. The prisoner also gave the location of the cocaine stash. The FJP told Peabody that they would hold the prisoner for 24 hours, and that he should come get him. Peabody took the next flight to Mexico.

Arriving at FJP headquarters, Peabody was disturbed to find that the prisoner was in very bad physical shape. Peabody asked what had happened, and the Mexican authorities explained that "El Tiburon" had resisted interrogation and that various forms of physical torture, including beatings with hoses and electric shocks from a cattle prod, were necessary to loosen his tongue. Peabody escorted "El Tiburon" and his signed confession back to the United States.

With the notes from Reyes's apartment, the conversations between Kassel and "El Tiburon," and the 250 kilograms of cocaine found in a storage unit in San Antonio, Peabody was able to charge all three suspects with conspiracy to deliver cocaine.

Question: Discuss the merits of any challenges to the searches and seizures based on the Fourth Amendment that the defendants could raise.

PROBLEM 2–27

Leshaundra Jefferson, a cocktail waitress at the Rockin' Rodeo bar in Reno, Nevada, disappeared one night during her shift. Her body was discovered a week later in a small pond about 10 miles from the bar. Tests indicated that her death was caused by drowning and that she had engaged in sexual intercourse before her death. Police suspected that she had been the victim of foul play, but they were unable to develop leads on the case until several months later, when FBI agents investigating a suspected terrorist in Mexico came upon her wallet hidden under the floorboards of the terrorist's house. Investigating, the agents learned about the still-open case file in Reno, and they forwarded the wallet and information about the terrorist to Reno police. Reno detectives quickly learned that the suspected terrorist's brother, Alex, had visited Mexico and stayed with his brother a week after Jefferson's disappearance. Furthermore, Alex had worked before that time in Reno and had quit his job the day after Jefferson's disappearance. Finally, a review of his credit card records revealed that he had used his credit card at the Rockin' Rodeo about an hour before Jefferson's co-workers noticed that she was missing. Using this information, Reno police arrested Alex. A blood test confirmed that his DNA matched that identified in the semen found in Jefferson's body. He was indicted on murder charges.

Alex filed a motion to suppress the results of the DNA test and all other information derived from the discovery of the wallet in Mexico, on the ground that the agents' search of his brother's house violated the Fourth Amendment. Unlike Alex, who is a resident alien of the United States, his brother is a Mexican national and has never visited the United States. Also unlike Alex, he is an ardent foe of U.S. policies affecting Mexican laborers. The agents had been investigating the brother after receiving a tip that he was planning to launch a suicide bombing campaign in U.S. factories along the Mexico–Texas border. The agents' search of his house was clandestine and warrantless, and even the Mexican government had not been informed of it.

Question: What is Alex's best argument for suppression of the wallet and the information discovered as a result of it? How will the prosecution respond?

Searches outside of United States territory must be compared to searches at the border, to which the Fourth Amendment unquestionably applies, but in a highly attenuated manner given the need to protect the border. There is some degree of ambiguity governing the substance of the search and seizure rules at the border. Understanding the likely rules—and the uncertainty about their meaning—requires distinguishing searches of the person from searches of property and, within the former category, arguably separating "routine" from "non-routine" searches of the person. Routine, suspicionless, warrantless seizures of the person and of property are generally permitted at the border. Here, we do not explore the border search cases in detail but do turn to a recent case in which the Court addressed the rules controlling searches of property at the border and, along the way, summarized and distinguished the rules governing other sorts of border searches, albeit while still leaving much uncertainty in the constitutional doctrinal scheme.

In *United States v. Flores–Montano*,[114] the Court had the opportunity to consider the appropriate scope of a border search. There, customs inspectors removed and disassembled the gas tank of a car entering the United States from Mexico at the international border in Southern California. The inspectors seized 37 kilograms of marijuana from Flores–Montano's gas tank. The gas tank removal procedure and the events leading up to it (including waiting for the mechanic) took about an hour.

Flores–Montano was indicted for unlawfully importing marijuana and for possession of marijuana with intent to distribute. The District Court granted defendant's motion to suppress on the ground that the government needed reasonable suspicion—which it did not rely on—to disassemble the gas tank. The Court of Appeals affirmed, declaring that reasonable suspicion is indeed required for "non-routine" border searches, with the degree of a search's intrusiveness being the "critical factor" in determining whether the search was routine.

The United States Supreme Court reversed, rejecting the reasonable suspicion test. The Court held instead that the "Government's authority to conduct suspicionless inspections at the border includes the authority to remove, disassemble, and reassemble a vehicle's fuel tank."[115] "While it may be true that some searches of property are so destructive as to require a different result," the Court noted, "this was not one of them."[116]

Central to the Court's holding was that a search of property, particularly of a car, rather than of a person, was involved. The Court explained: "Complex balancing tests to determine what is a 'routine' search of a vehicle, as opposed to a more 'intrusive' search of a person, have no place in border searches of vehicles."[117]

After noting its frequent recognition that the Government's interest in preventing unwanted entry of persons or property is at its zenith at the

---

114. 541 U.S. 149 (2004).

115. *Id.* at 155.

116. *Id.* at 155–56.

117. *Id.* at 153.

border, the Court found that interest strongly implicated in the case before it:

> That interest in protecting the borders is illustrated in this case by the evidence that smugglers frequently attempt to penetrate our borders with contraband secreted in their automobiles' fuel tank. Over the past 5–1/2 fiscal years, there have been 18,788 vehicle drug seizures at the Southern California ports of entry.... Of those, 18,788, gas tank drug seizures have accounted for 4,619 of the vehicle drug seizures, or approximately 25%. ... In addition, instances of persons smuggled in and around gas tank components are discovered at the ports of entry of San Ysidro and Otay Mesa at a rate averaging 1 approximately every 10 days.[118]

The Court concluded that Flores–Montano's privacy interest was small, the expectation of privacy being "less at the border than it is in the interior."[119] The Court noted that it had long recognized that automobiles seeking to enter the United States may be searched. Said the Court, "It is difficult to imagine how the search of a gas tank, which should be solely a repository for fuel, could be more of an invasion of privacy than the search of the automobile's passenger compartment."[120]

But, argued Flores–Montano, the Fourth Amendment "protects property as well as privacy."[121] Granted, said the Court, but noting, in an incredulous tone, that on this record he "cannot truly contend that the procedure of removal, disassembly, and reassembly of the fuel tank in this case or any other has resulted in serious damage to, or destruction of, property."[122] Indeed, noted the Court, in the 348 gas tank searches in which no contraband was found during fiscal year 2003, the vehicles continued on their way into the country without incident. Moreover, emphasized the Court, Flores–Montano cited not one accident in the many thousands of border gas tank disassembly cases. His reliance on exploratory drilling cases was therefore misplaced, explained the Court, for gas tank disassembly was obviously a very different situation from "potentially destructive drilling," though the Court made clear that it was leaving for another day the question whether, and under what circumstances, a border search of property might be unreasonable because of the "particularly offensive manner"[123] in which it was carried out. Finally, the Court readily dismissed Flores–Montano's claimed right not to be subjected to delay at the international border, finding no case supporting such a right, but also noting that a delay of one to two hours (the Government conceding at oral argument that gas tank searches could take up to two hours) was to be expected at the international border.

---

118. *Id.* at 154–55.

119. *Id.* at 155.

120. *Id.*

121. *Id.*

122. *Id.*

123. *Id.* at 155 n.2.

Justice Breyer offered a brief concurring opinion, which reads in its entirety as follows:

> I join the Court's opinion in full. I also note that Customs keeps track of the border searches its agents conduct, including the reasons for the searches. This administrative process should help minimize concerns that gas tank searches might be undertaken in an abusive manner.[124]

NOTES AND QUESTIONS

1.   How important was empirical data to the Court's opinion, that is, what if the Court had lacked any data on the number of border searches or their consequences? Could that have affected the outcome of the case? When should such empirical data about the broader history and impact of search and seizure practices and rules play a role in broader Fourth Amendment search and seizure doctrine more generally? For what sorts of purposes might such data be relevant? Should anecdote count, or only supposedly "hard" statistical evidence? Social science research? Who should have the burden of offering such data: the state or the defendant?

2.   Does Justice Breyer's concurring opinion suggest that the state may sometimes have a duty to create data-collection systems concerning the nature and impact of search and seizure practices and policies, at least in the sense that the existence of such systems may be a relevant factor in determining whether a search is reasonable? If so, can requiring the state to collect data on the racial identity of persons searched and seized and the intrusiveness and results of those activities be constitutionally mandated as a way to combat racial profiling? What would be the real-world costs and benefits of such a racial identity data-collection system?

3.   If it is relevant to Fourth Amendment analysis that empirical data exists concerning a search and seizure practice's historical success or failure in discovering and preventing crime, does that mean that other data is relevant as well? For example, should the Court consider relevant a practice's history of disparate racial impact? Does it matter whether the Court has declared that officers' subjective racial animus has no role in the reasonableness determination? Would the result in *Flores–Montano* have been different if there was evidence of an unjustified disparate racial or ethnic impact—for example, that only cars driven by Latinos were selected for gas tank disassembly?

4.   Whether a search is "routine" or not seems still to matter for searches of the person. What criteria should be used to distinguish routine from non-routine border searches? How should the terms "routine" and "non-routine" be defined? What purpose does this routine/non-routine distinction serve, and why is that purpose not served for property searches, according to the Court? "Intrusiveness" still seems to matter in determining the reasonableness of property searches at the border. Does or should intrusiveness be an important factor in defining what is "routine" for

---

124.   *Id.* at 156 (Breyer, J., concurring).

searches of the person? Should the routine nature of a search of property be relevant in determining how intrusive the search is, even if the absence of a property search's "routine" nature is not determinative after *Flores–Montano?*

VII.   REASONABLENESS BALANCING: AN INTRODUCTION AND SLIDING SCALES

A.   REASONABLENESS BALANCING DEFINED

Once a court determines that the Fourth Amendment applies, it must determine whether the search or seizure was reasonable. According to the Court, this requires weighing the government's interests against the individual's interests. The Court has used this balancing process to establish several bright-line rules:

- If government actors engage in a traditional law enforcement search or seizure, then the warrant clause applies. The warrant clause requires a warrant or a recognized exception to the warrant requirement *as well as* reasonable government conduct. The reasonableness of the government actors' conduct is evaluated by balancing the government's interests against the individual's interests.

- If instead government actors engage in a search or seizure in order to further a special governmental need, the warrant clause does not apply. The search or seizure is evaluated only under the reasonableness clause, which requires only reasonable government conduct. Once again, the reasonableness of the government actors' conduct is evaluated by balancing the government's interests against the individual's interests.

Regardless of the circumstances, then, courts must evaluate Fourth Amendment claims by balancing interests in order to determine whether government conduct was reasonable. We refer to this process as "reasonableness balancing."

In addition, the Court engages in what we call "categorical balancing." When faced with a new set of facts, it uses balancing to craft a rule to govern that category of facts. In future cases courts employ a two-step analysis: first, determining the applicable category, and second, deductively applying the Court's categorical rule to the facts. If the case does not fit an existing category, then the court must engage in balancing to craft a new categorical rule.

The Court uses balancing to analyze constitutional questions of all sorts. Constitutional balancing has been criticized for a number of reasons. Among the major criticisms are these two. First, judges may use balancing to implement their subjective value judgments, because the constitution does not define the interests to be balanced or the weights of those interests. Second, balancing requires the comparison of incommensurables—in the Fourth Amendment context, for example, the government's interest in solving crimes cannot easily be compared to an individual's interest in privacy or liberty.

Balancing has been defended on a number of grounds, however. First, judges may be able to define and weigh interests by relying on sources other than their own values—for example, history, empirical proof, and economics. Second, balancing may be no more subjective than other analytical methods. For example, reasoning by analogy to precedent also requires judges to implement value choices. Third, balancing may ensure that the constitution remains flexible and adaptable to modern circumstances. As an example, Professor Akhil Reed Amar[125] contends that a rigid, unchanging definition of probable cause would prevent the government from meeting society's changing law enforcement needs—for instance, a rigid definition of probable cause might prevent the use of metal detectors in airports. Amar argues that reasonableness balancing, rather than adherence to a rigid definition of probable cause, is the better approach:

> ... probable cause cannot be a fixed standard. It would make little sense to insist on the same amount of probability regardless of the imminence of the harm, the intrusiveness of the search, the reason for the search, and so on. Also, probable cause cannot be a high standard. It would make no sense to say that I may not be searched via metal detectors and x-ray machines at JFK [airport] unless there is a high likelihood—over fifty percent, or at least more than one percent—that I am toting a gun.
>
> In effect, this approach reads "probable cause" as "reasonable cause." Is it not easier to read the words as written, and say that warrantless searches must simply be "reasonable"? For unlike the seemingly fixed and high standard of "probable cause," reasonableness obviously does require different levels of cause in different contexts, and not always a high probability of success, if, say, we are searching for bombs on planes.

Whoever has the better argument about balancing, that kind of analysis is unavoidable under the Court's current Fourth Amendment jurisprudence. Scholars attempt to improve balancing by exposing the sources from which courts derive the interests to be balanced and the weights those interests should be given. In the Fourth Amendment context, courts typically describe the government's interest as the need to enforce criminal laws in order to protect life, liberty, and property. Professor Kate Stith[126] argues that this interest can be supported by the constitution's text. She points to the Preamble, which speaks of the need to "insure domestic tranquility" and to "establish justice" in order to "secure the blessings of Liberty"; the constitution's structure, which reveals the states' responsibility to ensure certain liberties, including personal safety; the Bill of Rights,

---

125. Akhil Reed Amar, *Fourth Amendment First Principles*, 107 Harv. L. Rev. 757, 784–85 (1994).

126. Kate Stith, *The Government Interest in Criminal Law: Whose Interest Is It Anyway?*, in Public Values in Constitutional Law 137, 145 (Stephen E. Gottlieb ed., 1993).

which acknowledges that the government may deprive a person of life, liberty, or property for adequate reasons; and, most importantly, the Fourteenth Amendment:

> In important ways, the Fourteenth Amendment altered the original understandings of 1789 and 1791. First, it greatly expanded the interests that the federal government could pursue. Second, it explicitly or by later interpretation constructed additional limitations on the interests that states might pursue, but nothing in the Fourteenth Amendment is inconsistent with the original understanding that protection against private threats to life, liberty and property is a fundamental interest (or, as some recent commentators assert, an affirmative obligation) of government.
>
> Indeed, the privileges and immunities clause of the Fourteenth Amendment may be understood to underscore that enforcement of the criminal law is a fundamental public value. As John Hart Ely has pointed out, the framers of that clause of the Fourteenth Amendment drew heavily upon Justice Bushrod Washington's construction, sitting as a circuit judge in *Corfield v. Coryell*, of the privileges and immunities clause of article IV. Professor Ely argues that *Corfield* permits inference of a "virtually infinite reference" of constitutional rights in addition to those specifically listed in the Constitution. But most interesting about *Corfield* for our current purposes is this: in giving examples of the "fundamental privileges" of citizenship under a free government, the very first "general" category *Corfield* mentions is "protection by the government." That is, among the rights ensured is the right to protection not against the government, but by the government. Moreover, there is no reason to suppose that this "protection by the government" is limited to protection through civil processes, for criminal laws and law enforcement were indispensable means of "government protection" then as now. (Indeed, *Corfield* mentions as a separate category of privilege the right to "acquire and possess property of every kind.") At the time the Fourteenth Amendment was ratified, as at the founding of the Republic, it was understood that state governments had a foremost political obligation to protect their residents from violence and unlawful takings. The argument may be made that the Fourteenth Amendment embedded this obligation in the text of the Constitution and extended its benefit to all citizens.

Professor Stith concludes that courts can evaluate the weight of government interests pursuant to an escalating scale: (1) interests of public officials have least weight; (2) interests in administrative efficiency have greater weight; and (3) interests of the general public have still greater weight.

Professor Scott Sundby[127] takes a different approach. Sundby argues that Fourth Amendment balancing is problematic because it defines the individual's interests as privacy ones. Sundby would shift the focus to trust:

---

127.   Scott Sundby, *"Everyman's" Fourth Amendment: Privacy or Mutual Trust Between Government and Citizen?*, 94 COLUM. L. REV. 1751, 1777–1802 (1994). Professor Paris makes a

I would characterize the jeopardized constitutional value underlying the Fourth Amendment as that of "trust" between the government and the citizenry. This vision of the Fourth Amendment's purpose is founded upon the idea that integral to the Constitution and our societal view of government is a reciprocal trust between the government and its citizens. Government action draws its legitimacy from the trust that the electorate places in its representatives by choosing them to govern. This mandate from the citizenry legitimates government action, however, only if the citizenry's decision itself is an informed and free choice such that the government can claim that it has the true consent of the governed. To achieve this legitimatizing mandate, therefore, the government itself must act so that it does not imperil the citizenry's ability to give its consent in an informed and free manner. Such governmental behavior will include trusting the People's ability to deal properly with information and materials that the government otherwise might ban as well as trusting the People to act responsibly and in accord with properly enacted laws and societal standards.

The first area of trust, of course, falls mainly within the purview of the First Amendment and the need to trust the citizenry to choose wisely in the marketplace of ideas. It is the second area of trust—trust that the citizenry will exercise its liberties responsibly—that implicates the Fourth Amendment and is jeopardized when the government is allowed to intrude into the citizenry's lives without a finding that the citizenry has forfeited society's trust to exercise its freedoms responsibly.

Even a rudimentary comparison of democratic to totalitarian and anarchist states demonstrates the central role that government-citizen trust plays in a free society. Totalitarian regimes maintain power not through the consent of the governed but by physical, economic, and psychological control over the populace. Such governments exercise control through a variety of means, but among the most essential is the use of the police power to reinforce the message that the government is superior and in control of the individual. Measures such as identification check-points, random searches, the monitoring of communications, and the widespread use of informants not only are means of keeping track of the citizenry, but also act as continuous symbolic reminders that the citizenry is dominated by the government. Far from fostering trust, the government's actions convey a message of distrust in order to perpetuate control of the citizenry.

To think of the Constitution and, especially, the Bill of Rights as means of enhancing the legitimacy of government and society through acknowledgment of the citizenry's dignity and value requires some readjustment of traditional thinking about the Founders' purposes. The time-honored story most often taught is that of a Lockean "rights" viewpoint: the Constitution was a social contract that pre-

---

similar argument about the value of trust in the context of interrogations. *See generally* Margaret L. Paris, *Trust, Lies, and Interrogation*, 3 Va. J. Soc. Pol'y & L. 3 (1995).

served certain natural rights, such as the right to accumulate private property, while setting up the basic frame-work necessary for society to function.

In this context, "rights" become enclaves from government interference, and one simply reads down the Bill of Rights to identify where those enclaves exist: the right to say and think what one chooses, the right to associate with whom one desires, the right to practice one's religious beliefs free from government dictates, and on through the amendments one proceeds. Using this perspective, when one reaches the Fourth Amendment, Justice Brandeis's depiction of the Amendment's purpose as being the protection of the "right to be let alone" fits perfectly, identifying yet another enclave where the individual is free from government interference.

While it may be true that the Bill of Rights creates enclaves of individual freedom, such a vision captures only part of the reason why the Bill of Rights is so important. Of equal, if not greater, importance is the acknowledgment accompanying the granting of such rights that the recipient is someone deserving of the respect and dignity that comes with their bestowal and the trust that the right will be exercised responsibly.

Despite its stated preference for the Warrant Clause, the Court has been quick to find a "special need" justifying departure. Such willingness to find a "need" might not be too surprising if one considers the magnitude of the social problems that the government can place on its side of the ledger. How can anyone possibly discount the importance of the war on drugs, the integrity of the educational system, or the saving of lives? With a little imagination, even the lowly Vehicle Identification Number can be made to sound as if it is crucial to civilized society.

Missing in the Court's consideration of the "special need" to move from the Warrant Clause into the reasonableness analysis, however, is an express evaluation of how switching clauses also has "special costs." Without such express consideration, the move is especially easy since the reasonableness test still will provide some potential protections for what is currently the primary focus of the Amendment—privacy. This is true because the Court's reasonableness analysis expressly takes into account privacy interests. The Court is thus relieved when choosing between the clauses from making an all-or-nothing choice between protecting privacy and allowing the government intrusion.

Moreover, because the current focus is on privacy, the Court in assessing the government's "special need" need not attach any special significance to the fact that the intrusion, from the citizen's viewpoint, is by the government rather than a non-government entity. A privacy interest in giving a urine sample can be diminished by pointing out that providing such a sample is a common medical procedure. A privacy interest in one's backyard can be downplayed by noting that passengers on a commercial aircraft might glance out of the window while munching on their peanuts. A privacy interest in one's employment space can be lessened by positing the overbearing boss constantly overseeing one's work or an office with a steady flow of visitors. Privacy is treated as a unitary concept that is equally invaded whether it be by canine, homeless person, tourist, fellow employee, or law enforcement agent. A look beyond privacy, though, reveals that switching to the Reasonableness Clause from the Warrant Clause does cause the loss of an important Fourth Amendment value—the special guaranty of traditional probable cause that an intrusion will take place only where an individual's actions give rise to a belief that she has breached the trust that she is law-abiding. Indeed, one way to think of traditional probable cause is as a constitutional mechanism requiring the government to trust the citizenry: only articulable reasons to believe that the trust has been violated will justify an intrusion. This quality is lost, of course, when the government is allowed to engage in an initiatory intrusion without individualized suspicion: the individual becomes powerless to avoid the intrusion other than by foregoing what is otherwise a legal activity.

Additionally, relying on government-citizen trust as a defining value recognizes that a government intrusion has special implications for the Fourth Amendment. From this perspective, a difference in kind does exist between voluntarily giving a urine sample for medical purposes and the government demanding a sample for urinalysis because it wishes to randomly check whether its citizens are obeying the law. The former context does not remotely implicate the government-citizen relationship, whereas in the latter setting, the intrusion's very purpose is the government's assertion of its power over the citizenry to ensure that the law is not being violated.

Looked at in this light, a court's reasonableness determination normally would require two findings beyond the current inquiry. First, because the starting presumption would be that the citizenry should be trusted absent evidence of wrongdoing, the government would have to affirmatively prove the existence of a serious problem that justified the government's breaching its trust to those subjected to the intrusion. For example, where the government wanted to randomly test employees for drug use, the burden would be on the government to demonstrate that an actual problem existed that justified requiring the intrusion's subjects to forfeit their right to be trusted. Asked in this fashion, the Court could not, as it did in *National Treasury Employees Union v. Von Raab*, simply point to a general societal problem with drugs and claim a symbolic need for the testing of Customs agents although no evidence existed that the targeted group was engaged in drug use.

Second, because probable cause would now be understood as a means of protecting the citizenry's right to be trusted, the government also would have to show as part of its special need why reliance on probable cause would defeat its purposes. The Court's present approach approximates a loose rational basis standard: if the intrusion arguably advances the government interest, the Court will not second-guess the government's judgment. Consequently, in cases like *Von Raab* and *Michigan Department of State Police v. Sitz*, the majority was willing to approve the challenged suspicionless intrusions even though they had little noticeable impact on the societal problem beyond that which conventional reliance on individualized suspicion had produced, and perhaps had even been counterproductive.

But if trust is used as a guiding value, then the deference should not be to the government's judgment as to the "need" for the particular intrusion, but to the Constitution's judgment that the citizenry is to be trusted to act in an informed and responsible manner. The burden of justification would rest with the government to show that the intrusion substantially furthered the government's goal beyond conventional enforcement means.

In the end, what is being sought is a Fourth Amendment inquiry requiring the government to demonstrate either that the citizen has forfeited her right to be trusted through misbehavior (i.e., through a showing of traditional probable cause), or that, if probable cause is to be dispensed with, trusting the citizenry is simply too costly given the immediacy and importance of the government interest. A classic example of the latter would be weapons screening at airports, which was instituted in response to a recurring problem with skyjackings. The opportunity to observe passengers for suspicious behavior prior to boarding is extremely limited, and once in the air, the place is effectively isolated from law enforcement personnel. Given these factors, the only realistic means of preventing a serious danger to passenger safety is to dispense with individualized suspicion and screen all passengers for weapons. Adding trust into the Fourth Amendment equation would not eliminate intrusions based on less than probable cause, but it would make clear that the burden rests with the government to demonstrate affirmatively why the presumption of trust should not apply.

PROBLEM 2–28

Professor William Stuntz also would redefine the individual's interest. Stuntz focuses on preventing government coercion.[128] Using the seven sources of constitutional data examined in Chapter 1, what arguments could you craft to support a balancing test that defined the individual's interest as "minimizing coercion"? What does coercion mean? How would a court resolve the issues in Problem 1–1 using a coerciveness approach as compared to the privacy and trust approaches? How would Professor Stith's analysis of governmental needs enter into the balancing process under each of these three approaches?

---

128. William J. Stuntz, *Privacy's Problem and the Law of Criminal Procedure*, 93 MICH. L. REV. 1016 (1995).

B. THE LIMITS OF REASONABLENESS BALANCING

In *Whren v. United States*,[129] the Court imposed limits on reasonableness balancing. There, officers observed a car violate minor traffic ordinances. The officers stopped the car and approached the driver's window, through which one of the officers observed crack cocaine. The driver and passenger were prosecuted for several federal drug offenses, and moved to suppress the cocaine, arguing that the traffic violations were a pretext for what would otherwise be an illegal investigatory stop for drugs. The Court rejected this argument. It also rejected a separate argument about reasonableness balancing. The defendants argued that the Court should use balancing to ban minor traffic stops by plainclothes officers. According to the defendants, the individual's interests in such stops are large, because stops result in an unsettling show of authority, inconvenience, time consumption, and citizen confusion. On the other hand, argued the defendants, the government has a minimal interest in enforcing minor traffic ordinances. In a unanimous opinion, the Court refused to re-balance interests that had already been subjected to categorical balancing:

> It is of course true that in principle every Fourth Amendment case, since it turns upon a "reasonableness" determination, involves a balancing of all relevant factors. With rare exceptions, not applicable here, however, the result of that balancing is not in doubt where the search or seizure is based upon probable cause....

> Where probable cause has existed, the only cases in which we have found it necessary actually to perform the "balancing" analysis involved searches or seizures conducted in an extraordinary manner, unusually harmful to an individual' s privacy or even physical interest—such as, for example, seizure by means of deadly force, *see Tennessee v. Garner*, 471 U.S. 1 (1985), unannounced entry into a home, *see Wilson v. Arkansas*, 514 U.S. 927 (1995), entry into a home without a warrant, *see Welsh v. Wisconsin*, 466 U.S. 740 (1984), or physical penetration of the body, *see Winston v. Lee*, 470 U.S. 753 (1985). The making of a traffic stop out-of-uniform does not remotely qualify as such an extreme practice, and so is governed by the usual rule that probable cause to believe the law has been broken "outbalances" private interest in avoiding police contact.

NOTES AND QUESTIONS

In *Whren*, all nine justices acknowledged that the Court balances interests when analyzing Fourth Amendment cases. Yet it refused to engage in balancing in that case. Do you agree with the defendants' argument that the interests at stake required balancing? Why did the Court reject their request for a ban on traffic stops? Does its rejection mean that the Court is less likely to engage in balancing when individual interests outweigh those of the government?

---

129. 517 U.S. 806 (1996).

As we note in the text on page 9, the text of the Fourth Amendment is less than crystal clear. One of the most difficult questions that it leaves unanswered is this: does the amendment's warrant clause modify its reasonableness clause—in other words, is a search without a warrant, or without probable cause, presumptively unreasonable? We further explain in the text (on page 176) that the Court traditionally has applied a bright-line rule to determine the relationship between the Fourth Amendment's warrant clause and its reasonableness clause. That bright-line rule states that where the government engages in law enforcement searches, it must satisfy the warrant clause's requirements—by obtaining a valid warrant or acting pursuant to a recognized warrant exception—before a search can be found to have been reasonable.

To put this another way, in traditional law enforcement searches the Court engages *not* in reasonableness balancing, but in categorical balancing—invalidating searches if the warrant requirement is not satisfied, or a recognized exception to that requirement is not met, despite case-specific indicia of reasonableness. Unlike *Whren*, then, this is a situation in which categorical balancing favors individual interests over those of law enforcement.

Some justices would like to rebalance these interests by decoupling the warrant clause from the reasonableness clause. If the two clauses were decoupled, a valid warrant would no longer be the presumptive requirement. Rather, whether a warrant is required would turn on a case-specific inquiry into what "reasonableness" demands in the particular circumstances of the case. Indeed, according to these justices, the bright-line rule we describe above has never been as bright as is claimed. Justice Thomas recently stated that the Court "has vacillated between imposing a categorical warrant requirement and applying a general reasonableness standard." The statement came in his dissent in *Groh v. Ramirez*,[130] where a majority of the Court held a search unconstitutional because it was based on an obviously invalid warrant. According to the majority in that case, a residential search is presumed to be unconstitutional if based on an invalid warrant. Categorical balancing applies, in other words, and the individual interests are held categorically to outbalance those of law enforcement. But Justice Thomas, joined by Justice Scalia and the Chief Justice in dissent, suggested in *Groh* that the Court has and should engage in case-by-case reasonableness balancing in these situations:

> The Fourth Amendment provides: "The right of the people to be secure in their persons, houses, papers, and effects, against unreasonable searches and seizures, shall not be violated, and no Warrants shall issue, but upon probable cause, supported by Oath or affirmation, and particularly describing the place to be searched, and the persons or things to be seized." The precise relationship between the Amendment's Warrant Clause and Unreasonableness Clause is unclear. But neither Clause explicitly requires a warrant. While "it is of course

---

130.   540 U.S. 551, 572 (2004) (Thomas, J., dissenting).

textually possible to consider [a warrant requirement] implicit within the requirement of reasonableness," the text of the Fourth Amendment certainly does not mandate this result. Nor does the Amendment's history, which is clear as to the Amendment's principal target (general warrants), but not as clear with respect to when warrants were required, if ever. Indeed, because of the very different nature and scope of federal authority and ability to conduct searches and arrests at the founding, it is possible that neither the history of the Fourth Amendment nor the common law provides much guidance.

As a result, the Court has vacillated between imposing a categorical warrant requirement and applying a general reasonableness standard. The Court has most frequently held that warrantless searches are presumptively unreasonable, but has also found a plethora of exceptions to presumptive unreasonableness. That is, our cases stand for the illuminating proposition that warrantless searches are per se unreasonable, except, of course, when they are not.

. . . I would turn to first principles in order to determine the relationship between the Warrant Clause and the Unreasonableness Clause. . . .

The view expressed in Justice Thomas's dissent, that the Court has not (and should not) rely on categorical balancing to invalidate searches where the warrant clause is not satisfied, does not yet carry the day. In his majority opinion, Justice Stevens insisted that the Court's "cases have firmly established the basic principle of Fourth Amendment law that searches and seizures inside a home without a warrant are *presumptively* unreasonable."[131]

We will discuss the *Groh* case in more detail later. In the meantime, consider these questions:

1. Based on what you have read about the Fourth Amendment's text and about other tools with which courts interpret that amendment, should the Court employ categorical balancing where the warrant clause is not satisfied, or should it engage in case-by-case reasonableness balancing?

2. If the Court abandoned categorical balancing for case-by-case reasonableness balancing in the warrant clause context, would you expect outcomes to change–in other words, would reasonableness balancing result in more pro-law enforcement decisions or more pro-defendant decisions?

Concluding Comment: This section provided background about the Court's Fourth Amendment balancing. The arguments for and against balancing are valuable to the practicing lawyer. For example, while it is unlikely that the Court will soon abandon the "privacy" concept as central to Fourth Amendment law, it is plausible that lawyers might persuade it to add considerations of trust or government coercion when it evaluates individual interests, because the Court recognizes that constitutional provisions serve multiple values and has been influenced by legal scholars in

---

131.   540 U.S. at 572 (emphasis added).

shaping constitutional law. Moreover, state courts may find those concepts useful when interpreting state constitutional issues. From the advocate's perspective, it is helpful to keep the balancing arguments in mind when evaluating how to best advance the client's interests.

This text returns repeatedly to the balancing theme, but shifts its focus now to the definition of probable cause.

VIII.   "PROBABLE CAUSE"

Checklist 2: When Is There Probable Cause?

1.   Was probable cause based upon a tip? If yes:
    a.   Is the informant credible—likely to be telling the truth?
       (i) Has he given previous accurate tips?
       (ii) Is he an "ordinary citizen" or a "stoolie," part of the world of criminality?
       (iii) Is his statement against his interest, implicating him in criminal activity?
       (iv) Does he have a reputation for truthfulness?
       (v) Does the accused have a reputation for engaging in the sort of crime alleged?
       (vi) Is there corroborating evidence? If so, does it corroborate innocent facts, facts more consistent with criminality, facts true at the time of the tip, or facts predicted by the tip to come true?
    b.   Is the informant reliable—likely to have had an adequate basis of knowledge?
       (i) Did the informant personally observe, or participate in, the criminal activity?
       (ii) Did the informant set out such detailed information as to suggest that he must have an adequate basis of knowledge?
       (iii) Is there corroborating evidence? If so, does it corroborate innocent facts, facts more consistent with criminality, facts true at the time of the tip, or facts predicted by the tip to come true?
    c.   Are there other reasons to credit the tip?
2.   Does the totality of the circumstances establish probable cause—a substantial chance of guilt?

A.   A SHORT HISTORY OF "PROBABLE CAUSE"

Before the Bill of Rights was drafted, the concept of probable cause had "migrated" to the law of arrest, search, and seizure from the grand jury context, where it formed the basis of a grand jury indictment. It is impossible to determine what the framers meant by probable cause, because there was no commonly accepted definition at the time the Fourth

Amendment was written. The evolution of the concept in America from colonial days to the present—or, more specifically, the direction of that evolution—does provide meaning, although that meaning remains vague. Barbara J. Shapiro summarizes that evolution as follows:[132]

> For several centuries the legal literature had listed causes of suspicion. The notion of probable or reasonable cause for suspicion eventually enters the literature either to summarize or supplement the lists, but it enters without much concern for the precise meaning of probable and reasonable. The concept was that well entrenched in connection with arrest before there were any attempts to define the meaning of those terms. [T]he specific causes of suspicion . . . gradually were replaced by a more generalized notion of suspicion which might be evaluated for reasonableness and probability. Hale's probable cause of suspicion was becoming the rule—but a rule lacking the substance that had been provided by the now vanished lists of causes of suspicion.

> The original causes which were thought to render suspicion probable eroded gradually. The notion disappeared that one's life-style, common fame, or the frequenting of ale houses was alone sufficient to render one liable for arrest for a felony. No alternate list was created, but the idea of an adequate basis for arrest remained. Most of the nineteenth-century American decisions which involve discussion of probable cause do not really deal with arrest but instead consider what is needed to justify a prosecuting attorney's decision to go forward.

> Thus what began as a list of oratorical strategies and then became a concrete list of indicia of suspicion gradually becomes probable or reasonable cause to suspect and then simply probable cause. . . . Gradually probable cause floats free of subjective suspicion and moves toward objective guilt. Our attention focuses less on the tentative decisions that take place at the very beginning of the criminal process and more on the final judgment that eventually will be rendered. The question becomes not "why do you suspect him?" but "what reasons do you have to believe that a conviction is warranted?" Once we understand the migration of probable cause away from personal suspicion and toward impersonal judgment of guilt by an official, the current uncertainties about probable cause to arrest become more comprehensible. . . . In the context of arrest, probable cause must live somewhere between suspicion and prediction of ultimate trial outcome. It has moved quite far toward the latter. As it does so, however, it encounters the problem of having the trial before the trial that we encounter in all pretrial determinations. And when it encounters that problem, it draws back a little toward suspicion. . . .

In 1878, the U.S. Supreme Court indicated that probable cause did not concern itself with the subjective belief of the arresting officer. The

---

132. Barbara J. Shapiro, Beyond Reasonable Doubt and Probable Cause: Historical Perspectives on the Anglo-American Law of Evidence (1991).

law was concerned with whether "the facts and circumstances before the officer are such to warrant a man of prudence and caution in believing that the offense had been committed." Shortly after, in *Carroll v. United States*, the Supreme Court declared that probable cause existed where "the facts and circumstances within their knowledge and of which they have reasonably trustworthy information were sufficient in themselves to warrant a man of reasonable caution in the belief" that an offense had been committed. The *Carroll* decision became the classic definition of probable cause in the United State....

The American probable cause standard represents the latest stage in a long historical evolution in which the justification for arrest moves from the personalized suspicion of a directly involved party, through the generalized suspicions of a more distanced party based as much on the suspect's life-style as on particular events, to the rough estimate of a very distanced official of the chances that a suspect will be convicted if tried.

1.   QUANTIFYING PROBABLE CAUSE

Other sources assist our understanding of the vague term. Professor Joseph Grano argues that in both England and America, at least until the 1940s, probable cause meant something less than more-likely-than-not: a loose "suspicion" standard applied.[133] A survey of judges in 1982 described probable cause on average as 44.52%. This standard may be higher than the "suspicion" standard described by Professor Grano, but it is lower than the more-likely-than-not standard that the language suggests.[134] Conversely, Professors LaFave and Israel, in their well-known treatise, state that probable cause may sometimes connote a greater-than-even certainty, depending upon the circumstances.[135] They point out that some of the Supreme Court's decisions may be read as adopting a more-probable-than-not test—requiring that the information at hand provide a basis for singling out one person.

However, the lower courts generally require less. Cases reveal that probable cause exists where information narrows the scope of suspicion to a fairly small group, although it does not exist where information permits suspicion of large numbers of people. The more relaxed approach of the lower courts has been defended on the ground that it strikes a fair balance between the interests of privacy and effective law enforcement, because arrests for investigative purposes sometimes must be based on general descriptions provided by crime victims and witnesses. Professors LaFave and Israel distinguish cases in which there is certainty about the crime, but uncertainty about the perpetrator's identity, from those in which there is

---

133. *See* Joseph Grano, *Probable Cause and Common Sense: A Reply to the Critics of Illinois v. Gates*, 17 U. MICH. J.L. REF. 465, 478–95 (1984).

134. C.M.A. McCauliff, *Burdens of Proof: Degrees of Belief, Quanta of Evidence, or Constitutional Guarantees?*, 35 VAND. L. REV. 1293, 1331–32 (1982).

135. WAYNE R. LAFAVE & JEROLD ISRAEL, CRIMINAL PROCEDURE § 3.3(b), at 141–42.

uncertainty about whether any crime has occurred—for example, when the police observe a person engaging in suspicious activity. As to the latter situation, courts disapprove of probable cause that is based on information as consistent with innocence as with guilt. In other words, if the observed pattern of events occurs just as frequently or even more frequently in innocent transactions, then it is too equivocal to constitute probable cause. LaFave and Israel's bottom line: probable cause is a more-likely-than-not test where we are uncertain whether a crime has occurred, but it is a less-than-50–percent test where the crime's occurrence is clear but the perpetrator's identity is not.

According to Professors LaFave and Israel, utilizing the more-probable-than-not test here but not in the first situation is defensible on two grounds: (1) permitting arrests for equivocal conduct would result in more frequent interference with innocent persons than would permitting arrests upon a somewhat general description from a crime victim or witness, which typically are fairly specific in terms of time and location; and (2) the law enforcement need is greater in the victim/witness description situation, because these cases often involve much more serious criminal activity as to which experience has shown that the likelihood of apprehending the offender is slight unless he is promptly arrested in the vicinity of the crime.

The Court's most recent attempt to define probable cause occurred in the 1983 case of *Illinois v. Gates*, which is reproduced below.[136] Some commentators argue that the Court's opinion in *Gates* identified probable cause as something clearly less than 50%. The most that can be said today, therefore, is that probable cause hovers somewhere just over or just under the 50% mark, depending upon the court and the situation. Probable cause is more than "reasonable suspicion" (a term we will see has great modern significance[137]), arguably less than preponderance, and certainly less than clear and convincing or beyond a reasonable doubt.

The Court may have muddied the quantification question further in *Maryland v. Pringle*,[138] despite the Court's unanimous opinion there. Understanding why this is so first requires examining the lower court opinion for comparison. In *Pringle*, an officer stopped a car for speeding at about 3:00 a.m. There were three occupants in the car: the driver and owner; the front-seat passenger, Joseph Jermaine Pringle; and a back-seat passenger. When the driver, in response to the officer's request to produce his license and registration, opened the glove compartment, the officer saw inside it a large amount of rolled-up cash. When the computer check revealed no outstanding violations, the officer asked the driver to get out, issued him an oral warning, and a second patrol car arrived. The driver, in answering the officer's question on the point, denied having weapons or narcotics in the car and next consented to a vehicle search. That search

---

136. 462 U.S. 213 (1983).

137. Judges surveyed about the meaning of this term pegged it at about a 30% certainty. *See* McCauliff, *Quanta of Evidence, supra* note 134, at 1331–32.

138. 540 U.S. 366 (2003).

uncovered $763 from the glove compartment and five glassine plastic baggies containing cocaine from behind the back-seat armrest. As the Court of Appeals of Maryland explained:

> The armrest in the back seat was the type that goes up and down. At the time of the stop, the armrest was in the upright position and flat against the seat. When Officer Snyder pulled down the armrest he found the drugs, which had been placed between the armrest and the back seat of the car and, absent the pulling down of the armrest, *were not visible*.[139]

The officer questioned all three men, telling them that he would arrest them all unless someone admitted to ownership of the drugs. None of the men admitted ownership of either the drugs or the money, and all three were arrested and taken to the police station. Later that morning, Pringle waived his *Miranda* rights and gave oral and written confessions that the cocaine was his and that he meant to sell it, though he denied that the other occupants knew anything about the drugs, and they were therefore released.

The trial court denied Pringle's motion to suppress the confession as the fruit of an illegal arrest, concluding that the arrest was done with probable cause. After a jury convicted Pringle of possession of cocaine and possession with intent to distribute it, he appealed his sentence of ten years without the possibility of parole. The Court of Appeals of Maryland reversed, finding insufficient evidence of probable cause. Central to that court's decision was the absence of evidence that the drugs, and, for that matter, the money, were visible to all occupants before the officer stopped the car. Probable cause for an arrest, explained that court, had to involve adequate proof that Pringle specifically committed the crimes of simple possession and possession with intent to sell. The substantive criminal law of Maryland concerning "possession" required proof that Pringle knew that the drugs were present and that the defendant singly or jointly exercised an actual or potential restraining or directing influence over the drugs, that is, had dominion and control over them. Although the court relied primarily on cases on the sufficiency of the evidence to take the possession question to the jury at trial, the court recognized that probable cause involved a significantly lower "quantum" of evidence. Nevertheless, concluded the Maryland Court, there was *no* evidence here available to the officer at the time of the arrest that Pringle was specifically aware of the cocaine's presence, much less of his influence over it; Pringle's mere presence in the car, in close proximity to the cocaine, was insufficiently individualized evidence of *his* wrongdoing. The Maryland Court explained:

> Under respondent's reasoning, if contraband was found in a twelve-passenger van, or perhaps a bus or other kind of vehicle, or even a place, i.e., a movie theater, the police would be permitted to place everyone in such a vehicle or place under arrest until some person confessed to being in possession of the contraband. Simply stated, a

---

139.   Pringle v. State, 370 Md. 525, 531 n. 2 (2002) (emphasis added).

policy of arresting everyone until somebody confesses is constitutionally unacceptable.[140]

The state court likewise rejected the relevance of the large wad of money in the glove compartment because the officer also lacked evidence of the money's visibility to Pringle at the time of his arrest. Thus, concluded the Maryland court:

> The money in the case at bar was not in the plain view of the police officer or petitioner; rather it was located in a closed glove compartment and was opened by the car's owner/driver in response to the officer's request for the car's registration. There are insufficient facts that would lead a reasonable person to believe that *petitioner* at the time of his arrest, had prior knowledge of the money or had exercised dominion and control over it. We hold that a police officer's discovery of money in a closed glove compartment and cocaine concealed behind the rear armrest of a car is insufficient to establish probable cause for an arrest of a front seat passenger, who is not the owner or person in control of the vehicle, for possession of the cocaine.[141]

The United State Supreme Court reversed, thoroughly rejecting the logic of the Court of Appeals of Maryland. In doing so, the Court stressed that the "probable-cause standard is incapable of precise definition or quantification into percentages because it deals with probabilities and depends on the totality of the circumstances."[142] Moreover, "the *quanta* . . . of proof appropriate in ordinary judicial proceedings are inapplicable to the decision to issue a warrant. . . . Finely tuned standards such as proof beyond a reasonable doubt or by a preponderance of the evidence, useful in formal trials, have no place in the [probable-cause] decision."[143] Rather, said the Court, it looks at all the events leading up to the arrest to decide whether, "viewed from the standpoint of an objectively reasonable police officer, [they] amount to probable cause."[144] At the same time, the Court recognized that the "long-prevailing standard of probable cause protects citizens from rash and unreasonable interferences with privacy and from unfounded charges of crime, while giving fair leeway for enforcing the law in the community's protection."[145] Moreover, while the probable cause concept is a "fluid," non-technical one, "turning on the assessment of probabilities in particular factual contexts—not readily, or even usefully, reduced to a neat set of legal rules"—"the *belief of guilt must be particularized with respect to the person to be searched or seized.*"[146]

The high Court focused not so much on the *visibility* of the drugs and money as on their *accessibility*:

---

140. *Id.* at 545, n. 12.

141. *Id.* at 546.

142. 540 U.S. at 371.

143. *Id.*

144. *Id.*

145. *Id.* at 370.

146. *Id.* at 371 (emphasis added).

In this case, Pringle was one of three men riding in a Nissan Maxima at 3:16 a.m. There was $763 of rolled-up cash in the glove compartment *directly in front of Pringle*. Five plastic glassine baggies of cocaine were behind the back-seat armrest and *accessible to all three men*. Upon questioning, the three men failed to offer any information with respect to the ownership of the cocaine or the money.[147]

The Court criticized the state appellate court's declaration that "[m]oney, without more, is innocuous,"[148] complaining that the state court's "consideration of the money in isolation, rather than as a factor in the totality of the circumstances, is mistaken in light of our precedents."[149] Accordingly, said the Court,

> We think it an entirely reasonable inference from these facts that any or all three of the occupants had knowledge of, and exercised dominion and control over, the cocaine. Thus a reasonable officer could conclude that there was probable cause to believe Pringle committed the crime of possession of cocaine, either solely or jointly.[150]

Finally, the Court rejected Pringle's argument that this was a mere "guilt-by-association case."[151] Pringle relied for this argument in part on *Ybarra v. Illinois*.[152] In *Ybarra*, police executing a warrant to search a tavern and its bartender for evidence of possession of a controlled substance conducted pat down searches of all the customers present, including Ybarra, and seized six tinfoil packets containing heroin from a cigarette pack retrieved from Ybarra's pocket. The Court invalidated the search, stressing that it was based on insufficiently individualized suspicion as to Ybarra and noting that "[a] person's mere propinquity to others independently suspected of criminal activity does not, without more, give rise to probable cause to search that person."[153] The *Pringle* Court distinguished *Ybarra* and another case relied upon by *Pringle, United States v. DiRe*, thus:

> This case is quite different from *Ybarra*. Pringle and his two companions were in a relatively small automobile, not a public tavern. In *Wyoming v. Houghton*, we noted that "a car passenger—unlike the unwitting tavern patron in *Ybarra*—will often be engaged in a common enterprise with the driver, and have the same interest in concealing the fruits or the evidence of their wrongdoing." Here we think it was reasonable for the officer to infer a common enterprise among the three men. The quantity of drugs and cash in the car indicated the likelihood of drug dealing, an enterprise to which a dealer would be

---

147. *Id.* at 371–72 (emphasis added).

148. *Id.* at 372.

149. *Id.*

150. *Id.*

151. *Id.*

152. 444 U.S. 85 (1979).

153. *Id.* at 91.

unlikely to admit an innocent person with the potential to furnish evidence against him.

In *DiRe*, a federal investigator had been told by an informant, Reed, that he was to receive counterfeit gasoline ration coupons from a certain Buttitta at a particular place. The investigator went to the appointed place and saw Reed, the sole occupant of the rear seat of the car, holding gasoline ration coupons. There were two other occupants in the car: Buttitta in the driver's seat and DiRe in the front passenger seat. Reed informed the investigator that Buttitta had given him counterfeit coupons. Thereupon, all three men were arrested and searched. After noting that the officers had no information implicating DiRe and no information pointing to DiRe's possession of coupons, unless presence in the car warranted that inference, we concluded that the officer lacked probable cause to believe that DiRe was involved in the crime. We said "[a]ny inference that everyone on the scene of a crime is a party to it must disappear if the Government singles out the guilty person." No such singling out occurred in this case; none of the three men provided information with respect to the ownership of the cocaine or money.

We hold that the officer had probable cause to believe that Pringle had committed the crime of possession of a controlled substance.[154]

NOTES AND QUESTIONS

1. The Court's conclusion is that a reasonable inference is warranted that "any *or* all three of the occupants had knowledge of, and exercised dominion and control over, the cocaine." The "or" suggests that the Court is saying that there are two plausible inferences: first, that at least *one* of the occupants possessed the cocaine; second, that all three jointly possessed the cocaine. Approving of the first inference as sufficient for probable cause, as the Court arguably seems to be doing, however, is confusing. Although the Court denies, and has long denied, that probable cause can be quantified, we have seen that both lower court judges and scholars try to do precisely that, and it is hard to see how probable cause can usefully be defined unless we have at least an approximate ballpark range of acceptable degrees of probability, even if the required range might vary with certain circumstances. But the probability that any one of three car occupants possessed the cocaine is 1/3, or 33–1/3%, a degree of confidence more akin to that assigned by judges and scholars to "reasonable suspicion" rather than to probable cause. If this is right, then how can we distinguish "probable cause" from "reasonable suspicion" after *Pringle*? Is the Court implicitly lowering the required degree of probability for both concepts while keeping "reasonable suspicion" as some undefined degree of probability less than "probable cause" but more than mere suspicion?

---

154. 540 U.S. at 373–74.

2.   The alternative inference suggested by the Court—that all three occupants jointly possessed the drugs—would overcome any mathematical concern, for if *all* possess the drugs as if they are one person, then it is logically the same as if there were in fact only one person in the car. The Court has clearly said that mere presence in a location where drugs are found is insufficient to establish probable cause. The influence of joint possession, therefore, seems to turn significantly on the *accessibility* of the money and the drugs to each of the occupants, that is, that each could have physically taken control over the drugs or money. But how can the Court make this question turn on "accessibility" when Maryland state law defines possession as *knowing* that the illegal substance is present and that you have some control over it? If what is required is probable cause to believe that a particular crime or crime has been committed, then does not the nature of that belief necessarily turn on relating it to what the elements of the crime require? Or can there simply be "free-floating" probable cause—a belief by the officer that something illegal is going on, but he does not know what? If "free-floating" probable cause is arguably inconsistent with the idea of individualized suspicion, then how can the Court substitute its judgment of the things that must be suspected as to a specific crime for the state's judgment when it defined the elements of the offense?

The dissent to the Court of Appeals of Maryland case chastised that Court's majority for looking to decisions on the sufficiency of the evidence at trial—a higher standard than "probable cause"—for precedent. But the state court majority did so, it maintained, solely to identify the elements of the crimes of possession and possession with intent to sell, readily agreeing that the quantum of proof required for probable cause was much lower than for sufficiency of the evidence. Who was right: the majority or the dissenters?

3.   The Court also found it significant that the occupants were in a "relatively small automobile, not a public tavern," and that a dealer would not likely admit an innocent person into the car in the first place for fear that the former might testify against the dealer. Concerning this second point: (a) How is it any different, if at all, from the "guilt-by-association" inference that the Court rejects?; (b) Does not this point *assume* that the drugs are visible so that the "innocent" occupant would have personal knowledge of the presence of the drugs about which he could testify?; (c) Are there not many plausible scenarios in which an innocent person could find himself in a car with drug possessors, users, or dealers? If there are, what would they be?

Concerning the first point—the small size of the car: (a) Where do we draw the line on size? Is it the physical size of the vehicle—so that a bus with two passengers and a driver, under circumstances where it is obvious that all three are friends, would somehow be different from the *Pringle* case? (b) Or is it the number of passengers and, if yes, again, where do you draw the line? What if there were four passengers? Five? Six? What if it were a mini-van with eight passengers? The state court majority had challenged the logic that there could be probable cause where there was no evidence that it was Pringle himself who possessed the drugs *as an individual* (whether solely or jointly) precisely on the grounds that it would logically entail holding large numbers of people present on a van or a bus where drugs were found on grounds of "probable cause." Who is right on this point—the state court or the Supreme Court?

4.   The Supreme Court also considered it a relevant circumstance that none of the car's occupants confessed to the crime before the arrest, thus disabling the officer from "singling out" the guilty person. How is this inference consistent with the Fifth Amendment privilege against self-incrimination? Does not this inference penalize Pringle and his co-occupants for the exercise of that constitutional privilege in that their silence requires them to pay a heavy toll—being arrested? Is it fair to argue as well that the absence of any "singling out" of one or more individuals as wrongdoers is precisely what demonstrates the absence of probable cause, that is, the absence of an adequate degree of *individualized* suspicion?

5.   Is the Court changing the meaning of probable cause across-the-board? Altering its meaning (in the sense of the necessary degree of probability) with the circumstances? Not changing its meaning at all? Does the Court's approach give adequate guidance to law enforcement and to lower courts about when and how they should find that probable cause does or does not exist?

2.   PROBABLE CAUSE AS AN OBJECTIVE, USUALLY INDIVIDUALIZED, DETERMINATION THAT TURNS ON THE COLLECTIVE KNOWLEDGE OF LAW ENFORCEMENT

Aside from the issue of quantification, there are other important aspects to the meaning of probable cause. Probable cause is an objective, not a subjective, test. Probable cause depends on what a reasonable police officer (or other government agent) has a right to believe under the circumstances. A classic formulation of the objective test can be found in *Beck v. Ohio*: "whether, at the moment the arrest was made . . . the facts and circumstances within their [the officers'] knowledge and of which they had reasonably trustworthy information were sufficient to warrant a prudent man in believing that the petitioner had committed or was committing an offense."[155] As with any objective test, a key difficulty is which circumstances should be considered. Considering too many circumstances may render the test subjective. Certainly, the experience of the officer is a relevant part of the circumstances. But more troubling questions will be raised below.

In *Devenpeck v. Alford*,[156] the United States Supreme Court reaffirmed its stance that probable cause is a highly objective measure. Police in that case had probable cause to arrest Alford for impersonating an officer, but at the time they arrested him they mistakenly believed that he was violating

---

155.   379 U.S. 89, 91 (1964).

156.   543 U.S. 146 (2004).

the Washington Privacy Act by making an audio recording of his interaction with them, and in the arrest papers they cited that Act. The Supreme Court upheld the arrest, emphasizing that "an officer's state of mind (except for the facts that he knows) is irrelevant to the existence of probable cause."[157] In other words, because the officers had probable cause to arrest Alford for impersonating an officer, the arrest was legal even though they arrested and intended to charge him on a different offense.

Another important question to keep in mind in reviewing the material below is this: does probable cause refer only to what is known to the individual officer, or does it include the knowledge of the entire police department? *Whiteley v. Warden* established that "officers called upon to aid other officers in executing arrest warrants are entitled to assume that the officers requesting aid offered the magistrate the information requisite to support an independent judicial assessment of probable cause."[158] The Court's opinion in *Whiteley* is generally understood to mean that an arresting officer acts appropriately if he makes an arrest: (1) based on a valid warrant obtained by another officer who had probable cause for the warrant, or (2) based on orders from an officer who had probable cause. The arresting officer need not himself be aware of the facts establishing probable cause. The same rule should apply to searches, stops, and other intrusions: the collective, institutional knowledge of the police will generally govern.

One possible justification for such a rule is that the police function as an institution, not as an unconnected group of individuals. Police work would grind to a halt if the officer who obtained information establishing probable cause or reasonable suspicion could not rely upon his fellow officers, or if arresting officers could not trust their colleagues. As one obvious example, suppose one police officer receives information that a fleeing suspect is in an area far from his location. He puts out a radio bulletin and another officer makes the arrest. If the latter officer could not rely on the former, the arrest could not take place.

However, this does not necessarily mean that probable cause should always include collective knowledge. Consider this hypothetical. Officer A has a hunch that Suspect committed a crime, but Officer A does not have probable cause. Officer A orders Officer B to arrest Suspect. While Officer B is looking for Suspect, Officer C, unbeknownst to A and B and quite accidentally, obtains information establishing probable cause to arrest Suspect. Officer C does not convey that information to A or B. If Officers A or B arrest Suspect, should Officer C's happy accident save the otherwise invalid arrest? Most courts and commentators would say "no," for a contrary result encourages illegal action by police who may gamble that

---

157. *Id.* at 153.

158. 401 U.S. 560, 568 (1971). For a summary of the case law on the limits of *Whiteley,* *see* WAYNE R. LaFAVE, SEARCH AND SEIZURE: A TREATISE ON THE FOURTH AMENDMENT § 3.5(c) (2004). *See also* United States v. Hensley, 469 U.S. 221 (1985) (investigatory stop of a suspect in reliance on another police department's "wanted flyer," which had been issued based upon specific and articulable facts establishing reasonable suspicion, was valid).

their fellow officers, working independently, will gather enough information in the aggregate to constitute probable cause.

"Probable cause" generally requires individualized suspicion—suspicion that this suspect is guilty of a crime or that this place harbors contraband, fruits, evidence, or instrumentalities of crime. For example, if police arrest Suspect for a marijuana offense, they must have information about Suspect's guilt, not just information that Suspect's group of friends uses marijuana. Similarly, if police search Suspect's house for marijuana, they must have information that marijuana will be found there, not just information that most homes in Suspect's neighborhood harbor marijuana.

There are exceptions to this general rule, but they are rare. One example involves housing code inspections, where the Court defines probable cause in generalized terms requiring only that the government demonstrate that homes in a particular area must be inspected. The text addresses this exception in the next chapter. "Drug courier profiles" may provide another example of generalized suspicion. These profiles are comprised of typical characteristics of drug dealers. When profiles rely heavily on typifications, especially group characteristics like race, they create nothing more than generalized suspicion. The Supreme Court has not decided whether such profiles give rise to probable cause, although it has indicated that officers may rely on characteristics listed in profiles, together with their own experiences, when evaluating whether individualized probable cause exists.

Finally, probable cause determinations are highly fact-sensitive, so sensitive that courts sometimes declare that precedent cannot be helpful because every situation is unique (*see Illinois v. Gates*, below). More often at the trial level, however, analogy to precedent is important, because cases applying the probable cause concept to particular fact situations provide meaning to the otherwise vague concept. In practice, therefore, lawyers carefully review precedent in their jurisdictions, looking for cases with facts similar to the ones at issue and finding ways to support or distinguish the results in those cases.

B. PROVING PROBABLE CAUSE: THE GATES TEST

The probable cause concept creates difficult proof problems. What information should be considered in making the probable cause determination? How much weight does that information deserve? These questions are particularly acute when police rely on informants for information.

1. INFORMANT'S TIPS AND THE AGUILAR–SPINELLI TWO–PRONGED TEST

Police often base their probable cause determinations on reports from crime victims, witnesses, and informants, who typically are small-fry criminals willing to provide information to the police in exchange for leniency or money. These third-party reports become the subject of police officer testimony when defendants file suppression motions challenging whether probable cause existed. Testimony about those reports is not inadmissible hearsay (which is defined by evidence law as an out-of-court statement offered for the truth of the matter asserted) because it is not offered to prove that those reports were true, but rather to prove that the officers had an objectively reasonable basis to believe that probable cause existed. Nevertheless, two of the values that the hearsay rule protects—testing credibility and testing reliability (or adequate substitutes for such tests)—are very important to the determination of probable cause.

Questions about the credibility and reliability of third-party reports abound in police work. Officers often have little time to question witnesses or informants in order to ascertain whether they are telling the truth. However, officers must verify third-party reports somewhat, because reviewing courts are required to determine whether the information from those reports constituted probable cause, either alone or in combination with corroborating details. Officer verification is especially important when police rely on tips from confidential informants, whose identity is not revealed to courts or defendants.

The Supreme Court recognized the importance of this verification process and established a test for courts reviewing probable cause determinations that depended on informants' tips. The test, now known as the "*Aguilar-Spinelli* test," was created in two cases, *Aguilar v. Texas*,[159] and *Spinelli v. United States*.[160] It required a two-part inquiry. First, was the informant credible—was he or she likely to be telling the truth? Second, was the informant reliable—was it likely that he or she had a sound basis of knowledge? These questions were not to be used simply as common sense guides to gauging the weight of informants' tips, but also as exclusionary rules of evidence. If police testimony failed to establish either prong, the tip could not be used in the probable cause determination.

Using principles analogous to evidence law, the Court made clear that neither prong could be satisfied by conclusory assertions—for example, "I received a tip from a credible informant" or "the informant told me narcotics were sold at this location." Instead, the police needed to provide specific, concrete information from which a magistrate deciding whether to issue a warrant, or a judge hearing a suppression motion, could independently assess whether each prong had been met. Police could bolster their informants' tips by gathering corroborating facts that "permit the suspicions engendered by the informer's tip to ripen into a judgment that a crime was probably being committed." "Innocent" facts could corroborate tips, although logic suggests that innocent details are often less significant than details inconsistent with innocence.[161] Finally, Justice White's concurring opinion in *Spinelli* noted that an informant may base his information on hearsay, but, if he does, there must be "good reason for believing it—

---

159. 378 U.S. 108 (1964).

160. 393 U.S. 410 (1969).

161. When you read Illinois v. Gates, identify the corroborating facts and determine whether the Court weighed the innocent facts less heavily than the suspicious ones.

perhaps one of the usual grounds for crediting hearsay information." While Justice White was not using hearsay in its strict evidentiary sense, his statement confirmed that analogy to the policies and precedents underlying the hearsay rule are instructive.

In addition to setting forth a two-pronged test, the Court's opinions in *Aguilar*, *Spinelli*, and subsequent cases provided guidance about each prong:

a. The Credibility Prong

Factors relevant to the informant's credibility included: (a) whether the tip was against interest, that is, whether it implicated the informant in criminal activity; (b) whether the informant had given prior accurate tips; and (c) whether the informant had a reputation for truthfulness.[162]

The first factor demonstrates the helpful nature of evidence law analogy. Rule 803(b)(3) of the Federal Rules of Evidence excepts from the hearsay rule "a statement which ... at the time of its making ... so far tended to subject the declarant to ... criminal liability ... that a reasonable person in the declarant's position would not have made the statement unless believing it to be true."[163] The basic principle underlying this rule forms the basis of the first factor and was important to the Court's opinion in *Williamson v. United States*.[164] There, police officers stopped Reginald Harris in a rental car while he was driving on a highway. Harris consented to a search of the car, which revealed a quantity of cocaine in two suitcases in the trunk. At first Harris claimed that an unnamed Cuban had given him the cocaine to place in a dumpster for a pickup. After the arresting officer suggested making a controlled buy, however, Harris changed his story, saying that he had in fact been transporting the cocaine to Atlanta for Fredel Williamson, who had witnessed Harris's arrest and therefore would not be caught in a phony buy. Harris's statements easily might be used in a search or arrest warrant affidavit concerning Williamson. The analytical difficulty was that Harris's statements had both an inculpatory aspect (he admitted to the crime of transporting cocaine) and an exculpatory aspect (he pinned most of the responsibility on Williamson as the mastermind). So, was the statement one against penal interest or not?

The actual issue in *Williamson* did not involve warrant affidavits but rather the admissibility of Harris's statements against Williamson at trial, but the analogy is clear. The Justices issued numerous opinions, so in many respects it is hard to identify the view of the Court, and the details need not concern us here. What matters is that the Court did clearly hold that Rule 803(b)(3) does not allow for the admission of non-self-inculpatory statements, even when they are made as part of a broader, generally self-inculpatory narrative. "One of the most effective ways to lie is to mix

---

162. Lower courts have also tended to credit tips by "citizen-informants," those not involved in crime but merely acting as good citizens and therefore having no reason to lie.

163. FED. R. EVID. 804(b)(3).

164. 512 U.S. 594 (1994).

falsehood with truth, especially truth that seems particularly persuasive because of its self-inculpatory nature." However, a majority of the Justices apparently recognized that many statements are not clear-cut, requiring a balancing of self-serving against disserving aspects.[165] One strong indicator that a statement is primarily self-serving, noted a majority of the Justices, is that it is made to "curry favor" with the authorities rather than to a third party from whom the speaker cannot expect any reward. *Williamson* thus highlights the complexities of determining whether an informant's tip is credible because against self-interest and emphasizes the close connection between evidentiary and criminal procedure concepts.

The third factor in the credibility prong, established by a plurality opinion in *United States v. Harris*,[166] also illustrates the helpful analogy to evidentiary principles: since a witness's reputation for truthfulness is often deemed relevant at trial, it makes sense that reputation should also be relevant to the less demanding probable cause determination.[167] It also makes sense to consider the suspect's reputation for criminal behavior, and several of the justices in *Harris* agreed, despite language in *Spinelli* that "the allegation that Spinelli was 'known' to the affiant and to other federal and local law enforcement officers as a gambler and an associate of gamblers is but a bald and unilluminating assertion of suspicion that is entitled to no weight in apprising the apprising the magistrate's decision."[168] This statement may not be a complete rejection of the role of the suspect's reputation but rather a requirement that the specific bases for the reputation be recited.[169]

b.   The Reliability Prong

Factors relevant to the reliability prong included: (1) whether the informant personally observed or participated in the activities reported in the tip; (2) whether the tip was so detailed that the informant must have

---

165.   For detailed analyses of the Justices' opinions, *see* Andrew E. Taslitz, *Daubert's Guide to the Federal Rules of Evidence: A Not–So–Plain–Meaning Jurisprudence*, 32 HARV. J. LEG. 3, 68–75 (1995).

166.   403 U.S. 573, 583 (1971).

167.   *See* FED. R. EVID. 404, 608.

168.   393 U.S. at 414. The *Spinelli* Court further noted that the "magistrate must rely on something more substantial than a casual rumor circulating in the underworld or an accusation based merely on an individual's general reputation." *Id.* at 416.

169.   Chief Justice Burger, in an opinion joined by Justices Black and Blackmun, in United States v. Harris, 403 U.S. 573 (1971), declared:

We cannot conclude that a policeman's knowledge of a suspect's reputation-something that policemen frequently know and that impressed such a "legal technician" as Mr. Justice Frankfurter—is not a "practical consideration of everyday life" upon which an officer (or a magistrate) may properly rely in assessing the reliability of an informant's tip. To the extent that Spinelli prohibits the use of such probative information, it has no support in our prior cases, logic, or experience and we decline to apply it to preclude a magistrate from relying on a law enforcement officer's knowledge of a suspect's reputation.

Id. at 582–83. Again, Justices Harlan, Douglas, Brennan, and Marshall appeared not to be persuaded by evidence of the suspect's reputation. *See id.* at 597–98.

first-hand knowledge; and (3) whether the nature of the information contained in the tip, or the manner it which it was gathered, indicate that it could have come only from personal knowledge or a highly reliable source.

2.   THE PROBLEM OF ANONYMOUS TIPS

If it was burdensome to establish the credibility and reliability of informants, it was even more difficult to do so in the case of confidential informants and almost always impossible in the case of anonymous tipsters. If a tipster were truly anonymous, how could an officer provide facts demonstrating the tipster's credibility? Reliability conceivably could be established in some circumstances, but the courts had made it clear after *Aguilar* and *Spinelli* that even an abundance of evidence on one prong could not make up for a lack of evidence on the other. So matters stood until the Court accepted certiorari in *Illinois v. Gates*.

3.   THE GATES TEST FOR PROBABLE CAUSE

In *Illinois v. Gates,*[170] the Court abandoned the *Aguilar/Spinelli* approach in favor of a "totality of the circumstances" approach. While informants' tips sometimes still are evaluated using the credibility and reliability factors articulated in *Aguilar/Spinelli*, much has changed because of *Gates*. *Gates* is a classic of criminal procedure worth extended analysis. Its approach applies to *all* probable cause inquiries—not just those involving informants' tips.

Illinois v. Gates

462 U.S. 213 (1983).

■ REHNQUIST, C.J. Respondents Lance and Susan Gates were indicted for violation of state drug laws after police officers, executing a search warrant, discovered marijuana and other contraband in their automobile and home. Prior to trial the Gates' moved to suppress evidence seized during this search. The Illinois Supreme Court affirmed the decisions of lower state courts, granting the motion. It held that the affidavit submitted in support of the State's application for a warrant to search the Gates' property was inadequate under this Court's decisions in *Aguilar v. Texas*, 378 U.S. 108 (1964), and *Spinelli v. United States*, 393 U.S. 410 (1969).

We granted certiorari to consider the application of the Fourth Amendment to a magistrate's issuance of a search warrant on the basis of a partially corroborated anonymous informant's tip. . . .

Bloomingdale, Ill., is a suburb of Chicago located in DuPage County. On May 3, 1978, the Bloomingdale Police Department received by mail an anonymous handwritten letter which read as follows:

---

170.   462 U.S. 213 (1983).

This letter is to inform you that you have a couple in your town who strictly make their living on selling drugs. They are Sue and Lance Gates, they live on Greenway, off Bloomingdale Road in the condominiums. Most of their buys are done in Florida. Sue his wife drives their car to Florida, where she leaves it to be loaded up with drugs, then Lance flies down and drives it back. Sue flies back after she drops the car off in Florida. May 3 she is driving down there again and Lance will be flying down in a few days to drive it back. At the time Lance drives the car back he has the trunk loaded with over $100,000.00 in drugs. Presently they have over $100,000.00 worth of drugs in their basement. They brag about the fact they never have to work, and make their entire living on pushers. I guarantee if you watch them carefully you will make a big catch. They are friends with some big drug dealers, who visit their house often. Lance & Susan Gates Greenway in Condominiums.

The letter was referred by the Chief of Police of the Bloomingdale Police Department to Detective Mader, who decided to pursue the tip. Mader learned, from the office of the Illinois Secretary of State, that an Illinois driver's license had been issued to one Lance Gates, residing at a stated address in Bloomingdale. He contacted a confidential informant, whose examination of certain financial records revealed a more recent address for the Gates, and he also learned from a police officer assigned to O'Hare Airport that "L. Gates" had made a reservation on Eastern Airlines flight 245 to West Palm Beach, Fla., scheduled to depart from Chicago on May 5 at 4:15 p.m.

Mader then made arrangements with an agent of the Drug Enforcement Administration for surveillance of the May 5 Eastern Airlines flight. The agent later reported to Mader that Gates had boarded the flight, and that federal agents in Florida had observed him arrive in West Palm Beach and take a taxi to the nearby Holiday Inn. They also reported that Gates went to a room registered to one Susan Gates and that, at 7:00 a.m. the next morning, Gates and an unidentified woman left the motel in a Mercury bearing Illinois license plates and drove northbound on an interstate frequently used by travelers to the Chicago area. In addition, the DEA agent informed Mader that the license plate number on the Mercury registered to a Hornet station wagon owned by Gates. The agent also advised Mader that the driving time between West Palm Beach and Bloomingdale was approximately 22 to 24 hours.

Mader signed an affidavit setting forth the foregoing facts, and submitted it to a judge of the Circuit Court of DuPage County, together with a copy of the anonymous letter. The judge of that court thereupon issued a search warrant for the Gates' residence and for their automobile. The judge, in deciding to issue the warrant, could have determined that the modus operandi of the Gates had been substantially corroborated. As the anonymous letter predicted, Lance Gates had flown from Chicago to West Palm Beach late in the afternoon of May 5th, had checked into a hotel room registered in the name of his wife, and, at 7:00 a.m. the following morning, had headed north, accompanied by an unidentified woman, out of West Palm Beach on an interstate highway used by travelers from South Florida to Chicago in an automobile bearing a license plate issued to him.

At 5:15 a.m. on March 7th, only 36 hours after he had flown out of Chicago, Lance Gates, and his wife, returned to their home in Bloomingdale, driving the car in which they had left West Palm Beach some 22 hours earlier. The Bloomingdale police were awaiting them, searched the trunk of the Mercury, and uncovered approximately 350 pounds of marijuana. A search of the Gates' home revealed marijuana, weapons, and other contraband. The Illinois Circuit Court ordered suppression of all these items, on the ground that the affidavit submitted to the Circuit Judge failed to support the necessary determination of probable cause to believe that the Gates' automobile and home contained the contraband in question. This decision was affirmed in turn by the Illinois Appellate Court and by a divided vote of the Supreme Court of Illinois.

The Illinois Supreme Court concluded—and we are inclined to agree— that, standing alone, the anonymous letter sent to the Bloomingdale Police Department would not provide the basis for a magistrate's determination that there was probable cause to believe contraband would be found in the Gates' car and home. The letter provides virtually nothing from which one might conclude that its author is either honest or his information reliable; likewise, the letter gives absolutely no indication of the basis for the writer's predictions regarding the Gates' criminal activities. Something more was required, then, before a magistrate could conclude that there was probable cause to believe that contraband would be found in the Gates' home and car.

The Illinois Supreme Court also properly recognized that Detective Mader's affidavit might be capable of supplementing the anonymous letter with information sufficient to permit a determination of probable cause. In holding that the affidavit in fact did not contain sufficient additional information to sustain a determination of probable cause, the Illinois court applied a "two-pronged test," derived from our decision in *Spinelli*. The Illinois Supreme Court, like some others, apparently understood *Spinelli* as requiring that the anonymous letter satisfy each of two independent requirements before it could be relied on. According to this view, the letter, as supplemented by Mader's affidavit, first had to adequately reveal the "basis of knowledge" of the letter writer—the particular means by which he came by the information given in his report. Second, it had to provide facts sufficiently establishing either the "veracity" of the affiant's informant, or, alternatively, the "reliability" of the informant's report in this particular case.

The Illinois court, alluding to an elaborate set of legal rules that have developed among various lower courts to enforce the "two-pronged test," found that the test had not been satisfied. First, the "veracity" prong was not satisfied because, "there was simply no basis [for] ... conclud[ing] that the anonymous person [who wrote the letter to the Bloomingdale Police Department] was credible." The court indicated that corroboration by police of details contained in the letter might never satisfy the "veracity" prong, and in any event, could not do so if, as in the present case, only "innocent" details are corroborated. In addition, the letter gave no indication of the basis of its writer's knowledge of the Gates' activities. The Illinois court understood *Spinelli* as permitting the detail contained in a tip to be used to infer that the informant had a reliable basis for his statements, but it thought that the anonymous letter failed to provide sufficient detail to permit such an inference. Thus, it concluded that no showing of probable cause had been made.

We agree with the Illinois Supreme Court that an informant's "veracity," "reliability" and "basis of knowledge" are all highly relevant in determining the value of his report. We do not agree, however, that these elements should be understood as entirely separate and independent requirements to be rigidly exacted in every case, which the opinion of the Supreme Court of Illinois would imply. Rather, as detailed below, they should be understood simply as closely intertwined issues that may usefully illuminate the common sense, practical question whether there is "probable cause" to believe that contraband or evidence is located in a particular place.

III

This totality of the circumstances approach is far more consistent with our prior treatment of probable cause than is any rigid demand that specific "tests" be satisfied by every informant's tip. Perhaps the central teaching of our decisions bearing on the probable cause standard is that it is a "practical, nontechnical conception." . . .

. . . [P]robable cause is a fluid concept—turning on the assessment of probabilities in particular factual contexts—not readily, or even usefully, reduced to a neat set of legal rules. Informants' tips doubtless come in many shapes and sizes from many different types of persons. As we said in *Adams v. Williams*, 407 U.S. 143 (1972), "Informants' tips, like all other clues and evidence coming to a policeman on the scene may vary greatly in their value and reliability." Rigid legal rules are ill-suited to an area of such diversity. "One simple rule will not cover every situation."

Moreover, the "two-pronged test" directs analysis into two largely independent channels—the informant's "veracity" or "reliability" and his "basis of knowledge." There are persuasive arguments against according these two elements such independent status. Instead, they are better understood as relevant considerations in the totality of circumstances analysis that traditionally has guided probable cause determinations: a deficiency in one may be compensated for, in determining the overall reliability of a tip, by a strong showing as to the other, or by some other indicia of reliability.

If, for example, a particular informant is known for the unusual reliability of his predictions of certain types of criminal activities in a locality, his failure, in a particular case, to thoroughly set forth the basis of his knowledge surely should not serve as an absolute bar to a finding of probable cause based on his tip. Likewise, if an unquestionably honest citizen comes forward with a report of criminal activity—which if fabricated would subject him to criminal liability—we have found rigorous scrutiny of the basis of his knowledge unnecessary. Conversely, even if we entertain some doubt as to an informant's motives, his explicit and detailed description of alleged wrongdoing, along with a statement that the event was observed first-hand, entitles his tip to greater weight than might otherwise be the case. Unlike a totality of circumstances analysis, which permits a balanced assessment of the relative weights of all the various indicia of reliability (and unreliability) attending an informant's tip, the "two-pronged test" has encouraged an excessively technical dissection of informants' tips, with undue attention being focused on isolated issues that cannot sensibly be divorced from the other facts presented to the magistrate.

As early as *Locke v. United States*, 7 Cranch. 339 (1813), Chief Justice Marshall observed, in a closely related context, that "the term 'probable cause,' according to its usual acceptation, means less than evidence which would justify condemnation. . . . It imports a seizure made under circumstances which warrant suspicion." More recently, we said that "the quanta . . . of proof" appropriate in ordinary judicial proceedings are inapplicable to the decision to issue a warrant. *Brinegar v. United States*, 338 U.S. 160 (1949). Finely-tuned standards such as proof beyond a reasonable doubt or by a preponderance of the evidence, useful in formal trials, have no place in the magistrate's decision. While an effort to fix some general, numerically precise degree of certainty corresponding to "probable cause" may not be helpful, it is clear that "only the probability, and not a prima facie showing, of criminal activity is the standard of probable cause." *Spinelli*, 393 U.S. at 419.

We also have recognized that affidavits are normally drafted by non-lawyers in the midst and haste of a criminal investigation. Technical requirements of elaborate specificity once exacted under common law pleading have no proper place in this area. Likewise, search and arrest warrants long have been issued by persons who are neither lawyers nor judges, and who certainly do not remain abreast of each judicial refinement of the nature of "probable cause." *See Shadwick v. City of Tampa*, 407 U.S. 345 (1972). The rigorous inquiry into the *Spinelli* prongs and the complex superstructure of evidentiary and analytical rules that some have seen implicit in our *Spinelli* decision, cannot be reconciled with the fact that many warrants are—quite properly—issued on the basis of nontechnical, common-sense judgments of laymen applying a standard less demanding than those used in more formal legal proceedings. Likewise, given the informal, often hurried context in which it must be applied, the "built-in subtleties" of the "two-pronged test" are particularly unlikely to assist magistrates in determining probable cause.

Similarly, we have repeatedly said that after-the-fact scrutiny by courts of the sufficiency of an affidavit should not take the form of de novo review. A magistrate's determination of probable cause should be paid great deference by reviewing courts. A grudging or negative attitude by reviewing courts toward warrants is inconsistent with the Fourth Amendment's strong preference for searches conducted pursuant to a warrant; . . . courts should not invalidate warrants by interpreting affidavits in a hyper technical, rather than a common sense, manner.

If the affidavits submitted by police officers are subjected to the type of scrutiny some courts have deemed appropriate, police might well resort to warrantless searches, with the hope of relying on consent or some other exception to the warrant clause that might develop at the time of the search. In addition, the possession of a warrant by officers conducting an arrest or search greatly reduces the perception of unlawful or intrusive police conduct, by assuring "the individual whose property is searched or seized of the lawful authority of the executing officer, his need to search, and the limits of his power to search." *United States v. Chadwick*, 433 U.S. 1 (1977). Reflecting this preference for the warrant process, the traditional standard for review of an issuing magistrate's probable cause determination has been that so long as the magistrate had a "substantial basis for . . . conclud[ing]" that a search would uncover evidence of wrongdoing, the Fourth Amendment requires no more. *Jones v. United States*, 362 U.S. 257 (1960). We think reaffirmation of this standard better serves the purpose of encouraging recourse to the warrant procedure and is more consistent with our traditional deference to the probable cause determinations of magistrates than is the "two-pronged test."

Finally, the direction taken by decisions following *Spinelli* poorly serves "the most basic function of any government": "to provide for the security of the individual and of his property." *Miranda v. Arizona*, 384 U.S. 436 (1966) (White, J., dissenting). The strictures that inevitably accompany the "two-pronged test" cannot avoid seriously impeding the task of law enforcement. If, as the Illinois Supreme Court apparently thought, that test must be rigorously applied in every case, anonymous tips seldom would be of greatly diminished value in police work. Ordinary citizens, like ordinary witnesses, see Federal Rules of Evidence 701, Advisory Committee Note (1976), generally do not provide extensive recitations of the basis of their everyday observations. Likewise, as the Illinois Supreme Court observed in this case, the veracity of persons supplying anonymous tips is by hypothesis largely unknown, and unknowable. As a result, anonymous tips seldom could survive a rigorous application of either of the *Spinelli* prongs. Yet, such tips, particularly when supplemented by independent police investigation, frequently contribute to the solution of otherwise "perfect crimes." While a conscientious assessment of the basis for crediting such tips is required by the Fourth Amendment, a standard that leaves virtually no place for anonymous citizen informants is not.

For all these reasons, we conclude that it is wiser to abandon the "two-pronged test" established by our decisions in *Aguilar* and *Spinelli*. In its place we reaffirm the totality of the circumstances analysis that traditionally has informed probable cause determinations. The task of the issuing magistrate is simply to make a practical, common-sense decision whether, given all the circumstances set forth in the affidavit before him, including the "veracity" and "basis of knowledge" of persons supplying hearsay information, there is a fair probability that contraband or evidence of a crime will be found in a particular place. And the duty of a reviewing court is simply to ensure that the magistrate had a substantial basis for concluding that probable cause existed. We are convinced that this flexible, easily applied standard will better achieve the accommodation of public and private interests that the Fourth Amendment requires than does the approach that has developed from *Aguilar* and *Spinelli*.

Our earlier cases illustrate the limits beyond which a magistrate may not venture in issuing a warrant. A sworn statement of an affiant that "he has cause to suspect and does believe that" liquor illegally brought into the United States is located on certain premises will not do. *Nathanson v. United States*, 290 U.S. 41 (1933). An affidavit must provide the magistrate with a substantial basis for determining the existence of probable cause, and the wholly conclusory statement at issue in *Nathanson* failed to meet this requirement. An officer's statement that "affiants have received reliable information from a credible person and believe" that heroin is stored in a home, is likewise inadequate. *Aguilar v. Texas*, 378 U.S. 108 (1964). As in *Nathanson*, this is a mere conclusory statement that gives the magistrate virtually no basis at all for making a judgment regarding probable cause. Sufficient information must be presented to the magistrate to allow that official to determine probable cause; his action cannot be a mere ratification of the bare conclusions of others. In order to ensure that such an abdication of the magistrate's duty does not occur, courts must continue to conscientiously review the sufficiency of affidavits on which warrants are issued. But when we move beyond the "bare bones" affidavits present in cases such as *Nathanson* and *Aguilar*, this area simply does not lend itself to a prescribed set of rules, like that which had developed from *Spinelli*. Instead, the flexible, common-sense standard . . . better serves the purposes of the Fourth Amendment's probable cause requirement.

Justice Brennan's dissent suggests in several places that the approach we take today somehow downgrades the role of the neutral magistrate, because *Aguilar* and *Spinelli* "preserve the role of magistrates as independent arbiters of probable cause. . . ." Quite the contrary, we believe, is the case. The essential protection of the warrant requirement of the Fourth Amendment . . . is in "requiring that [the usual inferences which reasonable men draw from evidence] be drawn by a neutral and detached magistrate instead of being judged by the officer engaged in the often competitive enterprise of ferreting out crime." Nothing in our opinion in any way lessens the authority of the magistrate to draw such reasonable inferences as he will from the material supplied to him by applicants for a warrant; indeed, he is freer than under the regime of *Aguilar* and *Spinelli* to draw such inferences, or to refuse to draw them if he is so minded.

The real gist of Justice Brennan's criticism seems to be a second argument, somewhat at odds with the first, that magistrates should be restricted in their authority to make probable cause determinations by the standards laid down in *Aguilar* and *Spinelli*, and that such findings "should not be authorized unless there is some assurance that the information on which they are based has been obtained in a reliable way by an honest or credible person." However, under our opinion magistrates remain perfectly free to exact such assurances as they deem necessary, as well as those required by this opinion, in making probable cause determinations. Justice Brennan would apparently prefer that magistrates be restricted in their findings of probable cause by the development of an elaborate body of case law dealing with the "veracity" prong of the *Spinelli* test, which in turn is broken down into two "spurs"—the informant's "credibility" and the "reliability" of his information, together with the "basis of knowledge" prong of the *Spinelli* test. That such a labyrinthine body of judicial refinement bears any relationship to familiar definitions of probable cause is hard to imagine. Probable cause deals "with probabilities. These are not technical; they are the factual and practical considerations of everyday life on which reasonable and prudent men, not legal technicians, act," *Brinegar v. United States*, 338 U.S. 160 (1949).

Justice Brennan's dissent also suggests that "words such as 'practical,' 'nontechnical,' and 'common sense,' as used in the Court's opinion, are but code words for an overly-permissive attitude towards police practices in derogation of the rights secured by the Fourth Amendment." An easy, but not a complete, answer to this rather florid statement would be that nothing we know about Justice Rutledge suggests that he would have used the words he chose in *Brinegar* in such a manner. More fundamentally, no one doubts that "under our Constitution only measures consistent with the Fourth Amendment may be employed by government to cure [the horrors of drug trafficking]," but this agreement does not advance the inquiry as to which measures are, and which measures are not, consistent with the Fourth Amendment. "Fidelity" to the commands of the Constitution suggests balanced judgment rather than exhortation. The highest "fidelity "is achieved neither by the judge who instinctively goes furthest in upholding even the most bizarre claim of individual constitutional rights, any more than it is achieved by a judge who instinctively goes furthest in accepting the most restrictive claims of governmental authorities. The task of this Court, as of other courts, is to "hold the balance true," and we think we have done that in this case.

IV

Our decisions applying the totality of circumstances analysis outlined above have consistently recognized the value of corroboration of details of an informant's tip by independent police work. . . .

Even standing alone, the facts obtained through the independent investigation of Mader and the DEA at least suggested that the Gates were involved in drug trafficking. In addition to being a popular vacation site, Florida is well-known as a source of narcotics and other illegal drugs. Lance Gates' flight to Palm Beach, his brief, overnight stay in a motel, and apparent immediate return north to Chicago in the family car, conveniently awaiting him in West Palm Beach, is as suggestive of a pre-arranged drug run, as it is of an ordinary vacation trip.

In addition, the magistrate could rely on the anonymous letter, which had been corroborated in major part by Mader's efforts.[171] ... The corroboration of the letter's predictions that the Gates' car would be in Florida, that Lance Gates would fly to Florida in the next day or so, and that he would drive the car north toward Bloomingdale all indicated, albeit not with certainty, that the informant's other assertions also were true. "Because an informant is right about some things, he is more probably right about other facts," *Spinelli*, 393 U.S. at 427 (White, J., concurring)—including the claim regarding the Gates' illegal activity. This may well not be the type of "reliability" or "veracity" necessary to satisfy some views of the "veracity prong" of *Spinelli*, but we think it suffices for the practical, common-sense judgment called for in making a probable cause determination. It is enough, for purposes of assessing probable cause, that "corroboration through other sources of information reduced the chances of a reckless or prevaricating tale," thus providing "a substantial basis for crediting the hearsay." *Jones v. United States*, 362 U.S. at 269.

Finally, the anonymous letter contained a range of details relating not just to easily obtained facts and conditions existing at the time of the tip, but to future actions of third parties ordinarily not easily predicted. The letter writer's accurate information as to the travel plans of each of the Gates was of a character likely obtained only from the Gates themselves, or from someone familiar with their not entirely ordinary travel plans. If the informant had access to accurate information of this type a magistrate could properly conclude that it was not unlikely that he also had access to reliable information of the Gates' alleged illegal activities. Of course, the Gates' travel plans might have been learned from a talkative neighbor or travel agent; under the "two-pronged test" developed from *Spinelli*, the character of the details in the anonymous letter might well not permit a sufficiently clear inference regarding the letter writer's "basis of knowledge." But, as discussed previously, probable cause does not demand the certainty we associate with formal trials. It is enough that there was a fair probability that the writer of the anonymous letter had obtained his entire story either from the Gates or someone they trusted. And corroboration of

---

171. The Illinois Supreme Court thought that the verification of details contained in the anonymous letter in this case amounted only to "the corroboration of innocent activity," and that this was insufficient to support a finding of probable cause. We are inclined to agree, however, with the observation of Justice Moran in his dissenting opinion that "In this case, ... seemingly innocent activity became suspicious in the light of the initial tip." ... This is perfectly reasonable. As discussed previously, probable cause requires only a probability or substantial chance of criminal activity, not an actual showing of such activity. By hypothesis, therefore, innocent behavior frequently will provide the basis for a showing of probable cause; to require otherwise would be to sub silentio impose a drastically more rigorous definition of probable cause than the security of our citizens demands. We think the Illinois court attempted a too rigid classification of the types of conduct that may be relied upon in seeking to demonstrate probable cause. In making a determination of probable cause the relevant inquiry is not whether particular conduct is "innocent" or "guilty," but the degree of suspicion that attaches to particular types of non-criminal acts.

major portions of the letter's predictions provides just this probability. It is apparent, therefore, that the judge issuing the warrant had a "substantial basis for . . . conclud[ing]" that probable cause to search the Gates' home and car existed. The judgment of the Supreme Court of Illinois therefore must be reversed.

■ STEVENS, J. (with whom Justice Brennan joins), dissenting. The fact that Lance and Sue Gates made a 22–hour nonstop drive from West Palm Beach, Florida, to Bloomingdale, Illinois, only a few hours after Lance had flown to Florida provided persuasive evidence that they were engaged in illicit activity. That fact, however, was not known to the magistrate when he issued the warrant to search their home.

What the magistrate did know at that time was that the anonymous informant had not been completely accurate in his or her predictions. The informant had indicated that "Sue drives their car to Florida where she leaves it to be loaded up with drugs. . . . Sue flies back after she drops the car off in Florida." Yet Detective Mader's affidavit reported that she "left the West Palm Beach area driving the Mercury northbound."

The discrepancy between the informant's predictions and the facts known to Detective Mader is significant for three reasons. First, it cast doubt on the informant's hypothesis that the Gates already had "over $100,000 worth of drugs in their basement." The informant had predicted an itinerary that always kept one spouse in Bloomingdale, suggesting that the Gates did not want to leave their home unguarded because something valuable was hidden within. That inference obviously could not be drawn when it was known that the pair was actually together over a thousand miles from home.

Second, the discrepancy made the Gates' conduct seem substantially less unusual than the informant had predicted it would be. It would have been odd if, as predicted, Sue had driven down to Florida on Wednesday, left the car, and flown right back to Illinois. But the mere facts that Sue was in West Palm Beach with the car, that she was joined by her husband at the Holiday Inn on Friday, and that the couple drove north together the next morning[172] are neither unusual nor probative of criminal activity.

Third, the fact that the anonymous letter contained a material mistake undermines the reasonableness of relying on it as a basis for making a forcible entry into a private home.[173]

---

172. Detective Mader's affidavit hinted darkly that the couple had set out upon "that interstate highway commonly used by travelers to the Chicago area." But the same highway is also commonly used by travelers to Disney World, Sea World, and Ringling Brothers and Barnum and Bailey Circus World. It is also the road to Cocoa Beach, Cape Canaveral, and Washington, D.C. I would venture that each year dozens of perfectly innocent people fly to Florida, meet a waiting spouse, and drive off together in the family car.

173. The Court purports to rely on the proposition that "if the [anonymous] informant could predict with considerable accuracy the somewhat unusual travel plans of the Gates, he probably also had a reliable basis for his statements that the Gates kept a large quantity of drugs in their home." Even if this syllogism were sound, its premises are not met in this case.

Of course, the activities in this case did not stop when the magistrate issued the warrant. The Gates drove all night to Bloomingdale, the officers searched the car and found 400 pounds of marijuana, and then they searched the house. However, none of these subsequent events may be considered in evaluating the warrant, and the search of the house was legal only if the warrant was valid. *Vale v. Louisiana*, 399 U.S. 30 (1970). I cannot accept the Court's casual conclusion that, before the Gates arrived in Bloomingdale, there was probable cause to justify a valid entry and search of a private home. No one knows who the informant in this case was, or what motivated him or her to write the note. Given that the note's predictions were faulty in one significant respect, and were corroborated by nothing except ordinary innocent activity, I must surmise that the Court's evaluation of the warrant's validity has been colored by subsequent events.

NOTES AND QUESTIONS

1. Does the *Gates* test function as an admissibility rule at suppression hearings or as a guide to determining the weight of informants' tips? What is the continuing role, if any, of the *Aguilar–Spinelli* test? Which test is wiser as a matter of policy?

2. Did *Gates* alter the definition of probable cause—judging how much cause is enough—and, if so, how? Pay close attention to the "substantial chance" language in footnote a. Also, what is the post-*Gates* standard of review by an appellate court of a magistrates' judgment that an officer indeed had probable cause? Does this standard, when combined with the "substantial chance" language in that footnote, further alter the meaning of "probable cause" as a practical matter?

3. In *Massachusetts v. Upton,*[174] a per curiam opinion reversing the state supreme court's rejection of the adequacy of an officer's affidavit recounting an informant's tip, the Court relied on the Gates totality of the circumstances analysis. In reviewing the facts excerpted from the Upton opinion below, ask yourself three questions: (1) Would the affidavit have survived the *Aguilar/Spinelli* test as originally understood? (2) What reasoning supports the Court's conclusion that the affidavit was sufficient to support a warrant? (3) Was the Court right?

The Court summarized the *Upton* facts thus:

> At noon on September 11, 1980, Lt. Beland of the Yarmouth Police Department assisted in the execution of a search warrant for a motel room reserved by one Richard Kelleher at the Snug Harbor Motel in West Yarmouth. The search produced several items of identification, including credit cards, belonging to two persons whose homes had recently been burglarized. Other items taken in the burglaries, such as jewelry, silver and gold, were not found at the motel.
>
> At 3:20 p.m. on the same day, Lt. Beland received a call from an unidentified female who told him there was "a motor home full of

---

174. 466 U.S. 727 (1984).

stolen stuff" parked behind #5 Jefferson Ave., the home of respondent George Upton and his mother. She stated that the stolen items included jewelry, silver and gold. As set out in Lt. Beland's affidavit in support of a search warrant:

> She further stated that George Upton was going to move the motor home any time now because of the fact that Ricky Kelleher's motel room was raided and that George Upton had purchased these stolen items from Ricky Kelleher. This unidentified female stated that she had seen the stolen items but refused to identify herself because "he'll kill me," referring to George Upton. I then told this unidentified female that I knew who she was, giving her the name of Lynn Alberico, who I had met on May 16, 1980, at George Upton's repair shop off Summer St., in Yarmouthport. She was identified to me by George Upton as being his girl friend, Lynn Alberico. The unidentified female admitted that she was the girl that I had named, stating that she was surprised that I knew who she was. She then told me that she'd broken up with George Upton and wanted to burn him. She also told me that she wouldn't give me her address or phone number but that she would contact me in the future, if need be.

Following the phone call, Lt. Beland went to Upton's house to verify that a motor home was parked on the property. Then, while other officers watched the premises, Lt. Beland prepared the application for a search warrant, setting out all the information noted above in an accompanying affidavit. He also attached the police reports on the two prior burglaries, along with lists of the stolen property. A magistrate issued the warrant, and a subsequent search of the motor home produced the items described by the caller and other incriminating evidence. The discovered evidence led to Upton's conviction on multiple counts of burglary, receiving stolen property, and related claims.

4. Several states have rejected the *Gates* test, preferring continued adherence to the *Aguilar–Spinelli* test. Notably, in *Commonwealth v. Upton*,[175] the state court, on remand from the Supreme Court decision in note 3 above, summarized its reasoning:

> We conclude that art. 14 provides more substantive protection to criminal defendants than does the Fourth Amendment in the determination of probable cause. We reject the "totality of the circumstances" test now espoused by a majority of the United States Supreme Court. That standard is flexible, but is also "unacceptably shapeless and permissive." The Federal test lacks the precision that we believe can and should be articulated in stating a test for determining probable cause. The "totality of the circumstances" test is used in deciding several constitutional questions, but it has been applied where no more definite, universal standard could reasonably be developed.

---

175.   476 N.E.2d 548 (Mass. 1985).

The test we adopt has been followed successfully by the police in this Commonwealth for approximately twenty years. It is a test that aids lay people, such as the police and certain magistrates, in a way that will continue to encourage more careful police work and thus will tend to reduce the number of unreasonable searches conducted in violation of art. 14. We reject the argument that the higher standard will cause police to avoid seeking search warrants. We have no sense, and certainly we have no factual support for the proposition, that in recent years police in this Commonwealth have risked conducting warrantless searches because of the unreasonable strictures of the *Aguilar–Spinelli* test.

We also do not believe that the *Aguilar-Spinelli* test has interfered or will interfere with the deference that a reviewing court should show to the issuing magistrate's determination. "Once a magistrate has determined that he has information before him that he can reasonably say has been obtained in a reliable way by a credible person, he has ample room to use his common sense and to apply a practical nontechnical conception of probable cause." *Illinois v. Gates* (Brennan, J., dissenting).

The New Mexico Supreme Court in *State v. Cordova*[176] added this:

We simply do not believe this tradition [of *Aguilar–Spinelli*] to be one of unthinking rigidity or overly technical application of the [relevant] principles.... Moreover, we believe these principles to be firmly rooted in the fundamental precepts of the constitutional requirement that no warrant issue without a written showing of probable cause before a detached and neutral magistrate. We are convinced that our rules, while providing a flexible, common sense framework, also provide structure for the inquiry into whether probable cause has been demonstrated. The fact that "non-lawyers" are involved in drafting applications for search warrants underscores rather than obviates the need for such structure.

5. Proving probable cause can be a problem when police officers submit search warrant applications based only on standard form affidavits—or standard form criminal complaints, in the case of arrest warrant applications. The Court has indicated that a form criminal complaint, into which the prospective arrestee's name is inserted, does not support a finding of probable cause for purposes of an arrest warrant, because it sets forth neither the source of the complainant's knowledge nor individualized facts about the arrestee's conduct. In such a situation, said the Court in *Giordenello v. United States*,[177] a magistrate cannot "assess independently the probability that the [arrestee] committed the crime charged."

There are indications that police continue to obtain warrants based on standard forms, despite the Court's decision in *Giordenello*. In the 2001

---

176. 784 P.2d 30 (N.M. 1989).

177. 357 U.S. 480, 486 (1958).

Term, the Court examined a certiorari petition in *Overton v. Ohio*,[178] a case alleging that Ohio police used a form criminal complaint, with only the name and address of the arrestee inserted, in order to obtain warrant for Overton's arrest. The arrest led to the discovery of drugs, which the prosecution used to prove its case against Overton. After the trial court denied her motion to suppress the drugs, she was convicted and appealed on the ground that the arrest warrant was not based on probable cause. The Ohio appellate courts gave her no relief. The United States Supreme Court denied her petition for writ of certiorari, but in an unusual written statement, Justice Breyer, joined by Justices Stevens, O'Connor, and Souter, stated that the Court should have summarily reversed Overton's conviction:

> The probable-cause determination must be made by a neutral magistrate in order to insure that the deliberate, impartial judgment of a judicial officer will be interposed between the citizen and the police, to assess the weight and credibility of the information which the complaining officer adduces as probable cause.

> As far as the record before us reveals, the only evidence in this case offered to the Magistrate to show "probable cause" for issuing the warrant consisted of a "complaint" presented to the Magistrate, signed by Detective Andre Woodson. That complaint sets forth Overton's name, the date of the offense, the name of the offense ("permitting drug abuse"), and the statutory reference. It further reads:

>> "[T]he defendant, being the owner, lessee, or occupant of certain premises, did knowingly permit such premises to be used for the commission of a felony drug abuse offense, to-wit: **Desarie Overton** being the lessee, owner, or occupant of **620 Belmont, Toledo, Ohio 43607**, knowingly permitted Cocaine, a Schedule Two controlled substance to be sold and possessed by the occupants, there, both being in violation of the Ohio Revised Code, a felony drug abuse offense. This offense occurred in Toledo, Lucas County, Ohio."

> This "complaint" sets forth the relevant crime in general terms, it refers to Overton, and it says she committed the crime. But nowhere does it indicate *how Detective Woodson knows, or why he believes, that Overton committed the crime.*

> This Court has previously made clear that affidavits or complaints of this kind do not provide sufficient support for the issuance of an arrest warrant.

6. We see in the next chapter that under certain circumstances, for example, certain seizures of the person less intrusive than full-blown arrests ("stops") and certain searches of the person less intrusive than full-blown searches ("frisks"), police action may be justified by "reasonable suspicion," something less than probable cause. As noted earlier, "reason-

---

178.   534 U.S. 982 (2001).

able suspicion" is estimated by many judges to establish about one-third chance of guilt. Note the importance of this conclusion: there can be "reasonable suspicion" of crime even where it is far more likely that there was no crime at all.

In determining whether "reasonable suspicion" exists, the Court also apparently now follows a totality of the circumstances weighing process, guided by concerns about an informant's credibility and reliability, similar to the approach in *Gates*. However, in *Alabama v. White*,[179] the Court noted:

> Reasonable suspicion is a less demanding standard than probable cause not only in the sense that reasonable suspicion can be established with information that is different in quantity or content than that required to establish probable cause, but also in the sense that reasonable suspicion can arise from information that is less reliable than that required to show probable cause.

We will address the meaning of "reasonable suspicion" in greater detail later. For now, however, it is useful to consider the concept in relationship to probable cause as a way of getting a better grasp on both concepts.

7. What are the two types of corroboration discussed in *Gates*? Why do they deserve different weights? In considering the role of police observations and corroboration, remember that probable cause must exist at the time of a search or seizure. Information that is "stale," that is, that establishes, for example, probable cause to believe that something was once at a location but not necessarily that it is there now will not be sufficient.

8. Is race ever relevant to the probable cause determination? What if an officer observed a white male, dressed in expensive clothes, standing outside an expensive car on a street corner, talking to six African–American teenagers in a predominantly African–American neighborhood at 2:00 a.m.? Would the white male's race be relevant to either probable cause or reasonable suspicion?

9. *Warrants and Prosecutor Ethics:* Richard Ceballos, a supervising deputy district attorney, upon the request of defense counsel, conducted an investigation that led him to conclude that evidence had been obtained by the police pursuant to a search warrant that had been based upon an affidavit containing serious misrepresentations. Ceballos recommended to his superiors that the case be dismissed, but they proceeded with the prosecution. At a subsequent suppression hearing, Ceballos testified as a witness for the defense. He later filed a lawsuit alleging that his First and Fourteenth Amendment rights had been violated by retaliation against him by his superiors for his efforts to dismiss the case, including reassigning him to a different position and courthouse and denying him a promotion.

In *Garcetti v. Ceballos*,[180] the United States Supreme Court reversed a Ninth Circuit decision that Ceballos had a cause of action, thus letting

---

179. 496 U.S. 325, 330 (1990).

180. 547 U.S. 410 (2006).

stand a district court grant of summary judgment against Ceballos. The high Court concluded that Ceballos had no constitutional free speech protection because he spoke pursuant to the duties of his official role as an employee, not his independent status as a citizen, thus being subject to discipline by his employer without violating the First and Fourteenth Amendments. A contrary rule, maintained the Court, would subject managerial discretion to routine judicial oversight, interfering with management's ability to achieve its objectives and failing to recognize the employer's need to have control over what the employer itself has commissioned or created. Furthermore, argued the Court, although exposing governmental inefficiency and misconduct is important, federal and state whistleblower protection laws, labor codes, and, for government attorneys, rules of conduct and constitutional obligation apart from the First Amendment provide ample protection.

Justices Stevens, Souter, and Breyer filed dissenting opinions, with Justices Ginsburg and Stevens joining Souter's dissent. Of particular note is Justice Breyer's view that lawyers, particularly prosecutors, are different from other public employees:

> First, the speech at issue is professional speech–the speech of a lawyer. Such speech is subject to independent regulation by canons of the profession. Those canons provide an obligation to speak in certain instances. And where that is so, the government's own interest in forbidding that speech is diminished.

> Second, the Constitution itself here imposes speech obligations upon the government's professional employee. A prosecutor has a constitutional obligation to learn of, to preserve, and to communicate with the defense about exculpatory and impeachment evidence in the government's possession.[181]

Does the majority or Justice Breyer have the better of the argument here?

PROBLEM 2–29

Reprinted below is the officer's affidavit supporting the request for a search warrant in *Spinelli*. After reviewing this affidavit, ask yourself these questions: (1) Does the affidavit establish probable cause (the Court concluded "no") as now defined? (2) If not, does the affidavit establish reasonable suspicion? (3) Is *Gates* a stronger or weaker case than *Spinelli* for probable cause? reasonable suspicion? Why?

AFFIDAVIT IN SUPPORT OF SEARCH WARRANT

I, Robert L. Bender, being duly sworn, depose and say that I am a Special Agent of the Federal Bureau of Investigation, and as such am authorized to make searches and seizures.

That on August 6, 1965, at approximately 11:44 a.m., William Spinelli was observed by an Agent of the Federal Bureau of Investiga-

---

181.   *Id*. at 446–49 (Breyer, J., dissenting).

tion driving a 1964 Ford convertible, Missouri license HC3B649, onto the Eastern approach of the Veterans Bridge leading from East St. Louis, Illinois, to St. Louis, Missouri.

That on August 11, 1965, at approximately 11:16 a.m., William Spinelli was observed by an Agent of the Federal Bureau of Investigation driving a 1964 Ford convertible Missouri license HC3B649, onto the Eastern approach of the Eads Bridge leading from East St. Louis, Illinois, to St. Louis, Missouri.

Further, at approximately 11:18 a.m. on August 11, 1965, I observed William Spinelli driving the aforesaid Ford convertible from the Western approach of the Eads Bridge into St. Louis, Missouri.

Further, at approximately 4:40 p.m. on August 11, 1965, I observed the aforesaid Ford convertible, bearing Missouri license HC3B649, parked in a parking lot used by residents of The Chieftain Manor Apartments, approximately one block east of 1108 Indian Circle Drive.

On August 12, 1965, at approximately 12:07 p.m., William Spinelli was observed by an Agent of the Federal Bureau of Investigation driving the aforesaid 1964 Ford convertible onto the Eastern approach of the Veterans Bridge from East St. Louis, Illinois, in the direction of St. Louis, Missouri.

Further, on August 12, 1965, at approximately 3:46 p.m., I observed William Spinelli driving the aforesaid 1964 Ford convertible onto the parking lot used by the residents of The Chieftain Manor Apartments approximately one block east of 1108 Indian Circle Drive.

Further, on August 12, 1965, at approximately 3:49 p.m., William Spinelli was observed by an Agent of the Federal Bureau of Investigation entering the front entrance of the two-story apartment building located at 1108 Indian Circle Drive, this building being one of The Chieftan Manor Apartments.

On August 13, 1965, at approximately 11:08 a.m., William Spinelli was observed by an Agent of the Federal Bureau of Investigation driving the aforesaid Ford convertible onto the Eastern approach of the Eads Bridge from East St. Louis, Illinois, heading towards St. Louis, Missouri.

Further, on August 13, 1965, at approximately 11:11 a.m., I observed William Spinelli driving the aforesaid Ford convertible from the Western approach of the Eads Bridge into St. Louis, Missouri.

Further, on August 13, 1965, at approximately 3:45 p.m. I observed William Spinelli driving the aforesaid 1964 Ford convertible onto the parking area used by residents of The Chieftain Manor Apartments, said parking area being approximately one block from 1108 Indian Circle Drive.

Further, on August 13, 1965, at approximately 3:55 p.m., William Spinelli was observed by an Agent of the Federal Bureau of Investigation entering the corner apartment located on the second floor in the southwest corner, known as Apartment F, of the two story apartment building known and numbered as 1108 Indian Circle Drive.

On August 16, 1965, at approximately 3:22 p.m., I observed William Spinelli driving the aforesaid Ford convertible onto the parking lot used by the residents of The Chieftain Manor Apartments approximately one block east of 1108 Indian Circle Drive.

Further, an Agent of the F.B.I. observed William Spinelli alight from the aforesaid Ford convertible and walk toward the apartment building located at 1108 Indian Circle Drive.

The records of the Southwestern Bell Telephone Company reflect that there are two telephones located in the southwest corner apartment on the second floor of the apartment building located at 1108 Indian Circle Drive under the name of Grace P. Hagen. The numbers listed in the Southwestern Bell Telephone Company records for the aforesaid telephones are Wydown 4–0029 and Wydown 4–0136.

William Spinelli is known to this affiant and to federal law enforcement agents and local law enforcement agents as a bookmaker, an associate of bookmakers, a gambler, and an associate of gamblers.

The Federal Bureau of Investigation has been informed by a confidential reliable informant that William Spinelli is operating a handbook and accepting wagers and disseminating wagering information by means of the telephones which have been assigned the numbers Wydown 4–0029 and WY down 4–0136.

_____/s/
Robert L. Bender
Special Agent
Federal Bureau of Investigation.

Subscribed and sworn to before me this 18th day of August, 1965, at St. Louis, Missouri.

_____/s/
William R. O'Toole.

PROBLEM 2–30

Officer Wayne Kalker, a District of Columbia police officer with two years' experience, was patrolling in uniform in a marked police cruiser in Northwest Washington. Shortly after midnight, he heard a radio report, based on an anonymous telephone tip, about an individual said to be selling drugs at the corner of 17th and Euclid Streets, N.W. The report described the individual as a black male, approximately 5'6″ in height, wearing blue jeans and a white shirt with dark writing on the front. Officer Kalker testified at a later suppression hearing that he was already in the immediate vicinity when he heard the report. He saw about 50 people in the area, but he quickly ruled out all but two suspects. He asked for a re-broadcast over police radio of the description, and, based on the re-broadcast, eliminated one of the two remaining suspects because he was 6'2" tall, wearing a white shirt and white shorts.

Officer Kalker approached the remaining suspect, Jerrold Towne, at about 12:10 a.m., and called out "Sir!" Towne, testified the officer later, looked back, saw the officer, then walked away at a crisp pace. The officer called out twice more, but Towne continued briskly walking. Officer Kalker stopped Towne, explained that he fit the description of someone alleged to be selling drugs, and asked for identification. Towne said he had none. Officer Kalker then noticed an object, about four inches long, that "just extruded from his pocket a little bit." The officer asked Towne what the object was, but receiving no reply pulled it from Towne's pocket. The object turned out to be a film canister. Kalker later testified that in 50 or 60 of the 70 drug arrests in which he had participated, drugs had been discovered in film canisters. Kalker also stated that at one point he thought the object was a knife, because in the past he had discovered knives in lipstick containers, which this object might have been. After pulling the object from Towne's pocket, Kalker opened it and extracted four tin-foil packets which later proved to contain PCP and marijuana. He then arrested Towne. Kalker noted in his police report that Towne was wearing maroon pants, although the report did not say whether they were long or short. No mention was made of writing on Towne's shirt.

Towne is your client, and in your initial interview of him, he said he was 5'8" to 5'9" tall. He told you that on the night of the arrest he was wearing a tan shirt with no writing on it and blue shorts. The police have been unable to locate Towne's booking photo, so you cannot confirm your client's recollection.

Question: You are about to meet with Towne to counsel him about his options. Among the possibilities is filing a motion to suppress the drugs and tin packets. In gauging what you will counsel Towne concerning the likely success of such a motion, you must consider the following questions:

(1) If Kalker is telling the truth, what, as a matter of law, are your chances of success in a suppression motion arguing lack of probable cause for the search and for any arrest that may have preceded the search?

(2) What questions will you ask Kalker on cross examination in the suppression hearing, and how likely, and in what way, are you to succeed in damaging his credibility? What will your theory be about the "true" facts, and how likely are you to prevail under this "true" set of affairs? If you need additional information, specify what that information is and how you will get it.

(3) If there was no probable cause, did the officer at least have "reasonable suspicion"—a standard lower than probable cause? At what point? Why?

PROBLEM 2–31

At about 3:45 p.m. on Saturday, April 28, the dispatcher for the Johnson County Sheriff's office at Buffalo received a telephone call from an anonymous informant who claimed knowledge of illegal drug activity. The informant then told the dispatcher that Don Toeg, John Toeg's brother, had "a lot of acid" and that Don and John were going to Sheridan to sell it. John had come from Colorado to visit his brother Don, and John had brought the LSD to Wyoming with him. The informant advised the dispatcher that the Toeg brothers planned to transport the drugs in Don's silver Volvo automobile, bearing Colorado license UKB 606. The informant stated that the vehicle was parked at 178 Western Avenue, in Buffalo, which was Don's address. Additionally, the informant told the dispatcher that the Toeg brothers were going along with others; they were getting ready to leave; and they would be leaving soon. Finally, the informant said, "If you don't believe me, ask Detective Johnson. I'm the guy who broke the Ex–X and Ramsey cases." "Ex–X" was a major drug case that Detective Johnson had broken based on an accurate anonymous tip. The same tipster gave bad information on the Ramsey case, but Johnson managed to bust Ramsey anyway based on independent investigation. Both cases had been kept hush and resulted in guilty pleas, so information about the tips never made it to the press.

The dispatcher then contacted an officer of the Buffalo Police Department and relayed the tip to him. About 4:00 p.m., the officer went to Don Toeg's house at 178 Western Avenue to attempt to verify the information the anonymous informant had furnished. The officer saw a Volvo bearing Colorado license plate UKB 606 parked in the driveway of Don Toeg's residence with the passenger door open. The make, license number, and location all matched the information on the tip. The officer then left that neighborhood and drove to the north exit on the route from Buffalo leading to Sheridan. In about 20 minutes, the officer saw the same silver Volvo traveling north on Highway 87 toward the interstate. He could see at least four people in the Volvo. At the time he saw the car with the people in it, the officer was at a pay phone talking to an agent of the drug task force. The agent then contacted Kevin Jordan, supervisor of the Northeast Drug Enforcement Team, at about 4:15 p.m., and reported the information that he had received from the Buffalo police officer. The information given to Jordan consisted of the substance of what the informant had told the dispatcher, including a description of the vehicle, together with the observations of the Buffalo police officer.

Agent Jordan then left Sheridan toward Buffalo and, after five miles, saw the Volvo, followed it, and stopped it. Don Toeg was the driver, but John Toeg and his wife, Laura Toeg, were also in the car. Don Toeg produced a suspended license, and he was quickly arrested for driving without a valid license. A search of the car revealed a large number of illegal weapons in the trunk but no drugs. All three were arrested for illegal possession of firearms.

Question: Assume that the Wyoming courts have interpreted their state constitution to permit vehicle stops only based on probable cause, not reasonable suspicion. Was there probable cause for the stop of the car? The search of the trunk? The arrest of the two passengers? If a stop can be based on reasonable suspicion, was the stop here justified? Any of the officer's subsequent conduct?

PROBLEM 2–32

Officer Tepel testified at a suppression hearing that on October 7, he was in a patrol car at 8 p.m. near Figueroa and 65th Streets in Los Angeles, California, when he noticed an odor similar to ether. Ether is one of many chemical ingredients required to manufacture PCP and related drugs. The officer conceded, however, that ether has many legitimate uses around the home—as a common solvent and a helpful aid in starting engines, for example. Nevertheless, the officer exited his car and followed the odor toward 6507 South Figueroa Street, approximately 35 yards from the patrol car. The odor became increasingly strong as he approached the house. Believing that the odor was emanating from a laboratory, he summoned the fire department, police chemists, and backup units.

While awaiting their arrival, Officer Tepel walked up an outside stairway to the house and tried to open a wrought iron gate that was five feet in front of the front door. The gate was locked, but the front door was open. From outside the gate, he saw bottles, jars, and different types of equipment "consistent with a PCP lab," although not necessarily unique to them; indeed, each of the items that he observed had potential perfectly legal uses.

When the backup units arrived, Officer Tepel and his fellow officers approached the wrought iron gate when John Etson appeared at the front door. The officers ordered him to open the gate, which he did. They entered the home and found a PCP lab.

QUESTIONS

1. Assume you represent Etson in a suppression motion and the prosecution has just completed the above direct examination of Officer Tepel. What questions will you ask on cross, and why?

2. What legal arguments in support of the suppression motion did you outline in preparation for the suppression hearing?

PROBLEM 2–33

In a small university town, with a total population (counting students) of about 5,000 persons, a college sophomore was raped. She promptly reported the crime, and semen was found in her vagina. She had struggled violently, repeatedly scratching her attacker, and blood other than hers was found under her fingernails. Her only description of her attacker was a white male between ages 18 and 25.

The officers then approached every white male in the town, asking each to consent to a DNA blood test to determine whether his DNA matched that of the assailant. If an individual agreed, blood was taken and a DNA test done. If not, investigation would immediately focus on that person. Moreover, each white male was told that he had the right to refuse, but if he did so, he would become a primary focus of investigation.

Question: Should a person's refusal to submit to such a blood test be a permissible ground for police focusing their investigation on that person? A permissible factor in the probable cause determination? Decisive in that determination? Would any of your answers change if the person fled immediately upon hearing the request? We will later study consent to search as a substitute for either a warrant or probable cause. For now, however, using your common-sense understanding of consent, are the officers' statements to the men they stopped relevant factors in the consent determination? Decisive? Would you want any further information and, if so, what? Should the search warrant in the Boson case in Chapter 1 have been issued? What is the likely success at a suppression hearing? Would your answer differ if there had not been a photo identification before submitting the warrant affidavit? It may be relevant to your analysis that deliberate lies or information obtained in reckless disregard for its truth must be ignored in the probable cause analysis, a rule we will address in greater depth in the next chapter.

4. THE PROBLEM WITH INFORMANTS, REVISITED: INFORMANTS AND WRONGFUL CONVICTIONS

There have been a significant number of cases, some of them infamous, in which innocent persons have been wrongfully convicted based primarily upon the testimony of lying or mistaken informants. Even where conviction did not result, innocent persons suffered the humiliation of wrongful arrest and sometimes extensive pre-trial incarceration until they were able to demonstrate their innocence at trial.

Informants may lie to receive a monetary benefit for providing information or to receive leniency or immunity in their own cases. Sloppy police work can inadvertently feed information to informants that enables them to lie convincingly or can fail to uncover the lies. Prosecutors may similarly mishandle informants. Reliance on jailhouse informants—inmates who snitch on others to gain privilege while in custody or to lessen their sentences—can be especially troubling. These dangers of wrongful prosecution and convictions require, in the view of many commentators, caution at the earliest stages of the criminal process (at the time of an arrest, search, or seizure), as well as at trial, when relying on tipsters. Numerous proposals have been made to promote such caution, among them a group of reforms suggested by Professor Clifford Zimmerman.[182] Zimmerman recommends that all jurisdictions enact the following changes in procedure:

---

182.   This discussion of informants and wrongful convictions draws heavily on Clifford Zimmerman, *Back From the Courthouse: Corrective Measures to Address the Role of Infor-*

1. There should be a flat bar on monetary or other compensation for being a tipster. Charging and sentencing concessions, such as dropped or reduced charges, should therefore be inadmissible.

2. There should be a rebuttable presumption that any given informant is unreliable, and the prosecution should bear a high burden of showing that an informant is trustworthy in a particular case. Because warrants are issued ex parte, "a new ombudsman-like position should be created to represent the interests of society in ferreting out unreliable informants. Without such a position, the Court must fulfill this role and view the evidence presented accordingly." The Court or ombudsman should consider numerous factors, including the circumstance under which the witness became an informant; the informant's motivations, past informant history, past criminal history, and the consistency, detail, and accuracy of prior informant statements.

3. If informant testimony is allowed, it should be permitted at trial only if corroborative, non-informant-based evidence is offered so that any resulting conviction does not stem solely from the informant's testimony. Furthermore, the Court must instruct the jury about the historic unreliability of informant testimony, noting it has led to wrongful convictions in the past, and the prosecutor should be required to present all reliability information necessary for jurors fairly to evaluate the witness. Defense counsel must have wide latitude to question the informant witness by exploring his reliability.

4. The court system must abandon the assumption of risk and informant-handler distancing doctrines; all informants must rebuttably be presumed to be government agents. Lying informants should face perjury prosecutions, and police and prosecutors should be punished by dismissal of cases using unreliable informants. Additionally, the harmless error rule should be abandoned in informant cases.

5. Ethical guidelines should be established for handling informants, strict record keeping requirements should be imposed, and national registries of tainted informers, including a blacklist of perjurers, should be widely accessible, with penalties created for violations of any of these requirements.

Do you agree with Professor Zimmerman's proposed reforms, or do they go too far? How would you handle the problem of perjurious or mistaken informers? Should gatekeeping rules to screen out bad informants be as strict at the warrant stage as at the trial stage?

Perhaps the facts of a recent United States Supreme Court case, *Kaupp v. Texas*,[183] will help in answering these questions. In *Kaupp*, after police discovered that a missing 14–year–old girl had been having a sexual relationship with her 19–year–old half brother, they questioned her brother

---

mants in *Wrongful Convictions*, in Wrongly Convicted: Perspective on Failed Justice 199 (Saundra D. Westerrelt and John A. Humphrey, eds., 2001); Robert M. Bloom, Ratting: The Use and Abuse of Informants In the American Justice System (2002).

183. 538 U.S. 626 (2003).

at police headquarters. The brother had been in the company of then 17–year–old Kaupp, so he too was brought to headquarters for questioning. Kaupp was cooperative and was allowed to leave. But the brother thrice failed a polygraph examination and eventually confessed to stabbing his half-sister, then placing her body in a drainage ditch. He implicated Kaupp in the crime.

The detectives failed to obtain a "pocket warrant" but brought Kaupp in for further questioning anyway. The Supreme Court later explained the detectives' efforts this way:

> The detectives applied to the district attorney's office for a "pocket warrant," which they described as authority to take Kaupp into custody for questioning.... The detectives did not seek a conventional arrest warrant, as they did not believe they had probable cause for Kaupp's arrest.... As the trial court later explained, the detectives had no evidence or motive to corroborate the brother's allegations of Kaupp's involvement ... ; the brother had previously failed three polygraph examinations, while, only two days earlier, Kaupp had voluntarily taken and passed one, in which he denied his involvement....[184]

Kaupp, once confronted with the brother's confession, admitted having some part in the crime and was thus indicted, convicted, and eventually sentenced to 55 years' imprisonment. On appeal, the issue that ultimately made it to the Court was whether Kaupp's admissions were the fruit of an arrest without probable cause, an issue discussed later in this book. The important point for now is that neither the detectives nor the state on appeal challenged Kaupp's claim that he had been brought to the station without probable cause. (The state did challenge whether probable cause was required, however, arguing that Kaupp was not "arrested"; alternatively, maintained the state, Kaupp fit within an exception to the exclusionary rule.) Whether these facts established probable cause for an arrest was thus not before the Court, and any statements on that subject would unquestionably be *dicta*. Nevertheless, the "pocket warrants" quote from the Court's opinion excerpted above can arguably be interpreted as expressing the Court's approval of the detectives' own judgment that they in fact lacked probable cause.

Consider: If this interpretation is right, how broadly should that *dicta* be read? Should an uncorroborated statement by a suspect who implicates another in the crime never be sufficient to establish probable cause for the arrest? Was it the polygraph results—showing lies by the informant, but truthful statements by Kaupp—that were the problem? If corroboration is needed, what sort of corroboration and how much? Would evidence of Kaupp's motive for the killing be sufficient, or would more direct evidence of Kaupp's involvement be necessary? When, if ever, would permitting ready use of uncorroborated statements by potential co-defendants create an unacceptable risk of convicting the innocent? Was there such a risk for

---

184.   *Id.* at 628 n. 1.

Kaupp? Could that fear have been relevant to the Court's ultimate conclusions?

PROBLEM 2–34

A woman in a restaurant overhears three "Arabic-looking young Muslim men" (these are her words) in a restaurant. The woman hears one of the men say, "If they thought September 11 was horrible, wait until they see September 13th." September 13, in the early morning, was the date when the woman overheard this conversation. She calls the police, telling them her name and address and recounting what she has heard. The police arrive as a van with the three men identified by the caller are leaving the restaurant. The police stop the van, based solely on this woman's tip, and question the three men for 17 hours, ultimately releasing them.

Question: As a matter of sound policy, should the police have so acted? What about as a matter of constitutional law? Would you want the police to obtain any of the additional information noted in Professor Zimmerman's reliability factors and, if so, what information and why?

PROBLEM 2–35

To fight terrorism, the President of the United States proposes urging every meter reader, delivery person, and neighbor to report any "suspicious activity" by local residents. Is this a wise course of action? Does it create any of the dangers about which Professor Zimmerman worries?

PROBLEM 2–36

Roland Largemouth is an inmate in the local jail. Largemouth offers to reveal certain statements made in his presence by his cellmate, Owen Roxbury, to the warden in exchange for a favorable parole recommendation. The warden agrees, Largemouth reports statements by Roxbury implicating him in a rape, and, based largely on Largemouth's testimony, Roxbury is convicted of rape. Would you, as a judge, have signed the warrant to arrest Roxbury on the rape charge? Have permitted the case to go to trial? Taken certain precautions in presenting the evidence at trial? What additional information, if any, would help you in answering these questions?

PROBLEM 2–37

Did Detective Mandelevoy have probable cause to obtain the warrant on which he based his search of Boson's apartment in Chapter 1? Did Officer Glemp have reasonable suspicion or probable cause to stop the car Boson was driving? To search the glove compartment and trunk?

PROBLEM 2–38

The Center City police have a policy of not investigating minor crimes, such as vandalism, to conserve scarce policing resources to address more serious offenses. Even if a vandalism or graffiti suspect is caught in the act, police generally recommend that the suspect, if a first offender, be granted pretrial probation, wiping his record clean as if he had never been arrested if he stays out of trouble for two years after his arrest. The only exception to these practices occur with hate crimes. If a hate crime is suspected, no matter how minor, the police will expend substantial effort on investigation. If that investigation establishes probable cause to believe that a hate crime has been committed, police will arrest the suspect, prosecute vigorously, and, upon conviction, seek the maximum sentence. The local prosecutor's office has signed onto these policies.

A hate crime is defined in this jurisdiction as follows: "Any crime committed by reason of the actual or perceived race, color, religion, national origin or sexual orientation of another individual or group of individuals." The state's courts have interpreted this statute to require proof that a crime was committed because of dislike of, resentment toward, hatred of, or desire to hurt or humiliate any individual because of his membership in a particular racial, ethnic, or other listed group. It is *not* sufficient under this language simply to prove that an offender selected his victim because the offender believed that members of the victim's racial or other specified group are "easy marks," that is, unlikely to resist or to prosecute. Graffiti or vandalism ordinarily has a maximum penalty of three months in a county jail, but, if the act of graffiti or vandalism meets the definition of a hate crime, the maximum sentence is two years in state prison.

Recently, Rabbi Moshe Aaron awoke to find a swastika painted on the door to his home. Rabbi Aaron immediately called the police. Rabbi Aaron explained that, the day before this incident, he saw a young man named Timothy Ennis, whom the rabbi knew from the neighborhood, wearing a swastika armband and walking by the rabbi's synagogue. The rabbi yelled, "Get off our property Aryan scum!" Timothy replied, "Never talk to your betters that way. You'll regret this, I promise" and walked away. The next day, the rabbi found the swastika on his door.

The police used an undercover agent the next day to tail Ennis to a Young Americans' Nazi Party membership rally, where the police saw Ennis sign up for membership in the Party. Additionally, several Jewish neighbors of Ennis reported that he had on several occasions hurled anti-Semitic epithets at them. But Ennis had no criminal record, not even of arrests. Finally, an 82–year–old member of the synagogue said that she saw from her apartment window (which is across the street from the rabbi's home) Ennis spray-painting the swastika on the rabbi's door about 5 a.m. on the morning of the incident.

Question: Do the police have probable cause to arrest Ennis for a hate crime or only for ordinary graffiti-writing? If the latter, should the police follow their usual pretrial probation policy or not? What sorts of additional information or investigation would you like before making your decision? Are there constitutional provisions that are relevant in addition to the Fourth Amendment?

C. SUPPRESSION MOTIONS

1. DEFINITION AND MECHANICS

A suppression motion is a written request, filed pretrial, that unconstitutionally obtained evidence be excluded (thus, the "exclusionary rule") from trial, never to be heard or seen by the jury. Seized physical evidence (e.g., drugs, money, stolen property, blood), the results of a photo identification or a lineup, and confessions are among the many types of evidence that can be suppressed. Moreover, evidence that is the "fruit" of a constitutional violation may often be suppressed. For example, if a murder suspect was arrested without probable cause, subsequently confessed, and, in that confession, identified the location of his victim's body, which was later dug up by the police, both the confession and the location and appearance of the body (as well as any laboratory tests done using samples taken from the body) might be suppressed as the "fruit" of the illegal arrest, subject to certain well-recognized exceptions to be studied later.

The prosecutor or defense lawyer preparing for a motion to suppress must identify which party has the burden of proof (the prevailing practice is to allocate the burdens of "production" and "persuasion" to the same party, so we simply use the more inclusive term "burden of proof"). Most burden of proof issues are left to the discretion of the state courts or the federal circuit courts of appeal. These courts hold generally that the defense has the burden of proof for searches and seizures performed pursuant to warrant, while the prosecution has the burden of proof for warrantless searches.[185] Some jurisdictions depart from the general rule, however. A few place the burden of proof on the prosecution for all searches or seizures, whether warrantless or not, and a few place burdens of proof primarily on the defendant. Despite a few differences, most courts are in agreement that the burden of proof should be on the defense for the following matters: whether the defendant has standing, whether the government engaged in a search or seizure, whether there was government action, and whether the evidence sought to be suppressed is the fruit of the poisonous tree. The prosecution ordinarily has the burden of proving exceptions to the fruit of the poisonous tree doctrine—for example, that there was an independent source for evidence or that it inevitably would have been discovered even without the illegal search.

The Supreme Court has spoken about burdens in a few situations. It held in *Bumper v. North Carolina*[186] that the prosecution has the burden of proving that consent was freely and voluntarily given in cases involving

---

185. For more detailed background on burdens and standards of proof in suppression hearings, *see* WAYNE R. LaFAVE, SEARCH AND SEIZURE: A TREATISE ON THE FOURTH AMENDMENT § 11.2(b) (2004).

186. 391 U.S. 543 (1968).

warrantless searches that the government claims were consensual. Conversely, in *Franks v. Delaware,*[187] the Court held that the defense has the burden of proving that a search or arrest warrant affidavit contains deliberate falsehoods or falsehoods in reckless disregard of the truth.

Regardless of who holds the burden of proof, it is ordinarily satisfied by a preponderance of the evidence, although some courts require prosecutors to meet the clear and convincing standard for consent searches or claims of voluntary abandonment. This higher standard is also required in motions predicated on the Sixth Amendment right to counsel (which this book addresses in a later chapter), in which the government attempts to salvage in-court identification as based upon independent observations of the suspect and not upon observations made during an uncounseled lineup that violated the Sixth Amendment.[188]

You may wonder how defendants can meet their burdens of proof, since they often are the only witnesses to the events at issue aside from law enforcement officers. The fact is that many defendants cannot win their suppression motions unless they testify. Obviously, though, their testimony might incriminate them. For example, defendants attempting to establish standing often must admit to ownership of illegal substances or privacy interests in places in which contraband was found. In order to facilitate factfinding at the suppression motion stage, the Court has set forth a rule barring the government from using incriminating suppression hearing testimony as substantive evidence in its case in chief at trial.[189] However, the Court appears to permit the government to use suppression hearing testimony in order to impeach defendants who take the stand at trial.[190] We will return to the issue of impeachment in another chapter.

Before we can worry about suppression hearing and trial testimony and impeachment, however, the defense must usually first draft a suppression motion. In the following excerpt from his Fourth Amendment treatise,[191] Professor Wayne LaFave offers helpful strategic and stylistic advice for drafting suppression motions:

> The motion, which in many jurisdictions must be made in writing, must of course identify the items which the defendant seeks to suppress. From the defense perspective, it might be desirable to limit the motion to such identification and a generalized claim that those items are the fruit of a Fourth Amendment violation. As one commentator has noted:
>
> > Even more than other pretrial motions . . . , motions to suppress evidence should be carefully drafted so as not to disclose the factual theories of the defense that underlie the motion. Police are

---

187.   438 U.S. 154 (1978).

188.   United States v. Wade, 388 U.S. 218 (1967).

189.   *See* Simmons v. United States, 390 U.S. 377 (1968) (barring such use where defendant testifies in order to establish standing).

190.   *See* United States v. Havens, 446 U.S. 620 (1980).

191.   LaFave, TREATISE, *supra* note 185, at § 11.2(a).

deeply interested in sustaining their arrests, searches, and confessions and will frequently conform their testimony to fit whatever theories validate their conduct. They should be educated as little as possible in advance.

However, it is unlikely that an unelaborated motion will pass muster.

For one thing, it is commonly required that the motion "must specify with particularity the grounds upon which it is based." The requirement is one of "specificity in the statement of defendant's legal theory," and may be met, for example, by alleging that the evidence in question was obtained from the defendant incident to an arrest which was not made upon probable cause. If there are several grounds upon which the objection might be based, they should all be enumerated, for the prevailing rule is that the failure to assert a particular ground operates as a waiver of the right to challenge the admissibility of the evidence on that ground. Illustrative is *United States v. Neumann*, holding that a motion to suppress which only alleged that a search warrant did not issue on probable cause did not preserve questions concerning the manner of execution of that warrant.

The nature and purpose of this requirement that the grounds for suppression must be particularized are helpfully elaborated in *State v. Johnson*. After noting that the attorneys for defendants Johnson and Imel "filed 'shot-gun' motions to suppress" which "contained only conclusory language—'illegal arrest,' 'violation of constitutional rights,' etc.," and "failed to specify with any particularity exactly why the arrests and resulting searches were supposedly invalid," the court commented:

> Neither the case law nor the statute defines the minimum specificity required in such motions. However, illuminating analogies are available. First, a motion to suppress can be compared to a pleading. Second, a motion to suppress can be compared to an oral objection to the admissibility of evidence made during the course of a trial. . . .
>
> A motion to suppress is, in effect, a pleading to the extent that it frames the issues to be determined in a pretrial hearing on the motion. The fundamental role of a pleading is to give an opposing party notice of the pleader's position concerning the facts and law so that the opposing party can begin to prepare his defense. A pleading thus both defines and limits the areas of consideration at a trial or other evidentiary hearing. Furthermore, the pleading assists the court in the conduct of the trial, for example, by enabling the court to determine the relevance of offered evidence. . . .
>
> We do not suggest that the analogy between a motion to suppress and a pleading is a perfect one. Nor do we intend that the measure of specificity used to test a pleading would be appropriate to also measure a motion to suppress. The principal difference, we

believe, is that when motions to suppress are filed, defendants possibly are not and in some instances cannot be aware of all the facts. With this in mind, we conclude that a motion to suppress should be as reasonably specific as possible under the circumstances in order to give the state as much notice as possible of the contentions it must be prepared to meet at the suppression hearing. For example, as noted above, the arguments of counsel in Johnson indicate counsel's contentions were: (1) there was no probable cause to arrest; and (2) the misdemeanor arrest was invalid because any violation was not committed in the arresting officer's presence. If these were, in fact, the contentions advanced by the motion, then the motion could have and should have so stated. . . .

Oral objections at trial must be accompanied by a reasonably definite statement of the grounds upon which they are made. . . . Examples of oral objections made during the course of trial that have been held not sufficiently definite are: "I object"; the evidence is "inadmissible"; or the evidence is "illegal." . . .

At least as much specificity should be required in a pretrial objection to the admissibility of evidence, i.e., a motion to suppress, as is required in an oral objection made during the course of a trial. In fact, even more specificity could reasonably be required because the pretrial objection can be researched and written under relatively calm circumstances, as distinguished from an extemporaneous objection made in the heat of trial. We merely point out, however, that broadly worded and vague objections are inappropriate in either context.

In some jurisdictions even more is required; the defendant must set out his grounds and in addition the facts which support them. Sometimes, for example, it is necessary that the motion itself "state facts showing wherein the search and seizure were unlawful." Or, it may be required that the motion be accompanied by "an affidavit or affidavits on behalf of the defendant setting forth all facts within his knowledge upon which he intends to rely in support of the motion." It has been held that this requirement is constitutional, which perhaps it is so long as the holding in *Simmons v. United States*—that testimony given by the defendant at the hearing on his motion is not admissible against him at trial on the question of guilt or innocence—is extended to such affidavits. But whether it is sound as a matter of policy to call upon the defendant to set out facts showing the Fourth Amendment violation is certainly not beyond debate. This question is much like that of whether it is wise to impose upon the defendant the initial burden of going forward with the evidence at the suppression hearing, discussed below.

Some indication of what will and will not suffice in terms of factual allegations is provided by *People v. Mendoza*, actually involving three separate appeals involving this question. The court there concluded "that the sufficiency of defendant's factual allegations should be evaluated by (1) the face of the pleadings, (2) assessed in conjunction with the context of the motion, and (3) defendant's access to information." As for the first of these, the court in *Mendoza* noted the extremes "are easy to identify": a defendant's assertion that while he was waiting for a bus at a particular place and time an officer approached, said he didn't like the defendant, and then "reached into my jacket pocket and removed a one-inch vial of cocaine" is a sufficient factual allegation; while "my Fourth Amendment rights were violated" is an insufficient legal conclusion. "More problematic," the court noted, "are those pleadings framed in terms of mixed issues of law and fact," but even here it is necessary that sufficient facts be set out so that the suppression court can determine whether a hearing is necessary. Thus, a defendant's claim that the police found marijuana "within the 'curtilage'" of defendant's home is insufficient, while a claim "the marijuana was growing 25 feet from my front door and was surrounded by a white picket fence" passes muster.

As for the second point in *Mendoza*, that defendant's allegations must be considered in context, the basic point is that certain fact assertions may or may not carry the day, depending upon what the papers in the case earlier filed by the prosecution indicate is the nature of the issue on the motion to suppress. As an example, the court considered how the context could affect the sufficiency of an allegation by the defendant that he was "merely standing on the street doing nothing wrong" when the police approached and searched him. This allegation will suffice when the case is one in which the police claim they were frisking defendant because of his supposedly "suspicious" or "furtive" behavior, but "the identical pleading" would be inadequate when the police claim this was a "buy-and-bust" situation in which a backup officer was arresting the defendant because of his recent sale of drugs to an undercover agent. Finally, the third point in *Mendoza* is simply this: "the degree to which the pleadings may reasonably be expected to be precise" will depend upon the amount of "information available to the defendant."

2. DRAFTING EXERCISE

If your teacher instructs you, draft a motion to suppress based on the facts presented in the problem below. Following the problem, there is a sample motion to suppress that you may use as a form.

PROBLEM 2–39

In two public housing projects in Chicago, in just four days, there were more than thirty shooting incidents, causing eight deaths, all from gang warfare. Attempts at deterring gangs had failed, so the projects hired private security guards. Despite that, crews sent to repair vacant apartments used by the gangs were driven off by them.

In response to these and similar events in public housing projects, the president announced a new anti-gang policy, articulated by the Secretary of Housing and Urban Development (HUD), on April 16. The policy included installing metal detectors in the lobbies; conducting weapons sweeps of post boxes, mail boxes, stairwells, air vents, and electrical outlets; doing similar sweeps of vacant units; and permitting exigent circumstances frisks and searches of apartments. Additionally, consent to search was required to be secured from tenants as a condition of obtaining or renewing a lease. This last term was analogized by HUD to typical lease terms granting consent to search for maintenance problems. However, the consent to search here required a majority of the project's current residents to vote for the new lease consent provision, which they did.

According to HUD's Secretary, similar sweeps had been "effective" elsewhere at reducing the number of weapons in the projects. For example, one "sweep" of vacant units and common areas had recovered tens of rifles, and close to 40 automatic weapons and revolvers. While thousands of tenants signed a petition supporting the sweeps and other searches authorized by the new HUD regulations, hundreds of other tenants sought an injunction to prevent what they viewed as outrageous violations of their privacy.

On October 30, police received an anonymous phone call saying the following:

> Apartment 11 G, Co-op Projects, small back bedroom, will be receiving five plugs and a large shipment of cocaine on November 8th. The supplier will confirm this by dropping a note in 11G's mail box saying "Christmas is coming early this year. Your toys will arrive tomorrow, signed Toys–R–Us," on November 7th, by 8 a.m. I know this is so because I buy coke from 11G, and he tried to convince me to buy some plugs too. You know you can trust me 'cause I'm the guy who gave you the tips on Tony G. and Philco.

"Plugs," the police knew, was slang for plastic guns, ones that could kill but would not set off metal detectors. Tony G. and Philco were two Co-op Project drug dealers. An anonymous tip about Tony G. making a big sale at a certain location had turned out to be 100 percent correct. But the same tipster's information on Philco had proved to be wrong about the time (off by two days), although right about the location of the sale. Luckily, police surveillance independently revealed the correct time, and Philco, like Tony G., was caught in the act, captured, and pled guilty. The records were sealed, so no one but the judge, the lawyers, the police, and Tony G. and Philco knew how they had been caught.

Pursuant to the HUD policy, the police opened up 11G's mailbox at 8 a.m. on November 7, finding nothing. They waited, however, until after the 10 a.m. mail delivery, opened the box, and found word-for-word the note mentioned by the telephone informant. The police immediately went to 11G, leased by the Johnsons, knocked and announced who they were and why they were there. Fearing that plugs might be distributed throughout the building, 100 police also simultaneously searched numerous other apartments and common areas, and the approach to the Johnson's apartment was part of this sweep. Mrs. Johnson had been a tenant on a year-to-year lease for ten years. Last year, she was one of 5,000 tenants who attended the meeting to vote on HUD's proposal to make consent to search a condition of all new leases. Mrs. Johnson had voted against the proposal, but a narrow majority, 2,501 tenants, had voted in favor, so all new leases contained the consent-to-search clause, including the new lease just signed by Mrs. Johnson.

The police search included the bedroom of Mrs. Johnson's 15–year-old son, Sean. The door to Sean's room was closed with a sign on it reading, "Stay out! No adults allowed, including parents! This means you! Don't believe my mom if she tells you differently. It's my room, not hers! DANGER!!!" The police ignored the room's sign, entered, searched, and found a duffel bag containing two plugs and two large bags of cocaine. The bag had two compartments, one labeled "Johnny B." the other, "Sean Johnson." "Johnny B." was Sean's best friend, and the bag was one they jointly used each day to carry their gym clothes to school. They traded who would keep the bag each night, and this night was Sean's. One plug and one cocaine bag were found in each compartment.

The police arrested both Sean and Johnny B. Mrs. Johnson wanted to ride with Sean in the police car to the police station, but they told her there was no room in the car. She would have to get to the station on her own. Sean and Johnny B. were in separate police cars. Both teens had been fully and properly Mirandized. Neither teen said anything at all after hearing the warnings. On the drive over with Sean, one officer said to another, "Well, now that Johnny B.'s told us that Sean was the mastermind, I guess this poor kid's going to spend a lot of time behind bars. It's a shame too. His mom's kind of frail; I'm not sure she could take it. Why would a kid do something like this to his mom?"

Sean then burst into tears and said, "He's lying. He was the supplier. I just did what he said. But I don't want to say anything more. Don't talk to me about it and don't discuss it in front of me. Just leave me alone!" He sobbed quietly, and the police said nothing further. Sean's mom was quite ill, and he feared she might die, but he did not understand how the police could have known. At the station, Sean was placed alone in a room for two hours. Two new police officers showed up around midnight, re-Mirandized Sean, and questioned him again. By this time, the prosecutor was signing the complaint against Sean, who was about to be preliminarily arraigned. Tired, Sean said simply, "I did it to get money to help my mom, but Johnny B. was the supplier. Now get me a lawyer." Questioning stopped immediately.

Question: Assume you are an associate in a firm that is representing Sean. Another firm represents Johnny B. For the first cut of a suppression motion, however, both firms have agreed to draft the motion jointly because it may be possible to have all the evidence excluded. Please prepare such a joint draft of a motion to suppress the mailbox letter, the two plugs and two bags of cocaine, and Sean's statement. Do so, focusing solely on Fourth Amendment and related fruit of the poisonous tree issues. Be prepared to argue either side of the motion.

As a guide to form, a sample suppression motion follows. While this sample is based on the Fifth, not the Fourth, Amendment (the point of the exercise is for you to craft the Fourth Amendment arguments on your own), the sample is typical of the style of a suppression motion in a simple case:

SUPERIOR COURT OF THE DISTRICT OF COLUMBIA
Criminal Division—Felony Branch

UNITED STATES OF AMERICA)
)   Criminal No. 6660–90
)   Judge Steffan Graae
)   Trial: April 10, 1990
JOHN v. BURNETTE   )

MOTION TO SUPPRESS STATEMENTS

Mr. John Burnette, through counsel, respectfully moves this Honorable Court, pursuant to Superior Court Rule of Criminal Procedure 12, D.C. Code § 23–561 (1989 Repl.), and the Fifth Amendment of the United States Constitution, to suppress all statements allegedly made to the police by Mr. Burnette. A hearing is requested on this motion.

In support of this motion, counsel states:

1. On June 16, Mr. Burnette was presented before this Court and charged with one count of First Degree Murder while Armed.

2. According to the government, on June 15, Cedric Francis was stabbed in an alley behind 2705 13th Street, Northeast. Mr. Francis was taken by ambulance to Medstar where he was pronounced dead.

3. On that same day, members of the Metropolitan Police Department entered the home of John Burnette at 1356 Bryant Street, Northeast, seized Mr. Burnette and transported him to the Homicide Branch, 300 Indiana Avenue, Northwest.

4. After being arrested and while in custody, Mr. Burnette was questioned by an officer of the Metropolitan Police Department. In response to questioning, Mr. Burnette allegedly gave a written statement. In the early morning hours of June 16th, while in a highly agitated state, and awaiting transportation to the hospital, Mr. Burnette allegedly made an oral statement. In both statements Mr. Burnette stated that he stabbed Cedric Francis.

5. At the time he allegedly made the statements, Mr. Burnette had not knowingly and intelligently waived his right to remain silent or his right to counsel. Mr. Burnette was under the influence of two potent prescription medications, dilantin and phenobarbital. Mr. Burnette was also intoxicated.

6. At the time he allegedly made statements to the police, Mr. Burnette's condition was such that he could not have comprehended and appreciated the waiver of rights.

7. The statements made by Mr. Burnette were also involuntary. The combination of drugs and alcohol and the stress of his arrest severely hampered Mr. Burnette's ability to act voluntarily.

8. Mr. Burnette's statements were not the product of a rational intellect and free will. *Culombe v. Connecticut*, 367 U.S. 568 (1961).

9. Because Mr. Burnette's statements were not voluntarily made, they are inadmissible for all purposes, including impeachment. *Mincey v. Arizona*, 437 U.S. 385 (1978).

WHEREFORE, for the foregoing reasons and for such reasons as may appear at a hearing on this Motion, Mr. Burnette respectfully requests that this motion be granted.

Respectfully submitted,

_____

Ramona Wu
Counsel for Mr. Burnette
Public Defender Service
451 Indiana Avenue, N.W.
Washington, D.C. 20001
(202) 628–1200

CERTIFICATE OF SERVICE

This is to certify that a copy of the foregoing Motion has been served by hand upon the Office of the United States Attorney, Felony Division, 555 Fourth Street, Northwest, Washington, D.C. 20001, attention Larry Parkinson, Esquire, this 7th day of October.

_____/s/
Ramona Wu

CHAPTER 3

SEARCHES AND SEIZURES: WARRANTS AND DETENTIONS

- SEARCH AND ARREST WARRANTS • WARRANT EXECUTIONS
- COMPUTER SEARCHES • ARRESTS • *TERRY* STOPS

I. WARRANT CONTENT

Checklist 3: When Has a Warrant Been Properly Issued and Executed?

1. Was the warrant application sufficient?

    a. Was the application accompanied by an affidavit made under oath?

    b. Did the affidavit establish probable cause?

2. Was the warrant proper?

    a. Was the warrant issued by a neutral and detached magistrate?

    b. Did the warrant describe the places to be searched, and the items or person to be seized, with reasonable particularity, based on facts learned after reasonable investigation?

3. Was the warrant execution reasonable?

    a. Was the warrant executed during daytime hours and within 10 days of its issuance, or if not, were there objectively reasonable grounds for the manner of execution?

    b. Did the officers knock and announce their presence, or if not, were there objectively reasonable grounds for their failure to do so?

    c. Did the officers act reasonably in dealing with individuals encountered during the warrant execution?

A. OVERVIEW OF SEARCH AND ARREST WARRANTS

There is a debate concerning the relationship of the Fourth Amendment's warrant clause to its "reasonableness" clause. While the Supreme Court has not taken a unified position on the matter, it is increasingly clear that law enforcement activity in many circumstances need not be accompanied by a warrant. Indeed, studies reveal that searches and seizures are more often warrantless than accompanied by warrants.[1] Nevertheless, the warrant requirement continues to be the centerpiece of the Fourth Amendment, creating a presumption that wherever possible, a judicial officer should authorize searches and seizures in advance.

The warrant clause contains unusually clear prescriptions concerning the warrant application process and the warrant itself. First, let us examine how a warrant is obtained consistent with the Fourth Amendment. Recall that the warrant clause states that "no Warrants shall issue, but upon probable cause, supported by Oath or affirmation, and particularly describing the place to be searched, and the persons or things to be seized." The information conveyed to the judicial officer, then, must demonstrate probable cause, and must be supported by an affidavit—a statement made under oath. In addition, the information must meet the "particularity" requirement, which will be discussed in the next subsection below.

The traditional justifications for the warrant requirement are twofold: first, that a neutral and detached magistrate is better equipped to make reliable probable cause judgments than a police officer involved in the "competitive enterprise of ferreting out crime"; second, that the warrant itself helps to limit police officer discretion when the officer conducts a search or seizure. Professor Christopher Slobogin has suggested another warrant function: avoiding the post-hoc, de facto weakening of the probable cause requirement. His argument runs roughly like this: if a judicial officer reviews a warrantless search *after* the search discovered evidence of crime, the judge will be likely to find that the search was based on probable cause. However, if a warrant is sought *before* the search takes place, the judicial officer cannot be certain that evidence of crime will be found and is more likely to require a meaningful showing of probable cause before approving the warrant.

Another commentator[2] has suggested two additional functions served by warrants:

> ... A warrant requirement forces police officers to rationalize and articulate the grounds for a search. The warrant process encourages the officer to think through the bases for his search before he decides to search a suspect's property or person. This rationalization process helps to prevent precipitous actions by police. The process also helps to dissuade officers from acting on vague impressions, hunches, or stereotypes.
>
> The warrant requirement mandates not only that police think through the justifications for a search, but also that police must articulate those justifications. The process of writing out a warrant application and presenting the application to a magistrate is not simply a bureaucratic hassle. Instead, this process forces the officer to critical-

---

1. *See* Christopher Slobogin, Criminal Procedure: Regulation of Police Investigation 105 (1993).

2. David E. Steinberg, *The Drive Toward Warrantless Auto Searches: Suggestions from a Back-Seat Driver*, 80 B.U. L. Rev. 545, 561–62 (2002).

ly analyze the justifications for his proposed search and to confront any weaknesses inherent in the case.

Practically speaking, the law enforcement officer seeking the warrant prepares an application for the warrant. According to Federal Rule of Criminal Procedure 41, a warrant may be sought for:

(1) evidence of a crime;

(2) contraband, fruits of crime, or other items illegally possessed;

(3) property designed for use, intended for use, or used in committing a crime; or

(4) a person to be arrested or a person who is unlawfully restrained.

In the case of a search warrant, the officer attaches a sworn affidavit to the application, setting forth in the affidavit all information necessary to establish probable cause to believe that the items sought in the search warrant constitute one of the first three items listed above.[3] In addition, the affidavit also must establish probable cause to believe that the items sought will be found in the place specified.[4] The affidavit may be, and usually is, based on hearsay "in whole or in part."[5] Moreover, most jurisdictions make provision for the rare instance in which the judicial officer wishes to question the affiant personally. For example, Rule 41 of the Federal Rules of Criminal Procedure states that:

(A) Warrant on an Affidavit. When a federal law enforcement officer or an attorney for the government presents an affidavit in support of a warrant, the judge may require the affiant to appear personally and may examine under oath the affiant and any witness the affiant produces.

(B) Warrant on Sworn Testimony. The judge may wholly or partially dispense with a written affidavit and base a warrant on sworn testimony if doing so is reasonable under the circumstances.

(C) Recording Testimony. Testimony taken in support of a warrant must be recorded by a court reporter or by a suitable recording device, and the judge must file the transcript or recording with the clerk, along with any affidavit.

Finally, the officer prepares the search warrant itself, so that all the judicial officer need do is evaluate the application and affidavit, and, if they comply with the Fourth Amendment, sign the warrant.

---

3. In Boyd v. United States, 116 U.S. 616, 641 (1886), the Supreme Court held that the government could not, consistent with the Fourth Amendment, obtain "mere evidence" from the accused, but the "mere evidence" rule was overturned in Warden v. Hayden, 387 U.S. 294, 309 (1967).

4. Sometimes a search warrant directs the officer to search a certain place in order to seize a person. As we will discuss below, law enforcement officers must have a search warrant before they may enter premises to execute an arrest warrant, unless the premises are those of the person named in the arrest warrant.

5. *See* Fed. R. Crim. Proc. 41.

Of course, officers sometimes do not have time to go back to headquarters, prepare a warrant application, and find a judge to sign the warrant. As telephone access from remote locations has become widespread, it has become more common for law enforcement officers to obtain warrants by submitting testimony over the telephone or by facsimile. Indeed, telephone (and fax) warrants may be changing the way in which warrantless searches are evaluated. As you will see in the next chapter, warrantless searches commonly were upheld where police established that they did not have time to obtain a warrant. Today, before upholding a search on the basis of such "exigent circumstances," courts increasingly expect officers to demonstrate that they did not have sufficient time even to obtain a telephone warrant.

While telephone warrants may be obtained more quickly than traditional warrants, they require nonetheless the formalities articulated in the Fourth Amendment. That is, they still must be based on statements made under oath that establish probable cause, and they still describe with particularity the places to be searched and the persons and items to be seized. Moreover, the record-keeping demands of a legal system are not relieved in the telephonic setting. As a result, statutes authorizing telephonic warrants typically contain detailed requirements. Here, for example, is the federal authorizing legislation, which is found in Rule 41 of the Federal Rules of Criminal Procedure:

(3) Requesting a Warrant by Telephonic or Other Means.

(A) In General. A magistrate judge may issue a warrant based on information communicated by telephone or other appropriate means, including facsimile transmission.

(B) Recording Testimony. Upon learning that an applicant is requesting a warrant, a magistrate judge must:

(i) place under oath the applicant and any person on whose testimony the application is based; and

(ii) make a verbatim record of the conversation with a suitable recording device, if available, or by a court reporter, or in writing.

(C) Certifying Testimony. The magistrate judge must have any recording or court reporter's notes transcribed, certify the transcription's accuracy, and file a copy of the record and the transcription with the clerk. Any written verbatim record must be signed by the magistrate judge and filed with the clerk.

(D) Suppression Limited. Absent a finding of bad faith, evidence obtained from a warrant issued under Rule 41(d)(3)(A) is not subject to suppression on the ground that issuing the warrant in that manner was unreasonable under the circumstances.

Warrant applications contain detailed information on which the issuing magistrate relies. The magistrate can question officers about the information in the application, and can discount information that does not seem credible, but once a warrant is issued the statements in the application are presumed to be accurate. But what if a person affected by a warrant later comes to believe that the application contained false information? Police lying, after all, is a phenomenon sufficiently common to have been given its own name: "testilying." There is a procedural remedy of questionable effectiveness for a criminal defendant who believes that a police officer lied in the warrant application: under *Franks v. Delaware*,[6] if the defendant can establish an intentional (or reckless) falsity in the warrant application, and if the falsity was necessary to the finding of probable cause, then evidence discovered during execution of the warrant must be suppressed. Proving that a police officer lied, of course, is not easy. Simply in order to get an evidentiary hearing (called a "*Franks* hearing") on the matter, the defendant must make out a substantial preliminary showing with an offer of proof. In the words of one court in the case of *United States v. Strube*,[7] "[a]ffidavits or otherwise reliable statements of witnesses should be furnished" during the preliminary showing. One of the issues in the *Strube* case was a search warrant affidavit that related statements made by several informants. At a hearing on his motion to suppress evidence discovered during the execution of the search warrant, the defendant asked for a *Franks* hearing so that he could establish that the affidavit was false. In support of his request, the defendant stated that two of the informants would testify at such a hearing that they had never made the statements attributed to them in the affidavit. However, the defendant failed to support this promise of testimony with affidavits from the informants, and indeed the informants refused to testify at the suppression hearing. In light of the defendant's failure to make out a "substantial preliminary showing necessary to overcome the presumption that a search warrant affidavit is valid," the trial court refused to hold the requested *Franks* hearing.

The court's decision illustrates the enormous difficulty that the *Franks* rule creates in uncovering police lies. That difficulty might be justified (imagine the burden courts would face in litigating every defense claim of police deceit) were adequate discovery tools available prior to the suppression hearing so that the defense could gather proof of police misrepresentations. But such tools are too often missing in many jurisdictions.[8]

The Oklahoma City bombing case generated multiple search warrants.[9] We reproduce on the next few pages a search warrant and its accompanying

---

6.   438 U.S. 154 (1978).

7.   1997 WL 33482969 (M.D. Pa. 1997).

8.   *See* Andrew E. Taslitz, *Slaves No More: The Implications of the Informed Citizen Idea for Discovery Before Fourth Amendment Suppression Hearings*, 15 GA. ST. L. REV. 709 (1999) (arguing that a holistic reading of the constitution suggests that meaningful pre-suppression-hearing discovery tools are required).

9.   On April 19, 1995, a huge explosion destroyed the Alfred P. Murrah Federal Building in Oklahoma City, Oklahoma. The explosion killed 167 people, including a number of children in the building's day care center. *See* generally, *e.g.*, Note, *The Comprehensive Terrorism Prevention Act of 1995*, 20 SETON HALL LEGIS. J. 201 (1996) (collecting newspaper reports). Timothy McVeigh and Terry Nichols, both allegedly tied to right-wing anti-government militia groups, were arrested and charged with the bombing. McVeigh was convicted and executed. Nichols was convicted of some charges and acquitted of others. He remains incarcerated.

application and affidavit, all from that case. As you review these, identify the parts that are constitutionally required and the sufficiency of those parts. Pay special attention to how the officer seeking the warrant established probable cause.

IN THE UNITED STATES DISTRICT COURT
FOR THE EASTERN DISTRICT OF MICHIGAN

In the Matter of the Search of)
3616 North Van Dyke Road,) NO. 95X71665
Decker, Michigan.   )

APPLICATION AND AFFIDAVIT FOR SEARCH WARRANT

I, Arthur Radford Baker, being duly sworn depose and say:

I am a Special Agent, Federal Bureau of Investigation, and have reason to believe that on the property or premises known as:

3616 North Van Dyke, also known as M–53, in Decker, Evergreen Township, Sanilac County, Michigan. The residence is located approximately 1/4 mile north of Deckerville Road on the east side of M–53. The house is a two-story wood frame farmhouse, white in color. East of the house is a wooden pole barn, faded red in color. East of the wooden pole barn is a metal pole barn, which is white with green trim. Southeast of the metal pole barn is a large hip-roof style barn, red in color. The property also contains three large metal grain bins and two above ground fuel storage tanks. There is one common driveway which leads to the house and by which all outbuildings can be accessed. The house sits approximately 100 to 130 feet off the road. Neither the house nor the mailbox contain any address numbers.

in the Eastern District of Michigan, there is now concealed certain property, namely:

Fertilizer, fuel oil, chemicals, dynamite, military explosives, detonators (blasting caps), electrical or non-electrical fusing systems, wires, batteries, timing devices, burning type fuse, mixing and other containers.

Sales receipts, invoices, shipping records, literature relating bomb-making or explosive manufacturing, or improved explosive or incendiary mixes, components of fusing and firing systems material from which explosives or devices can be made from any related chemicals, or any evidence of any explosive manufacturing or bomb-making operations.

Documents and all other information pertaining to the Michigan Militia, including but not limited to, goals of the organization, propaganda, literature, membership, history, identity of members, telephone numbers and addresses of members.

Various types of trace evidence transfer, including but not limited to hair, saliva, blood, fibers, fingerprints, and other trace evidence. Documentary evidence, such as bank records and telephone toll records.

which is property that constitutes evidence of the commission of a criminal offense, concerning a violation of Title 18 United States code, Section(s) 844(f).

The facts to support a finding of Probable Cause are as follows:

[See attached Affidavit]

Continued on the attached sheet and made a part hereof.

_____/s/
Signature of Affiant

Sworn to before me, and subscribed in my presence on May 3, 1995

_____/s/
Signature of Judicial Officer

AFFIDAVIT

Arthur Radford Baker, being duly sworn, states as follows:

1. I am a Special Agent of the Federal Bureau of Investigation assigned to the Detroit Field Office and an agent for 8 years.

2. On April 21, 1995 United States Magistrate Judge Steven Pepe issued a warrant authorizing the search of 3616 N. Van Dyke Road, Decker, Michigan, the residence of James Douglas Nichols (the property is also a working farm). On April 28, 1995 United States Magistrate Judge Thomas Carlson issued an additional warrant to search a pole barn located at 3616 N. Van Dyke. The April 21st and 28th search warrant applications and affidavits are attached and incorporated by reference.

3. The search warrants for Nichols' farm were issued as the result of an investigation regarding the bombing of a United States Federal Building in Oklahoma City, Oklahoma on April 19, 1995. This bombing resulted in the death of at least 120 individuals, the wounding of several hundred individuals, and substantial damage to the Albert P. Murrah Federal Building.

4. The search of Nichols farm pursuant to the April 21st warrant spanned three days and resulted in the seizure of numerous items and documents relating to the manufacture of improvised explosive devices. The April 28th warrant authorized, and resulted in, the seizure of a specific item, a 55 gallon blue plastic barrel. The agents conducting the seizure of the barrel did not engage in any additional search of the farm.

5. In the course of executing the April 21st warrant, agents observed a large volume of documents in the residence and barn (workshop) areas of the Nichols' farm; a cursory examination of those documents showed that they had been accumulated over the course of several years. However, agents did not seize the documents because they did not appear to have an immediately apparent link to the manufacture of explosive devices or the bombing of the Murrah Building.

6. Since the conclusion of the initial search of Nichols' farm, FBI agents have interviewed a cooperating individual who has requested the protection

of his/her identity (hereafter, the "CI.") During the period August 1987 through May 1990, the CI visited James Nichols at Nichols' farm on a regular basis, approximately 3–4 times a year. During the course of the CI's contacts with Nichols, Nichols frequently expressed hatred for the United States Government, blaming the government for the worlds' problems. Nichols also told the CI that he (Nichols) had "fun" making bombs.

7. On or about December 22 or December 23, 1988, the CI visited Nichols shortly after the terrorist bombing of Pan Am Flight 103 in Locherbie, Scotland. Nichols blamed the bombing on the U.S. government and told the CI that a small bomb could cause such a disaster. Nichols then explained to the CI that a "megabomb" capable of leveling a building could be built. Nichols then made a specific reference to a Federal Building in Oklahoma City and began looking through the toolshed and workbench for a newspaper clipping depicting the Oklahoma City building. Unable to immediately locate the newspaper clipping, Nichols drew the CI a diagram of the building. This diagram of the building was similar to the construction of the Murrah Federal Building in Oklahoma City. Nichols later located a newspaper article containing a reference to the Murrah Federal Building in Oklahoma City and showed it to the CI.

8. After learning the above information, FBI agents showed the CI several diagram type documents seized from Nichols' farm. The CI informed the agents that these were not the diagrams Nichols had made depicting the Oklahoma City building. Because they were unaware of the information regarding this diagram and the newspaper clipping, the agents conducting the search did not specifically look for these items; moreover, given the large volume of documents located at the Nichols' farm, the agents may not have recognized the significance of the diagram in the course of the search.

9. In the course of executing the April 21st warrant, agents observed several weapons in Nichols' residence. One weapon observed was an SKS 7.62, .39 caliber rifle.

10. During a robbery in November, 1994, of an Arkansas residence, a number of weapons were stolen. The owner did not have a complete list of the serial numbers, but he did have a description of the weapons. Although he filed a police report of the robbery, the owner did not file an insurance claim. The owner believes that Tim McVeigh may have been involved in the robbery, in that he had visited the owner on several occasions and was familiar with the gun collection. One of the weapons stolen was an SKS Chinese 7.62, .39 caliber rifle, similar to the one seen by the agents during the execution of the April 21st warrant. Also stolen in the Arkansas robbery was a safety deposit box key, which was recovered during the recent searches at Terry Nichols' residence.

11. During the execution of the April 21st warrant, agents seized a note addressed to James Nichols which apparently was written by Terry Nichols. The note stated: "Enclosed are 2 SKS 30 round magazines [sic] so you can try out your SKS. If you want me to get some ammo for you let me know." Also observed during the search was a letter addressed to James Nichols at the Decker, Michigan, address, postmarked March 8, 1995. The

return address was "T. Nichols, 1228 Westloop #197, Manhattan, Kansas 66502." The letter, which was signed Terry, stated that the Manhattan, Kansas address was just a mail drop location. In the letter, the author, believed to be Terry Nichols, stated that he had sent a package to James Nichols by Priority Mail, and told James that the author had forgotten to let James Nichols know the price of the two SKS magazines.

12.   Investigation by the FBI has revealed that on April 21, 1995, five telephone calls of a duration of one minute or less were placed from the residence of Terry Nichols to the residence of James Nichols. It is believed that these calls may have been recorded on James Nichols' answering machine while James was out, just prior to the execution of the search warrant. During that time period, there was heavy media coverage, which showed the Nichols farm and the presence of law enforcement officers preparing to execute the search warrant. It is believed that these calls may still be on the answering machine and may contain information relating to this investigation.

13.   Based on the facts set forth above, his training and experience, your affiant is of the opinion that there is probable cause to believe that the items set forth in the attachment will be found on the listed premises, and will constitute fruits or instrumentalities of the crimes listed.

_____/s/
Signature of affiant

Duly sworn and Subscribed to before me this 2nd day of May, 1995.

_____/s/
United States Magistrate Judge

IN THE UNITED STATES DISTRICT COURT
FOR THE EASTERN DISTRICT OF MICHIGAN

In the Matter of the Search of)
3616 North Van Dyke Road,   ) NO. 95X71665
Decker, Michigan.   )

SEARCH WARRANT

TO: any Federal Agent and any Authorized Officer of the United States

Affidavit having been made before me by Arthur Radford Baker, who has reason to believe that on the premises known as

> 3616 North Van Dyke, also known as M–53, in Decker, Evergreen Township, Sanilac County, Michigan. The residence is located approximately 1/4 mile north of Deckerville Road on the east side of M–53. The house is a two-story wood frame farmhouse, white in color. East of the house is a wooden pole barn, faded red in color. East of the wooden pole barn is a metal pole barn, which is white with green trim. Southeast of the metal pole barn is a large hip-roof style barn, red in color. The property also contains three large metal grain bins and two

above ground fuel storage tanks. There is one common driveway which leads to the house and by which all outbuildings can be accessed. The house sits approximately 100 to 130 feet off the road. Neither the house nor the mailbox contain any address numbers.

in the Eastern District of Michigan, there is now concealed certain property, namely:

Fertilizer, fuel oil, chemicals, dynamite, military explosives, detonators (blasting caps), electrical or non-electrical fusing systems, wires, batteries, timing devices, burning type fuse, mixing and other containers.

Sales receipts, invoices, shipping records, literature relating bomb-making or explosive manufacturing, or improved explosive or incendiary mixes, components of fusing and firing systems material from which explosives or devices can be made from any related chemicals, or any evidence of any explosive manufacturing or bomb-making operations.

Documents and all other information pertaining to the Michigan Militia, including but not limited to, goals of the organization, propaganda, literature, membership, history, identity of members, telephone numbers and addresses of members.

Various types of trace evidence transfer, including but not limited to hair, saliva, blood, fibers, fingerprints, and other trace evidence. Documentary evidence, such as bank records and telephone toll records.

which is property that constitutes evidence of the commission of a criminal offense, concerning a violation of Title 18 United States code, Section(s) 844(f).

I am satisfied that the affidavit and any recorded testimony establish probable cause to believe that the property so described is now concealed on the premises above-described and establish grounds for the issuance of this warrant.

YOU ARE HEREBY COMMANDED to search on or before May 12, 1995 (not to exceed 10 days) the place named above for the property specified, serving this warrant and commencing the search (in the daytime—6:00 A.M. to 10:00 P.M.) and continuing thereafter until completed, and if the property be found there to seize same, leaving a copy of this warrant and receipt for the property taken, and prepare a written inventory of the property seized, and promptly return this warrant to the duty magistrate judge, U.S. Judge, or Magistrate as required by law.

May 3, 1996, 1:30 PM

_____/s/

U.S. Judge or Magistrate

———

How does an arrest warrant differ from a search warrant? Examine the following and look for distinguishing characteristics.

————

IN THE UNITED STATES DISTRICT COURT
FOR THE WESTERN DISTRICT OF OKLAHOMA

United States of America, Plaintiff,	)	
	)	
v.	)	No. M–95–105–H
	)	
Terry Lynn Nichols, Defendant.	)	

CRIMINAL COMPLAINT

I, the undersigned complainant, being duly sworn, state the following is true and correct to the best of my knowledge and belief.

On or about April 19, 1995, in Oklahoma City, Oklahoma County, in the Western District of Oklahoma, defendant did maliciously damage and destroy by means of fire and an explosive, a building, vehicle, and other personal and real property in whole and in part owned, possessed, and used by the United States, and departments and agencies thereof, in violation of Title 18, United States Code, Section(s) 844(f) and 2.

I further state that I am a Special Agent of the Federal Bureau of Investigation and that this complaint is based on the following facts: See attached Affidavit of Special Agent Henry C. Gibbons, Federal Bureau of Investigation, which is incorporated and made a part hereof by reference. Continued on the attached sheet and made a part hereof.

————————————/s/
Signature of Complainant

Sworn to before me and subscribed in my presence, on this 9 day of May, 1995, at Oklahoma City, Oklahoma.

————————————/s/
Signature of Judicial Officer

STATE OF OKLAHOMA	)	
	)	ss:
COUNTY OF OKLAHOMA	)	

AFFIDAVIT

I, Henry C. Gibbons, being duly sworn, do hereby state as follows:

1. I am a Special Agent (SA) of the Federal Bureau of Investigation, have been so employed for approximately 26 years, and as such am vested with the authority to investigate violations of Title 18, United States Code, Section 844(f). I am presently assigned to the Oklahoma City Field Office, Oklahoma City, Oklahoma, and have been working on the investigation of

the April 19, 1995, bombing of the Alfred P. Murrah Federal Building. This Affidavit is submitted in support of a criminal complaint against Terry Lynn Nichols. The following information was received by the Federal Bureau of Investigation during the period April 19, 1995, to May 9, 1995:

2. On April 19, 1995, a massive explosive device was detonated outside the Alfred P. Murrah Federal Building in Oklahoma City, Oklahoma, at approximately 9:00 a.m., causing numerous deaths and injuries, and extensive damage.

3. Investigation by Federal agents at the scene of the explosion has determined that the explosive was contained in a truck owned by Ryder Rental Company.

a. A partial vehicle identification number (VIN) was found at the scene of the explosion and determined to be from a part of the truck that contained the explosive.

b. The VIN, which was reconstructed, was traced to a truck owned by Ryder Rentals of Miami, Florida.

c. Ryder Rentals informed the FBI that the truck was assigned to a rental company known as Elliott's Body Shop, a Ryder truck rental establishment in Junction City, Kansas.

4. An employee at Elliott's Body Shop has advised the FBI that two persons rented the truck on April 17, 1995. The rental agreement contained the following information:

a. The person who signed the rental agreement identified himself as Bob Kling, Social Security No. 962–42–9694, South Dakota driver's license number YF942A6, and provided a home address of 428 Maple Drive, Omaha, Nebraska. The destination was reflected as Omaha, Nebraska.

b. Subsequent investigation conducted by the FBI determined the information to be false.

5. An employee of Elliott's Body Shop in Junction City, Kansas, identified Timothy McVeigh from a photographic array as the person who rented the Ryder truck on April 17, 1995, and signed the rental agreement.

6. The Alfred P. Murrah Federal Building is used by various agencies of the United States, including the Agriculture Department, Department of the Army, the Defense Department, Federal Highway Administration, General Accounting Office, General Services Administration, Social Security Administration, Housing and Urban Development, Drug Enforcement Administration, Labor Department, Marine Corps, Small Business Administration, Transportation Department, United States Secret Service, Bureau of Alcohol, Tobacco, and Firearms, and Veterans Administration.

7. The detonation of the explosives in front of the Federal Building constitutes a violation of 18 U.S.C. Section 844(f), which makes it a crime to maliciously damage or destroy by means of an explosive any building or real property, in whole or in part owned, possessed or used by the United States, or any department or agency thereof.

8. On April 21, 1995, a federal criminal complaint was filed charging Timothy James McVeigh with a violation of Title 18, United States Code, Section 844(f), based on his involvement in the bombing of the Alfred P. Murrah Federal building on April 19, 1995.

9. On April 21, 1995, investigators learned that at approximately 10:20 a.m., on April 19, 1995, Timothy James McVeigh was arrested in Noble County, Oklahoma, on traffic and weapon offenses, and was thereafter incarcerated on those charges in Perry, Oklahoma. McVeigh's arrest occurred approximately 60–70 miles north of Oklahoma City, Oklahoma, approximately one hour and 20 minutes after the April 19, 1995, explosion that damaged the Alfred P. Murrah Federal Building. When booked into jail following that arrest, McVeigh listed 3616 North Van Dyke Road, Decker, Michigan, as his address and James Nichols of Decker, Michigan, as a reference. The property at 3616 N. Van Dyke Road, Decker, Michigan is owned by the Nichols family. James Nichols is the brother of Terry Nichols.

10. On April 27, 1995, a preliminary hearing was held on the federal criminal complaint against McVeigh, evidence was presented, and the federal magistrate judge found that there was probable cause to believe that an offense had been committed and that McVeigh committed it.

11. Supervisory Special Agent (SSA) James T. Thurman, Chief, Explosives Unit—Bomb Data Center, FBI Laboratory, Washington, D.C., has advised as follows:

> a. The bomb which detonated in front of the Murrah Federal Building on April 19, 1995, contained a high explosive main charge initiated by methods as yet unknown;
>
> b. An explosive device of the magnitude which exploded in Oklahoma City on April 19, 1995, would have been constructed over a period of time utilizing a large quantity of bomb paraphernalia and materials, which may have included, among other things, fertilizer, fuel oil, boosters, detonators (blasting caps), detonation cord, fusing systems, and containers;
>
> c. The construction of the explosive device that caused the damage to the Alfred P. Murrah Federal building would necessarily have involved the efforts of more than one person.

12. On April 21, 1995, at approximately 3:00 p.m., after hearing his name on the radio in connection with the Oklahoma City bombing, Terry Nichols voluntarily surrendered to the Department of Public Safety in Herington, Kansas. Herington authorities took no action and awaited the arrival of the FBI. Thereafter, a Special Agent of the FBI arrived and advised Nichols of his Miranda rights, which Nichols agreed to waive.

13. Terry Nichols was subsequently interviewed and provided the following information:

> a. He first met McVeigh at U. S. Army Basic Training in 1988 in Georgia. He later served with McVeigh at Fort Riley, Kansas. Over the years they have occasionally lived together, operated a business togeth-

er involving the sale of army surplus items and firearms at gun shows throughout the United States, and otherwise stayed in close contact.

b.   Nichols was with McVeigh in downtown Oklahoma City, on April 16, 1995.

c.   On Tuesday, April 18, 1995, McVeigh and Nichols met in Junction City, Kansas, where Nichols said he loaned his dark blue 1984 GMC half-ton diesel pickup to McVeigh. Nichols said McVeigh had the vehicle for approximately 5 hours while Nichols attended an auction.

d.   On Tuesday, April 18, 1995, McVeigh told Nichols he had items in a storage unit in Herington, Kansas, and that if McVeigh did not pick them up, Nichols should do it for him. On April 20, 1995, Nichols did pick up items, including a rifle, from the storage unit. Nichols described the location of the storage unit, which is further identified in paragraph 18.

e.   Nichols knows how to make a bomb by blending ammonium nitrate with diesel fuel which could be detonated by blasting caps. Nichols also stated that he had ammonium nitrate at his residence until Friday, April 21, 1995, at which time he placed it on his yard as fertilizer. Nichols said that he did this after reading in several different newspapers that ammonium nitrate was used in the Oklahoma City bombing.

f.   He had a fuel meter in his garage which he said he had purchased for resale.

g.   Nichols stated several times that if they searched his residence, he hoped that agents "would not mistake household items" for bomb-producing materials. In particular, Nichols told agents that he had several containers of ground ammonium nitrate which he said he sells as plant food fertilizer at gun shows.

h.   Nichols said he possessed numerous weapons scattered throughout his house and detached garage.

i.   Nichols also stated that he has in the past rented storage facilities in Kansas and Nevada.

j.   Nichols denied involvement in or knowledge of the bombing.

14.   While Terry Nichols was being interviewed, he gave consent for agents to search his residence, 109 South Second Street, Herington, Kansas, and his pickup truck, VIN #2GTEC14C9E1511984, described as a dark blue 1984 GMC Sierra Classic with a white topper, or camper shell. A search warrant was obtained and executed on Terry Nichols' residence in Herington, Kansas, on April 22, 1995. During that search, agents seized the following items:

a.   Five 60–foot #8 primadet cords with non-electric blasting caps. According to FBI bomb experts, such cord can be used to initiate the explosion of a fertilizer-fuel oil bomb.

b.   Four white barrels with blue lids made from material resembling the blue plastic fragments found at the bomb scene in Oklahoma City, Oklahoma.

c.   One fuel meter (referred to in paragraph 13(f)). According to information provided by ATF bomb experts, such a device could be used to obtain the proper volume of diesel fuel to ammonium nitrate for a bomb.

d.   One receipt from Mid–Kansas Cooperative Association, McPherson, Kansas, for 40 fifty-pound bags of 34–0–0 ammonium nitrate fertilizer.

e.   Five gas cans of various sizes.

f.   Several containers of ground ammonium nitrate. According to FBI bomb experts, this substance can be used as one ingredient of a booster for a fertilizer-fuel oil bomb.

15.   On September 30, 1994, forty (40) fifty-pound bags of 34–0–0 ammonium nitrate fertilizer were purchased from Mid–Kansas Cooperative Association in McPherson, Kansas, by a "Mike Havens." A receipt for that purchase, referred to in paragraph 14(d), was found at the residence of Terry Nichols. The FBI has identified a fingerprint on the receipt, as belonging to Timothy McVeigh.

16.   On October 18, 1994, forty (40) additional fifty-pound bags of 34–0–0 ammonium nitrate fertilizer were purchased from Mid–Kansas Cooperative Association, McPherson, Kansas, by a "Mike Havens," who was driving a dark-colored pickup with a light-colored camper shell.

17.   SSA Wallace Higgins, FBI Laboratory Explosives Unit, advises that 34–0–0 ammonium nitrate, fuel oil and #8 primadet cords can be used in the manufacture of a fertilizer-fuel oil bomb.

18.   On September 22, 1994, a storage unit, identified as unit #2, was rented at Herington, Kansas, in the name Shawn Rivers. Unit #2 was rented approximately one week prior to the purchase of the ammonium nitrate fertilizer described in paragraph 15. This is the same storage unit described in paragraph 13(d).

19.   On October 17, 1994, a storage unit identified as unit #40, was rented at Council Grove, Kansas, in the name Joe Kyle. Unit #40 was rented one day prior to the purchase of the ammonium nitrate fertilizer described in paragraph 16. The FBI has obtained from Terry Nichols' home a document with the location of this storage unit and the name Joe Kyle.

20.   On November 7, 1994, an additional storage unit, identified as unit #37, was rented at Council Grove, Kansas, in the name Ted Parker. The FBI has obtained from Terry Nichols' home a document with the location of this storage unit and the name Ted Parker.

21.   The FBI has obtained a letter from Terry Nichols to Tim McVeigh, dated on or about November 22, 1994, the day Nichols left the United States for a visit to the Philippines. In the letter, Terry Nichols tells Timothy McVeigh that he will be getting this letter only in the event of Nichols' death. Nichols instructs McVeigh to "clear everything out of CG

37" and to "also liquidate 40." Terry Nichols also tells McVeigh he is on his own and to "Go for it!!"

22.   Further investigation has revealed that "CG 37" refers to the Council Grove storage unit #37, rented by Terry Nichols on November 7, 1994, and that "Liquidate 40" refers to the Council Grove storage unit #40 rented by Terry Nichols on October 17, 1994.

23.   On April 15, 1995, Terry Nichols purchased diesel fuel from a Conoco service station in Manhattan, Kansas.

24.   On April 16, 1995, Terry Nichols purchased an additional 21.59 gallons of diesel fuel from a Conoco service station in Junction City, Kansas.

25.   On April 17, 1995, a call was placed from Room 25 at the Dreamland Hotel to the residence of Terry Nichols in Herington, Kansas. Timothy McVeigh stayed at the Dreamland Hotel, in Room 25, from April 14, 1995, through April 18, 1995.

26.   During the evening of April 17, 1995, a Ryder truck was seen parked behind the residence of Terry Nichols, 109 South 2nd Street, Herington, Kansas.

27.   On April 17 or 18, 1995, an older model pickup with a camper shell was seen backed up to the second garage door on the east end of the storage shed in Herington. This unit is #2. This is the storage unit which was previously discussed in paragraph 18.

28.   During the week of April 17th, a Ryder truck was seen backed up to the east end of the storage shed in Herington near storage unit #2. This is the storage unit which was previously discussed in paragraph 18.

29.   On the morning of April 18, 1995, a witness at the Geary State Fishing Lake, approximately six miles south of Junction City, Kansas, observed a yellow Ryder truck parked next to a pickup truck for several hours. Both vehicles were parked in an area which was not paved. The witness described the pickup truck as a dark blue or brown 1980–1987 Chevrolet or GMC truck and recalled that there was something white, possibly a camper shell, on the back of the pickup truck.

30.   On April 28, 1995, the witness accompanied an FBI agent to Geary State Fishing Lake and took him to the area where the two vehicles had been parked. In that area, the agent observed a circular area of brown vegetation surrounded by green vegetation. Upon inspecting the area of brown vegetation, he noticed an oily substance and detected the distinct odor of diesel fuel.

Further your affiant sayeth not.

_____/s/

HENRY C. GIBBONS
Special Agent Federal Bureau of
Investigation

Subscribed and sworn to before me this 9 day of May, 1995.

————————————/s/

RONALD L. HOWLAND
UNITED STATES MAGISTRATE
JUDGE

————

IN THE UNITED STATES DISTRICT COURT
FOR THE WESTERN DISTRICT OF OKLAHOMA

United States of America, Plaintiff,)
)
v.   ) No. M–95–105–H
)
Terry Lynn Nichols, Defendant.   )

WARRANT FOR ARREST

To: The United States Marshal and any Authorized United States Officer

YOU ARE HEREBY COMMANDED to arrest TERRY LYNN NICHOLS and bring him forthwith to the nearest magistrate to answer a Complaint charging him with maliciously damaging and destroying by means of fire and an explosive, a building, vehicle and other personal and real property in whole and in part owned, possessed, and used by the United States, and departments and agencies thereof, in violation of Title 18, United States Code, Sections 844(f) and 2.

————————————/s/

RONALD L. HOWLAND
United States Magistrate Judge

May 9, 1995, at Oklahoma City, Oklahoma

Bail fixed at $_____ by_____ [Name of Judicial Officer]

————

Notice several differences in the arrest warrant papers. First, the arrest warrant application typically is entitled a "complaint," rather than an application.[10] Moreover, the probable cause set forth in the arrest warrant differs from that found in a search warrant. In order to obtain an arrest warrant, the affiant must establish probable cause to believe that this particular *person* committed this particular *crime*. Finally, the arrest warrant does not specify the place in which the arrest should occur. This is

---

10. The complaint also serves as the beginning of the charging process. It will be filed with a judge in an initial appearance in order to establish probable cause against the arrested individual. *See* Federal Rule of Criminal Procedure 5. Eventually, it will be replaced with an indictment or information.

a significant fact, because the arrest warrant conveys no "searching" authority upon law enforcement officers. If officers wish to enter premises in order to effectuate an arrest, they must have a search warrant in addition to the arrest warrant.[11] The only exception to this rule covers the dwelling in which the person named in the arrest warrant lives.[12]

These differences aside, the basic structure of the warrant process is the same for both arrest and search warrants. Both must establish probable cause by means of a statement made under oath. Moreover, both require the executing law enforcement officer to bring to the judicial officer who issued the warrant either the person arrested or an inventory of the items seized. This requirement is conveyed in the form of a "return," which is typically printed on the back of the warrant. After the officer has executed the warrant, the officer fills out the return and signs the accompanying certification. The original warrant, which includes the return, is then filed with the court. The return ensures that judicial control is retained over the search, seizure, and arrest process—in other words, that an official record be made and kept of all law enforcement activity conducted pursuant to a warrant. A copy of the return, which includes an inventory of any items seized, is also left at the premises in order to notify interested persons of the law enforcement activity.

The requirement of a return is codified in the federal system as part of Rule 41 of the Federal Rules of Criminal Procedure. That rule requires, in part, that:

(1) Noting the Time. The officer executing the warrant must enter on its face the exact date and time it is executed.

(2) Inventory. An officer present during the execution of the warrant must prepare and verify an inventory of any property seized. The officer must do so in the presence of another officer and the person from whom, or from whose premises, the property was taken. If either one is not present, the officer must prepare and verify the inventory in the presence of at least one other credible person.

(3) Receipt. The officer executing the warrant must:

(A) give a copy of the warrant and a receipt for the property taken to the person from whom, or from whose premises, the property was taken; or

(B) leave a copy of the warrant and receipt at the place where the officer took the property.

(4) Return. The officer executing the warrant must promptly return it—together with a copy of the inventory—to the magistrate judge designated on the warrant. The judge must, on request, give a

---

11. Steagald v. United States, 451 U.S. 204, 211 (1981). In that case, the search warrant would direct the officer to enter the described premises in order to search for and seize the person named in the arrest warrant.

12. *See* Payton v. New York, 445 U.S. 573 (1980).

copy of the inventory to the person from whom, or from whose premises, the property was taken and to the applicant for the warrant.

The rules further provide that "[t]he magistrate judge to whom the warrant is returned must attach to the warrant a copy of the return, of the inventory, and of all other related papers and must deliver them to the clerk in the district where the property was seized." States have similar provisions requiring that law enforcement actors inventory the property they seize and provide notice of the seizure. Does the failure to follow such measures render a search "unreasonable" under the Fourth Amendment? Justice Thomas has suggested that it might, citing historical sources on common law warrants,[13] while at the same time acknowledging that lower courts are "nearly unanimous" in holding that the Fourth Amendment does not contain a notice requirement. The issue remains to be decided by the Court. Here is a copy of a typical return:

RETURN

Date Warrant Received _____

Date and Time Warrant Executed _____

Copy of Warrant and Receipt for Items Left With _____ at Residence

Inventory Made in the Presence of _____

Inventory of Person or Property Taken Pursuant to the Warrant: [this is usually a separate attachment]

CERTIFICATION

I swear that this inventory is a true and detailed account of the person or property taken by me on the warrant.

_____/s/

Subscribed and sworn to, and returned before me this date.

_____/s/
U.S. Judge or Magistrate

———

You probably noticed several other details in the warrants, including a direction in the search warrant that it be executed within 10 days, and that execution take place during daytime hours. We will flesh out these features below. In the meantime, what do you suppose is their significance? Are they constitutionally required? If so, why?

B.   PARTICULARITY

The Fourth Amendment prohibits warrants that do not "particularly describ[e] the place to be searched, and the persons or things to be seized."

---

13.   *See* City of West Covina v. Perkins, 525 U.S. 234 (1999) (Appendix).

The particularity requirements appears to have been a response to the "general warrants" that the colonists abhorred. The idea is that warrants grant limited authority to law enforcement officers, who may conduct only those searches and seizures whose "reasonableness" has already been established by the judicial officer who made the probable cause determination. In executing a warrant calling for the search and seizure of particular items, for example, the search must end once the items are found.[14]

As you might imagine, whether or not a warrant's descriptions meet the particularity requirement is a fact-bound inquiry. And, as in most other Fourth Amendment contexts, "reasonableness" reigns. The standard applied in each case is whether the warrant contains sufficient particularities so that the officer can be *reasonably* certain of executing it correctly. Moreover, as the Supreme Court made clear in *Maryland v. Garrison*,[15] the warrant is to be evaluated at the time it was issued and according to the information that the officers disclosed, or should have disclosed, to the issuing judicial official. There, the Court explained this test in the following manner:

> [W]e must judge the constitutionality of [law enforcement officers'] conduct in light of the information available to them at the time they acted. Those items of evidence that emerge after the warrant is issued have no bearing on whether or not a warrant was validly issued. Just as the discovery of contraband cannot validate a warrant invalid when issued, so is it equally clear that the discovery of facts demonstrating that a valid warrant was unnecessarily broad does not retroactively invalidate the warrant. The validity of the warrant must be assessed on the basis of the information that the officers disclosed, or had a duty to discover and to disclose, to the issuing Magistrate.

To illustrate, suppose that a magistrate issues a search warrant authorizing the search of a "9x12 storage locker located at the 'U–Store–It' facility at 123 Main Street." Is this warrant sufficiently particular? The answer depends in part on the facts disclosed to the magistrate in the affidavit. Suppose the affidavit disclosed that the "U–Store–It" facility contained only one 9x12 storage locker. In that case, the warrant would be sufficiently particular to permit the executing officer to be reasonably certain of executing it correctly.[16] If, on the other hand, the affidavit revealed nothing about the number of 9x12 lockers at the facility, or indicated that the facility included multiple lockers of that size, then a warrant issued with only the description noted above would not meet the particularity requirement because, at the time it was issued, one could not

---

14. Horton v. California, 496 U.S. 128, 136 (1990) (citing Coolidge v. New Hampshire, 403 U.S. 443, 466 (1971)).

15. 480 U.S. 79, 85 (1987).

16. If the executing officer discovered when arriving at the "U–Store–It" facility that there are many 9'x12" lockers, however, then the issue becomes not whether the warrant was sufficiently particular (it was, according to the information disclosed to the magistrate), but whether the executing officer acted reasonably once he or she discovered the existence of multiple lockers.

conclude that the executing officer would be reasonably able to execute it correctly.

The particularity issue arises frequently with "residual clauses" in search warrants. These clauses typically are added to a specific list of items and call for the search and seizure of "all other evidence." Generally, these clauses are upheld so long as the "all other evidence" language is limited to the specific crime detailed in the warrant. In other words, a warrant may not direct officers to look for evidence of unspecified crimes. The Supreme Court addressed this issue in *Andresen v. Maryland*,[17] and it is worth reading a short excerpt of Justice Blackmun's opinion for the Court. As you do so, pay special attention to Blackmun's reliance on one of the interpretive techniques that you learned about in Chapter 1. On what technique does he rely? Do you agree with Blackmun's conclusion that the challenged portion of the warrant is consistent with the Fourth Amendment?

Andresen v. Maryland

427 U.S. 463 (1976).

■ BLACKMUN, J. In early 1972, a Bi–County Fraud Unit, acting under the joint auspices of the State's Attorneys' Offices of Montgomery and Prince George's Counties, Md., began an investigation of real estate settlement activities in the Washington, D.C., area. At the time, petitioner Andresen was an attorney who, as a sole practitioner, specialized in real estate settlements in Montgomery County. During the Fraud Unit's investigation, his activities came under scrutiny, particularly in connection with a transaction involving Lot 13T in the Potomac Woods subdivision of Montgomery County. The investigation, which included interviews with the purchaser, the mortgage holder, and other lienholders of Lot 13T, as well as an examination of county land records, disclosed that petitioner, acting as settlement attorney, had defrauded Standard–Young Associates, the purchaser of Lot 13T. Petitioner had represented that the property was free of liens and that, accordingly, no title insurance was necessary, when in fact, he knew that there were two outstanding liens on the property. In addition, investigators learned that the lienholders, by threatening to foreclose their liens, had forced a halt to the purchaser's construction on the property. When Standard–Young had confronted petitioner with this information, he responded by issuing, as an agent of a title insurance company, a title policy guaranteeing clear title to the property. By this action, petitioner also defrauded that insurance company by requiring it to pay the outstanding liens.

The investigators, concluding that there was probable cause to believe that petitioner had committed the state crime of false pretenses against Standard–Young, applied for warrants to search petitioner's law office and the separate office of Mount Vernon Development Corporation, of which petitioner was incorporator, sole shareholder, resident agent, and director.

---

17.   427 U.S. 463, 465–82 (1976).

The application sought permission to search for specified documents pertaining to the sale and conveyance of Lot 13T. A judge of the Sixth Judicial Circuit of Montgomery County concluded that there was probable cause and issued the warrants.

The searches of the two offices were conducted simultaneously during daylight hours on October 31, 1972. Petitioner was present during the search of his law office and was free to move about. Counsel for him was present during the latter half of the search. Between 2% and 3% of the files in the office were seized. A single investigator, in the presence of a police officer, conducted the search of Mount Vernon Development Corporation. This search, taking about four hours, resulted in the seizure of less than 5% of the corporation's files.

Petitioner eventually was charged . . . with the crime of false pretenses, based on his misrepresentation to Standard–Young concerning Lot 13T. . . . Before trial began, petitioner moved to suppress the seized documents. The trial court held a full suppression hearing. At the hearing, the State returned to petitioner 45 of the 52 items taken from the offices of the corporation. The trial court suppressed six other corporation items on the ground that there was no connection between them and the crimes charged . . . .

With respect to all the items not suppressed or returned, the trial court ruled that admitting them into evidence would not violate the . . . Fourth Amendment[]. It reasoned that the . . . search warrants were based on probable cause, and the documents not returned or suppressed were either directly related to Lot 13T, and therefore within the express language of the warrants, or properly seized and otherwise admissible to show a pattern of criminal conduct relevant to the charge concerning Lot 13T. . . .

After a trial by jury, petitioner was found guilty . . . and the Court of Special Appeals rejected petitioner's Fourth Amendment Claim[]. Specifically, it held that the warrants were supported by probable cause, that they did not authorize a general search in violation of the Fourth Amendment, and that the items admitted into evidence against petitioner at trial were within the scope of the warrants or were otherwise properly seized. . . . We granted certiorari [to address, in part] . . . petitioner's contention that rights guaranteed him by the Fourth Amendment were violated because the descriptive terms of the search warrants were so broad as to make them impermissible "general" warrants, and because certain items were seized in violation of the principles of *Warden v. Hayden*, 387 U.S. 294 (1967).

. . . Although petitioner concedes that the warrants for the most part were models of particularity, he contends that they were rendered fatally "general" by the addition, in each warrant, to the exhaustive list of particularly described documents, of the phrase "together with other fruits, instrumentalities and evidence of crime at this [time] unknown." The quoted language, it is argued, must be read in isolation and without reference to the rest of the long sentence at the end of which it appears.

When read "properly," petitioner contends, it permits the search for and seizure of any evidence of any crime.

General warrants of course, are prohibited by the Fourth Amendment. "[T]he problem [posed by the general warrant] is not that of intrusion Per se, but of a general, exploratory rummaging in a person's belongings. . . . [The Fourth Amendment addresses the problem] by requiring a 'particular description' of the things to be seized." *Coolidge v. New Hampshire*, 403 U.S. 443 (1971). This requirement "makes general searches . . . impossible and prevents the seizure of one thing under a warrant describing another. As to what is to be taken, nothing is left to the discretion of the officer executing the warrant." *Stanford v. Texas*, 379 U.S. 476 (1965).

In this case we agree with the determination of the Court of Special Appeals of Maryland that the challenged phrase must be read as authorizing only the search for and seizure of evidence relating to "the crime of false pretenses with respect to Lot 13T." The challenged phrase is not a separate sentence. Instead, it appears in each warrant at the end of a sentence containing a lengthy list of specified and particular items to be seized, all pertaining to Lot 13T.[a] We think it clear from the context that the term "crime" in the warrants refers only to the crime of false pretenses with respect to the sale of Lot 13T. The "other fruits" clause is one of a series that follows the colon after the word "Maryland." All clauses in the series are limited by what precedes that colon, namely, "items pertaining to

---

a.   [T]he following items pertaining to sale, purchase, settlement and conveyance of lot 13, block T, Potomac Woods subdivision, Montgomery County, Maryland:

. . . title notes, title abstracts, title rundowns; contracts of sale and/or assignments from Raffaele Antonelli and Rocco Caniglia to Mount Vernon Development Corporation and/or others; lien payoff correspondence and lien pay-off memoranda to and from lienholders and noteholders; correspondence and memoranda to and from trustees of deeds of trust; lenders instructions for a construction loan or construction and permanent loan; disbursement sheets and disbursement memoranda; checks, check stubs and ledger sheets indicating disbursement upon settlement; correspondence and memoranda concerning disbursements upon settlement; settlement statements and settlement memoranda; fully or partially prepared deed of trust releases, whether or not executed and whether or not recorded; books, records, documents, papers, memoranda and correspondence, showing or tending to show a fraudulent intent, and/or knowledge as elements of the crime of false pretenses, in violation of Article 27, Section 140, of the Annotated Code of Maryland, 1957 Edition, as amended and revised, together with other fruits, instrumentalities and evidence of crime at this [time] unknown.

Petitioner also suggests that the specific list of the documents to be seized constitutes a "general" warrant. We disagree. Under investigation was a complex real estate scheme whose existence could be proved only by piecing together many bits of evidence. Like a jigsaw puzzle, the whole "picture" of petitioner's false-pretense scheme with respect to Lot 13T could be shown only by placing in the proper place the many pieces of evidence that, taken singly, would show comparatively little. The complexity of an illegal scheme may not be used as a shield to avoid detection when the State has demonstrated probable cause to believe that a crime has been committed and probable cause to believe that evidence of this crime is in the suspect's possession. The specificity with which the documents are named here contrasts sharply with the absence of particularity in Berger v. New York, 388 U.S. 41, 58–59 (1967), where a state eavesdropping statute which authorized eavesdropping "without requiring belief that any particular offense has been or is being committed; nor that the 'property' sought, the conversations, be particularly described," was invalidated.

... lot 13, block T." The warrants, accordingly, did not authorize the executing officers to conduct a search for evidence of other crimes but only to search for and seize evidence relevant to the crime of false pretenses and Lot 13T.[b]

What happens when the warrant *application* is adequately particular, but the warrant itself fails to include sufficient detail? The Supreme Court recently suggested that unless the warrant expressly incorporates and appends the application, its silence violates the Fourth Amendment.

In the situation giving rise to the Court's opinion in *Groh v. Ramirez*,[18] Jeff Groh (a Special Agent for the federal Bureau of Alcohol, Tobacco and Firearms) submitted an application for a warrant to search Mr. and Mrs. Joseph Ramirez's Montana ranch for "any automatic firearms or parts of automatic weapons, destructive devices to include but not limited to grenades, grenade launchers, rocket launchers, and any and all receipts pertaining to the purchase or manufacture of automatic weapons or explosive devices or launchers." The warrant itself did not specify these or any other items that law enforcement officers were authorized to seize. Instead, in the particularity portion of the warrant, Groh merely described the Ramirezes' residence. The warrant did not incorporate by reference the items identified in the application. Moreover, the application was not attached to the warrant when it was executed—indeed, it remained in court under seal. Writing for a 5–person majority, Justice Stevens held the warrant invalid, reiterating that "[t]he Fourth Amendment by its terms requires particularity in the warrant, not in the supporting documents." The requirement serves a "high function," according to Justice Stevens:

> and that high function is not necessarily vindicated when some other document, somewhere, says something about the objects of the search, but the contents of that document are neither known to the person whose home is being searched nor available for her inspection. We do not say that the Fourth Amendment forbids a warrant from cross-referencing other documents. Indeed, most Courts of Appeals have held that a court may construe a warrant with reference to a supporting application or affidavit if the warrant uses appropriate words of incorporation, and if the supporting document accompanies the warrant.

---

b. The record discloses that the officials executing the warrants seized numerous papers that were not introduced into evidence. Although we are not informed of their content, we observe that to the extent such papers were not within the scope of the warrants or were otherwise improperly seized, the State was correct in returning them voluntarily and the trial judge was correct in suppressing others. We recognize that there are grave dangers inherent in executing a warrant authorizing a search and seizure of a person's papers that are not necessarily present in executing a warrant to search for physical objects whose relevance is more easily ascertainable. In searches for papers, it is certain that some innocuous documents will be examined, at least cursorily, in order to determine whether they are, in fact, among those papers authorized to be seized. Similar dangers, of course, are present in executing a warrant for the "seizure" of telephone conversations. In both kinds of searches, responsible officials, including judicial officials, must take care to assure that they are conducted in a manner that minimizes unwarranted intrusions upon privacy.

18.   540 U.S. 551 (2004).

But in this case the warrant did not incorporate other documents by reference, nor did either the affidavit or the application (which had been placed under seal) accompany the warrant.

The Court concluded that the warrant "did [not] make what fairly could be characterized as a mere technical mistake or typographical error." Instead, it was "so obviously deficient" that the Court had to regard the subsequent search as "warrantless."

Interestingly, Groh had conceded in the Supreme Court the invalidity of the warrant. Nevertheless, he urged the Court to evaluate the case based on the circumstances in which his search was carried out, rather than to decide it based simply on the presence or absence of a valid warrant. The search, he argued, was reasonable because it was "functionally equivalent to a search authorized by a valid warrant." Among the circumstances viewed by Groh as bearing on the search's reasonableness were (1) the Magistrate's determination that the application established probable cause, (2) the fact that during his execution of the warrant Groh told Mrs. Ramirez what he was looking for, and (3) the fact that Groh's search and seizure did not exceed the particulars contained in the application.

Justice Stevens rejected Groh's efforts to decouple the Fourth Amendment's warrant clause from its reasonableness clause. The Court's cases "have firmly established," he stated, "the basic principle of Fourth Amendment law that searches and seizures inside a home without a warrant are presumptively unreasonable." He explained further that this "presumptive rule against warrantless searches applies with equal force to searches whose only defect is a lack of particularity in the warrant."

Justice Stevens went further to explain that he saw no reason in this situation to deviate from the categorical rule:

> Petitioner asks us to hold that a search conducted pursuant to a warrant lacking particularity should be exempt from the presumption of unreasonableness if the goals served by the particularity requirement are otherwise satisfied. He maintains that the search in this case satisfied those goals—which he says are "to prevent general searches, to prevent the seizure of one thing under a warrant describing another, and to prevent warrants from being issued on vague or dubious information,"—because the scope of the search did not exceed the limits set forth in the application. But unless the particular items described in the affidavit are also set forth in the warrant itself (or at least incorporated by reference, and the affidavit present at the search), there can be no written assurance that the Magistrate actually found probable cause to search for, and to seize, every item mentioned in the affidavit. *See McDonald*, 335 U.S., at 455 ("Absent some grave emergency, the Fourth Amendment has interposed a magistrate between the citizen and the police. This was done . . . so that an objective mind might weigh the need to invade [the citizen's] privacy in order to enforce the law"). In this case, for example, it is at least theoretically possible that the Magistrate was satisfied that the search for weapons and explosives was justified by the showing in the affidavit, but not

convinced that any evidentiary basis existed for rummaging through respondents' files and papers for receipts pertaining to the purchase or manufacture of such items. Or, conceivably, the Magistrate might have believed that some of the weapons mentioned in the affidavit could have been lawfully possessed and therefore should not be seized. *See* 26 U.S.C. § 5861 (requiring registration, but not banning possession of, certain firearms). The mere fact that the Magistrate issued a warrant does not necessarily establish that he agreed that the scope of the search should be as broad as the affiant's request. Even though petitioner acted with restraint in conducting the search, "the inescapable fact is that this restraint was imposed by the agents themselves, not by a judicial officer."

We have long held, moreover, that the purpose of the particularity requirement is not limited to the prevention of general searches. A particular warrant also "assures the individual whose property is searched or seized of the lawful authority of the executing officer, his need to search, and the limits of his power to search." *See . . . Illinois v. Gates*, 462 U.S. 213, 236 (1983) ("[P]ossession of a warrant by officers conducting an arrest or search greatly reduces the perception of unlawful or intrusive police conduct").*

It is incumbent on the officer executing a search warrant to ensure the search is lawfully authorized and lawfully conducted.** Because petitioner did not have in his possession a warrant particularly describing the things he intended to seize, proceeding with the search was clearly "unreasonable" under the Fourth Amendment. The Court of Appeals correctly held that the search was unconstitutional.

In addition to the five justices who joined Justice Stevens's opinion, two others agreed that the Fourth Amendment had been violated. Justices Thomas and Scalia, however, dissented from that holding. Both would decouple the warrant clause from the reasonableness clause and apply reasonableness balancing rather than categorical balancing to situations

---

* It is true, as petitioner points out, that neither the Fourth Amendment nor Rule 41 of the Federal Rules of Criminal Procedure requires the executing officer to serve the warrant on the owner before commencing the search. Rule 41(f)(3) provides that "[t]he officer executing the warrant must: (A) give a copy of the warrant and a receipt for the property taken to the person from whom, or from whose premises, the property was taken; or (B) leave a copy of the warrant and receipt at the place where the officer took the property." Quite obviously, in some circumstances—a surreptitious search by means of a wiretap, for example, or the search of empty or abandoned premises—it will be impracticable or imprudent for the officers to show the warrant in advance. Whether it would be unreasonable to refuse a request to furnish the warrant at the outset of the search when, as in this case, an occupant of the premises is present and poses no threat to the officers' safe and effective performance of their mission, is a question that this case does not present.

** The Court of Appeals' decision is consistent with this principle. Petitioner mischaracterizes the court's decision when he contends that it imposed a novel proofreading requirement on officers executing warrants. The court held that officers leading a search team must "mak[e] sure that they have a proper warrant that in fact authorizes the search and seizure they are about to conduct." That is not a duty to proofread; it is, rather, a duty to ensure that the warrant conforms to constitutional requirements.

like the one presented in *Groh*. Moreover, according to Justice Thomas, the search should not be treated as a "warrantless" one:

> ... [A] search conducted pursuant to a defective warrant is constitutionally different from a "warrantless search." Consequently, despite the defective warrant, I would still ask whether this search was unreasonable and would conclude that it was not. ...

> "[A]ny Fourth Amendment case may present two separate questions: whether the search was conducted pursuant to a warrant issued in accordance with the second Clause, and, if not, whether it was nevertheless 'reasonable' within the meaning of the first." *United States v. Leon*, 468 U.S. 897, 961 (1984) (STEVENS, J., dissenting). By categorizing the search here to be a "warrantless" one, the Court declines to perform a reasonableness inquiry and ignores the fact that this search is quite different from searches that the Court has considered to be "warrantless" in the past. Our cases involving "warrantless" searches do not generally involve situations in which an officer has obtained a warrant that is later determined to be facially defective, but rather involve situations in which the officers neither sought nor obtained a warrant. By simply treating this case as if no warrant had even been sought or issued, the Court glosses over what should be the key inquiry: whether it is always appropriate to treat a search made pursuant to a warrant that fails to describe particularly the things to be seized as presumptively unreasonable. ...

> [I]n contrast to the case of a truly warrantless search, if a warrant (due to a mistake) does not specify on its face the particular items to be seized but the warrant application passed on by the magistrate judge contains such details, a searchee still has the benefit of a determination by a neutral magistrate that there is probable cause to search a particular place and to seize particular items. In such a circumstance, the principal justification for applying a rule of presumptive unreasonableness falls away.

> In the instant case, the items to be seized were clearly specified in the warrant application and set forth in the affidavit, both of which were given to the Magistrate. The Magistrate reviewed all of the documents and signed the warrant application and made no adjustment or correction to this application. It is clear that respondents here received the protection of the Warrant Clause. Under these circumstances, I would not hold that any ensuing search constitutes a presumptively unreasonable warrantless search. Instead, I would determine whether, despite the invalid warrant, the resulting search was reasonable and hence constitutional.

———

PROBLEM 3–1

Notice that in the Oklahoma City bombing case search warrant, reproduced above, the officers are directed to search for and seize "[d]ocumentary evidence, such as bank records and telephone toll records." Under the Supreme Court's reasoning in *Andresen*, does this language violate the particularity requirement?

PROBLEM 3–2

In early 1999, Detective Lewis Drahm of the Elm Grove Police Department began an investigation following the discovery of photographs of a local 14–year-old boy engaged in sexual acts. Drahm was able to locate and interview the boy and his father. The boy told the detective that the photographs were taken during a sexual encounter with a man who contacted him in an Internet chat room. Upon learning of the situation, the victim's father allowed Drahm to transport the family computer to the police department for further investigation and provided permission to access his son's AOL account. The boy provided Drahm with the password. Using the boy's Internet account, Drahm logged on to AOL and received an e-mail from someone with the screen name "Capnjeffry," who was listed in the boy's AOL instant messenger "Buddy List." Following several emails with Capnjeffry in which Drahm posed as the boy, Drahm obtained a warrant to search AOL's records for information regarding Capnjeffry. AOL informed the detective that the screen name "Capnjeffry" belonged to Jeffery Lesinger. After several more email conversations in which Lesinger continued to solicit sex from the boy, Drahm applied for search and arrest warrants, detailing in the warrant applications his investigations to date and identifying the suspected crime as "using or attempting to use the Internet to induce a minor to engage in sexual activity." After obtaining the warrants and arresting Lesinger, Drahm searched Lesinger's computer, discovering numerous pieces of evidence supporting the prosecution.

Lesinger filed a motion to suppress the fruits of the computer search, alleging that the warrant lack sufficient particulars. The warrant specified, among the places to be searched, "computer equipment including computer hard drives, digital and magnetic storage devices, computer printouts, and computer software." Describing the items to be seized, the warrant listed "sexually explicit material or paraphernalia used to lower the inhibition of children, child pornography, material related to past molestation such as photographs, communication with children relating to sexual activity, and journals recording sexual encounters with children." Lesinger contended that the warrant provided insufficient objective limits on where in his computer hard drive the detective was authorized to search. He also claimed that the warrant authorized the seizure of virtually every document and file on his hard drive. Lesinger specifically referenced the Court's decision in *Groh* in his motion—stating that, after *Groh*, a warrant lacks particularity "unless it clearly establishes, through a specific list of places to be searched and items to be seized, the magistrate's control over the scope of the search."

Question: Assume you are the judge evaluating Lesinger's suppression motion. How should you rule? How will you explain the application of *Groh* to Lesinger's situation?

C.   NEUTRAL AND DETACHED MAGISTRATES

Although the Fourth Amendment does not specify the officials who may authorize warrants, the Supreme Court has long held that the issuing official must be a "neutral and detached magistrate"—meaning, in most cases, a judicial officer who has no stake in the investigation for which the warrant is sought. Rule 41 of the Federal Rules of Criminal Procedure grants authority to issue warrants as follows:

(b) Authority to Issue a Warrant. At the request of a federal law enforcement officer or an attorney for the government:

(1) a magistrate judge with authority in the district—or if none is reasonably available, a judge of a state court of record in the district—has authority to issue a warrant to search for and seize a person or property located within the district;

(2) a magistrate judge with authority in the district has authority to issue a warrant for a person or property outside the district if the person or property is located within the district when the warrant is issued but might move or be moved outside the district before the warrant is executed; and

(3) a magistrate judge—in an investigation of domestic terrorism or international terrorism (as defined in 18 U.S.C. § 2331)—having authority in any district in which activities related to the terrorism may have occurred, may issue a warrant for a person or property within or outside that district.

Although the federal rules permit only judicial officers to issue warrants, the Supreme Court has indicated that, for minor offenses at least, warrants may be issued by lay people who are neither judges nor lawyers. In *Shadwick v. City of Tampa*,[19] the Court upheld a municipal ordinance that permitted court clerks to issue arrest warrants in misdemeanor traffic cases, observing that no special competence was needed to evaluate the existence of probable cause in such cases.

The crucial issue from a constitutional perspective appears to be that of "detachment." While law enforcement is an executive branch function, the warrant clause in essence requires the executive branch to seek judicial approval for its warrant authority. For that reason, prosecutors and other members of law enforcement agencies cannot issue warrants. Even judicial officers who become overly involved in a case may lose their neutrality or detachment. In *Lo–Ji Sales, Inc. v. New York*,[20] for example, a New York "Town Justice" reviewed two films purchased from an adult bookstore by a New York State Police investigator. The Town Justice agreed that the films were obscene and issued a warrant authorizing seizure of other copies of those two films. The investigator's search warrant affidavit contained "an assertion that 'similar' films and printed matter portraying similar activities" could be found in the bookstore, and the warrant application request-

---

19.   407 U.S. 345, 347 (1972).

20.   442 U.S. 319 (1979).

ed that the Town Justice accompany the investigator to the bookstore for the execution of the warrant. As the Court explained,

> ... the stated purpose was to allow the Town Justice to determine independently if any other items at the store were possessed in violation of law and subject to seizure. The Town Justice agreed.
>
> Accordingly, the warrant also contained a recital that authorized the seizure of "[t]he following items that the Court independently [on examination] has determined to be possessed in violation of Article 235 of the Penal Law...." However, at the time the Town Justice signed the warrant there were no items listed or described following this statement. As noted earlier, the only "things to be seized" that were described in the warrant were copies of the two films the state investigator had purchased. Before going to the store, the Town Justice also signed a warrant for the arrest of the clerk who operated the store for having sold the two films to the investigator.
>
> The Town Justice and the investigator enlisted three other State Police investigators, three uniformed State Police officers, and three members of the local prosecutor's office—a total of 11—and the search party converged on the bookstore. The store clerk was immediately placed under arrest and advised of the search warrant. He was the only employee present; he was free to continue working in the store to the extent the search permitted, and the store remained open to the public while the party conducted its search mission which was to last nearly six hours....
>
> After the search and seizure was completed, the seized items were taken to a State Police barracks where they were inventoried. Each item was then listed on the search warrant, and late the same night the completed warrant was given to the Town Justice. The warrant, which had consisted of 2 pages when he signed it before the search, by late in the day contained 16 pages. It is clear, therefore, that the particular description of "things to be seized" was entered in the document after the seizure and impoundment of the books and other articles.

The Court held the warrant invalid. Not only was the particularity requirement violated ["the Fourth Amendment [does not] countenance open-ended warrants, to be completed while a search is being conducted and items seized or after the seizure has been carried out"], but also the Town Justice failed to be neutral and detached. The Court stated:

> We have repeatedly said that a warrant authorized by a neutral and detached judicial officer is "a more reliable safeguard against improper searches than the hurried judgment of a law enforcement officer engaged in the often competitive enterprise of ferreting out crime." ...
> The Town Justice did not manifest that neutrality and detachment demanded of a judicial officer when presented with a warrant application for a search and seizure. We need not question the subjective belief of the Town Justice in the propriety of his actions, but the objective facts of record manifest an erosion of whatever neutral and

detached posture existed at the outset. He allowed himself to become a member, if not the leader, of the search party which was essentially a police operation. Once in the store, he conducted a generalized search under authority of an invalid warrant; he was not acting as a judicial officer but as an adjunct law enforcement officer. When he ordered an item seized because he believed it was obscene, he instructed the police officers to seize all "similar" items as well, leaving determination of what was "similar" to the officer's discretion. Indeed, he yielded to the State Police even the completion of the general provision of the warrant. Though it would not have validated the warrant in any event, the Town Justice admitted at the hearing to suppress evidence that he could not verify that the inventory prepared by the police and presented to him late that evening accurately reflected what he had ordered seized.

In another case, the Court invalidated warrants issued by a magistrate who was paid a fee for each warrant he issued, but who received no fee for warrant applications that he declined to approve.[21]

D.   ANTICIPATORY SEARCH WARRANTS

Ordinary search warrants are generally based on affidavits establishing probable cause to believe that evidence of a crime is at a specified location at, or shortly before, the time that the affidavit is prepared. The evidence is also expected to be at that location at a later time: the time that the warrant is executed. The Federal Rules of Criminal Procedure indeed require execution of a warrant within no more than ten days precisely to avoid the problem of the warrant's turning "stale,"[22] that is, the passage of time rendering it less likely that the items once there will still be so. Moreover, if officers having a warrant learn that the specified items have left the location before the search actually occurs, they are no longer entitled to execute the warrant because the supposition of continued presence no longer holds.[23]

Anticipatory warrants are instead based on affidavits purportedly establishing probable cause to believe that evidence of crime will be at the specified location at the time of the search. But the affiant does not declare that the items are already there at, or about, the time of the affidavit's preparation. Anticipatory warrants are thus issued based upon more thorough predictions of the future than are traditional warrants. Although traditional warrants do reflect one future supposition–that the evidence will still be there at the time of warrant execution–the basis for issuing the warrant is past-oriented: the evidence was at the location at some point.[24]

---

21.   *See* Connally v. Georgia, 429 U.S. 245, 251 (1977).

22.   *See* FED. R. CRIM. P. 41(e)(2)(A); United States v. Wagner, 989 F.2d 69, 75 (2d Cir. 1993) (staleness).

23.   *See, e.g.,* United States v. Bowling, 900 F.2d 926, 932 (6th Cir. 1990).

24.   *See* Andrew E. Taslitz, *Fortune–Telling and the Fourth Amendment: Of Terrorism, Slippery Slopes, and Predicting the Future*, 58 RUTGERS L. REV. 195, 202 & n. 31 (2005) (briefly summarizing the nature of anticipatory warrants and the constitutional concerns they raise).

This relative difference in future orientation raises questions about the constitutionality of anticipatory warrants. Are they ever constitutional? A useful analogy can be made to electronic surveillance warrants, which are also issued based on the belief that conversations will occur in the future, though they may not have occurred in the past. The Court has upheld their constitutionality under certain conditions that refine the probable cause and warrant requirements to limit police discretion in this more amorphous (relative to traditional warrants) situation, and Congress has passed legislation to implement the Court's conditions (these matters are discussed in detail in a forthcoming chapter on electronic surveillance).[25] Justice Black's dissent in *Katz* (a case involving warrantless electronic eavesdropping of expected public telephone conversations) captures the constitutional difficulty of future-oriented searches like electronic ones:

> [T]he language of the second clause indicates that the [Fourth] Amendment refers not only to something tangible so it can be seized but to something already in existence so it can be described. Yet the Court's interpretation would have the Amendment apply to overhearing future conversations which by their very nature are nonexistent until they take place. How can one "describe" a future conversation, and, if one cannot, how can a magistrate issue a warrant to eavesdrop one in the future? It is argued that information showing what is expected to be said is sufficient to limit the boundaries of what later can be admitted into evidence; but does such general information really meet the specific language of the Amendment which says "particularly describing"? Rather than use language in a completely artificial way, I must conclude that the Fourth Amendment simply does not apply to eavesdropping.[26]

Black's conclusion was that electronic surveillance was constitutional because its future orientation rendered it entirely outside Fourth Amendment regulation, a position that the *Katz* majority implicitly rejected.[27] Yet Black's analysis mattered even more if the Amendment does apply: How do we gauge probable cause when we are fortune-telling the future? How do you describe what does not exist? The Court and Congress have offered detailed answers to those questions in the electronic surveillance context. But anticipatory warrants seek to extend this future orientation to all evidence, including ordinary physical evidence. Does the Fourth Amendment ever permit such an extension and, if so, under what conditions?

Lower courts have mostly said "yes" to the constitutionality of the extension but have often required a strong guarantee that the affiant's prediction will indeed come to pass, for example, requiring probable cause to believe that contraband is on a "sure course" to its intended destination. These courts have also often specified "triggering conditions"–post-warrant events that must come to pass before the anticipatory warrant may actually

---

25. *See id.* at 201–02 (summarizing the statutory and case law).

26. Katz v. United States, 389 U.S. 347, 365–66 (1967) (Black, J., dissenting).

27. *See* Taslitz, *Fortune-Telling, supra* note 24, at 201–02.

be executed, such as actually seeing a package ultimately delivered to a home that fits the warrant description of the expected package.[28] The United States Supreme Court recently had its first opportunity to weigh in on these questions of the constitutionality of anticipatory warrants in *United States v. Grubbs*.[29]

Jeffrey Grubbs had been arrested pursuant to a federal search warrant of his home on the basis of an anticipatory warrant issued by a magistrate judge, the affidavit of which indicated that the warrant was only to be executed after a "controlled delivery" of contraband to Grubbs' home. The contraband was a videotape of child pornography that he had ordered from an undercover federal postal inspector via the Internet. The warrant affidavit clearly recited a triggering condition:

> [e]xecution of this search warrant will not occur unless and until the parcel has been received by a person(s) and has been physically taken into the residence.... At that time, and not before, this search warrant will be executed by me and other United States Postal inspectors, with appropriate assistance from other law enforcement officers in accordance with this warrant's command.[30]

The affidavit also contained two attachments describing Grubbs' home and the items to be seized. These attachments were incorporated into the warrant, though the affidavit was not. The affidavit mentioned the attachments, however:

> "Based upon the foregoing facts, I respectfully submit there exists probable cause to believe that the items set forth in Attachment B to this affidavit and the search warrant, will be found at [Grubbs' residence], which residence is further described at Attachment A."[31]

Two days later, an undercover postal inspector delivered the package containing the videotape to Grubbs' home; Grubbs' wife signed for the package and took it, unopened, into the home. When Grubbs left his home a few minutes later, police detained him and searched his home. Approximately half an hour into the search, Grubbs was provided a copy of the warrant that included the attachments but not the supporting affidavit containing the warrant's "triggering" condition.

Grubbs subsequently consented to interrogation and admitted ordering the videotape. He was arrested. The videotape and other items were seized. A grand jury indicted him on one count of "receiving a visual depiction of a minor engaged in sexually explicit conduct," a violation of 18 U.S.C. Section 2252(a) (2).[32] Grubbs moved to suppress the evidence, arguing that the warrant was invalid "because it failed to list a triggering condition."[33]

---

28.   *See id.* at 202 & n.31–32.

29.   547 U.S. 90 (2006).

30.   *Id.* at 92.

31.   *Id.*

32.   *Id.* at 93.

33.   *Id.*

Grubbs' motion was denied by the district court; he pleaded guilty, reserving his right to appeal the denial.

On appeal, the Ninth Circuit reversed, holding that the Fourth Amendment's particularity requirement "applies with full force to the conditions precedent to an anticipatory search warrant." The Ninth Circuit reasoned that an anticipatory warrant suffering from such a defect "may be 'cured' if the conditions precedent are set forth in an affidavit that is incorporated in the warrant and 'presented to the person whose property is being searched.' " Because the postal inspectors " 'failed to present the affidavit—the only document in which the triggering conditions were listed'—to Grubbs and his wife, the 'warrant was . . . inoperative, and the search was illegal.' "

The Supreme Court granted certiorari based on two challenges to the search warrant: 1) the "antecedent question" of whether anticipatory search warrants are "categorically unconstitutional" (failing to satisfy the Fourth Amendment requirement that "no Warrants shall issue, but upon probable cause") and 2) whether listing the "triggering condition" in the warrant is necessary to " 'assure the individual whose property is searched or seized of the lawful authority of the executing officer, his need to search, and the limits of his power to search.' "[34]

The Court, in an opinion authored by Justice Scalia, reversed the Ninth Circuit. In discussing the first question, the Court determined that because probable cause "exists when 'there is a fair probability that contraband or evidence of a crime will be found in a particular place,' "and because this requirement necessarily "looks to whether evidence will be found when the search is conducted, all warrants are, in a sense, anticipatory."[35] Granted, said the Court, with ordinary warrants police seek authority to search for what is already there. But the magistrate's determination in that ordinary case that there is probable cause for the search nevertheless "amounts to a prediction that the item will still be there when the warrant is executed."[36] The anticipatory aspect of all warrants is even clearer, said the Court, with electronic surveillance. Accordingly, "[a]nticipatory warrants are . . . no different in principle from ordinary warrants."[37] Moreover (and like ordinary warrants), anticipatory warrants:

> require the magistrate to determine (1) that it is now probable that (2) contraband, evidence of a crime, or a fugitive will be on the described premises (3) when the warrant is executed. It should be noted, however, that where the anticipatory warrant places a condition (other than the mere passage of time) upon its execution, the first of these determinations goes not merely to what will probably be found if the condition is met. (If that were the extent of the probability determination, an anticipatory warrant could be issued for every house in the

---

34. *Id.* at 94–95, 98.

35. *Id.* at 95–96.

36. *Id.* at 95.

37. *Id.* 96.

country, authorizing search and seizure if contraband should be delivered—though for any single location there is no likelihood that contraband will be delivered.) Rather, the probability determination for a conditioned anticipatory warrant looks also to the likelihood that the condition will occur, and thus that a proper object of seizure will be on the described premises. In other words, for a conditioned anticipatory warrant to comply with the Fourth Amendment's requirement of probable cause, two prerequisites of probability must be satisfied. It must be true not only that if the triggering condition occurs "there is a fair probability that contraband or evidence of a crime will be found in a particular place . . ." but also that there is probable cause to believe the triggering condition will occur. The supporting affidavit must provide the magistrate with sufficient information to evaluate both aspects of the probable-cause determination.[38]

Thus, "when an anticipatory warrant is issued, 'the fact that the contraband is not presently located at the place described in the warrant is immaterial, so long as there is probable cause to believe that it will be there when the search warrant is executed.' "[39] Because the anticipatory warrant's affidavit explained that "execution of the search warrant will not occur unless and until the parcel [containing child pornography] has been received by a person(s) and has been physically taken into the residence," execution of the warrant before said triggering condition would give the government "no reason to believe the item described in the warrant could be found at the searched location; by definition, the triggering condition which establishes probable cause has not yet been satisfied when the warrant is issued." The Court found that the magistrate judge had a substantial basis for concluding that the triggering condition would be satisfied (Grubbs' refusal of delivery of the videotape was deemed "unlikely" by the Court) and the government had probable cause to conduct the search of Grubbs' home, given that the warrant's triggering condition occurred prior to the search warrant's execution.[40]

With respect to Grubbs' assertion that the anticipatory search warrant lacked sufficient particularity, thereby invalidating the government's search, the Court determined that the Fourth Amendment "specifies only two matters that must be 'particularly described' in the warrant": "the place to be searched" and "the persons or things to be seized." It does not address "unenumerated matters" such as "conditions precedent" to a warrant's execution.[41]

Regarding the government's "failure" to present either Grubbs or his wife with a copy of the full warrant containing the triggering condition, the Court noted that there is no such Constitutional requirement of warrant presentment in the Fourth Amendment's particularity provision.

---

38. *Id.*

39. *Id.*

40. *Id.* at 97.

41. *Id.*

NOTES AND QUESTIONS

1.   Is the Court right that in principle there is no distinction between an ordinary warrant and an anticipatory warrant? If there is such a distinction, does the Court's test adequately address the differences? Does the Court's test seem different from the "on a sure course" test of many lower courts? If yes, how?

2.   Does the absence of an express requirement in the Fourth Amendment's text of a warrant's containing "triggering conditions" necessarily exhaust what may be required in a warrant's text to render a search or seizure pursuant to that warrant "reasonable"? In connection with this question, consider the following language in Justice Souter's opinion in *Grubbs* concurring in part and concurring in the judgment (Souter being joined by Justices Stevens and Ginsburg):

> The Court notes that a warrant's failure to specify the place to be searched and the objects sought violates an express textual requirement of the Fourth Amendment, whereas the text says nothing about a condition placed by the issuing magistrate on the authorization to search (here, delivery of the package of contraband). That textual difference is, however, no authority for neglecting to specify the point or contingency intended by the magistrate to trigger authorization, and the government should beware of banking on the terms of a warrant without such specification. The notation of a starting date was an established feature even of the objectionable 18th-century writs of assistance. . . . And it is fair to say that the very word "warrant" in the Fourth Amendment means a statement of authority that sets out the time at which (or, in the case of anticipatory warrants, the condition on which) the authorization begins.[42]

Souter considered including the intended condition in the warrant as necessary to inform an executing officer, who may not have been the one obtaining the warrant, of the magistrate's intended limits on police authority. Souter also suggested that a government officer obtaining what the magistrate says is an anticipatory warrant "must know or should realize when it omits the condition on which authorization depends," thereby depriving the state of raising any good faith exception to the exclusionary rule should the search in fact be executed in a way that exceeds the authority the magistrate intended to confer.[43]

3.   The Ninth Circuit in *Grubbs* had asserted that a property owner must receive notice of the triggering condition before the search or he would "stand no real chance of policing the officers' conduct."[44] The majority noted, however, that this argument "assumes that the executing officer must present the property owner with a copy of the warrant before

---

42.   *Id.* at 100 (Souter, J., concurring). Five Justices were thus in the majority and three in the Souter opinion, Justice Alito having taken no part in the decision.

43.   *See id.* at 100–101 (Souter, J., citing Groh v. Ramirez, 540 U.S. 551, 554–55, 563 & n. 6.).

44.   377 F.3d at 1079 n. 9.

conducting his search."[45] But, continued the Court, "neither the Fourth Amendment nor Rule 41 of the Federal Rules of Criminal Procedure imposes such a requirement." Said the Court, "[t]he Constitution protects property owners not by giving them license to engage the police in a debate over the basis of the warrant, but by interposing ... the deliberate, impartial judgment of a judicial officer ... between the citizen and the police" and by providing for damages actions and suppression of evidence improperly obtained.[46]

Despite this apparently clear majority statement of a no-warrant-presentment rule, Justice Souter declared that "the right of an owner to demand to see a copy of the warrant before making way for the police" "remains undetermined today."[47] Yet Souter seemed to envision a role for the affected citizen, not only the magistrate, in policing the police, contrary to the vision of relative citizen passivity declared by the majority. Thus, Souter said,

> [I]f a later case holds that the homeowner has a right to inspect the warrant on request, a statement of the condition of authorization would give the owner a right to correct any misapprehension on the police's part that the condition had been met when in fact it had not been. If the police were then to enter anyway without a reasonable (albeit incorrect) justification, the search would certainly be open to serious challenge as unreasonable within the meaning of the Fourth Amendment.[48]

Which vision of the citizenry's role under the Fourth Amendment makes more sense as a matter of constitutional law? As a matter of sound policy to guide the crafting of statutes, regulations, or executive policies?

PROBLEM 3–3

Detective John O'Malley received an anonymous phone tip declaring that "Robert Obean at 1408 Luna Drive, Los Angeles, is going to be receiving a visit tomorrow from Paula Birnbaum around 4 p.m. ... Paula will just be returning from a trip to Mexico and will have smuggled large quantities of cocaine across the border in plastic bags in her alimentary canal. She will stay at Obean's home until she 'passes' the baggies. I know this because Paula shared this information with her new boyfriend–my brother–promising to shower him with gifts from the money she will receive for her efforts. I don't like seeing my baby brother mixed up in anything like this, so I'm calling you to put a stop to it." O'Malley is uncertain whether he has enough information to get a warrant and turns to you, a new Assistant District Attorney, to advise O'Malley on whether he can get a warrant and what, if any, conditions should be recited in the

---

45. 547 U.S. at 98–99.

46. *Id.* at 99.

47. *Id.* at 101 (Souter, J., concurring).

48. *Id.* at 101–02.

warrant. Advise him. If you think more investigation is needed, specify what, why, and how. Your supervisor, learning of O'Malley's request, has also asked you to draft a brief set of policy guidelines to regulate when and how your office should obtain anticipatory warrants and what the warrants should provide. Draft those guidelines.

II. Executing the Warrant

Many motions to suppress in criminal cases are based on the manner in which law enforcement officers execute search and arrest warrants. There are three major issues with which lawyers should be familiar: (1) law enforcement mistakes in executing warrants; (2) the time and manner of execution; and (3) the treatment of individuals encountered during warrant executions. We will discuss these separately below.

A. Mistakes in Executing Warrants

It is easy to imagine how law enforcement officers might encounter in the field problems that they did not anticipate during the warrant application process. A common problem involves the particularity requirement: an officer might have applied for a warrant to search what the officer believed to be a single-family residence, but what happens if the officer discovers while executing the warrant that the building contains multiple residences? The answer, not surprisingly, is that the officer must act reasonably and within the scope of the warrant. If the officer can determine which residence is covered by the warrant, the warrant may be executed. Otherwise, the officer must go back to the drawing board, obtain more information, and apply for a more particular warrant.

Officers make mistakes, however, and often the question for lawyers and courts is whether evidence obtained during mistaken executions must be suppressed. In our multi-unit dwelling situation, for example, the officer might enter the wrong dwelling before realizing the mistake. If the officer seizes evidence of a crime there, should that evidence be suppressed? The Supreme Court's answer has been: it depends on the reasonableness of the mistake and the officer's ensuing actions. Read the following excerpt from Justice Stevens's majority opinion in *Maryland v. Garrison*,[49] and evaluate the factors that entered into the Court's assessment of reasonableness.

Maryland v. Garrison

480 U.S. 79 (1987).

■ Stevens, J. Baltimore police officers obtained and executed a warrant to search the person of Lawrence McWebb and "the premises known as 2036 Park Avenue third floor apartment." When the police applied for the warrant and when they conducted the search pursuant to the warrant, they

---

49. 480 U.S. 79, 80–88 (1987).

reasonably believed that there was only one apartment on the premises described in the warrant. In fact, the third floor was divided into two apartments, one occupied by McWebb and one by respondent Garrison. Before the officers executing the warrant became aware that they were in a separate apartment occupied by respondent, they had discovered the contraband that provided the basis for respondent's conviction for violating Maryland's Controlled Substances Act. The question presented is whether the seizure of that contraband was prohibited by the Fourth Amendment.

. . . There is no question that the warrant was valid and was supported by probable cause. The trial court found, and the two appellate courts did not dispute, that after making a reasonable investigation, including a verification of information obtained from a reliable informant, an exterior examination of the three-story building at 2036 Park Avenue, and an inquiry of the utility company, the officer who obtained the warrant reasonably concluded that there was only one apartment on the third floor and that it was occupied by McWebb. When six Baltimore police officers executed the warrant, they fortuitously encountered McWebb in front of the building and used his key to gain admittance to the first-floor hallway and to the locked door at the top of the stairs to the third floor. As they entered the vestibule on the third floor, they encountered respondent, who was standing in the hallway area. The police could see into the interior of both McWebb's apartment to the left and respondent's to the right, for the doors to both were open. Only after respondent's apartment had been entered and heroin, cash, and drug paraphernalia had been found did any of the officers realize that the third floor contained two apartments. As soon as they became aware of that fact, the search was discontinued. All of the officers reasonably believed that they were searching McWebb's apartment. No further search of respondent's apartment was made.

. . . In our view, the case presents two separate constitutional issues, one concerning the validity of the warrant and the other concerning the reasonableness of the manner in which it was executed. . . .

I

The Warrant Clause of the Fourth Amendment categorically prohibits the issuance of any warrant except one "particularly describing the place to be searched and the persons or things to be seized." The manifest purpose of this particularity requirement was to prevent general searches. By limiting the authorization to search to the specific areas and things for which there is probable cause to search, the requirement ensures that the search will be carefully tailored to its justifications, and will not take on the character of the wide-ranging exploratory searches the Framers intended to prohibit. Thus, the scope of a lawful search is "defined by the object of the search and the places in which there is probable cause to believe that it may be found. Just as probable cause to believe that a stolen lawnmower may be found in a garage will not support a warrant to search an upstairs bedroom, probable cause to believe that undocumented aliens are being transported in a van will not justify a warrantless search of a suitcase." *United States v. Ross*, 456 U.S. 798 (1982).

In this case there is no claim that the "persons or things to be seized" were inadequately described or that there was no probable cause to believe that those things might be found in "the place to be searched" as it was described in the warrant. With the benefit of hindsight, however, we now know that the description of that place was broader than appropriate because it was based on the mistaken belief that there was only one apartment on the third floor of the building at 2036 Park Avenue. The question is whether that factual mistake invalidated a warrant that undoubtedly would have been valid if it had reflected a completely accurate understanding of the building's floor plan. . . .

Plainly, if the officers had known, or even if they should have known, that there were two separate dwelling units on the third floor of 2036 Park Avenue, they would have been obligated to exclude respondent's apartment from the scope of the requested warrant. On the basis of that information, we agree with the conclusion of all three Maryland courts that the warrant, insofar as it authorized a search that turned out to be ambiguous in scope, was valid when it issued.

II

The question whether the execution of the warrant violated respondent's constitutional right to be secure in his home is somewhat less clear. We have no difficulty concluding that the officers' entry into the third-floor common area was legal; they carried a warrant for those premises, and they were accompanied by McWebb, who provided the key that they used to open the door giving access to the third-floor common area. If the officers had known, or should have known, that the third floor contained two apartments before they entered the living quarters on the third floor, and thus had been aware of the error in the warrant, they would have been obligated to limit their search to McWebb's apartment. Moreover, as the officers recognized, they were required to discontinue the search of respondent's apartment as soon as they discovered that there were two separate units on the third floor and therefore were put on notice of the risk that they might be in a unit erroneously included within the terms of the warrant. The officers' conduct and the limits of the search were based on the information available as the search proceeded. While the purposes justifying a police search strictly limit the permissible extent of the search, the Court has also recognized the need to allow some latitude for honest mistakes that are made by officers in the dangerous and difficult process of making arrests and executing search warrants.

In *Hill v. California*, 401 U.S. 797 (1971), we considered the validity of the arrest of a man named Miller based on the mistaken belief that he was Hill. The police had probable cause to arrest Hill and they in good faith believed that Miller was Hill when they found him in Hill's apartment. As we explained: "The upshot was that the officers in good faith believed Miller was Hill and arrested him. They were quite wrong as it turned out, and subjective good-faith belief would not in itself justify either the arrest or the subsequent search. But sufficient probability, not certainty, is the touchstone of reasonableness under the Fourth Amendment and on the record before us the officers' mistake was understandable and the arrest a reasonable response to the situation facing them at the time.''

While *Hill* involved an arrest without a warrant, its underlying rationale that an officer's reasonable misidentification of a person does not invalidate a valid arrest is equally applicable to an officer's reasonable failure to appreciate that a valid warrant describes too broadly the premises to be searched. Under the reasoning in *Hill*, the validity of the search of respondent's apartment pursuant to a warrant authorizing the search of the entire third floor depends on whether the officers' failure to realize the overbreadth of the warrant was objectively understandable and reasonable. Here it unquestionably was. The objective facts available to the officers at the time suggested no distinction between McWebb's apartment and the third-floor premises.

. . . Prior to the officers' discovery of the factual mistake, they perceived McWebb's apartment and the third-floor premises as one and the same; therefore their execution of the warrant reasonably included the entire third floor. Under either interpretation of the warrant, the officers' conduct was consistent with a reasonable effort to ascertain and identify the place intended to be searched within the meaning of the Fourth Amendment.

———

The Court suggested it would not have upheld the search if the officers had known in advance that the third floor contained two apartments. What is the difference in the two situations? Was the Court right to condition its holding on what the officers knew and when they knew it? What kind of incentives might this rule create?

The officers in *Maryland v. Garrison* were able to see into the interior of both apartments from the third floor vestibule, because the doors were open. Justice Stevens suggested the officers could not, consistent with the constitution, enter Garrison's apartment if they became aware of the fact that it was separate from the apartment identified in the warrant. What would have happened if, while standing in the vestibule looking into Garrison's apartment, the officers had realized that his apartment was separate while at the same time seeing heroin and drug paraphernalia just inside of his door? Could the officers ''secure'' Garrison's apartment—guarding the door and prohibiting him from entering—while obtaining a search warrant? It appears that they could. In *Illinois v. McArthur*,[50] the Court upheld a police decision to prevent a man from entering his home for two hours while they obtained a search warrant. The homeowner claimed that the ''temporary seizure'' was unconstitutional, but the Supreme Court

---

50. 531 U.S. 326 (2001).

found that it was reasonable, given that the officers had probable cause and a strong interest in maintaining the status quo while obtaining a warrant. The decision reflects the Court's preference for home searches accompanied by warrants. As Justice Souter said in his concurrence, "[t]he law can hardly raise incentives to obtain a warrant without giving the police a fair chance to take their probable cause to a magistrate and get one."

Mistakes sometimes result from typographical errors in the warrant itself. Courts reviewing these situations generally hold that a typographic error does not render the ensuing search illegal, so long as the premises actually searched were the intended objects of the search.[51] And, since many search warrants are executed by the same officer or group of officers who prepared the application and affidavit, the proper premises usually are searched. What if a different officer executes the search warrant and, because of the typographical error, searches the wrong premises? Presumably the rule of *Maryland v. Garrison* would apply, and the search would be valid. Note also that the "good faith" exception to the exclusionary rule, which we will review in Chapter 5, also should salvage the search.

B. Time and Manner of Execution

You may have noticed in the Oklahoma City bombing case search warrant reproduced above that the warrant specified both the time of its execution ["in the daytime—6:00 A.M. to 10:00 P.M."] and the duration of its authority ["You are hereby commanded to search on or before May 12, 1995 (not to exceed 10 days)"]. The warrant, which was issued by a federal magistrate judge, was consistent with Rule 41 of the Federal Rules of Criminal Procedure, which provides in pertinent part:

The warrant must command the officer to:

(A) execute the warrant within a specified time no longer than 10 days;

(B) execute the warrant during the daytime, unless the judge for good cause expressly authorizes execution at another time; and

(C) return the warrant to the magistrate judge designated in the warrant.

In a later provision of the same rule, the term "daytime" is defined as "the hours between 6:00 a.m. to 10:00 p.m. according to local time."

Why these limitations? Are they constitutionally required? The answer to the first question is that the limitations are traditional common law ones now codified in the laws of most jurisdictions. Whether they are constitutionally required is not entirely clear. The 10–day limit prevents officers from executing "stale" warrants, that is, warrants that may no longer be supported by accurate facts. Although the Supreme Court has not ad-

---

51. *See, e.g.*, United States v. Arenal, 768 F.2d 263, 267 (8th Cir. 1985) (typographical error changing street address from 3028 Third Avenue to 3208 Third Avenue); United States v. Christopher, 546 F.2d 496, 497 (2d Cir. 1976) (unintentional transposition of room numbers); United States v. Larracuente, 740 F.Supp. 160, 165 (E.D.N.Y. 1990) (same).

dressed the issue of "stale" warrants, it has recognized that "stale" information cannot be used to establish probable cause. The daytime hours restriction also may have constitutional echoes in that it represents a balance between individual privacy interests (which, presumably, are heightened during nighttime hours) and government needs.

Many jurisdictions also require that officers "knock and announce" before entering premises pursuant to a search warrant.[52] The constitutional status of these "knock and announce" rules was in question for many years, but in *Wilson v. Arkansas*,[53] the Court held that a "knock and announce" execution sometimes is constitutionally required. In so doing, Justice Thomas relied on history as an interpretive method, holding that the Fourth Amendment incorporates a common law requirement that police officers entering a home must knock and announce their identity and purpose before attempting to enter the home forcibly. Thomas's opinion stated, however, that the knock-and-announce procedure is not always constitutionally required: it may be reasonable to dispense with it if, for example, it would endanger officer safety or the preservation of evidence.

The Court faced that issue in *Richards v. Wisconsin*[54] when it reviewed whether a state can establish categorical exceptions to the knock-and-announce procedure, as did the state courts of Wisconsin when they determined that law enforcement officers need not knock and announce when executing warrants in felony drug investigations. In affirming that exception, the Wisconsin Supreme Court had reasoned that all felony drug crimes involve "an extremely high risk of serious if not deadly injury to the police as well as the potential for the disposal of drugs by the occupants prior to entry by the police."[55] In *Richards*, the Court rejected Wisconsin's categorical approach and insisted that the reasonableness of a no-knock search must be determined on a case-by-case basis. Writing for a unanimous court, Justice Stevens observed that categorical exceptions overgeneralize, because they may encompass situations that do not pose risks to officer safety or to the preservation of evidence. Moreover, the categorical approach "impermissibly insulates these cases from judicial review." Furthermore, the Court feared the slippery slope: "If a per se exception were allowed for each category of criminal investigation that included a considerable—albeit hypothetical—risk of danger to officers, or destruction of evidence, the knock-and-announce element of the Fourth Amendment's reasonableness requirement would be meaningless." However, a probable cause standard would not give state interests appropriate weight. Consequently, the Court crafted this rule: to justify a no-knock entry, police must

---

52.   The federal system has such a requirement. *See* 18 U.S.C. section 3109:

The officer may break open any outer or inner door or window of a house, or any part of a house, or anything therein, to execute a search warrant, if, after notice of his authority and purpose, he is refused admittance or when necessary to liberate himself or a person aiding him in the execution of the warrant.

53.   514 U.S. 927 (1995).

54.   520 U.S. 385 (1997).

55.   549 N.W.2d 218, 219 (1996).

have reasonable suspicion that knocking and announcing their presence, under the circumstances, would be dangerous or futile, or that it would inhibit the effective investigation of the crime by, for example, allowing the destruction of evidence. The Court affirmed that the police officers who engaged in the particular no-knock entry at issue had acted with reasonable suspicion, because they had knocked and the suspect had slammed his door shut after observing their presence. At that point the officers could enter forcibly, said the Court, because they reasonably believed that the suspect was attempting to destroy evidence of drug activity.

The Court returned to the issue of no-knock entries a year later, in a case entitled *United States v. Ramirez*.[56] Officers in that case had obtained a "no-knock warrant" after establishing reasonable suspicion to believe that "knocking and announcing their presence might be dangerous to themselves or to others." While executing the warrant, the officers broke through a garage window. The Ninth Circuit held that the entry violated the Fourth Amendment, stating "while a 'mild exigency' is sufficient to justify a no-knock entry that can be accomplished without the destruction of property, 'more specific inferences of exigency' are necessary when property is destroyed." The Supreme Court disagreed. Writing for a unanimous court, Chief Justice Rehnquist pointed out that the reasonable suspicion standard announced in *Richards* "depends in no way on whether police must destroy property in order to enter." Rehnquist added, however, that:

> [t]his is not to say that the Fourth Amendment speaks not at all to the manner of executing a search warrant. The general touchstone of reasonableness which governs Fourth Amendment analysis governs the method of execution of the warrant. Excessive or unnecessary destruction of property in the course of a search may violate the Fourth Amendment, even though the entry itself is lawful and the fruits of the search not subject to suppression.

Reviewing the facts in *Ramirez*, the Court concluded that the officers had broken a single window "because they wished to discourage [any occupants] from rushing to the weapons that the informant had told them respondent might have kept there. Their conduct was clearly reasonable and we conclude that there was no Fourth Amendment violation." As it had in *Wilson*, the Court declined to elaborate on the exclusionary rule implications of no-knock entries and warrant executions that violate the Fourth Amendment, although in a footnote it indicated that the exclusionary rule might have applied in *Ramirez* if there had been a Fourth Amendment violation and if "there was sufficient causal relationship between the breaking of the window and the discovery of the gun to warrant suppression of the evidence."

In a follow-up to the Supreme Court's knock-and-announce cases, the Supreme Court of Pennsylvania held that the purpose of its own state knock-and-announce rule can be achieved "only if the police officer awaits

---

56. 523 U.S. 65 (1998).

a response for a reasonable period of time after his announcement of identity, authority, and purpose."[57] In the Pennsylvania case, detectives served a search warrant on Jean Martinelli's home. One of the detectives knocked, and when Mrs. Martinelli asked from within "who's there," the detective answered "Dave." The detective admitted that he responded in this fashion in order to get Mrs. Martinelli to open her door. When she opened her door part way, the detective pushed the door further open, walked in with his gun drawn, and announced his identity. The Pennsylvania court held that the knock-and-announce rule had been violated by the officer's failure to wait a reasonable time to permit Martinelli "to surrender her residence voluntarily," and it affirmed the suppression of evidence found during the search.

In *United States v. Banks,*[58] the United States Supreme Court likewise faced the question of how long a period of time the police must wait after knocking and announcing before they may forcibly enter a residence. Agents arrived at Banks's two-bedroom apartment at 2:00 p.m. on a weekday afternoon to execute a search warrant for cocaine. Officers at the front door called out "police search warrant" and rapped hard enough on the door to be heard by officers at the back door. After waiting 15 to 20 seconds with no answer, and, given no indication whether anyone was home, the officers broke down the front door with a battering ram. Banks had been in the shower and did not hear the police knocking and was just exiting the shower as the police entered. Their search produced weapons, crack cocaine, and other evidence of drug dealing. Banks moved to suppress the evidence on the ground that the police waited an unreasonably short time before forcing entry, violating both the Fourth Amendment and the federal knock-and-announce statute.

The District Court denied the motion, and Banks pled guilty while reserving his right to challenge the search on appeal. The Ninth Circuit reversed, ordering suppression, after detailing a list of numerous factors to guide the reasonableness inquiry and dividing the possible knock-and-announce circumstances into four categories, each with its own test of reasonableness, placing the current case in category four, entries in which no exigent circumstances exist and in which forced entry by destruction of property is required. That category, the Circuit Court concluded, mandated an "explicit refusal of admittance or a lapse of an even more substantial amount of time" than for cases in the other three categories.

The United States Supreme Court reversed, rejecting the Ninth Circuit's categorical, multi-factor approach. Said the Court, "it is too hard to invent categories without giving short shrift to details that turn out to be important in a given instance, and without inflating marginal ones."[59] Indeed, continued the Court, "no template is likely to produce sounder

---

57.   Commonwealth v. Martinelli, 729 A.2d 628 (Pa.Super. 1999).

58.   540 U.S. 31 (2003).

59.   *Id.* at 36.

results than examining the totality of the circumstances in a given case.''[60] There was no evidence that the police knew that Banks was in the shower, and, given the risk that cocaine might be flushed down the toilet or otherwise disposed of quickly, the 15 to 20 second wait was appropriate, even without an express refusal of entry:

> On the record here, what matters is the opportunity to get rid of cocaine, which a prudent dealer will keep near a commode or kitchen sink. The significant circumstances include the arrival of the police during the day, when anyone inside would probably have been up and around, and the sufficiency of 15 to 20 seconds for getting to the bathroom or the kitchen to start flushing cocaine down the drain. That is, when circumstances are exigent because a pusher may be near the point of putting his drugs beyond reach, it is imminent disposal, not travel time to the entrance, that governs when the police may reasonably enter.... And 15 to 20 seconds does not seem an unrealistic guess about the time someone would need to get in a position to rid his quarters of cocaine.[61]

In weighing the totality of these case-specific circumstances, the Court applied a reasonable suspicion test, in which the question was whether there was adequate evidence to establish reasonable suspicion of exigent circumstances that therefore required prompt entry. That test was analogous to the one used in determining whether the knock-and-announce requirement could be foregone entirely. Thus the Court stressed that the usual, non-technical, flexible test for reasonable suspicion, which the Court articulated in its preceding term in *United States v. Arvizu*,[62] applied:

> [W]e recently disapproved a framework for making reasonable suspicion determinations that attempted to reduce what the [Ninth] Circuit described as "troubling ... uncertainty" in reasonableness analysis, by "describ[ing] and clearly delimit[ing]" an officer's consideration of certain factors.... Here, as in *Arvizu*, the Court of Appeal's overlay of a categorical scheme on the general reasonableness analysis threatens to distort the "totality of the circumstances" principle, by replacing a stress on revealing facts with [a] resort to pigeonholes.... Attention to cocaine rocks and pianos tells a lot about the chances of their respective disposal and its bearing on reasonable time. Instructions couched in terms like "significant amount of time," and "an even more substantial amount of time" ... tell very little.[63]

Recently, in *Hudson v. Michigan*,[64] however, the United States Supreme Court held that the exclusionary rule does not apply to violations of the knock-and-announce rule, or at least not where the violation is a failure to wait a sufficient amount of time after announcing their presence but

---

60. *Id.*

61. *Id.* at 38.

62. 534 U.S. 266 (2002).

63. 540 U.S. at 42.

64. 547 U.S. 586 (2006).

before entering. The Court found that the social costs of applying the exclusionary rule in this context outweighed the social benefits. (A more detailed discussion of the case follows in Chapter 7).

C.   TREATMENT OF INDIVIDUALS DURING WARRANT EXECUTIONS

Imagine yourself sitting in a neighborhood restaurant enjoying the company of your friends. Without warning, armed officers enter the restaurant and order you and other patrons to the floor, threatening you at gunpoint. You are required to lie flat on the floor with your hands behind your head while other officers sweep through the premises. You are forced to remain on the floor, under constant surveillance, for over an hour until you are finally permitted to get up. Police officers then place you against the wall and pat you down. Eventually, you are permitted to leave the restaurant. Later, you learn that the officers had been executing a search warrant of the premises, out of which the owner allegedly had conducted drug transactions. Were the officers permitted to treat you in this manner while executing the warrant?

The answer is "probably not," but it depends on whether there were facts making the officers' actions objectively reasonable.[65] The Supreme Court addressed similar, although less egregious facts, in *Ybarra v. Illinois*.[66] That case involved the search of a tavern pursuant to a warrant that also directed the officers to search the tavern owner. While executing the warrant, the officers frisked the patrons, including Ybarra. The frisk of Ybarra revealed drugs. Ybarra was prosecuted for the drug possession and moved to suppress the evidence on the basis of the frisk, which he contended was illegal. The Supreme Court agreed. It explained, first, that the warrant to search the tavern and its owner did not give the officers authority to search anyone else on the premises. Second, although warrantless frisks are sometimes permissible under the rule of *Terry v. Ohio* (as you will learn in the next chapter), the frisk here was unconstitutional because there were no facts giving rise to a reasonable suspicion that Ybarra was involved in any criminal activity and was armed or dangerous.

These two pieces of the *Ybarra* holding are important. Recall that a warrant grants limited authority to law enforcement officers—they may search and seize only as the warrant directs them. A warrant to search a tavern and its owner does not convey the authority to search its patrons. Conversely, a warrant to search the tavern and "all individuals found on its premises" would be invalid for lack of particularity, unless there were unusual facts set forth in the affidavit that established probable cause to believe that "all individuals found on its premises" were involved in the criminal activity.

On the other hand, an entirely distinct doctrine (the *"Terry* rule") permits officers in all situations to frisk individuals for weapons if reason-

---

65.   These facts are taken from Swint v. Chambers, 5 F.3d 1435, 1439–40 (11th Cir. 1993), an action for damages by the restaurant patrons.

66.   444 U.S. 85, 90–94 (1979).

able suspicion exists to believe that those individuals are armed and dangerous. This rule suggests that law enforcement activity may depend in part on whether the warrant execution takes place in a public setting or in private. In the public tavern setting, Ybarra's mere presence did not create reasonable suspicion to believe that he posed a danger to the officers. In more private settings, however, officers might have reason to believe that persons present during the execution of a search warrant might be dangerous. For example, an officer executing a search warrant on the secluded farm of an anti-government militia member might reasonably suspect that family members present during the search may pose a danger to the officer, because the family members might be involved in the illegal activities themselves or at least have such a close connection with the targeted individual as to try to harm the officers.

The Supreme Court has been especially solicitous of officer safety concerns that arise when warrants are executed in private places. For example, the Court has held that officers executing an arrest warrant in a private home may conduct a "protective sweep" for individuals who might be concealed on the premises if they are in areas immediately adjacent to the location of the arrest or if there is reasonable suspicion that they are present and might pose a danger to the officers.[67] In another holding, the Court has authorized the practice of temporarily detaining individuals who occupy a residence that is the subject of a search warrant, at least if the search is for contraband.[68] The Court explained that in these circumstances, it is reasonable to detain the occupants, who might pose a danger of harm or of fleeing, and who might be able to assist the officers by opening locked containers and doors.

Once again, the cases in this area reflect the Court's attempt to reconcile the Fourth Amendment's protections with law enforcement needs. Consider the problems below in this light. How might those interests be reconciled, given the facts of the problems?

In some circumstances officers may handcuff home residents during search warrant executions. In *Muehler v. Mena*,[69] the United States Supreme Court upheld against a Fourth Amendment claim the handcuffing of a woman during a two-to three-hour search of her residence. The Court analyzed the situation for its "objective reasonableness," a test that it had articulated in *Graham v. O'Connor* (see page 308 and note 106, *infra*). The Court reasoned that law enforcement interests "in not only detaining, but using handcuffs, are at their maximum when, as here, a warrant authorizes a search for weapons and a wanted gang member resides on the premises." On the other hand, the individual's interests were less weighty because the restraint constituted a "minor intrusion." Justice Stevens disagreed with the majority's application of the *Graham* test, arguing that it did not give enough weight to the fact that the woman was very small, posed no flight

---

67. Maryland v. Buie, 494 U.S. 325, 327 (1990).

68. Michigan v. Summers, 452 U.S. 692, 704–05 (1981).

69. 544 U.S. 93 (2005).

risk to the two armed officers guarding her, and did not appear to be involved with the gang activity under investigation.

More recently, the Court upheld officers' ordering the occupants of a home at which a search warrant was being executed to stand nude before the officers for a limited period of time. In *Los Angeles County v. Rettele*,[70] police investigating four African–American suspects in a fraud and identity-theft crime ring, one of which suspects had a registered 9–millimeter Glock handgun, obtained a valid search warrant to search two houses for the suspects and for documents and computer files, as well as searching the suspects themselves for these items. The affidavit filed in support of the warrant cited various sources to show that the suspects resided at one of the homes. These sources included Department of Motor Vehicle reports, mailing address lists, an outstanding warrant, and an internet telephone directory. What the affidavit did not say, and the affiant did not know, was that that house had been sold to Max Rettele, who had resided there for three months with his wife and seventeen-year-old son. The Retteles were White. When the officers executed the warrant and entered the bedroom with guns drawn, they ordered Rettele and his wife to get out of their bed and show their hands, but they protested that they were not wearing any clothes. When Rettele tried to put on sweatpants, they told him not to move. Both husband and wife stood up, while the wife unsuccessfully tried to cover herself with a sheet. After one or two minutes, Rettele was allowed to get a robe for his wife, and he was himself allowed to get dressed. Shortly thereafter, the police realized they had made a mistake, apologized, and left.

The Retteles filed a section 1983 civil suit alleging that the warrant was obtained in a reckless fashion and the search conducted in an unreasonable manner. The district court granted summary judgment for the defendants, finding the warrant and subsequent search reasonable and, in the alternative, that if any rights were violated, they were not clearly established ones, thus entitling the officers to qualified immunity. The Ninth Circuit reversed, finding that a reasonable jury could find a cause of action because, under the facts alleged, the affiant failed to conduct an ownership inquiry to discover the sale of the house three months earlier, African–American suspects were sought, but there was no evidence that African–Americans lived at that address, no crime requiring an emergency search was alleged, and the Retteles being required to stand naked at gunpoint could be found to have exposed them to an unnecessarily painful, degrading or prolonged search, causing an undue invasion of privacy. The Ninth Circuit also held that the rights involved were sufficiently well-established that any reasonable officer should have known that the search and detention were unlawful.

The Supreme Court sided with the district court's grant of summary judgment to the defendants. The Court concluded that the officers had no way of knowing whether the African–American suspects might be else-

---

70.   550 U.S. 609 (2007).

where in the house, and people of different races can work together, live together, and commit crime together. The police believed that an armed suspect might be present, giving them authority to secure the scene. Furthermore,

> the orders by the police to the occupants, in the context of this lawful search, were permissible, and perhaps necessary, to protect the safety of the deputies. Blankets and bedding can conceal a weapon, and one of the suspects was known to own a firearm, factors which underscore this point. The Constitution does not require an officer to ignore the possibility that an armed suspect may sleep with a weapon within reach. The reports are replete with accounts of suspects sleeping close to weapons.[71]

Of course, added the Court, that does not mean that the police could unduly prolong their treatment of the Retteles, but they acted quickly here, allowing the Retteles to dress as soon as it was clear there was no threat. As for the harm done to the Retteles,

> the Fourth Amendment allows warrants to issue on probable cause, a standard well short of absolute certainty. Valid warrants will issue to search the innocent, and people like Rettele and Sadler unfortunately bear the cost. Officers executing search warrants on occasion enter a house when residents are engaged in private activity; and the resulting frustration, embarrassment, and humiliation may be real, as was true here. When officers execute a valid warrant and act in a reasonable manner to protect themselves from harm, however, the Fourth Amendment is not violated.[72]

Given that the Court found no Fourth Amendment violation, the Court did not reach the qualified immunity question. Justice Souter would have denied the writ of certiorari, while Justices Stevens and Ginsburg merely concurred in the judgment.

PROBLEM 3–4

During an FBI investigation of Mountaintop Mining, Inc., Special Agent Jones sought a search warrant for business records located at "Mountaintop Mining, Inc., 1245 Pikes Peak Drive, Suite B, Colorado Springs, Colorado." Jones used the address found on a sheet of Mountaintop's corporate stationery. He also checked the telephone directory and a Colorado Business Directory, and determined that he had the right address. He had never been to the corporate office.

At 2:30 p.m. Agent Jones obtained the needed warrant from a U.S. Magistrate in Denver and immediately drove to Colorado Springs. The warrant authorized him to seize "all business records and documents of Mountaintop Mining, Inc." and specified various types of records that Agent Jones expected to find. Traffic was heavy in Denver, and it took him about an hour and a half to make the 70 mile trip.

---

71. *Id.* at 614.

72. *Id.* at 615–16.

Upon arrival, Agent Jones and his partner Agent Smith identified themselves and presented a copy of the warrant to Randy Rex, president and owner of Mountaintop. The two began their search, but discovered that most of the records they wanted were not there. Agent Jones approached Rex and asked him where the records were kept. Rex asked his assistant, Bob, to show Agent Jones where the records were kept.

Bob led Agents Jones and Smith outside, walked about 35 feet down a breezeway to another building, and opened a door. Agent Smith noted that the number 1247 was above the entrance to this building, but decided that this building was simply part of Mountaintop's suite. Once inside, Bob explained that they had very recently leased this space to house their records.

Agent Jones found the records he needed. The two agents thanked Bob for his help and left with the records. With these records, Agent Jones was able to put together a case against Rex for skimming funds from federal assistance money to injured miners and using it to buy a reserved box of seats at the new Colorado Rockies baseball stadium in Denver.

Questions: (1) What is Rex's best argument for suppression of the financial records Agent Jones seized? What arguments would you make on behalf of the government against suppression? (2) Would your analysis change if telephonic warrants are routinely requested in this district, but that such a warrant takes 45 minutes to obtain?

PROBLEM 3–5

On January 3, third year law student Roxanne Grundel discovered that her apartment had been ransacked. Her front door had been forced open, apparently by a crowbar or some other sort of prying instrument. She called the local police and reported the theft to Detective Dash and described the damage. Among the items missing were a microwave, a 27' television, a VCR, a legal dictionary, and her laptop computer. Roxanne told Dash that a neighbor had seen an unfamiliar black Monte Carlo and a grey Nissan truck driving through the neighborhood the day of the theft.

Moments after taking Roxanne's report, Dash was contacted by Sarah Pence, who was calling to report the theft of her Monte Carlo automobile. Pence told Dash that she had looked out of her apartment window and had seen the car drive away, followed by a grey Nissan truck. Pence described her car as a black, 1996 model with the license plate "MNT–CAR." Dash called the police dispatcher and told him to put out an alert for a stolen car with the description Pence had given him.

The next day, Detective Oswalt stopped a Monte Carlo matching the description of the stolen vehicle. The driver, Clyde Stamps, was arrested and taken to the police station for questioning. After waiving his *Miranda* rights, Clyde told Oswalt that he had gotten the car from Sam Harrison. On a hunch, Dash asked Clyde about the burglary at Roxanne's apartment. Clyde said that he had nothing to do with it, but that Mark Verulrud did.

Clyde admitted he was friends with Mark and that he knew where Mark lived.

Clyde continued by explaining that Sam had come to his house the previous day, driving the Monte Carlo. Soon after he arrived, Mark showed up in the truck. Clyde said that Sam had told him that both vehicles were stolen and that all the property in the back of the truck had been taken from an apartment. Clyde said he saw a television, a microwave, and some other things that he couldn't identify in the back of the truck. Clyde explained that Sam and Mark had divvied up the goods among themselves at his house. He saw Mark take the television and some other things. Mark had told Clyde that he was going home.

Dash sought a warrant to search Mark's house. The application for the warrant and the warrant itself describe the items which were the object of the search as: (1) 27' SuperTek television; (2) DigiMax Laptop computer; (3) Brown's Legal Dictionary, Student Travel Edition, blue softcover; (4) burglar's tools.

Dash and Oswalt went to Mark's home and knocked on the door. A woman answered and identified herself as Marlene, Mark's sister. Dash asked if she lived there and she said she did. Dash explained he had a warrant to search the house for items related to a burglary and proceeded to enter the building. Dash found a 27' television in a bedroom. Marlene claimed it was her bedroom. She said that the television had "appeared out of nowhere" the other day. Oswalt found a legal dictionary in a garbage can in the living room. She also found a laptop computer matching the description in the warrant.

Dash began searching the kitchen. After noticing several rounds of 9mm ammunition on the counter, he opened a drawer located near the ammunition and discovered a loaded 9mm pistol. Dash asked Marlene about the pistol, and she said that it wasn't hers but that she had seen Mark with it a couple of days earlier. Dash asked if she had a permit for the pistol, which she denied. Dash seized the pistol since he was unable to determine if anybody had a permit to own it. A local ordinance prohibits the possession of a handgun without a permit.

Dash eventually tracked down Mark and arrested him. While booking Mark on burglary charges, Dash discovered that he had a previous felony conviction for forgery. Consequently, Mark was charged with being a felon in possession of a firearm.

Question: Assume you are Mark's attorney. Eliminating the pistol as evidence means that Mark will not face a prison sentence for the weapons charge. What is the best argument for suppression? Later on in this course you will learn about the "plain view" doctrine. For now, all you need to know is that officers executing a valid search warrant are allowed to seize items not described in the warrant if there is probable cause to believe that the item(s) constitutes contraband or the fruit, instrumentality, or evidence of a crime. The incriminating nature must be readily apparent to the officer on the basis of what she can observe without moving the item. Suppose that the government asserts that the seizure of the pistol was valid under the plain view doctrine. They press two claims: 1) no one present at the time of the search was legally able to possess the pistol, so its presence in the house was a probable violation of the firearms laws; and 2) that the pistol was probably used in the burglary and would thus be evidence of the crime they were investigating. Address each of these claims. Assuming that the court would find that a pistol is evidence of the crime of burglary, does that make it a "burglar's tool" and thus admissible as an item listed in the warrant?

———

The Court has addressed another question relating to the reasonableness of warrant executions: may the media accompany police officers when they execute search or arrest warrants in homes? The Court answered in the negative, holding that "it is a violation of the Fourth Amendment for police to bring members of the media or other third parties into a home during the execution of a warrant when the presence of the third parties in the home was not in aid of the execution of the warrant."[73] The two cases before the Court, *Wilson v. Layne* and *Hanlon v. Berger*, involved similar facts: law enforcement personnel allowed reporters and photographers to accompany them as they executed warrants in private homes. The media crews captured on film scenes from the warrant executions. Some of the scenes were embarrassing to the homeowners. For example, in the *Wilson* case, the warrant execution began at 6:45 AM, and the Wilsons were filmed coming out of their bedroom in sleeping attire. Writing for a unanimous court, Chief Justice Rehnquist reiterated that the scope of a warrant execution cannot exceed the terms of the warrant. The Chief Justice went on to state that,

> [w]hile this does not mean that every police action while inside a home must be explicitly authorized by the text of the warrant, ... the Fourth Amendment does require that police actions in execution of a warrant be related to the objectives of the authorized intrusion. ... Certainly the presence of reporters inside the home was not related to the objectives of the authorized intrusion. ... [A]lthough the presence of third parties during the execution of a warrant may in some circumstances be constitutionally permissible, ... the presence of these third parties was not.

Both cases had been brought as civil lawsuits seeking damages for the Fourth Amendment violations. Accordingly, the Court did not address the exclusionary rule implications of its holding. Chief Justice Rehnquist's opinion did suggest, however, that because the Fourth Amendment was violated by the presence of the media, and not by the presence of law enforcement officers, only evidence "discovered or developed by the media

---

73.   Wilson v. Layne, 526 U.S. 603 (1999) (invalidating media presence during execution of arrest warrant); Hanlon v. Berger, 526 U.S. 808 (1999) (same holding applied to execution of search warrant).

representatives'' would raise a potentially viable claim for application of the exclusionary rule.

D.   Exercise: Drafting and Executing a Warrant

You are a prosecutor for the Montgomery County, Maryland, district attorney's office. You learned yesterday that Montgomery County police had received information a month ago that Gregory Wayne Clutchette had absconded from parole in California, where he had been convicted of armed robbery, and might be living in Maryland. You also learned the following about the police investigation that took place in the ensuing month. The investigation revealed that a man driving a black Mercedes and identifying himself as ''Greg Clutch'' had been arrested in Maryland in March for assaulting an officer and resisting arrest. A subsequent check revealed that Clutch's fingerprints matched Clutchette's. He had given an address that turned out to be that of a mail receiving service at which Clutch had rented a mail box.

Montgomery County police, who had a warrant for Clutchette's arrest, began watching this mail box and in the past two weeks observed various persons collecting its contents and driving to two residences: one on Foxlair Road in Gaithersburg, Maryland, and one on Walnut Creek Court in Germantown, Maryland. A Walnut Creek neighbor told police last week that a man living there fit Clutchette's description and drove a black Mercedes.

You have just gotten a call from Detective Patterson, the officer in charge of the investigation. Patterson related that police saw a black Mercedes at the Foxlair address an hour ago. They staked out the home and radioed for assistance. Five officers are now present at the Foxlair address. Five others have surrounded the Walnut Creek home. Patterson would like to get a search warrant to enter the two homes, but his assessment of what he believes to be a volatile situation is that none of the officers on the scene can be spared to leave to obtain a warrant in person. He asks you whether he can get a warrant via telephone to search the two residences. He also wants to know whether he can obtain a ''no knock'' warrant given what he believes to be Clutchette's violent history. Patterson has a fax machine in his squad car and can receive fax transmissions from you.

Based on what Patterson has related to you, draft a ''duplicate original warrant'' seeking whatever you believe to be constitutionally permissible. In addition, draft for Detective Patterson an affidavit that he can read to the judge when he applies for the telephone warrant.

III.   Computer Searches

With increasing frequency, law enforcement officers need to search computers to discover evidence of crime. What issues arise concerning warrants for computer searches? A preliminary one often is standing, because many computer searches involve the workplace setting. Review the materials in Chapter 2 about standing in a corporate context. Moreover, as the excerpt below reveals,[74] the existence of probable cause is especially critical.

The government often includes merely hypothetical computers in a warrant's list of the items to be seized via boiler-plate, catch-all language. And the probable cause asserted in support of a warrant to search or seize computers is often based solely upon an agent's blanket assertion that persons engaged in crime "frequently keep records of both legitimate and illegitimate sources of income, such as, computer records, etc." But the government often fails to present evidence in search warrant affidavits which is particular to a certain person to believe the person possesses a computer or that a computer will even be found in a certain place. Even so, courts often defer to the experience and expertise of law enforcement agents. And in the business context, at least, courts have fairly rationally accepted agents' assumptions that records are regularly are kept on computers in order to justify searches or seizures of computers.

Such generalized assumptions are arguably insufficient to support a finding of probable cause to seize any and all computers that hypothetically may found in a person's home. But it may be difficult to convince a court to arrive at this conclusion. For example, an agent's assertion by affidavit that those engaged in illegal drug activity regularly keep in their homes documents indicating the telephone numbers of customers and suppliers will typically establish probable cause to search for such documents in a suspect's home. Nevertheless, defense attorneys should challenge warrants authorizing searches of computers when affidavits supporting those warrants fail to establish probable cause to believe evidence of a criminal activity is likely to be found within a computer. Given the uncertainty of the law in this area, it is important to at least preserve this argument. . . .

Particularity is also a significant issue both for prosecutors drafting computer warrants and for defense lawyers evaluating their clients' suppression claims:

A search warrant must be sufficiently particular in its description of the items to be seized to prevent a general exploratory rummaging in a person's belongings. Thus, "a warrant must clearly state what is sought, and its scope must be limited by the probable cause on which the warrant is based." Courts considering motions to suppress evidence on overbreadth grounds generally apply a three-factor test: (1) whether the warrant set out objective standards by which executing officers could differentiate items subject to seizure from those which

---

74. These excerpts are taken from Carla Rhoden, *Challenging Searches & Seizures of Computers at Home or in the Office: From a Reasonable Expectation of Privacy to Fruit of the Poisonous Tree and Beyond*, 30 AM. J. CRIM. L. 101 (2002).

were not; (2) whether probable cause existed to seize all items described in the warrant; and (3) whether the government was able to describe the items more particularly in light of the information available to it at the time the warrant was issued. Three distinct questions, discussed below in turn, arise under this test in evaluating the merits of an overbreadth argument in the computer search and seizure context.

A.   Did the warrant authorize agents to seize computers for subsequent search without clear limits to any probable cause established in the affidavit?

United States v. Hunter[75] is illustrative of a common overbreadth problem in warrants authorizing searches and seizures of computers:

> Attachment C described the property to be searched. Computer disks were included in the illustrative list for Sections II and III; those disks were appropriately particularized. All other computers and related equipment, however, were listed in Section IV, without limitation and without reference to the limitations in the other sections. Section IV did not indicate the specific crimes for which the equipment was sought, nor were the supporting affidavits or the limits contained in the searching instructions incorporated by reference.

Though Sections II and III in the warrant properly limited almost all the other items authorized for seizure by the suspected crimes, the warrant failed to do so expressly in connection with its authorization in Section IV to seize all computers, all computer storage devices, and all computer software systems. Thus, the court found that the warrant's authorization to seize any and all computers was a "catch-all paragraph, which lack[ed] sufficient limitation." In holding that this paragraph violated the Fourth Amendment's particularity requirement, the *Hunter* court explained that "[t]o withstand an overbreadth challenge, the search warrant itself, or materials incorporated by reference, must have specified the purpose for which the computers were seized and delineated the limits of their subsequent search."

However, applying a so-called "common sense" approach to interpretation of search warrants, several lower courts have held to the contrary. In *United States v. Evans*, for example, the search warrant authorized seizure of:

> Documents concerning cocaine trafficking including but not limited to records, books, notes, and/or ledgers showing amounts sold, "fronted," amounts owed, money collected and identities of distributors; bank records, and all other books, records, receipts, notes, or other records evidencing the acquisition transfer, or expenditure of monies since January 1, 1994; photographs of controlled substances, assets, or co-conspirators.

---

75.   13 F. Supp.2d 574, 584 (D. Vt. 1998).

All forms of computer hardware, software, and memory devices associated with the computer systems.

Memory typewriters, electronic address books and personal computers and laptop computers.[76]

After failing to engage in analysis regarding the warrant's facially overbroad authorization to seize any and all computer equipment found at the defendant's home, the court merely concluded: "The description of the computer equipment was as specific as possible since officers executing the warrant could not determine what information was contained in them until an evaluation was later conducted." Similarly, the warrant in *United States v. Lloyd* authorized agents to seize:

> (1) stolen motor vehicles; (2) all motor vehicle documents, titles and registrations; (3) correspondence to and from George Lloyd, also known as "Lex" related to the sale and transport of stolen motor vehicles; (4) all motor vehicle transport logs and records; (5) computer equipment, including hard drives, modems, floppy diskettes, and all other peripheral devices.[77]

And the court in *Lloyd* likewise failed to engage in any meaningful Fourth Amendment analysis as to the warrant's overbroad authorization to seize any and all computers. Instead, it simply reasoned: "[T]he warrant and supporting affidavit justif[ied] a search for documents relating to criminal activity at the office of defendant. The fact that defendant had a computer system d[id] not insulate him from a search of that system."

Defense attorneys should be quick to expose cases like *Evan* and *Lloyd* as ignoring significant constitutional problems. The Fourth Amendment requires express, not implied, limits as to what may be seized. The fact that virtually every remaining category of items to be seized is followed by a limiting statement, therefore, does not modify a warrant's independent authorization via boiler-plate language to seize any and all computers that may be found in a specified place. Rather, under a common-sense reading, such provisions stand out as plainly authorizing outright seizure of any and all computers for subsequent wholesale rummaging without limit to any suspected crime, relevant dates, or suspects. Warrants using this type boiler-plate provisions thus fail to properly limit agents' off-site search of computers to any probable cause established in the affidavit.

B.   The "all records" exception: did the affidavit allege sufficient facts to establish that all computer-related information was likely to evidence criminal activity?

It is fairly well-settled that, unless the government has established probable cause to believe that an entire business is a fraud, search

---

76.   994 F.Supp. 1340, 1343 (D. Kan. 1998).

77.   1998 WL 846822, *1 (E.D.N.Y. 1998).

warrants cannot authorize "all records" searches at commercial premises. The Ninth Circuit in *United States v. Kow* explained that "[a] generalized seizure of business documents may be justified if the government establishes probable cause to believe that the entire business is merely a scheme to defraud or that all of the business's records are likely to evidence criminal activity."[78] This includes seizure of all records from computers located at a business. For the "all records" exception to apply, the affidavit must establish probable cause to believe that the target business "conducted no legitimate business activities at all, and every action they took at every stage of their operations was designed only to further their fraudulent objectives." Courts have properly applied this exception where the affidavit in support of the search warrant shows that the company involved is merely a "boilershop" operation that markets only scams.

However, the government will generally fail to establish probable cause to seize all business records, including computer-related material, where the corporation appears to be engaged in some legitimate activity. The warrant in *Solid State Devices*, for example, authorized the seizure of all computers and computer-related material at a corporation under investigation for fraud relating to government contracts. But the corporation was engaged in legitimate activity, as evidenced by "awards and certificates from a variety of clients, commending its contributions to their projects." The court explained that the probable cause to believe the corporation had "routinely engaged in fraudulent practices" did not provide probable cause to believe that the "majority of its operations were fraudulent." Thus, while the affidavit would have provided probable cause for a narrow, more carefully defined search, it provided insufficient probable cause for the broad scope of the warrant.

The general rule against "all records" searches at commercial premises should similarly apply to computers located in a person's home. "A typical home computer with a modest 100–megabyte storage capacity can contain the equivalent of more than 100,000 typewritten pages of information. This information can include business and personal documents, financial records, address and phone lists, and electronic mail communications." Home computers are, therefore, like a "massive file cabinet, or even . . . an entire record center." The Fourth Amendment's prohibition against seizing all of a company's records without probable cause to believe the entire business is permeated with fraud should, therefore, apply to prevent an outright seizure of a home computer for subsequent search without limit.

This difficult to establish exception, however, has not been rigorously applied to searches of computers found in a suspect's home. The court in *United States v. Lacy*, for example, applied this exception to the warrant's blanket authorization to seize the defendant's entire

---

78. 58 F.3d at 427.

computer system. There, the affidavit "stated Lacy downloaded at least two [files containing computerized pictures] depicting minors engaged in sexual activity from [a computer bulletin board system]. . . ." Because the government "knew Lacy had downloaded computerized depictions of child pornography," the court held that the affidavit "established probable cause to believe his entire computer system was likely to evidence criminal activity." But it can be argued that *Lacy's* reasoning is flawed because it ignores the enormous storage capacity of modern computers. Moreover, . . . cases involving child internet pornography, like *Lacy*, can be distinguished, because in such cases computers are themselves instrumentalities of crime which can be seized outright under Federal Rule of Criminal Procedure 41(b).

In sum, where the government has probable cause to believe an entire business is nothing but a fraud, it may seek a warrant authorizing outright seizure of computers under the "all records" exception. Similarly, where the government seeks to seize a person's home computer for subsequent search without clear limits, it should be required to establish probable cause to believe that the entire contents of such a computer is permeated with evidence of crime. The government should plainly fail to establish this exception where a search warrant authorizes seizure of any and all hypothetical computers that may be found in a person's home via catch-all language but there are no facts in the affidavit to indicate that he or she had ever used or even possessed a computer. And, . . . such an affidavit may even fail to establish probable cause to perform any search of computers.

C.   Could the government have described the computer-related evidence to be seized more particularly?

In cases involving internet child pornography courts have indicated a consistent willingness to accept the government's post-hoc assertion that it was simply not practical to define computer-related information more particularly. For example, because the affidavit established probable cause to believe that the computer at issue had been used to transmit images depicting child pornography over the internet, the First Circuit in *United States v. Upham* explained:

> As a practical matter, the seizure and subsequent off-premises search of the computer and all available disks was about the narrowest definable search and seizure reasonably likely to obtain the images. A sufficient chance of finding some needles in the computer haystack was established by the probable cause showing in the warrant application; and a search of a computer and co-located disks is not inherently more intrusive than the physical search of an entire house for a weapon or drugs.[79]

The court acknowledged, however, that "there might be legitimate doubt whether a warrant authorizing a search of a house for a murder weapon would permit the police to cart off the entire contents of the

---

79.   168 F.3d 532, 535 (1st Cir. 1999) (citing *Lacy*, 119 F.3d at 746–47).

house, including the refrigerator, for purposes of a later search." And significantly, the *Upham* decision also noted: "Of course, if the images themselves could have been easily obtained through an on-site inspection, there might have been no justification for allowing the seizure of all computer equipment, a category potentially including equipment that contained no images of and had no connection to the crime."

The fact that the government could have described computer-related evidence more particularly in light of the information it had before executing a search of your client's home or office may often be evidenced by the clear guidelines provided by the United States Department of Justice to prosecutors and agents planning to execute search warrants on computers in its manual, SEARCHING AND SEIZING COMPUTERS AND OBTAINING ELECTRONIC EVIDENCE IN CRIMINAL INVESTIGATIONS ("The Manual").[80] The Manual prescribes several steps for federal agents to follow so as to ensure compliance with the Fourth Amendment and Federal Rule of Criminal Procedure 41. Before applying for a warrant to search a computer, the Manual advises agents to formulate a search strategy—such as the use of targeted "key word" searches where possible—for inclusion in the affidavit or other attachment in support of the warrant in order to optimize their ability to confine the search to the permissible scope of the warrant. A "key word" search contemplates that agents will search a computer by using search engines to pull only documents which contain certain words related to the probable cause established in the affidavit.

In *Grand Jury Subpoena Duces Tecum*, for example, the court quashed a subpoena for computer hardware where the government acknowledged that a "key word" search of the information stored on the computers would have revealed which of the documents were likely to be relevant to the grand jury's investigation. There, the court quite logically concluded, a subpoena demanding documents containing specified key words would identify relevant documents without requiring the production of irrelevant documents. Similarly, a search warrant explaining the need for an off-site search of computer equipment could limit such a search to "key word" type searches without authorizing the seizure of irrelevant documents. In this respect, it can often be far easier to perform narrowly tailored searches for documents stored on computers than when searching for documents stored in large filing cabinets, or even when searching for a suspected murder weapon in a home. Defense attorneys can challenge warrants authorizing unlimited searches of computer hardware where a "key word" or program specific search would have been practical.

Furthermore, where computer hardware is merely a storage device for evidence of a suspected crime, the Manual makes it clear that Federal Rule of Criminal Procedure 41 does not technically authorize

---

80. *See Searching and Seizing Computers and Obtaining Electronic Evidence in Criminal Investigations*, Chapter 2 (2001) http://www.cybercrime.gov/ssmanual/index.html ("The Manual").

agents to seize the hardware that contains the evidence. In contrast, the Manual explains that computers used to transmit child pornography may be seized outright under Federal Rule of Criminal Procedure 41(b) as an instrumentality of crime:

> The strategy for conducting a computer search is significantly different if the computer hardware is merely a storage device for evidence of crime. In such cases, Rule 41(b) authorizes agents to obtain a warrant to seize the electronic evidence, but arguably does not authorize the agents to seize the hardware that happens to contain the evidence. Cf. United States v. Tamura, 694 F.2d 591, 595 (9th Cir. 1982) (noting that probable cause to seize specific paper files enumerated in the warrant technically does not permit the seizure of commingled innocent files).... This does not mean that the government cannot seize the equipment; rather, it means that the government generally should only seize the equipment if a less intrusive alternative that permits effective recovery of the evidence is infeasible in the particular circumstances of the case.

Indeed, the Manual recognizes that "[w]hen agents obtain a warrant authorizing the seizure of equipment, defendants may claim that the description of the property to be seized is facially overbroad." In addition, the Manual advises that the "single most important consideration [in determining a search strategy] is the role of the computer hardware in the offense." In other words, the "single most important consideration" in determining how to avoid overbreadth problems guiding agents in cases involving internet child pornography (where the computer is an instrumentality of the crime) is altogether different from any role computers are suspected to play in offenses where the evidence sought is information that is merely stored on a computer. Given cases like *Lacy* and *Upham*, this is an important distinction.

The Manual goes on to describe four basic strategies for searching computers that are not themselves contraband, evidence, instrumentalities, or fruits of crime. Agents should attempt first to search the computer on-site and print out a hard copy of the particular information for which there is probable cause. If that is untenable, agents next should search the computer and make an electronic copy of such information. And if this is not feasible, agents should create a mirror-image copy of the entire computer storage device on-site and then later create a working copy for off-site review, subject to pre-set express limits in the warrant or attachments incorporated by reference. Only when necessary does the Manual contemplate that agents should seize computer equipment itself for review off-site. "Whatever search strategy is chosen," the Manual repeatedly stresses, "should be explained fully in the affidavit supporting the warrant application."

Significantly, the Manual's guidelines are based on well-established Fourth Amendment principles. Searches and seizures of computers present the same problem of intermingled documents noted by the

Supreme Court in *Andresen v. Maryland*, and by the Ninth Circuit in *United States v. Tamura*. The Court in *Andresen* stressed that courts must assure that such searches are conducted so as to minimize unjustified intrusions on Fourth Amendment rights:

> We recognize that there are grave dangers inherent in executing a warrant authorizing the search and seizure of a person's papers that are not necessarily present in executing a warrant to search for physical objects whose relevance is more easily ascertainable. In searches for papers, it is certain that some innocuous documents will be examined, at least cursorily, in order to determine whether they are, in fact, among those papers authorized to be seized.... Responsible officials, including judicial officials, must take care to assure that [such searches] are conducted in a manner that minimizes unwarranted intrusions upon privacy.

In *Tamura*, the Ninth Circuit articulated a rule for searches involving intermingled documents: where officers come across relevant documents so intermingled with irrelevant documents that they cannot feasibly be sorted at the site, they may seal or hold the documents pending approval by a magistrate of the conditions and limitations on a further search.

The *Tamura* rule should be applied to searches of computers "because it effectively balances individual privacy interests against law enforcement's need to conduct searches in the course of investigating criminal activity." Indeed, both the Ninth and Tenth Circuits have expressly approved of the procedure set out in *Tamura* in the computer search and seizure context. In *United States v. Hay*, for example, the Ninth Circuit explained that outright seizure of computers was justified because the agent stated in the affidavit why he believed it would be necessary to seize computers for search off-site, and because attachments to the warrant expressly incorporated by reference provided clear search techniques and limitations to the scope of the probable cause.[81] Similarly, the Tenth Circuit in *United States v. Walser* recently stated:

> [W]hen officers come across relevant computer files intermingled with irrelevant computer files, they may "seal or hold" the computer pending "approval by a magistrate of the conditions and limitations on a further search" of the computer. Officers must be clear as to what it is they are seeking on the computer and conduct the search in such a way that avoids searching files of types not identified the warrant.[82]

In sum, it may often be feasible for the government to describe computer-related material more particularly by articulating in the affidavit a targeted search strategy that is limited to probable cause. If the government foresees a need to seize computer hardware outright

---

81.   231 F.3d 630, 637 (9th Cir. 2000).

82.   275 F.3d 981, 986 (10th Cir. 2001).

rather than performing targeted searches on-site, it should explain this need in the affidavit and request the magistrate to authorize seizure of such hardware for subsequent off-site searching subject to express pre-set limits in the warrant.

————

At a time when rules governing the warrant process are struggling to evolve with the requirements of digital evidence searches, Professor Orin S. Kerr argues that "the warrant process must be reformed in light of the new dynamics of computer searches and seizures."[83] While it is clear that courts across the country have been particularly divided as to the appropriate particularity requirements of digital evidence search warrants, Kerr points out four specific doctrinal puzzles that have accompanied the emergence of a two-step digital evidence search:

> First, what should the warrant describe as the property to be seized: the physical hardware seized during the first physical search, or the digital evidence obtained during the electronic search? Second, what should the warrant describe as the place to be searched: the location of the hardware, the hardware itself, or the location where the electronic search will occur? Third, when must the electronic search occur—is the timing governed by the same rules that govern the physical warrant execution, by some other rules, or by no rules at all? And fourth, what recordkeeping requirements apply to the electronic search, and when must seized computer equipment be returned?

Focusing on statutory rules rather than the Fourth Amendment, Kerr goes on to "propose a series of changes to the law of the warrant process to update it for the era of digital evidence."

A)   *The Thing to Be Seized*

> The first change I would propose is to modify Rule 41's current requirement that "[t]he warrant must identify the person or property to be searched, and identify any person or property to be seized." In digital evidence cases, more specific language should be used. The language should require the police to state what physical evidence they plan to seize on-site, and then indicate what kind of evidence that they plan to search for in the subsequent electronic search. In other words, agents should be required to describe the goal for *both* the physical search stage *and* the electronic search stage. . . . Under this approach, a computer warrant would require the officers to name the specific evidence they are searching for twice, correlating with the two stages of criminal investigations.

B)   *The Place to Be Searched*

> Statutory warrant rules could also be amended to consider the case of computers in government custody. Alternatively, courts could simply

---

83.   Orin S. Kerr, *Search Warrants in an Era of Digital Evidence*, 75 MISS. L.J. 85 (2005).

approve descriptions of computers that name the place to be searched as the computer itself, held in the custody of whatever government agency presently held custody of that machine. . . .

C) *When Can the Search Be Executed*

Significant changes should be made to Rule 41 and equivalent state provisions to specify when each stage of the two-step warrant process should be executed. . . . One obvious change would be to amend [the language of Rule 41(e)(2)(A) and (B)] to clarify that the 10–day and daytime rules do not apply to the subsequent electronic search. . . . More importantly, Rule 41 should be amended to create an express provision, along with specific standards, on the question of when a computer must be searched and when it should be returned. . . . The standard should consider . . . backlogs and delays at government forensic laboratories . . . [and] the government's interest in the property, . . . [which sometimes] can be satisfied by generating a bitstream copy of the storage device. . . .

In cases where the computer is merely a storage device for evidence, the government should be required to seize the computer, create a bitstream copy of its files, and then return the property to its proper owner in a reasonable period of time such as 30 days. . . . When the computer hardware is believed to be a fruit, instrumentality of a crime, or contraband, the warrant should contain a different set of requirements. In these cases, the key question is whether the physical computer storage device already seized *actually* is a fruit, instrumentality of crime, or contraband. . . . If the material is discovered on the computer, then the person from whom the property has [sic] taken has no legal right to the property; it need never be returned. . . .

D) *What Are the Oversight and Recordkeeping Requirements, and When Must Property Be Returned?*

The question of what record keeping requirements to mandate is difficult to answer at this time because the underlying Fourth Amendment rules remain unclear. . . . Until we know more about what Fourth Amendment standards apply, it is too early to settle on the proper Rule 41 standard. . . . One rule that does not need to be changed concerns the inventory requirement for the return of the warrant. The inventory requirement is limited to physical hardware, and in my view it should remain so limited. . . .

I find [an approach requiring a listing of files that details the file name, creation date, access date, file size, and the location of the file on the disk] problematic. The inventory requirement is designed to make the government accountable and permit judicial review of the warrant process. The suspect needs to know what was taken if he wishes to challenge the seizure. Accessing computer storage devices and compiling a list of each device's contents does not seem to serve this function, however; the owner of the computer knows what is on the storage device, and taking the physical device obviously takes the contents of the device as well. Further, such an inventory requirement would have the perverse effect of expanding the government's power to search the computer. Completing the inventory would enable the government to find out all the file names and sizes of the material on the hard drive, which might then provide clues to unrelated crimes.

PROBLEM 3–6

Based on information provided by two confidential informants, Special Agent Markita Loving of the United States Secret Service submitted a thirty-three page affidavit on March 12 to Magistrate Judge Jensen. The affidavit summarized a bank fraud scheme alleged to have been undertaken by Carmine Solonski along with the two informants. The affidavit recounted information given to Loving by the informants regarding several automobile loans secured fraudulently from BankTucson, as well as other funds obtained from the bank by using false checks in the name of "George Flurnoy" created on Solonski's computer. The affidavit sought the issuance of an arrest warrant for Solonski and a search warrant for his residence at 15 Mason Street, Tucson, Arizona. Judge Jensen issued the warrants. On March 16, federal agents arrested Solonski at his residence and then executed the search warrant. They seized numerous items, including two computers: a Compaq Presario 4660 and an IBM Thinkpad. After taking the computers to a crime lab, they searched them thoroughly and discovered evidence of the bank frauds detailed in the affidavit, as well as additional federal crimes.

Question: If you represented Solonski in the subsequent federal case, would you be able to suppress the evidence of bank fraud discovered on his computers? On what grounds? Would you be able to suppress evidence of the additional crimes?

PROBLEM 3–7

SemiTor, Inc. supplies semiconductor devices to the Department of Defense and to a number of Department of Defense contractors. Because SemiTor's semiconductors are used in sophisticated military, aerospace, and space programs, the Government requires that they be manufactured in conformity with exacting standards and tested to assure a high degree of reliability. Gail Gennette is President and Chief Executive Officer of SemiTor, and she maintains an office at its corporate headquarters.

For the past few years, SemiTor has been under investigation by agents of the Defense Criminal Investigative Service ("DCIS"), an investigative agency within the Department of Defense. On May 17 Craig Schmidt, a DCIS Special Agent, presented an affidavit to United States Magistrate Judge Virginia Restall in support of the issuance of warrants to search SemiTor. Based on interviews with SemiTor employees and clients, as well as government experts, Schmidt alleged that SemiTor had acquired commercial-grade semiconductors that did not comply with the standards and specifications required under SemiTor's government contracts. He alleged that SemiTor then falsely labeled these parts as SemiTor-manufactured components, falsified test results certifying that the parts had undergone the necessary quality inspections, and sold the parts to the government at "high reliability" component prices.

On May 23 federal agents of the FBI, DCIS and NASA executed search warrants on the premises of SemiTor. The warrants authorized the seizure of a broad array of documents and data storage equipment, including the following:

> a.   Contracts, subcontracts, purchase orders, sales orders, invoices and correspondence, Certificates of Quality Conformance/Compliance (COQC), and memoranda relating to agreements between SemiTor, Inc., and any governmental or non-governmental entity regarding the manufacture, testing or inspection of semi-conductor devices supplied for U.S. Department of Defense or other governmental programs.

> b.   Electronic data processing and storage devices, computers and computer systems including central processing units; internal and peripheral storage devices such as fixed disks, floppy disk drives and diskettes, tape drives and tapes, optical storage devices or other memory storage devices; peripheral input/output devices such as keyboards, printers, video display monitors, optical readers, and related communications devices such as modems; together with system documentation, operating logs and documentation, software and instruction manuals, all passwords, test keys, encryption codes or similar codes that are necessary to access computer programs, data or other information or to otherwise render programs or data into a usable form.

Pursuant to the search warrants, the agents seized computers, computer storage media, and more than 2,000 file drawers and file boxes containing business records. Among other computers seized was one in Gennette's office. SemiTor claims that nearly ninety percent of all of the documents and items at SemiTor dealing with contracts over a five-year period were seized. These items have been stored since their seizure at DCIS offices in El Toro, California.

Question: Were the search warrants based on probable cause, and did they state the items to be seized with particularity? What, if anything, could or should the federal agents have done during their search to limit the exposure of matters not covered in the affidavit? Is it likely that Gennette will be able to assert a claim for the return of her computer? Under what federal provision may she seek relief?

PROBLEM 3–8

Examine Problem 3–2 above. Does the search warrant described in that problem satisfy the "overbreadth" concerns that arise in computer searches, as described in the text?

IV. ARRESTS

Checklist 4: Arrests

1. Definition of Arrest

    a. Was there a seizure of the suspect—would a reasonable person in the suspect's situation believe that he was not free to leave, and did police physically stop the suspect or by a show of authority cause the suspect to submit?

    b. If yes, did it so intrude on the suspect's freedom of movement as to constitute an arrest?

2. Justification for Arrest

    a. Was the arrest based on probable cause?

    b. If yes, did the police have an arrest warrant?

    c. If yes, did the arrest occur in the suspect's home?

    d. If the arrest occurred in the home of a third party, did police have a search warrant or other justification to enter that home?

    e. If the police did not have an arrest warrant, did the arrest occur on a public street?

3. Manner of Arrest

    a. Did the police use deadly force to arrest?

    b. If yes, did the police have probable cause to believe that the suspect

        (i) was fleeing; and

        (ii) posed an immediate threat of serious physical harm to the officer or others?

    c. If the police did not use deadly force, was their force reasonable considering

        (i) the severity of the crime;

        (ii) the threat to police officer and public safety; and

        iii) the suspect's flight or resistance?

4. Prompt Probable Cause Determination

    a. Was the arrested suspect given a judicial determination of probable cause within 48 hours of arrest?

        (i) If yes, can the arrested suspect demonstrate that the determination was nonetheless unreasonably delayed?

        (ii) If no, can the government demonstrate a bona fide emergency or other extraordinary circumstance justifying the delay?

b. Was any evidence, such as a confession, obtained because of the delay?

A. THE REQUIREMENT OF REASONABLENESS

The rules for when an arrest warrant is needed are fairly simple. Like any other government action under the Fourth Amendment, arrests must be *reasonable*. The Court has dealt with various components of reasonableness in the context of arrests. Chief among these are (1) the seriousness of the offense for which an arrest is made; (2) the level of suspicion necessary; (3) the requirement of a warrant; and (4) the use of force. We will discuss each of these below.

1. SERIOUSNESS OF OFFENSE

The authority to arrest is given by statute, and each jurisdiction instructs law enforcement officers as to which offenses are arrestable. The Fourth Amendment, however, serves as a check on this authority, because jurisdictions may not authorize arrests if such intrusive invasions of individual liberty would be unreasonable given the jurisdiction's interests. For example, it may be unreasonable under the Fourth Amendment for jurisdictions to authorize officers to arrest first-time parking offenders. Of course, arrests have long been considered reasonable for serious offenses, including felonies and breach-of-the-peace misdemeanors. In *Atwater v. City of Lago Vista*,[84] the Court confirmed that the Fourth Amendment also permits arrests—even warrantless ones—for traffic misdemeanors committed in their presence. You may have read this case in Chapter 1. If you did not, here are the basic facts and the Court's holding: a police officer had arrested Gail Atwater for violating a Texas law mandating the use of seatbelts for children and passengers in the front seat. Texas punishes violations of this law with a maximum $50 fine. Atwater claimed that an arrest for such a minor offense constituted an unreasonable seizure. Justice Souter, writing for a 5–justice majority, disagreed. Basing his opinion on an analysis of conditions existing at the time the Fourth Amendment was drafted, Justice Souter found no reason to believe that the Framers would have viewed such an arrest as unreasonable. Moreover, the majority explained that its holding would create a bright-line rule and thus provide greater guidance to police and lower courts than Atwater's proposed rule, which would prohibit arrests "when conviction could not ultimately carry any jail time and when the government shows no compelling need for immediate detention."

Recently, in a 9–0 decision, the Court relied upon *Atwater* to reverse a Virginia Supreme Court determination that suppression of evidence obtained illegally under state law violated the Fourth Amendment. In *Virginia v. Moore*,[85] the defendant was arrested for a citation-only offense

---

84. 532 U.S. 318 (2001).

85. 553 U.S. 164, 128 S.Ct. 1598 (2008).

committed in the officer's presence.[86] A search purportedly incident to arrest led to the discovery of cocaine and, eventually, the defendant's conviction.[87] The defendant's motion to suppress was denied, and he was convicted of possession with intent to distribute cocaine.[88] The Virginia Supreme Court reversed the defendant's conviction, given officers' violation of Virginia's citation-only law, prohibiting arrest for this minor offense, and the lack of a Fourth Amendment "search incident to citation" exception.[89] The Court, in a 9–0 decision, reversed the Virginia Supreme Court.[90] The Court found that the arrest did not offend the Fourth Amendment, as governmental violations of state law do not thereby violate *federal* constitutional law, and any contrary rule would impose the harsh federal constitutional remedy of exclusion under the Fourth Amendment on a state that, while adopting a statute that barred arrest for this minor offense, did not provide for such an extreme remedy when an arrest nevertheless takes place.[91] (The statute was in fact silent about remedy.) Central to the Court's decision was its insistence that the Fourth Amendment's protection may not vary from place to place. Accordingly, the Court recited the following rule: When officers have probable cause to believe that a person has committed a crime in their presence, the Fourth Amendment permits them to make an arrest, and to search the suspect in order to safeguard the evidence and ensure their own safety.[92]

Question: Is the Court right that the Fourth Amendment's protections cannot vary from "place to place?" For example, police may not have free-floating probable cause to believe something bad happened. Instead, they must have probable cause to believe that a specific state or federal criminal law has been violated. Given that the criminal laws of the states vary so widely, the same conduct might provide probable cause to arrest in one state but not another. We will, moreover, soon see that the validity of "administrative searches" turns on the adequacy of local governmental regulations constraining police discretion, but these regulations will also vary across local governmental units. Likewise, we will study "inventory searches," which can be done without probable cause and a warrant, but an inventory search first requires a valid seizure of the item (usually, but not always, a car), a seizure generally authorized by state or local statutes, again leading to local variation of a federal right. Is the Court implicitly overruling all these other doctrines? If not, what did the Court mean by its "place to place" statement, and does it make sense?

---

86. *Id.* at 1601.
87. *Id.*
88. *Id.*
89. *Id.*
90. *Id.* at 1606.
91. *Id.* at 1605–06.
92. *Id.* at 1608.

2. LEVEL OF SUSPICION

Probable cause is always required for full-blown arrests, which are highly intrusive seizures of the person, as opposed to brief stops on the street. The distinction between arrests and brief stops is discussed later in this Chapter.

3. WARRANT REQUIREMENT

The warrant requirement in the context of arrests and other seizures is governed by the location of the action. If the arrest is in a public place, the police can arrest without a warrant, so long as they have probable cause. Police also can seize contraband in a public place without a warrant.[93] On the other hand, if the arrest or seizure takes place in a place protected by the Fourth Amendment, a warrant is required. For the arrest of a defendant in his home, an arrest warrant is all that is necessary, because it authorizes the intrusion on the defendant's liberty and privacy interests.[94] If the arrest takes place in the home or premises of a third party, the police must also have a search warrant to protect the privacy expectations of that third party.[95] In such a situation, of course, the search warrant must be based on an affidavit establishing probable cause to believe that the defendant will be found in the home of the third party at the time of the search. Sometimes it is difficult to distinguish between a defendant's home and that of a third-party. The general rule is that the defendant's "home" includes any residence where the defendant is an overnight guest.[96] A defendant's brief, temporary stay in a home—for example, having dinner, chatting, or sharing a few drinks—is not enough to treat that home as the defendant's.[97]

The Court has suggested in *dicta*, however, that it might consider permitting modestly extended seizures of a person from a home or from the street on less than probable cause, albeit under a narrow set of circumstances. In *Kaupp v. Texas*,[98] discussed in more detail elsewhere in this book, the Court held that three police officers' awakening a 17–year old boy in his bedroom at 3 a.m. with a flashlight, then bringing him handcuffed, shoeless, and in his boxer shorts to a police station in a police car, was a de facto "arrest," thus requiring probable cause. The Court explained: "[W]e have never sustained against Fourth Amendment challenge the involuntary removal of a suspect from his home to a police station and his detention there for investigative purposes ... absent probable cause or judicial authorization."[99] Dropping a footnote at this point, and in the same breath, the Court continued: "We have, however, left open the possibility that,

---

93. Florida v. White, 526 U.S. 559 (1999).
94. Payton v. New York, 445 U.S. 573 (1980).
95. Steagald v. United States, 451 U.S. 204 (1981).
96. *See* Minnesota v. Olson, 495 U.S. 91 (1990).
97. *See* United States v. McNeal, 955 F.2d 1067 (6th Cir. 1992).
98. 538 U.S. 626 (2003).
99. *Id.* at 630.

under circumscribed procedure, a court might validly authorize a seizure on less than probable cause when the object is fingerprinting,"[100] citing *Hayes v. Florida*.[101] In *Hayes*, the Court found the *warrantless* transport of a rape suspect to the stationhouse for fingerprinting on less than probable cause violative of the Fourth Amendment. But the Court noted that it did not necessarily bar reasonable suspicion detentions for fingerprinting where the judiciary authorized them by issuing a warrant, even though based on less than probable cause. Sixteen years before *Hayes*, the Court had condemned as unconstitutional a roundup of 25 African–Americans for questioning and fingerprinting in an effort to identify a rapist.[102] Again, however, the Court had noted that "because of the unique nature of the fingerprinting process, such detentions might, under narrowly defined circumstances, be found to comply with the Fourth Amendment even though there is no probable cause in the traditional sense."[103] The Court seems to be suggesting that certain sorts of seizures of the person are less intrusive than "arrests," thus requiring only reasonable suspicion, but are more intrusive than "stops," thus requiring judicial supervision via a warrant. The Court's repeatedly returning to this concept, albeit in *dicta*, over the course of 35 years suggests that it may be inviting someone to bring the fingerprint warrant issue before the Court.

Consider: If the Court did approve of fingerprint warrants, would it necessarily follow that warrants for brief detention for DNA testing would also be constitutional? Are fingerprint and DNA warrants consistent with the text of the Fourth Amendment? With any of the other data sources for constitutional interpretation?

The warrant requirement is excused in exigent circumstances, but the Court has not defined exigency in any great detail. In *Warden v. Hayden*,[104] the Court had noted that the Fourth Amendment "does not require police officers to delay in the course of an investigation if to do so would gravely endanger their lives or the lives of others." And in *Minnesota v. Olson*,[105] the Court noted in dictum that warrants may be dispensed with if there is "hot pursuit of a fleeing felon, or imminent destruction of evidence, . . . or the need to prevent a suspect's escape, or the risk of danger to the police or to other persons inside or outside the dwelling." The exigent circumstances exception to the warrant requirement will be addressed in more detail later in this chapter.

PROBLEM 3–9

Review the warrant drafting exercise above.

---

100.   *Id.* at 631.

101.   470 U.S. 811 (1985).

102.   *See* Davis v. Mississippi, 394 U.S. 721 (1969).

103.   *Id.* at 727.

104.   387 U.S. 294 (1967).

105.   495 U.S. 91 (1990).

Question: Did the officers need a search warrant? Analyze the issue separately for each residence. Why or why not?

PROBLEM 3–10

The police received this anonymous tip: "Jonathan Norr robbed the 7–11 at Connors and Connecticut Streets last night, about 2 a.m. I was asleep in my apartment, which is just above the 7–11, when I was awakened about 2 a.m. by the sound of a gun firing. I looked out my front window and saw someone running away from the 7–11, on the street in front of the store. I was surprised, because I recognized the guy as my neighbor, Jonathan Norr." Police Officer Kripke, who received the tip, recognized Norr as Theresa Albogado's boyfriend. Albogado lived in a town home on Kripke's beat. The officer sometimes saw a white Chevy parked in front of Albogado's house and twice saw Norr leaving that house early in the morning, entering the Chevy, and driving off. On the many other occasions when Kripke saw the Chevy, it had been parked in front of Albogado's home all night. This night, at about 7 p.m., shortly before receiving the anonymous tip, Officer Kripke noticed the white Chevy in front of Albogado's home. Officer Kripke recited all these facts in an affidavit accompanying applications for an arrest warrant for Norr and a search warrant to search for Norr in Albogado's home.

After obtaining both warrants, Kripke, accompanied by two other officers, went to Albogado's home at 10 p.m., knocked, and announced who they were. When Albogado opened the door, the officers entered, found Norr in the kitchen, and arrested him, searching Norr's person incident to the arrest. Officer Kripke found an illegal handgun in Norr's right front pants pocket. Norr then pointed toward Albogado and blurted out, "She was in it with me; it was her idea, and she got me the gun to do it!" Albogado sprang up and ran into the street. One of Kripke's fellow officers caught and arrested her. A search of her person revealed a large quantity of cocaine in her fanny pack.

QUESTIONS

1. Will Norr succeed in his motion to suppress the gun and his statement to the police at his trial for robbery and unlicensed possession of a handgun? Would the result differ if the arrest had been done with only an arrest warrant? If it had been in Norr's own home, rather than Albogado's?

2. Will Albogado succeed in her motion to suppress the gun and the cocaine at her trial for robbery and possession of cocaine? Would the result be any different if Albogado had eluded the police when she fled on the day of Norr's arrest, but, two days later, Officer Kripke arrested Albogado without a warrant when he happened to see her walking on the street, one mile from her home? Do you need any further information to answer this question?

4. USE OF FORCE

In making any arrest, with or without a warrant, the arresting officer may be required to use force if the suspect flees or resists. Because an arrest is a "seizure," the force used must be "reasonable," which depends on:

> [a] careful balancing of the nature and quality of the intrusion on the individual's Fourth Amendment interests against the countervailing governmental interests at stake.... Our Fourth Amendment jurisprudence has long recognized that the right to make an arrest or investigatory stop necessarily carries with it the right to use some degree of physical coercion or threat to effect it.... [B]ecause [t]he test of reasonableness under the Fourth Amendment is not capable of precise definition or mechanical application, ... however, its proper application requires careful attention to the facts and circumstances of each particular case, including the severity of the crime at issue, whether the suspect poses an immediate threat to the safety of the officers or others, and whether he is actively resisting arrest or attempting to evade arrest by flight.[106]

Furthermore, the "reasonableness" of a particular use of force must be "judged from the perspective of a reasonable officer on the scene, rather than with the 20/20 vision of hindsight."

A more precise rule applies where police use deadly force. The deadly force rule was articulated in *Tennessee v. Garner*,[107] where officers were dispatched to answer a "prowler inside call." One officer heard a door slam in the house identified by a neighbor as the one with the prowler and saw someone run across the backyard. Using a flashlight, the officer perceived a youth, apparently 17 or 18 years old, who appeared in height to be between 5′5″ and 5′7″. The officer asked the youth (who turned out to be Garner) to halt, but, when Garner tried to climb over a fence, the officer shot Garner, who later died from the gunshot wound. The officer was reasonably sure that Garner was unarmed but feared Garner's escape. Garner's father brought an action seeking damages for violation of Garner's constitutional rights. The Court held that:

> The use of deadly force to prevent the escape of all felony suspects, whatever the circumstances, is constitutionally unreasonable. It is not better that all felony suspects die than that they escape. Where the suspect poses no immediate threat to the officer and no threat to others, the harm resulting from failing to apprehend him does not justify the use of deadly force to do so. It is no doubt unfortunate when a suspect who is in sight escapes, but the fact that the police arrive a little late or are a little slower afoot does not always justify killing the suspect. A police officer may not seize an unarmed, nondangerous suspect by shooting him dead. The Tennessee statute is unconstitu-

---

106.   Graham v. Connor, 490 U.S. 386, 396 (1989).

107.   471 U.S. 1 (1985).

tional insofar as it authorized the use of deadly force against such fleeing suspects.

It is not, however, unconstitutional on its face. Where the officer has probable cause to believe that the suspect poses a threat of serious physical harm, either to the officer or to others, it is not constitutionally unreasonable to prevent escape by using deadly force. Thus, if the suspect threatens the officer with a weapon or there is probable cause to believe that he has committed a crime involving the infliction or threatened infliction of serious physical harm, deadly force may be used if necessary to prevent escape, and if, where feasible, some warning has been given. As applied in such circumstances, the Tennessee statute would pass constitutional muster.

The Court rejected the argument that the common-law rule at the time the Fourth Amendment was adopted, allowing the use of whatever force was necessary to stop a fleeing felon, should control. "Because of sweeping change in the legal and technological context," concluded the Court, "reliance on the common-law rule in this case would be a mistaken literalism that ignores the purposes of a historical inquiry." Those changes were two-fold. First, at that time, most felonies were punishable by death, so killing a fleeing felon had no greater consequences than conviction. Second, the common-law rule developed when most weapons were so rudimentary that deadly force could be inflicted almost solely in a hand-to-hand struggle, placing the arresting officer at risk. Neither of these two facts hold true today.

Moreover, the long-term trend in the states has been away from the common-law rule, which now holds in less than half the states. "This trend is more evident and impressive when viewed in light of the policies adopted by the police departments themselves. Overwhelmingly, these are more restrictive than the common-law rule." This suggests that abandoning the common law rule is unlikely to hamper law enforcement severely, particularly because there has been no suggestion that in states doing so crime has worsened. Similarly, there has been no indication that in states allowing use of deadly force only against dangerous suspects, the standard has been difficult for the police to apply. Accordingly, the balance tipped in favor of the Court's newly-adopted rule, and, in applying that rule, the Court held that burglary is not an inherently violent crime and rarely involves physical violence. Given that there were no other indicators of Garner's dangerousness, the officer engaged in an unreasonable seizure in using deadly force to frustrate Garner's escape.

NOTES AND QUESTIONS

1. Three Justices dissented from the holding in *Garner*. What arguments do you think they did or should have raised? What techniques of constitutional interpretation did the majority apply? Did they apply those techniques persuasively? What other techniques did they ignore?

2.   The Court held in *California v. Hodari D.*[108] that a fleeing suspect has not been seized unless he stops, either because he is physically forced to do so or because he submits to an officer's show of authority. Similarly, if an officer shoots at an individual and misses, the Fourth Amendment does not apply because the person was not seized. And if a person is accidentally injured during the course of a high-speed police chase, the Fourth Amendment is inapplicable because the injury was not a result of government action "intentionally applied." The Court dealt with this situation in *County of Sacramento v. Lewis*,[109] where it held that the Fourth Amendment did not apply to an action for damages under 42 U.S.C. § 1983, where the damages were caused by a high-speed police chase and ensuing vehicular crash. The Court explained as follows:

> The Fourth Amendment covers only "searches and seizures," neither of which took place here. No one suggests that there was a search, and our cases foreclose finding a seizure. We held in *California v. Hodari D.*, 499 U.S. 621 (1991), that a police pursuit in attempting to seize a person does not amount to a "seizure" within the meaning of the Fourth Amendment. And in *Brower v. County of Inyo*, 489 U.S. 593 (1989), we explained "that a Fourth Amendment seizure does not occur whenever there is a governmentally caused termination of an individual's freedom of movement (the innocent passerby), nor even whenever there is a governmentally caused and governmentally desired termination of an individual's freedom of movement (the fleeing felon), but only when there is a governmental termination of freedom of movement through means intentionally applied." We illustrated the point by saying that no Fourth Amendment seizure would take place where a "pursuing police car sought to stop the suspect only by the show of authority represented by flashing lights and continuing pursuit," but accidentally stopped the suspect by crashing into him. That is exactly this case.

The Court went on to review plaintiff's claim that the police chase violated a different right—the Fourteenth Amendment substantive due process right against arbitrary action. Government action that "shocks the conscience" violates that right, but the Court in *Lewis* held that government action in the context of a high-speed police chase would have to be more than merely negligent or even "deliberately indifferent" in order to implicate the substantive due process right. Instead, officers would have to be acting with a "purpose to cause harm" before resulting injuries would be redressible under the Fourteenth Amendment. The United States Court of Appeals for the Ninth Circuit has held that the "purpose to cause harm" requirement applies when innocent by-standers, as well as pursued suspects, sustain injuries.[110]

---

108.   499 U.S. 621 (1991).

109.   523 U.S. 833 (1998).

110.   Onossian v. Block, 175 F.3d 1169 (9th Cir. 1999).

3. Assume that a police officer chases a speeding motorist who was clocked at 73 mph in a 55 mph zone and refuses to submit to the officer's show of authority when she activates her lights and sirens in reaction to the minor traffic offense. The chase continues with the fleeing speeder (who, as far as the police were aware, had no criminal record) driving upwards of 85 mph, weaving in and out of highway traffic, endangering other motorists, the chasing officer, and her colleagues who have joined the pursuit. The officer, in order to stop the speeder, purposely rams the back of his car, causing it to crash and rendering the speeding driver a quadriplegic. For the purpose of this question, assume that the pursuing officer's use of force constitutes a Fourth Amendment seizure. On these facts, is the ramming reasonable? Why? If the chase occurred on a rural stretch of unmarked road, would your answer change? What if it occurred in a major city, during rush hour? If, as a result of the ramming, the fleeing driver was killed, would that change your reasonableness analysis?

These questions arise in the context of the Court's recent decision in *Scott v. Harris*,[111] where the Court determined that a law enforcement official may, consistent with Fourth Amendment reasonableness, "take actions that place a fleeing motorist at risk of serious injury or death" in order to prevent that flight "from endangering the lives of innocent bystanders."[112] There, a Georgia county deputy pursued Harris after Deputy Timothy Scott clocked Harris's vehicle speed at 73 mph, a violation of the 55 mph limit.[113] The deputy activated his lights and siren and followed Harris, who did not stop. A six mile, ten minute long, high-speed chase ensued. It involved a number of law enforcement officers and ended when Scott "applied his push bumper to the rear of respondent's vehicle," causing it to veer off the road and crash at the bottom of an embankment.[114]

The deputy received permission from his supervisor during the chase to employ a "Precision Intervention Technique" maneuver that would have resulted in the driver's vehicle spinning to a complete stop.[115] The deputy decided, however, that the vehicle's speed made such a maneuver too dangerous. He chose instead to use the "push bumper" tactic, which caused the fleeing car to run off the road, careen down an embankment, and crash. As a result of injuries suffered in the crash, Harris was rendered a quadriplegic.[116]

Harris filed suit under 42 U.S.C.S. Section 1983, alleging that Scott's "push bumper" use of force was excessive, violating the Fourth Amendment's proscription against unreasonable seizures. Scott did not contest that his termination of the chase by ramming Harris's car constituted a

---

111. 550 U.S. 372 (2007).

112. *Id.* at 373.

113. *Id.* at 374.

114. *Id.* at 374–75.

115. *Id.* at 375 n.1 (citation omitted).

116. *Id.* at 375.

"seizure."[117] Instead, Scott moved for summary judgment, based on quali-fied immunity.[118]

Scott's motion was denied. On interlocutory appeal, the Court of Appeals for the Eleventh Circuit affirmed, relying upon Harris's rendition of the facts, in accordance with the applicable standard of review for summary judgment denials. The circuit affirmed the district court, finding Scott's use of force could constitute excessive deadly force under *Tennessee v. Garner*,[119] given that the extant law was "sufficiently clear to give reasonable law enforcement officers fair notice that ramming a vehicle under these circumstances was unlawful," as well as determining that a reasonable jury could find Scott violated Harris's Fourth Amendment right against unreasonable seizures.[120]

Scott petitioned the Court for a writ of certiorari, which was granted. The Court reversed, holding Scott's actions reasonable under the Fourth Amendment, even though he "placed [Harris] at risk of serious injury or death." Key to the Court's determination was videotaped evidence of the chase that utterly discredited Harris's version of the facts. The tape was so compelling, the Court refused to apply the normal standard of judicial review[121]—which requires reviewing courts to adopt Harris's version of the facts. Instead, the Court considered reliance upon Harris's version of events inappropriate:

> [r]eading the lower court's opinion, one gets the impression that respondent, rather than fleeing from the police, was attempting to pass his driving test.... The videotape tells quite a different story. There we see respondent's vehicle racing down narrow, two-lane roads in the dead of night at speeds that are shockingly fast. We see it swerve around more than a dozen other cars, cross the double-yellow line, and force cars traveling in both directions to their respective shoulders to avoid being hit. We see it run multiple red lights and travel for considerable periods of time in the occasional center left-turn-only lane, chased by numerous police cars forced to engage in the same hazardous maneuvers just to keep up. Far from being the cautious and controlled driver the lower court depicts, what we see on the video more closely resembles a Hollywood-style car chase....[122]

Additionally and given the videotape, the Court determined that it had to "slosh [its] way through the factbound morass of 'reasonableness,' " to

---

117.   *Id.* at 375–76.

118.   *Id.* at 376.

119.   *Id.* 471 U.S. 1 (1985).

120.   550 U.S. at 376 (citation omitted).

121.   Fed. Rule Civ. Proc. 56(c) requires that during a summary judgment motion, when there is a genuine issue of material fact, facts must be viewed in the light most favorable to the nonmoving party.

122.   550 U.S. at 378–80. There were no allegations or suspicions indicating that the videotape was altered, incomplete, or in any way unreliable. *Id.* at 378.

determine whether Scott's ramming of Harris's car under the circumstances was constitutionally reasonable:

> [s]o how does a court go about weighing the perhaps lesser probability of injuring or killing numerous bystanders against the perhaps larger probability of injuring or killing a single person? We think it appropriate in this process to take into account not only the number of lives at risk, but also their relative culpability. It was respondent, after all, who intentionally placed himself and the public in danger by unlawfully engaging in the reckless, high-speed flight that ultimately produced the choice between two evils that Scott confronted. Multiple police cars, with blue lights flashing and sirens blaring, had been chasing respondent for nearly 10 miles, but he ignored their warning to stop. By contrast, those who might have been harmed had Scott not taken the action he did were entirely innocent. We have little difficulty in concluding it was reasonable for Scott to take the action that he did.[123]

Harris invoked the Court's *Garner* analysis and preconditions for using deadly force, claiming that the ramming was an unreasonable use of deadly force. The Court rejected his claim, stating that *"Garner* did not establish a magical on/off switch that triggers rigid preconditions whenever an officer's actions constitute deadly force."[124] Instead, *Garner* represents only an application of the Fourth Amendment's reasonableness test to the use of a certain type of force in a certain type of situation. There, the use of deadly force was unreasonable; here, the Court determined that it did not matter: "[w]hether or not [the officer's] actions constituted application of 'deadly force,' all that matters is whether [his] actions were reasonable."[125]

Under those circumstances, Scott's termination of the chase with the level of force employed was found to be reasonable. The lower court decision was reversed and Scott was entitled to summary judgment.

Comment on Statutory and Administrative Regulations: Constitutional regulation of police use of force is supplemented in two ways.[126] First, state criminal law often prohibits use of excessive force, for example, through the Model Penal Code's prohibition on using deadly force to effect felony arrests unless "there is a substantial risk that the person to be arrested will cause death or serious bodily harm if his apprehension is delayed."[127] However, in the view of some commentators, the vagueness of state rules has made them relatively ineffective.

---

123. *Id*. at 384.

124. *Id*. at 382.

125. *Id*. at 383.

126. The following discussion of non-constitutional methods for controlling police use of force is drawn from Edwin Delattre, *Character & Cops, Ethics* in POLICING LAW: POLICE AND THE USE OF EXCESSIVE FORCE 1–2, 13, 37–42 (1993); JEROME SKOLNICK & JAMES FYFE, ABOVE THE LAW: POLICE AND THE EXCESSIVE USE OF FORCE (1993); SAMUEL WALKER, TAMING THE SYSTEM: THE CONTROL OF DISCRETION IN CRIMINAL JUSTICE, 1950–1990, 25–33 (1993).

127. Model Penal Code (3.07)(2)(h)(iv)(B). The additional complexities of that provision are not considered here.

Second, because of this vagueness and that of the *Garner* rule, well-run police departments generally have adopted clearer and more easily enforceable administrative guidelines. For example, an Omaha, Nebraska, rule states in relevant part that "[a] locally stolen vehicle that is not connected with any other felonious crime should not be considered a violation which would permit the use of deadly force."[128] These regulations have, on average, been surprisingly effective. Thus, the number of people shot and killed by the police in Omaha was reduced at least 30 percent between the 1970s and 1980s. During this same period, the disparity between black and white citizens shot was cut in half. These statistics led one commentator to conclude that the "control of deadly force is arguably the great success story in the long effort to control police discretion. It is the one decision point where we have persuasive evidence documenting a positive impact of new rules without any unintended and undesirable consequences."

This conclusion may seem surprising in light of wide media coverage of such horrors as the Rodney King case. King was videotaped on his hands and knees, struggling on the ground, impaled by TASER guns, repeatedly beaten about the head, neck, back, kidneys, ankles, legs, and feet by two police officers wielding two-foot black metal truncheons, while a third officer stomped King and numerous others simply watched. The comments of some of the officers involved suggested that the incident was far from an isolated one for the L.A.P.D. Indeed, numerous recent incidents of police abuse have hit the media, many consistent in particular with the impressions and experiences of minority group members, who often assume the reality of police brutality.[129]

The significance of incidents like the King beating can be reconciled with the relative success of departmental guidelines on police use of force when the politics of abuse is taken into account. Thus, Professor Walker notes that the consensus reflected in departmental use-of-force policies:

> was not reached through dispassionate deliberation by any means. Each change in a police department shooting policy was the result of conflict. The common scenario involved a highly questionable shooting, community protests, and often a lawsuit. In some cases, a lower court decision forced a change in policy. In other cases a police chief revised the department's shooting policy only after several controversial shooting incidents.[130]

Adoption and enforcement of these policies thus turned on sustained political pressure. While these policies can in many instances bring about permanent changes in police practices that may in turn alter police sub-cultures, such sub-cultures are hard to change. Many officers conceive of themselves as "urban adventurers, willing to put up with a tough job for

---

128. WALKER, TAMING, *supra* note 126, at 28.

129. *See, e.g.*, JOHN DESANTIS, THE NEW UNTOUCHABLES (1994) (collecting stories of abuse).

130. WALKER, TAMING, *supra* note 126, at 26.

minimal compensation for the same reasons other men may have volunteered for military service."[131]

Thus, too many officers still feel that to do their job well they must break down doors, engage in risky, high-speed pursuits, and participate in dangerous gun play. Unless educational requirements (at least two years of college) are adopted as a national standard for police officers, then innovative ideas will fall on deaf ears at the most important level—the street level.[132]

A law-and-order atmosphere, awareness of decreasing vigilance by ever more conservative courts, a top police leadership willing to tolerate hiding abuses from the light of day, and declining political pressure for change can, therefore, lead to the reassertion of the cowboy mentality and the rise of brutal beatings like King's.

Finally, understanding the difficulties inherent in controlling police use of force requires understanding the options available to the police and the ways in which misguided departmental policies can lead to abuse of those options. Jerome H. Skolnick and James J. Fyfe[133] offer a thorough discussion and analysis of this issue:

> ... The most critical [issue] is the question of escalating force: how much and with what instrumentality is force appropriate in the myriad situations officers confront on the street? State criminal laws distinguishing criminal conduct from acceptable use of force attempt to operationalize the distinction with admonitions to the effect that officers should use no more than is *necessary or reasonable*, or that force should be used only as a *last resort*. Such provisions, however, are too vague to serve as meaningful guidelines for cops in street situations. Hence, where officers are adequately trained (and not all are), the parameters of the police license to use force generally are conceptualized in training and policy as a scale from which officers should pick the least severe degree of force likely to accomplish the job at hand.
>
> Police use force to affect civilians' conduct. On a day-to-day basis, they do so most often by employing the least degree of force available to them, their *mere presence*. Cops wear uniforms and drive distinctly marked cars so that, without saying a word, they may have an effect on citizens' behavior. Indeed, the police tradition of *preventive patrol*—the single most expensive U.S. police activity—is based on the premise that the presence of uniformed cops and marked police cars will send would-be criminals elsewhere, will keep jaywalkers on the sidewalk, and will cause motorists to check their speedometers.
>
> When officers' mere presence fails to produce desired conduct, police resort to *verbalization*, second step on their ladder. For miscreant drivers, police verbalization typically begins with a red light or

---

131. DeSantis, Untouchables, *supra* note 129, at 251.

132. *Id.* at 253–54.

133. Skolnick & Fyfe, Above the Law, *supra* note 126, at 38–42.

siren signal to pull to the side of the road. Then, when officers actually do speak, they are instructed to do so *persuasively* and in tones that are resolute but not commanding: "Good morning, Sir, I'm afraid that you were traveling at 66 miles per hour. The speed limit here is 45. May I see your license, registration, and proof of insurance, please?" If this type of *adult-adult* interaction fails to get the desired results, or, in officers' reasonable assessments, would be inappropriate, they may proceed to, or begin, their interactions with more forcible options. The scale describes increasingly severe degrees of force but is not a suggestion that officers must start at the bottom and work their way higher until they find out what works. No cop is expected to say, "Pardon me, Sir. I'm afraid that we have a law against armed robbery in this state. May I have that sawed-off shotgun, please?" Instead, officers begin confrontations in such situations well up the scale of force.

One step up the scale from persuasion is another type of verbalization that the police call *command* voice. Motorists who reply with snappy comments to officers' requests for their drivers' licenses ("Why aren't you out catching a crook instead of harassing taxpayers?") are likely to hear command voices, "Sir, I asked you for your vehicle papers once. Now I'm *telling* you that you had better give them to me *now*!"

The first force option beyond verbalization is what police call *firm grips*. These consist of grips on parts of the body that let their subject know that an officer is present and that he or she wants the subject to remain still or to move in a certain direction, but that do not cause pain. An officer's grip on the elbow or shoulder of the drunk driving suspect he is trying to coax into a police station is a good example. So, too, are most of the means by which, without causing pain, officers cart off protestors at sit-in demonstrations.

The next level of forcible officer-to-citizen contact is *pain compliance*. This consists of grips designed to gain subjects' submission by inflicting pain without causing lasting physical injury. Cops are trained in a variety of *come-along* holds—hammerlocks, wristlocks, finger grips, and the like—which are very useful in breaking up bar fights and domestic battles and in arresting demonstrators whose protests have gone beyond mere passive resistance.

Next, officers put into action *impact techniques*, which, whether involving actual physical contact (kicks or batons, for example) or the use of chemical sprays or stunning electronic weapons, are designed to overcome resistance that is forcible, but less than imminently life-threatening. It is at this point that serious public misunderstandings arise regarding what may be legally and professionally—and reasonably—expected of police officers.

Most cops are not martial arts experts. Nor, unlike Secret Service Agents, are they expected by their employers to sacrifice their own lives unhesitatingly to save someone else's—*anybody* else's. In a jargon police trainers know well, cops simply are not paid enough to put their own lives on the line in order to avoid hurting somebody else—especially when that other person is attacking the cops. Thus, while cops should never force confrontations that might be avoided (as, unfortunately, they sometimes do with the growing population of mentally disturbed street people), they are under no obligation to counter force directed against them with a lesser degree of force.

Cops are trained not to try to use nightsticks to defend themselves against attacking knife-wielders, no matter how little the knife or how drunk its wielder. Instead, officers are taught to try to keep a safe distance between themselves and knife-wielders and to shoot when there is no other way to keep the distance from shrinking to unsafe ranges. Officers learn that trying to *play hero* by attempting to overcome force with lesser force allows no room for mistakes. The primary police obligation—to protect life—dictates that they not put themselves in harm's way to avoid using an appropriate degree of force.

In recent years traditional police impact methods—"intermediate force," in the language of the LAPD—have been supplemented by nonlethal devices. Perhaps the oldest of these are chemical sprays such as Mace, which has been available since the 1960s. More recently, police have been issued hand-held electronic "stun guns" that inflict a shock, and the Taser, a gunlike device that allows officers to shock subjects through wires hooked to two electronic darts. It is capable of shooting at close ranges. Careful viewers of the Rodney King tape were able to see Taser wires running from King's torso to the Taser with which Sergeant Stacey Koon had shot him.

The theory behind introducing these weapons was that they would provide officers with degrees of force midway between nightsticks and guns. Consequently, it was anticipated, police could use them to resolve confrontations that would otherwise end in shooting. In well-administered police departments, this theory has been borne out, and decreases in use of officers' firearms over the last two decades probably owe something to the new weapons. A constant temptation, however, is for officers to employ such devices as easier ways out of situations that, with only slightly more effort and no more danger, they could handle with lesser degrees of force. Thus, these devices have been a mixed blessing for police. If officers are to adhere to the principle of using no more force than necessary, their use of the newer technology must be monitored carefully.

The most extreme use of force is *deadly force*, which, in policing, most often involves the discharge of firearms. Deadly force is defined in law as force capable of killing or likely to kill, a description that certainly applies when officers fire their guns at other people. This definition also applies, however, to other varieties of force. In 1985 the Philadelphia Police Department dropped an incendiary bomb on a house occupied by a militant cult, an act that proved deadly when it resulted in eleven deaths, including those of four children.

Police in some departments also are trained in two neck holds that have proved capable of taking life. The first is the *carotid control hold*, the purpose of which is to induce unconsciousness by cutting off the flow of blood to the brain through the carotid artery, which runs up the side of the neck. In the emotions of street confrontations, this *sleeper* hold has resulted in fatalities. The second neck hold is the *bar arm control hold*, an extremely dangerous grip in which the forearm is forcibly squeezed in a viselike manner against the front of the neck in order to cut off air flow.

Police use of deadly force is governed by the criminal laws of individual states, which authorize officers to resort to this level of coercion in the imminent defense of their own lives or the lives of others. Until a 1985 challenge to the constitutionality of the fatal police shooting of an unarmed fifteen-year-old who was fleeing from a $10 burglary, police in about half the states also were authorized to use deadly force to apprehend all "fleeing felony" suspects. The Supreme Court's decision in *Tennessee v. Garner*, however, ruled that shootings in these situations violated the Fourth Amendment's protections against unreasonable seizures. Since then, the prevailing rules on police deadly force have permitted officers to shoot in order to apprehend only those fleeing suspects who are demonstrably dangerous (e.g., armed with a weapon; fleeing from a violent crime). Again, because of the vagueness of criminal laws defining justifiable use of deadly force by officers—and because proceedings against cops who have shot people in apparent violation of law are such political hot potatoes for prosecutors—well-run police departments generally have supplemented them with clearer and more easily enforceable administrative guidelines and policies.

The issue of when cops should *draw* guns is less clearly understood than the question of when they should *fire* them. We have run into unsophisticated police chiefs who argue that if a cop is able to return a drawn gun to its holster without having fired it, the gun should never have been drawn in the first place. Thankfully, we have found this twisted logic—a permutation of the principle that cops should never draw their guns unless they are prepared to fire them—only among police in small, quiet police departments where it is likely that guns are unholstered only for target practice.

In reality, the difference between drawing a gun and firing it is as big as the difference between showing the fleet and using it to launch an invasion. Police officers in well-run departments are trained to draw their guns only when circumstances present a reasonable expectation that they will encounter life-threatening violence. In the best police jurisdictions, this means that police officers draw their guns far more often than they are fired. Guns sometimes are discreetly drawn when officers respond to reports of violent crimes in progress. When, as is usually the case, it is discovered that reports were false or that criminals are long gone, the guns are just as discreetly put away. When officers make arrests for serious crime, guns sometimes are displayed more prominently as a means of inducing quick compliance by suspects. When the subjects of police concern are mentally disturbed or otherwise irrational, however, the display of guns may stimulate violence rather than defuse it. Similarly, officers generally are discouraged from approaching suspected dangerous people too closely while carrying unholstered weapons. Each year, about a quarter of U.S. Police officers shot in the line of duty are wounded or killed by people who have disarmed them and turned their own weapons against them. The fear of disarming also is the reason that corrections officers in even the most dangerous prisons do not carry guns while they are on duty among inmate populations. . . .

Clearly, questions of how much and when force is justified present some complex policy and training issues. Often these are matters of judgment rather than simple dichotomies split by what lawyers call a *bright line* distinguishing the permissible from the impermissible. Still, in lawyers' terms, some instances of use of force are so unambiguously excessive that they shock the consciences of all reasonable people. Like the King incident, most of the brutality cases that have drawn wide public attention and have led to expensive litigation have been characterized by truly outrageous police conduct rather than by borderline misbehavior. Further, some of the most sensational of such cases have involved officers who were following obnoxious policies rather than individual cops who acted out on their own.

The use of chokeholds in Los Angeles offers a prime and disastrous example of a misguided policy that tacitly encouraged vigilante justice and fostered public hostility toward the police. Virtually alone among large American police departments, the LAPD instructed officers that carotid control holds were pain compliance techniques rather than a form of deadly force. Hence, according to the LAPD, such holds could permissibly be used to gain the compliance of such offenders as loudmouth traffic violators or unruly black teenagers. These grips— referred to as "departmentally approved upper body control holds"— are mentioned in hundreds of LAPD reports dismissing complaints that they had been used unnecessarily. The LAPD reclassified them as a form of deadly force only when Adolph Lyons, a traffic offender who had been choked unconscious by an LAPD officer, brought a legal challenge that went as far as the U.S. Supreme Court. Lyons proved in court that, during the five years preceding his encounter with Los Angeles police, sixteen people had died after LAPD officers applied this hold to them, twice as many chokehold-related deaths as the combined total of the other twenty largest U.S. Police departments. The fact that fourteen blacks were included among the victims stimulated Chief Gates's speculation about the relative vulnerability of blacks' circulatory systems. The consequences of such policies and the philosophies and beliefs underlying them as an aspect of so-called "professional" policing, has raised deep concerns among thoughtful police as well as civilians, over how far we have actually progressed from our vigilante past.

———

QUESTIONS

1. What respective roles should constitutional, statutory, and administrative regulation play in the control of excessive use of force by police officers? How, if at all, would you improve upon the existing arrangement?

2. Are the constitutional tests in *Graham* and *Garner* adequate? How would you improve upon them, if at all? What techniques of interpretation were at work, and were they properly applied? What assumptions, if any, were made by the Court? Was there overt or covert legislative fact finding? If so, what legislative facts were found and how? What evidence supported those facts, and was the evidence adequate? Would you have wanted additional evidence? If so, where would you find it?

PROBLEM 3–11

In the Boson case set forth in Chapter 1, assume that Boson runs away from Officer Glemp, who is unaware of Boson's involvement in the Susan Oldham murder. Because Glemp has found a kilo of cocaine in Boson's car, however, he has probable cause to believe that Boson is a major drug distributor.

Question: In his effort to capture Boson, may Glemp use deadly force? If not, what level of force would be reasonable?

PROBLEM 3–12

Officers Kelley and Van Hall, parked in a police squad car at 2 a.m. in a small farming community in Minnesota, noticed a pick-up truck towing a gravity box wagon filled with soybean seed. Finding it odd that this activity would be going on at that hour, the officers speculated that a grain theft was in progress. Officer Kelley, noting that he "thought" a reflector was missing, suggested pulling the pickup truck over, so Officer Van Hall turned out the squad car's sirens and flashing lights.

The pickup driver reacted by speeding up. The officers chased the pickup at high speed for many blocks. During the chase, the pickup driver threw a large plastic bag out of the truck, onto the side of the road. Shortly thereafter, Van Hall managed to pass the pickup, skidding the car to face the speeding pickup at a right angle. Officer Kelley then fired several shots at the pickup's tires, flattening two of them, which sent the pickup careening off the road into a tree. Officer Kelley approached the driver's side of the pickup, pointed a gun at the driver and said, "Get your hands up or I'll shoot." The driver, Donovan Johnson, then said, "O.K., don't shoot; the stuff's mine; it's back the road a piece." Kelley ordered Johnson out of the truck, and Johnson complied. As Kelley was getting ready to cuff Johnson, however, Johnson kicked back, hitting Kelley in the groin. Officer Hall responded by punching Johnson three times in the face, then placing him in a chokehold. As a result of the chokehold, Johnson suffered permanent injury to his larynx and can no longer speak. An immediate search of Johnson's person revealed an unlicensed palm-size gun in his left boot. A later search up the road revealed that the bag that Johnson had thrown out of his truck contained a large quantity of marijuana.

QUESTIONS

1. At Johnson's trial for unlawful possession of an unlicensed weapon and for possession of marijuana to distribute, should any of the evidence be suppressed? Should Johnson recover damages in a civil rights suit for violation of his constitutional rights? In thinking about these questions, include in your analysis the usefulness of Minnesota's then-controlling definition of deadly force as:

> force which the actor uses with the purpose of causing, or which the actor should reasonably know creates a substantial risk of causing death or great bodily harm. The intentional discharge of a firearm in the direction of another person, or at a vehicle in which another person is believed to be, constitute deadly force.

2. Would your answers to the above questions differ if, before the officers turned on the squad car lights and sirens, Officer Kelley recognized Johnson as the driver and knew that Johnson was wanted for burglary, a burglary in which the crime Johnson allegedly intended to commit once inside the home (he did not succeed) was rape?

B. THE REQUIREMENT OF PROMPT ARRAIGNMENT

That a warrantless arrest may be reasonable does not mean that a defendant has no right to a judicial determination of probable cause. In *Gerstein v. Pugh*,[134] the Court held that the officer's probable cause judgment justifies only "a brief period of detention to take the administrative steps incident to arrest." Once there is no longer a danger that the defendant will escape or commit further crimes, the Fourth Amendment requires a judicial determination of probable cause "promptly after arrest." This rule is clearly required for defendants in custody, although it may not apply to those promptly released, perhaps by posting bail. The probable cause hearing need not be adversarial but can instead be decided by a magistrate based upon hearsay and written testimony—in short, a procedure much like that for obtaining a warrant before arrest. A full-scale adversarial hearing may come much later, if a pre-trial suppression motion is filed, thus triggering a suppression hearing.

---

134. 420 U.S. 103 (1975).

How "prompt" must a *Gerstein* hearing be? In *County of Riverside v. McLaughlin*,[135] the Court held that a *Gerstein* hearing's taking place within 48 hours of arrest is presumptively reasonable. But a particular defendant may show that such a delay was done "for the purpose of gathering additional evidence to justify the arrest, a delay motivated by ill will against the arrested individual, or delay for delay's sake," thereby rendering the delay unreasonable. The Court further held that a post–48–hour *Gerstein* hearing is presumptively *un*reasonable, in which case "the burden shifts to the government to demonstrate the existence of a bona fide emergency or other extraordinary circumstance."

What is the consequence of a *Gerstein* violation? Presumably, if the state fails to provide a probable cause determination promptly and an arrestee complains (by filing a petition for habeas corpus, or through some other proceeding), the appropriate remedy is an immediate probable cause determination or, failing that, immediate release. The issue is more problematic, however, when the complaint occurs long after the violation—for example, in a motion to suppress evidence. Courts have not been consistent about whether evidence obtained in violation of *Gerstein* should be suppressed.[136] The question comes up most frequently in the context of confessions taken in violation of the 48–hour period discussed in *County of Riverside v. McLaughlin*. At least one court has held that the Fourth Amendment balancing test requires that such statements be suppressed, because

> [i]gnoring the requirements of *McLaughlin* is functionally the same as making warrantless searches or arrests when a warrant is required. In both situations, law enforcement officials act without necessary judicial guidance or objective good faith. The cost of applying the exclusionary sanction to a violation of *McLaughlin* is that evidence obtained as a result of the illegal detention will be suppressed. The benefit is the same as that gained from the application of the exclusionary rule to certain warrantless arrests. It will deter law enforcement officials from ignoring the Fourth Amendment mandate of a judicial determination of probable cause. Violations of *McLaughlin* can be easily avoided, and applying the exclusionary rule to evidence obtained as a result of the illegal detention will deter further violations.[137]

The defendant in that case, Benjamin Huddleston, had been arrested without a warrant in the early afternoon of Friday, January 11, 1991, for his suspected involvement in an armed robbery. Officers took him into custody and questioned him. He was detained in jail over the weekend and was not taken before a magistrate until Tuesday, January 15, more than 72 hours after his arrest. Meanwhile, police obtained from Huddleston a waiver of his *Miranda* rights and a confession. The court held that while

---

135.   500 U.S. 44 (1991).

136.   The Supreme Court has not yet determined the issue. In Powell v. Nevada, 511 U.S. 79 (1994), the Court declined to rule on it, stating that application of the exclusionary rule to *Gerstein* violations "remains an unresolved question."

137.   State v. Huddleston, 924 S.W.2d 666, 673 (Tenn. 1996).

the confession was voluntary and thus not violative of the Fifth Amendment, it violated the Fourth Amendment principles embodied in *Gerstein* and the balance of interests struck in *McLaughlin*. As a result, Huddleston's confession was held inadmissible.

C.   Expiration of Fourth Amendment Interest After Arrest

As you can see from the discussion above, the Fourth Amendment not only governs the reasonableness of arrests, but also it requires a prompt post-arrest determination of probable cause in the case of a warrantless arrest. Does the Fourth Amendment also govern conditions of detention after arrest? For example, can individuals held in jail or in prison file Fourth Amendment complaints about deprivations of liberty caused by their confinement? There is, thus far, no definitive answer to this question, but some case law and commentary support the idea that Fourth Amendment interests expire once the seizure is completed, forcing arrestees complaining about conditions of confinement to rely primarily on the due process clause or (in the case of post-conviction confinement) the cruel and unusual punishment clause. Other cases and commentary find that the Fourth Amendment may have some role to play even after confinement, though a substantially modified and reduced one. The latter view seems more sensible, for it is hard to understand why a continued intentional interference with a person's freedom of movement is not definitionally a "seizure" as defined by the Supreme Court's Fourth Amendment precedents. Too often this point is missed, with sorry consequences, as in the case of the internment of Japanese–Americans during World War II, which was not recognized at the time as involving Fourth Amendment interests, despite the effective arrest and then detention of large numbers of individuals without probable cause, warrants, or any recognized or even newly-minted exceptions to these requirements.[138]

V.   Stop and Frisk

While full custodial arrests and searches ordinarily require probable cause, and sometimes warrants, the Supreme Court has recognized situations in which the government intrudes on liberty and privacy interests in such a minimal fashion as not to require much justification. In these less intrusive interactions, the Court requires a level of suspicion it calls "reasonable suspicion," which is less demanding than probable cause.

Checklist 5: Evaluating Stops and Frisks

1.   Was there a stop?

---

138.   Andrew E. Taslitz, *Stories of Fourth Amendment Disrespect: from Elian to the Internment*, 70 Fordham L. Rev. 2257, 2302–16 (2002).

     a. Did the officer act in a way that would permit an individual reasonably to believe that his or her freedom of movement was significantly restricted?

     b. If so, was the restriction limited in duration, location, and intensity?

2. Was the stop justified by reasonable suspicion that the person was about to commit (or had committed) a crime?

3. Was there a frisk?

     a. Did the officer invade the individual's reasonable expectation of privacy in his or her person?

     b. If so, was the invasion limited to a brief patdown of the surfaces of outer clothing?

4. Was the frisk justified by a reasonable suspicion that the person was armed and dangerous?

A.   THE LANDMARK CASE OF TERRY V. OHIO

Terry v. Ohio

392 U.S. 1 (1968).

■ WARREN, C.J. This case presents serious questions concerning the role of the Fourth Amendment in the confrontation on the street between the citizen and the policeman investigating suspicious circumstances.

    Petitioner Terry was convicted of carrying a concealed weapon. Following the denial of a pretrial motion to suppress, the prosecution introduced in evidence two revolvers and a number of bullets seized from Terry and a codefendant, Richard Chilton, by Cleveland Police Detective Martin McFadden. At the hearing on the motion to suppress this evidence, Officer McFadden testified that while he was patrolling in plain clothes in downtown Cleveland at approximately 2:30 in the afternoon of October 31, 1963, his attention was attracted by two men, Chilton and Terry, standing on the corner of Huron Road and Euclid Avenue. He had never seen the two men before, and he was unable to say precisely what first drew his eye to them. However, he testified that he had been a policeman for 39 years and a detective for 35 and that he had been assigned to patrol this vicinity of downtown Cleveland for shoplifters and pickpockets for 30 years. He explained that he had developed routine habits of observation over the years and that he would "stand and watch people or walk and watch people at many intervals of the day." He added: "Now, in this case when I looked over they didn't look right to me at the time."

    His interest aroused, Officer McFadden took up a post of observation in the entrance to a store 300 to 400 feet away from the two men. "I get more purpose to watch them when I seen their movements," he testified. He saw one of the men leave the other one and walk southwest on Huron Road, past some stores. The man paused for a moment and looked in a store window, then walked on a short distance, turned around and walked back toward the corner, pausing once again to look in the same store window. He rejoined his companion at the corner, and the two conferred briefly. Then the second man went through the same series of motions, strolling down Huron Road, looking in the same window, walking on a short distance, turning back, peering in the store window again, and returning to confer with the first man at the corner. The two men repeated this ritual alternately between five and six times apiece—in all, roughly a dozen trips. At one point, while the two were standing together on the corner, a third man approached them and engaged them briefly in conversation. This man then left the two others and walked west on Euclid Avenue. Chilton and Terry resumed their measured pacing, peering and conferring. After this had gone on for 10 to 12 minutes, the two men walked off together, heading west on Euclid Avenue, following the path taken earlier by the third man.

By this time Officer McFadden had become thoroughly suspicious. He testified that after observing their elaborately casual and oft-repeated reconnaissance of the store window on Huron Road, he suspected the two men of "casing a job, a stick-up," and that he considered it his duty as a police officer to investigate further. He added that he feared "they may have a gun." Thus, Officer McFadden followed Chilton and Terry and saw them stop in front of Zucker's store to talk to the same man who had conferred with them earlier on the street corner. Deciding that the situation was ripe for direct action, Officer McFadden approached the three men, identified himself as a police officer and asked for their names. At this point his knowledge was confined to what he had observed. He was not acquainted with any of the three men by name or by sight, and he had received no information concerning them from any other source. When the men "mumbled something" in response to his inquiries, Officer McFadden grabbed petitioner Terry, spun him around so that they were facing the other two, with Terry between McFadden and the others, and patted down the outside of his clothing. In the left breast pocket of Terry's overcoat Officer McFadden felt a pistol. He reached inside the overcoat pocket, but was unable to remove the gun. At this point, keeping Terry between himself and the others, the officer ordered all three men to enter Zucker's store. As they went in, he removed Terry's overcoat completely, removed a .38–caliber revolver from the pocket and ordered all three men to face the wall with their hands raised. Officer McFadden proceeded to pat down the outer clothing of Chilton and the third man, Katz. He discovered another revolver in the outer pocket of Chilton's overcoat, but no weapons were found on Katz. The officer testified that he only patted the men down to see whether they had weapons, and that he did not put his hands beneath the outer garments of either Terry or Chilton until he felt their guns. So far as appears from the record, he never placed his hands beneath Katz' outer garments. Officer McFadden seized Chilton's gun, asked the proprietor of the store to call a police wagon, and took all three men to the station, where Chilton and Terry were formally charged with carrying concealed weapons.

On the motion to suppress the guns the prosecution took the position that they had been seized following a search incident to a lawful arrest. The trial court rejected this theory, stating that it "would be stretching the facts beyond reasonable comprehension" to find that Officer McFadden had had probable cause to arrest the men before he patted them down for weapons. However, the court denied the defendants' motion on the ground that Officer McFadden, on the basis of his experience, "had reasonable cause to believe ... that the defendants were conducting themselves suspiciously, and some interrogation should be made of their action." Purely for his own protection, the court held, the officer had the right to pat down the outer clothing of these men, who he had reasonable cause to believe might be armed. The court distinguished between an investigatory "stop" and an arrest, and between a "frisk" of the outer clothing for weapons and a full-blown search for evidence of crime. The frisk, it held, was essential to the proper performance of the officer's investigatory duties, for without it "the answer to the police officer may be a bullet, and a loaded pistol discovered during the frisk is admissible."

After the court denied their motion to suppress, Chilton and Terry waived jury trial and pleaded not guilty. The court adjudged them guilty, and the Court of Appeals for the Eighth Judicial District, Cuyahoga County, affirmed.... We granted certiorari to determine whether the admission of the revolvers in evidence violated petitioner's rights under the Fourth Amendment, made applicable to the States by the Fourteenth. *Mapp v. Ohio*, 367 U.S. 643 (1961). We affirm the conviction.

I

The Fourth Amendment provides that "the right of the people to be secure in their persons, houses, papers, and effects, against unreasonable searches and seizures, shall not be violated...." This inestimable right of personal security belongs as much to the citizen on the streets of our cities as to the homeowner closeted in his study to dispose of his secret affairs.... We have recently held that "the Fourth Amendment protects people, not places," *Katz v. United States*, 389 U.S. 347 (1967), and wherever an individual may harbor a reasonable "expectation of privacy," he is entitled to be free from unreasonable governmental intrusion. Of course, the specific content and incidents of this right must be shaped by the context in which it is asserted. For "what the Constitution forbids is not all searches and seizures, but unreasonable searches and seizures." *Elkins v. United States*, 364 U.S. 206 (1960). Unquestionably petitioner was entitled to the protection of the Fourth Amendment as he walked down the street in Cleveland. The question is whether in all the circumstances of this on-the-street encounter, his right to personal security was violated by an unreasonable search and seizure.

We would be less than candid if we did not acknowledge that this question thrusts to the fore difficult and troublesome issues regarding a sensitive area of police activity—issues which have never before been squarely presented to this Court. Reflective of the tensions involved are the practical and constitutional arguments pressed with great vigor on both sides of the public debate over the power of the police to "stop and frisk—as it is sometimes euphemistically termed—suspicious persons."

On the one hand, it is frequently argued that in dealing with the rapidly unfolding and often dangerous situations on city streets the police are in need of an escalating set of flexible responses, graduated in relation to the amount of information they possess. For this purpose it is urged that distinctions should be made between a "stop" and an "arrest" (or a "seizure" of a person), and between a "frisk" and a "search." Thus, it is argued, the police should be allowed to "stop" a person and detain him briefly for questioning upon suspicion that he may be connected with criminal activity. Upon suspicion that the person may be armed, the police should have the power to "frisk" him for weapons. If the "stop" and the "frisk" give rise to probable cause to believe that the suspect has committed a crime, then the police should be empowered to make a formal "arrest," and a full incident "search" of the person. This scheme is justified in part upon the notion that a "stop" and a "frisk" amount to a mere "minor inconvenience and petty indignity," which can properly be imposed upon the citizen in the interest of effective law enforcement on the basis of a police officer's suspicion.[a]

On the other side the argument is made that the authority of the police must be strictly circumscribed by the law of arrest and search as it has developed to date in the traditional jurisprudence of the Fourth Amendment. It is contended with some force that there is not—and cannot be—a variety of police activity which does not depend solely upon the voluntary cooperation of the citizen and yet which stops short of an arrest based upon probable cause to make such an arrest. The heart of the Fourth Amendment, the argument runs, is a severe requirement of specific justification for any intrusion upon protected personal security, coupled with a highly developed system of judicial controls to enforce upon the agents of the State the commands of the Constitution. Acquiescence by the courts in the compulsion inherent in the field interrogation practices at issue here, it is urged, would constitute an abdication of judicial control over, and indeed an encouragement of, substantial interference with liberty and personal security by police officers whose judgment is necessarily colored by their primary involvement in "the often competitive enterprise of ferreting out crime." *Johnson v. United States*, 333 U.S. 10 (1948). This, it is argued, can

---

a.   The theory is well laid out in the *Rivera* opinion: "[T]he evidence needed to make the inquiry is not of the same degree of conclusiveness as that required for an arrest. The stopping of the individual to inquire is not an arrest and the ground upon which the police may make the inquiry may be less incriminating than the ground for an arrest for a crime known to have been committed.... And as the right to stop and inquire is to be justified for a cause less conclusive than that which would sustain an arrest, so the right to frisk may be justified as an incident to inquiry upon grounds of elemental safety and precaution which might not initially sustain a search. Ultimately the validity of the frisk narrows down to whether there is or is not a right by the police to touch the person questioned. The sense of exterior touch here involved is not very far different from the sense of sight or hearing—senses upon which police customarily act." People v. Rivera, 201 N.E.2d 32, 34, 35 (N.Y. 1964), *cert. denied*, 379 U.S. 978 (1965).

only serve to exacerbate police-community tensions in the crowded centers of our Nation's cities.

In this context we approach the issues in this case mindful of the limitations of the judicial function in controlling the myriad daily situations in which policemen and citizens confront each other on the street. The State has characterized the issue here as "the right of a police officer ... to make an on-the-street stop, interrogate and pat down for weapons (known in street vernacular as 'stop and frisk')." But this is only partly accurate. For the issue is not the abstract propriety of the police conduct, but the admissibility against petitioner of the evidence uncovered by the search and seizure. . . .

The exclusionary rule has its limitations, however, as a tool of judicial control. It cannot properly be invoked to exclude the products of legitimate police investigative techniques on the ground that much conduct which is closely similar involves unwarranted intrusions upon constitutional protections. Moreover, in some contexts the rule is ineffective as a deterrent. Street encounters between citizens and police officers are incredibly rich in diversity. They range from wholly friendly exchanges of pleasantries or mutually useful information to hostile confrontations of armed men involving arrests, or injuries, or loss of life. Moreover, hostile confrontations are not all of a piece. Some of them begin in a friendly enough manner, only to take a different turn upon the injection of some unexpected element into the conversation. Encounters are initiated by the police for a wide variety of purposes, some of which are wholly unrelated to a desire to prosecute for crime. Doubtless some police "field interrogation" conduct violates the Fourth Amendment. But a stern refusal by this Court to condone such activity does not necessarily render it responsive to the exclusionary rule. Regardless of how effective the rule may be where obtaining convictions is an important objective of the police, it is powerless to deter invasions of constitutionally guaranteed rights where the police either have no interest in prosecuting or are willing to forgo successful prosecution in the intorest of serving some other goal.

Proper adjudication of cases in which the exclusionary rule is invoked demands a constant awareness of these limitations. The wholesale harassment by certain elements of the police community, of which minority groups, particularly Negroes, frequently complain,[b] will not be stopped by

---

b. The President's Commission on Law Enforcement and Administration of Justice found that "[i]n many communities, field interrogations are a major source of friction between the police and minority groups." President's Commission on Law Enforcement and Administration of Justice, Task Force Report: The Police 183 (1967). It was reported that the friction caused by "[m]isuse of field interrogations" increases "as more police departments adopt 'aggressive patrol' in which officers are encouraged routinely to stop and question persons on the street who are unknown to them, who are suspicious, or whose purpose for being abroad is not readily evident." While the frequency with which "frisking" forms a part of field interrogation practice varies tremendously with the locale, the objective of the interrogation, and the particular officer, it cannot help but be a severely exacerbating factor in police-community tensions. This is particularly true in situations where the "stop and frisk" of youths or minority group members is "motivated by the officers' perceived need to maintain

the exclusion of any evidence from any criminal trial. Yet a rigid and unthinking application of the exclusionary rule, in futile protest against practices which it can never be used effectively to control, may exact a high toll in human injury and frustration of efforts to prevent crime. No judicial opinion can comprehend the protean variety of the street encounter, and we can only judge the facts of the case before us. Nothing we say today is to be taken as indicating approval of police conduct outside the legitimate investigative sphere. Under our decision, courts still retain their traditional responsibility to guard against police conduct which is overbearing or harassing, or which trenches upon personal security without the objective evidentiary justification which the Constitution requires. When such conduct is identified, it must be condemned by the judiciary and its fruits must be excluded from evidence in criminal trials. And, of course, our approval of legitimate and restrained investigative conduct undertaken on the basis of ample factual justification should in no way discourage the employment of other remedies than the exclusionary rule to curtail abuses for which that sanction may prove inappropriate.

Having thus roughly sketched the perimeters of the constitutional debate over the limits on police investigative conduct in general and the background against which this case presents itself, we turn our attention to the quite narrow question posed by the facts before us: whether it is always unreasonable for a policeman to seize a person and subject him to a limited search for weapons unless there is probable cause for an arrest. Given the narrowness of this question, we have no occasion to canvass in detail the constitutional limitations upon the scope of a policeman's power when he confronts a citizen without probable cause to arrest him.

II

Our first task is to establish at what point in this encounter the Fourth Amendment becomes relevant. That is, we must decide whether and when Officer McFadden "seized" Terry and whether and when he conducted a "search." There is some suggestion in the use of such terms as "stop" and "frisk" that such police conduct is outside the purview of the Fourth Amendment because neither action rises to the level of a "search" or "seizure" within the meaning of the Constitution. We emphatically reject this notion. It is quite plain that the Fourth Amendment governs "seizures" of the person which do not eventuate in a trip to the station house and prosecution for crime—"arrests" in traditional terminology. It must be recognized that whenever a police officer accosts an individual and restrains his freedom to walk away, he has "seized" that person. And it is nothing less than sheer torture of the English language to suggest that a careful exploration of the outer surfaces of a person's clothing all over his or her body in an attempt to find weapons is not a "search." Moreover, it is simply fantastic to urge that such a procedure performed in public by a policeman while the citizen stands helpless, perhaps facing a wall with his

---

the power image of the beat officer, an aim sometimes accomplished by humiliating anyone who attempts to undermine police control of the streets."

hands raised, is a "petty indignity."[c] It is a serious intrusion upon the sanctity of the person, which may inflict great indignity and arouse strong resentment, and it is not to be undertaken lightly.[d]

The danger in the logic which proceeds upon distinctions between a "stop" and an "arrest," or "seizure" of the person, and between a "frisk" and a "search" is twofold. It seeks to isolate from constitutional scrutiny the initial stages of the contact between the policeman and the citizen. And by suggesting a rigid all-or-nothing model of justification and regulation under the Amendment, it obscures the utility of limitations upon the scope, as well as the initiation, of police action as a means of constitutional regulation. This Court has held in the past that a search which is reasonable at its inception may violate the Fourth Amendment by virtue of its intolerable intensity and scope. The scope of the search must be "strictly tied to and justified by" the circumstances which rendered its initiation permissible.

The distinctions of classical "stop-and-frisk" theory thus serve to divert attention from the central inquiry under the Fourth Amendment— the reasonableness in all the circumstances of the particular governmental invasion of a citizen's personal security. "Search" and "seizure" are not talismans. We therefore reject the notions that the Fourth Amendment does not come into play at all as a limitation upon police conduct if the officers stop short of something called a "technical arrest" or a "full-blown search."

In this case there can be no question, then, that Officer McFadden "seized" petitioner and subjected him to a "search" when he took hold of him and patted down the outer surfaces of his clothing. We must decide whether at that point it was reasonable for Officer McFadden to have interfered with petitioner's personal security as he did. And in determining whether the seizure and search were "unreasonable" our inquiry is a dual one—whether the officer's action was justified at its inception, and whether it was reasonably related in scope to the circumstances which justified the interference in the first place.

III

If this case involved police conduct subject to the Warrant Clause of the Fourth Amendment, we would have to ascertain whether "probable cause" existed to justify the search and seizure which took place. However,

---

c. Consider the following apt description: "[T]he officer must feel with sensitive fingers every portion of the prisoner's body. A through search must be made of the prisoner's arms and armpits, waistline and back, the groin and area about the testicles, and entire surface of the legs down to the feet." Priar & Martin, *Searching and Disarming Criminals*, 45 J. CRIM. L. CRIMINOL. & POLICE SCIENCE 481 (1954).

d. We have noted that the abusive practices which play a major, though by no means exclusive, role in creating this friction are not susceptible of control by means of the exclusionary rule, and cannot properly dictate our decision with respect to the powers of the police in genuine investigative and preventive situations. However, the degree of community resentment aroused by particular practices is clearly relevant to an assessment of the quality of the intrusion upon reasonable expectations of personal security caused by those practices.

that is not the case. We do not retreat from our holdings that the police must, whenever practicable, obtain advance judicial approval of searches and seizures through the warrant procedure, or that in most instances failure to comply with the warrant requirement can only be excused by exigent circumstances. But we deal here with an entire rubric of police conduct—necessarily swift action predicated upon the on-the-spot observations of the officer on the beat—which historically has not been, and as a practical matter could not be, subjected to the warrant procedure. Instead, the conduct involved in this case must be tested by the Fourth Amendment's general proscription against unreasonable searches and seizures.

Nonetheless, the notions which underlie both the warrant procedure and the requirement of probable cause remain fully relevant in this context. In order to assess the reasonableness of Officer McFadden's conduct as a general proposition, it is necessary first to focus upon the governmental interest which allegedly justifies official intrusion upon the constitutionally protected interests of the private citizen, for there is no ready test for determining reasonableness other than by balancing the need to search (or seize) against the invasion which the search (or seizure) entails. And in justifying the particular intrusion the police officer must be able to point to specific and articulable facts which, taken together with rational inferences from those facts, reasonably warrant that intrusion. The scheme of the Fourth Amendment becomes meaningful only when it is assured that at some point the conduct of those charged with enforcing the laws can be subjected to the more detached, neutral scrutiny of a judge who must evaluate the reasonableness of a particular search or seizure in light of the particular circumstances. And in making that assessment it is imperative that the facts be judged against an objective standard: would the facts available to the officer at the moment of the seizure or the search "warrant a man of reasonable caution in the belief" that the action taken was appropriate? Anything less would invite intrusions upon constitutionally guaranteed rights based on nothing more substantial than inarticulate hunches, a result this Court has consistently refused to sanction. And simple good faith on the part of the arresting officer is not enough.... If subjective good faith alone were the test, the protections of the Fourth Amendment would evaporate, and the people would be secure in their persons, houses, papers and effects, only in the discretion of the police.

Applying these principles to this case, we consider first the nature and extent of the governmental interests involved. One general interest is of course that of effective crime prevention and detection; it is this interest which underlies the recognition that a police officer may in appropriate circumstances and in an appropriate manner approach a person for purposes of investigating possibly criminal behavior even though there is no probable cause to make an arrest. It was this legitimate investigative function Officer McFadden was discharging when he decided to approach petitioner and his companions. He had observed Terry, Chilton, and Katz go through a series of acts, each of them perhaps innocent in itself, but which taken together warranted further investigation. There is nothing unusual in two men standing together on a street corner, perhaps waiting for someone. Nor is there anything suspicious about people in such circumstances strolling up and down the street, singly or in pairs. Store windows, moreover, are made to be looked in. But the story is quite different where, as here, two men hover about a street corner for an extended period of time, at the end of which it becomes apparent that they are not waiting for anyone or anything; where these men pace alternately along an identical route, pausing to stare in the same store window roughly 24 times; where each completion of this route is followed immediately by a conference between the two men on the corner; where they are joined in one of these conferences by a third man who leaves swiftly; and where the two men finally follow the third and rejoin him a couple of blocks away. It would have been poor police work indeed for an officer of 30 years' experience in the detection of thievery from stores in this same neighborhood to have failed to investigate this behavior further.

The crux of this case, however, is not the propriety of Officer McFadden's taking steps to investigate petitioner's suspicious behavior, but rather, whether there was justification for McFadden's invasion of Terry's personal security by searching him for weapons in the course of that investigation. We are now concerned with more than the governmental interest in investigating crime; in addition, there is the more immediate interest of the police officer in taking steps to assure himself that the person with whom he is dealing is not armed with a weapon that could unexpectedly and fatally be used against him. Certainly it would be unreasonable to require that police officers take unnecessary risks in the performance of their duties. American criminals have a long tradition of armed violence, and every year in this country many law enforcement officers are killed in the line of duty, and thousands more are wounded. Virtually all of these deaths and a substantial portion of the injuries are inflicted with guns and knives.

In view of these facts, we cannot blind ourselves to the need for law enforcement officers to protect themselves and other prospective victims of violence in situations where they may lack probable cause for an arrest. When an officer is justified in believing that the individual whose suspicious behavior he is investigating at close range is armed and presently dangerous to the officer or to others, it would appear to be clearly unreasonable to deny the officer the power to take necessary measures to determine whether the person is in fact carrying a weapon and to neutralize the threat of physical harm.

We must still consider, however, the nature and quality of the intrusion on individual rights which must be accepted if police officers are to be conceded the right to search for weapons in situations where probable cause to arrest for crime is lacking. Even a limited search of the outer clothing for weapons constitutes a severe, though brief, intrusion upon cherished personal security, and it must surely be an annoying, frightening, and perhaps humiliating experience. Petitioner contends that such an intrusion is permissible only incident to a lawful arrest, either for a crime involving the possession of weapons or for a crime the commission of which led the officer to investigate in the first place. However, this argument must be closely examined.

Petitioner does not argue that a police officer should refrain from making any investigation of suspicious circumstances until such time as he has probable cause to make an arrest; nor does he deny that police officers in properly discharging their investigative function may find themselves confronting persons who might well be armed and dangerous. Moreover, he does not say that an officer is always unjustified in searching a suspect to discover weapons. Rather, he says it is unreasonable for the policeman to take that step until such time as the situation evolves to a point where there is probable cause to make an arrest. When that point has been reached, petitioner would concede the officer's right to conduct a search of the suspect for weapons, fruits or instrumentalities of the crime, or "mere" evidence, incident to the arrest.

There are two weaknesses in this line of reasoning however. First, it fails to take account of traditional limitations upon the scope of searches, and thus recognizes no distinction in purpose, character, and extent between a search incident to an arrest and a limited search for weapons. The former, although justified in part by the acknowledged necessity to protect the arresting officer from assault with a concealed weapon, is also justified on other grounds, and can therefore involve a relatively extensive exploration of the person. A search for weapons in the absence of probable cause to arrest, however, must, like any other search, be strictly circumscribed by the exigencies which justify its initiation. Thus it must be limited to that which is necessary for the discovery of weapons which might be used to harm the officer of others nearby, and may realistically be characterized as something less than a "full" search, even though it remains a serious intrusion.

A second, and related, objection to petitioner's argument is that it assumes that the law of arrest has already worked out the balance between the particular interests involved here—the neutralization of danger to the policeman in the investigative circumstance and the sanctity of the individual. But this is not so. An arrest is a wholly different kind of intrusion upon individual freedom from a limited search for weapons, and the interests each is designed to serve are likewise quite different. An arrest is the initial stage of a criminal prosecution. It is intended to vindicate society's interest in having its laws obeyed, and it is inevitably accompanied by future interference with the individual's freedom of movement, whether or not trial or conviction ultimately follows. The protective search for weapons, on the other hand, constitutes a brief, though far from inconsiderable, intrusion upon the sanctity of the person. It does not follow that because an officer may lawfully arrest a person only when he is apprised of facts sufficient to warrant a belief that the person has committed or is committing a crime, the officer is equally unjustified, absent that kind of evidence, in making any intrusions short of an arrest. Moreover, a perfectly reasonable apprehension of danger may arise long before the officer is possessed of adequate information to justify taking a person into custody for the purpose of prosecuting him for a crime. Petitioner's reliance on cases which have worked out standards of reasonableness with regard to "seizures" constituting arrests and searches incident thereto is thus misplaced. It assumes that the interests sought to be vindicated and the invasions of personal security may be equated in the two cases, and thereby ignores a vital aspect of the analysis of the reasonableness of particular types of conduct under the Fourth Amendment.

Our evaluation of the proper balance that has to be struck in this type of case leads us to conclude that there must be a narrowly drawn authority to permit a reasonable search for weapons for the protection of the police officer, where he has reason to believe that he is dealing with an armed and dangerous individual, regardless of whether he has probable cause to arrest the individual for a crime. The officer need not be absolutely certain that the individual is armed; the issue is whether a reasonably prudent man in the circumstances would be warranted in the belief that his safety or that of others was in danger. And in determining whether the officer acted reasonably in such circumstances, due weight must be given, not to his inchoate and unparticularized suspicion or "hunch," but to the specific reasonable inferences which he is entitled to draw from the facts in light of his experience.

IV

We must now examine the conduct of Officer McFadden in this case to determine whether his search and seizure of petitioner were reasonable, both at their inception and as conducted. He had observed Terry, together with Chilton and another man, acting in a manner he took to be preface to a "stick-up." We think on the facts and circumstances Officer McFadden detailed before the trial judge a reasonably prudent man would have been warranted in believing petitioner was armed and thus presented a threat to the officer's safety while he was investigating his suspicious behavior. The actions of Terry and Chilton were consistent with McFadden's hypothesis that these men were contemplating a daylight robbery—which, it is reasonable to assume, would be likely to involve the use of weapons—and nothing in their conduct from the time he first noticed them until the time he confronted them and identified himself as a police officer gave him sufficient reason to negate that hypothesis. Although the trio had departed the original scene, there was nothing to indicate abandonment of an intent to commit a robbery at some point. Thus, when Officer McFadden approached the three men gathered before the display window at Zucker's store he had observed enough to make it quite reasonable to fear that they were armed; and nothing in their response to his hailing them, identifying himself as a police officer, and asking their names served to dispel that reasonable belief. We cannot say his decision at that point to seize Terry and pat his clothing for weapons was the product of a volatile or inventive imagination, or was undertaken simply as an act of harassment; the record evidences the tempered act of a policeman who in the course of an investigation had to make a quick decision as to how to protect himself and others from possible danger, and took limited steps to do so.

The manner in which the seizure and search were conducted is, of course, as vital a part of the inquiry as whether they were warranted at all. The Fourth Amendment proceeds as much by limitations upon the scope of governmental action as by imposing preconditions upon its initiation. . . .

We need not develop at length in this case, however, the limitations which the Fourth Amendment places upon a protective seizure and search for weapons. These limitations will have to be developed in the concrete factual circumstances of individual cases. Suffice it to note that such a search, unlike a search without a warrant incident to a lawful arrest, is not justified by any need to prevent the disappearance or destruction of evidence of crime. The sole justification of the search in the present situation is the protection of the police officer and others nearby, and it must therefore be confined in scope to an intrusion reasonably designed to discover guns, knives, clubs, or other hidden instruments for the assault of the police officer.

The scope of the search in this case presents no serious problem in light of these standards. Officer McFadden patted down the outer clothing of petitioner and his two companions. He did not place his hands in their pockets or under the outer surface of their garments until he had felt weapons, and then he merely reached for and removed the guns. He never did invade Katz' person beyond the outer surfaces of his clothes, since he discovered nothing in his patdown which might have been a weapon. Officer McFadden confined his search strictly to what was minimally necessary to learn whether the men were armed and to disarm them once he discovered the weapons. He did not conduct a general exploratory search for whatever evidence of criminal activity he might find.

V

We conclude that the revolver seized from Terry was properly admitted in evidence against him. At the time he seized petitioner and searched him for weapons, Officer McFadden had reasonable grounds to believe that petitioner was armed and dangerous, and it was necessary for the protection of himself and others to take swift measures to discover the true facts and neutralize the threat of harm if it materialized. The policeman carefully restricted his search to what was appropriate to the discovery of the particular items which he sought. Each case of this sort will, of course, have to be decided on its own facts. We merely hold today that where a police officer observes unusual conduct which leads him reasonably to conclude in light of his experience that criminal activity may be afoot and that the persons with whom he is dealing may be armed and presently dangerous, where in the course of investigating this behavior he identifies himself as a policeman and makes reasonable inquiries, and where nothing in the initial stages of the encounter serves to dispel his reasonable fear for his own or others' safety, he is entitled for the protection of himself and others in the area to conduct a carefully limited search of the outer clothing of such persons in an attempt to discover weapons which might be used to assault him. Such a search is a reasonable search under the Fourth

Amendment, and any weapons seized may properly be introduced in evidence against the person from whom they were taken.

■ DOUGLAS, J., dissenting. I agree that petitioner was "seized" within the meaning of the Fourth Amendment. I also agree that frisking petitioner and his companions for guns was a "search." But it is a mystery how that "search" and that "seizure" can be constitutional by Fourth Amendment standards, unless there was "probable cause" to believe that (1) a crime had been committed or (2) a crime was in the process of being committed or (3) a crime was about to be committed.

The opinion of the Court disclaims the existence of "probable cause." If loitering were in issue and that was the offense charged, there would be "probable cause" shown. But the crime here is carrying concealed weapons; and there is no basis for concluding that the officer had "probable cause" for believing that that crime was being committed. Had a warrant been sought, a magistrate would, therefore, have been unauthorized to issue one, for he can act only if there is a showing of "probable cause." We hold today that the police have greater authority to make a "seizure" and conduct a "search" than a judge has to authorize such action. We have said precisely the opposite over and over again.

In other words, police officers up to today have been permitted to effect arrests or searches without warrants only when the facts within their personal knowledge would satisfy the constitutional standard of probable cause. At the time of their "seizure" without a warrant they must possess facts concerning the person arrested that would have satisfied a magistrate that "probable cause" was indeed present. The term "probable cause" rings a bell of certainty that is not sounded by phrases such as "reasonable suspicion." Moreover, the meaning of "probable cause" is deeply imbedded in our constitutional history. . . .

The infringement on personal liberty of any "seizure" of a person can only be "reasonable" under the Fourth Amendment if we require the police to possess "probable cause" before they seize him. Only that line draws a meaningful distinction between an officer's mere inkling and the presence of facts within the officer's personal knowledge which would convince a reasonable man that the person seized has committed, is committing, or is about to commit a particular crime. In dealing with probable cause, . . . as the very name implies, we deal with probabilities. These are not technical; they are the factual and practical considerations of everyday life on which reasonable and prudent men, not legal technicians, act.

To give the police greater power than a magistrate is to take a long step down the totalitarian path. Perhaps such a step is desirable to cope with modern forms of lawlessness. But if it is taken, it should be the deliberate choice of the people through a constitutional amendment. Until the Fourth Amendment, which is closely allied with the Fifth, is rewritten, the person and the effects of the individual are beyond the reach of all government agencies until there are reasonable grounds to believe (probable cause) that a criminal venture has been launched or is about to be launched.

There have been powerful hydraulic pressures throughout our history that bear heavily on the Court to water down constitutional guarantees and give the police the upper hand. That hydraulic pressure has probably never been greater than it is today.

Yet if the individual is no longer to be sovereign, if the police can pick him up whenever they do not like the cut of his jib, if they can "seize" and "search" him in their discretion, we enter a new regime. The decision to enter it should be made only after a full debate by the people of this country.

————

NOTES AND QUESTIONS

Pay close attention to the reasoning of Chief Justice Warren's majority opinion. If you were to diagram the syllogism he used, what would it look like? On what interpretive techniques did Warren rely? Where would he stand on the debate over the relationship between the Fourth Amendment's warrant clause and its reasonableness clause? Warren's reputation as a strong advocate of Fourth Amendment rights might seem at odds with his decision in *Terry*. Why do you suppose he decided the case the way he did? What did he identify as the possible consequences of requiring probable cause for the kind of activity in which Officer McFadden engaged? Notice that Warren acknowledged in his opinion that police activity is a "major source of friction between the police and minority groups." Having acknowledged this problem, why did Warren decide the case as he did? Why would the deterrent principles of the exclusionary rule not be served by a rule prohibiting police from stopping individuals on something less than probable cause?

What about Justice Douglas's opinion? What are the steps in his logical syllogism? On what interpretive techniques does he rely? Where would he stand on the debate about the warrant clause and the reasonableness clause?

In your answers to the above questions, you will no doubt have highlighted the significance of the majority's reliance on the Fourth Amendment's reasonableness clause. A search or seizure, according to the Court, may be effectuated without a warrant so long as it is "reasonable." The Court was careful to explain that the kind of warrantless search and seizure at issue in *Terry*—that is, a search or seizure supported only by "reasonable suspicion" as opposed to probable cause—must be strictly confined in terms of its duration and intrusiveness.

In fact, a seizure under the *Terry* doctrine must be no more than a "stop"—a brief, on-the-scene detention that is strictly limited in time. An officer is justified in making such a stop only if the officer reasonably suspects that the person is engaging in (or, as in *Terry*, is about to engage in) criminal activity. During the brief period of the stop, the officer may ask questions in order to confirm or dispel suspicions, but if the officer's suspicions are not confirmed within a very brief period of time, the detention must end. We will address the distinction between such a "stop" and an arrest below.

A search justified by the *Terry* doctrine is frequently referred to as a "frisk." Recall from *Terry* that a frisk is justified only if the officer reasonably suspects that the person is armed and dangerous. According to the opinion in *Terry*, a frisk is a patdown of a person's outer clothing. The patdown is limited in scope and intensity to its justification—the officer's purpose is to discover weapons. Lingering even a few seconds over a package that feels like it contains drugs goes beyond the scope of the justification.[139] In addition to frisking a person, an officer also may frisk an *area* if the officer has reasonable suspicion that a person within the area is armed and dangerous. The Court applied this rule to the passenger compartment of a car in *Michigan v. Long*[140] and, in *Maryland v. Buie*,[141] to a residence in which police were executing an arrest warrant.

Cautionary Reminder: Remember that there are two types of reasonable suspicion: reasonable suspicion that criminal activity is afoot, justifying only a stop, and reasonable suspicion that a suspect is armed and dangerous, justifying a frisk for weapons. Reasonable suspicion to stop does not necessarily establish reasonable suspicion to frisk. Moreover, keep in mind that with any *Terry* stop other Fourth Amendment doctrines might come into play. For example, during an automobile stop, further investigation might establish grounds for a frisk, probable cause for an arrest, or probable cause for a full-blown search. For example, a stop based on reasonable suspicion that a driver committed forgery probably would not establish reasonable suspicion that the driver is armed and dangerous, so no *Terry* frisk of the passenger compartment would be appropriate. However, if the officer observed a gun on the front seat during the course of the stop, the officer would probably be justified in frisking the passenger compartment for weapons. If the stop developed probable cause for a custodial arrest and if the officer effected such an arrest, then the officer would be justified in conducting a search incident to arrest—searching the passenger compartment (the area within the driver's "immediate control")—as we will explain in a later chapter. And while the *Terry* frisk permits the officer to look only for weapons, the search incident to arrest permits the officer to look for weapons or evidence of the crime on which the custodial arrest was based. In practice, the frisk and the search may often lead to the same result, because the officer doing the *Terry* frisk can seize items meeting the requirements of the plain view doctrine described in a later chapter. Keep in mind that although police need not offer additional cause to believe any occupant of a vehicle be involved in criminal activity to justify seizure of passengers during a traffic stop, "[t]o justify a patdown of the driver or a passenger during a traffic stop, however, just as in the case of a pedestrian reasonably suspected of criminal activity, the

---

139. *See* Minnesota v. Dickerson, 508 U.S. 366 (1993).

140. 463 U.S. 1032 (1983).

141. 494 U.S. 325 (1990).

police must harbor reasonable suspicion that the person subjected to the frisk is armed and dangerous."[142] Neither the *Terry* frisk nor the search incident to arrest, however, would permit searching the trunk. A trunk search requires probable cause to believe that fruits, contraband, or evidence of a crime will be found in the trunk, as we will see later in this book.

B. Defining the Levels of Interaction

Terry v. Ohio is one of the most important search and seizure cases decided by the Supreme Court because it created an entirely new category of police activity—the "stop and frisk"—that can be conducted without probable cause. *Terry* creates, in effect, a three-level description of the interactions between individuals and law enforcement officials. The lowest level is a voluntary "encounter," in which (theoretically, at least) the individual is free to leave without answering any questions and in which no Fourth Amendment search or seizure occurs.[143] The second level involves the "stop and frisk," in which the individual, for a brief period, is not free to terminate the encounter. Because a "stop" temporarily restricts the individual's freedom to leave, a seizure is said to have occurred, and if the individual is "frisked," the frisk is classified as a minimally-intrusive search.[144] It is important to remember that a proper stop does not automatically justify a frisk. Finally, the third level evolves into an "arrest" where the invasion of an individual's freedom is so intrusive—for example, where that freedom is restricted for more than a brief period of time—that we require probable cause as a justification; and it evolves into a full search where the invasion of privacy is so great that we demand probable cause. This third level of activity constitutes the paradigmatic "search and seizure" under the Fourth Amendment.[145]

The distinctions among these types of encounters are subtle. Consider the following.

1. VOLUNTARY ENCOUNTERS VERSUS SEIZURES

The Court stressed in *Terry* that "[o]bviously, not all personal intercourse between policemen and citizens involves 'seizures' of persons. Only when the officer, by means of physical force or show of authority, has in some way restrained the liberty of a citizen may we conclude that a seizure has occurred." An officer who casually approaches an individual on the street and remarks, "Hello, how are you today?" is not effectuating a stop. Similarly, an officer's request to "ask a few questions" does not turn the encounter into a stop unless the officer's words, conduct, or demeanor would signal to an objectively reasonable person that the person is not free

---

142. *Arizona v. Johnson*, 129 S.Ct. 781, 784 (2009).

143. United States v. Mendenhall, 446 U.S. 544, 545–46 (1980).

144. Florida v. Bostick, 501 U.S. 429 (1991).

145. Florida v. Royer, 460 U.S. 491, 499–500 (1983).

to leave. This standard was articulated in *United States v. Mendenhall*,[146] where the Court stated that "a person has been 'seized' within the meaning of the Fourth Amendment only if, in view of all of the circumstances surrounding the incident, a reasonable person would have believed that he was not free to leave." It is important to note that the relevant perspective is that of the individual, not that of the officer. The officer's subjective intentions, therefore, are irrelevant. Moreover, note the Court's use of the objective "reasonable person" standard. As we will discuss later in this chapter, the Court has never acknowledged that the particular characteristics of the defendant—such as race, ethnicity, gender, or age— are pertinent to this test. Moreover, in one case, the Court stated that the "reasonable person" is an innocent person.[147]

What sorts of circumstances give rise to a reasonable belief that one is not free to leave? The Court has identified a number of factors that might be relevant in a given case. In *Mendenhall*, for example, the Court mentioned these: "the threatening presence of several officers, the display of a weapon by an officer, some physical touching of the person of the citizen, or the use of language or tone of voice indicating that compliance with the officer's request might be compelled." In that case, Sylvia Mendenhall had been approached by federal agents as she walked through an airport concourse. The agents identified themselves, requested her identification and airline ticket, and asked her some questions about herself. The Court did not answer definitively whether she had been seized, because only two justices in the majority reached the issue, but the explanation of those two justices is interesting:

> On the facts of this case, no "seizure" of the respondent occurred. The events took place in the public concourse. The agents wore no uniforms and displayed no weapons. They did not summon the respondent to their presence, but instead approached her and identified themselves as federal agents. They requested, but did not demand to see, the respondent's identification and ticket. Such conduct, without more, did not amount to an intrusion upon any constitutionally protected interest. The respondent was not seized simply by reason of the fact that the agents approached her, asked her if she would show them her ticket and identification, and posed to her a few questions. Nor was it enough to establish a seizure that the person asking the questions was a law enforcement official. In short, nothing in the record suggests that the respondent had any objective reason to believe that she was not free to end the conversation in the concourse and proceed on her way, and for that reason we conclude that the agents' initial approach to her was not a seizure.
>
> Our conclusion that no seizure occurred is not affected by the fact that the respondent was not expressly told by the agents that she was

---

146. 446 U.S. 544 (1980). The Court's opinion in *Mendenhall* was fragmented. Later, in *Florida v. Royer*, 460 U.S. 491 (1983), a majority of the Court approved the *Mendenhall* standard.

147. *See* Florida v. Bostick, 501 U.S. 429 (1991).

free to decline to cooperate with their inquiry, for the voluntariness of her responses does not depend upon her having been so informed. We also reject the argument that the only inference to be drawn from the fact that the respondent acted in a manner so contrary to her self-interest is that she was compelled to answer the agents' questions. It may happen that a person makes statements to law enforcement officials that he later regrets, but the issue in such cases is not whether the statement was self-protective, but rather whether it was made voluntarily.

Some situations make the "free to leave" test difficult to apply. In *Florida v. Bostick*,[148] for example, the Court reviewed a Florida county's practice of "routinely board[ing] buses at scheduled stops and ask[ing] passengers for permission to search their luggage." Passengers in buses are not ordinarily "free to leave," and Terrance Bostick found himself in just that predicament when:

> Two officers, complete with badges, insignia and one of them holding a recognizable zipper pouch, containing a pistol, boarded a bus bound from Miami to Atlanta during a stopover in Fort Lauderdale. Eyeing the passengers, the officers, admittedly without articulable suspicion, picked out the defendant passenger and asked to inspect his ticket and identification. The ticket, from Miami to Atlanta, matched the defendant's identification and both were immediately returned to him as unremarkable. However, the two police officers persisted and explained their presence as narcotics agents on the lookout for illegal drugs. In pursuit of that aim, they then requested the defendant's consent to search his luggage. Needless to say, there is a conflict in the evidence about whether the defendant consented to the search of the second bag in which the contraband was found and as to whether he was informed of his right to refuse consent. However, any conflict must be resolved in favor of the state, it being a question of fact decided by the trial judge.
>
> Two facts are particularly worth noting. First, the police specifically advised Bostick that he had the right to refuse consent. Bostick appears to have disputed the point, but, as the Florida Supreme Court noted explicitly, the trial court resolved this evidentiary conflict in the State's favor. Second, at no time did the officers threaten Bostick with a gun. The Florida Supreme Court indicated that one officer carried a zipper pouch containing a pistol—the equivalent of carrying a gun in a holster—but the court did not suggest that the gun was ever removed from its pouch, pointed at Bostick, or otherwise used in a threatening manner.

Bostick consented to a search of his luggage and the search revealed cocaine. He moved to suppress the cocaine after he was indicted for drug offenses, arguing that his consent was involuntary because he had been "seized." However, the Court stated that the appropriate test for seizure

---

148.   501 U.S. 429 (1991).

was not whether a reasonable person in his situation would have felt free to leave, but whether such a person would "feel free to decline the officers' requests or otherwise terminate the encounter." The Court remanded the case for a determination of the seizure issue under that standard.

Even after *Bostick*, bus searches continue to challenge the judiciary because they are (arguably, at least) inherently coercive. Nevertheless, the Court continues to state that the presence of inquisitive officers on a bus does not necessarily create a Fourth Amendment seizure. In *United States v. Drayton*,[149] a six-person majority reiterated:

> Law enforcement officers do not violate the Fourth Amendment's prohibition of unreasonable seizures merely by approaching individuals on the street or in other public places and putting questions to them if they are willing to listen. Even when law enforcement officers have no basis for suspecting a particular individual, they may pose questions, ask for identification, and request consent to search luggage—provided they do not induce cooperation by coercive means. If a reasonable person would feel free to terminate the encounter, then he or she has not been seized. ... The reasonable person test ... is objective and "presupposes an *innocent* person."

The *Drayton* case involved questioning of bus passengers by three police officers. The officers stepped onto the bus after passengers had disembarked at a rest stop and then reboarded to continue their trip. The officers wore no uniforms, but they did have visible badges. Their weapons were concealed. According to the record, one officer (Hoover) knelt on the driver's seat, facing the passengers. Two other officers (Lang and Blackburn) went to the rear of the bus, where Blackburn remained while Lang worked his way toward the front, questioning individual passengers. Lang inquired about travel plans and luggage, seeking, in the Court's words, "to match passengers with luggage in the overhead racks." Respondents, Drayton and Brown, were seated next to each other with Brown at the window and Drayton the aisle. Here is how the Court described what happened next:

> ... Lang approached respondents from the rear and leaned over Drayton's shoulder. He held up his badge long enough for respondents to identify him as a police officer. With his face 12–to–18 inches away from Drayton's, Lang spoke in a voice just loud enough for respondents to hear: "I'm Investigator Lang with the Tallahassee Police Department. We're conducting bus interdiction [sic], attempting to deter drugs and illegal weapons being transported on the bus. Do you have any bags on the bus?" Both respondents pointed to a single green bag in the overhead luggage rack. Lang asked, "Do you mind if I check it?," and Brown responded, "Go ahead." Lang handed the bag to Officer Blackburn to check. The bag contained no contraband.

> Officer Lang noticed that both respondents were wearing heavy jackets and baggy pants despite the warm weather. In Lang's experi-

---

149.   536 U.S. 194 (2002).

ence drug traffickers often use baggy clothing to conceal weapons or narcotics. The officer thus asked Brown if he had any weapons or drugs in his possession. And he asked Brown: "Do you mind if I check your person?" Brown answered, "Sure," and cooperated by leaning up in his seat, pulling a cell phone out of his pocket, and opening up his jacket. Lang reached across Drayton and patted down Brown's jacket and pockets, including his waist area, sides, and upper thighs. In both thigh areas, Lang detected hard objects similar to drug packages detected on other occasions. Lang arrested and handcuffed Brown. Officer Hoover escorted Brown from the bus.

Lang then asked Drayton, "Mind if I check you?" Drayton responded by lifting his hands about eight inches from his legs. Lang conducted a pat-down of Drayton's thighs and detected hard objects similar to those found on Brown. He arrested Drayton and escorted him from the bus. A further search revealed that respondents had duct-taped plastic bundles of powder cocaine between several pairs of their boxer shorts. Brown possessed three bundles containing 483 grams of cocaine. Drayton possessed two bundles containing 295 grams of cocaine.

Drayton and Brown filed motions to suppress, alleging, among other things, that they had been seized before they consented to the pat-downs. Although the trial court disagreed with their claim, the Court of Appeals for the Eleventh Circuit reversed their convictions, stating that bus passengers do not feel free to terminate officer questions without being told that they can refuse to cooperate. In the United States Supreme Court, the appellate court's *per se* approach did not fare well. Writing for the majority, Justice Kennedy held that the "free to terminate" test "necessitates a consideration of all of the circumstances surrounding the encounter and is not susceptible of *per se* rules." The Court then reviewed the facts of the case to determine whether respondents were seized:

> ... [W]e conclude that the police did not seize respondents when they boarded the bus and began questioning passengers. The officers gave the passengers no reason to believe that they were required to answer the officers' questions. When Officer Lang approached respondents, he did not brandish a weapon or make any intimidating movements. He left the aisle free so that respondents could exit. He spoke to passengers one by one and in a polite, quiet voice. Nothing he said would suggest to a reasonable person that he or she was barred from leaving the bus or otherwise terminating the encounter.

> ... There was no application of force, no intimidating movement, no overwhelming show of force, no brandishing of weapons, no blocking of exits, no threat, no command, not even an authoritative tone of voice. It is beyond question that had this encounter occurred on the street, it would be constitutional. The fact that an encounter takes place on a bus does not on its own transform standard police questioning of citizens into an illegal seizure. Indeed, because many fellow passengers are present to witness officers' conduct, a reasonable per-

son may feel even more secure in his or her decision not to cooperate with police on a bus than in other circumstances.

Respondents make much of the fact that Officer Lang displayed his badge. . . . [W]hile neither Lang nor his colleagues were in uniform or visibly armed, those factors should have little weight in the analysis. Officers are often required to wear uniforms and in many circumstances this is a cause for assurance, not discomfort. Much the same can be said for wearing sidearms. That most law enforcement officers are armed is a fact well known to the public. The presence of a holstered firearm thus is unlikely to contribute to the coerciveness of the encounter absent active brandishing of the weapon.

Officer Hoover's position at the front of the bus also does not tip the scale in respondents' favor. Hoover did nothing to intimidate passengers, and he said nothing to suggest that people could not exit and indeed he left the aisle clear. . . .

Finally, the fact that in Officer Lang's experience only a few passengers have refused to cooperate does not suggest that a reasonable person would not feel free to terminate the bus encounter. In Lang's experience it was common for passengers to leave the bus for a cigarette or a snack while the officers were questioning passengers. And of more importance, bus passengers answer officers' questions and otherwise cooperate not because of coercion but because the passengers know that their participation enhances their own safety and the safety of those around them. While most citizens will respond to a police request, the fact that people do so, and do so without being told they are free not to respond, hardly eliminates the consensual nature of the response.

Drayton contends that even if Brown's cooperation with the officers was consensual, Drayton was seized because no reasonable person would feel free to terminate the encounter with the officers after Brown had been arrested . . . The arrest of one person does not mean that everyone around him has been seized by police. If anything, Brown's arrest should have put Drayton on notice of the consequences of continuing the encounter by answering the officers' questions. Even after arresting Brown, Lang addressed Drayton in a polite manner and provided him with no indication that he was required to answer Lang's questions.

Justice Souter, joined by Justices Stevens and Ginsburg, disagreed with the Court's conclusion, and in doing so he explained the facts in a different light. Here is Justice Souter's view:

. . . [F]or reasons unexplained, the driver with the tickets entitling the passengers to travel had yielded his custody of the bus and its seated travelers to three police officers, whose authority apparently superseded the driver's own. The officers took control of the entire passenger compartment, one stationed at the door keeping surveillance of all the occupants, the others working forward from the back. With one officer right behind him and the other one forward, a third officer accosted each passenger at quarters extremely close and so cramped that as many as half the passengers could not even have stood to face the speaker. None was asked whether he was willing to converse with the police or to take part in the enquiry. Instead the officer said the police were "conducting bus interdiction," in the course of which they "would like ... cooperation." The reasonable inference was that the "interdiction" was not a consensual exercise, but one the police would carry out whatever the circumstances; that they would prefer "cooperation" but would not let the lack of it stand in their way. There was no contrary indication that day, since no passenger had refused the cooperation requested, and there was no reason for any passenger to believe that the driver would return and the trip resume until the police were satisfied. The scene was set and an atmosphere of obligatory participation was established by this introduction. Later requests to search prefaced with "Do you mind ..." would naturally have been understood in the terms with which the encounter began.

It is very hard to imagine that either Brown or Drayton would have believed that he stood to lose nothing if he refused to cooperate with the police, or that he had any free choice to ignore the police altogether. No reasonable passenger could have believed that, only an uncomprehending one. It is neither here nor there that the interdiction was conducted by three officers, not one, as a safety precaution. The fact was that there were three, and when Brown and Drayton were called upon to respond, each one was presumably conscious of an officer in front watching, one at his side questioning him, and one behind for cover, in case he became unruly, perhaps, or "cooperation" was not forthcoming. ... While I am not prepared to say that no bus interrogation and search can pass the Bostick test without a warning that passengers are free to say no, the facts here surely required more from the officers than a quiet tone of voice. A police officer who is certain to get his way has no need to shout.

If police conduct a traffic stop of a vehicle for an expired registration, are **passengers** "free to leave?" The Court had held in *Brendlin v. California* (discussed *infra*) that they are not. In *Arizona v. Johnson*,[150] the Court reaffirmed Brendlin's reasoning on this point. In *Johnson*, police ordered Johnson, a passenger in a lawfully stopped vehicle, out of the car and conducted a *Terry* frisk upon his person. Justice Ginsburg, writing for a unanimous Court, questioned why the prosecutor characterized officers' detention of Johnson as a consensual encounter, especially given that traffic stops effectively seize not merely the driver, but everyone in the vehicle:

[Officer] Trevizo ... never advised Johnson he did not have to answer her questions or otherwise cooperate with her.... Trevizo did not disagree when defense counsel asked in fact you weren't seeking

---

150.   129 S.Ct. 781 (2009).

[Johnson's] permission ...? As the dissenting [court of appeals] judge observed, consensual is an unrealistic characterization of the Trevizo–Johnson encounter: [T]he encounter ... took place within minutes of the stop; the patdown followed within mere moments of Johnson's exit from the vehicle; beyond genuine debate, the point at which Johnson could have felt free to leave had not yet occurred.[151]

The Court concluded that "a traffic stop of a car communicates to a reasonable passenger that he or she is not free to terminate the encounter with the police and move about at will."[152] The *Johnson* Court also clarified *Brendlin,* emphasizing that where there was at least reasonable suspicion to stop a car, the *Terry* "stop" test was automatically met as to the car's passengers. However, the *Terry* "frisk" test was not automatically met. Instead, the police had to have reasonable suspicion that the person frisked was herself armed and dangerous. A state appellate court had, contrary to the trial court's position, resolved a suppression motion in the case unfavorably to Johnson on other grounds, so the United States Supreme Court, after so clarifying the law, remanded the case for resolution under the now-clarified rule.

In doing so, the Court also made clear that: (1) an officer's inquiries into matters unrelated to the reason for the traffic stop (in this case, driving a car with a suspended registration) do not convert the encounter into something other than a lawful seizure, so long as such inquiries do not appreciably extend the stop's duration (the officer here had noticed passenger Johnson's wearing clothes consistent with Crips membership and carrying a scanner in his back pocket, scanners often being used when going about criminal activity, and so had asked Johnson to exit the car—the officer's goal being to question Johnson about what gang he might be in; as soon as Johnson exited, the officer frisked him, finding and seizing a gun, later leading to Johnson's being charged with, and convicted of, possession of a weapon by a prohibited possessor; all this occurred in mere moments); (2) accordingly, no new justification was needed for such inquiries, at least on the facts before the Court, thus making a frisk acceptable upon proof of individualized reasonable suspicion that the person frisked was armed and dangerous; and (3) "Officer Trevizo surely was not constitutionally required to give Johnson an opportunity to depart the scene after he exited the vehicle without first ensuring that, in so doing, she was not permitting a dangerous person to get behind her."[153] The Court also recognized that the Arizona Court of Appeals had assumed, without deciding, that Trevizo had reasonable suspicion that Johnson was armed and dangerous. Thus, on remand, the Arizona appellate court was free, if it chose, to reconsider the validity of that assumption.

---

151. *Id.* at 787–88 (citations and internal quotation marks omitted). The Court cited its recent decision in *Brendlin v. California,* 551 U.S. 249, 255 (2007) (confirming driver and all passengers are effectively seized under the Fourth Amendment for the duration of a traffic stop).

152. *Id.* at 788.

153. *Id.*

In *Hiibel v. Sixth Judicial District Court of Nevada*,[154] the Court faced a different sort of question whether a suspect stopped under *Terry* can refuse an officer's request. There, the specific request was for the suspect to identify himself by name. A deputy sheriff had been dispatched to investigate a telephone call by someone who reported seeing a man assault a woman in a red and silver GMAC truck on Grass Valley Road. When the officer arrived on the scene, he found a man standing by a parked truck, a woman sitting inside it, and skid marks in the gravel behind the vehicle, suggesting to the officer that the car had stopped suddenly.

The officer approached the man, who appeared to be intoxicated, and told him that the officer was investigating a report of a fight. The officer requested identification, and the as-yet-unidentified man asked him why he wanted to see it. The officer explained that he was conducting an investigation and wanted to find out who the unidentified man was and what he was doing there. After continued refusals to comply, the man taunted the officer, telling him to arrest the man and take him to jail. After eleven total requests for identification, and the passage of several minutes, and after warning the man that he would be arrested if he continued to refuse to comply, the officer did exactly that.

A Nevada statute authorized any peace officer to detain anyone under circumstances reasonably indicating that he had committed, was committing, or was about to commit a crime; the officer may so detain the person, however, only to ascertain his identity and the suspicious circumstances "surrounding his presence abroad." The statute further obligated the detainee to identify himself but declared that he "may not be compelled to answer any other inquiry of any peace officer."

Relying on this statute, the state charged the man, later identified as Larry Dudley Hiibel, with willfully obstructing a public officer in discharging a legal duty of his office. Hiibel was convicted of this charge, and the Sixth Judicial Circuit affirmed, rejecting Hiibel's Fourth and Fifth Amendment challenges. The Supreme Court of Nevada on further review also rejected the Fourth Amendment challenge, while denying without opinion Hiibel's request for a hearing to resolve his Fifth Amendment challenge. The United States Supreme Court granted certiorari on both issues, though here we address only the Fourth Amendment question (the Fifth Amendment challenge is addressed later in this text). The Court affirmed Hiibel's conviction.

The Court acknowledged that stop-and-identify statutes, like the one before it, could not be unduly vague and must involve an initial stop based on specific, objective facts establishing reasonable suspicion to believe that the suspect was involved in criminal activity. Hiibel's situation, said the Court, involved neither problem but rather whether, under the Fourth Amendment, officers cannot only ask one specific question—what is the suspect's name?—but also coerce an answer to that question upon threat of

---

154. 542 U.S. 177 (2004).

criminal prosecution. The Court found ample justification for upholding a state legislature's choice to give the police such authority:

> Obtaining a suspect's name in the course of a *Terry* stop serves important government interests. Knowledge of identity may inform an officer that a suspect is wanted for another offense, or has a record of violence or mental disorder. On the other hand, knowing identity may help clear a suspect and allow the police to concentrate their efforts elsewhere. Identity may prove particularly important in cases such as this, where the police are investigating what appears to be a domestic assault. Officers called to investigate domestic disputes need to know whom they are dealing with in order to assess the situation, the threat to their own safety, and possible danger to the potential victim.[155]

The Court brushed aside Hiibel's argument that statements in the Court's earlier opinions, including *Terry* itself, emphasized that a person detained can be questioned but is "not obligated to answer," saying those statements meant only that the Fourth Amendment itself imposed no obligations on the citizen. Here, by contrast, a statute created such an obligation. The statute had "an immediate relation to the purpose, rationale, and practical demands of a *Terry* stop" because the "threat of criminal sanction helps ensure that the request for identity does not become a legal nullity."[156] Nor does the statute significantly add to the intrusiveness of a *Terry* stop: "[T]he Nevada statute does not alter the nature of the stop itself: it does not change its duration ... or its location...."[157] Furthermore, explained the Court:

> Petitioner argues that the Nevada statute circumvents the probable cause requirement, in effect allowing an officer to arrest a person for being suspicious. According to petitioner, this creates a risk of arbitrary police conduct that the Fourth Amendment does not permit.... These are familiar concerns; they were central to the opinion in *Papachristou*, and also to the decisions limiting the operation of stop and identify statutes in *Kolender* and *Brown*. Petitioner's concerns are met by the requirement that a *Terry* stop must be justified at its inception and "reasonably related in scope to the circumstances which justified" the initial stop.... Under these principles, an officer may not arrest a suspect for failure to identify himself if the request for identification is not reasonably related to the circumstances justifying the stop. The Court noted a similar limitation in *Hayes*, where it suggested that *Terry* may permit an officer to determine a suspect's identity by compelling the suspect to submit to fingerprinting only if there is "a reasonable basis for believing that fingerprinting will establish or negate the suspect's connection to that crime." ... It is clear in this case that the request for identification was "reasonably related in scope to the circumstances which justified" the stop. The

---

155. *Id.* at 186.

156. *Id.* at 188.

157. *Id.*

officer's request was a commonsense inquiry, not an effort to obtain an arrest for failure to identify after a *Terry* stop yielded insufficient evidence. The stop, the request, and the State's requirement of a response did not contravene the guarantees of the Fourth Amendment.[158]

Justice Breyer, joined by Justices Souter and Ginsburg in dissent, took the position that *requiring* a suspect to answer an officer's questions—even if only seeking the suspect's name—went beyond the limited intrusion justified by *Terry*.[159] For the dissenters, the precedent was clear. Most particularly, Justice White, in his concurring opinion in *Terry*, said: "Of course, the person stopped is not obliged to answer, answers may not be compelled, and refusal to answer furnishes no basis for an arrest, although it may alert the officer to the need for continued observation."[160] Sixteen years later, in *Berkemer v. McCarty*,[161] the full Court had also declared that "an officer may ask the [*Terry*] detainee a moderate number of questions to determine his identity and try to obtain information confirming or dispelling the officer's suspicions. *But the detainee is not obliged to respond*."[162] Even more recently, in *Illinois v. Wardlow*,[163] the Court explained that allowing officers to stop and question a fleeing person is "quite consistent with the individual's right to go about his business or to stay put and remain silent in the face of police questioning."[164] The dissenters summarized their argument thus:

> This lengthy history—of concurring opinions, of references, and of clear explicit statements—means that the Court's statement in *Berkemer,* while technically *dicta*, is the kind of strong *dicta* that the legal community typically takes as a statement of law. And that law has remained undisturbed for more than 20 years.

> There is no good reason to reject this generation-old statement of the law. There are sound reasons rooted in Fifth Amendment considerations for adhering to the Fourth Amendment legal condition circumscribing police authority to stop an individual against his will.... Administrative considerations also militate against change. Can a state, in addition to requiring a stopped individual to answer "What's your name?" also require an answer to "What's your license number?" or "Where do you live?" Can a police officer, who must know how to make a *Terry* stop, keep track of the constitutional answers? After all, answers to any of these questions may, or may not, incriminate, depending upon the circumstances.

---

158. *Id.* at 188–89.

159. *Id.* at 197–99 (Breyer, J., dissenting).

160. *Terry*, 392 U.S. at 34.

161. 468 U.S. 420 (1984).

162. *Id.* at 439 (emphasis added by *Hiibel* dissenters).

163. 528 U.S. 119 (2000).

164. *Id.* at 125.

Indeed, as the majority points out, a name itself—even if it is not "Killer Bill" or "Rough 'em up Harry"—will sometimes provide the police with "a link in the chain of evidence needed to convict the individual of a separate offense." . . . The majority reserves judgment about whether compulsion is permissible in such instances. . . . How then is a police officer in the midst of a *Terry* stop to distinguish between the majority's ordinary case and this special case where the majority reserves judgment?

The majority presents no evidence that the rule enunciated by Justice White and then by the *Berkemer* Court, which for nearly a generation has set forth a settled *Terry*-stop condition, has significantly interfered with law enforcement. Nor has the majority presented any other convincing justification for change. I would not begin to erode a clear rule with special exceptions.[165]

The Court has also held that a purported *Terry* stop of a car is ordinarily a seizure not only of the car and its driver but of any passengers. In *Brendlin v. California*,[166] two officers stopped a car to see if its temporary operating permit matched the car, even though one of the officers admitted that "there was nothing unusual about the permit or the way it was affixed." That officer recognized the front seat passenger as "one of the Brendlin brothers," one of whom, the officer recalled, had dropped out of parole supervision. The officer confirmed that Brendlin was a parole violator wanted on a warrant and called for backup. When backup arrived, the officer ordered Brendlin out of the car at gunpoint, declared him under arrest, and conducted a search incident to arrest, finding on his person an orange syringe cap and, upon a patdown of the driver, finding on his person syringes and a plastic bag of a "green leafy substance," leading to the driver's arrest. Upon searching the car, the officers found tubing, a scale, and other things used to produce methamphetamine. Brendlin was charged with possession and manufacture of methamphetamine and, after losing a motion to suppress on the grounds that there was neither reasonable suspicion nor probable cause for the stop, pled guilty, subject to appeal on the suppression issue. When the case reached the United States Supreme Court, the Court came down unanimously in Brendlin's favor. Under these circumstances, though not necessarily under all circumstances, Brendlin was unquestionably seized. Explained the Court:

> A traffic stop necessarily curtails the travel a passenger has chosen just as much as it halts the driver, diverting both from the stream of traffic to the side of the road, and the police activity that normally amounts to intrusion on "privacy and personal security" does not normally (and did not here) distinguish between passenger and driver. *United States v. Martinez–Fuerte*, 428 U.S. 543, 554, 96 S.Ct. 3074, 49 L.Ed.2d 1116 (1976). An officer who orders one particular car to pull over acts with an implicit claim of right based on fault of some sort, and a sensible

---

165. *Id.* at 199 (Breyer, J., dissenting).

166. 551 U.S. 249 (2007).

person would not expect a police officer to allow people to come and go freely from the physical focal point of an investigation into faulty behavior or wrongdoing. If the likely wrongdoing is not the driving, the passenger will reasonably feel subject to suspicion owing to close association; but even when the wrongdoing is only bad driving, the passenger will expect to be subject to some scrutiny, and his attempt to leave the scene would be so obviously likely to prompt an objection from the officer that no passenger would feel free to leave in the first place.

. . .

It is also reasonable for passengers to expect that a police officer at the scene of a crime, arrest, or investigation will not let people move around in ways that could jeopardize his safety.[167]

The Court rejected arguments that the intent of the police mattered (it did not; the test is an objective one from the point of view of a reasonable passenger); that there was not an adequate show of authority aimed at the passenger (there was, for the reasons noted in the quote above); that Brendlin did nothing to show his submission to the police (under these circumstances, remaining seated, rather than running away, was a sufficient show of submission); and that cars having to slow down because this car was stopped would also be seized if the passenger—who was not the goal of the original stop—were considered seized, an absurd result (again, no reasonable driver who was slowed down or halted because of a traffic backup caused by another car's being stopped by the police would perceive that the police were also seizing all the other cars in the resulting traffic jam). Moreover, any contrary rule would encourage police to stop cars without even reasonable suspicion, knowing that they could obtain evidence from the passengers without fear of suppression. Because the state conceded that it had no justifiable grounds for stopping the car, and because Brendlin, the passenger, was indeed seized at the moment the car was stopped, his seizure was illegal and all its fruits should therefore be suppressed.

NOTES AND QUESTIONS

1. Are you persuaded by the majority's effort to distinguish *Hiibel* from earlier case law on the ground that *Hiibel* involved a statute mandating the suspect to answer, while no such statute existed in the preceding cases? Or was the *Hiibel* Court in effect overruling clear precedent (though "technically" *dicta*) without admitting that it was doing so? If the latter, why not be candid? Is the dissent correct in arguing that such overruling goes against underlying policies of *stare decisis* as applied to the *Hiibel* facts?

2. Is there, or should there be, a connection between the Fourth and Fifth Amendments such that Fifth Amendment invasions should be relevant to gauging Fourth Amendment intrusiveness? Should the converse apply, that

---

167. Id. at 257–58.

is, should a finding that a search violates (or does not violate) the Fourth Amendment be relevant to whether there has been a violation of the Fifth Amendment privilege against self-incrimination (a privilege to be studied in detail later)?

3. Twice in one term—in the *Hiibel* case and in *Kaupp v. Texas* (discussed later in this chapter)—the Court went out of its way to cite *Hayes's* dicta suggesting that warrants to pick someone up solely for fingerprinting may be issued based solely on reasonable suspicion. Could the Court be laying the groundwork for addressing the constitutionality of more highly techno-logical identification techniques than fingerprinting that might be useful in the War on Terrorism? How does this approach of using "reasonable suspicion warrants" under certain circumstances square with the text of the Constitution?

4. Would the analysis have changed if the officer had asked Hiibel specifically for the vehicle's registration papers? Whether Hiibel was carry-ing a gun and, if so, whether he had a permit to carry it with him? Whether he was married to the woman accompanying him and, if so, whether they were on the same health plan and whether he would produce his health insurance card?

5. There is a debate raging over whether it would be constitutional to require all Americans to carry electronic identification cards, including their name, address, social security number, visa status, passport usage, and medical history on the cards, to aid in the War on Terrorism. What, if anything, does *Hiibel* suggest about the constitutionality of such identifica-tion cards?

PROBLEM 3–13

Several years before the Supreme Court decided *Drayton*, two trial judges had to decide motions to suppress involving bus searches that, in the view of the defendants, were not voluntary encounters but seizures. In *United States v. Cuevas–Ceja*, a judge suppressed evidence found during a bus search in Oregon.[168] Within a few weeks of the *Cuevas-Ceja* decision, a trial judge in *Commonwealth v. Smith* refused to suppress evidence found during a search of a bus in Pennsylvania.[169] Using the following chart, analyze these cases under *Drayton*. What is the significance of each set of facts? Did either or both courts come out the right way? Would either or both cases be decided differently after *Drayton*?

United States v. Cuevas–Ceja	*Commonwealth v. Smith*
Five or six officers boarded the bus or stood just outside of the bus.	Two officers boarded the bus.
Officers stated that no one was to leave the bus, including the driver.	Officers said nothing about leaving but permitted people to exit the bus.

---

168. United States v. Cuevas–Ceja, 58 F. Supp. 2d 1175 (D. Or. 1999).

169. Commonwealth v. Smith, 732 A.2d 1226 (Pa. Super. 1999).

United States v. Cuevas–Ceja	*Commonwealth v. Smith*
Officers were intimidating.	Officers were calm and polite.
Officers interrupted the activities of passengers and delayed the bus's scheduled departure by one-half hour.	Officers did not interrupt passenger activities and let the bus leave on time.
Officers began at front of bus and blocked passengers from exiting.	Officers began questioning at the back of bus and left the aisle clear.
Officers collected and retained all IDs, tickets, and baggage claims.	Officers examined ID, ticket, and baggage claim of each passenger and immediately handed them back.

Let us address a final matter involving the line of demarcation between voluntary encounters and stops: what if the police try to seize an individual but fail to do so? If the police discover evidence left by that individual, is the evidence admissible? Had a seizure taken place? This question reached the Court in *California v. Hodari D.*[170] Hodari, a juvenile, was being chased by a police officer when he threw a package to the ground. The package was found to contain cocaine and Hodari was prosecuted. Hodari claimed that the cocaine was discovered during the course of an illegal seizure, arguing that he had been seized when he saw the officer chasing him. The Court did not find his argument persuasive. Instead, it held that the word "seizure" for Fourth Amendment purposes means "a laying on of hands or application of physical force to restrain movement . . . [as well as] submission to the assertion of authority." The fact that the police officer neither grabbed Hodari, nor got him to submit to his show of authority, meant that Hodari had not been seized when he threw down the cocaine.

Comment on State Constitutions: States may interpret their own constitutions to provide additional civil liberties. At least two states have refused to adhere to the rule in *Hodari D*. Both Massachusetts and New York consider a pursuit "the equivalent of a seizure" and require the suppression of evidence obtained during a pursuit unless the police had reasonable suspicion for the seizure.[171] The Massachusetts court reasoned that a "[p]ursuit that appears designed to effect a stop is no less intrusive than a stop itself." As a result, such a pursuit is the "functional equivalent of a seizure," because it "infringes considerably on the person's freedom of action."

PROBLEM 3–14

Police developed probable cause to believe that Raymond Royan had solicited the murder of his wife, Lisa. Knowing that Royan was extremely

---

170. 499 U.S. 621 (1991).

171. *See* Commonwealth v. Stoute, 665 N.E.2d 93, 97 (1996); People v. Martinez, 80 N.Y.2d 444, 446–47 (N.Y. App. 1992).

volatile, they developed an elaborate plan to arrest him without violence. The plan required three officers—Barbara Wilson, Fernando Bernal, and Mervin Soloby—to wait for Royan to leave his house and then to pose as stranded motorists in Wilson's car, blocking the driveway leading to the house. The plan assumed that when Royan arrived home, he would get out of his car to speak with the motorists. Wilson would explain their plight and ask him to look at her engine, and when he did so, Bernal would shine a flashlight in his eyes, announce that the three were police, and place him under arrest. Two other officers, Valerie Morey and Louise McKinley, planned to stay in their car a short distance from the scene and wait for a signal indicating that Royan had been arrested.

When Royan returned, it was dark. He stopped his car approximately 20 to 25 feet behind the "stranded car," but instead of getting out of his car, he remained in the driver's seat with the motor on and the car in gear. While Bernal and Soloby waited by the hood of Wilson' car, Wilson walked back to Royan's car alone, leaned down to talk with him through the driver's window and tried to persuade him to take a look at her engine. According to Wilson, Royan appeared nervous. Apparently impatient with Wilson' progress, Bernal came back to Royan's car and stood behind Wilson. Drawing his police flashlight, Bernal shone it into Royan's eyes and announced, "state police."

Royan responded by drawing an automatic weapon and shooting over Wilson' shoulder striking Bernal in the chest. As Bernal fell to the ground, Wilson drew her weapon and began to fire at Royan through the rear side window and then through the rear window of the car. As the gunfire erupted, Soloby rushed toward Royan's car, but Royan shot at him three times through the windshield, and Soloby fell to the ground wounded. Royan then turned his weapon on Wilson who was still firing at him through his rear window. Kicking his car door open, Royan spun out of the car and fired another round at Wilson, and Wilson fired her last round in return. As Royan stepped toward Wilson and raised his gun again, Soloby appeared from a ditch behind Royan's car. Startled, Royan shot at Soloby. Meanwhile, Morey and McKinley arrived on the scene. Morey fired her shotgun, striking Royan in the chest. Royan collapsed, but when he reached for the handgun he had dropped, McKinley grabbed it and fired once more at Royan. At the end of the shootout, which had lasted approximately a minute, Royan and Bernal lay dead and Soloby lay bleeding on the side of the highway.

Nearly two years later, Lisa Royan, the intended victim of Royan's murder plot and now the administrator of his estate, filed a $3,000,000 civil rights action against the police officers under 42 U.S.C. section 1983, alleging that by reason of their ill-conceived plan to arrest Royan along a dark street, "the defendants provoked a situation whereby unreasonable deadly force was used in the attempt to seize his person in violation of the Fourth Amendment."

Question: Was Raymond Royan ever seized? If not, can Lisa Royan recover using any other theory?

2.   STOPS VERSUS ARRESTS

Having decided that an individual has been "seized" for purposes of the Fourth Amendment is often not the end of the inquiry. For if the police had only reasonable suspicion to support their actions, it must be determined whether the seizure was a *Terry* stop, which can be based on reasonable suspicion, or whether it was a full-blown arrest, which requires probable cause. Stops and arrests are distinguished primarily on the basis of two factors: the length and the place of detention. Generally, *Terry* stops must be brief, and they must be conducted at the scene of the stop. Once the individual is detained for a considerable length of time or removed to another location, a reviewing court is likely to hold that the encounter escalated into an arrest.

a.   *Length of Detention*

The Court has not created a bright-line time limit on *Terry* stops, but it has provided some guidance. In *United States v. Sharpe*[172] it upheld a 20–minute detention as a *Terry* stop, emphasizing that during the detention officers were pursuing their investigation diligently and effectively. On the other hand, in *United States v. Place*,[173] the detention of a suitcase (yes, items may be subjected to a *Terry* stop) for 90 minutes was deemed too long. Its detention had "ripened" into a full-blown seizure and was no longer amenable to a *Terry* justification.

b.   *Place of Detention*

The place of the detention is less fuzzy than the issue of the detention's duration. In *Pennsylvania v. Mimms*,[174] the Court created a bright-line rule permitting officers to order drivers out of their vehicles after *Terry* traffic stops, as a matter of officer safety. Similarly, it held in *Maryland v. Wilson* that passengers may be ordered out as well.[175] But detentions that move beyond the immediate vicinity of the stop are likely to be considered arrests. The Court overturned a 15–minute stop in *Florida v. Royer* in part because Royer was taken from an airport concourse to an office about 40 feet away.[176] Suspects forcibly taken to police headquarters will undoubtedly be viewed as having been arrested.[177] For example, in *Hayes v. Florida*,[178] the Court held that a suspect had been arrested after he was picked up on reasonable suspicion of rape and taken to a stationhouse for fingerprinting.

In *Kaupp v. Texas*,[179] the Court reaffirmed its rule that, with very rare exceptions, forcible transportation to police headquarters constitutes an

---

172.   470 U.S. 675, 687 (1985).

173.   462 U.S. 696, 709–10 (1983).

174.   434 U.S. 106, 110 (1977).

175.   519 U.S. 408 (1997).

176.   460 U.S. 491, 494–95 (1983).

177.   *See* Dunaway v. New York, 442 U.S. 200 (1979).

178.   470 U.S. 811 (1985).

179.   538 U.S. 626 (2003). In *dicta*, the *Kaupp* Court left open the possibility of seizure of a person on less than probable cause for fingerprinting.

arrest. The Court used the same factors identified in *Mendenhall*[180] for distinguishing voluntary encounters from seizures as also relevant to determining whether a seizure is so intrusive as to constitute an arrest, for which probable cause is required:

> The state does not claim to have had probable cause here, and a straightforward application of the test just mentioned shows beyond cavil that Kaupp was arrested within the meaning of the Fourth Amendment, there being evidence of every one of the probative circumstances mentioned by Justice Stewart in *Mendenhall*. A 17–year-old boy was awakened in his bedroom at three in the morning by at least three police officers, one of whom stated "we need to go and talk." He was taken out in handcuffs without shoes, dressed only in his underwear in January, placed in a patrol car, driven to the scene of the crime and then to the sheriff's offices, where he was taken into an interrogation room and questioned. This evidence points to arrest even more starkly than the facts in *Dunaway v. New York*, where the petitioner "was taken from a neighbor's home to a police car, transported to a police station, and placed in an interrogation room." There we held it clear that the detention was "in important respects indistinguishable from a traditional arrest" and therefore required probable cause or judicial authorization to be legal. The same is, if anything, even clearer here.[181]

Keep in mind that although police need not offer additional cause to believe any occupant of a vehicle be involved in criminal activity to justify seizure of passengers during a traffic stop, "[t]o justify a patdown of the driver or a passenger during a traffic stop, however, just as in the case of a pedestrian reasonably suspected of criminal activity, the police must harbor reasonable suspicion that the person subjected to the frisk is armed and dangerous."[182] So, for example, recall the facts of the Court's recent decision in *Arizona v. Johnson*[183] (*see supra*), a member of Arizona's gang task force had ordered Johnson, a passenger in a lawfully stopped vehicle (the driver's registration had expired), out of the car and conducted a *Terry* frisk upon his person after noticing Johnson's attire, conduct, potential ties to gang activity, and scanner.[184] A unanimous Court held that a *Terry* frisk of a passenger ordered to exit a lawfully stopped vehicle for further questioning would not violate the Fourth Amendment, if the officer reasonably concluded that Johnson could be armed and dangerous.[185]

---

180.   446 U.S. 544 (1980). Although the *Mendenhall* opinions were fractured, a majority of the Court approved the *Mendenhall* standards for seizure in Florida v. Royer, 460 U.S. 491 (1983).

181.   538 U.S. at 630–31.

182.   *Arizona v. Johnson*, 129 S.Ct. 781, 784 (2009).

183.   *Id.*

184.   *See id.* at 784–85.

185.   *Id.*

C.   SUFFICIENCY OF FACTS FOR STOP AND FRISK

The Court in *Terry* emphasized that stop and frisk activity, like full blown searches and seizures, must be justified by facts that give rise "objectively" to a certain level of suspicion that "criminal activity may be afoot." Ordinary searches and seizures, of course, must be supported by probable cause. Stops and frisks, which the Court in *Terry* characterized as less intrusive, can be justified by a lower level of suspicion, which is typically described as "reasonable suspicion." Like probable cause, reasonable suspicion must be supported by "articulable facts": "the officer ... must be able to articulate something more than an inchoate and unparticularized suspicion or hunch." Additionally, the assessment must consider "the totality of the circumstances." The totality standard requires courts to consider all facts and circumstances identified by the officer, as well as deference to the officer's expertise in interpreting those facts and circumstances. In *United States v. Arvizu*,[186] for example, the Court reversed a Ninth Circuit decision attempting to define the weight due certain facts in the totality analysis. The case involved a border patrol agent's *Terry* stop of a minivan on an Arizona back road. The agent justified the stop on the basis of a number of facts that he claimed gave rise to reasonable suspicion to believe that the occupants of the van were trafficking in drugs. The appellate court held that some of the facts on which the agent relied were entitled to little or no weight because they were consistent with innocent behavior. These included the van's sudden slowing upon encountering the border patrol agent's vehicle and the fact that the driver did not make eye contact with the agent as the van passed the agent's vehicle. Other facts that did carry weight—prior use of the back road and minivans by drug smugglers and the fact that the minivan's travel coincided with a shift change among border patrol agents—did not raise sufficient inferences of guilt to create reasonable suspicion. Chief Justice Rehnquist, writing for a unanimous court, disavowed what he termed the appellate court's "divide-and-conquer analysis." Reasonable suspicion, wrote Rehnquist, requires reviewing courts to:

> look at the totality of the circumstances of each case to see whether the detaining officer has a particularized and objective basis for suspecting legal wrongdoing. This process allows officers to draw on their own experience and specialized training to make inferences from and deductions about the cumulative information available to them that might well elude an untrained person. .... Although an officer's reliance on a mere "hunch" is insufficient to justify a stop, the likelihood of criminal activity need not rise to the level required for probable cause, and it falls considerably short of satisfying a preponderance of the evidence standard.

The Chief Justice continued by stating that the appellate court's approach would "seriously undercut the totality of the circumstances principle which governs the existence *vel non* of reasonable suspicion."

---

186.   534 U.S. 266 (2002).

Take, for example, the court's positions that respondent's deceleration could not be considered because "slowing down after spotting a law enforcement vehicle is an entirely normal response that is in no way indicative of criminal activity" and that his failure to acknowledge [the agent's] presence provided no support because there were "no special circumstances rendering innocent avoidance improbable." We think it quite reasonable that a driver's slowing down, stiffening of posture, and failure to acknowledge a sighted law enforcement officer might well be unremarkable in one instance (such as a busy San Francisco highway) while quite unusual in another (such as a remote portion of rural southeastern Arizona). [The agent] was entitled to make an assessment of the situation in light of his specialized training and familiarity with the customs of the area's inhabitants. To the extent that a totality of the circumstances approach may render appellate review less circumscribed by precedent than otherwise, it is the nature of the totality rule.

The Court concluded by applying its version of the totality of the circumstances analysis and finding the stop properly based on reasonable suspicion. The *Arvizu* Court's deference to the officer's expertise is confusing because the Court has held that the reasonable suspicion assessment is a mixed question of law and fact, invoking the de novo standard of review for appellate courts. In other words, appellate courts supposedly do not defer to lower court determinations, but review the historical facts and make their own determinations.[187] Yet, according to *Arvizu*, an appellate court must give significant weight to the officer's view of the facts, and appellate review must be "less circumscribed by precedent than otherwise."

Deference aside, evaluating whether reasonable suspicion exists, like evaluating facts for probable cause, requires an assessment both of the *quantity* of available information and the *quality* of that information.

1. QUANTUM OF EVIDENCE FOR "REASONABLE SUSPICION"

Unlike probable cause, the term "reasonable suspicion" is not supported by a long common law history that might narrow the range of understandings about its meaning. It obviously, however, involves a lower level of suspicion than probable cause. The Court has remarked that the level of suspicion "is considerably less than proof of wrongdoing by a preponderance of the evidence" and less than a "fair probability that contraband or evidence of a crime will be found."[188] The Court has declined to clarify reasonable suspicion any further, but a survey of federal judges quantified reasonable suspicion as an average certainty of 31%.[189]

---

187.   *See* Ornelas v. United States, 517 U.S. 690 (1996).

188.   United States v. Sokolow, 490 U.S. 1 (1989) (citing Illinois v. Gates, 462 U.S. 213 (1983)).

189.   *See* C. M. A. McCauliff, *Burdens of Proof: Degrees of Belief, Quanta of Evidence, or Constitutional Guarantees?*, 35 VAND. L. REV. 1293, 1325 (1982).

Obviously, courts differ on how many, and what sorts of, facts and inferences are necessary in order to satisfy the reasonable suspicion standard. And facts may be susceptible of suspicious inferences in one situation while not so susceptible in another. For example, in *Brown v. Texas*,[190] the Court overturned a finding of reasonable suspicion that was based solely on the defendant's presence in a "high crime area." Years later, however, in *Illinois v. Wardlow*,[191] a defendant's flight from officers in a high crime area was enough to give rise to reasonable suspicion. In *Brown*, officers in a patrol car observed Brown and another man in an alley. Although the men were walking away from each other, the officers later testified that they believed the two had "been together or were about to meet until the patrol car appeared." The officers stopped and frisked Brown and asked him to explain who he was and what he was doing there. They later claimed that the situation "looked suspicious and we had never seen that subject in that area before." Moreover, the officers asserted that the area had a "high incidence of drug traffic." The Court held that the officers' actions constituted a seizure and that they lacked reasonable suspicion for the seizure. According to Chief Justice Burger, writing for the Court,

> none of the circumstances preceding the officers' detention of appellant justified a reasonable suspicion that he was involved in criminal conduct. Officer Venegas testified at appellant's trial that the situation in the alley "looked suspicious," but he was unable to point to any facts supporting that conclusion. There is no indication in the record that it was unusual for people to be in the alley. The fact that appellant was in a neighborhood frequented by drug users, standing alone, is not a basis for concluding that appellant himself was engaged in criminal conduct. In short, the appellant's activity was no different from the activity of other pedestrians in that neighborhood.

In *Wardlow*, the Court held that, in an "area of heavy narcotics trafficking," an individual's "unprovoked flight upon noticing the police" gave rise to reasonable suspicion justifying a *Terry* stop. Police on a narcotics patrol had conducted a *Terry* stop of Wardlow after he looked in their direction and fled. The officers frisked Wardlow and found a gun, and Wardlow later was prosecuted and convicted for unlawful use of the weapon. The Illinois Supreme Court struck down the conviction, holding that sudden flight in a high crime area does not create reasonable suspicion. Writing for a 5–justice majority, Chief Justice Rehnquist disagreed. The Chief Justice acknowledged that an individual's presence in a high crime area does not, by itself, create reasonable suspicion that the individual is engaging in criminal behavior. But presence in such an area, he wrote, is "among the relevant contextual considerations in a *Terry* analysis." Similarly, the Chief Justice stated, nervous or evasive behavior is a relevant consideration, and flight is the "consummate act of evasion." Taken together, he concluded, the two factors—presence in a high crime area and

---

190. 443 U.S. 47 (1979).

191. 528 U.S. 119 (2000).

unprovoked flight—supported in Wardlow's case a finding of reasonable suspicion.

Justice Stevens, joined by Justices Souter, Ginsburg, and Breyer, dissented from the majority's holding in *Wardlow*, although Justice Stevens lauded the majority for applying a fact-specific "totality of the circumstances" analysis, rather than creating a bright-line rule. Inferences to be drawn from flight vary from case to case, Justice Stevens asserted. And given the paucity of facts in the record, he wrote, it was unclear whether Wardlow's flight was an act of evasion—the officers did not remember whether they were in uniform or whether they were driving in marked cars. As a result, the dissenters found reasonable suspicion lacking.

Professor Lenese Herbert[192] has offered a novel spin on *Wardlow* opinion. Professor Herbert argues that residents of high crime areas have ample reasons to distrust the police yet little opportunity to express their displeasure or to obtain an effective hearing of their grievances. Accordingly, they protest by exit—by openly refusing to cooperate with the police and by blatantly challenging their authority over neighborhood residents. To Professor Herbert, therefore, flight from the police in a high crime neighborhood accompanied by no other evidence of wrongdoing is expressive, an act of protest sheltered by the Free Speech Clause of the First Amendment. Professor Herbert explains:

> Unfortunately, for those in high-crime areas who choose to protest the police via reactive flight, society seems incapable of recognizing that which in a low-or-no-crime area would be protected speech. In a high-crime area, the forum, the method of speaking and the speaker are commonly assumed to be less intelligent or intelligible. Ironically, in these neighborhoods, reactive flight may be the most effective way for residents to communicate their distaste of the police and to exercise their choice to remove themselves from the police presence without compromising the safety of themselves or others—especially when the speakers perceive disdain by society. Of all places where protest politics and expressive dissent occur, the high-crime area, with the tension that comes from aggressive policing and an oppressed citizenry, is likely to have a disproportionate amount of such expression. Yet the police, who enforce society's assessment of those in high-crime areas as subordinate and deviant, are allowed to define what is being said, to maintain their grip on their constituents' ability to speak, and to preserve their role as the only speakers in these areas who deserve a voice. Thus, the police have the ability via recasting expressions of protest as criminal conduct to deny members of these disparaged areas rights commensurate with full citizenship.

QUESTIONS

Do you think that Professor Herbert is right to see flight in high-crime areas as involving expressive conduct implicating the First Amendment. If

---

192. Lenese Herbert, *Can't You See What I'm Saying? Making Expressive Conduct a Crime in High–Crime Areas*, 9 GEO. J. POVERTY & THE LAW 135, 153 (2001).

so, does the state's interest in crime control outweigh these free speech concerns? Moreover, if Professor Herbert's position is indeed correct, what sorts of changes in police practice or in the design of other institutions might give the community a greater voice in police crafting and implementation of search and seizure power? If alternative means of expression are provided to the community, should that alter the role of flight in establishing reasonable suspicion? Would such institutional means for the expression of community protest simply be good policy, or would they be constitutionally required? Are these questions First Amendment issues, Fourth Amendment issues, or both?

PROBLEM 3–15

Larry Wills, age 25, works in a dry-cleaning store and lives in a 3-bedroom home with his wife and two children in a predominantly African–American neighborhood. While leaving his corner deli one day, eight officers jumped out of an unmarked van, frisked Wills, and shoved a camera in his face. One officer said, as he took Wills's photograph, "We are taking your picture now for anything you might do in the future." The police then let Wills go without charging him with any crime.

Wills's photo was taken pursuant to "Operation Jumpout," in which 18 police officers began stopping individuals, usually African–Americans, at drug-infested street corners to search for guns, crack, and heroin. The police would digitally photograph each person stopping, placing the photo into the police database for easy access should it be needed in the future. Of the more than 600 people detained thus far in this operation, only 20% were charged with a crime.

QUESTIONS

1. Can Wills make out a prima facie case of a Fourth Amendment violation if he brings a civil suit against the police department? What additional information, if any, would help you in making that decision?

2. If the officer had reasonable suspicion to stop, and to frisk Wills, was taking his photograph in itself a Fourth Amendment violation? If the police had never stopped Wills but had surreptitiously snapped his picture, would he then have a case for violation of the Fourth Amendment? Fully explain your answers.

2. QUALITY OF EVIDENCE FOR "REASONABLE SUSPICION"

As we noted above, the Court in *Terry* stressed that reasonable suspicion must be founded on "specific and articulable facts." Professors LaFave and Israel have remarked that although reasonable suspicion does not require the same *quantity* of information as probable cause, one would expect that the information would have to be of the same reliable *quality*.[193]

---

193. *See* WAYNE R. LAFAVE AND JEROLD H. ISRAEL, CRIMINAL PROCEDURE 210 (2d ed. 1992).

Not so, however. In *Alabama v. White*,[194] the Court stated:

> [r]easonable suspicion is a less demanding standard than probable cause not only in the sense that reasonable suspicion can be established with information that is different in quantity or content than that required to establish probable cause, but also in the sense that reasonable suspicion can arise from information that is less reliable than that required to show probable cause.

Reasonable suspicion, like probable cause, is dependent upon both the content of information possessed by police and its degree of reliability. Both factors—quantity and quality—are considered in the totality of the circumstances—the whole picture, that must be taken into account when evaluating whether there is reasonable suspicion. Thus, if a tip has a relatively low degree of reliability, more information will be required to establish the requisite quantum of suspicion than would be required if the tip were more reliable.

In that case, the Court upheld a stop based on an anonymous tip stating that Vanessa White "would be leaving 235–C Lynwood Terrace Apartments at a particular time in a brown Plymouth station wagon with the right taillight lens broken, that she would be going to Dobey's Motel, and that she would be in possession of about an ounce of cocaine inside a brown attaché case." The officers corroborated the fact that a brown Plymouth station wagon with a broken right taillight was parked at the apartments, and they observed White enter the station wagon (with nothing in her hands) and drive to a highway on which Dobey's Motel was located. They stopped her "just short" of the motel. The Court acknowledged that this was "a close case" but concluded that "when the officers stopped [White], the anonymous tip had been sufficiently corroborated to furnish reasonable suspicion that [she] was engaged in criminal activity."

On the extreme end of the unreliable information scale, an anonymous tip that lacks all indicia of reliability does *not* satisfy the reasonable suspicion standard. In *Florida v. J.L.*,[195] a unanimous Court held an anonymous tip that a person is carrying a gun to be insufficient, by itself, to justify a *Terry* stop and frisk. Police had conducted the *Terry* stop of J.L., a juvenile, after an anonymous caller informed them that "a young black male standing at a particular bus stop and wearing a plaid shirt" was carrying a gun. Arriving at the bus stop, police observed three black males, one of whom, J.L., was wearing a plaid shirt. The police noticed nothing suspicious about the individuals, but based on the tip stopped and frisked J.L., finding a gun. The Florida Supreme Court held the search invalid. Justice Ginsburg, writing for the unified Court, agreed that the anonymous tip lacked sufficient indicia of reliability to give rise to reasonable suspicion. Justice Ginsburg compared the paucity of details in the tip to the more detailed tip in *White*. She noted that the Court's decision in *White* depended on the fact that the tipster accurately predicted future movements of the

---

194.   496 U.S. 325, 330 (1990).

195.   529 U.S. 266 (2000).

suspect. By contrast, the tip in *J.L.* lacked even those "the moderate indicia of reliability." Justice Ginsburg cautioned, however, that the Court's holding was fact-specific and would not necessarily apply if, for example, police were to receive an anonymous "man with a bomb" tip, or in situations—such as airports and schools—in which 4th Amendment privacy is diminished.

The holding in *J.L.* also would not preclude a stop and frisk if police receive a "man with a gun tip" from a known informant. Indeed, shortly after it decided *Terry* the Court had reviewed just such a non-anonymous "man with a gun" tip, in *Adams v. Williams.*[196] In *Adams*, a police officer was told by an informant, who had previously given the officer information in the past, that a person seated in a nearby car was carrying narcotics and had a gun "at his waist." The officer approached the car and asked the driver to open the door. When the driver rolled down his window instead of opening the door, the officer reached into the car and immediately removed a gun from the driver's waistband. The Supreme Court treated the officer's actions as a frisk and suggested that the officer had reasonable suspicion to believe that the driver was armed and dangerous, considering that the tip had come from a known informant (who could have been subjected to an immediate arrest for false complaint, if he had lied), which made the case stronger than if it had come from "an anonymous telephone tip." Moreover, the seizure of the gun was proper given the officer's reasonable fear for his safety in a "high crime area" in the middle of the night. Said the Court, "the policeman's action in reaching to the spot where the gun was thought to be hidden constituted a limited intrusion designed to insure his safety, and we conclude that it was reasonable." That the intrusion was not based on the officer's personal observation was irrelevant: "some tips, completely lacking in indicia of reliability, would either warrant no police response or require further investigation before a forcible stop of a suspect would be authorized. But in some situations—for example, when the victim of a street crime seeks immediate police aid and gives a description of his assailant, or when a credible informant warns of a specific impending crime—the subtleties of the hearsay rule should not thwart an appropriate police response." Accordingly, the intrusion was reasonable, and the gun's presence established probable cause for an arrest.

D. PROFILES

1. HISTORY

At times, stop and frisk activity is conducted on the basis of "profiles" that supposedly assist police by identifying characteristics peculiar to persons engaging in criminal behavior. Law enforcement agencies began developing profiles years ago, and the practice increased in the late 1960s when they tackled the increasing threat of airplane hijacking (or "skyjacking"). At that time, the Federal Aviation Administration ("FAA") began to

---

196.   407 U.S. 143 (1972).

compile a profile that would help officials identify potential skyjackers.[197] Through the use of experts, field tests, and studies, the FAA developed a skyjacker profile that consisted of 25 to 35 characteristics not typically associated with the general public.[198] When the FAA's new profile was compared to 30 hijackings from 1969, 90 percent of the hijackers fit the profile.

Six years after the birth of the skyjacker profile, a Drug Enforcement Agency ("DEA") Special Agent by the name of Paul Markonni began to compile a profile for airport narcotics smugglers.[199] Markonni's profile contained seven primary characteristics:

- arrival from or departure to an identified source city;
- carrying little or no baggage, or large quantities of empty suitcases;
- unusual itinerary, such as a rapid turnaround time for a lengthy airplane trip;
- use of an alias;
- carrying unusually large amounts of currency in the many thousands of dollars, usually on the person, in briefcases, or in bags;
- purchasing airline tickets with a large amount of small denomination currency; and
- unusual nervousness beyond that ordinarily exhibited by passengers.

The profile contained four additional characteristics, which were characterized as "secondary":

- the almost exclusive use of public transportation, particularly taxicabs in departing from the airport;
- immediately making a telephone call after deplaning;
- leaving a false or fictitious call-back telephone number with the airline being utilized; and
- excessively frequent travel to source or destination cities.[200]

2. DRUG COURIER PROFILES

Markonni's "drug courier profile" became the model for profiles developed by other law enforcement agencies. Drug courier profiles are now so various that their characteristics include many traits that conflict with each other.[201] For example, profiles identify the following as suspicious characteristics: the suspect may be the first off the plane, the last, in the middle, after fifteen, twenty-five or thirty passengers, or even two-thirds of

---

197. Thomas J. Andrews, *Screening Travelers at the Airport to Prevent Hijacking: A New Challenge to the Unconstitutional Conditions Doctrine*, 16 ARIZ. L. REV. 657, 712 (1974).

198. United States v. Lopez, 328 F.Supp. 1077, 1082–86 (E.D.N.Y. 1971).

199. United States v. Berry, 636 F.2d 1075, 1080 n. 6 (5th Cir. 1981).

200. United States v. Elmore, 595 F.2d 1036, 1039 n. 3 (5th Cir. 1979), *cert. denied,* 447 U.S. 910 (1980).

201. *See, e.g.,* Charles L. Becton, *The Drug Courier Profile: "All Seems Infected That Th' Infected Spy, As All Looks Yellow To The Jaundiced Eye,"* 65 N.C. L. REV. 417, 431–38 (1987).

the way back. The suspect may be "sloppily dressed" or "smartly dressed"; the suspect may be young or old, male or female, an "individual traveling alone" or "two or more people traveling together." Profiles cast suspicion on individuals who carry no luggage, or new suitcases, or large, medium, or small bags. Suspicious baggage may be heavily laden or nearly empty, and it may be heavily perfumed or heavily insulated (American Tourister luggage is often singled out in drug courier profiles due to its heavy insulation).[202] Suspicious passenger behavior ranges from walking quickly to walking slowly, bumping into people, rushing to a restroom after deplaning, frequently looking over one's shoulder while walking, staring at one's luggage, appearing "cool," perspiring profusely, having calm demeanor, or having "tell-tale eyes." Tickets purchased with cash are immediately suspect but additionally suspicious characteristics include one-way tickets, round-trip tickets, first-class tickets, and tickets purchased with large denominations, small denominations, or even a combination of large and small denominations.

Drug courier profiles are troubling because their broad, often-conflicting characteristics encompass many individuals who are not engaged in criminal activity. To put it another way, they may fail to create sufficient inferences of criminal activity as to give rise to reasonable suspicion. As Justice Marshall put it, profiles have a "chameleon-like way of adapting to any particular set of observations."[203]

More troubling are the racial and ethnic overtones to the use of drug courier profiles. While one rarely finds reference in the cases to profiles containing explicit racial or ethnic characteristics, many do contain arguable "code words" for race or ethnicity: the suspect's presence in a "high crime area," for example. African–Americans and Hispanics in particular have argued that they are targeted by drug courier profiles.[204] In one recent drug prosecution, the defendants filed a motion seeking the suppression of evidence seized during a traffic stop, alleging that they had been stopped for the "crime" of "DWH"—"Driving While Hispanic."[205] On the other

---

202. Authors' note: One of Professor Paris's law students received a form letter from a travel company offering congratulations to the student for being selected "to receive at no cost a vacation for two to fabulous Reno Nevada." The letter contains a postscript as follows:

> P.S.S. Congratulations on being selected! In addition to your Reno getaway, you will receive an authentic American Tourister Carry–All just right to take along on your getaway!

203. *Sokolow*, 490 U.S. at 13 (Marshall, J., dissenting).

204. *See generally* United States v. Caicedo, 85 F.3d 1184, 1190 (6th Cir. 1996) (officer denied allegations that he targeted defendant because he was Mexican; claimed defendant demonstrated "extreme nervousness upon seeing him"); United States v. Rosales, 60 F.3d 835 (9th Cir. 1995) (unpublished opinion) (defendants claimed that Oregon State Police target Hispanic men driving "American-made luxury or performance automobiles . . . for pretextual traffic stops"; state trooper denied knowledge that the men were Hispanic until after pulling them over for weaving and speeding); United States v. Jennings, 985 F.2d 562 (6th Cir. 1993) (unpublished opinion) (defendant argued that drug courier profiles in Cincinnati airport target "Hispanics and Blacks").

205. *See Report of the Oregon Supreme Court Task Force on Racial/Ethnic Issues in the Judicial System*, 73 OR. L. REV. 823, 853 (1994).

hand, immigration profiles may lawfully contain explicit references to race or ethnicity,[206] which sometimes results in harassment, as was the case when the INS threatened the mayor of Pomona, California with deportation after his clothing and vehicle fit the profile of an illegal Mexican immigrant.[207]

3. CONSTITUTIONALITY

The Supreme Court has not articulated a clear position on profiles. However, these three points can arguably be inferred from its holdings: (1) the fact that a person matches a profile probably does not, in and of itself, give rise to reasonable suspicion; but (2) officers (and reviewing courts) may rely in part on the cumulative law enforcement wisdom embodied in profiles when assessing the inferences that may be drawn from a person's conduct or attributes; and (3) the fact that a person matches a profile does not detract from the inferences that might reasonably be drawn. The first of these points was made in *Reid v. Georgia*:[208]

The petitioner arrived at the Atlanta Airport on a commercial airline flight from Fort Lauderdale, Fla., in the early morning hours of August 14, 1978. The passengers left the plane in a single file and proceeded through the concourse. The petitioner was observed by an agent of the DEA, who was in the airport for the purpose of uncovering illicit commerce in narcotics. Separated from the petitioner by several persons was another man, who carried a shoulder bag like the one the petitioner carried. As they proceeded through the concourse past the baggage claim area, the petitioner occasionally looked backward in the direction of the second man. When they reached the main lobby of the terminal, the second man caught up with the petitioner and spoke briefly with him. They then left the terminal building together.

The DEA agent approached them outside of the building, identified himself as a federal narcotics agent, and asked them to show him their airline ticket stubs and identification, which they did. The airline tickets had been purchased with the petitioner's credit card and indicated that the men had stayed in Fort Lauderdale only one day. According to the agent's testimony, the men appeared nervous during the encounter. The agent then asked them if they would agree to return to the terminal and to consent to a search of their persons and their shoulder bags. The agent testified that the petitioner nodded his head affirmatively, and that the other responded, "Yeah, okay." As the three of them entered the terminal, however, the petitioner began to run and before he was apprehended, abandoned his shoulder bag. The bag, when recovered, was found to contain cocaine.

---

206. *See* United States v. Brignoni–Ponce, 422 U.S. 873, 877 (1975).

207. *See generally* Kevin C. Wilson, *And Stay Out! The Dangers of Using Anti–Immigrant Sentiment as a Basis for Social Policy: America Should Take Heed of Disturbing Lessons from Great Britain's Past*, 24 GA. J. INT'L & COMP. L. 567 (1995).

208. 448 U.S. 438 (1980) (per curiam).

The Superior Court granted the petitioner's motion to suppress the cocaine, concluding that it had been obtained as a result of a seizure of him by the DEA agent without an articulable suspicion that he was unlawfully carrying narcotics. The Georgia Court of Appeals reversed. It held that the stop of the petitioner was permissible, citing *Terry v. Ohio*, since the petitioner, "in a number of respects, fit a profile of drug couriers compiled by the [DEA]."

The Court held that these facts were not sufficient to give rise to reasonable suspicion required for the stop. The Court acknowledged that the agent suspected Reid of wrongdoing because he "appeared to the agent to fit the so-called 'drug courier profile,' a somewhat informal compilation of characteristics believed to be typical of persons unlawfully carrying narcotics." The Court concluded:

> the agent could not as a matter of law, have reasonably suspected the petitioner of criminal activity on the basis of these observed circumstances. Of the evidence relied on, only the fact that the petitioner preceded another person and occasionally looked backward at him as they proceeded through the concourse relates to their particular conduct. The other circumstances describe a very large category of presumably innocent travelers, who would be subject to virtually random seizures were the Court to conclude that as little foundation as there was in this case could justify a seizure.
>
> Nor can we agree, on this record, that the manner in which the petitioner and his companion walked through the airport reasonably could have led the agent to suspect them of wrongdoing. Although there could, of course, be circumstances in which wholly lawful conduct might justify the suspicion that criminal activity was afoot, this is not such a case. The agent's belief that the petitioner and his companion were attempting to conceal the fact that they were traveling together, a belief that was more an "inchoate and unparticularized suspicion or 'hunch,'" than a fair inference.

Notice that the Court evaluated for itself the inferences, or lack thereof, that it believed could be fairly drawn from the conduct and appearance of the defendant in *Reid*. In later cases, the Court has appeared more willing to accept law enforcement assessments concerning the suspiciousness of certain behavior or characteristics. For example, in *United States v. Sokolow*,[209] the Court upheld an airport stop that took place in circumstances not all that different from *Reid*. The government argued that the stop was justified because Sokolow was making a quick round trip to a drug "source city," had paid for his tickets in cash, had checked no baggage, and appeared nervous. These characteristics fit a drug courier profile, and the Court agreed that they combined to paint a suspicious picture—one that gave rise to reasonable suspicion to believe that Sokolow was trafficking in drugs. The Court stated that "the fact that these factors

---

209. 490 U.S. 1 (1989).

may be set forth in a 'profile' does not somehow detract from their evidentiary significance as seen by a trained agent.''

The lesson of *Reid* and *Sokolow* appears to be that courts reviewing *Terry* stops cannot rely exclusively on the fact that an individual matched a profile, but they may defer to accumulated law enforcement experience, embodied in profiles, when they evaluate for themselves the suspiciousness of certain behaviors and characteristics that form the asserted basis for the stop.[210]

4. PROFILING IN RESPONSE TO TERRORISM

There were substantial legal and attitudinal responses to the terrorist attacks of September 11, 2001. We discuss many of these in a later chapter. In terms of evaluating the uses of profiles, consider these two excerpts and answer the questions that follow them:

> . . . Congress adopted the Uniting and Strengthening America by Providing Appropriate Tools Required to Intercept and Obstruct Terrorism Act of 2001, popularly known as the ''Patriot Act.'' The Patriot Act is a lengthy and complex piece of legislation, and its provisions create significant changes in the federal criminal justice system. Those changes include: (1) authorizing the detention for questioning for up to seven days of individuals who are certified by the U.S. attorney general or the commissioner of immigration as immigrants suspected of involvement in terrorism; (2) ''roving wiretaps,'' permitting law enforcement authorities to obtain from a special intelligence court taps on any telephone used by a person suspected of involvement in terrorism; (3) the availability of nationwide search warrants for terrorism investigations; and (4) the sharing among intelligence and criminal justice officials of certain information on investigations. Other provisions permit officials to subpoena the addresses and times of e-mail messages sent by terrorism suspects. . . .

> Meanwhile, President Bush signed an executive order permitting trial before a special military tribunal, rather than a civilian court, of members of al-Qaeda; of people involved in acts of international terrorism against the United States; and of people knowingly harboring such terrorists. . . .

> Furthermore, Attorney General John Ashcroft issued an order permitting the attorney general to monitor communications between a client-inmate and his or her attorney when the attorney general has ''reasonable suspicion'' to ''believe that a particular inmate may use communications with attorneys or their agents to further or facilitate acts of violence or terrorism.'' The order provides a number of limitations on who may use these communications, for what purpose, and how they may be obtained. The order's perceived authorization of an

---

210. For a discussion of the theories defendants can use to challenge profiling, *see* Margie Paris, *A Primer in Profiling: The Merger of Civil Rights and Criminal Defense*, 15 CRIM. JUST. 4 (Fall 2000).

incursion into the traditional attorney-client relationship sparked significant protest in the legal community.

Further legal and attitudinal changes were sparked at the local level as well. Notably, protests against the growing use of video surveillance in public places, which had been loud before September 11, now became more muted. Consequently, Washington, D.C., joined the list of cities embarking on such surveillance programs. Similarly, . . . the growing sentiment against racial profiling reversed course with many Americans, including a significant percentage of the African-American community, supporting the profiling of those of apparent "Middle Eastern" ancestry as a helpful tool in the war on terrorism.[211]

Professor David Harris argued after September 11th that profiling is not only an insulting law enforcement technique, but also an ineffective one.[212] In fact, in the context of the war on terrorism, he argued that such ineffective techniques are dangerous to lives and property because they make it less likely that wrongdoers will be caught:

> The results of . . . hit rate studies were striking, all the more so for their consistency across many different jurisdictions and law enforcement agencies. The data on hit rates show that targeting law enforcement using racial or ethnic appearance does not, in fact, improve policing. It actually makes policing worse—less successful, less productive, less likely to find guns, drugs, and bad guys. Contrary to what the proponents of profiling might expect, hit rates were not higher using racial profiling. In fact, hit rates for race-based stops were lower—significantly lower—than the hit rates for traditional, nonprofile-based policing. That is, when police used racial and ethnic profiling to target black and brown populations as suspicious, the results they got were uniformly poorer than the results they got when they stopped whites simply on the basis of suspicious behavior. Racial profiling, then, doesn't improve policing; it pulls it down, delivering less bang for the law enforcement buck. Even if we ignore the high social costs—distrust of all government, including police and the legal system; exacerbation of existing problems such as residential segregation and employment discrimination; and destruction of valuable law enforcement initiatives such as community policing—racial profiling as a means to crime reduction simply does not deliver.

QUESTIONS

1. If Professor Harris is correct, does his argument affect the validity of racial profiling under the Fourth Amendment? Does it matter to the constitutionality of profiling whether it is done to catch terrorists or run-of-

---

211. Andrew E. Taslitz, *Terrorism and the Citizenry's Safety*, 17 Crim. Just. 4 (2002).

212. *See* David A. Harris, *Racial Profiling Revisited: "Just Common Sense" in the Fight Against Terror?*, 17 Crim. Just. 36 (2002).

the-mill suspects? Should profiling be ended by the courts, or instead by the legislative or the executive branches?

2. If Professor Harris is wrong and racial profiling is an effective law enforcement technique, does that mean that profiling is necessarily consistent with the Fourth Amendment?

3. What sort of evidence might the federal government need to establish "reasonable suspicion" that an inmate's communications to his attorney will be used to facilitate acts of violence or terrorism?

4. Is there a Fourth Amendment privacy interest in the addresses and times of a person's e-mails?

5. Why would "roving wiretaps" be desirable for prosecutors, and why is their use limited to a narrow category of cases? Answer these same questions concerning nationwide search warrants. What level of justification should be required to obtain either roving wiretaps or nationwide search warrants? Do these sorts of powers pose any dangers to Fourth Amendment freedoms?

6. Should a state of emergency or a war alter the test for Fourth Amendment reasonableness or its application? Why or why not? If so, how?

5.   LAWYERING STRATEGIES IN A PROFILING CASE

Professor Paris wrote the following primer[213] for beginning lawyers facing cases in which their clients suspected they had been profiled. The primer reviews what the lawyer should do in order to raise the Fourth Amendment issues created by profiling, as well as how a lawyer can raise an equal protection claim about profiling.

A Primer in Profiling: The Merger of Civil Rights and Criminal Defense

by Margaret Paris.

"The police stopped me because I'm black," explains the new client. "They can't do that, can they?" Such questions are becoming common as criminal defense lawyers increasingly find themselves representing defendants who believe they have been "profiled"—stopped and searched because of their race or ethnicity. Recent, well-supported studies back these claims, and the resulting growth in public awareness is matched by a surge in demands on the part of defendants that their lawyers address not only the criminal charges, but the potential civil rights infringement as well.

When defense lawyers represent clients who have been profiled, they face the challenging task of pursuing remedies in the criminal case using constitutional theories with which they may not have much experience and that require access to statistical data. To add to the difficulty, the client

---

213. Paris, *Primer, supra* note 210, pp. 4–9.

probably will need information on how to report police misconduct and pursue civil remedies.[214]

In order to fulfill the dual role of criminal defense attorney and civil rights advocate, a lawyer must learn a new body of case law and new methods of proof. Fortunately, there is the pioneering work of other lawyers and a wealth of information on the Web and in print. This article will focus on federal constitutional provisions because they provide powerful exclusionary remedies and sometimes result in the dismissal of charges.

Fourth Amendment concerns

Profiling runs afoul of the Fourth Amendment's search and seizure protections when law enforcement officers make a decision to stop or search a person based on the individual's apparent race or ethnicity, rather than on conduct or a close match with an eyewitness description. Profiling is "formal" when officers use a specific list of factors that describe individuals likely to be involved in a particular kind of criminal activity. Informal profiling takes place when officers act on the basis of malleable factors that they claim to have accumulated through their own experience or the experience of others in their units. Most profiling cases involve informal profiling and do not explicitly include race or ethnicity as factors, though these factors may play a big role. As a result, it is often difficult to challenge profiling using Fourth Amendment theories. Nevertheless, in most cases a lawyer must attempt to do so, if only to preserve a client's claims.

Identifying police actions

Although recent attention has focused on profiling in customs searches and traffic stops, profiling occurs whenever law enforcement officers make decisions based on race or ethnicity rather than on behavioral characteristics (except in those cases involving eyewitness description). For example, narcotics officers engage in profiling when they focus their use of drug-sniffing dogs on members of minority groups. Similarly, traffic police are guilty of profiling when they search the vehicles of minority drivers at a higher rate than cars driven by whites, or when they target minority drivers for computer checks.

In order to isolate the potential profiling claim, ask the client to describe the incident in a detailed narration. Then ask specific questions designed to clarify the potentially discriminatory police actions. For example, in a traffic stop situation ask whether police:

- questioned the client about his/her destination;
- demanded registration, license, and insurance papers;
- sought permission to search;

---

214. For a more detailed discussion on seeking civil remedies, *see* William H. Buckman & John Lamberth, *Challenging Racial Profiles: Attacking Jim Crow on the Interstate*, 23 CHAMPION 14, 18 (1999).

- employed drug-sniffing dogs;

- ran a computer check;

- issued a citation

If the profiling situation involved more than one individual, ask the client to describe the others affected by the police encounter and which of them were stopped, questioned, or searched.

Having identified the ways in which the client may have been treated differently than other individuals, the next step is to become familiar with the ways in which profiling violated the client's legal rights and what relief should be sought. There are two federal constitutional provisions that are potentially implicated by profiling: the Fourth Amendment's prohibition against unreasonable searches and seizures and the Fourteenth Amendment's guaranty of equal protection of the laws. (The Fifth Amendment provides this guaranty in cases involving federal actors.) Although federal remedies may be the first line of defense, state constitutional provisions, statutes, and regulations may also apply.

Crafting the motion

In crafting a Fourth Amendment motion, the ultimate goal is to obtain an order suppressing all evidence that was derived from Fourth Amendment violations. If possible, defense also seeks an order dismissing charges if tainted evidence is clearly the basis of the charge. The motion will identify the tainted evidence and the police actions that led to its discovery. It will also explain how the police ran afoul of the Fourth Amendment.

The central argument will concern the lack of individualized probable cause or reasonable suspicion by the police. If race or ethnicity was involved, argue that such factors are improper in the "guilt calculus." Ask the judge to disregard those factors and evaluate the existence of legitimate suspicion based on the remaining facts. If the profile does not explicitly contain race or ethnicity, determine whether it contains proxies or code terms such as "high crime area." Courts must examine such terms carefully to ensure they are not used to target "entire neighborhoods or communities in which members of minority groups regularly go about their daily business." Although the Supreme Court recently allowed the use of such a factor in *Illinois v. Wardlow*, defense should caution the court to ensure that the factor "is limited to specific, circumscribed locations where particular crimes occur with unusual regularity." Aside from impermissible factors such as race and ethnicity, defense must ask whether the factors in the profile are broad enough to describe a large group of innocent people. If so, they should be disregarded and the officer's decision should be evaluated only on legitimate factors. If the remaining factors are insufficient to give rise to individualized suspicion, the court must grant the motion to suppress. It's helpful to determine whether experts created the profile, if its accuracy can be verified, and whether police were trained to use the profile. The motion is more likely to be granted if defense can show the profile is an accumulation of police hunches and/or the officers received no specialized training.

If no profile was used and police simply targeted minorities, preserve the argument that pretextual stops violate the Fourth Amendment by referencing *Whren v. United States*, and argue that *Whren* was wrongly decided. Cite other cases in your jurisdiction in which similar pretext stops have been challenged, and raise the possibility that they reflect a pattern of stops that abuse the authority granted police by *Whren*. In addition, research the state's constitution and laws because some prohibit pretext policing.

In a pretext case, defense should also challenge the suspicion that police claim to have developed. The Sixth Circuit found no probable cause when police on I 40 in Tennessee pulled over a Winnebago that strayed 20 to 30 feet outside its lane—a distance that would take the trailer a third of a second to travel.[215] Police claimed probable cause based on a belief that the driver was intoxicated and had violated a state law requiring vehicles to be "driven as nearly as practicable entirely within a single lane." In a search, police found marijuana.

The trial court denied the defendant's motion to suppress the marijuana, but the reviewing court held that the driver's "failure to follow a perfect vector" did not give rise to probable cause to believe that the driver had violated either law. Writing separately to concur, Sixth Circuit Judge Clay suggested that the police had used the lane violation as a subterfuge, noting that "[i]n making credibility determinations as to an officer's purported reason for initially stopping a vehicle, the Court may use the record in the case before it, what has been learned from similar cases, all reasonable inferences that can be drawn therefrom, as well as its own common sense."

Today's judges are more likely to give credence to equal protection theories in criminal cases, but subjective intention is a vital element of such claims under the Fourteenth and Fifth Amendments—both of which prohibit purposeful discrimination by governmental actors. When there is clear evidence that the government has discriminated intentionally on the basis of a "suspect" classification, the actions must be justified by compelling government interests, and courts must strictly scrutinize the justification. In most profiling contexts, however, compelling government interest cannot be claimed and the case is won by proving intentional discrimination.

Intentional discrimination

But therein lies the rub: This kind of proof is not easy and it doesn't come cheaply. In an equal protection claim, a lawyer must make a prima facie case having two prongs. First, demonstrate that a government actor treated similarly situated people differently on the basis of a suspect classification. Second, establish that the governmental actor did so purpose-

---

215. United States v. Freeman, 209 F.3d 464 (6th Cir. 2000).

ly. Once the prima facie case is made, the burden shifts to the government to rebut with race-neutral explanations.

Three things help the lawyer to make such a case. First, establish a "colorable basis" for the belief that police engaged in purposeful discrimination and the court will order discovery. The "colorable basis" standard requires "some evidence," but not a prima facie case, on both of the prongs of the equal protection claim.

Second, establish proof of differential treatment at both the preliminary stage and in the prima facie case by using statistical surveys as the primary evidence. For example, black defendants, alleging they were targeted for traffic stops on the New Jersey Turnpike, produced a traffic survey showing African–American motorists were stopped on the turnpike at rates that far exceeded their representation in the overall population of drivers and of traffic violators.[216] Although the *Soto* defendants also introduced other evidence, the traffic survey was the principal evidence on which the judge relied.

Third, the most difficult prong of an equal protection claim—discriminatory intent—can be proven by inference where the pattern of differential treatment is "stark." The *Soto* case again serves as a useful example. The court sustained the defendants' prima facie case, holding that the strong statistical showing raised a presumption of purposeful discrimination.

What relief is available based on an equal protection theory? Defendants in the Soto case were successful in suppressing evidence because police were enforcing the laws in a discriminatory fashion. A motion to dismiss based on selective prosecution may also be appropriate. Defense should explain to the client that damages and injunctive relief might be available in a civil lawsuit. Aggrieved motorists have used class action mechanisms to gain settlements in Maryland and Pennsylvania, and other suits are still pending.

Once constitutional doctrines and available relief have been identified, a lawyer should examine the discovery needed to advance a client's claims. Because discovery laws differ among jurisdictions, this article will look at broad categories of useful information.

The most important data in many cases will be statistical evidence revealing differential law enforcement treatment of minorities and whites. In traffic stop situations, some data can be gleaned from traffic tickets issued on specific dates. More revealing data can be gleaned from spot checks over a broader time period. For example, in the *Soto* case, defendants stopped on the New Jersey Turnpike between 1988 and 1991 compiled a database of stops on 35 randomly selected days within that time period. The database was constructed with information obtained from the state, including arrest reports, patrol charts, radio logs, and traffic tickets. From the database, the defendants were able to identify the percentage of vehicles stopped on those days that had occupants identified by police as

---

216.   *See* State v. Soto, 734 A.2d 350, 352–53 (1996).

"black." They then conducted their own survey to determine the percentage of black travelers on the turnpike and the percentage of those who violated traffic laws. Spot checks of other kinds of data may also prove important. If defense believes the client was targeted for a pretextual stop and search, counsel should request "consent to search" forms for a number of days in the relevant period of time.

Other categories of useful information include:

- profiles, written or unwritten, used by relevant police units, including the sources of those profiles, data concerning their accuracy or inaccuracy, and information about stop and arrest rates by officers using the profiles;

- surveys, reports, training manuals, teaching videos, and any other materials from any source that were used to train police in the relevant jurisdiction. In the Soto case, the defense introduced training videos that consistently depicted drug traffickers as Hispanic. In addition, the state made reference to reports made by the state police and to annual traffic surveys conducted by New Jersey's Department of Transportation in an unsuccessful effort to rebut the defendants' statistical showing;

- regulations and policies governing the police unites, paying particular attention to any mission statements and the amount of discretion exercised. In Soto, the discretion exercised by different types of traffic enforcers was important to statistical differences in the "stop" rates. Certain radar patrol units, that were not permitted to choose their targets, stopped black drivers at far lower rates than police units that exercised more discretion in choosing targets. Moreover, Soto and other cases have verified what minorities have long known: Police units that participate in drug enforcement efforts tend to target minorities;

- information identifying current and former members of police units. Interviews may prove useful in discovering informal methods of training and unwritten profiling policies.

- personnel files, records of complaints against officers, records of investigating bodies, and records of lawsuits and motions to suppress involving similar police conduct. In connection with this information, research case law thoroughly for cases in your jurisdiction in which motions to suppress were filed concerning similar police conduct. In the *Freeman* case, the concurring judge relied on a record of motions to suppress (even though most of them were denied) to suggest that police were engaging in a disturbing pattern of pretextual stops;

- document retention policies in the relevant jurisdiction. This information not only determines what kinds of information are available, but also will help demonstrate ways in which the jurisdiction failed to investigate claims of discrimination. The judge in the Soto case questioned the credibility of a state police commander who claimed there was insufficient evidence of discrimination, but had neglected available sources of information.

Where else to search

There is a wealth of information available on the Web. The most useful websites are those created by the American Civil Liberties Union (ACLU) () and the Civil Rights Division of the U.S. Department of Justice (). The ACLU's site contains a lengthy and informative report by Professor David A. Harris, one of the country's leading experts on profiling. The report, "Driving While Black: Racial Profiling on Our Nation's Highways", is available at . In addition to information available on the Web, lawyer publications and law journal articles can provide you with more background information about profiling and discriminatory policing.

Finally, it may be appropriate to help a client report police profiling and advocate for better laws to control this practice. The client should first complain to the police department or the agency that has jurisdiction over the officers involved in the profiling. Many jurisdictions do not make the complaint process easy, but the effort is necessary. Not only are such complaints useful evidence for the next victim of profiling, but also police agencies themselves are paying more attention to the volume of profiling complaints; some have volunteered to collect data about profiling. Encourage the client to report profiling to the Department of Justice, which enforces antidiscrimination provisions found in the Civil Rights Act of 1964 and the Omnibus Crime Control and Safe Streets Act of 1968. The Justice Department has acted upon profiling complaints in several instances, and its enforcement activity has resulted in orders and consent decrees requiring law enforcement units to collect data about profiling. The state's attorney general's office and other state officials may be involved in monitoring activities. There are ways that a client can assist nongovernmental groups in monitoring profiling activity. The ACLU's website has a "driver profiling complaint form." The organization has taken a leading role in measuring and combating profiling, and the client's report assists in that effort. Also consider contacting the National Association for the Advancement of Colored People (NAACP) and other groups active in fighting profiling.

Profiling has been a pernicious law enforcement practice for many years. Acting as a civil rights lawyer—even for limited purposes—the criminal defense attorney helps a client find relief and combats profiling at the same time.

PROBLEM 3–16

Officer Guthrie, an Alabama State Policeman, spotted an early model Ford LTD approaching him on an interstate highway outside of Birmingham. The car had Texas license plates and the driver appeared to Guthrie to be Hispanic. The officer's suspicions were aroused because the interstate was (according to police department lore) a major source of drug trafficking that originated in Mexico and moved through Texas. As the Ford passed Officer Guthrie's car, its driver made eye contact with him and then looked away. The officer quickly turned around, pursued the Ford, and pulled it over to the side of the highway. As Officer Guthrie approached the vehicle, he noticed a passenger in the car. The passenger, who also appeared to Guthrie to be Hispanic, had apparently been lying down in the back seat until the car was pulled over.

Officer Guthrie asked the driver for his license and was handed a Texas license bearing the name of Arturo Tapia. Upon request, the passenger produced his own license with the name Bernard Tapia. Arturo explained that he and Bernard were going to Atlanta to find work. During this conversation, Officer Guthrie noticed that Arturo Tapia seemed nervous and that his hands were shaking. The officer also noticed that there was no luggage in the car—a curious development if the men were moving to a new city. Although both driver's licenses appeared to be in order, Officer Guthrie asked to see the car's registration papers. Bernard retrieved them from the glove compartment and closed its door quickly, but before he did so Officer Guthrie observed inside the glove compartment five or six plastic baggies filled with a dark substance. The officer ordered the men out of the car and searched the vehicle. Aside from the baggies, which contained marijuana, the officer discovered two illegal switchblades inside a duffle bag in the trunk.

The Tapia brothers were charged with drug offenses and possession of illegal weapons. They moved to suppress the items that Officer Guthrie found during his search of the car.

Question: As the prosecutor, argue that the search was valid and that the evidence should not be suppressed. What arguments will the defendants make in response? How would a court rule?

PROBLEM 3–17

Police officers received an anonymous telephone call alerting them to suspicious activity at 138 Jackson Street. According to the officers' later testimony, the caller "reported seeing a blue car in the driveway at 138 Jackson Street with six young white males inside. The caller also stated that he observed a handgun inside the motor vehicle and that it was wrapped in a towel." In response to this call, police went to 138 Jackson Street where they observed a blue motor vehicle containing a number of people backing out of the driveway. One of the officers parked his vehicle in the driveway, thereby blocking the blue vehicle from leaving, and turned on his blue police lights. Another officer approached the driver of the car and explained that the officers were responding to a report of a handgun. The driver denied that he had a gun and invited the police to search the vehicle. The police found the gun, and the driver was arrested.

Question: Was there a stop? If so, on what grounds will the prosecution attempt to justify the stop? What will the defense argue, and how should the court rule?

PROBLEM 3–18

In the Boson case in Chapter 1, assume that instead of driving out of Exum, Boson bought an airplane ticket. Two DEA agents, each holding a large drug-sniffing dog, spotted him in the airport concourse and noticed that he fit three out of seven characteristics of a drug courier profile: first, Boson appeared to be extremely nervous; second, he had checked no luggage; and third, he acted oddly at the security check-point, placing his carry-on bag on the conveyor belt and then standing back so that it would pass through the x-ray machine before he crossed the checkpoint.

After developing what they believed to be reasonable suspicion, the agents approached Boson, flashed their badges, and explained their suspicions. They asked Boson if they could look at his ticket and driver's license, and he promptly handed them over. By this time, Boson had put down his carry-on bag. One of the agents picked it up and placed it against the wall approximately 10 feet away from Boson. The dogs expressed a keen interest in the bag, straining their leashes to sniff the air from its direction. Meanwhile, the agents asked Boson why the names on his ticket and his driver's license did not correspond—a characteristic of the drug courier profile. They also noticed that Boson's ticket indicated he was traveling to Seattle, a known distribution center for drugs. The agents continued to question Boson about his travel plans for approximately 10 minutes. They then asked him to accompany them to a private room, but at that point he confessed to carrying cocaine in his bag. The agents handcuffed him and turned him over to the nearest U.S. Marshal's office.

Question: At what point did this contact escalate from a voluntary encounter to a stop? When did it escalate from a stop to an arrest? Was each escalation justified? Alternatively, consider this: on the original Boson facts, did the matching of three out of seven of the elements of the drug courier profile establish reasonable suspicion to stop the car?

CHAPTER 4

SEARCHES AND SEIZURES: WARRANT EXCEPTIONS

- SEARCH INCIDENT TO ARREST • EXIGENT CIRCUMSTANCES
  • PLAIN VIEW • AUTOMOBILES • SPECIAL NEEDS • CONSENT

WARRANTLESS SEARCHES AND SEIZURES

Checklist 6: Is a Warrantless Search or Seizure Permissible?

1. Is a warrantless search and seizure justified as part of a search incident to arrest?

    a. Did the warrantless search accompany a lawful custodial arrest?

    b. Was the search limited to the "wingspan" of the arrestee, that is, the area from which he might grab weapons or destroy evidence?

        (1) If yes, and if the law enforcement encounter was initiated while the arrestee was in a vehicle, was the search within the passenger compartment of the vehicle?

        (2) If no, was the search confined to the areas from which an attack on the officers might immediately be launched? If not, did the officers have reasonable suspicion to believe that a confederate in the criminal activity who poses a danger to the officer or others might be hiding in the area searched?

    c. Was the search substantially contemporaneous with the arrest—did it occur shortly before or after the arrest?

    d. For items seized as a result of the search, did the police have probable cause to believe that those items were contraband, fruits, evidence, or instrumentalities of a crime?

2. Is a warrantless search justified by exigent circumstances?

    a. Were the police pursuing a fleeing felon? If not,

    b. Did the police have probable cause to believe that the search would uncover contraband, fruits, evidence, or instrumentalities of a crime?

        (1) Did the circumstances present a threat to officer or public safety or to the integrity of evidence?

        (2) Was the government interest in the warrantless activity of sufficient gravity to outweigh the individual interests at stake?

3. Is a warrantless seizure justified by the plain view doctrine?

    a. Did the police view (or feel or smell or hear) the items seized from a lawful vantage point?

    b. Was the incriminating nature of the items immediately apparent—in other words, did the police have probable cause to believe that the items were contraband, fruits, evidence, or instrumentalities of a crime?

    c. Did the police have a lawful right of access to the items?

4. Is a warrantless search justified by the automobile exception?

    a. Was the search limited to a motorized vehicle that is presently capable of mobility?

    b. Did the police have probable cause to believe that the vehicle contained contraband, fruits, evidence, or instrumentalities of a crime?

5. Is a warrantless search and seizure justified by special governmental needs?

    a. Was the warrantless activity undertaken to advance a non-criminal investigation-related purpose?

    b. Was the warrantless activity reasonably necessary and effective in advancing that purpose?

    c. Was the government's interest of sufficient gravity to outweigh the individual interests at stake?

      (1) Did the government have a special need?

      (2) Did the search involve a pervasively regulated industry or another area with a low expectation of privacy?

      (3) Did the search involve a minimal amount of officer discretion and a minimal intrusion on privacy interests?

6. Is a warrantless search and seizure justified by consent?

    a. Did an individual voluntarily consent to the search or seizure?

    b. Was the search or seizure confined to the scope of the consent—in other words, to what a reasonable person would have understood the consent to mean?

    c. Was the consent given by an individual with actual or apparent authority?

A.   INTRODUCTION

The warrant requirement occupies a central role in Fourth Amendment jurisprudence. It remains disputed, however, whether warrants are a prerequisite to a "reasonable" search or seizure. While some scholars argue that warrants are presumptively required for almost all searches and seizures, others (including a majority of the Supreme Court justices) construe the "reasonableness clause" as the core standard of the Fourth Amendment—a construction that reduces warrants to only one of many factors in the determination of whether a particular search or seizure was reasonable. The argument remains heated among scholars as well. Professor Akhil Reed Amar has argued that the Framers disfavored warrants, and that warrants should not be considered a prerequisite to a reasonable search or seizure.[1] Amar contends that during the colonial period, trespass actions seeking to recover damages for unreasonable searches and seizures provided important protection against the enormous power of the Crown. Juries on occasion assessed huge damages against Crown officials who had, in the jurors' view, unreasonably trespassed upon the homes and papers of English citizens. But warrants effectively insulated officers of the Crown from trespass liability, because as a matter of law they rendered the officers' conduct reasonable. The broad issuance of general warrants, then, greatly diminished the power of citizen juries to regulate official behavior. The Framers, argues Amar, trusted those citizen juries far more than judges who were empowered to issue warrants, and their foremost intention was to limit the circumstances under which judges were permitted to issue warrants so that juries would remain the guardians of reasonableness—the touchstone of the Fourth Amendment, according to Amar.

Professor Tracey Maclin, among others, has challenged both Amar's historical analysis and his conclusion that the Framers did not prefer warrant-authorized searches to warrantless ones.[2] First, Maclin argues that the Framers did not view trespass suits as a bulwark against official oppression because there were substantial procedural bars to such suits (for example, unsuccessful plaintiffs would be assessed damages) that shielded officers to a great extent. Second, by the time that the Fourth Amendment was drafted, the practice of issuing general warrants had already declined, and specific warrants were the customary method of intrusion. Third, in the decades leading up to the ratification of the Fourth Amendment, "[e]xample after example illustrates discontent over promiscuous searches without warrants." Consequently, Maclin concludes that a warrant-preference rule is consistent with the Framer's intentions. He also argues that history should be read for what it tells us about Fourth Amendment values. Maclin quotes another scholar in order to explain those values: " 'A significant part of the historical record . . . is consistent with logic: the Framers acted to eliminate search and seizure methods that permitted the

---

1. *See* AKHIL REED AMAR, THE CONSTITUTION AND CRIMINAL PROCEDURE: FIRST PRINCIPLES 3–20 (1997).

2. *See* Tracey Maclin, *The Complexity of the Fourth Amendment: A Historical Review*, 77 B.U. L. REV. 925 (1997) (quoting Morgan Cloud, *Searching Through History; Searching For History*, 63 U. CHI. L. REV. 1707, 1729 (1996)). Maclin also relies on a detailed historical analysis found in William J. Cuddihy, *The Fourth Amendment: Origins and Original Meaning* (1990) (unpublished Ph.D. dissertation, Claremont Graduate School) (available from UMI Dissertation Services, 300 N. Zeeb Road, Ann Arbor, Michigan). Cuddihy's dissertation has been described by Justice O'Connor as "one of the most exhaustive analyses of the original meaning of the Fourth Amendment ever undertaken." *See also* Thomas Y. Davies, *Recovering the Original Fourth Amendment*, 98 MICH. L. REV. 547 (1999) (re-interpreting the Fourth Amendment's history as demonstrating an original intent only to ban general warrants but not to address warrantless searches at all, while concluding that such an original intent analysis would undermine the Framers' larger purpose of curbing the exercise of discretionary authority by officers); David A. Sklansky, *The Fourth Amendment and Common Law*, 100 COLUM. L. REV. 1739 (2000) (arguing that the Court has moved toward a new Fourth Amendment originalism in which analysis begins by determining whether the challenged action would have been condemned by the common law in 1791, a new approach unjustified by text or the intentions of the Framers).

arbitrary exercise of discretion and were conducted without good cause, whether or not warrants were employed.' " Thus, Professor Maclin concludes, a probable-cause preference rule is also consistent with the Framers' intentions.

Regardless of who wins the argument, there is no question that many, if not most, lawful searches and seizures are effectuated without warrants. This is because the Court has identified a number of circumstances in which warrants cannot practicably be obtained. Notice that these circumstances are popularly referred to as "exceptions to the warrant requirement," although the present-day Supreme Court often identifies them simply as circumstances in which law enforcement activity can be reasonably undertaken without a warrant. These circumstances can be gathered generally into six categories, and they are set forth below.

B. SIX CATEGORIES OF WARRANTLESS SEARCHES AND SEIZURES

1. SEARCHES INCIDENT TO ARREST

a. *Traditional Rule*

One of the oldest and most frequently used exceptions to the warrant requirement involves searches "incident" to—during or immediately after—an arrest.[3] For many years, it was assumed that the Fourth Amendment permitted warrantless searches of arrestees and areas in which arrests took place—an entire house, for example, might be searched after officers arrested a person on those premises. In *Chimel v. California*,[4] the Court limited the scope of the search incident to arrest doctrine, constraining it to searches of (1) the arrestee's person and (2) areas within the arrestee's immediate reach. Identifying the two central reasons for restricting such searches, the Court stated:

> When an arrest is made, it is reasonable for the arresting officer to search the person arrested in order to remove any weapons that the latter might seek to use in order to resist arrest or affect his escape. Otherwise, the officer's safety might well be endangered, and the arrest itself frustrated. In addition, it is entirely reasonable for the arresting officer to search for and seize any evidence on the arrestee's person in order to prevent its concealment or destruction. And the area into which an arrestee might reach in order to grab a weapon or evidentiary items must, of course, be governed by a like rule.

The dual purposes articulated in *Chimel*—officer safety and evidence preservation—remain the basis for the doctrine today.[5]

---

3. The search might even precede the arrest, so long as the arrest "follow[s] quickly on the heels of the ... search" and the results of the search are not necessary in order to establish probable cause for the arrest. *See* Rawlings v. Kentucky, 448 U.S. 98, 111 (1980).

4. 395 U.S. 752 (1969).

5. After its decision in Terry v. Ohio, the Supreme Court reaffirmed that the safety rationale underlying the search incident to arrest doctrine permits arresting officers to engage in more thorough searches than *Terry* would allow. *See, e.g.*, United States v. Robinson, 414

The search incident to arrest doctrine applies to all custodial arrests, that is, a seizure of the person with the intention of thereafter having him transported to the police station or other place to be dealt with according to law. In *Knowles v. Iowa* the Court unanimously held that the doctrine applies only when a police officer actually effectuates a custodial arrest.[6] There, a police officer had issued Mr. Knowles a traffic citation for speeding, conducted a full search of the car, and arrested Knowles after finding a bag of marijuana. The Court held that the search of Knowles' car was unconstitutional even though state law permitted the officer to arrest Knowles for speeding. Chief Justice Rehnquist's opinion pointed out that the two underlying rationales for the search incident to arrest doctrine—officer safety and preservation of evidence—are not present to the same extent when an officer declines to arrest.

An arresting officer may conduct a search incident to arrest without analyzing whether it is likely, given the facts of the individual case, that the arrestee possesses a dangerous weapon or will destroy evidence. Simply put, the authority to search flows from the arrest itself—which must be lawful or the results of the search will be suppressed. The nature of the search-incident-to-arrest authority is illustrated in *United States v. Robinson*.[7] Mr. Robinson had been stopped and arrested for driving with a revoked license. After the arrest, the officer searched Robinson and found heroin concealed in a crumpled cigarette packet in his pocket. Robinson claimed that the search was unconstitutional, arguing that the nature of the violation for which he was arrested did not provide any reason to believe that he was armed or carrying contraband. The Court disagreed, however, holding that:

> [the] authority to search the person incident to a lawful custodial arrest, while based upon the need to disarm and to discover evidence, does not depend on what a court may later decide was the probability in a particular arrest situation that weapons or evidence would in fact be found upon the person of the suspect. A custodial arrest of a suspect based on probable cause is a reasonable intrusion under the Fourth Amendment; that intrusion being lawful, a search incident to the arrest requires no additional justification. It is the fact of the lawful arrest which establishes the authority to search, and we hold that in the case of a lawful custodial arrest a full search of the person is not only an exception to the warrant requirement of the Fourth Amendment, but is also a "reasonable" search under that Amendment.

The search incident to arrest doctrine often is cited as an example of a "bright-line rule," and it does reduce the number of ad hoc judgments that

---

U.S. 218 (1973). The Court explained why a custodial arrest justifies a more far-reaching search than a *Terry* frisk: "[Because] the danger to an officer is far greater in the case of the extended exposure which follows the taking of a suspect into custody and transporting him to the police station than in the case of the relatively fleeting contact . . . [in] the typical Terry-type stop."

6. 525 U.S. 113 (1998).

7. 414 U.S. 218 (1973).

law enforcement officers must make. But bright-line rules often raise issues of definition and the search incident to arrest doctrine is no exception. Initially, what is the "area into which the arrestee might reach?" Typically referred to as the "wingspan" of the arrestee, the Court in *Chimel* defined it functionally as "the area from within which [the arrestee] might gain possession of a weapon or destructible evidence." This definition limits a search incident to arrest to the area immediately surrounding the arrested party—an area that must be determined on a case-by-case basis. It would not be constitutional, for instance, for an officer to search areas outside the room where an arrest takes place. Even a search of drawers and cabinets in the room where the arrest occurs may be invalid on the grounds that the storage areas were not within the immediate control of the arrestee and therefore not justified by the rationales for the exception.

Does the search incident to arrest doctrine permit officers to open closed containers found on the arrestee's person or within the arrestee's wingspan? Apparently so. Such a container might contain a weapon or evidence. Where it applies, the doctrine trumps any reasonable expectation of privacy that the arrestee might have in closed containers. Even a container too small to contain a weapon may conceal evidence, and the bright-line nature of the *Chimel* rule suggests that all container searches within the arrestee's wingspan are constitutional.

May arresting officers conduct a search incident to arrest after they have immobilized the arrestee? Yes. In fact, many searches take place after the arrestee is secured in handcuffs.[8] The rationale appears to be that there is always a possibility—however remote—that the arrestee might get free. But the doctrine applies regardless of the level of that risk. Thus, the search incident to arrest doctrine neither requires officers to make judgments about the risk that a particular arrestee poses, nor requires a court to evaluate such a judgment after the fact.

On the other hand, the arrest and search must be "contemporaneous"—they cannot be too remote in time from each other. In *United States v. Chadwick*,[9] the Supreme Court invalidated the search of a footlocker that had been removed to a government building from the place of arrest. The Court explained that "[o]nce law enforcement officers have reduced luggage or other personal property not immediately associated with the person of the arrestee to their exclusive control, and there is no longer any danger that the arrestee might gain access to the property to seize a weapon or destroy evidence, a search of that property is no longer an incident of the arrest." Although the *Chadwick* rule has been tempered by later decisions that permit searches incident to arrest even where the immobilized arrestee clearly poses no danger, the requirement that the search be closely related in time to the arrest remains important.

---

8. *See, e.g.,* United States v. Litman, 739 F.2d 137, 138–39 (4th Cir. 1984) (upholding search of shoulder bag even though arrestee had been secured and held against wall at gunpoint).

9. 433 U.S. 1, 13–15 (1977).

In *United States v. Robbins*,[10] for example, the Eighth Circuit Court of Appeals invalidated the search of a wallet that police had left at the place of arrest and returned for after the arrest was completed. The facts were these: when police arrested Robbins, he took out his wallet and gave it to a colleague, who placed the wallet in his desk. The police came back for the wallet "later." The court held that under the circumstances, the government was unable to establish that the search of the wallet was contemporaneous with the arrest. The "close-in-time" rule is also illustrated in *United States v. Clemons*,[11] in which the Ninth Circuit Court of Appeals upheld a suitcase search that took place "two or three minutes" after Clemons' arrest, even though Clemons was approximately 300 yards from the suitcase when he was arrested. When DEA agents approached him at an airport, Clemons dropped the locked suitcase and attempted to flee the scene. After he was captured and arrested, he was taken immediately to the DEA office at the airport—a walk that took two or three minutes. The agent who had retrieved his suitcase arrived at the DEA office at about the same time and proceeded to search the suitcase. Later, the court held that the search was incident to the arrest because the two were closely related in time.

In *United States v. Edwards*,[12] the Supreme Court upheld the seizure of an arrestee's clothing under the search incident to arrest doctrine, even though it occurred in the jail some ten hours after the arrest. There appeared to be extenuating circumstances justifying the delay: the arrest had happened late at night, the officers had no immediate way to provide the arrestee with other clothing, and the arrestee might have destroyed his clothing at any time once he realized their incriminating nature. Professors Charles H. Whitebread and Christopher Slobogin believe that *Edwards* did not change the close-in-time rule for searches incident to arrest, but rather should be viewed as a narrow exception for situations in which "an immediate search is virtually impossible and exigency still exists at the time of the later search."[13]

Finally, may an officer seize any item found during a search incident to arrest? Not necessarily. In order to justify seizing an item found during a search incident to arrest, the officer must have probable cause to believe that the item is contraband, or a fruit, instrumentality, or evidence of a crime.[14] If not, the item must be returned to the arrestee eventually, although it may be placed in a locker for safekeeping while the arrestee is detained.[15]

---

10. 21 F.3d 297 (8th Cir. 1994).

11. 72 F.3d 128 (4th Cir. 1995) (unpublished opinion; for full text of opinion, *see* 1995 WL 729479).

12. 415 U.S. 800 (1974).

13. CHARLES H. WHITEBREAD & CHRISTOPHER SLOBOGIN, CRIMINAL PROCEDURE: AN ANALYSIS OF CASES AND CONCEPTS 169 (1993).

14. The seizure authority stems from the plain view doctrine, discussed below.

15. This "safekeeping" function is discussed in the later section on inventory searches.

b.   Application to Automobiles

After *Chimel*, lower courts struggled to apply the search incident to arrest doctrine to automobile arrests. Automobile interiors, however, contain a wide variety of spaces that may or may not be within the immediate area of the arrestee's control, and the rules established by the courts were just as varied. As the Supreme Court observed of these rulings, "[w]hile the *Chimel* case established that a search incident to an arrest may not stray beyond the area within the immediate control of the arrestee, courts have found no workable definition of 'the area within the immediate control of the arrestee' when that area arguably includes the interior of an automobile and the arrestee is its recent occupant."[16]

The Court resolved this problem in *New York v. Belton* by creating a per se rule: when a police officer lawfully makes a custodial arrest of an automobile occupant, the officer may search the entire passenger compartment of the vehicle incident to the arrest. Further, the arresting officer may examine the contents of any containers within the passenger compartment since those containers and their contents would have been within that area of per se control. The Supreme Court emphasized that its holding "encompasses only the interior of the passenger compartment of an automobile and does not encompass the trunk." Applying its new rule, the Court approved the automobile search involved in the case, even though the occupants had been removed at the time of their arrest.

The dissent in *Belton* complained that the majority's decision marked a departure from the rationales articulated in *Chimel*—the safety of the arresting officer and the preservation of evidence. According to the dissent, after an arrestee is removed from the vehicle, there exists very little, if any, danger that evidence within the passenger compartment will be destroyed or that the arrestee will obtain a weapon from that area. The dissent concluded that the Court had "adopt[ed] a fiction—that the interior of a car is always within the immediate control of an arrestee who has recently been in the car."

It is hard to quarrel with the dissent's characterization of the rule as a fiction, but the fictional nature of the rule is what makes it so appealing: it provides police officers with a clear explanation of what they may search in connection with an automobile arrest. In fact, it provides more guidance than *Chimel*, which requires a case-by-case analysis of what areas are within the arrestee's wingspan. *Belton* is not immune, however, from definitional problems. For example, *Belton* applies to automobile "occupants." Would it apply to a person arrested just before entering an automobile? What about a person who exits an automobile as police approach? Many courts have construed *Belton* to cover all situations in which an officer initiates contact with a person in an automobile. For example, the following is the Sixth Circuit's articulation of such a construction of the *Belton* rule:

---

16.   New York v. Belton, 453 U.S. 454, 460 (1981).

Where the officer initiates contact with the defendant, either by actually confronting the defendant or by signaling confrontation with the defendant, while the defendant is still in the automobile, and the officer subsequently arrests the defendant (regardless of whether the defendant has been removed from or has exited the automobile), a subsequent search of the automobile's passenger compartment falls within the scope of *Belton* and will be upheld as reasonable.... However, where the defendant has voluntarily exited the automobile and begun walking away from the automobile before the officer has initiated contact with him, the case does not fit within *Belton's* bright-line rule, and a case-by-case analysis of the reasonableness of the search under *Chimel* becomes necessary.[17]

The Supreme Court has since disavowed this "initiation rule," however. In *Thornton v. United States*,[18] it held that the *Belton* rule applies regardless of whether the police interaction was initiated before or after the suspect left the vehicle. Instead, the Court adopted a rule linking *Belton's* applicability to temporal and physical proximity between the arrestee and the vehicle, explaining that "the arrest of a suspect who is next to a vehicle presents identical concerns regarding officer safety and the destruction of evidence as the arrest of one who is inside the vehicle." As a result of these concerns, and its desire to maintain a bright-line rule, the Court held that "[s]o long as an arrestee is the sort of 'recent occupant' of a vehicle as petitioner was here, officers may search that vehicle incident to arrest." In the case at hand, Marcus Thornton had pulled into a parking lot and gotten out of his car before a police officer initiated contact with him, although the officer suspected that Thornton had been aware of him and had parked in an effort to evade contact with him.

Despite the clear five-justice majority supporting *Thornton's* holding, the case revealed a surprising amount of disagreement on the Court about *Belton's* continued viability. Justice Scalia concurred in the judgment upholding the search, but he refused to join the Court's opinion and rationale. Justice Scalia would abandon *Belton's* rule and underlying rationales (ensuring officer safety and preventing destruction of evidence), which he viewed as not really at issue in most situations in which *Belton* applies, and substitute this rule: officers may search vehicles upon arrest if they have reason to believe that evidence "relevant to the crime of arrest" might be found in the vehicle. Justice Scalia acknowledged that his proposed rule "is a return to the broader sort of search incident to arrest that we allowed before *Chimel*," but he found support for it in the constitution and in prior case law, and he would limit it "to searches of motor vehicles, a category of 'effects' which give rise to a reduced expectation of privacy." Explaining his proposed rule, he stated:

There is nothing irrational about broader police authority to search for evidence when and where the perpetrator of a crime is lawfully

---

17. United States v. Hudgins, 52 F.3d 115, 119 (6th Cir. 1995).

18. 541 U.S. 615 (2004).

arrested. The fact of prior lawful arrest distinguishes the arrestee from society at large, and distinguishing a search for evidence of his crime from general rummaging. Moreover, it is not illogical to assume that evidence of a crime is most likely to be found where the suspect was apprehended.

Justice Ginsburg joined Justice Scalia's opinion. Justice O'Connor indicated that she found Scalia's reasoning compelling, but she did not endorse his proposed rule outright because of her "reluctan[ce] to adopt it in the context of a case in which neither the Government nor the petitioner has had a chance to speak to its merit." Justice Stevens, joined by Justice Souter, dissented. He favored retention of the "initiation rule," explaining that *Belton* "is not needed for cases in which the arrestee is first accosted when he is a pedestrian, because *Chimel* itself provides all the guidance that is necessary."

In *Arizona v. Gant*,[19] the Court modified (or perhaps the Court might say it "clarified") *Belton* and embraced much of Justice Scalia's concurring opinion in *Thornton* to craft this two-part currently-governing rule: (1) *Chimel* and *Belton* authorize a search of a vehicle incident to a *recent occupant's* arrest when the following is true: the arrestee is unsecured and within reach of the passenger compartment *at the time of the search*; accordingly, the fiction that an arrest of a recent automobile occupant automatically justifies a search incident to that arrest of the entire passenger compartment because, in theory, the recent occupant, though handcuffed and secured, still poses a danger to officers and evidence is no more; and (2) the entire passenger compartment of a vehicle of a current arrestee may be searched incident to arrest as well when it is "reasonable to believe that evidence relevant to the crime of arrest might be found in the vehicle."[20] If this last test is met, the search may proceed even if the arrestee is fully secured at the time of the search, thus posing no danger any longer to persons or evidence.

The first part of this test narrows *Belton*, as it was arguably later interpreted by the Court, by requiring that the risk of the recent occupant's obtaining weapons or destroying evidence be a real one *at the time of the search*, not at the time of the arrest. The second part broadens *Chimel* and *Belton* by authorizing a search even under circumstances where there is no danger of the recent occupant's grabbing weapons or destroying evidence if—and this may be an entirely new legal standard (more on this last point below)—there is "reason to believe" that evidence relevant to the crime of arrest will be found. This second part is limited to the "unique" motor vehicle context. Although the Court repeatedly, as to the second part of the rule, speaks of searching "the vehicle," it seems still to be using this

---

19.   129 S.Ct. 1710 (2009).

20.   *Id.* at 1714.

shorthand phrase to mean, "the passenger compartment of the vehicle," and at least one dissenting Justice so read the majority opinion.[21]

The facts of *Gant* itself illustrate the new rule. Based on an anonymous tip that a certain residence was being used to sell drugs, Officers Griffith and Reed knocked on the residence's front door, which was answered by Gant. The officers asked to speak to the owner, but they left when Gant replied that the owner would return later. The officers conducted a records check, which revealed that Gant had his driver's license suspended and had an outstanding warrant for his arrest for driving with a suspended license.

When the officers returned to the residence, they found a man near the back of the house and a woman in a car parked in front of it and, upon arrival of a third officer, handcuffed both suspects (the man for providing a false name, the woman for possessing drug paraphernalia) and secured each in separate police cars, when Gant himself arrived by car. Gant got out of his car, shut the door, and met Officer Griffith about ten to twelve feet away from Gant's car. Griffith immediately arrested and handcuffed Gant. When backup officers arrived, they locked Gant in the backseat of their vehicle. Two officers then searched his car, one finding a gun, the other discovering a bag of cocaine in the pocket of a jacket on the backseat.

Gant was charged with possession of a narcotic drug for sale and possession of drug paraphernalia (the plastic bag containing the cocaine). He unsuccessfully sought to suppress the evidence at the trial level, arguing in part that the *Belton* search incident to arrest exception for motor vehicles did not apply because he posed no threat to the officers at the time of the search. At the suppression hearing, Officer Griffith, when asked why the search was conducted, answered: "Because the law says we can do it."[22]

The Court agreed with Gant's argument, finding that the original fictional rules were inconsistent with the justifications for the *Chimel* and *Belton* decisions, namely, the need for a search of the grabbing area because of the danger posed of violence or evidence destruction, dangers that evaporate where, as in *Gant*, the offender is safely secured at the time of the search. The Court worried that many lower courts' broader interpretation of *Belton* as creating a police "entitlement" to search rather than an exception justified by *Chimel*'s twin rationales unmoored the doctrine from its underlying logic.

Indeed, Justice Stevens began the analytical portion of his opinion on behalf of the Court by stressing the "basic rule that 'searches conducted outside the judicial process, without prior approval by judge or magistrate are *per se* unreasonable under the Fourth Amendment—subject only to a few specifically established and well-delineated exceptions' "[23]—a rule not routinely recited by the Court (which in other opinions often takes reasonableness balancing as the starting point rather than articulating a presumptive rule against warrantless searches or ones lacking probable cause)

---

21. *Id.* at 1726, 1731 (Alito, J., dissenting) (so describing the majority's rule).

22. *Id.* at 1715.

23. *Id.* at 1716.

or that is, according to some critics, honored in the breach. But Stevens' opinion took this "basic rule" seriously, narrowing the Court's interpretation of *Belton* to maintain the search incident exception's "narrow" and "well-delineated" status as an exception.

The State had argued, however, that, even without the twin *Belton* rationales applying, the broad interpretation given *Belton* by many lower courts should be adopted for different reasons: the bright-line nature of the rule (if you arrest a current or recent occupant, you can search the passenger compartment every time) aids sound law enforcement more than it invades the limited privacy interest in cars. The Court rejected this argument. First, said the Court, although one's privacy interest in a car less than in a home, it is still substantial, and the permitted invasion of that interest is likewise substantial because the broad rule permits searching not only the passenger compartment but "every purse, briefcase, or other container within that space."[24] Giving the state such power for arrests involving mere traffic offenses "creates a serious and recurring threat to the privacy of countless individuals."[25] Indeed, Stevens declared, "the character of that threat implicates the central concern underlying the Fourth Amendment—the concern about giving police officers unbridled discretion to rummage at will among a person's private effects."[26]

Second, continued the Court, the state overestimates the clarity of its proposed rule, for lower courts have struggled with how close in time and space the occupant must be to the stopped vehicle at the time of the search and whether it continues to be reasonable if it is conducted after the suspect has been removed from the scene.

Third, the Court emphasized, the state was just wrong to suggest that a broad reading of *Belton* was needed to protect law enforcement safety and evidentiary interests. The Court's narrower reading of *Belton* still permits a search incident whenever the dangers to physical safety or evidence are *real* ones. Moreover, the *Terry* stop and frisk doctrine, as interpreted in application to cars in *Michigan v. Long*, permits an officer search of a passenger compartment for weapons whenever there is "reasonable suspicion" to believe that anyone, arrestee or not, is dangerous and might gain immediate access to weapons in the car. Furthermore, if there was probable cause to believe that the car harbored evidence of criminal activity, a warrantless search of the car for weapons is permitted under the "auto exception" to the warrant requirement. Indeed, such searches can be done concerning offenses other than the offense of arrest. Additionally, should, for example, a house be nearby, the protective sweeps doctrine permits suspicionless, warrantless arrests of areas immediately adjacent to the place of arrest from which an attack might be launched and searches of other areas where there is reasonable suspicion to believe that a dangerous person might be hiding. The combination of these exceptions amply pro-

---

24. *Id.* at 1720.

25. *Id.*

26. *Id.*

tected law enforcement's interests, particularly in light of Scalia's *Thornton* concurrence rule, which the Court also adopted.

Fourth, *stare decisis* deserved little weight, concluded the Court, especially given this situation's easy distinction from the facts of earlier Court precedent in this area; the weak police reliance interests, given that other rules have not congealed into "routine practice" in a way that would make the new rules burdensome to the police; the "checkered history" of change, interpretation, and misinterpretation of the search incident to arrest rule for automobiles, which suggests the existence of no stable body of precedent anyway; and the twenty-eight years of experience with *Belton*, which has revealed "that articles inside the passenger compartment are rarely within the area into which an arrestee might reach...."[27]

Yet, offering little explanation other than citing Scalia's concurring opinion in *Thornton* as justification for doing so, the Court also adopted Scalia's alternative and additional search incident to arrest exception for motor vehicles—one that permitted searches where neither of the twin *Belton* rationales applied, namely, where there was reason to believe that evidence relevant to the crime of arrest might be found. That test, however, could not be met for most traffic violations and was not met in *Gant*. Other than the police seeing Gant drive while he lacked a license—and see him so drive they did—there simply was no other physical evidence needed to prove the crime of driving with a suspended license. Because no evidence "relevant to the crime of arrest" could exist, much less be found in the car, this newly-created test was not, therefore, met in the case before the Court.

Implicitly, the Court found that the police officers' prior investigations of suspected drug sales at the residence where they found Gant was irrelevant to the search incident question because the offense *of arrest*— driving with a suspended license—had nothing to do with drugs. Moreover, it was unlikely that the anonymous informant's tip about drug sales at a residence where Gant was found but did not own was adequate to establish probable cause to arrest him on a drug-related crime. Consequently, the police could not legally charge him with, and arrest him for, a drug offense—or, at least they could not do so at the time of arrest for the traffic violation. Under the Court's new rule inspired by Scalia's *Thornton* concurrence, however, the police could have searched the passenger compartment of Gant's car for drugs even if they lacked a reason to fear that he would hurt them or destroy their evidence, so long as he police had "reason to believe" the drugs would be in the car. They simply lacked such a reason on the facts before the Court.

Justice Scalia,[28] in his concurring opinion, expressed his view that the first part of the Court's rule invited police to leave crime scenes unsecured so that they retain the option of a passenger compartment search incident to arrest of a recent occupant. Accordingly, he would prefer to abandon the *Chimel/Belton* line of cases entirely, replacing them solely with the rule he

---

27. *Id.* at 1723.

28. *Id.* at 1724 (Scalia, J., concurring).

articulated in *Thornton* (what we have called the second part of the *Gant* rule). But since no other Justice shared his view, rather than permit the broad interpretation of *Belton* to stand, thus permitting "plainly unconstitutional searches—which is the greater evil,"[29] Scalia joined the majority opinion.

Justice Alito,[30] joined by Chief Justice Roberts and Justice Kennedy as to Alito's entire opinion, and by Justice Breyer for most of Alito's opinion, dissented. The bulk of Alito's opinion argued that, contrary to the majority's claim, it was overruling, not merely clarifying, *Belton* and that *stare decisis* counseled against going down that road. Alito also maintained that the first part of the new rule would endanger officers by creating perverse incentives for them to leave scenes unsecured, and that the second part of the new rule would confuse law enforcement officers and judges for some time to come. Concerning the second part of the new rule, Alito queried why the test was "reason to believe" rather than "probable cause"; why, if there was "reason to believe" that evidence of crime was present, the search should be restricted to the crime of arrest; and why, if there was such reason to believe, the search should be limited to the passenger compartment. Alito also saw confusion arising from the majority's failure to counsel officers about what to do if they arrest only one of several occupants, but the remaining occupants raise a risk of danger or evidence destruction.

Justice Breyer[31] wrote a separate dissent to emphasize the *stare decisis* grounds for his vote. However, he did not join Part E of Justice Alito's dissenting opinion (the portion defending *Belton*'s reasoning), offering no explanation for this position.

The "reason to believe" language of part two of the new *Gant* rule is likely to worry commentators as well as the *Gant* dissenting Justices. The "reason to believe" phrase or its variants has occasionally appeared in a smattering of earlier opinions by the Court, sometimes as a synonym for probable cause, other times as a synonym for "reasonable suspicion."[32] But the Court has most recently resurrected variants of the phrase in its exigent circumstances jurisprudence and now in *Gant*. At least one commentator worries that the Court is now inching toward a four-tier, rather than a three-tier, spectrum of justifications for searches and seizures, the four tiers being: (1) probable cause; (2) reasonable suspicion; (3) reason to believe; and (4) no suspicion.[33]

One final point of clarification. Although the *Gant* rule is now the law, we have given you background on the development of the search incident to

---

29.   *Id.* at 1725.

30.   *Id.* at 1726 (Alito, J., concurring).

31.   *Id.* at 1725 (Breyer, J., dissenting).

32.   *See generally* Kit Kinports, *Diminishing Probable Cause and Minimalist Searches*, 6 OHIO ST. J. CRIM. L. 649 (2009) (making the arguments discussed in this paragraph of our text but as to recent pre-*Gant* case law).

33.   *See id.* at 660.

arrest doctrine as applied to automobiles to enable you better to understand the *Gant* rule's meaning. Moreover, the first part of *Gant* merely changes the old apparent *Belton* rule, which required assuming danger to officers and evidence *at the time of arrest* as justifying a relatively contemporaneous suspicionless, warrantless search of a passenger compartment, to a rule in which there must be a real risk of those events *at the time of the actual search itself*. Otherwise, prior case law applies. Furthermore, the *Gant* rule's second part, which adopts Scalia's *Thornton* concurrence, does not so much change prior law as add to it. Finally, it is plausible that some state courts will under their state constitutions invalidate searches done under part two of the *Gant* rule because doing so would provide more, not less, protection than the federal Constitution, and states are always free to add to federal constitutional rights under state constitutional equivalents.

NOTES AND QUESTIONS

1. Do you agree that the majority's "reason to believe" phrase is a new level of justification different from "reasonable suspicion"? If yes, is it higher or lower than "reasonable suspicion"? What, if anything, would justify such a new tier, and when should it apply?

2. Note that even if "reason to believe" is a new tier, it is triggered by the "offense of arrest," and arrest still requires probable cause. Was there probable cause to arrest Gant for possession or sale of drugs under the facts before the Court at the time of the arrest? What if, instead of an anonymous tip, the officers had received a tip from an ordinary citizen identifying himself and claiming that while at the residence noted in Gant for a dinner party, this citizen saw the residence's owner—who was not Gant—sell cocaine to someone (again, not Gant) at the party, although Gant was a guest? Would that create probable cause to arrest Gant on drug charges?

Even more strongly, what if, in the immediately preceding question, we instead were told in the citizen tip that Gant himself sold the drugs; would the police now have probable cause to arrest Gant on drug charges? If they did have probable cause to arrest him on drug charges, would they have "reason to believe" that his car contained drugs? Would it matter whether they told him they were arresting him for driving with a suspended license, although they had probable cause at the time to arrest him on a drug charge?

3. What if Gant had a passenger in the car but the police only arrested Gant; could they frisk the passenger? Detain her for questioning on the scene? Take her to the station? Search her person incident to arrest? Does it matter whether Gant was arrested for driving with a suspended license, as he was, or on a drug charge, as the hypotheticals in question number two above posit?

4. *Stare decisis*'s force usually turns on these factors: (1) Was there reasonable reliance on the existing rule by any class of persons or entities, and would they thereby be harmed by a sudden change in the law?; (2)

Have relevant circumstances changed since the existing rule was adopted such that the rule's justifications no longer hold or no longer hold with such force?; (3) Has experience shown the rule to be unworkable?; (4) Have later cases been implicitly so inconsistent with the earlier precedent as to undermine its force?; and (5) Was the original precedent badly reasoned?[34] Some Justices argue as well that *stare decisis* should generally have less force in constitutional law.[35]

Given these factors, who do you think had the better argument on "overruling"? *Belton* (if it was overruled), Justice Stevens or Justice Alito? Was *Belton* overruled? Modified? Clarified? Retained but more fully explained to reject misunderstandings of the precedent by lower courts? How do we distinguish among these things, if at all, and why should we care? How can the distinctions affect advocates' arguments before trial judges? Appellate judges?

5. Alito's opinion cites an empirical study showing that police almost always handcuff an arrestee and remove him to a secure place before conducting a search incident to arrest.[36] Alito concluded that this argued in favor of the broad reading of *Chimel/Belton* because the narrow reading adopted by the Court would mean that searches incident to arrest of an automobile's passenger compartment would rarely be justified and thus rarely occur. In other words, infrequency of searches of recent occupants of automobiles and of their passenger compartments incident to arrest was a bad thing. Do you agree? Can you argue that this empirical study cuts just the opposite way, that is, in favor of the majority rule?

Another issue concerns the meaning of "passenger compartment." The *Belton* rule created, in effect, an irrebuttable presumption that a vehicle's "passenger compartment," and the containers within, are within the wingspan of the arrestee. It did so based on its assumption that arrestees conceivably can reach any area within an automobile's passenger compartment. But some cars have more "reachable areas" than others. Station wagons and hatchbacks, for instance, contain areas that would not ordinarily be described as "passenger compartments" but that nevertheless might be accessible to someone in the car. Are those areas searchable under the *Belton* rule? Most courts would answer yes, construing the rule broadly to include "whatever area is within a passenger's reach."[37] On the other

---

34. *See* Gant, 129 S.Ct. at 1726, 1728–30 (Alito, J., concurring) (outlining the factors to consider in deciding whether to depart from *stare decisis*).

35. *See id.* at 1724–25 (Scalia, J., concurring) ("Justice ALITO insists that the Court must demand a good reason for abandoning prior precedent. That is true enough, but it seems to me ample reason that the precedent was badly reasoned and produces erroneous (in this case unconstitutional) results.").

36. *See id.* at 1725, 1730 n.1 (Alito, J., concurring) (citing Myron Moskovitz, *A Rule in Search of a Reason: An Empirical Reexamination of* Chimel *and* Belton, 2002 WIS. L. REV. 657, 665).

37. United States v. Thompson, 906 F.2d 1292, 1298 (8th Cir. 1990); *see also, e.g.,* United States v. Pino, 855 F.2d 357, 364 (6th Cir. 1988), *cert. denied*, 493 U.S. 1090 (1990) (rear section of a mid-sized station wagon); United States v. Russell, 670 F.2d 323, 327 (D.C. Cir.), *cert. denied*, 457 U.S. 1108 (1982) (hatchback).

hand, officers are generally not permitted to dismantle the passenger compartment by ripping out door panels and other fixtures, although they may open glove compartments and examine objects—such as removable stereos—"capable of holding another object."[38] The rationale for this limitation is that such areas are ordinarily not accessible to an automobile occupant, unless facts indicate otherwise.[39]

6. One major justification for the search incident to arrest doctrine is that a suspect's awareness that he is facing custodial arrest gives him a strong incentive for grabbing a weapon or destroying evidence. But this justification assumes that arrestees will also have the ability to act on this incentive. Professor Myron Moskowitz,[40] in an empirical examination of what police actually do when they make an arrest, challenged the accuracy of this assumption:

> Is there anything about the facts of an arrest *qua* arrest that tends to justify a search? Well, yes. An arrest is often a traumatic event for a suspect. One moment he is free, and the next moment he is in the custody of the police. And he might realize that this custody can turn into a lengthy prison term if the police obtain more evidence to convict or add further charges. In this emotional state, the arrestee might seek to harm the arresting officers in order to escape, and he might try to dispose of any evidence that might enhance the likelihood of conviction or lead to further charges. But the police are neither stupid nor helpless. They can and will prevent these actions—first and foremost by restraining and removing the suspect from any area that might contain a weapon or evidence. If they arrest him in the home, they will handcuff him and remove him from the home. If they arrest him in a car, they will remove him from the car and then handcuff him. Common sense tells us this, and the police themselves tell us that this is what they in fact do. There might be occasional exceptions. But if the Court honors its purported commitment to the Fourth Amendment even slightly, it should form its general rule based on what the police normally do, not on the exceptions.

7. Even if Professor Moskowitz's empirical analysis is correct, does that necessarily undermine the wisdom of the search incident to arrest doctrine in its entirety? In part?

---

38. *See, e.g.,* United States v. Patterson, 65 F.3d 68, 71 (7th Cir. 1995) (search incident to arrest doctrine does not extend to dismantling portions of vehicle); United States v. Veras, 51 F.3d 1365, 1371 (7th Cir. 1995) (doctrine permits search of secret compartment in back seat); United States v. Willis, 37 F.3d 313, 317 (7th Cir. 1994) (doctrine permits search of removable stereo).

39. Where, for example, an officer perceives that a door panel is detached, the likelihood increases that a court will uphold a search behind that panel on the ground that the area was accessible to the arrestee.

40. Moskowitz, *supra*, n. 36 at 657, 697.

8. Is Moskowitz's argument strongest for (a) searches of the arrestee's person; (b) wingspan searches in the arrestee's home; (c) wingspan searches in a third party's home; (d) wingspan searches in the arrestee's car; or (e) wingspan searches in a third party's car? Can an officer arresting a suspect in a home or a car search a third individual's person if that individual is within the arrestee's wingspan?

c. Protective Sweeps

When making an arrest at a private residence, various factors may combine to create a more dangerous situation for the arresting officers. Unfamiliar floor plans, close quarters, and the possibility of hidden confederates arguably increase the threat of an ambush to arresting officers. Against this danger, however, is posed the arrestee's expectation of privacy in all rooms of the home and the Court's decision in *Chimel* to limit the search incident to arrest doctrine to areas within the arrestee's wingspan. Attempting to reconcile these interests, the Court has created a rule permitting in every in-home arrest a protective check of areas adjacent to the arrest from which an attack might immediately be launched against the arresting officer and broader protective sweeps of specific areas in which the officer has a reasonable suspicion that confederates who pose a danger to the officer or others may be lurking.

The protective sweep rule was created in *Maryland v. Buie*,[41] where the Court evaluated a search that took place during an in-home arrest for an armed robbery suspect. Police entered Buie's residence armed with a warrant for his arrest and apprehended him as he was leaving his basement. An officer went into the basement to see if an accomplice was hiding there. Although the officer found no one inside, he spotted and seized a red running suit that had been described by an eyewitness to the robbery. Later, that suit was introduced as evidence against Buie, who challenged its seizure. Upholding the protective sweep, the Court stated:

> We should emphasize that such a protective sweep, aimed at protecting the arresting officers, if justified by the circumstances, is nevertheless not a full search of the premises, but may extend only to a cursory inspection of those spaces where a person may be found. The sweep lasts no longer than is necessary to dispel the reasonable suspicion of danger and in any event no longer than it takes to complete the arrest and depart the premises.

Question: Recall Cal and Bart in Chapter 2 (at page 121, question 4). Assume that after police entered Cal's trailer home upon Bart's signal, officers searched Cal, the confidential informant, and two others who happened also to be inside Cal's trailer home. Officers retrieved from Cal's front pants pocket the marked currency Bart used to purchase the methamphetamines. Additionally, officers located a significant quantity of methamphetamines in Cal's home. Cal is subsequently charged with felony drug distribution: methamphetamine. Cal's defense counsel files a motion to

---

41.   494 U.S. 325 (1990).

suppress the drugs in the government's case against Cal. Would a trial judge find constitutional the officers' actions inside Cal's home under *Chimel*? *Buie*? Why?

PROBLEM 4–1

In the Boson case in Chapter 1, assume that the back seat of Boson's Mustang has been modified to fold down, permitting access to the trunk, although the seat was not folded down at the time of the stop. Assume also that Boson is charged with drug offenses after Officer Glemp finds the cocaine in his trunk, and that he moves to suppress the cocaine.

Question: If the trial court finds that Boson did not consent to the search of his trunk, must it suppress the cocaine? Can the prosecution successfully argue that the search incident to arrest doctrine should apply? Does it matter whether Glemp knew about the car's modified, fold-down back seat?

PROBLEM 4–2

As part of an undercover operation, DEA agents purchased a small sample of heroin from Julian Hurtado. The undercover agents discussed with Hurtado the possibility of purchasing additional, larger quantities of heroin. Hurtado said he had a new source of supply in Chicago and agreed to make a transfer to the undercover agents on September 7th in the parking lot of a Shell gas station in Racine, Wisconsin. On that date, Hurtado supplied the agents with five ounces of heroin. He was arrested and immediately agreed to cooperate in the investigation. He identified his source of supply as a "German fellow" from Illinois known to him as "Carl." He gave the agents Carl's electronic pager number, which reflected a Chicago-area telephone number. He also gave the agents a physical description of Carl.

The undercover agents immediately began calling the pager number, eventually making a connection. Hurtado, at the agents' request, spoke with "Carl" and arranged a meeting to obtain more heroin. The meeting was to take place later that day in the parking lot of a McDonald's restaurant in the Chicago area. Hurtado stated that Carl would be driving a blue Buick and that the meeting would take place in approximately an hour and a half.

Based on this information, the agents traveled to the parking lot near Chicago and soon observed a blue Buick driven by a man matching the description of "Carl." According to the agents, the driver of the automobile drove around the parking lot two or three times, left the parking lot, and then drove around a second parking lot. The agents stopped the Buick and asked the driver if he was "Carl." The driver, who turned out to be Carl Oberdorn, said yes. The officers asked Oberdorn to get out of the car and patted him down for weapons. Oberdorn was then placed in handcuffs and moved to the front of his vehicle. At the front of the car, the agents searched Oberdorn and found an electronic pager, which they seized. While looking for drugs in the car, the agents pried open two concealed compartments in the rear area of the vehicle, and inside one they found a loaded .25 caliber Beretta pistol. After the gun was found, one of the agents noticed that Oberdorn's wristwatch was also an electronic data bank capable of storing telephone numbers. The agent recognized this function of the watch because he owned a similar electronic telephone directory. The agents removed the wristwatch/electronic telephone directory from Oberdorn's wrist and retained it as evidence.

While still at the parking lot, one of the agents pushed a button on Oberdorn's digital pager, which revealed the numeric messages previously transmitted to the pager. Among the digital messages recovered was the telephone number of the phone at the Shell gas station in Racine where the agents had called the pager number provided by Hurtado. The following day, the agents retrieved various telephone numbers stored in Oberdorn's wristwatch.

Question: Assume that you are the Assistant United States Attorney assigned to prosecute Oberdorn. You know from experience that Oberdorn's lawyer will move to suppress the pager and its numbers, the gun and ammunition, and the watch and the numbers the officers retrieved from it. What arguments do you anticipate the defense lawyer making for each item, and what is your assessment of the lawyer's success?

PROBLEM 4–3

Officer J. D. Birch of the Memphis Police Department observed Freddie Mann pull out of an alley in an automobile. Officer Birch recognized Mann from prior arrests and knew that his driver's license had been revoked. Mann saw Officer Birch and immediately backed his car down the alley into a small automotive repair garage. Just as Mann got out of his car, Officer Birch turned into the alley after him. Officer Birch ordered Mann to stop. Mann walked away, but Officer Birch overtook him and requested Mann's driver's license. During this encounter, Officer Birch saw in Mann's shirt pocket a hand-rolled cigarette that he suspected was marijuana. He removed the cigarette, smelled the odor of marijuana, and placed Mann under arrest for possession of marijuana. After securing Mann in his squad car, Birch called for additional officers and, upon their arrival, proceeded to search the vehicle. The search of the interior revealed approximately $8,000 in cash under the front seat and the trunk contained a set of scales and clear cellophane—both items commonly used to package cocaine.

Question: Among other things, Mann is prosecuted for conspiracy to distribute cocaine. As his attorney, on what grounds would you move to suppress the items found in Mann's vehicle? What are your chances of success?

2.   EXIGENT CIRCUMSTANCES

The rationales underlying the search incident to arrest doctrine partly relate to exigency—or at least the possibility of exigency. The doctrine protects officer safety and the integrity of evidence in circumstances in which time is of the essence. The Court has recognized that in situations other than arrests, the presence of exigent circumstances may demand immediate action from the police and permit no time to obtain a warrant. Like the search incident to arrest doctrine, those exigencies involve safety risks to officers or the possibility that evidence might be destroyed. They include other dangers as well—for example, the possibility that a felon might evade arrest by fleeing into a private place.

The Court has crafted a doctrine that permits warrantless searches and seizures if: (1) probable cause for the search or seizure exists and (2) there are sufficient exigent circumstances to justify the warrantless activity. This doctrine is often referred to as the "exigent circumstances," or "emergency," exception to the warrant requirement. Some analysts further subdivide the doctrine to include a subcategory known as "hot pursuit of a fleeing felon." We refer to the doctrine in its entirety as the "exigent circumstances" exception to the warrant requirement.

As a general rule, the doctrine applies "to those situations in which law enforcement agents will be unable or unlikely to effectuate an arrest, search or seizure, for which probable cause exists, unless they act swiftly."[42] From the outset, it is important to recognize that this doctrine requires case-by-case analysis, unlike the search incident to arrest doctrine.[43] The officer in the field must make a quick judgment about whether probable cause and sufficient exigencies exist, and afterwards lawyers and judges must evaluate the facts that informed that judgment, comparing them with the facts in other cases in which warrantless searches have been permitted. To complicate matters, the doctrine requires balancing because the issue of sufficient exigencies depends in part on the severity of the warrantless intrusion on protected interests and the severity of the criminal activity. Given the need to balance interests, the doctrine does not provide clear guidelines to officers, lawyers, or judges.[44]

We begin with a brief examination of the balancing issue. The Court addressed the balance in *Welsh v. Wisconsin*,[45] where it invalidated a warrantless entry into Welsh's home to search for evidence of drunk

---

42. United States v. Campbell, 581 F.2d 22, 25 (2d Cir. 1978).

43. There have been efforts to create bright-line rules in the area. For example, in Mincey v. Arizona, 437 U.S. 385 (1978), the state argued for a per se "murder scene exception" to the warrant requirement. There, police had conducted a four-day search of a suspect's apartment after his arrest in connection with the fatal shooting of a police officer at that location. The Court refused to create a categorical exception to the warrant requirement in homicide cases, observing that "a four-day search that included opening dresser drawers and ripping up carpets can hardly be rationalized in terms of the legitimate concerns that justify an emergency search." *Id.* at 393.

44. The circuits differ greatly as to how they apply the doctrine. The variations in application may result in some circuits expanding the exception beyond its intended and appropriate limits. *See* Barbara C. Salken, *Balancing Exigency and Privacy in Warrantless Searches to Prevent Destruction of Evidence: The Need for a Rule*, 39 Hastings L.J. 283, 287–88, 300–24 (1988).

45. 466 U.S. 740 (1984).

driving. Police had received reports that Welsh had been driving erratically and had driven his car off the road and abandoned it. On this information, the police went to Welsh's home, forcibly entered without a warrant, and arrested him. The State argued that the warrantless entry and arrest were necessary in order to obtain a sample of his blood, which would have lost its alcohol content in the time it would have taken police to obtain a warrant. The Court rejected that argument, suggesting that the warrantless home entry—a major invasion of privacy—could not be justified by the government's interest in solving a relatively minor crime.

Likewise, in a narcotics case, the government cannot justify a warrantless entry and search on the risk that narcotics will be destroyed unless they demonstrate that the narcotics were in the process of destruction or about to be removed. In *Vale v. Louisiana,*[46] police officers arrested Vale in front of his home after observing him engage in what appeared to be a narcotics transaction. The officers entered his home and searched it, later claiming that the warrantless search was justified by the risk that the drugs would have been destroyed if they had waited for a search warrant. The Court disagreed, stating that "[w]e decline to hold that an arrest on the street can permit its own 'exigent circumstance' so as to justify a warrantless search of the arrestee's home."

Professors LaFave and Israel point out that *Vale* was the first case after *Chimel* to test the exigent circumstances doctrine. Prior to *Chimel,* they explain, the Court had not clarified what, if any, circumstances would justify a warrantless entry and search because police officers were able to use the then-broad search incident to arrest doctrine to avoid the issue. After *Chimel,* their searching authority pursuant to an arrest was much curtailed. *Vale* is now interpreted as one of the first Supreme Court cases "recognizing that a warrantless search of a dwelling for evidence may be undertaken in 'an exceptional situation.' "[47] Thus, the result in *Vale* notwithstanding, the lower courts interpreted it as a signal that exigent circumstances could justify a warrantless home entry and search.

Searches of homes implicate special privacy interests that affect the balance of government versus individual interests. In situations in which the challenged search implicates a lesser privacy interest, the Court has not been reluctant to acknowledge that law enforcement needs may outweigh individual interests. For example, consider *Cupp v. Murphy,*[48] in which the Court validated the seizure of blood, tissue, and fiber samples from under the fingernails of a murder suspect. The suspect had voluntarily submitted to questioning regarding the recent strangulation of his wife. Shortly after his arrival at the police station, police noticed a dark stain on one of his fingers and began to ask him about it. As soon as he became aware of the officer's suspicions, the suspect "put his hands behind his back and appeared to rub them together. He then put his hands in his pockets and a

---

46.   399 U.S. 30 (1970).

47.   WAYNE R. LAFAVE AND JEROLD H. ISRAEL, CRIMINAL PROCEDURE 186–87 (2d ed. 1992).

48.   412 U.S. 291 (1973).

'metallic sound, such as keys or change rattling' was heard.'' Fearing that the evidence on his hands might be destroyed, the police took incriminating samples of blood, tissue, and fiber from under his fingernails without his consent. The Court held that:

> On the facts of this case, considering the existence of probable cause, the very limited intrusion undertaken incident to the station house detention, and the ready destructibility of the evidence, we cannot say that this search violated the Fourth and Fourteenth Amendments.

The severity of the crime involved in *Cupp* and the minimal intrusion occasioned by the search and seizure clearly influenced the Court's decision. Had the crime been less serious or had the required intrusion been entry to a private residence, the Court might have refused to allow a warrantless search. Similarly, in *Schmerber v. California*,[49] the Court upheld warrantless blood sampling activity. Schmerber was in a hospital at the time, and police did not need to effectuate a warrantless entry into a home in order to obtain the blood sample. Upholding the seizure, the Court stated that:

> The officer in the present case . . . might reasonably have believed that he was confronted with an emergency, in which the delay necessary to obtain a warrant, under the circumstances, threatened ''the destruction of evidence.'' We are told that the percentage of alcohol in the blood begins to diminish shortly after the drinking stops, as the body functions to eliminate it from the system.

Issues of balancing are always resolved in favor of the government in cases involving the ''hot pursuit'' of a fleeing felon. The rule is an old common law principle that permits officers to enter premises without a warrant if (1) they are in pursuit of a fleeing felon and (2) that pursuit began in a public place, in which officers could have made a warrantless arrest. For example, in *United States v. Santana*,[50] officers had probable cause, although not a warrant, to arrest Santana for a narcotics felony. The officers saw her standing ''in the doorway'' of her house—one of the officers testified that ''she was standing directly in the doorway [so that] one step forward would have put her outside, [and] one step backward would have put her in the vestibule of her residence.'' They approached within 15 feet of her, got out of their vehicle, and identified themselves as police. Santana ''retreated into the vestibule of her house,'' and the officers followed, arresting her in the vestibule and seizing heroin pursuant to a search incident to arrest. In the subsequent criminal case, she moved to suppress the heroin and the Court held as follows:

> While it may be true that under the common law of property the threshold of one's dwelling is ''private,'' as is the yard surrounding the house, it is nonetheless clear that under the cases interpreting the Fourth Amendment Santana was in a ''public'' place. She was not in an area where she had any expectation of privacy. . . . She was not

---

49. 384 U.S. 757 (1966).

50. 427 U.S. 38 (1976).

merely visible to the public but was as exposed to public view, speech, hearing, and touch as if she had been standing completely outside her house. Thus, when the police, who concededly had probable cause to do so, sought to arrest her, they merely intended to perform a function which we have approved in *Watson*.

The only remaining question is whether her act of retreating into her house could thwart an otherwise proper arrest. We hold that it could not. In *Warden v. Hayden*, 387 U.S. 294 (1967), we recognized the right of police, who had probable cause to believe that an armed robber had entered a house a few minutes before, to make a warrant-less entry to arrest the robber and to search for weapons. This case, involving a true "hot pursuit,"[51] is clearly governed by *Warden*; the need to act quickly here is even greater than in that case while the intrusion is much less. The District Court was correct in concluding that "hot pursuit" means some sort of a chase, but it need not be an extended hue and cry in and about the public streets. The fact that the pursuit here ended almost as soon as it began did not render it any the less a "hot pursuit" sufficient to justify the warrantless entry into Santana's house. Once Santana saw the police, there was likewise a realistic expectation that any delay would result in destruction of evidence. See *Vale v. Louisiana*, 399 U.S. 30 (1970). Once she had been arrested, the search incident to that arrest, which produced the drugs and money, was clearly justified. *United States v. Robinson*, 414 U.S. 218 (1973); *Chimel v. California*, 395 U.S. 752 (1969).

We thus conclude that a suspect may not defeat an arrest which has been set in motion in a public place, and is therefore proper under *Watson*, by the expedient of escaping to a private place.

Where an exigent circumstances claim does not involve the hot pursuit of a fleeing felon, there is far less unanimity among the state and lower federal courts on what circumstances are sufficient to justify warrantless law enforcement activity. Nevertheless, a review of opinions reveals several factors that recur in successful exigent circumstances claims. For example, in *United States v. MacDonald*,[52] the Second Circuit Court of Appeals provided a detailed list of factors that convinced it to uphold a warrantless search:

> . . . (1) the grave nature of the ongoing crimes; (2) the presence of loaded weapons; (3) a likelihood that the suspects were themselves using narcotics; (4) a clear and immediate threat of danger to law enforcement agents and to the public at large; (5) not only more than the minimum probable cause to believe, but actual knowledge, that the suspect committed the crime; (6) at least strong reason to believe the

---

51. *Warden* was based upon the "exigencies of the situation," and did not use the term "hot pursuit" or even involve a "hot pursuit" in the sense that that term would normally be understood. That phrase first appears in Johnson v. United States, 333 U.S. 10 (1948), where it was recognized that some element of a chase will usually be involved in a "hot pursuit" case.

52. 916 F.2d 766 (2d Cir. 1990).

suspects were on the premises; (7) a likelihood . . . that a suspect might escape if not quickly apprehended; (8) an urgent need to prevent the loss of evidence; (9) the additional time required to obtain a warrant [given the time of day]; and (10) an attempt by the agents to enter peacefully.

Pay particular attention to the ninth factor identified by the court in *MacDonald*. Evaluating the time pressure on the officers provides considerable insight into how a court will decide the case. If the officers clearly had sufficient time to obtain a warrant, their claim of exigent circumstances should fail. Even in situations in which the officers have limited time to act, courts will review warrantless activity more critically if it takes place during the day, when warrants can be obtained more quickly. During the nighttime hours, however, and in isolated areas, the officers' judgment will carry more weight due to the longer period of time necessary to obtain a warrant.

Of similar importance to the analysis is the nature of the criminal activity. When that activity relates to illegal drugs, courts more readily approve warrantless searches and seizures despite the Supreme Court's holding in *Vale*. This is due in part to the courts' willingness to take judicial notice of the dangerousness of drug law enforcement: persons involved in illegal drug operations are assumed to be armed and desperate, because their activities involve commodities worth thousands—sometimes millions—of dollars, and because the penalties for dealing in illegal drugs are very severe. Moreover, courts emphasize the uniquely evanescent nature of the fruits, evidence, and instrumentalities of illegal drug operations, much of which might easily be flushed down toilets or put down sinks. Finally, there is a possibility that persons involved in illegal drug operations may themselves be using narcotics, a factor that courts assume heightens the danger to officers and others. As a result of these factors, warrantless searches and seizures are frequently approved in drug cases based on claims of exigent circumstances.

Let us examine two cases in order to observe how courts work with these general rules in the context of narcotics operations. In *United States v. Rubin*,[53] federal narcotics agents received information that a shipping crate contained hashish. They later observed the crate as it was delivered to the suspect's home. Later, when the suspect was arrested near a neighborhood gas station, he yelled out to the station attendant, "Call my brother." According to the agents, the statement indicated a strong possibility that the evidence at the house would be destroyed by the brother absent intervention. The agents immediately entered the house, found other men preparing the hashish for sale, and arrested them. Upholding the warrantless entry and search, the court crafted its own rule for narcotics cases:

> When Government agents . . . have probable cause to believe contraband is present and, in addition, based on the surrounding circum-

---

53. 474 F.2d 262 (3d Cir. 1973).

stances or the information at hand, they reasonably conclude that the evidence will be destroyed or removed before they can secure a search warrant, a warrantless search is justified. The emergency circumstances will vary from case to case, and the inherent necessities of the situation at the time must be scrutinized. Circumstances which have seemed relevant to courts include (1) the degree of urgency involved and the amount of time necessary to obtain a warrant; (2) reasonable belief that the contraband is about to be removed; (3) the possibility of danger to police officers guarding the contraband while a search warrant is sought; (4) information indicating the possessors of the contraband are aware that the police are on their trail; and (5) the ready destructibility of the contraband and the knowledge that efforts to dispose of narcotics and to escape are characteristic behavior of persons engaged in the narcotics traffic.

Reviewing the circumstances of the case in light of this general rule, the court concluded that the agents had acted reasonably when they entered the house without a warrant. The mere fact that they knew contraband existed within the house was not sufficient to allow them warrantless entry. However, the statement suggesting that the contraband might be destroyed did create sufficient exigencies to justify the warrantless entry.

We mentioned that danger to officers or others in narcotics cases also frequently justifies warrantless law enforcement activity. In *United States v. Crespo*,[54] the court considered a failed narcotics sting that created dangerous circumstances for an informant and officers. The danger convinced the court to uphold a warrantless home entry. Summarizing the reasons for its decision, the court noted that:

> Crespo already believed Polkowski to be a federal informant; her arrival at his door confirmed the discovery of both his identity and his address, information which Crespo logically could assume would be passed on immediately to the Government. Although we would be hesitant to hold that exigent circumstances sufficient to justify a warrantless arrest in the home exist whenever law enforcement officials make a narcotics suspect aware of their presence and intent to enter that home, our conclusion here is supported by more compelling evidence of the urgent need to make such an arrest.

Not infrequently, in narcotics cases and in other kinds of cases, defendants oppose the government's showing of exigent circumstances by alleging that the law enforcement officers themselves caused the exigency. Generally, if exigent circumstances arise as a direct result of irresponsible conduct by law enforcement officers, or as a direct result of conduct that the officers intended to create the exigent circumstances, their search and seizure activity will not be approved. But if the exigencies arise because suspects respond in a criminal fashion to routine police actions, the courts

---

54.   834 F.2d 267 (2d Cir. 1987).

are not reluctant to uphold the resulting search or seizure. The courts' approval is especially assured if the exigencies could not have been predicted at the outset of the encounter.[55]

When evaluating a warrantless search whose justification is exigent circumstances, bear in mind the Court's opinion in *Illinois v. McArthur*. There, the Court held that police acted constitutionally when they prohibited a resident from entering his home for two hours while they obtained a search warrant for marijuana. In light of *McArthur*, will it be more difficult for police to establish exigent circumstances sufficient to justify a warrantless entry? What if police had encountered McArthur while he was inside of his home, rather than outside? Justice Souter, who wrote a concurrence in the case, addressed this hypothetical, opining that police would have acted constitutionally had they entered the residence to prevent him from destroying the marijuana.

May police enter a home without a warrant when responding to a 3:00 a.m. noise complaint and, on the scene, witnessing (through the home's kitchen window) a tumultuous fracas that included a landed punch, bloody mouth, and several adults restraining a minor (the puncher)? What if the officer is not interested in breaking up the fight or investigating the situation, but "primarily motivated by intent to arrest and seize evidence?" The Court's answer to both these questions was "yes" in *Brigham City v. Charles W. Stuart*,[56] finding an objectively reasonable basis under these circumstances for police to believe an occupant was seriously injured or imminently threatened with serious injury, thus justifying a warrantless entry into the home, "regardless of an individual officer's state of mind."

In a concurring opinion, Justice Stevens characterized as "peculiar" that despite the Utah trial judge, the intermediate state appellate court, and the Utah Supreme Court all finding a Fourth Amendment violation, "neither trial counsel nor the trial judge bothered to identify the Utah Constitution as an independent basis for the decision because they did not expect the prosecution to appeal."[57] Said Stevens,

> [o]ur holding today addresses only the limitations placed by the Federal Constitution on the search at issue; we have no authority to decide whether the police in this case violated the Utah Constitution.[58]

As you work through the problems below, be sure to identify precisely which factors are present, or absent, and why those factors make a difference to the exigent circumstances analysis.

---

55. *See generally* United States v. MacDonald, 916 F.2d 766 (2d Cir. 1990). For a critical discussion of the *MacDonald* decision, *see* Peter E. Donohue, *The Second Circuit's Interpretation of Exigent Circumstances in* United States v. MacDonald*: The Erosion of the Warrant Requirement*, 65 ST. JOHN'S L. REV. 1163 (1991).

56. 547 U.S. 398 (2006).

57. *Id.* at 407–08 (Stevens, J., concurring).

58. *Id.* at 408.

PROBLEM 4–4

Dennis and Steven Kranig were brothers who shared a hobby: they were both bank robbers. The brothers always followed the same routine, with Dennis entering and robbing the bank, while Steven stayed outside as a lookout. They robbed a number of banks in the Hollywood area, always getting away but once leaving behind a very important clue: a surveillance photo showing both the thief and the lookout man.

One day as the pair was leaving a bank after another hit, they were spotted by Officer Jones, who had investigated several previous robberies and thought he recognized them from the surveillance photo. Officer Jones followed the brothers to a nearby hotel, into which they disappeared. Jones, joined by his partner Smith, spoke with the hotel manager and received permission to search for the two suspects. They progressed through the hallways of the hotel, knocking on each door in turn. The officers would identify themselves and order the occupants to open the door.

Finally, Officer Jones knocked on the door to room 222 and Dennis answered. Jones immediately recognized him from the photo. Dennis backed away from the door and the officers followed him in, guns drawn, and arrested him. While Jones dealt with Dennis, Officer Smith began searching the room and questioning Steven. Steven refused to give his name, claimed to have no I.D., and denied knowing Dennis.

Finally, Officer Jones approached Steven, recognized him from the photo, and placed him under arrest. Meanwhile, Officer Smith continued searching the room, turning up several pieces of evidence, including stolen money. Both suspects were properly advised of their rights upon arrest, and once in custody both gave full confessions.

Dennis eventually pled guilty to robbery and Steven went to trial. He now contends that the facts of the case reveal both an unlawful seizure of his person and an unlawful search of his room. Therefore, both the physical evidence and his statements should be suppressed.

Question: Assess Steven's claims. Can the search be justified by the "hot pursuit" doctrine? If not, were the officers still justified in their actions, or did they violate the suspects' Fourth Amendment rights?

PROBLEM 4–5

Mark Donohough was wanted for giving false information in connection with acquiring a firearm. Agents from the Bureau of Alcohol, Tobacco and Firearms, assisted by Oklahoma City Police officers, went to the home of Mark's parents with a valid arrest warrant. Upon entering the home, the officers found Mark in the doorway of his bedroom. Within two minutes of entry, Mark was handcuffed, placed in the custody of a BATF agent, and taken away.

After the arrest, the officers noticed a can of black powder and a hand grenade (later shown to be a souvenir paperweight) on top of the work-bench. They called a bomb technician and continued their search, later claiming as justification for the search a fear that the explosives threatened the neighborhood. For the next two hours, without a warrant or consent from either Mark or his parents, the officers systematically searched his bedroom and seized items. Three items were instrumental in charging Mark with possession of parts to convert a firearm into an illegal machine gun in violation of federal law. Mark now moves to suppress all evidence found in the search.

The first item, a rifle, was located in a closed, hard plastic case under a workbench. The officers observed this case close to Mark at the time of arrest and seized it immediately after he was handcuffed. They claim to have recognized it as a gun case, but the court notes that from its outward appearance it could have contained camera equipment or a musical instrument.

The second item was an M–16 bolt carrier assembly, found on top of an envelope on the workbench. The assembly was observed in plain view at the time of the arrest, but was not seized until later.

The final item was an envelope containing two sear kits (used to convert the rifle into an automatic weapon), found in a small file box on top of the workbench. These sear kits were discovered only after the bedroom had been secured and Mark had been taken away. The sear kits were not in plain view at the time of Mark's arrest and could not have been found without the prolonged search.

The government advances several arguments to contest Mark's motion to suppress. The government claims that exigent circumstances justified the search that led to finding the sear kits. As for the other items, the government claims that the rifle was seized properly incident to arrest. In addition, it claims that the plain view doctrine justifies the seizure of both the rifle and the M–16 bolt carrier assembly.

Question: As the judge in Mark's case, consider the government's arguments and assess any counter-arguments Mark might raise. For each item, decide whether the motion to suppress should be granted.

3.   PLAIN VIEW, TOUCH, AND SMELL

Police officers are permitted to seize contraband, fruits, evidence, and instrumentalities of crime that they find in "plain view." This widely-used doctrine increases the efficiency of law enforcement work by eliminating the warrant requirement in situations in which that requirement would serve no purpose. Application of the plain view doctrine depends on the presence of three elements. First, "[i]t is ... essential ... that the officer did not violate the Fourth Amendment in arriving at the place from which the evidence could be plainly viewed...." [Second,] its incriminating character "must ... be 'immediately apparent.' " "Third, the officer 'must also have a lawful right of access to the object itself.' "[59] After discussing

---

59.   Horton v. California, 496 U.S. 128, 140 (1990).

each of these elements, we will return to explain why the warrant requirement is considered expendable in plain view cases.

The first requirement limits the plain view doctrine to situations in which the officer observes the item from a lawful vantage point. In *Horton*, for example, an officer lawfully executing a search warrant for proceeds of an armed robbery viewed weapons that had been used to perpetrate the crime. Although the warrant did not authorize him to seize the weapons, he could do so pursuant to the plain view doctrine, in part because he was lawfully on the premises in which he viewed them.

The second limitation requires the officer to have probable cause to believe that the item is contraband, or a fruit, evidence, or instrumentality of crime. If the officer has only a hunch about the item, or even reasonable suspicion, it cannot be seized. In *Arizona v. Hicks*,[60] officers lawfully inside an apartment pursuant to a warrant observed stereo equipment that they believed to be stolen. Their belief was nothing more than a hunch, however, because they lacked specific facts about the equipment that would give rise to probable cause. One of the officers moved a piece of equipment to see its serial numbers, which he radioed back to headquarters. When the officer received confirmation that the serial numbers matched those of stolen equipment, he seized the equipment. The Supreme Court held the seizure invalid because the equipment's incriminating nature was not immediately apparent. Moreover, when the officer moved the equipment to observe serial numbers, he engaged in a warrantless search that was without justification.

In most situations, the incriminating nature of the item is immediately apparent through the use of the visual sense. The officer sees the item and recognizes it as contraband, or a fruit, evidence, or instrumentality of criminal activity. But the incriminating nature of the item may be recognized through other sensory organs as well. For example, the officer might conceivably feel, hear, or smell an item and immediately recognize its incriminating nature. The Court has recognized that the plain view doctrine is not limited to situations involving sight. In *Minnesota v. Dickerson*,[61] the Court explicitly extended the doctrine to situations involving "plain feel." In *Dickerson*, an officer had lawfully subjected the defendant to a *Terry* pat-down for weapons. The officer felt no weapons, but he did feel, in the pocket of Dickerson's thin jacket, a bag containing lumps of crack cocaine. The officer testified, "As I pat-searched the front of his body, I felt a lump, a small lump, in the front pocket. I examined it with my fingers and it slid and it felt to be a lump of crack cocaine in cellophane." The officer seized the cocaine and arrested Dickerson.

The Supreme Court held that "plain feel" seizures are consistent with the rationales underlying the plain view doctrine:

> The rationale of the plain view doctrine is that if contraband is left in open view and is observed by a police officer from a lawful vantage

---

60.   *See* Arizona v. Hicks, 480 U.S. 321 (1987).

61.   508 U.S. 366, 370 (1993).

point, there has been no invasion of a legitimate expectation of privacy and thus no "search" within the meaning of the Fourth Amendment— or at least no search independent of the initial intrusion that gave the officers their vantage point. The warrantless seizure of contraband that presents itself in this manner is deemed justified by the realization that resort to a neutral magistrate under such circumstances would often be impracticable and would do little to promote the objectives of the Fourth Amendment. The same can be said of tactile discoveries of contraband. If a police officer lawfully pats down a suspect's outer clothing and feels an object whose contour or mass makes its identity immediately apparent, there has been no invasion of the suspect's privacy beyond that already authorized by the officer's search for weapons; if the object is contraband, its warrantless seizure would be justified by the same practical considerations that inhere in the plain view context.

The Court went on to find, however, that the "plain feel" doctrine did not apply to the seizure in the case because the incriminating nature of the substance in Dickerson's pocket was not immediately apparent. Instead, "the officer determined that the item was contraband only after conducting a further search, one not authorized by *Terry* or by any other exception to the warrant requirement." The "further search" consisted of the officer's manipulation of the substance in the pocket *after* he realized that the pocket did not contain a weapon. That activity, which took only a few seconds, went "beyond what is necessary to determine if the suspect [was] armed, [and was] . . . no longer valid under *Terry*."

The third factor—that the officer is lawfully in a position to seize the item—reflects the rule that a warrantless entry into a private place cannot be justified without exigent circumstances, even when it is accompanied by probable cause. One can easily come up with a hypothetical in which the third factor is not present. Imagine that as an officer walks down the street she observes through a window the crown jewels, which had been stolen earlier that day. Does the plain view doctrine permit the officer to make a warrantless entry in order to seize the jewels? No. Although she occupied a lawful vantage point when she viewed the jewels, and although their incriminating nature was immediately apparent, she cannot seize them without crossing the threshold of the home—something that the plain view doctrine does not permit. The officer has the choice of obtaining a warrant to enter the home or of justifying a warrantless entry by another doctrine— the exigent circumstances exception, most likely.

Now that you are familiar with the doctrine's requirements, let us return to the question of its justification. Notice that the three requirements limit the doctrine to situations in which police activity implicates no privacy interests. As the Court observed, "[t]he 'plain-view' doctrine is often considered an exception to the general rule that warrantless searches are presumptively unreasonable, but this characterization overlooks the important difference between searches and seizures. If an article is already in plain view, neither its observation nor its seizure would involve any invasion of privacy.''[62] The only constitutionally protected interest at stake is the individual's possessory interest in the item seized, and the warrant requirement does little to protect that interest under the circumstances. The warrant requirement would substitute a magistrate's neutral judgment for that of the officer, but if the officer's judgment is incorrect, the item can be returned without much harm done to the owner: arguably, possessory interests, unlike privacy interests, are not irrevocably lost.

PROBLEM 4–6

In the Boson case in Chapter 1, assume that Boson is charged with drug offenses because of the cocaine Officer Glemp found in his trunk. Boson files a motion to suppress the cocaine arguing, among other things, that Officer Glemp's inspection of his glove compartment (and discovery of the rolling papers) was illegal.

Question: Can the prosecution argue that the plain view doctrine justifies the glove compartment search? Would the situation be different if Glemp had asked Boson for his vehicle registration and had seen the rolling papers when Boson opened the glove compartment to retrieve the registration?

PROBLEM 4–7

The Utah County Police Department initiated an investigation into Doug Weinberg's business. The business, which was known as Search Investigations, specialized in serving process and performing investigations. The police had learned that Doug was illegally using Utah County stationery to obtain business and was performing illegal wiretaps. Further, an informant told them that he had been involved in a kidnapping incident.

A search warrant obtained by the police allowed them to search Doug's home for four types of items: (1) letters or documents bearing the official Utah County seal; (2) letters or documents inscribed by any insignia which suggests affiliation with a government agency; (3) surveillance equipment such as electronic listening devices, radios, and cameras; and (4) business records and personal files. A team of several officers went to Doug's home to execute the warrant.

In the course of the search, one of the officers entered a closet containing rows of cardboard boxes. While looking behind the first row of boxes, he observed a double-barreled shotgun with a barrel approximately twelve to thirteen inches long. Possession of an unregistered sawed off shotgun (a shotgun having a barrel shorter than eighteen inches) is illegal. The officer seized the gun, along with several files found in the closet. The shotgun was later found to be unregistered.

At a subsequent criminal proceeding, Doug moved to suppress the shotgun. He argued that the shotgun was inappropriately seized, since it

---

62. Horton, 496 U.S. at 133.

was not in plain view, but was found during a "fishing expedition" by the officer. Doug also claims that since owning a sawed-off shotgun is illegal only if the gun is unregistered, the seizure did not fall within the plain view doctrine.

Question: Assess Doug's arguments for suppression of the shotgun. What is the best way to articulate these arguments? What are the best arguments with which the prosecution might counter Doug's motion?

PROBLEM 4–8

Review Problem 4–3 above, in which Officer Birch seized a hand-rolled cigarette from Freddie Mann's pocket.

Question: On what lawful basis could Officer Birch make the seizure? As Mann's lawyer, what argument(s) would you make to suppress the marijuana cigarette? What are the chances of your motion's success? If your motion is successful, what are the potential consequences to the automobile search?

4.   VEHICLE AND CONTAINER SEARCHES

a.   *Vehicle Searches: General Rules*

The Fourth Amendment protects against "unreasonable" searches and seizures wherever they may occur—in the home, office, or a vehicle. The Court has decided, however, that one's expectation of privacy differs in degree between a structure (be it home or office) and a vehicle.[63] Moreover, the mobility of vehicles makes them more problematic for law enforcement. For these reasons, the Court has fashioned a broad rule known as the "automobile exception" to the warrant requirement. The exception permits warrantless searches of motorized vehicles whenever law enforcement officials have probable cause to believe that fruits, evidence, or instrumentalities of criminal activity will be found therein. The exception extends to containers within vehicles as well. In short, vehicle searches require only probable cause in order to satisfy the Fourth Amendment.

Early Prohibition-era cases provide the backdrop for this doctrine. Typically, the cases involved seizures of bootlegged alcohol that smugglers transported by car or truck. These Prohibition-era searches and seizures (usually accomplished by agents from the Treasury Department, known popularly as "T–Men") were upheld by the Supreme Court in a series of cases beginning with *Carroll v. United States*.[64] Agents developed probable cause to believe that Carroll was transporting alcohol in his car. They stopped and searched the car without a warrant, and they then arrested Carroll and another individual after they found alcohol concealed within the backseat upholstery. The defendants asserted that the search and

---

63.   Whether this distinction is recognized by most citizens will be examined later in this section.

64.   267 U.S. 132, 146 (1925).

seizure violated their Fourth Amendment rights, but the Court disagreed. In rendering the decision that formed the basis for the automobile exception, the Court emphasized that warrantless vehicle searches did not violate the reasonableness requirement of the Fourth Amendment:

> On reason and authority the true rule is that if the search and seizure without a warrant are made upon probable cause, that is, upon the belief, reasonably arising out of circumstances known to the seizing officer, that an automobile or other vehicle contains that which by law is subject to search and seizure and destruction, the search and seizure are valid. The Fourth Amendment is to be construed in the light of what was deemed an unreasonable search and seizure when it was adopted, and in a manner which will conserve public interests as well as the interests and rights of individual citizens.

b.   *Mobility and Privacy Rationales*

The Court has articulated two rationales—mobility and privacy—as support for the automobile exception to the warrant requirement. To begin with mobility, there undoubtedly is a mobility inherent to vehicles that is unmatched in structures such as residences or offices. The Court has made much of this difference, contrasting in *Carroll* the "necessity for a search warrant between goods subject to forfeiture, when concealed in a dwelling house or similar place, and like goods in course of transportation and concealed in a movable vessel where they readily could be put out of reach of a search warrant." According to the Court, the Fourth Amendment does not require warrants for vehicles because they may disappear before a warrant can be obtained.

The mobility rationale remains an important underpinning of the automobile exception. In *California v. Carney,*[65] for example, the Court suggested that fixed, immovable "mobile homes" might not be subject to the exception even though they might technically be considered "vehicles." The Court suggested in that case that courts consider the following factors in distinguishing mobile homes from residences: "location, whether the vehicle is licensed, whether it is connected to utilities, and whether it has convenient access to a public road." On the other hand, movable vehicles are subject to the exception even where they have been taken into police control and no longer pose a threat of mobility. This rule was established in *Chambers v. Maroney.*[66] There, police officers stopped a vehicle which they had probable cause to believe contained fruits, evidence, and instrumentalities of an armed robbery, took it to the police station, and searched it thoroughly without a warrant. The Court held the search to be valid under the automobile exception, and interestingly enough, maintained that one reason for allowing the warrantless search at the station house was that cars are inherently mobile. Many scholars have questioned the Court's reasoning in *Chambers*, and its consequences remain unclear. One thing

---

65.   471 U.S. 386 (1985).

66.   399 U.S. 42 (1970).

appears to be certain: it cannot be argued that mobility is the only rationale underlying the automobile exception. Something else has influenced the Court's decision to exempt vehicles from the warrant requirement, and that obviously is the Court's assessment that vehicles do not invoke the same kind of privacy interests as do structures.

On numerous occasions the Court has stated that individuals have lesser expectations of privacy in vehicles as opposed to homes or offices:

> One has a lesser expectation of privacy in a motor vehicle because its function is transportation, and it seldom serves as one's residence or as the repository of personal effects. A car has little capacity for escaping public scrutiny. It travels public thoroughfares where both its occupants and its contents are in plain view.... This is not to say that no part of the interior of an automobile has Fourth Amendment protection; the exercise of a desire to be mobile does not, of course, waive one's right to be free from unreasonable intrusion. But insofar as Fourth Amendment protection extends to a motor vehicle, it is the right of privacy that is the touchstone of our inquiry.[67]

In addition to the inherently less private nature of vehicles, the Court has observed that vehicles are heavily regulated: they are subject to state licensing requirements that further limit their owners' and occupants' privacy interests,[68] as you will see later in this chapter when we discuss the "special needs" exception to the warrant requirement.

The Court's approach to vehicle searches has caused many to wonder whether the average citizen realizes that he or she loses some constitutional protections when operating a motor vehicle. Some scholars have argued that the average citizen would not distinguish vehicles from structures in terms of the privacy expected in each.[69] Nevertheless, the doctrine of reduced expectations of privacy in vehicles appears to be firmly ensconced in the Court's Fourth Amendment jurisprudence. The Court relied on this doctrine recently to uphold the warrantless search of two cars.[70] Police had probable cause to believe that the cars contained drugs, but there was no risk that the drugs would be moved or destroyed. The Court stated that exigent circumstances were not needed because individuals enjoy reduced expectations of privacy in automobiles. According to the Court, so long as a vehicle is readily mobile, nothing more than probable cause is required to justify a search.

c. Containers Within Vehicles

In *California v. Acevedo*,[71] the Court held that containers in cars may be searched under the automobile exception whether probable cause relates

---

67. Cardwell v. Lewis, 417 U.S. 583, 590–91 (1974).

68. Cady v. Dombrowski, 413 U.S. 433, 441 (1973).

69. For an interesting discussion of warrantless searches as applied to camping tents and recreational vehicles, *see* Robert J. Leibovich, *Privacy Goes Camping: Staking a Claim on the Fourth Amendment*, 26 U. MEM. L. REV. 293 (1995).

70. Pennsylvania v. Labron, 518 U.S. 938 (1996).

71. 500 U.S. 565 (1991).

to the entire car or only to the container. *Acevedo* involved a sting operation in which officers observed a package of marijuana taken into an apartment. Later, they saw the defendant enter the apartment and emerge, after about ten minutes, carrying a brown paper bag that looked full. The defendant placed the bag into the trunk of a car and began to drive away, but officers stopped him and recovered marijuana from the bag. Moving to suppress the fruits of the search, the defendant argued that the officers should have detained the bag until they could obtain a warrant, but the Court disagreed. Under the automobile exception, the Court held that there are no boundaries on container searches other than probable cause. That is, officers may search containers in vehicles so long as they have probable cause to believe that the objects of those searches may be found therein.

The Court held in *Wyoming v. Houghton*[72] that police may search containers within the scope of the probable cause they have developed, regardless of who owns those containers. In *Houghton*, a police officer stopped an automobile for traffic offenses. During the stop, the officer noticed a syringe in the driver's pocket, and the driver acknowledged that he used the syringe to take drugs. The officer then searched the car. On the back seat, he found a purse, which was identified by one of the passengers as hers. A search of the purse revealed drugs. The passenger, Sandra Houghton, was prosecuted. She filed a motion to suppress, contending that the search of her purse had violated the Fourth Amendment because the officer knew the purse was hers and had no reason to suspect its contents or to connect her with any illegal activity. Applying the automobile exception, the Wyoming Supreme Court agreed with her, but the United States Supreme Court reversed. Writing for a 6–person majority, Justice Scalia stated "[w]hen there is probable cause to search for contraband in a car, it is reasonable for police officers—like customs officials in the Founding era—to examine packages and containers without a showing of individualized probable cause for each one. A passenger's personal belongings, just like the driver's belongings or containers attached to the car like a glove compartment, are 'in' the car, and the officer has probable cause to search for contraband in the car." Justice Scalia commented that he would reach the same result ... because of the passenger's reduced expectation of privacy and the heightened needs of law enforcement to deal with a vehicle of ready mobility.

PROBLEM 4–9

In the *Boson* case in Chapter 1, assume that Officer Glemp did not search Boson's car after seeing the rolling papers in the glove compartment. Instead, he returned to his police car, where he heard over his radio that a warrant for Boson's arrest had been issued for the Susan Oldham murder. Glemp arrested Boson and transported him to the lock-up. Meanwhile, a police tow-truck towed Boson's car to a police lot, where it was

---

72.   526 U.S. 295 (1999).

thoroughly searched. Boson is charged with drug offenses based on the cocaine found in his trunk, and he moves to suppress the cocaine.

Question: Can Boson successfully argue that the automobile exception does not apply? Why or why not? Is there another warrant exception that might apply?

PROBLEM 4–10

Ishmael Johansson is a retired sea captain who lives alone on the edge of town. Johansson suffers from the early stages of Alzheimer's disease and has been known to engage in violence. Rumors abound that years ago, on a tropical island, he viciously murdered his first mate by impaling him with a harpoon. Recently, Johansson has been seen driving around town with a six-foot harpoon in his car, and police fear that he poses a threat to the safety of the community. Officer Montgomery unearths a little-known statute prohibiting the possession of "knives, switchblades, or any sharpened metal blade, which is in excess of 18 inches in length."

Montgomery observes Johansson park his car in front of the local grocery store. While Johansson is inside the store, Montgomery takes the opportunity to search the vehicle. When he fails to locate the harpoon in the passenger compartment, he opens the glove compartment and discovers a severed human ear. Moving his search to the trunk, Montgomery locates the harpoon and a large quantity of home-made wormwood, an illegal spirit.

A crime lab analysis reveals that the ear belonged to a murder victim in a nearby county, and Johansson is charged with the murder, along with charges relating to the wormwood. Despite his mental condition, the judge rules him fit for trial.

Question: You have been assigned to prosecute Johansson, who has filed a motion to suppress the ear and the wormwood. What is your response? How should the court rule?

PROBLEM 4–11

At approximately 2:00 a.m., Officer Ireniac was conducting a routine police patrol of a state park. He observed a mobile home parked at a campsite at the top of a steep hill. Ireniac could see that the mobile home was connected to an electrical outlet at the site but easily could be unplugged. He checked the electrical connection to make sure that it was fully plugged in, since it was raining hard and was expected to freeze. As he did so, he noticed that the vehicle was licensed for road travel.

Ireniac's inspection of the mobile home exterior was cut short when a call from Bob Farcus, a fellow officer, came through on the squad car radio. Farcus informed Ireniac that he had stopped a car carrying two men on a highway a few miles from the state park. Farcus explained that he had smelled methamphetamine and marijuana on driver's licenses that the men displayed, and that his observations prompted a search uncovering a small bag of marijuana. Farcus stated that both men were in custody. He asked Ireniac to stop by a mobile home where the men claim to be staying—the same mobile home at which Ireniac had stopped on patrol—because the men admitted that "there might be" drug paraphernalia there.

Ireniac returned to the mobile home and knocked on the door. When no one answered, he pushed its door open and searched it thoroughly. In a box under a table, he found glassware, chemicals, and books all used for methamphetamine production.

Question: The men Farcus arrested were charged with various drug offenses. They move for suppression of the items seized from the mobile home on the basis that Ireniac did not have the right to search the mobile home without a warrant. Analyze the motion.

PROBLEM 4–12

A confidential informant tells police that Maurice Kronin, who works at the local barbershop, carries a loaded pistol of "an illegal variety" in his brown backpack to and from work every day. Further, the informant tells them that next Tuesday at 3:00 p.m., Maurice will be picked up from the barbershop by a man driving a dark blue Nissan Sentra, license number WYA–094. Since the informant has provided reliable information on ten to fifteen previous occasions, the police send two undercover detectives to investigate the tip. The detectives park across the street from the barber shop at the hour indicated by the informant. They observe Maurice leaving the shop with a brown backpack. He is picked up by a car that exactly matches the informant's description. Maurice places the brown backpack in the trunk of the car.

The detectives follow the car for several blocks and pull it over. They pat down the men and ask the driver to open the trunk. In the backpack, they find a fully-loaded 9mm Glock handgun. Maurice is arrested on charges of possession of a firearm and possession of unregistered ammunition.

Question: Assume that the stop of the vehicle was lawful. Maurice argues that the search of the backpack was illegal since the detectives had neither warrant nor probable cause. He seeks to have the evidence of the handgun suppressed and the charges dismissed. As his attorney, what arguments would you raise? What would a court probably decide?

5.   "SPECIAL NEEDS" SEARCHES AND SEIZURES

"Special needs" searches and seizures are those conducted for a non-criminal investigation-related purpose. These are sometimes referred to as regulatory or administrative searches and seizures, because they further regulatory or administrative interests of state and federal governments. For such searches and seizures, the Court eliminates or modifies both the warrant requirement and the probable cause requirement. Instead, reasonableness balancing is undertaken to come up with a new rule—for example: "no warrant but reasonable suspicion," or a "warrant but one justified by certain administrative criteria (e.g., a safety inspection of any uninspected building over a certain age) and not requiring probable cause." While many new special needs cases are likely to be unique in some significant respects and thus not within a previously-decided rule for a certain class of cases, the Court will at least analogize to aspects of, and justifications for, earlier rules in crafting a new one.

There are always two steps in the analysis of special needs cases: first (a threshold issue) a court must determine whether the governmental purpose truly is regulatory rather than criminal law enforcement; and second, if the purpose is regulatory, the court must balance that regulatory interest against the individual interest infringed upon.

a. Determining Governmental Purpose

Since only non-criminal-investigation interests may be advanced by the search or seizure, there is a "no pretext" requirement: if the purported administrative purpose is just a smokescreen to circumvent the usual warrant and probable cause requirements, the search or seizure will not fall into the special needs category and will be subjected to ordinary Fourth Amendment analysis.[73] Logic would suggest, therefore, that whether the activity is engaged in by the police or, instead, by government agents unconnected with law enforcement should be critical in determining whether to treat a search or seizure as advancing special needs. While this factor indeed seems to carry weight in the inquiry, it is clearly not decisive because the Court has upheld arguable special needs searches and seizures conducted by the police under circumstances likely to result in someone's criminal prosecution—most notably drunk driver roadblocks.

b. Balancing the Interests

Once a court determines that a search or seizure advances special governmental needs, then it must balance those needs against the interests of individuals affected by the government action. Several factors will enter into the courts' balancing process. First, the weight of the state's purported non-criminal-investigation interest must be determined. Related to this inquiry are two others: (a) the effectiveness of the chosen means in attaining the states' goals; and (b) the availability of other, less restrictive (not necessarily the least restrictive) alternative means for pursuing those goals.

Second, the degree of the individual's interest must be gauged. Generally, searches and seizures of cars or businesses are viewed as less invasive than are searches and seizures of homes or persons. Additionally, individuals involved in "pervasively regulated industries" and heavily monitored people (children, for example), are considered to enjoy lower protections, because a history of extensive government supervision has exposed their

---

73. *See* Whren v. United States, 517 U.S. 806 (1996).

activities to public view. You may find this line of reasoning troubling, because it arguably makes the constitutionality of special needs searches and seizures a self-fulfilling prophecy: if the government extends its regulatory reach widely, it will reduce expectations of privacy or liberty interests and corresponding Fourth Amendment protections. The solution here may be the length of time that government regulation has existed in a particular area. If long tolerated by legislators and private citizens, such regulation and the corresponding reductions in individual interests may simply reflect the will of the people. To the extent that "reasonableness" is a majoritarian concept, or at least includes majority views as a relevant factor, a history of extensive government regulation may make much sense as part of the reasonableness inquiry. Moreover, the willingness of legislatures and administrative agencies to adopt such regulations may indicate a majority sentiment that there is a grave problem for the government to address, thus making the extent of government regulation an indicator of the importance of the government's need as well as the size of the individual's interest. Finally, even after the size of the interest is determined, the degree to which the regulation in fact invades that interest must be measured, for some invasions may be relatively small. Thus, taking urine samples as part of a drug-screening program is invasive of privacy, but that invasiveness can be reduced in many ways, such as having same-sex observers.

Third, limitations must be placed on the discretion of government actors. While warrants ordinarily serve this purpose, in special needs cases there usually are strong government justifications for rejecting the traditional warrant requirement. But in its place, there must be other adequate procedures designed to avoid abuse of government discretion. Clear rules in statutes, regulations, or internal administrative policies telling government actors when and how to conduct their searches may be one way to limit such discretion.

c.   Recognized Areas of Special Needs

Below are summaries of special governmental needs that the Court has evaluated. As you explore these, make sure to identify (1) the threshold issue of governmental purpose, and (2) the factors that affected the Court's balancing process.

(I) HEALTH AND SAFETY INSPECTIONS

Federal, state, and local governments often pursue health and safety goals through regulations. For example, local fire codes require the installation of smoke detectors in residences and certain other types of buildings, and local inspectors typically are authorized to conduct searches to ensure compliance with the requirement. It would be burdensome and dangerous to require inspectors to obtain a warrant, based on probable cause to believe that a building lacks compliance, before engaging in such an inspection. On the other hand, the public would not be happy with a regulatory regime that permitted inspectors to demand entrance to residences at will. As a compromise among these interests, most local fire codes modify or eliminate the traditional probable cause justification while requiring "area-wide warrants" giving inspectors permission to conduct searches at certain intervals. Courts generally uphold these types of regulatory searches. But they are careful to point out that Fourth Amendment interests remain important considerations in these sorts of regulatory schemes. For example, in *Camara v. Municipal Court*,[74] a homeowner claimed Fourth Amendment protection against a warrantless inspection of his home by a health inspector acting pursuant to the San Francisco Housing Code. The Court held that the Fourth Amendment applied, saying "even the most law-abiding citizen has a very tangible interest in limiting the circumstances under which the sanctity of his home may be broken by official authority, for the possibility of criminal entry under the guise of official sanction is a serious threat to personal and family security." Furthermore, a warrant was needed because otherwise "the occupant has no way of knowing whether enforcement of the municipal code involved requires inspection of his premises, no way of knowing the lawful limits of the inspector's power to search, and no way of knowing whether the inspector himself is acting under proper authorization." However, a weighing of government and individual interests required substantially modifying the usual warrant rules:

> [T]here can be no ready test for determining reasonableness other than by balancing the need to search against the invasion which the search entails.... [W]e think that a number of persuasive factors combine to support the reasonableness of area code-enforcement inspections. First, such programs have a long history of judicial and public acceptance. Second, the public interest demands that all dangerous conditions be prevented or abated, yet it is doubtful that any other canvassing technique would achieve acceptable results. Many such conditions— faulty wiring is an obvious example—are not observable from outside the building and indeed may not be apparent to the inexpert occupant himself. Finally, because the inspections are neither personal in nature nor aimed at the discovery of evidence of crime, they involve a relatively limited invasion of the urban citizen's privacy.

Consequently, "probable cause" was met "if reasonable legislative or administrative standards for conducting an area inspection," such as passage of time, nature of the building, and condition of the overall area, were met, but individualized knowledge about the interior condition of a particular dwelling was not required.

PROBLEM 4–13

Animal Control Officer Frank Wagon received an anonymous telephone tip that a dog bite had occurred earlier that day at the residence of Daniel and Beverly Quackenbush. When officer Wagon approached the Quackenbushes at their residence, they told him they did not own the dog

---

74. 387 U.S. 523 (1967).

but were simply watching it until the owners returned. Because Wagon could not determine whether the dog had been vaccinated for rabies, he ordered it quarantined. Beverly Quackenbush signed an agreement to keep the dog quarantined at her home for ten days and to notify the authorities immediately if the dog escaped, became ill, or died. Later, Wagon was told by his supervisor that the dog could not be quarantined at the Quackenbush home because they were not the dog's owners. The next day, Wagon returned to the Quackenbush residence and ordered Daniel Quackenbush to turn over the dog to him. Daniel insisted the dog was healthy and had bitten no one. Daniel refused to produce the dog without a search warrant. Officer Wagon thereupon immediately obtained and executed an administrative warrant pursuant to the following statute:

> Any person who, after notice, violates any order of a local health officer concerning the isolation or quarantine of an animal of a species subject to rabies, which has bitten or otherwise exposed a person to rabies or who, after that order, fails to produce the animal upon demand of the local health officer, is guilty of a misdemeanor. Upon such refusal, an Animal Control Officer may obtain a search of a home or business to locate the animal. The warrant shall be issued based upon an affidavit attesting to the violation of the health officer's order noted above in this section. Upon such proof, the local Health Commissioner may issue a warrant specifying the animal to be searched for, the location, time, and duration of the search.

Officer Wagon searched the Quackenbush home and found the dog in the basement. The dog was tested and found not to be rabid.

Question: The District Attorney has asked you to prepare a memorandum advising him whether to proceed with prosecuting Daniel Quackenbush for violating the above statute. Specifically, you must advise the D.A. of two things: first, the likelihood that Quackenbush will succeed in a motion to suppress; and, second, if he will, whether that is based on the specific facts of this case or on constitutional flaws in the statute. If the latter, the D.A. wants you to advise him on what changes he should seek from the legislature. What will you tell him?

PROBLEM 4–14

Review Problem 2–39 concerning the housing project residents who voted to permit certain warrantless searches. Could those searches be justified as administrative searches. Why or why not?

(II) PERVASIVELY REGULATED INDUSTRIES

Where the government's special needs concern pervasively regulated industries, the Court has not generally required regulatory searches to be authorized by warrants, in part because of the lesser expectation of privacy in that setting. In addition, the Court has recognized that the traditional notice requirement is relaxed because it may defeat the purposes of the inspection.

Below is a brief excerpt from *New York v. Burger*[75] reciting the facts of the case. *Burger* was the first Supreme Court case overtly raising the problem of "dual purposes:" a search or seizure that seems to serve regulatory goals as well as the goals of criminal law enforcement. We delete the reasoning because in later cases the Court clarified its dual purposes rule: where the *primary purpose* is regulatory, a dual purpose search or seizure will be treated as a special needs action. Nevertheless, the *Burger* facts are useful to examine and highlight the nature of the problem.

New York v. Burger

482 U.S. 691 (1987).

■ Blackmun, J. This case presents the question whether the warrantless search of an automobile junkyard, conducted pursuant to a statute authorizing such a search, falls within the exception to the warrant requirement for administrative inspections of pervasively regulated industries. The case also presents the question whether an otherwise proper administrative inspection is unconstitutional because the ultimate purpose of the regulatory statute pursuant to which the search is done—the deterrence of criminal behavior—is the same as that of penal laws, with the result that the inspection may disclose violations not only of the regulatory statute but also of the penal statutes.

I

Respondent Joseph Burger is the owner of a junkyard in Brooklyn, N.Y. His business consists, in part, of the dismantling of automobiles and the selling of their parts. His junkyard is an open lot with no buildings. A high metal fence surrounds it, wherein are located, among other things, vehicles and parts of vehicles. At approximately noon on November 17, 1982, Officer Joseph Vega and four other plainclothes officers, all members of the Auto Crimes Division of the New York City Police Department, entered respondent's junkyard to conduct an inspection pursuant to N.Y.Veh. & Traf.Law § 415–a5 (McKinney 1986).[a] On any given day, the

---

75.   482 U.S. 691 (1987).

a.   This statute reads in pertinent part: "Records and identification. (a) Any records required by this section shall apply only to vehicles or parts of vehicles for which a certificate of title has been issued by the commissioner [of the Department of Motor Vehicles] or which would be eligible to have such a certificate of title issued. Every person required to be registered pursuant to this section shall maintain a record of all motor vehicles, trailers, and major component parts thereof, coming into his possession together with a record of the disposition of any such motor vehicle, trailer or part thereof and shall maintain proof of ownership for any motor vehicle, trailer or major component part thereof while in his possession. Such records shall be maintained in a manner and form prescribed by the commissioner. The commissioner may, by regulation, exempt vehicles or major component parts of vehicles from all or a portion of the record keeping requirements based upon the age of the vehicle if he deems that such record keeping requirements would serve no substantial value. Upon request of an agent of the commissioner or of any police officer and during his regular and usual business hours, a vehicle dismantler shall produce such records and permit said agent or police officer to examine them and any vehicles or parts of vehicles which are

Division conducts from 5 to 10 inspections of vehicle dismantlers, automobile junkyards, and related businesses.

Upon entering the junkyard, the officers asked to see Burger's license[b] and his "police book"—the record of the automobiles and vehicle parts in his possession. Burger replied that he had neither a license nor a police book. The officers then announced their intention to conduct a § 415–a5 inspection. Burger did not object. In accordance with their practice, the officers copied down the Vehicle Identification Numbers (VINs) of several vehicles and parts of vehicles that were in the junkyard. After checking these numbers against a police computer, the officers determined that respondent was in possession of stolen vehicles and parts. Accordingly, Burger was arrested and charged with five counts of possession of stolen property and one count of unregistered operation as a vehicle dismantler, in violation of § 415–a1.

In the Kings County Supreme Court, Burger moved to suppress the evidence obtained as a result of the inspection, primarily on the ground that § 415–a5 was unconstitutional. After a hearing, the court denied the motion. It reasoned that the junkyard business was a "pervasively regulated" industry in which warrantless administrative inspections were appropriate; that the statute was properly limited in "time, place and scope," and that, once the officers had reasonable cause to believe that certain vehicles and parts were stolen, they could arrest Burger and seize the property without a warrant.

... When respondent moved for reconsideration ... the court ... reaffirmed its earlier determination in the instant case that § 415–a5 was constitutional. For the same reasons, the Appellate Division affirmed. The New York Court of Appeals, however, reversed. In its view, § 415–a5 violated the Fourth Amendment's prohibition of unreasonable searches and seizures. According to the Court of Appeals, "the fundamental defect [of § 415–a5] ... is that [it authorize[s]] searches undertaken solely to uncover evidence of criminality and not to enforce a comprehensive regulatory scheme. The asserted 'administrative schem[e]' here [is], in reality, designed simply to give the police an expedient means of enforcing penal sanctions for possession of stolen property." In contrast to the statutes authorizing warrantless inspections whose constitutionality this Court has upheld, § 415–a5, it was said, "do[es] little more than authorize general searches, including those conducted by the police, of certain commercial premises." To be sure, with its license and recordkeeping requirements, and with its authorization for inspections of records, § 415–a appears to be administrative in character. "It fails to satisfy the constitutional requirements for a valid, comprehensive regulatory scheme, however, inasmuch as

---

subject to the record keeping requirements of this section and which are on the premises.... The failure to produce such records or to permit such inspection on the part of any person required to be registered pursuant to this section as required by this paragraph shall be a class A misdemeanor."

b. An individual operating a vehicle-dismantling business in New York is required to have a license.

it permits searches, such as conducted here, of vehicles and vehicle parts notwithstanding the absence of any records against which the findings of such a search could be compared." Accordingly, the only purpose of such searches is to determine whether a junkyard owner is storing stolen property on business premises.

NOTES AND QUESTIONS

1. The *Burger* Court upheld the validity of the search on the facts before it, viewing the search as an administrative one. In assessing the reasonableness of the search, the Court relied in part on the nature of the junkyard business as long "pervasively-regulated," although its manifestation here in the form of vehicle dismantling was a relatively new type of commercial venture. The Court also saw the search as serving the state's "substantial interest in eradicating automobile theft" given that automobile junkyards and vehicle dismantlers "provide the major market for stolen vehicles and vehicle parts." Moreover, said the Court, unannounced, even frequent, inspections were necessary to serve as a credible deterrent to dealing in stolen automobile parts. Furthermore, the statute authorizing the search informed vehicle dismantlers that they could be subject to inspection on a regular basis, a form of notice and statement of authority akin to that obtained via a search warrant. Finally, searches were limited to regular and usual business hours, and their scope was limited to examining pertinent records and vehicle parts on the premise. The Court apparently conceded that the search had dual purposes, but noted that nothing prevents the state from adopting both regulatory and penal means for addressing a social problem.

2. Only later did the Court clearly and expressly adopt a "primary purpose" test, though the *Burger* Court arguably did so implicitly. Was the Court correct to conclude implicitly that the "primary purpose" in the legislation before it was administrative? What criteria should distinguish a "primary" from a "secondary" purpose? What particular facts are central to your decision and why? Can you conceive of an auto-dismantling inspections statute that the court would characterize as serving primarily crime-control purposes?

3. If the Court was right to treat this search as a special needs one, was the Court also correct in finding the search "reasonable"? Why?

PROBLEM 4–15

A Maine statute provides that the commissioner of the Department of Agriculture, Food, and Rural Resources or his duly authorized representative:

> shall have free access, ingress and egress to any place ... wherein potatoes are packed, stored, transported, sold, offered or exposed for sale or for transportation. He may ... open any container and may take samples therefrom.

Question: The Maine Commissioner of the Department of Agriculture, Food, and Rural Resources is concerned that potato quality and disease inspections pursuant to this statute may be unconstitutional, and he wonders whether adopting regulations may help to cure the constitutional problem by modifying when and how such searches shall be done. You are his general counsel. What advice will you give him?

(III) DRUG TESTING

The leading cases involving special needs searches of individuals have usually involved searches of persons or personal items seeking evidence of tobacco, alcohol, or drug usage. These cases can be subdivided into three categories: those involving children, those involving adults working in safety-sensitive contexts, and those involving adults in non-sensitive contexts. The Court has dealt with these differently.

The Court generally defers to governmental judgments about searches of children. In *New Jersey v. T.L.O.*,[76] for example, a high school teacher reported T.L.O. to the Vice–Principal for smoking in the lavatory, in violation of a school rule. The Vice–Principal opened T.L.O.'s purse, removed a pack of cigarettes, and, in the process, saw cigarette rolling papers, which he associated with marijuana usage. He therefore searched her purse thoroughly, finding a small amount of marijuana, a pipe, a number of plastic index cards, a substantial quantity of money, and an index card that appeared to be a list of students who owed T.L.O. money, as well as two letters implicating T.L.O. in marijuana dealing. The Vice–Principal turned this evidence over to the police, and T.L.O. subsequently confessed to selling marijuana. In a later delinquency proceeding, she moved to suppress both the evidence found in her purse and the confession. The Supreme Court held the warrantless search valid even though based only on reasonable suspicion. In doing so, the Court emphasized the need for discipline in the schools; the reality that a warrant would interfere with the swift and informal disciplinary procedures needed in schools; and the importance of achieving a balance that did not ignore the legitimate privacy expectations of school children. The warrantless reasonable suspicion standard, in the Court's view, struck the appropriate balance.

In *Vernonia School District 47J v. Acton*,[77] the Court upheld the constitutionality of a suspicionless random drug testing program required for students participating in high school or grade school interscholastic athletics in Vernonia, Oregon. The policy resulted from rising disciplinary incidents, rudeness, and profanity among all students, and injuries to student athletes, who were both admired and perceived as drug culture leaders. Students wanting to participate in athletics were required to sign a form consenting to the testing, with the parents' written permission. Each week 10 percent of athletes' names were drawn for urine testing by same sex-monitors. Boys remained fully clothed at the urinal, their backs to the

---

76.   469 U.S. 325 (1985).

77.   515 U.S. 646 (1995).

monitors. Girls produced samples in an enclosed stall, with the monitor outside, listening for the normal sounds of urination and then testing the vial for temperature and tampering. James Acton, a seventh-grader who wanted to play football, refused to sign the consent form and was therefore denied participation. The Actons brought suit seeking declaratory and injunctive relief for violation of Fourth and Fourteenth Amendment rights.

Upholding the school district's actions, the Court stressed the school's "custodial and tutelary responsibility for children," which routinely required, for example, that students submit to invasive medical examinations and vaccinations for their own good, thus reducing the children's' legitimate privacy expectations. For athletes, these expectations were sharply reduced:

> Legitimate privacy expectations are even less with regard to student athletes. School sports are not for the bashful. They require "suiting up" before each practice or event, and showering and changing afterwards. Public school locker rooms, the usual sites for these activities, are not notable for the privacy they afford. The locker rooms in Vernonia are typical: no individual dressing rooms are provided; shower heads are lined up against a wall, unseparated by any sort of partition or curtain; not even all the toilet stalls have doors.

> There is an additional respect in which school athletes have a reduced expectation of privacy. By choosing to "go out for the team," they voluntarily subject themselves to a degree of regulation even higher than that imposed on students generally. In Vernonia's public schools, they must submit to a pre-season physical exam ... , they must acquire adequate insurance coverage or sign an insurance waiver, maintain a minimum grade point average, and comply with any "rules of conduct, dress, training hours and related matters as may be established for each sport by the head coach and athletic director with the principal's approval." Somewhat like adults who choose to participate in a "closely regulated industry," students who voluntarily participate in school athletics have reason to expect intrusions upon normal rights and privileges, including privacy.

The Court concluded that, while excretory functions are shielded by great privacy, the procedures followed here (males fully clothed while observed, females alone in private stalls during urination) minimized privacy invasion. Furthermore, no testing was done for epilepsy, diabetes, pregnancy, or other private conditions, and test results were disclosed only to a limited class of school personnel and were not given to law enforcement authorities. Moreover, the nature and immediacy of the government interests were great. While conceding it had previously suggested that governmental interests in special needs cases must be "compelling," the Court defined "compelling interests" flexibly:

> It is a mistake, however, to think that the phrase "compelling state interest," in the Fourth Amendment context, describes a fixed, minimum quantum of governmental concern, so that one can dispose of a case by answering in isolation the question: Is there a compelling state

interest here? Rather, the phrase describes an interest which appears important enough to justify the particular search at hand, in light of other factors which show the search to be relatively intrusive upon a genuine expectation of privacy. Whether that relatively high degree of government concern is necessary in this case or not, we think it is met.

The compelling interest in *Vernonia*, the Court concluded, was sufficient because the school years are the time when the "physical, psychological, and addictive effects of drugs are most severe," impairing "maturing nervous systems" and leading to quicker and more lasting addiction than is true for adults. These evils are visited on those for whom the state has undertaken a special responsibility for care, and athletes in particular faced substantial physical risks from impaired performance. Regarding the efficacy of the programs, the Court noted its repeated refusal "to declare that only the 'least intrusive' search practicable can be reasonable under the Fourth Amendment." Consequently the Court rejected the defense argument that a "less intrusive alternative," namely drug testing on suspicion, should have been followed, for that alternative may be impracticable because, among other reasons, it added to the "ever-expanding diversionary duties of schoolteachers the new function of spotting and bringing to account drug abuse, a task for which they are ill prepared." The random testing program is better suited to the job, concluded the Court, and was sufficiently efficacious given the "self-evident [truth] that a drug problem largely fueled by the 'role model' effect of athletes' drug use, and of particular danger to athletes, is effectively addressed by making sure that athletes do not use drugs."[78]

The Court took its holding in *Vernonia* one step further in *Board of Education v. Earls*,[79] where it upheld suspicionless drug testing of students involved in any competitive extracurricular activity. Writing for a 5–person majority, Justice Thomas declared that the testing policy "reasonably serves the School District's important interest in detecting and preventing drug use among its students." Engaging in a "fact-specific balancing of the intrusion on the children's Fourth Amendment rights against the promotion of legitimate governmental interests," Justice Thomas found that (1) student privacy interests were limited in the context of extracurricular activities, (2) the intrusion on those interests was negligible, and (3) the school district's interest was important. Thomas specifically rejected the lower court's "novel test that 'any district seeking to impose a random

---

78. The Court cautioned, however, against the assumption that suspicionless drug testing would pass muster in other contexts. The most significant element in this case, said the Court, was that the testing was done "in furtherance of the government's responsibilities, under a public school system, as guardian and tutor of children entrusted to its care." Consequently, just as when government in its role as employer searches employees, the relevant question is "whether the intrusion is one a reasonable employer might engage in, so here the question was whether 'the search is one that a reasonable guardian and tutor might undertake.' "Additionally, the Court stressed the importance of the "primary guardians of Vernonia's school children"—the parents—supporting the program, with no parents other than the Actons objecting.

79. 536 U.S. 822 (2002).

suspicionless drug testing policy as a condition to participation in a school activity must demonstrate that there is some identifiable drug abuse problem among a sufficient number of those subject to the testing, such that testing that group of students will actually redress its drug problem.'" Thomas remarked, "[I]t would be difficult to administer such a test," and "we refuse to fashion what would in effect be a constitutional quantum of drug use necessary to show a 'drug problem.'" Justice Breyer, concurring, noted that the Court's decision "preserves an option for a conscientious objector. He can refuse testing while paying a price (nonparticipation) that is serious, but less severe than expulsion from the school."

But "[e]ven with the high degree of deference that courts must pay to the educator's professional judgment," school administrators can go too far in their judgments about searches of children, as evidenced by the Court's decision in *Safford v. Redding*,[80] which held that the strip searching of a thirteen year old's bra and panties for the forbidden (by school policy), over-the-counter drugs ibuprofen and naproxen, by school administrators violated the Fourth Amendment.[81]

In *Safford*, middle school administrators received information from another student that Savana Redding had distributed school-prohibited, over-the-counter drugs to one of her schoolmates. Based on the information, the assistant principal summonsed Savana to his office, showed her an opened confiscated day planner, which contained, several knives, lighters, and a cigarette.[82] Savana admitted ownership of the day planner; however, she denied the items were hers, explaining that she had loaned the day planner to a friend.[83] The assistant principal then confronted Savana with four 400 mg. pills of ibuprofen and one 200 mg. naproxen pill.[84] Savana denied knowledge of the pills; she also denied giving the drugs to students. Savana agreed to allow the assistant principal to search her backpack; he and an administrative assistant searched, but found nothing.[85]

At that point, the assistant principal instructed the administrative assistant to take Savana to the nurse's office to search her further for pills.[86] The administrative assistant and the nurse asked Savana to remove her jacket, socks, shoes, and then her pants and shirt, which she did.[87] She was finally told to "pull her bra out and to the side and shake it, and to pull out the elastic on her underpants, thus exposing her breasts and pelvic area."[88] No pills were found on Savana.[89] Her mother, April Redding, sued

---

80. 129 S.Ct. 2633 (2009).

81. *See id.* at 2637–38.

82. *See id.* at 2638.

83. *See id.*

84. *See id.*

85. *See id.*

86. *See id.*

87. *See id.*

88. *See id.*

89. *See id.*

Safford Unified School District #1, the assistant principal, the administrative assistant, and the nurse, claiming that their "strip search" of her daughter violated her Fourth Amendment rights.[90]

The Supreme Court agreed with April Redding, noting the reasonableness of the thirteen year old's expectation of privacy

> [i]s indicated by the consistent experiences of other young people similarly searched, whose adolescent vulnerability intensifies the patent intrusiveness of the exposure .... The common reaction of these adolescents simply registers the obviously different meaning of a search exposing the body from the experience of nakedness or near undress in other school circumstances. Changing for gym is getting ready for play; exposing for a search is responding to an accusation reserved for suspected wrongdoers and fairly understood as so degrading that a number of communities have decided that strip searches in schools are never reasonable and have banned them no matter what the facts may be.
>
> . . .
>
> The indignity of the search does not, of course, outlaw it, but it does implicate the rule of reasonableness as stated in T.L.O., that "the search as actually conducted [be] reasonably related in scope to the circumstances which justified the interference in the first place...". The scope will be permissible, that is, when it is "not excessively intrusive in light of the age and sex of the student and the nature of the infraction."[91]

The intrusiveness of the administrators' search troubled the Court's majority, particularly considering the non-lethal, nearly innocuous nature of the offending, restricted substances: "nondangerous school contraband does not raise the specter of stashes in intimate places, and there is no evidence in the record of any general practice among Safford Middle School students of hiding that sort of thing in underwear." Moreover, because neither student who had implicated Savana did so while revealing this predilection, nor had the administrators located these or similar contraband in the underwear of students, the lack of such evidence "weigh[s] heavily against any reasonable conclusion that [Savana] presently had the pills on her person, much less in her underwear."[92]

---

90. *Id.* Writing for the majority, Justice Souter noted that "[t]he exact label for this final step in the intrusion is not important, though strip search is a fair way to speak of it:"

> The very fact of [Savana] pulling her underwear away from her body in the presence of the two officials who were able to see her necessarily exposed her breasts and pelvic area to some degree, and both subjective and reasonable societal expectations of personal privacy support the treatment of such a search as categorically distinct, requiring distinct elements of justification on the part of school authorities for going beyond a search of outer clothing and belongings.

Id. at 2641.

91. *Id.* at 2641–42 (citations omitted).

92. *Id.* at 2642 (citations omitted).

What was missing in facts favorable to the school administrators was "any indication of danger to the students from the power of the drugs or their quantity, and any reason to suppose that [Savana] was carrying pills in her underwear." This lack "was fatal to finding the search reasonable."[93] Citing *T.L.O.*, Justice Souter noted that even the well-meaning, properly motivated assistant principal here was, nevertheless, still limited by reasonableness, *i.e.*, those that require "the support of reasonable suspicion of danger or of resort to underwear for hiding evidence of wrongdoing before a search can reasonably make the quantum leap from outer clothes and backpacks to exposure of intimate parts."[94] Given "the content of the suspicion," the administrators' search of Savana failed to match the degree of intrusion, given "the content of the suspicion." There was "no reason to suspect that large amounts of the drugs were being passed around, or that individual students were receiving great numbers of pills."[95] Justice Thomas, who concurred in part and dissented in part, would have found the search constitutional, as a matter of law.[96]

Question: What if the assistant principal discovered banned (versus restricted) drugs in Savana's day planner; would the Court's analysis change? What if Savana's day planner contained "Hemp Oil Gelcaps"[97] or a nearly empty bag of "Hemp Crunch"?[98] If you do not know, hemp (also most generally known as *cannabis sativa*) is the actual plant from which marijuana is derived and is gaining in popularity for its multiple, non-illicit uses in manufacturing clothing, medicine, food, paper, and beauty products.[99] Might this information influence the Court's analysis or the outcome? Why?

Moving from searches of children to the safety-sensitive context, the Court has exhibited a similar deference to governmental drug-testing policies. In *Skinner v. Railway Labor Executives' Ass'n*,[100] the Court upheld the validity of Federal Railroad Administration regulations that mandate blood and urine testing of employees involved in certain train accidents to uncover drug usage and authorize breath and urine tests for employees violating certain safety rules. While the Court thought it clear that reason-

---

93. *Id*. at 2643 (citations omitted).

94. *Id*. (citations omitted).

95. *Id*. at 2642 (citations omitted).

96. *Id*. at 2646 (Thomas, J., concurring in part and dissenting in part).

97. http://everything.hemp.com/detail.aspx?PRODUCT=111 (last visited October 10, 2009).

98. http://everything.hemp.com/detail.aspx?PRODUCT=302http://everything.hemp.com/detail.aspx?PRODUCT=302 (last visited October 10, 2009).

99. *See, e.g. http://www.thehia.org/* (detailing mission statement to, *inter alia*, represent the hemp industry and industrial uses of hemp), http://www.hemp.org/mission.php (discussing nonprofit organization's efforts to "remove unjust cannabis prohibition" and "educate people about the medicinal and industrial uses of cannabis"); *see also* http://everything.hemp.com/ (an online distributor of products derived from the hemp plant) (last visited October 10, 2009).

100. 489 U.S. 602 (1989).

able expectations of privacy had been invaded, special needs balancing tipped in favor of the state. First, the governmental interest in ensuring the safety of the traveling public was great. Second, the standardized nature of the tests and, in the Court's view, the minimal discretion given those charged with enforcing the regulation meant there were "virtually no facts for a neutral magistrate to evaluate"; a warrant was, therefore, unnecessary. Third, the evidence (drugs in the blood) might dissipate during the delay needed to get a warrant, thus impeding the government's achievement of its objectives. Fourth, an employee consents to significant restrictions on his freedom of movement where necessary for his employment; the additional interference required for blood, breath, or urine testing is minimal. Fifth, the privacy expectations of the employees were reduced by their "participation in an industry that is regulated pervasively to ensure safety," and the regulations minimized the intrusiveness of urine testing. Sixth, the means chosen was sufficiently effective to deter employees engaged in safety-sensitive tasks from using controlled substances or alcohol in the first place. Moreover, the testing procedures helped railroads to obtain valuable information about the causes of major accidents:

> A requirement of particularized suspicion of drug or alcohol use would seriously impede an employer's ability to obtain this information, despite its obvious importance. Experience confirms the FRA's judgment that the scene of serious rail accidents is chaotic.... Obtaining evidence that might give rise to the suspicion that a particular employee is impaired, a difficult endeavor under the best of circumstances, is most impracticable in the aftermath of a serious accident.

In a companion case, *National Treasury Employees Union v. Von Raab*,[101] the Court also upheld a United States Customs Service program requiring mandatory urinalysis for applicants for three types of jobs or promotions: those involving drug interdiction, those requiring the carrying of firearms, and those in which the employee would handle classified documents. The employee was allowed to produce the sample privately, while a same-sex monitor listened for the "normal sounds of urination." The authorizing regulations expressly provided, unlike in *Skinner*, that test results could not be turned over to criminal prosecutors without an employee's consent.

The Court found suspicionless testing reasonable for the first two classes of employees because of the state's compelling interest in ensuring the physical fitness and integrity of those involved in drug interdiction and preventing drug users from carrying firearms. Furthermore, these employees had a diminished expectation of privacy because these jobs uniquely required "judgment and dexterity." The regulations made the testing process automatic, so that officials had no discretion whatsoever and minimized the degree of intrusion.

Perhaps the most important part of the Court's opinion, however, was its analysis of the admitted absence of proof of a drug problem among

---

101.   489 U.S. 656 (1989).

customs employees, in sharp contrast to *Skinner*, where both the existence of such a problem and the risks it created were well documented. The Court found this to be a distinction without a difference under the particular facts of *Von Raab*:

> Petitioners' ... contention evinces an unduly narrow view of the context in which the Service's testing program was implemented. Petitioners do not dispute, nor can there be doubt, that drug abuse is one of the most serious problems confronting our society today. There is little reason to believe that American workplaces are immune from this pervasive social problem, as is amply illustrated by our decision in *Railway Labor Executives*. Detecting drug impairment on the part of employees can be a difficult task, especially where, as here, it is not feasible to subject employees and their work product to the kind of day-to-day scrutiny that is the norm in traditional office environments. Indeed, the almost unique mission of the Service gives the Government a compelling interest in ensuring that many of these covered employees do not use drugs even off duty, for such use creates risks of bribery and blackmail against which the Government is entitled to guard. In light of the extraordinary safety and national security hazards that would attend the promotion of drug users to positions that require the carrying of controlled substances, the Service's policy of deterring drug users from seeking such promotions cannot be deemed unreasonable.
>
> The mere circumstance that all but a few of the employees tested are entirely innocent of wrongdoing does not impugn the program's validity. The same is likely to be true of householders who are required to submit to suspicionless housing code inspections, see *Camera v. Municipal Court of San Francisco*, and of motorists who are stopped at the checkpoints we approved in *United States v. Martinez–Fuerte*, 428 U.S. 543 (1976). The Service's program is designed to prevent the promotion of drug users to sensitive positions as much as it is designed to detect those employees who use drugs. Where, as here, the possible harm against which the Government seeks to guard is substantial, the need to prevent its recurrence furnishes an ample justification for reasonable searches calculated to advance the Government's goal.

In situations not involving school children and adults whose jobs involve the safety of others, the Court has signaled that it may be unwilling to defer greatly to governmental judgments. In *Chandler v. Miller*, the Court struck down a Georgia statute that required drug testing for designated state employees.[102] Writing for an eight-person majority, Justice Ginsburg began by emphasizing that the Fourth Amendment's "restraint on government conduct generally bars officials from undertaking a search or seizure absent individualized suspicion." Citing *Skinner*, *Von Raab*, and *Vernonia*, the majority acknowledged that it had relaxed this requirement in cases of special governmental need, but it stated that such a need must be "substantial—important enough to override the individual's acknowl-

---

102. 520 U.S. 305, 309 (1997).

edged privacy interest, sufficiently vital to suppress the Fourth Amendment's normal requirement of individualized suspicion." According to the majority, Georgia failed to demonstrate a substantial need for suspicionless drug testing. First, the state had failed to demonstrate a prior problem of drug abuse by state officials, a showing "not in all cases necessary to the validity of a testing regime", but one that would "shore up a need for a suspicionless general search program." Second, the state had made no showing that ordinary law enforcement methods would not suffice to apprehend addicted candidates. Third, unlike the situation in *Von Raab*, candidates for public office were subject to "relentless scrutiny" likely to reveal a drug problem. Fourth, the state's desire to portray an image of a commitment against drug abuse could not justify a suspicionless search, for that would "diminish . . . personal privacy for a symbol's sake."

Justice Rehnquist filed the sole dissent. Rehnquist complained that the majority asked too much of the state: the rule established in *Skinner* and *Von Raab* did not require, in his view, a governmental need of "especially great importance." Rather, a "special need" exists if the state can articulate any proper governmental purpose other than law enforcement. Rehnquist argued that drug use among state employees gives rise to a risk of bribery and blackmail—a risk that satisfies the special needs requirement. Moreover, Rehnquist stated that the state need not prove that its concerns are based on previous harms. Therefore, in his view, the majority was misguided when it demanded that the state prove a history of drug use among the employees covered by the mandatory testing regime.

Finally, another example of the Court's refusal to read the special needs exception broadly in the adult drug testing category can be found in *Ferguson v. City of Charleston*,[103] where the Court struck down drug screening of maternity patients suspected of using cocaine. A state agency (the Medical University of South Carolina, or MUSC) had designed the drug screening (known as Policy M–7) for implementation in a Charleston public hospital. The stated purpose of the policy was to "identify/assist pregnant patients suspected of drug use." Under Policy M–7, the Charleston hospital, which obtained urine samples from maternity patients without clarifying the uses to which the samples would be put, would test the urine of those patients suspected of using cocaine. If a patient tested positive twice, police were notified and the patient was arrested or threatened with arrest unless she consented to substance abuse treatment. The policy listed the offenses for which the patient should be charged, depending on the age of her fetus and whether a positive test occurred after childbirth. Ten maternity patients who were arrested after they tested positive for cocaine brought suit challenging the constitutionality of the policy.

The Supreme Court held the drug screening unconstitutional, holding that the urine testing constituted a search and declining to apply the special needs doctrine because Policy M–7's purpose was "indistinguish-

---

103.   532 U.S. 67 (2001).

able" from the general public interest in crime control. Searches and seizures motivated by that interest, according to the Court, are subject to the Fourth Amendment requirement of individualized suspicion. In this excerpt from the majority opinion, pay careful attention to what facts were important to the Court's determination of the "programmatic purpose" of Policy M–7, and how and why the Court distinguished that purpose from the policy's "ultimate goal:"

Because the hospital seeks to justify its authority to conduct drug tests and to turn the results over to law enforcement agents without the knowledge or consent of the patients, this case differs from the four previous cases in which we have considered whether comparable drug tests "fit within the closely guarded category of constitutionally permissible suspicionless searches." In three of those cases, we sustained drug tests for railway employees involved in train accidents, *Skinner v. Railway Labor Executives' Assn.*, 489 U.S. 602 (1989), for United States Customs Service employees seeking promotion to certain sensitive positions, *Treasury Employees v. Von Raab*, 489 U.S. 656 (1989), and for high school students participating in interscholastic sports, *Vernonia School Dist. 47J v. Acton*, 515 U.S. 646 (1995). In the fourth case, we struck down such testing for candidates for designated state offices as unreasonable. *Chandler v. Miller*, 520 U.S. 305 (1997).

In each of those cases, we employed a balancing test that weighed the intrusion on the individual's interest in privacy against the "special needs" that supported the program. As an initial matter, we note that the invasion of privacy in this case is far more substantial than in those cases. In the previous four cases, there was no misunderstanding about the purpose of the test or the potential use of the test results, and there were protections against the dissemination of the results to third parties. The use of an adverse test result to disqualify one from eligibility for a particular benefit, such as a promotion or an opportunity to participate in an extracurricular activity, involves a less serious intrusion on privacy than the unauthorized dissemination of such results to third parties. The reasonable expectation of privacy enjoyed by the typical patient undergoing diagnostic tests in a hospital is that the results of those tests will not be shared with nonmedical personnel without her consent. In none of our prior cases was there any intrusion upon that kind of expectation.

The critical difference between those four drug-testing cases and this one, however, lies in the nature of the "special need" asserted as justification for the warrantless searches. In each of those earlier cases, the "special need" that was advanced as a justification for the absence of a warrant or individualized suspicion was one divorced from the State's general interest in law enforcement. ... In this case, however, the central and indispensable feature of the policy from its inception was the use of law enforcement to coerce the patients into substance abuse treatment. This fact distinguishes this case from circumstances in which physicians or psychologists, in the course of ordinary medical procedures aimed at helping the patient herself, come across information that under rules of law or ethics is subject to reporting requirements, which no one has challenged here.

Respondents argue in essence that their ultimate purpose—namely, protecting the health of both mother and child—is a beneficent one. In *Chandler*, however, we did not simply accept the State's invocation of a "special need." Instead, we carried out a "close review" of the scheme at issue before concluding that the need in question was not "special," as that term has been defined in our cases. In this case, a review of the M–7 policy plainly reveals that the purpose actually served by the MUSC searches is ultimately indistinguishable from the general interest in crime control.

In looking to the programmatic purpose, we consider all the available evidence in order to determine the relevant primary purpose. In this case, as Judge Blake put it in her dissent below, "it . . . is clear from the record that an initial and continuing focus of the policy was on the arrest and prosecution of drug-abusing mothers. . . ." Tellingly, the document codifying the policy incorporates the police's operational guidelines. It devotes its attention to the chain of custody, the range of possible criminal charges, and the logistics of police notification and arrests. Nowhere, however, does the document discuss different courses of medical treatment for either mother or infant, aside from treatment for the mother's addiction.

Moreover, throughout the development and application of the policy, the Charleston prosecutors and police were extensively involved in the day-to-day administration of the policy. Police and prosecutors decided who would receive the reports of positive drug screens and what information would be included with those reports. Law enforcement officials also helped determine the procedures to be followed when performing the screens. In the course of the policy's administration, they had access to . . . medical files on the women who tested positive, routinely attended the substance abuse team's meetings, and regularly received copies of team documents discussing the women's progress. Police took pains to coordinate the timing and circumstances of the arrests with MUSC staff. . . .

While the ultimate goal of the program may well have been to get the women in question into substance abuse treatment and off of drugs, the immediate objective of the searches was to generate evidence for law enforcement purposes in order to reach that goal. The threat of law enforcement may ultimately have been intended as a means to an end, but the direct and primary purpose of MUSC's policy was to ensure the use of those means. In our opinion, this distinction is critical. Because law enforcement involvement always serves some broader social purpose or objective, under respondents' view, virtually any nonconsensual suspicionless search could be immunized under the special needs doctrine by defining the search solely in terms of its ultimate, rather than immediate, purpose. Such an approach is inconsistent with the Fourth Amendment. Given the primary purpose of the Charleston program, which was to use the threat of arrest and prosecution in order to force women into treatment, and given the extensive involvement of law enforcement officials at every stage of the policy, this case simply does not fit within the closely guarded category of "special needs."

The fact that positive test results were turned over to the police does not merely provide a basis for distinguishing our prior cases applying the "special needs" balancing approach to the determination of drug use. It also provides an affirmative reason for enforcing the strictures of the Fourth Amendment. While state hospital employees, like other citizens, may have a duty to provide the police with evidence of criminal conduct that they inadvertently acquire in the course of routine treatment, when they undertake to obtain such evidence from their patients for the specific purpose of incriminating those patients, they have a special obligation to make sure that the patients are fully informed about their constitutional rights, as standards of knowing waiver require.

As respondents have repeatedly insisted, their motive was benign rather than punitive. Such a motive, however, cannot justify a departure from Fourth Amendment protections, given the pervasive involvement of law enforcement with the development and application of the MUSC policy. The stark and unique fact that characterizes this case is that Policy M–7 was designed to obtain evidence of criminal conduct by the tested patients that would be turned over to the police and that could be admissible in subsequent criminal prosecutions. While respondents are correct that drug abuse both was and is a serious problem, the gravity of the threat alone cannot be dispositive of questions concerning what means law enforcement officers may employ to pursue a given purpose. The Fourth Amendment's general prohibition against nonconsensual, warrantless, and suspicionless searches necessarily applies to such a policy.

Justice Kennedy, who filed a separate concurring opinion, disagreed with the Court's distinction between "immediate" and "ultimate" purposes. According to Justice Kennedy, no such distinction is found in the Court's precedents. Rather, previous cases had "turned upon what the majority terms the policy's ultimate goal." Nevertheless, Justice Kennedy agreed that Policy M–7 was unconstitutional because it had "a penal character with a far greater connection to law enforcement than other searches sustained under our special needs rationale."

Justice Scalia, joined in dissent by the Chief Justice and Justice Thomas, argued that there were no constitutional problems with the policy because the maternity patients had consented to the taking of their urine. The dissent also stated that, even in the absence of consent, the special needs doctrine covered the policy because it was motivated by the desire "to refer pregnant drug addicts to treatment centers, and to prepare for necessary treatment of their possibly affected children." The fact that medical personnel agreed to use law enforcement as "a strong incentive for their addicted patients to undertake drug-addiction treatment" makes no difference to Fourth Amendment analysis, said Justice Scalia.

Professor Taslitz[104] has argued that the Court's ambiguity concerning the meaning of "programmatic purpose" can be clarified thus:

> The ... majority opinion continued to embrace the idea that the state's purpose is what distinguishes an administrative search from an ordinary criminal investigatory one. Yet the Court rejected the notion that the subjective purposes of state actors control. Instead, what matters is the state's "programmatic purpose," which the Court concluded was, in the case before it, criminal investigation. This conclusion is at first surprising, because it contradicts the likely subjective intentions at work. The Hospital and the police very likely see themselves as protecting the health and safety of the pregnant women and their soon-to-be-children rather than as wreaking retribution. The credible threat of punishment may thus have been seen by these state actors simply as a motivator to ensure that parent and future child received medical help. Yet the Court found the "programmatic purpose" to be pursuit of criminal investigation. What explains this apparent contradiction? The Court never clearly defined "programmatic purpose." But the Court did consider the extent of police involvement in creating and implementing the hospital's search program to be critically relevant in determining whether such a purpose existed.

> ... [T]he apparent contradiction can be resolved, and the "programmatic purpose" phrase sensibly defined, by embracing the radical feminist insight that the meaning of human actions both partly constitutes and contributes to the functioning of social systems. The Ferguson majority was right to categorize the hospital's searches as ordinary criminal ones because that is the social meaning most fairly ascribed to the state's actions. The heavy involvement of the police sent the message that the program's purpose was punitive and retributive. The program created the sort of stigma associated with the criminal justice system, a stigma amplified by the twin aspects of the conduct involved: the alleged use of drugs and the violation of governing conceptions of "good" motherhood.

QUESTIONS

Recall the *Earls* case, which upheld suspicionless, warrantless drug testing of students involved in competitive extracurricular activities. Was that case properly decided under Taslitz's "social meaning" approach to the "programmatic purpose" determination? Would your answer change depending upon whether test results are turned over to the police? What

---

104. Andrew E. Taslitz, *A Feminist Fourth Amendment?: Consent, Care, Privacy, and Social Meaning in Ferguson v. City of Charleston*, 9 DUKE J. GENDER & L. 1 (2002).

factual distinctions, if any, are there between *Earls* and *Ferguson* that make a difference to the social meaning of each program?

PROBLEM 4–16

Associate Dean George Johanson of the Harrod University School of Law received the following anonymous tip:

> I'm a student at Harrod and so is Bobby McKnight. McKnight has been making his way through law school by dealing dope to the kids at the nearby high school. I've seen McKnight selling weed to these kids, and I've seen him store it in his law school locker. Just this morning, I saw him put a plastic bag of weed in his locker. You've got to stop him. He's dealt bad stuff to some older kids, some gang members. I overheard one of them at the law school this morning saying "Tell me when you see McKnight, and I'll get the guns from the car. We'll keep it parked at the law school until McKnight gets his." I don't know what their car looks like, but if you don't stop McKnight now, he and some others may get hurt bad.

The caller then hung-up. Johanson, along with some security guards, immediately opened and searched McKnight's locker, finding a large quantity of marijuana inside. Immediately thereafter, Johanson and the guards started opening and searching all the cars on the student lot. They found an Uzi in one car, a car that, it turned out, did not belong to high school kids but to McKnight, who has now been arrested for illegal possession of an unlicensed weapon and of marijuana.

Question: You represent McKnight. What arguments will you raise in a motion to suppress the Uzi and the marijuana? What if the tip had never mentioned any weapons, but Johanson informed all students by letter that, as a condition of continued enrollment, they had to sign a form consenting to a random search for weapons or drugs of any cars that they park on campus? How, if at all, would that change the analysis? Would your analysis differ if this were a high school rather than a law school? Why?

(IV) SEARCHES OF PROBATIONERS AND PROBATIONERS' RESIDENCES

In *Griffin v. Wisconsin*,[105] the Court showed deference to local authorities' judgments about "special needs" involving probationers. The decision in *Griffin* upheld a Wisconsin regulation permitting warrantless searches of probationers' homes, so long as the searching officer had "reasonable grounds" to suspect the presence of contraband—a violation of probationary terms. According to the Court, the regulation and ensuing searches were reasonable in order to satisfy the state's need to ensure compliance with probationary terms.

More recently, in *United States v. Knights*,[106] the Court unanimously approved the warrantless search of a probationer's home for purposes *other*

---

105. 483 U.S. 868 (1987).

106. 534 U.S. 112 (2001).

than ensuring compliance with probationary terms. In doing so, the Court broadened considerably the rationale for such searches. In *Knights*, an officer developed reasonable suspicion that Knights had engaged in a crime unrelated to the offense of conviction. The officer searched Knights's residence without a warrant, knowing that Knights's probation order included a condition requiring him to "submit his ... person, property, place of residence, vehicle, personal effects, to search at anytime, with or without a search warrant, warrant of arrest or reasonable cause by any probation officer or law enforcement officer." Knights had signed the order, a fact the government used to argue that Knights had, in effect, consented to the search. The Supreme Court sidestepped the consent issue altogether, remarking that the search was reasonable under the Fourth Amendment balancing test. Knights's status as a probationer, said the Court, was a factor that weighed on both sides of the balance. The condition of probation reduced his expectations of privacy and liberty (particularly because he was "unambiguously informed of it"). And his probationary status heightened the state's interest in his activities. The Court concluded,

> We hold that the balance of these considerations requires no more than reasonable suspicion to conduct a search of this probationer's house. The degree of individualized suspicion required of a search is a determination of when there is a sufficiently high probability that criminal conduct is occurring to make the intrusion on the individual's privacy interest reasonable. Although the Fourth Amendment ordinarily requires the degree of probability embodied in the term "probable cause," a lesser degree satisfies the Constitution when the balance of governmental and private interests makes such a standard reasonable. Those interests warrant a lesser than probable-cause standard here. When an officer has reasonable suspicion that a probationer subject to a search condition is engaged in criminal activity, there is enough likelihood that criminal conduct is occurring that an intrusion on the probationer's significantly diminished privacy interests is reasonable.

> The same circumstances that lead us to conclude that reasonable suspicion is constitutionally sufficient also render a warrant requirement unnecessary.

Knights had argued that the probationary condition made reasonable only those searches having to do with the terms of his probation. The Supreme Court disagreed: "Because our holding rests on ordinary Fourth Amendment analysis that considers all the circumstances of a search, there is no basis for examining official purposes." The Court declined to decide whether the search would have been reasonable without any individualized suspicion.

Should law enforcement be permitted to sample individuals' DNA? "All fifty states currently have legislation requiring that DNA profiles of certain categories of individuals be [created]," and "appellate courts in this country are virtually unanimous in upholding [those] statutes."[107] Some states

---

107.   Nason v. State, 102 P.3d 962, 964 (Alaska Ct. App. 2004).

have "increased the number of individuals eligible for inclusion in these databases" by enacting provisions allowing the taking and analysis of DNA samples from certain categories of arrestees. While the Supreme Court has not addressed the constitutionality of taking DNA samples from persons subject to arrest, Tracey Maclin suggests that "forcibly obtaining and testing DNA samples of arrestees, absent judicial authorization or probable cause for the search, cannot be justified under the special needs exception."[108]

After determining that the Court will likely find that states' forcibly obtaining and testing DNA samples of arrestees constitutes a search under the Fourth Amendment, Maclin goes on to argue that "[b]ecause the so-called 'special needs exception' permits suspicionless searches in a variety of contexts, it would seem to be the most appropriate category for analyzing the constitutionality of taking an arrestee's DNA." However, predicting whether the Court will uphold states' taking arrestees' DNA is not an easy task. "While the Court has issued several rulings under its 'special needs' analysis, these cases do not form a coherent doctrine." Maclin derived four criteria from these rulings that the Court will likely use to determine whether taking arrestees' DNA samples is constitutional. "The criteria include: the purpose of the search; whether law enforcement officials will have access to the results of the search; the extent of police involvement in conducting the search; and finally, whether the search can be characterized as serving civil and criminal law interests." Maclin uses these four criteria to predict whether the Court would uphold taking DNA from arrestees as a valid special needs search.

First, because the purpose behind some states' DNA laws is "to use DNA samples from arrestees to assist law enforcement officials 'in criminal investigations' and to enhance states' 'chances of solving crimes,' such searches would not fit within the special needs exception." Second, many states "make the test results of DNA samples 'available directly to federal, and local law-enforcement officers.'" When law enforcement has access to search results, the Court has been reluctant to uphold those searches under the special needs exception. Third, "the fact that police officials are intimately involved in the implementation of DNA searches strongly suggests that such searches do not satisfy the special needs exception." Finally, "[w]hile DNA searches may advance the states' secondary or ultimate interest in determining the identification of persons held in custody or charged with a crime, 'the immediate objective of the searches [is] to generate evidence *for law enforcement purposes* ...'" Therefore, under the Court's current precedents, forcibly obtaining and testing DNA samples of arrestees ... cannot be justified under the special needs exception."

Relevant to the question whether individualized suspicion should be required to search probationers and parolees is this underlying inquiry: are

---

108. *See* Tracey Maclin, *Is Obtaining an Arrestee's DNA a Valid Special Needs Search Under the Fourth Amendment? What Should (and Will) the Supreme Court Do?*, 33 J.L. Med. & Ethics 102 (2005).

full Fourth Amendment privacy interests restored after a convicted person has completely and successfully served his sentence in accordance with the requirements of his conviction? According to at least one state, the answer is, at best, "not so fast:"

> [t]he California legislature has determined that "the period immediately following incarceration is critical to successful reintegration of the offender into society and to positive citizenship." Cal. Pen. Code § 3000(a)(1). In order to "provide for the supervision of and surveillance of parolees," and "to provide educational, vocational, family and personal counseling necessary to assist parolees in the transition between imprisonment and discharge," California law requires that "[a] sentence pursuant to Section 1168 or 1170 [the general sentencing provisions of the California Penal Code] shall include a period of parole, unless waived as provided in this section."
>
> The period of parole lasts up to three years for certain offenses, and up to five years for others. Id. § 3000(b)(1), (2). If a person receives a life sentence and is subsequently paroled, the period of parole is five years, and may be extended for an additional five years. Id. § 3000(b)(3). In the case of a person sentenced for first or second degree murder, "the period of parole, if parole is granted, shall be the remainder of the person's life." Id. § 3000.1(a).
>
> Parolees may be discharged from parole before their periods of parole have been completed. Discharge occurs after one year if the parolee was convicted of a nonviolent felony, and after two or three years for most other felonies, unless the Board of Prison Terms determines that the person should be retained on parole for a longer period. Id. § 3001(a), (b). Persons subject to lifetime parole are discharged after five years (in the case of second-degree murder) or seven years (in the case of first-degree murder), unless the Board determines that they should be retained on parole. Id. § 3000.1(b).[109]

The application of parole and its requirements should come as no surprise. However, there is more:

> California law provides for a "notice of parole," which is "a general description of rules and regulations governing parole." Cal. Code Regs. tit. 15, § 2511(a). By statute, "the notice of parole shall read as follows: ... Search. **You and your residence and any property under your control may be searched without a warrant at any time by any agent of the Department of Corrections or any law enforcement officer.**" Id. § 2511(b).[110]

According to the California Supreme Court, "parole is not a matter of choice ... there can be no voluntary consent to inclusion of the search condition."[111]

---

109. Samson v. California, Brief for the Petitioner, 2004 U.S. Briefs 9728 at *1–3.

110. *Id.* at **9 (emphasis added).

111. People v. Reyes, 968 P.2d 445, 448 (Cal. 1998) (citation omitted).

Is this as oppressive as it sounds? Ask Donald Curtis Samson and Deborah Watson:

> On September 6, 2002, at about 5:30 in the afternoon, Officer Alex Rohleder of the San Bruno, California Police Department was driving his patrol vehicle when he observed two adults and a little baby walking down the street. The two adults were Petitioner and his friend Deborah Watson; the baby was Ms. Watson's three-year-old son.... Officer Rohleder was not actively looking for Petitioner, but just happened to run across him.... Officer Rohleder was aware that Petitioner was on parole, and was under the impression that he might have a parolee at large warrant (issued when a parolee's whereabouts are "unknown" or s/he "remains unavailable for supervision").... The officer conducted a pat-down search of Petitioner for weapons and found nothing. The officer asked Petitioner whether he had an outstanding warrant. Petitioner responded no he didn't.... The officer called his dispatcher and confirmed that Petitioner's statements were correct.
>
> The police officer then proceeded to search Petitioner more thoroughly. The officer conducted this second search of Petitioner solely because it's a condition of his parole.... Nothing about Petitioner's conduct gave rise to any suspicion that he was engaged in wrongdoing....
>
> The officer explained that, being [a] parolee, Petitioner needs to make sure he's still obeying the laws. It's a privilege for him to be out there. The officer searched Petitioner's pockets and found a cigarette box in his left breast pocket. The officer searched inside the cigarette box and found a plastic baggy containing Methamphetamine.[112]

When this case reached the United States Supreme Court, the Court, in an opinion by Justice Scalia, found the search constitutional. Parolees, said the Court, had fewer privacy expectations than probationers because parole is more akin to imprisonment than is probation. A parolee is released *before his sentence of incarceration ends* on condition that he abide by certain rules for the balance of his sentence. A probationer is never incarcerated. Parolees' severely diminished privacy expectations, said the Court, were outweighed by the overwhelming state's interest in supervising parolees because they are so likely to re-offend. The state may not be rendered powerless to combat recidivism by promoting reintegration and positive citizenship, goals that may require privacy intrusions that would not otherwise be tolerated under the Fourth Amendment, maintained the Court. Nor need there be concern about arbitrary application given the state's prohibition on harassing, capricious or arbitrary searches. Additionally, concluded the Court, it was irrelevant that many other states and the federal government require individualized suspicion before searching parolees, for the question is whether the program is drawn to meet California's needs and is reasonable given the parolee's reduced privacy expectations.

---

112. Samson v. California, Brief for the Petitioner, 2004 U.S. Briefs 9728 at *4–5 (internal quotations and citations omitted).

Said the Court, "The touchstone of the Fourth Amendment is reasonableness, not individualized suspicion."[113]

Justice Stevens, joined by Justices Souter and Breyer in dissent, emphasized that " '[t]he suspicionless search is the very evil the Fourth Amendment was intended to stamp out,' " and exceptions to its prohibition should be " 'jealously guarded,' " limited primarily to special needs searches, yet the Court had not relied on any argument that the parolee search fit the special needs category. Furthermore, the special needs cases required "programmatic safeguards designed to ensure evenhandedness in application; if individualized suspicion is to be jettisoned, it must be replaced with measures to protect against state actors' unfettered discretion." Importantly, Justice Stevens also found the attitudes of the rest of the country, not just Californians, to be critical to the analysis:

> Nor is it enough, in deciding whether someone's expectation of privacy is "legitimate," to rely on the existence of the offending condition or the individual's notice thereof. . . . The Court's reasoning in this respect is entirely circular. The mere fact that a particular State refuses to acknowledge a parolee's privacy interest cannot mean that a parolee in that State has no expectation of privacy that society is willing to recognize as legitimate—especially when the measure that invades privacy is both the *subject* of the Fourth Amendment challenge and a clear outlier. With only one or two arguable exceptions, neither the Federal Government nor any other State subjects parolees to searches of the kind to which petitioner was subjected. And the fact of notice hardly cures the circularity; the loss of a subjective expectation of privacy would play "no meaningful role" in analyzing the legitimacy of expectations, for example, if the Government were suddenly to announce on nationwide television that all homes henceforth would be subject to warrantless entry.[114]

NOTES AND QUESTIONS

1. The majority and dissenting opinions seem to raise this question: Should what privacy expectations "society" is willing to recognize as reasonable, and the weight of those expectations, be decided based upon the attitudes of "American society" as a whole or the attitudes of those within the state where the search or seizure takes place? Is your answer affected by the Fourth Amendment's statement that the right it recites is one of "the People"? What about each opinion suggests these questions are involved? Are reasonable expectations of privacy and their weight really empirical questions about attitudes, or are they normative questions about what we should expect, or are they both?

2. What about Ms. Watson, who was in Samson's company at the time of the search?:

---

113.   Samson v. California, 547 U.S. 843, 855 (2006).

114.   547 U.S. 843, 862–63 (2006) (Stevens, J., dissenting).

The officer also searched Petitioner's companion.... According to the officer, Ms. Watson consented to the search. According to Ms. Watson, the officer did not ask permission to search her, but instead told her to empty her pockets and asked if she had any weapons or drugs. After the officer went through Watson's belongings on top of the hood of the car, he told her to go home.[115]

As Ms. Watson was not on parole nor was she a criminal convict, should she have received different treatment? Why? The majority did not consider this precise question but did address a related point: "Likewise, petitioner's concern that California's suspicionless search law frustrates reintegration efforts by permitting intrusions into the privacy interests of third parties is also unavailing because that concern would arise under a suspicion-based regime as well."

(V) SEARCHES AND SEIZURE BY CUSTOMS AND BORDER PATROL OFFICERS

The Court has always exhibited great deference to governmental policy decisions in circumstances involving national borders and customs. In *United States v. Martinez–Fuerte,*[116] the Court approved a suspicionless border checkpoint. The Court stated that border checkpoints advance the government's interest in controlling the influx of illegal aliens. In reaching this conclusion, the Court noted that thousands of illegal immigrants were stopped at such checkpoints each year. Moreover, the permanent checkpoint was minimally intrusive: drivers were not surprised because three signs warned drivers of the impending checkpoint, and the field officers' discretion was limited, for they were not the ones who decided where to put the checkpoint. Instead, high-ranking Border Patrol officials chose the location and timing of checkpoints based on effectiveness and safety, with field officers operating in a regularized manner, using a fixed set of written guidelines to ask questions. Nor was individualized suspicion necessary because these were neither ordinary searches nor invasions of the "sanctuary of private dwellings."

Far more intrusive governmental actions than checkpoints are tolerated when they advance the national government's interest in patrolling borders and monitoring items brought into the country. In *United States v. Montoya de Hernandez,*[117] for example, the Court upheld a 19–hour detention of a person suspected of smuggling drugs in her alimentary canal. While the customs agents holding did not have probable cause, they did have reasonable suspicion. The Court concluded that reasonable suspicion sufficiently justified the stop and the search. Here is an excerpt from the Court's opinion. Note how the Court portrayed the government's interest as uniquely weighty:

> Respondent arrived at Los Angeles International Airport shortly after midnight, March 5, 1983, on Avianca Flight 080, a direct 10–hour

---

115.   Samson v. California, Brief for the Petitioner, 2004 U.S. Briefs 9728 at *5.

116.   428 U.S. 543 (1976).

117.   473 U.S. 531 (1985).

flight from Bogota, Colombia. Her visa was in order so she was passed through Immigration and proceeded to the customs desk. At the customs desk she encountered Customs Inspector Talamantes, who reviewed her documents and noticed from her passport that she had made at least eight recent trips to either Miami or Los Angeles. Talamantes referred respondent to a secondary customs desk for further questioning. At this desk, Talamantes and another inspector asked respondent general questions concerning herself and the purpose of her trip. Respondent revealed that she spoke no English and had no family or friends in the United States. She explained in Spanish that she had come to the United States to purchase goods for her husband's store in Bogota. The customs inspectors recognized Bogota as a "source city" for narcotics. Respondent possessed $5,000 in cash, mostly $50 bills, but had no billfold. She indicated to the inspectors that she had no appointments with merchandise vendors, but planned to ride around Los Angeles in taxicabs visiting retail stores such as J.C. Penney and K–Mart in order to buy goods for her husband's store with the $5,000.

Respondent admitted that she had no hotel reservations, but stated that she planned to stay at a Holiday Inn. Respondent could not recall how her airline ticket was purchased. When the inspectors opened respondent's one small valise, they found about four changes of "cold weather" clothing. Respondent had no shoes other than the high-heeled pair she was wearing. Although respondent possessed no checks, waybills, credit cards, or letters of credit, she did produce a Colombian business card and a number of old receipts, waybills, and fabric swatches displayed in a photo album.

At this point Talamantes and the other inspector suspected that respondent was a "balloon swallower," one who attempts to smuggle narcotics into this country hidden in her alimentary canal. Over the years Inspector Talamantes had apprehended dozens of alimentary canal smugglers arriving on Avianca Flight 080.

The inspectors requested a female customs inspector to take respondent to a private area and conduct a patdown and strip search. During the search the female inspector felt respondent's abdomen area and noticed a firm fullness, as if respondent were wearing a girdle. The search revealed no contraband, but the inspector noticed that respondent was wearing two pairs of elastic underpants with a paper towel lining the crotch area.

When respondent returned to the customs area and the female inspector reported her discoveries, the inspector in charge told respondent that he suspected she was smuggling drugs in her alimentary canal. Respondent agreed to the inspector's request that she be x-rayed at a hospital but in answer to the inspector's query stated that she was pregnant. She agreed to a pregnancy test before the x-ray. Respondent withdrew the consent for an x-ray when she learned that she would have to be handcuffed en route to the hospital. The inspector then gave respondent the option of returning to Colombia on the next available flight, agreeing to an x-ray, or remaining in detention until she produced a monitored bowel movement that would confirm or rebut the inspectors' suspicions. Respondent chose the first option and was placed in a customs office under observation. She was told that if she went to the toilet she would have to use a wastebasket in the women's restroom, in order that female customs inspectors could inspect her stool for balloons or capsules carrying narcotics. The inspectors refused respondent's request to place a telephone call.

Respondent sat in the customs office, under observation, for the remainder of the night. During the night, customs officials attempted to place respondent on a Mexican airline that was flying to Bogota via Mexico City in the morning. The airline refused to transport respondent because she lacked a Mexican visa necessary to land in Mexico City. Respondent was not permitted to leave, and was informed that she would be detained until she agreed to an x-ray or her bowels moved. She remained detained in the customs office under observation, for most of the time curled up in a chair leaning to one side. She refused all offers of food and drink, and refused to use the toilet facilities. The Court of Appeals noted that she exhibited symptoms of discomfort consistent with "heroic efforts to resist the usual calls of nature."

At the shift change at 4 o'clock the next afternoon, almost 16 hours after her flight had landed, respondent still had not defecated or urinated or partaken of food or drink. At that time customs officials sought a court order authorizing a pregnancy test, an x-ray, and a rectal examination. The Federal Magistrate issued an order just before midnight that evening, which authorized a rectal examination and involuntary x-ray, provided that the physician in charge considered respondent's claim of pregnancy. Respondent was taken to a hospital and given a pregnancy test, which later turned out to be negative. Before the results of the pregnancy test were known, a physician conducted a rectal examination and removed from respondent's rectum a balloon containing a foreign substance. Respondent was then placed formally under arrest. By 4:10 a.m. respondent had passed 6 similar balloons; over the next four days she passed 88 balloons containing a total of 528 grams of 80% pure cocaine hydrochloride. ...

Here the seizure of respondent took place at the international border. Since the founding of our Republic, Congress has granted the Executive plenary authority to conduct routine searches and seizures at the border, without probable cause or a warrant, in order to regulate the collection of duties and to prevent the introduction of contraband into this country. This Court has long recognized Congress' power to police entrants at the border. As we stated recently:

> Import restrictions and searches of persons or packages at the national border rest on different considerations and different rules of constitutional law from domestic regulations. The Constitution

gives Congress broad comprehensive powers "[t]o regulate Commerce with foreign Nations," Art. I, § 8, cl. 3. Historically such broad powers have been necessary to prevent smuggling and to prevent prohibited articles from entry.

Consistently, therefore, with Congress' power to protect the Nation by stopping and examining persons entering this country, the Fourth Amendment's balance of reasonableness is qualitatively different at the international border than in the interior. Routine searches of the persons and effects of entrants are not subject to any requirement of reasonable suspicion, probable cause, or warrant, and first-class mail may be opened without a warrant on less than probable cause. Automotive travelers may be stopped at fixed checkpoints near the border without individualized suspicion even if the stop is based largely on ethnicity, and boats on inland waters with ready access to the sea may be hailed and boarded with no suspicion whatever.

These cases reflect longstanding concern for the protection of the integrity of the border. This concern is, if anything, heightened by the veritable national crisis in law enforcement caused by smuggling of illicit narcotics, and in particular by the increasing utilization of alimentary canal smuggling. This desperate practice appears to be a relatively recent addition to the smugglers' repertoire of deceptive practices, and it also appears to be exceedingly difficult to detect. Congress had recognized these difficulties. Title 19 U.S.C. § 1582 provides that "all persons coming into the United States from foreign countries shall be liable to detention and search authorized ... [by customs regulations]." Customs agents may "stop, search, and examine" any "vehicle, beast or person" upon which an officer suspects there is contraband or "merchandise which is subject to duty."

Balanced against the sovereign's interests at the border are the Fourth Amendment rights of respondent. Having presented herself at the border for admission, and having subjected herself to the criminal enforcement powers of the Federal Government, respondent was entitled to be free from unreasonable search and seizure. But not only is the expectation of privacy less at the border than in the interior, the Fourth Amendment balance between the interests of the Government and the privacy right of the individual is also struck much more favorably to the Government at the border. ...

We hold that the detention of a traveler at the border, beyond the scope of a routine customs search and inspection, is justified at its inception if customs agents, considering all the facts surrounding the traveler and her trip, reasonably suspect that the traveler is smuggling contraband in her alimentary canal.

PROBLEM 4–17

Sonya Sheffield and Jacqueline Daltre live and work in Canton, Ohio. On August 26, they purchased same-day tickets to fly together to Miami.

Later that day, at Miami International Airport, they purchased tickets on Air Jamaica for a same-day flight to Jamaica. Both paid for their tickets in cash. Sheffield and Daltre returned to Miami on August 28, via Air Jamaica Flight Number 33, having spent only two days in Jamaica. The plane landed in Miami at approximately 3:30 p.m. and was greeted by U.S. Customs inspectors, including Inspector Rachel Tambord, a customs inspector on the "Miami Rover Team." The Rover Team consists of a select group of plain clothes officers charged solely with screening international passengers for narcotics. Tambord had received 11 weeks basic training at the U.S. Customs School in Glenco, Georgia, and was nearing completion of her one year status as a "trainee." She was aware that Jamaica was a source country of drugs imported into the United States.

As passengers from Air Jamaica Flight 33 disembarked from the plane, Inspector Tambord asked Sheffield and Daltre to step aside. Prior to meeting the aircraft she had received a "tip" that certain individuals traveling from Ohio may be carrying narcotics. While at the gate, she preliminarily questioned the two women, checked and retained their documentation and Customs declarations, and discovered they were on a two-day trip from a source country. The women told Tambord they were traveling together, and they appeared nervous as she escorted them from the gate upstairs to the Immigration checkpoint. There, she let them retrieve their luggage at the baggage carousel while she located another customs agent, Laura Arnold, to assist her. She and Arnold then went off with the women to a nearby private inspection area to conduct a luggage search.

The search of the luggage revealed no evidence of narcotics, and a lengthy session of questioning likewise was fruitless. After conferring, the two inspectors agreed to request permission from their supervisor—Alexis Joseph—to conduct patdown searches of the women. In accordance with U.S. Customs procedures, the inspectors informed Supervisor Joseph of the following articulable facts that led them to believe a patdown search was warranted: 1) the continued nervousness of the women; 2) the fact that the women had been on a short trip to a source country; and 3) the fact that the women were wearing loose fitting clothing. Supervisor Joseph granted permission for the pat-down searches. The women were taken individually behind a partition in the inspection room, accompanied by both inspectors. Each woman was informed of the procedures for a patdown search. Each was searched by one of the female inspectors while the other inspector stood nearby as a witness. No evidence of narcotics was found, but Inspector Arnold found three gold watches in a pouch under Daltre's shirt. The watches had not been declared on Daltre's Customs form and exceeded the value of merchandise that could lawfully be brought into the country without paying duties. Daltre was charged with a misdemeanor and was released from the airport, 3 hours after her plane had landed.

Question: If Daltre challenges the actions of the Customs inspectors, will she likely succeed in convincing the court: (a) that the inspectors were required to have reasonable suspicion that she was smuggling drugs before detaining her for 3 hours and conducting a search of her luggage and her person; and (b) that the facts known to the inspectors did not give rise to reasonable suspicion? What if Inspector Tambord had had a hunch that Sheffield was carrying explosives concealed on her person when she de-planed. Would Tambord have to justify a patdown by articulating facts giving rise to reasonable suspicion? What if Tambord did not suspect Daltre and Sheffield of doing anything illegal but had such a load of passengers from whom to collect Customs declarations that she required the two women to wait for 90 minutes until she was able to process their forms. Would that 90–minute detention violate the constitutional rights of the women?

(VI) ROADBLOCKS

The constitutionality of roadblocks has never been completely settled, and the permissibility of each must be decided on a fact-intensive basis. In *Delaware v. Prouse*,[118] an officer made a suspicionless stop to check license and registration, a stop the Court condemned as "the unconstrained exercise of discretion." There were better ways, such as yearly inspections, the Court noted, to achieve the state's interest in vehicle registration and safety. Nevertheless in *Michigan Department of State Police v. Sitz*[119] the Court upheld a sobriety checkpoint that permitted suspicionless stops to check for drunk driving. In *Sitz*, the checkpoints were placed at selected sites along state roads. Officers in the field were to choose sites based on specified guidelines, including the safety of the location and minimizing inconvenience to the drivers. All vehicles passing through a checkpoint were stopped and their drivers briefly checked for signs of intoxication. Where there were such signs, police directed the motorist out of the traffic flow, where another officer would check the driver's license and registra-tion, also conducting further sobriety tests if warranted. Of 126 vehicles stopped at the single checkpoint operated under the program, one arrest was made for drunk driving.

In upholding the checkpoint program, the Court applied a three-prong test, drawn from *Brown v. Texas*,[120] balancing: (1) the gravity of the public concerns served by the seizure; (2) the degree to which the seizure advanced the public interest; and (3) the severity of the interference with individual liberty. The respondents in *Sitz* had argued that reasonableness balancing could be applied only where there were special interests beyond criminal law enforcement, a justification that did not extend to checkpoints used solely to enforce criminal law prohibitions on drunk driving. But the majority relied instead on the *Terry* line of cases, which employed reason-ableness balancing in the criminal law enforcement context. Of course, the

---

118.   440 U.S. 648 (1979). Although the point might be debatable, we treat roadblocks as administrative searches, as do LAFAVE & ISRAEL, CRIMINAL PROCEDURE, *supra* note 47, at 214 and STEPHEN A. SALTZBURG & DANIEL J. CAPRA, AMERICAN CRIMINAL PROCEDURE 327–31 (5th ed. 1996). We draw heavily on both these texts in this section.

119.   496 U.S. 444 (1990).

120.   443 U.S. 47 (1979).

Court in *Sitz* went beyond the reduced level of justification permitted by *Terry* and its progeny to justify an entirely suspicionless search. In doing so, the Court stressed the relatively minor severity of the intrusion:

> At traffic checkpoints the motorist can see that other vehicles are being stopped, he can see visible signs of the officers' authority, and he is much less likely to be frightened or annoyed by the intrusion. ... Here, checkpoints are selected pursuant to the guidelines, and uniformed police officers stop every approaching vehicle. The intrusion resulting from the brief stop at the sobriety checkpoint is for constitutional purposes indistinguishable from the checkpoint stops we upheld in *Martinez-Fuerte*.

The gravity of the public concern also favored the procedure because of the state's heavy interest in eradicating drunk driving. The effectiveness of the program in eradicating drunk driving may have been thought by many to be especially problematic. Not so, however, for the Court. While the Court seemed to require some supporting empirical data, it emphasized that earlier cases, like *Prouse*, were not meant to "transfer from politically accountable officials to the courts the decision as to which among reasonable alternative law enforcement techniques should be employed to deal with a serious public danger." Such a transfer would be unwise because "the choice among such alternatives remains with the government officials who have a unique understanding of, and responsibility for, limited public resources."

In an important recent opinion, the Supreme Court confirmed that the constitution forbids highway checkpoints whose "primary purpose" is the "discovery and interdiction of illegal narcotics." The case, *City of Indianapolis v. Edmond*,[121] involved a checkpoint program initiated by the City of Indianapolis for that purpose. The location for each checkpoint was selected on the basis of crime statistics and traffic flow. Checkpoints operated during daytime hours and were identified by signage as "Narcotics Checkpoints." Approximately 30 officers were stationed at the checkpoints, and following written procedures they stopped a predetermined number of vehicles and examined each in order. After a vehicle was stopped, its driver would be advised that "he or she is being stopped briefly at a drug checkpoint," and each would be asked to produce license and registration. An officer would evaluate the driver for "signs of impairment," visually examine the vehicle, and lead a drug-sniffing dog around its perimeter. After operating six roadblocks, the City claimed a "hit rate" of nine percent, because stops of 1,161 vehicles led to 104 arrests. Of those arrests, however, only 55 were for drug-related offenses.

The Court accepted the case on certiorari after two motorists brought a class action lawsuit challenging the constitutionality of the checkpoint program. Striking down the program on Fourth Amendment grounds, Justice O'Connor stressed that searches and seizures motivated by "the

---

121. 531 U.S. 32 (2000).

general interest in crime control" ordinarily must be based on individual-ized suspicion.

Chief Justice Rehnquist, joined by Justices Scalia and Thomas, dissent-ed. The dissenters explained that the case "follows naturally" from *Martinez-Fuerte* and *Sitz*, because the checkpoint program served significant and appropriate state interests ("preventing drunken driving and ensuring the proper licensing of drivers and registration of their vehicles") with minimal intrusions on motorists. As far as the drug interdiction purpose was concerned, the dissenters would hold irrelevant the "subjective expec-tations of those responsible for [the program]." Justice Thomas, who reads the constitution from an originalist position, wrote a separate dissent. Justice Thomas suggested that the Court's decisions in *Sitz* and *Martinez-Fuerte* were wrongly decided, because they permit searches and seizures without individualized suspicion. "I rather doubt," he wrote, "that the Framers of the Fourth Amendment would have considered 'reasonable' a program of indiscriminate stops of individuals not suspected of wrongdo-ing." Nevertheless, Justice Thomas was not prepared to consider overrul-ing *Sitz* and *Martinez-Fuerte* "without the benefit of briefing and argu-ment." In light of his belief that those cases controlled the present case, he would uphold the Indianapolis checkpoint program.

Reproduced below is an excerpt from Justice O'Connor's majority opinion in the *Edmond* case. The excerpt will help you put the Court's checkpoint cases into a coherent framework and also to evaluate the Court's position on the Fourth Amendment relevance of the subjective intent of police and policy makers.

City of Indianapolis v. Edmond
531 U.S. 32 (2000).

■ O'CONNOR, J. The Fourth Amendment requires that searches and sei-zures be reasonable. A search or seizure is ordinarily unreasonable in the absence of individualized suspicion of wrongdoing. While such suspicion is not an "irreducible" component of reasonableness, we have recognized only limited circumstances in which the usual rule does not apply. For example, we have upheld certain regimes of suspicionless searches where the pro-gram was designed to serve "special needs, beyond the normal need for law enforcement." *See, e.g., Vernonia School Dist. 47J v. Acton*, 515 U.S. 646 (1995) (random drug testing of student-athletes); *Treasury Employees v. Von Raab*, 489 U.S. 656 (1989) (drug tests for United States Customs Service employees seeking transfer or promotion to certain positions); *Skinner v. Railway Labor Executives' Assn.*, 489 U.S. 602 (1989) (drug and alcohol tests for railway employees involved in train accidents or found to be in violation of particular safety regulations). We have also allowed searches for certain administrative purposes without particularized suspi-cion of misconduct, provided that those searches are appropriately limited. *See, e.g., New York v. Burger* (warrantless administrative inspection of premises of "closely regulated" business); *Michigan v. Tyler*, 436 U.S. 499

(1978) (administrative inspection of fire-damaged premises to determine cause of blaze); *Camara v. Municipal Court of City and County of San Francisco*, 387 U.S. 523 (1967) (administrative inspection to ensure compliance with city housing code).

We have also upheld brief, suspicionless seizures of motorists at a fixed Border Patrol checkpoint designed to intercept illegal aliens, *United States v. Martinez–Fuerte*, 428 U.S. 543 (1976), and at a sobriety checkpoint aimed at removing drunk drivers from the road, *Michigan Dept. of State Police v. Sitz*, 496 U.S. 444 (1990). In addition, in *Delaware v. Prouse*, 440 U.S. 648 (1979), we suggested that a similar type of roadblock with the purpose of verifying drivers' licenses and vehicle registrations would be permissible. In none of these cases, however, did we indicate approval of a checkpoint program whose primary purpose was to detect evidence of ordinary criminal wrongdoing.

In *Martinez-Fuerte*, we entertained Fourth Amendment challenges to stops at two permanent immigration checkpoints located on major United States highways less than 100 miles from the Mexican border. We noted at the outset the particular context in which the constitutional question arose, describing in some detail the "formidable law enforcement problems" posed by the northbound tide of illegal entrants into the United States. These problems had also been the focus of several earlier cases addressing the constitutionality of other Border Patrol traffic-checking operations. In *Martinez-Fuerte*, we found that the balance tipped in favor of the Government's interests in policing the Nation's borders. In so finding, we emphasized the difficulty of effectively containing illegal immigration at the border itself. We also stressed the impracticality of the particularized study of a given car to discern whether it was transporting illegal aliens, as well as the relatively modest degree of intrusion entailed by the stops. . . .

In *Sitz*, we evaluated the constitutionality of a Michigan highway sobriety checkpoint program. The *Sitz* checkpoint involved brief suspicionless stops of motorists so that police officers could detect signs of intoxication and remove impaired drivers from the road. Motorists who exhibited signs of intoxication were diverted for a license and registration check and, if warranted, further sobriety tests. This checkpoint program was clearly aimed at reducing the immediate hazard posed by the presence of drunk drivers on the highways, and there was an obvious connection between the imperative of highway safety and the law enforcement practice at issue. The gravity of the drunk driving problem and the magnitude of the State's interest in getting drunk drivers off the road weighed heavily in our determination that the program was constitutional.

In *Prouse*, we invalidated a discretionary, suspicionless stop for a spot check of a motorist's driver's license and vehicle registration. The officer's conduct in that case was unconstitutional primarily on account of his exercise of "standardless and unconstrained discretion." We nonetheless acknowledged the States' "vital interest in ensuring that only those qualified to do so are permitted to operate motor vehicles, that these vehicles are fit for safe operation, and hence that licensing, registration, and vehicle inspection requirements are being observed." Accordingly, we suggested that "[q]uestioning of all oncoming traffic at roadblock-type stops" would be a lawful means of serving this interest in highway safety.

We further indicated in *Prouse* that we considered the purposes of such a hypothetical roadblock to be distinct from a general purpose of investigating crime. The State proffered the additional interests of "the apprehension of stolen motor vehicles and of drivers under the influence of alcohol or narcotics" in its effort to justify the discretionary spot check. We attributed the entirety of the latter interest to the State's interest in roadway safety. We also noted that the interest in apprehending stolen vehicles may be partly subsumed by the interest in roadway safety. We observed, however, that "[t]he remaining governmental interest in controlling automobile thefts is not distinguishable from the general interest in crime control." Not only does the common thread of highway safety thus run through *Sitz* and *Prouse*, but *Prouse* itself reveals a difference in the Fourth Amendment significance of highway safety interests and the general interest in crime control.

. . . [W]hat principally distinguishes these checkpoints from those we have previously approved is their primary purpose. As petitioners concede, the Indianapolis checkpoint program unquestionably has the primary purpose of interdicting illegal narcotics. . . .

We have never approved a checkpoint program whose primary purpose was to detect evidence of ordinary criminal wrongdoing. Rather, our checkpoint cases have recognized only limited exceptions to the general rule that a seizure must be accompanied by some measure of individualized suspicion. We suggested in *Prouse* that we would not credit the "general interest in crime control" as justification for a regime of suspicionless stops. Consistent with this suggestion, each of the checkpoint programs that we have approved was designed primarily to serve purposes closely related to the problems of policing the border or the necessity of ensuring roadway safety. Because the primary purpose of the Indianapolis narcotics checkpoint program is to uncover evidence of ordinary criminal wrongdoing, the program contravenes the Fourth Amendment.

Petitioners propose several ways in which the narcotics-detection purpose of the instant checkpoint program may instead resemble the primary purposes of the checkpoints in *Sitz* and *Martinez-Fuerte*. Petitioners state that the checkpoints in those cases had the same ultimate purpose of arresting those suspected of committing crimes. Securing the border and apprehending drunk drivers are, of course, law enforcement activities, and law enforcement officers employ arrests and criminal prosecutions in pursuit of these goals. If we were to rest the case at this high level of generality, there would be little check on the ability of the authorities to construct roadblocks for almost any conceivable law enforcement purpose. Without drawing the line at roadblocks designed primarily to serve the general interest in crime control, the Fourth Amendment would do little to prevent such intrusions from becoming a routine part of American life.

Petitioners also emphasize the severe and intractable nature of the drug problem as justification for the checkpoint program. There is no doubt that traffic in illegal narcotics creates social harms of the first magnitude. The law enforcement problems that the drug trade creates likewise remain daunting and complex, particularly in light of the myriad forms of spin-off crime that it spawns. The same can be said of various other illegal activities, if only to a lesser degree. But the gravity of the threat alone cannot be dispositive of questions concerning what means law enforcement officers may employ to pursue a given purpose. Rather, in determining whether individualized suspicion is required, we must consider the nature of the interests threatened and their connection to the particular law enforcement practices at issue. We are particularly reluctant to recognize exceptions to the general rule of individualized suspicion where governmental authorities primarily pursue their general crime control ends.

Nor can the narcotics-interdiction purpose of the checkpoints be rationalized in terms of a highway safety concern similar to that present in *Sitz*. The detection and punishment of almost any criminal offense serves broadly the safety of the community, and our streets would no doubt be safer but for the scourge of illegal drugs. Only with respect to a smaller class of offenses, however, is society confronted with the type of immediate, vehicle-bound threat to life and limb that the sobriety checkpoint in *Sitz* was designed to eliminate.

Petitioners also liken the anticontraband agenda of the Indianapolis checkpoints to the antismuggling purpose of the checkpoints in *Martinez-Fuerte*. Petitioners cite this Court's conclusion in *Martinez-Fuerte* that the flow of traffic was too heavy to permit "particularized study of a given car that would enable it to be identified as a possible carrier of illegal aliens," and claim that this logic has even more force here. The problem with this argument is that the same logic prevails any time a vehicle is employed to conceal contraband or other evidence of a crime. This type of connection to the roadway is very different from the close connection to roadway safety that was present in *Sitz* and *Prouse*. Further, the Indianapolis checkpoints are far removed from the border context that was crucial in *Martinez-Fuerte*. While the difficulty of examining each passing car was an important factor in validating the law enforcement technique employed in *Martinez-Fuerte*, this factor alone cannot justify a regime of suspicionless searches or seizures. Rather, we must look more closely at the nature of the public interests that such a regime is designed principally to serve.

The primary purpose of the Indianapolis narcotics checkpoints is in the end to advance "the general interest in crime control." We decline to suspend the usual requirement of individualized suspicion where the police seek to employ a checkpoint primarily for the ordinary enterprise of investigating crimes. We cannot sanction stops justified only by the generalized and ever-present possibility that interrogation and inspection may reveal that any given motorist has committed some crime.

Of course, there are circumstances that may justify a law enforcement checkpoint where the primary purpose would otherwise, but for some emergency, relate to ordinary crime control. For example, . . . the Fourth Amendment would almost certainly permit an appropriately tailored road-block set up to thwart an imminent terrorist attack or to catch a dangerous criminal who is likely to flee by way of a particular route. The exigencies created by these scenarios are far removed from the circumstances under which authorities might simply stop cars as a matter of course to see if there just happens to be a felon leaving the jurisdiction. While we do not limit the purposes that may justify a checkpoint program to any rigid set of categories, we decline to approve a program whose primary purpose is ultimately indistinguishable from the general interest in crime control.

Petitioners argue that our prior cases preclude an inquiry into the purposes of the checkpoint program. For example, they cite *Whren v. United States*, 517 U.S. 806 (1996) and *Bond v. United States*, 529 U.S. 334 (2000), to support the proposition that "where the government articulates and pursues a legitimate interest for a suspicionless stop, courts should not look behind that interest to determine whether the government's 'primary purpose' is valid." These cases, however, do not control the instant situation.

In *Whren*, we held that an individual officer's subjective intentions are irrelevant to the Fourth Amendment validity of a traffic stop that is justified objectively by probable cause to believe that a traffic violation has occurred. We observed that our prior cases "foreclose any argument that the constitutional reasonableness of traffic stops depends on the actual motivations of the individual officers involved." In so holding, we expressly distinguished cases where we had addressed the validity of searches conducted in the absence of probable cause.

Whren therefore reinforces the principle that, while "[s]ubjective intentions play no role in ordinary, probable-cause Fourth Amendment analysis," programmatic purposes may be relevant to the validity of Fourth Amendment intrusions undertaken pursuant to a general scheme without individualized suspicion. Accordingly, *Whren* does not preclude an inquiry into programmatic purpose in such contexts. It likewise does not preclude an inquiry into programmatic purpose here.

Last Term in *Bond*, we addressed the question whether a law enforcement officer violated a reasonable expectation of privacy in conducting a tactile examination of carry-on luggage in the overhead compartment of a bus. In doing so, we simply noted that the principle of *Whren* rendered the subjective intent of an officer irrelevant to this analysis. While, as petitioners correctly observe, the analytical rubric of *Bond* was not "ordinary, probable-cause Fourth Amendment analysis," nothing in *Bond* suggests that we would extend the principle of *Whren* to all situations where individualized suspicion was lacking. Rather, subjective intent was irrelevant in *Bond* because the inquiry that our precedents required focused on the objective effects of the actions of an individual officer. By contrast, our cases dealing with intrusions that occur pursuant to a general scheme absent individualized suspicion have often required an inquiry into purpose at the programmatic level.

Petitioners argue that the Indianapolis checkpoint program is justified by its lawful secondary purposes of keeping impaired motorists off the road and verifying licenses and registrations. If this were the case, however, law enforcement authorities would be able to establish checkpoints for virtually any purpose so long as they also included a license or sobriety check. For this reason, we examine the available evidence to determine the primary purpose of the checkpoint program. While we recognize the challenges inherent in a purpose inquiry, courts routinely engage in this enterprise in many areas of constitutional jurisprudence as a means of sifting abusive governmental conduct from that which is lawful. As a result, a program driven by an impermissible purpose may be proscribed while a program impelled by licit purposes is permitted, even though the challenged conduct may be outwardly similar. While reasonableness under the Fourth Amendment is predominantly an objective inquiry, our special needs and administrative search cases demonstrate that purpose is often relevant when suspicionless intrusions pursuant to a general scheme are at issue.

It goes without saying that our holding today does nothing to alter the constitutional status of the sobriety and border checkpoints that we approved in *Sitz* and *Martinez-Fuerte* or of the type of traffic checkpoint that we suggested would be lawful in *Prouse*. The constitutionality of such checkpoint programs still depends on a balancing of the competing interests at stake and the effectiveness of the program. When law enforcement authorities pursue primarily general crime control purposes at checkpoints such as here, however, stops can only be justified by some quantum of individualized suspicion.

PROBLEM 4–18

In *Edmond*, the majority declined to decide the constitutionality of checkpoints that have "the primary purpose of checking licenses or driver sobriety and a secondary purpose of interdicting narcotics." The majority also cautioned that it was not taking any view "on the question whether police may expand the scope of a license or sobriety checkpoint seizure in order to detect the presence of drugs in a stopped car."

Question: Suppose that Indianapolis had designed a checkpoint program that defined its "primary purpose" as driver sobriety. In support of the program, the City cited statistics suggesting that driver insobriety was causing a number of highway deaths. The City also indicated as a secondary purpose of the program its interest in discovering and confiscating illegal drugs. The program's written documentation instructed officers to stop cars, evaluate each driver for impairment, and then conduct a thorough dog sniff of the outside of each car. In practice, total stopped time for the driver impairment check averaged 5 minutes; each dog sniff added, on average, 5 minutes to the stop of a vehicle. Would the Court uphold this program? Why or why not?

The Court's most recent case on this question, *Illinois v. Lidster*,[122] further clarifies the point. In *Lidster*, one week after a fatal hit-and-run accident, police set up a checkpoint to locate witnesses to the crime. As each car approached the checkpoint, an officer would stop the car for 10 to 15 seconds to ask whether its occupants had seen the crime and would hand the driver a flyer asking for assistance. When Robert Lidster approached the checkpoint in his minivan, his van swerved, nearly hitting one of the officers. That officer subsequently smelled alcohol on Lidster's breath, administered a sobriety test, and arrested him. Lidster was convicted of driving under the influence of alcohol and appealed on the ground that much of the evidence against him should have been suppressed as the fruit of an illegal checkpoint seizure. Although the trial court rejected this claim, two Illinois appellate courts accepted it, and the United States Supreme Court accepted certiorari.

At first blush, there was ample reason to support the Illinois appellate court decisions. Unlike in the drunk driving cases, and many of the urine drug-testing cases, there was no imminent danger to public safety, indeed no "civil" purpose at all. The sole reason for the roadblock—one run by the police alone—was to investigate crime. Indeed, the Court had recently held in *City of Indianapolis v. Edmond*,[123] discussed immediately above, that a roadblock to find those transporting—but not necessarily then using—illicit drugs served no immediate safety purpose and was therefore a traditional criminal search requiring probable cause and a warrant or a recognized exception to the warrant requirement.

But, in *Lidster,* the Supreme Court held otherwise, upholding the conviction and the constitutionality of the search. Not all criminal enforcement objectives, explained the Court, are the sort that demand presumptive unconstitutionality absent individualized suspicion. "The stop's primary law enforcement purpose," concluded the Court, was "*not* to determine whether a vehicle's occupants were committing a crime, but to ask vehicle occupants, as members of the public, for their help in providing information about a crime in all likelihood committed by others."[124] The Court continued: "The police expected the information elicited to help them apprehend, not the vehicle's occupants, *but other individuals*."[125] Moreover, in such a situation, requiring individualized suspicion makes no sense, for no individual is stopped because he or she is suspected of, or even potentially sought for, involvement in any crime. "Like certain other forms of police activity, say, crime control or public safety, an information-seeking stop is not the kind of event that involves suspicion, or lack of suspicion, of the relevant individual."[126] Additionally, concluded the Court:

---

122.   540 U.S. 419 (2004).

123.   531 U.S. 32 (2000).

124.   540 U.S. at 419.

125.   *Id.* at 423.

126.   *Id.* at 425.

[I]nformation-seeking highway stops are less likely to provoke anxiety or to prove intrusive. The stops are likely brief. The police are not likely to ask questions designed to elicit self-incriminating information. And citizens will often react positively when police simply ask for their help as "responsible citizen[s]" to "give whatever information they may have to aid in law enforcement."[127]

Furthermore, said the Court, the law ordinarily allows police to seek voluntary public cooperation in solving crime; the Fourth Amendment "does not treat a motorist's car as his castle;" the traffic delay was brief; and proliferation of similar checkpoints was unlikely given "limited police resources and community hostility to related traffic tie-ups...."[128] Therefore, the Court declared that a more flexible reasonableness balancing test like that in the drunk-driving roadblock cases was appropriate, indeed classifying those latter cases as another example of "special law enforcement concerns ... justify[ing] highway stops without individualized suspicion."[129] The suspicionless, warrantless information roadblock in *Lidster* survived reasonableness balancing because the stop was tailored to serve a grave public concern (finding a killer) in that it was located where there was a good chance of finding drivers knowledgeable about the crime; the delay (including time waiting in a line of cars) was brief—a few minutes at most—and the contact provided little reason for anxiety or alarm, for all cars were temporarily stopped, and there were no allegations of discriminatory or other unlawful police behavior during questioning.

The Court never expressly explained *why* information-seeking stops are less likely to provoke anxiety than many other stops and *why* the *Lidster* stop was more like sobriety checkpoints and even pure public safety measures (like crowd control) than like checkpoints for drug traffickers. Implicitly, however, the level of stigma arguably seemed to be an important factor. A driver stopped to be questioned about witnessing a crime is treated like a respectable citizen rather than a potential criminal. Neither he nor knowing observers are likely to see the investigation as even potentially stigmatizing. To the contrary, the Court seems right in suggesting that expecting presumably honest citizens to help in finding the killer of a 70–year-old bicyclist (the hit-and-run driver's victim) is a sign of respect. Categorizing the stop, therefore, as one whose primary purpose was other than the "general interest in crime control" might therefore be correct.

Whether the more flexible resulting balancing test for administrative seizures was met on the *Lidster* facts, however, may be more debatable, as Justice Stevens, joined by Justices Souter and Ginsburg, argued in their opinion concurring in part and dissenting in part. Justice Stevens agreed with the majority's primary purpose analysis but favored a remand for additional factfinding on the application of the reasonableness balancing

---

127. *Id.*

128. *Id.* at 426.

129. *Id.* at 424.

test. Justice Stevens questioned whether there were less intrusive but equally or even more effective alternatives, such as placing flyers on Post Office employee cars, the victim having just finished work there before the fatal accident. Stevens also questioned whether the annoyance of delay for drivers at a location where many were leaving a factory at the end of a shift and the accompanying large surge of vehicles could be justified by an investigatory method so likely to be ineffective. Because the roadblock was unpublicized, he also speculated that waiting drivers, who would not know the purpose of the search until reaching the checkpoint, might be alarmed at being ensnared in an unexpected midnight roadblock—facts and possibilities entirely ignored by the majority.

PROBLEM 4–19

In *Edmond*, the majority stated that "while subjective intentions play no role in ordinary, probable-cause Fourth Amendment analysis, programmatic purposes may be relevant to the validity of Fourth Amendment intrusions undertaken pursuant to a general scheme without individual suspicion."

Question: What does the Court mean by "programmatic purposes?" Perhaps you will find some assistance from this language in the lower court opinion[130] in the *Edmond* case:

> It is necessary . . . to distinguish between two kinds of purpose, that of the program's designers and that of the police officers manning the roadblocks. The test for the lawfulness of a particular search or seizure is an objective one; the motives of the officer carrying out the search or seizure are irrelevant. *Whren v. United States*. But the purpose behind the program is critical to its legality. The program must be a bona fide effort to implement an authorized regulatory policy rather than a pretext for a dragnet search for criminals.

PROBLEM 4–20

In late 2002 and early 2003, two snipers shot and killed a number of people in Washington, D.C. and its suburbs. The killings terrorized the community. At the time, nothing was known about the killers other than a description of the vehicle out of which they operated and in which they fled each crime scene. That was described by one tipster as a white truck, with a vertical accordion rear door, an old paint job, a dented fender, and black-lettered words on both sides. Police, in an effort to find the killer, stopped every truck that they could find fitting the description just noted.

Question: Was roadblock justified under the special needs doctrine or was it a traditional search for the purposes of criminal investigation? If the latter, was the description adequate to establish reasonable suspicion to stop white trucks fitting the fleeing truck's description? Whether the

---

130.   Edmond v. Goldsmith, 183 F.3d 659 (7th Cir. 1999) (opinion by Posner, J.).

seizure was a special needs search or a traditional criminal seizure, under what circumstances should the police have been able to search each stopped truck and its passengers? Would the roadblock have been justified if, instead of asking permission to search each driver's trunk, the police had asked each occupant of each car whether he or she had any information helpful in finding the snipers? What if the snipers had been caught and the police set up a roadblock questioning vehicle occupants about whether they had information useful in prosecuting and convicting the snipers?

PROBLEM 4–21

Assume the following changes in the Boson case in Chapter 1. On April 13, in Franklin County, Missouri, a police officer stopped defendant Daniel Boson's car pursuant to a drug enforcement checkpoint. The checkpoint had been conceived by Deputy Kenneth Hotsen and Corporal Michael Shutz, with the approval of the local sheriff. The plan called for erecting an intentionally misleading sign stating, "DRUNK DRIVING CHECKPOINT 3 MILES AHEAD" on eastbound I–44. No checkpoint was, however, established on I–44. Rather, the checkpoint was located at the top of exit ramp 242, the only ramp between the sign and the 3–mile point where the fictional checkpoint would have been located. Exit ramp 242 was chosen because of its "remote location . . . nothing there except a few isolated residences." The officers believed that a light flow of traffic would simplify checkpoint operation and that suspected drug traffickers would exit in an attempt to avoid the fictional drunk driving checkpoint.

Approaching drivers could not see any police presence until the cars were stopped. Police cars with lights turned off were parked across the street on the entrance ramp to I–44. A single uniformed officer would stop all exiting vehicles at the top of the ramp. The officer would not speak to the driver. A police officer dressed in camouflage would then approach the car, tell the driver the reason for the stop, ask that he exhibit a driver's license, and ask why he exited at that location. The questioning officers were instructed to "look for signs of drunk driving or drug trafficking." If an officer believed that he had reasonable suspicion of either, he was required to seek permission to search the car. The plan did not include a drug courier profile or a list of signals giving rise to reasonable suspicion of drug trafficking. If permission were granted, a search would be conducted. If permission were denied, then another camouflaged officer would lead a drug sniffing dog around the exterior of the car. No motorist was expected to be stopped more than a few minutes.

That day, the checkpoint lasted eight hours. Sixty-two cars, roughly one every seven minutes, passed through the off ramp. Only one person, Boson, was arrested. Boson was stopped and refused consent to search, but a drug sniffer dog then alerted to the trunk. A search of the trunk revealed a large quantity of cocaine.

Question: You are Boson's counsel. What arguments will you raise in any motion to suppress, and what is the likelihood that you will succeed?

Would your conclusions differ and, if so, how and why, if (a) the police looked only for signs of drunk driving, (b) the police looked only for signs of drug trafficking, and (c) the initial sign read, "drug enforcement checkpoint 3 miles ahead."

PROBLEM 4–22

In August, Captain Wilhelm Camper, in conjunction with a small committee, prepared guidelines for a sobriety checkpoint to be conducted by the Kettering, Ohio, police department on September 4th and 5th. Camper told the committee that the checkpoint was planned both to raise public awareness of the seriousness of drunk driving violations and to arrest anyone caught breaking the law. The site of the checkpoint was selected based on traffic flow, safety, illumination, drunk driving arrests in the area, and the availability of public property to use in operating the checkpoint. The planned average delay of each car at the checkpoint was less than 45 seconds. The plan was publicized via television news and local newspapers in August.

Before conducting the checkpoint, the police distributed written guidelines to participating officers at a formal briefing session. Those guidelines were that police were to stop: (1) every third vehicle traveling east and west on Dorothy Lane between 10:30 p.m. and 11:00 p.m., (2) every second vehicle between 11:00 p.m. and midnight, and (3) every car between midnight and 3:30 a.m. The guidelines permitted deviation from this stopping pattern if approved by the on-scene commander for safety reasons and required resumptions of the designated pattern as soon as the exigency ended. On September 4, the police deviated twice from the designated pattern for westbound traffic because of traffic congestion resulting from the showing of a popular movie at a nearby theatre. On both occasions, the police waved all cars through the checkpoint. The deviations lasted only as long as the traffic jam.

For motorists westbound on Dorothy Lane, the checkpoint was set up so that signs for the checkpoint were visible on the right side of the road 400 feet before the initial stopping point. Designated cars were stopped at an initial contact point, about 100 feet west of Oakmont Road, where a police officer would "greet the driver," explain the stop's purpose, and engage in "innocuous conversation" while making a cursory examination of the driver for no more than 30 seconds to identify any signs of impairment. If such signs were not detected, the driver would be waved on. But if signs of intoxication were detected (e.g., the smell of alcohol plus other indicators, such as slurred words), the driver would be asked to submit to a rapid horizontal gaze nystagmus test, which seeks to identify intoxication based upon eye movements. If that test suggested intoxication, the driver would be moved to a secondary checkpoint for other forms of sobriety testing.

On September 4 and 5, the police screened 374 out of 699 travelers on westbound Dorothy Lane, tested 22 drivers, and arrested 11. From eastbound traffic, police screened 194 out of 492 cars, tested 11 drivers, and arrested 2. Overall, out of 568 screened motorists, 13 were arrested, a 2.3% detection and arrest rate for all cars screened.

Thomas Eggie was stopped on September 4, at 2:00 a.m., pursuant to the above guidelines. Patrolman Thatcher, who did the stop, noticed defendant had a flushed face, bloodshot eyes, and a strong odor of alcohol. His horizontal gaze nystagmus number was high (6 points), suggesting intoxication, so he was waved on for field sobriety tests, all of which he flunked; he was then arrested. When first stopped by the examining officer, the defendant was ordered to extinguish his cigarette. Moreover, the defendant's examination and arrest were filmed by a media film crew, covering the incident for a T.V. news story on the checkpoint. Furthermore, there was no place for a car to exit between the sign announcing the checkpoint and the location of the initial stop.

Question: The defense has filed a motion to suppress the results of the various sobriety tests and the examining officer's observations. You are the judge who has heard the motion, at a hearing establishing the above facts. How will you rule and why?

(VII) INVENTORY SEARCHES

An inventory search is one conducted by the police not for purposes of criminal investigation but rather to protect the owner's property from loss or theft, and the police from unjustified lawsuits arising from such loss and theft while the property is in police custody. Also, inventories protect the safety of the police and the public by locating things in seized property that might pose a danger to police or the public. Because inventory searches are done to serve a special need other than criminal law enforcement, specifically protecting life and property, they appear to be administrative searches. The most common types of inventory searches are of properly seized and impounded cars and of property on an arrestee's person.

An inventory search may itself be justified, however, only if the initial seizure of the property being inventoried was permissible. Statutes might, for example, provide for impounding cars abandoned on public highways or subject to repeated parking violations. A general Fourth Amendment seizure analysis might also justify a seizure of a car under particular circumstances, such as where it blocks the entrance to a hospital emergency room or when it might be subject to theft or damage if left at the site where its driver is arrested.

If the seizure is itself justified, an inventory search of a car may be justified by these noninvestigative state interests: (1) ensuring protection of the police department from false claims, (2) protecting inventoried items from theft or vandalism, (3) protecting the police and public from potential danger, and, for abandoned cars, permitting the police to investigate who owns the car or whether it has been abandoned. The Court in *South Dakota v. Opperman*[131] upheld an inventory search of a locked car that had been impounded after receiving two tickets for being illegally parked. The

---

131. 428 U.S. 364 (1976).

warrantless search uncovered marijuana in the glove compartment. The Court concluded that the search, which had been done pursuant to standard procedures to protect valuables first observed through the car's window, was permissible because it was effectuated: (1) pursuant to lawful impoundment; (2) of a routine nature, following standard police procedures; and (3) for noninvestigative reasons, and not as a "mere pretext concealing an investigatory police motive." Justice Powell explained in a concurring opinion that the requirement of standard departmental procedures meant that "no significant discretion . . . [was] placed in the hands of the individual officer."

It is not clear how much is left of *Opperman's* non-pretext rule. In *Arkansas v. Sullivan*,[132] the Court held that results of an inventory search could not be suppressed on the basis of an allegedly pretextual arrest. Police had stopped Sullivan for speeding and having an improperly tinted windshield. He was unable to produce car registration or insurance documentation, but he handed over his driver's license. Upon reviewing this, the officer recognized him as someone with a reputation for narcotics dealing. He also noticed what was described as a "rusted roofing hatchet" in the car. Thereupon the officer arrested him for the speeding and windshield offenses, as well as for failure to produce required paperwork and carrying a weapon (the hatchet), and he conducted an inventory search of the car, finding methamphetamine. An Arkansas trial court and that state's supreme court held that the methamphetamine should be suppressed because the arrest was merely a pretext motivated by a desire to search Sullivan's car.

The United States Supreme Court overruled the Arkansas courts in a *per curiam* opinion. Emphasizing that Sullivan's claim focused on the officer's motivation for the stop and arrest, the Court reiterated its position in *Whren* that "subjective intentions play no role in ordinary, probable-cause Fourth Amendment analysis." Is there a difference between challenging the pretextual nature of the arrest (which implicates "ordinary, probable-cause Fourth Amendment analysis") and challenging the pretextual nature of the inventory search? The Court did not say, but consider this hypothetical: suppose Sullivan discovered that the Arkansas inventory search policy gave discretion to the arresting officer to decide whether or not to impound and search the car. Could Sullivan successfully suppress the methamphetamine by claiming that the officer's decision to conduct the inventory search was motivated by a desire to find narcotics? Under these circumstances, would Sullivan have any other argument with which to challenge the inventory search?

The remaining parts of *Opperman* appear viable still. Its analysis was extended to the search of items found on an arrestee, specifically a shoulder bag carried by a man arrested for disturbing the peace and found to contain drugs, in *Illinois v. Lafayette*.[133] The same rationale applied as in *Opper-*

---

132. 532 U.S. 769 (2001).

133. 462 U.S. 640 (1983).

man—protecting police, the owner, and the public from theft, damage, or injury. Furthermore, there may be less of an invasion for a station house search than for a publicly embarrassing street search. Once again, the Court rejected the argument that less intrusive alternatives, such as storing rather than searching the bag, could have been followed:

> [T]he real question is not what "could have been achieved," but whether the Fourth Amendment requires such steps; it is not our function to write a manual on administering routine, neutral procedures at the station house. . . . Even if less intrusive means existed of protecting some particular types of property, it would be unreasonable to expect police officers in the everyday course of business to make fine and subtle distinctions in deciding which containers or items may be searched and which must be sealed as a unit.

While police thus need not follow the least restrictive alternative, there still must be some restrictions on their discretion. *Colorado v. Bertine*[134] makes it clear, however, that these limits are quite broad. In *Bertine*, police department regulations gave police officers discretion whether to impound a vehicle or park it in a public lot. However, those same regulations prohibited the parking alternative if that option raised a reasonable risk of damage to the vehicle or the arrestee would not agree. The defendant had been arrested for driving under the influence of alcohol, and the police then towed his van to a secure, lighted location. The Court rejected the defense argument that the safety of the property could not justify an inventory because the police could have offered the driver a chance to arrange for the property's safekeeping, because "reasonable police regulations relating to inventory procedures administered in good faith satisfy the Fourth Amendment, even though courts might as a matter of hindsight be able to devise equally reasonable rules requiring a different procedure." The broad limits on police officer discretion were adequate, for "[n]othing in *Opperman* or *Lafayette* prohibits the exercise of police discretion so long as that discretion is exercised according to standard criteria and on the basis of something other than suspicion of criminal activity." The Court, again rejecting a least intrusive means analysis, also dismissed the defendant's claim that containers in his vehicle could not be opened absent a weighing of the privacy invasion against the risk that each container might hold dangerous or valuable items. It was sufficient that "the police department procedures mandated the opening of closed containers and the listing of their contents."

Nevertheless, there must be at least some restrictions on the exercise of police officer discretion. Thus, the Court in *Florida v. Wells*[135] unanimously rejected the state's effort to apply the inventory search exception to opening a locked suitcase where the Florida Highway Patrol had no policy at all concerning when to open closed containers. However, in doing so the

---

134. 479 U.S. 367 (1987).

135. 495 U.S. 1 (1990).

Court stressed that, while some regulations were needed, those regulations could still vest officers with considerable discretion:

> While policies of opening all containers are unquestionably permissible, it would be equally permissible, for example, to allow the opening of closed containers whose contents officers determine they are unable to ascertain from examining the contents' exteriors. The allowance of the exercise of judgment based on concerns related to the purpose of an inventory search does not violate the Fourth Amendment.

Comment on State Constitutions: State courts may establish more stringent standards than the United States Supreme Court's for determining whether administrative searches survive constitutional scrutiny. Of particular interest is *People v. Keta*,[136] where a New York State appellate court held that the statute at issue in the *Burger* case was inconsistent with the New York State constitution:

> ... we adhere to the view ... that the so-called "administrative search" exception to the Fourth Amendment's probable cause and warrant requirements cannot be invoked where, as here, the search is "undertaken solely to uncover evidence of criminality" and the underlying regulatory scheme is "in reality, designed simply to give the police an expedient means of enforcing penal sanctions." This principle was a fundamental assumption in administrative-search jurisprudence before *Burger*. And, notwithstanding *Burger*, it remains analytically sound, since, without such a limitation, what was originally conceived as a narrow exception would swallow up the rule and permit circumvention of the traditional probable cause and warrant requirements where their protections are most needed.
>
> Further, the administrative search provisions of Vehicle and Traffic Law sec. 415–a(5)(a) cannot pass constitutional muster because the essential element of pervasive governmental supervision is lacking. While the Supreme Court found this element to be satisfied by analogy to what it deemed "related" industries such as junkyards, which, according to that Court, are highly regulated, we conclude that more is required to permit an exception to the warrant and probable cause requirements embodied in article I, sec. 12. Once again, our insistence upon close analysis in this context is motivated by our belief that the administrative search exception should remain a narrow and carefully circumscribed one. ...
>
> Although the Supreme Court in *Burger* placed great weight on the fact that the statute is supported by a "substantial" governmental interest and that warrantless inspections are "necessary to further [the] regulatory scheme," we deem these factors in themselves to be insufficient justification for departing from article I, sec. 12's general prohibition against warrantless, suspicionless searches. Such arguments are always available when the regulatory activity in question

---

136.   593 N.E.2d 1328 (N.Y. 1992).

has a law enforcement-related goal. Obviously, the government's interest in law enforcement is always, by definition, "substantial," and tools such as unannounced general inspections, without judicial supervision or regularity and accountability, are always helpful in detecting and deterring crime. If these were the only criteria for determining when citizens' privacy rights may be curtailed there would be few, if any, situations in which the protections of article I, sec. 12 would operate. Indeed, the very purpose of including such protections in our Constitution was to provide a counterbalancing check on what may be done to individual citizens in the name of governmental goals.

For the same reasons, the dissent's reliance on the "staggering" statistics attesting to the growth of automobile theft in New York and the economic burdens such crime imposes are hardly a persuasive ground for relaxing article I, sec. 12's proscription against unreasonable searches and seizures. The alarming increase of unlicensed weapons on our urban streets and the catastrophic rise in the use of crack cocaine and heroin are also matters of pressing social concern, but few would seriously argue that those unfortunate facets of modern life justify routine searches of pedestrians on the street or any other suspension of the privacy guarantees that are there to protect all of our citizens. The fact is that, regrettably, there will always be serious crime in our society, and there will always be upsurges in the rate of particular crimes due to changes in the social landscape. Indeed, the writs of assistance were themselves a response of the colonial government to an unprecedented wave of criminal smuggling—a crime that also led to "intolerable" economic losses.

Our responsibility in the judicial branch is not to respond to these temporary crises or to shape the law so as to advance the goals of law enforcement, but rather to stand as a fixed citadel for constitutional rights, safeguarding them against those who would dismantle our system of ordered liberty in favor of a system of well-kept order alone. As has recently been observed, the present crisis will, undoubtedly, abate, but the precedents we create now will long endure. Accordingly, in response to the dissent's appeal to our citizens' legitimate fears about rising crime, it suffices to observe, as Benjamin Franklin did some 200 years ago, that "those who give up essential liberty to purchase a little temporary safety deserve neither liberty nor safety."

———

Oregon also has adopted more stringent standards, implementing what Judge (formerly professor) David Schuman argues are communitarian principles.[137] To communitarians, searches and seizures raise "questions of general public policy," rather than "questions of a particular individual's rights," and consequently they prefer "categorical, prospective, legislative

---

137. *See* David Schuman, *Taking Law Seriously: Communitarian Search and Seizure*, 27 AM. CRIM. L. REV. 583, 611 (1990).

restraints on official discretion, instead of ad hoc judicial limitations cast as rights-based claims against the government.'' Schuman argues that in the administrative search area, Oregon courts have encouraged legislative bodies to enact rules defining the search and seizure authority of officers. For example, in *Nelson v. Lane County*,[138] the Oregon Supreme Court explained that an administrative search unaccompanied by warrant or individualized suspicion could be valid if it was permitted by ''a law or ordinance providing sufficient indications of the purposes and limits of executive authority, and if it were carried out pursuant to a properly authorized administrative program, designed and systematically administered to control the discretion of non-supervisory officers.'' According to Schuman, *Nelson* and other Oregon cases indicate that administrative searches will be held unlawful under Oregon constitutional law if ''they do not find their source in some rational deliberative policy choice made by the people or their elected representatives.''

PROBLEM 4–23

The Reston, Virginia, Police Department has no written policy concerning impoundment and inventory searches of cars. However, general, if not universal, police practice has been to impound cars of suspected drug dealers or gang members and cars blocking traffic or otherwise creating an immediate risk of harm to persons or property. Only impounded cars in the first group, those of suspected drug dealers or gang members, were routinely subjected to an inventory search. For cars blocking traffic or creating a hazard, owners were given a significant opportunity to reclaim their cars or have friends or relatives do so. Only if the cars were not reclaimed would they be subjected to an inventory search. Community minority group members complained that this policy was discriminatorily applied against minority groups. For example, they maintained, largely minority suspected drug dealers or gang members, but not white suspects, had their cars impounded and inventoried. Similarly, they maintained, cars impounded for blocking traffic or creating other hazards were, contrary to the asserted policy, immediately impounded and inventoried if owned by a minority group member but not if owned by a white. The asserted policy was, however, the one routinely taught in the police academy and in every precinct as standard police policy.

John Arat, a 22–year-old African–American male and a resident of Baltimore, Maryland, was stopped in Reston, Virginia, for speeding 20 m.p.h. over the posted limit. A Virginia statute permitted the arrest of any out-of-state resident stopped for a traffic violation, such arrest being seen as a way to ensure payment of any fines. Accordingly, the officer arrested John Arat and told Arat that his car would be impounded. Arat protested the arrest and the impoundment, asking permission to park the car in a legal space or, if not, to call his cousin, who lived only blocks away, to do so. The officer refused. The officer has seen Arat in the neighborhood often

---

138.   743 P.2d 692 (Or. 1987).

and, the officer would later admit to others, suspected Arat-based on his clothes, his expensive car, and his cruising the streets at early morning hours far from his home-to be a drug dealer. Moreover, Arat wore a jacket with a skull and crossbones on the back, the mark of a local gang.

When Arat's impounded car was subjected to an inventory search, 1 pound of marijuana was found in the trunk, marijuana that Arat, as your client, maintains was planted there by the arresting officer.

Question: What are your chances of succeeding on a motion to suppress the marijuana? What additional discovery will you do, either formal or informal, and why? What witnesses, if any, will you call to the stand at the suppression hearing? Whom do you expect the prosecution to call, and what do you expect those witnesses to say?

6. CONSENT

a. *Requirement of Voluntariness*

In their efforts to control crime, police often are faced with suspicious situations that do not justify Fourth Amendment search and seizure activity. The state has an obvious interest in investigating these situations in order to prevent or discover criminal activity. On the other hand, the constitution protects individuals from such investigative activity. By permitting individuals to "consent" to searches and seizures, those constitutional impediments are removed. Consent might be seen, therefore, as a vehicle promoting cooperative relations between individuals and their governments. Consent also might be characterized as a decision on the part of the individual to waive the protections of the Fourth Amendment. The Court has refused to view consent as a waiver of rights, however, because such a view entails consequences that the Court has found unacceptable, including a requirement of detailed warnings before a valid consent may be given. Here is the Court's discussion of the waiver issue from the landmark case of *Schneckloth v. Bustamonte*:[139]

> ... The argument is that by allowing the police to conduct a search, a person "waives" whatever right he had to prevent the police from searching. It is argued that under the doctrine of *Johnson v. Zerbst*, 304 U.S. 458, to establish such a "waiver," the State must demonstrate "an intentional relinquishment or abandonment of a known right or privilege." But these standards were enunciated in *Johnson* in the context of the safeguards of a fair criminal trial. Our cases do not reflect an uncritical demand for a knowing and intelligent waiver in every situation where a person has failed to invoke a constitutional protection....
>
> Almost without exception, the requirement of a knowing and intelligent waiver has been applied only to those rights which the Constitution guarantees to a criminal defendant in order to preserve a fair trial. Hence ... the standard of a knowing and intelligent waiver

---

139. 412 U.S. 218 (1973).

has most often been applied to test the validity of a waiver of counsel, either at trial, or upon a guilty plea. And the Court has also applied the *Johnson* criteria to assess the effectiveness of a waiver of other trial rights such as the right to confrontation, to a jury trial, and to a speedy trial, and the right to be free from twice being placed in jeopardy. . . . The guarantees afforded a criminal defendant at trial also protect him at certain stages before the actual trial, and any alleged waiver must meet the strict standard of an intentional relinquishment of a "known" right. But the "trial" guarantees that have been applied to the "pretrial" stage of the criminal process are similarly designed to protect the fairness of the trial itself. Hence, . . . the Court held "that a post-indictment pretrial lineup at which the accused is exhibited to identifying witnesses is a critical stage of the criminal prosecution; that police conduct of such a lineup without notice to and in the absence of his counsel denies the accused his Sixth (and Fourteenth) Amendment right to counsel. . . ." Accordingly, the Court indicated that the standard of a knowing and intelligent waiver must be applied to test the waiver of counsel at such a lineup. The Court stressed the necessary interrelationship between the presence of counsel at a post-indictment lineup before trial and the protection of the trial process itself . . . And . . . the Court found that custodial interrogation by the police was inherently coercive, and consequently held that detailed warnings were required to protect the privilege against compulsory self-incrimination. The Court made it clear that the basis for decision was the need to protect the fairness of the trial itself. . . .

There is a vast difference between those rights that protect a fair criminal trial and the rights guaranteed under the Fourth Amendment. Nothing, either in the purposes behind requiring a "knowing" and "intelligent" waiver of trial rights, or in the practical application of such a requirement suggests that it ought to be extended to the constitutional guarantee against unreasonable searches and seizures. . . . The Constitution requires that every effort be made to see to it that a defendant in a criminal case has not unknowingly relinquished the basic protections that the Framers thought indispensable to a fair trial.

The protections of the Fourth Amendment are of a wholly different order, and have nothing whatever to do with promoting the fair ascertainment of truth at a criminal trial. Rather, as Mr. Justice Frankfurter's opinion for the Court put it in *Wolf v. Colorado*, 338 U.S. 25, the Fourth Amendment protects the "security of one's privacy against arbitrary intrusion by the police . . ." [T]he Court emphasized that "there is no likelihood of unreliability or coercion present in a search-and-seizure case."

Nor can it even be said that a search, as opposed to an eventual trial, is somehow "unfair" if a person consents to a search. While the Fourth and Fourteenth Amendments limit the circumstances under which the police can conduct a search, there is nothing constitutionally suspect in a person's voluntarily allowing a search. The actual conduct of the search may be precisely the same as if the police had obtained a warrant. And, unlike those constitutional guarantees that protect a defendant at trial, it cannot be said every reasonable presumption ought to be indulged against voluntary relinquishment. We have only recently stated: "[I]t is no part of the policy underlying the Fourth and Fourteenth Amendments to discourage citizens from aiding to the utmost of their ability in the apprehension of criminals." Rather, the community has a real interest in encouraging consent, for the resulting search may yield necessary evidence for the solution and prosecution of crime, evidence that may insure that a wholly innocent person is not wrongly charged with a criminal offense. . . .

It would be unrealistic to expect that in the informal, unstructured context of a consent search, a policeman, upon pain of tainting the evidence obtained, could make the detailed type of examination demanded by Johnson. And, if for this reason a diluted form of "waiver" were found acceptable, that would itself be ample recognition of the fact that there is no universal standard that must be applied in every situation where a person forgoes a constitutional right.

Rather than analyze consent as a waiver, the Court turned to the voluntariness test. That test, according to the Court, "reflects a fair accommodation of the constitutional requirements involved" by "reconciling the recognized legitimacy of consent searches with the requirement that they be free from any aspect of official coercion." The Court went on in *Schneckloth* to explain that

in examining all the surrounding circumstances to determine if in fact the consent to search was coerced, account must be taken of subtly coercive police questions, as well as the possibly vulnerable subjective state of the person who consents. Those searches that are the product of police coercion can thus be filtered out without undermining the continuing validity of consent searches. In sum, there is no reason for us to depart in the area of consent searches, from the traditional definition of "voluntariness."

To prove that the consent was given voluntarily, the state must show that the consent was obtained without coercion. In making this determination, the "traditional definition of voluntariness" requires the reviewing court to examine the totality of all the surrounding circumstances, including the characteristics of the accused and the details of the police-citizen interaction. Similar to the voluntariness assessment that takes place when a suspect has confessed, some of the factors taken into account "include the youth of the accused, his lack of education or his low intelligence, [and] the lack of any advice to the accused of his constitutional rights." Other factors include whether the individual was in custody when consent was given, the nature of the requests for consent, and the use of physical punishment such as the deprivation of food or sleep. We will discuss a few of the more important factors below.

A factor frequently mentioned is the individual's lack of awareness that consent may be refused. Most courts hold that lack of knowledge regarding the right to refuse is only one element to be considered, and in *Schneckloth* itself, the fact that the suspect was not informed of his right to refuse to consent did not invalidate the consent. The Court explained that the prosecution should not be burdened with having to prove the suspect's subjective understanding of the situation. Nor, according to the Court, should police be required to give a standard warning in every police-citizen encounter. The suspect's knowledge of the right to withhold consent, therefore, is not always determinative or even important. In *United States v. Drayton*,[140] the Court confirmed its rejection of "the suggestion that police officers must always inform citizens of their right to refuse when seeking permission to conduct a warrantless consent search." Moreover, the Court explained, a presumption of invalidity does not attach "if a citizen consented without explicit notification that he or she was free to refuse to cooperate. Instead, the Court has repeated that the totality of the circumstances must control, without giving extra weight to the absence of this type of warning." In *Drayton*, the Court held that, under a totality of circumstances analysis, bus passengers voluntarily consented to requests by police to search their bags and their persons.

Interestingly, sociology professor Illya Lichtenberg[141] has done a statistical study to determine whether warning motorists about their right to withhold consent affects the rate at which they consent to post-traffic stop searches. Lichtenberg used data provided by the Ohio Highway Patrol and the Maryland Chapter of the American Civil Liberties Union. His conclusion: the rates of consent after warnings actually *increased* modestly. Lichtenberg explains this result as consistent with psychological research demonstrating that most people feel great pressure to comply with the requests of someone in authority, even when those requests are contrary to an individual's moral standards and personal desires. He concludes further that warnings are an inadequate means for obtaining truly voluntary consent. Yet warnings may offer police further incentives to seek consent because the mere giving of them may convince a trial court that the consent was indeed voluntary.

QUESTIONS

1. If Professor Lichtenberg is right, what steps (in addition to warnings) could be taken to improve the likelihood that consent to search or seizure is voluntarily given?

2. If you have trouble crafting an answer to the preceding question, are there other solutions to the problem—for example, written rules that discourage consent searches, banning such searches altogether, or redefining "consent"?

---

140. 536 U.S. 194 (2002).

141. Illya Lichtenberg, *Miranda in Ohio: The Effects of Robinette on the "Voluntary" Waiver of Fourth Amendment Rights*, 44 HOWARD L.J. 349, 357, 361–74 (2001).

Sometimes government actors obtain consent from prison inmates under circumstances raising questions about voluntariness. For example, prison inmates are routinely required to sign forms acknowledging that their telephone conversations may be taped. Having made that acknowledgment, their use of telephone facilities constitutes their "implied consent" to any taping.[142] Here is the language from one such federal form:

> The Bureau of Prisons reserves the authority to monitor (this includes recording) conversations on any telephone located within its institutions, said monitoring to be done to preserve the security and orderly management of the institution and to protect the public. An inmate's use of institutional telephones constitutes consent to this monitoring. A properly placed phone call to an attorney is not monitored ... I understand that telephone calls I make from institution telephones may be monitored and recorded.

In *United States v. Lombardo*, an inmate's telephone calls were recorded without an intercept order under the Federal Wiretap Act, and the recorded conversations revealed evidence that would be used against him. The inmate made a motion to suppress the contents of the calls, but the trial court denied the motion after finding that the inmate (1) had signed the form upon arrival at the prison and (2) had consented to the recording by his use of the telephone. Can you make a good argument that the inmate's consent was involuntary?

In the *Ferguson* case (discussed in the section on special needs searches), the Court struck down a drug-screening program that targeted maternity patients receiving obstetrical care in a public hospital in Charleston, South Carolina. Under the program, the hospital obtained urine samples from maternity patients and subjected some to drug testing. Positive results were revealed to police. While the maternity patients did not know that results of their urine tests would be turned over to law enforcement agents, they did know that their urine was being taken for medical purposes, and they had signed a consent form that authorized hospital staff to perform all necessary tests, including drug tests. The Court remanded on the question whether patients had consented to the taking of their urine. While the majority had little to say on the consent issue, it suggested that the circumstances might require a knowing, intelligent, and voluntary waiver of rights, as opposed to simple consent (which requires only voluntariness): "when [state employees] undertake to obtain ... evidence from their patients for the specific purpose of incriminating those patients, they have a special obligation to make sure that the patients are fully informed about their constitutional rights, as standards of knowing waiver require. *Cf. Miranda v. Arizona*, 384 U.S. 436 (1966)." Justice Scalia dissented, arguing that the taking of the urine, which he characterized as the only act that could possibly be considered a search for Fourth Amendment purposes, was lawful because the maternity patients had consented to it. But consent, to Justice Scalia, does not require information. Rather,

---

142.   *See* United States v. Lombardo, 1999 WL 305096 (S.D.N.Y. 1999).

consent is simply the absence of coercion. As he observed, "[t]here is no contention . . . that the urine samples were extracted forcibly." Moreover, citing *Hoffa*, Justice Scalia urged that "information obtained through violation of a relationship of trust is obtained consensually, and is hence not a search." Finally, Justice Scalia discounted any argument that the maternity patients were coerced into giving urine samples by their need for medical treatment. "If that was coercion, it was not coercion applied by the government."

It appears that both the majority and Justice Scalia agreed in *Ferguson* that "simple consent" is nothing more than voluntariness—in other words, the absence of coercion. The majority, however, suggested that something more than voluntariness was required under the circumstances. Professor Taslitz explains:

> The Court applied a new consent definition specific to this case, leaving open the possibility of applying this new definition to selected other cases as well. This new definition required, in addition to voluntariness, that consent to search be "knowingly and intelligently made." In other words, the patients must understand more precisely what it was they were consenting to and what were its consequences. Moreover, the Court cited as support for this conclusion Miranda v. Arizona, a Fifth Amendment case embracing a more vibrant notion of consent, a notion that the Court had earlier rejected as too limiting for the state in the Fourth Amendment context.
>
> . . . The Court's rationale is best understood as reflecting various insights from feminist theory. Specifically, the Court saw the definition of consent as turning on context rather than on a universal notion identical under all circumstances. Critical aspects of that context were the nature of the human relationships involved—primarily the doctor-patient and mother-child relationships—as well as the complexity of human emotion, the power inequalities between the parties, and the social meanings of their actions. The Court at least implicitly gave patient and parental autonomy great weight, and was offended by paternalistic notions that a more powerful social actor, here, the Hospital, knows what is best for, and therefore can take advantage of, the less powerful social actors, the patients.[143]

Another important factor—the nature of police presence—relates to the coercive nature of the police-individual encounter. Courts generally acknowledge that police presence can be intimidating. The number of officers on the scene, their physical presence measured against the severity of the situation, the use or brandishing of weapons, and the tone of voice used by the officer during the encounter, are evaluated for their potential impact on any consent eventually given. Police actions that would cause a reasonable person to become frightened or upset may invalidate the consent. Moreover, at some point the police presence may cause a reasonable belief that the person is in custody. If there is no justification for custody, it

---

143. Taslitz, *Feminist Fourth*, *supra* note 104, at 3.

will constitute an illegal seizure. Should an illegal seizure render subsequent consent involuntary? The United States Supreme Court has not yet decided the issue definitively. However, in *United States v. Drayton*, the Court indicated that an unlawful seizure has bearing on the consent analysis, stating:

> Law enforcement offices do not violate the Fourth Amendment's prohibition of unreasonable seizures merely by approaching individuals on the street or in other public places and putting questions to them if they are willing to listen. Even when law enforcement officers have no basis for suspecting a particular individual, they may pose questions, ask for identification, and request consent to search luggage—provided they do not induce cooperation by coercive means. If a reasonable person would feel free to terminate the encounter, then he or she has not been seized.

In an earlier case, *Ohio v. Robinette*,[144] the Ohio Supreme Court stated that an illegal seizure invalidates consent unless the prosecution can prove that the consent was freely given and was not tainted by the illegality. The *Robinette* case involved a traffic stop for speeding, after which the officer decided not to ticket the driver. Nevertheless, the officer continued the stop, ordering the driver out of his car and obtaining consent to search. The Ohio court concluded that the continued interaction constituted a seizure because an ordinary person would not have discerned that the stop had evolved into a voluntary encounter. Moreover, because the continued seizure was illegal (the officer had neither reasonable suspicion nor probable cause aside from the speeding violation), the Ohio court held the consent involuntary absent additional proof that it was untainted by the illegality. In support of this proposition, the Ohio court cited a United States Supreme Court case, *Florida v. Royer*,[145] but *Royer* was only a plurality decision, and it was unclear whether the proposition would command a majority of the current justices. The United States Supreme Court took the *Robinette* case on certiorari, but it did not decide the consent issue. In his opinion for the majority, Chief Justice Rehnquist concluded that *Robinette* was lawfully detained when he gave his consent. The Chief Justice reasoned that the officer's subjective intention not to issue a ticket was irrelevant under *Whren*, and "in light of the admitted probable cause to stop Robinette for speeding, [the officer] was objectively justified in asking Robinette to get out of the car." The majority then rejected the Ohio court's per se rule that required officers to indicate that a traffic stop is over before asking for consent.[146]

Writing in dissent, Justice Stevens disagreed with the majority's holding on the issue of detention. Stevens stated, "[W]hen the officer had completed his task of either arresting or reprimanding the driver of the speeding car, his continued detention of that person constituted an illegal

---

144.   653 N.E.2d 695, 696 (Ohio 1995).

145.   460 U.S. 491 (1983).

146.   519 U.S. 33 (1996).

seizure." Once having made that determination, Stevens asserted that "a consent obtained during an illegal detention is ordinarily ineffective to justify an otherwise invalid search." Because Robinette's consent to the search was the product of an unlawful detention, "the consent was tainted by the illegality" and was invalid. As did the Ohio Supreme Court, Stevens relied on *Royer*. In that case, officers had taken Royer from an airport concourse to an office about 40 feet away for questioning. Justice White, writing for a plurality, determined that the 15–minute interaction constituted an arrest, not a *Terry* stop, and that the arrest was illegal because the officers did not have probable cause. Moreover, Royer's consent to a luggage search was ineffective, because "statements given during a period of illegal detention are inadmissible even though voluntarily given if they are the product of the illegal detention and not the result of an independent act of free will." Justice Stevens noted in *Robinette* that Justice Brennan had concurred in the *Royer* result and had indicated his agreement "with this much of the plurality's decision, diverging on other grounds." Argued Justice Stevens, "Justice Brennan's agreement on that narrow principle represents the holding of the Court."

In *Kaupp v. Texas*,[147] the Court more recently concluded first, that an initial police interaction was non-consensual; second, that, in the alternative, if it was consensual, later events even more clearly were not. *Kaupp* involved a 17–year-old boy suspected of complicity in the murder of a 14–year-old girl. The police admittedly lacked probable cause for an arrest. Nevertheless, they awakened the teenager in his bedroom at 3:00 a.m. with a flashlight, after having been admitted to the boy's home by his father. One of the officers, a Detective Pinkins, identified himself and said, "[W]e need to go and talk."[148] Kaupp said, "Okay." Two officers handcuffed Kaupp, leading him shoeless and in boxer shorts to a police car, driving him to the crime scene, then to the police station, where he admitted some part in the crime.

After his motion to suppress his confession as the fruit of an illegal arrest was denied, he appealed. The Texas Court of Appeals affirmed the conviction, concluding that Kaupp consented to accompany the officers to the crime scene and to the police station. Nor, said the Court of Appeals, was this conclusion altered by Kaupp's being handcuffed and driven to the station in a police car because these practices were "routinely" done to protect officer safety when transporting individuals, and Kaupp "did not resist the use of handcuffs or act in a manner consistent with anything other than full cooperation."[149] The Court of Criminal Appeals of Texas denied discretionary review, but the Supreme Court accepted certiorari. The Court rejected the Texas appellate court's conclusion that Kaupp consented to being transported to the police station:

---

147.   538 U.S. 626 (2003).

148.   *Id.* at 628.

149.   *Id.* at 629.

Kaupp's "Okay" in response to Detective Pinkins statement is no showing of consent under the circumstances. Pinkins offered Kaupp no choice, and a group of police officers rousing an adolescent out of bed in the middle of the night with the words "we need to go and talk" presents no option but "to go." There is no reason to think Kaupp's answer was anything more than "a mere submission to a claim of lawful authority." . . . If reasonable doubt were possible on this point, the ensuing events would resolve it: removal from one's house in handcuffs on a January night with nothing on but underwear for a trip to a crime scene on the way to an interview room at law enforcement headquarters. Even an "initially consensual encounter . . . can be transformed into a seizure or detention within the meaning of the Fourth Amendment." . . . *See Hayes* ("[A]t some point in the investigative process, police procedures can qualitatively and quantitatively be so intrusive with respect to a suspect's freedom of movement and privacy interests as to trigger the full protection of the Fourth and Fourteenth Amendments"). It cannot seriously be suggested that when the detectives began to question Kaupp, a reasonable person in his situation would have thought he was sitting in the interview room as a matter of choice, free to change his mind and go home to bed.

Nor is it significant, as the state court thought, that the sheriff's department "routinely" transported individuals, including Kaupp on one prior occasion, while handcuffed for [the] safety of the officers, or that Kaupp "did not resist the use of handcuffs or act in any manner consistent with anything other than full cooperation." The test is an objective one, and stressing the officers' motivation of self-protection does not speak to how their actions would reasonably be understood. As for the lack of resistance, failure to struggle with a cohort of deputy sheriffs is *not a waiver of Fourth Amendment protection*, which does not require the perversity of resisting arrest or assaulting a police officer.[150]

Here the Court seems simultaneously to be saying that there was no voluntary consent and that, therefore, a reasonable person in Kaupp's position *would have understood* that he was not free to leave, thus rendering the police action a "seizure"—and a quite intrusive one at that—within the meaning of the Fourth Amendment. Interestingly, though by no means necessary to its decision, the Court here uses "waiver" language, as it also did in *Ferguson*. Yet in *Schneckloth* the Court had rejected waiver—which would require a "knowing, voluntary, and intelligent" relinquishment of rights—as the justification for the consent-to-search doctrine. No one seriously believes that the Court has yet, as a general principle, modified the *Schneckloth* mere "voluntariness" requirement as the sole pre-condition to finding "consent" to search or seize. Still, the application of a waiver test in *Ferguson* and the appearance of waiver language in *dicta* in *Kaupp* may suggest the Court's willingness to move toward the heightened standard of knowing, voluntary, and intelligent "waiver" as the true

---

150. *Id.* at 631–32 (emphasis added).

definition of Fourth Amendment "consent" in some narrow, as-yet-to-be-specified, range of circumstances, even if "consent" remains equated simply with "voluntariness" in the run-of-the-mill case.

Police deception is important also. The courts are likely to find the consent invalid if the police misrepresent their ability to make the search. For example, if officers falsely claim that they have a search warrant and the person submits on the basis of that authority, then the evidence obtained during the search will be suppressed.[151] Alternatively, if the officers actually have a warrant, but use that warrant to obtain consent, any fruits of the search will be suppressed if the warrant turns out to be invalid.[152] These kinds of threats cause the individual to comply with a show of authority when none is lawfully present. However, if an officer threatens to get a warrant and actually possesses sufficient facts so that a warrant could be obtained, the threat does not vitiate the consent. Thus, some situations involving threats may prove coercive and some may not, depending on the totality of the circumstances.

One kind of deception that never invalidates consent involves undercover operations. For example, an informant may conceal the fact that he is working as an agent of the government to obtain the confidence of the suspect. In both *On Lee v. United States*[153] and *Hoffa v. United States*,[154] the Court held that the Fourth Amendment did not protect individuals against their own misplaced confidence in "false friends." One assumes the risk that friends will turn out to be government agents.

We will explore in depth in a later chapter the problem of racism in law enforcement. The problem is especially troubling in consent searches. Because voluntariness depends on coercion, and because African–Americans and other minorities might be more likely to perceive coercion in a police-individual interaction, race should be a factor in determining the voluntariness of a person's consent to search. Professor Devon Carbado[155] has elaborated on this point thus:

> This upside-down conception of the Fourth Amendment has profound racial implications given existing racial stereotypes about crime and criminality. In the context of a police encounter with a black person, for example, the officer's starting point likely will be that this person is a criminal or a potential criminal. This burden of presumed criminality—a significant part of the burden of blackness—will not be easy to disprove. An officer's racial bias might lead him to ignore stereotype-disconfirming data. In other words, an officer's ex ante investment in seeing black people as criminal might racially blind him to the possibility of their innocence. The tension between stereotypes

---

151.   Go–Bart Importing Co. v. United States, 282 U.S. 344, 358 (1931).

152.   Bumper v. North Carolina, 391 U.S. 543, 549–50 (1968).

153.   343 U.S. 747 (1952).

154.   385 U.S. 293 (1966).

155.   Devon Carbado, *[E]racing the Fourth Amendment*, 100 MICH. L. REV. 946, 1017–20 (2002).

about blackness, on the one hand, and the perception of innocence necessary to avoid or easily terminate police encounters, on the other, creates a "racial incentive system" for blacks to signal noncriminality. That is, in the context of a police encounter, a black person will need to find ways to demonstrate to the police officer that stereotypes about blackness are wrong (all or most black people are not criminals) or that they do not apply to him (this black person is not a criminal).

With respect to consent searches, one way for a black person to present counter-stereotypical information in response to the racial incentive system is to say yes to an officer's request for permission to conduct a search. As the *Bustamonte* Court explains: "If the search is conducted and proves fruitless that in itself may convince the police that an arrest with its possible stigma and embarrassment is unnecessary." The problem, however, is that because of racial stereotypes there is greater pressure for blacks to say yes to consent searches than there is for whites. Consenting to a search may be the only way a black person can demonstrate his innocence, particularly if the black person is young, male, "unprofessionally" dressed, and in a high crime (read: black neighborhood) or predominantly white (read: low crime) area. Thus assuming that consent searches are a means by which any person can establish his innocence, the extent, to which one perceives the need to do this—that is, to give up privacy to prove innocence—is a function of race. . . .

Quite apart from the theoretical incentive for blacks, in the context of police encounters, to signal cooperation via privacy and dignity-compromising identity performances, is the fact that they are encouraged to do both as a matter of socialization and formal or political advice. Consider, for example, Dr. Robert L. Johnson's and Dr. Steven Simring's *The Race Trap: Smart Strategies for Effective Racial Communication in Business and In Life*. In it, Johnson and Simring offer the following strategies for people who are racially profiled:

- Don't argue the Fourth Amendment . . . [A]t the point you are stopped it is important to maintain control of your emotions and your behavior.

- Don't be sarcastic or condescending to the officer. Always be cooperative and polite.

- Don't display anger—even if justified. Most police officers resent challenges to their authority, and may overreact to any real or perceived affront.

- Don't lose sight of your goal. The objective in most racial profiling scenarios is to end the encounter as quickly as possible with a minimum of potential trauma. Getting stopped for no good reason is inconvenient. But being jacked up against your car and searched is an experience that can stay with you for years. Getting handcuffed and taken into custody escalates the nightmare.

Johnson and Simring conclude their discussion with the suggestion that "[r]acial profiling" by the police is a reality in a system that often treats minorities unfairly. However, the immediate issue isn't fairness. Rather, it's your ability to negotiate the encounter you are facing at the time. The negotiation to which Johnson and Simring refer is between a suspect's sense of self (as a rights-bearing person of worth and dignity) and the suspect's sense of what he needs to do to manage the police encounter (establish that he is not a criminal). Conduct engaged in to demonstrate the latter often will compromise the former.

Yet blacks make this compromise or strike this bargain all the time. Indeed, their parents, family members, and community leaders teach them how—when, if at all, to speak, when and how to say "Sir," or "Officer, or Trooper, whether or not to move," and when, if at all, to assert rights. In short, blacks grow up with the expectation that they will be called upon to negotiate their dignity and privacy in the context of police encounters. Part of what I am suggesting here is that one way to perform this negotiation is to say "yes" to an officer's request for permission to conduct a search. Not only does this strategy signal cooperation and obedience, it can also establish innocence.

It bears mentioning again that whites are subject to pressures to comply with requests from the police as well. That is, whites are also subject to the racial incentive system I have described. However, the pressure/incentive for whites to comply with police orders is not as great as the pressure/incentive for blacks to comply; because white people are not presumed to be criminals. Because of stereotypes, black people are subject to a kind of surplus compliance. They are more vulnerable to compliance requests, more likely to comply, and have to give up more privacy to do so.

b.   *The Requirement of Authority or Apparent Authority*

Can a third party furnish consent for another person? Yes, if that third party has actual or apparent authority to do so.[156]

(1) ACTUAL AUTHORITY

Actual authority depends on whether the third party shares access to or control over the premises at issue. For example, in *United States v. Matlock*,[157] a woman sharing a bedroom with the defendant consented to a search of that room after the defendant's arrest. The Court held that the consent was valid under the doctrine of common authority. That doctrine "rests . . . on mutual use of the property by persons generally having joint access or control for most purposes, so that it is reasonable to recognize that any of the co-inhabitants has the right to permit the inspection in his

---

156.   This discussion relies in part on the excellent discussion in WAYNE R. LAFAVE AND JEROLD H. ISRAEL, CRIMINAL PROCEDURE 239–43 (2d ed. 1992).

157.   415 U.S. 164 (1974).

own right and that the others have assumed the risk that one of their number might permit the common area to be searched.''

The *Matlock* decision raises many questions. For instance, what happens if the owner refuses to give consent, and the police discover a third party who has the independent authority to grant a consent to search? In such a case, the police might be tempted to seek consent from the third party, even though their request has already been rebuffed by the owner. Courts sometimes frown on this practice since it appears manipulative and evidences a lack of respect for the individual's right to withhold consent. On the other hand, cases which allow searches under such circumstances do not appear to violate *Matlock* since the Court stated there that each party with authority may grant consent. An even more difficult situation arises when both roommates are present and one consents and the other objects to the search.

The Supreme Court has recently addressed a similar question in *Georgia v. Randolph*.[158] In *Randolph*, police responded to a domestic dispute complaint filed by Randolph's estranged wife, Janet, who reported that her husband, a cocaine user, had taken the couple's son. While the police were on the scene, Scott returned, explained that he had removed his son to a neighbor's home to prevent Janet from taking the son out of the country, disputed his wife's accusation regarding the cocaine, and insisted that she was the one with the substance abuse problem.

Once police retrieved the son with Janet's assistance, she renewed her accusations against her husband, adding that there were "items of drug evidence" within their home. Police Sergeant Murphy asked Scott for permission to search the marital home; he unequivocally refused. Sergeant Murphy then asked Janet for permission. Not only did she give permission, she escorted police to a location identified as Scott's bedroom, where a straw with a white powdery substance suspected of being cocaine was discovered. Sergeant Murphy went to his vehicle, where he contacted the local district attorney, who instructed that the search should be stopped and advised Sergeant Murphy to seek a search warrant. Upon Sergeant Murphy's return to the Randolph home, Janet withdrew her consent. Sergeant Murphy seized the straw and the couple, returned to the station, obtained a search warrant, executed the warrant, and subsequently charged Scott with possession of cocaine.

At trial, Scott moved to suppress the evidence. The motion to suppress was denied, on the basis that his wife, Janet, had common authority to consent to the search of their home. The Georgia intermediate and high courts reversed the trial court's denial, noting that Scott's presence and refusal invalidated Janet's consent and made police entry and search of the marital home unreasonable.[159] The Supreme Court granted certiorari to resolve a split in the authority on whether one occupant may give law

---

158.   547 U.S. 103 (2006).

159.   *Id.* at 107–08.

enforcement effective consent to search shared premises, as against a co-tenant who is present and announces his refusal to consent to the search.

According to the majority, prior to *Randolph*, the Court had not dealt directly with the reasonableness of police entry "in reliance on consent by one occupant subject to immediate challenge by another:"[160]

> the Fourth Amendment rule ordinarily prohibiting the warrantless entry of a person's house as unreasonable *per se*, ... [has] one "jealously and carefully drawn" exception, *Jones v. United States,* [357 U.S. 493, 499 (1958) which] recognizes the validity of searches with the voluntary consent of an individual possessing authority, *Rodriguez, 497 U.S., at 181* .... That person might be the householder against whom evidence is sought, *Schneckloth v. Bustamonte,* [412 U.S. 218 (1973)], or a fellow occupant who shares common authority over property, when the suspect is absent, *Matlock, supra,* ... and the exception for consent extends even to entries and searches with the permission of a co-occupant whom the police reasonably, but erroneously, believe to possess shared authority as an occupant, *Rodriguez, supra,* at 186.... None of our co-occupant consent-to-search cases, however, has presented the further fact of a second occupant physically present and refusing permission to search, and later moving to suppress evidence so obtained. The significance of such a refusal turns on the underpinnings of the co-occupant consent rule, as recognized since *Matlock.*[161]

According to the majority, however, the Court did take "a step toward the issue" in *Minnesota v. Olson.*[162] There, police arrested Olson on the basis of evidence that he was involved in the murder of a gas station attendant. Police arrested Olson in the home of two women with whom he stayed. Olson claimed that police violated his Fourth Amendment expectation of privacy in the women's home when they entered and searched it. There, the Supreme Court held that overnight houseguests have a legitimate expectation of privacy in their temporary quarters because "it is unlikely that [the host] will admit someone who wants to see or meet with the guest over the objection of the guest."[163]

"Longstanding social custom" accepts that those who visit the homes of friends and relatives as temporary, overnight guests have a privacy interest in the premises, based on their status. So, for the majority in *Randolph*, if "that customary expectation of courtesy or deference is a foundation of Fourth Amendment rights of a houseguest, it presumably should follow that an inhabitant of shared premises may claim at least as much, and it turns out that the co-inhabitant naturally has an even stronger claim."[164]

---

160. *Id.* at 113.
161. *Id.* at 108–09.
162. 495 U.S. 91 (1990).
163. *Id.* at 99.
164. *Randolph,* 547 U.S. at 113.

Thus, when the police obtain voluntary consent to search the premises of an occupant who shares (or is reasonably believed to share)[165] common authority over the searched premises and no physically present co-tenant objects, the Fourth Amendment's reasonableness requirement is not offended.

In the present case, however, Scott's presence on the premises and his stated refusal to consent to the warrantless governmental entry and search of the shared home invalidated the government's evidence against him. According to the majority, where a co-tenant is present, vocal, and refusing to consent, police may still decide to enter, search, and seize incriminating evidence as against the consenting co-tenant, but not against the demurring one, over and above that individual's refusal to consent. Justice Souter found persuasive social expectations regarding disputed permission between co-tenants, given that these expectations are a constant element in assessing Fourth Amendment reasonableness in the Court's consent cases:

> [t]o begin with, it is fair to say that a caller standing at the door of shared premises would have no confidence that one occupant's invitation was a sufficiently good reason to enter when a fellow tenant stood there saying, "stay out." Without some very good reason, no sensible person would go inside under those conditions. Fear for the safety of the occupant issuing the invitation, or of someone else inside, would be thought to justify entry, but the justification then would be the personal risk, the threats to life or limb, not the disputed invitation.
>
> . . .
>
> The visitor's reticence without some such good reason would show not timidity but a realization that when people living together disagree over the use of their common quarters, a resolution must come through voluntary accommodation, not by appeals to authority. Unless the people living together fall within some recognized hierarchy, like a household of parent and child or barracks housing military personnel of different grades, there is no societal understanding of superior and inferior, a fact reflected in a standard formulation of domestic property law, that "[e]ach cotenant . . . has the right to use and enjoy the entire property as if he or she were the sole owner, limited only by the same right in the other cotenants". . . . The want of any recognized superior authority among disagreeing tenants is also reflected in the law's response when the disagreements cannot be resolved. The law does not ask who has the better side of the conflict; it simply provides a right to any co-tenant, even the most unreasonable, to obtain a decree partitioning the property (when the relationship is one of co-ownership) and terminating the relationship. . . . And while a decree of partition is not the answer to disagreement among rental tenants, this situation resembles co-ownership in lacking the benefit of any understanding that

---

165. Illinois v. Rodriguez, 497 U.S. 177 (1990) holds valid warrantless searches where an objectively reasonable police officer would have believed under the circumstances that the consenting party had actual authority to consent to a search, even if s/he did not.

one or the other rental co-tenant has a superior claim to control the use of the quarters they occupy together. In sum, there is no common understanding that one co-tenant generally has a right or authority to prevail over the express wishes of another, whether the issue is the color of the curtains or invitations to outsiders.[166]

. . .

Since the co-tenant wishing to open the door to a third party has no recognized authority in law or social practice to prevail over a present and objecting co-tenant, his disputed invitation, without more, gives a police officer no better claim to reasonableness in entering than the officer would have in the absence of any consent at all. Accordingly, in the balancing of competing individual and governmental interests entailed by the bar to unreasonable searches, *Camara v. Municipal Court of City and County of San Francisco*, [387 U.S. 523, 536–537 (1967)], the cooperative occupant's invitation adds nothing to the government's side to counter the force of an objecting individual's claim to security against the government's intrusion into his dwelling place. Since we hold to the "centuries-old principle of respect for the privacy of the home," *Wilson v. Layne,* [526 U.S. 603 (1999)], "it is beyond dispute that the home is entitled to special protection as the center of the private lives of our people," *Minnesota v. Carter,* [525 U.S. 83 (1998) (Kennedy, J., concurring)]. We have, after all, lived our whole national history with an understanding of "the ancient adage that a man's home is his castle [to the point that t]he poorest man may in his cottage bid defiance to all the forces of the Crown," *Miller v. United States,* [357 U.S. 301 (1958)] (internal quotation marks omitted).[167]

Chief Justice Roberts, along with Justices Thomas and Scalia dissented. The dissenters regarded the issue as a straightforward one, asserting that the Court's cases reflect the understanding that "[e]ven in our most private relationships, our observable actions and possessions are private at the discretion of those around us:"[168]

[i]f an individual shares information, papers, or places with another, he assumes the risk that the other person will in turn share access to that information or those papers or places with the government. And just as an individual who has shared illegal plans or incriminating documents with another cannot interpose an objection when that other person turns the information over to the government, just because the individual happens to be present at the time, so too someone who shares a place with another cannot interpose an objection when that person decides to grant access to the police, simply because the objecting individual happens to be present.[169]

---

166.   *Randolph,* 547 U.S. at 113–15.

167.   *Id.* at 114–15.

168.   *Id.* at 133 (Roberts, Chief J., dissenting).

169.   *Id.* at 128 (Roberts, Chief J., dissenting).

Accordingly, the dissenting Justices would rule as reasonable the warrantless search in *Randolph*, as the police obtained voluntary consent to enter and search from someone authorized to give it, Scott's wife:

> [t]he majority suggests that "widely shared social expectations" are a "constant element in assessing Fourth Amendment reasonableness," . . . , but that is not the case; the Fourth Amendment precedents the majority cites refer instead to a "legitimate expectation of *privacy*. . . ." Whatever social expectation the majority seeks to protect, it is not one of privacy. The very predicate giving rise to the question in cases of shared information, papers, containers, or places is that privacy has been shared with another. Our common social expectations may well be that the other person will not, in turn, share what we have shared with them with another—including the police—but that is the risk we take in sharing. If two friends share a locker and one keeps contraband inside, he might trust that his friend will not let others look inside. But by sharing private space, privacy has "already been frustrated" with respect to the lockermate. . . . If two roommates share a computer and one keeps pirated software on a shared drive, he might assume that his roommate will not inform the government. But that person has given up his privacy with respect to his roommate by saving the software on their shared computer.
>
> A wide variety of often subtle social conventions may shape expectations about how we act when another shares with us what is otherwise private, and those conventions go by a variety of labels—courtesy, good manners, custom, protocol, even honor among thieves. The Constitution, however, protects not these but privacy, and once privacy has been shared, the shared information, documents, or places remain private only at the discretion of the confidant.[170]

In addition to balking at the majority's characterization of Court precedent, the dissenting Justices regarded as troubling the "costs" of the majority's decision. Specifically, the dissenting minority argued that the Court's decision would thwart abused spouses' consent to warrantless police entry and search of homes which contain nonconsenting criminal spouses:

> [w]hile the majority's rule protects something random, its consequences are particularly severe. The question presented often arises when innocent cotenants seek to disassociate or protect themselves from ongoing criminal activity. . . . Under the majority's rule, there will be many cases in which a consenting co-occupant's wish to have the police enter is overridden by an objection from another present co-occupant. What does the majority imagine will happen, in a case in which the consenting co-occupant is concerned about the other's criminal activity, once the door clicks shut? The objecting co-occupant may pause briefly to decide whether to destroy any evidence of wrongdoing or to inflict retribution on the consenting co-occupant first, but there

---

170. *Id.* at 131 (Roberts, Chief J., dissenting).

can be little doubt that he will attend to both in short order. It is no answer to say that the consenting co-occupant can depart with the police; remember that it is her home, too, and the other co-occupant's very presence, which allowed him to object, may also prevent the consenting co-occupant from doing more than urging the police to enter.

Perhaps the most serious consequence of the majority's rule is its operation in domestic abuse situations, a context in which the present question often arises.... While people living together might typically be accommodating to the wishes of their cotenants, requests for police assistance may well come from coinhabitants who are having a disagreement. The Court concludes that because "no sensible person would go inside" in the face of disputed consent, ... and the consenting cotenant thus has "no recognized authority" to insist on the guest's admission, ... a "police officer [has] no better claim to reasonableness in entering than the officer would have in the absence of any consent at all...." But the police officer's superior claim to enter is obvious: Mrs. Randolph did not invite the police to join her for dessert and coffee; the officer's precise purpose in knocking on the door was to assist with a dispute between the Randolphs—one in which Mrs. Randolph felt the need for the protective presence of the police. The majority's rule apparently forbids police from entering to assist with a domestic dispute if the abuser whose behavior prompted the request for police assistance objects.[171]

The dissent further explained: "One element that can make a warrantless government search of a home ' "reasonable" ' is voluntary consent.... Proof of voluntary consent 'is not limited to proof that consent was given by the defendant,' but the government 'may show that permission to search was obtained from a third party who possessed common authority over or other sufficient relationship to the premises.'[172] Thus, according to the dissenting Justices' reading of Court precedent, co-occupants have 'assumed the risk that one of their number might permit [a] common area to be searched.' Just as Mrs. Randolph could walk upstairs, come down, and turn her husband's cocaine stash over to the police, so 'she can consent to police entry and search of what is, after all, her home, too.' "[173]

NOTES AND QUESTIONS

1. What type of data source does the majority rely on to justify its interpretation of the Fourth Amendment?

2. Is the majority right to rely on social expectations in the consent context rather than in the reasonable expectations of privacy for a search

---

171. *Id.* at 139 (Roberts, Chief J., dissenting).

172. *Id.* at 128–29 (Roberts, Chief J., dissenting, citing *Matlock*).

173. *Id.* at 128 (Roberts, Chief J., dissenting).

context? Do you agree that social expectations are as the majority describes them?

3.   Is the dissent's reliance on assumption of risk a normative judgment or an alternative analysis of social expectations?

4.   Do you agree with the dissent that the majority's approach will leave domestic abuse victims at the mercy of their abusers? What if the *Randolph* facts differed in this one respect: Mrs. Randolph's complaint was that her husband had just been beating her, that there was a bloody dress in the bedroom to prove it, and that she feared that he was about to beat her again. How would the majority's rule approach this situation?

Relationships between the parties affect issues of third-party consent. Where property law governs the relationship, it usually governs the authority to consent as well. Take the landlord-tenant relationship. Property law generally does not afford a landlord the authority to consent to a search, because the landlord has granted exclusive possession of the premises to the tenant and has retained a right to re-enter the premises only at the end of the leasehold or under certain defined circumstances.[174] Typically, though, the landlord can lawfully grant consent to search common areas such as vestibules, hallways, and staircases, because leases do not grant tenants the right to exclusive possession of common areas. Similarly, condominium associations generally control the common areas of condominium buildings, but not individual units.

Familial relationships can present more vexing problems. In almost all situations, either spouse may consent to a search of the family residence. What about children? Most courts are reluctant to uphold consent obtained from children, fearing that children will be manipulated against their parents' wishes. The closer the child is to the age of majority, the more likely the court is to presume the child understands the situation and to uphold the consent. Some courts analyze parent-child relationships in terms of "rights," finding the parents' rights in the house to be superior to those of the child regardless of age. Courts sometimes use this rule against the child and permit parents to consent to a search of the child's room over the objections of the child.

Finally, what happens if a third party consents to a search that includes the owner's personal closet into which the third party has never gone and placed no belongings? Individuals living in a shared premises can retain areas of exclusive personal control. Most likely, the result would depend on the degree of separation of the private area from the common area being searched. The result might also depend on the doctrine of apparent authority.

5.   Prior to the Court's decision in *Randolph* and within several of the federal circuits, the doctrine of "consent once removed" applied. That doctrine authorized an undercover law enforcement officer's entrance into a house at the express invitation of an individual with authority to consent

---

174.   Chapman v. United States, 365 U.S. 610, 616–17 (1961).

to the officer's entry. Such consent allowed the undercover officer an ability to enter, establish probable cause to arrest or search, and summons *other officers* for assistance.[175] The consent for the latter officers came, therefore, from the initial, undercover officer, not the house's resident or owner, thus consent "once removed." However, what if the party authorizing law enforcement's entrance into another's home is not an undercover police officer, but a confidential informant? Recall Cal and Bart in Chapter 2 (at page 121). Is there a constitutional basis upon which a court might distinguish Bart from an undercover police officer?[176] That question has just been decided by the Court and is discussed elsewhere in this Casebook.[177]

(II) APPARENT AUTHORITY

Apparent authority looks at the consent from the perspective of the objectively reasonable police officer. The pertinent question is this: would a reasonable police officer under the circumstances have believed that the third party had actual authority to consent? If so, then the third-party consent is valid. If a reasonable officer would have realized that the third party lacked authority to consent, then a search based on that consent will be held invalid.

The Court established this test in *Illinois v. Rodriguez*,[178] where police made a warrantless entry of Rodriguez's apartment accompanied by his former girlfriend. The girlfriend had complained to police that Rodriguez had beaten her and offered to let them into the apartment (she referred to it as "our" apartment and indicated that she had personal possessions there) with her key. After they entered, they discovered evidence of drug possession and arrested Rodriguez. Later it was discovered that the former girlfriend had vacated the apartment and had no legal authority to consent to the search. The Court remanded the case to determine whether the officers' mistake was an objectively reasonable one. So long as the circumstances would have permitted a reasonable officer to believe that the girlfriend had authority, her consent validated the search.

Might the doctrines of "assumption of the risk" and "apparent authority" inadvertently collude against a criminal defendant's Fourth Amendment privacy interests? Absolutely, as evidenced by the Court's recent decision in *Pearson v. Callahan*, where the Court was asked to determine whether qualified immunity extended to Utah police officers who relied upon the doctrine of "consent-once-removed" to justify the warrantless search of the home of an arrestee who sold methamphetamine to an

---

175. *See Callahan v. Millard County*, 494 F.3d 891, 896 (10th Cir. 2007) (citations omitted), *cert. granted, Pearson v. Callahan*, 128 S.Ct. 1702 (2008).

176. The Court of Appeals for the 10th Circuit indicates that there is. *See Callahan*, 494 F.3d at 896 ("'[w]e find the distinctions between an officer and an informant summoning additional officers to be significant").

177. *See Pearson v. Callahan*, 129 S.Ct. 808 (2009).

178. 497 U.S. 177, 179 (1990).

undercover informant.[179] "Consent-once-removed" authorizes warrantless entry into a home "when consent to enter has already been granted to an undercover officer or informant who has observed contraband in plain view."[180] Callahan did not allow the informant in; instead, Callahan's daughter let him inside their home.[181] How does this square with the Court's decision in *Georgia v. Randolph*[182] (discussed in the Casebook at pages 479–82), particularly if the daughter granted entry that the father might have denied?

Callahan was subsequently convicted of possession and distribution of methamphetamine.[183] The conviction was vacated. Callahan filed a federal lawsuit in the district court under 42 U.S.C. § 1983, alleging that the officers' entry into his home violated the Fourth Amendment, in that "consent-once-removed" had not been accepted by the Tenth Circuit. The Supreme Court determined that because the officers' unlawfulness was not clearly established at the time they gained entry to his home, they were entitled to qualified immunity, given that the doctrine of consent-once-removed had gained acceptance in two states and in three federal courts of appeals.[184] However, the Supreme Court itself neither accepted nor rejected the consent-once-removed doctrine embraced by some of the lower courts. All that mattered was that the state of the law on the doctrine was not clearly established.

c. *Scope of Consent*

Even if officers obtain a valid consent to search, they must conduct their search within the scope of the consent. The consent, after all, releases the officers from complying with the requirements of the Fourth Amendment, but those requirements remain effective in all areas except for those covered by the consent. So, for example, if a suspect agrees to permit officers to search her car, the officers cannot use that consent to justify a search of her home. In that situation, the scope of the consent is limited to the car.

Of course, issues of scope usually are much more complex than the example above. They involve more than just the physical area searched: the intensity and duration of the search are important as well. Scope issues are avoided where officers identify the scope of their intended search when they ask for consent—naming what is to be searched and what they expect to find.

---

179. *See Pearson*, 129 S.Ct. at 813–14.

180. *Id.* at 813.

181. *Id.*

182. 547 U.S. 103 (2006).

183. *See Pearson v. Callahan,* 129 S.Ct. 808, 814 (2009).

184. *See id.* at 822–23. According to the Court, law enforcement officers "are entitled to rely on existing lower court cases without facing personal liability for their actions.... [i]f judges thus disagree on a constitutional question, it is unfair to subject police to money damages for picking the losing side of the controversy." *Id.* at 823 (citation omitted).

Where the scope of consent is disputed, the test is an objective one: what would the reasonable person have understood by the exchange between the officer and the suspect?[185] Imagine if a border patrol officer obtains consent after asking, "May I search your trunk for persons illegally on U.S. soil?" A reasonable person would understand that consent to mean that the officer may open the trunk and look inside for objects large enough to be human beings. The officer will have exceeded the scope of the consent if he dismantles door panels or opens small compartments.

The issue of the intensity of the search arises frequently in narcotics cases. Police rather commonly obtain consent to search an automobile for drugs and proceed to pry open door panels or cut through carpeting. Would a reasonable person understand the consent to extend to such a search? Courts are not unanimous on this issue. In one case, a judge held that a reasonable person would not understand the consent to extend so far because the law in that circuit prohibited police from dismantling the car bodies during an otherwise valid search unless they had probable cause to believe the car's panels contain narcotics.[186] For another example, consider *United States v. Dichiarinte*,[187] in which the defendant consented to a search of his house for narcotics, but the detectives opened files and read documents leading to charges of income tax evasion. The defendant had not consented to a search of the documents, and the document search had nothing to do with the narcotics search. While the detectives would have been permitted to flip through the files for hidden packages of drugs, they exceeded the scope of the defendant's consent when they read the documents.

d.   Withdrawing Consent

An individual may withdraw consent to search at any time. Of course, if an officer finds incriminating items before consent is withdrawn, the plain view doctrine permits its seizure, and any subsequent withdrawal of consent would be to no avail.

A major issue concerning withdrawal is whether it casts suspicion on the individual, furnishing the basis for a continued search. In other words, can the withdrawal be used to create reasonable suspicion or probable cause?[188] Most likely not. Since one has a right not to consent, neither an initial refusal nor a subsequent withdrawal of consent create inferences of guilt. Few courts have addressed this issue, however. In *United States v. Carter*,[189] a suspect consented to a search of his duffel bag, but when a lunch bag was found within it, he withdrew consent. He then claimed that the lunch bag contained food. He offered to show the officer the food, but

---

185.   Florida v. Jimeno, 500 U.S. 248, 250 (1991).

186.   *See* United States v. Garcia, 897 F.2d 1413, 1419–20 (7th Cir. 1990).

187.   445 F.2d 126, 129–30 (7th Cir. 1971).

188.   For an excellent discussion of this issue, *see* Rachel Karen Laser, *Unreasonable Suspicion: Relying on Refusals to Support Terry Stops*, 62 U. CHI. L. REV. 1161 (1995).

189.   985 F.2d 1095, 1097 (D.C. Cir. 1993).

he removed nothing but his empty hand from the bag. The suspect explicitly objected to a continued search of the bag. Rather than stop the search, the officer seized the bag and discovered cocaine. The court upheld the search, concluding that Carter's offer to show the detective the contents of his bag and his peculiar way of retracting that offer, quite apart from his earlier withdrawal of consent, gave rise to a reasonable suspicion that he was concealing drugs in his bag. The court observed in dictum that a person's withdrawal of consent, standing alone, cannot be used to support a finding of reasonable suspicion, since the right to withdraw consent would be of little value if its very exercise could be used in such a fashion.

PROBLEM 4–24

In the Boson case in Chapter 1, recall that Boson said nothing in response to Officer Glemp's request to search the car. Yet Boson did not object or stop Officer Glemp from searching.

Question: As the prosecutor, how would you make the argument that Boson consented? Do you think your argument will be successful?

PROBLEM 4–25

Delinda Montgomery, a 19–year-old college student returning from her parent's residence in Canada, is driving through Michigan on her way back to school. Police officers observe her failure to signal when making a lane change. After following the car for several minutes, the officers decide to stop her and issue a citation. Before leaving the cruiser, the officers request back-up since the interstate is deserted due to the early morning hour and unusually cold weather. The first officer approaches Delinda and in a harsh tone of voice says: "You aren't from around here, are you?" Delinda immediately notices the officer's standard-issue firearm as well as the officer's habit of placing his hand on the gun's butt when talking. The officer explains the reason for stopping her, takes her license and registration, and asks her to step out of the car.

Delinda has been driving for sixteen hours and is quite tired. All she wants to do is go to sleep. Unfortunately, the officers pulled her over twenty miles from the hotel at which she planned to spend the night. Further, she needs to take her prescription medication for severe depression. After stepping out of the car, she notices the other officer watching carefully from behind the door of the cruiser. The first officer asks if he can "have a look" in the car for illegal drugs. Delinda does not want them to search the car because she has a box of Cuban cigars (which she remembers are illegal in the United States) in a locked suitcase in the backseat, but she remembers that the officer has her license and registration. She also remembers a television program that said the police cannot search without probable cause or a warrant, but she is not sure whether that means she can refuse to consent. Timidly, she asks if the officers have a form that specifically describes where they are going to search. The officer laughs and says, "Miss, that's not the way we do things around here." Delinda responds, "I guess you can do it then."

The officer begins searching the passenger compartment, finding a folded newspaper in the front seat. After shaking it, a blank check and a state driver's license fall out. The officer notices that the license and check belong to "Lisa Jackson" even though Delinda's picture appears on the license. The officer suspects that the material is being used for fraudulent purposes and continues the search. By this time, the second officer has approached Delinda and is asking her numerous questions. Delinda wants to keep an eye on the first officer, but she is prevented from doing so by the second officer's questions. The first officer finds the locked suitcase in the back seat and begins tugging at the clasp. When the suitcase opens, the Cuban cigars fall out.

The entire traffic stop takes forty minutes. Delinda is charged with possession of a check to be used for fraudulent purposes, possession of false identification, and possession of illegal contraband (the cigars).

Question: Did Delinda consent to the search? What are the factors bearing on her consent? Did the situation change from the time the search began? If so, how will those changes likely affect the admissibility of evidence?

PROBLEM 4–26

Brenda Ackerman owns several pieces of property in the town of Gaston. On one parcel, Jim Wallerstrom resides in his mobile home next to a stream. He pays rent to Brenda for the right to park the trailer on the property, but both parties have access to the area since Brenda desires to fish in the stream at her discretion. Brenda possesses a key to Jim's trailer since she sometimes borrows fishing supplies from inside the trailer when he is away. One day as she is leaving Jim's trailer after paying him a social visit, Brenda is approached by two Gaston police officers seeking entrance to the trailer. One of the officers makes a sweeping motion in the direction of the trailer with her arm, asking: "You own this?" Brenda responds that she does. After the officers explain that they received a "tip" about illegal weapons being stored inside the trailer, Brenda consents to a search of the trailer. The officers enter and find several illegally modified shotguns inside. Jim is charged with possession of illegal firearms after the officers discover that he is the true owner of the trailer.

After receiving several threats from Jim's friends regarding her decision to allow the search, Brenda decides that staying by herself would not be the safest move. One of her friends, Peggy Aryeh, is in town on business and invites Brenda to share her hotel room. Brenda accepts the invitation and moves many of her personal effects into the room. After staying in the hotel room for several days, Brenda answers the door while Peggy is at a meeting downstairs. Two police officers ask Brenda if they can search the room for illegal drugs as part of a community random search program. Brenda consents to the search. Peggy returns to the room and is arrested for possession of cocaine, but vehemently protests Brenda's authority to consent to the search.

Brenda, distraught from the events, leaves the hotel only to be kidnapped by Tom Gorey, a friend of Jim's, who has decided to exact revenge on Brenda for allowing the search of the mobile home. Tom takes Brenda to his mountain cabin where he confines her against her will. The cabin is so isolated that Tom convinces Brenda that she cannot escape by running away and due to inclement weather would probably freeze to death before finding help. Tom figures that telling Brenda that she cannot run away will save him the trouble of tying her up and confining her to one area of the cabin.

One month later, two police officers arrive at the cabin door. Tom, out gathering wood, is not home to answer the door. Brenda, relieved to see the police, quickly consents to their request to search the cabin for tools of the counterfeiting operation that they suspect Tom is operating out of his cabin. The police find several thousand dollars in twenties upstairs in a clothes dryer with several engraving plates nearby. Tom is arrested for counterfeiting and kidnapping.

Question: Analyze Brenda's authority to consent to each of the searches. What arguments will the owners raise and how will the prosecution respond? Remember the reasons underlying the third-party consent doctrine.

PROBLEM 4–27

State trooper Dennis Bruger stopped Bill Wallace for a broken taillight on the boat trailer he was towing. Bruger knew Wallace well from previous drug offenses and was advised by dispatch to approach the subject "with extreme care" because he might be armed. Bruger approached Wallace's pickup truck and asked to see Wallace's license and registration. Wallace surrendered the documents but explained that he was hurrying home from Lake Montimute and demanded to know why he had been stopped. Bruger informed him of the broken taillight and told Wallace that he would issue him a citation for the light. Bruger then placed the license and registration in his own front pocket. "I'll just hang onto these," Bruger said, patting the documents.

Bruger asked Wallace if he could search the vehicle for illegal weapons and missing Indian burial artifacts, because Bruger was aware of recent Indian grave robberies in the Lake Montimute area. The robbers had stolen, among other things, small but priceless artifacts. Wallace said, "Whatever," and at Bruger's request stepped out of the truck to observe the search.

Bruger searched the passenger compartment of the truck, concentrating on the opaque film vials in Wallace's camera bag, thinking that they might contain cocaine. After finding only film inside, the officer looked through a checkbook lying on the floor, thinking that small artifacts like arrowheads might be tucked inside. There were no arrowheads inside, but he quickly scanned the ledger to find out to whom Wallace had written checks. Bruger noticed several checks written to "Grand Cayman Islands Bank, Acct. #34096." Bruger knew that many Americans used bank accounts in the Cayman Islands to evade their income taxes, and he wrote down the number of the account for referral to the local Internal Revenue Service field office. Bruger also pulled up the carpet to search for weapons. Instead of weapons, he found a blank check that later turned out to have been recently stolen.

Finally, Bruger turned to Wallace, pointed at the covered boat on the trailer, and said: "That must be a nice boat under that tarp." Wallace, eager to show off his new boat, quickly removed the tarp, which had been tied down in numerous places. Bruger noticed a pair of sneakers and a large taped box in the boat. He began to inspect the box as if he wanted to open it. Wallace immediately expressed his concern over potential damage to the contents of the box, which he claimed were gift-wrapped. Bruger told Wallace that he had been conducting these searches for years and was very good at them—"Relax, nothing will get hurt," he said. He opened the box and saw several firearms inside. Although he knew these to be illegal, he closed the box and pretended to be disinterested in them, because his attention had been drawn to the sneakers, which appeared to have a false heel. Knowing that drug dealers use such devices to conceal drugs, Bruger pried open the sneaker's heel, causing damage to the shoe. As he did so, Wallace said, "I don't want you looking around any more." At that same moment, Bruger peered into a small compartment inside the shoe's heel and saw three bags of white powder that later proved to be heroin.

Bruger stopped searching and placed Wallace under arrest. Wallace was later indicted for narcotics and weapons violations, for charges involving the stolen check, and for federal income tax evasion relating to money he had funneled through the Cayman Islands bank account.

Question: As Wallace's lawyer on all charges, will you be able to suppress any or all of the evidence that the prosecution will seek to introduce?

PROBLEM 4–28

Joe and Lucille Gutman were driving a rented Cadillac with Florida license plates on the interstate through New Mexico. Joe was driving the car at a lawful speed. He was not, however, wearing his safety belt—a violation of New Mexico law. The Gutmans' vehicle passed Officer Keane, who noticed that Joe did not appear to be wearing the shoulder strap part of his safety belt. Keane followed the car for about three miles and at one point drove alongside it to confirm that Joe was not wearing his safety belt. He then pulled the car over and determined that Joe's driver's license and the car rental agreement were in order. Keane informed Joe that he had been stopped for a safety belt violation.

By that time, Keane had all the information he needed to write a citation for the safety belt violation. Rather than issue the citation, however, he continued to question the Gutmans in a leisurely fashion. In response to his questions about their travel plans, Lucille explained that she and Joe were en route from their home in Florida to vacation in Las Vegas and that they had saved $5,000 for the trip. Lucille, who was eight months pregnant, was perspiring heavily. She appeared to Keane to be avoiding eye contact. These facts, combined with the Gutmans' travel plans, aroused the officer's suspicions that the Gutmans were transporting drugs or contraband. In order to confirm his suspicions, he tried to get a good view into the car. He peered through the window at the car's dashboard under the pretext that he was checking the car's mileage. He also glanced around the passenger compartment while making conversation with Lucille about her pregnancy. Finally, he asked the couple whether they were carrying drugs or contraband, which they denied.

After about fifteen minutes of conversation, Keane handed Joe a consent to search form, which Joe signed. The officer searched the trunk and found $5,000 hidden in a shoe. In the interior of the car, he found a packet of cocaine behind the rear seat. Keane arrested Joe and Lucille, who were charged with narcotics offenses.

Question: The Gutmans have moved to suppress the cash and cocaine. Their motions challenge the legality of the initial stop, the extent of the subsequent investigation, and the validity of the consent to search. Assess their arguments. How should the court rule?

CHAPTER 5

SEARCHES AND SEIZURES: RACISM IN LAW ENFORCEMENT

- TAKING RACE INTO ACCOUNT THROUGH THE 14TH AMENDMENT
- USING RACE AND CULTURE IN SUPPRESSION MOTIONS

I. THE PROBLEM

It has been widely recognized that law enforcement in the United States has a disparate impact on minority groups—especially (although certainly not exclusively) African–Americans[1]—and on poor people. This disparate impact stems, in part, from intentional discrimination. More of the impact, however, is likely due to subconscious stereotyping (for example, law enforcement suspicion of young minority group males) and to complex systemic forces having to do with poverty, culture, and history. And some of the impact is due to differences among the groups themselves—for example, in their attitudes toward privacy intrusions and in how they evaluate the adequacy and reliability of evidence of crime. Regardless of the reasons for the disparate impact, there is no question that it exists—and that, ironically, the groups affected most negatively by law enforcement are also the groups most victimized by crime.

The disparate impact of law enforcement creates a serious problem. Law enforcement is one of government's most important functions. At its best, it brings people together in the task of keeping communities safe. But where law enforcement divides people—vesting power in one group and imposing oppression on others—it becomes one of government's biggest failures. This—the political nature of Fourth Amendment doctrine—is the subject of this chapter.

A. PROFILING

Among the various ways that law enforcement has a disparate impact on minorities, racial profiling gets the most media attention. Racial profil-

---

1. Anyone interested in the issues of race and criminal procedure that are addressed in this chapter should also read RANDALL KENNEDY's book, RACE, CRIME, AND THE LAW (1997), as well as DAVID COLE, NO EQUAL JUSTICE: RACE AND CLASS IN THE AMERICAN CRIMINAL JUSTICE SYSTEM (1999); KATHERYN K. RUSSELL, RACIAL HOAXES, WHITE FEARS, BLACK PROTECTIONISM, POLICE HARASSMENT, AND OTHER MACROAGGRESSIONS (1998); Andrew E. Taslitz, *Stories of Fourth Amendment Disrespect: From Elian to the Internment*, 70 FORDHAM L. REV. 2257 (2002).

ing occurs when officers consciously or subconsciously rely on race as the sole or substantial basis for their decision to stop, arrest, or search an individual. Profiling does not occur if race is part of the description of an offender. Rather, profiling occurs when an officer's decision is based on assumptions or stereotyping.

Efforts to justify racial profiling usually involve an argument that profiling works—that certain groups really are more likely to commit certain crimes. Opponents argue that, for the most part, there is no evidence of group-related crime rates, that profiling is less effective than other law enforcement techniques focusing on behavior, and that profiling damages all Americans. Opponents also argue that profiling is prohibited by the notion of equality embedded in our constitution, even in those rare situations in which offense rates for certain groups exceed those of others. The debate has become more heated as ethnic profiling of persons believed to be Muslim or of "Middle Eastern" ancestry has increased in the aftermath of the September 11, 2001, terrorist attacks on the United States.

Profiling claims are difficult to advance in court because available doctrines are inadequate. Nevertheless, state and municipal governments recently have settled high visibility profiling lawsuits, perhaps to foster better relationships among law enforcement and communities, or perhaps simply to do the right thing. One settled lawsuit arose in California between the American Civil Liberties Union and the California Highway Patrol. The Patrol agreed to a ban on using minor traffic violations as a pretext for drug searches of cars. It also agreed to halt its practice of asking stopped drivers for consent to search. The *New York Times*[2] explained:

> ... Mr. [Curtis] Rodriguez [the primary plaintiff] of San Jose, a lawyer, was stopped and searched by patrol officers in June 1998. He said he saw a number of other Latino drivers stopped in the same area of Highway 152 just before he was pulled over.
>
> Officials of the civil liberties union said the highway patrol agreement to stop asking drivers' permission to search their cars was a first in the nation. Civil liberties lawyers say the so-called consent searches, although the United States Supreme Court has ruled them permissible, are inherently coercive because of the disparity in power between an officer and a motorist.
>
> Commissioner Helmick stopped such searches in 2001, after studies showed that Latinos in parts of California were about three times as likely to be searched by C.H.P. officers as whites ...
>
> Mark Schlosberg, director of police practices at the A.C.L.U. of Northern California, said he hoped that the agreement would set a standard for police departments across the state.

---

2. John M. Broder, *California Ending Use of Minor Traffic Stops as Search Pretext*, NEW YORK TIMES, Feb. 28, 2003.

"Already data collected locally, even by police departments in diverse and progressive cities such as San Francisco and Sacramento, demonstrates large disparities in the rates at which African–American and Latino motorists are stopped and searched," Mr. Schlossberg said.

B. PRETEXT

Having reviewed the *Terry* doctrine, you have the background with which to understand the problem of "pretext." For years, defendants and civil rights groups have argued that police officers frequently manipulate their authority under the *Terry* doctrine in order to circumvent individual rights. Most often, this complaint has been heard in the context of traffic stops, where police officers may stop automobiles for minor traffic violations (based on probable cause or reasonable suspicion) and then develop authority to search the automobile by means of one of the exceptions to the warrant requirement that will be addressed in the next chapter. These exceptions include search incident to arrest, the automobile exception, plain view, or consent. Opponents of these practices contend that officers use their lawful traffic enforcement authority as a "pretext" to gain access to the interior of automobiles. In cases involving minor traffic offenses, they argue, officers would not ordinarily stop vehicles unless they desired to search them. And the vehicles most often targeted for "pretext" traffic stops, according to these groups, are those holding blacks, Hispanics, or individuals from other targeted ethnic minorities.

In response to the "pretext" problem, defendants urged courts to exclude evidence if the circumstances revealed subjective bad faith on the part of the officer. Alternatively, defendants proposed an objective test: evidence should be admitted only if a reasonable officer would have engaged in the law enforcement activity at issue. Courts responded variously, but most of them rejected these proposals. The Supreme Court followed suit by resoundingly refusing in *Whren v. United States* to adopt the "reasonable officer" requirement.[3]

Whren involved the traffic stop of a truck occupied by two black men in a "high drug area." Plainclothes officers in an unmarked car stopped the truck after it remained at an intersection for "an unusually long time"— more than 20 seconds—and then took off at an "unreasonable" rate of speed after a police car approached it. The truck had also turned without signaling. During the traffic stop, an officer observed crack cocaine in the car. The occupants were arrested, the car searched, and charges brought for drug violations. The defendants moved to suppress the fruits of the search on the grounds that the stop had been a "pretext," but the trial court denied the motion because the stop had been accompanied by probable cause to believe that the driver had violated traffic ordinances. After conviction and an unsuccessful appeal, the defendants petitioned the Supreme Court for certiorari.

---

3.   Whren v. United States, 517 U.S. 806 (1996).

Justice Scalia, writing for a unanimous Court, emphasized that traffic stops are reasonable under the Fourth Amendment so long as police have probable cause to believe that a traffic violation has occurred. The officers unquestionably had probable cause to stop Whren's vehicle for violations of multiple provisions of the District of Columbia traffic code, and the presence of probable cause, said the Court, was determinative. The Court acknowledged the defendants' concern that:

> "in the unique context of civil traffic regulations" probable cause is not enough. Since, they contend, the use of automobiles is so heavily and minutely regulated that total compliance with traffic and safety rules is nearly impossible, a police officer will almost invariably be able to catch any given motorist in a technical violation. This creates the temptation to use traffic stops as a means of investigating other law violations, as to which no probable cause or even articulable suspicion exists. Petitioners, who are both black, further contend that police officers might decide which motorists to stop based on decidedly impermissible factors, such as the race of the car's occupants. To avoid this danger, they say, the Fourth Amendment test for traffic stops should be, not the normal one (applied by the Court of Appeals) of whether probable cause existed to justify the stop; but rather, whether a police officer, acting reasonably, would have made the stop for the reason given.

But the Court concluded that its prior case law "foreclose[s] any argument that the constitutional reasonableness of traffic stops depends on the actual motivations of the individual officers involved. We of course agree with petitioners that the Constitution prohibits selective enforcement of the law based on considerations such as race. But the constitutional basis for objecting to intentionally discriminatory application of laws is the Equal Protection Clause, not the Fourth Amendment. Subjective intentions play no role in ordinary, probable-cause Fourth Amendment analysis."

Finally, the Court disagreed with the defendants' contention that the Fourth Amendment required it to balance the "governmental and individual interests implicated in a traffic stop." The defendants argued that such a balancing test would prohibit the use of traffic stops for minor traffic offenses, at least if the stops were occasioned by plainclothes officers in unmarked cars, because:

> such investigation only minimally advances the government's interest in traffic safety, and may indeed retard it by producing motorist confusion and alarm.... And as for the Fourth Amendment interests of the individuals concerned, petitioners point out that our cases acknowledge that even ordinary traffic stops entail "a possibly unsettling show of authority"; that they at best "interfere with freedom of movement, are inconvenient, and consume time" and at worst "may create substantial anxiety." That anxiety is likely to be even more pronounced when the stop is conducted by plainclothes officers in unmarked cars.

The Court stated that while "in principle every Fourth Amendment case, since it turns upon a 'reasonableness' determination, involves a balancing of all relevant factors" ..., [w]ith rare exceptions not applicable here ... the result of that balancing is not in doubt where the search or seizure is based upon probable cause. Elaborating on this point, the Court observed that:

> Petitioners urge as an extraordinary factor in this case that the "multitude of applicable traffic and equipment regulations" is so large and so difficult to obey perfectly that virtually everyone is guilty of violation, permitting the police to single out almost whomever they wish for a stop. But we are aware of no principle that would allow us to decide at what point a code of law becomes so expansive and so commonly violated that infraction itself can no longer be the ordinary measure of the lawfulness of enforcement. And even if we could identify such exorbitant codes, we do not know by what standard (or what right) we would decide, as petitioners would have us do, which particular provisions are sufficiently important to merit enforcement.

> For the run-of-the-mine case, which this surely is, we think there is no realistic alternative to the traditional common-law rule that probable cause justifies a search and seizure.

Whren leaves little doubt that, under the federal constitution, pretext is not a viable objection to searches and seizures, except those effectuated under the administrative and inventory search doctrines. Of course, states may provide differently in their own constitutions and laws.

PROBLEM 5–1

Recall *Maryland v. Wilson*,[4] in which the Court held that police may order a passenger in a lawfully stopped car to exit the car, even absent individualized suspicion that the passenger represents a danger to the officer. Dissenting in that case, Justice Kennedy argued that, coupled with *Whren*, the holding which allows police to stop vehicles in "almost countless circumstances" would put "tens of millions of passengers ... at risk of arbitrary control by the police." Recall also *Atwater v. City of Lago Vista*,[5] where the Court held that the Fourth Amendment permits police to make full custodial arrests even for minor offenses.

Questions: Do you believe that Justice Kennedy's concerns will be heightened after Atwater? Consider this scenario: an officer patrolling an interstate known to be a major drug trafficking route observes a car traveling 5 miles per hour over the speed limit. The driver is a Hispanic male. The officer believes that Hispanic males engage in most of the drug trafficking in that area. The officer stops the car, arrests the driver, and engages not only in a search incident to arrest, but also in a full inventory search of the car. Does the Fourth Amendment provide any basis for

---

4.   519 U.S. 408 (1997).

5.   532 U.S. 318 (2001).

challenging the searches? Is an effective remedy provided by the equal protection clause of the Fourteenth Amendment?[6]

C. Police Culture

The undoubted disparate impact of law enforcement on minority groups raises questions about whether some of that impact is a result of intentional discrimination in the law enforcement profession. Social scientists disagree about whether, or the extent to which, police officers are racially prejudiced. At least five perspectives have been defended: (1) the police are not racially prejudiced; (2) the police are racially prejudiced; (3) police practices reflect the admittedly often racist attitudes of the larger society; (4) the police response is related to the socio-economic status, not the race, of the suspect; and (5) the police differential response to minorities reflects cultural biases.[7] Each of these positions has problems. Position one defies common sense, given that the police are drawn from a larger society in which large percentages of whites still admit to racial prejudice toward many minorities, especially African–Americans. Positions two through four offer different explanations for the same outcome: differential treatment of minorities by the police. These four positions concede a certain amount of ill will by the police toward minorities, whether articulated as racial hatred, class hatred of a class that happens to be disproportionately minority, or cultural animosity.

There is little dispute that some police departments display more racial prejudice than others; that some police actions are racially motivated; that there are racial disparities in some aspects of police treatment of minorities in many cities, whether or not motivated by racial prejudice (for example, higher rates of stopping and questioning blacks, arresting blacks on the basis of less stringent legal standards, and shooting and killing blacks at a disproportionate rate); that there has been a long history of tension between many minority communities and the police; and that many minorities, especially African–Americans, perceive police departments to be racist. Each of these facts has Fourth Amendment implications.[8]

Moreover, police culture may promote differential treatment of minorities. Police work requires officers to work in dangerous conditions. It also requires them to invoke their authority and sometimes to use force. These conditions encourage police solidarity—what Jerome Skolnick and James Fyfe call the "brotherhood" of the police.[9] Some police exhibit distrust and

---

6. For more on using the Fourteenth Amendment in these circumstances, *see* Margie Paris, *A Primer in Profiling: The Merger of Civil Rights and Criminal Defense*, 15 Crim. Just. 4 (Fall 2000). As Professor Paris's article describes, an equal protection claim must be supported by proof of discriminatory intent. Ironically, then, officer intent is irrelevant for Fourth Amendment purposes but vitally important to a Fourteenth Amendment equal protection claim.

7. Coramae Richey Mann, Unequal Justice: A Question of Color 143 (1993).

8. *See id.* at 138–49.

9. Jerome H. Skolnick and James J. Fyfe, Above the Law: Police and the Excessive Use of Force 92 (1993).

suspicion of civilians, "macho" attitudes, a tendency toward conservatism, and a desire for tidiness and order.

Police training supports these traits, according to Skolnick and Fyfe. Typical police recruits are young, athletic males who enjoy weight-lifting. They receive training in the use of deadly weapons and other forms of self-defense—some learning to kill with their bare hands. Police training fosters suspicion and skepticism by encouraging police to distinguish between the "normal" and the "abnormal," the latter requiring prompt investigation, often based on snap decisions. To maintain the necessary degree of readiness, police look for "symbolic assailants, those who display gestures, language, or other behaviors that, from training or experience, police have come to associate with criminal activity." Stereotyping is thus an essential aspect of police behavior.[10]

Police work reinforces police culture. Police often need to assert authority (sometimes as a way to avoid violence), and this may lead them to react testily when their authority is challenged. Many officers form intense dislike for citizens who challenge their authority, a troubling fact when the citizen involved is a minority group member whom the officer assumes is a potential offender. Skolnick and Fyfe cite a study of police behavior in the 1960s, which noted a further difficulty:

> ... Chevigny notes that it ... may be more difficult for members of minority groups to show the submissive qualities middle-class people learn to use when dealing with authorities. He further observes that the words "Sorry, Officer" often feel like galling words of submission to the downtrodden and are especially hard for African–Americans to say. "The combination of being an outcast," he writes, "and refusing to comply ... is explosive."[11]

These problems are accentuated in poorly managed departments. Such departments may reward officers for the numbers of calls handled and arrests made and for being "hard nosed." This kind of management promotes a siege mentality.

The combination of police culture and minority group apprehension has significant implications for much of the law of pre-trial constitutional criminal procedure.

II.   A POSSIBLE SOLUTION: TAKING RACE INTO ACCOUNT

We have noted earlier the argument that the meaning of the Fourth Amendment was altered—"mutated"—when it was incorporated by the

---

10. *Id.* Human reasoning processes inevitably involve some degree of comparison to stereotypes and group norms, but some judgments are so much toward the pure, stereotypical, group-based end of the spectrum as to violate notions of individualized justice. *See* Andrew E. Taslitz, *Myself Alone: Individualizing Justice Through Psychological Character Evidence*, 52 MD. L. REV. 1, 18–30 (1993). We have seen earlier that notions of individualized justice—for example, the individualized suspicion usually required for probable cause—play at least some role in Fourth Amendment analysis.

11. *See* SKOLNICK & FYFE, EXCESSIVE USE, *supra* note 9, at 103.

Fourteenth Amendment against the states. That argument suggests that the Court should create a race-conscious Fourth Amendment jurisprudence, taking race into account when it decides, for example, when a reasonable person would believe that he or she has been seized. This section will address the broad implications of that argument to a wide array of problems concerning the role of race in Fourth Amendment analysis.

A. MUTATING THE FOURTH AMENDMENT

The African–American experience has had a profound effect on the United States Constitution. After the Civil War, the Reconstruction Amendments—abolishing slavery, defining citizenship, and prohibiting states from discriminating among their citizens—committed the nation to an aspiration of equality. Through one of these amendments (the Fourteenth), the notion of due process was imposed on the states, requiring them to observe the governmental limits found in the Bill of Rights. Among those limits, of course, is the Fourth Amendment's prohibition against unreasonable searches and seizures. Consequently, the Fourth Amendment's meaning can be informed by search and seizure practices under the slavery and Reconstruction periods, and it would be most helpful to learn about practices directed at African–Americans whose suffering was the primary animating force behind the Fourteenth Amendment's ratification. Therefore, today, an attorney representing a criminal defendant of *any* background should understand the African–American experience.

1. SCHOLARSHIP CASTING LIGHT ON THE FOURTEENTH AMENDMENT

We begin by reproducing a fairly lengthy excerpt from an article by Professor Akhil Reed Amar. In this excerpt, Professor Amar does not make the precise argument made here, nor does he suggest that race is central to his position. Nevertheless, a close reading of Amar's piece, combined with a review of the Fourteenth Amendment's history, supports the notion that the Fourth Amendment was mutated by the Fourteenth Amendment to require a race-conscious law of search and seizure in some circumstances. Professor Amar[12] writes:

> To recast the textual point as an historical one, the core applications and central meanings of the right to keep and bear arms and other key rights were very different in 1866 than in 1789. Mechanical incorporation obscured all this and, indeed, made it easy to forget that when we "apply" the Bill of Rights against the states today, we must first and foremost reflect on the meaning and the spirit of the Amendment of 1866, not the Bill of 1789. . . .

> As a matter of constitutional text and structure, these [First Amendment] clauses are indeed easy cases for full application against states via the Fourteenth Amendment. An ounce of history here

---

12. Akhil Reed Amar, *The Bill of Rights and the Fourteenth Amendment*, 101 YALE L.J. 1193, 1266, 1275–81 (1992).

provides powerful confirmation. From the 1830's on, the abolitionist crusaders had understood that freedom of speech for all men and women went hand in hand with freedom of bodily liberty for slaves. The Slave Power posed a threat to Freedom—of all kinds—and could support itself only through suppression of opposition speech, with gag rules on antislavery petitions, bans on "incendiary" publications, intrusions on the right of peaceable assembly, and so on. This global theory of Freedom was not limited to a few lawyers or theorists spearheading the crusade, but was quite literally the popular platform of the antislavery movement, perhaps best exemplified by an 1856 Republican Party campaign slogan: "Free Speech, Free Press, Free Men, Free Labor, Free Territory, and Fremont."

During the Thirty-eighth and Thirty-ninth Congresses, Republicans invoked speech, press, petition, and assembly rights over and over—more frequently than any other right, with the possible exception of due process. These invocations occurred in a variety of overlapping contexts: as glosses on the "civil rights" to be protected by the Civil Rights and Freedman's Bureau Acts; as part of the definition of republican government (whose violation justified continued Southern exclusion from the national legislature); as "fundamental rights" of all citizens; and as paradigmatic "privileges or immunities" of national citizenship and/or interstate comity.

Once again, the centrality of these rights was not an ideal limited to a few leading lawyers or theorists, but was widely understood by the polity. Various petitions from ordinary constituents to Congress in 1866 stressed the importance of the rights of "speech," "press," and "assembly" (while of course embodying the interrelated right of petition); the New York Evening Post noted that the freedoms of speech and of the press were guaranteed by the Civil Rights Act (even though the Act did not explicitly speak of those freedoms) and later read Section One of the proposed Amendment as covering the same ground; the Philadelphia North American and United States Gazette in September 1866 listed freedoms of speech, press, and assembly as paradigmatic "privileges and immunities" of citizenship within the meaning of the then pending Amendment; various prominent Congressmen on the campaign trail in 1866 (including Bingham, Wilson, and Speaker of the House Schuyler Colfax) emphasized the Amendment's protection of freedom of speech; state politicians in leading Northern states—Wisconsin, Pennsylvania, Ohio, Massachusetts, New York, and so on—linked the Amendment to freedom of discussion; and various popular 1866 conventions, both Northern and Southern, not only embodied the right to peaceably assemble, but used these occasions to reaffirm the importance of speech, press, petition, and assembly rights.

Thus far, the refined incorporation model and Black's total incorporation approach appear to converge. But refined incorporation can help us to see what Black's approach obscured: how the very meaning of freedom of speech, press, petition, and assembly was subtly redefined in the process of being incorporated. In the eighteenth century the paradigmatic speaker was someone like John Peter Zenger or James Callender, a relatively popular publisher saying relatively popular things critical of less popular government officials. In the mid-nineteenth century the paradigm shifted to the Unionist, the abolitionist, and the freedman: to speakers like Samuel Hoar, Harriet Beecher Stowe, and Frederick Douglass. Hoar was a Massachusetts lawyer who in 1844 went to South Carolina with his daughter to defend the rights of free blacks, only to be literally ridden out of town on a rail by an enraged populace after the South Carolina legislature passed an act of attainder and banishment. A generation later, Hoar's cause célèbre still burned brightly in the memories of members of Congress who repeatedly cited the incident. Stowe, of course, authored the "incendiary" bestseller Uncle Tom's Cabin in the 1850's—a novel that outraged the pro-slavery South and inspired the anti-slavery North, leading Lincoln to describe her as "the little woman who wrote the book that made this great war." Frederick Douglass escaped from slavery in Maryland in 1838, published a daring autobiography in 1845, founded and edited a leading abolitionist newspaper over the next two decades, and became a preeminent orator on behalf of civil rights and suffrage for both women and freedmen.

The shift from Zenger and Callender to Hoar, Stowe, and Douglass was subtle but significant. All can be seen as "outsiders," but with an important difference. As representatives of the Fourth Estate, Zenger and Callender were "outside" the government that sought to censor them, but Hoar, Stowe, and Douglass were outsiders in a much deeper sense. Vis-a-vis the Southern society trying to suppress the speech, Hoar, Stowe, and Douglass were geographic, cultural, and ethnic outsiders who were critical of dominant social institutions and opinions. Put another way, this shift directs us away from Madison's first concern in the Federalist No. 51 (the "agency" problem of protecting the people against unrepresentative government), toward his second concern (protecting minorities from "factional" majority tyranny). The new First/Fourteenth amendment tradition is less majoritarian and more libertarian. To recast this point in a temporal frame, the abolitionist experience dramatized why even majoritarians should logically support strong First Amendment protection for offensive and provocative speech of fringe groups. For if allowed to freely preach their gospel, a zealous fringe group in one era (like proponents of abolition, equality, and black suffrage in 1830) could conceivably convert enough souls to their crusade to become a respectable or even dominant political force over the next generation (like the Republican Party of the 1860's).

My language here—"preach," "gospel," "zealous," "convert," "souls," and "crusade"—reflects the religious inspiration of many abolitionists. For example, Stowe's husband, father, and many brothers were famous New England clergymen. The well publicized martyrdom of Elijah Lovejoy also dramatized the centrality of religious speech.

Lovejoy, a Presbyterian minister, used his church weekly to condemn slavery. His writings cost him his life in 1837 when he was murdered by an angry mob bent on silencing his press.

Republicans naturally understood the religious roots of abolitionism, and often stressed the need to protect religious speech. We have already noted Bingham's 1859 speech proclaiming the centrality of the right to "utter according to conscience," and on the campaign trail in 1866 he reminded his audience that men had been imprisoned in Georgia for teaching the Bible, and made clear that the Fourteenth Amendment would put an end to such state action, a theme to which he returned in a key speech on the Amendment before the House in 1871. In early 1866, Lyman Trumbull introduced his Civil Rights Bill by stressing the need to protect the freedom "to teach" and "to preach," citing a Mississippi Black Code punishing any "free negroes and mulattoes" who dared to "exercis[e] the functions of a minister of the Gospel." Similarly, in 1865, Representative James M. Ashley linked religion to freedom of speech in the following way: "[The Slave Power] has silenced every free pulpit within its control ... And made free speech and a free press impossible within its domain...."

In 1789, the freedoms of speech and press had been yoked with religious freedoms largely for reasons of federalism: both religious regulation and press censorship were seen as beyond Congress' enumerated powers. This federalism-based reading of the original First Amendment draws support from the dramatic fact that no previous state constitution had linked these two sets of rights in a single provision. But once yoked together in the federal Bill, these clauses helped reinforce a libertarian theory of freedom of all expression—political, religious, and even artistic (Uncle Tom's Cabin was of course all three). By the 1860's, libertarianism had displaced federalism and majoritarianism as the dominant, unifying theme of the First Amendment's freedoms.

The centrality of religious speech in the 1860's proved especially significant for women. Though excluded from exercising the formal political rights of voting, holding public office, and serving on juries or militias, women could and did play leading roles in religious organizations. Moreover, these organizations engaged in moral crusades with obvious political overtones: temperance, abolition, and (eventually) suffrage. As a result, the voice of women was much harder to ignore in the 1860's than it had been in the 1790's. In the debates over the Constitution and Bill of Rights, only one woman—Mercy Otis Warren—had participated prominently, and even then under a pseudonym. (Indeed, her most important pamphlet during the ratification debates was long ascribed to Elbridge Gerry, and was not credited to her until 1932.) In 1866, however, the most widely read condemnation of slavery had been authored by a woman (Stowe); and in a campaign orchestrated by Susan B. Anthony and Elizabeth Cady Stanton, thousands and thousands of women flooded the Thirty-ninth Congress with petitions on the issue of women's suffrage, which had been largely a nonissue for the Founding Fathers. At least five petitions from women on the suffrage issue were presented on the floor of Congress in the first two months of 1866 alone. Women were therefore central exercisers of First Amendment freedoms in the Reconstruction era in a way they had not been at the Founding—yet another example of the rising importance of "outsider" speech. Interestingly, in discussing the Hoar affair before the Thirty-eighth Congress, Representative William D. Kelley pointedly spoke of not only Samuel Hoar, but also his "beautiful and accomplished daughter." So, too, Representative John Kasson noted that "innocent ladies, cultivated, intelligent, Christian women, have been driven from the cities and States of the South ... Because they had dared to say something offensive to this intolerant spirit of slavery," and Representative Morris reminded his audience that Southern states had "incarcerated Christian men and women for teaching the alphabet."

Just as the centrality of religious speech helped bring women into the core of the First Amendment, it also helped blacks. As with women, the exclusion of blacks from formal political rights like voting underscored the importance of their participation in other organizations like churches, that could help focus the voice of the community. Southern governments, of course, were all too aware of the "incendiary" dangers posed by any assembly of blacks, even (or perhaps especially) an assembly of God. After all, Nat Turner, who had led a famous slave revolt in the 1830's, had been a black preacher—hence the Mississippi Black Code cited by Trumbull, prescribing thirty-nine lashes for any black exercising the functions of a minister. But Republicans like Trumbull strongly affirmed the "civil" rights of blacks to assemble and preach, even as these same Republicans disclaimed an intent to confer "political" rights like the franchise upon blacks. Charles Sumner provided the Joint Committee on Reconstruction yet another dramatic example of black speech, laying before the Committee a petition "from the colored citizens of South Carolina," claiming to represent "four hundred and two thousand citizens of that State, being a very large majority of the population." Unsurprisingly, the petition prayed for "constitutional protection in keeping arms, in holding public assemblies, and in complete liberty of speech and of the press."

The gloss of the Fourteenth Amendment experience on the First Amendment text has important doctrinal implications. As the paradigmatic speech in need of constitutional protection shifts from a localist criticizing the central government to a Unionist defending its Reconstruction policies, carpetbagging federal judges appointed in Washington, D.C. become more trustworthy guardians of First Amendment freedoms than localist juries. When the core of the Amendment was protection of the people collectively from unrepresentative government, perhaps an unelected federal judge on the federal payroll was a more suspect sentry; but when the central mission of free speech shifted to protection of currently unpopular ideas from a current majority, an

Article III officer with life tenure, sheltered from current political winds and sensitive to the long-term value of free speech, enjoyed certain advantages over a jury structured to reflect today's dominant community sentiment. If women and blacks were central speakers in the Reconstruction paradigm, would a jury of twelve white men be in every sense a jury of their "peers"? And if not, there was less reason to expect that such a jury would represent their interests and rights any better than would a federal judge.

Thus, it is largely the Fourteenth Amendment experience, I submit, that best justifies the emphasis in modern First Amendment doctrine on federal judges, rather than juries, as guardians of free speech. Yet the reigning doctrinal approach of jot for jot incorporation has obscured the significance of the Fourteenth Amendment, which all but drops out of the free speech picture. Advocates and scholars focus all their analytic and narrative attention on the Founding, not the Reconstruction. Thus, in championing the rights of Communists and Jehovah's Witnesses in the twentieth century, the ACLU has analogized to Zenger more than to the abolitionists—who are the truer forebears of modern political and religious speakers perceived as "nuts" and "cranks" by the dominant culture. Similarly, in the landmark First Amendment case of our era, *New York Times Co. v. Sullivan,* Justice Brennan quoted Madison and thoughtfully reflected on the lessons of the Alien and Sedition Act controversy, but said virtually nothing about the Reconstruction Amendment except that it incorporated the First Amendment against states (presumably jot for jot). Yet the facts before the Court in Sullivan almost cried out for comparison with the Reconstruction era. Southern followers of the Reverend Martin Luther King, many of them black and many of them religious, had used a Northern newspaper to criticize Southern officials; and a Southern jury composed of good ole boys had socked the speakers with massively punitive damages. Many of the doctrinal rules crafted by Sullivan and its progeny reflect obvious suspicion of juries—resulting, for example, in various issues being classified as legal questions or mixed questions of law and fact inappropriate for unconstrained jury determination—yet that suspicion is much better justified by the Reconstruction experience than by the Founding.

Professor Taslitz's summary of search and seizure practices during slavery and Reconstruction may help to clarify how Amar's theory applies to the Fourth Amendment:[13]

Free Movement and Southern Fears

. . . [R]epressive searches and seizures were not directed solely at those engaged in blatant political speech. The South had a growing fear

---

13. Andrew E. Taslitz, *Slaves No More: The Implications of the Informed Citizen Idea for Discovery Before Fourth Amendment Suppression Hearings*, 15 GA. ST. L. REV. 709 (1999). For those interested in a far more detailed revisionist history of the Fourth Amendment and its modern implications, *see* ANDREW E. TASLITZ, RECONSTRUCTING THE FOURTH AMENDMENT: A HISTORY OF SEARCH AND SEIZURE, 1789–1868 (N.Y.U. Press 2006).

of slave revolt and violent retribution. That fear was magnified in 1831, after Virginia slave Nat Turner led a revolt in which 60 Whites died before the insurrection was repressed. John Brown's raid in Harper's Ferry in 1859 in the hope of sparking widespread slave rebellion yet again heightened Southern fears. Southerners understood that slave resistance was also expressive conduct. Every slave who successfully fled North sent a message to his brethren that freedom was in their grasp. And who knew which of such escaped slaves could become a Frederick Douglass using their freedom to speak out in the abolitionist cause. Every slowdown, breach of rules, minor theft, or other acts of "insolence" came to be seen as a direct threat to the entire social order. Repression thus increased at all levels, taking the form of brutal and legally sanctioned interference with free movement and privacy.

Thus every Southern state but Delaware established legislation to create and regulate countywide slave patrols. These patrols had keeping order among slaves, especially in preventing runaways and thefts, as their primary duty. While the importance of the patrols waxed and waned over the antebellum period, they attained special importance during the Civil War. In some states, patrollers could even arrest and summarily punish White persons for keeping company with slaves.

Southern jails also became warehouses for runaways and even for slaves thought likely to try an escape. Many states provided procedures to imprison runaways, such as Mississippi, which in 1846 required close confinement but permitted jailers to take them out to have them work on public projects. The Fugitive Slave Act of 1850, which made capture of runaways easier, spread Southern repression more visibly into the North.

Anti-literacy laws spread, making it a crime to teach slaves to read and write. In 1833, Florida authorized White citizen patrols to search the homes of slaves and free Blacks, seizing any firearms found and summarily punishing Blacks who could not offer a proper explanation for the firearms' presence. In 1846 and 1861, the Florida legislature again provided for such citizen patrols but in addition enforced a pass system for free Blacks and slaves. The primary function of the searches and passes was to terrorize Blacks into accepting their subordination.

Whipping quickly became in practice the "disciplinary center-piece" of plantation slavery. The law frequently gave sanction to these beatings as necessary to social order.

Assemblages of slaves, often regardless of the purpose, were prohibited as giving rise to "such circumstances of terror as cannot but endanger the public peace...." Other states prohibited assemblages for certain purposes, such as teaching reading and writing, but often made an exception for religious activities.

The crime of slave "insolence" more directly linked slave speech and arrest. Frederick Douglass explained that a slave committed this crime "in the tone of an answer, in answering at all; in not answering; in the expression of countenance; in the motion of the head; in the gait, manner and bearing of the slave." One example was the 1851 trial of the slave Sole or Solomon for insolence to patrollers. One patroller testified that Sole used "some very improper or unbecoming language such as asserting his Equality with any man and that he would die before he would submit to being whipped to death." The magistrates sentenced Sole to 200 lashes.

The Slave Power sought to justify its repression of speech, press, and slave resistance and dissension in varying ways. John Calhoun represented one line of defense. Calhoun was skeptical about the existence of inalienable equal human rights, describing the Declaration of Independence's ethical appeal as "the most dangerous of all political errors." Calhoun instead embraced a philosophy in which communities, not the individual, were at the core, and it was the White community's preservation that mattered. Jefferson Davis, on the other hand, embraced the Declaration of Independence, but saw Blacks as outside its ambit. To challenge slavery was to challenge the inalienable White right to property. Moreover, argued some Southern rights theorists, slavery fortified the White spirit of freedom, and states, not the Federal government, were best institutionally equipped to protect those freedoms. What all these strands of thought shared, however, was a conception of Black moral incapacity to engage in reasoned debate and thus to be the bearers of any rights.

Abolitionism and Northern Reaction

Southern repression of free speech and growing rights skepticism did much for the abolitionist's cause. The Slave Power came to be perceived as a direct threat to the very concept of inalienable equal rights. Free Whites, not only slave or free Blacks, were being attacked, gagged, searched, and imprisoned in the name of preserving slavery. Furthermore, the Slave Power's belief in Black moral incapacity challenged the Lockean notion of toleration that was at the core of his concept of equal inalienable rights. All persons in Lockean theory were entitled to equal respect by virtue of their moral powers rationally to assess and pursue ends and thus be equal bearers of rights. This notion of tolerance contrasted with its opposite: the moral status of persons differing and specified in advance by nature or a hierarchical social structure. Such a hierarchical social theory rejected the idea that it needed to be justified in a crucial testing by other ideas and worldviews; the result would be a repressive orthodoxy. While perhaps not thought of in such sophisticated Lockean terms, however, much of the Northern public increasingly came to understand that the practice of slavery justified widespread repression of dissenters of all races and ultimately the rejection of the Declaration of Independence's generous version of a rights-based philosophy. Thus the 1856 Republican Party campaign slogan: "Free Press, Free Men, Free Labor, Freemont."

Republicans increasingly invoked rights to free speech, press, petition, and assembly as part of the definition of "republican government." But they understood too that the Slave Power repressed these rights, primarily by offending the privacy and free movement of slaves, free Blacks, resident Southern anti-slavery Whites, and visiting Northern abolitionist Whites. Republican condemnation of slavery after the Civil War drew on a variation of Madison's theory of faction. Madison favored a large republic to allow the war of so many factions that no one could gain dominance. He feared too oppression of minorities from unjust combinations of the majority. To Madison, slavery created a property-based faction in which "the mere distinction of colour ... [was] made a ground of the most oppressive dominion ever exercised by man over man."

Before the War, some Northern Republican Constitutional theorists believed that slavery would die of its own accord. But by the end of the Civil War, many came to understand that race-based slavery had survived and grown because it bred its own faction that entrenched the institution. That faction bred two political evils: slavery, which led to general intolerance and oppression, and "unreasonable" racial prejudice, which led to a caste-based philosophy inimical to the very notion of Republican government. This does not mean that most Republicans were not, by modern standards, racist. They were. But, by the end of the Civil War, that racism focused on a denial of social status but not of the moral capacity necessary for equal civil and political rights.

The most glaring evidence of the continuing factional power of the slaveocracy was the adoption of Black Codes to replace the pre-Civil War Slave Codes. Again, the Black Codes sought to re-institute the functional equivalent of slavery by impinging upon Black privacy, property, and freedom of movement. The Codes provided for the arrest and return to their employers of Blacks who breached labor contracts, prohibited Black servants from leaving their masters' premises, and authorized hiring out Black children and Blacks unable to pay vagrancy fines. The Codes made certain conduct criminal for Blacks but not Whites. These crimes were powerfully reminiscent of the Southern law of slavery. The Mississippi Black Code thus made it a crime for Blacks to make "insulting gestures" or to function as ministers of the gospel without a license from some White church. South Carolina created a separate court system for Blacks accused of crimes. Senator Trumbull, in proposing national legislation, which eventually became the Civil Rights Act of 1866, described the Black Codes thus:

> They provided that if any colored person, any free Negro or Mulatto, shall come into that State for the purpose of residing there, he shall be sold into slavery for life. If any person of African descent residing in the State travels from one county to another without having a pass or a certificate of his freedom, he is liable to be committed to jail and to be dealt with as a person who is in the State without authority ... and one provision of the statute

declares that for "exercising the functions of the Gospel free Negroes and Mulattoes, on conviction, may be punished by any number of lashes not exceeding thirty-nine on the bare back, and shall pay the costs." The statutes of South Carolina make it a high penal offense for any person, White or Colored to teach [former] slaves.

The Codes thus sought to repress Black enjoyment of freedom of movement, privacy, and property as an expression of an intolerable idea of equality. Apart from the Codes, other governmental and pseudo-governmental conduct served similar functions. For example, in 1866 various Southern White militias, "composed of Confederate veterans still wearing their gray uniforms ... frequently terrorized the Black population, ransacking their homes to seize shotguns and other property and abusing those who refused to sign labor contracts." The Ku Klux Klan, in action by 1866, played a particularly brutal role in intimidating, whipping, and beating blacks into signing onerous labor contracts with their landlords, contracts that, once signed, worked in conjunction with the Black Codes to limit Black freedom of movement. When Blacks in 1866 and their White Republican allies gathered in a New Orleans hall to convene a convention to discuss extending the franchise to freedmen, "they were attacked and slaughtered by a mob led by the city police, a force largely made up of militant Confederate veterans." Similarly, in Memphis, city police played a key role in triggering racial violence against former Black servicemen. A similar wave of violence against White Republicans and friends of the freedmen swept the South.

The Republicans who debated the Fourteenth Amendment understood the close connection among the kinds of rights that the Fourth Amendment protected. Free speech, press, the nature of free movement and privacy were central aspects of the expression of a message of equality. When persons can be subject to arbitrary search and seizure at all, but especially because of their race or political views, there can be no debate among an informed citizenry. The Lockean philosophy of tolerance, the deliberation necessary to sound political judgment, and the respect for all persons' moral reasoning powers the notion that the idea of equal inalienable human rights entailed required protection from unreasonable and arbitrary arrest, search, and seizure. The Fourteenth Amendment was partly intended to ensure the constitutionality of the 1866 Civil Rights Act in effectively outlawing the Black Codes. The Reconstruction Congress meant precisely by doing so to halt the designation of Blacks as special targets for various searches and seizures. Privacy protection and equality values became inseparably linked. John Bingham, the author of Section 1 of the Fourteenth Amendment, clearly saw protection of Fourth Amendment values against state action as necessary to protecting against the Madisonian fear of majority tyranny over minorities. He pointedly listed the Fourth Amendment, during House debates over the Fourteenth Amendment, as among the privileges and immunities of United

States citizenship. Similarly, Senator Howard quoted *Corfield v. Coryell* on the Senate floor and listed the "right to be exempt from unreasonable searches and seizures" as among the privileges of national citizenship. There is little serious doubt that the Fourteenth Amendment was meant to ensure the application of the Bill of Rights, including the Fourth Amendment, to the States.

The procedural question remained, however, of how search and seizure rights would be enforced. The North had long thought juries critical to that role, echoing many of the themes sounding at the time of adoption of the fourth amendment. In particular, the jury's role shaped the battle over the fugitive slave law. Thus Salmon P. Chase, an abolitionist lawyer (later Chief Justice) had argued in 1837 that surely his client, Matilda Lawrence, a free Black woman in Ohio, "was entitled to a jury before her liberty could be snatched away ... [by] some greedy White man [who] called her his slave." Chase lost the case, leading various Northern states to respond with personal liberty laws guaranteeing alleged fugitive slaves a jury trial. The Supreme Court ultimately struck down a personal liberty law in *Priggs v. Pennsylvania*, and in 1850 Congress adopted the Fugitive Slave Act, denying alleged fugitive slaves the benefits of the jury trial. The jury, we have seen, was long viewed as essential to the monitoring function of an informed citizenry. Senator Charles Sumner railed against the interference with this function by the abomination of separating the seizure decision from the jury's hands. Said Summer:

> In denying the Trial by Jury [this act] is three times unconstitutional; first as the Constitution declares "the right of the people to be secure in their persons against unreasonable seizures;" secondly as it further declares, that "No person shall be deprived of life, liberty or property without due process of law;" and thirdly, because it expressly declares that "in suits at common law ... the right of jury trial shall be preserved." By this triple cord did the framers of the Constitution secure the Trial by Jury in every question of Human Freedom.

Immediately after the Civil War, Republicans had a similar faith in the jury trial, but they viewed it, unlike the framers did, solely as a civil, not a political, right. They came again to recognize the jury's political nature as their understanding grew that Southern juries could not be counted on to protect free Blacks. For an informed citizenry to function effectively in the jury's monitoring function, all citizens needed representation on the jury. Similarly, the Republicans had come to understand that informed citizens could not choose wise leaders or monitor their rulers' abuses unless all citizens had a say. Thus the Republicans pressed for passage of the fifteenth amendment, which Akhil Amar has argued must be understood as guaranteeing Blacks the right to vote both as electors and as jurors.

While the Fifteenth Amendment aimed in part to create a properly functioning jury to serve an informed citizenry, the Fourteenth Amendment's incorporation of the Bill of Rights should not be understood in cramped terms. The amendment's sponsors and ratifiers likely understood themselves primarily as engaged in the political task of enacting broad moral principles rather than in the bureaucratic task of enacting particular solutions. Among the major moral principles enacted were these: (1) there is an important link between Fourth Amendment and informed citizenry concepts; (2) in incorporating the Bill of Rights against the States, the Fourteenth Amendment shifted the Bill's emphasis from libertarian concerns toward a greater concern with protecting minorities from majority tyranny—including the tyranny of suppressing ideas in a way that aids minority subordination; and (3) monitoring governmental abuses of the power of search and seizure is necessary to guard against such subordination. These values should be kept in mind in interpreting the Fourth Amendment today. As we will shortly see, the suppression hearing before a judge may today more effectively secure these purposes than would sole reliance on the jury.

2. FOURTH AMENDMENT IMPLICATIONS

a.   *Defining a "Seizure"*

An important part of the Fourth Amendment test for the seizure of a person is whether a reasonable person under the circumstances would feel that he or she was not free to leave. The key is what counts as part of the reasonable person's circumstances. Different circumstances create different reasonable persons. Professor Tracey Maclin reminds us that black men may perceive a degree of coercion in police encounters that white men would not:

> Why do black men fear the police? As one commentator noted, "[w]ith reason, African–Americans tend to grow up believing that the law is the enemy, because those who are sworn to uphold the law so often enforce it in a biased way." Black males learn at an early age that confrontations with the police should be avoided; black teenagers are advised never to challenge a police officer, even when the officer is wrong. Even if a police officer has arguable grounds for stopping a black male, such an encounter often engenders distinct feelings for the black man. Those feelings are fear of possible violence or humiliation.[14]

Significant empirical data suggest that these perceptions are based on actual unequal treatment.[15] The central point, however, is that the mythical "reasonable man" of seizure law always has a race, the "default" race (if race is not otherwise expressly addressed) being the views of the white majority. But because the whole point of the Fourth Amendment is to require an adequate justification for coercive police action, and because race affects perceptions of coercion, it only seems right that race must be

---

14. Tracey Maclin, *Black and Blue Encounters: Some Preliminary Thoughts About Fourth Amendment Seizures: Should Race Matter?*, 26 VALPARAISO U.L. REV. 243, 255 (1991).

15. *See, e.g.*, SAMUEL WALKER, THE POLICE IN AMERICA: AN INTRODUCTION 234 (1992).

part of the "reasonable man's" circumstances. Current law ignores this distinction.

b. Distinguishing Stops From Arrests

Distinguishing between a stop and an arrest turns at least implicitly on the reasonable person's perception of the degree to which freedom of movement has been restricted. Once again, the detainee's race should be relevant in determining whether a stop became so intrusive as to become an arrest, requiring probable cause.[16] A rule taking race into account would be especially sensible given the likelihood, discussed earlier, that minority resentment of police conduct will lead to escalating tension and increase the chance that police will engage in intrusive conduct such as frisks and custodial arrests.[17]

c. Reasonable Suspicion and Probable Cause Determinations

Consciously or unconsciously, police may consider race in making judgments about whether they have reasonable suspicion for a stop and frisk or probable cause for an arrest or full-blown search or seizure. Race may enter the calculation as simple animus, but it may also be used in a more subtle way. For example, an officer's suspicions might be aroused by a black person's presence in a white neighborhood or vice versa, because such presence is assumed to be unusual and police are taught to suspect the unusual. Or an officer might depend on stereotyping to conclude that a black person is engaging in suspicious activity:

> Several factors explain the tendency of the police to stop and question racial minorities at a disproportionate rate. Police officers are trained to be suspicious, to look for criminal suspects. To do this, they develop a visual "shorthand" for suspects, based on visual clues. Inevitably, this involves a certain amount of stereotyping. Skolnick argues that "a disposition to stereotype is an integral part of the policeman's world." A police officer's experience indicates that young black men engage in robbery at a higher rate than young white men. Data on participation in crime supports this perception.[18]

Drug courier profiles are an example of such stereotyping.

Sheri Lynn Johnson argues that stereotyping is unjustifiable from a social science perspective. She explains that without significant empirical or

---

16. See MANN, UNEQUAL JUSTICE, *supra* note 7, at 160–65 (summarizing data showing very negative minority perceptions of police and police-citizen encounters).

17. Whether the higher *arrest* rate for African–Americans reflects discrimination or their relatively higher rate of participation in certain crimes has been subject to some dispute, although powerful arguments favor the former explanation; nevertheless, most concede the reality of the heightened tensions in all pre-trial police contacts. *See, e.g.,* Walker, IN AMERICA, *supra* note 15, at 234–42; JEFFREY REIMAN, THE RICH GET RICHER AND THE POOR GET PRISON: IDEOLOGY, CRIME, AND CRIMINAL JUSTICE 100–08 (4th ed. 1995); Mann, UNEQUAL JUSTICE, *supra* note 7, at 149–52.

18. WALKER, IN AMERICA, *supra* note 15, at 234–35.

other trustworthy data, race is not a logical predictor of crime and is irrelevant to probable cause or reasonable suspicion.[19] She identifies and rejects five ways in which race is used in probable cause/reasonable suspicion determinations:

(1) Race establishes general criminal propensity. This assumption may be in part a product of disparities in participation rates or arrest rates among racial and ethnic groups. In either event, there is no way to determine with any confidence how much weight race or ethnicity deserves in probable cause or reasonable suspicion determinations, and it should not be so used.

(2) Race is a factor in some drug courier profiles, which help to identify suspicious behavior. There is little empirical support for profiles. Law enforcement agencies keep much of the allegedly supporting data secret, and arrest rates, rather than participation rates, may explain the presence of race in profiles.

(3) Race identifies suspicious behavior through incongruity. incongruity is usually supported by an officer's testimony that members of a particular race are rarely seen in a particular neighborhood. The problem with incongruity is that the rarity of an event does not necessarily make it a good predictor of criminality. Even an officer's testimony that most minority group members in a particular neighborhood have engaged in crime is insufficient because an individual officer's experience is not extensive enough from which to draw conclusions—in social science terms, the sample size is inadequate.

(4) Race helps to identify illegal aliens. One might argue that race or ethnicity would be relevant if, for example, INS statistics show that most arrested illegal aliens are "Hispanic." There are at least two problems with such an argument, however. First, it is questionable whether someone can be identified as "Hispanic" based on appearance, especially given Anglo stereotyping. Second, Anglo officers may have cultural biases that lead them to view Hispanic behaviors as suspicious ones indicating illegal alien status.

(5) Race helps to identify particular offenders. Using race in this way is legitimate only in this sense: if eyewitnesses describe the perpetrator as white, then police should be investigating only white suspects, and vice versa.

Race should not be a factor in probable cause and reasonable suspicion determinations for reasons aside from social science. The Fourteenth Amendment's textual reference to equality, and the intention of its drafters to provide equal treatment to the newly freed slaves, suggest that courts should not permit race to be considered in the objective determination of probable cause.[20] A rule prohibiting racial considerations would also help

---

19. *See* Sheri Lynn Johnson, *Race and the Decision to Detain a Suspect*, 93 YALE L.J. 214 (1983).

20. Professor Johnson has crafted a slightly different argument, specifically that use of race in the probable cause determination is an equal protection, not a Fourth Amendment,

police departments eliminate racism from police culture. Finally, such a rule will help alleviate minority mistrust of the police and the criminal justice system, a factor that both logic and the Court's opinion in *Terry v. Ohio*[21] suggest must be part of the Fourth Amendment reasonableness determination.

d. Acknowledging Pretext

The Supreme Court's opinion in *Whren v. United States* reveals that the present Court is unwilling to invalidate pretextual police conduct. Instead, the Court suggested that such claims be raised using equal protection principles, but by doing so, the Court effectively ensured no remedy for racial disparity at all, because equal protection selective prosecution claims are notoriously difficult to prove, as we discuss below. At most, the Court may be willing to examine claims of "fabricated pretext," when police rely on a legally sufficient justification for Fourth Amendment activity but provide no facts to support the justification. According to some scholars, though, the Court has ignored instances of fabricated pretext.

The Court's refusal to acknowledge the problem of pretext may encourage racist police behavior. For example, it encourages officers to engage in traffic stops of African–Americans, even though those officers would not be inclined to stop whites in the same circumstances. Moreover, condoning such activity sends powerful and hurtful messages about inferiority, amplifying perceptions that the justice system is racist.

Professor Tracey Maclin[22] points to empirical data showing that Black and Hispanic motorists constitute a disproportionately large segment of those subjected to arbitrary traffic stops. Given the magnitude of the problem, Maclin argues that the "reasonableness" of stops should involve a flexible inquiry into multiple factors, rather than a wooden application of the probable cause and reasonable suspicion standards. Maclin also argues that in several pre-*Whren* cases the Supreme Court recognized the relevance to Fourth Amendment analysis of factors such as disparate racial impact and minority perceptions. Maclin goes on to explain that adding race-consciousness to the "reasonableness" inquiry helps to promote Fourth Amendment values by limiting police discretionary power, discouraging police perjury, and improving state-citizen trust. Therefore, Maclin urges that *Whren* be overruled. In its place, Maclin proposes a rule requiring the prosecution to provide a race-neutral justification whenever a defendant raises an inference of a race-based traffic stop.

---

problem. *See id.* at 241–51. We will soon see that the Court likely agrees that the problem is one of equal protection but, unlike Professor Johnson, the Court is very unlikely to find an equal protection violation.

21. *See* Robin Magee, *The Myth of the Good Cop and the Inadequacy of Fourth Amendment Remedies for Black Men: Contrasting Presumptions of Innocence and Guilt*, 23 CAP. L. REV. 151, 167–68 (1994).

22. Tracey Maclin, *Race and the Fourth Amendment*, 51 VANDERBILT L. REV. 333, 342–54 (1998).

e. Sub–Arrests

A "sub-arrest" is a seizure of the person that is more intrusive than a stop but less intrusive than a custodial arrest.[23] Examples of sub-arrests include taking an individual to the stationhouse for a brief period in order to place him in a lineup or to take his fingerprints. Although the term has not yet been given Fourth Amendment significance, the Court has suggested that sub-arrests based on reasonable suspicion may be reasonable under certain circumstances.[24] This suggestion is troublesome, because reasonable suspicion can be established on less reliable evidence than is needed for probable cause[25] and often involves fairly general descriptions.[26] Professor Maclin again raises the spectre of police abuse:

> A tragic and controversial case in Boston illustrates how constitutional freedoms can be lost when society responds aggressively to a horrible crime. On October 24, 1989, a white couple, Carol and Charles Stuart, were found shot after attending a birthing class at a hospital in the Mission Hill section of Roxbury, a predominantly black neighborhood. The initial description of the alleged assailant was that he was a black male, about 6 feet tall and approximately 30 years old. After the shooting, many black men were stopped, questioned and searched by police, often in blatant disregard of constitutional norms. The shooting also brought renewed interest in (and support for) the Boston police of indiscriminately stopping and frisking members of youth gangs.

> The description provided in the Stuart case is a slim reed to support—for example—on-site fingerprinting of tall, black men in their late 20's or early 30's found in Roxbury. There are hundreds of persons who fit that description. Any investigative detention, including police forcibly stopping and questioning young black men, based on this description would run afoul of the constitutional requirement of specificity. Indeed, amidst public furor and pressure to find the killer, the events in the Stuart case took a bizarre turn. Several weeks after the attack and after the police had produced several suspects, one of whom Mr. Stuart identified in a lineup as the assailant, new developments led

---

23. Tracey Maclin, *Book Review: Seeing the Constitution From the Backseat of a Police Squad Car*, 70 B.U. L. REV. 543 (1990).

24. *See* Davis v. Mississippi, 394 U.S. 721, 727 (1969), which held that a round-up of 25 African–Americans for questioning and fingerprinting in an effort to match the crime scene prints of a rape suspect was unconstitutional. In doing so, however, the Court noted that "[i]t is arguable . . . that because of the unique nature of the fingerprinting process, such detentions might, under narrowly defined circumstances, be found to comply with the Fourth Amendment even though there is no probable cause in the traditional sense." In Hayes v. Florida, 470 U.S. 811 (1985), the Court found a Fourth Amendment violation when police, acting on only reasonable suspicion, took rape suspect Hayes to the stationhouse for fingerprinting. But the Court noted that it did not necessarily bar reasonable suspicion detentions for fingerprinting or the judiciary from authorizing by warrant a fingerprinting seizure on less than probable cause.

25. Alabama v. White, 496 U.S. 325, 330 (1990).

26. Maclin, *Backseat*, *supra* note 23, at 570.

the police to focus on Mr. Stuart himself. And, just as the police were prepared to arrest Mr. Stuart, he committed suicide.

f. Consensual Searches

A consensual search is valid if the consent was voluntarily given.[27] Voluntariness depends on coercion. If African–Americans or other minorities are more likely to perceive coercion in a citizen-police officer encounter, then common sense (and the Fourteenth Amendment) suggest that race and ethnicity should be factors, though not determinative ones, in determining voluntariness.

B. Lessons From Equal Protection Analysis

Will any of these race-based arguments be accepted by the current Court? Answering this question requires dividing those arguments into two categories: (1) those involving minority perceptions of police conduct; and (2) those involving police conduct that reveals discriminatory intentions and effects.

The Court has not articulated a coherent approach to the first group of cases, but its decision in *Whren* suggests that it is likely to insist on a "colorblind" jurisprudence. The second category, however, employs a well-recognized equal protection approach. For example, defendants can get relief from racially motivated prosecutions if they can demonstrate (1) that they were intentionally singled out for prosecution on the basis of race; and (2) that similarly situated persons of a different race were not prosecuted.[28] Courts are reluctant to grant selective prosecution claims such as these because those claims result in dismissal of the entire case, rather than the suppression of evidence. Moreover, selective prosecution claims are notoriously difficult to prove because most defendants cannot obtain the proof they need from the government. Before a defendant may obtain discovery to support a selective prosecution claim, he or she must already have a "colorable basis" for the claim—some evidence tending to show the existence of the two essential elements—as well as a colorable basis to believe that the government possesses probative documents.

The Supreme Court's treatment of the colorable basis requirement in *United States v. Armstrong*[29] highlights the difficulty of proving selective prosecution. There, defendants filed a motion for discovery in a federal crack cocaine prosecution. The motion sought information pertinent to the defendants' selective prosecution claim, which contended that the federal government had chosen to prosecute black defendants while referring white defendants to state prosecutors operating under more lenient sentencing laws. Accompanying the motion for discovery was an affidavit from a

---

27. *See* Schneckloth v. Bustamonte, 412 U.S. 218 (1973).

28. John S. Herbrand, *What Constitutes Such Discriminatory Prosecution or Enforcement of Law as to Provide a Valid Defense in Federal Criminal Proceedings*, 45 A.L.R. Fed. 732, § 2a (1996).

29. 517 U.S. 456 (1996).

federal public defender ("FPD") alleging that in each of the FPD office's crack cases in 1991, the defendant was black. The motion also was accompanied by a study listing those defendants, their race, and status.

After the district court ordered discovery, the government moved for reconsideration, submitting its own affidavits claiming that its decisions in each case rested on reasons other than race, such as the quantity of crack, the strength of evidence, and the number of sales. Additionally, the government submitted portions of a 1989 Drug Enforcement Administration report concluding that large-scale crack distribution networks were controlled by Jamaican, Haitian, and African–American street gangs. In response, defendants submitted an affidavit alleging that a drug treatment center intake coordinator had told defense counsel that there are equal numbers of Caucasian and minority users and dealers. The defendants also submitted an affidavit from a criminal defense attorney, who stated that, in his experience, many nonblacks had been prosecuted in state court for crack offenses, and a newspaper article reporting that federal crack criminals, all of whom were black, were punished far more severely than if they had possessed powder.

The district court denied the reconsideration motion and dismissed the case when the government refused to comply with the discovery order. The Ninth Circuit, sitting en banc, affirmed the dismissal, holding that a defendant is not required to demonstrate that the government failed to prosecute those similarly situated. The Supreme Court reversed and remanded for proceedings consistent with its opinion.

The Court stressed that "the showing necessary to obtain discovery should itself be a significant barrier to the litigation of insubstantial claims." This "significant barrier" required some evidence tending to show the existence of the essential elements of the defense. But, concluded the Court, the Ninth Circuit was wrong in starting from the presumption, for which it cited no authority, that all races commit all types of crimes and that no type of crime is the exclusive province of any particular racial or ethnic group. The Court concluded that United States Sentencing Commission statistics, showing that more than 90 percent of persons sentenced in 1994 for crack trafficking were black, while over 93 percent of convicted LSD dealers were white, were "at war" with the Ninth Circuit's presumption. Furthermore, the Court concluded that it would "not have been an insuperable task" to prove that similarly situated defendants of other races were known to federal prosecutors but were not prosecuted in federal court. The Court was unconvinced by the defense study, which had not addressed non-blacks, or by the newspaper article, which addressed discriminatory sentencing rather than prosecution. Similarly, the Court characterized the defense affidavits as "hearsay and reported personal conclusions based on anecdotal evidence," an insufficient showing to meet the test for discovery.

The Court's decision in *Armstrong* illustrates the difficulty of addressing problems of racism using the equal protection clause. When defendants use equal protection theory to claim that police used improper racial considerations in determining probable cause or reasonable suspicion, they cannot even obtain discovery to support their claim without first showing the two essential elements addressed in Armstrong. For example, they would have to establish a colorable basis for the proposition that similarly suspicious whites were not stopped or searched. This high burden renders race-based challenges of little concern to the police. Success in such challenges may depend on the receptivity of state courts.

C.   Using Race and Culture in Suppression Motions

Cultural Factors in Motions to Suppress

James G. Connell, III and Rene L. Valladares.[30]

Cultural issues can permeate every aspect of a criminal case. From the first meeting with the client, through trial, sentencing, and appeal, the defense of a client from another culture poses unique problems. The importance off cultural issues is magnified by the unprecedented number of individuals from other countries who are currently prosecuted and incarcerated in the United States.

Litigating cultural issues can be fascinating because defense counsel is challenged to think creatively and borrow from disciplines such as anthropology and cultural psychology. However navigating the waters of cultural issues without a compass can be treacherous. For instance, a client can be seriously harmed by a criminal defense lawyer who gives her erroneous information regarding the impact of her guilty plea on her immigration status. Likewise, a criminal defense lawyer who fails to adequately understand cultural psychological syndromes can miss critical trial defenses or mitigation arguments.

One of the areas where cultural issues play a major role is in motions to suppress physical evidence or statements. A client who was raised in a repressive regime that commands strict submission to authority may believe that he has absolutely no choice but to consent to a request to have his automobile searched by a highway patrol officer making a casual traffic stop. . . .

In both examples, the cultural difficulties can be exacerbated by the inability of the defendants to speak English. This article describes opportunities for counsel to strengthen Fourth . . . Amendment motions to suppress by incorporating cultural factors into the traditional constitutional analysis.

Applicability of the Fourth Amendment to Undocumented Aliens

One threshold issue in the application of the Fourth Amendment to non-citizens is whether the Fourth Amendment protects such non-citizens at all. The Supreme Court held in *United States v. Verdugo–Urquidez* that

---

30.   James G. Connell, III & Rene L. Valladares, *Cultural Factors in Motions to Suppress*, The Champion 18 (March 2001).

non-resident aliens confined in the United States are not protected by the Fourth Amendment against unreasonable extraterritorial searches, and the Ninth Circuit has questioned whether resident aliens are protected by the Fourth Amendment in similar circumstances. More disturbingly, the Supreme Court has questioned *in dicta* whether the Fourth Amendment protects undocumented aliens residing in the United States against unreasonable searches in U.S. territory.

Notwithstanding these ominous portents, the case for Fourth Amendment protections against unreasonable domestic searches and seizures remains strong. A number of Supreme Court decisions have held that the Constitution is fully applicable everywhere within the incorporated territory of the United States. Although the issue has not arisen recently, the Supreme Court repeatedly held in the 19th century that the Constitution applied fully to the continental Territories.

In a series of cases regarding U.S. holdings overseas collectively known as the *Insular Cases,* the Supreme Court held that where territory is part of the United States, the inhabitants of that territory are entitled to the guarantees of the Constitution. In its most recent case regarding the territorial reach of the Constitution the Court unanimously held in 1979 that the Fourth Amendment governs searches conducted in Puerto Rico.

Indeed each of the opinions in *Verdugo–Urquidez* support or are at least consistent with the principle that the Fourth Amendment governs all searches within the United States, regardless of the immigration status of the target.

In his "Opinion of the Court," Chief Justice Rehnquist interpreted the Fourth Amendment phrase "the people" to refer to "a class of persons who are part of a national community or who have other wise developed sufficient connection with this country to be considered part of that community" and questioned the assumption that an earlier opinion, *INS v. Lopez–Mendoza*, stood for the proposition that undocumented aliens in the United States were protected by the Fourth Amendment.

Otherwise, however Chief Justice Rehnquist focused his analysis on the extraterritoriality of the search: he repeatedly emphasized the location of the search, and explained that "if there was a constitutional violation, it occurred solely in Mexico."

Justice Kennedy was the fifth member of Rehnquist's majority, but he wrote separately that, "If the search had occurred in a residence in the United States, I have little doubt that the full protections of the Fourth Amendment would apply."

Justice Stevens, concurring in the judgment, wrote that "comment on illegal aliens' entitlement to the protections of the Fourth Amendment [is not] necessary to resolve this case." He emphasized the extraterritorial location of the search, and concluded that the Warrant Clause does not apply to foreign searches because American magistrates cannot authorize such searches.

Justice Blackmun, dissenting, argued the Fourth Amendment was applicable because the U.S. exercised sovereign power over the defendant, but that the Warrant Clause was inapplicable for the same reason.

Finally, Justice Brennan reasoned in his dissent that "the majority implies that respondent would be protected by the Fourth Amendment if the place searched were in the United States." Lower Courts applying *Verdugo–Urquidez* have arrived at the conclusion that the decision, taken as a whole, does not deny fourth Amendment rights to undocumented aliens. Each court to consider the question has concluded that the Fourth Amendment protects undocumented aliens. *United States v. Guitterez* illustrates both sides of the debate. In *Guitterez*, a district court initially denied a motion to suppress on the basis that the Fourth Amendment did not protect the defendant, an undocumented alien who had lived in the United States for twelve years, because he lacked substantial, voluntary connections to the United States. Later, the district court reversed itself *sua sponte*, and held that aliens have no obligation to demonstrate connections to the United States. Later, the district court reversed itself *sua sponte*, and held that aliens have no obligation to demonstrate connections to the United States in order to claim standing to challenge domestic searches and seizures under the Fourth Amendment. In doing so, the district court reasoned that the Fourth Amendment may not protect undocumented aliens against unreasonable domestic searches or seizures was *dicta* supported by only four justices, and that such a rule would be confusing and unworkable. This "near miss" demonstrates both the danger of misapplication of the Fourth Amendment, and the proper analysis that the Fourth Amendment governs all searches conducted within the territory of the United States.

In litigating the applicability of the Fourth Amendment to aliens, counsel should both emphasize her client's ties to the United State and stress the difficulty of evaluating various levels of connection to the Untied States. Family, employment, trade or driver's licenses, payment of sales and income taxes, rent or mortgage payment, consumer debt, voluntary presence in the United State, and other connections between the individual and society may demonstrate the significant connections discussed in *Verdugo–Urquidez*. At the same time, the multiplicity of factors, as well as the varieties of status under immigration law, may demonstrate to the court the unworkability of litigating the ties of each and every alien to come before the court.

Ethnic Appearance in Stops

One issue which has recently gained new currency is the extent to which law enforcement officers may rely on ethnic appearance as one factor among other in articulating reasonable suspicion for a stop. It is clearly established that ethnic appearance alone cannot provide reasonable suspicion for a stop. Twenty-five years ago, the Supreme Court noted in *United States v. Brignoni–Ponce*, that although Mexican appearance alone would not justify reasonable suspicion that the occupants of a car were undocumented aliens or involved in other illegal activity, "[t]he likelihood that any given person of Mexican ancestry is an alien is high enough to make Mexican appearance a relevant factor."

The Ninth Circuit has recently revisited the question of whether ethnic appearance is a relevant factor in reasonable suspicion analysis, and held *en banc* that it is not. In *United States v. Montero–Camargo*, the Ninth Circuit directly contradicted *Brignoni–Ponce*, explaining that "[t]he likelihood that in an area in which the majority—even a substantial part of the population is Hispanic, any given person of Hispanic ancestry is in fact an alien, let alone an illegal alien, is not high enough tot make Hispanic appearance a relevant factor in the reasonable suspicion calculus." The Ninth Circuit reasoned that the Supreme Court's statement in *Brignoni–Ponce*, which the Ninth Circuit characterized as *dictum*, has been undermined by demographic changes over the past 25 years. The court concluded that "Hispanic appearance is, in general, of such little probative value that it may not be considered as a relevant factor where particularized or individualized suspicion is required."

In addition to the doubtful empirical relevance of ethnicity to crime, the Equal Protection Clause may provide a basis for challenging the use of ethnic appearance as a factor in reasonable suspicion or probable cause analysis. In the context of pretextual stops, the Supreme Court agreed "that the Constitution prohibits selective enforcement of the law based considerations such as race." The Court has noted, however that "the constitutional basis for objecting to intentionally discriminatory applications of law is the Equal Protection Clause, not the Fourth Amendment."

Over the past decade, equal protection law has become increasingly strict about the use of racial or ethnic characteristics in governmental decision-making. The Supreme Court has held that the government may not use race as a factor in awarding benefits such as government contracts, or in drafting legislative districts. In its decisions, the Supreme Court has relied heavily on the idea of "stigmatic harm": that governmental use of racial or ethnic classifications, even for benign purposes, "may in fact promote notions of racial inferiority and lead to a politics of racial hostility."

The Ninth Circuit adopted the jurisprudence of stigmatic harm as an independent basis for precluding ethnic appearance as a factor in *Montero–Camargo*. The court explained that, "Stops based on race or ethnic appearance send the underlying message to all our citizens that those who are not white are judged by the color of their skin alone. Such stops also send a clear message that those who are not white enjoy a lesser degree of constitutional protection—that they are in effect assumed to be potential criminals first and individuals second." Accordingly, use of racial or ethnic appearance as a factor in reasonable suspicion or probable cause analysis does not survive the strict scrutiny applied to race or national origin-base classifications.

This area of the law will continue to evolve as more courts struggle with the impact of the Supreme Court's new equal protection jurisprudence on law enforcement activities. Counsel should point out strict race-neutral decision-making as the mandate of the Supreme Court's affirmative action and voting district cases; if the law cannot rely on ethnicity to assist minorities, surely law enforcement cannot rely on ethnicity to stop or arrest minorities.

Meaning of Seizure

Counsel may incorporate cultural factors into the question of whether a person has been seized as well as the basis for seizing them. Of course, a person is not seized within the meaning of the Fourth Amendment unless given the totality of the circumstances, a reasonable person would not have felt free to leave.

Notwithstanding the reasonable person standard, courts are occasionally willing to examine the cultural background of the defendant in deterring whether she felt free to leave. In *United States v. Moreno*, the leading case on the issue, the Ninth Circuit held that the defendant's "lack of familiarity with police procedures in this country, his alienage and his limited ability to speak and understand the English language contributed significantly to the quantum of coercion present" in the police encounter.

Even courts and judges who strictly adhere to the reasonable person standard have acknowledged that trial courts may consider factors which are apparent to police, such as language difficulties. For example, in *United States v. Zapate*, the Tenth Circuit held that subjective factors are irrelevant, "other than to the extent that they may have been know to the officer and influenced his conduct."

Of course, a court need not incorporate language difficulties or cultural fear of police as formal factors in order to consider them relevant to whether a reasonable person would have felt free to leave. Rather than focus on the fact that the defendant did not speak English well, counsel can argue that a reasonable person who did not fully understand law enforcement questions or demands would not have understood what was going on.

Consent to Search

Unlike the issue of seizure the validity of a consent to search is determined on the basis of subjective factors. A court examines the totality of the circumstances surrounding the defendant to determine whether she has voluntarily consented to a search. The court considers the characteristics of the individual defendant, including her age, educations and awareness of the protections the American legal system affords to criminal suspects.

Many defendants, especially aliens, genuinely do not understand that they have the right to refuse a search. Less than fluent English may complicate this problem. Speakers of English as a second language may understand the phrase " ... I search the car." but not the preceding phrase "Do you mind if...." An officer's colloquial English usage may also be at fault; the answer to the question "Can I search the car?" is literally "yes" whether or not the suspect gives her permission. Hand gestures or raise voices add to the confusion. Courts have repeatedly found consent to search to be invalid if law enforcement officers had to communicate with the suspect in such rudimentary ways that the suspect did not understand that she had the right to refuse to consent.

D.   IMPLICATIONS FOR OTHER AMENDMENTS

1.   FIFTH AMENDMENT

In *Miranda*, the Court established certain warnings that must be given before a suspect in custody may be interrogated. For *Miranda* purposes, the question whether a suspect is in custody is an objective one that depends in part on the perceptions of a reasonable person in the suspect's position. Race and ethnicity should be part of this inquiry because those factors affect the degree to which a citizen will feel the kind of coercion inherent in a "police-dominated" atmosphere about which the *Miranda* Court was concerned.

2.   DUE PROCESS

Under the Due Process Clause, the government must prove that a confession was made voluntarily before it can use that confession in court. Just as race and ethnicity should be relevant to the voluntariness of consent, they should also be relevant in the context of confessions. The text will address this argument in later chapter. The text also will reveal due process problems with cross-racial eyewitness identifications, which are often not trustworthy.

E.   ETHICS AND RACE

Professor Taslitz, with Professor Sharon Styles–Anderson, has proposed the following amendment to the Model Rules of Professional Conduct:

It is professional misconduct for a lawyer to:

(1) Commit, in the course of representing a client, any verbal or physical discriminatory act, on account of race, ethnicity, or gender, if intended to intimidate litigants, jurors, witnesses, court personnel, opposing counsel, or other lawyers, or to gain a tactical advantage; or

(2) Engage, in the course of representing a client, in any continuing course of verbal or physical discriminatory conduct, on account of race, ethnicity, or gender, in dealings with litigants, jurors, witnesses, court personnel, opposing counsel, or other lawyers if such conduct constitutes harassment.[31]

This rule has, with minor modifications, been endorsed by both the American Bar Association Criminal Justice Section's governing council and

---

31.   Andrew E. Taslitz and Sharon Styles–Anderson, *Still Officers of the Court: Why the First Amendment Is No Bar to Challenging Racism, Sexism and Ethnic Bias in the Legal Profession*, 9 GEO. J. LEG. ETHICS 781, 785 (1996).

its Committee on Race and Racism in the Criminal Justice System. Ultimately, however, the ABA as a whole did not endorse the proposed rule. But debate over the proposal did lead the ABA to modify the Comments to Rule 8.4 of the Model Rules of Professional Conduct. Comment 2 now reads as follows:

> A lawyer who, in the course of representing a client, knowingly manifests by words or conduct, bias or prejudice based upon race, sex, religion, national origin, disability, age, sexual orientation or socioeconomic status, violates paragraph (d) when such actions are prejudicial to the administration of justice. Legitimate advocacy respecting the foregoing factors does not violate paragraph (d). . . .

If this comment is widely adopted by the states, or if the original proposal makes more progress at the state level than it did in the ABA house of Delegates, then the comment or the proposal might affect the behavior of prosecutors in several ways relevant to this text.

Consider the following problem in light of this rule. Keep in mind also that the "duty of the prosecutor is to seek justice, not merely to convict."[32] The meaning of this duty is subject to wide debate, but it may obligate the prosecutor to strive for fair procedures that are consistent with the Constitution and that promote accurate fact finding.[33]

PROBLEM 5–2

An officer stopped and frisked a young African–American male looking into a store window at 6 p.m. The frisk uncovered evidence of a crime for which the suspect was charged. The prosecutor suspects (although she is not sure) that the officer would not have stopped and frisked the suspect had he been white, although there are other facts that arguably support reasonable suspicion.

QUESTIONS

1. Under the proposed rule, does the prosecutor engage in a "discriminatory act" intended to gain a tactical advantage based on race, or under the adopted comment to Rule 8.4(d) does she manifest bias prejudicial to the administration of justice, if she argues at a suppression hearing: (a) that race is a relevant factor that pushes an otherwise close case over the line into the zone of reasonable suspicion; or (b) that there was reasonable suspicion without considering race and that the officer did not consider race when he decided to stop and frisk? Would your answer differ if the prosecutor did not mention race at the suppression hearing?

---

32. American Bar Association Standards Relating to the Administration of Criminal Justice, The Prosecution Function, Standard 3–1.1.

33. Fred C. Zacharias, *Structuring the Ethics of Prosecutorial Trial Practice: Can Prosecutors Do Justice?*, 44 VAND. L. REV. 45 (1991).

2. Would it matter if the prosecutor had investigated the facts and uncovered evidence convincingly demonstrating that the stop was a pretextual one, and that the officer wanted to harass the suspect because he assumed most young black males are up to no good? Would you want more specific facts? What facts?

3. Would it matter if the prosecutor's investigation revealed that the officer had coerced the suspect to confess because the officer did not like the defendant's race? What if the prosecutor believed that an eyewitness claiming to recognize the defendant at a line-up did so primarily because of the defendant's race? Could the prosecutor use the eyewitness's testimony at trial?

4. Would it matter if the prosecutor and the defendant shared the same race? For a discussion of the ethical obligations of a Black prosecutor in the American criminal justice system, see Lenese Herbert, "Et in Arcadia Ego: A Perspective On Black Prosecutors' Loyalty Within the American Criminal Justice System," 49 Howard L.J. 495 (2006).

PROBLEM 5–3

Consider the following case histories.[34] Can you identify Fourth Amendment problems in each?

Case History 11: While cruising his beat, a patrolman recognized the brother of a man he had arrested earlier in the year for murder driving down the street. The time was about 2:00 a.m. The patrolman decided to stop him to see what he was doing. He was a Mexican–American youth and a young white girl was in the car with him. He had neither identification nor any proof that the car was his. The officer informed the youth that he could be arrested for no identification (sec. 40302A C.V.C.) and Grand Theft Auto, but since he (the patrolman) knew him, he would not be arrested. The youth was released after being given a stern warning. Later the patrolman said that "the kid's problem was that he was just plain dumb," and that one had to "get on him once in a while in order to keep him in line."

Case History 12: Driving down a residential street an officer noticed some people, Mexican–Americans, moving some belongings from a house to a truck parked adjacent to the curb. It was about 9 o'clock in the evening. The patrolman asked what was going on and was told that the people were moving. The patrolman frisked several of them and then checked one of them for warrants. The man had no warrants and the officer decided to stop. Before leaving he told the people that burglars often tell the police they are moving and this was why they were questioned.

Case History 13: A car with a discontinued out-of-state license plate was stopped (there was also a minor equipment violation). All three occupants in the car were ordered out, patted down for weapons, and questioned separately. The driver had no identification and said the car

---

34. These case histories appear in MICHAEL K. BROWN, WORKING THE STREET (1981).

belonged to a girl friend; they were driving home. There was no registration in the car, but the officers did find an insurance slip with the girl's name on it. Each occupant gave the same story, and the officers believed them. They were released with a warning. . . .

Case History 15: As two officers drove by a cut-rate gas station, they noticed a black man, bent over, standing in front of the front door. A Cadillac with a woman and several children in it was parked next to the gas pumps. Suspecting a burglary, they stopped and questioned him. He said he worked at the station, but when he gave the wrong address of the station, they checked his identification, ran him through the computer for warrants. The man said that he misunderstood the question and the officers believed him. He was released.

Case History 16: A young Mexican–American man walking down the street was stopped and questioned. He was checked for warrants but none were found. The officer said later that the man was stopped because he "looked suspicious."

Case History 17: Late at night a black youth was observed standing near an automobile on a residential street. As the patrol car drove by, he turned and walked away. The patrolmen went back and stopped and questioned him. The youth explained that he was waiting for a friend to pick him up. One officer examined the car and found no evidence of any attempt to break into it. The youth had poor identification, but he said that he had been with friends in a nearby apartment building. The people in the apartment verified the story and the youth was released.

Case History 18: A young black man walking down the street with a large portable radio to his ear was stopped and asked where he had gotten the radio. He replied that it belonged to his sister, and when he demanded to know why he had been stopped, he was spread-eagled on the hood of the car and frisked. He had some identification and said he was on his way to work at a local elementary school where he was a janitor. One officer examined the radio and discovered that the serial number had been removed. The officers were about to book him when the man's supervisor at the school, who happened to be driving by, stopped and certified that the man worked at the school and that the radio belonged to him. The man was released into the custody of his supervisor.

PROBLEM 5–4

In the Boson case in Chapter 1, assume that one of the three drug courier profile factors that led to Boson's car being stopped was race. What arguments can you craft under the Fourth Amendment, Equal Protection Clause, and any relevant state constitutions to suppress all fruits, dismiss the case, or receive damages for civil rights violations?

PROBLEM 5–5

The issues raised in this chapter are sometimes best understood via a role-play. Your professor will distribute secret instructions for prosecution and defense, to be used in a role-play involving the defendant, Adair Robinson. That role-play will require you to engage in one of the following: plea negotiation, presentation of testimony at a suppression hearing, or presentation of an oral argument. If your professor instructs you to engage in plea negotiation, read the following hints on negotiation in order to prepare.

Hints on Negotiating:[35] There are two primary theories for negotiating: competitive and problem-solving. Competitive theory assumes that egocentric self-interest dominates human behavior. Effective competitive negotiators are dominating, competitive, forceful, tough, arrogant, and uncooperative. They make high demands and few concessions. They use exaggeration, ridicule, threat, bluff, and accusation to win by intimidation. The competitive approach carries risks. Because competitive negotiators rely primarily on tension, fear, and threat—techniques that require special communication skills as opposed to sophisticated legal knowledge—they are often less well prepared to discuss the law and the facts of their case than negotiators who use problem-solving techniques. In addition, because competitive negotiators do not consider deeply the opposing party's needs, they may also miss many opportunities for agreement. Impasse may be the result.

By contrast, the problem-solving theory assumes people are dominated by enlightened (rather than egocentric) self-interest. Enlightened self-interest acknowledges that the needs of one party often cannot be satisfied unless those of the other party are met as well. The problem-solving negotiator, employing the concept of enlightened self-interest, often works to unearth the needs of all parties to the conflict, creating a greater range of solutions than the competitive negotiator who assumes that the parties' needs are mutually exclusive. Furthermore, the problem-solving negotiator recognizes that different people value things differently and thus exploits differential or complementary needs.

Carrie Menkel–Meadow provides the example of a married couple planning a vacation. The husband prefers the mountains, the wife the seaside. Applying a competitive theory, one might assume that either the husband or the wife must win and that the other must lose. At best, the couple might compromise by choosing to spend one week in each location. The compromise makes each happy during one week and unhappy during the other. Applying a problem-solving theory, one would look more deeply into the needs of this couple. The husband might prefer the mountains because he likes hiking, fishing, and breathing the mountain air. The wife might desire a seaside vacation because she prefers swimming, sunbathing, and seafood. But suppose the wife's preference for seafood is relatively unimportant to her and the husband can be happy without the mountain

---

35.   These negotiating hints are based on John S. Murray, *et al.*, NEGOTIATION (1996), and sources cited therein; Carrie Menkel–Meadow, *Toward Another View of Legal Negotiation: The Structure of Problem Solving*, 31 UCLA L. REV. 754, 795, 798–801, 809–10 (1984); GERALD R. WILLIAMS, LEGAL NEGOTIATION AND SETTLEMENT 24–25, 41–42, 49 (1983); and our own experience as negotiators in legal practice.

air. In that case, the couple can find a location other than the mountains where the husband can hike and fish and the wife can swim and sunbathe. Both parties give up something relatively unimportant to them and gain a vacation in which both are reasonably happy for the entire time. The problem-solving approach has created a win-win situation.

Although popular opinion holds that most lawyers are competitive, the fact is that most negotiate using a problem-solving method. Moreover, some studies find no difference in the degree of effectiveness between effective competitive negotiators and those using cooperative, problem-solving strategies. Perhaps even more importantly, a substantially higher percentage of effective lawyers is cooperative. We hope we can persuade you to try the problem-solving theory, although your preference for one theory or another will be influenced powerfully by your personality. No matter which theory comes naturally to you, you should learn to switch theories based on the circumstances.

Once you have chosen a negotiating theory, you must also choose a specific strategy or cluster of strategies. For example, think carefully about how you open the negotiations. You might choose to open with a very high offer, or an extremely low one. An extremely high or low bid might be beneficial in that it conceals the result that you really want—i.e., your "bottom line." An extreme bid may have negative consequences as well: it may convey the message that you are not negotiating in good faith, thus encouraging impasse. You may need to strategize about whether to make an opening bid at all, or whether to wait for the other party to make its first move. It may be that the other party's opening bid will be better than your bottom line. Furthermore, the other party's opening bid conveys information to you, and one strategic goal in negotiating is information-gathering. New information may give you powerful arguments with which you might improve your negotiating position. Furthermore, you might be able to use new information at a trial (evidence rules make some exceptions) if the negotiation fails to result in an agreement.

Strategically, the art of persuasion will be one of your primary tools. A strong knowledge of the law and case-specific facts gives you the means with which to persuade the other party. Pointing out weaknesses in that party's arguments can reduce its perception that it will prevail, making it willing to take less and give more. Persuasive arguments should address policy-based and legitimate emotional appeals as well as pure fact and law-based appeals. And of course, if you are experimenting with competitive negotiation, you might want to use intimidation (but only ethical intimidation!) as a means of persuasion as well.

An additional strategy that you might want to employ involves effective communication with the other party about the reasons for any concessions that you choose to make. If you do not offer principled reasons for concessions, the other party will assume that your position is weak or that you are erratic. Consequently, that party may press for further advantage. An example of communicating a principled reason for a concession might be this: "I believe that your case analogy is weak, but there is a small possibility that it might appeal to Judge X; to compensate for the risk that Judge X will agree with you, I am willing to concede Y."

Finally, remember to pay attention to your own body language and that of the lawyer for the other party. Body language can convey confidence or fear, surprise or recognition, resistance or acceptance. Controlling how you convey these emotions, and becoming aware of the emotional response of the other party's lawyer, are vitally important strategies for effective negotiation.

F. CLIENT INTERVIEWS AND SUPPRESSION MOTIONS

When a defense lawyer prepares for a suppression motion, a key task is developing information sufficient to raise all pertinent issues. Matters not raised in suppression motions typically are waived.[36] In many situations, the defendant is the only witness to alleged Fourth Amendment violations, aside from the police. The defense lawyer must employ sound interviewing techniques in order to uncover critical information in support of the suppression motion.

Legal interviewing is distinct from legal counseling. The goals of the two are different: the two major goals of interviewing are gathering information and building a relationship of trust between lawyer and client (or lawyer and witness), while the goal of counseling is to impart advice. The two processes also differ in when they occur in the lawyer-client relationship: interviewing is the preliminary stage, while counseling happens later, after the lawyer has gathered information and developed legal theories.[37]

The material below discusses methods lawyers employ to ensure they gather the information that they need. Prosecutors use these methods as well when they interview police officers and other potential witnesses. In the material below, the word "client" refers to such witnesses as well.

1. WHAT IS A GOOD INTERVIEW

In the paragraph above, we identified the two major goals of interviewing as gathering information and building a relationship of trust between lawyer and client. In order to accomplish these goals, the lawyer often divides an interview into three stages: (1) preliminary problem identification, (2) chronological overview, and (3) theory development.[38] The three-

---

36. *See, e.g.*, Fed. R. Crim. Proc. 12(f).

37. HARROLD A. FREEMAN, LEGAL INTERVIEWING AND COUNSELING 5 (1964).

38. This section relies on DAVID A. BINDER & SUSAN C. PRICE, LEGAL INTERVIEWING AND COUNSELING: A CLIENT-CENTERED APPROACH (1977). In a later revision of this text, the authors modestly modify their approach. *See* DAVID A. BINDER, ET AL., LAWYERS AS COUNSELORS: A CLIENT-CENTERED APPROACH (1991). We rely on the original text for the excerpts reproduced in this section. This section also derives from our experiences in practice. Additional useful background can be found in THOMAS L. SCHAFFER & JAMES R. ELKINS, LEGAL INTERVIEWING AND COUNSELING IN A NUTSHELL (1987).

stage approach encourages thoroughness, helps the client to tell his tale completely and accurately, and builds trust.

In the preliminary problem identification stage, the lawyer asks for a general description of the events that caused the problem. The lawyer imposes minimal order on the client's responses and seldom asks for details, to avoid imposing on the client the lawyer's own assumptions about the events and silencing the client's voice.[39] The lawyer also asks the client about what relief is desired, again without imposing the lawyer's own views. The lawyer makes brief notes of key words during this process but also remains responsive to the client by concentrating on the client's explanation, providing verbal encouragement, and maintaining eye-contact. Most lawyers make a detailed memorandum of the interview immediately after it is over. This approach enables the lawyer to maintain a rapport with the client while making an adequate record of the interview.

During the chronological overview, the lawyer elicits a step-by-step chronology. The lawyer asks the client to go over the events a second time, this time beginning when the problem started. The lawyer encourages the client to talk about the events in chronological fashion. At this stage, the lawyer still does not seek detailed elaboration of the points raised by the client. The lawyer's note-taking and responsiveness are similar to those practiced during the preliminary problem identification stage, and the client's explanation during this stage will become part of the lawyer's post-interview memorandum.

The final stage requires the lawyer to question the client more closely in order to distill legal theories from the client's information. By this time, the lawyer probably has identified several possible theories. Now the lawyer focuses his or her questions in order to search for missing details. For example, if the lawyer believes that evidence may be suppressed on the theory that the client's consent was involuntary, the lawyer must seek details from the client about the atmosphere surrounding the client's consent, the client's feelings at the time, and the conduct of the police. The lawyer will consciously and systematically explore these areas, taking more detailed notes than the lawyer took in the first two stages.

The "T–Funnel Sequence" is a helpful technique to use in the theory development stage:

> ... The T–Funnel pattern explores a topic by employing a series of open-ended questions at the beginning. These questions are used to get at the facts the client recalls. When these questions are no longer productive, the lawyer employs a series of narrow questions. The latter

---

39. *See* Clark D. Cunningham, *The Lawyer as Translator, Representation as Text: Towards an Ethnography of Legal Discourse*, 77 Cornell L. Rev. 1298, 1301 (1992). Cunningham provides a thought-provoking perspective on legal representation. The article begins with this statement: "This is a true story. It is the story of how the law punished a man for speaking about his legal rights; of how, after punishing him, it silenced him; of how, when he did speak, he was not heard. This pervasive and awful oppression was subtle and, in a real way, largely unintentional. I know because I was one of his oppressors. I was his lawyer." *Id.* at 1299.

are used to ask about those possibilities the lawyer has thought of but which were not mentioned in response to the open-ended questions. In using the T–Funnel, the lawyer should make more than one attempt to determine what the client can remember before narrowing down and attempting to get a picture of the subject by asking about specific items.[40]

Binder and Price offer an example of the T–Funnel sequence in a case involving a commercial transaction:

Lawyer	Tell me everything he said about the car.
Client	He said it was in good condition, had new tires, and that it had always been serviced regularly at their shop.
Lawyer	What else did he say?
Client	That's about it; he said there had been just one previous owner.
Lawyer	Okay, he mentioned the condition, the tires, the one owner, the regular service; what else did he tell you?
Client	That's all.
Lawyer	I know it's difficult to remember, but it's really important to your case that you try. Go back in your mind's eye. Try to picture yourself there with the salesman. Think very carefully, what else did he say?
Client	He said the car had new tires, not because of a lot of mileage, but because the prior owner had just let it sit around a lot; I think he said it had only 23,000 miles.
Lawyer	Okay, that's helpful. What else did he say?
Client	That's all, really.
Lawyer	Did he say anything about the engine?
Client	Sure, when he was talking about the car being in good condition. He said the engine has just been tuned up and there were new spark plugs and something else.
Lawyer	New points?
Client	Yes, that's it.
Lawyer	Did he say anything about the transmission?
Client	No.
Lawyer	Did he say anything about the heating or radiator?
Client	No.
Lawyer	Did he say anything about gas mileage?
Client	He said it got good mileage, but he didn't say how much.
Lawyer	Did he say anything about prior accidents?
Client	No.

The advantage of the T–Funnel is that while open-ended questions permit free association and thus retrieve a wide scope of information, narrow questions may jog memories otherwise blocked.

The three-stage technique helps develop information and establish a trusting relationship between lawyer and client. These goals also are furthered when lawyers engage in "active listening," described by Binder and Price as "the process of picking up the client's message and sending it back in a reflective statement which mirrors what the lawyer has heard":

---

40.   Binder & Price, LEGAL INTERVIEWING, *supra* note 38, at 92.

Client   When I asked him for the money, he had the nerve to tell me not to be uptight.

Lawyer   Rather than telling you about the money, he suggested you were somehow wrong for asking. I imagine that made you angry.

Note the lawyer does not simply repeat or "parrot" what was said. Rather, the lawyer's response is an affirmative effort to convey back the essence of what was heard. It is a response which, by mirroring what was said, affirmatively demonstrates understanding. Further, since the statement only mirrors, it does not in any way "judge" what has been said. In short, it is a completely empathetic response.

By demonstrating non-judgmental understanding, active listening builds rapport and encourages the client to talk openly and expansively. The technique can be used to uncover the client's feelings as well as the client's recollection of factual events.

2.   THE ETHICS OF CLIENT INTERVIEWS

Every lawyer is tempted to make the client's version of events more favorable to the legal theories that the lawyer will raise. These temptations arise during the client interview, when the lawyer can easily influence the client's recollection of events by asking leading questions and making suggestive remarks. Techniques designed to influence the client's recollection are unethical, however, as are efforts to change the client's story. Model Rule 3.3 of the Model Rules of Professional Responsibility prohibits the lawyer from knowingly using false testimony, and Model Rule 1.2 prohibits the lawyer from counseling or assisting the client to engage in fraudulent conduct.[41]

There is a fine line between facilitating the client's recollections and encouraging the client to alter those recollections. Some lawyers and commentators argue that it is appropriate for a lawyer to tell the client the law before beginning the interview. Others disapprove of that technique on the ground that it provides clients with an irresistible motive to lie. Those who disapprove of the technique argue that it is as imprudent as it is unethical, because it may encourage the client to conceal information that the lawyer needs to know. The best interview, according to these lawyers and commentators, includes a "non-judgmental" warning against perjury that makes the client feel the lawyer is "helping [the client] protect himself rather than demonstrating some kind of moral superiority."[42]

---

41. *See, e.g.*, Deborah L. Rhode, Professional Responsibility: Ethics by the Pervasive Method 210–14 (1994) (citing the Model Rules). This section relies on Professor Rhode's discussion of interview techniques that help clients "present what they know" as opposed to helping clients "know new things." *Id.* at 212.

42. *Id.* at 212.

3. ROLE–PLAYING EXERCISE: CLIENT INTERVIEW IN WARRANTLESS SEARCH CASE

Your instructor will ask you to play the roles of lawyer and/or client in the case of Adair Robinson, the defendant in Problem 5–5. Your instructor will distribute secret information to students playing the client role. As Adair's lawyer, you must decide whether to file a motion to suppress and determine what grounds should be raised in such a motion. Interview your client and write a memorandum of the interview. Specify what theories you believe should be raised in a motion to suppress and what theories the interview caused you to reject.

4. ROLE–PLAYING EXERCISE: SUPPRESSION HEARING

Your instructor may ask you to participate in a role-play hearing on Adair Robinson's motion to suppress and instruct you about the bases for Robinson's motion. You may be asked to participate as judge, witness, defense lawyer, or prosecutor. Whatever the role, inhabit it completely for purposes of the exercise.

CHAPTER 6

SEARCHES AND SEIZURES:

- ● TERRORISM, SURVEILLANCE, & SPECIAL STATUTORY POWERS

I. INTRODUCTION

The increasing desire of law enforcement officials to uncover terrorism and other dangerous activities motivates them to engage in eavesdropping and surveillance. While some of this activity is of the old-fashioned physical type—listening to people talk in a restaurant, following people on the street, and so on—of greater value is electronic surveillance that enables government agents to overhear conversations in homes and offices, and over the telephone, to read email communications, to monitor telephone, email, Internet, and banking records, and so on.

Courts and legislatures have long been concerned about eavesdropping and surveillance, especially electronic surveillance. In the following excerpt from the Supreme Court's 1967 opinion in *Berger v. State of New York*,[1] you can discern how troubled it was as it described the growing technology of surveillance:

Eavesdropping is an ancient practice which at common law was condemned as a nuisance. At one time the eavesdropper listened by naked ear under the eaves of houses or their windows, or beyond their walls seeking out private discourse. The awkwardness and undignified manner of this method as well as its susceptibility to abuse was immediately recognized. Electricity, however, provided a better vehicle and with the advent of the telegraph surreptitious interception of messages began. As early as 1862 California found it necessary to prohibit the practice by statute. During the Civil War General J. E. B. Stuart is reputed to have had his own eavesdropper along with him in the field whose job it was to intercept military communications of the opposing forces. Subsequently newspapers reportedly raided one another's news gathering lines to save energy, time, and money. Racing news was likewise intercepted and flashed to bettors before the official result arrived.

The telephone brought on a new and more modern eavesdropper known as the "wiretapper." Interception was made by a connection with a telephone line. This activity has been with us for three-quarters of a century. Like its cousins, wiretapping proved to be a commercial as

---

1. 388 U.S. 41 (1967).

well as a police technique. . . . During prohibition days wiretaps were the principal source of information relied upon by the police as the basis for prosecutions. . . .

Sophisticated electronic devices have now been developed (commonly known as "bugs") which are capable of eavesdropping on anyone in most any given situation. They are to be distinguished from "wiretaps" which are confined to the interception of telegraphic and telephonic communications. Miniature in size—no larger than a postage stamp—these gadgets pick up whispers within a room and broadcast them half a block away to a receiver. It is said that certain types of electronic rays beamed at walls or glass windows are capable of catching voice vibrations as they are bounced off the surfaces. Since 1940 eavesdropping has become a big business. Manufacturing concerns offer complete detection systems which automatically record voices under almost any conditions by remote control. A microphone concealed in a book, a lamp, or other unsuspected place in a room, or made into a fountain pen, tie clasp, lapel button, or cuff link increases the range of these powerful wireless transmitters to a half mile. Receivers pick up the transmission with interference-free reception on a special wave frequency. And, of late, a combination mirror transmitter has been developed which permits not only sight but voice transmission up to 300 feet. Likewise, parabolic microphones, which can overhear conversations without being placed within the premises monitored, have been developed.

Of course, these days the government has even more sophisticated techniques available to it. For several years the FBI used a system called "Carnivore" that enabled it to conduct direct surveillance of the Internet, picking out emails and other communications (including instant messaging) by certain individuals or containing certain words from the billions of pieces of electronic data sent through the vast interconnected web of that medium. Although that system has reportedly been abandoned, the agency is reputed to be using other software to accomplish similar surveillance.[2]

The legality of government surveillance is the subject of this chapter. We will first review the constitutional limitations on government surveillance and then examine the complex statutory structures governing surveillance that were put in place during the 1930s by the United States Congress and supplemented after several crucial events in American history, most recently the September 11, 2001 terrorist attacks.

II.   CONSTITUTIONAL LIMITS ON SURVEILLANCE

Checklist 7: Was the government surveillance constitutional under the Fourth Amendment?

1. Was there a search or seizure?

---

2. *See, e.g., FBI Abandons Carnivore,* http://www.msnbc.msn.com/id/6841403/ [last visited March 4, 2010]; and *EFF Sues for Information on Electronic Surveillance Systems,* http://www.eff.org/press/archives/2006/10/03 [last visited March 4, 2010].

    a. Was there a search—an invasion of a reasonable expectation of privacy?

    b. Had the person given up his or her reasonable expectation of privacy?

    c. Did the person engage in activities that are open to observation by others?

    d. Did the person's activities generate records held by third parties?

    e. Did the person assume the risk of searches by entering certain designated areas such as airports?

2. Does the statute authorizing government surveillance meet substantive Fourth Amendment requirements?

    a. Probable cause?

    b. Particularity?

    c. Neutral and detached magistrate?

    d. Reasonable warrant execution?

A.   Fourth Amendment

A constitutional analysis of government surveillance involves two strands of Fourth Amendment doctrine. The first is the foundational threshold test of *Katz v. United States*, in which the Supreme Court established that the government violates Fourth Amendment rights only when its agents interfere with reasonable expectations of privacy. The second is the requirement that government activity that does implicate reasonable expectations of privacy be justified by probable cause or reasonable suspicion, and that any warrants satisfy particularity and executional requirements.

1.   SURVEILLANCE AND THE *KATZ* TEST

The "reasonable expectation of privacy" test announced in *Katz* has created a threshold that exempts much government surveillance from Fourth Amendment scrutiny. Although you are familiar with the *Katz* test, a complete understanding of how it has shaped surveillance law requires some historical background.

For many years before *Katz*, electronic surveillance was considered to invoke principles of property law, rather than of privacy rights. When the Supreme Court decided *Olmstead v. United States*[3] in 1928, it employed a trespass analysis to determine whether electronic surveillance violated the Fourth Amendment. At issue in *Olmstead* was the admissibility of evidence that was largely obtained by wiretaps of telephone lines running from the defendants' businesses and homes. The wiretaps had been installed in the basements of the office buildings that housed the defendants' business and on external telephone lines that ran from the defendants' homes, so the

---

    3. 277 U.S. 438 (1928).

insertions were made "without trespass upon any property of the defendants." This fact was critical, because in the absence of a physical trespass, the Court in *Olmstead* held that the Fourth Amendment was not violated. The Court reasoned that the Fourth Amendment applies only to searches of "material things—the person, the house, his papers, or his effects[,]"and not intangibles such as oral communications. As a result of the *Olmstead* ruling, subsequent electronic surveillance decisions focused on property law concepts as opposed to privacy concerns for almost forty years.[4]

In 1967, the Supreme Court gave a strong signal that it was ready to revise its method of analyzing electronic surveillance cases. In *Berger v. New York*, defendant Berger challenged the admissibility of evidence acquired through the use of a recording device installed in an attorney's office. The device had been installed pursuant to a warrant issued under a New York eavesdropping statute. The Supreme Court struck down the New York statute as overbroad, implicitly holding that intangibles such as private conversations fall within the scope of the Fourth Amendment and that electronic surveillance should be scrutinized for its intrusion upon protected privacy, rather than its physical intrusion onto protected property.

Later in the same term during which *Berger* was decided, the Supreme Court issued its opinion in *Katz*. As you know from our earlier discussion of that case, the FBI had placed a wiretap on the outside of a telephone booth, from which it was able to record Katz's conversation. Because the FBI had not occasioned a physical trespass onto any of Katz's property, following *Olmstead*, the evidence should have been admitted. The Court in *Katz*, however, declined to use the *Olmstead* approach. Instead it announced that the Fourth Amendment "protects people, not places[,]" and found the intrusion to have been an unconstitutional search because it "violated the privacy upon which [Katz] justifiably relied while using the telephone booth."

Although the Court in both *Berger* and *Katz* ruled that the challenged actions in those cases were unconstitutional, neither opinion held that electronic surveillance was unconstitutional *per se*. In fact, both cases contained dicta in which the Court suggested that electronic surveillance could be constitutional if properly conducted.

Even more significantly, the Court subsequently narrowed the reach of Fourth Amendment protections by holding that people forfeit reasonable expectations of privacy in many situations. Among others circumstances, as

---

4. *See, e.g.,* Michael Goldsmith, *The Supreme Court and Title III: Rewriting The Law of Electronic Surveillance*, 74 J. CRIM. LAW & CRIMINAL. 1, 24–25 (1983); Goldman v. United States, 316 U.S. 129, 134–35 (1942) (use of a detectaphone placed against an office wall in order to hear private conversations in the office next door did not violate the Fourth Amendment because there was no physical trespass); On Lee v. United States, 343 U.S. 747, 751 (1952) (conversation between Lee and a federal agent occurring in Lee's laundry and electronically recorded by the agent did not violate the Fourth Amendment because no trespass was committed); Silverman v. United States, 365 U.S. 505, 511–12 (1961) (insertion of a "spike mike" into a partition wall was unconstitutional under the Fourth Amendment).

you learned in an earlier chapter, people give up expectations of privacy when they engage in activities that are open to observation by others (e.g., traveling on public roads), when their activities result in records held by third parties (e.g., pen registers and bank records), and when they assume the risk of searches by entering certain places (e.g., airports). Thus, the *Katz* test, while embracing privacy concepts over trespass ones, actually limits the situations in which surveillance activities are considered "searches" for Fourth Amendment purposes. Based on these limitations, in the electronic realm courts have concluded, among other things: senders of email (like senders of mail) assume the risk that recipients may share those communications with others, and users of online bulletin boards assume the risk that their postings will be read by undercover agents.

2.   SUBSTANTIVE FOURTH AMENDMENT REQUIREMENTS

As a result of *Katz* and its progeny, much government surveillance does not implicate the Fourth Amendment. But some surveillance remains within the Fourth Amendment's scope. For example, although individuals cannot claim privacy in telephone company records, they can make good Fourth Amendment claims about the contents of their private telephone conversations. Thus any statute governing surveillance must take into account substantive Fourth Amendment requirements. Moreover, those requirements—probable cause, particularity, neutral and detached magistrate, reasonable warrant executions, and so on—may have special meaning in the surveillance context. Indeed, when the Court reached its decision in *Berger* that the New York eavesdropping statute was unconstitutionally broad, it discussed some of those requirements in a manner that has since shaped federal statutes. In *Berger*, the Court contrasted the "eavesdropping warrants" permitted by the New York statute with the safeguards attending a traditional search warrant, and it concluded that the former did not stack up well against the latter:

> ... First, ... eavesdropping is authorized without requiring belief that any particular offense has been or is being committed; nor that the "property" sought, the conversations, be particularly described. ... It is true that the statute requires the naming of "the person or persons whose communications, conversations or discussions are to be overheard or recorded." But this does no more than identify the person whose constitutionally protected area is to be invaded rather than "particularly describing" the communications, conversations, or discussions to be seized. As with general warrants this leaves too much to the discretion of the officer executing the order. Secondly, authorization of eavesdropping for a two-month period is the equivalent of a series of intrusions, searches, and seizures pursuant to a single showing of probable cause. Prompt execution is also avoided. ... Third, the statute places no termination date on the eavesdrop once the conversation sought is seized. ... Finally, the statute's procedure, necessarily because its success depends on secrecy, has no requirement for notice as do conventional warrants, nor does it overcome this defect by

requiring some showing of special facts. . . . Nor does the statute provide for a return on the warrant thereby leaving full discretion in the officer as to the use of seized conversations of innocent as well as guilty parties. In short, the statute's blanket grant of permission to eavesdrop is without adequate judicial supervision or protective procedures.

The Court in *Berger* made extensive reference to its holding in *Osborn v. United States*,[5] where recordings of conversations were found admissible only because "[t]he recording device was . . . authorized 'under the most precise and discriminate circumstances, circumstances which full met the requirement of particularity' of the Fourth Amendment." The Court specifically noted:

> the order [in *Osborn*] described the type of conversation sought with particularity, thus indicating the specific objective of the Government in entering the constitutionally protected area and the limitations placed upon the officer executing the warrant. Under it the officer could not search unauthorized areas; likewise, once the property sought, and for which the order was issued, was found the officer could not use the order as a passkey to further search. In addition the order authorized one limited intrusion rather than a series or a continuous surveillance . . . , [and] the order was executed by the officer with dispatch, not over a prolonged and extended period. In this manner no greater invasion of privacy was permitted than was necessary under the circumstances. Finally, the officer was required to and did make a return on the order showing how it was executed and what was seized. Through these strict precautions the danger of an unlawful search and seizure was minimized.

According to the Court, "[t]hrough these 'precise and discriminate' procedures the order authorizing the use of the electronic device afforded similar protections to those that are present in the use of conventional warrants authorizing the seizure of tangible evidence."

In *Katz*, the Court once again cited *Osborn* with approval, finding that the electronic surveillance of Katz conducted by the FBI satisfied the "precise and discriminate circumstances" test articulated in *Osborn*, and was unconstitutional only because the government had not obtained a warrant.

Later in this chapter, we will review the details of the federal Wiretap Act, which was enacted after *Katz*. As you read those materials, keep in mind the Court's emphasis in *Berger* and *Katz* on substantive Fourth Amendment concerns, and ask yourself whether the Wiretap Act addresses the Court's concerns adequately.

B.   FIRST AMENDMENT

The Fourth Amendment is not the only Bill of Rights guaranty to apply potentially to government surveillance. Such activities may implicate

---

5.   385 U.S. 323 (1966).

First Amendment protected freedoms as well, most clearly the freedoms of speech, assembly, and association. Out of a concern that First Amendment freedoms would be chilled if surveillance records were kept about the views and activities of individuals, most law enforcement agencies eschew dossier-collection practices. Indeed, during the 1960s and 1970s, lawsuits forced many police departments to enter into consent decrees forbidding them to collect and maintain information about individuals without some reason to suspect those individuals of criminal conduct. Indeed, at least one state has prohibited these practices by statute. Oregon laws state:

> No law enforcement agency ... may collect or maintain information about the political, religious or social views, associations or activities of any individual, group, association, organization, corporation, business or partnership unless such information directly relates to an investigation of criminal activities, and there are reasonable grounds to suspect the subject of the information is or may be involved in criminal conduct.[6]

The Federal Privacy Act of 1974, while providing weaker protection than Oregon's statute, states that "[e]ach agency that maintains a system of records shall ... maintain no record describing how any individual exercises rights guaranteed by the First Amendment ... unless pertinent to and within the scope of an authorized law enforcement activity."

Needless to say, in the wake of September 11, 2001, law enforcement agencies have come under pressure once again to collect and retain information about individuals. While this book does not focus on the First Amendment implications of surveillance practices, good lawyering suggests that you research these in any surveillance situation in which you may become professionally involved.

III. STATUTORY REGULATION OF SURVEILLANCE

Checklist 8: What level of protection does the Wiretap Act provide for the communication?

1. Did the communication require a "Super Search Warrant" under Title I?

   a. Did someone intercept of an oral, wire, or electronic communication?

      i. If the communication was oral, does it meet the *Katz* test—were the words "uttered by a person exhibiting an expectation that such communication is not subject to interception under circumstances justifying such expectation"?

   b. Was the interception accomplished by means of an "electronic, mechanical, or other device" that was sent through interstate or foreign commerce?

---

6. Oregon Revised Statutes § 181.575.

   c. If the interception was of an oral or wire communication, was it contemporaneous, i.e., in transit; or if not, does the interception meet the exception for communications temporarily stored in an electronic system before being heard by the recipient?

   d. If the interception was of an electronic communication, was it contemporaneous?

   e. If the communication meets the above requirements, did the government obtain an intercept order that makes the stringent showings?

2. Was the communication a stored electronic communication, covered by Title II?

   a. Was the communication stored electronically, for example in a stored email, voicemail, or a subscriber record maintained by communications services providers?

   b. If the communication was stored for 180 days or less, did the government have a court order based on probable cause?

   c. If the communication was stored for more than 180 days, did the government have a subpoena for the communications?

3. Is the government surveillance a pen register or a trap and trace device that would be governed by Title III?

   a. Did the government certify that the information is "relevant" to an ongoing investigation?

   b. Did the government obtain court permission for the pen register or trap and trace device?

A. HISTORICAL BACKGROUND

While these days we might think of federal statutes governing surveillance (such as the USA PATRIOT Act, discussed below) as enlarging governmental powers, the original such statute apparently had as its motivation Congress's desire to restrict certain kinds of eavesdropping, including eavesdropping by nongovernmental actors. That statute, known as the Federal Communications Act, was passed in 1934, in the wake of the Supreme Court's decision in *Olmstead*. From the discussion of the *Olmstead* opinion above, you may recall that the Court there disclaimed any Fourth Amendment violation where the government attached wiretaps to telephone lines outside of defendants' property. Applying a trespass doctrine, the Court thus left telephones open to government wiretapping, so long as the wiretapping devices did not physically invade dwellings or office spaces. But Congress was not happy with this kind of wiretapping, and it criminalized it in the Federal Communications Act, declaring that no person "shall intercept any [wire] communication and divulge [it] . . . to any person, . . . and no person having received such intercepted communication . . . shall divulge [it]." As construed by the Court, the Act was limited to telephone communications, so its reach was rather limited.

Moreover, the Act did not apply to agents of state governments. As a result, much eavesdropping remained lawful.[7]

In the 1960s, Congress broadened its coverage of eavesdropping. Concerned about increasing eavesdropping practices, as well as by the rising crime, civil disobedience, and revolutionary activity that had reignited government desires to eavesdrop, it enacted the Omnibus Crime Control and Safe Streets Act of 1968. Title III of that act, referred to commonly as the Wiretap Act, relies on the Supreme Court's decisions in *Berger* and *Katz*, which, while sounding caution with respect to electronic surveillance, suggested that carefully crafted and monitored surveillance practices could satisfy the Fourth Amendment.[8] The Wiretap Act criminalizes the interception of "aural" communications—in other words, communications that can be overheard by ear. The Wiretap Act applies to all government actors— state and federal—because Congress used its Commerce Clause power to enact the statute. Moreover, the Wiretap Act applies to private actors, who can be charged criminally and/or sued civilly for violating some of its provisions. Thus, the Act reaches far more conduct than the Fourth Amendment.

The Wiretap Act has been supplemented by the Electronic Communications Privacy Act of 1986 [ECPA] and the Digital Telephony Act of 1994 to cover the intentional interception by *any* means (including electronic) of wire, oral, or electronic communications. As amended, the Wiretap Act governs eavesdropping on person-to-person conversations, as well as on communications via telephone, cordless telephone, cellular telephone, email, and other devices. It remains the dominant statute regulating the use of mechanical devices to intercept oral, wire, and electronic communications. It also remains, in the words of one court, a statute "famous (if not infamous) for its lack of clarity."[9]

In 2001, after the September 11th terrorist attacks, Congress quickly passed an act enlarging government surveillance powers in some respects. Formally titled the "Uniting and Strengthening America by Providing Appropriate Tools Required to Intercept and Obstruct Terrorism Act," the USA PATRIOT Act will be discussed in a separate section below.

Finally, Congress established a separate statutory framework to regulate surveillance by foreign intelligence gathering agencies. This framework, created in 1978 in the Foreign Intelligence and Surveillance Act [FISA], governs domestic surveillance of foreign powers, their agents, and groups that engage in international terrorism. FISA makes surveillance easier, and as a result it cannot be used for ordinary criminal investiga-

---

7. For more information about federal surveillance statutes and their history, *see, e.g.*, DANIEL J. SOLOVE & MARC ROTENBERG, INFORMATION PRIVACY LAW (2003); Richard C. Turkington & Anita L. Allen, PRIVACY LAW: CASES & MATERIALS (1999); and JAMES G. CARR, THE LAW OF ELECTRONIC SURVEILLANCE (1994).

8. *Katz* was decided on December 18, 1967; The Wiretap Act was enacted on June 19, 1968 and codified at 18 U.S.C. sections 2510 et seq.

9. Steve Jackson Games, Inc. v. United States Secret Service, 36 F.3d 457, 462 (5th Cir. 1994).

tions. FISA powers originally could be used only where foreign intelligence gathering was the "primary purpose" of the government's activities, but in 2002 the USA PATRIOT Act amended FISA to lower that threshold. As a result, the government now may use its broad FISA powers if foreign intelligence gathering is merely "a significant purpose" of its investigation. We will discuss FISA briefly in a later section of this chapter.

Notice that in this discussion of statutory regulation there has been no mention of surveillance cameras and other technologically-assisted physical surveillance. There currently is no legislative framework with which to analyze the legality of physical surveillance, except under FISA. And of course, if physical surveillance, such as video cameras, is conducted public spaces, the Fourth Amendment presumably would not apply. This gap in protection has prompted many to urge policymakers to evaluate the wisdom of unbridled physical surveillance. We will acquaint you with that policy debate later in this chapter.

B.   THE WIRETAP ACT AND ITS AMENDMENTS

The broad reach of the Wiretap Act requires lawyers to have a good working knowledge of its basic provisions. In the discussion below, we will highlight the important aspects of the Act.

1.   HIERARCHY OF PROTECTIONS

a.   *"Super Search Warrants" for Contemporaneous Interceptions*

The Wiretap Act, as amended, consists of three sections that describe a hierarchy of protections. The first section, and the top level of the hierarchy, is now known as Title I. This part of the Wiretap Act bans the interception of oral, wire, and electronic communications by means of "any electronic, mechanical, or other device." Oral communications (i.e., face-to-face conversations) are protected only if they meet the *Katz* test. As the Act puts it, the words must be "uttered by a person exhibiting an expectation that such communication is not subject to interception under circumstances justifying such expectation." In addition, oral communications are protected only if the device used to intercept them has been sent through interstate or foreign commerce. Wire communications are those that transfer human voices from points of origin to points of reception by means (at least in part) of wires, cables, and "like connection[s]" that affect interstate or foreign commerce. Electronic communications are:

> transfers of signs, signals, writing, images, sounds, data, or intelligence of any nature transmitted in whole or in part by a wire, radio, electromagnetic, photoelectronic or photooptical system that affects interstate or foreign commerce, but does not include . . . any wire or oral communication.

Title I of the Act covers only the *contemporaneous* interception of these three types of communications—in other words, the capture of communications while they are "in flight" or being transmitted. The requirement of contemporaneity applies to the interception of oral communications, wire communications (these typically are telephone conversations), and electronic communications such as email. The only exception to the contemporaneity requirement is for oral and wire communications that have been temporarily stored in an electronic system before they have been heard by the recipient. This exception implicates primarily voicemail messages that have been left on an answering system and not yet accessed by the recipient. Once these communications are listened to by the recipient, however, they are no longer covered by Title I. Because of this limited exception to the contemporaneity requirement, it is important to distinguish wire communications (such as telephone calls) from electronic ones (such as email), because the latter enjoy Title I protection *only* from contemporaneous interceptions—in other words, only from capture while they are *in transit*.

When the government engages in contemporaneous interceptions protected by Title I, it must first obtain an intercept order, which requires stringent showings beyond those required by the Fourth Amendment. A traditional search warrant would not satisfy the provisions of Title I. For this reason, Professor Orin S. Kerr[10] says that an intercept order is really a "super search warrant." Violation of the super search warrant requirement may result in exclusion of evidence. We will describe these super search warrants and the exclusionary remedy below. Before doing that, however, we will briefly review the other two Titles in the Act.

b. Lower Protection for Stored Electronic Communications

Title II of the Wiretap Act, sometimes called the Stored Communications Act, governs communications in electronic storage, including stored email, voicemail, and subscriber records maintained by communications services providers. The government need not obtain a super search warrant for these communications. Instead, a court order based on probable cause will suffice in the case of communications that have been stored for 180 days or less (except for oral and wire communications not yet in the hands of the recipient, as the discussion of Title I relates). For communications stored more than 180 days, the requirements are lower: a subpoena, which requires no showing of probable cause, will do if the stored communications are in the hands of a third party (such as an Internet Service Provider [ISP]). Of course, if stored communications are sought in a computer in which an individual has a reasonable expectation of privacy, then the search also must be accompanied by a search warrant or the search will violate the Fourth Amendment.

The Act does not provide an exclusionary remedy for violations of the stored communications provision. In other words, if the Fourth Amendment is not violated, these communications may be admitted in court even if their interception violated the Wiretap Act.

---

10. Orin S. Kerr, *Internet Surveillance Law after the USA PATRIOT Act: The Big Brother That Isn't*, 97 Nw. U. L. Rev. 607 (2003).

c.   *Lowest Protection for Pen Registers and Trap and Trace Devices*

Title III of the Wiretap Act governs pen registers as well as trap and trace devices. You may recall that pen registers are records of outgoing calls from a particular telephone. Trap and trace devices can capture the telephone numbers of incoming calls. Under Title III of the Wiretap Act (this title is called, not surprisingly, the "Pen Register Act"), the government can obtain pen registers and trap and trace records with court permission, which must be granted if the government certifies that the information is "relevant" to an ongoing investigation. There is no exclusionary remedy for violations of this part of the Wiretap Act.

d.   *Wiretap Act Distinguished From Fourth Amendment*

When you are faced with a situation in which eavesdropping or surveillance took place, remember to analyze the Fourth Amendment issues and Wiretap Act issues separately. While the Wiretap Act protects some things that are also protected by the Fourth Amendment, it goes beyond the Fourth Amendment in some respects—notably because it applies to private actors. Conversely, it leaves other things unprotected by its terms that are protected by the Fourth Amendment. Hence, for each person affected by eavesdropping or surveillance, the lawyer must analyze (1) whether Fourth Amendment violations occurred; and (2) regardless of the presence or absence of Fourth Amendment violations, whether the Wiretap Act was violated. Also, the appropriate remedy for each type of violation must be analyzed.

Although the amendment and the statute must be analyzed separately, remember that they do have a relationship at least in one respect: a valid intercept order permits the government to enter private places in secret, without having a separate search warrant.

PROBLEM 6–1

Bradford Calhoun worked for BookLook, Inc., which ran an online rare and out-of-print book listing service. BookLook's customers were book dealers. As part of its service to dealers, BookLook gave them an e-mail address at the domain "BkLk.com" and acted as the e-mail provider. Calhoun managed the e-mail server—the hard drive through which the email service was provided. Wanting to get information about customer business practices, Calhoun began to intercept and copy all incoming communications to them from Amazon.com. He accomplished his interceptions by modifying the email server so that, before delivering any message from Amazon.com to the recipient's mailbox, BkLk.com would automatically copy the message and place the copy in a separate mailbox that Calhoun could access. Through these means, he intercepted thousands of messages.

Questions: Did Calhoun's actions violate the Wiretap Act? If so, which provision?

PROBLEM 6–2

Jamila Reppe was involved in litigation against her former employer, Karsten Bloume. In order to get damaging information from Bloume, Reppe snuck into his office one night and installed a device, called a KeyKatcher, on his desktop computer. Specifically, she placed the Key-Katcher on the cable that connected his keyboard to his computer's central processing unit (CPU). As he composed e-mails and other messages by depressing keys on the keyboard, the KeyKatcher recorded and stored, on its memory, the electronic impulses traveling down the cable between the keyboard and the computer to which it was attached. Later, Reppe was able to read the content of messages that Bloume had typed on the keyboard.

Questions: Did Reppe's actions violate the Wiretap Act? If so, which provision?

2. EXCEPTIONS TO THE WIRETAP ACT'S TITLE I COVERAGE

The Wiretap Act exempts a few communications from Title I, its most protective provision. The most powerful exception, and the only important one for our purposes, permits the warrantless interception of a communication if one of the parties to that communication has given prior consent to the interception. Notice that the consent of only one of the parties is necessary, and that party may be someone "acting under color of law." So, for example, an undercover agent may call a suspect on the telephone and tape the conversation. Since the agent consents to the interception, it is not unlawful under the Wiretap Act. And, as we have seen, the suspect would have no Fourth Amendment claim because he knowingly "revealed" his words to another person—the undercover agent—bearing the risk that the agent would not keep them private.

While federal law permits the interception of communications so long as one party consents, some states have statutes forbidding interceptions unless all parties consent. Maryland is one such state—it does not permit the taping of telephone conversations, for example, unless all parties to the conversation agree. Further, Maryland's wiretap law makes it a crime to tape a telephone conversation without the knowledge and consent of the other parties, and violations of the law carry a possible sentence of 5 years in prison. In 1997, Linda Tripp taped approximately 25 telephone conversations she had with Monica Lewinsky, during which Ms. Lewinsky described her relationship with President Clinton. At the time of the taping, Ms. Lewinsky lived in Washington, D.C.—a jurisdiction that permits taping with one-party consent. Nevertheless, in July 1999, a Maryland grand jury indicted Ms. Tripp for alleged violations of the Maryland wiretap law. The indictment was dismissed after the Maryland trial court suppressed much of the prosecution's evidence because it violated an immunity agreement between Ms. Tripp and Independent Counsel Kenneth Starr.[11]

---

11. *See* State v. Tripp, 2000 WL 675492 (Md. Cir. Ct. 2000).

PROBLEM 6–3

Carmelo Williams, a pilot for NorthCentral Airlines, created and maintained a website where he posted bulletins critical of his employer, its officers, and the incumbent union, Professional Pilots Association ("PPA"). Many of those criticisms related to Williams's opposition to labor concessions that NorthCentral sought from PPA. Because PPA supported the concessions, Williams, via his website, encouraged NorthCentral employees to consider alternative union representation.

Williams controlled access to his website by requiring visitors to log in with a user name and password. He created a list of people, mostly pilots and other employees of NorthCentral, who were eligible to access the website. Pilot Aaron Wong was included on this list. Williams programmed the website to allow access when a person entered the name of an eligible person, created a password, and clicked the "SUBMIT" button on the screen, indicating acceptance of the terms and conditions of use. These terms and conditions prohibited any member of NorthCentral's management from viewing the website and prohibited users from disclosing the website's contents to anyone else.

NorthCentral vice president James Douglass was concerned about untruthful allegations that he believed Williams was making on the website. He asked Wong for permission to use Wong's name to access Williams's website. Wong agreed. Wong had not previously logged into the website to create an account. When Douglass accessed the website using Wong's name, he typed in Wong's name, created a password, and clicked the "SUBMIT" button indicating acceptance of the terms and conditions. Douglass then viewed the website.

Based on the website's contents, NorthCentral fired Williams. Williams filed suit alleging claims under the Wiretap Act and state tort law arising from Douglass's viewing and disclosure of Williams's secure website.

Questions: Did Douglass's activity violate the Wiretap Act? If so, which provision(s)?

3. REQUIREMENTS FOR "SUPER SEARCH WARRANTS"

Aside from the communications that are excepted from the Wiretap Act's coverage, the lawful interception of oral, wire, and electronic communications under Title I can occur only upon issuance of an intercept order—Professor Kerr's "super search warrant"—to a government law enforcement official. Requirements for these orders fall into three categories: jurisdictional, documentary, and executional.[12] As you examine these categories, consider their rationales. Which are constitutionally required? What public policy informed Congress's decision to include those (if any) that are not constitutionally required? Do the requirements reflect Congress's attention to the Supreme Court's opinions in *Berger* and *Katz*?

---

12. Goldsmith, *Supreme Court, supra* note 4, at 41.

a. Jurisdictional Requirements

The Wiretap Act imposes three jurisdictional requirements for a lawful intercept order. First, the application must be for surveillance concerning a crime for which surveillance is allowed under the statute. If the request is by a federal agency, the list of interceptable crimes is quite extensive, but these generally are serious felonies. If the application is by a state agent, the crime must be one designated in a state statute authorizing electronic surveillance. Moreover, the Wiretap Act limits state jurisdiction to the crimes of "murder, kidnapping, gambling, robbery, bribery, extortion, or dealing in narcotic drugs, marihuana or other dangerous drugs, or other crime dangerous to life, limb, or property, and punishable by imprisonment for more than one year."

The second jurisdictional requirement is that the application must be authorized by a statutorily designated official. A police officer or low-level prosecutor, for example, must seek authorization from such an official before applying for an intercept order.

Finally, the application must be made to "a judge of competent jurisdiction." If a federal agent makes application for an intercept order, the application must be heard by a federal judge with territorial jurisdiction over the point of interception, although the order may authorize interception anywhere within the United States if the surveillance will occur over a large area by use of a "mobile interception device." Only federal district court and appellate court judges can issue orders authorizing interceptions outside of their territorial jurisdictions. Applications by state agents must be made to those state court judges who are authorized by state statute to issue such orders.

b. Documentary Requirements

The Wiretap Act sets out documentary requirements for both the application and the intercept order itself. These requirements are lengthy, specific and more comprehensive than the requirements of a traditional warrant. They illustrate the seriousness with which electronic intrusions are to be evaluated.

Consistent with the Fourth Amendment, all applications must be made upon oath or affirmation; in addition, they must be in writing and state the applicant's authority to make such an application. The application must also include, in the words of the Act:

(a) the identity of the investigative or law enforcement officer making the application, and the officer authorizing the application;

(b) a full and complete statement of the facts and circumstances relied upon by the applicant, to justify his belief that an order should be issued, including (i) details as to the particular offense that has been, is being, or is about to be committed, (ii) a particular description of the nature and location of the facilities from which or the place where the communication is to be intercepted, (iii) a particular description of the type of communications sought to be intercepted, (iv) the identity of the person, if known, committing the offense and whose communications are to be intercepted;

(c) a full and complete statement as to whether or not other investigative procedures have been tried and failed or why they reasonably appear to be unlikely to succeed if tried or to be too dangerous [this is referred to as the "necessity requirement"];

(d) a statement of the period of time for which the interception is required to be maintained. If the nature of the investigation is such that the authorization for interception should not automatically terminate when the described type of communication has been first obtained, a particular description of facts establishing probable cause to believe that additional communications of the same type will occur thereafter;

(e) a full and complete statement of the facts concerning all previous applications known to the individual authorizing and making the application, made to any judge for authorization to intercept, or for approval of interceptions of, wire or oral communications involving any of the same persons, facilities or places specified in the application, and the action taken by the judge on each such application; and

(f) where the application is for the extension of an order, a statement setting forth the results thus far obtained from the interception, or a reasonable explanation of the failure to obtain such results.

Moreover, Title I specifies that "the issuing judge is free to require the applicant to furnish additional information."

Once an application is submitted to a judge of competent jurisdiction, the judge must determine if: (a) there is probable cause to believe that the stated crime has been, is being, or is about to be committed; (b) there is probable cause to believe that communications concerning the offence will be intercepted; (c) the government has satisfied the necessity requirement by showing that normal investigative techniques have been tried and failed or are reasonably likely to fail or are too dangerous; and (d) there is probable cause to believe that the point of interception will be used in the commission of the offense, or is leased to or commonly used by a person committing the offense. The judge may issue an intercept order if and only if these determinations are made.

Finally, each intercept order must specify: (a) the person, if known, whose communications are to be intercepted; (b) the location of interception; (c) a description of the communication to be intercepted and the offense to which it relates; (d) the agency authorized to intercept the communications and the person authorizing the application; (e) the length of time for which surveillance is authorized; and (f) that the surveillance must be executed as soon as practicable and in a way which minimizes the interception of nonpertinent communications. The Wiretap Act does provide a limited exception to the requirement that the application and the order specify the location of interception. The requirement is waived in a federal application for interception of an oral communication (one not transmitted by wire or cable) where it is determined that specification of point of interception is "not practical." The requirement is also waived in a federal application for interception of a wire or electronic communication if it is found that the targeted person is purposely trying to thwart interception by changing facilities. There is no corresponding waiver provision for applications made by a state agent.

c.   *Executional Requirements*

The final set of requirements imposed by Title I of the Wiretap Act relate to the execution of the intercept order. First, surveillance may be conducted only by the agency authorized by the order to intercept the communications. Moreover, the surveillance must be done in such a way "as to minimize the interception of communications not otherwise subject to interception under this chapter." If possible, the intercepted communication must be recorded in a way that will prevent alterations. Finally, upon attainment of the authorized objective or expiration of the order, the surveillance must cease and any recordings made must be turned over to the judge issuing the order and sealed according to judicial directions. Duplicates of the recordings may be made, and the information contained therein can be used by law enforcement officers for investigative purposes.

The execution requirements contain a notice provision to those whose communications have been intercepted. Within a reasonable time, but not later than ninety days after expiration of the wiretap order or denial of the wiretap application, the issuing judge must serve the persons named in the application or order a notice that includes an inventory of intercepted matter. Other overheard parties may also be given such an "inventory notice" at the judge's discretion. In addition, both the issuing judge and the official authorizing the intercept application must provide the Administrative Office of the United States Court a summary of each surveillance case, and a "full and complete report" of the surveillance cases occurring over the past year must be submitted to Congress each April.

As the discussion above reveals, Title I of the Wiretap Act is impressive in the scope and precision of its requirements. How do these requirements fare in practice? As one would expect, the courts walk a fine line between construing the statute strictly and providing the government with reasonable leeway. In *United States v. Donovan*,[13] the Supreme Court was rather exacting in interpreting the Act's documentary requirements, holding that a wiretap application cannot simply name those whom the government is "targeting" for prosecution. Instead, the application must include the names of all individuals as to whom the government has probable cause and whose conversations it expects to intercept conversations over the "target telephone." But the Tenth Circuit in *United States v. VanMeter*[14] was more relaxed in interpreting the Act's necessity requirement, under

---

13.   429 U.S. 413 (1977).

14.   United States v. VanMeter, 278 F.3d 1156 (10th Cir. 2002).

which the government must show that it has tried other methods of investigation, or that those methods would fail, before it is entitled to an intercept order:

> . . . Congress has required investigators to show the "necessity" of any wiretap application by providing "a full and complete statement as to whether or not other investigative procedures have been tried and failed or why they reasonably appear to be unlikely to succeed if tried or to be too dangerous." 18 U.S.C. § 2518(1)(c). This section of the federal wiretap statute serves to insure that wiretapping is not used in situations where traditional investigative techniques would suffice to expose the crime. Our case law establishes normal investigative procedures subject to 18 U.S.C. § 2518(1)(c) include: (1) standard visual and aural surveillance; (2) questioning and interrogation of witnesses or participants (including the use of grand juries and the grant of immunity if necessary); (3) use of search warrants; and (4) infiltration of conspiratorial groups by undercover agents or informants. . . . We add pen registers and trap and trace devices to this list because they possess a logical relationship and close affinity to wiretaps and yet are less intrusive.

In this case, federal agents used normal investigation procedures or reasonably explained why those procedures would fail or be too dangerous. Agents conducted visual surveillance of Mr. VanMeter and other suspects at several locations. Investigators also explained that further visual observation would not establish the extortionate subject matter of conversations held in private locations or on the telephone. Agents conducted aural surveillance by obtaining the consent of confidential informants to listen to telephone conversations with suspects. To obtain the cooperation of these informants, federal agents questioned and interrogated witnesses and participants. However, because the cooperating informants were outside the circle of trusted conspirators, they could obtain only limited information. The government reasonably feared approaching other potential witnesses would alert the principal suspects of the investigation. Moreover, the government reasonably believed Oklahoma State Department of Health employees and nursing home operators would not risk retaliation from Mr. VanMeter.

Similarly, agents reasonably explained their choice to not use grand jury investigation or grants of immunity. Under the circumstances investigators believed the risk that witnesses would lie to the grand jury, claim their Fifth Amendment privilege, or inform principal suspects of the investigation outweighed modest potential evidentiary gains. Agents also explained search warrants were not reasonably likely to produce physical evidence of the verbal communications at the heart of the extortion investigation. Furthermore, the government explained infiltrating undercover agents or informants was unreasonable under the circumstances. . . . Finally, agents used pen registers and toll records to establish the number and duration of calls. . . .

Because federal agents used normal investigation procedures or reasonably explained why those procedures would fail or be too dangerous, Mr. VanMeter has not overcome the presumption the wiretap authorizations were proper. . . .

NOTES AND QUESTIONS

1. As the *Vanmeter* case confirms, the Wiretap Act's necessity requirement requires the government to show in its application that wiretapping is necessary. what is the purpose of this requirement? does the Fourth Amendment impose a similar burden on the government? Why or why not?

2. The Wiretap Act also has a "minimization requirement"—that is, the government is required to establish in advance a plan for minimizing the impact of an intercept order on communications not covered by the order. Moreover, in executing a wiretap the government must effectuate its minimization plan. What is the purpose of this requirement? Does the Fourth Amendment impose a similar requirement on the government?

———

4. REMEDIES FOR TITLE I VIOLATIONS

What remedies exist for Wiretap Act violations? The statute provides for the criminal prosecution of violators in certain circumstances and for civil damages, but neither of these is available if the violator establishes "good faith reliance" on a court order or other reasonably official authorization. The most sought-after remedy in many instances is exclusion from a criminal case of evidence gained by an illegal wiretap. Title I of the Wiretap Act expressly requires suppression of evidence obtained in violation of its provisions:

> Whenever any wire or oral communication has been intercepted, no part of the contents of such communication and no evidence derived therefrom may be received in evidence in any trial, hearing, or other proceeding in or before any court, grand jury, department, officer, agency, regulatory body, legislative committee, or other authority of the United States, a State, or a political subdivision thereof if the disclosure of that information would be in violation of this chapter.

Not all violations of Title I warrant the exclusionary remedy, however. First, notice from the statutory language above that the interception of electronic communications does not merit an exclusionary remedy—only wire and oral communications are subject to suppression. Moreover, even with wire and oral communications, suppression is authorized only if: (a) the communication was unlawfully intercepted; (b) the order of authorization or approval under which it was intercepted was insufficient on its face; or (c) the interception was not made in conformity with the order of authorization or approval.

Most of the debate over these three grounds for suppression has centered around what it means for a communication to be "unlawfully intercepted." The Supreme Court struggled with this issue for several years. Then, in *United States v. Donovan*,[15] the Court held that an interception is "unlawful" only if it undermines the purpose of the Wiretap Act. Thus, failures to comply fully with the Act do not result in an exclusionary remedy unless they involve statutory requirements that play "a central role" in the statutory framework.

PROBLEM 6–4

SoftwareGames, Inc. was a software design firm with headquarters in Orange County, California. Shares in SoftwareGames were publicly traded on the National Association of Securities Dealers Exchange (commonly referred to as "NASDAQ"). Richard Snersen served as SoftwareGames's Vice President for North American Sales and worked in SoftwareGames's Nashville, Tennessee, office. After nearly three years with SoftwareGames, Snersen had accumulated 51,445 shares of SoftwareGames stock.

In a series of transactions between June 10 and June 18, Snersen liquidated his entire position in SoftwareGames. In addition to selling his own shares, Snersen "sold short" 25,000 shares on July 8, and another 10,000 shares on July 20. Short selling is a device whereby an individual sells stock which he does not own, expecting that the price will decline before he has to deliver the shares and that he will thereby be enabled to cover by purchasing the stock at the lesser price. If the decline takes place, the short seller pockets the difference between the sales price and the lower purchase price.

Amidst this flurry of sales activity, on June 19, Snersen telephoned his girlfriend, Angela Brache, an employee in the Los Angeles office of SoftwareGames, and left her the following voicemail message:

> Hi, Angie, Rich.... I talked to Tom last night after I left you some messages and he and Lou discovered that there was about a million and a half dollar mistake in the budget, so now we're back at ground zero and we've got to scramble for the next few days. Anyway, I sold all my stock off on Friday and I'm going to short the stock because I know its going to go down a couple of points here in the next week as soon as Lou releases the information about next year's earnings. You might want to do the same.

Snersen was correct in his estimation that the price of SoftwareGames's stock would decline. Following the company's release of its fourth-quarter sales figures on August 19, SoftwareGames stock dropped roughly 38%, from approximately eight dollars ($8) per share to approximately five dollars ($5) per share. In addition to the substantial losses he avoided by selling his own stock—somewhere in the neighborhood of $150,000—Snersen's short sales netted him approximately $50,000.

---

15.   429 U.S. 413 (1977).

Unbeknownst to either Snersen or Brache, another Los Angeles-based SoftwareGames employee, Linda Govinda, suspected that Snersen and Brache were profiting by sales of stock. She decided to do some investigating. Guessing correctly Brache's voicemail password, she accessed Brache's voice mailbox. When Govinda encountered Snersen's message, which remained on Brache's voice mailbox because she had not yet listened to it, Govinda forwarded it to her own mailbox. In order to retrieve it, she then called her own voicemail from her home telephone, played the message, and recorded it with a handheld audiotape recorder. After recording the message, Govinda approached a co-worker, Robert Tsongas. She informed him of the general nature of the communication and provided him with a copy of the recording.

Tsongas listened to the message and telephoned the United States Attorney's Office for the Central District of California, where he spoke to Assistant United States Attorney Bailey Williams ("Williams"). Tsongas told Williams that he believed he had information, in the form of an audiotape, that indicated possible criminal activity. He played the tape for Williams approximately four times and attempted to answer several questions about the contents of the recording. He informed Williams that he believed that the speaker on the tape was Snersen and that the references in the message to "Tom" and "Lou" were probably to Tom Cristy and Lou Delmenico, both corporate officers at SoftwareGames. Tsongas offered to send Williams a copy of the tape itself, but Williams declined. Tsongas never spoke to Williams again.

Williams referred the matter to Special Agent Maura Konstans of the Federal Bureau of Investigation ("FBI"). Konstans contacted the Pacific Regional Office of the Securities and Exchange Commission ("SEC") and relayed to a staff attorney that an "anonymous informant had told [Williams] about insider trading in the stock of a company called Software-Games by a person named Richard Snersen and that the anonymous informant had a tape of a conversation involving an individual purporting to be Snersen discussing insider trading." In November, the SEC issued a formal order of investigation against Snersen. Over the course of the ensuing eight months, the SEC obtained documentary evidence from various sources and deposed a number of witnesses. Sometime during its investigation, the SEC obtained via administrative subpoena an audiotape copy of the recorded voicemail message.

The SEC then referred the matter back to the United States Attorney in Los Angeles for possible criminal prosecution. Throughout the next eighteen months, the United States Attorney's Office and the FBI conducted substantial additional investigation, during which they interviewed fifteen individuals and subpoenaed sixteen additional boxes of documents.

Snersen was indicted on eleven counts of insider trading. He moved to suppress all the evidence supporting the indictment, alleging that it was "derived from" an illegal interception of his voicemail.

Questions: Was the voicemail message on Brache's voice mailbox unlawfully intercepted? If so, should the exclusionary remedy apply in snersen's case?

PROBLEM 6–5

On February 18, Buckminster County law enforcement officials informally delivered a 195–page application and supporting affidavit to Buckminster County Judge Moira Chouvrant. The application sought an ex parte order permitting installation of a wiretap on the telephone located at Full City Auto, the business of Eric J. Mulvihill and Craymond Robinson. The next day, after Judge Chouvrant had studied the application and affidavit, Officer Wanda Sneed of the County Police Department, County Attorney Gray Wooley, and Assistant United States Attorney Theodore Pagni returned to the judge's chambers to formally apply for the wiretap order pursuant to state statute.

After a brief conversation with Judge Chouvrant, Officer Sneed signed the original affidavit, Wooley signed the original application, and they handed the original set of papers to Judge Chouvrant, who signed portions of them that the other three could not see. The law enforcement officers asked for copies of the signature pages, and Judge Chouvrant arranged for photocopying. Officer Sneed did not look at the copies she received and put in her file. A few minutes later, at 9:00 a.m. on February 19, the original papers as signed in chambers were filed with the clerk of court. Buckminster police then instructed the local phone company to begin intercepting and recording calls to and from Full City Auto's telephone.

Because wiretap orders are limited by statute to a maximum of thirty days, Wooley and Pagni submitted an application for an extension order in mid-March. On March 19, Judge Chouvrant signed and filed an extension order which provided, "said authorization shall continue day and night for a period of thirty (30) days from the end of the 30–day period of prior authorization." On March 26, Pagni applied for permission to disclose the wiretap evidence for law enforcement purposes. Judge Chouvrant signed and filed an order permitting disclosure of "any information concerning wire communications, or evidence derived therefrom, pursuant to the order of this Court, dated February 19, and March 19."

Information obtained through this wiretap led to the seizure of two shipments of cocaine and to other evidence of drug trafficking. A federal grand jury then indicted Mulvihill and Robinson for conspiracy to distribute cocaine. Following disclosure of the wiretap application and order, defense counsel learned that Judge Chouvrant had signed the original February 19 application and supporting affidavit as attesting witness, but had not signed the filed February 19 wiretap order. When the government could not produce a signed copy of that order, defendants moved to suppress all evidence obtained from the wiretap.

Questions: Assume that you work in the united states attorney's office that is prosecuting the cocaine charges. on what grounds can you argue against suppression of the evidence? are you likely to be successful?

C. THE USA PATRIOT ACT

The USA PATRIOT Act is a long and complex document amending many other federal statutes. The discussion here will be limited to those provisions affecting criminal investigations.

1. PROVISIONS AFFECTING FOURTH AMENDMENT SEARCHES

One of the more controversial of the PATRIOT Act's provisions affects search warrants issued under traditional Fourth Amendment standards. As a result, the constitutionality of that provision remains in question. The provision endorses what are known as "sneak and peak" warrants— warrants that remain secret even after their execution. Recall that officers ordinarily must notify residents that a search warrant has been executed by leaving a copy of the warrant and an inventory of items seized. Under section 213 of the Act, the government can put off giving this sort of notice if a court finds that there is reasonable cause to believe that notice will create an "adverse result" in the form of danger to persons or evidence, flight from the jurisdiction.

2. PROVISIONS AFFECTING STATUTORY POWERS

Most of the controversy surrounding the PATRIOT Act concerned changes it made to FISA. But it also affected statutory surveillance powers under the Wiretap Act. These changes can be summarized in six categories:

(a) Recall from the discussion above that temporarily stored wire communications (e.g., voice mail messages not yet delivered to recipients) enjoyed Title I protection. Under the PATRIOT Act, these are now treated under Title II like other communications in electronic storage. In other words, if such communications have been stored for 180 days or less, the government must obtain a warrant or order based on probable cause but need not obtain a super search warrant. If the communications have been stored for more than 180 days, the government can intercept them with a subpoena.

(b) Warrants or orders for stored email communications are effective nationwide, and not just in the jurisdiction in which they were issued. According to the government, this provision makes its work much more efficient, because Internet service providers [ISPs] often are located in places unconnected with an investigation. According to ISPs, however, the nationwide jurisdiction provision makes it impossible in many cases for them to challenge intercept orders, because courts of issuance may be far from the ISPs and costs therefore prohibitive.

(c) The government now is entitled to greater information about ISP customers. Under Title II of the Wiretap Act, the government could obtain certain ISP records that fell within the definition of communications in electronic storage. These included customer names and addresses and duration of customers' accounts. The PATRIOT Act adds other records, including the customer's electronic aliases, times and duration of online sessions, and credit card and bank accounts with which ISP was paid.

(d) Recall that the government has access to pen registers and trap and trace devices only upon a statement of relevance. The PATRIOT Act has added the Internet equivalent of these devices, so that the government can have access to email addressing data and routing information. In other words, the government can monitor to whom an individual is sending email, and from whom the individual receives email.

(e) Under the PATRIOT Act, courts with jurisdiction over the investigation can issue nationwide orders authorizing the release of pen registers, trap and trace records, and their Internet equivalents. Again, the government contends that it can fight crime more effectively with this nationwide jurisdictional provision; ISPs complain that they cannot meaningfully challenge (and thus monitor) the validity and execution of orders.

(f) Intelligence officials may now share broadly the information they gather under FISA. The sharing of information need only "assist the official who is to receive that information in the performance of his official duties." Arguably, this information sharing provision, while making law enforcement more effective, provides incentives for agencies to use its aggressive FISA powers in order to help criminal investigators who otherwise must respect the more burdensome responsibilities of the Wiretap Act.

D.   THE FOREIGN INTELLIGENCE SURVEILLANCE ACT

The government is granted considerably more leeway when it is investigating the activities of foreign powers than when it is engaging in traditional domestic criminal law enforcement. In part this leeway stems from the deference granted the executive branch in matters of foreign affairs by the legislative and judicial branches. The Foreign Intelligence Surveillance Act [FISA] exemplifies this deference. It applies whenever federal law enforcement agents investigate foreign intelligence gathering within the borders of the United States. As we mentioned above, the USA PATRIOT Act widened some of FISA's scope.

FISA enables the government to engage in some information gathering without judicial authorization. Even more significantly, where judicial oversight is necessary, a special court is invoked that operates in secret. Orders of this court, which is comprised of federal trial judges, are reviewed by a special FISA court of appeals comprised of federal appellate judges. These courts are empowered to authorize surveillance without a showing of probable cause to believe that criminal activity is afoot, so long as the government demonstrates that it is investigating a foreign power or an agent of a foreign power, including terrorist organizations. Information that the government gains through a FISA investigation may be shared with law enforcement officers working in traditional criminal law enforcement.

The secrecy of the FISA court apparently convinced President Bush and his administration to trust that body to oversee its "Terrorist Surveillance Program." The program, created by a secret order issued by President Bush in October 2001, directed the National Security Agency [NSA] to monitor telephone and email communications between persons believed to be linked to al Qaeda and other terrorist groups, even if they were United States citizens. The American public did not know about the secret NSA surveillance until December 2005, when it was reported by the New York Times. After a firestorm of criticism and an ACLU lawsuit filed in the United States Court of Appeals for the Sixth Circuit, the administration acquiesced to FISA court involvement. The extent of the program, its duration, and the fate of the lawsuit, are still unknown.

E. Technologically-Assisted Physical Surveillance

We mentioned above that legislatures have not yet regulated the use of technology to enhance physical surveillance. For example, video cameras are used more and more frequently in public places for surveillance and safety. In response to this regulatory gap, the American Bar Association promulgated Standards on Technologically–Assisted Physical Surveillance. These Standards contain recommendations "concerning government use of physical surveillance technology such as video surveillance, tracking devices, magnification and illumination devices, and detection devices that can discern items through opaque surfaces."[16] The Standards mirror the Fourth Amendment in some circumstances and go farther in others. For example, they state that "technologically-assisted physical surveillance should be regulated not only when it diminishes privacy, but also when it diminishes 'freedom of speech, association and travel, and the openness of society.'" They would limit surveillance in public areas unless it is "reasonably likely to achieve a legitimate law enforcement objective." They would require both oversight by high-level or politically accountable officers and the opportunity for public comment.

F. Other Special Statutory Powers

1. MAIL SURVEILLANCE

The Fourth Amendment protects the contents of first class mail sent through the United States Postal Service. Congress also has protected the mail through a federal criminal statute.[17] As a result, the government cannot open a sealed envelope sent through the mail, unless it has a warrant. But what if the government wishes not to open envelopes, but simply to keep track of the addresses on mail sent by, or to, a particular individual? Obviously, the information written on the outside of envelopes is open to public view and therefore not protected by the Fourth Amend-

---

16. Martin Marcus and Christopher Slobogin, *Meeting the Challenges of the Technological Revolution: The ABA Standards for Electronic Surveillance of Private Communications and for Technologically-assisted Physical Surveillance*, Crim. Just. (2003).

17. *See* Ex Parte Jackson, 96 U.S. (6 Otto) 727 (1877); 18 U.S.C. § 1703.

ment. Nevertheless, a postal service regulation prohibits this sort of "envelope surveillance" without an authorized "mail cover."[18] A mail cover may be issued upon the written request of a law enforcement agent specifying "reasonable grounds to demonstrate that the mail cover is necessary to . . . [o]btain information regarding the commission or attempted commission of a crime." Professor Kerr points out that the regulation does not contain much strength, because it does not require a court order or a return of service and it does not provide an exclusionary remedy—or any other remedy, for that matter.

2.   MATERIAL WITNESS WARRANTS

What happens when the government wishes to obtain the testimony of a reluctant witness who may flee the jurisdiction rather than testify at trial or before a grand jury? In such a case, it might be desirable from the government's perspective to be able to "seize" the witness, but an arrest warrant would not be available if there existed no probable cause to believe that the witness had committed a crime. By statute, law enforcement officers in many jurisdictions have the authority to seize such witnesses as "material witnesses." In the federal system, the authorizing statute is part of the Bail Reform Act of 1984. Section 3144 of that Act provides:

> If it appears from an affidavit filed by a party that the testimony of a person is material in a criminal proceeding, and if it is shown that it may become impracticable to secure the presence of the person by subpoena, a judicial officer may order the arrest of the person. . . . No material witness may be detained because of inability to comply with any condition of release if the testimony of such witness can adequately be secured by deposition, and if further detention is not necessary to prevent a failure of justice. Release of a material witness may be delayed for a reasonable period of time until the deposition of the witness can be taken pursuant to the Federal Rules of Criminal Procedure.

Courts construing this provision have held that before issuing a material witness warrant, a judicial officer must be satisfied that probable cause exists to believe (1) that testimony of the witness is material and (2) that it may become impracticable to secure his presence by subpoena or other court process.[19] Once the witness is arrested pursuant to the warrant, the Act clearly requires that the witness be released once his or her testimony has been taken by deposition, unless detention is justified on some other basis.

Since the terrorist attacks of September 11, 2001, the United States government has appeared to use the material witness statute aggressively. For example, in May, 2004, the FBI arrested Portland, Oregon lawyer Brandon Mayfield as a material witness to a Madrid, Spain train station

---

18.   This discussion is based in part on Kerr, *Internet Law*, *supra* note 10.

19.   *See*, *e.g.*, United States v. Coldwell, 496 F.Supp. 305, 307 (E.D. Okl. 1979); United States v. Feingold, 416 F.Supp. 627, 628 (S.D.N.Y. 1976).

bombing. Mayfield was held for two weeks before the government acknowledged that a fingerprint it had thought was his in fact belonged to someone else. A reporter for the Portland Oregonian, analyzing Mayfield's situation, reported that "[t]he Justice Department reported to Congress that as of January 2003, nearly 50 people had been detained as material witnesses in connection with the investigation of the Sept. 11 attacks. Since then, however, it has refused to update the statistics, saying they are covered by grand jury secrecy rules."[20]

The *Mayfield* case prompted this editorial from The Washington Post:[21]

> When Portland, Ore., lawyer Brandon Mayfield was taken into federal custody two weeks ago under a material-witness warrant, an indictment seemed likely to follow. A fingerprint belonging to Mayfield, who had converted to Islam, reportedly had been found on a bag of detonators connected to the deadly Madrid bombing, and Mr. Mayfield had done legal work for an Islamic radical successfully prosecuted in Oregon. Yet this week Mr. Mayfield walked out of detention a free man; Spanish police had reportedly tied the fingerprint on the bag to an Algerian. And the Justice Department now finds itself with some explaining to do.

> A gag order on the case makes information scant, and the court, in releasing him, noted that his "release will be supervised" and that there will be "further grand jury proceedings wherein he remains a material witness." Many more facts may yet emerge. It isn't too soon, however, to ask whether someone misread a fingerprint, and if so who and why; or to worry that federal authorities might have arrested someone without the evidence to bring a responsible case.

> The case is the latest example of the Justice Department's aggressive use of the power to detain "material witnesses"—people with evidence in a court proceeding who might flee if left at large. The statute, which authorizes such detentions under court supervision for "a reasonable period of time" in order to secure testimony, is not new. It has long been used with relatively little controversy in organized-crime cases.

> But since the Oklahoma City bombing investigation and particularly since Sept. 11, 2001, designation of material witnesses has become a more routine tool in the government's legal arsenal and has been deployed at an earlier stage of criminal proceedings. Rather than being used merely to ensure that witnesses are available for trial after an indictment has been issued, it has been employed to hold suspects who are themselves under investigation. The result is that dozens of people across the country have been detained for varying periods of time while the government seeks to compile evidence against them. The circumstances of these detentions are shrouded in secrecy, as are the names

---

20. Mark Larabee, *Portland Case Fuels Rights Debate*, THE OREGONIAN (May 31, 2004).

21. *Arresting Witnesses*, THE WASHINGTON POST (Editorial, May 22, 2004).

of the detainees and even the raw number of them. The Justice Department at times has seemed to use the statute as a kind of preventive detention law.

Congress, which has shown little interest in legislating on difficult matters involving liberty and security, has failed to clarify the new circumstances under which the material-witness law should apply. The result is a detention authority for which the parameters are dangerously undefined. How long is a "reasonable period of time" for the government to hold someone without charge while digging around to see if it can make a case? In typical criminal cases, the government is required to bring charges in order to hold any suspect. If that is to change in terrorism cases, the change should come as a result of a deliberate legislative decision, not the mission creep of an old statute envisioned for other problems.

Even if Mr. Mayfield's case does not prove to be an example of an abuse of the power, the use of the material-witness law needs careful attention and a healthy dose of sunlight.

G.   EXTENDED DETENTION OF PERSONS IN THE WAR ON TERRORISM

In addition to detaining persons pursuant to material witness warrants, the United States has engaged in extended detentions of individuals in the War on Terrorism on a variety of other grounds.[22] Although the United States Supreme Court has chosen not to rest its very recent and few decisions in this area on Fourth Amendment grounds, it has recognized important due process and related protection for these detainees that merit at least brief mention. These cases also matter because at least one of them recognizes the importance of the right to counsel in preventing governmental excess in a perhaps indefinite war.

Hamdi v. Rumsfeld[23] raised the question whether Yaser Hamdi, an American citizen captured in a combat zone in Afghanistan, then taken to the U.S. naval base at Guantanamo Bay, Cuba, and finally jailed in a naval brig on the east coast of the United States, could be held indefinitely without serious judicial review, in solitary confinement, with no visitors and no access to lawyers, because he was designated by the Executive as an "enemy combatant." The Court, in a fractured set of opinions, answered this question with a resounding "no."

Hamdi's father had filed a habeas corpus petition on Hamdi's behalf. The Justice Department sought summary dismissal on the ground that the court could not "second guess" the Executive's "enemy combatant" designation. The Fourth Circuit ultimately dismissed the petition, finding that Hamdi's own legal papers conceded that Hamdi was seized in a zone of

---

22. *See generally* BARBARA OLSHANSKY, AMERICA'S DISAPPEARED: SECRET IMPRISONMENT, DETAINEES, AND THE WAR ON TERROR (2004).

23. 542 U.S. 507 (2004).

overseas combat and that that was sufficient to justify deference to the President's decision.

In the United States Supreme Court, only Justice Thomas agreed with the Government's position. The plurality opinion, signed on to by Justices O'Connor, Rehnquist, Kennedy, and Breyer, held that "due process demands that a citizen held in the United States as an enemy combatant be given a meaningful opportunity to contest the factual basis for that detention before a neutral decisionmaker. ... Plainly, the 'process' Hamdi has received is not that to which he is entitled under the Due Process Clause."[24] The plurality thus not only rejected the Government's claim that the judiciary owed virtually unquestioned deference to the Executive on this matter, but also rejected the Government's fallback position that production of but "some evidence" from the Department of Defense demonstrating that the detention was not wholly arbitrary—a burden met by the affidavit of a Pentagon official—was adequate to support the President's decision.[25] The plurality likewise rejected the Government's blockade of Hamdi's access to counsel, unequivocally declaring that Hamdi "unquestionably has the right to access to counsel."[26] The Court remanded the case to the Fourth Circuit for further proceedings in which Hamdi will have the opportunity to show that the Executive's enemy designation was wrong.

Justice Scalia, in an opinion joined by Justice Stevens, would have gone further, issuing the writ of habeas corpus and discharging Hamdi without remanding the case for unnecessary further proceedings. Justice Scalia read the history of habeas corpus as demonstrating that the Great Writ could be suspended only by congressional, not executive, action while the courts were open and that "Citizens aiding the enemy have been treated as traitors subject to criminal process."[27] Furthermore, said Justice Scalia, the Non–Detention Act was intended to prohibit precisely such executive detentions. That Act, passed by Congress in 1971 to prevent the recurrence of events like the Japanese–American internment camps during World War II, declared that "[n]o citizen shall be imprisoned or otherwise detained by the United States except pursuant to an Act of Congress."[28] Justice Scalia rejected the argument, articulated in the plurality opinion, that the Authorization for Use of Military Force Act (authorizing the President to use "all necessary and appropriate force against nations, organizations, or persons he determines planned, authorized, committed, or aided the terrorist attacks that occurred on September 11, 2001 ... to prevent any future acts of international terrorism against the United States"[29]) constituted adequate congressional action because detention is a "necessary and appropriate" use of force.[30] Justice Scalia did "not think this statute even authorizes

---

24. *Id.* at 509, 538 (O'Connor, J., plurality opinion).

25. *See id.* at 537–39 (O'Connor, J., plurality opinion).

26. *Id.* at 539 (O'Connor, J., plurality opinion).

27. *Id.* at 559 (Scalia, J., dissenting).

28. 18 U.S.C. § 4001(a).

29. 115 Stat. 224.

30. *Hamdi*, 542 U.S. at 575 n.5 (Scalia, J., dissenting).

detention of a citizen with the clarity necessary to satisfy the interpretive canon that statutes should be construed so as to avoid grave constitutional concerns."[31] Moreover, he said, the statute was "not remotely a congressional suspension of the writ, and no one claims that it is."[32] Therefore, in the view of Justices Scalia and Stevens, the Government had only two choices absent clear congressional action suspending the writ of habeas corpus: release Hamdi or process him through the ordinary criminal justice system.

Justices Souter and Ginsburg likewise agreed that remand was unnecessary because the Non–Detention Act barred detention of citizens on United States soil without explicit congressional authorization. Justice Souter explained:

> The fact that Congress intended to guard against a repetition of the World War II internments when it repealed the 1950 [Cold War statute authorizing the Attorney General in time of emergency to detain anyone reasonably thought likely to engage in sabotage or espionage] and gave us § 4001(a) provides a powerful reason to think that § 4001(a) was meant to require clear congressional authorization before any citizen can be placed in a cell. It is not merely that the legislative history shows that § 4001(a) was thought necessary in anticipation of times just like the present, in which the safety of the country is threatened. To appreciate what is most significant, one must recall that the internments of the 1940s were accomplished by Executive action. Although an Act of Congress ratified and confirmed an Executive order authorizing the military to exclude individuals from defined areas and to accommodate those it might remove, . . . the statute said nothing whatever about the detention of those who might be removed, . . .; internment camps were creatures of the Executive, and confinement in them rested on assertion of Executive authority. . . . When, therefore, Congress repealed the 1950 Act and adopted § 4001(a) for the purpose of avoiding another *Korematsu*, it intended to preclude reliance on vague congressional authority (for example, providing "accommodations" for those subject to removal) as authority for detention or imprisonment at the discretion of the Executive (maintaining detention camps of American citizens, for example). In requiring that any Executive detention be "pursuant to an Act of Congress," then, Congress necessarily meant to require a congressional enactment that clearly authorized detention or imprisonment. . . .
>
> Under this principle of reading § 4001(a) robustly to require a clear statement of authorization to detain, none of the Government's arguments suffices to justify Hamdi's detention.[33]

---

31. *Id.* at 574 (Scalia, J., dissenting).

32. *Id.* (Scalia, J., dissenting).

33. *Id.* at 544–45 (Souter, J., concurring in part, dissenting in part, concurring in the judgment).

Nevertheless, Justices Souter and Ginsburg joined in the plurality's remand "to give practical effect to the conclusions of eight members of the Court [in] rejecting the Government's position."[34]

Despite the majority signing onto a remand, however, there were important limitations on the plurality's opinion. First, a clear majority (Chief Justice Rehnquist and Justices O'Connor, Breyer, Kennedy, and Thomas) explicitly recognized the President's authority to designate both citizens and non-citizens as enemy combatants and, though less clear on the point, should the War on Terrorism prove to be a conflict of near-indefinite duration, this same majority arguably agreed for now that such individuals can be held in custody without criminal charge or trial for the entire duration of the conflict.[35] Second, five Justices also concluded that the Authorization for Use of Military Force Act overcame any objection that the detention of American citizens violated the Non–Detention Act. Third, the plurality's opinion and at least that of Justice Scalia and Stevens were limited to "*citizen*-detainees."

Fourth, although the citizen-detainee can turn to the courts or to other sorts of tribunals to challenge an enemy-combatant designation, the process due is limited. Said the plurality, that process must include the detainee's receiving "notice of the factual basis for his classification, and a fair opportunity to rebut the government's factual assertions before a neutral decisionmaker."[36] However, the plurality suggested that the "standards we have articulated could be met by an appropriately authorized and constituted military tribunal" like the Article V tribunals already governed by Army regulation where the Geneva Convention applies.[37] Article III courts might, therefore, not necessarily be involved. Further, the burden can be shifted to the detainee to prove that he is *not* an enemy combatant once the Government "puts forth credible evidence that the habeas petitioner meets the enemy combatant criteria," a standard highly deferential to the Government.[38] Explained the plurality, such burden-shifting would still "meet the goal of ensuring that the errant tourist, embedded journalist, or local aid worker has a chance to prove military error while giving due regard to the Executive once it has put forth meaningful support for its conclusion that the detainee is in fact an enemy combatant."[39] However, the plurality and at least three other Justices (the total lineup including Justices O'Connor, Kennedy, Breyer, Souter, Ginsburg, and Chief Justice Rehn-

---

34. *Id.* at 553 (Souter, J., concurring in part, dissenting in part, concurring in the judgment).

35. *Cf.* Timothy Lynch, *No Blank Check*, pamphlet published by The Federalist Society for Law and Policy Studies (July 2004) (counting votes and reaching similar conclusion); Lee A. Casey, David B. Rivkin, Jr., and Darin R. Bartram, *The Supreme Court's 2004 "War on Terror" Cases*, pamphlet published by The Federalist Society for Law and Policy Studies (July 2004) (similar).

36. *Hamdi*, 542 U.S. at 533 (O'Connor, J., plurality opinion).

37. *Id.* at 538 (O'Connor, J., plurality opinion).

38. *Id.* at 534 (O'Connor, J., plurality opinion).

39. *Id.* (O'Connor, J., plurality opinion).

quist) insisted that the detainees would be entitled to the assistance of counsel, offering no clear rationale, perhaps on the apparent assumption that the centrality of counsel to due process was self-evident.[40]

Rumsfeld v. Padilla[41] had in some ways been the most eagerly anticipated of the Court's opinions on detention of suspected terrorists because it involved an American citizen initially detained on United States soil. Padilla was allegedly trained abroad by Al Qaeda, re-entering the U.S. with the goal of detonating a radiological "dirty" bomb. He was taken into custody at Chicago's O'Hare International Airport, and then transferred to New York City on the basis of a material witness warrant, where he was assigned counsel. He was, however, transferred to military custody, now being held at the Naval brig at Charleston, South Carolina, when, only a few days after being assigned counsel, his status was re-designated by the President as an enemy combatant.

When Padilla's lawyer filed a habeas petition in the Southern District of New York, the District Court rejected the Government's claim that Padilla was not entitled to counsel but held that the President had authority to designate Padilla an enemy combatant, a decision entitled to substantial deference by the judiciary. The Second Circuit reversed, concluding that, as an American citizen, Padilla could not be held as an enemy combatant but must be released or be processed through the regular criminal justice system. The Second Circuit relied on a reading of the Non–Detention Act, similar to that later articulated by Justice Scalia in *Hamdi*, forbidding prolonged detention of American citizens absent contrary congressional enactment.

However, the high Court disappointed observers by not resolving the substantive issue, instead ruling that the petition had been filed in the wrong court and needed to be re-filed in the District of South Carolina, where Padilla's "immediate custodian" held Padilla in detention. Justice Stevens, joined by Justices Souter, Ginsburg, and Breyer, dissented, arguing that the case's merits should have been addressed because of their "profound importance."[42] Given the Court's decision on *Hamdi*, however, when Padilla re-files, he will likely be accorded access to present his case to a "neutral decisionmaker."[43]

Finally, *Rasul v. Bush*[44] involved *non*-citizen detainees at the United States Naval Station, Guantanamo Bay, Cuba ("Gitmo"), purportedly beyond U.S. territory because of Cuba's retention over Guantanamo's "ultimate sovereignty" when leasing the area to the U.S. in 1903. The Government had argued that the courts lacked habeas jurisdiction over non-citizen detainees held outside United States territory, relying on *Johnson v.*

---

40.   *See* Lynch, *Blank Check, supra* note 35; Casey, et al., *supra* note 35.

41.   542 U.S. 426 (2004).

42.   *Id.* at 540 (Stevens, J., dissenting).

43.   *See* Lynch, *supra* note 35; Casey, *et al.*, *Terror Cases, supra* note 35.

44.   542 U.S. 466 (2004).

Eisentrager,[45] in which the Court rejected petitions by German nationals captured in China at the end of World War II and held under American authority in post-war Germany because those claimants were outside U.S. territory and thus beyond the federal court's jurisdiction. The United States Court of Appeals for the District of Columbia Circuit agreed with the Government's position that *Eisentrager* controlled in *Rasul* and that the Gitmo detainees could not challenge their detention.

The Court reversed in a 5–4 split, with the majority's opinion authored by Justice Stevens and joined by Justices O'Connor, Souter, Ginsburg, and Breyer, with Justice Kennedy concurring in the result. Justice Stevens found no inherent constitutional right to habeas review beyond U.S. territory, at least for aliens. However, he distinguished *Eisentrager* on the ground that the Court had there *assumed* that statutory habeas review was unavailable. But, said Justice Stevens, subsequent Supreme Court decisions clarified that even non-citizens held overseas can obtain review under the habeas corpus statute, 28 U.S.C. § 2241. Accordingly, the Gitmo detainees could challenge the legality of their detention via the federal habeas process. Given the statutory basis of the majority's decision, however, Congress may remain free to amend the habeas statute to alter this result.[46] And given *Hamdi's* decision on the limited due process rights of citizen-detainees, it is also unlikely that the aliens in the *Rasul* case will be accorded any greater process.[47]

Justice Scalia, joined by Chief Justice Rehnquist and Justice Thomas, dissented on a number of grounds, including that the majority misread *Eisentrager* and effectively extended the habeas statute "to the four corners of the earth."[48]

Military commissions, tribunals "neither mentioned in the Constitution nor created by statute [were] born of military necessity."[49] Over a half-century ago, the Supreme Court recognized that trial by military commission " 'is an extraordinary measure raising important questions about the balance of powers in our constitutional structure.' "[50]That message bore reiteration most recently in *Hamdan v. Rumsfeld*.[51] In *Hamdan*, petitioner, Salim Ahmed Hamdan, a Yemeni national, was captured and turned over to the U.S. military during the invasion of Afghanistan pursuant to Congress's adoption of legislation that authorized the president, George W. Bush, to

> [u]se all necessary and appropriate force against those nations, organizations, or persons he determines planned, authorized, committed, or aided the terrorist attacks ... in order to prevent any future acts of

---

45. 339 U.S. 763 (1950).

46. *See* Lynch, *supra* note 35 Casey, et al., *supra* note 35.

47. *See* Casey, *supra*.

48. Rasul, 542 U.S. at 498 (Scalia, J., dissenting).

49. Hamdan v. Rumsfeld, 548 U.S. 557, 590 (2006).

50. *Id.* at 567 (*citing* Ex parte Quirin, 317 U.S. 1, 19 (1942)).

51. *Id.* at 567–68.

international terrorism against the United States by such nations, organizations, or persons.[52]

The joint resolution was enacted shortly after the September 11, 2001, al Qaeda terror attacks on the World Trade Center and the Pentagon. As a result of the joint resolution, hundreds of individuals, including Hamdan, were captured and transported as detainees/prisoners in Guantánamo Bay, Cuba. On November 13, 2001, President Bush issued a military order, which vested in the Secretary of Defense the power to appoint military commissions to try individuals subject to the order, which also governed how non-American detainees in the so-called "War Against Terrorism" would be treated. Hamdan, deemed by the President of the United States to be eligible for trial by military commission, was regarded as an "enemy combatant," *i.e.,* "part of or supporting Taliban or al Qaeda forces, or associated forces that are engaged in hostilities against the United States or its coalition partners."[53] Ultimately, Hamdan was charged with conspiracy "to commit . . . offenses triable by military commission" that spanned 1996 to November 2001.

Hamdan asserted that the military commission lacked authority to try him because: (1) neither congressional Act nor the common law of war supports trial by this commission for conspiracy, an offense that, Hamdan says, is not a violation of the law of war; and (2) the procedures adopted to try him violate basic tenets of military and international law, including but not limited to, the principle that a defendant must be permitted to see and hear the evidence against him. Attorneys for the Bush administration argued the contrary, asserting further that Hamdan and other Guantánamo detainees were not covered by the Geneva Conventions on treatment of prisoners of war.

The Supreme Court, in a 5–to–3 decision, agreed with Hamdan. Justice Stevens, writing for the majority, determined that the commission convened to try Hamdan lacks power to proceed because its structure and procedures violate both the Uniform Code of Military Justice and the Geneva Conventions:

> [t]he charge against Hamdan . . . alleges a conspiracy extending over a number of years, from 1996 to November 2001. All but two months of that more than 5–year-long period preceded the attacks of September 11, 2001, and the enactment of the AUMF—the Act of Congress on which the Government relies for exercise of its war powers and thus for its authority to convene military commissions. Neither the purported agreement with Osama bin Laden and others to commit war crimes, nor a single overt act, is alleged to have occurred in a theater of war or on any specified date after September 11, 2001. None of the overt acts that Hamdan is alleged to have committed violates the law of war. . . . The offense alleged must have been committed both in a theater of war

---

52. *Id.* at 568 (quoting Authorization for Use of Military Force, 115 Stat. 224, note following 50 U.S.C. § 1541 (2000 ed., Supp. III)).

53. *Id.* at 571 n.1.

and *during*, not before the relevant conflict . . . [t]he deficiencies in the time and place allegations also underscore—indeed are symptomatic of—the most serious defect of this charge: The offense it alleges is not triable by law-of-war military commission.

. . .

At a minimum, the Government must make a substantial showing that the crime for which it seeks to try a defendant by military commission is acknowledged to be an offense against the law of war. That burden is far from satisfied here. The crime of conspiracy has rarely if ever been tried as such in this country by any law-of-war military commission not exercising some other form of jurisdiction, and does not appear in either the Geneva Conventions or the Hague Conventions–the major treaties on the law of war.[54]

As a result of the Court's decision, lawyers for other Guantánamo detainees are considering whether to file habeas corpus petitions to challenge their detentions. These and other lawyers may also use *Hamdan* to challenge detentions at other locations worldwide that house "high value" U.S.-held detainees (including senior al Qaeda officials) in secret jails run by the U.S. Central Intelligence Agency.[55] As for the governmental response, President Bush could request specific, *Hamdan*-responsive legislation that would allow his administration to create a detainee-specific criminal justice system that would conform with the Court's ruling.[56]

---

54. *Id.* at 598–600, 603–04.

55. *See* Neil A. Lewis, "Detainees May Test Reach of Guantánamo Ruling," New York Times (July 1, 2006), located at http://www.nytimes.com/2006/07/01/us/01geneva.html?ex=1309406400&en=a18c62059cc35f1d&ei=5088&partner=rssnyt&emc=rss (last visited March 4, 2010).

56. *See* Linda Greenhouse, *Justices, 5–3, Broadly Reject Bush Plan to Try Detainees*, N.Y. TIMES, June 30, 2006, at A1, available at http://www.nytimes.com/2006/06/30/washington/30hamdan.html?r=1 (last visited March 4, 2010).

CHAPTER 7

SEARCHES AND SEIZURES: THE EXCLUSIONARY RULE

- LIMITATIONS AND EXCEPTIONS

- EVALUATING THE EXCLUSIONARY RULE

I. EXCLUSIONARY RULE BALANCING

The Court held in *Mapp v. Ohio* that evidence seized in violation of a person's Fourth Amendment rights cannot be used against that person in a criminal trial. The Court made clear that the exclusionary rule applies not only to the illegally obtained evidence itself, but also to other material derived from that evidence—in other words, to the fruit of the poisonous tree. In subsequent cases, the Court extended the exclusionary rule to require suppression of evidence obtained through violations of Fifth and Sixth Amendment rights as well.[1]

At the same time the Court began limiting the rule to situations in which its application would significantly further its purposes, although the Court has not always been consistent as to what those purposes are. The "significantly further" requirement stems from the balancing test that the Court employs to determine whether the rule should apply: weighing the constitutional interests at stake against the public's interest in effective law enforcement. Critics of this formula observe that the public's interest almost always appears to be the weightier and that constitutional rights will be increasingly compromised as a result.

As you read the materials below, keep this balancing formula in mind. Consider how the Court defines the constitutional interests at stake and how the balancing process affects those interests. Consider also the law enforcement interests that are affected by these decisions. Is it appropriate to consider these interests when adjudicating constitutional rights? If so, are they adequately described? Adequately protected? Are the rules fashioned by the Court likely to result in more effective law enforcement practices?

---

1. *See* Murphy v. Waterfront Comm'n, 378 U.S. 52 (1964) (applying exclusionary rule to Fifth Amendment violations) and United States v. Wade, 388 U.S. 218 (1967) (applying exclusionary rule to Sixth Amendment violations).

Checklist 9: Does the Exclusionary Rule Require Suppression?

1. Did the police violate a constitutional right?

    a. If yes, as a result, did they discover evidence that is offered in a criminal case, but not to impeach a testifying defendant?

    b. If yes, is the evidence the direct product of the constitutional violation or is it a fruit of the poisonous tree?

2. If the evidence is fruit of the poisonous tree, can the prosecution establish by a preponderance:

    a. That the evidence would have been discovered inevitably if the violation had not occurred? OR

    b. That the evidence was discovered from an independent source? OR

    c. That the taint of the constitutional violation was so attenuated when the evidence was discovered that suppression would not further the purposes of the exclusionary rule?

        (i) Was the causal connection between the constitutional violation so remote that the costs of exclusion are not worth its benefits? OR

        (ii) Will the specific interests protected by the particular constitutional guarantee violated (generally meaning the particular doctrinal rule crafted) be too little served to justify the costs of exclusion to the truth-finding process?

3. Regardless of whether the evidence is the direct product of the constitutional violation or a fruit of the poisonous tree, did the police act in objective good faith reliance on a facially valid warrant?

4. Will suppression of the evidence adequately redress the government's violation?

    a. If not, why not?

    b. If not, what alternatives to the exclusionary rule and/or suppression of the evidence may be available as a remedy?

II. LIMITATIONS ON EXCLUDING FRUITS OF THE POISONOUS TREE

The Supreme Court has limited the exclusionary rule in two ways. First, it has narrowed the reach of the fruit-of-the-poisonous-tree doctrine—the doctrine under which courts exclude evidence indirectly discovered by means of a constitutional violation. In this section we will elaborate on three limitations to the fruit-of-the-poisonous tree doctrine. Second, the Court has created several broad exceptions to the exclusionary rule itself. We will explain those exceptions in the next section.

A. INEVITABLE DISCOVERY

In *Nix v. Williams*,[2] the Court articulated the fruit-of-the-poisonous-tree limitation that is generally known as the "inevitable discovery" exception. In doing so, it also explained another limitation, the "independent source" exception. As you read *Nix*, make sure that you examine carefully the Court's explanation of the purposes of the exclusionary rule.

Nix v. Williams

467 U.S. 431 (1984).

■ BURGER, C.J. We granted certiorari to consider whether, at respondent Williams' second murder trial in state court, evidence pertaining to the discovery and condition of the victim's body was properly admitted on the ground that it would ultimately or inevitably have been discovered even if no violation of any constitutional or statutory provision had taken place.

I

A

On December 24, 1968, 10–year–old Pamela Powers disappeared from a YMCA building in Des Moines, Iowa, where she had accompanied her parents to watch an athletic contest. Shortly after she disappeared, Williams was seen leaving the YMCA carrying a large bundle wrapped in a blanket; a 14–year–old boy who had helped Williams open his car door reported that he had seen "two legs in it and they were skinny and white."

Williams' car was found the next day 160 miles east of Des Moines in Davenport, Iowa. Later several items of clothing belonging to the child, some of Williams' clothing, and an army blanket like the one used to wrap the bundle that Williams carried out of the YMCA were found at a rest stop on Interstate 80 near Grinnell, between Des Moines and Davenport. A warrant was issued for Williams' arrest.

Police surmised that Williams had left Pamela Powers or her body somewhere between Des Moines and the Grinnell rest stop where some of the young girl's clothing had been found. On December 26, the Iowa Bureau of Criminal Investigation initiated a large-scale search. Two hundred volunteers divided into teams began the search 21 miles east of Grinnell, covering an area several miles to the north and south of Interstate 80. They moved westward from Poweshiek County, in which Grinnell was located, into Jasper County. Searchers were instructed to check all roads, abandoned farm buildings, ditches, culverts, and any other place in which the body of a small child could be hidden.

Meanwhile, Williams surrendered to local police in Davenport, where he was promptly arraigned. Williams contacted a Des Moines attorney who arranged for an attorney in Davenport to meet Williams at the Davenport

---

2.   467 U.S. 431 (1984).

police station. Des Moines police informed counsel they would pick Williams up in Davenport and return him to Des Moines without questioning him. Two Des Moines detectives then drove to Davenport, took Williams into custody, and proceeded to drive him back to Des Moines.

During the return trip, one of the policemen, Detective Leaming, began a conversation with Williams, saying: "I want to give you something to think about while we're traveling down the road. . . . They are predicting several inches of snow for tonight, and I feel that you yourself are the only person that knows where this little girl's body is . . . and if you get a snow on top of it you yourself may be unable to find it. And since we will be going right past the area [where the body is] on the way into Des Moines, I feel that we could stop and locate the body, that the parents of this little girl should be entitled to a Christian burial for the little girl who was snatched away from them on Christmas [E]ve and murdered. . . . [A]fter a snow storm [we may not be] able to find it at all." Leaming told Williams he knew the body was in the area of Mitchellville—a town they would be passing on the way to Des Moines. He concluded the conversation by saying "I do not want you to answer me. . . . Just think about it. . . ."

Later, as the police car approached Grinnell, Williams asked Leaming whether the police had found the young girl's shoes. After Leaming replied that he was unsure, Williams directed the police to a point near a service station where he said he had left the shoes; they were not found. As they continued to drive to Des Moines, Williams asked whether the blanket had been found and then directed the officers to a rest area in Grinnell where he said he had disposed of the blanket; they did not find the blanket. At this point Leaming and his party were joined by the officers in charge of the search. As they approached Mitchellville, Williams, without any further conversation, agreed to direct the officers to the child's body.

The officers directing the search had called off the search at 3 p.m., when they left the Grinnell Police Department to join Leaming at the rest area. At that time, one search team near the Jasper County—Polk County line was only two and one-half miles from where Williams soon guided Leaming and his party to the body. The child's body was found next to a culvert in a ditch beside a gravel road in Polk County, about two miles south of Interstate 80, and essentially within the area to be searched.

B

First Trial

In February 1969 Williams was indicted for first-degree murder. Before trial in the Iowa court, his counsel moved to suppress evidence of the body and all related evidence including the condition of the body as shown by the autopsy. The ground for the motion was that such evidence was the "fruit" or product of Williams' statements made during the automobile ride from Davenport to Des Moines and prompted by Leaming's statements. The motion to suppress was denied.

The jury found Williams guilty of first-degree murder; the judgment of conviction was affirmed by the Iowa Supreme Court. Williams then sought release on habeas corpus in the United States District Court for the Southern District of Iowa. That court concluded that the evidence in question had been wrongly admitted at Williams' trial; a divided panel of the Court of Appeals for the Eighth Circuit agreed.

We granted certiorari, and a divided Court affirmed [in *Brewer v. Williams*], holding that Detective Leaming had obtained incriminating statements from Williams by what was viewed as interrogation in violation of his right to counsel. This Court's opinion noted, however, that although Williams' incriminating statements could not be introduced into evidence at a second trial, evidence of the body's location and condition "might well be admissible on the theory that the body would have been discovered in any event, even had incriminating statements not been elicited from Williams."

C

Second Trial

At Williams' second trial in 1977 in the Iowa court, the prosecution did not offer Williams' statements into evidence, nor did it seek to show that Williams had directed the police to the child's body. However, evidence of the condition of her body as it was found, articles and photographs of her clothing, and the results of post mortem medical and chemical tests on the body were admitted. The trial court concluded that the State had proved by a preponderance of the evidence that, if the search had not been suspended and Williams had not led the police to the victim, her body would have been discovered "within a short time" in essentially the same condition as it was actually found. The trial court also ruled that if the police had not located the body, "the search would clearly have been taken up again where it left off, given the extreme circumstances of this case and the body would [have] been found in short order."

In finding that the body would have been discovered in essentially the same condition as it was actually found, the court noted that freezing temperatures had prevailed and tissue deterioration would have been suspended. The challenged evidence was admitted and the jury again found Williams guilty of first-degree murder; he was sentenced to life in prison.

On appeal, the Supreme Court of Iowa again affirmed.

In 1980 Williams renewed his attack on the state-court conviction by seeking a writ of habeas corpus in the United States District Court for the Southern District of Iowa. The District Court conducted its own independent review of the evidence and concluded, as had the state courts, that the body would inevitably have been found by the searchers in essentially the same condition it was in when Williams led police to its discovery. The District Court denied Williams' petition.

... [After the Court of Appeals for the Eighth Circuit reversed the federal trial court,] we granted the State's petition for certiorari. ...

II

A

The Iowa Supreme Court correctly stated that the "vast majority" of all courts, both state and federal, recognize an inevitable discovery exception to the exclusionary rule. We are now urged to adopt and apply the so-called ultimate or inevitable discovery exception to the exclusionary rule.

Williams contends that evidence of the body's location and condition is "fruit of the poisonous tree," i.e., the "fruit" or product of Detective Leaming's plea to help the child's parents give her "a Christian burial," which this Court had already held equated to interrogation. He contends that admitting the challenged evidence violated the Sixth Amendment whether it would have been inevitably discovered or not. Williams also contends that, if the inevitable discovery doctrine is constitutionally permissible, it must include a threshold showing of police good faith.

B

... The core rationale consistently advanced by this Court for extending the exclusionary rule to evidence that is the fruit of unlawful police conduct has been that this admittedly drastic and socially costly course is needed to deter police from violations of constitutional and statutory protections. This Court has accepted the argument that the way to ensure such protections is to exclude evidence seized as a result of such violations notwithstanding the high social cost of letting persons obviously guilty go unpunished for their crimes. On this rationale, the prosecution is not to be put in a better position than it would have been in if no illegality had transpired.

By contrast, the derivative evidence analysis ensures that the prosecution is not put in a worse position simply because of some earlier police error or misconduct. The independent source doctrine allows admission of evidence that has been discovered by means wholly independent of any constitutional violation. That doctrine, although closely related to the inevitable discovery doctrine, does not apply here; Williams' statements to Leaming indeed led police to the child's body, but that is not the whole story. The independent source doctrine teaches us that the interest of society in deterring unlawful police conduct and the public interest in having juries receive all probative evidence of a crime are properly balanced by putting the police in the same, not a worse, position that they would have been in if no police error or misconduct had occurred. When the challenged evidence has an independent source, exclusion of such evidence would put the police in a worse position than they would have been in absent any error or violation. There is a functional similarity between these two doctrines in that exclusion of evidence that would inevitably have been discovered would also put the government in a worse position, because the police would have obtained that evidence if no misconduct had taken place. Thus, while the independent source exception would not justify admission of evidence in this case, its rationale is wholly consistent with and justifies our adoption of the ultimate or inevitable discovery exception to the exclusionary rule.

It is clear that the cases implementing the exclusionary rule begin with the premise that the challenged evidence is in some sense the product of illegal governmental activity. Of course, this does not end the inquiry. If the prosecution can establish by a preponderance of the evidence that the information ultimately or inevitably would have been discovered by lawful means—here the volunteers' search—then the deterrence rationale has so little basis that the evidence should be received. Anything less would reject logic, experience, and common sense.

The requirement that the prosecution must prove the absence of bad faith, imposed here by the Court of Appeals, would place courts in the position of withholding from juries relevant and undoubted truth that would have been available to police absent any unlawful police activity. Of course, that view would put the police in a worse position than they would have been in if no unlawful conduct had transpired. And, of equal importance, it wholly fails to take into account the enormous societal cost of excluding truth in the search for truth in the administration of justice. Nothing in this Court's prior holdings supports any such formalistic, pointless, and punitive approach.

More than a half century ago, Judge, later Justice, Cardozo made his seminal observation that under the exclusionary rule "[t]he criminal is to go free because the constable has blundered." *People v. Defore*, 150 N.E. 585 (1926). Prophetically, he went on to consider "how far-reaching in its effect upon society" the exclusionary rule would be when "[t]he pettiest peace officer would have it in his power through overzeal or indiscretion to confer immunity upon an offender for crimes the most flagitious." Some day, Cardozo speculated, some court might press the exclusionary rule to the outer limits of its logic—or beyond—and suppress evidence relating to the "body of a murdered" victim because of the means by which it was found.... But when, as here, the evidence in question would inevitably have been discovered without reference to the police error or misconduct, there is no nexus sufficient to provide a taint and the evidence is admissible.

C

The Court of Appeals did not find it necessary to consider whether the record fairly supported the finding that the volunteer search party would ultimately or inevitably have discovered the victim's body. However, three courts independently reviewing the evidence have found that the body of the child inevitably would have been found by the searchers. Williams challenges these findings, asserting that the record contains only the "post hoc rationalization" that the search efforts would have proceeded two and one-half miles into Polk County where Williams had led police to the body.

When that challenge was made at the suppression hearing preceding Williams' second trial, the prosecution offered the testimony of Agent Ruxlow of the Iowa Bureau of Criminal Investigation. Ruxlow had organized and directed some 200 volunteers who were searching for the child's body. The searchers were instructed "to check all the roads, the ditches, any culverts.... If they came upon any abandoned farm buildings, they were instructed to go onto the property and search those abandoned farm buildings or any other places where a small child could be secreted." Ruxlow testified that he marked off highway maps of Poweshiek and Jasper Counties in grid fashion, divided the volunteers into teams of four to six persons, and assigned each team to search specific grid areas. Ruxlow also testified that, if the search had not been suspended because of Williams' promised cooperation, it would have continued into Polk County, using the same grid system. Although he had previously marked off into grids only the highway maps of Poweshiek and Jasper Counties, Ruxlow had obtained a map of Polk County, which he said he would have marked off in the same manner had it been necessary for the search to continue.

The search had commenced at approximately 10 a.m. and moved westward through Poweshiek County into Jasper County. At approximately 3 p.m., after Williams had volunteered to cooperate with the police, Detective Leaming, who was in the police car with Williams, sent word to Ruxlow and the other Special Agent directing the search to meet him at the Grinnell truck stop and the search was suspended at that time. Ruxlow also stated that he was "under the impression that there was a possibility" that Williams would lead them to the child's body at that time. The search was not resumed once it was learned that Williams had led the police to the body, which was found two and one-half miles from where the search had stopped in what would have been the easternmost grid to be searched in Polk County. There was testimony that it would have taken an additional three to five hours to discover the body if the search had continued; the body was found near a culvert, one of the kinds of places the teams had been specifically directed to search.

On this record it is clear that the search parties were approaching the actual location of the body, and we are satisfied, along with three courts earlier, that the volunteer search teams would have resumed the search had Williams not earlier led the police to the body and the body inevitably would have been found....

The judgment of the Court of Appeals is reversed, and the case is remanded for further proceedings consistent with this opinion.

■ STEVENS, J. (concurring in the judgment). This litigation is exceptional for at least three reasons. The facts are unusually tragic; it involves an unusually clear violation of constitutional rights; and it graphically illustrates the societal costs that may be incurred when police officers decide to dispense with the requirements of law. Because the Court does not adequately discuss any of these aspects of the case, I am unable to join its opinion.

I

In holding that respondent's first conviction had been unconstitutionally obtained, Justice Stewart, writing for the Court, correctly observed:

"The pressures on state executive and judicial officers charged with the administration of the criminal law are great, especially when the crime is murder and the victim a small child. But it is precisely the predictability of those pressures that makes imperative a resolute loyalty to the guarantees that the Constitution extends to us all."

There can be no denying that the character of the crime may have an impact on the decisional process. As the Court was required to hold, however, that does not permit any court to condone a violation of constitutional rights. ... The rule of law that the Court adopts today has an integrity of its own and is not merely the product of the hydraulic pressures associated with hard cases or strong words. ...

III

The majority is correct to insist that any rule of exclusion not provide the authorities with an incentive to commit violations of the Constitution. If the inevitable discovery rule provided such an incentive by permitting the prosecution to avoid the uncertainties inherent in its search for evidence, it would undermine the constitutional guarantee itself, and therefore be inconsistent with the deterrent purposes of the exclusionary rule. But when the burden of proof on the inevitable discovery question is placed on the prosecution, it must bear the risk of error in the determination made necessary by its constitutional violation. The uncertainty as to whether the body would have been discovered can be resolved in its favor here only because, as the Court explains, petitioner adduced evidence demonstrating that at the time of the constitutional violation an investigation was already under way which, in the natural and probable course of events, would have soon discovered the body. This is not a case in which the prosecution can escape responsibility for a constitutional violation through speculation; to the extent uncertainty was created by the constitutional violation the prosecution was required to resolve that uncertainty through proof. Even if Detective Leaming acted in bad faith in the sense that he deliberately violated the Constitution in order to avoid the possibility that the body would not be discovered, the prosecution ultimately does not avoid that risk; its burden of proof forces it to assume the risk. The need to adduce proof sufficient to discharge its burden, and the difficulty in predicting whether such proof will be available or sufficient, means that the inevitable discovery rule does not permit state officials to avoid the uncertainty they would have faced but for the constitutional violation.

The majority refers to the "societal cost" of excluding probative evidence. In my view, the more relevant cost is that imposed on society by police officers who decide to take procedural shortcuts instead of complying with the law. What is the consequence of the shortcut that Detective Leaming took when he decided to question Williams in this case and not to wait an hour or so until he arrived in Des Moines? The answer is years and years of unnecessary but costly litigation. Instead of having a 1969 conviction affirmed in routine fashion, the case is still alive 15 years later. Thanks to Detective Leaming, the State of Iowa has expended vast sums of money and countless hours of professional labor in his defense. That expenditure surely provides an adequate deterrent to similar violations; the responsibility for that expenditure lies not with the Constitution, but rather with the constable.

––––––

NOTES AND QUESTIONS

The constitutional right at issue in *Nix* was the Sixth Amendment right to counsel, which protects different interests than the Fourth Amendment right against unreasonable searches and seizures. This text will address the Sixth Amendment in a later chapter. For now, focus on the rationales underlying the exclusionary rule and not the constitutional right that the rule is designed to protect.

According to Chief Justice Burger's majority opinion, what rationales require application of the exclusionary rule? Does Justice Stevens suggest a different view of the exclusionary rule? Reexamine the majority's opinion in *Mapp v. Ohio*, which is reproduced in Chapter 1. Are there rationales offered in that opinion for the exclusionary rule that do not appear in *Nix*? If so, do you think those other rationales would have made a difference to the Court's opinion in *Nix*? Should they have?

Notice from *Nix* that once again the Court is engaging in balancing. Chief Justice Burger states that "[t]he independent source doctrine teaches us that the interest of society in deterring unlawful police conduct and the public interest in having juries receive all probative evidence of a crime are properly balanced by putting the police in the same, not a worse, position than they would have been in if no police error or misconduct had occurred." Do you agree? Does the Court accurately articulate the interests on each side of the balance? Are you satisfied that the inevitable discovery doctrine "properly balances" those interests?

Justice Stevens addressed the issue of the incentives that these doctrines provide police officers. Is he correct in concluding that the rule announced in *Nix* will not lessen the deterrence value of the exclusionary rule? About the fact that a "good faith" rule is not necessary? What was the point of Justice Stevens' concurrence? Justice Stevens repeats Justice Stewart's words from the original opinion in *Brewer v. Williams*: "The pressures on state executive and judicial officers charged with the administration of the criminal law are great, especially when the crime is murder and the victim a small child. But it is precisely the predictability of those pressures that makes imperative a resolute loyalty to the guarantees that the Constitution extends to us all." Does the inevitable discovery rule pressure judges in hard cases to uphold the prosecution's showing? Is the fear of such pressure an appropriate factor to apply when balancing the interests described above?

B. INDEPENDENT SOURCE

Although Justice Stevens agreed in *Nix* that the inevitable discovery exception would not weaken the deterrent properties of the exclusionary rule, he has expressed a worry that the independent source exception poses a far greater risk of law enforcement disregard for constitutional rights. The Court has addressed the independent source exception in two more recent cases. The first was *Segura v. United States*.[3] In that case, federal agents unlawfully entered Segura's apartment and remained there until a search warrant was obtained. The search warrant itself was valid and "untainted" by the unlawful entry, that is, no information discovered during the unlawful search had been mentioned in the warrant affidavit. The admissibility of what the agents discovered while waiting in the apartment was not before the Court, but the Court held that the evidence found for the first time during the execution of the warrant was admissible because it was discovered pursuant to an "independent source" unconnected with the invalid entry.

Segura left unanswered the question of the admissibility of evidence the agents discovered before they obtained the search warrant. Four years later, in *Murray v. United States*,[4] the Court answered that question. The evidence would be admissible, the Court said, so long as the products of the illegal search were not used to obtain the warrant. The facts of *Murray* were as follows: informants advised federal agents that Murray and another individual, Carter, were trafficking in illegal drugs. On April 6, 1983, agents observed Murray and Carter each drive a vehicle into a warehouse in South Boston. Twenty minutes later, the two men drove the vehicles out of the warehouse, and when they did so, the agents were able to observe within the warehouse two other individuals and a tractor-trailer rig bearing a long, dark container. The vehicles driven by Murray and Carter were stopped and lawfully searched, and they were found to contain marijuana. After receiving this information, the agents forced their way into the warehouse, where they saw a number of marijuana bales. They left without disturbing the bales and kept the warehouse under surveillance until they reentered with a search warrant. In applying for the warrant, the agents did not mention their illegal entry into the warehouse[5] or the observations they had made during that entry. Only the informants' tips, the lawful pre-entry surveillance, and the results of the vehicle searches were used to support the warrant application. The agents later admitted, however, that they had not begun to prepare a warrant affidavit, or even engaged in any discussions of obtaining a warrant, until after their illegal entry into the warehouse.

---

3. 468 U.S. 796 (1984).

4. 487 U.S. 533 (1988).

5. It was assumed throughout appellate review in *Murray* that the initial warrantless entry was not justified by exigent circumstances and that the search therefore violated the Fourth Amendment.

In moving to suppress the evidence found in the warehouse, Murray and Carter contended that the independent source exception "applies only to evidence obtained for the first time during an independent lawful search." In response, the government argued that the exception "applies also to evidence initially discovered during, or as a consequence of, an unlawful search, but later obtained independently from activities untainted by the initial illegality." The Court agreed with the government, commenting that "[o]ur cases have used the concept of 'independent source' in a more general and a more specific sense. The more general sense identifies all evidence acquired in a fashion untainted by the illegal evidence-gathering activity. Thus, where an unlawful entry has given investigators knowledge of facts x and y, but fact z has been learned by other means, fact z can be said to be admissible because derived from an 'independent source.' This is how we used the term in *Segura v. United States*." The Court went on to observe that "[t]he original use of the term, however, and its more important use for purposes of these cases, was more specific. It was originally applied in the exclusionary rule context . . . with reference to that particular category of evidence acquired by an untainted search which is identical to the evidence unlawfully acquired—that is, in the example just given, to knowledge of facts x and y derived from an independent source."

The majority noted that this "specific" application of the independent source exception was consistent with *Nix*. According to the Court in *Murray*, the "inevitable discovery" doctrine applied in *Nix*:

> obviously assumes the validity of the independent source doctrine as applied to evidence initially acquired unlawfully. It would make no sense to admit the evidence because the independent search, had it not been aborted, would have found the body, but to exclude the evidence if the search had continued and had in fact found the body. The inevitable discovery doctrine, with its distinct requirements, is in reality an extrapolation from the independent source doctrine: Since the tainted evidence would be admissible if in fact discovered through an independent source, it should be admissible if it inevitably would have been discovered.

The Court was not troubled by Murray's argument that application of the independent source exception in these circumstances would give law enforcement officers an incentive to disregard Fourth Amendment rights. The Court stated:

> [a]n officer with probable cause sufficient to obtain a search warrant would be foolish to enter the premises first in an unlawful manner. By doing so, he would risk suppression of all evidence on the premises, both seen and unseen, since his action would add to the normal burden of convincing a magistrate that there is probable cause the much more onerous burden of convincing a trial court that no information gained from the illegal entry affected either the law enforcement officers' decision to seek a warrant or the magistrate's decision to grant it. Nor would the officer without sufficient probable cause to obtain a search

warrant have any added incentive to conduct an unlawful entry, since whatever he finds cannot be used to establish probable cause before a magistrate.

Justices Marshall, Stevens and O'Connor disagreed. Writing for the dissent, Justice Marshall argued:

[t]he incentives for . . . illegal conduct are clear. Obtaining a warrant is inconvenient and time consuming. Even when officers have probable cause to support a warrant application, therefore, they have an incentive first to determine whether it is worthwhile to obtain a warrant. Probable cause is much less than certainty, and many "confirmatory" searches will result in the discovery that no evidence is present, thus saving the police the time and trouble of getting a warrant. If contraband is discovered, however, the officers may later seek a warrant to shield the evidence from the taint of the illegal search. The police thus know in advance that they have little to lose and much to gain by forgoing the bother of obtaining a warrant and undertaking an illegal search.

Do you agree that the exclusionary rule limits developed in *Segura* and *Murray* provide police with incentives to disregard the constitution?

C.   ATTENUATION OF THE TAINT

Chief Justice Burger in *Nix* repeated a famous statement from *Wong Sun v. United States*: "We need not hold that all evidence is fruit of the poisonous tree simply because it would not have come to light but for the illegal actions of the police. Rather, the more apt question in such a case is whether, granting establishment of the primary illegality, the evidence to which instant objection is made has been come at by exploitation of that illegality or instead by means sufficiently distinguishable to be purged of the primary taint." This statement spawned a third exception to the fruit-of-the-poisonous-tree exclusionary rule—the "attenuation of the taint" doctrine.

In *Brown v. Illinois*, the Court applied the attenuation doctrine to a case involving violations of both the Fourth and Fifth Amendments. Pay close attention to Justice Blackmun's explanation of why the taint of the original Fourth Amendment violation was not "attenuated" by the giving of *Miranda* warnings. According to the Supreme Court in *Brown*, a piece of evidence that can be linked causally to the constitutional violation nevertheless may be admissible if that causal link is so "attenuated" that the deterrent purpose of the exclusionary rule would not be served by suppressing the evidence. The question of "attenuation" is one of degree, as Justice Powell pointed out in his concurrence in *Brown*. In their exhaustive treatise, Wayne LaFave and Jerold Israel acknowledge that there is no "litmus-paper test" for determining when the attenuation doctrine should apply.[6] They quote a law review article, however, that sets forth three criteria that should be considered:

---

6.   WAYNE R. LAFAVE AND JEROLD H. ISRAEL, CRIMINAL PROCEDURE 473 (2d ed. 1992). The quote is from Comment, 115 U.PA. L. REV. 1136, 1148–51 (1967).

(1) "Where the chain between the challenged evidence and the primary illegality is long or the linkage can be shown only by 'sophisticated argument,' exclusion would seem inappropriate. In such a case it is highly unlikely that the police officers foresaw the challenged evidence as a probable product of their illegality; thus it could not have been a motivating force behind it. It follows that the threat of exclusion could not possibly operate as a deterrent in that situation."

(2) The same may be said where evidence "is used for some relatively insignificant or highly unusual purpose. Under these circumstances it is not likely that, at the time the primary illegality was contemplated, the police foresaw or were motivated by the potential use of the evidence, and the threat of exclusion would, therefore, effect no deterrence."

(3) "Since the purpose of the exclusionary rule is to deter undesirable police conduct, where that conduct is particularly offensive the deterrence ought to be greater and, therefore, the scope of exclusion broader."

In *Brown*, Justice Blackmun analyzed a situation in which a Fourth Amendment violation was causally linked to a subsequent confession. According to Blackmun, in such a situation relevant factors in the attenuation analysis are "[1] the temporal proximity of the arrest and the confession, [2] the presence of intervening circumstances, and, ... [3] the purpose and flagrancy of the official misconduct." Are these factors the same or similar to the ones quoted above? What might be the significance of the fact that the evidence sought to be suppressed in *Brown* is a confession, rather than a physical item discovered as a result of a constitutional violation? How does that difference affect the attenuation analysis, which depends on an assessment of whether the deterrent purposes of the exclusionary rule will be served by suppression?

The Court recently applied the *Brown* factors to determine whether to suppress a confession resulting from an arrest of a juvenile without probable cause in *Kaupp v. Texas*.[7] The police brought the 19–year–old half brother of a 14–year–old missing girl in for questioning. They also brought Kaupp to the police station for the same purpose because he had been in the *half-brother's* company on the date of the disappearance. Kaupp was cooperative and permitted to leave, but the half-brother thrice failed a polygraph test, eventually admitting that he had stabbed his half sister and placed her body in a drainage ditch. The half-brother also implicated Kaupp in the crime.

Detectives immediately tried, but failed, to obtain a warrant to question Kaupp. Detective Pinkins, hoping to confront Kaupp with the half-brother's statement, and accompanied by two other plain clothes detectives and three uniformed officers, went to Kaupp's house and were admitted by his father a 3 a.m. on a January morning. Pinkins, with at least two other officers, awakened Kaupp in his bedroom by shining a flashlight, identified

---

7. 538 U.S. 626 (2003).

himself, and said, " '[W]e need to go and talk.' " Kaupp said " 'Okay,' " and two officers handcuffed him, leading him shoeless and still in boxer shorts and a T-shirt, to a police car. The car stopped for 5 or 10 minutes where the victim's body had been found, then continued on to the sheriff's headquarters. There, police placed Kaupp in an interview room, removed his handcuffs, and *Mirandized* him.

Although he initially denied any involvement in the crime, within 10 or 15 minutes of interrogation, and after being confronted with the half-brother's confession, Kaupp admitted having some part in the crime, without confessing to the murder itself or acknowledging causing the fatal wound. He was subsequently indicted and convicted of murder, having lost his motion to suppress his statements as fruits of an illegal arrest. Texas appellate courts affirmed the conviction, concluding that no arrest had yet taken place, thus no probable cause was required.

When the case reached the Supreme Court, the state conceded that the detectives lacked probable cause. But they argued that Kaupp voluntarily consented to accompany the officers to the station for questioning and that, therefore, no "arrest" had been made by the time of questioning. The Court rejected these claims without dissent. However, though expressing doubt that the state could succeed in avoiding suppression of Kaupp's confession, the Court remanded the case to the trial court to determine whether Kaupp's statements fit within *Brown's* attenuation exception to the exclusionary rule. The Court reasoned thus:

> Since Kaupp was arrested before he was questioned, and because the state does not even claim that the sheriff's department had probable cause to detain him at that point, well-established precedent requires suppression of the confession unless that confession was "an act of free will [sufficient] to purge the primary taint of the unlawful invasion." Demonstrating such purgation is, of course, a function of circumstantial evidence, with the burden of persuasion on the state. Relevant considerations include observation of *Miranda*, "[t]he temporal proximity of the arrest and the confession, the presence of intervening circumstances, and, particularly, the purpose and flagrancy of the official misconduct...."
>
> The record before us shows that only one of these considerations, the giving of *Miranda* warnings, supports the state, and we held in *Brown* that "*Miranda* warnings, *alone* and *per se*," cannot always ... break, for Fourth Amendment purposes, the casual connection between the illegality and the confession.... All other factors point the opposite way. There is no indication from the record that any substantial time passed between Kaupp's removal from his home in handcuffs and his confession after only 10 or 15 minutes of interrogation. In the interview, he remained in his partially clothed state in the physical custody of a number of officers, some of whom, at least, were conscious that they lacked probable cause to arrest. In fact, the state has not even alleged "any meaningful intervening event" between the illegal arrest and Kaupp's confession. Unless, on remand, the state can point to

testimony undisclosed on the record before us and weighty enough to carry the State's burden despite the clear force of the evidence shown here, the confession must be suppressed.[8]

Consent searches frequently raise attenuation issues. Although the Supreme Court has not been entirely clear on the relationship between a Fourth Amendment violation and a subsequent search pursuant to consent, some lower courts have held that an illegal search or seizure "invalidates consent unless the government bears its burden of showing that the taint of the illegal [activity] had dissipated before the consent was given."[9] The most frequent scenario is that of an allegedly illegal stop that precedes consent. The courts generally consider four factors in determining whether the taint of such a stop has sufficiently dissipated: "[1] whether a *Miranda* warning was given, [2] the temporal proximity of the stop and the consents, [3] the presence of intervening circumstances, and [4] the purpose and flagrancy of the illegal stop." Presumably similar factors would be used to analyze whether the taint of an unlawful search had dissipated before consent was given.

Nearly ten years after it issued its opinion in *Brown*, the Court was asked to deal with the Fifth Amendment question left undecided in *Brown*: where the original violation is a failure to render *Miranda* warnings, rather than a Fourth Amendment violation, does the later provision of *Miranda* warnings purge subsequent statements of the taint? The Court responded in the affirmative in *Oregon v. Elstad*. We reproduce that opinion later in this book. In the meantime, why do you suppose the result in that case was different than the result in *Brown*? Are the results reconcilable?

Recently, the Court gave a new spin to the attenuation doctrine as well as to the independent source doctrine in *Hudson v. Michigan*,[10] which addressed the propriety of suppression as a remedy for "knock-and-announce" violations. There, Detroit, Michigan police obtained and executed a search warrant for drugs and firearms in Hudson's home in violation of the Fourth Amendment's "knock-and-announce" rule (when they arrived to execute the warrant, they announced their presence and waited "three to five seconds" before turning the unlocked front door knob and entering Hudson's home). Hudson moved to suppress all inculpatory evidence seized, arguing that the "premature entry" violated his Fourth Amendment right against unreasonable search and seizure.

The Supreme Court determined that violation of the knock-and-announce rule does not require as a remedy suppression of the seized evidence. Even if there were a "but-for" connection between the violation and the discovery of the evidence, said the Court, attenuation occurs in two circumstances: first, when the causal connection is remote; second, when the *specific interests* protected by the particular constitutional guarantee

---

8. *Id.* at 633.

9. *See, e.g.,* United States v. Restrepo, 890 F.Supp. 180 (E.D.N.Y.1995), and cases cited therein.

10. 547 U.S. 586 (2006).

violated would not be served by suppression. (The Court argued that both sorts of attenuation were rooted in precedent, but this second sort had not been so clearly identified before as a distinct form of attenuation). Three specific interests were protected by the knock-and-announce rule, in the Court's view: (1) the protection of life and limb "because an unannounced entry may provoke violence in supposed self-defense by the surprised resident."; (2) the protection of property because individuals have the opportunity to comply with the law rather than suffer forcible damage to their dwelling; and (3) "those elements of privacy and dignity that can be destroyed by a sudden entrance," in short, "assur[ing] the opportunity to collect oneself before answering the door." Concluded the Court:

> What the knock-and-announce rule has never protected, however, is one's interest in preventing the government from seeing or taking evidence described in a warrant. Since the interests that *were* violated in this case have nothing to do with the seizure of the evidence, the exclusionary rule is inapplicable.[11]

The Court continued, however, declaring: "Quite apart from the requirements of unattenuated causation, the exclusionary rule has never been applied except 'where its deterrence benefits outweigh its substantial social costs.'" Accordingly, the remedy "has always been our last resort, not our first impulse." Concerning the knock-and-announce rule violation, the Court found the costs of suppression to be considerable:

> In addition to the grave adverse consequence that exclusion of relevant incriminating evidence always entails (viz., the risk of releasing dangerous criminals into society), imposing that massive remedy for a knock-and-announce violation would generate a constant flood of alleged failures to observe the rule, and claims that any asserted *Richards* justification for a no-knock entry.... The cost of entering this lottery would be small, but the jackpot enormous: suppression of all evidence, amounting in many cases to a get-out-of-jail-free card. Courts would experience as never before the reality that "[t]he exclusionary rule frequently requires extensive litigation to determine whether particular evidence must be excluded."[12]

The Court also found little benefit in deterrence, a "necessary ... [but not] sufficient condition" for applying the exclusionary rule. Ignoring the knock-and-announce requirement, said the Court, would achieve nothing but the destruction of property or physical injury when officers (having a warrant) are entitled to enter anyway. The officers thus already have a strong incentive to comply. Even were that not sufficient deterrence, said the Court, not all constitutional violations can or should be deterred by the exclusionary rule (e.g., suppression makes no sense where an already-confessed suspect has his sixth amendment rights violated by thereafter denying him prompt access to counsel). Importantly, the Court, using sweeping language not clearly limited to the case before it, emphasized that

---

11. *Id.* at 594.

12. *Id.* at 595.

legal and cultural changes may have obviated, or at least significantly minimized, the deterrent value of the exclusionary rule today relative to what it was a half-century ago:

> We cannot assume that exclusion in this context is necessary deterrence simply because we found that it was necessary in different contexts and long ago. That would be forcing the public today to pay for the sins and inadequacies of a legal regime that existed almost half a century ago. Dollree Mapp could not turn to 42 U.S.C § 1983 for meaningful relief; *Monroe v. Pape*, 365 U.S. 167 (1961), which began the slow but steady expansion of that remedy, was decided the same term as *Mapp*. It would be another 17 years before the § 1983 remedy was extended to reach the deep pockets of municipalities.... Citizens whose Fourth Amendment rights were violated by federal officers could not bring suit until 10 years after *Mapp*....
>
> Hudson complains that "it would be very hard to find a lawyer to take a case such as this," ... but 42 U.S.C. § 1988(b) answers this objection. Since some civil rights violations would yield damages too small to justify the expense of litigation, Congress has authorized attorney's fees for civil-rights plaintiffs. This remedy was unavailable in the heydays of our exclusionary-rule jurisprudence.... The number of public-interest law firms and lawyers who specialize in civil-rights grievances has [also] greatly expanded.[13]

Furthermore, said the Court, police professionalism has significantly increased over the last few decades, with a new emphasis on discipline, improved training, enhanced citizen review, and the possibility that failure to teach and enforce constitutional requirements can expose municipalities to civil liability. "[W]e now have increasing evidence," the Court insisted, "that police forces across the United States take the constitutional rights of citizens seriously." The Court was further unpersuaded that the few published decisions announcing huge damages awards for knock-and-announce violations suggested such suits were not succeeding, for "we do not know how many claims have been settled, or indeed how many violations have occurred that produced anything more than nominal injury." The cost-benefit analysis thus weighed squarely against suppression.

Although a majority of the Court supported the attenuation and cost-benefit analyses, only a plurality joined in the final part of the Court's opinion on the independent source doctrine (Justice Kennedy refused to join this portion). The plurality relied on *Segura*, where, you will recall, police had entered an apartment without a warrant or consent and remained there for 19 hours awaiting a search warrant. Once the warrant had been obtained, the police conducted the search. The Court refused to apply the exclusionary rule, holding that the valid search with a warrant constituted an "independent source" based on information mentioned in the warrant affidavit that was obtained prior to entering the apartment,

---

13. *Id.* at 597–98.

thus rendering the search "wholly unrelated" to the prior illegal entry. The Hudson plurality concluded that:

> [I]t would be bizarre to treat more harshly the actions in this case [than those in *Segura*], [for here] the only entry was *with* a warrant. If the probable cause backing a warrant that was issued *later in time* could be an "independent source" for a search that proceeded after the officers illegally entered and waited, a search warrant obtained *before* going in must have at least this much effect.[14]

The plurality also cited dicta in *United States v. Ramirez*, where the Court said, "[D]estruction of property in the course of a search may violate the Fourth Amendment, even though the entry itself is lawful and the fruits of the search are not subject to suppression." The *Ramirez* Court had not found entry by breaking a window illegal but said had it done so, it would have been necessary to determine whether there was a sufficient causal nexus between that breaking and the discovery of guns to warrant suppression. Concluded the *Hudson* plurality: "What clearer expression could there be of the proposition that an impermissible manner of entry does not necessarily trigger the exclusionary rule?"[15]

Justice Kennedy, though concurring in the attenuation and cost-benefit portions of the Court's opinion, was apparently sufficiently troubled by that opinion's tone to issue this caution:

> [T]he continued operation of the exclusionary rule, as settled and defined by our precedents, is not in doubt. Today's decision determines only that in the specific context of the knock-and-announce requirement, a violation is not sufficiently related to the later discovery of evidence to justify suppression.
>
> As to the basic right in question, privacy and security in the home are central to the Fourth Amendment's guarantees as explained in our decisions and as understood since the beginnings of the Republic. This common understanding ensures respect for the law and allegiance to our institutions, and it is an instrument for transmitting our Constitution to later generations undiminished in meaning and force. It bears repeating that it is a serious matter if law enforcement officers violate the sanctity of the home by ignoring the requisites of lawful entry. Security must not be subject to erosion by indifference or contempt.[16]

Kennedy also raised the tantalizing prospect that affirmative evidence offered of a "demonstrated [widespread] pattern of knock-and-announce violations" might be "grave cause for concern," "particularly if those violations were committed against persons who lacked the means or voice to mount an effective protest...." At the same time, he conceded that even were such evidence offered, to allow suppression to return as a remedy would require substantial revisions in the causation requirement "that

---

14. *Id.* at 600.

15. *Id.* at 602.

16. *Id.* at 603 (Kennedy, J., concurring).

limits our discretion in applying the exclusionary rule" and would raise difficult practical implications.

Dissenting Justices Breyer, Stevens, Souter, and Ginsburg characterized the majority's decision as "a significant departure from the Court's precedents." First, argued the dissent, the Court had misconceived the nature of the injury done, for more was at stake than physical injury to body or property or the chance to prepare oneself. In particular, the dissent cited with approval this language from the 120 year old case, *Boyd v. United States*, which declared that the Fourth Amendment's prohibitions apply:

> "to all invasions on the part of the government and its employees of the sanctity of a man's home and the privacies of his life. It is not the breaking of his doors, and the rummaging of his drawers, that constitutes the essence of the offence; but it is the invasion of his indefeasible right of personal security, personal liberty and private property."[17]

The costs of the exclusionary rule cited by the majority, said the dissent, are ones general to the rule itself and not specific to the knock-and-announce situation. In fact, the availability of "no-knock warrants" in many states can help to diminish those costs. Accordingly, "[t]he majority's 'substantial social costs' argument is an argument against the Fourth Amendment's exclusionary principle itself. And it is an argument that this Court, *until now*, has consistently rejected."[18]

The dissent rejected the majority's argument that there was no "but-for" causation, arguing that the majority wrongly separated the manner of entry from the fact of entry and misunderstood the independent source and inevitable discovery doctrines. Those doctrines, argued the dissent, do not address "what *hypothetically could* have happened had the police acted lawfully in the first place" but rather what occurred or would have occurred "*despite* (not simply *in the absence of*) that unlawful behavior." Complying with the knock-and-announce rule was a necessary condition of police entering the home, and entering the home was a necessary precondition to finding and seizing the evidence.

The dissent also rejected the majority's creating a "policy-related variant of the causal connection scheme" that constitutes an unwarranted departure from prior law, in part by its emphasis on the kind of harm caused by the specific Fourth Amendment violation. That there is a violation has always been enough to merit suppression absent well-recognized exceptions. The Court thus adds to the meaning of "attenuation" a new, second meaning in which "the interest protected by the constitutional guarantee that has been violated would not be served by suppression of the evidence obtained." The majority's focus on a narrow set of interests, concluded the dissent:

---

17. *Id*. at 606 (Breyer, J., dissenting).

18. *Id*. at 614.

does not fully describe the constitutional values, purposes, and objectives underlying the knock-and-announce requirement. That rule does help to protect homeowners from damaged doors; it does help to protect occupants from surprise. But it does more than that. It protects the occupants' privacy by assuring them that government agents will not enter their home without complying with those requirements (among others) that diminish the offensive nature of any such intrusion. Many years ago, Justice Frankfurter wrote for the Court that the "knock at the door, . . . as a prelude to a search, without authority of law . . . [i]s inconsistent with the conception of human rights enshrined in [our] history" and Constitution. . . . How much the more offensive when the search takes place without any knock at all.[19]

Additionally, the dissent worried that suppression was sorely needed to achieve deterrence. Unlike in other cases where the Court had not worried that an exception to the exclusionary rule would undermine deterrence because police could not in advance count on the assumption that the exception would be available, officers will now "almost always know that they can ignore the knock-and-announce requirement without risking the suppression of evidence discovered after their unlawful entry." Relatedly, the cases reporting violations are "legion," something that alone should be sufficient to meet Justice Kennedy's concern that a "widespread pattern" be shown. Moreover, Michigan's amici "concede that civil immunities prevent tort law from being an effective substitute for the exclusionary rule at this time," civil actions also being "expensive, time-consuming, not readily available, and rarely successful."

For the dissent, precedent supported only two well-recognized exceptions to the exclusionary rule, one where there was specific reason to believe the rule would not achieve appreciable deterrence, notably the good faith and impeachment exceptions as examples, a second where admissibility occurred in proceedings other than criminal trials. The second exception did not apply because this was a criminal case. The first exception did not apply both because there was a need for deterrence generally and because these officers had not acted in good faith because they did not act as a " 'reasonable officer would and should act in similar circumstances.' "

Furthermore, said the dissent, although there may be areas "where text or history or tradition leaves room for a judicial decision that rests upon little more than an unvarnished judicial instinct," "this is not one of them" because our "Fourth Amendment traditions place high value upon protecting privacy in the home" and assuring that constitutional protections are effective; absent good reason not to give practical reality to these protections via the exclusionary rule, violations must prod exclusion "lest the Amendment 'sound the promise to the ear but break it to the hope.' "[20]

---

19. *Id.* at 620.

20. *Id.* at 629–30.

NOTES AND QUESTIONS

1. We have devoted so much space to the *Hudson* case because of the arguable intimation that four Justices (a plurality consisting of Justices Scalia, Roberts, Thomas, and Alito) are ready to abandon the exclusionary rule entirely or to severely cut back its scope and bite. Certainly the dissenters expressed this worry, and even Justice Kennedy in concurrence seemed concerned that that may be where the plurality plans to go. Is this a fair reading of the plurality's views? Do you think that the Court's arguments support elimination of the exclusionary rule, or do the dissenters have the better argument?

2. There now seem to be two distinct attenuation doctrines. It is a bit unclear whether the Court's cost-benefit approach is part of its attenuation analysis or something separate. Would the logic of the harm-specific approach prevent suppression in other contexts, for example, if the police obtain a confession as the result of using excessive force to stop a fleeing suspect, should an argument that the confession was obtained in violation of the Fourth Amendment and therefore requires suppression be rejected? Has the *Brown* analysis for attenuation of confessions obtained via Fourth Amendment violations been altered by *Hudson*?

3. The majority and Justice Kennedy in concurrence seem to demand that the defense produce evidence of a widespread problem before suppression should be allowed, the majority speculating that there may be many successful civil suits without evidence of such success. Are they right to put the burden of proof of this question on the defense?

4. The dissent seems to see the real injury as one to intangible interests in privacy, security, and liberty. The majority focuses more on physical harm to persons or property or narrow privacy harms from psychologically preparing oneself for an invasion of one's home. Which view makes more sense in a criminal case aimed at vindicating injuries to the public versus a civil case aimed at making injured individuals whole? Is your answer affected by the Fourth Amendment's text purporting to vest rights in "the People"?

5. The Court argues that police professionalism has improved, reducing the need for the exclusionary rule. Is it plausible, however, that the exclusionary rule may account for such increased professionalism and that the absence of the rule might encourage backsliding? Or are there cultural and political forces that would prevent backsliding even without a rule?

6. Are civil and regulatory actions likely to be effective deterrents in the absence of the exclusionary rule? Generally? In the context of the knock-and-announce requirement?

7. What different methods of constitutional interpretation did each opinion use and what different data sources did it rely upon? What respective roles did history play versus concern about future real-world effects?

8. Justice Kennedy thought evidence of widespread injury to those without voice or unable effectively to protest might require a rethinking of the

Court's exclusionary rule jurisprudence. Such an approach seems to invite an exploration by the Court of the political forces involved to see who has and who lacks political power effectively to protest against police abuses. Is this concern with the impact of search and seizure practices on the politically powerless an appropriate one for Fourth Amendment analysis, or is it more properly limited to places where it has traditionally had more pride of place, such as under the Fourteenth Amendment? Is such a sharp separation between the two amendments viable?

9. Is the dissent right that the plurality has altered the independent source and inevitable discovery doctrines by imagining what the police might do or might have done rather than looking to what they have in fact done? If yes, might that expand those doctrines so much that they swallow much of what remains of the exclusionary rule? Could this be why Justice Kennedy hesitated to join the independent source/inevitable discovery portion of the Court's opinion?

Fruit-of-the-Poisonous–Tree Problems

PROBLEM 7–1

One evening police in St. Paul, Minnesota, received a report of a "big yellow car" with three "unkempt teenagers" in it, "prowling" in a shopping center that was near a bank. The following day, a "dirty" young male robbed the bank using a gun. The robber reportedly escaped in a "white-and-yellow Oldsmobile" driven by another person. Shortly after the robbery, the police received a report of two "disheveled and suspicious-looking" males in jeans getting out of a "light-colored Olds" a short distance from the bank.

A police dog tracking scent from the bank led Officer Marris and his partner to an apartment complex with nine apartment buildings that share one parking lot. At least three people from the apartment complex stated that a white-and-yellow Oldsmobile had been seen in the area of the parking lot outside one particular apartment building. The caretaker for the apartment complex then told Marris that the apartment in question was a "problem" apartment. Moments later, outside that apartment building, the officers stopped a white-and-yellow Oldsmobile driven by a juvenile male. Two other juvenile males and a woman were passengers. The officers questioned the foursome, obtained their names, and learned that one of the young men, Carl Nickerson, had been staying in the "problem" apartment "for a couple of days" as a guest. After receiving evasive answers to questions regarding lack of personal identification and ownership documents for the car and after finding a substantial amount of cash in Nickerson's pocket, the police detained the four people until witnesses from the bank could arrive.

Within approximately fifteen minutes (about two hours after the robbery), four witnesses from the bank arrived and identified Nickerson as the robber. The police then arrested Nickerson and the other two young men and searched the car. In the back, between the seat and the backrest, they found a set of keys. Officer Marris went to the apartment identified by the caretaker as the "problem" apartment and tried the keys in that apartment door. One of the keys unlocked the door, and the officer entered the apartment. While checking to see if anyone was in the apartment, he saw an envelope addressed to the woman who had been in the car. Marris went back to the squad car and asked the woman to accompany him to the apartment. There, she gave him consent to search the premises. Rather than search, however, Marris left the apartment and prepared a search warrant application. In the application, he referred to the envelope he had seen in the woman's apartment, citing the connection between the apartment, the woman, and the presence in the same car of Nickerson—who had been positively identified by witnesses as one of the bank robbers. Marris obtained a search warrant for the apartment, and during his execution of the warrant he found a gun and $20,000 in cash.

After he was charged with bank robbery, Nickerson moved to suppress the gun and cash found in the apartment. Nickerson argues that it was unlawful under the Fourth Amendment for the police (1) to try in the apartment door the keys found in a search of the car in which Nickerson was riding and (2) to enter the apartment upon finding that one of the keys unlocked the apartment door. Nickerson also contends that the search warrant was invalid because it was based in part on what Officer Marris observed (primarily the envelope) during the allegedly illegal entry into the apartment. Finally, Nickerson argues that the woman's consent was invalid because it too was a product of the initial illegality.

Question: Should Nickerson's motion be granted? Why or why not?

PROBLEM 7–2

On December 10th, the managers of Woodward Apartments in Lundwick, North Carolina, notified their tenants in writing that an exterminating company would begin spraying apartments on December 15th. Apartment B–2 of Woodward Apartments was leased to Tiffany Darstraum. On December 15th, while working in Darstraum's apartment, the exterminator discovered a locked closet in an upstairs bedroom. Brent Andrews and Carol Kencik, the apartment managers, unlocked the closet to allow extermination of the area inside. After gaining entry to the locked closet, Andrews, Kencik, and the exterminator observed artificial light devices, plant food, plant tools, and approximately thirty plants in individual planters which they recognized to be marijuana. The Woodward managers immediately contacted police about their discovery.

In response to the call, the Lundwick Police Department dispatched Patrolman Clay Polgers to the scene. Patrolman Polgers, accompanied by Andrews and Kencik, entered Darstraum's apartment and observed the marijuana plants inside the closet. Afterwards, Patrolman Polgers removed everyone from the apartment and called detectives in the vice-narcotics unit. When the detectives arrived, Patrolman Polgers was standing at the front door. Also present were Andrews, Kencik, and the exterminator.

After interviewing Andrews, Kencik, the exterminator, and Patrolman Polgers, the detectives presented the magistrate with an affidavit in support of their request for a search warrant. The affidavit related that Andrews, Kencik, and the exterminator had observed approximately thirty marijuana plants, plant food, artificial lights, and plant tools inside the locked closet. The affidavit also included Patrolman Polgers' corroborative observations of the marijuana plants. After obtaining the warrant, the detectives conducted a search of Darstraum's apartment and seized marijuana plants and paraphernalia.

Darstraum was charged with drug offenses and moved to suppress all evidence seized as a result of the search. The judge held a hearing on the motion, and at the hearing, one of the detectives testified that she would have attempted to obtain a warrant based solely on her conversation with the apartment managers and the exterminator.

Question: How should the judge rule on Darstraum's suppression motion?

PROBLEM 7–3

Review the prosecution memorandum in the Boson case in Chapter 1. Assume that at the time Officer Glemp stopped Boson's car, there was a warrant out for Boson's arrest on suspicion of murder. Boson is charged with drug offenses and makes a motion to suppress the cocaine found in his trunk.

Question: What arguments might the prosecution make in response? How should the court rule?

III. EXCEPTIONS TO THE EXCLUSIONARY RULE

A. THE GOOD FAITH EXCEPTION

Checklist 10: Does the Good Faith Exception Apply?

1. Did the police rely on an invalid warrant to conduct a search or seizure?

2. If yes, can the prosecution establish that there was no culpability on the part of the individual officers involved—i.e., that they did not know that the warrant was invalid and were not aware of facts that would have made them reckless or negligent with respect to the warrant's invalidity?

3. If yes, can the prosecution establish that a "reasonably well trained officer" would have believed the warrant to be valid?

    a. Was the warrant not based on an affidavit "so lacking in indicia of probable cause as to render official belief in its existence entirely unreasonable"?

    b. Was the warrant not so facially deficient that a reasonable officer would recognize its invalidity?

4. If yes, can the defendant establish that the warrant was issued on the basis of an affidavit containing false statements, or statements made in reckless disregard for the truth, or that the warrant was issued by a magistrate who was not "neutral and detached"?

5. If yes, was either systemic negligence involved or, if not, did individual officers act deliberately, recklessly or with gross negligence in violating the Constitution? (This last question clearly arises where an officer believes that a current warrant exists when it does not and has the potential to extend to searches where police know that they proceed without a warrant, though the Court has never yet so held.)

———

One of the most significant and active areas of exclusionary rule jurisprudence is known as the "good faith exception." The Court initiated this exception in the companion cases of *United States v. Leon*, 468 U.S. 897 (1984), and *Massachusetts v. Sheppard*, 468 U.S. 981 (1984), and its work in the area continues to the present, with its recent issuance of *Herring v. United States*, 129 S.Ct. 695 (2009). Below we will discuss these cases, and several important decisions handed down between them. As you read these materials, pay attention to the debate about the appropriate balance between furthering the exclusionary rule's purposes and safeguarding the public's interest in law enforcement.

In *Leon* and *Sheppard*, the Court upheld the admission of evidence that had been derived from illegal police activity. Key to the Court's judgments was the fact that in both cases the police were not culpable in any sense; that is, they had not caused the illegality and had acted reasonably ("in good faith") in relying on what appeared to be valid warrants.

Leon involved a residential search warrant, the execution of which resulted in evidence of drug trafficking. After Leon and others were charged with federal crimes on the basis of that evidence, they filed motions to suppress it, claiming that the evidence was the product of an illegal search. According to the defendants, the search warrant was invalid because it was based on stale and insufficient information. The federal trial court agreed, finding that the affidavit was insufficient to establish probable cause. Moreover, responding to a request from the government, the court found that the officer who executed the warrant had done so "in good faith." After the Court of Appeals for the Ninth Circuit affirmed, the Supreme Court accepted the government's petition for writ of certiorari and reversed the suppression.

The majority framed the question as whether "the exclusionary rule can be modified somewhat without jeopardizing its ability to perform its intended functions," and it answered that question in the affirmative for a category of situations (which we will examine below) exemplified by the facts before it. Its method of analysis involved "weighing the costs and benefits of preventing the use in the prosecution's case in chief of inherently trustworthy tangible evidence obtained in reliance on a search warrant issued by a detached and neutral magistrate that ultimately is found to be defective." The majority stated that it did not question that the balance required exclusion where the Fourth Amendment violation was "substantial and deliberate." But it concluded that the balance came out differently where evidence was obtained "in the reasonable good-faith belief that a search or seizure was in accord with the Fourth Amendment."

Two matters from the majority opinion are critical to a thorough understanding of the case: its analysis of the exclusionary rule's deterrent effects; and its definition of "good faith."

1. *Analysis of deterrent effects.* The majority believed no deterrent benefits could be achieved by applying the exclusionary rule in a "good faith reliance" situation. It began by explaining that the exclusionary rule is sensibly applied where courts "hope to instill in [police officers], or in their future counterparts, a greater degree of care toward the rights of an accused," and it noted that where police have been "willful, or at the very least negligent," they can strive for better behavior in the future. But if police officers acted "in complete good faith," there is nothing to deter because they already were exercising an appropriate degree of care. The Court also analyzed the exclusionary rule's deterrent potential on another important set of actors—the judiciary, which had issued the invalid warrant on which police had relied. The majority stated that the threat of exclusion cannot be expected to deter judges and magistrates from wrongdoing, because they are not "adjuncts to the law enforcement team . . . and have no stake in the outcome of particular criminal prosecutions."

2. *Definition of "good faith."* The majority's opinion in *Leon* created a category of cases in which the exclusionary rule would not apply. That category is exemplified by situations in which an objectively reasonable officer would have believed the warrant to be valid. Trial courts are to determine objective reasonableness on a case-by-case basis by (i) considering all of the facts and circumstances known to the individual officers involved in the case, and then (ii) asking whether a reasonable officer, who possesses these facts and "reasonable knowledge of what the law provides," would have relied on the warrant. The Court identified three situations where objective reasonableness should not be found: where a judge or magistrate wholly abandons his or her role as a neutral and detached actor, where the warrant application is completely lacking in indicia of probable cause, and where the warrant is facially deficient in failing to particularize the place to be search or the things seized.

In addition, the situation must not involve a warrant application containing statements known by the officer to be false or misleading, or about which the officer recklessly disregarded the truth.

The same day that it decided *Leon*, the Court issued a second opinion applying the newly minted good faith exception. In *Massachusetts v. Shep-*

pard[21] police officers applied for a warrant to search Sheppard's residence for evidence of his involvement in a murder. The officers' affidavit established probable cause, but they used a preprinted warrant form referring to "controlled substances" as the items to be seized. When they alerted the issuing judge to the preprinted form, he told them that he would make the necessary changes. He did make some changes, but not in the substantive portion of the warrant, which continued to authorize only a search for controlled substances (the warrant failed to state that it incorporated the items listed in the affidavit). After the officers searched the residence and seized the items listed in the affidavit, Sheppard moved to suppress the resulting evidence, claiming that the warrant did not particularly describe the items to be seized. A majority of the Supreme Court upheld the grounds.

In *Groh v. Ramirez*,[22] a majority of the Court held that an officer's execution of a warrant that failed to list the particulars of what was to be searched for and seized, and failed to incorporate by reference its supporting application, would not satisfy the good faith exception. Writing for the Court, Justice Stevens began by pointing out that, in contrast to the situation in *Sheppard*, here the officer himself had prepared the warrant and knew that it was defective when he submitted it to the magistrate:

> In *Massachusetts v. Sheppard*, we suggested that "the judge, not the police officers," may have committed "[a]n error of constitutional dimension," because the judge had assured the officers requesting the warrant that he would take the steps necessary to conform the warrant to constitutional requirements. Thus, "it was not unreasonable for the police in [that] case to rely on the judge's assurances that the warrant authorized the search they had requested." In this case, by contrast, petitioner did not alert the Magistrate to the defect in the warrant that petitioner had drafted. . . .

Stevens went on to observe, citing *Leon*, "Nor would it have been reasonable for petitioner to rely on a warrant that was so patently defective, even if the Magistrate was aware of the deficiency." He explained:

> Given that the particularity requirement is set forth in the text of the Constitution, no reasonable officer could believe that a warrant that plainly did not comply with that requirement was valid. Moreover, because petitioner himself prepared the invalid warrant, he may not argue that he reasonably relied on the Magistrate's assurance that the warrant contained an adequate description of the things to be seized and was therefore valid. In fact, the guidelines of petitioner's own department placed him on notice that he might be liable for executing a manifestly invalid warrant. An ATF directive in force at the time of this search warned: "Special agents are liable if they exceed their

---

21.   468 U.S. 981 (1984).

22.   540 U.S. 551 (2004). The pertinent issue in *Groh* was whether, in a lawsuit under 42 U.S.C. § 1983, the officer was entitled to qualified immunity when he conducted an illegal search, but that analysis is identical to the *Leon* good faith analysis. *Id.*

authority while executing a search warrant and must be sure that a search warrant is sufficient on its face even when issued by a magistrate." Searches and Examinations, ATF Order O 3220.1(7)(d) (Feb. 13, 1997). *See also id.*, at 3220.1(23)(b) ("If any error or deficiency is discovered and there is a reasonable probability that it will invalidate the warrant, such warrant shall not be executed. The search shall be postponed until a satisfactory warrant has been obtained"). And even a cursory reading of the warrant in this case—perhaps just a simple glance—would have revealed a glaring deficiency that any reasonable police officer would have known was constitutionally fatal.

No reasonable officer could claim to be unaware of the basic rule, well established by our cases, that, absent consent or exigency, a warrantless search of the home is presumptively unconstitutional. Indeed, as we noted nearly 20 years ago in *Sheppard*: "The uniformly applied rule is that a search conducted pursuant to a warrant that fails to conform to the particularity requirement of the Fourth Amendment is unconstitutional." Because not a word in any of our cases would suggest to a reasonable officer that this case fits within any exception to that fundamental tenet, petitioner is asking us, in effect, to craft a new exception. Absent any support for such an exception in our cases, he cannot reasonably have relied on an expectation that we would do so.

Petitioner contends that the search in this case was the product, at worst, of a lack of due care, and that our case law requires more than negligent behavior before depriving an official of qualified immunity. But as we observed in [*Leon*,] the companion case to *Sheppard*, "a warrant may be so facially deficient—i.e., in failing to particularize the place to be searched or the things to be seized—that the executing officers cannot reasonably presume it to be valid." This is such a case.

Justice Kennedy disagreed with the majority's application of the *Leon* test. Kennedy believed the officer's reliance on the warrant to be reasonable:

> . . . [It] is obvious from the record below that the officer simply made a clerical error when he filled out the proposed warrant and offered it to the Magistrate Judge. The officer used the proper description of the property to be seized when he completed the affidavit. He also used the proper description in the accompanying application. When he typed up the description a third time for the proposed warrant, however, the officer accidentally entered a description of the place to be searched in the part of the warrant form that called for a description of the property to be seized. No one noticed the error before the search was executed. Although the record is not entirely clear on this point, the mistake apparently remained undiscovered until the day after the search when respondents' attorney reviewed the warrant for defects. The officer, being unaware of his mistake, did not rely on it in any way. It is uncontested that the officer trained the search team and executed the warrant based on his mistaken belief

that the warrant contained the proper description of the items to be seized.

The question is whether the officer's mistaken belief that the warrant contained the proper language was a reasonable belief. In my view, it was. . . . .

In *Arizona v. Evans*,[23] the Court reversed the suppression of evidence that had been seized pursuant to a previously quashed warrant. In that case, after a trial judge had invalidated a warrant for Evans' arrest, a court clerk neglected to inform the sheriff's office to remove the warrant from its computer. When Evans subsequently was stopped for a traffic violation, a police officer ran a computer inquiry, which erroneously indicated that the arrest warrant was still valid. While arresting Evans pursuant to that warrant, the officer discovered a small quantity of marijuana, for which Evans was prosecuted. Evans moved to suppress the marijuana, and the Arizona Supreme Court held that it should have been suppressed because the good faith exception did not apply.

The United States Supreme Court held that the evidence need not be suppressed, because the officer had executed the arrest warrant in good faith reliance on the apparently valid warrant. The Court relied in part on the fact that the error in failing to remove the warrant from the computer had been that of the court clerk, and not that of the police department. The Court expressly declined to decide whether a similar error made by the police department would negate the good faith exception.

Comment on State Constitutions: The good faith exception has not been endorsed unanimously in the state courts. For example, if a criminal defendant in an Oregon proceeding moves to suppress evidence based on a violation of the Oregon constitution, the good faith exception probably does not apply.[24] Similarly, the states of Connecticut, Michigan, New Jersey, New York, North Carolina, Pennsylvania, and Vermont have refused to recognize a good faith exception to the exclusionary rule.[25]

A Note on Burdens of Proof: Prior to *Leon*, the Court had held in *Franks v. Delaware* that warrant affidavits are presumed valid and that the burden of invalidating a warrant based on the affiant's lies or reckless disregard for the truth was on the defense. Yet such lies or disregard for the truth are listed in *Leon* as instances in which objectively reasonable good faith is lacking. And *Leon* suggests that the burden of showing good faith is on the prosecution. Therefore, the Court seems to have created a

---

23. 514 U.S. 1 (1995).

24. *See* State v. Buffington, 743 P.2d 738, 745 (Or.App.1987) (Van Hoomissen, dissenting).

25. *See, e.g.*, State v. Marsala, 579 A.2d 58 (Conn.1990) (pointing out that Michigan, New Jersey, New York, and North Carolina had already rejected the good faith exception; and acknowledging that California, Florida, Indiana, Kansas, Louisiana, Missouri, and Ohio had adopted the good faith exception for their state constitutions); State v. Novembrino, 519 A.2d 820 (N.J.1987); Commonwealth v. Edmunds, 586 A.2d 887 (Pa.1991); State v. Oakes, 598 A.2d 119 (Vt.1991).

contradiction regarding burdens of proof in this area. Can you resolve this contradiction?

Question: Decide whether the good faith exception applies to the following facts:

On November 17, 2003, the city clerk's office issued an arrest warrant for Bennie for failure to appear in court. Per usual arrest warrant procedure, the city clerk's office forwarded the arrest warrant to the county sheriff's department for execution. County sheriff's department staffers logged the warrant information into the office computer. Bennie's home bordered the boundary of three counties; accordingly, the county sheriff's department enlisted the help of the other two neighboring departments in serving the arrest warrant.

On February 2, 2004, the city clerk's office recalled the arrest warrant, which had been erroneously initiated and entered. The county sheriff's department physically removed the warrant from the department's files and returned the warrant to the city clerk's office. Accordingly, as of February 2, 2004, there was no longer an outstanding warrant for Bennie's arrest.

Unfortunately, due to a breakdown that occurred someplace within the county sheriff's department, the department failed to update its computerized records when it acted on the city clerk's office recall order. As a result of this failure, the computer database that the county sheriff's department used for its active warrants did not reflect the city clerk's office recall. Instead, the computer database continued to indicate incorrectly that Bennie had an outstanding arrest warrant.

On July 7, 2004, Bennie visited a county impound office to reclaim her recently impounded car. Officer Sponsler recognized Bennie and decided to run a records check on her. Sponsler learned that Bennie had an outstanding warrant for her arrest; he asked that it be faxed to him; however, it could not be located. After a couple of phone calls between offices, the city clerk's office informed Sponsler that the warrant had been recalled. Meanwhile, Sponsler's partner, Officer Royster, followed Bennie, who had driven away. Royster affected a traffic stop and informed Bennie she was under arrest, based on a county warrant for her arrest. Bennie protested, was arrested immediately, and patted down. Royster found a small bag in her pocket that contained powder residue which tested positive for methamphetamine. Royster's search incident to arrest also uncovered an illegal handgun. Should the evidence of Bennie's criminality be suppressed, given the government's recordkeeping errors?

––––––

The Court decided a case on nearly identical facts in its most recent salvo on the good faith exclusionary rule debate. That decision was handed down in *Herring v. United States*,[26] where a five-justice majority held the

––––––

26.   129 S.Ct. 695 (2009).

exclusionary rule inapplicable in a situation in which police had not acted "culpably" despite the fact that they had arrested Herring on the basis of a law enforcement error. According to the majority, something more than simple negligence is needed before evidence can be excluded on the ground of a police error. Instead, police must act with at least gross negligence, or as a result of the "systemic negligence" of their departments. This seems to be a new standard, and it arguably imposes a significantly higher burden on defendants (assuming it is they, and not the prosecution, who will bear the burden of proof–a matter that is still unclear but that may follow from *Herring*'s logic). Now, in order to gain the application of the exclusionary rule, the burden-holder must probably satisfy a two-part test, proving, first, that the individual police officers' error rose beyond simple negligence, or that the department or perhaps a relevant sub-unit of it, engaged in "systemic negligence"; and second, that, even if the first prong were met, excluding evidence would contribute to deterrence significantly enough to justify the social costs of exclusion.

A review of *Herring's* facts demonstrates the difficulty facing defendants. In that case, a county sheriff's employee had failed to update the sheriff's database to reflect the recall of a warrant for Herring's arrest. A police officer in a neighboring county relied on that database five months later to arrest Herring and, in the accompanying search incident to arrest, found drugs that were used to prosecute him. The Court observed that the employee's error was a matter of "isolated negligence attenuated from the arrest," and it held that the exclusionary rule did not apply, explaining that the rule "serves to deter deliberate, reckless, or grossly negligent conduct, or in some circumstances recurring or systemic negligence," and that the error in *Herring* did not "rise to that level."[27]

Aside from the additional burden it may impose on defendants, *Herring* has several interesting features. First, its emphasis on culpability seems to invite at least sometimes an analysis of subjective officer mental states. Although "gross negligence," an objective mental state, may suffice, the Court also specifically stated that deliberate or reckless conduct, two at least partially subjective mental states, may suffice as well. In the past, the Court has purportedly favored almost entirely objective standards for good faith, seeking to avoid serious scrutiny of the mental states of individual government actors.

Second, the mention of "systemic negligence" undoubtedly will produce defense efforts to inquire into departmental practices. Courts will have to develop standards for discovery, perhaps requiring defendants to produce a "showing" of systemic negligence before enabling them to get discovery from police departments. If courts do not do so, or if the Supreme Court ultimately concludes that they lack authority to do so, then it will be extraordinarily difficult to avoid the application of the exclusionary rule on the grounds that systemic negligence showed the absence of good faith. Likewise, "gross negligence" and subjective mental states on the part of

---

27. *Id.* at 702.

individual officers are much harder to prove than simple negligence, so, absent statutory, rule-based, or constitutionally-based arguments resulting in expanded discovery procedures, it will also be very difficult to prove that individual officers failed to act in good faith.

Third, *Herring's* apparent logic was that the exclusionary rule should apply only if there is police culpability to punish *and* if exclusion's deterrent value is worth its cost (the Court uses inconsistent language, some suggesting that "culpability" is just another word for "deterrable," or perhaps simply one factor relevant to the likely presence of effective deterrence,[28] other language expressly stating conjunctively that both culpability *and* deterrence justifying exclusion are required;[29] the authors of this casebook read the tenor of the opinion as a whole as more consistent with these latter, conjunctive statements.). To date, the good faith exception has been applied only to searches based on statutes specifically authorizing a warrantless search or on actual or apparent warrants doing so (e.g., the officer in *Herring* believed, but *incorrectly,* that a valid warrant existed that authorized the arrest). But if the Court is convinced that only culpable police conduct that is sufficiently "deterrable" by exclusion should be subject to the exclusionary rule, then it is hard to see why the good faith exception should be so limited. If the exception is indeed one day extended to warrantless searches and seizures, then the "exception" will likely become the rule, that is, few Fourth Amendment violations will be in "bad faith," so exclusion will in practice become a rarity, whatever may be said about it on paper.

Indeed, the Court cited as a critical analogy *Franks v. Delaware,*[30] which held that *the defense* has the burden of proving that the affiant lied or acted in reckless disregard of the truth in obtaining a warrant if a search or seizure resulting from the warrant is to be suppressed. Moreover, elsewhere this most recent term, the Court has emphasized that inadmissibility pursuant to the Fourth Amendment exclusionary rule is "not ... automatic."[31] We have said earlier in this text that the burden of proof that an exception to the exclusionary rule applies is usually on the prosecution,[32] but the tenor of the Court's opinions increasingly criticizing or limiting the exclusionary rule might (or might not) signal that the Court is prepared to put the burden of proving the *in*applicability of at least the good faith exception on the defense. If that comes to pass, the rarity of the exclusionary rule's application is even more likely to become a reality, especially if the good faith exception is indeed extended to warrantless searches (some

---

28. *See id.* at 701 ("The extent to which the exclusionary rule is justified by these deterrence principles varies with the culpability of the law enforcement conduct.").

29. *See id.* at 702 ("To trigger the exclusionary rule, police conduct must be sufficiently deliberate that exclusion can meaningfully deter it, *and* sufficiently culpable that such deterrence is worth the price paid by the justice system.").

30. 438 U.S. 154 (1978).

31. Kansas v. Ventris, 129 S.Ct. 1841, 1845 (2009).

32. *See infra* page 227.

argue that suppression is already quite rare, but, even if this is so, the changes considered here would make suppression still more rare).

Fourth, and on the other hand, the *Herring* Court also repeatedly described both the culpability inquiry in other portions of the opinion, and the question of deterrence, as "objective" determinations, while citing and approving much of its earlier good faith exception case law. Such language may suggest that the Court is not departing from the specific holdings of its earlier good faith cases in any important way (for example, *Leon*'s listing of four situations that cannot constitute good faith). Nevertheless, the Court's express introduction for the first time of the concept of "culpability"[33] may suggest that, once roaming beyond the specific factual situations identified in its earlier good faith precedent, it may apply what seems to be a new test more rigorously, making it harder to extend the exception to new situations—though the Court is likely to insist that its new and old precedent are indeed consistent. Furthermore, many commentators were convinced in the pre-*Dickerson* world that the Court would use that case to overrule *Miranda*. It did not. It may, therefore, turn out that, contrary to the suggestions in the first three points above, *Herring* will turn out to be less a radical departure from the past than a modest one, or perhaps even *Herring* might conceivably be limited to its facts.

Justice Ginsburg, writing in a dissent joined by Justices Stevens, Souter, and Breyer, however, was not sanguine. Ginsburg insisted that the exclusionary rule, while serving deterrence, also served to avoid tainting the judiciary with "partnership in official lawlessness" and assured "the people—all potential victims of unlawful government conduct—that the government would not profit from its lawless behavior," an assurance "minimizing the risk of seriously undermining popular trust in government."[34] Additionally, in an age of computers, Ginsburg thought it crucial to give police departments and their employees an incentive to get it right, an effort that would not be unduly expensive.

Simple negligence was the only standard that would do this effectively because any higher standard renders a remedy an "empty promise: How is an impecunious defendant to make the required showing? If the answer is that a defendant is entitled to discovery (and, if necessary, to an audit of police databases), . . . then the Court has imposed a considerable administrative burden on courts and law enforcement."[35] Civil remedies, insisted Justice Ginsburg, were also a fanciful remedy because of the substantial hurdles to recovery. Moreover, the risks of police errors were high, thereby most seriously impacting innocent persons, " 'wrongfully arrested based on erroneous information [carelessly maintained] in a computer database.' "[36]

---

33. We say "expressly" because one of us argued well before *Herring* that a culpability requirement was already implicit in the Court's good faith jurisprudence. *See* Andrew E. Taslitz, *The Expressive Fourth Amendment: Rethinking the Good Faith Exception to the Exclusionary Rule*, 76 MISS. L.J. 483 (2006).

34. *Herring*, 129 S.Ct. at 704, 707.

35. *Id.* at 701.

36. *Id.* at 705.

These costs, said Justice Ginsburg, were unacceptable: " 'The offense to the dignity of the citizen who is arrested, handcuffed, and searched on a public street simply because some bureaucrat has failed to maintain an accurate computer data base' is evocative of the use of general warrants that so outraged the authors of our Bill of Rights."[37]

Moreover, puzzled Ginsburg, "[i]t is not clear how the Court squares its focus on deliberate conduct with its recognition that application of the exclusionary rule does not require inquiry into the mental state of the police."[38] For Ginsburg, the majority's opinion represented nothing less than a further "erod[ing] of the exclusionary rule" that renders exclusion as a remedy for Fourth Amendment violations a mere " 'chimera.' "[39]

Justice Breyer, joined by Justice Souter, wrote his own dissent too, merely to emphasize what he saw as the importance of the distinction between *police* recordkeeping errors and *judicial* ones, concluding that the exclusionary rule should apply to the former but not the latter. This bright line, Breyer insisted, would be "far easier for courts to administer than The Chief Justice's case-by-case, multifactored inquiry into the degree of police culpability."[40]

For a topical comparison of U.S. evidence suppression under *Mapp v. Ohio* with other nations' treatment of law enforcement error, see Adam Liptak's "U.S. Is Alone in Rejecting All Evidence if Police Err," The New York Times (July 19, 2008), located at http://www.nytimes.com/2008/07/19/us/19exclude.html (last visited March 4, 2010)(which also features booking photos of Dollree Mapp, Booker T. Hudson, and Bennie Herring).

Good Faith Exception Problems

PROBLEM 7–4

Review Problems 3–4 and 3–5 in Chapter 3, involving computer searches. Assuming each search warrant was defective in some manner, analyze whether the ensuing execution of each would be protected by the good faith exception. Why or why not?

PROBLEM 7–5

Terrence K. Werthner moves to suppress evidence seized from his home. Werthner shares his residence with his stepson, Leonard Dyer, who was seventeen years old at the time of the search and seizure. Werthner's residence is in Aberdeen, Grays Harbor County.

On January 21, a deputy prosecutor in Pierce County charged Dyer with felony assault committed in Pierce County. The deputy prosecutor

---

37. *Id.* at 709.

38. *Id.* at 710 n.7.

39. *Id.* at 710.

40. *Id.* at 710, 711.

filed the charge in the adult division of the Pierce County Superior Court. He also prepared and proposed an arrest warrant that showed on its face, in capital letters, Dyer's date of birth. A judge of the adult division ordered that the warrant issue, and the warrant was forwarded to Aberdeen for service. At the time the warrant for Dyer was issued, a state statute provided: "The juvenile courts in the several counties of this state, shall have exclusive original jurisdiction over all proceedings relating to juveniles alleged or found to have committed offenses." The statute defined "juvenile" as any person under eighteen. Because of this statute, the adult division of the Pierce County Superior Court lacked jurisdiction to issue the arrest warrant.

On February 12, at about 6:30 a.m., uniformed Aberdeen police officers went to Werthner's residence to serve the warrant. Dyer answered the door and was immediately arrested. Being in his underwear, he asked if he could get dressed before going to jail. The officers agreed and followed him into the house. Inside, the officers smelled the odor of marijuana and surmised that a marijuana grow was in progress. They had not smelled the odor before entering, and they had not previously been suspicious about the residence. The officers chose not to investigate further at that time. Rather, they allowed Dyer to get dressed and took him to jail.

An hour and a half later, one of the officers returned to the house and knocked. Werthner answered the door. The officer asked to "look through his house to satisfy my curiosity that I believed he had a marijuana grow in his home." Werthner did not reply. The officer said he could attempt to obtain a search warrant, and Werthner responded, "Get a warrant."

The officer returned to his patrol car and began to drive away. As he did, he saw Werthner get into a van and back it from the street into the driveway of the residence. The officer drove around the block and parked where Werthner could not observe him. From his new vantage point, he saw Werthner make several hurried trips from the house to the van, carrying objects the officer was too far away to identify. The officer suspected the objects were marijuana plants, based on what he had smelled while in the house earlier. The officer left his patrol car and approached the residence on foot. As he went nearer, he saw in the van, which was about 20 feet away from him at the time, marijuana plants or boxes containing marijuana plants.

As the officer approached the house, a taxi pulled up and Dyer's mother got out. The officer told her that he needed to speak with Werthner, and she entered the house. Werthner came out a moment later, threw his hands in the air, and said, "You guys got me, I give up." The officer then asked if there were more marijuana plants inside. Werthner said yes, and that officers could search if they wanted to. He signed a consent-to-search form, and officers soon found a marijuana grow operation.

Still on February 12, the deputy prosecutor back in Pierce County moved to dismiss the charge against Dyer without prejudice. The motion stated: "The defendant is a juvenile and, therefore, this court does not have jurisdiction over him. I am referring this case to juvenile court." A judge of the adult division granted the motion and quashed the arrest warrant.

Four days later, on February 16, a deputy prosecutor in Grays Harbor County charged Werthner with manufacture of marijuana and possession of marijuana with intent to deliver. Werthner then filed a motion to suppress the evidence seized on February 12th, as well as the statement he made when he came out of the house.

Questions: (1) Were Werthner's Fourth Amendment rights violated when the police entered his house to arrest Dyer? (2) If so, should the violation be remedied by applying the exclusionary rule?

B.   THE "CRIMINAL CASE" EXCEPTION

The Court desires to confine the reach of the exclusionary rule to those situations in which deterrent effects of the rule outweigh the rule's costs. As a result, the Court has declared that the exclusionary rule applies only in criminal trials.[41] In other words, the Fourth Amendment does not require the exclusion of illegally seized evidence from ordinary civil cases, or administrative or deportation proceedings. Nor does it apply ordinarily in quasi-criminal proceedings.[42] For example, the Court recently affirmed in *Pennsylvania Board of Probation and Parole v. Scott* that the exclusionary rule does not apply in parole revocation hearings.[43] Such hearings involve allegations that a convicted person placed on parole has committed a new crime or has violated some condition of parole. If the prosecution proves the violation, the judge can revoke the person's parole and impose a prison term equal to the time remaining on the term of parole. Writing for a five-justice majority, Justice Thomas observed, "Application of the exclusionary rule would both hinder the functioning of state parole systems and alter the traditionally flexible, administrative nature of parole revocation proceedings. The rule would provide only minimal deterrence benefits in this context, because application of the rule in the criminal trial context already provides significant deterrence of unconstitutional searches." Justice Souter, joined by Justices Ginsburg and Breyer, disagreed with Justice Thomas's conclusion about "minimal deterrence benefits." Justice Souter argued that when parolees commit new crimes, prosecutors often pursue parole revocation instead of prosecution "as the course of choice," because the

---

41. For cases dealing with these limitations, *see, e.g.*, I.N.S. v. Lopez–Mendoza, 468 U.S. 1032 (1984) (exclusionary rule does not apply in deportation proceedings); United States v. Janis, 428 U.S. 433 (1976) (exclusionary rule does not apply in civil tax case). The one exception to this rule is civil forfeiture proceedings, which, for the present at least, are treated like criminal trials for exclusionary rule purposes. In 1965, the Supreme Court ruled that evidence should have been suppressed in a civil forfeiture case, *see* One 1958 Plymouth Sedan v. Pennsylvania, 380 U.S. 693 (1965) (applying the exclusionary rule in civil forfeiture on the basis of the "quasi-criminal" nature of civil forfeiture proceedings); *see also, e.g.*, United States v. Certain Real Property 566 Hendrickson Blvd., 986 F.2d 990 (6th Cir.1993) (same).

42. The exclusionary rule probably does apply in juvenile court proceedings. The Supreme Court has not addressed this issue directly, but lower federal courts have assumed that it would apply. *See, e.g.*, United States v. Sechrist, 640 F.2d 81 (7th Cir.1981).

43. 524 U.S. 357 (1998).

balance of time to be served "may well be long enough to render recommitment the practical equivalent of a new sentence for a separate crime" and because recommitment "may be accomplished without shouldering the burden of proof beyond a reasonable doubt." Justice Souter concluded from this, "Suppression in the revocation proceeding cannot be looked upon, then, as furnishing merely incremental or marginal deterrence over and above the effect of exclusion in criminal prosecution. Instead, it will commonly provide the only deterrence to unconstitutional conduct when the incarceration of parolees is sought."

On the other hand, courts do apply the exclusionary rule in some quasi-criminal cases, such as some (but not all) civil tax proceedings and civil forfeiture cases.

What are the bases for deciding whether deterrence would be served by application of the exclusionary rule in a particular proceeding? Courts have identified these:

- The nature of the proceeding.
- Whether the search and the proceeding were initiated by the same agency, or the same sovereign.
- An indication of an explicit understanding between two law enforcement bodies—the one that conducted the search and the one that initiated the proceeding.
- A statutory regime in which both the searching agency and the prosecuting agency share resources—particularly resources derived from one of the proceedings.
- A strong relationship between the law enforcement interests of the searching agency and the type of proceeding at which the seized material is being offered.

A federal court[44] explained this last factor—called the "zone of primary interest"—in a tax case, as follows:

> Where the relationship between the objectives of the law enforcement agency to which the officer belongs and the secondary proceedings is close, an inference may be drawn that the officers had the use of the evidence in the subsequent proceeding in mind when they made the seizure. The zone of primary interest of an IRS agent, for example, has been held to encompass both criminal and civil tax enforcement proceedings. Hence, the exclusionary rule has been applied to bar the use of illegally seized evidence in civil tax proceedings where that evidence was seized by agents of the IRS.

Second, even where the rule applies, it requires the suppression of evidence from the trial itself, but no more. Grand juries are permitted to examine evidence that was illegally obtained, and judges are permitted to consider illegally obtained evidence for sentencing purposes.[45] Moreover,

---

44. Wolf v. Commissioner of Internal Revenue, 13 F.3d 189, 195 (6th Cir.1993).

45. *See, e.g.,* United States v. Calandra, 414 U.S. 338 (1974) (grand jury); Nichols v. United States, 511 U.S. 738 (1994) (sentencing under Federal Sentencing Guidelines).

within the criminal trial itself, evidence that was obtained through constitutional violations may be admitted for the limited purpose of impeaching a testifying defendant.[46] The rationale for the impeachment exception is that the "shield" provided by the exclusionary rule "cannot be perverted into a license to use perjury by way of a defense."[47] In other words, if a defendant takes the stand and says things that are deceptive or untrue, the prosecutor is permitted to undermine the defendant's credibility by demonstrating the falsity of the testimony, even if that means displaying inadmissible evidence. The impeachment exception applies to fruits of Fourth Amendment violations, *Miranda* violations, and violations of the Massiah right to counsel (which are discussed in Chapter 3), though not to involuntary statements. The latter are inadmissible for any purpose because their reliability is so questionable.

C.   THE IMPEACHMENT EXCEPTION

The impeachment exception has two important limitations. First, the impeachment must relate either to the defendant's testimony on direct examination or to questions asked by the prosecutor on cross-examination that are "reasonably suggested" by the defendant's testimony on direct examination.[48] That is to say, the prosecution cannot manipulate cross-examination in order to get inadmissible evidence before the jury.

To illustrate, suppose Mary Lackerby is on trial for theft of the Hope diamond from the Cleveland Museum on March 1st. Suppose further that police had found the Hope diamond in her apartment during an unconstitutional search, and that the court excluded it as the fruit of a Fourth Amendment violation. On direct examination, Mary explicitly denies having committed the theft or ever having seen the Hope diamond. The prosecutor may, using the Hope diamond and the illegal search, demonstrate the untruth of her testimony—it may place the diamond in front of her, ask her to acknowledge that it was found in her apartment, and so on, in order to prevent her from "hiding behind the exclusionary rule." The trial judge probably would give a limiting instruction to the jury, permitting the jury to consider the impeaching evidence only on the issue of Mary's credibility, and not as substantive evidence of her guilt.

Suppose Mary does not say anything directly about her guilt or innocence, but rather takes the stand to explain that she spent March 1st in Columbus. In that case, the prosecutor will have to ask further questions on cross-examination in order to set up a proper impeachment, because impeachment is permitted only if it directly contradicts the defendant's testimony. The prosecutor may ask, for example, "So if you were in Columbus on March 1st, you weren't in Cleveland at all that day? And you had nothing to do with the theft of the Hope diamond? You have never

---

46.   *See, e.g.*, Harris v. New York, 401 U.S. 222 (1971); Walder v. United States, 347 U.S. 62 (1954).

47.   Harris v. New York, 401 U.S. 222, 226 (1971).

48.   United States v. Havens, 446 U.S. 620, 627–28 (1980).

even seen the Hope diamond?" If Mary answers these questions in a manner directly inconsistent with the presence of the Hope diamond in her apartment, then the prosecutor may impeach her with the diamond.

Moreover, the prosecutor may ask her these questions in order to set up the impeachment only if the questions are "reasonably suggested" by her testimony on direct examination, or, in other words, if the questions are reasonably related to the issues the defendant put in dispute by his or her testimony on direct.[49] In the example above, Mary's direct testimony offered an alibi, and therefore she put in dispute the issue of whether she committed the theft. Thus, the prosecutor's questions are "reasonably suggested" by her direct testimony. On the other hand, if Mary limited her direct testimony to something collateral to the issue of guilt or innocence, the prosecutor's questions would be improper. Obviously there is much gray area between these two situations, and the propriety of the questions and the impeachment is left to the discretion of the trial judge.

Trial Hint: From the foregoing, you can see that the impeachment exception affects the defendant's decision whether or not to testify. A defendant who has successfully suppressed evidence might be hesitant to take the stand, for fear that the suppressed evidence might become admissible during cross-examination. Do you suppose that this practical impact of the impeachment exception affects the deterrent value of the exclusionary rule? Is it implausible to think that police officers might calculate that an illegal search will nonetheless help the prosecution win its case?

The second major limitation to the impeachment exception is that it applies only to testifying defendants: other defense witnesses cannot be impeached with evidence suppressed by operation of the exclusionary rule. In *James v. Illinois*,[50] the Court explained the limitation in this way:

> ... The [impeachment] exception ... generally discourages perjured testimony.... [E]xpanding the impeachment exception to encompass the testimony of all defense witnesses would not have the same beneficial effects. First, the mere threat of a subsequent criminal prosecution for perjury is far more likely to deter a witness from intentionally lying on a defendant's behalf than to deter a defendant, already facing conviction for the underlying offense, from lying on his own behalf....
>
> More significantly, expanding the impeachment exception to encompass the testimony of all defense witnesses likely would chill some defendants from presenting their best defense—and sometimes any defense at all—through the testimony of others. Whenever police obtained evidence illegally, defendants would have to assess prior to trial the likelihood that the evidence would be admitted to impeach the otherwise favorable testimony of any witness they call. Defendants might reasonably fear that one or more of their witnesses, in a position to offer truthful and favorable testimony, would also make some

---

49. United States v. Miranda–Uriarte, 649 F.2d 1345, 1353 (9th Cir.1981).

50. 493 U.S. 307 (1990).

statement in sufficient tension with the tainted evidence to allow the prosecutor to introduce that evidence for impeachment. . . .

Given the potential chill created by expanding the impeachment exception, the conceded gains to the truthseeking process from discouraging or disclosing perjured testimony would be offset to some extent by the concomitant loss of probative witness testimony. Thus, the truthseeking rationale supporting the impeachment of defendants in Walder and its progeny does not apply to other witnesses with equal force.

Impeachment Problems

PROBLEM 7-6

You are an Assistant United States Attorney in Nevada. One of your assignments is to prosecute Dr. Robert Palmeri, a dentist with a small practice in the sleepy rural town of Lakeport, Nevada. As a practicing dentist, Palmeri was registered with the Drug Enforcement Administration [DEA] to purchase Schedule II narcotic controlled substances, including cocaine. Between January and April Palmeri purchased 10 ounces of cocaine, ostensibly for use in his practice. This was such a large quantity as to evoke the suspicion that he was diverting it to non-dental uses. Ultimately, the DEA obtained a search warrant to search his office and patient records. The search of Palmeri's patient records found only six references to cocaine use in the course of patient treatment.

Meanwhile, DEA agents had been surveilling Palmeri and a friend, who was later identified as Peter Ceccholini. Palmeri and Ceccholini met nearly every day at a riding stable outside of town. Agents observed that several times during each ride, the two would position their horses close together. Palmeri would remove something from his saddle bag, and he and Ceccholini would then hunch over with their hands to their faces. The agents could not clearly see what Palmeri and Ceccholini were doing, but they suspected that the two men were snorting cocaine. One day, after Palmeri and Ceccholini had dismounted at the stables and walked away from their horses in order to speak with a stable employee, a DEA agent reached into Palmeri's saddle bag, from which he retrieved a cocaine snorting tube.

Palmeri was charged with federal drug offenses. He moved to suppress evidence, including the cocaine snorting tube, and his motion with respect to that item was successful. At trial, you decided to call Dr. Michael Barken, an eminent Denver dentist and professor, who calculated that to use 10 ounces of cocaine at its toxic limit, a dentist would have to see 1,500 patients; using it at its common dosage, a dentist would have to make 30,000 patient applications. You also called Mr. Ceccholini, who testified that he and Palmeri used cocaine almost daily on their rides. The drug was furnished by Palmeri from bottles similar to those which he could receive as a DEA registrant.

After the close of your case, Palmeri takes the stand to testify in his own defense. On direct examination, he states positively that all of the cocaine he had ordered was used in his practice. His lawyer does not ask him whether he had used any personally. You are about to rise to conduct your cross-examination.

Question: What question or questions should you ask Dr. Palmeri? Are those questions proper? Will you be able to confront Palmeri with the illegally seized cocaine snorting tube? Should you be?

PROBLEM 7–7

Edward Trzaska is a federal probationer completing the last part of a sentence for firearms violations. The probationary part of his sentence prohibits him from possessing firearms of any sort. Acting on a tip, government agents found firearms in a container in a garage that Trzaska had rented. The search of the garage was legal and accompanied by a warrant. Shortly after finding the firearms, however, the agents broke into Trzaska's apartment and searched it without a warrant. There, they found a rifle and ammunition.

After Trzaska was charged with substantive firearms offenses and with violating the terms of his probation, his Probation Officer asked him about the rifle and ammunition found in his apartment. In response to the Probation Officer's questions, and in the presence of one of the agents who had searched his apartment, Trzaska stated "I'm like a drug addict with these guns. It's a sickness."

Before trial, Trzaska successfully moved to suppress the rifle, ammunition, and the statement to the Probation Officer, as fruits of the unlawful search of his apartment.

Trzaska did not testify at trial, but his son, Kevin Trzaska, testified during the defense case. Kevin claimed that the firearms found in the garage were his and stated that, at his father's direction, he had obtained them from his father's friend Hank Weggman. The following exchange took place between defense counsel and Kevin on direct examination:

Q: Do you know why your father asked you to pick them up from Hank?

A: My dad didn't want nothing to do with them anymore.

Q: Did he tell you why didn't want to have anything to do with them?

A: Because he had too many problems in his past, and he—he wanted to put it down.

The government objected to these out-of-court statements, which were offered to prove that Edward Trzaska was no longer involved with guns and that he was, therefore, not illegally in possession of the firearms as charged. The judge permitted the testimony, however, and on cross-examination, the prosecutor sought to introduce Trzaska's statement in order to impeach the out-of-court statement he had made to his son regarding his intent to relinquish ownership of the firearms. The judge permitted the prosecutor to read the statement to Kevin and to ask Kevin whether his father had told him about it. In addition, the judge permitted the prosecutor, on rebuttal, to call the agent to testify about the statement and the context in which it was made—in other words, that Trzaska had made the statement in response to questions about the rifle and ammunition seized from his apartment.

After the agent testified, the judge gave the jury the following limiting instruction: "The limited purpose and the only purpose that I'm admitting this testimony is for you to evaluate the credibility of the statement that was attributed to the defendant by his son." Moreover, the judge warned the jury that the rifle and ammunition illegally seized from Trzaska's apartment could not be considered as evidence of his guilt, but that "the testimony about what the agent took or saw at that time is only being admitted to place in context the remark allegedly made by the defendant."

In summation, defense counsel made the following argument: "Kevin told you his father did not want to have anything to do with the guns. He knew it was trouble. He knew that he was a convicted felon, and therefore was in a different category than his son. He knew that if he took those guns into his possession and kept them, that not only was he risking the violation of parole, but he was also risking sitting right where he's sitting right now. So he tells his son, 'they're yours.' "

Question: On appeal, Trzaska claims that the admission of his statement violated his Fourth Amendment rights. How should the appellate court rule?

PROBLEM 7–8

On March 30, 1981, President Ronald Reagan, his Press Secretary (James Brady), a Secret Service agent, and a Metropolitan Police Department officer were shot in an assassination attempt in front of the Hilton Hotel in Washington, D.C. John W. Hinckley, Jr., was apprehended on the scene and taken into custody. Hinckley was charged with three federal offenses relating to the incident. He raised a motion to suppress evidence that the government sought to admit at trial under the impeachment exception to the exclusionary rule. Hinckley's motion was based in part on an allegedly unlawful search and seizure of his jail cell. Read the following description of the search and the theory under which the government seeks to introduce its fruits, and prepare to evaluate that theory:

> Hinckley was transferred to the Federal Correctional Institution at Butner, North Carolina, on April 2, 1981 to undergo psychiatric evaluation. Formidable security measures were instituted during Hinckley's stay there: he was held in solitary confinement, kept under round-the-clock supervision, personally checked by guards every fifteen minutes, accompanied by three officers every time he left a secured area, restricted in his access to prison personnel, and even prohibited from receiving mail except from designated individuals. Upon arrival, he was advised by the Manager of the Mental Health Unit, Jesse James, that his cell would be frequently searched, primarily for "items

with which he could harm himself," and that his mail (except for attorney-client mail and correspondence with certain officials) would be read. In May, after Hinckley ingested a large quantity of medication in an apparent suicide attempt, the security measures were further intensified. Searches were increased to twice daily, and he was transferred to a cell where he could be continually observed through a window in an adjoining guard station.

Under continual observation, in solitary confinement, and with knowledge that all his personal correspondence would be read, Hinckley's exclusive outlet for private expression was his writing. He maintained a diary and wrote notes on pads provided by the prison authorities. Some of the correctional officers assigned to guard him read these papers during the cell searches—which were conducted in Hinckley's absence—although they had not been instructed to do so by anyone at Butner. During a contraband search on Thursday, July 23, 1981, while correctional officer Donald Meece was looking through the contents of an unmarked envelope Hinckley had placed on an extra bed he normally used to store reading materials, correspondence, and personal writings, the officer's eye was caught by certain "trigger words" on folded sheets of personal notes. As a result of these "trigger words," Meece skimmed the complete document and showed it to Officer Elmer Stone, who was assisting the search. Stone read the document, replaced it in the envelope, and reported the matter to their supervisor. . . .

The next day, Stone conducted the morning cell search with Officer Ronald Graham. Stone again read the document and then showed it to Graham. The two reported on the contents of the document to Captain Paul Hungerford, who ordered the papers copied and replaced while Hinckley was at the gym. Hungerford testified that he took precautions to conceal the search and seizure from Hinckley because he expected that if Hinckley knew about it, he would be "bent out of shape" and would present a problem over the weekend when staff was at a minimum.

On Monday, July 27, Hungerford met with the acting warden, and they decided to contact the Federal Bureau of Investigation. That afternoon, Hungerford and an FBI agent seized the document and Hinckley's diary, and left a receipt for Hinckley indicating that "contraband" had been seized. . . .

We turn . . . to the government's contention that, even if the evidence that is the subject of this appeal was obtained in violation of Hinckley's constitutional rights, its use should be permitted at trial for what the government styles a limited purpose—namely, to rebut the insanity defense on which Hinckley is expected to rely. [T]he government's arguments in this regard are novel. . . .

The government urges, to begin with, that the exclusionary rule applies only when the government seeks to use evidence to prove the basic elements of a crime. Reasoning broadly that because insanity is an affirmative defense, and proof of sanity is therefore not part of the prosecution's case-in-chief, the government asserts that illegally obtained evidence can be used generally to rebut an insanity defense without jeopardizing constitutional principles. The government stresses the inherently difficult nature of an insanity defense determination, and the concomitant need of the court to consider all available evidence on the issue. . . .

The government's final argument for admission is based on a "testimony-by-proxy" theory. According to its view, if in the course of an insanity plea the defense puts forth testimony by expert witnesses on the defendant's mental state, that testimony is tantamount to the defendant taking the stand himself. Since it has been held permissible to use illegally obtained evidence to impeach testimony by the defendant, the government argues that it should also be possible to use the same testimony to rebut the expert psychiatric witnesses.

Question: Should the government have prevailed in the Hinckley case? Is the Trzaska case different? If so, why? If either of these cases were to undergo Supreme Court review, how would you expect the Court to rule?

D.   HABEAS REVIEW OF VIOLATIONS OF THE FOURTH AMENDMENT EXCLUSIONARY RULE

Pursuant to federal habeas corpus statutes,[51] individuals in state or federal custody may file petitions in federal court challenging the constitutionality of judicial rulings that led to their imprisonment.[52] For example, as we will discuss later, a person convicted of a crime may seek habeas relief on the ground that the trial court should have excluded an involuntary confession. However, the Supreme Court has restricted the availability of habeas relief for Fourth Amendment violations. In *Stone v. Powell*,[53] it held that a Fourth Amendment exclusionary rule violation may *not* form the basis for habeas relief if the proceedings that resulted in the conviction provided a "full and fair" opportunity to litigate Fourth Amendment claims. The Court's decision was based on a cost-benefit analysis in which it noted the high costs of the exclusionary rule and found, on the benefit side, "no reason to believe . . . that the overall educative effect of the exclusionary rule would be appreciably diminished if search and seizure claims could not be raised in federal habeas corpus review."[54]

IV.   DOES THE EXCLUSIONARY RULE WORK?

Whether the exclusionary rule "works" depends on what purposes one seeks to further by its use. You know from the opinions reproduced above

---

51.   28 U.S.C. § 2254 and 28 U.S.C. § 2255.

52.   There are many procedural hurdles to habeas relief that are not relevant to this discussion.

53.   428 U.S. 465 (1976).

54.   *Stone* involved habeas review of state court convictions under 28 U.S.C. Section 2254, but it has been applied to federal convictions as well. *See* United States v. Hearst, 638 F.2d 1190 (9th Cir.1980), *cert. denied*, 451 U.S. 938 (1981).

that members of the Supreme Court have disagreed about the purposes of the exclusionary rule, and that they continue to disagree to this day. The debate concerning the rule's rationales rages among legal scholars as well. The major positions appear to be these: (1) the rule is constitutionally required; (2) the rule protects judicial integrity; and (3) the rule deters police misconduct. We will address each of these below. In addition, we will address a fourth rationale suggested by scholars.

A. THE EXCLUSIONARY RULE IS CONSTITUTIONALLY REQUIRED

The Court in *Mapp v. Ohio* held in part that the Fourth Amendment's limitations on government activity implicitly contain remedial measures. According to this view, the exclusionary rule is not appropriately evaluated in terms of whether it "works"—it simply must be enforced as a part of the constitution.

A majority of the Supreme Court has explicitly moved away from this position, however. In *United States v. Calandra*,[55] the Court stated that the "use of illegally obtained evidence ... presents a question, not of rights, but of remedies," and it termed the exclusionary rule "a judicially created remedy designed to safeguard Fourth Amendment rights through its deterrence effect, rather than a personal constitutional right." The removal of constitutional underpinnings leaves the exclusionary rule vulnerable. If the rule is judicially created, it can be judicially taken away, or judicially narrowed. Moreover, the lack of constitutional grounding raises a grave question: by what authority can the Court enforce the exclusionary rule in state court proceedings, unless that rule is constitutionally required? Although the Court has not answered this question, at least one justice has expressed the belief that the exclusionary rule is unconstitutional as enforced against the states, and a leading scholar agrees.[56]

One scholar has sought to reclaim constitutional status for the exclusionary rule, arguing that it is rooted in "restorative justice." According to Professor Nortan, "The exclusionary rule is a just one because it puts both the State and the accused in the positions they would have been in had the Constitution not been violated—neither better nor worse."[57]

B. THE EXCLUSIONARY RULE PRESERVES JUDICIAL INTEGRITY

The second major rationale expressed in *Mapp* frequently is referred to as the "judicial integrity" principle. That is, the courts' refusal to admit

---

55. 414 U.S. 338 (1974).

56. *See* Mapp v. Ohio, 367 U.S. 643 (1961) (Harlan, J., dissenting); *see also, e.g.*, Joseph Grano, *Prophylactic Rules in Criminal Procedure: A Question of Article III Legitimacy*, 80 NW. U. L. REV. 100 (1985).

57. *See* Jerry E. Norton, *The Exclusionary Rule Reconsidered: Restoring the Status Quo Ante*, 33 WAKE FOREST L. REV. 261, 262, 283–94 (1994) (finding this principle in the Fourth Amendment's history and basic principles of justice).

evidence "enabl[es] the judiciary to avoid the taint of partnership in official lawlessness."[58] There are at least two corollaries to this position. The first is that the exclusionary rule fosters public trust in the judiciary. In the words of Justice Brennan, application of the exclusionary rule "assur[es] the people—all potential victims of unlawful government conduct—that the government [will] not profit from its lawless behavior, thus minimizing the risk of seriously undermining popular trust in government." Recent research into the nature of trust suggests that this is not an insignificant point.[59]

The second corollary is that by excluding evidence wrongfully obtained, courts themselves teach lawful behavior. Again, Justice Brennan's dissent in *Calandra* is instructive. Quoting Justice Brandeis's dissent in *Olmstead v. United States*,[60] he reminds us that " 'In a government of laws, existence of the government will be imperiled if it fails to observe the law scrupulously. Our government is the potent, the omnipresent teacher. For good or for ill, it teaches the whole people by its example. Crime is contagious. If the government becomes a lawbreaker, it breeds contempt for law; it invites every man to become a law unto himself; it invites anarchy.' "

These rationales have not greatly influenced the Court's exclusionary rule jurisprudence. The Court has not disavowed the judicial integrity rationale altogether, but it has relegated that rationale to a "limited" role.[61] Moreover, it suggested in *Leon* that suppressing probative evidence also creates disrespect for the judicial system.

C.   THE EXCLUSIONARY RULE DETERS POLICE MISCONDUCT

The deterrence rationale obviously forms the centerpiece of the Court's exclusionary rule cases. In order to question the success of the rule in terms of this rationale, one must ask whether it actually deters unconstitutional activity. But there is another side to the deterrence rationale: the Court seeks to deter wrongful police conduct, but not to "overdeter": that is, it has crafted the rule explicitly in order to avoid imposing large costs on the efficacy of the criminal justice system.[62] Thus, a proper measure of the exclusionary rule must take into account this cost-avoidance principle as well.

---

58.   *Calandra*, 414 U.S. at 357 (Brennan, J., dissenting).

59.   *See, e.g.*, SISSELA BOK, LYING: MORAL CHOICE IN PUBLIC AND PRIVATE LIFE (1978); R. Kent Greenawalt, *Silence as a Moral and Constitutional Right*, 23 WM. & MARY L.REV. 15 (1981); Margaret L. Paris, *Trust, Lies, and Interrogation*, 3 VA. J. SOC. POLICY & LAW 3 (1995).

60.   277 U.S. 438, 485 (1928) (Brandeis, J., dissenting).

61.   Stone v. Powell, 428 U.S. 465, 492–95 (1976).

62.   Among the potential costs are: lost convictions, disrespect for the judicial system, lack of a remedy for the "innocent" who are not charged with criminal offenses, creation of incentives for law enforcement officers and judges to engage in inappropriate behavior in order to reduce the impact of the exclusionary rule, loss of incentives to develop alternative remedies for police misconduct, and distortion of judicial resources. *See, e.g.*, CHRISTOPHER SLOBOGIN,

In light of the express emphasis on the deterrence rationale, it is surprising that empirical data concerning the effectiveness of the exclusionary rule is virtually nonexistent. Indeed, data concerning the efficacy of the Fourth Amendment exclusionary rule is very scanty; most of what exists with respect to the exclusionary rule focuses almost exclusively on the *Miranda* rule. In a groundbreaking study published in 1996, Richard Leo concludes that *Miranda* has had little effect on the kinds of interrogation techniques that the Supreme Court in *Miranda* found so abhorrent.[63] Thus, the rule appears to be a failure in terms of deterring police misconduct in interrogations. On the other side of the deterrence rationale, the *Miranda* rule seems to have had some effect on the numbers of suspects who either "prevent or terminate questioning," although police nevertheless are successful in eliciting incriminating information from suspects in a high percentage of cases. Leo's study appears to support the conclusion, therefore, that the *Miranda* rule has not overly discouraged effective police interrogation techniques.

Although it is unclear whether the exclusionary rule "works" in the sense of significantly deterring police misconduct, it certainly is effective in giving criminal defendants a special oversight role in our system of justice. Their self-interest makes them uniquely careful watchdogs for police mistakes or intentional wrongdoing which, when uncovered, lead to the exclusion of evidence. Professor Taslitz has argued that the Bill of Rights mandates institutions that promote an informed citizenry capable of monitoring governmental abuses. In a complex modern society, citizen monitors must specialize where their guardianship is most effective. Suppression hearings required by the exclusionary rule—enable highly motivated citizens (suspects fearing incarceration) armed with legal counsel to expose police abuses in a public fashion. Such hearings are likely to be more effective than other alternatives in exposing governmental wrongdoing.[64]

"Testilying," the tendency of many police officers to lie at suppression hearings, undermines the exclusionary rule's deterrent value. Two scholars have recently suggested addressing the problem through the law of evidence. These scholars propose that courts admit expert testimony about this tendency for the purpose of impeaching the testifying officers.[65]

CRIMINAL PROCEDURE: REGULATION OF POLICE INVESTIGATION 499–500 (2nd ed. 1998) (citing, among other studies, Office of Legal Policy, *U.S. Justice Department, Rep't to the Attorney General on the Search and Seizure Exclusionary Rule*, 22 MICH. J.L. REF. 573 (1989)).

63.   Richard A. Leo, *Inside the Interrogation Room*, 86 J. CRIM. LAW & CRIMINOL. 266 (1996). In a recent analysis of the Fourth Amendment and Fifth Amendment exclusionary rules, Samuel Walker concluded that they "have probably reduced some of the worst police behavior." SAMUEL WALKER, TAMING THE SYSTEM: THE CONTROL OF DISCRETION IN CRIMINAL JUSTICE, 1950–1990, 53 (1993).

64.   *See* Andrew E. Taslitz, *Slaves No More: The Implications of the Informed Citizen Idea for Discovery Before Fourth Amendment Suppression Hearings*, 15 GA. ST. L. REV. 709 (1999).

65.   *See* Gabriel J. Chin and Scott C. Wells, *The Blue Wall of Silence as Evidence of Bias and Motive to Lie: A New Approach to Police Perjury*, 59 U. PITT. L. REV. 233 (1998).

D.   Separation of Powers

Yet another rationale for the exclusionary rule, rooted in the concept of the separation of powers, has been suggested by the CATO Institute:[66]

> The drive to abolish the exclusionary rule is fundamentally misguided, on constitutional grounds, for the rule can and should be justified on separation-of-powers principles, which conservatives generally support. When agents of the executive branch (the police) disregard the terms of search warrants, or attempt to bypass the warrant-issuing process altogether, the judicial branch can and should respond by "checking" such misbehavior. The most opportune time to check such unconstitutional behavior is when prosecutors attempt to introduce illegally seized evidence in court. Because the exclusionary rule is the only effective tool the judiciary has for preserving the integrity of its warrant-issuing authority, any legislative attempt to abrogate the rule should be declared null and void by the Supreme Court.

Americans "Constitutionalize" Common–Law Principles

When the American revolutionaries sat down to draw up their plans for a new government, they were keenly aware of the shortcomings of the British Constitution. While they clearly admired the protections of the common law, they also knew that Parliament could easily sweep common-law principles aside—especially in the case of searches and seizures. The lesson the Founders took to heart was that the British Constitution was "only and whatever Parliament said it was."

Thus, the Framers of the American Constitution were determined to devise a better way to secure their hard-won liberties. Under the American Constitution, the powers of the government would be reduced to writing; they would be enumerated and divided among three separate branches, and the powers of the legislative body would be limited. As Chief Justice John Marshall noted in *Marbury v. Madison* (1803), "[T]he powers of the legislature are defined and limited; and that those limits may not be mistaken or forgotten, the constitution is written."

It is against that background that one must read and interpret the words of the Fourth Amendment. The purpose of the Fourth Amendment was to elevate the common-law principles of search and seizure so that they would be beyond the reach of the legislature. The amendment essentially constitutionalized four precepts of the English common law: (1) the judicial nature of the "warrant-issuing" process, (2) the "probable cause" requirement, (3) the "oath or affirmation" requirement, and (4) the "particularity" requirement. Much has been written about the last three precepts, but little attention has been paid to the first. Yet it is the warrant-issuing process that holds the key to

---

66. Timothy Lynch, *Policy Analysis No. 319: In Defense of the Exclusionary Rule*, CATO Institute 1, 11–14, 21–24 (October 1, 1998).

the controversy over whether the exclusionary rule can be constitutionally justified.

Under the common law, warrants would issue only "upon probable cause," and the determination of whether probable cause had been established was thought to be judicial in nature. Sir Matthew Hale, for example, said that the justice of the peace was to judge the reasonableness of suspicions or allegations. If the justice of the peace found the causes of the suspicions to be reasonable, the suspicions would then be his as well as the accuser's, and a warrant would accordingly be issued. Whether the warrant was or was not issued, the reasonableness of the accuser's suspicions would have been, in Hale's words, "adjudged." Similarly, Lord Mansfield wrote in 1765 that "under the principles of the common law . . . It is not fit, that the receiving or judging of the information should be left to the discretion of the officer. The magistrate ought to judge; and should give certain directions to the officer." Again, Blackstone wrote that it was the duty of the justice of the peace to "judge" the "ground of suspicion" before issuing a warrant. Thus, the fundamental point is this: the determination of probable cause belongs to the judiciary. That is the common-law principle that was constitutionalized through the Fourth Amendment.

Under the U.S. Constitution, then, the power to search is divided between the executive and judicial branches. That fact has enormous implications for the American criminal justice system. To begin with, police officers must apply for search warrants from judicial officers before they can lawfully invade the homes and businesses of citizens. Judicial officers, in turn, must remain within their sphere and respect the searching prerogatives of the executive branch. The judiciary, for example, cannot issue commands to executive officers with respect to which houses ought to be searched. Even if a judge has firsthand knowledge that a particular home holds contraband, he cannot issue a search warrant and order the police to search that home. That is because the "governmental investigation and prosecution of crimes is a quintessentially executive function." The judiciary can only react to the applications that are brought before it by agents of the executive branch; the judiciary cannot initiate an investigation or prosecution. Those are just a few of the implications of the Fourth Amendment's division of powers between the executive, and the judicial branch.

But for purposes of the exclusionary rule debate, what is most important is this: Whereas Parliament could tinker with, manipulate, and indeed pervert the common-law principles pertaining to searches and seizures, American legislatures must respect the warrant-issuing power the Constitution has lodged within the judicial branch. Under the U.S. Constitution, even a unanimous vote in Congress cannot alter the Bill of rights or constitutional procedures. The Supreme Court recognized that point in *Bram v. United States* (1897):

Both [the Fourth and Fifth Amendments] contemplated perpetuating, in their full efficacy, by means of a constitutional provision, principles of humanity and civil liberty, which had been secured in the mother country only after years of struggle, so as to implant them in our institutions in the fullness of their integrity, free from the possibilities of future legislative change.

Justice Antonin Scalia expressed the same sentiment in 1991 when he said, "It is the function of the Bill of Rights to preserve [the judgment of the Founders], not only against the changing views of Presidents and Members of Congress, but also against the changing views of Justices."

Thus the crux of the modern debate over the exclusionary rule is hidden within the basic constitutional question, Who issues search warrants? In America, judicial officers decide when search warrants are to be issued. Once the judicial nature of the warrant-issuing process is admitted, the constitutional debate over the exclusionary rule is essentially over, for any attempt by the legislative or executive branches to seize control of the warrant-issuing process amounts to a violation of the separation-of-powers principle.

. . . .

The Exclusionary Rule: A Response to Executive Branch Lawlessness

As noted earlier, one way in which the executive branch has sought to expand its search and seizure powers is by denying the legal necessity of search warrants. Regardless of the reasons offered, it is a fact that police officers frequently choose to proceed with a search without applying for a warrant. Because judges and judicial magistrates are not on the scene when such searches take place, only much later does the judicial branch become aware of the circumstances surrounding a warrantless search—when prosecutors are in court seeking to present the evidence that the police acquired during the search. If the attorney for the accused contends that the search was unlawful and objects to the admission of illegally seized evidence, how should a trial judge respond? Should the evidence be excluded or admitted?

The Supreme Court addressed those questions in *Weeks v. United States* (1912). Weeks, who was suspected of illegal gambling activity, was taken into custody at his place of employment, while a separate group of police officers went to his home and entered it without his permission and without a search warrant. The police seized various books, papers, and letters and turned those items over to prosecutors. When prosecutors tried to introduce some of those incriminating papers at Week's trial, the defense attorney cited the peculiar circumstances of the search and lodged an objection. The trial court overruled the objection, allowing the prosecution to introduce the seized papers. Weeks was convicted, but he appealed his case all the way to the Supreme Court, arguing that the trial court's failure to exclude the incriminating papers was a legal error.

Because a warrant is not required for every search, the Supreme Court began its analysis by reviewing the limited instances in which police may conduct searches without warrants. Finding none of those exceptions applicable to the case under review, the Court concluded that the search was unlawful and that the trial court should not have allowed prosecutors to introduce illegally seized evidence at trial.

The United States Marshal could only have invaded the house of the accused when armed with a warrant issued as required by the Constitution, upon sworn information and describing with reasonable particularity the thing for which the search was to be made. Instead, he acted without sanction of law, doubtless prompted by the desire to bring further proof to the aid of the Government, and under color of his office undertook to make a seizure of private papers in direct violation of the constitutional prohibition against such action. . . . To sanction such [methods of evidence gathering] would be to affirm by judicial decision a manifest neglect if not an open defiance of the prohibitions of the Constitution, intended for the protection of the people against such unauthorized action.

The *Weeks* precedent makes sense. The Fourth Amendment manifests a preference for a procedure of antecedent justification that the police must follow before they can invade American homes or businesses. The exclusionary rule is a logical and necessary corollary to the principle of antecedent justification. Enforcement of the rule puts executive branch agents in the position they would have been in had there been no violation of the warrant clause. Thus, the exclusionary rule restores the equilibrium that the Fourth Amendment established.

The exclusionary rule is also appropriate where executive branch agents obtain a search warrant but then disregard its terms and conditions. Such misconduct is more common than many people think. In 1994, for example, a state judge in Oklahoma issued a warrant that authorized a search of the residence of one Albert Foster. Consistent with the particularity requirement of the Fourth Amendment, the warrant specifically identified the items to be searched for and seized— four firearms (one Remington shotgun, one Taurus .38 special, and two 22–caliber Rugar carbines) and any marijuana they might find. But the officers executing the search seized the following items:

> several VCR machines, miscellaneous video equipment, a socket set, two bows and a sheath containing six arrows, a pair of green coveralls, a riding lawn mower, three garden tillers, a brown leather pouch containing miscellaneous gun shells, a holster, several stereo systems, a CB radio base station, two soft tip microphones, several televisions with remote controls, a Dewalt heavy duty drill, a Vivitar camera tripod, a Red Rider BB-gun Daisy model, a Corona Machete in brown leather case, an ASAHI Pentex Sportmatic Camera, a Bowie type knife in black sheath, a Yashica camera MAT–24, a black leather bag with tapes, a metal rod, a Westinghouse clock radio, five hunting knives, a box of pellets, a

screwdriver set, three vehicles, and a small box containing old coins, knives, watch, and jewelry.

When a court hearing was held to determine the legality of the search, one of the police officers admitted that it was standard practice for his department to conduct open-ended searches. Here is a telling excerpt from the transcript of the hearing:

COUNSEL: Would it be a fair statement that anything of value in that house was taken?

MARTIN: Yes, sir. . . .

COUNSEL: And would it be a fair statement that as long as you have been deputy in Sequoyah County that when you all do a search that this is the way in which it is conducted?

MARTIN: Yes, sir.

COUNSEL: You go in and look for everything that's there, for any leads or anything that might lead to something being stolen, or whatever?

MARTIN: Yes, sir.

Foster's defense attorney moved to suppress as evidence all of the property seized during the search. The trial court granted that defense motion because the police had "exhibited flagrant disregard for the terms of the warrant by conducting a wholesale seizure of Foster's property [which amounted] to a fishing expedition for the discovery of incriminating evidence."

The executive branch cannot be permitted to make a mockery of the search warrant. When law enforcement officers disregard the terms of a warrant, the Constitution's particularity requirement is undermined and a valid specific warrant is transformed into a general warrant. Since judicial officers are not on the scene when search warrants are flouted, the most opportune time to sanction such lawlessness is when executive branch representatives (prosecutors) come into court seeking the judge's permission to introduce the illegally obtained evidence. The only way the judiciary can maintain the integrity of its warrant-issuing process is by withholding its approval. The judicial branch cannot—and should not—rely on the executive branch to discipline its own agents.

The exclusionary rule fits neatly within the Constitution's separation-of-powers framework. The men who framed and ratified the Constitution recognized "the insufficiency of a mere parchment delineation of the boundaries" between the three branches of government. "The great security," wrote James Madison, against a gradual concentration of the several powers in the same department consists in giving those who administer each department the necessary constitutional means and personal motives to resist encroachments of the others. The provision for defense must in this, as in all other cases, be made commensurate to the danger of attack.

The exclusionary rule is a "commensurate" judicial response to the executive branch's attack on the judiciary's warrant-issuing prerogative. As the California Supreme Court has noted, since "the very purpose of an illegal search and seizure is to get evidence to introduce at trial, the success of the lawless venture depends entirely on the court's lending its aid by allowing the evidence to be introduced." Withholding such "aid" in appropriate cases is a measured response to executive branch encroachment.

E. CONCLUSION

The question of whether the exclusionary rule "works" is a difficult one for two reasons. First, there is inadequate empirical material on which to base conclusions one way or the other. Second, it may be unrealistic to assume that the Court's exclusionary rule jurisprudence is based on one articulated "rationale." While the Court speaks of the deterrence rationale as paramount, it also appears to be influenced by other public policy and political concerns.[67] It is difficult, if not impossible to gauge whether the Court's exclusionary rule cases have advanced these public policy concerns, and doubtless the debate over the efficacy of the exclusionary rule will continue for some time. To quote U.S. Supreme Court Justice Harry Blackmun:

> If a single principle may be drawn from this Court's exclusionary rule decisions, from Weeks through Mapp v. Ohio. To the decisions handed down [in United States v. Leon], it is that the scope of the exclusionary rule is subject to change in light of changing judicial understanding about the effects of the rule outside the confines of the courtroom.[68]

V. ALTERNATIVES TO THE EXCLUSIONARY RULE

By now, you certainly understand how the exclusionary rule penalizes governmental misconduct which yields evidence—direct or derivative—in violation of the Fourth Amendment. For exclusionary rule advocates, the only legitimate end for such governmental overreaching is juridical rejection of the evidence.

---

67. *Cf.* Andrew E. Taslitz, *Interpretive Method And The Federal Rules Of Evidence: A Call For A Politically Realistic Hermeneutics*, 32 HARV. J. ON LEGIS. 329 (1995) (arguing that courts interpret the Federal Rules of Evidence and, indeed, most legal texts, not merely on the basis of their purported "plain meaning," but also on a host of other factors, including considerations of politics and public policy).

68. United States v. Leon, 468 U.S. 897, 928 (1984) (Blackmun, J., concurring).

However, the Supreme Court has held that the exclusionary rule announced in *Weeks v. United States*[69] (evidence obtained in violation of the Fourth Amendment will be excluded from federal criminal prosecutions) and *Mapp v. Ohio*[70] (state criminal prosecutions) "is not a personal constitutional right. It is not calculated to redress the injury to the privacy of the victim of the search or seizure, for any '[r]eparation comes too late.'"[71] Instead, the exclusionary rule is a judicial sanction meant to deter unconstitutional searches and seizures by removing the incentive—admissible evidence—for law enforcement agents to violate the Fourth Amendment's prohibitions.

When unreasonable searches and seizures under the Fourth Amendment fail to yield evidence of criminality, the deterrent benefit of the exclusionary rule is lost. What remains is the constitutional violation. Although the person whose rights were violated may feel sufficiently vindicated at the lack of evidence and is pleased to go about his or her business, the fact remains that his/her Fourth Amendment rights were violated. Similarly, even if evidence of criminality was found but, subsequently, excluded at trial because it was discovered through an unreasonable search and seizure, the Fourth Amendment violation remains unanswered, despite suppression under the exclusionary rule, because the individual has not been made whole for the incursion upon his or her rights.

In light of its limitations, it is useful to examine alternatives to the exclusionary rule. We discuss some of them below, along with brief discussions of their costs and benefits.[72] But first, read the following description of what happened to Harvard Law student, Bryonn Bain. As you read, think about the exclusionary rule's utility as a remedy for Fourth Amend-

---

69. 232 U.S. 383 (1914).

70. 367 U.S. 643 (1961).

71. Stone v. Powell, 428 U.S. 465, 484–86 (1976) (quoting Linkletter v. Walker, 381 U.S. 618, 637 (1965)). *See* also United States v. Calandra, 414 U.S. 338, 347–48 (1974) (noting that the exclusionary rule safeguards constitutional rights "generally through its deterrent effect, rather than a personal constitutional right of the party aggrieved"). Yet, as discussed in an earlier chapter, only persons whose privacy, property, or locomotive interests have been invaded have "standing" to seek suppression.

72. There are others. For example, Some scholars have proffered varying **civil administrative processes** to redress those injured by police misconduct under the Fourth Amendment. Under these systems, "individuals injured by police misconduct would have access to a civil administrative process, which would include the availability of monetary recoveries for victims from police officers and their employers." Timothy Perrin, H. Mitchell Caldwell, Carol A. Chase, and Ronald W. Fagan, *If It's Broken, Fix It: Moving Beyond the Exclusionary Rule*, 83 IOWA L. REV. 669, 744 (1988) (modeling administrative remedies system after the California Fair Employment and Housing Act). Advocates of such systems assert that administrative systems will, *inter alia*, effectively deter police misconduct, as the processes would offer a remedy for all instances of police misconduct, regardless of criminal case dispositions; an effective incentive for victims to hold police accountable for abuse and misconduct; a fairer and more efficient forum; proportional remedies benefiting those with the worst injuries from official misconduct (versus those most culpable of the worst crimes); and an, overall, more trustworthy criminal justice system. *Id.*

ment violations given that no evidence was recovered from Bain and the case against him was ultimately dismissed.

After hundreds of hours and thousands of pages of legal theory in law school, I have finally had my first real lesson in the Law.... While home from school for the weekend, I was arrested for a crime I witnessed someone else commit.

We left the Latin Quarter nightclub that night laughing that Red, my cousin, had finally found someone shorter than his five-foot-five frame to dance with him. My younger brother, K, was fiending for a turkey sandwich, so we all walked over to the bodega around the corner, just one block west of Broadway. We had no idea that class was about to be in session....

As we left the store, armed only with sandwiches and Snapples, the three of us saw a group of young men standing around a car parked on the corner in front of the store. As music blasted by the wide-open doors of their car, the men around the car appeared to be arguing with someone in an apartment above the store. The argument escalated when one of the young men began throwing bottles at the apartment window. Several other people who had just left the club, as well as a number of random passersby, witnessed the altercation and began scattering to avoid the raining shards of glass....

My brother, cousin, and I abruptly began to walk up the street toward the subway to avoid the chaos that was unfolding. Another bottle was hurled. This time, the apartment window cracked, and more glass shattered onto the pavement. We were halfway up the block when we looked back at the guys who had been hanging outside the store. They had jumped in the car, turned off their music, and slammed the doors, and were getting away from the scene as quickly as possible. As we continued to walk toward the subway, about six or seven bouncers came running down the street to see who had caused all the noise. "Where do you BOYS think you're going?!" yelled the biggest of this muscle-bound band of bullies in black shirts. They came at my family and me with outstretched arms to corral us back down the block. "To the 2 train," I answered. Just then I remembered that there are constitutional restrictions on physically restraining people against their will. Common sense told me that the bouncers' authority couldn't possibly extend into the middle of the street around the corner from their club. "You have absolutely no authority to put your hands on any of us!" I insisted, with a sense of newly found conviction. We kept going.... The bouncer who appeared to be in charge warned us we would regret having ignored him. "You BOYS better stay right where you are!" barked the now seething bouncer. I told my brother and cousin to ignore him. We were not in their club. In fact, we were among the many people dispersing from the site of the disturbance, which had occurred an entire block away from their "territory." They were clearly beyond their jurisdiction (we spent weeks on the subject in Civil Procedure!). Furthermore, the bouncers had not bothered to ask anyone among the many witnesses what had happened before they attempted to apprehend us. They certainly had not asked us. . . .

Less than 10 minutes after we had walked by the bouncers, I was staring at badge 1727. We were screamed at and shoved around by Officer Ronald Connelly and his cronies. "That's them, officer!" the head bouncer said, indicting us with a single sentence. . . . "You boys out here throwin' bottles at people?!" shouted the officer. Asking any of the witnesses would have easily cleared up the issue of who had thrown the bottles. But the officer could not have cared less about that. My family and I were now being punished for the crime of thwarting the bouncers' unauthorized attempt to apprehend us. . . .

[W]e were up against the wall in a matter of minutes. Each of us had the legs of our dignity spread apart, was publicly frisked down from shirt to socks, and then had our pockets rummaged through. All while Officer Connelly insisted that we shut up and keep facing the wall or, as he told Red, he would treat us like we "were trying to fight back." The officers next searched through my backpack and seemed surprised to find my laptop and a casebook I had brought to the club so that I could get some studying done on the bus ride back to school.

We were shoved into the squad car in front of a crowd composed of friends and acquaintances who had been in the club with us and had by now learned of our situation. I tried with little success to play back the facts of the famous Miranda case in my mind. I was fairly certain these cops were in the wrong for failing to read us our rights. . . . We were never told that we had a right to remain silent. We were never told that we had the right to an attorney. We were never informed that anything we said could and would be used against us in a court of law. . . . [73]

NOTES AND QUESTIONS

1. Did the police act reasonably under the Fourth Amendment? Why? If not, should there be a legal remedy for Bryonn, his brother, and his cousin, Red? If so, should the remedy be identical or different for Bryonn, his brother, and cousin, Red?

2. Assume that police had unconstitutionally located evidence of criminality in Bryonn's backpack, his brother's socks, and Red's pockets. Would the evidence of criminality justify the police searches, or should the exclusionary rule operate on these facts in favor of the young men? Why?

---

73. Excerpted from Bryonn Bain, "Walking While Black: The Bill of Rights for Black Men," The Village Voice (April 26–May 2, 2000), located at http://www.villagevoice.com/gener ic/show_print.php?id=14362&page=bain&issue=0017&printcde=MzUwOTI0MzY4NQ= =&refpage=L25ld3MvaW5kZXguGhwP2lzc3VlPTAwMTcmcGFnZT1iYWluJmlk PTE0 MzYy. After four court appearances over five months, the D.A.'s case against Bryonn Bain, Kristofer Bain, and Kyle Vazquez was dismissed. No affidavits or other evidence were produced to support the charges against them. *Id.*

3. What if Bryonn and his relatives decided to forego a criminal trial and accept the government's offer that in exchange for a plea of "guilty," the government would not ask for jail time, a fine, or other penalty? What relief would the exclusionary rule provide the young men? As the overwhelming majority of criminal prosecutions are disposed of via guilty pleas and not jury trials, according to some scholars, "police officers know that a plea of guilty is the most likely case disposition, and so the issue of police misconduct or evidence suppression will never come to light." See Perrin, et al., *If It's Broken, supra*, n. 72.

4. The First Amendment states that "Congress shall make no law . . . abridging the freedom of speech, or of the press, or the right of the people peaceably to assemble, and to petition the Government for a redress of grievances." U.S. CONST. amend. I. According to Mr. Bain, the officers not only ignored his right to speak dissent at the governmental conduct, the officers seemed ready to punish exercise of that right. Is there a remedy for such a violation, if it occurred? Should there be?

5. What if, instead of the police, Immigration and Naturalization Service agents or FBI agents had engaged in the same sort of conduct? Would that change your answers to any of the above four questions?

A. Fourth Amendment Violations

1. TORT REMEDIES

a. *Common Law Tort Suits*

An aggrieved plaintiff who has suffered an unconstitutional violation of his Fourth Amendment rights has a number of legal options available. One option an aggrieved person may choose to pursue after suffering a Fourth Amendment violation would be to file a common law tort claim against the government. (The Federal Tort Claims Act, concerning tort suits against the federal government, adds complications to be discussed later in this Chapter.) Depending on the particulars of the violative conduct, such a lawsuit could sound in conversion, false arrest, false imprisonment, trespass to land, trespass to chattels, assault, battery, intentional infliction of emotional distress, negligent infliction of emotional distress, and invasion of privacy.[74] Generally, for those seeking redress for Fourth Amendment violations, common law tort claims are roundly considered to be "ineffective and remedially inadequate."[75] In addition to practical considerations (e.g., exorbitant costs of difficult litigation; nominal jury awards), procedural hurdles (e.g., governmental immunity of state actors and their employing

---

74. *See* Donald V. MacDougall, *Criminal Law: The Exclusionary Rule and Its Alternatives–Remedies for Constitutional Violations in Canada and the United States*, 76 J. CRIM. L. & CRIMINOLOGY 608, 643 (1985).

75. Perrin, et al., *If It's Broken, supra* n. 72, at 738 (citing Silas J. Wasserstrom and Louis Michael Seidman, *The Fourth Amendment as Constitutional Theory*, 77 GEO. L.J. 19, 83 (1988) ("civil suits against law enforcement officials . . . are wholly inadequate")).

entities), and tactical challenges (securing sympathetic police witnesses willing to testify against their coworkers):

> potential plaintiffs, after all, are individuals who are in contact with the criminal justice system, generally as suspects or defendants. Many are unlikely to bring suit for harm suffered, whether because of ignorance of their rights, poverty, fear of police reprisals, or the burdens of incarceration. Moreover, in many cases the harm suffered by individuals from the constitutional violation itself may be small, widely dispersed, and intangible, providing little incentive for potential plaintiffs to sue, especially given the lack of sympathy that this group of plaintiffs can expect from the trier of fact.[76]

b.   Section 1983

42 U.S.C. Section 1983 ("Section 1983")[77] is the most frequently used basis for police misconduct actions against state or local officers and provides a means by which an aggrieved person can enforce his/her rights against the police for unconstitutional searches and seizures. Section 1983 provides a civil rights enforcement remedy for a person who is deprived under color of state law of any rights, privileges, or immunities secured by the U.S. Constitution. It provides:

> [e]very person who, under color of any statute, ordinance, regulation, custom, or usage, of any State or Territory or the District of Columbia, subjects, or causes to be subjected, any citizen of the United States or other person within the jurisdiction thereof to the deprivation of any rights, privileges, or immunities secured by the Constitution and laws, shall be liable to the party injured in an action at law, suit in equity, or other proper proceeding for redress.[78]

Section 1983 was crafted " 'to deter state actors from using the badge of their authority to deprive individuals of their federally guaranteed rights' and to provide related relief."[79] It is the primary source of law for obtaining damages and equitable relief against state and local officials, and through them, municipalities who violate the Constitution. Section 1983 allows plaintiffs to sue state and local officials in state or federal courts (these courts exercise concurrent jurisdiction) for violating the plaintiff's constitutional rights. Although Section 1983 does not provide an aggrieved with a substantive basis for a claim or for relief for Fourth Amendment violations, it is a device that allows an aggrieved person the procedural means to file a civil claim against certain infringing governmental entities, primarily municipalities. Section 1983 does *not* apply, however, to states themselves, that is, not to states *as* states, even though municipalities are

---

76.   Daniel J. Meltzer, *Deterring Constitutional Violations By Law Enforcement Officials: Plaintiffs and Defendants as Private Attorneys General*, 88 COLUM. L. REV. 247, 284 (1988).

77.   28 U.S.C. § 1983 (2006).

78.   42 U.S.C. § 1983 (2006).

79.   Richardson v. McKnight, 521 U.S. 399, 403 (1997) (quoting Wyatt v. Cole, 504 U.S. 158, 161 (1992)).

entities that can be sued in their capacity as *municipalities*. State and municipal officials may also be subject to Section 1983 liability *as individuals*, though the government might choose, at times, to indemnify them.

Section 1983 does not require a specific state of mind for actionability.[80] A reviewing court must examine the nature of the constitutional right asserted to determine whether a deprivation of that right requires a particular state of mind.[81] Analysis of a plaintiff's Section 1983 claim(s), then, must begin with the identification of the specific and personal constitutional right allegedly infringed. For instance, deprivations of equal protection require proof of discriminatory intent on the part of the state actor,[82] deprivations under the Eighth Amendment require a showing of deliberate indifference,[83] and deprivations of First Amendment rights require proof that the state's action was intended to repress an individual's protected speech or association.[84]

In order to prevail under a Section 1983 claim, a plaintiff must establish that the violative conduct alleged: 1) was committed by a governmental official acting within the scope of that official's authority or misusing that authority and 2) deprived the plaintiff of constitutional or other federal rights. Under Section 1983, the plaintiff must allege and prove that the violative governmental actor acted under color of any statute, ordinance, regulation, custom, or usage. "Misuse of power, possessed by virtue of state law and made possible only because the wrongdoer is clothed with the authority of state law," constitutes action taken under color of state law.[85]

Two cases helped shape the law of municipal liability under Section 1983 in the United States. In *Monroe v. Pape*,[86] the Supreme Court held that government actors could be personally liable for Fourth Amendment violations under Section 1983. In *Monell v. Department of Social Services*,[87] civil relief pursuant to Section 1983 was extended to reach the deep pocket of municipalities. In *Monell*, the Supreme Court held that local governments may, in fact, be sued as "persons" under Section 1983. Also, pursuant to *Monell*, municipal liability attaches "for constitutional deprivations visited pursuant to governmental 'custom' even though such a custom has not received formal approval through the body's official decisionmaking channels."[88] Municipal liability may be imposed for a single decision by

---

80. *See* Parratt v. Taylor, 451 U.S. 527 (1981).

81. *Id.*

82. *See, e.g.*, Washington v. Davis, 426 U.S. 229 (1976).

83. *See, e.g.*, Estelle v. Gamble, 429 U.S. 97 (1976).

84. *See, e.g.*, Mt. Healthy City School District v. Doyle, 429 U.S. 274, 287 (1977).

85. Monroe v. Pape, 365 U.S. 167, 184 (1961) (quoting United States v. Classic, 313 U.S. 299, 326 (1941)).

86. *Id.*

87. 436 U.S. 658 (1978).

88. Monell v. Department of Social Servs., 436 U.S. 658, 690–91 (1978).

municipal policymakers under appropriate circumstances.[89] However:

> [e]ven though a single decision by municipal policymakers ... may be sufficient to establish that a municipal policy or custom caused the alleged deprivation, municipal liability may not be imposed pursuant to 42 USC § 1983 for a single incident of unconstitutional conduct ... without proof that the conduct was taken pursuant to a municipal policy or custom.[90]

There are also a wide variety of other limitations on suing municipalities that would take more space to describe than we have here.[91] Importantly, remedies for Section 1983 violations can include a variety of types of damages, as well as injunctive relief under appropriate circumstances.[92] Furthermore, Section 1988(b) of Title 42 of the United States Code provides that, for violations of Section 1981 and certain other specified civil right statutes, "the court, in its discretion, may allow the prevailing party, other than the United States, a reasonable attorney's fee as part of the costs."[93]

It is difficult to exaggerate the importance of filing a Section 1983 lawsuit within the statute of limitations. This point is illustrated in *Wallace v. Kato*.[94] There, Chicago police arrested without probable cause fifteen year old Andre Wallace during the investigation of a fatal shooting in 1994, subjected him to hours of custodial interrogation without the benefit of counsel, and obtained the teen's signed confession. Wallace was tried, convicted, and sentenced to 26 years' imprisonment.

On direct appeal, the appellate court determined that the officers arrested Wallace without probable cause and in violation of his Fourth Amendment right against unreasonable seizures.[95] Ultimately, in 2001, the

---

89. Pembaur v. City of Cincinnati, 475 U.S. 469, 480 (1986). *See also Safford Unified School District #1, et al. v. Redding,* 129 S.Ct. 2633 (2009) (finding strip search of thirteen year old student's bra and panties for forbidden over-the-counter drugs by Safford Unified School District #1 school administrators violated the Fourth Amendment). In *Safford*, the Court found the school district's officials were entitled to qualified immunity "where clearly established law does not show that the search violated the Fourth Amendment." *Id.* at 2644(citing *Pearson v. Callahan*, 129 S.Ct. 808 (2009)). The Court, however, did not rule on the school district's liability, as the Ninth Circuit failed to address that issue in its decision. Accordingly, the case was remanded "for consideration of the *Monell* [*v. Dep't of Soc. Servs.*, 436 U.S. 658, 694 (1978)] claim." Id.

90. *Id.* Important progeny of *Pembaur*, for those interested in researching the matter, include City of St. Louis v. Praprotnik, 485 U.S. 112 (1988); City of Canton v. Harris, 489 U.S. 378 (1989); and Board of County Commissioners of Bryan County v. Brown, 520 U.S. 397 (1997).

91. *See generally* JOHN C. JEFFRIES, ET AL., CIVIL RIGHTS ACTIONS: ENFORCING THE CONSTITUTION 134–216 (2000).

92. *See id.* at 303–34 (discussing compensatory and punitive damages), 745–897 (discussing injunctive relief); JOHN C. JEFFRIES, ET AL., 2006 SUPPLEMENT TO CIVIL RIGHTS ACTIONS: ENFORCING THE CONSTITUTION 45, 109–27 (2006) (updating same).

93. 42 U.S.C. § 1988(b). For details concerning this attorneys' fees statute, *see* JEFFRIES, *supra* note 91, at 335–403; JEFFRIES 2006 SUPPLEMENT, *supra* note 92, at 46–61.

94. 549 U.S. 384 (2007).

95. *Id.* at 386.

appellate court of Illinois concluded that the taint of the unconstitutional seizure was not sufficiently attenuated, making admission of the confession constitutionally improper. Wallace's criminal conviction was vacated and the case remanded. In 2002, prosecutors dropped all charges.[96]

In 2003, Wallace filed a Section 1983 lawsuit against the city of Chicago and several officers based on the unlawful arrest. The district court granted summary judgment for the defendants, which was affirmed by the Seventh Circuit. According to the courts, Wallace's lawsuit was time-barred. Specifically, the circuit court of appeals determined that Wallace's cause of action did not accrue when his conviction was vacated in 2002, but at the time of his 1994 arrest.

The Supreme Court affirmed. The Court determined that the statute of limitations began to run when Wallace first appeared before the examining magistrate and was bound over for trial on his underlying felony charge. The Court's rationale was based on application of both federal and state law, as well as common law treatment of the crimes of false arrest and false imprisonment.[97] The Court announced that, however, the accrual date for a Section 1983 claim is a matter of federal law.[98] Under federal law, accrual occurs when the plaintiff has "a complete and present cause of action."[99]

However, another consideration "ar[ose] from the common law's distinctive treatment of false arrest and false imprisonment," the common law causes of action most analogous to Wallace's Section 1983 claim.[100] Wallace's claim arose from his detention without legal process, *i.e.,* when he was arrested in 1994 without a warrant. The Court determined that the limitations period for a false imprisonment claim begins to run when the false imprisonment ends; after that, "any damages recoverable must be based on a malicious prosecution claim and on the wrongful use of judicial process rather than detention itself."[101] The Court did not find that Wallace's false imprisonment ended when he was released from custody after the charges against him were dropped, but when the legal process was initiated against him—when he was bound over for trial by the magistrate.[102]

Since Wallace's claim accrued before he had been convicted, he argued that the Court's decision in *Heck v. Humphrey*[103] applied to his case. The Court disagreed, characterizing the requested application as a "bizarre extension of *Heck*."[104] The Court also refused to adopt a rule applying

---

96. *Id.* at 387.

97. *Id.* at 389.

98. *Id.* at 388.

99. *Id.*

100. *Id.* at 388.

101. *Id.* at 389.

102. *Id.*

103. 512 U.S. 477 (1994).

104. Wallace, 549 U.S. at 393.

equitable tolling in cases where a false arrest claim accrued before the existence or setting aside of a conviction.[105]

Justices Stevens and Souter concurred in the Court's judgment that Wallace's action was time-barred.[106] However, they disagreed with the majority's reliance upon common-law tort analogies. Justices Breyer and Ginsberg dissented, arguing that equitable tolling should occur when a Section 1983 plaintiff reasonably claims that the government's unlawful behavior "was, or will be, necessary to a criminal conviction."[107]

Recently, the Court foreclosed plaintiffs' ability to bring Section 1983 actions and recover attorney's fees against police officers and municipalities for "false arrests," *i.e.,* full custodial arrests for "citation only" offenses. In a 9–0 decision, the Court reversed a Virginia Supreme Court determination that suppression of evidence obtained illegally under state law violated the Fourth Amendment. In *Virginia v. Moore*,[108] the defendant was arrested for the misdemeanor offense of driving on a suspended license and in violation of Virginia's "citation only" law.[109] As a result of the arrest, police affected a full custodial arrest and a search incident to arrest, which led to the discovery of cocaine and, eventually, the defendant's conviction of possession with intent to distribute cocaine.[110] The defendant's motion to suppress was denied, and he was convicted.[111] The Virginia Supreme Court reversed the defendant's conviction, given the officers' violation of Virginia's "citation only" law and the lack of a Fourth Amendment "search incident to citation" exception to the warrant "requirement."[112] The Court, reversed and remanded to the Virginia Supreme Court, holding that the arrest did not offend the Fourth Amendment, as governmental violations of state law do not mandate the federal constitutional remedy of evidence exclusion.[113]

c.   Bivens Actions and Qualified Immunity

Section 1983 lawsuits cannot be brought against federal officials; however, redress can be had pursuant to *Bivens v. Six Unknown Named Agents of the Federal Bureau of Narcotics*[114] ("*Bivens*"). In *Bivens*, federal officials forcibly entered the home of an innocent criminal suspect without a warrant, manacled him, searched and ransacked his apartment, and arrested him. In the face of the exclusionary rule's remedial ineffectiveness,

---

105. *Id.*

106. *Id.* at 397-400 (Stevens, J. and Souter, J., concurring in judgment).

107. *See id.* at 400-05 (Breyer, J., dissenting).

108. 128 S.Ct. 1598 (2008).

109. *Id.* at 1601.

110. *Id.*

111. *Id.* at 1602.

112. *Id.*

113. *See id.* at 1604-06.

114. 403 U.S. 388 (1971).

the Supreme Court created an implied private cause of action under the Fourth Amendment and permitted a lawsuit against the federal agents.[115]

Bivens and Section 1983 allow a plaintiff to seek damages from governmental agents who have violated his Fourth Amendment rights. But governmental agents performing discretionary functions generally are granted qualified immunity and are shielded from tort liability for all civil damages, so long as their conduct does not violate clearly established statutory or constitutional rights of which a reasonable person would have known. The qualified immunity analysis is identical under either *Bivens* or Section 1983. Courts evaluating a claim of qualified immunity "must first determine whether the plaintiff has alleged the deprivation of an actual constitutional right at all, and if so, proceed to determine whether that right was clearly established at the time of the alleged violation."[116] This order of procedure is designed to "spare a defendant not only unwarranted liability, but unwarranted demands customarily imposed upon those defending a long drawn-out lawsuit."[117] Deciding the constitutional question before addressing the qualified immunity question also promotes clarity in the legal standards for official conduct, to the benefit of both the officers and the general public.[118] Under a *Bivens* cause of action, the governmental official must have been acting "under color of authority" and the governmental official must have deprived the individual of his constitutional rights under the Fourth Amendment or some other constitutional provision.[119] Absolute immunity from any suit under *Bivens* or Section 1983 whatsoever may also be available to certain categories of persons while they are engaged in certain conduct, for example, to legislators while engaging in activities like voting on bills, holding hearings, or participating in committee debates and to judicial officers acting within the scope of the judicial functions of their office.[120]

---

115. *Id.*

116. Conn v. Gabbert, 526 U.S. 286 (1999).

117. Siegert v. Gilley, 500 U.S. 226, 232 (1991).

118. *See* County of Sacramento v. Lewis, 523 U.S. 833, 840–42, n. 5 (1998). Other important qualified immunity cases are Saucier v. Katz, 533 U.S. 194 (2001) (qualified immunity applied in a *Bivens* action challenging a military policeman's use of excessive force in removing a demonstrator protesting at a speech given by Vice President Gore at a military base; the application of the Fourth Amendment force rule to this situation did not involve a violation of "clearly established law" that would be apparent to a reasonable police officer); *But see* Pearson v. Callahan, 129 S.Ct. 808 (2009) (overruling *Saucier*); Groh v. Ramirez, 540 U.S. 551 (2004) (discussed elsewhere in this text, the *Groh* Court disallowed qualified immunity); Brosseau v. Haugen, 543 U.S. 194 (2004) (police officer sued under Section 1983 for allegedly shooting a fleeing felon in the back in violation of Fourth Amendment excessive force rules was entitled to qualified immunity); Hope v. Pelzer, 536 U.S. 730 (2002) (articulating the method that courts are to follow in assessing whether the law is "clearly established" in arguably unusual circumstances); Wilson v. Layne, 526 U.S. 603 (1999) (media ride along in executing an arrest warrant in a private home violated the Fourth Amendment, but the officers were entitled to qualified immunity because that rule was not then "clearly established").

119. A *Bivens* cause of action has been had on Fifth Amendment and Eighth Amendment claims. *See, e.g.*, Sonntag v. Dooley, 650 F.2d 904 (7th Cir.1981) (Fifth Amendment); Carlson v. Green, 446 U.S. 14 (1980) (Eighth Amendment).

120. *See* JEFFRIES, *supra* note 91, at 50–79.

Recently, however, the Court revisited *Saucier*'s two-step test and concluded that although often appropriate, "[it] should no longer be regarded as mandatory."[121] In *Pearson v. Callahan*, the Court was asked to determine qualified immunity of Utah police officers who relied upon the doctrine of "consent-once-removed" as legal justification for the warrantless search incident to arrest of a suspected dealer's home in which he sold methamphetamine to a cooperating undercover informant voluntarily admitted.[122] Callahan was subsequently convicted of possession and distribution of methamphetamine; however, the Utah Court of Appeals vacated the conviction.[123] Callahan then filed a federal lawsuit in the district court under 42 U.S.C. § 1983, alleging that the officers' entry into his home violated the Fourth Amendment.[124] At the time of the officers' entry, "consent-once-removed" had not been accepted by the Tenth Circuit.[125] Nevertheless, the district court granted summary judgment on behalf of the defendants, holding that the officers were entitled to qualified immunity, as they could have reasonably believed that "consent-once-removed" authorized their entry into Callahan's home.[126] The Tenth Circuit reversed the district court's decision (notwithstanding the other courts' and circuits' acceptance of "consent-once-removed"), finding that, under *Saucier*'s two-part test, the officers were not entitled to qualified immunity, as 1) Callahan had established a Fourth Amendment violation and 2) the officers' unconstitutionality was clearly established.[127]

In reversing the Tenth Circuit's decision, the Court determined that because the officers' unlawfulness was not clearly established, they were entitled to qualified immunity, given that the doctrine of consent-once-removed had gained acceptance in two states and in three federal courts of appeals "involving consensual entries by private citizens acting as confidential informants."[128]

---

121. Pearson v. Callahan, 129 S.Ct. 808, 815 (2009).

122. *See id*. at 813. "Consent-once-removed" authorizes warrantless entry into a home "when consent to enter has already been granted to an undercover officer or informant who has observed contraband in plain view." *Id*. at 814. Note that Callahan did not allow the informant inside his home; Callahan's daughter let the informant inside. *Id*. at 813.

123. *Id*. at 814.

124. *Id*.

125. *See id*. at 814.

126. *Id*.

127. *See id*. at 813. The Tenth Circuit's decision "took no issue with application of the doctrine when the initial consent was granted to an undercover law enforcement officer, but the majority disagreed with decisions 'that broade[n] this doctrine to grant informants the same capabilities as undercover officers.'" Id. at 814 (citation omitted).

128. *See id*. at 822–23. According to the Court, law enforcement officers "are entitled to rely on existing lower court cases without facing personal liability for their actions.... [i]f judges thus disagree on a constitutional question, it is unfair to subject police to money damages for picking the losing side of the controversy." *Id*. at 823 (citation omitted).

That "consent-once-removed" had not been accepted by the Tenth Circuit was of no import ("[t]he officers here were entitled to rely on these cases, even though their own Federal Circuit had not yet ruled on 'consent-once-removed' entries"[129]), nor was the court's adherence to the *Saucier* procedure. It is important to note that the Court itself neither accepted nor rejected the "consent-once-removed" doctrine. In the Court's rejection— although the *Pearson* Court characterizes its decision as "relaxation"[130]—of *Saucier*'s mandate, Justice Alito, writing for the majority, cited criticism by lower court judges, Justices, and the "considerable body of new experience to consider regarding the consequences of requiring adherence to this inflexible procedure."[131] Specifically, the Court determined that the two-step test fails to serve the purpose of qualified immunity when the test "forces the parties to endure additional burdens of suit—such as the costs of litigating constitutional questions and delays attributable to resolving them—when the suit otherwise could be disposed of more readily."[132] In other words, "[a]dherence to *Saucier*'s two-step protocol departs from the general rule of constitutional avoidance and runs counter to the older, wiser judicial counsel not to pass on questions of constitutionality ... unless such adjudication is unavoidable."[133] Relaxation of *Saucier*'s mandate allows lower court judges—those the Court deemed to be in the best position to do so—to determine if, and how, *Saucier* "will best facilitate the fair and efficient disposition of each case."[134]

Absolute immunity has also been extended to cover prosecutors in a number of circumstances. Recently, In *Van de Kamp v. Goldstein*,[135] the Court considered how immunity applies where a prosecutor is engaged in certain administrative activities. In 1980, Goldstein was convicted of murder after trial, sentenced, and incarcerated.[136] Eighteen years later, Goldstein filed a habeas corpus action in the Federal District Court for the Central District of California, claiming that he had been improperly convicted, based on the false testimony of aptly-named jailhouse informant, Edward Floyd Fink.[137] Fink not only gave the government useful testimony in Goldstein's prosecution, but had done so in others.[138] In exchange for his useful testimony, the government gave Fink "testimony-related rewards:"

---

129. *Id*. at 813.

130. *Id*. at 822. In fact, the Court had directed the parties to address whether *Saucier* should be overruled. *Id*. at 815.

131. *Id*. at 817. "Where a decision has been questioned by Members of the Court in later decisions and [has] defied consistent application by the lower courts, these factors weigh in favor of reconsideration." *Id*. at 818 (citations omitted).

132. *Id*. at 818 (citations omitted).

133. *Id*.

134. *Id*. at 813.

135. 129 S.Ct. 855 (2009).

136. *See id*. at 859.

137. *Id*.

138. *Id*.

reduced jail time.[139] Prosecutors in the Los Angeles County District Attorney's Office knew of Fink and his usefulness.[140] They were also aware of their office's role in securing less jail time in exchange for Fink's usefulness.[141] Still, no one in the office disclosed this impeachment evidence information to Goldstein's defense attorney before or during trial.[142]

Goldstein sued petitioners, John Van de Kamp and Kurt Livesay, the former Los Angeles County district attorney, and chief deputy district attorney under Section 1983, claiming, that the failure to disclose Fink's impeachment evidence—which the government was required to do, per *Giglio v. U.S.*[143]—led to Goldstein's conviction.[144] An evidentiary hearing in the district court revealed that Fink had lied when he testified that he received no favorable governmental treatment when, in fact, he had. The district court determined that disclosure might have made a difference in Goldstein's trial and ordered either a new trial or Goldstein's release. As Goldstein had already served 25 years of his sentence, the state chose to release him.[145]

In his Section 1983 claim, Goldstein sought damages for the office's chief supervisory attorneys' failure to train and supervise adequately its prosecutors and establish an information system about informants.[146] At Goldstein's trial, the trial deputy did not know of Fink's testimonial favors because the supervisors "failed to create any system for the Deputy District Attorneys handling criminal cases to access information pertaining to the benefits provided to jailhouse informants and other impeachment information."[147] The supervisors claimed absolute immunity and moved for dismissal.[148] The district court denied the motion, as the charged conduct amounted to "administrative," not "prosecutorial," conduct and, therefore, fell outside the scope of the prosecutor's absolute immunity to Section 1983 claims.[149] On interlocutory appeal, the Ninth Circuit affirmed the District Court's "no immunity" determination.[150] The Supreme Court disagreed. Even assuming, *arguendo* (as the Court did), that *Giglio* imposed training, supervision, or information-system management obligations on prosecutors

---

139. *See id.*

140. *Id.*

141. *Id.*

142. *See id.*

143. 405 U.S. 150, 154 (1972). In *Giglio*, the Supreme Court recognized the inherent danger in the use of "jailhouse snitches" and obligated the government to disclose whether testimonial favors are promised or given to those who provide useful prosecutorial testimony. In Goldstein, Fink lied about receiving testimonial favors.

144. *See Van de Kamp v. Goldstein*, 129 S.Ct. 855, 859 (2009).

145. *See id.*

146. *See id.* at 859.

147. *See id.* at 861.

148. *See id.* at 859.

149. *See id.*

150. *See id.*

like Goldstein's, the Court found that these government officials enjoy absolute immunity, akin to that enjoyed by those prosecutors they supervised.[151] The Court could not (consistent with *Imbler*'s concerns regarding line prosecutors) exempt discretionary supervisory decisions from absolute immunity. Supervisory decisions of the type challenged by Goldstein "necessarily require legal knowledge and the exercise of related discretion," even though they involve training and supervision generally or concerning the particular case in question. The Court posed the following hypothetical to make its point:

> [s]uppose that Goldstein had brought such a case, seeking damages not only from the trial prosecutor but also from a supervisory prosecutor or from the trial prosecutor's colleagues—all on the ground that they should have found and turned over the impeachment material about Fink. *Imbler* makes clear that all these prosecutors would enjoy absolute immunity from such a suit. The prosecutors' behavior, taken individually or separately, would involve "[p]reparation . . . for . . . trial," *424 U.S., at 431, n. 33, 96 S.Ct. 984, 47 L.Ed.2d 128*, and would be "intimately associated with the judicial phase of the criminal process" because it concerned the evidence presented at trial. *Id., at 430, 96 S.Ct. 984, 47 L.Ed.2d 128*. And all of the considerations that this Court found to militate in favor of absolute immunity in *Imbler* would militate in favor of immunity in such a case.

> The only difference we can find between *Imbler* and our hypothetical case lies in the fact that, in our hypothetical case, a prosecutorial supervisor or colleague might himself be liable for damages *instead of* the trial prosecutor. But we cannot find that difference (in the pattern of liability among prosecutors within a single office) to be critical. Decisions about indictment or trial prosecution will often involve more than one prosecutor within an office. We do not see how such differences in the pattern of liability among a group of prosecutors in a single office could alleviate *Imbler*'s basic fear, namely, that the threat of damages liability would affect the way in which prosecutors carried out their basic court-related tasks. Moreover, this Court has pointed out that it is the interest in protecting the proper functioning of the office, rather than the interest in protecting its occupant, that is of primary importance. *Kalina, 522 U.S., at 125, 118 S.Ct. 502, 139 L.Ed.2d 471*. Thus, we must assume that the prosecutors in our hypothetical suit would enjoy absolute immunity.[152]

Given the Court's conclusion that supervisory prosecutors are immune when sued for their actions regarding a specific or particular trial, the outcome in the instant matter was obvious to the Court:

> [o]nce we determine that supervisory prosecutors are immune in a suit directly attacking their actions related to an individual trial, we must find they are similarly immune in the case before us. We agree with

---

151. *See id.*

152. *Id.* at 862–63 (emphasis in the original).

the Court of Appeals that the office's *general* methods of supervision and training are at issue here, but we do not agree that that difference is critical for present purposes. That difference does not preclude an intimate connection between prosecutorial activity and the trial process. The management tasks at issue, insofar as they are relevant, concern how and when to make impeachment information available at a trial. They are thereby directly connected with the prosecutor's basic trial advocacy duties. And, in terms of *Imbler*'s functional concerns, a suit charging that a supervisor made a mistake directly related to a particular trial, on the one hand, and a suit charging that a supervisor trained and supervised inadequately, on the other, would seem very much alike.[153]

Accordingly, whither *Imbler* goes, so does *Goldstein*:

> We conclude that the very reasons that led this Court in *Imbler* to find absolute immunity require a similar finding in this case. We recognize, as Chief Judge Hand pointed out, that sometimes such immunity deprives a plaintiff of compensation that he undoubtedly merits; but the impediments to the fair, efficient functioning of a prosecutorial office that liability could create lead us to find that *Imbler* must apply here.[154]

d.   The Federal Tort Claims Act

The United States, as a sovereign, is immune from lawsuits and cannot be sued except to the extent that it has consented to suit by statute via an unequivocally expressed waiver of its sovereign immunity.[155] The Federal Tort Claims Act ("FTCA")[156] is such a waiver and serves as the exclusive remedy for tort claims against the United States government. (It is impor-

---

153.   *Id*. at 864. The Court handled separately, but not differently, Goldstein's claim that the Los Angeles County District Attorney's Office should have established a system that would have permitted line prosecutors to access information pertaining to testimony-related rewards. According to the Court, any differences do not require a different outcome. Deciding what to include and what not to include in an information system is little different from making similar decisions in respect to training. Again, determining the criteria for inclusion or exclusion requires knowledge of the law. *Id*. Justice Souter explained that were this claim allowed, a court would still have to review the prosecuting office's legal judgments

> not simply about *whether* to have an information system but also about *what kind* of system is appropriate, and whether an appropriate system would have included *Giglio*-related information *about one particular kind of trial informant*. Such decisions—whether made prior to or during a particular trial—are "intimately associated with the judicial phase of the criminal process." *Imbler, supra, at 430, 96 S.Ct. 984, 47 L.Ed.2d 128*; see *Burns, 500 U.S., at 486, 111 S.Ct. 1934, 114 L.Ed.2d 547*. And, for the reasons set out above, all *Imbler*'s functional considerations (and the anomalies we mentioned earlier, *supra, at ___, 172 L.Ed.2d, at 716–717*) apply here as well.

Id. at 864 (emphasis in the original).

154.   *Id*. at 864–65.

155.   *See* FDIC v. Meyer, 510 U.S. 471, 475 (1994); *see also* United States v. Mitchell, 445 U.S. 535, 538 (1980).

156.   28 U.S.C. § 1346(b).

tant to distinguish actions against the government itself from those against its agents which *Bivens*, for example, might permit.) Essentially, the FTCA allows individuals to bring lawsuit against the federal government for personal injuries and property damage "caused by the negligent or wrongful acts or omissions of . . . employees of the Government while acting within the scope of [their] offices or employment."[157] The government itself, not its agencies or employees, is the only proper defendant in an FTCA lawsuit.[158] An action against the United States brought pursuant to the FTCA is exclusive of any other civil action or proceeding for money damages. Thus, for those injured by the tortious actions of federal government employees, the FTCA is the exclusive means available to seek relief and redress.

Under the FTCA, the United States is liable only to the extent that it has waived sovereign immunity.[159] Thus, plaintiffs cannot state a Fourth Amendment claim against a federal employee in his official capacity because the FTCA does not waive sovereign immunity for constitutional violations.[160] The Supreme Court has determined that the United States' liability under the FTCA is to be based on the state law liability of a private party, not of a state or municipal entity. The United States waives sovereign immunity " 'under circumstances' where local law would make a 'private *person*' liable in tort."[161] The United States is entitled to all defenses available to its agents.[162] Any monetary judgment recovered from the defendant government is payable out of the public treasury of the United States.[163]

While the FTCA provides a limited waiver of the United States' sovereign immunity, this waiver does not apply to "any claim arising out of assault, battery, false imprisonment, false arrest, malicious prosecution, abuse of process, libel, slander, misrepresentation, deceit, or interference

---

157. 28 U.S.C. § 1346(b)(1). The FTCA does not provide redress for the following actions: United States employees acting within their discretionary authority; actions by U.S. Postal Service employees which affect the transmission of the mail; property seized pursuant to tax or customs duty; admiralty; the establishment of a quarantine; the intentional torts of actors that include "assault, battery, false imprisonment, false arrest, malicious prosecution, abuse of process, libel, slander, misrepresentation, deceit, or interference with contract rights;" fiscal operations of the U.S. Treasury; "combatant activities of the military or naval forces, or the Coast Guard, during time of war;" and "actions arising in a foreign country." *See* 28 U.S.C. §§ 2680(h), (i)–(k).

158. *See* 28 U.S.C. §§ 2674, 2679(a), (b).

159. *See* 28 U.S.C. §§ 1346(b), 2674. Congress has not waived sovereign immunity with respect to constitutional violations. Accordingly, constitutional claims against the United States and its employees in their official capacity under the Fourth Amendment should be dismissed for lack of subject matter jurisdiction, as the Fourth Amendment's mere existence does not waive sovereign immunity.

160. 28 U.S.C. § 2679(b). Plaintiffs may seek redress for Fourth Amendment violations against the employee in his individual capacity.

161. United States v. Olson, 546 U.S. 43, 44 (2005) (quoting 28 U.S.C. Section 1346(b)(1)).

162. 28 U.S.C. § 2674.

163. *See* Land v. Dollar, 330 U.S. 731, 738 (1947).

with contract rights,"[164] that is, the federal government does not consent to suit for these torts or for claims arising out of these torts. Accordingly, plaintiff's FTCA claims against the Government for false arrest and malicious prosecution are, <u>ostensibly</u>, barred by the doctrine of sovereign immunity. However, within the FTCA, there is an exception to the exception, which provides that the United States waives its sovereign immunity "with regard to acts or omissions of investigative or law enforcement officers of the United States Government . . . [on] any claim arising . . . out of assault, battery, false imprisonment, false arrest, abuse of process, or malicious prosecution."[165] "Investigative or law enforcement officers" are defined as "any officer of the United States who is empowered by law to execute searches, to seize evidence, or to make arrests for violations of Federal law."[166]

A successful action under the FTCA cannot lie "unless the claimant shall have first presented the claim to the appropriate Federal agency and his claim shall have been finally denied by the agency."[167] Failure to file an administrative claim may divest the court of subject matter jurisdiction. Plaintiffs must also comply with the two-year statute of limitations (which can be equitably tolled).[168]

For Fourth Amendment violations which occur on the federal level, plaintiffs are not limited to an FTCA lawsuit, but may also sue federal agents in their individual capacity for relief pursuant to *Bivens*.[169] Although an FTCA lawsuit may be regarded as superior to a *Bivens* lawsuit, both causes of action may be brought simultaneously. "Thus the plaintiff whose constitutional rights have been violated by a federal police officer in bad faith can be assured of monetary compensation at the same time he can exact direct 'revenge' against the official to the extent the official can afford it."[170]

e.   Section 1985

When police officers conspire among themselves or with other actors to deprive a person of his or her constitutional rights, 42 U.S.C. Section 1985(3)[171] may provide civil relief for an aggrieved plaintiff. Under 42 Section 1985(3), a plaintiff must prove the following four requirements: (1) the governmental actors conspired, (2) "for the purpose of depriving, either directly or indirectly, any person or class of persons of the equal protection of the laws, or of equal privileges and immunities under the laws," (3) one

---

164.   *See* 28 U.S.C. § 2680(h).

165.   *Id.*

166.   *Id.*

167.   28 U.S.C. § 2675.

168.   *See* Irwin v. Department of Veterans Affairs, 498 U.S. 89, 95–96 (1990).

169.   403 U.S. 388 (1971).

170.   CHARLES H. WHITEBREAD, CHRISTOPHER SLOBOGIN, CRIMINAL PROCEDURE: AN ANALYSIS OF CASES AND CONCEPTS (4TH Ed. University Textbook Series, 2000) 52.

171.   42 U.S.C. § 1985(3) (1988).

or more of the conspirators acted "in furtherance of the object of the conspiracy," and (4) the plaintiff was "injured in his person or property" or "deprived of having and exercising any right or privileged of a citizen of the United States."[172] Section 1985(3) reaches a broad range of conspiracies, as it contains no "under color of law" requirement. However, Section 1985(3) requires "some racial or . . . otherwise class-based, invidiously discriminatory animus behind the conspirators' action."[173] Lower courts have found that Section 1985(3) applies also where the conspiracy was motivated by the plaintiff's ethnicity, religious affiliation, gender, or attempt to exercise a fundamental right. Failure to prove such animus defeats a Section 1985(3) claim. Additionally, private conspiracies to violate constitutional guarantees (as against state interference or infringement) are not actionable under Section 1985(3).[174]

f. RICO

There is budding precedent for aggrieved plaintiffs to proceed under the civil arm of the Racketeer Influenced and Corrupt Organizations Act ("Civil RICO").[175] As thwarting organized crime was the primary impetus for the promulgation of RICO, the original goal of RICO was twofold: (1) augment police departments' abilities to fight organized crime and (2) provide new remedies for parties' injured as a result of organized criminal activities.[176]

Given Civil RICO's purpose —protecting legitimate enterprises from organized criminal corruption[177]—how might it be useful in the face of a Fourth Amendment violation? Civil RICO may not have been crafted to be used against the very agencies it was drafted to empower; however, its purposeful language provides tools which may be employed to build a federal cause of action.[178] The seeming proliferation of "bad cops" and departmental corruption suggest that Civil RICO's use against police officers is not an inconceivable stretch, particularly considering that Congress intended a liberal construction.[179] Using Civil RICO to battle the scourge of

---

172. *See* Griffin v. Breckenridge, 403 U.S. 88, 100–02 (1971).

173. *Id.* at 102 (citation omitted).

174. *See, e.g.,* United Brotherhood of Carpenters v. Scott, 463 U.S. 825 (1983) (holding conspiracy to violate First Amendment rights not actionable without state action).

175. 18 U.S.C. § 1964 (1994 & Supp. 2000).

176. *See* Congressional Statement of Findings and Purpose, Organized Crime Control Act, Oct. 15, 1970, 1, 84 Stat. 922, 923 (1970).

177. *See, e.g.,* Wesley Kobylak, *Annotation, Civil Action for Damages under 18 U.S.C.A. § 1964(c) of the Racketeer Influenced and Corrupt Organizations Act for Injuries Sustained by Reason of Racketeering Activity,* 70 A.L.R. Fed. 538, 544 (1984) (noting RICO's purpose was to prevent organized crime's invasion and corruption of legitimate enterprises).

178. *See* Rene Sanchez, *L.A. Police Misconduct Likened to Racketeering: Judge's Order Could Widen City's Liability,* Wash. Post. (Aug. 31, 2004) at A4 (quoting Professor Erwin Chemerinsky's reaction to the use of federal Civil RICO against the city of Los Angeles, CA).

179. Steven P. Ragland, *Using the Master's Tools: Fighting Persistent Police Misconduct with Civil RICO,* 51 Am. U.L. Rev. 139, 148 (2001).

police departmental misconduct may be appropriate. Civil RICO has been described as having "many benefits over [S]ection 1983 and provides a means to overcome the common barriers faced by injured plaintiffs suing errant officers."[180]

To state a claim under Civil RICO, a plaintiff must allege "(1) conduct (2) of an enterprise (3) through a pattern (4) of racketeering activity." Under Civil RICO, plaintiffs are entitled to damages only from an injury to business or property as a result of racketeering activities.[181] "Racketeering activity" is "any act or threat involving murder, kidnapping ... bribery, extortion ... or dealing in a controlled substance," as well as obstruction of justice or criminal investigations, tampering with or retaliating against witnesses, victims, or informants.[182] A plaintiff must establish a nexus between the violative acts and a lawful RICO enterprise via three elements: 1) the named defendant committed the violative acts, 2) doing so was facilitated by his position within the enterprise, and 3) the enterprise felt the effect of the commission of the violative acts.[183]

Civil RICO does not provide redress for personal injuries;[184] however, where such injuries lead to pecuniary loss, a Civil RICO cause of action may sound.[185] Civil RICO claims also must allege a "pattern of racketeering activity" which requires at least two acts of racketeering activity within a ten-year period.[186] The pattern requirement has been described as one of the more complicated elements of a RICO claim. Additionally, the Supreme Court requires that a plaintiff satisfy the "continuity plus relationship" test, which requires a showing that the predicate acts are related to each other and pose a threat of continued criminal activity.[187] The relationship element is met if the predicate acts have "the same or similar purposes, results, participants, victims, or methods of commission, or otherwise are interrelated by distinguishing characteristics and are not isolated events."[188] The continuity element is met if there is a series of related predicates extending "for such an extended period of time such that a threat of future harm is implicit," called closed-ended continuity, or if the predicates "by [their] nature project[] into the future with a threat of

---

180. Matthew V. Hess, *Good Cop–Bad Cop: Reassessing the Legal Remedies for Police Misconduct*, 1993 UTAH L. REV. 149, 167 (1993).

181. *See* 18 U.S.C. § 1964(c) (1994 & Supp. 2000).

182. 18 U.S.C. §§ 1961(1)(A), 1961(1)(B).

183. *See* United States v. Cauble, 706 F.2d 1322, 1333 (5th Cir.1983) (explaining the newly modified formulation for establishing a nexus under RICO).

184. *See* Oscar v. University Students Co-op. Ass'n, 965 F.2d 783, 785 (9th Cir.1992) (holding personal injuries not compensable).

185. Ragland, *Master's Tools*, *supra* note 179, at 153 (noting that "plaintiff's injury is his pecuniary loss resulting from injury and inability to work not his actual physical injury").

186. *See* 18 U.S.C. § 1961(5) (1994 & Supp. 2000).

187. *See* H.J. Inc. v. Northwestern Bell Tel. Co., 492 U.S. 229, 239 (1989); Midwest Grinding Co., Inc. v. Spitz, 976 F.2d 1016, 1022 (7th Cir.1992).

188. H.J. Inc., 492 U.S. at 240.

repetition," as when they "are part of an ongoing entity's regular way of doing business," called open-ended continuity.[189]

There is little case law on the use of Civil RICO against violative police officers and their employing departments. RICO does define "enterprise" to include legal entities as well as informal associations. However, RICO is silent on whether the definition applies to state and local entities. The Supreme Court has not yet reached this question. Nevertheless, it seems that federal courts construe "enterprise" under RICO as including state and local entities.[190]

The seminal case on Civil RICO's use in the realm of Fourth Amendment violations is *Guerrero v. Gates*.[191] In *Guerrero*, the plaintiff, Guerrero, alleged that members of the Los Angeles Police Department twice planted drugs on his person and arrested him illegally, once in 1995 and again in 1997. As a result of the governmental conduct in 1995, Guerrero pleaded guilty and was sentenced to probation. In 1997, Guerrero pleaded guilty to the second charge and was sentenced for two years. Guerrero named over 200 defendants in his lawsuit, including former LAPD police chiefs, police officers, city attorneys, the mayor, and a former district attorney under 42 U.S.C. Section 1983 and RICO for the alleged wrongful arrest, malicious prosecution, excessive force, and a general conspiracy of "bad behavior."[192]

What was interesting about Guerrero's case was that it was one of many that arose out of the LAPD Rampart scandal, which involved "a wide variety of misconduct by LAPD officers including the shooting of unarmed suspects, the planting of evidence to justify those shootings, the preparation of false police reports to cover up the misconduct and the presentation of perjured testimony resulting in the false convictions and imprisonment of a number of innocent citizens."[193] Although the majority of his Section 1983 claims were barred,[194] the circuit court of appeals declared that Guerrero did have standing to pursue his RICO claims, which alleged "injury due to lost employment prospects during his alleged wrongful incarceration."[195] Specifically, the appellate court held that an individual

---

189. *Id.* at 241–42; Midwest Grinding Co., Inc., 976 F.2d at 1023.

190. Ragland, *Master's Tools, supra* note 179, at 156 (citation omitted).

191. 110 F.Supp.2d 1287 (C.D.Cal.2000).

192. Guerrero v. Gates, 442 F.3d 697, 702 (9th Cir.2006).

193. *Id.* at 702 (quoting Ovando v. City of Los Angeles, 92 F.Supp.2d 1011, 1014 (C.D.Cal.2000)). *See also* Rene Sanchez, *L.A. Police Misconduct Likened to Racketeering: Judge's Order Could Widen City's Liability*, Wash. Post. (Aug. 31, 2004) at A4.

194. According to the circuit court, the Supreme Court's decision in Heck v. Humphrey, 512 U.S. 477 (1994), precluded Guerrero's recovery of damages under Section 1983, as a judgment in his favor " 'would necessarily imply the invalidity of his conviction;' he cannot show that his conviction has already been invalidated; and no exception to *Heck's* bar applies." *Id.* at 703 (citation omitted). *Heck* did not bar Guerrero's Section 1983 claim that the officers used excessive force during the arrest, as the claim did not "necessarily imply the invalidity of his conviction or sentence." *Id.* (citation omitted). However, the remaining excessive force claim was barred with respect to the 1995 (but not the 1997) arrest by the one year statute of limitations. *Id.* at 705.

195. *Id.* at 707.

"may bring a civil claim under RICO if he has been 'injured in his business or property by reason of a violation' of the statute."[196] To recover under RICO, however, the aggrieved plaintiff must prove "that the racketeering activity proximately caused the loss."[197] As Guerrero alleged that he was "unable to pursue gainful employment while defending [himself] against unjust charges and/or while unjustly incarcerated" and that he "suffered a material diminishment of [his] employment prospects by virtue of the unjust and unconstitutional conviction," he adequately alleged an injury to business or property under RICO.[198]

2.   INJUNCTIVE RELIEF

Injunctive relief for Fourteenth Amendment violations is not easily attained in police misconduct cases.[199] The U.S. Supreme Court set forth a two-part test in *City of Los Angeles v. Lyons.*[200] In *Lyons,* the Supreme Court denied the plaintiff standing to seek, *inter alia*, injunctive and declaratory relief that would bar police from indiscriminately using choke-holds. There, the plaintiff, Lyons, was placed without provocation and justification in a chokehold by a Los Angeles police officer during a minor traffic stop. The chokehold rendered Lyons unconscious and caused damage to his larynx.[201] Lyons argued that an injunction directed at the municipality was warranted, given his injury, the possibility of suffering a similar harm in the future at the hands of the police, and the fact that at least 15 other persons similarly treated had died as a result.[202]

While the Court determined that the past injury Lyons suffered as a result of the officer's actions provided a predicate for compensatory damages, it did not supply one for prospective equitable relief, since the fact that such practices had been used in the past did not translate into a real and immediate threat of future injury to Lyons.[203] The Court announced that in order to establish equitable relief standing, Lyons would have had not only to allege

> that he would have another encounter with the police but also to make the incredible assertion either (1) that all police officers in Los Angeles always choke any citizen with whom they happen to have an encounter, whether for the purpose of arrest, issuing a citation, or for questioning, or (2) that the City ordered or authorized police officers to act in such manner.[204]

---

196.   *Id.*

197.   *Id.*

198.   *Id.* at 707–08.

199.   *See* City of Riverside v. Rivera, 477 U.S. 561, 574–75 (1986).

200.   461 U.S. 95 (1983).

201.   Lyons, 461 U.S. at 97–98.

202.   *Id.* at 100.

203.   *See id.* at 105–06.

204.   *Id.* at 105–06.

Undoubtedly, given the virtually impossible legal standard, Lyons's attempt at injunctive relief was stillborn. Irrespective of the actuality of his recent encounter with the Los Angeles police, Lyons was "no more entitled to an injunction that any other citizen of Los Angeles; and a federal court may not entertain a claim by any or all citizens who no more than assert that certain practices of law enforcement are unconstitutional."[205]

A similar result was had in *Campbell v. Miller*.[206] There, the plaintiff, an attorney with no criminal record or prior arrests, was taken into custody by police and charged with misdemeanor possession of marijuana.[207] Before releasing Campbell, police strip-searched him (*i.e.,* conducted a body cavity search) for illegal drugs. None were found and no criminal prosecution ensued. Campbell subsequently sued ten police officers, the Chief of Police, and the City of Indianapolis under 42 U.S.C. Section 1983, seeking monetary damages as well as an injunction against the departmental practice of strip-searching misdemeanor arrestees.[208] The Court of Appeals for the Seventh Circuit affirmed the district court's denial of Campbell's request for injunctive relief. The appellate court found it "difficult to see how a court could issue an injunction at Campbell's behest:"

> [u]nless the same events are likely to happen again to him there is no controversy between him and the City about the City's future handling of other arrests. Campbell has sought to represent all persons arrested for misdemeanors, but the district court has not certified that class and may never do so. Thus Campbell cannot rely on the prospect that other arrested persons may be subjected to body-cavity searches.... He represents his own interests, not those of third parties. Only if he is apt to be arrested and searched again would prospective relief be apt, and nothing in this record suggests that Campbell is a repeat offender ... he is not the right party to pursue injunctive relief.[209]

The bottom line: Suits for injunctive relief can sometimes succeed, but the hurdles to such success are large.

3. CRIMINAL REMEDIES

Some may regard the mere suggestion of enforcing criminal law against law enforcement officers as extraordinary. For those, such use of criminal and civil laws may be regarded even as anathema, particularly when one considers that these very governmental officials are entrusted with enforcing the law. It would be wise to recall that "law enforcement officers are not above the law. They are subject to its demands like any other citizen."[210]

---

205. *Id.* at 111.

206. 373 F.3d 834 (7th Cir.2004).

207. *Id.* at 835.

208. *Id.* at 835–36.

209. *Id.* at 836.

210. Hess, *Good Cop, supra* note 180, at 177.

Reconstructionists at the country's helm actively worked to craft legislation to create a utopian vision of the new America: a country whose citizens possessed equal political, social, and civic rights, as secured by the federal government. This reality had never been the state of affairs in the United States before the Civil War and transformed the political life and history of the United States.[211]

The constitutional framework upon which Reconstruction was built consisted of the Thirteenth,[212] Fourteenth,[213] and Fifteenth[214] amendments, as well as a battery of federal statutory codes to dismantle state race-based laws and protect the civil rights of those newly freed, newly designated Black Americans. These Reconstruction Amendments underlie many of the political, civil, and social rights battles had in the 20th century and continue to remain relevant in recent 21st century legal history, as recent battles along these lines are often influenced by rights that were lost, never constitutionalized, or not clearly legislated.

In addition to constitutional and legislative fixes to eradicate slavery from the United States, the Reconstruction Congress also abolished a form of indentured servitude—peonage—that had an impact upon Native Americans and Mexicans who lived in the territory of New Mexico under Spanish rule. Two months after the passage of the Fifteenth amendment, Congress passed the Civil Rights Act of 1870, which shored up the substantive right to vote as well as, among other things, made it illegal to subject Chinese to unequal treatment.[215] Additionally, Congress passed the "Ku Klux Klan Act" in response to the violence leveled against the newly freed Blacks and whites who assisted or supported the new Americans.

In order further to dismantle state race-based laws and protect the civil rights of those newly designated Americans, numerous federal laws were also enacted. In 1870, Congress passed the Civil Rights Act of 1870, which shored up the substantive right to vote as well as, *inter alia*, made it

---

211. Fascinating understandings of the American Reconstruction can be found in Angela P. Harris's *Equality Trouble: Sameness and Difference in Twentieth–Century Race Law*, 88 CAL. L. REV. 1923 (2000); *see also* ERIC FONER, RECONSTRUCTION: AMERICA'S UNFINISHED REVOLUTION, 1863–1877 (1988).

212. The Thirteenth Amendment abolished slavery in the United States and gave Congress the ability to enforce the prohibition via legislation.

213. The Fourteenth Amendment made citizenship national for the first time in American history. It provided that "[a]ll persons born or naturalized in the United States, and subject to the jurisdiction thereof, are citizens of the United States and of the state wherein they reside." Additionally, the Fourteenth Amendment prohibited states from depriving U.S. citizens' privileges or immunities, due process, or equal protection of the law. Congress provided that Southern states could be re-admitted to the Union only if they ratified the Fourteenth Amendment.

214. The Fifteenth Amendment guaranteed the right to vote to all men, irrespective of race or color.

215. *See* Harris, *Equality Trouble*, *supra* note 211, at 1931–33 (noting that the Civil Rights Act of 1870 criminalized special taxes levied against Chinese as well as the practice of forbidding Chinese from testifying against whites in a court of law).

illegal to subject Chinese to unequal treatment.[216] In addition to constitutional and legislative fixes to eradicate slavery from the United States, the Reconstruction Congress also abolished a form of indentured servitude—peonage—that had an impact upon Native Americans and Mexicans who lived in the territory of New Mexico under Spanish rule.

18 U.S.C. Section 241 criminally punishes violations of federal civil rights. After ratification of the Thirteenth Amendment to the United States Constitution, the U.S. Congress passed the Civil Rights Act of April 9, 1866, which, among other things, provided criminal penalties for civil rights violations by any person who acts "under color of any law, statute, ordinance, regulation, or custom." The Act and other related statutes were promulgated to punish those who terrorized newly freed, formerly enslaved Blacks in the United States. Section 241 criminalizes conspiracies that interfere with individuals' civil rights. It provides:

> If two or more persons conspire to injure, oppress, threaten, or intimidate any person in any State, Territory, Commonwealth, Possession, or District in the free exercise or enjoyment of any right or privilege secured to him by the Constitution or laws of the United States, or because of his having so exercised the same; or

> If two or more persons go in disguise on the highway, or on the premises of another, with intent to prevent or hinder his free exercise or enjoyment of any right or privilege so secured—

> They shall be fined not more than $10,000 or imprisoned not more than ten years, or both; and if death results, they shall be subject to imprisonment for any term of years or for life.[217]

Section 241 is applicable to conspiracies involving either public or private actors. No actual deprivation of federal civil rights need be proven; proof of the conspiracy to deprive is enough. Section 241 does not entail a private cause of action; only federal prosecutors (from the United States Department of Justice or a United States Attorney's Office) may initiate and prosecute under this statute. To obtain a conviction for conspiracy to violate civil rights under Section 241, the government must prove that the defendant knowingly agreed with another person to injure the aggrieved party in the exercise of a right guaranteed under the Constitution.[218] Specific intent to deprive another of civil rights is an element of the offense that the government must prove beyond a reasonable doubt.

Similarly, 18 U.S.C. Section 242 provides criminal penalties for federal civil rights violations that occur under color of law. Like 18 U.S.C. Section 241, Section 242 was promulgated in the aftermath of passage of the Thirteenth, Fourteenth, and Fifteenth Amendments. Section 242 provides that:

---

216.   *See id.*

217.   18 U.S.C. § 241 (1988).

218.   Anderson v. United States, 417 U.S. 211, 223 (1974).

[w]hoever, under color of any law, statute, ordinance, regulation, or custom, willfully subjects any inhabitant of any State, Territory, Commonwealth, Possession, or District to the deprivation of any rights, privileges, or immunities secured or protected by the Constitution or laws of the United States, or to different punishments, pains, or penalties, on account of such inhabitant being an alien, or by reason of his color, or race, than are prescribed for the punishment of citizens, shall be fined not more than $1,000 or imprisoned not more than one year, or both; and if bodily injury results shall be fined under this title or imprisoned not more than ten years, or both; and if death results shall be subject to imprisonment for any term of years or for life.[219]

Section 242 does not forbid deprivations of constitutional or statutory rights. Rather, 18 U.S.C. Section 242 (similar to Section 1983) is an enforcement mechanism by which persons deprived of these rights may bring a claim for redress in the form of criminal prosecution. Section 242 is well-suited for those incidents of police misconduct where the goal is not law enforcement, "but to deprive a citizen of a right that is protected by the Constitution."[220] For example, in *United States v. Perkins*,[221] the conviction of a police officer under Section 242 for violating a motorist's right to be free from unreasonable force was affirmed when the evidence at trial proved that there was no legitimate law enforcement reason for the defendant to repeatedly (at least eleven times) stomp on the head of and deliver a number of forceful kicks to a motorist who had been secured (handcuffed and lying face-down on the ground by officers on the scene) after a traffic stop and foot chase.[222]

The seminal case interpreting 18 U.S.C. Section 242 is *Screws v. United States*.[223] In *Screws*, the sheriff of Baker County, Georgia, with the assistance of two other law enforcement officers, arrested a Black citizen of that state. They beat their prisoner to death with fists and a blackjack. The U.S. Supreme Court was faced with a strong challenge to the constitutionality of applying Section 242 (then Section 20 of the Criminal Code, 18 U.S.C. Section 52) to the deprivation of due process rights, on the grounds that the due process clause lacked the specificity which is constitutionally mandated for criminal statutes. To preserve the statute's constitutionality, the Court held that 18 U.S.C. Section 242 requires as one element of the offense the specific intent "to deprive a person of a right which has been made specific either by the express terms of the Constitution or laws of the United States or by decisions interpreting them."[224]

To convict under Section 242, a jury must find that (1) the defendant deprived the victim of a right secured by the Constitution or laws of the

---

219.   18 U.S.C. § 242 (1988).

220.   *See* Screws v. United States, 325 U.S. 91, 106 (1945).

221.   470 F.3d 150 (4th Cir.2006).

222.   Perkins, 470 F.3d at 152.

223.   325 U.S. 91 (1945).

224.   Screws, 325 U.S. at 104.

United States (in *Perkins*, it was the Fourth Amendment right to be free from the use of unreasonable force), (2) the defendant acted willfully, (3) the defendant acted under color of law, and (4) that the defendant's victim suffered bodily injury as a result of the defendant's conduct.[225] Accordingly, the plaintiff must prove that the defendant had the specific intent to deprive him or her of a right. It is enough that the aggrieved plaintiff show that the governmental actor acted in reckless disregard of the plaintiff's constitutional rights. Under Section 242, "the crucial question is not whether the officer has violated a state law, but whether the officer also deprived a citizen of a federal right."[226]

––––––––

As the above material should make clear, there are significant difficulties associated with alternative remedies, irrespective of the specific cause of action advanced. In practice, there are numerous hurdles to achieving success in such suits, including the doctrine of qualified immunity for police officers, sovereign immunity, standing, high substantive burdens of proof (such as showing intentional wrongdoing), obstacles to discovery, and evidentiary rules embracing narrow concepts of relevancy.[227]

Monetary damages are, however, often so low, and legal costs so high, that there is little motive for injured parties to bring suit. Lawyers, recognizing the hurdles, have little financial incentive to take on these cases. On the plus side, civil lawsuits can sometimes lead to consent decrees and court-ordered injunctive relief that impose widespread changes in police practices.[228] Moreover, damages help to make whole those citizens who are wrongly searched or seized but where no evidence of a crime is uncovered, at least in the rare instances where damages are substantial and procedural roadblocks overcome. Some scholars suggest procedural changes—including the appointment of counsel in civil cases and a guarantee of minimum liquidated damages—in order to minimize the costs and increase the benefits of civil lawsuits. At present, these proposals do not appear to be politically viable.

In addition to the exorbitant costs associated with such litigation, procedural hurdles, and tactical considerations:

> [t]he potential plaintiffs, after all, are individuals who are in contact with the criminal justice system, generally as suspects or defendants. Many are unlikely to bring suit for harm suffered, whether because of ignorance of their rights, poverty, fear of police reprisals, or the burdens of incarceration. Moreover, in many cases the harm suffered

––––––––

225. *See Perkins*, 470 F.3d at 153 n.3.

226. Hess, *Good Cop, supra* note 180.

227. Many of these obstacles are summarized in Sean P. Trende, *Why Modest Proposals Offer the Best Solution for Combating Racial Profiling*, 50 DUKE L.J. 331 (2000).

228. For a rousing defense of structural reform litigation as a means for regulating the police, *see* Myriam E. Gilles, *Reinventing Structural Reform Litigation: Deputizing Private Citizens in the Enforcement of Civil Rights*, 100 COLUM. L. REV. 1384 (2000).

by individuals from the constitutional violation itself may be small, widely dispersed, and intangible, providing little incentive for potential plaintiffs to sue, especially given the lack of sympathy that this group of plaintiffs can expect from the trier of fact.[229]

A common problem for plaintiffs who pursue tort remedies is the means by which their Fourth Amendment injury is assessed and measured. Ultimately, Section 1983 claims are judged in accordance with the same set of rules and standards that govern tort liability, *i.e.*, that a person should be compensated fairly for injuries caused by the violation of his or her guaranteed rights. Although quantifiable damages can include, e.g., loss of wages, loss of personal integrity, personal humiliation, personal emotional distress, filial injury, or loss and injury to consortium are harder to discern, assess, and value. All too often, damage awards will suffer because juries will determine that the plaintiffs in these lawsuits—usually not regarded highly, given their prior contacts with the criminal justice system—have suffered little injury, if any, and are merely seeking to profit from law-abiding, tax paying, "good citizens."[230]

Collateral estoppel may stymie an aggrieved plaintiff's ability to redress Fourth Amendment violations via tort remedies. The U.S. Supreme Court's decision in *Allen v. McCurry*[231] held that in certain circumstances, collateral estoppel will deprive certain plaintiffs the opportunity to litigate claims of constitutional deprivation in a federal forum. How might that occur? According to the Court, plaintiffs asserting federal rights are not entitled to unencumbered opportunities to litigate those federal rights in a federal forum, so long as there was a full and fair opportunity to do so in a state court proceeding, i.e., when the issues raised in the federal forum were previously decided in the state criminal proceeding.

Additionally, a wronged plaintiff's Section 1983 and *Bivens* claim may be limited by the doctrines of absolute or qualified immunity. Absolute immunity from Section 1983 claims shields certain governmental actors from any lawsuit. Absolute immunity is available for those governmental actors who are "intimately associated with the judicial phase of the criminal process." Absolute immunity attaches to the office or position, not the actor who holds the office or position. Absolute immunity attaches to these governmental actors so that they may freely participate in and contribute to the judicial process. Once attached, these actors receive absolute immunity for their testimony. Those typically protected by absolute immunity include judges, criminal prosecutors, and witnesses. Quali-

---

229. Daniel J. Meltzer, *Deterring Constitutional Violations By Law Enforcement Officials: Plaintiffs and Defendants as Private Attorneys General*, 88 COLUM. L. REV. 247, 284 (1988).

230. *See, e.g.*, STEPHEN A. SALTZBURG AND DANIEL J. CAPRA, AMERICAN CRIMINAL PROCEDURE CASES AND COMMENTARY 551 (6th ed. West Group 2000) (DISCUSSING TORT RECOVERY LIMITATIONS): " 'Respectable' persons have the greatest chance of recovering, since they will not be tainted by their past, but the 'respectable' person is probably least likely to be subject to arbitrary arrest and harassment, and thus least likely to require a tort remedy."

231. 449 U.S. 90, 103–05 (1980).

fied immunity has been characterized as "a substantive impediment to some section 1983 actions against police officers."[232] Qualified immunity shields officials from liability only for those discretionary acts that do not violate clearly established constitutional norms. Those governmental actors who perform their discretionary duties in good faith and with probable cause are not subject to personal civil liability if qualified immunity attaches to their acts.[233] The standard for qualified immunity—set forth in the Supreme Court's decision in *Harlow v. Fitzgerald*[234]—asks: at the time of the alleged violation, did the governmental actor's conduct violate "clearly established statutory or constitutional rights of which a reasonable person would have known?"[235] If the answer is "no"—that is, the law was not clearly established—qualified immunity applies. If the answer is "yes," qualified immunity will not attach to the governmental actor and it will not shield him or her personally from Section 1983 recovery. However, there may be instances where, despite clearly established law, qualified immunity may be had. Governmental actors may be able to show extraordinary circumstances that indicate either he or she "neither knew or should have known of the relevant legal standard."[236]

Complainants in criminal police misconduct cases "also must call police officers as key witnesses to the events in dispute and these witnesses are not eager to provide damaging testimony against their fellow officers, and indeed may provide false testimony."[237] Even when a complainant is successful, "[t]he damages for violations of privacy and proper police procedure can be difficult for juries to value.... mak[ing] it hard to find an attorney who is willing to take such cases on a contingent basis."[238]

> Given the above concerns, it is no wonder that the various legal doctrines and trial realities prevent civil tort claims from becoming a reliable alternative to the exclusionary rule. Although there are signs that civil tort lawsuits are effective in addressing police misconduct, ultimately, it remains difficult to determine what role, if any, civil tort suits play in regulating Fourth Amendment violations.[239]

---

232. Hess, *Good Cop, supra* note 180, at 158.

233. *Id.* at 159–60: "If an officer has probable cause to make an arrest, by definition, there is a reasonable good faith belief the defendant committed a crime. Therefore, the arresting officer is protected by good faith immunity. However, this does not mean that the absence of probable cause precludes immunity, assuming the officer had a reasonable belief that there was probable cause."

234. 457 U.S. 800 (1982).

235. *Id.* at 818.

236. *Id.* at 819. However, *Harlow* gives no explanation or example of what might constitute "extraordinary circumstances."

237. *See* Marc L. Miller and Ronald F. Wright, *Secret Police and the Mysterious Case of the Missing Tort Claims*, 52 BUFFALO L. REV. 757, 762 (2004).

238. *Id.* at 763.

239. *See id.* at 758 (asserting the difficulty of assessing the role tort suits play in regulating police abuse).

Despite its significant flaws and critics, the exclusionary rule remains intact, albeit significantly weakened, given the post-*Mapp* Supreme Court decisions which have "beaten and battered the rule:"[240]

> [a]lthough recognizing the [exclusionary] rules' imperfections, respondents believe it is the only mechanism that injects any restraint in the system, or any respect for rights. Though often evaded, the respondents believe that by creating a *possibility* of suppression, the rule makes the Fourth Amendment a factor in police and judicial thinking.
>
> . . .
>
> Critics might also argue that pervasive perjury is a cost of the exclusionary rule, and as such, outweighs any incremental benefit gained by the rule's uneven deterrent effect. Respondents ... nevertheless believe that the exclusionary rule has dramatically improved police behavior and should be retained.... Today, while police often perjure themselves, they also, because of the exclusionary rule, often obey the Fourth Amendment. By any measure, this is an improvement [over pre-*Mapp* days].[241]

A CAVEAT: The above discussion of alternative remedies to the exclusionary rule is neither a comprehensive summary of the relevant law nor of the many subtleties in interpreting and applying it. Rather, the goals of this chapter's section are to alert you to the options and give you a sense of their strengths and weaknesses, relative to the exclusionary rule. At a minimum, we want you to think critically and strategically about these options and to do more research where necessary. In connection with these goals, consider the following problem.

PROBLEM 7–9

Ted is a 50 year old African American male. One Friday night, at around 11:45 p.m., Ted and his thirteen year old son, Glenn, left their suburban home in Eugene, OR to take Glenn's friends, Hal and Dan, home. Hal and Dan lived approximately fifteen minutes away via automobile. After dropping off both boys, Ted and Glenn had a harrowing encounter with members of the Eugene Police Department. Glenn explains what happened that night, as Ted refuses to speak about it and, since the event, has refused to leave the family home:

> *Hal, Dan, and I went to the mall that afternoon and stayed all evening and into the night. We called my dad to pick us up; he did. It was getting late, so dad said that we needed to take Hal and Dan home. First, we dropped off Dan, whose mom waited for him in their driveway. Then we went to Hal's house to drop him off. Hal got out of my*

---

240. H. Mitchell Caldwell, *Fixing the Constable's Blunder: Can One Trial Judge in One County in One State Nudge a Nation Beyond the Exclusionary Rule?*, 2006 B.Y.U. L. REV. 1, 2 (2006).

241. Myron W. Orfield, Jr., *Deterrence, Perjury, and the Heater Factor: An Exclusionary Rule in the Chicago Criminal Courts*, 63 U. COLO. L. REV. 75, 123, 132 (1992).

dad's car, said goodbye, and headed up the path, through the hedges, and toward his home. My dad and I waited outside for him to get into his house. We waited for about 3 minutes, but the way we were positioned we couldn't see the front door because of a tree. We pulled around the corner when we thought Hal had gone inside, and then when we reached the corner, we had a better angle. We saw that Hal was not inside. We waited there for another 5 minutes for Hal to call Hal's father and for Hal's father to come downstairs and let Hal in.

During that time, a car pulled up next to us on the passenger side and the driver, a white male probably in [his] late fifties, rolled down the window as if to say something to us. I rolled down the window also, to respond, and he backed up. I thought this was strange, but I assumed that we were in the parking spot of one of the residents on the street. We pulled off, and the car followed us. It followed us for about 5 minutes, and then at one of the intersections in front of the college, a police car came out from the right and cut us off.

Two officers got out of the car and raised their guns at me and my father. They told us to put our hands up and we did. They came over and opened the doors and told us to un-strap our seat belts, which we also did. My father asked what this was about and they told him to get out of the car. I was pulled out of the car, and told to lie down on the ground with my hands on my head.

While I was on the ground, they searched me, and I told them that I had a DVD movie in my back pocket and a book under my right arm, in case they were suspicious. They made me lie on my side and checked my front pockets and asked if I had a pocket knife or anything like that and I said no, and told them that I have my keys in my left pocket and my cell phone in my right. I was picked up off of the ground and they asked if I had a wallet, and I told them it was in my back pocket. I was then guided to the curb where I was told to sit with my legs crossed. I watched from the curb as my father was frisked, and the car was searched. My father kept asking what this was about; I guess one of the cops didn't want to answer, so he slapped my father. Hard.

They searched in the front and back seats, and in the glove compartment. From the curb I saw that there were two other police cars behind us, not including the car that had originally followed us, which I discovered was an unmarked officer. Then they brought my father to sit next to me on the curb. They asked for his driver's license, which gave to one of the officers. He asked again what this was about and they told him as soon as they know, he will know. We waited for another 5 minutes while one officer asked my father if our family car was his car and the other officer checked to verify his ID.

After waiting, my father said he thought he knew what it was about and the officer asked him to explain. He then explained how we had dropped off my friend and waited for him to get into the house before we left. The officer said that's what it was about, and that they had received a call saying there was suspicious activity on that street. The officer in the unmarked car said he had radioed in our car information, and then said that his battery died which is why there were so many cars because they were making sure he was okay.

Finally, we were allowed to stand up, and the officer who had verified my father's ID wrote a receipt and handed it to him. One of the officers—an African American male—apologized, and we got back into our car and headed home.

NOTES AND QUESTIONS

1. Under the Fourth Amendment, were the officers' actions lawful? Why?

2. If this was an unreasonable seizure and search of Ted, Glenn, and their effects, which of the alternative remedies would best redress the injuries to Ted? Glenn?

3. Does it matter that the police (mis)conduct occurred in the presence of Ted's teen son, Glenn? Should it matter? Professor Lenese Herbert suggests that it should. Professor Herbert argues that when police conduct of this sort occurs in the presence of children, the government has compromised not only the person's Fourth Amendment rights against unreasonable searches and seizures, but also their Fourteenth Amendment right to parent. Moreover, as such policing seems to occur most frequently against specifically poor populations of color or Blacks irrespective of socio-economic status, Professor Herbert finds the governmental violations do more than inconvenience or annoy:

> [r]ace-based policing not only violates the African American parents' Fourth Amendment right to be let alone, but also violates their Fourteenth Amendment right to rear children when such policing takes place in the presence of their children.... [I]mposition of these constitutional violations <u>eviscerates</u> a parent's right to establish a positive foundation for their children's ego knowledge, irrespective of their racial status in society, resulting in a governmental "breeding" of race-based stigma and rendering impotent the African American parent.[242]

4. The Supreme Court has held that associational freedoms are anchored in the First Amendment.[243] Accordingly, unconstitutional deprivation of familial association under the First Amendment is compensable under 42 U.S.C. § 1983. See, e.g., Trujillo v. County of Santa Fe.[244] In *Trujillo*, Rose Trujillo and her daughter, Patricia Trujillo, appealed the dismissal of their Section 1983 action, which sought damages for the wrongful death of Richard Trujillo, who had been an inmate at the time of his death. Richard was Rose's son and Patricia's brother. The Tenth Circuit Court of Appeals

---

242. Lenese Herbert, *Plantation Lullabies: How Fourth Amendment Policing Violates the Fourteenth Amendment Right of African Americans to Parent*, 19 ST. JOHN'S J. OF LEGAL COMM'TARY 197, 203 (2005).

243. *See* Roberts v. United States Jaycees, 468 U.S. 609, 619 (1984).

244. 768 F.2d 1186, 1187 (10th Cir.1985).

determined that both Rose and Patricia alleged an injury "to their own personal constitutional rights [which] in no way derived from the decedent's personal rights."[245] The court of appeals also held that Rose and Patricia had constitutionally protected interests in their relationship with Richard: "[a]lthough the parental relationship may warrant the greatest degree of protection and requires a state to demonstrate a more compelling interest to justify an intrusion on that relationship, we cannot agree that other intimate relationships are unprotected and consequently excluded from the remedy established by [S]ection 1983."[246] Does Glenn have a viable cause of action under 42 U.S.C. § 1983? Would Ted's wife? If Ted forbade Glenn from associating in or around Hal and Dan's neighborhood, would Hal and/or Dan have a Section 1983 claim?

B. FIFTH AND SIXTH AMENDMENT VIOLATIONS: CONFESSIONS, LINEUPS, ASSISTANCE OF COUNSEL

Many of the views in the immediately preceding analysis hold true when applying the exclusionary rule in the context of the Fifth, Sixth, and Fourteenth Amendments as well. An additional justification for evidentiary exclusion arises in the context of the Fifth, Sixth, and Fourteenth Amendments, however: to protect the quality of the truth-finding process. Coerced, unwarned, or uncounseled confessions and suggestive lineups and photospreads raise the risk that the confession is false or that the lineup is unreliable. These errors, in turn, increase the chances of convicting the innocent.

Recent research has shown what, in the view of many observers, is an unacceptably high rate of mistaken convictions. For example, you may recall the infamous 1989 case of "The Central Park Jogger." In that notorious case, a lone woman jogger was attacked, beaten, raped, and left for dead in Central Park, New York. The jogger remained in a coma for nearly two weeks. In the interim, a group of African American boys,[247] were apprehended and interrogated regarding the crime. The boys were indicted on charges of, *inter alia*, attempted murder, rape, sodomy, and assault; ultimately, they were convicted and sentenced to prison. Key to the convictions were the five boys' "confessions" to crimes for which they were charged, but did not commit:

> There can be no doubt that in the absence of the confessions of the five
> defendants charged with the rape of the jogger, there would have been
> no case against them for that crime. From the very beginning of the
> investigation, the boys' confessions were the centerpiece of the prose-

---

245. *Id.*

246. *Id.* at 1189.

247. At the time of arrest, Wise was 16 years old; McGray and Salaam were 15 years old; Richardson and Santana were 14 years old. *See* Affirmation of Nancy E. Ryan, Assistant District Attorney, In Response to Motion to Vacate Judgment of Conviction, People v. Wise, 752 N.Y.S.2d 837 (Sup.Ct.2002) (No. 4762/89), available at http://news.findlaw.com/hdocs/docs/crim/nywise@ta1120502aff.pdf.

cution's proof. Due to the jogger's brain injuries, she was unable to identify her attackers, and no other eyewitness placed them at the scene. ... It was thus a great blow to the state's case when pretrial tests run on those blood and semen samples failed to link the boys to the jogger's rape and assault.[248]

Thirteen years later and after all but one of the boys had completely served their prison sentences, serial rapist and convicted killer, Matia Reyes, suddenly confessed to committing the crimes against the Central Park Jogger. DNA evidence at the scene of the crime confirmed the truth of the confession.[249]

DNA testing has vindicated significant numbers of inmates wrongly imprisoned.[250] Earlier chapters of this text have explored, and later ones will further explore, the various ways to reduce the risk of such errors in the future. It is important to stress here, however, that judicial solutions— in the form of the exclusionary rule—are not the only options available for the wrongful convictions problem. Moreover, the exclusionary rule's remedial or deterrent effects will not suffice under circumstances such as those present in the Central Park Jogger's case, save for administrative, legislative, or other policy changes to prevent such a miscarriage from occurring again. Many police departments have on their own, for example, adopted new guidelines for conducting lineups and interrogations, using administrative remedies to encourage officer compliance. The bottom line is that a combination of constitutional principles, policy concerns, and politics offer a wide range of solutions for preventing and remedying the sorts of substantive constitutional violations discussed in this text.

---

248.   Sharon L. Davies, *The Reality of False Confessions—Lessons of the Central Park Jogger Case,* 30 N.Y.U. REV. L. & SOC. CHANGE 209, 216–17 (2006).

249.   *Id.* at 220–21.

250.   For example, The Innocence Project, founded by lawyers Barry Scheck and Peter Neufeld in 1992, is a non-profit legal clinic and criminal justice resource center. The Innocence Project works to exonerate convicted prison inmates via post-conviction DNA testing where such testing can yield conclusive proof of innocence. Since its founding and as of the date this text went to press, the Innocence Project has been responsible for exonerating nearly 252 wrongly convicted individuals, a number of whom had received death sentences. The organization's website is located at http://www.innocenceproject.org/.

CHAPTER 8

CONFESSIONS AND SELF–INCRIMINATION

● VOLUNTARINESS ● *MIRANDA* DOCTRINE ● *MASSIAH* DOCTRINE

I. DUE PROCESS AND VOLUNTARINESS

A. HISTORICAL BACKGROUND OF DUE PROCESS AND CONFESSIONS

Some sixty years ago, in Mississippi, three African–American men were arrested for the murder of a white man. The men denied their involvement in the crime, but sheriff's deputies pressed them for confessions. The "pressure" was acute: one suspect was hanged by his neck three times and then tied to a tree and whipped. The rope marks on his neck were still visible at trial. He maintained his innocence until the next day, when the deputy again severely whipped him and declared "that he would continue whipping until he confessed." The two other men were stripped naked, laid over chairs in the county jail, and "cut to pieces" with a leather strap with buckles on it. Finally, each of the three men "confessed," and each was convicted of murder. No other evidence linked the accused men to the crime.

In the landmark case *Brown v. Mississippi*,[1] the Supreme Court held that the confessions of the three men were "involuntary" and overturned their convictions. The Court articulated a general rule: where a defendant's statement is obtained by the police through means of coercion that renders it "involuntary," the due process clause of the Fifth Amendment (or, in state trials, the Fourteenth Amendment) requires the trial court to exclude the statement from the defendant's criminal trial. The Court also has suggested that coerced statements may not be used for impeachment purposes.[2] In addition, an appellate court generally must reverse a conviction if an involuntary statement was admitted at trial, although admission of a coerced confession can sometimes be "harmless error."

---

1. 297 U.S. 278 (1936).

2. *See* Mincey v. Arizona, 437 U.S. 385, 398 (1978) (commenting that "*any* criminal trial use against a defendant of his *involuntary* statement is a denial of due process") (emphasis in original). As we will see, the Court has distinguished between confessions that violate the due process test for voluntariness, and those that violate the rule in Miranda v. Arizona. The latter *may* be used for impeachment purposes.

The Court has articulated several rationales for excluding coerced statements under the due process clause. First, excluding coerced confessions deters police misconduct, satisfying the "deep-rooted feeling that the police must obey the law while enforcing the law" and "that in the end life and liberty can be as much endangered from illegal methods used to convict those thought to be criminals as from the actual criminals themselves."[3] Second, the exclusionary remedy voices society's disapproval for techniques "so offensive to a civilized system of justice that they must be condemned."[4] Finally, exclusion protects the integrity of the courts from evidence that is "revolting to the sense of justice."

Revolting as coerced confessions are, they are inadmissible only if they are a product of state conduct. That is, a statement is not constitutionally excludable when obtained through "private" compulsion. For example, where a defendant is compelled by "command hallucinations" and the "voice of God" to confess to a crime, that confession is not rendered inadmissible by the fact of that compulsion. In *Colorado v. Connelly*,[5] the Court reasoned that:

> [such a] statement might be proved to be quite unreliable, but this is a matter to be governed by the evidentiary laws of the forum, and not by the Due Process Clause of the Fourteenth Amendment. "The aim of the requirement of due process is not to exclude presumptively false evidence, but to prevent fundamental unfairness in the use of evidence, whether true or false." ... [C]oercive police activity is a necessary predicate to the finding that a confession is not "voluntary" within the meaning of the Due Process Clause of the Fourteenth Amendment.

On the other hand, the voluntariness of a confession is sufficiently important to due process that the prosecution bears the burden of proving it in each case in which it seeks to use a confession.

In the following materials, we will discuss the elements of the due process voluntariness doctrine. We devote a good deal more attention to the due process voluntariness doctrine than do most texts for several reasons: first, the doctrine offers an excellent opportunity to examine fundamental questions of constitutional interpretation and policy; second, *Miranda* protections are declining, as you will learn later in this chapter, thus raising the relative importance of the voluntariness doctrine; third, a clear understanding of voluntariness will improve your comprehension of *Miranda*; and fourth, voluntariness highlights evidence-like concerns with accurate fact-finding.

---

3.   Spano v. New York, 360 U.S. 315, 320–21 (1959).

4.   Miller v. Fenton, 474 U.S. 104, 109 (1985). In overturning the convictions in Brown, for example, the Court addressed the blatant offensiveness of the police brutality and noted that "[c]oercing the supposed state's criminals into confessions and using such confessions so coerced from them against them in trials has been the curse of all countries. It was the chief inequity, the crowning infamy of the Star Chamber, and the Inquisition, and other similar institutions. The constitution recognized the evils that lay behind these practices and prohibited them in this country."

5.   479 U.S. 157, 167 (1986).

Checklist 11: Due Process Voluntariness

1. Was the statement the product of coercive governmental activity, such as force or the threat of injury, psychological pressures, police deception, or promises of leniency?

2. If yes, does the totality of the circumstances indicate that the coercive activity overcame the will of the person making the statement?

———

B. The Totality of Circumstances Test and Its Multiple Goals

The voluntariness standard requires a showing that, under the totality of the circumstances, the defendant's statement was a product of free will. The prosecution bears the burden of establishing voluntariness by a preponderance of the evidence. Generally, where the defense disputes the voluntariness of a statement, it will put in issue two facts: (1) whether the police subjected the defendant to coercion; and (2) whether the coercion was sufficient to overcome the will of the accused, considering his particular vulnerabilities and the conditions of the interrogation, and regardless of whether he was guilty or innocent.[6] In engaging in this two-pronged inquiry, courts must examine the "totality of the circumstances," because:

> [C]oercion can be mental as well as physical, and ... blood of the accused is not the only hallmark of an unconstitutional inquisition.... [T]he efficiency of the rack and the thumbscrew can be matched, given the proper subject, by more sophisticated modes of "persuasion." A prolonged interrogation of an accused who is ignorant of his rights and who has been cut off from the moral support of friends and relatives is not infrequently an effective technique of terror. Thus, the range of inquiry in this type of case must be broad, and ... the judgment in each instance [must] be based upon consideration of "the totality of the circumstances."[7]

Totality of the circumstances demands a flexible case-specific inquiry, because there is "[n]o single litmus-paper test for constitutionally impermissible interrogation."[8] Instead, the courts look to both "objective" factors, focusing on the conduct of the police (for example, the length of detention, its duration and intensity, and use of deception and promises of leniency), and "subjective" factors, focusing on the particular vulnerability of the individual suspect (for example, age, education, mental instability,

———

6. Professors Bloom and Brodin argue that only this second showing embodies the "totality of the circumstances" test, citing several cases adopting that view. Robert M. Bloom & Mark S. Brodin, Constitutional Criminal Procedure—Examples and Explanations 246 (2d ed. 1996). But the Court has never so stated, and the Court's continuing consideration of both objective and subjective factors in undertaking a totality of the circumstances analysis belies any sharp limitation of that analysis to the second showing.

7. Blackburn v. Alabama, 361 U.S. 199, 206 (1960).

8. Culombe v. Connecticut, 367 U.S. 568, 601 (1961).

sobriety, and familiarity with the criminal justice system). The inclusion of both objective and subjective factors reflects multiple goals:[9] reducing the risk of unreliable confessions, advancing fairness, respecting individual dignity, and enhancing individual trust of government. We will explore each of these below.

1. REDUCING THE RISK OF UNRELIABLE CONFESSIONS

Police interrogation techniques may induce false confessions and thus improper convictions. A 1986 study of wrongful convictions in felony cases, for example, conservatively estimated that nearly 6,000 false convictions occur every year in the United States, with false confessions being one of the leading sources of erroneous conviction of innocent individuals.[10] Another study concluded that confessions are second only to mistaken identity as causes of wrongful conviction.[11] In a path-breaking study, two false confession scholars have analyzed "125 recent cases of proven interrogation-induced false confessions (i.e., cases in which indisputably innocent individuals confessed to crimes they did not commit) and how these cases were treated by officials in the criminal justice system."[12] Their analysis was an attempt to confirm or dispel prior studies reporting that interrogation-induced false confession are a primary cause of wrongful convictions.[13] Carefully compiling and reviewing information about the 125 documented false confessions, they discovered that 35 percent of those who falsely confessed were convicted, and even of those not convicted, a fourth spent more than a year in pretrial detention before their cases were disposed of and almost 40 percent spent more than seven months in jail before a favorable disposition. The authors concluded,

> . . . confession evidence is inherently prejudicial and highly damaging to a defendant, even if it is the product of coercive interrogation, even if it is supported by no other evidence, and even if it is ultimately proven false beyond any reasonable doubt. . . . [I]n the overwhelming majority of cases that go to trial, confessions (even if they are demonstrably false) almost always seal the defendant's fate—either by leading the innocent defendant to choose to accept a plea bargain or, more commonly, by leading a judge or jury to wrongfully convict the factually innocent defendant. . . . It is remarkable that more than four-fifths of the false confessors in our sample who chose to take their case to trial were convicted. To put it another way, if our sample is representative of the underlying population of false confessors in America, a false confessor who chooses to take his case to trial stands more than an

---

9. *See* JOSEPH D. GRANO, CONFESSIONS, TRUTH, AND THE LAW 106 (1993).

10. JEROME H. SKOLNICK & JAMES J. FYFE, ABOVE THE LAW: POLICE AND THE EXCESSIVE USE OF FORCE 63 (1993).

11. M. Inman, *Police Interrogations and Confessions*, in Sally M. A. Lloyd–Bostock, PSYCHOLOGY IN LEGAL CONTEXTS 45–66 (1981).

12. Steven A. Drizin and Richard A. Leo, *The Problem of False Confessions in the Post–DNA World*, 82 N.C. L. REV. 891 (2004).

13. *Id.* at 920.

80% chance of conviction, despite the fact that he is officially presumed innocent, that he is in fact innocent, and that there is no reliable evidence confirming or supporting his false confession.[14]

The authors also found that certain populations were especially vulnerable to the problem of false interrogation-induced confessions: juveniles and the mentally ill and retarded.[15] Confessions are also often retracted with the same spontaneity and conviction as when they were made.[16]

Why would people confess to things they did not do, or to more than they did? One answer, according to social psychologists, is that certain interrogation tactics confuse people so much that they literally lose touch with the truth. For example, the "fabrication of evidence ploy" (putting a suspect in a lineup where a pretend eyewitness identifies him, or confronting him with a faked fingerprint match or a concocted lie detector test result),[17] may so confuse an innocent person that he will actually come to disbelieve his own recollection of events.[18] "Good cop-bad cop" questioning—the display of sympathy by one interrogator and an authoritarian manner by the other—may prompt confessions in a similar manner.[19] Once an accused person has confessed, he or she believes in the confession's truth. Some social scientists believe that:

> under appropriate conditions, most people can be induced to confess, whether or not they are guilty. The anxiety evoked by the procedure leads to an increased talkativeness—even when the accused is informed of his rights. "Get them to make the first admission, no matter how small: 'yes, I drink a lot.' You've immediately got them going." Both the conditions of the interrogation and the manner of the interrogator may increase the probability of a confession. The suspect is away from familiar and supportive surroundings, often in a stark room with a special arrangement of furniture, interrogator and suspect are in close proximity, and the power and the ability of the former to take the initiative are strongly emphasized. It is useful for the interrogator to feign sympathy, to express concern for the welfare of the suspect and to deceive him as to the strength of the evidence against him. Cautions as to silence may be delivered so as to minimize their impact, particularly if the suspect is poorly educated or overwrought.[20]

---

14. *Id.* at 961.

15. *Id.* at 963–74.

16. E. L. Hilgendorf and B. Irving, *A Decision—Making Model of Confessions*, in Psychology in Legal Contexts, *supra* note 11, at 67–84.

17. *See* Skolnick & Fyfe, Above the Law, *supra* note 10, at 61 (defining and illustrating the ploy).

18. Richard Ofshe, *The Internalized Coerced Confession*, Guggenheim Crime Seminar Lecture, Center for the Study of Law and Society (Berkeley, California, April 13, 1992).

19. Skolnick & Fyfe, Above the Law, *supra* note 10, at 65–66.

20. Philip M. Feldman, The Psychology of Crime: A Social Science Textbook 87 (1993). For an excellent and concise summary of the psychological literature, *see* Richard Leo, *False Confessions: Causes, Consequences, and Solutions*, in Wrongly Convicted: Perspectives on Failed Justice 36 (Saundra D. Westervelt & John A. Humphrey, eds., 2001). *See also generally*

Such concerns have led these social scientists to recommend the adoption of police procedures that will reduce the risk of false confessions. For example, many suggest that interrogations should be videotaped mandatorily. At least two states (Alaska and Minnesota) have enacted such a requirement, as has the United Kingdom. Prince George's County, Maryland, also enacted a videotaping requirement after an expose of multiple false confessions that had been obtained using psychological pressure and lengthy interrogations. Consider the techniques described in this article, one of four describing interrogation problems in Prince George's County:

Echoing arguments that have been made since at least the 1930s, Marissa J. Reich and Steven A. Drizin call for an end to the policies of many state and federal law enforcement agencies, which do not require that interrogations be recorded.[21] According to Drizin and Reich, "preventing false confessions, increasing effective administration of criminal justice, and improving relationships between the police and the public ... have consistently served as a foundation for the arguments laid out by the numerous legal scholars and law enforcement officials who have advocated for a rule requiring electronic recordings to be made during all custodial interrogations."

In 1961, Fred E. Inbau, an opponent of recorded interrogations, argued that "the key to a successful interrogation is privacy because it is a necessary precondition to a confession, and without it, suspects would be less likely to confess." For Drizin and Reich, this argument may be losing its persuasiveness "[i]n the post-DNA age ... and particularly in the past decade, as the number of wrongful convictions based on false confessions has continued to climb. ... [I]t is becoming increasingly difficult for jurors to accept the assertions of police officers that they did not tape interrogations because it was not their policy to do so." They conclude: "It is far too early to declare a victory in the war to end police secrecy in the interrogation room. ... One thing, however, is certain: We can no longer afford to ignore the voices of those who have advocated for an end to secrecy in the police interrogation process."

Allegations of Abuses Mar Murder Cases

April Witt[22]

The room is cramped and cold. The floor and walls are carpeted to muffle sound. A small table and two chairs are the only furnishings. There is no window, no clock, no clue to when night becomes day. After 28 hours in that interrogation room, Keith Longtin was so exhausted he wondered if

---

Welsh White, MIRANDA'S WANING PROTECTIONS: POLICE INTERROGATION PRACTICES AFTER DICKERSON (2001).

21.   Steven A. Drizin & Marissa J. Reich, *Heeding the Lessons of History: The Need for Mandatory Recording of Police Interrogations to Accurately Assess the Reliability and Voluntariness of Confessions*, 52 DRAKE L. REV. 619 (2004).

22.   WASHINGTON POST (June 3, 2001).

he'd lost his mind. "The detective said, 'Well, thanks for making a confession.' " Longtin recalled. "I'm like, 'What? I didn't admit to anything.' He said, 'Yes, you did.' "

Longtin spent the next eight months in jail, charged with the 1999 slaying of his wife while Prince George's County homicide detectives overlooked DNA evidence that would set him free. Eventually, other investigators—not the homicide squad—linked the DNA to a man they now say is the real killer. While Longtin was in jail, that man allegedly sexually assaulted seven women. . . .

Some Prince George's lawyers, including former prosecutors, said interrogation room abuse is the routine rather than the exception. "That's the name of the game: They hold people for as long as it takes until they say something, and they don't let them see a lawyer," said Steven D. Kupferberg, a former Prince George's prosecutor who is now a private defense lawyer in Rockville. "I haven't had that experience in any other county, and I practice law all over [Maryland] and in D.C." Prince George's Public Defender Joseph M. Niland said long and intimidating interrogations are part of the history of the Prince George's Police Department. "The culture is that not only is this okay, this is how you do it: You get in there and you make him give it up," Niland said. James Papirmeister said that when he was a top homicide prosecutor for the county, he accepted detectives' testimony about confessions at face value. After he became a defense lawyer, however, he said he was shocked by the frequency with which his clients' rights were violated in the interrogation room and detectives then lying about it on the witness stand. "Most of them want to get the right person," said Papirmeister, whose office is lined with laudatory mementos from his law enforcement days, including an honorary badge from Prince George's homicide detectives. "Some don't care about that. They just want to close a case. Job success: That's what it's all about. It's the ends justify the means. It's routine."

Homicide detectives have one of the most challenging and important jobs in law enforcement. They get out of bed in the middle of the night to canvass neighborhoods when someone is killed, attend autopsies before breakfast, sort lies from half-truths and spend hours trying to get killers to act against their best interest—to confess. Artful interrogators who win uncoerced confessions are agents of justice. Without them, many murders would never be solved. "The reason they are successful is that they are very diligent about what they do," said Lt. Col. Orlando D. Barnes, the Prince George's deputy chief. "If we can make any improvements, we will. Interrogation is not an exact science." Lt. Michael McQuillan, the homicide unit commander, said his detectives do a tough job well and never deny suspects attorneys or coerce confessions. "We are ethical. We are thorough. We are truthful," McQuillan said. "I stand behind every one of these investigations. . . . I can tell you that in each case, the allegations they are making are not true. People do confess to murders they don't do," he said. "People confess to crimes they don't do. Why? I don't know. You have to ask them." . . .

The detectives who work the interrogation rooms are proud of their record in gaining confessions. Suspects admitted their involvement to detectives in 68 percent of all 1999 murder investigations that resulted in an arrest, according to case summaries in an internal report prepared by the homicide commander. By contrast, only a few of the summaries mention physical evidence as leading to an arrest. The summaries provide only a snapshot of the investigations and are not comprehensive. . . .

Samuel L. Serio, a lawyer who defended Keith Longtin, said Prince George's homicide detectives rely on confessions because it spares them a lot of painstaking evidence gathering and interviewing. "If they got the confession: Case closed," said Serio, a former police officer who represented the Fraternal Order of Police for 17 years. "They are not going any farther. It's just a little box they check, cleared one arrest. The stats are, 'Did you close the case,' not 'Was justice done.' That's not even on the sheet. You know how many people who are behind bars that didn't do it?"

Longtin said that when Prince George's homicide detectives couldn't get a confession from him, they simply twisted his words to concoct one. "They tried to frame me," said Longtin, 45. "The police lie, and nobody holds them accountable for their lies." The officers directly involved in Longtin's interrogation did not respond to written requests for interviews. Their supervisor declined to discuss specifics of the case but said the detectives did nothing wrong. The following account is based on interviews with Longtin and police and on court documents.

When a homicide detective walked into the interrogation room and placed a stack of photographs face down on the small table, Keith Longtin feared that his wife must be dead. Crime scene photos, he recalls thinking. He tried to calm down and help the detectives do their job. He answered questions, waived his right to a lawyer and volunteered blood and hair samples. "They asked me different questions like, did I carry a knife," said Longtin, a welder who identifies himself as a born-again Christian. "I said yeah, I did. For my work. I didn't have anything to hide. I didn't fear I'd be implicated. You don't think something like that. All I'm doing is telling them the truth." He had been given a tag that said "visitor" when they took him into the room about 1:30 p.m. on a Tuesday, Oct. 5. He didn't emerge until Thursday. He began to fathom the depth of his troubles when a detective flipped the photographs. They showed the brutalized body of his once-beautiful blond wife. "To see her like that, it looked like someone took a Skil saw and went across her nose. It was just wild to me," Longtin said. "She's nude. She only has a top on. . . . Her eyes were open. I got broke down," he said. As he laid his head on the table and wept, he said, two detectives began accusing him and taunting him. While one detective shoved the hideous photos in his face, the other mocked his grief as phony and said he'd killed her.

The detectives believed they had reason to suspect Longtin. They knew that his brief marriage to Donna Zinetti had been in trouble. They knew that Longtin and Zinetti were living apart and that a church elder had separated them during a bitter argument in their Laurel church before she died. They knew that he had a bad temper and an arrest record for assault. And they knew that he had shown up—tearful and hysterical—as police worked the crime scene in a wooded area near her apartment complex. The 36–year–old Zinetti had been found strangled and stabbed to death, with her jogging shorts down around her ankles. The detectives knew that the medical examiner recovered semen during her autopsy.

When detectives briefly left Longtin alone in the interrogation room, he said, he made a futile attempt to call a lawyer on his cell phone. The detectives confiscated his cell phone when they returned, he said. By late Tuesday, reporters who had seen detectives hustle Longtin from the crime scene asked whether he was a suspect. No, said a police spokesman, in fact, Longtin already had gone home. Later, a spokesman would say he had been given "misinformation" by homicide detectives.

Longtin said there was no misunderstanding inside the interrogation room. He wasn't allowed to use the bathroom without two detectives escorting, records show. "They wouldn't let me leave," Longtin said. "They wouldn't get out of the way and let me out of the room. They said later that they offered to let me go. That's a lie. I'd have left, believe me." Longtin said one detective became angry when he stood up and asked to leave. "He said he was going to handcuff me to the wall and beat the crap out of me if I didn't sit down," Longtin said.

As the questioning continued through a sleepless night, Longtin grew wearier. The police interrogation log shows that fresh rounds of detectives came in and out of the room to question him. The interrogators dropped ever more details of the crime into their comments until he developed a pretty good idea of just what had happened to his wife, Longtin said. "There were so many of them," Longtin said. "One detective would leave and another one would come in. He would say, 'Well, what do you think happened? This is what I think happened.' He would give me a clue or information. Then another one would come in and ask me what happened, and I'd say things that I'd heard [from the detective] before."

One detective told Longtin that his wife had sex before she died. "She had a boyfriend," Longtin recalled the detective taunting him. "You killed her because you caught her with him, and that's why she had semen in her. It was consensual sex." "I kept telling him, 'Look, my wife walked with the Lord. She walked with Jesus. She wouldn't do that.'" He said one detective barked, "You did it!" over and over. "I'd say, 'No,'" Longtin said. "He'd say, 'We know you did it.' He was hammering at me, just constantly. Every time I would say something: 'You did it.' That's all he would say. 'You did it. You did it.'" ...

Longtin ... continued to insist that he had nothing to confess. Late Wednesday afternoon, about 28 hours into the questioning, one detective suggested he was insane and just couldn't remember that he had murdered his wife, he said. Longtin said he began to question his own sense of reality. "I didn't have no sleep from Sunday," he said. "I was burned out—period. With all the back-and-forth, my mind wasn't right. I remember him at one point saying, he said to me, 'You have a split personality.' I said, 'No, I don't think so.' But I thought about it. At that point, when you are tired like that, I thought, 'Well, maybe I do.' "

Longtin said the detective asked: "Didn't you go over to her house and have an argument with her, and she ran out of the house and you grabbed a knife? How big was the knife?" The detective "was trying to catch me that way," Longtin said. "I'd say, 'Well, if I did that in my other self. . . . But I couldn't have done it because I had no blood anywhere. I had no blood anywhere on my clothes or on me.' I'd say, 'It wasn't me. It wasn't me.' We went around with that for like 15 minutes. Then I remember saying something like, 'The guy who killed her, if he goes there and he grabbed a knife from the kitchen drawer, and he ran after her and he stabbed her . . .' The detective said, 'Well, thanks for making a confession. What can I do for you?' I'm like, 'What? I didn't admit to anything.' I said, 'No, I didn't do it.' He said, 'Yes, you did.' "

The police log indicates that Detective Bert Frankenfield was the only interrogator in the room between noon and 5 p.m. that Wednesday. His notes say that over those five hours, Longtin both maintained his innocence and "remembered" his wife being chased down her apartment hallway with a kitchen knife and grabbed from behind. Detective Glen Clark relieved Frankenfield and remained in the room until 10 p.m., the log shows. In his notes, Clark boiled that into five spare sentences: "Defendant goes to victim's house on Sunday night. They have an argument. She leaves to go run. He goes to kitchen, grabs a knife to follow her. Defendant will not talk any more."

Longtin never wrote or signed any statement incriminating himself, records show. He said he didn't go to this wife's apartment, he didn't grab a knife and chase her—and he never told detectives that he did. The police log indicated he slept about 50 minutes in more than 38 hours in the interrogation room. He said he hadn't slept at all. On Thursday afternoon, two days after he arrived at police headquarters, Longtin was taken before a magistrate. "The defendant admitted to having a verbal and physical altercation at the victim's apartment," Detective Ronald Herndon wrote in a sworn charging document. "The defendant gave details about this case that had not been released to the media and only the perpetrator would have known. He stated that during the altercation the victim ran out of her apartment and that he ran after her with a knife. The defendant knew that the victim had been stabbed several times and that the stabbing occurred in the wooded area near the victims apartment." . . .

The case against Keith Longtin began to unravel when a Prince George's County detective—from the sex crimes unit, not homicide—and a District detective noticed similarities between the Zinetti case and a series of unsolved sexual assaults. . . . A DNA analysis showed that the semen recovered from Zinetti's corpse was [from the suspect in those assaults], police said. . . .

On June 12, more than eight months after his interrogation by Prince George's homicide detectives, Longtin was released from jail. The state dropped all charges against him. Chief Farrell assessed the chain of events that set Longtin free: "I'd say the system worked. Another one of our investigators did what was supposed to be done. Other information came to light. It was taken forward ... and the right thing was done." ...

During the eight months Longtin spent in jail, he missed his wife's funeral. His bills went unpaid. His credit rating was destroyed. He said police sent his truck to a junkyard. They gave the wedding ring he'd bought for his wife to in-laws who never liked him. Longtin said all he had left was his faith. "I stood on the Lord, and he delivered me out of the mouth of the lion," Longtin said. He still struggles with depression. He finds it hard to get out of bed to go to work. A lot of days, he doesn't.

––––––

2. FAIRNESS

Professor Joseph Grano[23] points out that the Court's due process jurisprudence advances several notions of fairness. He characterizes these fairness notions as the "fox-hunter's, equality, and human dignity arguments." The "fox-hunter's argument" requires the government to conduct a thorough investigation of the facts, and not just rely on confessions, in order to give defendants a sporting chance to win at trial. The "equality argument" prevents the government from using its vastly greater resources to overwhelm the defendant. The "human dignity" argument demands that the government avoid undue pressure and cruelty. Each of these three arguments implicates reliability concerns and involves normative judgments.

3. DIGNITY AND DECENCY

Courts allow police to use confessions as a means to ferret out crime, but discourage them from using coercion to limit the suspect's options unreasonably. The Supreme Court explained that an admissible confession must be:

> ... the product of an essentially free and unconstrained choice by its maker[.] If it is, if he has willed to confess, it may be used against him. If it is not, if his will has been overborne and his capacity for self-determination critically impaired, the use of his confession offends due process. The line of distinction is that at which governing self-direction is lost and compulsion, of whatever nature or however infused, propels or helps to propel the confession.[24]

Courts make normative judgments about how much limitation on free choice is unreasonable, because "[e]xcept where a person is unconscious or drugged ... all incriminating statements, even those made under brutal treatment," reflect the suspect's choice among alternatives.[25]

––––––

23. *See* Grano, CONFESSIONS, *supra* note 9.

24. Culombe, 367 U.S. at 602.

25. Paul M. Bator & James Vorenberg, *Arrest, Detention, Interrogation and the Right to Counsel: Basic Problems and Possible Legislative Solutions*, 66 COLUM. L. REV. 62, 72 (1966).

4. INDIVIDUAL TRUST OF GOVERNMENT

Professor Paris[26] has suggested a final reason for the voluntariness doctrine. If police are permitted to interrogate suspects in a cruel fashion, she argues, important bonds of trust between government and individuals would be damaged. This would have profound consequences because democratic governments rely in large part on a foundation of trust as opposed to fear. We might add that common police questioning of subcommunities, such as African–Americans, will breed distrust and its ill consequences among that subgroup, an issue we visited in an earlier chapter in slightly different terms in our discussions of race.

NOTES AND QUESTIONS

1. Assume that you are arguing a case in a jurisdiction in which precedent has not yet determined the relevance or weight of police deception and promises of leniency in gauging whether a confession is involuntary. How would the social science data above help you in suggesting appropriate rules of law? Could you craft clearer guidelines than the general commitment to consider the "totality of the circumstances"? How would you get the data before the court? If you are the prosecutor and want to challenge this data, what information would you want that might enable you to mount such a challenge?

2. Assume that you are a defense attorney preparing for a hearing on a motion to suppress your client's confession as involuntary. Which witnesses might you call to the stand? What, if anything, might each of these types of witnesses offer: (a) experts on police tactics and training; (b) research psychologists who have studied the accuracy of confessions under particular circumstances; (c) a clinical psychologist who has examined your client?

3. Can you craft a set of police practice rules that would reduce the likelihood of false confessions? Can you craft an argument that due process requires the adoption of such rules? Is there a cost to doing so, and, if so, do the costs outweigh the benefits? Is such balancing relevant to due process? Why?

C. INTERPRETIVE APPROACHES TO DUE PROCESS

A grand, general phrase like "due process" must be given meaning by reference to extratextual sources. One possible extratextual source is the "original intent" of the Framers of the constitution. But the Court has not used original intent as its principal guide in crafting due process guidelines for limiting police conduct in obtaining confessions. History has been relevant in a broad sense: the Court generally invalidates investigatory techniques that were banned by the common law and the colonists. However, it has not indicated that the full scope of the due process clauses must find firm roots in history and tradition. Instead, it looks to other extratex-

---

26. Margaret L. Paris, *Trust, Lies, and Interrogation*, 3 VA. J. SOC. POL'Y & L. 3, 25–27 (1995).

tual sources, such as "immutable principles of justice, or principles of justice that, if not immutable and universal, at least are basic to the American system of justice."[27]

Some commentators have argued that this vague inquiry permits the justices simply to substitute their own values for those of the framers or of legislatures. According to these commentators, the Court should distinguish broadly contestable moral judgments (which should not be read into due process) from what Professor Grano calls "society's bedrock moral or political principles, which the due process clause may arguably protect." Such an inquiry requires the Court to pay heed to doctrines of federalism and separation of powers, as well as the basic functions, goals, and processes of our political structure. It also requires the Court to consider whether sufficient protections against police abuses can be provided by alternative institutions—for example, by legislative or executive agency rule-making—and alternative procedures—for example, by requiring mandatory videotaping of confessions.

In addition to examining original intent and fundamental principles, the Court implicitly considers current attitudes as one factor in the due process inquiry. Finally, social science may play a limited, if not a decisive, role in the Court's due process analysis.

NOTES AND QUESTIONS

1. Has the Court's due process voluntariness jurisprudence displayed the kind of restraint urged by some commentators? Is such restraint sound as a limitation on constitutional interpretation in this area?

2. How might the social science data recounted above, or similar data, have affected the Court's crafting of due process voluntariness guidelines in its leading cases? How might such data have affected the outcome of particular decisions?

3. Should present majority attitudes matter in giving due process meaning, given the purposes of the Bill of Rights? For example, should minority attitudes, particularly fear and distrust of the police by certain groups in certain areas, be relevant? How would you prove such attitudes?

4. Think back to the discussion in Chapter One concerning historical conceptions of due process in the criminal justice system at the time of the post-Civil War amendments. How, if at all, do and should those conceptions affect the crafting of the due process voluntariness doctrine today?

5. Would a knowledge of historical and present police practices be relevant to the due process analysis? Why?

6. How would we distinguish a "mutable" from an "immutable" principle of justice in this area? Principles "basic" to the American system of justice

---

27. Grano, CONFESSIONS, *supra* note 9, at 97.

from those that are "peripheral"? "Universal" justice principles from Anglo–American ones?

D.   THE TOTALITY TEST IN PRACTICE

We now turn to a brief review of how the courts have treated particular police tactics. Results in individual cases will turn not only on the particular tactic but also on the suspect's vulnerability and a weighing of how the goals outlined above are served in the particular case.

1.   USE OF FORCE AND FEAR OF PHYSICAL INJURY

The use or threatened use of force is highly determinative of involuntariness. Similarly, manipulating the defendant's fear of physical injury will in some circumstances result in coercion. For example, in *Arizona v. Fulminante*,[28] defendant Fulminante had been incarcerated in prison and was approached by an undercover informant, Anthony Sarivola, who presented himself as an organized crime figure. Sarivola offered to protect Fulminante from "some rough treatment" at the hands of fellow inmates, if Fulminante told the truth about a rumor that he had killed his eleven-year-old stepdaughter. Fulminante then confessed to Sarivola in considerable detail. The Court held that Fulminante's confession was involuntary because there was "a credible threat of physical violence" such that Fulminante's "will was overborne in such a way as to render his confession the product of coercion."

Dissenting, Chief Justice Rehnquist argued that the confession was not coerced in light of the following factors: Fulminante had been in prison on multiple occasions and was "presumably able to fend for himself"; he had stipulated during the hearing on his motion to suppress that he had never expressed a fear of other inmates to Sarivola or sought Sarivola's protection; Sarivola never threatened Fulminante or demanded the confession; the conversation between the two men was not lengthy; and Fulminante had been free to leave. In addition, Justice Rehnquist stated that because Fulminante was not aware that Sarivola was an FBI informant, there was no "danger of coercion result[ing] from the interaction of custody and official interrogation."

2.   LENGTHY INTERROGATIONS AND DEPRIVATION OF BODILY NEEDS

Sometimes interrogators obtain confessions by engaging in lengthy interrogations that break the suspect down even without physical force. In these situations, suspects become sleep deprived and may also be denied adequate food, water, and rest breaks. Courts factor the length of the interrogation, and its conditions, into the totality analysis, but criticisms

---

28.   499 U.S. 279 (1991).

abound that long interrogations remain fairly common. Consider the following newspaper article reporting on four false confessions obtained by the Prince George's County, Maryland police department:[29]

The methods allegedly used to gain those false confessions are not unusual, according to lawyers, former suspects and court and police documents. In the last three years, people have been convicted and imprisoned based on confessions they gave during interrogations conducted over 32, 35, 51, even 80 hours. Sometimes police document sleep deprivation in their own interrogation logs. For example, a log indicates that Keith Longtin slept about 50 minutes during more than 38 hours in the interrogation room when he allegedly implicated himself in his wife's 1999 slaying. Longtin spent more than eight months in jail before DNA evidence exonerated him.

The effects of prolonged lack of sleep during interrogation were underscored during the Korean War, when 36 of 59 captured U.S. airmen confessed to war crimes they had not committed. That immediately raised fears that the communists had developed terrible new drugs or methods of brainwashing. Their tactic proved more simple: sleep deprivation. "It was just one device used to confuse, bewilder and torment our men until they were ready to confess to anything," Louis West, a psychiatrist who served on a government panel that studied the confessions, once told an interviewer. "That device was prolonged, chronic loss of sleep."

Richard Schwab, medical director of the University of Pennsylvania's Center for Sleep Disorders, said depriving people of sleep during prolonged questioning can help extract confessions, even from the innocent. After one night of lost sleep, people's judgment is impaired, their reactions slow, they have trouble making decisions and they are prone to mistakes, Schwab said. After two nights, he said, people can become temporarily psychotic and hallucinate.

A respected textbook on law enforcement interrogations warns against "an unduly prolonged, continuous interrogation" that might be apt to make an innocent person confess. The authors of "Criminal Interrogation and Confession" suggest that competent interrogators should be able to obtain most confessions within about four hours.

Police departments in adjacent jurisdictions say their interrogations of suspects generally are far shorter than those in Prince George's County. "I don't think I've ever seen one more than six or seven hours, really," said Lt. Philip Raum, a former Montgomery County homicide detective who now works for the chief of the detectives bureau. "If somebody had to stay up 24 hours without sleep, how voluntary is that?" Detective Pamela Reed, who teaches interrogation tactics to District detectives, said she has kept murder suspects in the interrogation room for seven or eight hours while she alternately questions them and checks out information they've given her. In 23

---

29. April Witt, *No Rest for the Suspects*, THE WASHINGTON POST (June 4, 2001).

years on the force, she said, the longest interrogation she has participated in was of a man suspected of killing a police officer. She said it lasted between 16 and 18 hours. . . .

Rutgers law professor George C. Thomas, co-author of "The *Miranda* Debate: Law, Justice and Policing," contends that marathon interrogations are inherently coercive. "It's just not ethical policing," Thomas said in an interview, "and I'm pretty far right on these issues. I don't think it's wrong to trick or cajole an offender. But it's wrong to question a guy for 55 hours with relays of fresh officers. Whether it's unconstitutional or not, who knows, but it's wrong." The U.S. Supreme Court has left it to judges and juries to decide if "the totality of the circumstances" indicates that a confession was voluntary or whether the suspect's "will was overborne" by coercive police conduct. The length of time a suspect was questioned is just one factor judges and juries are supposed to consider, the court has said. They also should take into account the suspect's age, intelligence and character, where the questioning took place, whether the suspect had previous experience with police and whether police used violence, threats or promises, either direct or implied, to extract a confession.

In one high-profile case in 1988, Prince George's Circuit Court Judge Joseph S. Casula issued a blistering 53–page ruling that threw out the confession Prince George's homicide squad interrogators elicited from Jane F. Bolding. Bolding, a nurse, had come under scrutiny after a series of unexpected cardiac arrests in the intensive care unit of Prince George's Hospital Center. Casula found that detectives unlawfully held Bolding for 34 hours in an interrogation room, refused to let her see a lawyer, grilled her for more than 24 hours without letting her sleep and coerced her to confess that she had injected patients with lethal doses of potassium chloride. "There are simply no short-cuts around the Constitution," Casula wrote in suppressing the confession.

Thirteen years later, Prince George's homicide detectives "appear to operate under the thinking that they may interrogate a suspect for any length of time required to secure an inculpatory statement," attorney Michael S. Blumenthal told the Maryland Court of Appeals recently in an unsuccessful bid to overturn the murder conviction of a client who wept and wet his pants during an interrogation that lasted more than 30 hours. "No individual, even the innocent individual," Blumenthal said, "is without a breaking point."

3.   USE OF OTHER PSYCHOLOGICAL TECHNIQUES

a.   *Pressure Tactics*

The use of psychological pressures, aside from lengthy interrogations and deprivation of bodily needs, may render a confession involuntary. In determining whether such pressures overcame the defendant's will, courts consider characteristics such as the defendant's age, ability to understand,

and psychological profile. For example, in *Spano v. New York*,[30] Vincent Spano, a suspect in a murder case, was interrogated for hours by several officers despite his requests for an attorney and his manifest desire to remain silent. He was also questioned by a friend, whom Spano had earlier telephoned for help and who was directed by the police to play on Spano's sympathies. Finally, after succumbing to the friend's questioning and signing a statement, Spano was taken to the scene where he had thrown away the murder weapon, was questioned further, and made additional damaging statements. The Court considered the following factors in determining whether Spano's statements were involuntary given the totality of the circumstances:

> [Spano] was a foreign-born young man of 25 with no past history of law violation or of subjection to official interrogation.... He had progressed only one-half year into high school and ... had a history of emotional instability. He ... was subjected to the leading questions of a skillful prosecutor in a question and answer confession. He was subject[ed] to questioning not by a few men, but by many.... [T]he effect of such massive official interrogation must have been felt. [Spano] was questioned for virtually eight straight hours before he confessed.... Nor was the questioning conducted during normal business hours, but began in early evening, continued into the night, and did not bear fruition until the not-too-early morning.... The questioners persisted in the face of his repeated refusals to answer on the advice of his attorney, and they ignored his reasonable requests to contact the local attorney whom he had already retained and who had personally delivered him into the custody of these officers in obedience to the bench warrant.

> The use of ... a "childhood friend" ... is another factor which deserves mention in the totality of the situation. [The friend's] was the one face ... in which [Spano] could put some trust. There was a bond of friendship between them going back a decade into adolescence. It was with this material that the officers felt that they could overcome [Spano's] will. They instructed [the friend] falsely to state that [Spano's] telephone call had gotten him into trouble, that his job was in jeopardy, and that loss of his job would be disastrous to his three children, his wife and his unborn child....

We conclude that [Spano's] will was overborne by official pressure, fatigue and sympathy falsely aroused.... The undeviating intent of the officers to extract a confession ... is ... patent. When such an intent is shown, this Court has held that the confession obtained must be examined with the most careful scrutiny, and has reversed a conviction on facts less compelling than these. Accordingly, we hold that [Spano's] conviction cannot stand under the Fourteenth Amendment.

---

30. 360 U.S. at 321–24.

b. Deception

As the excerpt above suggests, courts pay considerable attention to "deceptive police tactics" when determining whether a confession is voluntary. The Court invalidated a confession given after a suspect was "subtly" questioned by a state-employed doctor who purported to be present in order to give the suspect medical relief but who was really a psychiatrist with considerable knowledge of hypnosis.[31] The measure of importance given to police deception varies from state to state. In most jurisdictions, deception alone does not render a confession involuntary, but constitutes one factor among many to be considered within the totality of the circumstances.

c. Promises of Leniency

Promises of leniency may also be considered in determining voluntariness. For example, in *Lynumn v. Illinois*,[32] the defendant, Beatrice Lynumn, underwent police interrogation during which she denied and then admitted having sold marijuana. She later testified that, after her initial denial, the officers warned her that if she did not "cooperate" she could get ten years in prison, suffer a termination of financial aid to her children, and have her children taken away from her. According to the defendant, she believed that if she answered the questions as the officers wanted her to answer, she would not be prosecuted. Lynumn testified that she asked the police what to say and was told to admit to the marijuana sale, which she did. The officers did not dispute Lynumn's version of the events. In reviewing the totality of the circumstances, the Court held that Lynumn's confession had been coerced, reasoning that

> There was no friend or adviser to whom [Lynumn] might turn. She had had no previous experience with the criminal law, and had no reason not to believe that the police had ample power to carry out their threats. We think it clear that a confession made under such circumstances must be deemed not voluntary, but coerced.

Some courts have imposed a strict prohibition against promises. Thus, one court reviewed a case in which a defendant, who was not a suspect at the time, was promised by a sheriff that if he would help solve a crime, the sheriff would "certainly try to help him." The court found that the promise was "susceptible of the interpretation that if the defendant would help him solve the . . . case and it developed that the defendant was involved, he, the Sheriff, would certainly try to help him."[33] Other courts prohibit only specific promises made in exchange for a confession, so that an officer's general statement that he will help a defendant "all that he can" will not

---

31.   Leyra v. Denno, 347 U.S. 556 (1954). On the other hand, the Court did not suppress a confession as involuntary where the police lied to a suspect, telling him that his accomplice had already confessed. That was insufficient, given that the "totality of the circumstances" included a short duration of questioning and a defendant who was a mature adult of normal intelligence. Frazier v. Cupp, 394 U.S. 731 (1969).

32.   372 U.S. 528 (1963).

33.   State v. Woodruff, 130 S.E.2d 641, 645 (N.C.1963).

render that defendant's subsequent confession involuntary.[34] Still other courts refuse to omit confessions unless they were induced by promises "of such character as would be likely to influence the defendant to speak untruthfully."[35] For example, a Texas court excluded a confession made by an employee whose employer promised not to press charges, contact the police, or discharge the employee as a result of the confession. The court reasoned that because of the promise the employee was "inclined to admit a crime he had not committed ... [because] he had reason to believe there was no danger in admitting it."

Generally speaking, however, an officer's words of comfort and frequent assurances made to make a defendant feel more comfortable about speaking will not render a confession involuntary, at least where the defendant has been given *Miranda* warnings and knows at the time of the confession that he may be prosecuted following the confession.[36] Similarly, an officer's statement that a defendant is not a criminal, combined with encouragement that the defendant unburden himself, is not by itself sufficient to overcome a suspect's will.

What if the defendant, rather than the officer, initiates the discussion about a promise of leniency? Under the totality of circumstances analysis, where a defendant sought a promise of leniency as a precondition for confession, the ensuing confession is less likely to be found involuntary than a confession made after police initiated the promise.[37] Another relevant fact is an officer's representation that he has authority to enforce the promise. If, for example, a government agent promises to relate the fact of the defendant's cooperation to appropriate officials, and the agent does not represent that he has authority to affect the outcome of the case, the promise likely will not render the ensuing confession involuntary.[38]

E. Proving Voluntariness

The prosecution bears the burden of establishing that a confession was voluntary by a preponderance of the evidence. The trial judge makes the voluntariness determination outside of the presence of the jury. If the judge finds the confession involuntary, then it must be excluded—the jury will not be permitted to hear of it, lest its deliberations be tainted by such powerful evidence of guilt.[39] If the judge finds the confession voluntary, then the defendant must be permitted to attack its veracity in front of the jury by introducing the circumstances in which it was given.[40] In some jurisdictions, a defendant in these circumstances is given the opportunity to

---

34. Hargett v. State, 357 S.W.2d 533, 534 (Ark.1962).

35. Fisher v. State, 379 S.W.2d 900, 902 (Tex.Crim.App.1964).

36. Miller v. Fenton, 796 F.2d 598 (3d Cir.), *cert. denied*, 479 U.S. 989 (1986).

37. Drew v. State, 503 N.E.2d 613 (Ind.1987). *See also* People v. Wright, 469 N.E.2d 351 (Ill.App.1984); State v. Hutson, 537 S.W.2d 809 (Mo.App.1976).

38. United States v. Fraction, 795 F.2d 12 (3d Cir.1986).

39. *See* Jackson v. Denno, 378 U.S. 368 (1964).

40. *See* Crane v. Kentucky, 476 U.S. 683 (1986).

go even further, by having the jury make a second determination on the voluntariness issue. If the jury finds the confession involuntary, then the judge instructs the jury to disregard it. This procedure is followed by a number of states, although it is not required by the United States constitution.[41]

F.   CAUSATION AND GOVERNMENT ACTION

The Court has repeatedly required that government action must have "induced," "brought about," "produced," "extracted," or "obtained" the confession. This is language suggestive of a causation requirement. Certainly this at least means that there must be "but-for" causation, as is illustrated by this example:

> Police officers arrested D for robbery and brought D to the station for interrogation. When D refused to acknowledge guilt, other officers went to D's home to interrogate D's spouse. Finding D's spouse equally uncooperative, the officers responded by beating the spouse. In the meantime, D, who was neither mistreated nor cognizant of the events at D's home, had a change of heart and confessed. At D's subsequent trial, the prosecutor relied on D's confession as well as other evidence.[42]

Because the defendant in the example was unaware of the wrongful police conduct, his confession must have resulted from factors other than the police conduct (that is, it cannot be said that "but-for" that conduct, he would not have confessed). Indeed, it was apparently his own guilty conscience that led him to confess.

In the vast majority of cases, the difficult question is not deciding whether the suspect would have remained silent "but-for" the police conduct, but choosing which cause, among all of the available "but-for" causes, matters most. This is a normative judgment based on due process values. For example, if a defendant is ninety-eight percent likely to confess before arrest, and, upon being arrested, is threatened by police with a beating if he does not confess, his ensuing confession probably is a product of both police misconduct and his guilty conscience. Whether to suppress the confession as "caused" by police threats cannot be resolved as a factual matter alone, although a factual inquiry may help. The normative portion of the inquiry thus draws on the same due process values we discussed above.

G.   DOES TORTURE VIOLATE THE DUE PROCESS CLAUSE?

1.   THE QUESTION

For criminal procedure purposes, the importance of the due process "voluntariness" doctrine is that an involuntary confession—one induced

---

41. The Court in Jackson v. Denno approved a procedure in which the defendant was not permitted to have a separate jury determination of voluntariness.

42. Grano, CONFESSIONS, *supra* note 9, at 75.

through too much coercion—cannot be used against the person in a criminal case. Recall that the doctrine had its inception in *Brown v. Mississippi*, and that the Court there crafted the doctrine as an exclusionary rule prohibiting the use at trial of involuntary statements. Recent events have caused many to ask whether the voluntariness doctrine goes further. Does it prohibit the use of coercive techniques altogether, or just the introduction at trial of the products of those techniques? In other words, does the due process violation take place immediately upon the application of coercion, or does it take place only when the fruits of coercion are introduced in the courtroom?

The question is an important one for several reasons. First, some victims of coercion may not want to rest with the exclusionary remedy. Because constitutional violations are remediable under federal statutes (principally the federal civil rights statute, 42 U.S.C. § 1983), these victims might want to pursue remedies for the harm they suffered at the hands of interrogators. Moreover, some suspects who have been victimized by coercive interrogations never face criminal charges, so the exclusionary rule supplied by the voluntariness doctrine is not available. In the latter camp are suspects detained and interrogated, but never charged, during the aftermath of September 11, 2001.

The question, then, put starkly, is whether torture alone violates the due process clause. The answer remains unclear. Here are some of the pieces of this constitutional puzzle.

2. SUBSTANTIVE DUE PROCESS

In *Chavez v. Martinez*,[43] the Court confronted an involuntary confession that the government never sought to introduce in a criminal case. The facts of the case were these: Oliverio Martinez sued police officer Ben Chavez under 42 U.S.C. § 1983 after Chavez interrogated him in a hospital emergency room. Martinez had just been shot in the head and body several times by two other officers. His injuries were so severe as to cause permanent blindness and paralysis. From a transcript of the interrogation, it is clear that Martinez was in agony and believed that life-saving measures would be withheld from him unless he talked to Chavez. In the words of Justice Stevens, the interrogation "was the functional equivalent of an attempt to obtain an involuntary confession from a prisoner by torturous methods." Martinez was never charged with a crime arising out of the incidents preceding his injuries, and the government never sought to use his statements against him.

Martinez's suit alleged that Chavez had violated his Fifth and Fourteenth Amendment rights to be free from coercive interrogations. In the lower courts, the case was thought to involve primarily the Fifth Amendment privilege against self-incrimination. In fact, court rulings in the case were eagerly anticipated because they were expected to clarify whether coercive interrogations constitute instant violations of the Fifth Amend-

---

43. 538 U.S. 760 (2003).

ment, or whether the privilege against self-incrimination is violated only when statements are introduced at trial. (We will discuss these aspects of the case in a later section of this supplement.) However, the case developed a Fourteenth Amendment substantive due process angle in the Supreme Court. This arose out of the lower court's decision on qualified immunity. Chavez had raised the qualified immunity defense as a shield, claiming that his conduct did not violate "clearly established" rights—as it would have to before he could be liable under § 1983. The trial court granted summary judgment to Martinez on the issue of qualified immunity, and the Ninth Circuit affirmed. Rather than confine its discussion to clearly established Fifth Amendment rights, however, the court also stated that "a police officer violates the Fourteenth Amendment when he obtains a confession by coercive conduct, regardless of whether the confession is subsequently used at trial." The court explained further that "the due process violation caused by coercive behavior of law-enforcement officers in pursuit of a confession is complete with the coercive behavior itself. . . . The actual use or attempted use of that coerced statement in a court of law is not necessary to complete the affront to the Constitution."

In the Supreme Court, those words were carefully scrutinized. Did the Ninth Circuit mean that due process was violated merely because the officer had violated the Fifth Amendment privilege against self-incrimination, and therefore also the clause in the Fourteenth Amendment that incorporates the Fifth Amendment against the states? Or did the Ninth Circuit mean something more—that the officer had violated *other* rights clearly established under the Fourteenth Amendment due process clause? Martinez had not raised the latter claim in front of the Ninth Circuit, but he did brief it in the Supreme Court, and the Court took it on. The justices issued *six* opinions and achieved little consensus, although this much is clear: a majority of the Court reversed the judgment of the Ninth Circuit and remanded on the issue of whether "Martinez may pursue a claim of liability for a substantive due process violation."

Here are the various positions that emerged from the opinions. We offer these with the suggestion that you first review the material in the text on pages 39 and 40 about the incorporation debate:

A.   The apparent majority position (written by Justice Thomas): the Fourteenth Amendment due process clause has two aspects: (a) it incorporates various provisions of the Bill of Rights against the states; and (b) it provides a few carefully limited "substantive" rights. The only substantive due process right pertinent to Martinez's case is the right against government conduct that "shocks the conscience," as described in *Rochin v. California* (see page 159 of the text) and *County of Sacramento v. Lewis* (see page 310 of the text). In order for Martinez to make out a claim involving the former kind of protection, he would have to establish that Chavez violated his privilege against self-incrimination (which he was unable to do because a majority of the Court viewed the privilege as arising only at trial, as we will see in a later section of this supplement). In order to invoke substantive due process, he would have to establish that Chavez's conduct shocked the conscience. This, according to Thomas and language from older cases, requires proof of "the most egregious official conduct"— most likely of the sort that was "intended to injure in some way *unjustifiable by any government interest*."[44] Thomas stated that the record did not support a finding that Chavez's conduct had shocked the conscience. The Chief Justice and Justice Scalia joined this part of Thomas's opinion. In a separate opinion, Justice Souter indicated that he also would apply substantive due process protection in this case only if Chavez's conduct were found to shock the conscience, but he stated that he believed Martinez "has a serious argument in support of such a position" and proposed a remand on that issue (he gained a majority on the remand). Justice Breyer joined Justice Souter's opinion.

Thus, a majority of 5 justices appears to take the position that coerced statements that are not introduced at trial *do* violate constitutional rights, but *only* if the conduct producing them shocks the conscience.

B.   Justice Stevens's position: the Fourteenth Amendment due process clause involves two kinds of protections: (a) it protects against government conduct that shocks the conscience; and (b) it protects against government conduct that interferes with rights "implicit in the concept of ordered liberty." "Unusually coercive police interrogation procedures" violate the second standard, which has as one source of protections the rights found in the Fifth Amendment. Martinez's claim under the second standard is strong, because the interrogation through torture constituted "an immediate deprivation of [Martinez's] constitutionally protected interest in liberty." Justice Stevens thus appears to take a broader position than the majority and would supporting a holding that "unusually" coerced statements that are not introduced at trial *do* violate constitutional rights, *regardless* of government interests.

C.   The minority position (written by Justice Kennedy): as compared with the Fifth Amendment, the Fourteenth Amendment is broader and "less specific." It protects the "fundamental right to liberty of the person." That right is violated by "the official imposition of severe pain or pressure for purposes of interrogation," and the violation in such a case is immediate. Kennedy recognized that interrogations must accommodate government interests, but he warned that "police should take the necessary steps to ensure that there is neither the fact nor the perception that the declarant's pain is being used to induce the statement against his will." In this case, Martinez's pain was not caused by Chavez, but Martinez demonstrated that the officer "exploited his pain and suffering with the purpose and intent of securing an incriminating statement." That conduct is remediable under § 1983. Justices Stevens and Ginsburg joined Justice

---

44.   Here Justice Thomas was quoting from *Lewis*. We added the emphasis because the language appears to require a balancing of the government's interests against those of the suspect. Actually, the full language from *Lewis* leaves open the theoretical possibility that even conduct justifiable by government interests may nevertheless shock the conscience: "conduct intended to injure in some way unjustifiable by any government interest is the sort of official action most likely to rise to the conscience-shocking level".

Kennedy. Three justices, then, appear to agree that coerced statements that are not introduced at trial *do* violate constitutional rights *if* the government produced them by intentionally manipulating pain.

The upshot of *Chavez v. Martinez* is this: eight justices[45] apparently accept the proposition that substantive due process protects individuals from certain forms of government conduct—at the bare minimum, from government conduct that shocks the conscience. But the "shocks the conscience" test may require victims to establish government conduct that is unjustifiable when viewed in light of any government interests animating it. Moreover, according to some scholars the "shocks the conscience" test is only the first part of the analysis: "[t]he conclusion that a constitutional right has been violated does not end with a finding that the police behavior shocks the conscience. Rather, the analysis only begins there. The Fourteenth Amendment's guarantee that the government will not deprive any person of due process of law, like virtually all constitutional provisions, is not absolute. The government may deprive a person of life, liberty or property if the government has a sufficiently valid justification for doing so."[46]

A coda to the *Martinez* case: we mentioned above that a majority remanded the case to determine whether Martinez's Fourteenth Amendment rights had been violated. On remand the Ninth Circuit answered in the affirmative.[47] Notice how it picked up on Justice Stevens's broader position:

> . . . We hold that, if the facts as alleged are proven true, [the conduct] did [violate the Fourteenth Amendment]. Accordingly, Chavez is not entitled to qualified immunity on Martinez's Fourteenth Amendment substantive due process claim.
>
> The Fourteenth Amendment's Due Process Clause protects individuals from state action that either "shocks the conscience" or interferes with rights "implicit in the concept of ordered liberty." Martinez alleges that Chavez brutally and incessantly questioned him, after he had been shot in the face, back, and leg and would go on to suffer blindness and partial paralysis, and interfered with his medical treatment while he was "screaming in pain . . . and going in and out of consciousness." Chavez allegedly continued this "interrogation" over Martinez's pleas for him to stop so that he could receive treatment. If Martinez's allegations are proven, it would be impossible not to be shocked by Sergeant Chavez's actions. A clearly established right, fundamental to ordered liberty, is freedom from coercive police interrogation. Because, under the facts alleged by Martinez, Chavez violated

---

45.   Justice O'Connor did not join any of the opinions on the due process issue.

46.   Marcy Strauss, *Torture*, 48 N.Y.L. Sch. L. Rev. 201 (2004) (citing Erwin Chemerinsky, Constitutional Law 700 (2d ed. 2001): "If a right is deemed fundamental [under the due process clause], the Government must present a compelling interest to justify an infringement. Alternatively, if a right is not fundamental, only a legitimate purpose is required for the law to be sustained.").

47.   Martinez v. City of Oxnard, 337 F.3d 1091 (9th Cir.2003).

Martinez's clearly established due process rights, we affirm the district court's denial of qualified immunity to Chavez. The ultimate resolution of the merits of Martinez's Fourteenth Amendment claim will depend upon the resolution of contested facts. We leave that resolution to the district court.

Chavez challenged this holding by filing a petition for writ of certiorari in the Supreme Court. But that petition has been denied.[48]

3. FOURTH AMENDMENT PROHIBITION AGAINST UNREASONABLE SEARCHES AND SEIZURES

As we saw in Chapter 3 of the text, members of "the people" have a constitutional right to be free from unreasonable searches and seizures. This right protects against the use of *unreasonable* means—including bodily invasions (which may be searches) and excessive force—to effect searches or seizures, and many litigants have successfully pursued remedies under these doctrines, primarily for the use of excessive force to arrest. Keep in mind three things, however. First, in § 1983 claims, if the Fourth Amendment applies, then substantive due process analysis is precluded, due to the Court's holding in *Graham v. Connor*[49] that in those cases the amendment providing "an explicit textual source of constitutional protection" applies, rather than "the more generalized notion of substantive due process." Second, the interests protected by the Fourth Amendment probably evaporate once a person has been arrested, although the Court in *Graham v. Connor* noted that the issue has not been settled. Some lower courts appear to reason that Fourth Amendment protections end when the seizure is completed; that substantive due process protections apply to pretrial detainees; and that 8th Amendment protections to convicted, imprisoned persons.[50] Third, under the terms of *United States v. Verdugo–Urquidez*,[51] the Fourth Amendment protects only "the people" of the United States—"a class of persons who are part of a national community or who have otherwise developed sufficient connection with this country to be considered part of that community."

Professor Russell D. Covey has argued that compelled custodial interrogations are themselves Fourth Amendment searches, violating privacy interests protected by that amendment. Accordingly, Professor Covey would presumptively permit such non-consensual interrogation only upon issuance of an "interrogation warrant" based upon probable cause to believe that questioning will produce evidence of crime and limiting the scope of the interrogation, subject perhaps to certain exceptions. **Question:** Would this be a suitable solution to the problem of torture? Does it make sense as a constitutional mandate? As a matter of policy? Note that Covey's

---

48. *See* Petition for Certiorari Filed, 72 U.S.L.W. 3643 (April 2, 2004) (No. 03–1381); 124 S.Ct. 2932 (2004) (petition for writ of certiorari denied).

49. 490 U.S. 386, 394–95 (1989).

50. *See* Wright v. Whiddon, 951 F.2d 297 (11th Cir.1992).

51. 494 U.S. 259 (1990).

idea is different from that of the "torture warrant," which would judicially authorize torture under certain conditions and subject to certain limits. Covey's warrant would authorize interrogation but not via torture. Is the torture warrant an acceptable alternative to Professor Covey's approach? Is Professor Covey's position inconsistent with the position of the Court in any of the cases we have earlier cited?

4.   EIGHTH AMENDMENT BAN ON CRUEL AND UNUSUAL PUNISHMENTS

The Eighth Amendment protects against cruel and unusual punishments, but that right applies only to persons actually convicted of a crime. The Court stated in *Ingraham v. Wright*[52] that the Eighth Amendment applies "only after the State has complied with constitutional guarantees traditionally associated with criminal prosecutions. . . . [T]he State does not acquire the power to punish with which the Eighth Amendment is concerned until after it has secured a formal adjudication of guilt in accordance with the due process of law. When the State seeks to impose punishment without such an adjudication, the pertinent constitutional guarantee is the Due Process Clause of the Fourteenth Amendment." Thus, convicted persons who are tortured in prison may sue based on Eighth Amendment doctrines. These require the claimant to "allege and prove the unnecessary and wanton infliction of pain."[53] Again, if the Eighth Amendment applies in a § 1983 case, substantive due process principles will be inapplicable.

5.   INTERNATIONAL LAW

International law prohibits torture, and the United States has ratified most of the treaties containing this law, but it is unclear to what extent American courts will enforce it or afford relief for violations of it. Marcy Strauss remarks that "the impact of these treaties on United States interrogation tactics, frankly is seemingly insignificant. Although the treaties, and international law generally, establish important international norms of conduct, there is no real enforcement."[54]

6.   THE PROBLEM OF EXTRATERRITORIALITY

In light of the "war on terrorism" and the war in Iraq, and the corresponding detention and interrogation by United States government agents of hundreds, perhaps of thousands, of people, claims of abuse are increasingly being brought in United States courts involving extraterritorial conduct. Do the constitutional doctrines discussed above apply in those situations? According to Diane Marie Amann, "[j]urisprudence respecting the degree to which U.S. constitutional guarantees apply abroad is, at best, inconsistent."[55] You are already familiar with the holding in *Verdugo–*

---

52.   430 U.S. 651, 671–72 n.40 (1977).

53.   Whitley v. Albers, 475 U.S. 312 (1986).

54.   Marcy Strauss, *Torture*, *supra* note 46, at 252.

55.   Diane Marie Amann, *Guantanamo*, 42 COLUM. J. TRANSNAT'L L. 263 (2004).

Urquidez restricting Fourth Amendment protections to members of "the people" of the United States. Further, Amann relates dicta stating that (1) "aliens are not 'entitled to Fifth Amendment rights outside the sovereign territory of the United States' "[56]; and (2) " 'certain constitutional protections available to persons inside the United States are unavailable to aliens outside of our geographic borders.' "[57] Amann points out, however, that "[c]ontaining no territorial limitation akin to that in the European Convention, the text of the U.S. Constitution constrains neither the political branches from acting abroad nor the judicial branch from reviewing their actions."[58] Whether the judicial branch will apply the doctrines we discuss above to review extraterritorial actions of the political branches remains to be seen.

H. Extraterritorial Interrogations and Non-Citizens

It is not yet clear whether interrogations by U.S. actors that take place abroad are covered by the due process clause. One federal trial court has applied the clause to statements made abroad by non-citizens under interrogation by U.S. actors, at least "insofar as [the suspect] is the present subject of a domestic criminal investigation."[59] That court pointed out that with unlawfully obtained confessions, the constitutional violation takes place at the trial, when the government seeks to introduce the statement, and not during the interrogation itself. Interrogations abroad may be covered by international treaties and conventions as well, but the enforceability of these is always in question. In any event, the applicability of constitutional or international restraints on interrogation techniques often is simply meaningless because the government has no intention of attempting to use the products of interrogation at trial. Consider this newspaper article reporting on interrogation techniques used by the United States in investigating terrorism:

Questioning Terror Suspects in a Dark and Surreal World
DON VAN NATTA Jr.[60]

CAIRO, March 8—The capture of Khalid Shaikh Mohammed provides American authorities with their best opportunity yet to prevent attacks by Al Qaeda and track down Osama bin Laden. But the detention also presents a tactical and moral challenge when it comes to the interrogation

---

56. Here Amann is quoting Chief Justice Rehnquists's opinion in *Verdugo–Urquidez*, 294 U.S. at 269.

57. Amann's quote is from Zadvydas v. Davis, 533 U.S. 678, 693 (2001).

58. Amann, *Guantanamo, supra* note 55, at 314.

59. United States v. Bin Laden, 132 F.Supp.2d 168 (S.D.N.Y.2001). The opinion explicitly rests on the privilege against self-incrimination under the Fifth Amendment, rather than the due process clause, but it mentions "involuntary" confessions at several points.

60. The New York Times (March 9, 2003).

techniques used to obtain vital information. Senior American officials said physical torture would not be used against Mr. Mohammed, regarded as the operations chief of Al Qaeda and mastermind of the Sept. 11 attacks. They said his interrogation would rely on what they consider acceptable techniques like sleep and light deprivation and the temporary withholding of food, water, access to sunlight and medical attention. . . .

But the urgency of obtaining information about potential attacks and the opaque nature of the way interrogations are carried out can blur the line between accepted and unaccepted actions, several American officials said. Routine techniques include covering suspects' heads with black hoods for hours at a time and forcing them to stand or kneel in uncomfortable positions in extreme cold or heat, American and other officials familiar with interrogations said. Questioners may also feign friendship and respect to elicit information. In some cases, American officials said, women are used as interrogators to try to humiliate men unaccustomed to dealing with women in positions of authority. . . .

Secretary of State Colin L. Powell and Defense Secretary Donald H. Rumsfeld have said that American techniques adhere to international accords that ban the use of torture and that "all appropriate measures" are employed in interrogations. Rights advocates and lawyers for prisoners' rights have accused the United States of quietly embracing torture as an acceptable means of getting information in the global antiterrorism campaign. "They don't have a policy on torture," said Holly Burkhalter, the United States director of Physicians for Human Rights, one of five groups pressing the Pentagon for assurances detainees are not being tortured. "There is no specific policy that eschews torture." Critics also assert that transferring Qaeda suspects to countries where torture is believed common—like Egypt, Jordan and Saudi Arabia—violates American law and the 1984 international convention against torture, which bans such transfers.

Some American and other officials subscribe to a view held by a number of outside experts, that physical coercion is largely ineffective. The officials say the most effective interrogation methods involve a mix of psychological disorientation, physical deprivation and ingratiating acts, all of which can take weeks or months. "Pain alone will often make people numb and unresponsive," said Magnus Ranstorp, deputy director of the Center for the Study of Terrorism and Political Violence at St. Andrews University in Scotland. "You have to engage people to get into their minds and learn what is there." . . .

Omar al-Faruq, a confidant of Mr. bin Laden and one of Al Qaeda's senior operatives in Southeast Asia, was captured last June by Indonesian agents acting on a tip from the C.I.A. Agents familiar with the case said a black hood was dropped over his head and he was loaded onto a C.I.A. aircraft. When he arrived at his destination several hours later, the hood was removed. On the wall in front of him were the seals of the New York City Police and Fire Departments, a Western official said. It was, said a former senior C.I.A. officer who took part in similar sessions, a mind game called false flag, intended to leave the captive disoriented, isolated and vulnerable. Sometimes the décor is faked to make it seem as though the suspect has been taken to a country with a reputation for brutal interrogation. In this case, officials said, Mr. Faruq was in the C.I.A. interrogation center at the Bagram [Afghanistan] air base. American officials were convinced that he knew a lot about pending attacks and the Qaeda network in Southeast Asia, which Mr. bin Laden sent him to set up in 1998.

The details of the interrogation are unknown, though one intelligence official briefed on the sessions said Mr. Faruq initially provided useless scraps of information. What is known is that the questioning was prolonged, extending day and night for weeks. It is likely, experts say, that the proceedings followed a pattern, with Mr. Faruq left naked most of the time, his hands and feet bound. While international law requires prisoners to be allowed eight hours' sleep a day, interrogators do not necessarily let them sleep for eight consecutive hours. Mr. Faruq may also have been hooked up to sensors, then asked questions to which interrogators knew the answers, so they could gauge his truthfulness, officials said. The Western intelligence official described Mr. Faruq's interrogation as "not quite torture, but about as close as you can get." The official said that over a three-month period, the suspect was fed very little, while being subjected to sleep and light deprivation, prolonged isolation and room temperatures that varied from 100 degrees to 10 degrees. In the end he began to cooperate. . . .

In a typical prison, where punishment is the aim, routine governs life. At Bagram, where eliciting information is the goal, the opposite is true. Disorientation is a tool of interrogation and therefore a way of life. To that end, the building—an unremarkable hangar—is lighted 24 hours a day, making sleep almost impossible, said Muhammad Shah, an Afghan farmer who was held there for 18 days. Colonel King said it was legitimate to use lights, noise and vision restriction, and to alter, without warning, the time between meals, to blur a detainee's sense of time. He said sleep deprivation was "probably within the lexicon." Prisoners are watched, moved and, according to some, manhandled by military police officials. Most detainees live on the hangar's bottom floor, a large area divided with wire mesh into group cells holding 8 to 10 prisoners each. Some are kept on the top floor in isolation cells. Former detainees have given disparate accounts of their treatment, with the harshest tales, predictably, emerging from the isolation cells. Those who have probably been subjected to the most thorough interrogations, and the greatest duress, have probably not been released. . . .

Colonel King said that an American military pathologist had determined that the deaths of two prisoners in December were homicides and that the circumstances were still under investigation. Two former prisoners said they had been forced to stand with their hands chained to the ceiling and their feet shackled in the isolation cells. One said he was kept naked except when he was taken to interrogation room or the bathroom. Mr. Shah, who was never in an isolation cell, said neither his hands nor feet were ever tied, but he had seen prisoners with chains around their ankles. Colonel King said that the building was heated and that the prisoners were fed a balanced diet under which most gained weight. Mr. Shah said he had received plentiful food—bread, biscuits, rice and meat—three times a day. . . .

Far less is known about the conditions for the suspected Qaeda members who have been turned over to foreign governments, either after the United States finished with them or as part of the interrogation procedure. Even the numbers and locations are a mystery. American . . . officials have acknowledged that suspects have been sent to Jordan, Syria and Egypt. . . .

In Cairo, leaders of several human rights organizations and attorneys who represent prisoners said torture by the Egyptian government's internal security force had become routine. They also said they believed that the United States had sent a handful of Qaeda suspects to Egypt for harsh interrogations and torture by Egyptian officials. "In the past, the United States harshly criticized Egypt when there was human rights violations, but now, for America, it is security first—security, before human rights," said Muhammad Zarei, a lawyer who had been director of the Cairo-based Human Rights Center for the Assistance of Prisoners. Egyptian officials denied that any Qaeda members or terror suspects had been moved to Egypt. An Egyptian government spokesman, Nabil Osman, blamed rogue officers for abuses and said there was no systematic policy of torture. "Any terrorist will claim torture—that's the easiest thing," Mr. Osman said. "Claims of torture are universal. Human rights organizations make their living on these claims. Their job is not to talk about the human rights of the victim but of the human rights of the terrorist or those in jail." Mr. Osman declined to say whether Egypt had assisted with interrogations of Qaeda suspects at the request of the Americans. He would say only that both governments had cooperated in sharing information about terrorists and potential terrorist activities. "We are providing them with a wealth of information," he said. He said many of Egypt's antiterrorism initiatives, like military tribunals, had been imitated by the Untied States. "We set the model," he said, "for combating terrorism."

NOTES AND QUESTIONS

1. Would the techniques described in the article above render any resulting confessions involuntary if they took place in the United States? Why or why not?

2. Should confessions obtained abroad through such techniques violate the constitution? How would you identify the interests at stake? How would you resolve them?

I. EXCLUSIONARY RULE AND FRUIT-OF-THE-POISONOUS-TREE

Involuntary confessions are inadmissible for any purpose, including impeaching a defendant on the witness stand. Once a court determines that a confession is inadmissible, the focus of the exclusion question shifts to evidence that police uncovered as a result of the confession. The fruit-of-the-poisonous tree doctrine presumably applies just as it does to Fourth Amendment violations, although the Supreme Court has not yet expressly so held. Assuming that the fruit-of-the-poisonous-tree doctrine applies, the admissibility of evidence discovered as a fruit of an involuntary confession would turn on the issues discussed in the exclusionary rule chapter: whether the evidence had an independent source, or would inevitably have been discovered, or is so attenuated from the tainted confession that it should be admitted. This chapter addresses the fruit-of-the-poisonous-tree doctrine in more detail after the discussion of *Miranda*.

———

A role-playing exercise and a series of problems follow. When you work on these, remember to: (a) analogize to the facts of similar cases; (b) consider the role of the values discussed earlier in this chapter as being embodied in the Court's cases; and (c) consider the role of social science in resolving the problems.

J. Role-Play on Voluntariness

John Chang is a recent immigrant to the United States from Hong Kong. He speaks broken English well enough to order groceries, find the correct buses for travel on public transportation, and make himself understood at his job, digging graves. Mr. Chang was well-educated in Hong Kong, having received undergraduate and graduate degrees in mechanical engineering, but he has had trouble finding work as an engineer in the United States. This failure has made him despondent, leading him to drink; he has been arrested twice for public drunkenness in the United States and once for simple assault. He pled guilty to the latter charge in exchange for probation, conditioned on his continuing successful participation in Alcoholics Anonymous.

In the early morning hours of August 16, Mr. Chang and two of his friends, both immigrants, consumed a pitcher of beer at a local bar, and all three experimented with psychedelic mushrooms while on their way to a second bar. Before they got to the second bar, however, Mr. Chang was arrested at 3:58 a.m. by the Jacksonville police on suspicion of burglarizing Tonn's grocery store in Jacksonville one week earlier. The only evidence police have that links Mr. Chang to the burglary is an identification by Mrs. Johnson, a seventy-two-year-old Caucasian woman. Mrs. Johnson, who is near-sighted, observed the ground-floor burglary from her sixth floor apartment across the street from the burglary site. The burglary took place at approximately 2:00 a.m.

Mr. Chang was taken to the police station and given *Miranda* warnings. He was questioned by Captain Jarvis in an interrogation room in which he sat with four detectives. The questioning continued for one-half an hour after he was advised of his rights. He repeatedly denied any guilt and was told, "If you cooperate in this country, the judge sometimes goes easier on you." He still denied his guilt. He was taken across the street to the county jail about 5:00 a.m., where he was put into the cell block for city prisoners.

While there, he became obstreperous, demanding to see Captain Jarvis, beating on a metal table with his cup, and swearing in a loud voice. When he refused to quiet down, the turnkey asked two officers to put him in a small cell called "the hole."

When the officers started to place Mr. Chang in the hole, he picked up an empty five-gallon bucket that was sitting on the floor and drew back his arms as though he were going to hit the officers with the bucket. Officer Williams then used tear gas on Mr. Chang by spraying him directly in the face. Officers Williams and Seymour then took Mr. Chang by the arms and led him into a small cell without resistance.

Half an hour later he asked to be released from the cell. He was still crying and the odor of tear gas was still in the air. Captain Jarvis asked Mr. Chang if he wanted to talk to him about the break-in at Tonn's grocery store and Mr. Chang stated, again in halting English, "I went in there. I done it." He was then released from "the hole" and allowed to wash the tear gas from his face. At about 6:00 a.m., he agreed to accompany the police on an automobile ride and pointed out a pry bar used in the burglary. He also named an accomplice.

Assignment: Your instructor will give you instructions for a role-play on voluntariness. In addition to those instructions, review the materials about interviewing in Chapter 5.

K.   REVIEW PROBLEMS

PROBLEM 8–1

Terry Walker was charged with first degree sexual assault on a child after a grand jury reviewed a confession that he had made during a "pretest interview" with a polygraph examiner. Walker had gone to the police station to take the polygraph at the request of police officers. Upon his arrival, a police officer explained that he had a right not to answer questions and to consult with an attorney. Walker stated that he understood these rights. He then took part in the "pretest interview" with Officer Richard Circo, who reiterated that Walker was free to leave at any time during the interview. Walker initially denied having had sexual contact with the victim. Officer Circo explained erroneously that if the victim had agreed to have sex with Walker, the conduct would not constitute sexual assault. Circo also stated that children often "lead adults on" about sex. Finally, Circo remarked, "I've seen someone who's in pain and who is under stress, and you're in a lot of emotional stress." Shortly thereafter, Walker admitted that he had engaged in sexual intercourse with the fifteen-year-old victim. No polygraph test was administered.

Question: Assuming that Walker moves to dismiss the confession at trial, how should the trial court rule?

PROBLEM 8–2

Witnesses observed James Albrecht near the scene of a murder. Police questioned Albrecht about the murder but did not bring charges against him. Six years later, Albrecht sold a "hot" stereo to Ron Jost, who was an undercover officer involved in a stolen property sting operation. Jost discussed this transaction with other officers and learned of Albrecht's possible involvement in the still-unsolved murder. Several months later, Jost contacted Albrecht and asked Albrecht to consider joining Jost's "criminal organization." Jost mentioned that the organization needed "muscle" and was interested in people with violent backgrounds. Jost asked whether Albrecht had ever committed any violent crimes, to which Albrecht responded that he had not. Jost then took Albrecht to meet a fictitious higher-up in the organization. On the way to the meeting, Jost stated that he was aware of Albrecht's involvement in the murder. He warned Albrecht that the organization needed to know truthfully if Albrecht had been involved and whether the police had any evidence against him. Again, Albrecht denied having had a role in the murder.

A week later, a police detective approached Albrecht and identified himself as the officer investigating the murder, for which Albrecht was still under investigation. The detective opined that advances in DNA testing would lead to new evidence about the murderer, and that the murderer would receive a long prison term. Finally, the detective stated that Albrecht was also under investigation for having sold stolen property, and he told Albrecht that the department was interested in information about others who had received stolen property, including Jost.

Albrecht called Jost that same day. Jost offered to have his organization help Albrecht leave the state, but he again stated that the organization needed to know whether Albrecht had been involved in the murder. Jost explained that the organization needed the information in order to determine how far away it should send Albrecht. Once again Albrecht denied having committed the murder, but hours later he called Jost back, admitted that he had been the killer, and provided details of the crime. He and Jost arranged to meet that evening. When he arrived at the prearranged time, police officers arrested him and charged him with the murder.

Question: Should the trial court exclude Albrecht's admissions?

PROBLEM 8–3

Paul Beckley was charged with six burglaries after he made oral and written confessions. The confessions were obtained after Beckley came to police headquarters for questioning about his involvement in the offenses. Officers read him *Miranda* warnings prior to the questioning, and Beckley signed a written waiver of those rights. One of the officers then told

Beckley that he would convey Beckley's cooperativeness to the prosecutor. During questioning, Beckley initially denied any wrongdoing but ultimately confessed to having committed the burglaries. The officer responded that if Beckley's information was "good," the department would lodge complaints against him for only three of the burglaries and would not ask for jail time. After the officer made those remarks, he asked Beckley to sign a written transcription of the confessions, which Beckley did.

Question: Should the trial court exclude the oral and written confessions?

PROBLEM 8–4

In the Brunell case in Chapter 1, review the prosecution memorandum that discusses a visit to Terry Marvoal's home by three FBI agents and a federal prosecutor. Assume that you represent Marvoal, whose version of the events is as follows. Marvoal lives with her three young children in a home that she purchased with her income from Brunell's Natural Foods, Inc. One evening at 11:30 p.m., when the family was sleeping, three federal agents and a federal prosecutor rang her doorbell. Marvoal admitted the four men after they identified themselves. The men explained that they needed to speak with her about the on-going investigation of Arthur Brunell and his company, and she asked that they do so in the kitchen because she did not want their voices to frighten the children. As they sat around the kitchen table in the small room, the men demanded that Marvoal cooperate in the investigation. They explained that others involved in the company were being interviewed that same night, and that any employees who did not assist the investigation would face criminal charges. Moreover, the prosecutor told Marvoal that if she chose not to cooperate he would charge her with violations of the Racketeer Influenced and Corrupt Organizations Act ("RICO") and would file for a RICO forfeiture, which would strip her of income she had earned from the company, as well as anything she bought with that income. "If I have to do that, you and your kids will be out on the street by next week, because you'll lose this house," he warned her tensely. He continued, "I really don't want to do that, but you have to choose now. Of course, you can always choose to keep your mouth shut and go to jail with Brunell. That's just what he wants you to do."

Marvoal felt her knees shaking with fear as she listened to the prosecutor. As a single mother, she was particularly afraid of losing her home or, even worse, going to jail, because she had no close relatives who would take care of her children. Just then, she thought she heard her youngest child crying in an upstairs bedroom, and she wanted to check on him. However, the agent nearest the kitchen door had tipped his chair in a way that prevented her from leaving the room, and she was too intimidated to ask him to move. Quickly, she said, "I want to do the right thing—I'll do whatever you want me to do." The four men appeared to relax when she said this, and Marvoal felt she could excuse herself to check on her child.

When she returned, she talked at length about her involvement with Brunell's tax fraud.

Question: If Marvoal is prosecuted, what motion should you make and on what grounds? What will be the substance of the prosecution's response? How will the court rule?

II. Custodial Interrogations and the Miranda Doctrine

Checklist 12: The *Miranda* Rule

1. Was a suspect in custody—deprived of freedom of action in any significant way, that is, held incommunicado in a police-dominated atmosphere?

2. If yes, was he subjected to interrogation, or did he instead spontaneously blurt out a statement?

3. If he was subjected to interrogation, was the interrogation by a government actor?

4. If yes, is there an applicable exception to the *Miranda* rule—such as public safety or routine booking?

5. If no, was the suspect read the following rights?

    a. You have the right to remain silent;

    b. Anything you say can and will be used against you in a court of law;

    c. You have the right to consult with a lawyer and to have the lawyer with you during the interrogation;

    d. If you cannot afford a lawyer, one will be appointed to represent you prior to any questioning.

6. If yes, did the suspect voluntarily, knowingly, and intelligently waive both his right to silence and his right to counsel?

7. If the suspect refused to waive his right to silence, did any subsequent questioning resume only after scrupulously honoring the suspect's right to silence, as determined by consideration of at least the following factors?

    a. Whether he was immediately left alone when he invoked his right to remain silent;

    b. Whether he was questioned by a different detective only after having been reminded of his right to remain silent and having been given an opportunity to exercise that right;

    c. Whether he was asked only about an unrelated crime.

8. If the suspect refused to waive his right to counsel, did all interrogation efforts fully cease, resuming only if and when the suspect himself initiated further communication, exchanges, or conversations with the

police, without his change of mind having been prompted by police action or **if** prompted by police action, only after more than two weeks' passage of time?

9. If there was a *Miranda* violation, has the suspect taken the stand at trial and testified inconsistently with his statement, thus subjecting the suspect to impeachment by the statement?

A. HISTORICAL BACKGROUND OF THE FIFTH AMENDMENT

The voluntariness requirement imposed by the due process clause must always be satisfied before a statement obtained by a government actor can be admitted in court against the maker of the statement. But in some situations specialized doctrines must be satisfied in addition to the requirement of voluntariness. The most important of these specialized doctrines is the *Miranda* rule. Created in the Supreme Court's landmark opinion in *Miranda v. Arizona*, the rule governs all custodial interrogations by state and federal law enforcement actors and is based on the Fifth Amendment's privilege against self-incrimination, rather than the due process requirement of voluntariness. In order for you to understand the *Miranda* opinion fully, consider the following brief background on the Fifth Amendment's privilege against self-incrimination.

For thousands of years and in many legal systems, the defendant's testimony formed the centerpiece of a criminal trial. In the highly-developed ancient Chinese legal system, for example, the judge could not sentence a defendant until the defendant confessed to the crime. The judge was permitted to use various forms of persuasion, including trickery and torture, in order to extract the all-important confession, although the judge himself faced serious penalties if an innocent person died under such torture.[61] Torture and forced testimony were features of the English legal system as well. During the religious upheavals of the early seventeenth century, the English Crown empowered ecclesiastical courts to investigate charges of religious heresy, or nonconformity. Persons brought before those courts were exposed to a "cruel trilemma": asked to swear an oath to testify truthfully, they had the unenviable choice of (1) refusing to take the oath, which constituted contempt and virtually guaranteed that the contemnors would be tortured in the infamous Court of Star Chamber; (2) taking the oath and telling the truth about their religious beliefs and practices, which were most likely considered heretical and punishable by death; or (3) taking the oath and lying about their religious beliefs and practices, which constituted perjury and was punishable by death and, perhaps more seriously, eternal damnation. Popular reaction to the inhu-

---

61. *See, e.g.,* CELEBRATED CASES OF JUDGE DEE xviii (Robert Van Gulik trans., Dover Pub. 1976). This volume is a translation of DEE GOONG AN, an 18th Century Chinese detective novel featuring the famous Judge Dee, a Seventh Century magistrate. In the pages cited, the translator (who himself went on to write a series of books and stories about Judge Dee) describes the Chinese Penal Code, which dates back to 650 A.D.

manity of these practices eventually forced the Crown to curtail the power of the ecclesiastical courts and abolish the Star Chamber. Moreover, according to some scholars, the experience formed the basis for the Fifth Amendment's guarantee that "[n]o person ... shall be compelled in any criminal case to be a witness against himself."[62]

The Fifth Amendment "privilege against self-incrimination" is viewed by many as one of the most important provisions in the Bill of Rights.[63] Yet the privilege is not uncontroversial. While few would disagree that using torture to force a confession from an unwilling person is cruel and intolerable, some judges and scholars have questioned a rule that discourages people from honestly acknowledging their guilt. Consider these two statements:

> [The privilege is founded on] our unwillingness to subject those suspected of crime to the cruel trilemma of self-accusation, perjury, or contempt; our preference for an accusatorial rather than an inquisitorial system of criminal justice; our fear that self-incriminating statements will be elicited by inhumane treatment and abuses; our sense of fair play which dictates a fair state-individual balance by requiring the government to leave the individual alone until good cause is shown for disturbing him and by requiring the government in its contest with the individual to shoulder the entire load; our respect for the inviolability of the human personality and of the right of each individual to a private enclave where he may lead a private life; our distrust of self-deprecatory statements; and our realization that the privilege, while sometimes a shelter to the guilty, is often a protection to the innocent.[64]

———

> [I]t is wrong, and subtly corrosive of our criminal justice system, to regard an honest confession as a mistake. While every person is entitled to stand silent, it is more virtuous for the wrongdoer to admit his offense and accept the punishment he deserves. Not only for society, but for the wrongdoer himself, admission of guilt, if not coerced, is inherently desirable because it advances the goals of both justice and rehabilitation.... We should, then, rejoice at the "poor fool" who has made [an honest confession]; and we should regret the attempted retraction of that good act, rather than seek to facilitate and encourage it. To design our laws on premises contrary to these is to abandon belief in either personal responsibility or the moral claim of just government to obedience.[65]

---

62. *See, e.g.*, Leonard Levy, ORIGINS OF THE FIFTH AMENDMENT 134 (1967).

63. *See, e.g.*, Sheri Lynn Johnson, *Confessions, Criminals and Community*, 26 HARV. C.R.-C.L. L. REV. 327 (1991).

64. Murphy v. Waterfront Comm'n, 378 U.S. 52, 55 (1964).

65. Minnick v. Mississippi, 498 U.S. 146, 167 (1990) (Scalia, J., dissenting). *See generally* David Dolinko, *Is There a Rationale for the Privilege Against Self–Incrimination?*, 33 UCLA L. REV. 1063 (1986) (arguing that the privilege serves no rational purpose).

PROBLEM 8–5

Your client, Margo Peters, tells you that she embezzled $40,000 two years ago from Feed the Hungry, a charitable organization to which she volunteered her bookkeeping skills. At the time, severe personal problems plagued her, and she was drinking heavily. She has since joined Alcoholics Anonymous and is undergoing counseling. She now deeply regrets her illegal actions. An FBI agent has asked Ms. Peters to contact him. She asks for your advice.

Question: What information would you like to have before you recommend a course of action (or inaction) to Ms. Peters? How would your recommendations change depending on the information you obtain? Would you permit your client to submit to an interview with the FBI agent? What warnings would you give her in advance of any such interview?

Note on Defense Ethics: Some scholars in the field of legal ethics believe that lawyers must assist their clients to be good people. For example, Professor Thomas Shaffer states that lawyers should be good moral influences on their clients and should provide them with moral leadership.[66] Shaffer might advise Ms. Peters to acknowledge her wrongdoing and accept the consequences. On the other hand, ethicists such as Monroe Freedman value the client's freedom of choice above all else. While Freedman acknowledges that "moral discourse between lawyer and client is an important element of . . . the lawyer's role," a lawyer who agrees to represent a client is committed "to provide zealous representation of the client's interests as the client perceives them."[67]

B. THE *MIRANDA* DECISION AND INTERPRETIVE CONTROVERSY

The privilege against self-incrimination protects individuals from making incriminating testimonial communications under compulsion by state and federal actors. Prior to *Miranda*, however, the privilege had never been applied in the interrogation setting. Rather, it applied only in the courtroom or in situations in which compulsion came in the form of official court process—for example, a court order compelling compliance with a subpoena. As you read the *Miranda* opinion, notice how the majority extends the privilege into the informal context of police questioning.

1. THE OPINION

Miranda v. Arizona
384 U.S. 436 (1966).

■ WARREN, C.J. The cases before us raise questions which go to the roots of our concepts of American criminal jurisprudence: the restraints society

---

66. Thomas Shaffer, *Legal Ethics and the Good Client*, 36 CATH. U. L. REV. 319, 322 (1987).

67. Monroe Freedman, *Legal Ethics and the Suffering Client*, 36 CATH. U. L. REV. 331, 332 (1987).

must observe consistent with the Federal Constitution in prosecuting individuals for crime. More specifically, we deal with the admissibility of statements obtained from an individual who is subjected to custodial police interrogation and the necessity for procedures which assure that the individual is accorded his privilege under the Fifth Amendment to the Constitution not to be compelled to incriminate himself. . . .

I

The constitutional issue we decide in each of these cases is the admissibility of statements obtained from a defendant questioned while in custody or otherwise deprived of his freedom of action in any significant way. In each, the defendant was questioned by police officers, detectives, or a prosecuting attorney in a room in which he was cut off from the outside world. In none of these cases was the defendant given a full and effective warning of his rights at the outset of the interrogation process. In all the cases, the questioning elicited oral admissions, and in three of them, signed statements as well which were admitted at their trials. They all thus share salient features—incommunicado interrogation of individuals in a police-dominated atmosphere, resulting in self-incriminating statements without full warnings of constitutional rights.

An understanding of the nature and setting of this in-custody interrogation is essential to our decisions today. The difficulty in depicting what transpires at such interrogations stems from the fact that in this country they have largely taken place incommunicado. From extensive factual studies undertaken in the early 1930's, including the famous Wickersham Report to Congress by a Presidential Commission, it is clear that police violence and the "third degree" flourished at that time. In a series of cases decided by this Court long after these studies, the police resorted to physical brutality—beatings, hanging, whipping—and to sustained and protracted questioning incommunicado in order to extort confessions. The Commission on Civil Rights in 1961 found much evidence to indicate that "some policemen still resort to physical force to obtain confessions." The use of physical brutality and violence is not, unfortunately, relegated to the past or to any part of the country. . . .

. . . [W]e stress that the modern practice of in-custody interrogation is psychologically rather than physically oriented. . . . This Court has recognized that coercion can be mental as well as physical, and that the blood of the accused is not the only hallmark of an unconstitutional inquisition.

Interrogation still takes place in privacy. Privacy results in secrecy and this in turn results in a gap in our knowledge as to what in fact goes on in the interrogation rooms. A valuable source of information about present police practices, however, may be found in various police manuals and texts which document procedures employed with success in the past, and which recommend various other effective tactics. These texts are used by law enforcement agencies themselves as guides. It should be noted that these texts professedly present the most enlightened and effective means presently used to obtain statements through custodial interrogation. By considering these texts and other data, it is possible to describe procedures observed and noted around the country. . . .

The manuals suggest that the suspect be offered legal excuses for his actions in order to obtain an initial admission of guilt. Where there is a suspected revenge-killing, for example, the interrogator may say: "Joe, you probably didn't go out looking for this fellow with the purpose of shooting him. My guess is, however, that you expected something from him and that's why you carried a gun—for your own protection." . . .

When the techniques described above prove unavailing, the texts recommend they be alternated with a show of some hostility. One ploy often used has been termed the "friendly-unfriendly" or the "Mutt and Jeff" act. . . .

The interrogators sometimes are instructed to induce a confession out of trickery. The technique here is quite effective in crimes which require identification or which run in series. In the identification situation, the interrogator may take a break in his questioning to place the subject among a group of men in a line-up. "The witness or complainant (previously coached, if necessary) studies the line-up and confidently points out the subject as the guilty party." Then the questioning resumes "as though there were now no doubt about the guilt of the subject." . . .

The manuals also contain instructions for police on how to handle the individual who refuses to discuss the matter entirely, or who asks for an attorney or relatives. The examiner is to concede him the right to remain silent. . . . [H]owever, the officer is told to point out the incriminating significance of the suspect's refusal to talk:

Joe, you have a right to remain silent. That's your privilege and I'm the last person in the world who'll try to take it away from you. If that's the way you want to leave this, O.K. But let me ask you this. Suppose you were in my shoes and I were in yours and you called me in to ask me about this and I told you, "I don't want to answer any of your questions." You'd think I had something to hide, and you'd probably be right in thinking that. That's exactly what I'll have to think about you, and so will everybody else. So let's sit here and talk this whole thing over.

Few will persist in their initial refusal to talk, it is said, if this monologue is employed correctly.

From these representative samples of interrogation techniques, the setting prescribed by the manuals and observed in practice becomes clear. In essence, it is this: To be alone with the subject is essential to prevent distraction and to deprive him of any outside support. The aura of confidence in his guilt undermines his will to resist. He merely confirms the preconceived story the police seek to have him describe. Patience and persistence, at times relentless questioning, are employed. To obtain a confession, the interrogator must "patiently maneuver himself or his quarry into a position from which the desired objective may be attained." When normal procedures fail to produce the needed result, the police may resort to deceptive stratagems such as giving false legal advice. It is important to keep the subject off balance, for example, by trading on his insecurity about himself or his surroundings. The police then persuade, trick, or cajole him out of exercising his constitutional rights.

It is obvious that such an interrogation environment is created for no purpose other than to subjugate the individual to the will of his examiner. This atmosphere carries its own badge of intimidation. To be sure, this is not physical intimidation, but it is equally destructive of human dignity.[a] The current practice of incommunicado interrogation is at odds with one of our Nation's most cherished principles—that the individual may not be compelled to incriminate himself. Unless adequate protective devices are employed to dispel the compulsion inherent in custodial surroundings, no statement obtained from the defendant can truly be the product of his free choice....

II

We sometimes forget how long it has taken to establish the privilege against self-incrimination, the sources from which it came and the fervor with which it was defended. Its roots go back into ancient times.[b] Perhaps the critical historical event shedding light on its origins and evolution was the trial of one John Lilburn, a vocal anti-Stuart Leveller, who was made to take the Star Chamber Oath in 1637. The oath would have bound him to answer to all questions posed to him on any subject. He resisted the oath and declaimed the proceedings, stating: "Another fundamental right I then contended for, was, that no man's conscience ought to be racked by oaths imposed, to answer to questions concerning himself in matters criminal, or pretended to be so."

On account of the Lilburn Trial, Parliament abolished the inquisitorial Court of Star Chamber and went further in giving him generous reparation. The lofty principles to which Lilburn had appealed during his trial gained popular acceptance in England. These sentiments worked their way over to the Colonies and were implanted after great struggle into the Bill of

---

a. The absurdity of denying that a confession obtained under these circumstances is compelled is aptly portrayed by an example in Professor Sutherland's article, Arthur E. Sutherland, *Crime and Confession*, 79 Harv. L. Rev. 21, 37 (1965):

Suppose a well-to-do testatrix says she intends to will her property to Elizabeth. John and James want her to bequeath it to them instead. They capture the testatrix, put her in a carefully designed room, out of touch with everyone but themselves and their convenient "witnesses," keep her secluded there for hours while they make insistent demands, weary her with contradictions of her assertions that she wants to leave her money to Elizabeth, and finally induce her to execute the will in their favor. Assume that John and James are deeply and correctly convinced that Elizabeth is unworthy and will make base use of the property if she gets her hands on it, whereas John and James have the noblest and most righteous intentions. Would any judge of probate accept the will so procured as the "voluntary" act of the testatrix?

b. Thirteenth-century commentators found an analogue to the privilege grounded in the Bible. "To sum up the matter, the principle that no man is to be declared guilty on his own admission is a divine decree." Maimonides, Mishneh Torah (Code of Jewish Law), Book of Judges, Laws of the Sanhedrin, c. 18, 6, III Yale Judaica Series 52–53. *See also* Lamm, *The Fifth Amendment and Its Equivalent in the Halakhah*, 5 Judaism 53 (Winter 1956).

Rights. Those who framed our Constitution and the Bill of Rights were ever aware of subtle encroachments on individual liberty. They knew that "illegitimate and unconstitutional practices get their first footing by silent approaches and slight deviations from legal modes of procedure." *Boyd v. United States*, 116 U.S. 616 (1886). The privilege was elevated to constitutional status and has always been "as broad as the mischief against which it seeks to guard." *Counselman v. Hitchcock*, 142 U.S. 547 (1892). We cannot depart from this noble heritage.

Thus we may view the historical development of the privilege as one which groped for the proper scope of governmental power over the citizen.... We have recently noted that the privilege against self-incrimination—the essential mainstay of our adversary system—is founded on a complex of values. All these policies point to one overriding thought: the constitutional foundation underlying the privilege is the respect a government—state or federal—must accord to the dignity and integrity of its citizens. To maintain a fair state-individual balance, to require the government to shoulder the entire load, to respect the inviolability of the human personality, our accusatory system of criminal justice demands that the government seeking to punish an individual produce the evidence against him by its own independent labors, rather than by the cruel, simple expedient of compelling it from his own mouth. In sum, the privilege is fulfilled only when the person is guaranteed the right to remain silent unless he chooses to speak in the unfettered exercise of his own will. ...

We are satisfied that all the principles embodied in the privilege apply to informal compulsion exerted by law-enforcement officers during in-custody questioning. An individual swept from familiar surroundings into police custody, surrounded by antagonistic forces, and subjected to the techniques of persuasion described above cannot be otherwise than under compulsion to speak. As a practical matter, the compulsion to speak in the isolated setting of the police station may well be greater than in courts or other official investigations, where there are often impartial observers to guard against intimidation or trickery....

III

Today, then, there can be no doubt that the Fifth Amendment privilege is available outside of criminal court proceedings and serves to protect persons in all settings in which their freedom of action is curtailed in any significant way from being compelled to incriminate themselves. We have concluded that without proper safeguards the process of in-custody interrogation of persons suspected or accused of crime contains inherently compelling pressures which work to undermine the individual's will to resist and to compel him to speak where he would not otherwise do so freely. In order to combat these pressures and to permit a full opportunity to exercise the privilege against self-incrimination, the accused must be adequately and effectively apprised of his rights and the exercise of those rights must be fully honored.

It is impossible for us to foresee the potential alternatives for protecting the privilege which might be devised by Congress or the States in the exercise of their creative rule-making capacities. Therefore we cannot say that the Constitution necessarily requires adherence to any particular solution for the inherent compulsions of the interrogation process as it is presently conducted. Our decision in no way creates a constitutional straitjacket which will handicap sound efforts at reform, nor is it intended to have this effect. We encourage Congress and the States to continue their laudable search for increasingly effective ways of protecting the rights of the individual while promoting efficient enforcement of our criminal laws. However, unless we are shown other procedures which are at least as effective in apprising accused persons of their right of silence and in assuring a continuous opportunity to exercise it, the following safeguards must be observed.

At the outset, if a person in custody is to be subjected to interrogation, he must first be informed in clear and unequivocal terms that he has the right to remain silent. For those unaware of the privilege, the warning is needed simply to make them aware of it—the threshold requirement for an intelligent decision as to its exercise. More important, such a warning is an absolute prerequisite in overcoming the inherent pressures of the interrogation atmosphere. . . . Further, the warning will show the individual that his interrogators are prepared to recognize his privilege should he choose to exercise it.

The Fifth Amendment privilege is so fundamental to our system of constitutional rule and the expedient of giving an adequate warning as to the availability of the privilege so simple, we will not pause to inquire in individual cases whether the defendant was aware of his rights without a warning being given. Assessments of the knowledge the defendant possessed, based on information as to his age, education, intelligence, or prior contact with authorities, can never be more than speculation; a warning is a clearcut fact. More important, whatever the background of the person interrogated, a warning at the time of the interrogation is indispensable to overcome its pressures and to insure that the individual knows he is free to exercise the privilege at that point in time.

The warning of the right to remain silent must be accompanied by the explanation that anything said can and will be used against the individual in court. This warning is needed in order to make him aware not only of the privilege, but also of the consequences of forgoing it. It is only through an awareness of these consequences that there can be any assurance of real understanding and intelligent exercise of the privilege. Moreover, this warning may serve to make the individual more acutely aware that he is faced with a phase of the adversary system—that he is not in the presence of persons acting solely in his interest.

The circumstances surrounding in-custody interrogation can operate very quickly to overbear the will of one merely made aware of his privilege by his interrogators. Therefore, the right to have counsel present at the interrogation is indispensable to the protection of the Fifth Amendment privilege under the system we delineate today. Our aim is to assure that the individual's right to choose between silence and speech remains unfettered throughout the interrogation process. A once-stated warning, delivered by those who will conduct the interrogation, cannot itself suffice to that end among those who most require knowledge of their rights.... Thus, the need for counsel to protect the Fifth Amendment privilege comprehends not merely a right to consult with counsel prior to questioning, but also to have counsel present during any questioning if the defendant so desires.

The presence of counsel at the interrogation may serve several significant subsidiary functions as well. If the accused decides to talk to his interrogators, the assistance of counsel can mitigate the dangers of untrustworthiness. With a lawyer present the likelihood that the police will practice coercion is reduced, and if coercion is nevertheless exercised the lawyer can testify to it in court. The presence of a lawyer can also help to guarantee that the accused gives a fully accurate statement to the police and that the statement is rightly reported by the prosecution at trial....

Accordingly we hold that an individual held for interrogation must be clearly informed that he has the right to consult with a lawyer and to have the lawyer with him during interrogation under the system for protecting the privilege we delineate today. As with the warnings of the right to remain silent and that anything stated can be used in evidence against him, this warning is an absolute prerequisite to interrogation. No amount of circumstantial evidence that the person may have been aware of this right will suffice to stand in its stead. Only through such a warning is there ascertainable assurance that the accused was aware of this right.

If an individual indicates that he wishes the assistance of counsel before any interrogation occurs, the authorities cannot rationally ignore or deny his request on the basis that the individual does not have or cannot afford a retained attorney. The financial ability of the individual has no relationship to the scope of the rights involved here. The privilege against self-incrimination secured by the Constitution applies to all individuals.... In fact, were we to limit these constitutional rights to those who can retain an attorney, our decisions today would be of little significance.[c]

In order fully to apprise a person interrogated of the extent of his rights under this system then, it is necessary to warn him not only that he has the right to consult with an attorney, but also that if he is indigent a lawyer will be appointed to represent him.... The warning of a right to counsel would be hollow if not couched in terms that would convey to the indigent—the person most often subjected to interrogation—the knowledge that he too has a right to have counsel present. As with the warnings of the right to remain silent and of the general right to counsel, only by effective

---

c. Estimates of 50–90% indigency among felony defendants have been reported. Herman I. Pollock, *Equal Justice in Practice*, 45 Minn. L. Rev. 737, 738–39 (1961); Paul Ivan Birzon, Robert Kasanof, & Joseph Forma, *The Right to Counsel and the Indigent Accused in Courts of Criminal Jurisdiction in New York State*, 14 Buffalo L. Rev. 428, 433 (1965).

and express explanation to the indigent of this right can there be assurance that he was truly in a position to exercise it.

Once warnings have been given, the subsequent procedure is clear. If the individual indicates in any manner, at any time prior to or during questioning, that he wishes to remain silent, the interrogation must cease. At this point he has shown that he intends to exercise his Fifth Amendment privilege; any statement taken after the person invokes his privilege cannot be other than the product of compulsion, subtle or otherwise. Without the right to cut off questioning, the setting of in-custody interrogation operates on the individual to overcome free choice in producing a statement after the privilege has been once invoked. If the individual states that he wants an attorney, the interrogation must cease until an attorney is present. At that time, the individual must have an opportunity to confer with the attorney and to have him present during any subsequent questioning. If the individual cannot obtain an attorney and he indicates that he wants one before speaking to police, they must respect his decision to remain silent.

This does not mean, as some have suggested, that each police station must have a "station house lawyer" present at all times to advise prisoners. It does mean, however, that if police propose to interrogate a person they must make known to him that he is entitled to a lawyer and that if he cannot afford one, a lawyer will be provided for him prior to any interrogation. If authorities conclude that they will not provide counsel during a reasonable period of time in which investigation in the field is carried out, they may refrain from doing so without violating the person's Fifth Amendment privilege so long as they do not question him during that time....

The warnings required ... in accordance with our opinion today are, in the absence of a fully effective equivalent, prerequisites to the admissibility of any statement made by a defendant. No distinction can be drawn between statements which are direct confessions and statements which amount to "admissions" of part or all of an offense.... Similarly, for precisely the same reason, no distinction may be drawn between inculpatory statements and statements alleged to be merely "exculpatory." ...

The principles announced today deal with the protection which must be given to the privilege against self-incrimination when the individual is first subjected to police interrogation while in custody at the station or otherwise deprived of his freedom of action in any significant way. It is at this point that our adversary system of criminal proceedings commences, distinguishing itself at the outset from the inquisitorial system recognized in some countries. Under the system of warnings we delineate today or under any other system which may be devised and found effective, the safeguards to be erected about the privilege must come into play at this point.

Our decision is not intended to hamper the traditional function of police officers in investigating crime. When an individual is in custody on probable cause, the police may, of course, seek out evidence in the field to be used at trial against him. Such investigation may include inquiry of persons not under restraint. General on-the-scene questioning as to facts surrounding a crime or other general questioning of citizens in the fact-finding process is not affected by our holding. It is an act of responsible citizenship for individuals to give whatever information they may have to aid in law enforcement. In such situations the compelling atmosphere inherent in the process of in-custody interrogation is not necessarily present.

In dealing with statements obtained through interrogation, we do not purport to find all confessions inadmissible. Confessions remain a proper element in law enforcement. Any statement given freely and voluntarily without any compelling influences is, of course, admissible in evidence. The fundamental import of the privilege while an individual is in custody is not whether he is allowed to talk to the police without the benefit of warnings and counsel, but whether he can be interrogated. There is no requirement that police stop a person who enters a police station and states that he wishes to confess to a crime, or a person who calls the police to offer a confession or any other statement he desires to make. Volunteered statements of any kind are not barred by the Fifth Amendment and their admissibility is not affected by our holding today. . . .

IV

A recurrent argument made in these cases is that society's need for interrogation outweighs the privilege. . . . The whole thrust of our foregoing discussion demonstrates that the Constitution has prescribed the rights of the individual when confronted with the power of government when it provided in the Fifth Amendment that an individual cannot be compelled to be a witness against himself. That right cannot be abridged. As Mr. Justice Brandeis once observed: "Decency, security, and liberty alike demand that government officials shall be subjected to the same rules of conduct that are commands to the citizen. In a government of laws, existence of the government will be imperilled if it fails to observe the law scrupulously. Our government is the potent, the omnipresent teacher. For good or for ill, it teaches the whole people by its example. Crime is contagious. If the government becomes a lawbreaker, it breeds contempt for law; it invites every man to become a law unto himself; it invites anarchy. To declare that in the administration of the criminal law the end justifies the means . . . would bring terrible retribution. Against that pernicious doctrine this court should resolutely set its face." *Olmstead v. United States*, 277 U.S. 438 (1928) (dissenting opinion). . . .

It is also urged upon us that we withhold decision on this issue until state legislative bodies and advisory groups have had an opportunity to deal with these problems by rule making. We have already pointed out that the Constitution does not require any specific code of procedures for protecting the privilege against self-incrimination during custodial interrogation. Congress and the States are free to develop their own safeguards for the privilege, so long as they are fully as effective as those described above in informing accused persons of their right of silence and in affording a continuous opportunity to exercise it. In any event, however, the issues presented are of constitutional dimensions and must be determined by the courts.... Judicial solutions to problems of constitutional dimension have evolved decade by decade. As courts have been presented with the need to enforce constitutional rights, they have found means of doing so.... Where rights secured by the Constitution are involved, there can be no rule making or legislation which would abrogate them.

■ Harlan, J. (joined by Stewart and White, JJ.), dissenting. I believe the decision of the Court represents poor constitutional law and entails harmful consequences for the country at large. How serious these consequences may prove to be only time can tell. But the basic flaws in the Court's justification seem to me readily apparent now once all sides of the problem are considered....

The Court's opinion in my view reveals no adequate basis for extending the Fifth Amendment's privilege against self-incrimination to the police station. Far more important, it fails to show that the Court's new rules are well supported, let alone compelled, by Fifth Amendment precedents. Instead, the new rules actually derive from quotation and analogy drawn from precedents under the Sixth Amendment, which should properly have no bearing on police interrogation.

The Court's opening contention, that the Fifth Amendment governs police station confessions, is perhaps not an impermissible extension of the law but it has little to commend itself in the present circumstances. Historically, the privilege against self-incrimination did not bear at all on the use of extra-legal confessions, for which distinct standards evolved; indeed, "the history of the two principles is wide apart, differing by one hundred years in origin, and derived through separate lines of precedents." 8 Wigmore, Evidence § 2266, at 401 (McNaughton rev. 1961). Practice under the two doctrines has also differed in a number of important respects. Even those who would readily enlarge the privilege must concede some linguistic difficulties since the Fifth Amendment in terms proscribes only compelling any person "in any criminal case to be a witness against himself."

Though weighty, I do not say these points and similar ones are conclusive, for, as the Court reiterates, the privilege embodies basic principles always capable of expansion. Certainly the privilege does represent a protective concern for the accused and an emphasis upon accusatorial rather than inquisitorial values in law enforcement, although this is similarly true of other limitations such as the grand jury requirement and the reasonable doubt standard. Accusatorial values, however, have openly been absorbed into the due process standard governing confessions.... Since extension of the general principle has already occurred, to insist that the privilege applies as such serves only to carry over inapposite historical details and engaging rhetoric and to obscure the policy choices to be made in regulating confessions....

Examined as an expression of public policy, the Court's new regime proves so dubious that there can be no due compensation for its weakness in constitutional law. The foregoing discussion has shown, I think, how mistaken is the Court in implying that the Constitution has struck the balance in favor of the approach the Court takes. Rather, precedent reveals that the Fourteenth Amendment in practice has been construed to strike a different balance, that the Fifth Amendment gives the Court little solid support in this context, and that the Sixth Amendment should have no bearing at all. Legal history has been stretched before to satisfy deep needs of society. In this instance, however, the Court has not and cannot make the powerful showing that its new rules are plainly desirable in the context of our society, something which is surely demanded before those rules are engrafted onto the Constitution and imposed on every State and county in the land.

Without at all subscribing to the generally black picture of police conduct painted by the Court, I think it must be frankly recognized at the outset that police questioning allowable under due process precedents may inherently entail some pressure on the suspect and may seek advantage in his ignorance or weaknesses. The atmosphere and questioning techniques, proper and fair though they be, can in themselves exert a tug on the suspect to confess, and in this light to speak of any confessions of crime made after arrest as being "voluntary" or "uncoerced" is somewhat inaccurate, although traditional. A confession is wholly and incontestably voluntary only if a guilty person gives himself up to the law and becomes his own accuser. Until today, the role of the Constitution has been only to sift out undue pressure, not to assure spontaneous confessions.

The Court's new rules aim to offset these minor pressures and disadvantages intrinsic to any kind of police interrogation. The rules do not serve due process interests in preventing blatant coercion since, as I noted earlier, they do nothing to contain the policeman who is prepared to lie from the start. The rules work for reliability in confessions almost only in the Pickwickian sense that they can prevent some from being given at all.[d] In short, the benefit of this new regime is simply to lessen or wipe out the inherent compulsion and inequalities to which the Court devotes some nine pages of description.

What the Court largely ignores is that its rules impair, if they will not eventually serve wholly to frustrate, an instrument of law enforcement that has long and quite reasonably been thought worth the price paid for it.[e] There can be little doubt that the Court's new code would markedly

---

d. The Court's vision of a lawyer "mitigat[ing] the dangers of untrustworthiness" by witnessing coercion and assisting accuracy in the confession is largely a fancy; for if counsel arrives, there is rarely going to be a police station confession. Any lawyer worth his salt will tell the suspect in no uncertain terms to make no statement to police under any circumstances.

e. This need is, of course, what makes so misleading the Court's comparison of a probate judge readily setting aside as involuntary the will of an old lady badgered and beleaguered by the new heirs. With wills, there is no public interest save in a totally free choice; with confessions, the solution of crime is a countervailing gain, however the balance is resolved.

decrease the number of confessions. To warn the suspect that he may remain silent and remind him that his confession may be used in court are minor obstructions. To require also an express waiver by the suspect and an end to questioning whenever he demurs must heavily handicap questioning. And to suggest or provide counsel for the suspect simply invites the end of the interrogation.

How much harm this decision will inflict on law enforcement cannot fairly be predicted with accuracy. Evidence on the role of confessions is notoriously incomplete.... We do know that some crimes cannot be solved without confessions, that ample expert testimony attests to their importance in crime control, and that the Court is taking a real risk with society's welfare in imposing its new regime on the country. The social costs of crime are too great to call the new rules anything but a hazardous experimentation....

PROBLEM 8–6

If your instructor assigns a deductive brief of *Miranda*, prepare the brief and be ready to discuss whether *Miranda* uses deduction, induction, balancing, or a combination of these methods. What are the major premises of the opinion? What are the proofs for each premise? Do this exercise before reading the next section. Then use the material in the next section to critique your deductive brief. What did you miss and why? What did the authors of this text miss that you spotted? How would the deductive brief help you in preparing for oral argument if the *Miranda* issue were re-argued before the Court today?

2. CRITICIZING AND QUESTIONING MIRANDA

a. *The Role of Text*

The Fifth Amendment guarantees that "[n]o person shall be compelled in any criminal case to be a witness against himself." Read literally, the amendment would seem to offer protection only against being called to testify at a trial, hearing, or possibly a pretrial deposition, for only then is someone asked to be a "witness." Arguably, therefore, a literal interpretation would not extend protection to pretrial interrogation by the police.

The Court in *Miranda* adopted a more practical, common sense reading of the language, recognizing that pretrial proceedings can sometimes virtually determine the outcome of the trial itself. A defendant's admission of guilt is remarkably powerful evidence. Even if the admission was the result of confusion, deception, psychological coercion, threats of violence, or actual violence, it will be hard to convince a jury not to give the statement great weight. The power of the confession will be even greater if it is tape-recorded or videotaped. What is the real difference between a defendant being called to the stand and asked to confess at trial, and his doing so to the police on a videotape that is later played at trial? The only real difference is that police interrogation may involve coercive aspects that can be hidden from the jury. The defendant who confessed to the police thus acted as a "witness against himself" as much as if he were he forced to testify at trial.

b. *Miranda and Original Intent*

While the Framers may not have expressly contemplated applying the privilege against self-incrimination to stationhouse confessions, they undoubtedly expected it to reach pretrial interrogations. The privilege was designed as a response to the oath *ex officio*, because that oath was demanded of those undergoing questioning.[68] Judges and magistrates, rather than police officers, performed the role of crime investigators and interrogators in the sixteenth and seventeenth centuries.[69] By extending the protection of the privilege to police interrogation, *Miranda* may be consistent with the framers' desire to protect suspects from the compulsion that accompanies interrogation.

Professor Schulhofer advances this view, subscribing to a "neo-originalist" position that looks to the values of the framers and how changing circumstances require that rules change to serve those values:[70]

> [I]t seems clear that the privilege was intended primarily to bar pretrial examination by magistrates, the only form of pretrial interrogation known at the time. The reasons for concern about that form of interrogation under formal process apply with even greater force to questioning under compelling informal pressures. As professor Edmund Morgan showed almost forty years ago, "the function which the police have assumed in interrogating the accused is exactly that of the early committing magistrates, and the opportunities for imposition and use are fraught with much greater danger.... Investigation by the police is not judicial, but when it consists of an examination of the accused, it is quite as much an official proceeding as the early English preliminary examination before a magistrate, and it has none of the safeguards of a judicial proceeding."

Professor Levy notes that the precise purposes of the privilege as recited in the Fifth Amendment cannot be proved because the framers left

---

68. GEORGE L. KIRKHAM & LAVRIN A. WOLLAN, JR., INTRODUCTION TO LAW ENFORCEMENT 28–39 (1980) (organized police forces charged with investigating crime did not exist in the eighteenth century).

69. While the privilege originated in the fear of being compelled to answer under oath, later suspects were prohibited from testifying under oath, even if doing so on their own behalf. Levy, ORIGINS, *supra* note 62, at 263. Nevertheless, judicial questioning at preliminary examinations continued, and a confession, even though not made under oath, sufficed to convict. The privilege thus "gradually came to be viewed as a bar to *judicial* questioning of the accused in the common law courts." Grano, CONFESSIONS, *supra* note 9, at 124.

70. Stephen J. Schulhofer, *Reconsidering Miranda and the Fifth Amendment*, in THE BILL OF RIGHTS: ORIGINAL MEANING AND ORIGINAL UNDERSTANDING 289 (Eugene W. Hickok, Jr. ed., 1991) (quoting in part E. M. Morgan, *The Privilege Against Self–Incrimination*, 34 MINN. L. REV. 1, 27–28 (1949)).

too few clues.[71] He argues that the privilege was a "self-evident truth," so its meaning was simply taken for granted by the framers. More importantly, he saw the purpose in writing a constitution as leaving room for growth: "To them the statement of a bare principle was sufficient, and they were content to put it spaciously, if ambiguously, in order to allow for expansion as the need might arise."

To accept that Fifth Amendment protection may extend to police interrogation does not necessarily establish that *Miranda* warnings are, even in the broadest sense, consistent with original intent. Thus Professor Grano argues that, at best, the Fifth Amendment protects against "compelling" a suspect to answer questions. That protection does not bar police from asking the questions in the first place, yet that, in Professor Grano's view, is what *Miranda* seeks to prohibit or at least discourage.

Professor Schulhofer argues the opposite: *Miranda* was the compromise designed by the Court to permit police officer questioning, despite the coercive aspects of such questioning, which would otherwise prohibit interrogation entirely. Compulsion under the Fifth Amendment means discouraging silence, a definition very different from the "overbearing the will" that due process voluntariness prohibits. Custodial interrogation is inherently compelling because it brings psychological pressures to bear for the specific purpose of overcoming the suspect's resistance to talk. However, rather than prohibit police questioning, the Court created rules that "actually work to sanitize the interrogation process and to permit the officer to continue questioning his isolated suspect."[72] This result was a compromise between the needs of law enforcement and the command of the Fifth Amendment to assure a measure of dignity to arrested suspects. *Miranda* warnings do not eliminate compulsion, but they arguably reduce it to a more acceptable level and express a symbolic commitment to doing so. This is a decidedly pro-law-enforcement conclusion, given that some significant amount of compulsion is unavoidable whenever police conduct an interrogation.

NOTES AND QUESTIONS

1. Assume that the suspect being questioned is a middle-aged professor who spends his life teaching the subject of criminal procedure, who thus knows perfectly well that he is entitled to remain silent and that no formal penalties can be imposed upon him for refusing to talk. Before *Miranda*, could it be argued that he was nevertheless "compelled" to speak by the very first police officer question?

2. Assume that you live in a state that adopted a new state constitution in 1970. The state constitutional analogue to the federal constitution's privilege against self-incrimination uses precisely the same language as appears in the federal constitution. Does the "original intent" of the state constitu-

---

71. Levy, Origins, *supra* note 62, at 258.

72. Schulhofer, *Reconsidering*, *supra* note 70, at 297–98.

tion's drafters mandate police provision of a series of code-like warnings similar to *Miranda*?

3.   *Miranda* also created a Fifth Amendment right to counsel, although counsel is nowhere mentioned in that amendment. This right is broader than the Sixth Amendment right to counsel, which only applies post-indictment. What would you want to know to determine whether this Fifth Amendment right to counsel is consistent with original intent? What sources would you examine? What, if anything, does this question suggest about whether original intent makes any sense as a way of interpreting the constitution?

4.   Which, if any, of the arguments that *Miranda* is or is not consistent with original intent outlined above makes the most sense to you? Would your opinion change if you discovered, as some commentators contend, that the history of the privilege is "clouded and ambiguous" and that the framers "left too few clues" as to its rationale? Would the wording of analogous state constitutional provisions at the time the Fifth Amendment was ratified be relevant? Who were the framers of the amendment anyway?

5.   If Professor Schulhofer is right that *Miranda* was a quintessential example of constitutional balancing, what gave the Court the authority to engage in such balancing? Is balancing consistent with original intent? Is there any way to make balancing more objective? How can the weights of the various interests be determined here? Did the Court strike the right balance? Is there a better procedure than *Miranda* that would show greater respect for the appropriate balance of power between the state and the individual?

c.   *"Involuntariness" Versus "Compulsion"*

Suppose that the police have just arrested and are questioning a well-known criminal defense attorney on suspicion of murder. The attorney is thirty-five years old, has been a defense attorney for ten years, is sober, fed, and well-rested. He is in an interrogation room with only one detective, whom the attorney has long known and liked, although their relationship had been purely professional. The detective gently says, "Look, you know your rights, and you know we suspect you of being the murderer. Do you want to talk?" The attorney responds "yes" and tearfully recounts the details of the murder. *Miranda* warnings were, however, never recited.

Such a confession would unquestionably be voluntary under the due process clauses of the Fifth and Fourteenth Amendments. Moreover, any *Miranda* warnings would arguably be a waste of time because the attorney obviously knows his rights. Yet the confession would be suppressed because of the failure to give *Miranda* warnings. If the kind of coercion prohibited by the due process clause and compulsion prohibited by the Fifth Amendment privilege against self-incrimination mean the same thing, then this suppression seems to make little sense.[73]

---

73.   This example is based on one in Stephen J. Schulhofer, *Reconsidering Miranda and the Fifth Amendment*, in THE BILL OF RIGHTS: ORIGINAL MEANING AND CURRENT UNDERSTANDING 293–94 (Eugene W. Hickok, Jr. ed., 1991).

Professor Grano criticizes *Miranda* on these grounds. He argues that any confession that is voluntary (i.e., not coerced) is also given without compulsion.[74] Grano acknowledges that the failure to warn a suspect of his rights is problematic and justifies a rebuttable presumption that compulsion exists unless warnings are given. But according to Grano, a per se rule such as *Miranda*—one that invalidates all unwarned confessions by establishing an unrebuttable rule—will exclude some confessions that are neither compelled nor involuntary.

It can be argued, however, that coercion and compulsion are in fact quite different. The coercion prohibited by the due process clause is fairly extreme—it must be sufficient to undercut the individual's free will—while the compulsion prohibited by the privilege need only be sufficient to make the privilege difficult to assert. What justifies such a difference? Perhaps an answer lies in the concept of human dignity that some argue forms an important foundation of the privilege. Of the many definitions of human dignity is this one by Professor Kent Greenawalt:[75]

> [D]ignity affects how people should act toward each other. Most especially, dignity precludes humiliating treatment. In a liberal democracy the concept of dignity is closely related to ideas of respect, individuality, autonomy, tolerance, and equality. To recognize the dignity of liberal citizens involves acknowledgement of their independence of choice, their power to define for themselves the kinds of persons they will be and the lives they will lead. Dignity is something that is to be accorded all citizens, not only some; and in some basic respect, equality of status is prerequisite for equal dignity.

Remember that Justice Earl Warren asserted in *Miranda* that "the constitutional foundation underlying the privilege is the respect a government must accord to the dignity and integrity of its citizens." The pressure to speak that is inherent in all custodial interrogations arguably offends human dignity because it makes a suspect's free choice more difficult. The individual becomes purely a means to an end—obtaining his conviction. Moreover, custodial interrogation has unfair effects, both on the psyches of the subjects and on the results of the interrogation. Professor Greenawalt has summarized these concerns effectively:

> From the moral point of view, pressures and tricks designed to get suspects to confess are much more questionable than inferences from silence and dismissal. When law enforcement officers browbeat suspects, play on their weaknesses, deceive them as to critically relevant facts, such as whether a suspected confederate has confessed, or keep them in a hostile setting, the officials intentionally manipulate the environment to make rational, responsible choice more difficult. Such tactics hardly accord with respect for autonomy and dignity, and they

---

74. *See* Grano, Confessions, *supra*, note 9, at 131–41.

75. R. Kent Greenawalt, *The Right to Silence and Human Dignity*, in the Constitution of Rights: Human Dignity and American Values 192, 193 (Michael J. Meyer and William A. Parent eds., 1992).

work unevenly by undermining the inexperienced and ignorant and by having little effect on the hardened criminal. These tactics can be defended only under some extreme version of the battle model of the criminal process or, more persuasively, with the argument that some compromise with ideal procedures is required because getting admissions from suspects is so essential to solving crimes. The *Miranda* rules . . . were formulated largely to curb the worst tactics of this sort, but the Supreme Court has not adopted constitutional principles that would effectively prevent admissions obtained by pressure and deceptions that would be considered immoral in private contexts.

Viewing *Miranda* as protecting fundamental concepts of human dignity still leaves two questions open. First, even if custodial interrogation in a police-dominated atmosphere offends human dignity under the circumstances posited by Professor Greenawalt, surely there are less coercive circumstances under which simple questioning would not offend human dignity—for example, if "the defendant is not young and inexperienced, the interrogator is not powerfully built and square-jawed, and the suspect actually knows his rights."[76] The second problem with the human dignity argument is finding a solid basis in the privilege for such a vague and essentially moral concept.

Scholars have noted that the framers explicitly endorsed dignity as a value underlying the constitution.[77] Thus Alexander Hamilton wrote in the Federalist Papers: "Yes, my countryman, I own to you that, that after having given it an attentive consideration, I am clearly of opinion, it is your interest to adopt it [the Constitution]. I am convinced, that this is the safest course for your liberty, your dignity, and your happiness."[78] He also urged New Yorkers to "take a firm stand 'for our safety, our tranquility, our dignity, our reputation.' "

If the Bill of Rights is read holistically, it can be viewed as protecting aspects of human dignity.[79] Professor Parent argues the following to document this: The First Amendment's protection of free speech "serves to prohibit unjust personal denigration in the form of coerced silence on despised minorities."[80] And the Fifth Amendment's self-incrimination clause similarly protects "citizens who already stand vulnerable to assaults on their dignity precisely because they are most likely to be victimized by unwarranted official harassment." The Thirteenth Amendment's prohibition of slavery, the Fifteenth and Nineteenth Amendments' guarantees of the right to vote to blacks and women also expands protection for the "moral dignity and therewith the freedom of long-oppressed groups." Indeed, the whole theory of recognizing rights, as embodied in the Bill of

---

76.   Schulhofer, *Reconsidering, supra* note 70, at 293.

77.   William A. Parent, *Constitutional Values and Human Dignity*, in THE CONSTITUTION OF RIGHTS: HUMAN DIGNITY AND AMERICAN VALUES 47, 69 (1992).

78.   *Id.*, citing THE FEDERALIST NO. 1, at 4 (Bantam 1982).

79.   Akhil Amar, *The Bill of Rights as a Constitution*, 100 YALE L.J. 1131, 1132–33 (1991).

80.   Parent, *Values, supra* note 77, at 69.

Rights, is arguably a ringing declaration that all citizens be treated with the same respect, recognizing them as full members of the human community, who cannot be held in arbitrary contempt by the government.

Justice Brennan also recognized the critical role of human dignity as a basic constitutional value, basing his argument primarily on the due process clauses.[81] He saw the framers as intending due process to be a flexible concept, one that changes over time as society changes.[82] Due process is unquestionably a protection against arbitrary conduct, and conduct is arbitrary if moral dignity is denigrated or ignored.[83] It may be this notion of human dignity that best supports the idea of a distinction between voluntariness and compulsion and thus best supports *Miranda*.

NOTES AND QUESTIONS

1. What interpretive techniques create and define a Fifth Amendment conception of dignity? How do these techniques differ from those used by Professor Grano to define involuntariness and compulsion?

2. Would social science—such as moral psychology—aid your quest to find a justification for the concept of dignity? How?

Professor Mark A. Godsey argues that the Supreme Court has wrongfully utilized a subjective voluntariness test when determining a confession's admissibility.[84] According to Godsey, "confession law should be regulated primarily by the self-incrimination clause [of the Fifth Amendment] rather than by the due process clauses . . . [and] . . . the touchstone for confession admissibility under the self-incrimination clause should be compulsion rather than voluntariness." Furthermore, "existing Supreme Court precedent suggests an objective standard that focuses on government conduct rather than the suspect's state of mind when determining the existence of compulsion."

Godsey attempts to lay out a workable test for compulsion that is based on the self-incrimination clause. The first step of this "objective penalties test" is to determine the baseline of the person being interrogated. "This baseline is highly a function of the environment in which the interrogation takes place and the rights the parties are generally allowed in this setting." For example, when officers are interrogating a person in her house, where that person has the right to smoke whenever she wants, the officers can not tell her to stop smoking because that would take away one of her rights. Under Godsey's test, impermissible compulsion exists any time an interrogator alters a person's status quo by removing one of his rights as established by the baseline.

---

81.   Peter Irons, BRENNAN V. REHNQUIST: THE BATTLE FOR THE CONSTITUTION 36–37 (1994).

82.   Parent, *Values*, *supra* note 77.

83.   Irons, BATTLE, *supra* note 81, at 37–38.

84.   Mark A. Godsey, *Rethinking the Involuntary Confession Rule: Toward a Workable Test for Identifying Compelled Self–Incrimination*, 93 CAL. L. REV. 465 (2005).

Two special circumstances are worth noting. First, although an interrogator's threat is an objective penalty, an offer is not. It may be difficult to determine the difference between the two, but Godsey suggests the simple rule that any offer made by a government actor must be genuine; an interrogator may only offer to do something he would otherwise not have done. For example, an officer may not offer to forego charging a defendant with rape in exchange for a murder confession if that officer did not have enough evidence to charged the defendant with rape. Second, prolonged interrogation can constitute an objective punishment if a reasonable suspect would feel that the questioning restrained his freedom.

3.   AFFIRMING MIRANDA'S CONSTITUTIONAL STATUS

For years after the Court announced the *Miranda* decision, its constitutional status remained in question on the basis of the interpretive issues discussed above. Moreover, in *Oregon v. Elstad*, which we reproduce in a later section of this chapter, the Court called *Miranda* a "prophylactic" rule, indicating that some confessions taken in violation of *Miranda* do not violate the constitution. Doubts about *Miranda* were finally put to rest, when the Court stated unambiguously that the decision is constitutionally based. The statement came in *Dickerson v. United States*,[85] a case involving the constitutionality of 18 U.S.C. § 3501. That federal statute had been enacted in 1968 as a conservative response to *Miranda*. It reestablished voluntariness as the sole test for the admissibility of confessions in federal prosecutions. Under the statute, a voluntary confession taken in violation of *Miranda* would be admissible in federal court. In other words, the statute would override *Miranda*—a result that would be possible only if *Miranda* were held to be unconstitutional or not constitutionally based. If a reviewing court found *Miranda* to be constitutionally based, then the statute would be ruled unconstitutional.

For twenty years, the statute was never used and so its constitutionality was never tested in court, because the United States Department of Justice—which prosecutes federal crimes—considered it unconstitutional. During the Clinton administration, conservatives criticized the Justice Department for its failure to invoke the statute and began looking for cases ripe for its application. Things came to a head in *Dickerson* after a federal trial court suppressed an alleged bank robber's confession. The trial court ruled the confession voluntary but found that it had not been preceded by *Miranda* warnings. The United States appealed, but the Justice Department directed the U.S. Attorney's Office not to invoke § 3501 in the appeal. Nevertheless, the United States Court of Appeals for the Fourth Circuit accepted *amicus* briefing by the conservative Washington Legal Foundation and the Safe Streets Coalition and took up the issue of § 3501, noting that "[f]ortunately, we are a court of law and not politics" and that "the Department of Justice cannot prevent us from deciding this case under the governing law simply by refusing to argue it." The Fourth Circuit panel voted two to one to reverse the trial court, holding in doing so

---

85.   530 U.S. 428 (2000).

that § 3501 rendered the confession admissible. According to the majority, "the irrebuttable presumption created by the Court in *Miranda*—that a confession obtained without the warnings is presumed involuntary—is . . . not required by the Constitution. Accordingly, Congress necessarily possesses the legislative authority to supersede the conclusive presumption created by *Miranda* pursuant to its authority to prescribe the rules of procedure and evidence in the federal courts." The Supreme Court then granted Dickerson's petition for writ of certiorari.

The Supreme Court's handling of the case was closely watched, and many expected it to overturn the venerable *Miranda* decision. The Court asked law professor Paul Cassell, a former clerk for Justice Scalia, to brief and argue in support of the opinion below. Representing the interests of the United States, the Solicitor General urged the Court not only to uphold *Miranda* and find the statute unconstitutional, but also to affirm the Fourth Circuit on the ground that *Miranda* had not been violated. The Supreme Court did not issue its decision until the very end of the term, on June 26, 2000—after George W. Bush was sworn in to succeed Clinton in the presidency. The decision was surprising to some, as was the identity of the opinion writer and the numerical strength of the majority. Writing for seven justices, Chief Justice Rehnquist stated: "We hold that *Miranda*, being a constitutional decision of this Court, may not be in effect overruled by an Act of Congress, and we decline to overrule *Miranda* ourselves. We therefore hold that *Miranda* and its progeny in this Court govern the admissibility of statements made during custodial interrogation in both state and federal courts." The Chief Justice conceded, "[T]here is language in some of our opinions that supports the view taken by" the Fourth Circuit, but he went on to list the factors indicating that *Miranda* is constitutionally based:

> . . . [F]irst and foremost . . . is that both *Miranda* and two of its companion cases applied the rule to proceedings in state courts—to wit, Arizona, California, and New York. Since that time, we have consistently applied *Miranda's* rule to prosecutions arising in state courts. It is beyond dispute that we do not hold a supervisory power over the courts of the several States. With respect to proceedings in state courts, our authority is limited to enforcing the commands of the United States Constitution. . . . Our conclusion regarding *Miranda's* constitutional basis is further buttressed by the fact that we have allowed prisoners to bring alleged *Miranda* violations before the federal courts in habeas corpus proceedings. Habeas corpus proceedings are available only for claims that a person "is in custody in violation of the Constitution or laws or treaties of the United States." 28 U.S.C. § 2254(a). Since the *Miranda* rule is clearly not based on federal laws or treaties, our decision allowing habeas review for *Miranda* claims obviously assumes that *Miranda* is of constitutional origin.

The *Miranda* opinion itself begins by stating that the Court granted certiorari "to explore some facets of the problems . . . of applying the privilege against self-incrimination to in-custody interrogation, and to give concrete constitutional guidelines for law enforcement agencies and courts to follow." In fact, the majority opinion is replete with statements indicating that the majority thought it was announcing a constitutional rule. Indeed, the Court's ultimate conclusion was that the unwarned confessions obtained in the four cases before the Court in *Miranda* "were obtained from the defendant under circumstances that did not meet constitutional standards for protection of the privilege."

Additional support for our conclusion that *Miranda* is constitutionally based is found in the *Miranda* Court's invitation for legislative action to protect the constitutional right against coerced self-incrimination. After discussing the "compelling pressures" inherent in custodial police interrogation, the *Miranda* Court concluded that, "[i]n order to combat these pressures and to permit a full opportunity to exercise the privilege against self-incrimination, the accused must be adequately and effectively apprised of his rights and the exercise of those rights must be fully honored." However, the Court emphasized that it could not foresee "the potential alternatives for protecting the privilege which might be devised by Congress or the States," and it accordingly opined that the Constitution would not preclude legislative solutions that differed from the prescribed *Miranda* warnings but which were "at least as effective in apprising accused persons of their right of silence and in assuring a continuous opportunity to exercise it."

The Court of Appeals also relied on the fact that we have, after our *Miranda* decision, made exceptions from its rule in cases such as *New York v. Quarles*, 467 U.S. 649 (1984), and *Harris v. New York*, 401 U.S. 222 (1971). But we have also broadened the application of the *Miranda* doctrine in cases such as *Doyle v. Ohio*, 426 U.S. 610 (1976). These decisions illustrate the principle—not that *Miranda* is not a constitutional rule—but that no constitutional rule is immutable. No court laying down a general rule can possibly foresee the various circumstances in which counsel will seek to apply it, and the sort of modifications represented by these cases are as much a normal part of constitutional law as the original decision.

The Court of Appeals also noted that in *Oregon v. Elstad*, 470 U.S. 298 (1985), we stated that "[t]he *Miranda* exclusionary rule ... serves the Fifth Amendment and sweeps more broadly than the Fifth Amendment itself." Our decision in that case—refusing to apply the traditional "fruits" doctrine developed in Fourth Amendment cases—does not prove that *Miranda* is a nonconstitutional decision, but simply recognizes the fact that unreasonable searches under the Fourth Amendment are different from unwarned interrogation under the Fifth Amendment.

As an alternative argument for sustaining the Court of Appeals' decision, the court-invited *amicus curiae* contends that the section complies with the requirement that a legislative alternative to *Miranda* be equally as effective in preventing coerced confessions. We agree with the *amicus'* contention that there are more remedies available for abusive police conduct than there were at the time *Miranda* was decided, *see, e.g., Wilkins v. May*, 872 F.2d 190, 194 (7th Cir.1989) (applying *Bivens v. Six Unknown Fed. Narcotics Agents*, 403 U.S. 388 (1971), to hold that a suspect may bring a federal cause of action under the Due Process Clause for police misconduct during custodial interrogation). But we do not agree that these additional measures supplement § 3501's protections sufficiently to meet the constitutional minimum. *Miranda* requires procedures that will warn a suspect in custody of his right to remain silent and which will assure the suspect that the exercise of that right will be honored. [Section] 3501 explicitly eschews a requirement of preinterrogation warnings in favor of an approach that looks to the administration of such warnings as only one factor in determining the voluntariness of a suspect's confession. The additional remedies cited by amicus do not, in our view, render them, together with § 3501, an adequate substitute for the warnings required by *Miranda*.

The dissent argues that it is judicial overreaching for this Court to hold § 3501 unconstitutional unless we hold that the *Miranda* warnings are required by the Constitution, in the sense that nothing else will suffice to satisfy constitutional requirements. But we need not go further than *Miranda* to decide this case. In *Miranda*, the Court noted that reliance on the traditional totality-of-the-circumstances test raised a risk of overlooking an involuntary custodial confession, a risk that the Court found unacceptably great when the confession is offered in the case in chief to prove guilt. The Court therefore concluded that something more than the totality test was necessary. As discussed above, § 3501 reinstates the totality test as sufficient. Section 3501 therefore cannot be sustained if *Miranda* is to remain the law.

Whether or not we would agree with *Miranda's* reasoning and its resulting rule, were we addressing the issue in the first instance, the principles of stare decisis weigh heavily against overruling it now. While stare decisis is not an inexorable command, particularly when we are interpreting the Constitution, even in constitutional cases, the doctrine carries such persuasive force that we have always required a departure from precedent to be supported by some special justification. We do not think there is such justification for overruling *Miranda*. *Miranda* has become embedded in routine police practice to the point where the warnings have become part of our national culture. While we have overruled our precedents when subsequent cases have undermined their doctrinal underpinnings, we do not believe that this has happened to the *Miranda* decision. If anything, our subsequent cases have reduced the impact of the *Miranda* rule on legitimate law enforcement while reaffirming the decision's core ruling that unwarned statements may not be used as evidence in the prosecution's case in chief.

The disadvantage of the *Miranda* rule is that statements which may be by no means involuntary, made by a defendant who is aware of his "rights," may nonetheless be excluded and a guilty defendant go free as a result. But experience suggests that the totality-of-the-circumstances test which § 3501 seeks to revive is more difficult than *Miranda* for law enforcement officers to conform to, and for courts to apply in a consistent manner. The requirement that *Miranda* warnings be given does not, of course, dispense with the voluntariness inquiry. But as we [have] said, cases in which a defendant can make a colorable argument that a self-incriminating statement was "compelled" despite the fact that the law enforcement authorities adhered to the dictates of *Miranda* are rare.

In sum, we conclude that *Miranda* announced a constitutional rule that Congress may not supersede legislatively. Following the rule of stare decisis, we decline to overrule *Miranda* ourselves. The judgment of the Court of Appeals is therefore reversed.

Justices Scalia and Thomas dissented, stating that *Miranda* is a non-constitutional rule and urging that the Court overrule it.

In *Miranda* and *Dickerson*, the Court acknowledged that the Fifth Amendment privilege against self-incrimination forbids the use of confessions produced by coercive interrogation techniques and that *Miranda* warnings are constitutionally required in order to dispel the inherent coercion present in the interrogation room. But a majority of the Court has since affirmed that *Miranda* is a prophylactic rule and not part of the "core" of rights embedded within the Fifth Amendment.[86] A majority of the Court also apparently agrees that *Miranda* violations take place only when *Miranda*-violative statements are introduced at trial.[87] In other words, a suspect interrogated without the requisite warnings may not obtain any relief other than exclusion of his statement at trial.[88]

Note on the McNabb–Mallory Rule: In *Corley v. United States*,[89] the Court had to consider whether the same statute that the prosecution had argued in *Dickerson* had overruled *Miranda* also overruled the "*McNabb-Mallory*" rule. The common law had required an arresting officer to bring the defendant before a magistrate promptly. The rule's purpose was to prevent secret detentions while also informing the defendant of the charges against him. Several federal statutes came to embody this common law rule. In *McNabb v. United States*,[90] the Court, exercising its supervisory

---

86. *See* Chavez v. Martinez, 538 U.S. 760 (2003); United States v. Patane, 542 U.S. 630 (2004); Missouri v. Seibert, 542 U.S. 600, 124 S.Ct. 2601 (2004).

87. *Chavez*, 538 U.S. at 772; *Patane*, 542 U.S. at 639–40.

88. Two justices pointed out in *Chavez*, however, that "[t]he question whether the absence of *Miranda* warnings may be a basis for a § 1983 action under any circumstances is not before the Court." *Chavez*, 538 U.S. at 779 (Souter, J., concurring in judgment), joined by Justice Breyer.

89. 129 S.Ct. 1558 (2009).

90. 318 U.S. 332 (1943).

power over the federal courts, held that violation of this prompt "presentment" requirement would be subject to the exclusionary rule were any statements obtained from the defendant as a result of the delay. That exclusionary rule applied even to statements that were otherwise "voluntary." Shortly after *McNabb*, Congress pulled the various presentment statutes together in Federal Rule of Criminal Procedure 5(a), which mandated that an arresting officer "take the arrested person without unnecessary delay before the nearest available commissioner or before any other nearby officer empowered to commit persons charged with offenses against the laws of the United States." The current version of Rule 5(a) is substantially similar. Thereafter, in *Mallory v. United States*,[91] the Court applied the *McNabb* exclusionary rule to a purported violation of Rule 5(a). The *Mallory* Court emphasized that "delay for the purpose of interrogation is the epitome of 'unnecessary delay.' "

In 1968, Congress passed 18 U.S.C. § 3501, in an effort to repeal *Miranda*. The *Dickerson* Court, of course, held that section 3501 failed in this endeavor because *Miranda* was rooted in the Constitution and thus could not be overruled by a statute. Subsection (a) was the one aimed at *Miranda* and had said, in essence, that voluntary confessions were admissible. But subsection (c) focused on *McNabb-Mallory*, declaring that in any federal prosecution "a confession made ... by ... a defendant therein, while such person was under arrest ..., shall not be inadmissible solely because of delay in bringing such person before a magistrate judge ... if such confession is found by the trial judge to have been made voluntarily ... and if such confession was made ... within six hours [of arrest] ...." In *Corley*, the state argued that subsection (c) overruled the *McNabb-Mallory* exclusionary rule, a rule rooted in earlier, now rejected statutes, and in the supervisory power of the courts, thus not a constitutional rule and therefore not controlled by logic like that in *Dickerson*. The Court mostly disagreed, concluding that the statute had *modified* but not overruled *McNabb-Mallory*. The new rule was this: confessions obtained because of unnecessary delay in bringing an arrested defendant before a magistrate judge shall be inadmissible, even if voluntary, *if and only if* the delay exceeded six hours. The Court found its conclusion supported by the statute's express language (declaring that voluntary confessions may not be made inadmissible solely because of presentment delay of *under six hours*) and by the supporting legislative history.

Several points must be emphasized. First, remember that *McNabb-Mallory* is not a constitutional rule, thus at least arguably subject to later change by Congress and the Court. Second, for this same reason, the rule applies only to federal, not state, prosecutions. Third, even if there is a delay of over six hours, that does not automatically result in exclusion. The delay still must be "unnecessary," most clearly including delay done for the specific purpose of thereby obtaining a confession.

---

91. 354 U.S. 449 (1957).

C.   *MIRANDA'S* IMPACT

There have been few studies of *Miranda's* impact, and most were completed in the immediate aftermath of the decision.[92] Many commentators agreed at the time that *Miranda* had little effect on the confession rate. For example, in a New Haven, Connecticut study, warnings ended interrogation in only eight of eighty-one cases in which their impact could be determined. In a Washington, D.C. study, forty-four percent of the suspects who received all or part of a *Miranda* warning talked, while forty-two percent of those who did not receive the warnings talked. The one study finding a modest decline was in Pittsburgh. This Pittsburgh study found that the percentage of cases where confessions were obtained fell after *Miranda* by twenty-five percent in robbery cases, eighteen percent in homicide cases, and fourteen percent in burglary cases, and were "probably necessary for conviction" in twenty percent of cases. Yet the conviction rate was largely unchanged.[93] A study in Wisconsin found that *Miranda* had the smallest effect on departments that were already professionalized, suggesting to one author that *Miranda's* impact may be limited simply because it was already compatible with professional police practices.[94] The author of the Wisconsin study speculated that, once longer-term studies were done, they would likely reveal that police regularly stop questioning as soon as a suspect asserts his rights because they fear otherwise losing the case.[95] Most commentators agreed, based upon available evidence, that *Miranda* had probably curtailed physical abuses, as well as shortening the length of interrogations.[96] Furthermore, commentators believed that *Miranda* served a valuable educational function in making the citizenry generally more aware of its rights.[97]

In the last decade, scholars reignited the debate about *Miranda's* impact. Professor Paul Cassell reassessed the existing studies, concluding that *Miranda* has resulted in lost convictions in 3.8 percent of all serious criminal cases, which he deems a serious social cost in terms of absolute

---

92. Samuel Walker, TAMING THE SYSTEM: THE CONTROL OF DISCRETION IN CRIMINAL JUSTICE 1950–1990, 46–47 (1993).

93. *See* Michael Wald, et al., *Interrogations in New Haven: The Impact of Miranda*, 76 YALE L.J. 1519, 1578 (1967); Richard J. Medalie, et al., *Custodial Police Interrogation in Our Nation's Capital: The Attempt to Implement Miranda*, 66 MICH. L. REV. 1347, 1373 (1968); Richard H. Seeburger & R. Stanton Wettick, Jr., *Miranda in Pittsburg: A Statistical Study*, 29 U. PITT. L. REV. 1, 13–20 (1967).

94. Walker, TAMING, *supra* note 92, at 46–47 (citing Neal Miller, THE COURT AND LOCAL LAW ENFORCEMENT: THE IMPACT OF MIRANDA (1971)).

95. More recent data suggests that this prediction has proven to be accurate. *See* Paul G. Cassell and Bret S. Hayman, *Police Interrogation in the 1990s: An Empirical Study of the Effects of Miranda*, 43 U.C.L.A. L. REV. 839, 836 (1996) (reporting on the results of a 1994 Salt Lake County, Utah study and commenting that "in none of our cases did the police continue questioning a suspect after an invocation of *Miranda* rights").

96. *See, e.g.*, Welsh S. White, *Defending Miranda: A Reply to Professor Caplan*, 39 VAND. L. REV. 1, 13–14 (1986). Stephen J. Schulhofer, *The Constitution and the Police: Individual Rights and Law Enforcement*, 66 WASH. U.L.Q. 11, 30–32 (1988).

97. *See* Lawrence M. Friedman, CRIME AND PUNISHMENT IN AMERICAN HISTORY 303–04 (1993).

numbers of guilty going unpunished.[98] Professor Stephen Schulhofer argues that Professor Cassell's analysis of the data is flawed, concluding that *Miranda* harmed law enforcement in fewer than one percent of the cases in the immediate post-*Miranda* period and that *"Miranda's* empirically detectable net damage to law enforcement is zero."[99] Even if 3.8 percent is the correct figure for lost convictions, Professor Shulhofer views this as a small number.[100] Professor Richard Leo disputes the assertion that *Miranda* has lowered the confession rate. In a study involving three jurisdictions, Professor Leo determined that police obtained confessions in sixty-four percent of the cases in which they used interrogation techniques.[101] Despite his conclusion that *Miranda* has not significantly affected the rate of confessions, Professor Leo argues that it remains an important feature of American criminal justice because of its profoundly positive impact on, among other things, the professionalization of police practices and the public's awareness of constitutional rights.[102]

Other sources suggest that the minimal change in the confession rate may be due to officers' becoming adept at mechanically reciting the warnings by rote, like a mantra, while more subtly and effectively inducing suspects to waive their rights and talk. One modern police officer training manual on interrogation, while paying lip service to *Miranda* and cautioning officers to use persuasion rather than compulsion, relays a bewildering array of techniques to be used to confuse, pressure, and deceive the suspect. Officers are told that "[c]ontrol is the foundation upon which the successful application of all inquiry techniques and skills must rest. The investigator must gain and continually maintain control." Control can be maintained by stories that "affect the feelings" or by suggestion. Key to control is recognizing that each person is "vulnerable at . . . a weak spot," such as his family, job, religion, or reputation, and then exploiting that vulnerability. The officer must "persuade" the suspect by "expressing confidence in the subject's guilt by pointing out the existence of overwhelming evidence (including evidence refuting an alibi), the futility of denial, and the physiological signs of guilt." The officer must switch from slow to rapid-fire questions, watching for emotional reactions that can be amplified.[103] Repe-

---

98. Paul G. Cassell, *Miranda's Social Costs: An Empirical Reassessment*, 90 Nw. U.L. Rev. 387 (1996). For a collection of readings concerning Miranda's wisdom, *see* The Miranda Debate: Law, Justice, and Policing (Richard A. Leo, George C. Thomas III, and George C. Thomas, eds.) (1998).

99. Stephen J. Shulhofer, *Miranda's Practical Effect: Substantial Benefits and Vanishingly Small Costs*, 90 Nw. U.L. Rev. 500, 545–48 (1996).

100. For Professor Cassell's reply, *see* Paul G. Cassell, *All Benefits, No Costs: The Grand Illusion of Miranda's Defenders*, 90 Nw. U.L. Rev. 1084 (1996).

101. Richard A. Leo, *Inside the Interrogation Room*, 86 J. Crim. L. & Criminol. 266, 300–01 (1996).

102. *See* Richard A. Leo, *The Impact of Miranda Revisited*, 86 J. Crim. L. & Criminol. 621, 668 (1996). *See also* George C. Thomas, *Is Miranda a Real–World Failure? A Plea for More (and Better) Empirical Evidence*, 43 U.C.L.A. L. Rev. 821 (1996); Richard A. Leo & Richard J. Ofshe, *The Truth About False Confessions and Advocacy Scholarship*, 37 Cr. L. Bull. 293 (2001).

103. *See generally* Don Rabon, Interviewing and Interrogation (1992).

tition, uncomfortably long silences, changes of scene, exploring emotionally sensitive matters from the suspect's past, hypothetical stories, the cold shoulder, playing one suspect against the other, the Good Cop/Bad Cop routine, exploiting minor admissions by the suspect, and striving in any available manner to intensify the suspect's emotions are identified as additional useful techniques. And all of this is to be done incommunicado in police custody. But, as an afterthought, the manual cautions the officer not to use techniques that would cause an "innocent person to confess or that would violate the legal or moral canons of the profession."

Professor Welsh White confirms that protections against police abuses have waned under the *Miranda* rule.[104] White attributes this problem to tactics that enable police to circumvent *Miranda* warnings, and as a partial solution he would bolster the voluntariness doctrine. In the following review by Professor Taslitz, White's reasoning and solutions are summarized:

Review of *Miranda's Waning Protections: Police Interrogation Practices After Dickerson*, by Welsh S. White

Andrew E. Taslitz[105]

The ... blockbuster movie, *Minority Report*, starring Tom Cruise, provides a useful entry point for discussing the content of Welsh White's outstanding new book.... In the film, Cruise is a detective of the future, assigned to a "Pre–Crime Unit" that uses the talents of three mutants who supposedly can foresee homicides with 100 percent accuracy. Accordingly, Cruise and his fellow cops arrest suspects for "future crimes" they have yet to commit.

The movie opens with Cruise and his fellow officers making an arrest just as a husband is purportedly preparing to kill his wife in a jealous rage. Cruise arrests the husband in the nick of time and then *Mirandizes* him. No trial is necessary, and Cruise quickly "halos" the husband, placing a device on his head that immobilizes him; he is then immediately warehoused in frozen stasis along with the many other pre-crime offenders. From a lawyer's perspective, the amusing part of this scene is the utter pointlessness of warning the suspect about his rights to remain silent and to have an appointed attorney when his conviction and punishment are guaranteed, with or without the warnings.

Later, Cruise is himself accused of a future homicide. He discovers, however, that there are sometimes secret "minority reports": dissents filed by one of the mutants who disagrees with the precognitive vision of the other two. Cruise frantically searches for his own minority report, only to

---

104. *See* WELSH WHITE, MIRANDA'S WANING PROTECTIONS: POLICE INTERROGATION PRACTICES AFTER DICKERSON (2001).

105. Andrew E. Taslitz, *Book Review: Miranda's Waning Protections: Police Interrogation Practices After Dickerson, by Welsh S. White*, 17 CRIM. JUST. (Winter 2002).

find that it does not exist: There is no evidence of his innocence. Yet when he's later faced with the situation—a setup that makes him want to kill a suspect—Cruise does not do so, though the suspect ends up committing suicide. Although Cruise looks guilty, even in his own mind, he was instead innocent. But given the presence of a dead body, Cruise has a difficult time convincing the state.

Like the opening sequence in Minority Report, Welsh White suggests that *Miranda* warnings are too often useless. The police have developed sophisticated techniques for getting suspects to confess, usually after waiving their *Miranda* rights entirely. But once the suspects confess, absent the most extreme circumstances, the confession will be admitted at trial, and the suspect's conviction will be guaranteed. And, like Cruise's own predicament in the movie, that conviction will come to pass despite a suspect's being entirely innocent, though the suspect may not always be certain that this is so. In short, contrary to what his book's title might suggest, Welsh White is less interested in defending the *Miranda* doctrine and its reaffirmance by the recent *Dickerson* case (though he does approve of the doctrine as a minimal first step) than he is in pointing out its failures as a way to protect against wrongful convictions. Having documented those failures, he has a positive project as well: suggesting a way to fix the problem.

Interrogators, says White, use a variety of methods to get suspects to waive *Miranda* rights. Officers deliver the warnings in a neutral, flat manner, or they de-emphasize the warning's significance after spending time building rapport with the suspect. The officers also offer suspects the opportunity to tell their side of the story, or they convince them that they are acting in their best interests. Even when suspects invoke their *Miranda* rights, interrogators try to encourage waiver by leaving suspects alone to stew or prompting them to change their minds. (For example, saying to the 17–year-old suspect in a rape case, "Well, the victim has told us her side of the story, so you just let me know if you change your mind and want to tell me your side too").

If these techniques fail to result in an eventual waiver, the police sometimes question anyway, knowing that under current law they can at least use the statement to impeach the defendant at trial if he or she takes the stand. Alternatively, if necessary, the police will falsely testify to facts establishing that a voluntary waiver took place. They will likely succeed in doing so because, absent corroborating evidence (which is usually unavailable given that the questioning takes place in secret), judges often resolve credibility questions in favor of the officers. Once a confession is admitted for any reason, however, the jury will convict. In White's view, the application of these troubling techniques will today likely survive constitutional challenge in many circumstances. But, he is at great pains to point out, the existence of these techniques and their impact is not shown by his mere unsupported opinion. Rather, he explains, his descriptions are undergirded by substantial empirical and anecdotal evidence. Indeed, one of his complaints throughout the book is that the courts too often ignore the empirical data that should inform the crafting of wise doctrine and its sound application.

For White, among *Miranda*'s great failings is that it does not provide procedural mechanisms to aid in accurate fact finding, to overcome the too often incorrect assumption of police credibility, and to supplement the limited information for judging voluntariness that arises from the isolated nature of secret interrogations taking place in police stations.

But White's even greater concern is not really with *Miranda* at all. *Miranda* permits interrogation once a voluntary waiver of rights is obtained without reciting any guidelines for what techniques the police may safely use in conducting their interrogations. The current version of due process doctrine does not fill this gap because due process violations are found only in extreme circumstances, such as when force or its threat, promises of protection from force, or excessively lengthy continuous interrogations are found. Current law therefore permits the use of "pernicious interrogation techniques," that is, those raising a substantial risk of a false conviction. Indeed, White offers empirical evidence that convictions resulting from false confessions are a substantial problem in serious cases, for it is in those cases that police seem to believe that obtaining a confession by questionable methods is worth the cost. White recounts a variety of techniques (a few of which will be discussed shortly) that he labels "pernicious." Indeed, it is one of the many strengths of his book that he uses a large number of transcripts from "real-world" cases to illustrate his point.

White's solution to all these problems lies not in *Miranda*'s Fifth Amendment rationale, but in the Due Process Clause. He does not seek to change current due process law much, arguing that it already implicitly embraces the following principle: the police may not use interrogation methods that are substantially likely to produce untrue statements. White argues that current application of this general principle has been distorted by the courts' ignoring the teachings of modern social science on the likelihood of certain interrogation techniques' leading to wrongful convictions and on the problem of factfinding accuracy concerning the circumstances under which confessions were taken.

White would strengthen due process rules in five circumstances:

1. *Questioning the mentally handicapped*: White recommends that a suspect's mental handicap be taken into account and heavily weighted in determining a confession's voluntariness under the totality of the circumstances, even where the police were unaware of the suspect's special vulnerability. White would therefore specifically overrule the High Court's decision in Colorado v. Connelly. White would do so because the empirical data demonstrate that "even the average level of stress built into an interrogation can be excessive and overbearing" for the mentally handicapped.

2. *Lengthy interrogations*: White would create the following bright-line rule: any confession resulting from more than six hours of questioning

must automatically be deemed involuntary given the substantial empirical data suggesting that the risk of false confessions is unacceptably high once that threshold is passed.

3. *Threats of punishment or promises of leniency*: White considers any confession involuntary in which the interrogator should be aware that either the suspect or a reasonable person in the suspect's position would perceive the officer's statements as expressing the likelihood that the suspect will receive leniency or avoid adverse consequences if only he or she will confess. This rule circumvents the problem of police using only implicit, subtle threats, while recognizing data showing the likelihood that even innocent people will confess rather than risk unpleasant consequences.

4. *Threats of adverse consequences to a friend or loved one*: White would flatly prohibit such threats because of the substantial evidence that people will lie about their own guilt to save loved ones. White would again use an objective test: Would a reasonable interrogator believe that the suspect would likely perceive the interrogator's conduct as embodying such a threat?

5. *Misrepresenting the evidence against a suspect*: Here White's general rule would be that questioners may not employ tactics likely to suggest to the suspect that the evidence against him or her is so overwhelming that continued resistance would be futile. He admits, however, that this test is a case-specific one, weighing many factors, such as the nature and quality of the misrepresentation; the extent to which it seemed to establish the suspect's guilt; and the suspect's apparent vulnerability. He therefore tries to supplement this general rule with two more specific per se rules: first, if the lie is about the existence of scientific evidence, such as a DNA match that purportedly proves the defendant's guilt, due process is violated; second, if the lie involves the use of fictitious lineups in which witnesses falsely claim to identify the defendant as the wrongdoer in the current case or in another, unrelated crime, that, too, violates due process. The data reveal that the risk of the innocent confessing in both situations is intolerable.

White would also address fact-finding problems concerning the voluntariness both of *Miranda* waivers and of the resulting confessions by again relying on the Due Process Clause. This time, White finds in that clause a constitutional mandate to record interrogations, preferably via video. White specifically roots his argument in an analogy to *Jackson v. Denno*. There, the Court invalidated the New York procedure allowing the same jury that determined a defendant's guilt or innocence to determine whether his confession was involuntary. If so, the jury was supposed to ignore the defendant's confession, even if truthful, as evidence of his guilt. The Court reasoned that it would be hard for a jury to understand the policy reasons for barring reliance on a coerced but otherwise truthful confession. Moreover, the jury's belief in a suspect's guilt or innocence would likely color its determination whether the confession was voluntary. Given that facts in suppression motions are often disputed, credibility critical, and the plausibility of inferences to be drawn from established facts key, the reliability of the judgment of the same jury's deciding guilt or innocence also deciding a confession's voluntariness was questionable. The voluntariness determination instead, explained the Court, "requires facing the issue squarely, in illuminating isolation and unclouded by other issues." Only the judge or a separate jury not deciding guilt or innocence could reliably perform that task. Furthermore, such alternative procedures would aid appellate review by offering a clear-cut determination on a central issue.

As well-known commentators later noted, *Jackson* did not portray the New York procedure as always or even more often than not resulting in the admission of involuntary confessions. Indeed, the Court relied on common sense assumptions rather than exploring empirical data. In White's words, it was sufficient for the Court majority that the procedure "posed substantial threats to a defendant's constitutional right to have a confession entirely disregarded and to have the coercion issue reliably determined." But, argues White, modern data show that a variety of forces make it hard for judges accurately to determine voluntariness themselves because of their undue willingness to believe the police. They are also keenly aware that a decision to suppress a confession might result in the acquittal of a perhaps guilty person. Neither judge nor jury is therefore likely reliably to determine the voluntariness of a confession or of a *Miranda* waiver. That problem could be substantially cured by recording, preferably videotaping, interrogations. Although there is no way to ensure that the police will tape all that happens, even what they choose to tape may aid the court's credibility judgment. Furthermore, apart from credibility disputes, there will be a fuller record, revealing an officer's loudness of voice and persistence and the suspect's reactions (such as signs of fear, wariness, or resignation). Videotaping cannot replace the substantive protections (rights to silence and counsel) provided by *Miranda* but can create a procedural mechanism to give that substance life.

All of Welsh White's suggestions are of immediate practical value to practicing lawyers. He argues for little change in the law, instead primarily insisting that current due process rules are weakly applied because they ignore the lessons of social science. Any criminal defense attorney can make ready use of the empirical data in White's book to support a suppression motion. White's strategy of focusing on the dangers of wrongful convictions, that is, of convicting the innocent, is also more likely to move policymakers to action in a law-and-order world than are pleas to respect the rights of the guilty. White's book is, therefore, likely over time to have a significant practical impact (his arguments can also be raised under state constitutions—which are sometimes more protective of defendants' rights than is the federal Constitution). Yet his book is concise, beautifully written, carefully argued, and well supported. His subtle prose will appeal to all educated readers, his creativity will excite academics, and his nuts-and-bolts practicality will have an impact on policymakers. It is no overstatement to say that this is one of the most accessible and yet important books on the law of confessions of the last 20 years. Failure to read and use it should be considered malpractice.

———

There are other sources of authority, besides *Miranda*, that may bolster its protections. Consider Article 36 of the Vienna Convention on Consular Relations, to which the United States is a signator, which requires that detained foreign nationals be notified that they are entitled to communicate with their consul.[106] Some lawyers have argued that Article 36 requires this warning: "If you are not a citizen of the United States, you have a right to contact your consul."[107] Although it had long been unclear whether the failure to provide this notification should result in the exclusion of any subsequent confession, the United States Supreme Court recently held in *Sanchez-Llamas v. Oregon* that suppression is not required.[108]

PROBLEM 8–7

Return to the file memorandum in the Boson case in Chapter 1. Would a motion to suppress Boson's statement come out differently under Professor Welsh White's rules? What additional information, if any, would you need to answer this question with confidence?

PROBLEM 8–8

Return to Problem 8–4 earlier in this chapter. Would the likely outcome of a motion to suppress Marvoal's confession come out differently under Professor White's rules? What additional information, if any, would you need to answer this question with confidence?

PROBLEM 8–9

Assume that you are representing a client who has confessed to a robbery and is about to be tried in state court. You want to argue that, under the state constitution, any confession given in police custody is violative of that constitution's analogue to the Fifth Amendment, even where proper *Miranda* warnings have been given. What arguments would you raise? Are you more likely to succeed if you argue only that there is a violation if questioning is outside the presence of counsel? As a backup position, can you argue for a compromise alternative to *Miranda* that would better reflect the proper balance of the interests of the state and the individual? What, if any, information would you want, or arguments would

---

106. *See* Vienna Convention on Consular Relations, April 24, 1963, 21 U.S.T. 77, 79.

107. *See* Victor M. Uribe, *Consuls at Work: Universal Instruments of Human Rights & Protection in the Context of Criminal Justice*, 19 HOUS. J. INT L. 375, 423 (1997).

108. *See* Sanchez–Llamas v. Oregon, 548 U.S. 331 (2006).

you raise, to support the notion that the state constitution should be interpreted to reach a different conclusion than is mandated by the federal constitution? To argue that a different approach to interpreting the state constitution is required compared to the federal one?

D.   *MIRANDA* THRESHOLDS: CUSTODY & INTERROGATION

1.   THE DEFINITION OF CUSTODY

As the Court made clear in its opinion, police are not required to give *Miranda* warnings unless they subject a person to "custodial interrogation." In this subsection and the next, we will explore what the terms "custody" and "interrogation" mean. Custodial interrogation, explained the Court in *Miranda*, is "questioning initiated by law enforcement officers after a person has been taken into custody or otherwise deprived of his freedom of action in any significant way." A person is in custody when formally arrested. If there has been no formal arrest, an objective test is used in determining whether a person has been taken into custody or significantly deprived of freedom: a court must determine "how a reasonable man in the suspect's position would have understood his situation."[109] Since our hypothetical reasonable man would not believe that an officer stopping him in order to ask the time is restraining him, a person stopped in those circumstances is not considered to be in custody even if the officer actually intended to arrest the person. An "unarticulated plan [to arrest a suspect] has no bearing on the question whether a suspect was 'in custody' at a particular time."

The irrelevance of police officers' subjective expectations was underscored in *Stansbury v. California*.[110] There, Stansbury agreed to accompany police to a stationhouse for questioning. The police questioned him without giving him *Miranda* warnings, and he admitted seeing the homicide victim that night. When he also admitted that he had several prior felony convictions, the police *Mirandized* him, and he requested an attorney. The trial court denied a suppression motion, concluding Stansbury was not in "custody" when first questioned, even though the officers subjectively may have thought otherwise. In a per curiam opinion, the Court concluded:

> Our decisions make clear that the initial determination of custody depends on the objective circumstances of the interrogation, not on the subjective views harbored by either the interrogating officers or the person being questioned. In *Beckwith v. United States*, 425 U.S. 341 (1976), for example, the defendant, without being advised of his *Miranda* rights, made incriminating statements to Government agents during an interview in a private home. He later asked that *Miranda* "be extended to cover interrogation in non-custodial circumstances after a police investigation has focused on the suspect." We found his argument unpersuasive, explaining that "it was the compulsive aspect

---

109.   Berkemer v. McCarty, 468 U.S. 420 (1984).

110.   511 U.S. 318 (1994).

of custodial interrogation, and not the strength or content of the government's suspicions at the time the questioning was conducted, which led the Court to impose *Miranda* requirements with regard to custodial questioning." As a result, we concluded that the defendant was not entitled to *Miranda* warnings. . . .

It is well settled, then, that a police officer's subjective view that the individual under questioning is a suspect, if undisclosed, does not bear upon the question whether the individual is in custody for purposes of *Miranda*. The same principle obtains if an officer's undisclosed assessment is that the person being questioned is not a suspect. In either instance, one cannot expect the person under interrogation to probe the officer's innermost thoughts. Save as they are communicated or otherwise manifested to the person being questioned, an officer's evolving but unarticulated suspicion do not affect the objective circumstances of an interrogation or interview, and thus cannot affect the *Miranda* custody inquiry.

A person is not considered to be in custody unless freedom of movement is restrained in some "significant way." Thus, if a person is not significantly restrained, that person is not in custody. For example, a person detained pursuant to a routine traffic stop is not considered to be in custody, so *Miranda* does not apply. The Court has justified this result by explaining why the concerns articulated in *Miranda* are not present in these circumstances:[111]

> Two features of an ordinary traffic stop mitigate the danger that a person questioned will be induced "to speak where he would not otherwise do so freely." First, detention of a motorist pursuant to a traffic stop is presumptively temporary and brief. The vast majority of roadside detentions last only a few minutes. A motorist's expectations, when he sees a policeman's light flashing behind him, are that he will be obliged to spend a short period of time answering questions and waiting while the officer checks his license and registration, that he may then be given a citation, but that in the end he most likely will be allowed to continue on his way. In this respect, questioning incident to an ordinary traffic stop is quite different from stationhouse interrogation, which frequently is prolonged, and in which the detainee often is aware that questioning will continue until he provides his interrogators the answers they seek.

Second, circumstances associated with the typical traffic stop are not such that the motorist feels completely at the mercy of the police. To be sure, the aura of authority surrounding an armed, uniformed officer and the knowledge that the officer has some discretion in deciding whether to issue a citation, in combination, exert some pressure on the detainee to respond to questions. But other aspects of the situation substantially offset these forces. Perhaps most importantly, the typical traffic stop is public, at least to some degree. Passersby, on foot or in other cars, witness the

---

111. Berkemer, 468 U.S. at 421.

interaction of officer and motorist. This exposure to public view both reduces the ability of an unscrupulous policeman to use illegitimate means to elicit self-incriminating statements and diminishes the motorist's fear that, if he does not cooperate, he will be subjected to abuse. The fact that the detained motorist typically is confronted by only one or at most two policemen further mutes his sense of vulnerability. In short, the atmosphere surrounding an ordinary traffic stop is substantially less "police dominated" than that surrounding the kinds of interrogation at issue in *Miranda* itself and in the subsequent cases in which we have applied *Miranda*.

Although relevant, location is not determinative when deciding whether a person is in custody. Questioning a suspect in the suspect's own home might constitute custodial interrogation, whereas questioning in police headquarters might not, depending on the circumstances. Thus, when a suspect voluntarily went to a police station for questioning, was informed he was not under arrest, and left the police station without any resistance, he was unable to argue later that his statements should have been excluded from trial because he was not read his *Miranda* rights.[112] Another suspect, however, was held to have been in custody after he was awakened at 4:00 a.m. and questioned by four officers who entered his bedroom at a boarding house.[113]

A jailed suspect generally is considered to be in custody, even if the questioning deals with charges unrelated to those for which the suspect is jailed. For example, a defendant incarcerated on state charges successfully sought to exclude incriminating statements he made after being questioned by an Internal Revenue Service investigator who failed to provide him with his *Miranda* rights.[114] Lower courts, however, have not read Mathis to mean that all incarcerated persons must be given *Miranda* warnings before questioning. Both the Ninth and the Fourth Circuit Courts of Appeals, for example, require a showing that the questioning officer placed further limitations on the individual's freedom than were imposed by general prison conditions.[115] The test in both these circuits is whether the officer's conduct "would cause a reasonable person to believe his freedom of movement had been further diminished."

Consider questioning by a probation officer, for example, a person on probation with the conditions that he meet with a probation officer whenever directed to do so and that he truthfully answer the probation officer's questions "in all matters." The probationer knows that failure to comply with these conditions might cause the court to revoke his probation. Is the probationer "in custody" when answering the probation officer's questions? In *Minnesota v. Murphy*,[116] the Court answered in the negative, holding

---

112.   Oregon v. Mathiason, 429 U.S. 492 (1977).

113.   Orozco v. Texas, 394 U.S. 324 (1969).

114.   Mathis v. United States, 391 U.S. 1 (1968).

115.   *See* Garcia v. Singletary, 13 F.3d 1487 (11th Cir.1994); United States v. Conley, 779 F.2d 970 (4th Cir.1985), *cert. denied*, 479 U.S. 830 (1986).

116.   465 U.S. 420 (1984).

that the Fifth and Fourteenth Amendments do not prohibit the introduction of the probationer's statements. The Court explained that Murphy was not in custody for purposes of *Miranda* because reporting to a probation officer does not involve a formal arrest or significant restraint on freedom. The Court found unpersuasive the facts that the probation officer intended to elicit incriminating responses, that Murphy did not expect to be questioned about criminal activity, and that he had not consulted with counsel before the meeting. The Court emphasized the lack of evidence suggesting that Murphy believed his probation would be revoked if he terminated the meeting with the probation officer.

A majority of a divided Court in *Yarborough v. Alvarado*[117] insisted that the custody inquiry is an objective one and that the suspect's age is not necessarily a factor to be considered. The suspect in that case, Michael Alvarado, was 17 years old at the time he was brought by his parents to a California police station for questioning about a homicide. Alvarado's parents remained in the lobby of the police station while a detective questioned him for about two hours. The detective did not *Mirandize* Alvarado, who ultimately acknowledged having had some involvement in the killing. When the interview was over, the detective escorted him back to where his parents were waiting, and the three drove away. Alvarado was later arrested, charged, and convicted of second-degree murder. The trial court denied his motion to suppress the statements he made during the interview, finding that he had not been in custody. Although state appellate courts and a federal district court (exercising habeas jurisdiction) agreed, the United States Court of Appeals for the Ninth Circuit ordered the conviction reversed, holding that "the state court erred in failing to account for Alvarado's youth and inexperience when evaluating whether a reasonable person in his position would have felt free to leave."[118] The Supreme Court overturned the Ninth Circuit's judgment, based primarily on the deferential standard with which federal courts in habeas cases must view state court findings—a standard that we will discuss later in this chapter. In another portion of its decision, however, the Court went farther, stating that "[t]he *Miranda* custody inquiry is an objective test." The Court explained:

> ... [T]he objective *Miranda* custody inquiry could reasonably be viewed as different from doctrinal tests that depend on the actual mindset of a particular suspect, where we do consider a suspect's age and experience. For example, the voluntariness of a statement is often said to depend on whether "the defendant's will was overborne," *Lynumn*, a question that logically can depend on "the characteristics of the accused." *Schneckloth*. The characteristics of the accused can include the suspect's age, education, and intelligence, as well as a suspect's prior experience with law enforcement. In concluding that there was "no principled reason" why such factors should not also apply to the *Miranda* custody inquiry, the Court of Appeals ignored the

---

117.   541 U.S. 652 (2004).

118.   *Id.* at 659–60.

argument that the custody inquiry states an objective rule designed to give clear guidance to the police, while consideration of a suspect's individual characteristics—including his age—could be viewed as creating a subjective inquiry. . . .

. . . In most cases, police officers will not know a suspect's interrogation history. Even if they do, the relationship between a suspect's past experiences and the likelihood a reasonable person with that experience would feel free to leave often will be speculative. True, suspects with prior law enforcement experience may understand police procedures and reasonably feel free to leave unless told otherwise. On the other hand, they may view past as prologue and expect another in a string of arrests. We do not ask police officers to consider these contingent psychological factors when deciding whether suspects should be advised of their *Miranda* rights.

Justice O'Connor, a member of the five-person majority, stated in a concurrence that "[t]here may be cases in which a suspect's age will be relevant to the *Miranda* 'custody' inquiry." She went on to observe that "Alvarado was almost 18 years old at the time of his interview. It is difficult to expect police to recognize that a suspect is a juvenile when he is so close to the age of majority."[119] A four-justice dissent argued that the definition of custody "has introduced the concept of a 'reasonable person' to avoid judicial inquiry into subjective states of mind, and to focus the inquiry instead upon objective circumstances that are known to both the officer and the suspect and that are likely relevant to the way a person would understand his situation."[120] In this case, urged the dissent, "Alvarado's youth is an objective circumstance that was known to the police" and should have been considered. We reproduce an excerpt of Justice Breyer's dissenting opinion below because it is the clearest statement yet of what it means to judge someone from the perspective of the "situated reasonable person" in the context of constitutional criminal procedure:

> In my view, Michael Alvarado clearly was "in custody" when the police questioned him (without *Miranda* warnings) about the murder of Francisco Castaneda. To put the question in terms of federal law's well-established legal standards: Would a "reasonable person" in Alvarado's "position" have felt he was "at liberty to terminate the interrogation and leave"? A court must answer this question in light of "all of the circumstances surrounding the interrogation." And the obvious answer here is "no." . . .

> What about Alvarado's youth? The fact that Alvarado was 17 helps to show that he was unlikely to have felt free to ignore his parents' request to come to the station. And a 17–year-old is more likely than, say, a 35–year-old, to take a police officer's assertion of authority to keep parents outside the room as an assertion of authority to keep their child inside as well.

---

119.   *Id.* at 669 (O'Connor, J., concurring).

120.   *Id.* at 674 (Breyer, J., dissenting).

The majority suggests that the law might prevent a judge from taking account of the fact that Alvarado was 17. I can find nothing in the law that supports that conclusion. Our cases do instruct lower courts to apply a "reasonable person" standard. But the "reasonable person" standard does not require a court to pretend that Alvarado was a 35–year-old with aging parents whose middle-aged children do what their parents ask only out of respect. Nor does it say that a court should pretend that Alvarado was the statistically determined "average person"—a working, married, 35–year-old white female with a high school degree. See U.S. Dept. of Commerce, Bureau of Census, Statistical Abstract of the United States: 2003 (123d ed.).

Rather, the precise legal definition of "reasonable person" may, depending on legal context, appropriately account for certain personal characteristics. In negligence suits, for example, the question is what would a "reasonable person" do "under the same or similar circumstances." In answering that question, courts enjoy "latitude" and may make "allowance not only for external facts, but sometimes for certain characteristics of the actor himself," including physical disability, youth, or advanced age. W. Keeton, D. Dobbs, R. Keeton, & D. Owen, Prosser and Keeton on Law of Torts § 32, pp. 174–179 (5th ed.1984); see also Restatement (Third) of Torts § 10, Comment b, pp. 128–130 (Tent. Draft No. 1, Mar. 28, 2001) (all American jurisdictions count a person's childhood as a "relevant circumstance" in negligence determinations). This allowance makes sense in light of the tort standard's recognized purpose: deterrence. Given that purpose, why pretend that a child is an adult or that a blind man can see? See O. Holmes, The Common Law 85–89 (M. Howe ed.1963).

In the present context, that of *Miranda's* "in custody" inquiry, the law has introduced the concept of a "reasonable person" to avoid judicial inquiry into subjective states of mind, and to focus the inquiry instead upon objective circumstances that are known to both the officer and the suspect and that are likely relevant to the way a person would understand his situation. This focus helps to keep *Miranda* a workable rule.

In this case, Alvarado's youth is an objective circumstance that was known to the police. It is not a special quality, but rather a widely shared characteristic that generates commonsense conclusions about behavior and perception. To focus on the circumstance of age in a case like this does not complicate the "in custody" inquiry. And to say that courts should ignore widely shared, objective characteristics, like age, on the ground that only a (large) minority of the population possesses them would produce absurd results, the present instance being a case in point. I am not surprised that the majority points to no case suggesting any such limitation.

Nor am I surprised that the majority makes no real argument at all explaining why any court would believe that the objective fact of a suspect's age could never be relevant. The majority does discuss a suspect's "history with law enforcement"—a bright red herring in the present context where Alvarado's youth (an objective fact) simply helps to show (with the help of a legal presumption) that his appearance at the police station was not voluntary. . . .

As I have said, the law in this case is clear. This Court's cases establish that, even if the police do not tell a suspect he is under arrest, do not handcuff him, do not lock him in a cell, and do not threaten him, he may nonetheless reasonably believe he is not free to leave the place of questioning—and thus be in custody for *Miranda* purposes.

Our cases also make clear that to determine how a suspect would have "gaug[ed]" his "freedom of movement," a court must carefully examine "all of the circumstances surrounding the interrogation," including, for example, how long the interrogation lasted (brief and routine or protracted?), how the suspect came to be questioned (voluntarily or against his will?), where the questioning took place (at a police station or in public?), and what the officer communicated to the individual during the interrogation (that he was a suspect? that he was under arrest? that he was free to leave at will?). In the present case, every one of these factors argues—and argues strongly—that Alvarado was in custody for *Miranda* purposes when the police questioned him.

Common sense, and an understanding of the law's basic purpose in this area, are enough to make clear that Alvarado's age—an objective, widely shared characteristic about which the police plainly knew—is also relevant to the inquiry. Unless one is prepared to pretend that Alvarado is someone he is not, a middle-aged gentleman, well versed in police practices, it seems to me clear that the California courts made a serious mistake.

NOTES AND QUESTIONS

1. One might argue that Justice O'Connor's concurrence and the four-person dissent, taken together, constitute a five-person majority for the proposition that youth *should* be considered if the suspect were substantially underage and the police obviously perceived that fact. But if the majority is to be taken at its word, should age *ever* be a factor in determining whether a reasonable person in the suspect's situation would have felt free to leave?

2. Can race, gender, or other characteristics, be distinguished from age for purposes of the custody determination? Is there room in the majority's decision for the proposition that some of these characteristics should be considered when determining whether a reasonable person in the suspect's situation would have felt free to leave? What about a person from another country who obviously believes that he or she will not be permitted to leave—if police admit they were aware of that fact, should it make a difference? Are the concerns about inherent coercion, recognized in *Miranda*, present in such a situation? Is the majority really rejecting Justice Breyer's definition of the reasonable man, and, if so, what definition is the majority applying? If not, how does the majority reach a different conclusion than Justice Breyer?

PROBLEM 8–10

In the Brunell case in Chapter 1, assume that you represent Terry Marvoal. She relates the facts of the late-night interview described in the prosecutor's memorandum.

Question: Was Marvoal in custody? Can you successfully raise a *Miranda* claim in order to exclude the statements she made that night?

PROBLEM 8–11

Based largely on Peter Holmes' confession to police, a grand jury indicted him for first degree murder and related felonies. His attorney moved to suppress the statements and presented the following facts at a hearing on the motion. Holmes was given his *Miranda* warnings before he confessed, but he had been in the presence of police officers for eight hours prior to that time. Police officers approached Holmes about the murder and told him that they hoped he could "assist in the investigation." Holmes had agreed to accompany the officers to the police station for that purpose. There, he answered questions in a seemingly informal setting. Intermittently, officers placed him in a small locked room. He was not handcuffed. He was not told that he was free to leave, but there was a bell in the room that he was told he could use to summon an officer. Holmes also accompanied officers in a squad car to and from his apartment, where they executed a search warrant. He was not told that he did not have to accompany the officers on their search warrant execution, nor that he did not have to return with them to the police station. After the search, he was formally arrested, booked, and given his *Miranda* warnings. After that time, he made a confession that was reduced to writing.

Question: Should the trial court suppress Holmes' confession?

PROBLEM 8–12

Using the facts of the preceding problem, change the facts as follows and determine whether the trial court should grant the motion to suppress:

a. Holmes drove his own car to the police station.

b. Holmes went to the police station in a squad car, but, after accompanying the officers during the search of his apartment, he drove his own car back to the police station.

c. The entire eight-hour period transpired at night.

d. Before asking Holmes whether he would accompany them to the station for questioning, the officers had solid evidence implicating him in the murder. They fully intended to arrest Holmes, but held off doing so in order to increase the chances that he would say something incriminating.

e. Approximately one hour into the eight-hour interaction, Holmes said, "Arrest me or let me go."

f. Early in the eight-hour period, Holmes overheard one officer say to another, "Watch that suspect."

g. Holmes had a felony record and a general distrust of police.

h. Holmes was an African–American male who had been harassed by police on numerous occasions and who had observed many situations in which police used force against other African–American males.

In connection with this last question, consider prophetic evangelist Jim Wallis's description[121] of his conversation with the mother of a young African–American janitor, "Butch":

> Butch's mother recounted a history of poverty and violence, especially at the hands of the police. I was stunned by what she said about the Detroit Police Department. She told of countless times that her husband or one of her sons had been picked up on the street for no apparent reason, taken down to the precinct, verbally abused, falsely accused, and even beaten.
>
> When she went down to the police station to find out what had happened and try to bring them home, she was often assaulted with vile and profane language. The police would tell her that they would "take care of" her husband or son, give her man what he deserved, and that she'd better "get her ass on home" or she was going to get the same treatment.
>
> I remember how my insides began to hurt and my eyes welled up with tears as one by one every person in the room told me stories of how they or close friends had been abused by the police, mostly for the crime of being at the wrong place at the wrong time, and for being black. I had never heard such things before, but I knew they were telling the truth.
>
> Butch's mother told me what she taught her children about the police. When they spotted a cop, they were to duck into an alley, crouch under some stairs, or hide behind a corner. When the policeman passed by, it was safe to come out and try to find their way home themselves. "So I tell my children," she said, "to watch out for the policeman."

PROBLEM 8–13

       James DeLaurier and his brother were involved in a serious accident when their car ran across an embankment into a ditch. They were both

---

121. JIM WALLIS, THE SOUL OF POLITICS: A PRACTICAL AND PROPHETIC VISION FOR CHANGE 78–79 (1994).

badly injured, and, when police arrived, their two bodies were positioned so that it could not be determined who had been the driver of the vehicle. As paramedics removed DeLaurier from the car, he became combative and resisted their efforts to put him into an ambulance. It appeared that he was extremely intoxicated. The paramedics asked Officer Dostanko to help them subdue DeLaurier. Dostanko yelled at DeLaurier to "lie back and let the paramedics do their job." He stayed close by and continued to shout at DeLaurier until paramedics were able to get him into the ambulance. Dostanko followed the ambulance to the hospital. In the emergency room, Dostanko asked DeLaurier whether he had been driving, to which DeLaurier responded, "No." Dostanko then walked into another part of the emergency room, where he spoke with the brother. The brother said that DeLaurier had been driving. When Dostanko related this information back to DeLaurier, the latter acknowledged, "All right, I was driving." The state seeks to use this statement against DeLaurier at his trial on drunk driving charges. He has filed a motion to suppress.

Question: Should DeLaurier's statement be admitted at trial?

PROBLEM 8–14

Stevie Patton flagged down a squad car at 4:55 a.m. and informed its occupants that there had been a stabbing in a nearby apartment. Patton was bleeding from a severe cut on his left hand and appeared highly emotional. Officers accompanied him to the scene, where they found a woman and a young girl, both dead from stab wounds. Patton remained in the apartment while police investigated the scene. Some time later, they noticed that he appeared to have lost a significant amount of blood, and they transported him to the hospital. An officer remained with Patton at the hospital and after his discharge transported him to the police station. He arrived there at approximately 10:00 a.m. and was taken to an interview room in the homicide office. There, a detective advised him that he was not under arrest and that he was free to leave, although the detective wanted to ask him a few questions. Patton responded that he would answer any questions and, in the course of doing so, implicated himself in the stabbings. After fifteen minutes of questioning, the detective notified Patton that he was under arrest and read him his *Miranda* rights. The trial court has taken under advisement Patton's motion to suppress his pre-*Miranda* statements from the murder trial.

Question: How should the trial court rule?

PROBLEM 8–15

Using the facts of the preceding problem, assume that when Patton arrived at the police station, he asked to call his father "because his father had an attorney he would refer to him." The officer who had transported him from the hospital said, "You'll have to talk to homicide about that," and turned Patton over to the detective in the homicide office. Patton said nothing to the detective about his desire to call his father, and the interview proceeded as detailed above. He now moves to suppress his statement.

Question: Should the court grant the motion to suppress?

PROBLEM 8–16

The Logan County Sheriff's Office received a tip indicating that marijuana was being grown on Steve Breidenbach's farm. After confirming details of the tip by several means, including a helicopter fly-over, police obtained a search warrant for the farm. During their execution of the warrant, they observed a young man run into a wooded area and crouch behind a tree. Officer Page drew his weapon and pursued the man. Approaching the man with his gun at firing position, Page asked, "Who are you and what are you doing here?" The man responded that he was Steve Breidenbach and that he was checking his irrigation ditches. Without holstering his gun, Page responded, "I think you're lying to me. I think you're trying to destroy your marijuana plants." Breidenbach acknowledged that there were four marijuana plants growing in the area and pointed them out to Page. At trial for cultivation and possession of marijuana, the court admitted Breidenbach's statements to Page, finding that he was not in custody, and Breidenbach was convicted.

Question: On appeal, how should the court rule?

2.   THE DEFINITION OF INTERROGATION

Where police officers question a suspect, it is obvious that the suspect has been subjected to "interrogation" for purposes of *Miranda*. In other situations, however, it is not so clear when a suspect's statements were in response to questioning. In these situations, determining whether the suspect was subjected to interrogation depends largely on the application of a rule developed by the Supreme Court in *Rhode Island v. Innis*.[122] There, the Court held that words or actions by a police officer may constitute a "functional equivalent" to express questioning. As the Court saw it, such words or actions create the kind of inherent compulsion that it undertook in *Miranda* to dispel. Determining precisely what constitutes the "functional equivalent" to express questioning is not always an easy task. In *Innis*, the Court suggested that the test is an objective one: words or actions constitute the "functional equivalent" to questioning if the police *should know* those words or actions are "reasonably likely to elicit an incriminating response." The Court noted that in determining whether the police should have known about the effects of their remarks, "[a]ny knowledge the police may have had concerning the susceptibility of a defendant to a particular form of persuasion might be an important factor."

The *Innis* test, with its objective standard, appears to cast a fairly broad net. In reality, the Court has applied it rather narrowly. In *Arizona*

---

122.   446 U.S. 291 (1980).

v. Mauro, it refused to find that interrogation occurred when police attended, and tape recorded, a meeting between a woman and her husband, who had been taken into custody for suspicion of killing their son.[123] The Court remarked that the event was not a "psychological ploy" intended by the officers to incriminate Mauro. More interesting is the fact that the Court showed little interest in analyzing whether the officers "should have known" that the situation was reasonably likely to elicit incriminating statements from him. Instead, the majority focused on the Arizona Supreme Court's finding that the officers were aware of a "possibility" that Mauro would incriminate himself during the meeting. According to the Court, a "possibility" does not indicate "a sufficient likelihood of incrimination to satisfy the legal standard articulated in ... *Rhode Island v. Innis.*"

Another narrowing device is characterizing brief interactions as "on the scene questioning," rather than interrogation. The Court had mentioned in *Miranda* itself that warnings would not be required when police officers were merely engaging in brief, on the scene questioning during the fact finding process. What of the common police-citizen interaction that occurs after an arrest for driving under the influence of alcohol? Before administering *Miranda* warnings, officers frequently perform "field sobriety tests" in order to establish probable cause that the arrestee is under the influence. In one such case, the arresting officer explained to the arrestee how the field sobriety tests would be administered. During this process, the arrestee made incriminating statements. The Court held that these statements were admissible because the officer's comments were "not likely to be perceived as calling for any verbal response."[124] At the same time, however, the Court recognized that a request that the arrestee compute the date of his fourth birthday did constitute interrogation, rendering inadmissible the arrestee's inept responses.

The drunk driving arrest and its accompanying sobriety tests may raise yet another *Miranda* interrogation problem. Many states have enacted "informed consent" laws that require drivers to submit to sobriety tests (which include breathalyzer tests, physical coordination tests, and mental ability tests) or risk losing their driving privileges. What of the driver who is informed of the negative consequences of her refusal to submit to sobriety tests[125] and who is shortly thereafter given *Miranda* warnings and questioned about the offense? Does the close proximity of these two, very different kinds of warnings, raise a constitutional issue? At least one state

---

123.   481 U.S. 520 (1987).

124.   Pennsylvania v. Muniz, 496 U.S. 582 (1990).

125.   Typical language of such a warning includes the following:

You are about to be asked to take a breath test to determine the alcohol content of your blood. Driving under the influence of intoxicants is a crime. You are subject to criminal penalties if the test or other evidence shows you are under the influence of intoxicants. If you refuse or fail the test, evidence of the refusal or failure may be offered against you. If you refuse or fail the test, your driving privileges will be suspended.

court believes that it does.[126] The appropriate solution, according to that court, is to require a "clear break" between the field sobriety warnings and the *Miranda* warnings. That is, sufficient time has to elapse so that it is reasonable that the compulsion created by the field sobriety warnings has been dispelled.

In *Hiibel v. Sixth Judicial District Court of Nevada Humboldt County*,[127] the Court faced a related but different sort of question than whether an officer had "interrogated" a suspect. There, an officer arriving on a scene in response to a tip asked a man on the scene for identification. The man refused eleven requests by the officer seeking the man's name. After warning the man that he would be arrested if he continued his refusal, the officer arrested the man, later identified as Larry Dudley Hiibel. Hiibel was charged with, and convicted for, obstructing a public officer's discharge of his duties. The charge was based on a statute requiring persons detained by an officer on reasonable suspicion of a crime to identify themselves by name, though the statute prohibited compelling answers to any other inquiry. Hiibel's challenge to his conviction included an objection that he was compelled to incriminate himself by being required to give his name, thus violating his constitutional privilege against self-incrimination. The Court affirmed the conviction, rejecting this Fifth Amendment claim.

Specifically, the Court concluded that Hiibel's giving his name under these particular circumstances would not "incriminate" him because it would not "furnish a link in the chain of evidence needed to prosecute him."[128] Said the court, "As best we can tell, petitioner refused to identify himself only because he thought his name was none of the officer's business. Even today, petitioner does not explain how the disclosure of his name could have been used against him in a criminal case."[129] The Court continued:

> The narrow scope of the disclosure requirement is also important. One's identity is, by definition, unique; yet it is, in another sense, a universal characteristic. Answering a request to disclose a name is likely to be so insignificant in the scheme of things as to be incriminating only in unusual circumstances. *See Baltimore City Dept. of Social Srvs.v. Bouknight* (suggesting that "fact[s] the State could readily establish" may render "any testimony regarding existence or authenticity [of them] insufficiently incriminating").... In every criminal case, it is known and must be known who has been arrested and who is being tried ... Even witnesses who plan to invoke the Fifth Amendment privilege answer when their names are called to the stand. Still, a case may arise where there is a substantial allegation that furnishing identity at the time of a stop would have given the police a link in the chain of evidence needed to convict the individual of a separate offense.

---

126.   *See, e.g.,* State v. Scott, 826 P.2d 71 (Or.App.1992).

127.   542 U.S. 177 (2004).

128.   *Id.* at 199.

129.   *Id.*

In that case, the court can then consider whether the privilege applies, and, if the Fifth Amendment has been violated, what remedy must follow. We need not resolve these questions here.[130]

Justice Stevens dissented. First, he concluded that Hiibel's revelation of his name was "testimonial," for a "testimonial communication" is "the extortion of information from the accused, the attempt to force him 'to disclose the contents of his own mind.'"[131] Questioning during a *Terry* stop, argued Justice Stevens, unquestionably qualifies as interrogation, so compelled responses to such questions, because they result from extorting information from the suspect, are therefore also testimonial in nature.

Nor would Justice Stevens accept the majority's core argument that Hiibel's compelled disclosure of his name would not have been "incriminating," for, in Stevens' view, one's name can readily provide the necessary link to inculpatory evidence:

> The Court reasons that we should not assume that the disclosure of petitioner's name would be used to incriminate him or that it would furnish a link in a chain of evidence needed to prosecute him.... But why else would an officer ask for it? And why else would the Nevada Legislature require its disclosure only when circumstances "reasonably indicate that the person has committed, is committing, or is about to commit a crime?" If the Court is correct, then petitioner's refusal to cooperate did not impede the police investigation. Indeed, if we accept the predicate for the Court's holding, the statute requires nothing more than a useless invasion of privacy. I think that, on the contrary, the Nevada Legislature intended to provide its police officers with a useful law enforcement tool, and that the very existence of the statute demonstrates the value of the information it demands....

> A name can provide the key to a broad array of information about the person, particularly in the hands of a police officer with access to a range of law enforcement database. And that information, in turn, can be tremendously useful in a criminal prosecution. It is therefore quite wrong to suggest that a person's identity provides a link in the chain to incriminating evidence "only in unusual circumstances."[132]

NOTES AND QUESTIONS

1. Under the majority's approach, would the privilege apply if the officer had asked Hiibel—upon penalty of arrest if he refused—to produce his insurance card, which, once produced, would reveal itself to be expired? If the officer instead requested Hiibel's registration card? Would the privilege apply to the officer's insisting, upon penalty of arrest, that Hiibel produce his national identification card, if such cards were distributed to all citizens and required to be produced by national legislation as a means for better

---

130.   *Id.*

131.   *Id.* at 194 (Stevens, J., dissenting).

132.   *Id.* at 196 (Stevens, J., dissenting).

fighting the War on Terrorism? Would the precise content of the information electronically contained on such a card (e.g., medical information, social security number, criminal history, visa and passport usage, etc.) affect your answer to this last question? In connection with these questions, consider this *dictum* from the majority opinion:

> Respondents urge us to hold that the statements . . . [that the statute] requires are nontestimonial, and so outside the Clause's scope. We decline to resolve the case on that basis. "[T]o be testimonial, an accused's communication must itself, explicitly or implicitly, relate a factual assertion or disclose information." . . . Stating one's name may qualify as an assertion of fact relating to identity. Production of identity documents might meet the definition as well. As we noted in *Hubbell*, acts of production may yield testimony establishing the "existence, authenticity, and custody of items [the police seek]."[133]

By "acts of production," the Court meant, for example, that a document, such as a business record, that you prepared on your own in the course of your everyday life rather than in response to a government command is not a "compelled" communication, therefore not being protected by the privilege. However, if the government compels you, perhaps by a subpoena, to hand over such a document to it, that handing over may be a compelled testimonial communication. Why? Because, simply by turning over the requested document, you admit: (1) that it exists; (2) that it is what the government requested and is therefore authentic; and (3) that it is in your possession, things that might all be incriminating at trial. Consequently, absent immunity for the information revealed by this "act of production," you can use your privilege against self-incrimination to refuse to produce the document, even though the document's contents are not themselves protected by the privilege. Obviously, if the government cannot get the document from you, as a practical matter, it cannot use its contents against you. (The details of the act of production doctrine are discussed further in Chapter 9).

Would you answer any of these questions differently under Justice Stevens' approach?

2. Who had the better argument—the majority or Justice Stevens? Would Justice Stevens's approach create any practical problems for the police? Could it sometimes work against a detainee's interests? What differences, if any, are there in the interpretive methods followed by the majority and Justice Stevens?

PROBLEM 8–17

In the Brunell case in Chapter 1, assume that you are an Assistant United States Attorney. You make a late-night visit to Terry Marvoal's home and make the statements described in the prosecution memorandum.

Question: Did you "interrogate" Marvoal?

---

133. *Id.* at 189.

PROBLEM 8–18

Thomas Voice is arrested for murder and taken to a squad car. During the long drive to the county jail, police officers turn on the radio, which broadcasts a news item relating to the murder. Voice becomes visibly upset, prompting one of the officers to state, "Settle down. Everything is going to be all right." Voice replies, "Leave me alone or I'll kill you too." He then makes additional incriminating statements in response to the news broadcast. After his indictment, his attorney makes a motion to suppress the statements.

Question: How should the trial court rule?

PROBLEM 8–19

After a bar shooting that resulted in the death of the shooting victim, Harold Medeiros was stopped by police officers as he drove away from the bar. Madeiros asked the police officers why they had stopped him, and they replied that his car matched the description given by a witness who had seen a car leaving the scene of the shooting. Without giving *Miranda* warnings, one of the officers asked Madeiros where he was coming from. Madeiros admitted he had just come from the bar and made inculpatory statements about the shooting. The trial court granted Madeiros's pretrial motion to suppress the statements about the shooting, holding that the officer had interrogated Madeiros, and the government appealed.

Question: How should the appellate court rule?

PROBLEM 8–20

Marco Garcia is incarcerated in a state prison. One day a prison guard observes him feeding a small fire in his cell. After extinguishing the flames, the guard, in a very accusatorial tone, asks Garcia why he had started the fire. In response, Garcia said, "I didn't get my canteen privileges, and I got my rights."

Question: Should the trial court exclude the statements?

PROBLEM 8–21

Officer Nason saw Jill O'Leary weaving her vehicle across the lane markings of the road over a distance of about eight blocks. Nason stopped O'Leary's car and asked her to perform a series of sobriety tests, all of which she failed. O'Leary's eyes were bloodshot, and she smelled of alcohol. Nason administered similar tests to O'Leary's passenger, who also smelled of alcohol, but the passenger passed all the tests. The following exchange then occurred between Nason and O'Leary:

Nason: I had to stop you to do my job. You were a danger and in danger.
O'Leary: I understand.

Nason:	As long as we're cool with each other. I know your dad, and I wouldn't do this unless it was necessary.
O'Leary:	We're not cool enough where I learned my lesson sitting in the back of this cop car?
Nason:	(laughs, then talks to dispatcher)
O'Leary:	I preach this stuff to my nieces and nephews and stuff.
Nason:	Yeah—I do the same thing with my own sister-in-law. Your friend is coming awful close to being arrested; he wasn't even driving. If he's intoxicated, I have to arrest him for public intoxication, you know that's our policy as far as passengers. Is he your boyfriend?
O'Leary:	Look, don't arrest him. He only had a couple of drinks, while I had quite a few more. He's my fiance, and I always thought I could handle liquor better than he, so I chose to drive. I made a judgment call when we left the party. I guess it probably wasn't the right one.

Nason then arrested O'Leary and gave her appropriate *Miranda* rights. Furthermore, unbeknownst to O'Leary, Nason had videotaped and sound-recorded the entire event.

Question: Should the trial court suppress O'Leary's statements to Nason?

PROBLEM 8–22

Toliver and a co-defendant were taken into custody on burglary charges. After reading Toliver his *Miranda* warnings, the police ask him whether he wishes to make a statement concerning the burglary. Toliver responds, "No." The officers leave Toliver in order to speak with the co-defendant. Upon their return, they inform Toliver that the co-defendant made statements implicating Toliver in the burglary. Toliver responds with ambiguous remarks and, ultimately, begins to answer questions. After thirty-five minutes, Toliver makes a complete confession. Toliver's confession is admitted into evidence and he is convicted. State appellate courts affirm his conviction, and he ultimately files a writ of habeas corpus in federal court.

Question: Should the court grant the writ?

E.   ADEQUACY OF WARNINGS

The Court in *Miranda* was unusually specific about what it was requiring of law enforcement officers. Refer back to the text of the case. What, precisely, did the Court say with respect to the content of the warnings? We can distill its holding to require at least the following:

- The suspect "must first be informed in clear and unequivocal terms that he has the right to remain silent."

- This warning "must be accompanied by the explanation that anything said can and will be used against the individual in court."

- The suspect "must be clearly informed that he has the right to consult with a lawyer and to have the lawyer with him during interrogation."

- The suspect must be warned "that if he is indigent a lawyer will be appointed to represent him" prior to any questioning.

Aside from its specificity concerning the information that officers are required to impart, the Court in *Miranda* was adamant that shortcomings in the required warnings could not be compensated by a showing that the suspect was in fact fully aware of his rights. Thus, warnings must be given to all suspects who are subjected to custodial interrogation—even, presumably, judges, lawyers, and law students.

In later years, the Court has declined to interpret *Miranda* as requiring a "talismanic incantation" of a rigid warnings formula. Rather, words that convey the rights articulated in *Miranda* are sufficient. Officers appear to use the Court's own language in warning a suspect of his right to remain silent—something many of us can confirm through television and movie exposure. Thus, most of the litigation has centered around warnings concerning the *Miranda* right to counsel. In *California v. Prysock*,[134] for example, officers warned Prysock as follows: "You have the right to talk to a lawyer before you are questioned, have him present with you while you are being questioned, and all during the questioning." The officers then went on to advise Prysock, "You ... have the right to have a lawyer appointed to represent you at no cost to yourself." Prysock argued that the language about the right to appointed counsel was inadequate because it failed to include the information that he could have an attorney appointed for him before and during questioning. The Court disagreed, holding that the warnings had to be interpreted as a whole and finding that, taken together, the warnings "conveyed ... his right to have a lawyer appointed if he could not afford one prior to and during interrogation."

A particularly vexatious problem arises when officers suggest that counsel will be appointed at some point in the future. The Court alleviated this problem in *Duckworth v. Eagan*,[135] in which a suspect was given the following warnings:

> You have a right to talk to a lawyer for advice before we ask you any questions, and to have him with you during questioning.

> We have no way of giving you a lawyer, but one will be appointed for you, if you wish, if and when you go to court.

A five-person majority approved the warning, reasoning that if police cannot provide appointed counsel, "*Miranda* requires only that the police not question a suspect unless he waives his right to counsel."

---

134. 453 U.S. 355 (1981).

135. 492 U.S. 195 (1989).

PROBLEM 8–23

After being arrested for possession of cocaine with intent to distribute, Sam Noti was given the following verbal warning:

> Sam, you have the right to remain silent, the right to the services of an attorney before questioning. If you desire an attorney, and cannot afford one, an attorney will be appointed by the Court with no charge to you. Any statement you do make can and will be used against you in a court of law. Do you understand each of these rights?

Noti then made an incriminating statement (to the effect that the cocaine was indeed his), which the government seeks to use against him at trial.

Noti contends that the statement should be suppressed because the warning was defective. Specifically, he argues that the arresting officer failed to inform him of his right to counsel during questioning as well as before questioning.

Question: Should Noti's statement be suppressed?

PROBLEM 8–24

Austin Winkler was arrested for murder. Following his arrest, Officer Forbin read him the following warning:

> You have the right to remain silent. Anything you say can and will be used against you in a court of law. You have the right to an attorney and to have the attorney present while you are being questioned if you want one. And if you can't afford one the court will appoint one to represent you before any proceedings free of charge.

Forbin then asked Winkler if he would discuss the matter "without the presence of your lawyer now." Winkler responded, "I know an attorney. If I feel at any point—I'll stop answering questions." During questioning, Winkler made an incriminating statement that the government wishes to use against him. Winkler seeks to suppress the statement. He argues that the *Miranda* warning that Forbin gave was inadequate because it could be interpreted to mean that an indigent is entitled to appointed counsel for court "proceedings" but not for police questioning. Since the warning was inadequate, the statement was taken in violation of his *Miranda* rights and thus inadmissible.

Question: Should the trial court grant Winkler's motion to suppress?

F. WAIVER OF RIGHTS VERSUS INVOCATION OF RIGHTS

1. COMPONENTS OF A VALID WAIVER

A suspect's statement, made during custodial interrogation, cannot be admitted without a showing (a) that s/he was given *Miranda* warnings; (b) that s/he waived *Miranda* rights in fact; and (c) that the waiver was effective. A great deal of court time is consumed in determining whether *Miranda* rights have been effectively waived in particular circumstances. In

Miranda, the Supreme Court anticipated this problem and devoted a substantial portion of its opinion to a discussion of waiver:

... The defendant may waive effectuation of [his] rights, provided the waiver is made voluntarily, knowingly and intelligently. If, however, he indicates in any manner and at any stage of the process that he wishes to consult with an attorney before speaking there can be no questioning. Likewise, if the individual is alone and indicates in any manner that he does not wish to be interrogated, the police may not question him. The mere fact that he may have answered some questions or volunteered some statements on his own does not deprive him of the right to refrain from answering any further inquiries until he has consulted with an attorney and thereafter consents to be questioned. ...

[A] heavy burden rests on the government to demonstrate that the defendant knowingly and intelligently waived his privilege against self-incrimination and his right to retained or appointed counsel. This Court has always set high standards of proof for the waiver of constitutional rights, *Johnson v. Zerbst*, 304 U.S. 458 (1938), and we reassert these standards as applied to in custody interrogation. Since the State is responsible for establishing the isolated circumstances under which the interrogation takes place and has the only means of making available corroborated evidence of warnings given during incommunicado interrogation, the burden is rightly on its shoulders.

An express statement that the individual is willing to make a statement and does not want an attorney followed closely by a statement could constitute a waiver. But a valid waiver will not be presumed simply from the silence of the accused after warnings are given or simply from the fact that a confession was in fact eventually obtained. ... The record must show, or there must be an allegation and evidence which show, that an accused was offered counsel but intelligently and understandingly rejected the offer. Anything less is not waiver. Moreover, where in-custody interrogation is involved, there is no room for the contention that the privilege is waived if the individual answers some questions or gives some information on his own prior to invoking his right to remain silent when interrogated.

Whatever the testimony of the authorities as to waiver of rights by an accused, the fact of lengthy interrogation or incommunicado incarceration before a statement is made is strong evidence that the accused did not validly waive his rights. In these circumstances the fact that the individual eventually made a statement is consistent with the conclusion that the compelling influence of the interrogation finally forced him to do so. It is inconsistent with any notion of a voluntary relinquishment of the privilege. Moreover, any evidence that the accused was threatened, tricked, or cajoled into a waiver will, of course, show that the defendant did not voluntarily waive his privilege. The requirement of warnings and waiver of rights is a fundamental with respect to the Fifth amendment privilege and not simply a preliminary ritual to existing methods of interrogation.

Despite the Court's emphasis on the prosecution's "heavy burden" of persuasion with regard to waiver, it later held that the prosecution "need prove waiver only by a preponderance of the evidence."[136] The Court reasoned that since the voluntariness of a confession can be established by a mere preponderance, "then a waiver of the auxiliary protections established in *Miranda* should require no higher burden of proof."

a. Waiver in Fact

What of the defendant who immediately makes a statement after having been given *Miranda* warnings? Is the fact of the statement a sufficient indication that the suspect made a voluntary, knowing, and intelligent waiver? The Court in *Miranda* said that "a valid waiver will not be presumed simply from the silence of the accused after warnings are given or simply from the fact that a confession was in fact eventually obtained." However, these words do not mean that an express verbal waiver is always required. For example, in *North Carolina v. Butler*,[137] the Court held that an express statement of waiver was not required. Butler had been arrested following an armed robbery. The FBI agents who arrested him determined that he had "an 11th grade education and was literate." He was given an "Advice of Rights" form to read and, when asked if he understood those rights, stated that he did. He refused, however, to sign the waiver at the bottom of the form, stating "I will talk to you but I am not signing any form." He then made damaging statements. In upholding the admission of those statements the Court emphasized that the question of waiver "is not one of form, but rather whether the defendant in fact knowingly and voluntarily waived" his *Miranda* rights. At least in some cases, the Court went on, "waiver can be clearly inferred from the actions and words of the person interrogated." Thus, a per se rule requiring an express waiver is inappropriate.

b. Voluntary

The substance of the waiver analysis has two parts: first, the waiver must have been voluntary, and second, it must have been knowingly and intelligently made. The first prong is similar to voluntariness in confession cases: considering the totality of the circumstances, the court must find that the waiver was a product of a free and deliberate choice.[138] Bear in mind that although the analysis mirrors the overall question of the voluntariness of the confession, certain facts may be especially important to the issue of the voluntariness of the waiver. For example, a long period of time between the rendering of *Miranda* warnings and the waiver might suggest

---

136. Connelly, 479 U.S. at 168.

137. 441 U.S. 369 (1979).

138. Connelly, 479 U.S. at 170; Moran v. Burbine, 475 U.S. 412, 421 (1986).

that the waiver was derived by overcoming the suspect's will to invoke his *Miranda* rights.

c. Knowing and Intelligent

The more interesting issue frequently is whether the waiver was knowing and intelligent. Courts must decide this issue based on the "particular facts and circumstances surrounding th[e] case, including the background, experience, and conduct of the accused."[139] Thus, the analysis focuses on the suspect's ability to understand the warnings and the consequences of speaking, although the Supreme Court has indicated that this analysis is not to be made too stringently. In *Connecticut v. Barrett*,[140] for example, defendant Barrett had been advised of his *Miranda* rights and signed a card stating that he understood those rights. Barrett then made verbal admissions to having committed sexual assault, although he insisted that he would not give a written statement unless his attorney was present. The Court found the "illogical" nature of this decision unimportant to the waiver analysis and refused to deem it an indication that Barrett had failed to understand that verbal statements could (and would) be just as damaging as written statements. It remarked, "we have never embraced the theory that a defendant's ignorance of the full consequences of his decisions vitiates their voluntariness."

Barrett is instructive for another purpose: it illustrates that a waiver can be limited in scope. Barrett obviously invoked his right to counsel for purposes of making a written statement, but he waived that right, and his right to remain silent, as to verbal admissions. So long as police officers honored the scope of his waiver, his statements were admissible.

PROBLEM 8–25

In the Brunell case in Chapter 1, Terri Marvoal made a statement to federal officials who visited her home, after they warned her that she would face serious charges if she did not cooperate.

Question: Assuming that the officials had given her *Miranda* warnings as well, does the fact that she responded with a statement mean that she waived her *Miranda* rights? Could her statement be viewed as an implied waiver?

PROBLEM 8–26

Detectives Simpson and Cleaver arrested Vance Terronova in his apartment on suspicion of murdering his stepfather, Gene. While in Terronova's apartment, Simpson had Terronova read aloud from a standard *Miranda* form. Simpson then asked if he understood what he had read. Terronova said, "Yeah. It means I'm under arrest." Simpson responded

---

139. North Carolina v. Butler, 441 U.S. 369, 374–75 (1979).

140. 479 U.S. 523 (1987).

that what Terronova had read meant that he had the right to an attorney and the right to remain silent. At no point did the detectives ask Terronova if he wished to waive those rights.

Cleaver told Terronova that his stepfather had died and asked him where he had been that evening. Terronova stated that he had been with friends. Meanwhile, other officers were sweeping the premises for weapons and people. Terronova objected to what he considered to be a warrantless search of his home. As the search and questioning continued, Terronova stated that he "didn't shoot Gene," intending to exculpate himself. Terronova quickly realized that he had just incriminated himself because the police had never mentioned a shooting. He then asked for an attorney and all questioning stopped at that point.

Terronova is described as an articulate, college-educated adult. He does not claim any lack of understanding of his *Miranda* rights, nor does he claim that he expressly refused to waive his rights. Nevertheless, he contends in a motion to suppress his statement that he did not waive his *Miranda* rights by responding to Cleaver's questions. Since Defendant's *Miranda* rights were not waived, but were in full effect at the time that he made the statement that he "didn't shoot Gene," Defendant argues that the statement should be excluded from evidence.

The state argues that the statement is admissible because at the time that Terronova made the incriminating statement he had yet to express any desire to remain silent. The fact that he had offered an alibi indicated a willingness to talk, thereby implicitly waiving his right to silence. Since he had waived his *Miranda* rights at the time of the statement in question, the statement is admissible.

Question: How should the trial court rule on the motion to suppress?

PROBLEM 8–27

Pursuant to a valid search warrant, DEA agents raided Elroy Teller's house. During the search they discovered Teller and another individual, Jane Michaels. The search also yielded:

- $30,000 in cash ($10,000 of which had previously been marked and used to make an undercover heroin buy);
- a hand scale;
- notes containing references to cocaine prices as well as the name Darlene Silver, a known street-level heroin distributor; and
- various items that could be used to process or distribute cocaine.

The search did not, however, uncover any illegal narcotics.

Teller and Michaels were arrested, given *Miranda* warnings, and transported in separate vehicles to the Marshall's office. On the car ride to the Marshall's office, DEA Agent Brown explained to Michaels the potential benefits of her opportunity to cooperate with the government, and asked Michaels some questions about the drug operation. Michaels remained silent for five to ten minutes, making no response to Brown's questions. Eventually, however, she responded to Brown's inquiries, stating "I didn't sell any heroin to Darlene."

Question: Should Michael's statement be suppressed?

2.   INVOCATION AND ITS CONSEQUENCES

a.   *Invocation in Fact*

Suspects do sometimes decide to invoke their *Miranda* rights—that is, to remain silent or to ask for the presence of counsel during questioning. The invocation of these rights has consequences to further questioning by police, as we will see. But first we must determine what constitutes an adequate invocation of rights. Obviously, a suspect who says, "I hereby invoke my right to remain silent," has effectively invoked that right. And a suspect who says, "I announce that I will not answer questions without counsel present," has successfully invoked the *Miranda* right to counsel. On the other hand, a suspect who says nothing—literally—has not invoked his or her *Miranda* rights. But what of the defendant who makes an ambiguous statement that might or might not indicate a desire for silence or for counsel? Should we be so solicitous of *Miranda* rights as to make effective even an ambiguous statement, or should we the burden on suspects to make their wishes perfectly clear.

In *Davis v. United States*, the Supreme Court opted to put the burden of clarity on suspects, at least in the context in which a suspect argues that he had invoked his *Miranda* right to counsel.[141] Davis had been arrested on suspicion of beating a sailor to death with a pool cue. Navy investigators read him his *Miranda* rights and obtained from Davis a signed waiver of those rights. Davis agreed to speak with the investigators, but about an hour into the interrogation said, "Maybe I should talk to a lawyer." The investigators then stopped their questioning and attempted to clarify whether Davis wished to consult an attorney. Davis responded that he did not wish to speak with a lawyer and made incriminating statements. About an hour later, Davis stated that he thought he wanted a lawyer before saying more. At his murder trial, the court admitted the statements made between Davis's first, tentative expression of interest in consulting counsel and his ultimate statement that he wanted a lawyer. The Supreme Court agreed that the statements were properly admitted. Justice O'Connor, writing for a five-member majority, stated that requiring questioning to cease upon ambiguous statements would establish unreasonable obstacles to legitimate police investigative activity. Instead, the majority determined, an appropriate balance is struck by requiring a suspect to "articulate his desire to have counsel present sufficiently clearly that a reasonable police officer in the circumstances would understand the statement to be a request for an attorney."

---

141.   512 U.S. 452 (1994).

Four concurring justices disagreed with the Court's rule, arguing that it created too great a risk that Fifth Amendment safeguards would be meaningless in the "real world." Suspects who make statements they believe to express their desire for counsel might be deterred from reiterating that desire if law enforcement officials are permitted to brush off their remarks and continue questioning. The concurring justices favored a rule that would require police to cease questioning and ask questions that would clarify whether the suspect wishes to consult with counsel before being interrogated further.

b. Resumption of Questioning After Invocation of Rights

(1) THE RIGHT TO REMAIN SILENT

A special kind of problem occurs when a suspect refuses to waive his *Miranda* rights—in other words, invokes the rights listed in *Miranda*—but later makes incriminating statements. The admissibility of those statements depends on several factors, including the specific right that the suspect invoked, the conduct of the police, and whether the incriminating statements concern the offense for which the suspect invoked his rights.

As a general rule of thumb, even after a defendant invokes his Fifth Amendment right to remain silent, police may question him with respect to another offense, provided that they "scrupulously honor" his original decision to remain silent. In *Michigan v. Mosley*,[142] a detective arrested Mosley in connection with some robberies and gave him appropriate *Miranda* rights. Mosley refused to discuss the robberies and was left alone. Two hours later, a different detective again gave him *Miranda* warnings and questioned him about an unrelated murder. Mosley then made incriminating statements about the murder. The Supreme Court held that these statements were not obtained in violation of *Miranda*. The Court reasoned that the main purposes of *Miranda* were to ensure that defendants will be informed of their right to remain silent and that police will scrupulously honor the exercise of that right, so as to dispel the inherently coercive atmosphere present during custodial interrogations.

In an effort to make a "reasonable and faithful" interpretation of *Miranda*, the Court held that "the admissibility of statements obtained after the person in custody has decided to remain silent depends under *Miranda* on whether his right to cut off questioning was scrupulously honored." Because Mosely was advised of his *Miranda* rights, immediately left alone when he invoked his right to remain silent, questioned by a different detective only after having been reminded of his right to remain silent and having been given an opportunity to exercise that right, and asked only about an unrelated crime, the subsequent questioning could not be said to have undercut Mosley's previous decision not to speak. Thus, the statements regarding the murder were not rendered inadmissible by the fact that Mosley had invoked his right to remain silent during a previous interrogation on another offense. It is unclear under what other circum-

---

142. 423 U.S. 96 (1975).

stances, if any, the Court will hold that subsequent questioning by the police "scrupulously honored" the right to remain silent.

(II) The Right to Counsel

While *Michigan v. Mosley* established a rule permitting further interrogation in some circumstances following a suspect's assertion of the right to remain silent, little such flexibility exists after the suspect invokes the right to consult with an attorney. Under the bright-line rule of *Edwards v. Arizona*,[143] all government questioning must cease once a suspect exercises the *Miranda* right to consult with an attorney. In *Edwards*, police gave the defendant his *Miranda* rights and left him alone after he stated that he wanted to speak with an attorney. The next morning the officers re-approached Edwards in his jail cell and read him his *Miranda* rights again. Edwards said he was willing to talk and made incriminating statements that he subsequently sought to suppress. The Court held that the later questioning violated Edward's right to the assistance of counsel. The Court set forth the following rule:

> [A]lthough we have held that after initially being advised of his *Miranda* rights, the accused may himself validly waive his rights and respond to interrogation, the Court has strongly indicated that additional safeguards are necessary when the accused asks for counsel; and we now hold that when an accused has invoked his right to have counsel present during custodial interrogation, a valid waiver of that right cannot be established by showing only that he responded to further police-initiated custodial interrogation even if he has been advised of his rights. We further hold that an accused, such as Edwards, having expressed his desire to deal with the police only through counsel, is not subject to further interrogation by the authorities until counsel has been made available to him, unless the accused himself initiates further communication, exchanges, or conversations with the police.

This right to counsel, first announced in *Miranda* and bolstered in *Edwards*, bears some special mention. The Court had long struggled with the obvious fact that providing counsel during police questioning would reduce inherently coercive police activity. Nevertheless, the language of the Fifth Amendment does not contain any reference to such a right. The Court found some assistance in the Sixth Amendment right to counsel "in all criminal prosecutions," which it interpreted, as we will see below, to preclude intrusive police activity without an attorney at any stage *after* indictment. In *Miranda*, the Court took the next step: it created a right to counsel that would apply even *before* the initiation of criminal proceedings. Under *Miranda*, then, a suspect is "protected by the prophylaxis of having an attorney present to counteract the inherent pressures of custodial interrogation, which arise from the fact of such interrogation and exist

---

143. 451 U.S. 477 (1981).

regardless of the number of crimes under investigation or whether those crimes have resulted in formal charges.''[144]

This right is sometimes referred to as the *''Miranda* right to counsel,'' and it has some special aspects of its own. Unlike a defendant's Sixth Amendment right to the assistance of counsel, the *Miranda* right to counsel is not ''offense-specific''—that is, it is not limited to the charge for which the suspect was arrested. Instead, it is ''custody-specific''—it extends throughout the entire ''incident of custody,'' until the suspect is released. In other words, incriminating statements obtained as a result of custodial questioning after a defendant has invoked the *Miranda* right to counsel will be inadmissible even if the questioning and statements relate to a different crime, so long as the invocation of rights and the subsequent interrogation take place within the same custodial incident. This is because the Court presumes that a defendant who invokes his *Miranda* right to counsel considers himself at that time unable to deal with the pressures of custodial interrogation without legal assistance. This presumption does not disappear just because officials have approached the suspect about a separate investigation, but it does disappear once custody has terminated.

(III) RESUMPTION OF QUESTIONING

Obviously, the above rules mean that police must be very careful once a suspect has invoked the right to silence or to counsel, because resumption of questioning can result in exclusion of a subsequent statement. But not all subsequent conversations are the result of a resumption of questioning. Some may have been initiated by the suspect, and these can ''open the door'' to further police questioning. The Court has warned police, however, that not all statements or inquiries made by a defendant to an officer should be considered an initiation of further discussion: there are some inquiries, such as a request for a drink of water or a request to use a telephone, that are so routine that they cannot be fairly said to represent a desire on the part of an accused to open up a more generalized discussion relating directly or indirectly to the investigation. Such inquiries or statements, by either an accused or a police officer, relating to routine incidents of the custodial relationship, will not generally ''initiate'' a conversation in the sense which that word was used in *Edwards*. On the other hand, when a defendant's statements or inquiries can reasonably be interpreted as evincing ''a willingness and a desire for a generalized discussion about the investigation'' at hand, an officer may reinitiate questioning.

An example of the latter is found in *Oregon v. Bradshaw*.[145] Bradshaw had been arrested and booked following a car wreck in which a person was killed. The police read Bradshaw his *Miranda* rights and later rearrested him for furnishing liquor to the minor who was killed in the car wreck. After that set of warnings, Bradshaw asked for a lawyer. As he arrived at the jail, he asked a police officer, ''Well, what is going to happen to me

---

144.   Arizona v. Roberson, 486 U.S. 675, 685 (1988).

145.   462 U.S. 1039, 1045 (1983).

now?'' The officer responded that he did not have to talk, that the officer was not attempting to talk with him, and that if he wanted to talk it had to be of his own free will. Bradshaw responded that he "knew" all of this and engaged in an incriminating conversation. The Court held that the defendant's inquiry, "Well, what is going to happen to me now?," initiated further conversation and that *Edwards* did not bar the officer from questioning Bradshaw after that point.

Does this mean that a defendant's initiation of a conversation with an officer automatically constitutes a waiver of that defendant's *Miranda* rights? According to *Bradshaw*, the answer is no. As we discussed above, the prosecution must prove that in fact the defendant made a waiver of *Miranda* rights. The defendant's initiation of a conversation, after first invoking his rights, does not constitute a waiver "per se," although it would seem to be an important factor. Thus, once a defendant initiates a conversation, and removes the bar of *Edwards*, officers must obtain a valid waiver of *Miranda* rights before the defendant's statements will be considered admissible.

Up until very recently, invocation of *Miranda* by incarcerated criminal suspects posed a unique problem for officers who would like to interrogate these individuals regarding other criminal acts. Given the protections afforded by *Edwards*, must police wait indefinitely for the incarcerated individuals to initiate a conversation and waive their *Miranda* rights before attempting interrogation anew? In *Maryland v. Shatzer*,[146] the Court considered whether the return of an incarcerated suspect to the general prison population qualifies as a break in *Miranda* custody that ends the *Edwards* presumption of involuntariness. Shatzer, an incarcerated inmate serving a prison sentence on an unrelated crime, invoked his *Miranda* rights and requested an attorney when a detective attempted a 2003 interview regarding suspected sexual abuse of Shatzer's three-year-old son. The detective ultimately terminated the interview and closed the case. In 2006, a different detective conducted a follow-up investigation with Shatzer regarding the same suspected sexual abuse. Armed with new information and details from Shatzer's son, the new detective interrogated the still-incarcerated Shatzer, who waived his *Miranda* rights and submitted to interrogation. Five days later and after being informed by the police that he had failed a polygraph test, Shatzer, again, waived his *Miranda* rights and inculpated himself regarding the suspected sexual abuse. The trial court denied Shatzer's motion to suppress his inculpatory 2006 statements, reasoning that *Edwards* did not apply, given the nearly three year break between the 2003 attempts and 2006 interrogations. Shatzer was convicted of sexual child abuse. Subsequently, the Court of Appeals of Maryland reversed and remanded, holding that passage of time alone is insufficient to end the protections *Edwards* affords. The appellate court also noted that to the extent a "break-in-custody exception" to *Edwards* existed, Shatzer's return to jail did not constitute a break in custody.[147]

---

146. 130 S.Ct. 1213 (2010).

147. *Id*. at **4-8 (citations omitted).

In a 7-2 decision, the Supreme Court reversed.[148] Writing for the majority, Justice Scalia held that *Edwards* does not mandate suppression of Shatzer's 2006 statements made after "a break in *Miranda* custody lasting more than two weeks between the first and second attempts at interrogation."[149] Scalia characterized the *Edwards* rule as "judicially prescribed prophylaxis," not "a constitutional mandate," and, therefore, "applies only when its benefits outweigh its costs."[150] On these facts, the cost of the *Edwards* rule outweighed its benefits, as the " 'inherently compelling pressures' of custodial interrogation" ended when Shatzer returned to "his normal life" in jail. Accordingly, Shatzer's continued incarceration between the 2003 attempts and 2006 custodial interrogations constituted a break in *Miranda* custody, as "lawful imprisonment imposed upon conviction of a crime does not create the coercive pressures identified in *Miranda*." The majority also announced a numerical rule to the *Edwards* presumption of involuntariness: fourteen days. According to the majority, fourteen days is enough to dissipate custodial interrogation's coercive effects and "provides plenty of time for the suspect to get reacclimated to his normal life, to consult with friends and counsel, and to shake off any residual coercive effects of his prior custody."[151]

Justice Thomas, concurring in part and in judgment, took issue with both the presumption of involuntariness recognized in *Edwards*, as well as the newly announced, "*ipse dixit*," and "arbitrary" fourteen day application of *Edwards* "to interrogations that occur after custody ends."[152] Justice Stevens also concurred in the judgment, given the nearly three-year gap between interrogations. However, Stevens was troubled by the Court's "cost-benefit" analysis that was "insufficiently sensitive to the concerns that motivated the *Edwards* line of cases." Specifically, Justice Stevens deemed the new numerical rule "overconfident:"

> A prisoner's freedom is severely limited, and his entire life remains subject to government control. Such an environment is not conducive to "shak[ing] off any residual coercive effects of his prior custody." . . . Nor can a prisoner easily "seek advice from an attorney, family members, and friends," [] especially not within 14 days; prisoners are frequently subject to restrictions on communications. Nor, in most cases, can he live comfortably knowing that he cannot be badgered by police; prison is not like a normal situation in which a suspect "is in control, and need only shut his door or walk away to avoid police badgering." *Montejo* v. *Louisiana*, 556 U.S. ___, ___ (2009) (slip op., at 16). Indeed, for a person whose every move is controlled by the State, it is likely that "his sense of dependence on, and trust in, counsel as the

---

148.   Justices Stevens and Thomas dissented in the Court's opinion. However, both concurred in its judgment.

149.   Shatzer, 130 S.Ct. 1213 at **32 (citations omitted).

150.   *Id*. at **12-13 (citations omitted).

151.   *Id*. at **21.

152.   *Id*. at **34-35 (Thomas, J., concurring in part and in judgment).

guardian of his interests in dealing with government officials intensified." *United States* v. *Green*, 592 A.2d 985, 989 (D.C. 1991); cf. *Minnick*, 498 U.S., at 153 (explaining that coercive pressures "may increase as custody is prolonged"). The Court ignores these realities of prison, and instead rests its argument on the supposition that a prisoner's "detention . . . is relatively disconnected from their prior unwillingness to cooperate in an investigation." . . . But that is not necessarily the case. Prisoners are uniquely vulnerable to the officials who control every aspect of their lives; prison guards may not look kindly upon a prisoner who refuses to cooperate with police. And cooperation frequently is relevant to whether the prisoner can obtain parole. See, *e.g.*, Code of Md. Regs., tit. 12, § 08.01.18(A)(3) (2008). Moreover, even if it is true as a factual matter that a prisoner's fate is not controlled by the police who come to interrogate him, how is the prisoner supposed to know that? As the Court itself admits, compulsion is likely when a suspect's "captors appear to control [his]fate," . . . But when a guard informs a suspect that he must go speak with police, it will "appear" to the prisoner that the guard and police are not independent. "Questioning by captors, who *appear* to control the suspect's fate, may create mutually reinforcing pressures that the Court has assumed will weaken the suspect's will." *Illinois* v. *Perkins*, 496 U.S. 292, 297 (1990) (emphasis added).[153]

Question: Why 14 days? When did Justice Scalia become "so legislative?"[154] One Supreme Court blogger opines:

If you're wondering how Justice Scalia could end up writing an opinion that sounds so legislative—picking 14 days out of thin air—you need to know Justice Scalia's history with *Miranda*. Justice Scalia intensely dislikes the entire line of *Miranda* cases. The Court has sometimes referred to the *Miranda* rules as "prophylactic." That is, they are rules created to protect the Constitution, and enforced as constitutional law, but not necessarily constitutional rules themselves. In his dissent in *Dickerson* v. *United States*, Justice Scalia argued that this entire approach was illegitimate. He would overthrow the entire line of cases as an illegitimate power grab.

It's not clear how many Justices continue to see *Miranda* as just "prophylactic" after *Dickerson*. But Justice Scalia still does. And he has long had a special dislike for the *Edwards* rule in particular.[155]

PROBLEM 8–28

John Scott was arrested on a charge of stealing an automobile. Before being given his *Miranda* warnings he said, "I don't want to talk." He was nevertheless then *Mirandized* and repeated, "I don't want to talk."

---

153. *Id.* at *50-52 (Stevens, J., concurring in judgment).

154. Orin Kerr, *"Does the Constitution Have a 14-Day Clause?,"* SCOTUSBlog.com, (Feb. 25, 2010), located at http://www.scotusblog.com/2010/02/does-constitutionthe--have-a-14-day-clause/.

155. *Id.*

He is brought to a cell and left alone for over three hours. When the police returned, they brought a Big Mac and fries for Scott from McDonald's, a meal Scott had earlier identified as his favorite. Scott said, "I don't want to talk right now, I'm hungry." The police gave Scott some cigarettes to smoke and left him alone for another two hours.

New police officers now came to the cell, however, and asked Scott, "Are you full and have you had plenty of smokes?" He said, "Yes, you guys are treating me fine." Detective Salmon then *Mirandized* Scott; Scott said he understood the warnings. Detective Salmon then said, "Look, we're not here to talk about the car theft. Rita Moran just picked your photo. She says you're the one who raped her last Friday night." Detective Salmon was lying. They had not had time to do a photo-spread (this was Scott's first arrest), but Salmon played a hunch. "If you don't want to talk to us, you don't have to, as you know, but we would like to get your side of the story."

Scott smiled and said, "Look, Detective, I'm very tired, but this is wrong. You have to believe me. I just took the car for a joyride because I was jealous of all my friends having cars, and I can't afford one. I was going to return it. But grabbing a car and rape are two different things. She wanted it, she said so, and she got scared when my condom broke, and now she's crying rape."

QUESTIONS

1. What are the chances of defense counsel's succeeding on the motion to suppress the confession in the car theft case? Are the chances for success any different in a motion to suppress the confession in the rape case?

2. If you are the prosecutor, what witnesses would you call to the stand at the suppression hearing, and what questions would you ask them?

PROBLEM 8–29

Charles Roe was arrested on an arson charge. A search incident to arrest revealed a blood-stained gun. He was *Mirandized* but not questioned. One officer recalls a faint smell of alcohol and Roe's having bloodshot eyes but another officer does not remember that being the case. Roe was re-*Mirandized* at the station, questioned, and denied participating in the offense. He was taken to a jail cell about 3 a.m. Six hours later, at 9 a.m., Roe was questioned by a new officer, Detective Bland. Roe was first re-*Mirandized*, and he said, "I want to see an attorney." Detective Bland responded:

If you want an attorney, you'll get one right away. But we have a strong case against you, and you'll almost certainly be convicted and sentenced to a minimum of four years in prison. Your cohort, Smelser, told us you planned the fire to get some insurance money for a friend of yours who owned the place and Smelser was just the lookout. We've got a signed written statement from him. If we get the lawyers involved, you won't be cooperating, so it's hard to believe you'll get the minimum. But that's your choice. You have an absolute right to counsel, and we're going to get you that representation right now. We can't make any promises, anyway, but, like I said, this means it won't look too good at sentencing in showing you cooperated.

But the Detective refused to produce the statement when Roe asked for it. Roe finally confessed.

A criminal complaint against Roe on the arson charge was filed against Roe by 5 p.m. that day. At 5:40 p.m., another Detective, Sam Hill, appeared in Roe's cell, *Mirandized* him, and said he wanted to question Roe about an armed robbery and assault. Hill told Roe that the victim had been pistol-whipped, and the blood on the gun found on Roe at his arrest on the arson charge matched the victim's. Roe promptly confessed.

QUESTIONS

1. What is the likelihood of a motion to suppress Roe's confession to the arson succeeding? Any difference in the likelihood of suppressing his confession to the robbery?

2. Assume the prosecutor has carefully monitored and approved the behavior of each of the detectives involved, keeping in frequent phone contact on the progress of the investigation. Would such behavior be ethical? Wise?

G. Scope of the Miranda Exclusionary Rule

1. FRUIT OF THE POISONOUS TREE

Prior to its confirmation that *Miranda* is constitutionally based, the Supreme Court characterized *Miranda* as a mere prophylactic rule and limited the breadth of the *Miranda* exclusionary rule. Most importantly, in *Oregon v. Elstad*, it limited the rule to the exact statements or evidence obtained as a direct result of a *Miranda* violation.[156] As a result of the *Elstad* rule, the indirect "fruit" of such a violation is not automatically excluded. In *Elstad*, a suspect made an incriminating statement during custodial interrogation before police officers gave him the required *Miranda* warnings. The statement was inadmissible, but the police failed to relate this information to the suspect. Later, police read the suspect his *Miranda* rights, and he made another confession. If the fruit-of-the-poisonous tree doctrine were applicable, the latter confession arguably would be an inadmissible "fruit" of the *Miranda*-violative statement, which had caused the suspect to believe that the "cat was out of the bag." But in her majority opinion, Justice O'Connor held that the second statement could be admitted, so long as the first was voluntary. According to Justice O'Connor, "the dictates of *Miranda* and the goals of the Fifth Amendment proscription against use of compelled testimony are fully satisfied in the circum-

---

156. 470 U.S. 298, 308–09 (1985).

stances of this case by barring use of the unwarned statement in the case in chief. No further purpose is served by imputing 'taint' to subsequent statements obtained pursuant to a voluntary and knowing waiver.''

The implicit reasoning of Justice O'Connor's opinion in *Elstad* seems to be this: if *Miranda* is not itself a constitutional right, but merely a rule designed to protect constitutional rights, then non-constitutional *Miranda* violations do not need the same degree of protection as do "true" constitutional violations. The minimal additional deterrent value that a fruits analysis would have in protecting against "true" constitutional violations is just not worth the further cost—in the form of excluding highly probative evidence—that a fruits analysis would impose. For apparently similar reasons, if police acquire the name of a potential witness from a defendant in the course of a *Miranda*-violative statement, the testimony of that witness will not necessarily be excluded even though the defendant's statements will be excluded.[157] Are you confident that *Elstad* will survive *Dickerson*? Why or why not?

The Court put speculation about *Oregon v. Elstad* to rest in *United States v. Patane*[158] and *Missouri v. Seibert*,[159] in which it affirmed that the fruit of the poisonous tree doctrine does not apply to police actions that violate *Miranda* but not "core" Fifth Amendment protections. *Patane* involved an unwarned confession followed by the discovery of physical evidence; *Seibert* a successive interrogation substantially similar to *Elstad*. Neither case produced a majority opinion, although majorities were reached on a few propositions.

In *Patane*, the Court, although fractured, mustered a bare majority for the rule that physical evidence obtained from an unwarned confession need not be excluded. The facts in question were these: Samuel Patane violated a restraining order by attempting to contact his ex-girlfriend, and officers who arrested him also wished to question him about his possible illegal possession of a firearm. After his arrest, the officers attempted to give him *Miranda* warnings, but he stated that he knew his rights and they did not complete the warnings. Patane then made inculpatory statements about the firearm, including instructions about where to find it, and was charged with unlawful possession. The government conceded the inadmissibility of his statements but contended that the firearm itself should be admitted. The United States Court of Appeals for the Tenth Circuit rejected the government's position, holding that *Elstad* did not survive *Dickerson*. Applying the fruit of the poisonous tree doctrine, that court held that the firearm should have been excluded.

But the Tenth Circuit's decision was short-lived. In the Supreme Court, five justices agreed that the trial court need not have excluded the firearm. There was no majority, however, as to the rule's rationale. A plurality (comprised of Justice Thomas, who wrote the plurality opinion,

---

157.   Michigan v. Tucker, 417 U.S. 433 (1974).

158.   542 U.S. 630 (2004).

159.   542 U.S. 600 (2004).

Chief Justice Rehnquist, and Justice Scalia) believed that there had been no constitutional violation or even a violation of the *Miranda* rule. Justice Thomas stated that the "core protection afforded by the Self–Incrimination Clause is a prohibition on compelling a criminal defendant to testify against himself at trial." This core protection "cannot be violated by the introduction of nontestimonial evidence obtained as a result of voluntary statements." The plurality also stated that "a mere failure to give *Miranda* warnings does not, by itself, violate a suspect's constitutional rights or even the *Miranda* rule," because violations of the right and the rule take place only when unwarned statements are admitted at trial. Further, "because police cannot violate the Self–Incrimination Clause by taking unwarned though voluntary statements, an exclusionary rule cannot be justified by reference to a deterrence effect on law enforcement" because there is nothing to deter.[160]

The remaining two justices who supported the Court's judgment—Justices Kennedy and O'Connor—urged narrower grounds similar to those underlying the *Elstad* ruling. Justice Kennedy based their concurrence on a "recognition that the concerns underlying [the *Miranda* rule] must be accommodated to other objectives of the criminal justice system"—i.e., truth-seeking. Said Justice Kennedy, "[i]n light of the important probative value of reliable physical evidence, it is doubtful that exclusion can be justified by a deterrence rationale." But he stated that it was unnecessary to decide whether there indeed was "nothing to deter," as the plurality insisted, or whether the failure to give *Miranda* warnings constituted a *Miranda* violation.[161]

Four justices dissented, expressing concerns about law enforcement incentives created by the rule. Said Justice Souter, "[t]here is no way to read this case except as an unjustifiable invitation to law enforcement officers to flout *Miranda* warnings when there may be physical evidence to be gained."[162] In a separate dissent Justice Breyer said that he would create a rule requiring exclusion of physical evidence obtained as a result of unwarned questioning "unless the failure to provide *Miranda* warnings was in good faith."[163]

Justice Breyer's "good faith" rule was derived from one he first proposed in *Seibert*. In that case, similar to *Elstad*, police had first obtained an unwarned confession and then, after giving *Miranda* warnings, "cover[ed] the same ground a second time."[164] But in a stunning contrast to *Elstad*, in which the police apparently believed that the suspect was not in custody during the first interrogation, the successive interrogation technique in *Seibert* was intentional—the result of a "police protocol" pursuant to which the interrogating officer had been taught to "question first, then

---

160.   *Patane*, 542 U.S. at 642 (plurality opinion of Thomas, J.).

161.   *Id.* at 645 (Kennedy, J., concurring).

162.   *Id.* at 647 (Souter, J., dissenting).

163.   *Id.* at 647 (Breyer, J., dissenting).

164.   *Seibert*, 542 U.S. at 604 (Souter, J., plurality opinion).

give the warnings, and then repeat the question 'until I get the answer that she's already provided once.' "[165] This "question-first" technique, said Justice Souter writing for a four-justice plurality, is designed to undermine the effectiveness of *Miranda* and should be tested on that basis:

> ... [W]hen *Miranda* warnings are inserted in the midst of coordinated and continuing interrogation, they are likely to mislead and deprive a defendant of knowledge essential to his ability to understand the nature of his rights and the consequences of abandoning them. By the same token, it would ordinarily be unrealistic to treat two spates of integrated and proximately conducted questioning as independent interrogations subject to independent evaluation simply because *Miranda* warnings formally punctuate them in the middle.

According to the plurality, the "question-first" technique used on Seibert thwarted *Miranda's* effectiveness and his post-warning statements, induced through use of that technique, had to be excluded. The plurality offered this explanation for how courts in future cases can distinguish between the permissible *Elstad* situation and the prohibited *Seibert* one:

> ... The inquiry is simply whether the warnings reasonably convey to a suspect his rights as required by *Miranda*. The threshold issue when interrogators question first and warn later is thus whether it would be reasonable to find that in these circumstances the warnings could function "effectively" as *Miranda* requires. Could the warnings effectively advise the suspect that he had a real choice about giving an admissible statement at that juncture? Could they reasonably convey that he could choose to stop talking even if he had talked earlier? For unless the warnings could place a suspect who has just been interrogated in a position to make such an informed choice, there is no practical justification for accepting the formal warnings as compliance with *Miranda*, or for treating the second stage of interrogation as distinct from the first, unwarned and inadmissible statement. ...

> The contrast between *Elstad* and this case reveals a series of relevant facts that bear on whether *Miranda* warnings delivered midstream could be effective enough to accomplish their object: the completeness and detail of the questions and answers in the first round of interrogation, the overlapping content of the two statements, the timing and setting of the first and the second, the continuity of police personnel, and the degree to which the interrogator's questions treated the second round as continuous with the first.[166]

The plurality thus created a multiple-factor objective approach designed to determine whether *Miranda* warnings were likely effective from the suspect's perspective, although one of the plurality's members, Justice Breyer, wrote separately to provide a different method of distinguishing *Elstad* from *Seibert*.

---

165. *Id.* at 606 (Souter, J., plurality opinion).

166. *Id.* at 611–15 (Souter, J., plurality opinion).

The plurality's renunciation of the "question-first" technique employed in *Seibert* was bolstered by a separate concurrence by Justice Kennedy, whose opinion can fairly be characterized as a fifth vote for prohibiting that technique and a second vote for applying an intent-based test:

> The technique used in this case distorts the meaning of *Miranda* and furthers no legitimate countervailing interest. The *Miranda* rule would be frustrated were we to allow police to undermine its meaning and effect. . . . When an interrogator uses this deliberate, two-step strategy, predicated upon violating *Miranda* during an extended interview, postwarnings statements that are related to the substance of prewarning statements must be excluded absent specific, curative steps.[167]

In a dissent written for four justices, Justice O'Connor reiterated her position in *Elstad* that, because the fruit of the poisonous tree doctrine does not apply to *Miranda* violations, the only appropriate analysis is the voluntariness of the first and second statements.[168]

PROBLEM 8–30

Four uniformed police officers appeared at the home of Adrian Bainbridge, who had recently been paroled following a brief incarceration on an assault conviction. One officer *Mirandized* Bainbridge but then said, "Look, we just want to talk to you to see what you know about the Jones murder." While that officer was asking this question, a second officer followed Bainbridge's spouse when she headed toward the kitchen, and a third officer ran to, and then stood by, the rear door. The fourth officer stood guard outside the front door.

Bainbridge replied to the first officer's question, "I don't want to talk until I've had a chance to speak to my parole officer, Roberto Unger." The first officer said, "Sure. Why don't we drive to the station house to make the call? Won't that be a better place to talk about these things than in front of your wife and kids?" Bainbridge said, "O.K."

The four officers and Bainbridge then drove down to the police station. During the twenty-minute ride, the first officer repeatedly stressed to Bainbridge that his cooperation could only work in his favor. But Bainbridge kept repeating that he wanted to speak to his parole officer first.

Upon arriving at the station, Bainbridge was promptly taken to the interrogation room. One officer left to call Bainbridge's parole officer. The parole officer arrived within fifteen minutes and met with Bainbridge alone. Bainbridge told his parole officer, "I didn't do it. I swear. I was at the bar that night, and I saw the fight and saw Jones stabbed, but I never saw the guy who stabbed him before. Honest. Ask Peter Sun, my friend. He was with me, and he'll vouch for me."

---

167. *Id.* at 622 (Kennedy, J., concurring).

168. *Id.* at 622–28 (O'Connor, dissenting).

The parole officer promptly reported the conversation to the police who in turn contacted Peter Sun. But Officer Ruiz, who contacted Sun, told Sun, "Your friend, Bainbridge, said he was at the bar that night, and he saw you stab Jones." Sun broke down in tears, denied doing the deed, and said Bainbridge was the real killer. He offered to wear a wire and get proof of Bainbridge's wrongful actions.

The next day, about twenty-four hours after the parole officer finished talking to Bainbridge, the police told Bainbridge, "You're free to go. We just talked to your friend, Sun, and he vouched for you. He's waiting for you outside to drive you home."

Bainbridge was then released and entered Sun's car. Immediately thereafter Bainbridge said to Sun, "The cops are getting hot. We've gotta go get that knife before they find it. They claim they believed your story, but I think they're lying." The two men then drove to an isolated location, dug into the ground, and pulled out a knife. The police then arrived and arrested Bainbridge for Jones's murder.

QUESTIONS

1. Will a motion to suppress Bainbridge's conversations with the police officers, the parole officer, and Sun, likely be granted? What about a motion to suppress the knife? To bar Sun from testifying? Before answering this question, you might want to review the material on fruit-of-the-poisonous tree analysis in the chapter on the Fourth Amendment.

2. Would your answers change if the facts were modified as follows: Bainbridge has an IQ of seventy, is sixteen years old, had no guardian present, and has a fourth-grade education. His only previous arrest was on the assault charge mentioned above. During the ride to the police station, the first officer said, "Look, we know you did it. We've got an eyewitness who saw you do it. But we know it was probably self-defense, so we think you should have a chance to tell your side of the story. If you don't, though, I can't be responsible for what happens. And before we can call your parole officer, we'll want you to talk to Officer Thomas alone for awhile. He has a real rapport with suspects and might be able to help you really understand that talking to us is in your best interest." Officer Thomas is 6' 5" tall and 250 pounds of solid muscle. He has a reputation on the street of being a particularly tough officer, someone who likes to hassle those he thinks are "suspicious-looking" just for the fun of it.

2. IMPEACHMENT

The breadth of the *Miranda* exclusionary rule is limited in other contexts as well. For example, statements obtained in violation of *Miranda* may be used for the purpose of impeaching the defendant's trial testimony, provided that those meet usual trustworthiness standards:

> It is one thing to say that the Government cannot make an affirmative use of evidence unlawfully obtained. It is quite another to

say that the defendant can turn the illegal method by which evidence in the Government's possession was obtained to his own advantage, and provide himself with a shield against contradiction of his untruths. . . .

[T]here is hardly justification for letting the defendant affirmatively resort to perjurious testimony in reliance on the Government's disability to challenge his credibility.[169]

On the other hand, the defendant's invocation of the *Miranda* right to remain silent cannot be used for impeachment purposes. The Court held in *Doyle v. Ohio*[170] that it is improper for a prosecutor to comment on a defendant's postarrest silence after being given *Miranda* warnings. It is permissible, however, for a prosecutor to comment on a defendant's postarrest silence when no *Miranda* warnings or their substantial equivalent are given to the defendant. The reasoning is that "because the *Miranda* warnings contain an 'implicit assurance' that silence will carry no penalty, it does not comport with due process to permit the prosecution during trial to call attention to [the defendant's] silence at the time of arrest and to insist that because he did not speak about the facts of the case at that time, as he was told he need not do, an unfavorable inference might be drawn as to the truth of his trial testimony."[171] Thus, "the use for impeachment purposes of petitioner's silence, at the time of arrest and after receiving *Miranda* warnings [violates] the Due Process Clause of the Fourteenth Amendment." Likewise, "absent some sort of affirmative assurances embodied in the *Miranda* warnings, the Constitution does not prohibit the use of a defendant's postarrest silence to impeach him at trial." This is because in such a case no governmental action induced the defendant to remain silent.

For similar reasons, a defendant may be impeached with his pre-arrest silence. Thus, if a defendant raises an alibi defense at trial, he may be cross-examined as follows:

Question:	Your best friend, Johnny, told you the police were looking for you in connection with a robbery?
Answer:	Yes.
Question:	And Johnny then said, "You did it, didn't you?"
Answer:	Yes.
Question:	And you looked at him, smiled, and said nothing, isn't that right?
Answer:	Yes.
Question:	You never told Johnny that you were innocent of this crime, did you?
Answer:	No.
Question:	You never told Johnny you had an alibi?
Answer:	That's right.

---

169. Walder v. United States, 347 U.S. 62, 65 (1954).

170. 426 U.S. 610 (1976).

171. Greer v. Miller, 483 U.S. 756, 762–63 (1987).

PROBLEM 8–31

Detective George Paul arrested John Durpo for the crime of attempted murder after Durpo's fellow mill-worker was found beaten and unconscious at the mill yard. Detective Paul gave Durpo *Miranda* warnings and questioned him about the crime. Durpo had only a third grade education and an IQ of sixty. Durpo was also a devout Christian.

Durpo admitted to having been in the mill yard on the day of the crime, but he denied having seen anyone there. Detective Paul said, "Look, this man was a good Christian man, and if we can't find his body, he'll never get a proper burial." Durpo burst into tears and admitted that he had met someone in the yard that day and had asked him for some beer, and, when he refused, had punched the stranger but that was all. He hadn't killed anyone. He then said, "I think I want to be quiet now. I don't want to talk anymore."

Paul replied, "Let's go to the Chapel together. Maybe that will give you the strength to go on." At that point, Durpo wept even harder, and Paul resumed his questioning. Durpo soon admitted that he in fact hit the guy in the yard that day with a pipe and the guy fell down and stopped moving. His answers to Paul's questions were short and often inaudible.

A pretrial motion to suppress the statement was granted in part. The trial court ruled that all statements made after Durpo said he wanted to be quiet were suppressed.

At trial, Durpo took the stand in his own defense and denied involvement in the crime. He said he confessed because he was confused, tired, and depressed, and he needed a place to stay and wanted his girlfriend to feel sorry for him. To buttress this statement, he asserted that he would not have been able to relate the events of the offense had Detective Paul not in fact provided the details of the crime.

The prosecutor began his cross-examination of Durpo as follows:

Question: He [the officer] led you around?
Answer: Yes, sir.
Question: He told you the answers?
Answer: Yes, sir.
Question: And you just agreed with him?
Answer: Mostly, yes.
Question: Mostly?
Answer: Right.
Question: You just agreed with him. So you wouldn't be able to tell Detective Paul things about that crime which were not known to anybody else but the police and the person who did it, could you?
Answer: Right, right.

The prosecutor now wants to continue his cross-examination by revealing the answers to the questions posed by Detective Paul to Durpo after Durpo had said he wanted to be quiet.

QUESTIONS

1. Under what circumstances, if any, should the prosecutor be able to reveal to the jury portions of Durpo's confession made after he expressed his desire to be silent? What details, if any, would you want concerning the content of Durpo's statements?

2. Under your state constitution, what arguments might you craft that statements suppressed under *Miranda* should not be used, even for impeachment?

H. *Miranda* Exceptions

Despite the Court's desire to maintain the bright-line nature of *Miranda*, it has recognized situations in which *Miranda* warnings are not required. There have been two recognized exceptions: for "public safety" and "routine booking practices." Another possible exception, for minor offenses, was rejected by the Court in *Berkemer v. McCarty*.[172] There, a motorist was stopped for a misdemeanor traffic offense. He was questioned during the roadside stop and made incriminating remarks. The Court ultimately determined that the motorist was not in custody during that period, and thus that *Miranda* warnings were not required. But along the way, it emphasized that the *Miranda* interests were applicable and that if the motorist had been in custody, the warnings would have been required. To rule otherwise, according to the Court, would muddy *Miranda*'s bright-line quality, leaving law enforcement officers unsure in many instances whether the seriousness of the offense was such that the warnings were required.

The Court did muddy *Miranda*'s bright-line quality in *New York v. Quarles*.[173] There, the Court created an exception to *Miranda*'s requirements where police must ask questions in order to prevent an immediate danger to public safety. In *Quarles*, police responded to a midnight report that a woman had been raped at gunpoint. Information provided to the police indicated that the assailant had fled into an all-night grocery store. Officers entered the store and spotted Quarles, who had run to the rear of the store. The officers discovered after frisking him that he had an empty shoulder holster. One of the officers asked the handcuffed man where the gun was, without first administering *Miranda* warnings. Quarles responded, "the gun is over there." The Court held that Quarles' statement was admissible despite the absence of the warnings. It reasoned that the custodial interrogation had occurred in circumstances posing a danger to the public, thus raising interests that outweighed Quarles' interest in being warned of his rights. Had the officers acted differently, the Court speculated, the gun might have become a dangerous weapon in the hands of an accomplice or might have been found by a store employee or customer.

---

172. 468 U.S. 420 (1984).

173. 467 U.S. 649 (1984).

The public safety exception has been applied occasionally by other courts, and in so doing those courts have helped supply standards for its use. For example, the Washington Supreme Court upheld use of the exception in a hostage situation. In *State v. Finch*,[174] the defendant had kidnapped his estranged wife and two others, and he held them hostage in a trailer as a SWAT team and an armored personnel carrier assembled outside. After he killed one of the kidnap victims and a police officer, Finch holed up for the night in the trailer. Early the next morning, a SWAT negotiator became concerned that Finch was becoming "increasingly agitated and upset." He established telephone contact and tried to calm Finch down by suggesting that the killings had been in self-defense. Finch replied, "[I]t wasn't no self-defense. It was premeditated, man." When the prosecution used that statement against him, Finch claimed that his *Miranda* rights had been violated. In upholding the trial court's denial of that claim, the Washington Supreme Court determined that there was "an objectively reasonable need" to dispense with *Miranda* warnings in order to protect the police and Finch, who appeared to be suicidal. The court observed that "[r]equiring the warnings in the present case could have further upset Mr. Finch and eroded the potential for a peaceful resolution."

The "routine booking exception" permits officers to ask general biographical questions during booking or pretrial services without first giving *Miranda* warnings. The exception was developed in *Pennsylvania v. Muniz*.[175] According to the Court, officers were not required to give Muniz *Miranda* warnings when they arrested him on drunk driving charges and asked him questions as part of a routine practice for receiving persons suspected of driving while intoxicated. The questions to which Muniz was asked to respond called for information about his name, address, weight, color of eyes, date of birth, and age. Because these questions were routine and were "reasonably related" to police administrative concerns, the Court held that Muniz's slurred responses could be admitted against him, even though he had not received *Miranda* warnings before making them.

PROBLEM 8–32

Two police offers were called to investigate an assault report at 6 p.m. The first officer to arrive at the scene exited his patrol car and was approached by a woman who said she had seen a man strike another woman on the head, force her into a black Thunderbird, and drive away. Just then, Madison Brady drove up in a black Thunderbird and, upon seeing the officer, slowed down. The officer drew his revolver and ordered Brady to step out of his car. After Brady did so, the officer frisked Brady and found no weapons. By this time, a crowd had gathered. The officer asked Brady whether he had a gun in the car and Brady replied, "In the trunk." The officer searched the trunk and found a revolver, two speed

---

174.   975 P.2d 967 (Wash.1999).

175.   496 U.S. 582 (1990).

loaders, ammunition, seal bombs, an electronic scale, a bag of methamphet-amine, and a powder that appeared to be a cutting agent.

At the subsequent suppression hearing, the officer testified, "I asked Brady where the gun was because I was nervous. I'd seen Johnny Lyndon in the crowd that was gathering, and I'd always suspected Lyndon was a motorcycle gang member. I saw Lyndon had a knife in his left boot, and I figured if this Brady kid was mixed up with Lyndon, Brady'd be dangerous and might hurt somebody, so I had to act fast. There wasn't time for *Miranda* warnings."

QUESTIONS

1. How credible is the officer's testimony? If you are defense counsel, what questions will you ask the officer on cross-examination at a suppression hearing? What other witnesses will you call to the stand?

2. Disregard the credibility of the officer; should *Miranda* warnings have been given? Does the officer's subjective mental state control? Is it relevant?

I. Undercover Activities

In *Illinois v. Perkins*, the Supreme Court was asked to address an issue that had been percolating in the lower courts for some time: is *Miranda* violated when a "suspect is unaware that he is speaking to a law enforcement officer and gives a voluntary statement?"[176] Perkins, who was incarcerated on battery charges, came under suspicion for a murder. In order to gather information against him, police placed an undercover agent in the cellblock with him. The agent engaged Perkins in conversation and asked whether "he had ever 'done' anybody." Perkins responded by describing "at length" the murder of which he was suspected. The trial court suppressed these statements, and the state appealed. After state appellate courts affirmed the suppression, the Court took the matter on the state's petition for a writ of certiorari. The Court held that there was no *Miranda* violation in these circumstances, explaining that "[c]onversations between suspects and undercover agents do not implicate the concerns underlying *Miranda*." Those concerns relate to the "inherently compelling pressures" generated by a police-dominated atmosphere. If a suspect does not know that he is in the presence of police, those pressures are absent.

PROBLEM 8–33

Johnny Waxman was arrested on a murder charge. While waiting for the police and prosecutors to complete the paperwork necessary for issuing a complaint and proceeding to preliminary arraignment, Waxman was placed in a cell with Bobo Boyee. Boyee told Waxman that Boyee was in for robbery and asked Waxman what he was in for. Waxman replied "murder."

---

176. 496 U.S. 292 (1990).

"Did you do it?" said Boyee. Waxman said, "That's for me to know alone." Boyee kept asking Waxman about the crime, and when Waxman refused to answer, Boyee, who was a good foot taller than Waxman and 70 lbs. heavier, grabbed Waxman by the collar and said, "Look, if I help out the Boys in Blue, they'll help me, and I ain't going away for 20 years if I can help it. You're gonna talk, and if you don't I'm gonna make you talk, and I can do it without leaving marks, ya unnerstan?" Waxman then confessed to the murder.

At the suppression hearing, police officers admitted that they had recently been helped by Boyee in three other cases in which Boyee reported to the police on what cellmates had told him. The officers further admitted that, because of this history, they put Waxman in Boyee's cell, hoping Waxman would in the course of chatting reveal important information to Boyee, who would in turn report that information to the police. The officers denied promising Boyee anything in exchange for information. They also denied that they urged him to ask questions or told him to use force. In fact, they denied talking to him at all about what he would do in the cell. They also denied knowing or even suspecting that he had ever used force to get the three earlier confessions. Indeed, the officers maintained that they always believed he just made small talk—about jail food and whether the inmate liked music—and otherwise acted like a fly on the wall, a passive listener reporting what he had heard from this cellmates.

Question: Should Waxman's confession be suppressed for violating *Miranda*? Sixth Amendment right to counsel? Due process voluntariness requirement?

J.   CULTURAL FACTORS IN THE *MIRANDA* MOTION TO SUPPRESS

Exploring cultural issues can help to clarify many *Miranda* issues, as is explained in the following article excerpt:

Cultural Factors in Motions to Suppress

James G. Connell, III and Rene L. Valladares[177]

Applicability of the Fifth Amendment in Undocumented Aliens

Unlike the Fourth Amendment, the Fifth Amendment applies to each "person" Accordingly, the Fifth Amendment applies to all persons within the United States, irrespective of their immigration status. The Supreme Court has recently reaffirmed that resident aliens in the United States "are entitled to the same protections under the [Self–Incrimination] Clause as citizens." Similarly, *Miranda* protects aliens, lawfully present or otherwise against the inherent pressures of custodial interrogation.

---

177. James G. Connell, III & Rene L. Valladares, *Cultural Factors in Motions to Suppress*, THE CHAMPION 18 (March 2001).

Meaning of Custody

A person is in custody for purposes of *Miranda* "as soon as a suspect's freedom of action is curtailed to a 'degree associated with formal arrest.'" Typically, whether a person is in custody "depends on the objective circumstances of the interrogation, not on the subjective views harbored by either the interrogating officers or the person being questioned."

Notwithstanding the objective focus of the test for custody, the Ninth Circuit has applied a "refined objective standard" which may incorporate factors such as alienage, threats of deportation, and language difficulties. In *United States v. Beraun–Panez*, the Ninth Circuit held that when government agents know of a subjective factor, such as alienage, the court may consider the element in determining whether a suspect was in custody. After analyzing "how a reasonable person who was an alien would perceive and react" to police questioning, the court held that the defendant was in custody when questioned by police.

Of course, other courts may not be willing to "refine" a clearly established rule. When arguing that a suspect was in custody, counsel should present the obvious, unique characteristics of a defendant as objective facts. For example, if police examined a defendant's genuine or suspected false immigration document, the defendant's alienage and possible deportability are objective circumstances to be considered under the traditional test. Likewise, counsel may demonstrate the objective fact of a defendant's limited knowledge of English by the officers' own actions, such as calling an interpreter or foreign language-speaking agent, or by evidence of the defendant's lack of proficiency, whether from an expert or those who know the defendant well. Even a court which has explicitly rejected the refined objective standard has acknowledged that "when a suspect's knowledge of English is clearly inadequate, it may be appropriate to refine the standard to account for this characteristic."

Interrogation Regarding Immigration Status

National origin may also have an impact on the determination of whether government agents have interrogated a person. Interrogation includes "express questioning or its functional equivalent," that is, "any words or actions on the part of the police (other than those normally attendant to arrest and custody) that the police should know are reasonably likely to elicit an incriminating response from the suspect."

Typically, government agents may obtain biographical data necessary to complete booking or pre-trial services without administering *Miranda* warnings under the "routine booking question" exception. The police, however, "may not ask questions, even during booking, that are designed to elicit incriminatory admissions."

This rule takes on special significance in the case of aliens, because alienage is an element of several immigration crimes. In addition to a direct status, statements about other biographical information, such as place of birth, may help the government establish that a defendant is an alien.

Accordingly, the routine booking question exception "is inapplicable ... where the elicitation of information regarding immigration status is reasonably likely to inculpate the respondent." Although asking an American citizen her place of birth may be a routine booking question, the same question may be interrogation when addressed to a Vietnamese speaker.

Language of Miranda Warnings

Once a court has determined that law enforcement authorities interrogated a suspect in custody, it must determine whether the language of the *Miranda* warnings, if any, reasonably conveyed the *Miranda* rights to the suspect. Of course, law enforcement need not use the precise language of *Miranda* to convey the warnings. Nevertheless, the language used must be sufficient to apprise the accused of the rights set forth in *Miranda*.

If law enforcement provide *Miranda* warnings in English, the question of whether the suspect understood the rights is an issue of the validity of the waiver. If law enforcement translate the warnings, however, the language of the warnings themselves is subject to challenge. Of course, "[t]he translation of a suspect's *Miranda* rights need not be a perfect one," but the translation must include each of the core *Miranda* rights in language that a suspect can understand.

If counsel does not speak the language under discussion fluently, and the language of the warnings is not reduced to writing prior to the suppression hearing, counsel will need to have an interpreter present who can devote her attention to the testimony. Generally, this will require two interpreters to be present: one to assist the defendant and facilitate communication between attorney and client, and one to listen to the foreign language testimony of law enforcement.

Counsel must also pay special attention to the problem of making a record for an effective challenge and an appeal. The court will almost certainly not have the capacity to transcribe foreign language warnings. Counsel should ask the person who administered the warnings to write down the exact words that they used to administer the warnings. If possible, counsel should have an interpreter provide the defense translation of the warnings in English.

In *State v. Santiago*, the Supreme Court of Wisconsin struggled with the question of a record for foreign-language warnings. Although defense counsel attempted to make a record, the police officer could not write Spanish, the court reporter could not transcribe in Spanish, the Spanish interpreter did not transcribe the officer's words, and the trial court prohibited the interpreter from interpreting the officer's words on the basis that the interpretation would become "official" without the Spanish in the record. The court resolved the dilemma by placing the burden on the government: it held "that an informing officer must, upon an accused's request, furnish testimony as to the foreign-language *Miranda* warnings given to the accused and that those words be preserved in the record." Counsel should encourage their courts to resolve the issue in a similar fashion.

One problem in translating the *Miranda* warnings is the problem of false cognates. The Spanish verb "apuntar" looks like the English world "to appoint." "Apuntar," however, does not mean "to appoint"; it means "to point to." The proper Spanish verb for "to appoint" is "otorgar."

Another problem in translation is that the target language may have two or more different words for two or more different meanings of an English word. In *State v. Ramirez*, the interpreter used the Spanish word for "the right hand side" ("derecha") instead of the Spanish word for "right" in the legal sense ("derecho"). Additionally, the interpreter told the suspect in Spanish that he had rights underneath ("bajo") the law in a physical sense rather than on the basis of ("de acuerdo con") the law.

Similarly, the Spanish word for "to furnish" in the sense of "to provide" ("nombrar") is different from the word for "to furnish" in the sense of "to provide with furniture." In one unpublished habeas case, law enforcement told the petitioner, "If you do not have funds with which to obtain the services of a lawyer, one will be given furniture for you to represent you before any questions are asked."

In addition, interpreters may add conflicting or erroneous statements to the *Miranda* warnings. In *People v. Mejia–Mendoza*, for example, an interpreter told the defendant "[n]othing is being used against you" and "[j]ust because you say something you'll be released" without the detective's knowledge. A literal translation of the Navajo words used to mean, "you have the right to remain silent" means "you should be respectful of authority." A Navajo, especially a young person, may believe that part of being respectful to an elder, or indeed to any police officer, involves answering all questions fully and with respect for the questioner.

Finally, translations of the *Miranda* rights may not convey all the *Miranda* rights simply because they omit one of the rights. As formulated in English, the *Miranda* warnings are succinct and draw to some extent on legal shorthand. Although no particular language must be used, the *Miranda* warnings must convey each of the following rights:

(1) That the suspect has the right to remain silent;

(2) That anything the suspect says can be used against her in a court of law;

(3) That the suspect has the right to an attorney;

(4) That the suspect has the right to have the attorney present during questioning; and

(5) That if the suspect cannot afford an attorney, an attorney will be furnished to her free of cost both prior to and during questioning.

Although this list may seem elementary, it is important to check the warnings as given against the list. It is not enough to tell a suspect that she has the right to remain silent; law enforcement must also tell the suspect the consequences of not remaining silent. Likewise, it is not enough to tell a suspect that she has the right to talk to an attorney prior to questioning;

law enforcement must tell her that she may have an attorney present during questioning.

In *Ramirez*, the Spanish language warnings did not inform the defendant that anything he said could be used as evidence against him. The interpreter also told the defendant in Spanish that "if you can't pay for a lawyer, it is possible to have a lawyer without paying before the questioning." The court indicated that this language did not inform the defendant "that he had the right to an attorney free of charge during all stages of questioning."

Similarly, in *United States v. Higareda–Santa Cruz*, law enforcement informed the defendant in Spanish that, "In case you do not have money, you have the right to petition an attorney from the court." The court held that the statement did not convey the defendant's *Miranda* rights both because it "impl[ied] that the defendant must be completely without money before he can obtain an appointed attorney" and "imp[lied] that even if a defendant has no money, he might not obtain counsel because he must 'petition' the court for an attorney."

Typically, the person who renders the *Miranda* warnings into another language need have no special qualifications. Courts are somewhat more sensitive to conflicts of interest, however, than to competency. Although the rule is most often honored in the breach, a number of courts have indicated that an interpreter should be neutral and disinterested.

Following this principle, a Washington court has held that the police violated the due process rights of a defendant by using a potential co-defendant to advise him of his *Miranda* rights. At least two jurisdictions, Minnesota and the District of Columbia, have statutes prohibiting police officers from serving as interpreters during custodial interrogation. When litigating this issue, counsel may wish to draw upon national or local interpreters' codes of ethics to demonstrate the problem of interpretation by biased interpreters.

Waiver of Miranda Rights

The government bears the burden to prove that any waiver of *Miranda* rights was knowing, voluntary, and intelligent. Counsel should be careful not to confuse the determination of whether a *Miranda* waiver is voluntary with the question of whether a statement is voluntary under the Due Process Clause; counsel can challenge a statement on both grounds separately. In order to be knowing and intelligent, a "waiver must have been made with a full awareness of both the nature of the right being abandoned and the consequences of the decision to abandon it?"

Two main cultural factors come into play in determining the knowing, voluntary, and intelligent character of a *Miranda* waiver. Both issues fundamentally relate to the question of whether a defendant actually understood that she did not have to speak with law enforcement authorities without counsel present. The D.C. Circuit has explained, "the focus must be on the plain meaning of the required warnings. A defendant must comprehend, for example, that he really does not have to speak; he must recognize that anything he says actually will be used by the state against him." Counsel should not forget that cultural inquiries into the defendant's background are not goals in themselves. In argument and evidence, counsel must relate any cultural issues to the fundamental question of whether the defendant knew what she was doing when she waived her *Miranda* rights.

Initially, "language difficulties may impair the ability of a person in custody to waive these rights in a free and aware manner." If a government agent gives warnings in English skills, any waiver may not be a knowing waiver simply because the suspect did not understand her rights. To native English speakers, the word "right" carries a bundle of meanings, including a corresponding duty of authorities to respect the exercise of the right. In another language, or to a non-English speaker, the word "right" or its analogue may not carry the critical importance that it signifies to the judge or other native English speakers.

The foreign language translation of the *Miranda* warnings can be important even where *Miranda* warnings are given in English to a speaker of English as a second language. Counsel should not forget that many non-native speakers mentally translate English into their native language to process it. Although presenting the argument that the defendant did not understand the language of the *Miranda* warnings to mean that she had the power not to speak without retribution may require testimony from the defendant, it may be effective in the proper circumstances.

Similarly, the court and counsel will clearly understand the warnings that the court will appoint counsel to represent the defendant to mean that an attorney will defend the client without charge. If a defendant does not understand the legal meaning of the word "represent," however, that warning sounds more like a threat to have a prosecutor examine the case than a promise of a free defense.

A second cultural factor in the waiver of *Miranda* rights is the suspect's familiarity with the American justice system, and, by extension, her rights to counsel and to remain silent. Police, paramilitary, or military forces in the defendant's home country may demand compliance on pain of imprisonment or violence. More fundamentally, some defendants may not understand that they have the right to remain silent because they have never imagined a legal system in which they actually have the right to remain silent.

In establishing lack of familiarity with the American criminal justice system as a factor, counsel should impress upon the court the difference between the legal culture of the defendant and the American adversarial system. Many foreign defendants are familiar with inquisitorial systems in which the examination of the defendant, often without counsel, is a major source of evidence. In the People's Republic of China, the criminal procedure law mandates that, "[t]he defendant shall answer the questions put by the investigation personnel according to the facts." Ethiopian law apparently also requires an accused to forgo silence. Even most European countries do not grant the accused the right to consult with counsel during pre-trial questioning, and, in "virtually all countries of Europe, . . . police may continue to question a suspect despite the suspect's refusal to make a statement or assertion of a desire to remain silent."

An obvious, but overlooked, approach to attacking the knowing, voluntary, and intelligent nature of a *Miranda* waiver is simply to ask a client why she thought she had to talk to the police. A client from another culture may explain a reason, or provide a level of detail, that counsel has never considered.

Main Issue

Although cultural issues offer some new avenues of defending clients, such as the Vienna Convention, these issues also present opportunities to give depth to traditional Fourth and Fifth Amendment motions to suppress. The central theme of cultural factors cases is not to lose focus on the main issues before the court. If counsel addresses the appropriate legal standard in the context of her clients' unique and diverse experience, she will both serve her client well and, hopefully win a few motions.

———

PROBLEM 8–34

John E. Lynn is a suspected Al–Qaeda operative arrested in the United States on a charge of complicity in the September 11, 2001 terrorist attack on the World Trade Center. Lynn allegedly gave flying lessons to members of an Al–Qaeda call knowing that they planned to fly a plane into the towers. Lynn's name is a pseudonym—he is in fact a citizen of Saudi Arabia, where he was born and raised. Lynn arrived in the United States in January 2001. He is described by the arresting FBI agents as speaking English poorly but clearly understanding every word that the agents said. Nevertheless, the agents included among their group an agent who had some familiarity with Arabic, and this agent served as an interpreter. This agent read the *Miranda* warnings to Lynn in both English and Arabic. After receiving the warnings, Lynn promptly confessed.

Question: Assume that you are Lynn's defense counsel and are considering filing a motion to suppress his confession. What investigation would you do? What additional information would you need? How would you prepare for litigating this motion in ways different than you would for a run-of-the-mill *Miranda* suppression hearing? What factors will affect your assessment of the likelihood of your succeeding on the motion?

PROBLEM 8–35

Return to the role-play on voluntariness immediately preceding Problem 8–1. Given what you have just read about cultural issues in motions to suppress confessions, what is the likelihood of defense counsel succeeding in a motion to suppress Mr. Chang's confession on the grounds of a *Miranda* violation? What additional information might you want, and how and from whom would you obtain it? Would you call Mr. Chang to the stand to testify at his suppression hearing, and, if so, what questions would you ask him on direct examination, and what questions would you anticipate the prosecution asking him on cross-examination? What questions would you ask in cross-examining the police? Would you call an expert to the stand? If so, who and why?

K. REVIEW EXERCISE: CRITIQUING PORTIONS OF A SUPPRESSION HEARING TRANSCRIPT RAISING *MIRANDA* ISSUES

At a hearing to suppress certain statements made by Andy Gavel to Officer Kurmand, who arrested Gavel on murder charges, Officer Kurmand testified as follows.

On June 15, he went to 555 S. 5th St., where he arrested Andy Gavel in apartment 3C on a murder charge. Several of Gavel's family members were in the apartment at the time. Officer Kurmand immediately asked Gavel, "Where's the knife?" and Gavel said, "Over there," and pointed to a knife on a nearby table.

Kurmand then transported Gavel to the Homicide Unit at the local police station. While exiting the police station elevator to reach the Homicide Unit, Gavel turned to Officer Kurmand and said, "What happened to that guy I stabbed? I boarded him twice." Officer Kurmand further testified that Gavel then said something that sounded like he was saying he acted in self-defense, but these words were softly mumbled and slurred. Other than the words "self-defense," however, the officer found it impossible to understand what Gavel was saying.

Kurmand then escorted Gavel in silence to an interrogation room in the Homicide Unit and handed Gavel over to the Homicide Detectives. Kurmand told the detectives, "He's in bad shape." But Kurmand did not remember smelling any alcohol on Gavel's breath.

Defense counsel then engaged in the following cross-examination:

Q. Okay. You were actually the arresting officer or participated in the arrest of Mr. Gavel?

A. Participated in the arrest.

Q. You did not read him his rights when you arrested him, did you?

A. No, I didn't.

Q. And when you transported him to come—well, you took him from his apartment to the scene of the crime, correct?

A. That's correct.

Q. And from the apartment to the scene of the crime, you did not read him his rights; is that correct?

A. That's correct.

Q. Although he had been placed under arrest?

A. That's correct.

Q. And he was handcuffed, yes?

A. He was handcuffed.

Q. And he was certainly in custody?

A. He was certainly in custody.

Q. And then from the scene of the crime, you took him—and when we—when we say "scene of the crime," just to be more specific, we're talking about 2705 13th Street?

A. That's correct.

Q. From the scene of the crime, you took him directly to Homicide?

A. Directly to Homicide.

Q. Now, when you arrested—were you actually the officer that handcuffed Mr. Gavel?

A. I was the one who was forced to subdue him.

Q. Was he cooperative or did you have to use force?

A. He was cooperative.

Q. So, you were pretty close to him; that's fair to say, right?

A. That's true.

Q. Did you smell alcohol on his breath?

A. No.

Q. Not at all?

A. No.

Q. It's fair to say that from the time that you took him into custody, you didn't—Mr. Gavel didn't drink while he was in your presence, correct?

A. No.

Q. Okay. Now, from the scene of the crime, 2705 13th Street, you went directly to Homicide? I think I've asked that already.

A. Yes.

Q. And during that transport, you did not read Mr. Gavel his rights, did you?

A. No.

Q. Were you alone when you were transporting him?

A. Yes, I was.

Q. Was there any—did you have any conversations with Mr. Gavel whatsoever between the time of his arrest at his apartment on Bryant Street and the time he went to the scene of the crime?

A. No conversation.

Q. What happened at the scene?

A. What scene?

Q.   When you went back to 2705 13th Street?

MR. ROBINSON [the prosecutor]: I'll object at this juncture, Your Honor.

THE COURT: I'll overrule it.

THE WITNESS: I had taken the defendant back to the scene. He was transported in my vehicle. I remained inside the vehicle as did the defendant.

BY MS. SMITH [defense counsel]:

Q.   And you just sat there?

A.   That's correct.

Q.   Who—

THE COURT: For how long?

THE WITNESS: I'd say approximately well over five minutes, well over five minutes.

BY MS. SMITH:

Q.   When you say "well over five minutes," was it as long as an hour?

A.   Less than ten.

Q.   Okay. So, between five and ten minutes?

A.   Yes.

Q.·   Okay. Did someone instruct you to go back to the scene?

A.   Yes.

Q.   Did any other officer or detective come over to the car and discuss the case with you while Mr. Gavel was sitting in the car?

A.   I don't believe we discussed the case. But I brought Mr. Gavel there for a showup identification, which another officer then conducted, and that officer told me that an eyewitness then identified Gavel.

Q.   So, in Mr. Gavel's presence, there was discussion about the case?

A.   Not in his presence.

Q.   Not in his presence? Well, you just indicated that you were sitting in the car with Mr. Gavel for a period of five to ten minutes alone with him, right?

A.   (Nodding head.)

Q.   Did you get out of the car while you were at the scene?

A.   I believe I got out once.

Q.   Okay. And are you saying that's when the discussion about the identification took place?

THE COURT: Well, he didn't say that that—

BY MS. SMITH:

Q. Let me—let me try to clarify it. When you got to the scene, 2705 13th Street—well, let me step back for a second. During the transport of Mr. Gavel from Bryant Street to the scene, was there any discussion over the radio about Mr. Gavel's case?

A. I wouldn't recall.

Q. You wouldn't recall. When you got to the scene—how were you instructed then to get—to go to the scene? Were you in his apartment when you received that instruction?

A. I knew to take him back to the scene.

Q. That was—was that your decision or had Homicide become involved at that point?

A. The command supervisor on the scene—I believe someone gave—indicated the ID. However, that would have been done if he hadn't said anything anyway.

Q. Okay. Well—but, he hadn't said anything anyway when—when you put him under arrest at his apartment, right? He didn't say anything then, did he, Mr. Gavel?

A. He said nothing.

Q. Okay. So, you're just—what I'm trying to ascertain, officer—

THE COURT: What I think—I think you two may have been on a different phases or maybe I'm on a different phase. When he said if he hadn't said anything anyway, I think he was referring to the supervisor, not your client.

MS. SMITH: That's what I thought he was talking about, Mr. Gavel.

THE COURT: Is that what—I thought he said his supervisor may have told him to take him back, but if he hadn't said anything, I would have taken him back anyway. I thought that's what he was referring to. Is that correct?

THE WITNESS: In that regard.

MS. SMITH: Okay.

THE COURT: Not the client. If—if the supervisor hadn't said anything, standard procedure, I guess, he's saying would have—he would have taken him back.

MS. SMITH: Okay. Okay.

BY MS. SMITH:

Q. At the apartment, was there any discussion about taking him back to the scene for identification or any discussion about the circumstances surrounding the stabbing before Mr. Gavel was transported back to the scene by police officers.

THE COURT: I thought that's what he just said he didn't remember.

MS. SMITH: No. I asked about radio communication.

THE COURT: Oh, radio. Oh.

THE WITNESS: I—I wouldn't recall the transmission of that information.

BY MS. SMITH:

Q.   Okay. But, I guess my—I'm talking about a different question, not just about the order to transport, but whether there was any discussion about the stabbing in Mr. Gavel's presence while you were in the apartment?

THE COURT: You mean by someone other—somebody else there in the apartment?

MS. SMITH: Yes.

THE WITNESS: Whether there was any information described in reference to the stabbing inside the apartment?

BY MS. SMITH:

Q.   Yes.

A.   The only thing that was said inside the apartment, we asked him where was the knife.

Q.   And you got an answer.

A.   Yes.

Q.   Okay.

A.   He said right—right on the table.

Q.   And that was after he was arrested or secured, right?

A.   Simultaneously.

Q.   All of that was done?

A.   All at the same time.

Q.   So, it's fair to say that he was in custody during this.

A.   He was being placed into custody at the same time.

Q.   And no rights were read to him at that point, right?

A.   No.

Q.   Now, Mr. Gavel's brother was present in the apartment when Mr. Gavel was placed under arrest, correct?

A.   There were several people in the apartment. I don't know who they were.

Q.   There were several—

A.   I'd say about three or four—

Q.   —nonpolice officers in the apartment?

A.   Nonpolice officers.

Q.   Prior to Mr. Gavel being transported to the scene, were any of those wit—were any of those persons questioned about whether or not they had any knowledge about the stabbing while Mr. Gavel was there?

MR. ROBINSON: I'll object.

THE COURT: Oh, I'll overrule that. Well, did you question any other people about the stabbing while—before you took Gavel away from the apartment?

THE WITNESS: I did not.

THE COURT: Okay.

BY MS. SMITH:

Q.   Did someone else?

A.   Unknown to me.

THE COURT: When you said where is the knife, to whom were you speaking?

THE WITNESS: The defendant.

THE COURT: Who said it's on the—it's right there on the table?

THE WITNESS: Mr. Gavel.

THE COURT: Okay.

BY MS. SMITH:

Q.   And how long did you stay in the apartment before you took him back to the scene?

A.   Could have been less—could have been five-minutes.

Q.   When Mr. Gavel started to speak to you in the elevator, you didn't stop and say, "Sir, you have a right to remain silent. You are under arrest. Anything you can say can be used against you," did you?

A.   No, I didn't say anything.

Q.   And, you know as a police officer that upon a suspect's arrest that you're required to give *Miranda* warnings, right?

MR. ROBINSON: I'll object.

THE COURT: Well, I'll overrule that.

BY MS. SMITH:

Q.   Yes?

A.   It depends.

Q.   It depends whether or not you're required to give *Miranda* warnings when someone is under arrest? Is that what you're saying?

A.   Sometimes it's done, sometimes not.

Q.   And in this case, it was not done?

A.   It was not done.

Q.   All right. Do you recall what time it was that you arrived at the Homicide Branch?

A.   It could have been about 7:30.

Q.   About 7:30. And is it fair to say that as soon as you arrived at the office, you left Mr. Gavel alone and spoke with Detective Jones and that was your last contact with him?

A.   Yes.

Q.   When you were transporting Mr. Gavel, did you detect whether or not he had any problems walking?

A.   I don't recollect that.

Q.   When you say that you could not understand what Mr. Gavel was saying about self-defense, was that because he was mumbling or— or was it because he was just difficult to understand?

A.   I think it was because he was difficult to understand. The end of that speech was difficult to understand.

Q.   And when you say "difficult to understand," are you—are you saying that's because he was speaking softer or because he was thick-tongued? Was it the manner of speech or the pitch or the tone of his speech that caused you not to be able to understand, if you recall?

A.   Now that I totally can't recollect.

Q.   Did he appear to be thick-tongued to you or slurring his words?

THE COURT: That's two separate questions.

BY MS. SMITH:

Q.   Did he appear to be slurring his words?

THE COURT: At what point in time, ma'am?

MS. SMITH: When he made the statement.

THE COURT: Which part of it cause he said—the first part or the self-defense part or the whole thing?

MS. SMITH: The entire.

THE COURT: Okay.

THE WITNESS: He was talking understandable.

BY MS. SMITH:

Q.   Except for that one?

A.   The end of that conversation.

Q.   Just lastly, sergeant, were you aware of the fact that Mr. Gavel's medication was seized or found at the scene of the crime and taken as evidence?

THE COURT: What's that got to do with what I got to decide. Whether he was aware of that or not is of no moment on this motion.

MS. SMITH: I would—I would respectfully disagree given the fact that he was aware that Mr. Gavel was taking medication—

THE COURT: Okay. I'll overrule it. I'll overrule it. Let him answer.

MS. SMITH: Then that would be something relevant to a voluntariness issue, yes.

THE WITNESS: I was not aware at the time.

MS. SMITH: Okay. Thank you.

THE COURT: Anything further of this witness?

MR. ROBINSON: No, Your Honor.

THE COURT: Okay. Thank you very much.

THE WITNESS: Thank you, sir.

(The witness was excused at approximately 11:50 a.m.)

QUESTIONS

1. Why did defense counsel ask the questions she did? What was her strategy? The legal bases for her questions?

2. Are there additional questions you think should have been asked? What? Why? What cases support your conclusions and why? Did defense counsel's questions clearly build toward particular points, or were they sometimes confusing and incomplete? How might you have done a better job?

3. Are there additional witnesses whom you would call to the stand? Who? Why?

4. What legal grounds were likely raised in the motion to suppress?

5. What do you think of the role of the trial judge? Did he leave the impression of being a neutral arbiter?

L.   REVIEW PROBLEMS

PROBLEM 8–36

Robert Brav, complaining of appetite and sleeping disturbances and that "everything has piled up on me, and I can't get it out," voluntarily admitted himself to the State Hospital for Mental Health. Brav met with staff psychologist George Johnson. Johnson knew at the time that Brav's girlfriend was missing and that the police suspected that Brav had something to do with that disappearance.

Brav, just before a later suppression hearing on a charge of murdering his girlfriend, told his lawyer that he assumed that all that he told Johnson would be confidential. Indeed, he says, based upon prior hospital admissions for mental health treatment, he knew there was a state statute recognizing a psychotherapist-patient privilege. He also says that at no time did Johnson mention that he would be revealing anything said to third parties. Finally, Brav says he was repeatedly questioned about, and badgered by Johnson about, the murder of Brav's girlfriend. Finally, Brav admitted the murder to Johnson.

But Johnson later told the prosecutor that Johnson had, before talking to Brav, told Brav, "I [Johnson] will have to tell my supervisor if you make any incriminating statements" and Brav had responded, "That's alright, I need to get this off my chest, real bad, and I deserve what happens." Both Brav and Johnson agreed at the subsequent suppression hearing, however, that after the interview Johnson reported the incriminating statements to his supervisor, who in turn called the police.

When the police arrived, they gave Brav a written statement of his *Miranda* warnings. At the bottom of the statement were two questions for the defendant to respond to by checking a "yes" or a "no" box. The first question read, "Do you understand each of these rights I have explained to you?" The second question read, "Having these rights in mind, do you wish to talk to us now?" Brav checked "yes" to the first question but failed to respond to the second one. Brav later told his lawyer that he did not respond to the second question because he was not sure whether he should have been talking to the police without his lawyer.

One of the detectives then read Brav his *Miranda* rights again, asking Brav whether he understood those rights and then whether he wished to talk to the police. Brav answered "yes" to the first question but hesitated before answering the second question, bit his lip, tears welling in his eyes, and said, "I guess so." Brav then confessed to the murder, and, after confession, read a typed version of his statement and checked "yes" this time to both the immediately-preceding questions.

QUESTIONS

1. Assume you represent Brav and have just filed a motion to suppress Brav's statement. Should you call Brav to the stand? What questions would you ask him? What additional information, if any, would you want and what other witnesses might you call at the suppression hearing and why?

2. Do you have any ethical concerns about calling Brav to the stand? What additional investigation, if any, might be necessary to resolve those concerns? What actions should you take?

3. If Johnson takes the stand, what questions would you ask him on cross-examination, and why, if you represent Brav? If you are the prosecutor and Brav takes the stand, what questions would you ask him on cross, why, and what additional information might you want to prepare, and how would you get it?

4. If you are the judge and Brav, the police officers, Johnson, and his supervisor all testify, how will you rule and why? Will your ruling, whatever it may be, survive on appeal?

5. Might any of the answers to the above questions affect plea negotiations? How? How would the prosecutor and defense counsel factor the above concerns into such negotiations and what tactics should each side follow? Are there any ethical or strategic limitations on what defense counsel may or should reveal during these negotiations? Keep in mind also that prosecutors are constitutionally obliged to turn over to the defense, prior to trial, all material, exculpatory evidence.[178] Some courts have interpreted this obligation to apply in the plea negotiation context.[179]

PROBLEM 8–37

Assume that after Brav's confession to the police in the preceding problem, Brav was arrested and incarcerated. The police executing a valid search warrant for Brav's body hairs, went to the prison to meet with Brav. Brav's attorney was present at the start of this meeting and advised Brav in the presence of the police not to talk to the police. Toward the end of the meeting, Brav's counsel left Brav alone with the police to execute the warrant. The police did so and left the prisoner's cell.

Two days earlier, Brav had sent a note to the police saying he wanted to talk and his lawyer need not be present. The police had not acted on that note. Immediately after executing the warrant, however, Brav said, "Did you get my note?" The police officers said "yes" and re-administered complete and correct *Miranda* warnings, and Brav clearly stated that he understood his rights and wanted to waive them. The police said nothing further but just let all parties stand in the cell, in silence. Brav then said, "Look, here's what happened" and confessed again to the crime, this time in great detail. Brav's lawyer files a motion to suppress this statement given in the cell.

Question: Will Brav's motion to suppress likely succeed?

PROBLEM 8–38

The police, investigating a charge of lewd and lascivious conduct upon a child, called John Cosby on the phone, asking him to drop by whenever he had time to answer some questions that they hoped might help them with their investigation. Cosby agreed and came by the police station to talk to Detective Gilbert. Gilbert had invited the twenty-year-old Cosby to drop by because the fourteen-year-old victim, having recently "recovered" some repressed memories of abuse while under hypnosis in therapy, remembered that he had been sexually abused six years earlier by a then-fourteen-year-old babysitter, and Cosby had indeed at that time been one of the victim's three usual babysitters.

Detective Gilbert told Cosby the victim had identified his assailant as one of his former babysitters, and Cosby had been mentioned as a former babysitter for the victim. Gilbert told Cosby that he was not under arrest but then read Cosby his *Miranda* rights and asked, "Do you understand

---

178.   *See* Brady v. Maryland, 373 U.S. 83 (1963).

179.   *See, e.g.*, Sanchez v. United States, 50 F.3d 1448 (9th Cir.1995).

your rights?" and "Do you want to make a statement?" Cosby said yes, and Gilbert asked, "What was the highest grade you completed in school?" Cosby said, "Eighth grade."

Gilbert questioned Cosby, who at first denied any sexual contact with the victim. Cosby denied any, but after being reminded he was "under oath," said he and the victim had engaged in some sexual touching. Cosby blushed and seemed embarrassed and Gilbert said:

> I realize this is embarrassing for you, but I talk to kids all the time about this sort of thing. All right? So anything that you say to me is not going to shock me or embarrass me because I've talked to a lot of kids before. So if you do have something to say and if something more happened, I don't want you to feel like you can't tell me. Okay? So why don't you take a deep breath and think back.

Cosby then admitted to sodomizing the victim on several occasions.

At the subsequent hearing on the defense motion to suppress these statements, Cosby admitted he went to the police of his own free will. But he maintained that he was not told what he might be charged with or what the interview was about. He described himself as a slow learner and said that he understood some but not all of his *Miranda* rights. He remembered being told he did not have to talk but thought it would be the best thing. He did not think he would be charged with a crime. A psychologist later testified that Cosby had an eighty I.Q. and would have a limited ability to understand *Miranda* warnings. Contrary prosecuting expert testimony, finding Cosby to be of "normal intelligence," was offered.

The trial court granted the motion to suppress, finding:

1. Cosby was not in custody at the start of the interview by Detective Gilbert.
2. Cosby was fully advised of his *Miranda* rights by Detective Gilbert.
3. Cosby has an eighth grade education and mentality.
4. Cosby did not invoke his *Miranda* rights during the course of the interview.
5. A person of normal intelligence would have invoked his *Miranda* rights.
6. Cosby is childlike and unable to comprehend being in jeopardy.
7. Cosby did not understand his *Miranda* rights and did not freely and voluntarily waive them.

The prosecution appealed the granting of the motion to an intermediate state appellate court, which overruled the trial court.

Question: Was the appellate court's decision correct? Why or why not?

PROBLEM 8–39

Eighteen-year-old Luther Pardo was arrested on suspicion of the murder of Robert Rider. That suspicion arose from a phone call received from an anonymous informant, who said:

I saw who killed Robert Rider. It was last night, at 2 a.m., in the woods behind the McDonald's on 18th street. I had been camping in the woods and saw Luther Pardo drop what looked like a body. I knew Pardo because we went to high school together. When Pardo left, I looked at the body. I didn't recognize the face until I saw Rider's photo in today's newspaper, in the story about the murder. I immediately recognized the face as the one of the dead man I'd seen in the woods. I'm afraid of Pardo. He was crazy in high school.

The informant then hung up.

Immediately after Pardo's arrest, John Gage appeared at the police station, told the police in Pardo's presence that he, Gage, represented Pardo and the police should not question him and left. After he left, Pardo said, "I don't know who that guy is. I didn't hire him."

Pardo was placed in a cell and was given *Miranda* warnings thirty hours later. His mother, Johnine, a local police officer, was also brought in. Three other police officers were present. One of the police officers said, in Pardo's presence, "Johnine, you're here as his mom, in your private capacity, not as a police officer," Johnine started to beg Pardo to "come clean," so she could help him. She then aggressively questioned her son, resting at times to let the other officers question. Johnine often cried, again begging her son to "help himself." One officer later described the scene as the "most emotionally intense interrogation I ever witnessed." Johnine also said that she had no idea who retained Gage. Pardo asked the police, "Will my statements to my mom incriminate me?" Johnine responded, "Anything you say, any cooperation, will help me, and you, and the police, and that's the right thing, that's what matters." Finally, Pardo agreed to give a statement and confessed to the murder.

QUESTIONS

1. On what grounds, if any, might a motion to suppress Pardo's statement be filed?

2. Assuming Gage did represent Pardo, did he do so effectively? What else, if anything, should he have done? For help in resolving these questions, see Chapter 5 for information about the right to effective assistance of counsel.

PROBLEM 8–40

Ben Harvey was arrested for the murder of John Bean. At 3:37 p.m., Harvey was given *Miranda* warnings, indicated he understood the warnings, and was questioned about a forgery scam. He denied involvement in that scam and in the murder and asked to be left alone awhile for time to think. The police did so. They returned forty minutes later, reminded him, "Remember your *Miranda* rights," and he cried and asked to talk to his mother-in-law, Ms. Pearl Davis.

Davis showed up an hour later and spoke with Harvey ten minutes alone. The police questioned Harvey, and he said, "I just didn't do anything." The police again left Harvey alone.

Fifteen minutes later Harvey asked a guard to let him speak to Detective Storm, the Chief Detective on the case. Storm showed up, again said, "Remember your *Miranda* rights," and Harvey promptly confessed to the forgery.

The next morning two officers drove Harvey to the murder scene. He was re-*Mirandized*, said again he didn't kill anyone, and said, "Look, feel free to search my house. You won't find anything." The police did go to Harvey's property, saw a watch that matched the murder victim's stolen watch on Harvey's car seat (the car was parked in Harvey's garage), and took the watch, which was identified by the victim's family as the victim's.

Four hours after taking Harvey to the murder scene, the police told Harvey about finding the watch. He said, "I didn't think you'd search the car. Let me talk to my dad." Fifteen minutes later, Harvey's dad appeared and spent an hour alone with Harvey. When the police returned, Harvey was re-*Mirandized*, stated he understood all his rights, and confessed to the murder.

QUESTIONS

1.   Should Harvey's confession to forgery be suppressed?

2.   Should Harvey's confession to the murder be suppressed?

PROBLEM 8–41

Assume that you are counsel for Boson in Chapter 1. What arguments will you raise to suppress Boson's statements, and how likely are you to succeed?

III.   THE SIXTH AMENDMENT RIGHT TO COUNSEL

Checklist 13: The Right to Counsel After Initiation of Formal Charges

1.   Was the statement made by a person after adversarial proceedings had begun?

2.   If yes, did a government actor deliberately elicit the statement in the absence of defense counsel or a valid waiver of counsel?

3.   If yes, did the statement concern the charged offense?

The Supreme Court's analysis of confessions implicates most directly the Fifth and Fourteenth Amendments. However, in 1964, the Court added another dimension when it decided, in *Massiah v. United States*,[180] that a criminal defendant's Sixth Amendment right to counsel protects the defendant during post-indictment interactions with government agents.

A.   THE *MASSIAH* DOCTRINE'S HISTORICAL BACKGROUND

The decision in *Massiah* appears to have grown out of the Court's increasing awareness that deprivation of legal advice is a significant factor in the voluntariness inquiry. As Professor LaFave explains, as early as the mid–1940s the Court began to take "special note" of the fact that defendants who confessed typically had been denied access to counsel.[181] Despite the Court's refusal to impose on the states a requirement that counsel be provided to all criminal defendants, a number of justices began to suggest that "the accused who wants a counsel should have one at any time after the moment of arrest."[182]

During the ensuing decade, the Court decided several confession cases involving police refusals to provide counsel. Most notable was *Spano v. New York*, in which police obtained a confession from an indicted defendant who had already retained a lawyer.[183] During interrogation, the defendant had asked for his lawyer, but the police ignored his requests. The Court held that the confession was involuntary, based on a number of factors, including the denial of counsel. Several years later, the Court finally held that states must provide counsel to indigent defendants in criminal cases.[184] The Court's emphasis on the importance of counsel has been explained as follows:

> The right to be heard would be, in many cases, of little avail if it did not comprehend the right to be heard by counsel. Even the intelligent and educated layman has small and sometimes no skill in the science of law. If charged with crime, he is incapable, generally, of determining for himself whether the indictment is good or bad. He is unfamiliar with the rules of evidence. Left without the aid of counsel he may be put on trial without a proper charge, and convicted upon incompetent evidence, or evidence irrelevant to the issue or otherwise inadmissible. He lacks both the skill and knowledge adequately to prepare his defense, even though he have a perfect one. He requires the guiding hand of counsel at every step in the proceedings against him.[185]

---

180.   377 U.S. 201 (1964).

181.   Wayne R. LaFave and Jerold H. Israel, CRIMINAL PROCEDURE 302 (2d ed. 1992).

182.   Crooker v. California, 357 U.S. 433, 437 (1958) (Douglas, J., dissenting).

183.   360 U.S. 315 (1959).

184.   Gideon v. Wainwright, 372 U.S. 335 (1963). To explore the details of the *Gideon* case, read Anthony Lewis's GIDEON'S TRUMPET (1964). In subsequent cases, the Court limited the right to counsel to cases in which the defendant received a sentence of "actual imprisonment." *See* Scott v. Illinois, 440 U.S. 367 (1979); Argersinger v. Hamlin, 407 U.S. 25 (1972).

185.   Powell v. Alabama, 287 U.S. 45, 68–69 (1932).

and as follows:

> [A]ny person haled into court ... cannot be assured a fair trial unless counsel is provided for him. This seems to us to be an obvious truth. Governments, both state and federal, quite properly spend vast sums of money to establish machinery to try defendants accused of crime. Lawyers to prosecute are everywhere deemed essential to protect the public's interest in an orderly society. Similarly, there are few defendants charged with crime, few indeed, who fail to hire the best lawyers they can get to prepare and present their defenses. That government hires lawyers to prosecute and defendants who have the money hire lawyers to defend are the strongest indications of the widespread belief that lawyers in criminal courts are necessities, not luxuries. The right of one charged with crime to counsel may not be deemed fundamental and essential to fair trials in some countries, but it is in ours.[186]

B.   THE DECISION IN *MASSIAH* AND INTERPRETIVE ISSUES

The Court's previous recognition that criminal defendants have a right to counsel even during the preliminary phases of the adversarial process, and that access to counsel is often a crucial factor in the voluntariness analysis, set the stage for *Massiah*. A federal grand jury had indicted Massiah and his friend, Colson, for narcotics offenses. Massiah hired a lawyer, pleaded not guilty at his arraignment, and was released on bail. Without his or his lawyer's knowledge, Colson had agreed to cooperate with government efforts to trap Massiah into making incriminating statements. Colson permitted the government to install a radio transmitter in his car. He then asked Massiah to get into the car and initiated a conversation with Massiah about the narcotics charges. Massiah made damaging admissions to Colson, which were intercepted by federal agents and recounted at Massiah's trial.

The government's subterfuge put Massiah in a difficult legal position on appeal. Obviously, his major contention was that the trial court should have excluded his statements from trial. He would have a difficult time persuading a court that his statements were "involuntary," since no coercion was apparent, even of the psychological variety. His claim, therefore, focused on his Sixth Amendment right to counsel, which applies "in all criminal prosecutions." According to Massiah, that right to counsel cloaked him with protection from the time of indictment through trial and was violated when the government obtained statements through trickery and in the absence of his lawyer.

The Supreme Court agreed. In a majority opinion joined by five other justices, Justice Stewart held that the Sixth Amendment precluded the government from "deliberately eliciting" damaging statements from the defendant without providing the defendant the opportunity to consult with counsel. According to Justice Stewart, the Sixth Amendment right to counsel arose when Massiah was indicted and applied during pretrial as

---

186.   *Gideon*, 372 U.S. at 344.

well as trial stages of the process. Justice Stewart said in general that the pretrial period is "the most critical period of the proceedings":

> [U]nder our system of justice the most elemental concepts of due process of law contemplate that an indictment be followed by a trial, in an orderly courtroom, presided over by a judge, open to the public, and protected by all the procedural safeguards of the law.... [A] Constitution which guarantees a defendant the aid of counsel at such a trial could surely vouchsafe no less to an indicted defendant under interrogation by the police in a completely extrajudicial proceeding. Anything less ... might deny a defendant effective representation by counsel at the only stage when legal aid and advice would help him. ...
>
> Any secret interrogation of the defendant, from and after the finding of the indictment, without the protection afforded by the presence of counsel, contravenes the basic dictates of fairness in the conduct of criminal causes and the fundamental rights of persons charged with crime.
>
> This view no more than reflects a constitutional principle established as long ago as Powell v. Alabama, where the Court noted that "... during perhaps the most critical period of the proceedings ... that is to say, from the time of their arraignment until the beginning of their trial, when consultation, thorough-going investigation and preparation [are] vitally important, the defendants ... [are] as much entitled to such aid [of counsel] during that period as at the trial itself."

Thus, according to Justice Powell, if the government were permitted to engage in surreptitious measures during the pretrial period in order to obtain damaging statements from the accused, the right to counsel would be rendered ineffective.

NOTES AND QUESTIONS

1. The Sixth Amendment by its terms declares that "the accused" in all criminal prosecutions shall have the right to the "assistance of counsel for his defense." Is a suspect an "accused"? Does he become an "accused" when arrested? When indicted? When arraigned? When he is the focus of police investigation? Most scholars agree that the Sixth Amendment was enacted to reject the prevailing rule in England that denied felony defendants the right to retained counsel at trial. Thus, an important purpose of the Sixth Amendment was to permit defendants the right to retain counsel for trial, an approach that most American states adopted even before the American Revolution.[187]

---

187. *See* William M. Beaney, The Right to Counsel in American Courts 27–36 (1955); J. B. Post, *The Admissibility of Defence Counsel in English Criminal Procedure*, 5 J. Legal Hist. 23 (1984); Note, *An Historical Argument for the Right to Counsel During Police Interrogation*, 73 Yale L.J. 1000, 1018–30 (1964); James J. Tomkovicz, *An Adversary System Defense of the Right to Counsel Against Informants: Truth, Fair Play, and the Massiah Doctrine*, 22 U.C. Davis L. Rev. 1, 2, 10–11 (1988).

2. While perhaps not contemplated by the framers, extending that right to indigents by means of appointed counsel is relatively uncontroversial, given that it serves the framers' goal of assisting defendants who could not on their own recognize and present all defenses.[188] Extending the right to pretrial events that might "appropriately be considered to be parts of the trial itself" is also relatively uncontroversial. But extending the right to police interrogations is another matter. Thus one court emphasized that the right to assistance of counsel begins when the "defense" begins—the point of time, according to that court, when the defendant is "put in jeopardy on his trial." According to that court, the right ensures "reasonable access to the prisoner for the purpose of preparing his defense."[189] Professor Grano, in an effort to ease constraints on the state's ability to obtain confessions, warns that providing counsel at interrogations subverts truthseeking by depriving the state of necessary evidence. He views as the heart of the Sixth Amendment providing counsel at trial in order to promote truth in the presentation of evidence. Grano ignores the possibility that counsel's presence during interrogations may promote truthful confessions, at least in certain cases.[190] Moreover, an approach to constitutional interpretation more sensitive to concerns that constitutional principles be given room to evolve would consider the Sixth Amendment values that counsel's presence at interrogation might serve. Those values would include the "fox-hunter's, equality, and dignity" arguments considered earlier.

3. *A Note on Formalism*: The start-of-adversarial-proceedings dividing line is arguably a "mere formalism," for it is hard as a practical matter to see why an uncharged suspect on whom the police are focusing has a less urgent need for counsel than the charged defendant. The line may be a product of a balance between state and individual interests. That is, the Court may have adopted the adversarial proceedings dividing line as a compromise fairly serving all interests. Driving this balance is the Court's fear on the one hand that providing a right to counsel too early in the process would destroy the effectiveness of interrogation as an investigatory tool, and its recognition on the other hand of the value of counsel.

4. As you prepare for class, think about how you would answer the following questions:

a. What arguments might you craft for a more flexible approach to interpreting the Sixth Amendment? How would the fox-hunter's, equality, and dignity arguments support the theory that there should be a pre-indictment right to counsel at interrogation? Might these arguments be more effective under state constitutions?

b. What arguments could you make for a pre-indictment right to counsel under due process, rather than the Sixth Amendment? Under what circumstances might such a case-specific right apply?

---

188. Grano, CONFESSIONS, *supra* note 9, at 156.

189. State v. Murphy, 94 A. 640, 646 (N.J.1915).

190. Grano, CONFESSIONS, *supra* note 9, at 157–58.

c.   Is the kind of balancing discussed above legitimate under the Sixth Amendment?

d.   If it is, why would the balance not be better served by requiring counsel at the point of arrest? When investigation has focused on a particular suspect?

e.   *Miranda* created a Fifth Amendment right to counsel for custodial interrogation. Why should the Fifth Amendment support a different result than the Sixth? If balancing was involved in *Miranda*, why was the balance there struck as it was, and why would not the same balance be appropriate under the Sixth Amendment?

C.   THRESHOLDS: FORMAL CHARGE AND DELIBERATE ELICITATION

1.   THE REQUIREMENT OF A FORMAL CHARGE

Massiah comes far closer to a bright-line rule than the "totality of the circumstances" approach used in the coerced confession cases. Rather than evaluate, on a case-by-case basis, the voluntariness of confessions, the *Massiah* doctrine sets up an automatic formula: any uncounseled statement "deliberately elicited" after indictment must be excluded from trial. On the other hand, the *Massiah* doctrine is limited to situations in which the adversarial process has begun. According to the Court, the Sixth Amendment right to counsel is triggered by "the initiation of adversary judicial criminal proceedings—whether by way of formal charge, preliminary hearing, indictment, information, or arraignment." This was the necessary dividing line because only at that point has the state fully committed all its resources to prosecution, thus immersing the suspect in the "intricacies of substantive and procedural criminal law."[191]

Recently, in *Rothgery v. Gillespie County, Texas,*[192] the Court held that the Sixth Amendment right to counsel attached at a post-arrest proceeding, entitled under Texas law an "article 15.7 hearing," that combined the initial bail determination, the Fourth Amendment *Gerstein* prompt probable cause determination, and the first formal apprisal of the defendant of the accusations against him—so holding even though no prosecutor was present nor yet playing any role in the case. However, the Court emphasized that it was holding only that the hearing marked the start of "formal adversarial proceedings" but was not deciding whether that hearing was a "critical stage," a term probably roughly meaning a "trial-like" confrontation at which counsel is needed to act as a "spokesperson or advisor,"[193] though the definition of the term "critical stage" is arguably ambiguous and contested.

---

191.   Kirby v. Illinois, 406 U.S. 682, 689–90 (1972). Although *Kirby* was a case dealing with line-ups, the logic of its analysis applies to confessions as well.

192.   128 S.Ct. 2578 (2008).

193.   *See* United States v. Ash, 412 U.S. 926 (1973) (so defining "critical stage," a term whose meaning is discussed in more detail in chapter 10 *infra*).

The Sixth Amendment guarantees the accused the presence of counsel *only* at "critical stages" occurring after the right has "attached," that is, after formal adversarial proceedings have begun. By not addressing the critical stage question, the Court has thus left open whether any Sixth Amendment guarantee of counsel's presence applies at hearings akin to Texas's article 15.7 hearing. *Miranda* rights probably do not apply at such hearings because the accused is not in a "police-dominated atmosphere" but rather involved in a public proceeding before a magistrate. Should the Court eventually hold that proceedings like Texas's article 15.7 hearings are not critical stages, a defendant might find himself with neither Fifth nor Sixth Amendment protections for any statements that he makes at the hearing. He would be reduced to relying for suppression of any such statements on a Fourth Amendment fruit-of-the-poisonous tree argument (if there was a Fourth Amendment violation and if no exception to the exclusionary rule applies) or on the hard-to-prove due process involuntariness argument. *Rothgery* is discussed in more detail in chapter 10 (concerning eyewitness identifications) of the text.

By confining the *Massiah* doctrine to situations in which the Sixth Amendment right to counsel had already attached, the Court left unprotected those confessions that police obtain during the investigatory, or precharge, phase of a case. During the same term in which it decided *Massiah*, the Court, in *Escobedo v. Illinois*,[194] took a small step toward providing unindicted suspects with a right to counsel, but that effort was eventually preempted by its later, more sweeping decision in *Miranda v. Arizona*. In *Escobedo*, the Court dealt with a confession by an incarcerated, but uncharged, murder suspect. The suspect, Escobedo, had retained counsel and repeatedly asked to see his lawyer, but police refused to honor his request. Moreover, his lawyer came to the police station but was denied access to his client. Despite the Court's recognition that the preindictment stage of a case is critical to a defendant, and that it could draw "no meaningful distinction" between pre- and post-indictment interrogations, it declined to create a broad right to counsel. Instead, it issued a very limited holding, as follows:

> [W]here, as here, the investigation is no longer a general inquiry into an unsolved crime but has begun to focus on a particular suspect, the suspect has been taken into police custody, the police carry out a process of interrogations that lends itself to eliciting incriminating statements, the suspect has requested and been denied an opportunity to consult with his lawyer, and the police have not effectively warned him of his absolute constitutional right to remain silent, the accused has been denied "The Assistance of Counsel" in violation of the Sixth Amendment to the Constitution ... and ... no statement elicited by the police during the interrogation may be used against him at a criminal trial.

---

194.   378 U.S. 478 (1964).

After its opinion in *Miranda v. Arizona*, which provided a much less fact-specific right to counsel during the investigatory phase—a right based on the Fifth Amendment privilege against self-incrimination—the Court itself recognized that the holding in *Escobedo* was limited to its own facts.

2.   DELIBERATE ELICITATION

As indicated above, the *Massiah* doctrine comes into play only where law enforcement personnel have "deliberately elicited" incriminating statements. An officer may be found to have deliberately elicited incriminating statements directly, by engaging the defendant in conversation about the charged conduct, or indirectly, by knowingly exploiting an opportunity to confront an accused without an attorney present. An example of the direct variety of deliberate elicitation is *Brewer v. Williams*,[195] in which a police officer encouraged a defendant to make incriminating admissions by playing on his emotions. In that case, Williams was seen, shortly after the disappearance of a ten-year-old girl on Christmas Eve, placing into his car a large wrapped bundle that had "two legs in it." After police obtained a warrant for his arrest, he was arrested in another county, where he consulted with an attorney and was arraigned before a judge on the warrant. The police arranged to have two detectives transport him to the appropriate jurisdiction. The attorney who had represented Williams at arraignment told the detectives that he was not to be questioned before he consulted with his attorney in the charging jurisdiction. En route, one of the two detectives, fully aware of the fact that Williams was a former mental patient and deeply religious, addressed him as "Reverend" and said:

> I want to give you something to think about while we're traveling down the road.... Number one, I want you to observe the weather conditions, it's raining, it's sleeting, it's freezing, driving is very treacherous, visibility is poor, it's going to be dark early this evening. They are predicting several inches of snow for tonight, and I feel that you yourself are the only person that knows where this little girl's body is, that you yourself have only been there once, and if you get a snow on top of it you yourself may be unable to find it. And, since we will be going right past the area on the way into Des Moines, I feel that we could stop and locate the body, that the parents of this little girl should be entitled to a Christian burial for the little girl who was snatched away from them on Christmas [E]ve and murdered. And I feel we should stop and locate it on the way in rather than waiting until morning and trying to come back out after a snow storm and possibly not being able to find it at all.

Williams then directed the detectives to the location of the murdered girl's body. The Court held that his statements were inadmissible because they had been deliberately elicited in the absence of his attorney and after the initiation of the criminal proceedings.

---

195.   430 U.S. 387 (1977).

In *Fellers v. United States*,[196] the Supreme Court held that officers who arrived at John Fellers' home with an arrest warrant and an indictment, and who informed him that "their purpose in coming was to discuss his involvement in the distribution of methamphetamine and his association with certain charged co-conspirators" had deliberately elicited his statements and thus implicated his Sixth Amendment rights. Fellers' statements, which were made outside the presence of counsel and without a waiver of his rights, could not be admitted. The Court declined to decide whether a subsequent statement, made after *Miranda* warnings and waivers, was admissible, or whether the rationale of *Elstad* would apply.

The *Massiah* doctrine also applies to less direct situations, including those in which a law enforcement officer intentionally creates a situation likely to induce a defendant to make incriminating statements to an informant. In *United States v. Henry*,[197] law enforcement agents contacted an informant/cellmate of the defendant, who had been indicted on a charge of armed robbery, and told the cellmate "to be alert to any statements made by [the defendant], but not to initiate any conversation with or question [him] regarding the ... robbery." Subsequently, the cellmate reported to the agents that the defendant had admitted to participating in the robbery. The cellmate was paid for providing the information. The Court held that the government had "deliberately elicited" the defendant's admissions. The Court emphasized that the cellmate had been an informant for more than a year, that he was paid only if he produced useful information, and that the agents knew that he had access to the defendant and would be able to converse with the defendant without raising suspicion. Under these circumstances, the Court concluded, the agents "must have known that such propinquity likely would lead" to incriminating statements. The Court also viewed as important the fact that the cellmate was not a "passive listener," but instead had some "conversations" with the defendant and that the defendant's incriminating statements were "the product" of these conversations.

By way of contrast, asking an informant merely to listen does not violate a defendant's right to counsel. Thus, in *Kuhlmann v. Wilson*,[198] the Court held that a defendant's incriminating statements, reported to the police by a cellmate who had been instructed to "keep his ears open," had not been "deliberately elicited" within the meaning of *Massiah*. It is important to note that in this case, the cellmate "at no time asked any questions of [the defendant] concerning the pending charges, and that he only listened to [the defendant's] spontaneous and unsolicited statements." Thus, the cellmate acted as a "listening post without participating in active conversation and prompting particular replies."

Finally, "knowing exploitation" by law enforcement officers of an "opportunity to confront the accused" without the assistance of counsel

---

196. 540 U.S. 519 (2004).

197. 447 U.S. 264 (1980).

198. 477 U.S. 436 (1986).

may violate the Massiah doctrine even when the officers did not intentionally create the situation. In *Maine v. Moulton*,[199] Moulton and Colson were indicted with four counts of theft and, assisted by counsel, were arraigned and released on bail. Moulton and Colson subsequently met in order to plan their trial strategy, and, according to Colson, Moulton proposed killing a witness. Colson then confessed to the police and consented to record any calls from Moulton. He also agreed to wear a body transmitter in order to record further conversations and meetings with Moulton regarding trial strategy. During one such meeting with Moulton, which had been requested by Moulton, Colson elicited several incriminating statements from Moulton. The Court held that the statements should have been excluded, rejecting the prosecution's contention that the fact that Moulton had initiated the telephone calls and the meetings meant that his Sixth Amendment rights had not been violated. The Court explained that "knowing exploitation by the State of an opportunity to confront the accused without counsel being present is as much a breach of the State's obligation not to circumvent the right to the assistance of counsel as is the intentional creation of such an opportunity." Thus, "the Sixth Amendment is violated when the State obtains incriminating statements by knowingly circumventing the accused's right to have counsel present in a confrontation between the accused and a state agent" and any statements acquired in such a manner may not be admitted at a trial of the accused.

PROBLEM 8–42

Jamie was arrested and charged with robbing a local convenience store. Jamie's cellmate, John, had been indicted on a charge of murder. John frequently cooperated with law enforcement by informing the police of incriminating statements made by other cellmates. John provided the information in the hopes of gaining favor with police and possibly obtaining a recommendation for a reduced sentence. Although police never specifically ask John to question Jamie about the robbery, they were aware that John had reported incriminating statements made by other cellmates. After several days in jail, John asked Jamie, "What are you in for?" Jamie replied, "I lost my job and needed some cash, so I thought I'd borrow some from the cashier at the corner market." John repeated the incriminating statements to the police.

Question: Should the trial court exclude the information about Jamie's statement to John?

D. INVOKING AND WAIVING SIXTH AMENDMENT RIGHTS

Once a defendant has been formally charged, his Sixth Amendment right to counsel "attaches." Nevertheless, it also must be invoked before it is fully effective. Many lower courts had until the recent decision in

---

199. 474 U.S. 159 (1985).

Montejo v. Louisiana,[200] discussed shortly, held that invocation occurs whenever counsel enters an appearance, though not all courts agreed. Often this happens simply when an appearance of defense counsel is entered on behalf of a defendant. After the right attaches, but *before it is invoked*, the right may be waived by the defendant. The government bears the burden of proof on waiver, and it must demonstrate "an intentional relinquishment or abandonment of a known right or privilege."[201] In other words, the government must prove that the defendant's waiver of the right to counsel was "voluntary" and "knowing and intelligent." Ordinarily, this analysis will mirror the *Miranda* analysis, and the same warnings will satisfy both *Miranda* and *Massiah*.

In *Iowa v. Tovar*,[202] the Supreme Court emphasized that the extent of warnings required by the Sixth Amendment varies according to context. The *Patterson* case, it said, involved the very early stages of a criminal case, where "the full dangers and disadvantages of self-representation . . . are less substantial and more obvious to an accused than they are at trial"— correspondingly the warnings could be "less rigorous." At later stages, a more extensive set of warnings and waivers might be required.

In 1986, the Court held that once the *Massiah* right had been invoked, however, there may be no finding of waiver if the waiver was made in response to government-initiated interrogation. This rule was developed for *Miranda* situations, but in *Michigan v. Jackson*,[203] the Court applied it to the Sixth Amendment context. There, Jackson was arrested and arraigned. He requested that counsel be appointed for him, and that request was granted. Before he was able to contact his appointed attorney, two officers advised him of his *Miranda* rights, and he confessed. The Court held the waiver invalid, holding that an accused person in custody, who has "expressed his desire to deal with the police only through counsel, is not subject to further interrogation by the authorities until counsel has been made available to him, unless the accused himself initiates further communication, exchanges, or conversations with the police." Thus, the Court held that the defendant's confession was taken without an adequate waiver and could not be used against him during the prosecution's case-in-chief at trial.

But the Court recently overruled *Michigan v. Jackson* in *Montejo v. Louisiana*.[204] There, Montejo had been arrested on robbery and murder charges, waived his *Miranda* rights, and ultimately confessed to the crime. At a hearing held within 72 hours, as required by Louisiana law, the court appointed counsel for the indigent Montejo, though Montejo had not himself requested counsel. Later that same day, two detectives asked Montejo to accompany them in an effort to locate the murder weapon.

---

200. 129 S.Ct. 2079 (2009).

201. Johnson v. Zerbst, 304 U.S. 458, 464 (1938).

202. 541 U.S. 77 (2004).

203. 475 U.S. 625 (1986).

204. *Montejo*, 129 S.Ct. at 2091.

Montejo agreed, and, during the excursion wrote an apology letter to the victim's widow, only meeting his defense lawyer upon returning to prison, a lawyer upset at interrogation of his client occurring during his absence. The letter was admitted at trial over Montejo's objection, and he was convicted of first-degree murder and sentenced to death.

When the case reached the United States Supreme Court, the Court concluded that the *Jackson* rule had proven "unworkable." Requiring defendants like Montejo actually to assert their rights to "invoke" them at preliminary arraignment seemed unfair because many states do not even ask an accused to do so but simply appoint counsel. Yet applying *Jackson* where a defendant has never affirmatively invoked his right also seemed inconsistent with *Jackson*'s rationale, which the Court described as "preclud[ing] the State from badgering defendants into waiving their previously asserted rights."[205] "The effect of this badgering," continued the Court, "might be to coerce a waiver, which would render the subsequent interrogation a violation of the Sixth Amendment."[206] But, explained the Court, "it would be completely unjustified to presume that a defendant's consent to police-initiated interrogation was involuntary or coerced simply because he had previously been appointed a lawyer."[207] *Jackson* required something more affirmative to justify that presumption. If something more affirmative were shown, rather than engaging in a case-by-case assessment of voluntariness, *Jackson* created a bright-line rule ensuring the automatic exclusion of confessions resulting after Sixth Amendment rights-invocation, a purposely overly-broad rule to avoid even the possibility of badgering-induced waivers resulting in statements used to convict at trial.

But, concluded the Court, the cost-benefit calculus underlying *Jackson* tipped the balance against retaining the rule. Most importantly, the Court had already provided substantial overlapping protection in its *Miranda* jurisprudence. *Miranda* itself was a prophylactic (purposely overly-broad) rule designed to protect the privilege against self-incrimination. The *Edwards* rule requiring interrogation to stop upon assertion of the *Miranda* right to counsel was a second level of prophylaxis to protect the first level. *Minnick*'s bar on further questioning or seeking of a waiver until counsel was present (or until the suspect re-initiated the conversation) once the *Miranda* right to counsel was asserted was a third layer of prophylaxis. Three such layers, concluded the Court, are sufficient to prevent "badgered" waivers. Granted, the Court conceded, *Edwards* applied only in the context of custodial interrogation while the Sixth Amendment right widely applies to all post-indictment interrogations. But, said the Court, these "uncovered situations are the *least* likely to pose a risk of coerced waivers." Indeed, "When a defendant is not in custody, he is in control, and need only shut his door or walk away to avoid police badgering."

---

205. *Id.* at 2089.

206. *Id.*

207. *Id.* at 2088.

Yet the costs of retaining the *Jackson* rule were, in the Court's eyes unacceptable, the principal cost being letting the guilty and dangerous go free under the exclusionary rule. The Court also rejected the argument that ending *Jackson* would render *Edwards* itself unworkable because courts will have to determine whether preliminary arraignment statements constituted *Edwards* violations. The Court said, for the very first time, that preliminary arraignment invocations of the *Miranda* right to counsel were *irrelevant* under *Miranda* and its progeny. "What matters for *Miranda* and *Edwards* is what happens when the defendant is approached for interrogation, and (if he consents) what happens during the interrogation not what happened at any preliminary hearing."[208] *Jackson's* rule thus no longer "pay[s] its way," and, given its young age (just over two decades old) and the absence of significant reliance interests, combined with the rule's unworkability, the force of *stare decisis* was limited. Accordingly, the rule lives no more.

However, the Court remanded to offer Montejo the opportunity to raise an *Edwards* claim, finding that he may not have done so because of *Jackson's* broader protection. In doing so, the Court stressed that a valid *Miranda* waiver may also constitute a valid Sixth Amendment waiver, and there is no reason for treating waivers differently based solely on whether the defendant was in fact represented or not at the time.

Justice Stevens, joined by Justices Ginsburg, Souter, and Breyer, dissented.[209] Stevens relied primarily on two concepts. First, he insisted that if *requesting* a lawyer constituted an invocation of Sixth Amendment rights, then surely *having* a lawyer surely must be treated in the same fashion because the existence of the lawyer-client relationship is at the core of what the fullest protection of Sixth Amendment rights is all about. Second, said Stevens, *Jackson's* purpose was *not* to prevent police badgering waivers but rather to " 'protect the unaided layman at critical confrontations with his adversary' " by "giving him 'the right to rely on counsel as a "medium" between him[self] and the State.' "[210] *Edwards,* decided under the Fifth Amendment, and *Jackson,* decided under the Sixth Amendment, thus served very different functions. For that reason, *Patterson,* holding that waiver of *Miranda* rights may constitute a waiver of Sixth Amendment rights, was wrongly decided. Furthermore, as read by Stevens, the clear rule for when to apply *Jackson*—whenever a post-indictment defendant requests *or* has counsel—made the rule perfectly workable. On the other hand, the majority insisted that *Jackson's* costs in freeing the guilty were substantial without citing "any empirical data or even anecdotal support...."[211] Indeed, to the contrary, several *amici* with an interest in law

---

208. *Id.* at 2091.

209. Justice Breyer did not, however, join one small portion of Stevens' dissent: footnote 5. That footnote addressed a concurring opinion in Montejo by Justice Alito, joined by Justice Kennedy, that compared Arizona v. Gant to Montejo on the question of the role of stare decisis.

210. *Id.* at 2096.

211. *Id.* at 2097 n.3.

enforcement conceded that *"Jackson*'s protective rule rarely impedes prosecution."[212] Accordingly, the balance of costs and benefits favored retaining *Jackson*, and there is little, if any, justification for departing from *stare decisis*. Finally, said Stevens, even if *Jackson* had never been decided, Montejo should prevail on these facts. The Sixth Amendment, even under the majority's reading, bars post-indictment interrogations absent waiver of rights under that amendment. But, because Stevens would reject *Patterson*'s holding, Montejo's waiver of his *Miranda* rights could not alone constitute a waiver of Sixth Amendment rights, and there was no other evidence of such a waiver. Absent waiver, post-indictment interrogation was prohibited even if Montejo never affirmatively invoked his Sixth Amendment rights.

It is too early to tell whether some state courts will find Stevens' dissent persuasive and retain or adopt the *Jackson* rule under their state constitutions. What is clear about this 5–4 decision is that *Jackson* no longer governs under the federal Constitution. A suspect's post-indictment invocation of his Sixth Amendment rights does not, therefore, flatly bar police from trying to get him to change his mind and waive those rights. However, that change of mind and waiver must still be "knowing, voluntary, and intelligent." Furthermore, if the suspect is facing "custodial interrogation" and asserts his *Miranda* right to counsel, *Edward*'s per se rule will still apply.

E.   *MASSIAH*'S OFFENSE–SPECIFIC NATURE

Because the *Massiah* right attaches only when a defendant is formally charged with a crime, it is "offense specific"—that is, it covers only communications about that particular crime. The Supreme Court affirmed its strict adherence to this characteristic in *McNeil v. Wisconsin*.[213] Paul McNeil was arrested for an armed robbery at location "A" and invoked his right to remain silent. McNeil was represented by an appointed attorney at a bail hearing on the charge. Two days later, officers approached McNeil in order to question him about a robbery at location "B" and read him his *Miranda* rights. He signed a waiver, agreed to talk, and made incriminating statements. The following day formal charges of armed robbery at location "B" were brought against him. McNeil sought to exclude the incriminating statements, arguing that "his courtroom appearance with an attorney ... constituted an invocation of the *Miranda* right to counsel, and ... any subsequent waiver of that right during police-initiated questioning regarding any offense was invalid."

The Supreme Court disagreed. McNeil's Sixth Amendment right to counsel had attached with regards to the robbery at location "A" in that he had been brought before a magistrate in a bail hearing. That right is offense-specific, and as of the time of the incriminating statements it had not attached to the robbery at location "B" because formal charges were

---

212.   *Id.*

213.   501 U.S. 171 (1991).

not brought until the following day. Accordingly, McNeil's Sixth Amendment right to counsel did not serve to keep out the statements regarding the robbery at location "B." Likewise, his *Miranda* right to counsel did not keep out the statements regarding the robbery at location "B" because he had not invoked that right to counsel—he had only invoked his right to counsel under the Sixth Amendment. The Court reasoned as follows:

> To invoke the Sixth Amendment interest is, as a matter of fact, not to invoke the *Miranda*-Edwards interest. One might be quite willing to speak to the police without counsel present concerning many matters, but not the matter under prosecution. It can be said, perhaps, that it is likely that one who has asked for counsel's assistance in defending against a prosecution would want counsel present for all custodial interrogation, even interrogation unrelated to the charge. That is not necessarily true, since suspects often believe that they can avoid the laying of charges by demonstrating an assurance of innocence through frank and unassisted answers to questions. But even if it were true, the likelihood that a suspect would wish counsel to be present is not the test for applicability of Edwards. The rule of that case applies only when the suspect "[h]as expressed" his wish for the particular sort of lawyerly assistance that is the subject of *Miranda*. It requires, at a minimum, some statement that can reasonably be construed to be expression of a desire for the assistance of an attorney in dealing with custodial interrogation by the police. Requesting the assistance of an attorney at a bail hearing does not bear that construction. "[T]o find that [the defendant] invoked his Fifth amendment right to counsel on the present charges merely by requesting the appointment of counsel at his arraignment on the unrelated charge is to disregard the ordinary meaning of that request."

Thus, there had been no violation of either McNeil's Sixth Amendment or *Miranda* right to counsel and the incriminating statements were properly admitted at trial.

The "offense-specific" rule has proven difficult to interpret in some cases. For example, in the hypothetical mentioned above, in which a person is implicated in both a robbery and a murder, does it matter if those two crimes occurred at the same time—and against the same victim? Some courts have held that "factually related" crimes are the same crime for *Massiah* purposes, so that a defendant charged with a crime enjoys the protection of *Massiah* on all factually related offenses even if he has not yet been charged with them. The Supreme Court disavowed this line of cases. In *Texas v. Cobb*,[214] the defendant was charged with burglary and received appointed counsel. Police also suspected him of having murdered the burglary victims, but despite several rounds of questioning (which had been authorized by defendant's attorney) they obtained no confession. Months later, the defendant told his father he had committed the murders, and when the father informed police, they arrested defendant and questioned

---

214. 532 U.S. 162 (2001).

him again. This time, the defendant waived his rights and confessed to the murders. Relying on the waiver-invalidating rule articulated in *Michigan v. Jackson* the defendant claimed that his confession should be excluded because he was represented by counsel on the factually related burglary charge and counsel had not authorized the questioning that resulted in the murder confession. Nor had defendant initiated that questioning. Quoting its opinion in *McNeil*, the Court made short shrift of his argument, reiterating, "The Sixth Amendment right to counsel is offense specific. It cannot be invoked once for all future prosecutions, for it does not attach until a prosecution is commenced, that is, at or after the initiation of adversary judicial criminal proceedings." The Court clarified that by "offense" it meant the charged offense plus any other crimes that would be considered the "same offense" for double jeopardy purposes—a narrow category including, for example, lesser included offenses. Because the defendant in *Cobb* had not been charged with murder, and because murder is not the same offense as burglary for double jeopardy purposes, the questioning did not violate *Massiah*, and the confession was admissible.

Note on Prosecution and Defense Ethics: Thus far, we have been talking about limitations that the constitution imposes when government agents question an indicted defendant. Do additional ethical restraints apply to government agents who are lawyers? Recall that prosecutors are subject to the same ethical rules that bind other lawyers. Many jurisdictions have a version of the American Bar Association's Model Code of Professional Responsibility, which includes the following provision:

> A. During the course of his representation of a client a lawyer shall not:
>
> 1. Communicate or cause another to communicate on the subject of the representation with a party he knows to be represented by a lawyer in that matter unless he has the prior consent of the lawyer representing such other party or is authorized by law to do so. . . .[215]

This rule obviously limits the communications of lawyers for private parties with other parties. For example, imagine that you represent a husband in a divorce proceeding. If you know that the wife is represented by counsel, the rule prohibits you from communicating with her about the divorce, unless one of the exceptions is present. Moreover, you cannot cause another person to communicate with her about the divorce—for example, by hiring an investigator to interview her.

Now imagine that you are a prosecutor. During the course of an investigation, you encounter an individual who is willing to serve as an informant. He agrees to record telephone conversations with the targets of your investigation, all of whom have retained counsel specifically for the investigation. If you permit the informant to record the conversations, have you not violated DR 7–104(A) by "causing another" to communicate with

---

215. *See* United States v. Hammad, 858 F.2d 834, 837 (2d Cir.1988) (quoting DR 7–104(A)(1)), *cert. denied*, 498 U.S. 871 (1990).

represented persons on the subject of the representation? Would it matter if the targets of the investigation had already been indicted?

Most courts would hold that recording the conversations of unindicted persons does not violate DR 7–104(A), while similar communications with indicted persons does violate the rule. Some commentators, and courts, contend that DR 7–104(A) does not apply to government lawyers, particularly to criminal prosecutors, while others acknowledge the rule's applicability but exempt preindictment investigative activity. With respect to the first position, DR 7–104(A) expressly depends on a lawyer's representation of a "client." The rule states that "[d]uring the course of the lawyer's representation of a client, a lawyer shall not ..." Prosecutors have no client in the sense that other lawyers do. Moreover, prosecutors are charged with the duty to seek justice, not just to advocate a partisan victory. At least theoretically, then, prosecutors operate differently than private lawyers, and perhaps the rule should not apply to them. During the Reagan administration, United States Attorney General William Thornburgh took this position, issuing a policy statement that "purport[ed] to exempt federal litigators from compliance with the rule."[216] Thornburgh's position was criticized sharply by the American Bar Association and other groups, and few courts have adopted the position that the rule does not apply at all to criminal prosecutors.[217]

The position that public policy requires an exemption for prosecutors only during the preindictment stage of a case has been more successful. The United States Department of Justice has adopted this position,[218] following a rule that modifies DR 7–104:

> An attorney for the government may communicate, or cause another to communicate, with a represented person concerning the subject matter of the representation if:
>
> (a) The communication-
>
>> (1) Is made in the course of an investigation, whether undercover or overt, of possible criminal activity; and
>>
>> (2) Occurs prior to the attachment of the Sixth Amendment right to counsel with respect to charges against the represented person arising out of the criminal activity that is the subject of the investigation; or
>
> (b) The communication is otherwise permitted by law.

Most courts have acknowledged in one way or another that prosecutors are exempt from DR 7–104 before indictment. The most common method is

---

216. *See* United States v. Lopez, 989 F.2d 1032, 1035 (9th Cir.1993) (characterizing Memorandum from Dick Thornburgh, Attorney General, to All Justice Department Litigators (June 8, 1989)).

217. *See Hammad*, 858 F.2d at 837–38 (rejecting government's position that DR 7–104(A) is "inapplicable to criminal investigations under any circumstances" and citing cases in accord).

218. 28 CFR Part 77, AG Order No. 1765–93 (7–26–93).

to hold that a preindictment communication during an investigation comes within the "authorized by law" exception to the rule. This same language gives prosecutors the ability to question represented persons in front of a grand jury.[219] Thus, most courts decline to apply DR 7–104 until after indictment.[220] At least one court has gone further, refusing to limit the application of the rule to situations in which the Sixth Amendment right to counsel has already attached.[221] Nevertheless, that court acknowledged that while DR 7–104 applies to prosecutors in preindictment situations, communications during that time generally will be approved under the "authorized by law" language. The court explained its holding as follows:

> The Constitution defines only the "minimal historic safeguards" which defendants must receive rather than the outer bounds of those we may afford them.... The Model Code of Professional Responsibility, on the other hand, encompasses the attorney's duty "to maintain the highest standards of ethical conduct." The Code is designed to safeguard the integrity of the profession and preserve public confidence in our system of justice. It not only delineates an attorney's duties to the court, but defines his relationship with his client and adverse parties. Hence, the Code secures protections not contemplated by the Constitution.

> [W]e resist binding the Code's applicability to the moment of indictment. The timing of an indictment's return lies substantially within the control of the prosecutor. Therefore, were we to construe the rule as dependent upon indictment, a government attorney could manipulate grand jury proceedings to avoid its encumbrances....

> The principal question presented to us herein is: to what extent does DR 7–104(A)(1) restrict the use of informants by government prosecutors prior to indictment, but after a suspect has retained counsel in connection with the subject matter of a criminal investigation? ... As we see it, under DR 7–104(A)(1), a prosecutor is "authorized by law" to employ legitimate investigative techniques in conducting or supervising criminal investigations, and the use of informants to gather evidence against a suspect will frequently fall within the ambit of such authorization.

There are other thorny ethical issues that may crop up when a defendant is interrogated. For example, if a prosecutor discovers that certain police officers routinely deny defendants their right to counsel during interrogations, does the prosecutor have an ethical obligation to intervene? If so, how should the prosecutor intervene, and what practical constraints are there on her efforts?

---

219.   *See, e.g.,* United States v. Schwimmer, 882 F.2d 22 (2d Cir.1989) (holding that DR 7–104(A)(1) does not prohibit a prosecutor from asking questions of a represented person before a grand jury), *cert. denied,* 493 U.S. 1071 (1990).

220.   The Ninth and Tenth Circuits appear to reason that DR 7–104 does not apply until indictment. *See* United States v. Ryans, 903 F.2d 731 (10th Cir.1990), *cert. denied,* 498 U.S. 855 (1990); United States v. Kenny, 645 F.2d 1323 (9th Cir.), *cert. denied,* 454 U.S. 828 (1981).

221.   *Hammad,* 858 F.2d at 839.

Consider the applicability of Model Rule of Professional Conduct 3.8(b), which declares that a prosecutor in a criminal case shall "make reasonable efforts to assure that the accused has been advised of the right to, and the procedure for obtaining, counsel and has been given reasonable opportunity to obtain counsel." A comment to the Rule further emphasizes that the prosecutor's responsibility as a minister of justice obliges him "to see that the defendant is accorded procedural justice." ABA Standard 3–1.2 for the Prosecution Function declares that "it is an important function of the prosecutor to seek to reform and improve the administration of criminal justice. When inadequacies or injustices in the . . . procedural law come to the prosecutor's attention, he or she should stimulate efforts for remedial action." Moreover, "a prosecutor should not knowingly use illegal means to obtain evidence or to employ or instruct or encourage others to use such means."[222] Does knowing "toleration" of an illegal police practice also constitute knowing "encouragement" of that practice? Despite the language quoted above, at least two commentators have concluded that "[t]here is no hint that the prosecutor has any duty to supervise police activity," other than the vague prohibition against encouraging use of illegal means to obtain evidence.[223] Nevertheless, these commentators go on to argue that prosecutors should have a supervisory function over the police.

The situation is not necessarily easier for defense counsel. A defendant has a right not merely to counsel but to the "effective" assistance of counsel. The scope and meaning of this right are examined in the last chapter of this text. Would an effective attorney ever counsel a client to submit to interrogation outside of the attorney's presence? Would an effective attorney ever counsel a client to confess? When? Why? What actions other than counseling total silence might a lawyer take to protect his client's interests?

PROBLEM 8–43

In the Brunell case in Chapter 1, assume that Terry Marvoal retained you in 1993 to represent her in the IRS investigation and any criminal matters arising out of that investigation. Assume also that the late-night visit described in Problem 8–4 occurred the day after the grand jury indicted Marvoal in 1996, but the day before she was to be arraigned.

Question: What motion should you bring and on what grounds? How will the prosecution respond, and what is the court's likely ruling?

F.   Scope of the Sixth Amendment Exclusionary Rule

Confessions and statements obtained in violation of a defendant's Sixth Amendment right to counsel are inadmissible under the *Massiah* doctrine.

---

222.   Standard 3–3.2(c).

223.   *See* Robert H. Aronson & Donald T. Wechstein, Professional Responsibility in a Nutshell 390 (2d ed. 1991).

But keep in mind that the doctrine is "offense-specific." That is, the rule excludes only those statements relating to an offense for which the adversarial process has been initiated. "[T]o exclude evidence pertaining to charges as to which the Sixth Amendment right to counsel had not attached at the time the evidence was obtained, simply because other charges were pending at the time, would unnecessarily frustrate the public's interest in the investigation of criminal activities." Accordingly, "[i]ncriminating statements pertaining to other crimes, as to which the Sixth Amendment right has not yet attached, are, of course, admissible at a trial of those offenses."[224]

The fruit of the poisonous tree doctrine excludes evidence discovered as a result of Sixth Amendment violations, and the traditional limitations on that doctrine—inevitable discovery, independent source, and attenuation of the taint—apply.[225] For example, recall the "Christian burial speech" in *Brewer v. Williams*. The defendant there, Williams, sought to exclude the body of the murdered girl on the ground that it was the "fruit" of incriminating statements deliberately elicited in the absence of counsel after the initiation of the adversarial process. While the Court agreed that William's statements should have been suppressed, it refused in its subsequent opinion in *Nix v. Williams*[226] (which involved the same case) to hold that the trial court should have excluded the body. The victim's body had been placed in a culvert, and when Williams identified the area, police had already initiated a search involving 200 volunteers who were specifically directed to search for the body in culverts in that area. Police testified that in the absence of William's confession they would have discovered the body within three to five hours. It was clear to the Court that "the evidence in question would inevitably have been discovered without reference to the police error or misconduct" and thus, there was "no nexus sufficient to provide a taint."

The applicability of the fruit of the poisonous tree doctrine to an *Elstad*-like situation was raised, but not decided, in *Fellers v. United States*.[227] There, the Court held that Fellers' Sixth Amendment rights were violated when the trial court admitted statements he made to police who came to his home to arrest him and who told him, without giving him *Miranda* rights, that they were there to discuss his involvement in drug crimes. Their conduct constituted deliberate elicitation, said the Court. But the Court declined to decide whether Fellers' later statements made at the jailhouse after he had waived his rights, could be admitted:

> ... [B]ecause of its erroneous determination that petitioner was not questioned in violation of Sixth Amendment standards, the Court of Appeals improperly conducted its "fruits" analysis under the Fifth Amendment. Specifically, it applied *Elstad* to hold that the admissibili-

---

224.   *Moulton*, 474 U.S. at 180.

225.   United States v. Wade, 388 U.S. 218 (1967).

226.   Nix v. Williams, 467 U.S. 431 (1984).

227.   540 U.S. 519 (2004).

ty of the jailhouse statements turns solely on whether the statements were "knowingly and voluntarily made." The Court of Appeals did not reach the question whether the Sixth Amendment requires suppression of petitioner's jailhouse statements on the ground that they were the fruits of previous questioning conducted in violation of the Sixth Amendment deliberate-elicitation standard. We have not had occasion to decide whether the rationale of *Elstad* applies when a suspect makes incriminating statements after a knowing and voluntary waiver of his right to counsel notwithstanding earlier police questioning in violation of Sixth Amendment standards. We therefore remand to the Court of Appeals to address this issue in the first instance.[228]

Question: How do you think this issue will be or should be decided?

Another central exclusionary problem involves the use of Sixth–Amendment violative statements for impeachment purposes. In *Michigan v. Harvey*,[229] the Court had held that prosecutors may impeach defendants with statements taken in violation of the old *Michigan v. Jackson* rule. Remember that that rule had precluded a finding of waiver where police initiate post-indictment interrogation after the defendant asserts his Sixth Amendment right to counsel. The logic of the *Harvey* case was essentially that the *Jackson* rule was a mere "prophylactic" rule designed to protect core Sixth Amendment rights and subject to a cost-benefit analysis. The costs of excluding a *Jackson*-violative statement for impeachment purposes did not seem worth the benefits because police could not count on a defendant taking the stand and lying, so the deterrent effect of excluding violative statements on direct would not be diluted by admitted them on cross. But recently, in Montejo v. Louisiana, as noted above, the Court overruled *Jackson* itself. Would the Court still permit impeachment for other types of Sixth Amendment violations given that *Jackson*'s prophylactic protection no longer applied?

The Court answered this question "yes," suggesting that its answer likely applied to at least one broad category of Sixth Amendment rights—those that apply pre-trial—in *Kansas v. Ventris*,[230] though *Ventris* itself more narrowly involved a jailhouse informant's deliberately eliciting a post-charge statement from the defendant. At trial, Ventris testified that his co-defendant, Theel, was entirely at fault for the alleged robbery and homicide. The government successfully called a jailhouse informant to impeach Ventris. The informant testified, over defense objection, that Ventris admitted both to being the shooter and taking the victim's money and car. The prosecution had conceded, however, that the statement was "probably" one obtained in violation of Ventris's Sixth Amendment rights but argued that that did not give Ventris license to commit perjury. Ventris was convicted of aggravated burglary and aggravated robbery but acquitted of felony

---

228. *Id.* at 520.

229. 494 U.S. 344 (1990).

230. 129 S.Ct. 1841 (2009).

murder, suggesting that the jury did not, or at least did not wholly, believe the informant's testimony.

When the case reached the United States Supreme Court, the Court, in an opinion written by Justice Scalia, distinguished the "core" right to counsel—a right that applies at trial—from "prophylactic" rights, such as the Sixth Amendment right to counsel during interrogations, which were created to ensure that police manipulation does not render counsel's representation "entirely impotent." A violation of that right, said the Court, occurred at the time of the interrogation, not at the time of admission of the statement at trial. At trial, the defendant here had counsel, although arguably counsel's trial representation is not "worth much" when the state has overwhelming evidence of guilt, so the trial right is necessarily distinct from the pre-trial one. Once having characterized the relevant right as a pre-trial prophylactic one violated only at the time of interrogation, the Court saw the question at trial as not one of preventing a constitutional violation but of what remedy it deserved. Applying logic strikingly similar to that it used in *Harvey*, the Court held that, although a statement obtained in violation of the Sixth Amendment could not be used in the prosecution's case-in-chief, it could be used to impeach the defendant should he testify inconsistently at trial. Said the Court, "[o]nce the defendant testifies [at trial] in a way that contradicts prior statements, denying the prosecution use of 'the traditional truth-testing devices of the adversary process' . . . is a high price to pay for vindication of the right to counsel at the prior [interrogation] stage."[231]

Finally, the Court rejected the argument of *amici* that jailhouse snitch testimony is so inherently unreliable that it required a special rule to protect the innocent. The Court refused to become a "rule-making organ for the promulgation of state rules of criminal procedure," particularly because, it said, "[o]ur legal system is built on the premise that it is the province of the jury to weigh the credibility of competing witnesses."[232] Moreover, creating a special rule seemed especially inappropriate in this case, where the jury apparently disbelieved the informant.

Justices Stevens and Ginsburg dissented, rejecting every one of the majority's premises. First, Justice Stevens rejected the distinction between inferior prophylactic rules and superior trial ones in this area, finding the violation to have begun during interrogation but to have continued by admission of the statement at trial: "The use of ill-gotten evidence during any phase of criminal prosecution does damage to the adversarial process— the fairness of which the Sixth Amendment was designed to protect."[233] This was no metaphysical assertion but a practical one, for when counsel "is excluded from a critical pretrial interaction between the defendant and the State, she may be unable to effectively counter the potentially devastat-

---

231. *Id.* at 1846.

232. *Id.* at 1847.

233. *Id.* at 1847, 1848.

ing, and potentially false, evidence subsequently introduced at trial."[234] Second, the Sixth Amendment protects more than counsel's mere presence but rather mandates her effective assistance, so Stevens rejected the majority's "stingy view" of the right as one met even where counsel's presence at trial is "not worth much."[235] Third, Stevens warned against the dangers of ignoring the likelihood that "evidence gathered by self-interested jailhouse informants may be false...."[236] Fourth, Stevens saw no inconsistency with protecting the right to counsel and the need to seek the truth because part of the purpose of effective "partisan advocacy" is to "best promote the ultimate objective that the guilty be convicted and the innocent go free."[237] Finally, said Stevens, by creating yet another occasion in which the Court "privileged the prosecution at the expense of the Constitution," the Court "taxes the legitimacy of the entire criminal process."[238] Permitting such "shabby tactics" by the prosecution, concluded Stevens, is "intolerable in all cases."[239]

G.   Review Problems

PROBLEM 8–44

At 7:00 a.m. on July 1, a court arraigned Vernon Jacoby on arson charges. Detective Johnson, who had arrested Jacoby, came to Jacoby's cell at 8 a.m. that day to question him. Johnson believed that Jacoby was still awaiting his arraignment and that no complaint had yet been filed. He gave Jacoby full and accurate *Miranda* warnings, and Jacoby clearly stated he wanted to waive his rights and talk. Detective Johnson then asked, "Do you want to tell me about the arson?" Jacoby responded, "I did a couple of arsons, but I would like to talk to my lawyer before I talk about all of them." Detective Johnson immediately ended the conversation, stating, "Well, that's it."

Question: Will the defense succeed in a motion to suppress Jacoby's statement to Detective Johnson? If the statement is suppressed and Jacoby takes the stand at trial, will the state be able to impeach Jacoby with his statements to Johnson?

PROBLEM 8–45

Police arrested John Marven for soliciting an unknown killer to murder Marven's wife. While awaiting trial, he was incarcerated in the same jail as John O'Hara, a convicted rapist. O'Hara had been awaiting sentence on his rape conviction for eighteen months. Throughout that time he had

234. *Id.* at 1848–49.
235. *Id.* at 1849 n.3.
236. *Id.* at 1849 n.2.
237. *Id.* at 1849.
238. *Id.* at 1849.
239. *Id.* at 1849.

frequently reported to the police incriminating statements made by his cellmates and other inmates. His reporting instincts were so good that prosecutors, without his knowledge, intervened several times to postpone sentencing on his rape conviction. The prosecutors had never spoken to O'Hara about his reporting, nor asked him why he did so.

Without telling O'Hara that they were doing so, prosecutors arranged for him to be transferred to Marven's cell. While in the cell, the following conversation took place:

O'Hara:	Watcha in for?
Marven:	Solicitation to kill my wife.
O'Hara:	Who do they claim you got to do it?
Marven:	They don't know me. If I'd wanted to do it, I'da done it myself. I'da wrung her scrawny neck.
O'Hara:	So you didn't pay anybody to do it? You're innocent?
Marven:	Nope. I didn't pay anybody. And I didn't ask anybody. But that doesn't mean I'm innocent, but that's all I'm going to say. I sure am glad she is gone. Cause they can't prove nothin, and I'm gonna have some fun!

O'Hara promptly reported this conversation to the police, and the next day Marven was arrested for the murder of his wife, and the solicitation charges were dropped.

Question: Assume that the defense has filed a motion to suppress Marven's statement to O'Hara as having been obtained in violation of the Sixth Amendment. What result? Next, assume you are the prosecutor at the suppression hearing. What questions will you ask O'Hara? What other witnesses will you call to the stand, why, and what will you ask them?

PROBLEM 8–46

George Ricardo was arrested and arraigned on October 1 for unauthorized use of an automobile and was promptly released on bond. On October 2, he was arrested again, this time for carrying a firearm without a license. At the police station, before booking was completed, Ricardo's mother appeared and asked to talk to Ricardo alone. The police agreed. Shortly thereafter, Ricardo's mother told the police, "He's willing to talk."

Detective Folklor gave Ricardo his *Miranda* rights and obtained a written waiver of those rights from Ricardo. Folklor then asked, "Ricardo, do you want to tell me about the pistol and the stolen cars?" Ricardo responded with a lengthy statement in which he admitted stealing cars, including the one for which he was arrested on October 1, and to carrying a stolen, unlicensed pistol.

Question: At his auto theft trial, will Ricardo succeed if he files a motion to suppress his statements to Detective Folklor? What about the same motion at his trial for carrying an unlicensed firearm? Would the result change if the police had completed their booking procedures on the firearm arrest before Ricardo had spoken? What if Ricardo had been arraigned on that charge before he made his statement?

PROBLEM 8–47

Boyer Raleigh, a reporter for the Washington Post, posed as an inmate to get a story on conditions in Washington, D.C. jails. While in a jail cell with Adam Kraymore, Raleigh overheard Kraymore mumble something about killing his own wife. Kraymore had been jailed on charges of threatening his brother-in-law. Kraymore took to Raleigh, quickly coming to see Raleigh as a real friend. Kraymore was then transferred to a nearby state mental health facility to be evaluated regarding whether he was competent to stand trial on the threats charges.

Raleigh subsequently approached the director of the mental health facility, identified himself as a reporter, and asked permission to meet with Kraymore to convince him to attend counseling sessions, something Kraymore had steadfastly refused to do. The director agreed. Raleigh met with Kraymore and offered, "as a friend," to sit in on Kraymore's sessions with the prison psychiatrist. Kraymore agreed.

Raleigh then advised the director that he planned to get Kraymore's story on tape, by secreting a tape-recorder on his person during the sessions with the psychiatrist. The mental health facility's written rules exclude third persons from psychiatric counseling sessions unless necessary to prevent patient violence. Nevertheless, the director made an exception and Raleigh sat in on Kraymore's first (and only) counseling session. During that session Kraymore denied threatening his brother-in-law but admitted killing his wife. A story on the killing appeared in the Post the next day.

Question: If defense counsel files a motion to suppress Raleigh's statements during the counseling session, how would you rule as the judge?

PROBLEM 8–48

Duane Webb was arrested on a burglary charge and placed in a holding cell. His girlfriend, Sharon, had seen him arrested and had called Webb's lawyer, Lawrence Tase. The lawyer showed up at the police station shortly after the arrest and handed an officer a business card that contained the following hand-written words: "Duane, don't say anything without me—Tase." Webb had by this time been in the holding cell several hours and had repeatedly asked for his lawyer. The officer who got Tase's card gave it to Webb saying, "This is from a visitor," but Webb just grabbed it, shoved it in his pocket, and said, "Get me my lawyer."

The officers had purposely postponed getting Webb to an arraignment and delayed the paperwork necessary for filing a complaint. They also postponed getting him his lawyer. They tried to delay because they wanted to get to Sharon, as they suspected that she and Webb had been involved in another, more serious crime—a mob-related hit. They succeeded in reaching Sharon and convinced her to help them in exchange for helping her get leniency.

At the urging of the police, Sharon called the station, asking to speak to Webb. Webb was brought to an area where suspects can receive phone calls. During the telephone call, which police recorded, Sharon told Webb that the police were sniffing around, and she wanted his permission to move their hidden "stash" of money, which included cash from the burglary and money obtained as a payoff for the hit. Webb agreed and made numerous statements implicating himself in both the burglary and the murder.

Question: Should any of Webb's statements be suppressed as having been obtained in violation of the Sixth Amendment?

In habeas corpus actions, in which individuals seek collateral federal review of their convictions, courts cannot grant relief on the ground that the Fourth Amendment exclusionary rule should have applied.[240] But this judicially-created limitation does not apply to habeas relief sought for Fifth and Sixth Amendment violations. According to the Court in *Withrow v. Williams*,[241] the Fifth and Sixth Amendments involve "personal trial rights," whereas *Stone* concerned the Fourth Amendment exclusionary rule, which is designed "to deter future constitutional violations" rather than to confer "a personal constitutional right." Thus, habeas relief is potentially available on the ground that a confession was wrongfully admitted in violation of the Fifth or Sixth Amendments.

But Congress has imposed many *statutory* restrictions on habeas relief that affect Fifth and Sixth Amendment claims. For example, in the Antiterrorism and Effective Death Penalty Act of 1996 ("AEDPA"), Congress restricted the circumstances in which state prisoners can gain habeas relief. Under AEDPA, relief can be granted only in a case in which a state court decision "was based on an unreasonable determination of the facts in light of the evidence presented in the State court proceeding."[242] As one federal judge has explained, this means that "a federal court may not second-guess a state court's fact-finding process unless, after review of the state-court record, it determines that the state court was not merely wrong, but actually unreasonable."[243] Although this standard is a challenging one, petitioners have satisfied it in a number of cases by establishing that a state court: (1) neglected to make required factual finding altogether; (2) made factual findings under an incorrect legal standard; (3) made factual findings without providing an opportunity for a hearing; or (4) obviously misunderstood, misstated, or ignored the record in making factual findings.

---

240. The limitation, created in Stone v. Powell, 428 U.S. 465 (1976), applies if the habeas petitioner had a full and fair opportunity to raise Fourth Amendment claims in trial court.

241. 507 U.S. 680 (1993).

242. 28 U.S.C. Section 2254(d)(2).

243. Taylor v. Maddox, 366 F.3d 992, 999 (9th Cir.2004).

Consider the following problem in light of AEDPA's standard for habeas relief:

PROBLEM 8–49

On May 30, Billy Sheldon was riding his bicycle through a beachside area in Long Beach, California when two assailants tried to take it from him. Billy resisted and the assailants fled. Billy then gave chase and the taller of the assailants turned and shot Billy twice, killing him. Three months later, Detectives Raymond and McClain came to suspect that sixteen-year-old Reef Baylor had been involved in the murder. The detectives obtained an arrest warrant and a search warrant for his apartment. On September 1, at 11:30 p.m., the detectives and three other officers executed the warrants. They found the small teen (Reef was 5' 3'' tall) asleep on the living room sofa; his mother, who was his only custodial parent, was not home. The five law enforcement agents woke him, guns drawn and flashlights shining. Reef was taken to the top floor of the police station and placed in an interrogation room alone for half an hour. At 12:15 a.m. the next morning, Detectives Raymond and McClain entered the interrogation room and began questioning him. There were no recording devices used during the interrogation. He was given no food, water, or rest, and after almost three hours of questioning, he confessed to the murder. Detective McClain then produced a tape recorder from his blazer pocket and recorded Reef's confession and waiver of his *Miranda* rights. At 3:30 a.m., he was permitted to call attorney Arthur Closs. Reef told Closs about his arrest, interrogation, and the details surrounding the interrogation. Closs explained to Reef that he would not be able to represent him since he may be called as a witness in Reef's case.

Before trial, Reef challenged the admissibility of his confession on the grounds that it was coerced and obtained in violation of *Miranda* and *Edwards*. His testimony at the suppression hearing was as follows:

Q: While you were being questioned, did you ask to speak with anyone?

A: I asked to speak with my attorney. I told the detectives that I knew an attorney that I could call to get some advice. They told me no, that it wouldn't be possible.

Q: Did you ask to speak with anyone else?

A: I then asked if I could speak with my mother, if I could call her. They told me, no.

Q: Did you ask to speak to a lawyer?

A: Yes.

Q: Did you ask to speak with a specific lawyer?

A: Yes, I did. Arthur Closs.

Q: Did you have the phone number of Mr. Closs?

A: Yes, I did.

Q: Did you want to talk to the detectives?

A: No, I didn't.

Q: Did you want to talk with Arthur Closs before you talked to the detectives?

A: Yes.

Q: Did you try to do that?

A: Yes, I did. But they wouldn't let me.

Q: Who wouldn't?

A: One of the detectives, I can't remember.

Q: How did they prevent you from doing that?

A: They told me it wouldn't be possible. They told me that they wanted me to tell them what they wanted to hear. They said to tell them what happened, and that then I could use the phone.

Q: After questioning you more, did you still want to speak with Arthur Closs or any lawyer?

A: Several times, I said I wanted to talk to Arthur.

Reef further testified that he confessed to the murder so that he could make a phone call. He said that he started agreeing with everything so that he could make a phone call and clear things up later. Attorney Closs also testified at the suppression hearing, stating that Reef had called him at approximately 4 a.m. on September 2, highly agitated and in tears. He recalled what Reef told him about the details of the interrogation and about his motivation for confessing. Closs's testimony matched Reef's in every respect. Detective Raymond testified at the suppression hearing as well, stating that he did not recall Reef asking for an attorney. Detective Raymond also could not recall Reef asking for his mother.

The trial court denied Reef's motion to suppress his confession, stating only that "I believe Officer Raymond and not the defendant in this case." The recorded confession was played for the jury, which found Reef guilty of first-degree murder. The appellate courts affirmed.

Question: Assume that you represent Reef in a federal habeas action challenging his conviction. How would you argue that Reef is entitled to relief?

CHAPTER 9

SELF-INCRIMINATION OUTSIDE THE INTERROGATION ROOM

- PRINCIPLES OF FIFTH AMENDMENT PRIVILEGE

- ACT OF PRODUCTION PRIVILEGE   • IMMUNITY

- USING THE FIFTH AMENDMENT IN CIVIL CASES

I.   GENERAL PRINCIPLES OF FIFTH AMENDMENT PRIVILEGE

The materials in the previous chapter have explained the protections afforded individuals who make incriminating statements under questioning by government actors. Those protections stem from both the due process guaranty and the privilege against self-incrimination. The privilege against self-incrimination also arises frequently outside of the interrogation room. For example, you may recall hearing about individuals invoking their Fifth Amendment rights in order to avoid testimony before the United States Congress. How have those rights against self-incrimination been interpreted? On what basis may a person invoke them? When are those rights considered to have been waived? Those questions and more will be addressed in this chapter.

———

Checklist 14: When Does the Privilege Apply?

1. Is the privilege asserted by a "natural person" rather than an entity such as a corporation?

2. If yes, is the privilege asserted on the person's own behalf?

3. If yes, is the person compelled—by custodial interrogation, court process, or threats of sanctions from a government actor—to communicate?

4. If yes, does the communication involve something testimonial in nature rather than physical acts or characteristics?

5. If yes, is there a "substantial and real" hazard that the testimonial communication could be used in a criminal prosecution or could lead to other evidence that might be so used?

6. If the person compelled is not a criminal defendant, does that person assert the privilege in response to specific questions?

7. Has the privilege been waived in the same proceeding by other communications on the same or a related subject?

8. If the compulsion involves pre-existing documents or items, would the act of producing them be incriminating?

    a. Would the act of production reveal the existence of the items?

    b. Would the act of production reveal the person's possession of the items?

    c. Would the act of production authenticate the items?

————

A.   BALANCING IN THE SELF-INCRIMINATION CONTEXT

At the beginning of the *Miranda* section of the last chapter, we quoted two Supreme Court views about the Fifth Amendment privilege against self-incrimination. One view lauded the privilege as a bulwark of government respect for the individual. The other lamented that the privilege encourages lawbreakers to avoid acknowledging personal responsibility for their deeds. To some extent, the cases and materials below reflect courts' attempts to accommodate both of these views. Additionally, Professor Adam Kurland has suggested that the Court often balances the concerns of the Fifth Amendment against the truth-seeking functions of the criminal trial.[1] But this (often implicit) balancing raises questions like these: what authority does the Court have for engaging in such balancing? How can the Court balance interests effectively and fairly, without simply substituting judicial value preferences for legislative ones?

For Discussion: To better understand the Court's Fifth Amendment analyses, you should briefly review the Chapter 1 discussion of balancing before continuing. In reading the cases excerpted in the following pages, contrast any implicit balancing with similar analyses under the Fourth Amendment, especially our discussion about administrative searches. Ask yourself the following questions. Is the Court's method of analysis similar under the Fourth and Fifth Amendments? What role does text play? History? Underlying constitutional values? Real-world consequences? Would social science aid our inquiry, and, if so, how and why? Is the Court striking a fair and proper balance between concerns about fairness and governmental oppression, on the one hand, and concerns about personal responsibility and truth, on the other? Why?

B.   WHO HAS A PRIVILEGE AGAINST SELF-INCRIMINATION?

The Supreme Court has established that only "natural persons" have a privilege against self-incrimination under the Fifth Amendment; no corre-

————

1.   *See* Adam H. Kurland, *Prosecuting Ol' Man River: The Fifth Amendment, the Good Faith Defense, and the Non–Testifying Defendant*, 51 U. PITT. L. REV. 841, 863–69 (1990).

sponding right can be claimed by entities such as corporations or partnerships, no matter how small or large.[2] The Court has articulated two justifications for this limitation. First, the privilege is designed to protect that "private enclave where [a person] may lead a private life," a value that is not implicated in the case of an entity. Second, placing the privilege in the hands of an entity would frustrate legitimate governmental regulation:

> The greater portion of evidence of wrongdoing by an organization or its representatives is usually to be found in the official records and documents of that organization. Were the cloak of the privilege to be thrown around these impersonal records and documents, effective enforcement of many federal and state laws would be impossible. The framers of the constitutional guarantee against compulsory self-disclosure, who were interested primarily in protecting individual civil liberties, cannot be said to have intended the privilege to be available to protect economic or other interests of such organizations so as to nullify appropriate governmental regulations.[3]

Sole proprietors may assert the privilege, however, since they are unstructured entities that conduct business as individuals. In determining whether an unstructured organization is small and personal enough to come within the Fifth Amendment guarantee, courts consider the following: How perpetual is the organization? Does it have a constitution, rules, or bylaws? Does it have books and records apart from the books and records of its members? The more personal an organization, the more likely that the privilege will apply. For example, the Supreme Court has suggested that a "small family partnership" also might be able to assert Fifth Amendment rights. Lower courts have not been generous with claims by such entities, however.

Note that the Court obviously is balancing public versus private interests here. It asserts that the framers intended this balancing, but there is no serious historical material supporting this assertion. Moreover, it is highly unlikely that the framers thought about the problem of government regulation. Perhaps the Court is identifying the values that the framers intended the privilege to serve, and then concluding that those values support the result. But deciding whether particular values are better served by one rule or another necessarily involves a balancing of the real-world impact of each rule: to what extent does it serve, and to what extent disserve, the underlying values?

In addition to the "natural person" limitation, the Court imposed a standing-like requirement in *Fisher v. United States*:[4] only the individual holding the privilege may assert it, and no one else may claim it on that person's behalf. However, an attorney may be able to withhold documents on the grounds of the attorney-client privilege. For other examples of this rule, consider the defendant at trial who wishes to object to a question put

---

2. Hale v. Henkel, 201 U.S. 43 (1906).

3. Bellis v. United States, 417 U.S. 85, 91 (1974).

4. 425 U.S. 391 (1976).

to a witness. Even if the witness's answer would incriminate the defendant, the Fifth Amendment is unavailable to the defendant in this circumstance, because only the witness can assert the privilege on his or her own behalf.[5] Similarly, the defendant may not appeal a conviction on the ground that the court erred in ruling that the witness was not entitled to assert the privilege.

PROBLEM 9–1

The *Brunell* case in Chapter 1 includes a grand jury subpoena to Boyd Gregory, the tax lawyer who prepared income tax returns for Brunell's Natural Foods, Inc. Assume that the subpoenaed records had been given to Gregory by Brunell.

Question: Can Gregory refuse to produce the documents? What is the best argument against production? How will the prosecutor respond? How will the judge rule?

C. How to Invoke and Waive the Privilege

A person asserts the privilege in different ways, depending on whether the person is a criminal defendant or not. A defendant in a criminal case invokes the privilege simply by choosing not to take the stand. In that situation, the prosecution cannot call the defendant to the stand, or make any reference to the defendant's silence.[6]

For those who are not criminal defendants, the assertion of the privilege is more complicated. Persons in this category include parties to civil lawsuits and anyone questioned as a witness in criminal or civil proceedings, whether by deposition, interrogatory, questioning before a grand jury, or questioning at trial. Such a witness cannot assert the privilege in a wholesale fashion by refusing to respond to all questioning, but only in response to specific questions. Similarly, persons responding to discovery requests must assert the privilege on a question-by-question basis. The witness must articulate something that can reasonably be interpreted as an attempt to invoke the privilege, although no magic words are required. If the witness's invocation of the privilege is challenged, the witness has the burden of establishing that the privilege applies, by demonstrating a "substantial and real" threat of criminal liability stemming from the testimony. It is not enough to claim that the answers would cause embarrassment or disgrace. If a court determines that the privilege does not apply, or if the witness is immunized, then the witness will be compelled to answer or risk being held in contempt of court.

---

5. *See, e.g.*, State v. Cota, 432 P.2d 428, 432 (Ariz.1967) (privilege not available to defendant as a third party).

6. Brown v. United States, 356 U.S. 148 (1958). There are some situations where prosecutors may call attention to a person's decision not to testify. These are discussed later in this chapter.

By this time, it should be apparent why civil practitioners need to know as much as their criminal counterparts about the privilege against self-incrimination: if a defendant in a civil proceeding answers a question instead of asserting the privilege, that answer can become a potent weapon for the prosecution in a subsequent criminal proceeding.[7] The same is true, of course, for statements made in a prior criminal proceeding. The fact that the defendant had an opportunity to assert the privilege, but did not do so, means that the privilege was waived as to that answer. In other words, that answer can be used against the defendant in any proceeding, and cannot be shielded by the Fifth Amendment. However, having made a statement in one proceeding does not mean that the defendant has forever waived his or her privilege. Generally, a waiver in one proceeding lasts only as long as the proceeding—the waiver does not carry over into the next.

A criminal defendant can never be forced to take the stand. If the defendant does take the stand, however, and chooses to answer questions on his or her own behalf, then the defendant will be required to answer questions on cross-examination that concern "matters reasonably related to the subject matter of [the] direct examination."[8] The rationale is that a defendant should not be allowed to create an inaccurate impression of the facts by picking and choosing which questions to answer.

PROBLEM 9–2

In the *Brunell* case in Chapter 1, assume that two weeks later after Brunell was initially contacted by the IRS, his wife filed for divorce. Her lawyer, Sarah Cunningham, contacted Brunell and stated that she would soon serve him with extensive discovery requests. Cunningham explained that she believed Brunell had removed cash from his business and concealed it in safe deposit boxes in order to avoid sharing it with his wife. Brunell soon received a large package of discovery requests and a notice of deposition. During his deposition, Brunell revealed information relevant to his income from the natural foods business.

Question: As the prosecutor in Brunell's tax fraud case, can you introduce at trial the answers Brunell gave during the deposition? Can you call Brunell to the stand in order to ask him about subjects covered during the deposition? Why or why not?

D. Thresholds: Compulsion, Incrimination, Testimony

The Fifth Amendment privilege against self-incrimination applies only to compelled, incriminating testimony. Three theshholds must be present, therefore, in order for a person to have a claim of privilege: compulsion (by

---

7. United States v. Kordel, 397 U.S. 1, 7–11 (1970). Most likely, any hearsay objection to the statement will be overruled on the ground that the statement is an admission. *See* Federal Rule of Evidence 801(d)(2) (admissions of a party-opponent are not hearsay).

8. McGautha v. California, 402 U.S. 183, 215 (1971); *see* also, *e.g.*, United States v. Hearst, 563 F.2d 1331, 1338–40 (9th Cir.1977), cert. denied, 435 U.S. 1000 (1978).

a government actor), incrimination, and testimony. Each of these will be addressed below.

1.   COMPULSION BY GOVERNMENT ACTOR

The Fifth Amendment prohibits only "compelled" testimonial self-incrimination:

> [I]t is ... axiomatic that the Amendment does not automatically preclude self-incrimination, whether spontaneous or in response to questions put by government officials. It does not preclude a witness from testifying voluntarily in matters which may incriminate him.... Indeed, far from being prohibited by the Constitution, admissions of guilt by wrongdoers, if not coerced, are inherently desirable. In addition to guaranteeing the right to remain silent unless immunity is granted, the Fifth Amendment proscribes only self-incrimination obtained by a genuine compulsion of testimony. Absent some officially coerced self-accusation, the Fifth Amendment privilege is not violated by even the most damning admissions.[9]

The issue of compulsion typically requires an after-the-fact inquiry. That is, in the usual case, the government seeks to introduce a statement made by the defendant, who claims that admission of the statement would violate the privilege. The court must determine whether the person was under compulsion by a government official when the statement was made. If such compulsion was present, the statement is inadmissible. If government compulsion was lacking, admission of the statement will not violate the privilege against self-incrimination, unless some other factor is present.

Three examples are useful here. First, consider the situation in which a lawful search and seizure uncovers incriminating material. The Fifth Amendment privilege does not protect that material because there is no compulsion—"the individual against whom the search is directed is not required to aid in the discovery ... of [the] incriminating evidence."[10] Second, imagine that an undercover government agent overhears a murder suspect mutter to himself, "I didn't mean to kill that guy." Under those circumstances, the Fifth Amendment does not require the statement's suppression because the suspect spoke freely, in the absence of pressure from anyone. The same rule applies to statements voluntarily made to a paid government informant. In *Hoffa v. United States*,[11] a paid government informant named Partin initiated discussions with Teamsters Union President James Hoffa, who was at the time on trial for violations of the Taft–Hartley Act. Hoffa was later charged with jury tampering in that trial. At the jury tampering trial, Partin testified against Hoffa and claimed that Hoffa had made several incriminating statements during their earlier discussions. In rejecting Hoffa's argument that use of the incriminating statements as evidence violated the Fifth Amendment, the Court concluded

---

9.   United States v. Washington, 431 U.S. 181, 186–87 (1977).

10.   Andresen v. Maryland, 427 U.S. 463, 474 (1976).

11.   385 U.S. 293 (1966).

that "no claim has been or could be made that [Hoffa's] incriminating statements were the product of any sort of coercion, legal or factual. [Hoffa's] conversations with Partin ... were wholly voluntary. For that reason, if for no other, it is clear that no right protected by the Fifth Amendment privilege against compulsory self-incrimination was violated." Now hypothesize a situation in which a suspect makes an incriminating statement in response to a death threat from a confederate. In this situation, compulsion is present, but the Fifth Amendment does not apply because the source of the compulsion was private. Just as the Fourth Amendment requires a government actor before its protections are implicated, so too the Fifth Amendment protects only against government compulsion.

Determining whether compulsion existed can be a complicated matter because the Supreme Court constantly must balance interests involved in the various circumstances in which the issue arises.

a. Questioning in Custody and During Court Proceedings

When a person is in official custody (under arrest, for example), any statement that the person makes may be treated as "compelled" unless special warnings are given before the person is questioned. This is the basis for the *Miranda* rule, which we discussed earlier in this chapter.

In many other situations, the Court does not require special warnings, so a person speaks at his or her peril—the privilege must be immediately claimed or the person "will not be considered to have been compelled within the meaning of the Amendment."[12] Consider, for example, the person who is subpoenaed to testify at trial. In a sense, the person's testimony is compelled by the subpoena, which carries the threat of legal sanction for non-compliance. At the very least, one might imagine that the person should be educated about his or her Fifth Amendment rights before deciding whether to testify, thus dispelling any compulsion to testify. Nevertheless, the Supreme Court does not require that the person be advised of the right against self-incrimination or make a knowing and intelligent waiver of the right. If the person responds to questioning, the statements are admissible even if the person was unaware of the right to remain silent.

The Court has not held that specific warnings are required when a grand jury issues a subpoena to a person who is likely to be indicted. However, some Justices have urged that the person should at least make a knowing and intelligent waiver of the privilege against self-incrimination, and the Court appears to recognize the danger of compulsion in these circumstances. In *United States v. Washington*, a prosecutor advised the target of a grand jury's investigation that "he had a right to remain silent and that any statements he did make could be used to convict him of

---

12. United States v. Monia, 317 U.S. 424, 430 (1943) (Frankfurter, J., dissenting).

crime." The Court reasoned that this advice "eliminated any possible compulsion to self-incrimination which might otherwise exist."[13]

b. The "No Comment" Rule

At trial, if a jury were encouraged to infer guilt because of the defendant's decision not to testify, defendants would be forced to forego their Fifth Amendment rights. As a result, it is often repeated that the Fifth Amendment forbids either comment by the prosecution on the accused's silence or instructions by the court that such silence is evidence of guilt. Thus, even where a defendant declines to testify as to matters that we would expect him to deny or explain because the facts are within his knowledge, the prosecutor or court is prohibited from commenting on that failure. The reason for the rule, articulated in *Griffin v. California*, is obvious: such a comment would constitute compulsion, because it would make the assertion of the privilege costly by impermissibly creating "a penalty . . . for exercising a constitutional privilege."[14] Indeed, fear of such a penalty is particularly justified, because even without adverse comment, the statistical reality is that juries do hold silence against defendants, convicting non-testifying defendants more often than those who take the stand.[15]

There are important caveats to the "no comment" rule. First, it applies only in criminal cases. In civil cases, a party who invokes the Fifth Amendment may be penalized by sanctions or by suffering adverse inferences of guilt. It is entirely constitutional, for example, for an attorney in such a case to argue to the jury that it should consider the party's refusal to answer questions as an indication that those answers would be damaging to the party.[16] However, state evidence rules, such as in California, may prohibit this, even providing an instruction to the jury that it should not take the party's refusal as a negative indication.

Second, a prosecutor may comment on the criminal defendant's decision not to testify when that comment is responsive to defense counsel's assertion that the defendant was not given the opportunity to tell his side of the story. For example, in *United States v. Robinson*,[17] the defense attorney made several statements in his closing argument accusing the government of unfairly denying the defendant the opportunity, before and during the trial, to explain his actions. In chambers, the prosecution argued that the defendant had "opened the door" to a comment on his decision not to testify.[18] The judge agreed, and the prosecutor's closing argument

---

13.   United States v. Washington, 431 U.S. 181, 188 (1977).

14.   380 U.S. 609, 614 (1965).

15.   *See Kurland, O' Man River, supra* note 1, at 866 (noting statistical reality); Valerie P. Hans and Neil Vidmar, Judging the Jury 144 (1986) (authors' psychological research revealed "many lay persons infer guilt when a defendant remains silent").

16.   Baxter v. Palmigiano, 425 U.S. 308 (1976).

17.   485 U.S. 25 (1988).

18.   The "open-door" doctrine, also known as the doctrine of "curative admissibility," is invoked to allow otherwise inadmissible evidence or cross-examination "on matters usually

included the following:

> [Defense counsel] has made comments to the extent the Government has not allowed the defendants an opportunity to explain. It is totally unacceptable. He explained himself away on tape right into an indictment. He explained himself to the insurance investigator, to the extent that he wanted to. He could have taken the stand and explained it to you, anything he wanted to. The United States of America has given him, throughout, the opportunity to explain.

The Court agreed that the prosecution's comments did not violate the defendant's Fifth Amendment rights. The Court recognized that the central purpose of a trial is to determine factually whether a defendant is guilty or innocent, and that in order to meet that goal "it is important that both the defendant and the prosecutor have the opportunity to meet fairly the evidence and arguments of one another."

Third, a judge may instruct a criminal jury not to draw any inferences from the defendant's decision not to testify. The instruction is mandatory whenever the defendant requests it,[19] and the judge may give such an instruction even if the defendant objects to it.[20] The Court has reasoned that the jury will probably notice the defendant's silence and draw adverse inferences from it: "Too many, even those who should be better advised . . ., readily assume that those who invoke it are . . . guilty of crime."[21]

Fourth, it should be noted that four members of the Supreme Court have questioned the viability of *Griffin's* prohibition on commenting on, or drawing adverse inferences from, a defendant's assertion of the privilege. In *Mitchell v. United States*,[22] Justice Scalia dissented from the majority's extension of *Griffin* to sentencing proceedings. Joined by three others, Justice Scalia argued that *Griffin* was neither well grounded in history nor supported by logic or public policy. The *Mitchell* dissenters did not call for *Griffin* to be overruled (although Justice Thomas stated that he would be "willing to reconsider" it), but they urged that it not be extended to new circumstances. Justice Scalia put forth another reason for withholding *Griffin* from sentencing proceedings: the Court has held that the constitu-

---

immune from inquiry." David W. Louisell & Christopher B. Mueller, Federal Evidence §§ 11, 336 (1977). The doctrine "rests upon a loose notion of waiver and holds that the adversary may try to disprove, usually by cross-examination but also by independent evidence, that which the witness testified to on direct." *Robinson* provides a variation on the open-door doctrine because the defendant did not testify. Defense counsel (as opposed to defendant or another witness) stated that defendant was somehow being denied the right to testify on his own behalf. This is the "door" that was "opened" to allow the government to comment on defendant's right to take the stand.

   19.   Carter v. Kentucky, 450 U.S. 288 (1981).

   20.   Lakeside v. Oregon, 435 U.S. 333, 339–41 (1978). The following is a typical instruction:

> There is no burden upon a defendant to prove that [he or she] is innocent. Accordingly, the fact that a defendant did not testify must not be considered by you in any way, or even discussed, in arriving at your verdict.

   21.   *Carter,* 450 U.S. at 302.

   22.   526 U.S. 314 (1999).

tion affords fewer procedural rights at sentencing than in the guilt phase. For example, facts at sentencing may be established by a preponderance of the evidence, defendants do not enjoy the right to confront all witnesses, and judges exercise wide discretion to consider information from a variety of sources. This dichotomy in treatment refutes, in Justice Scalia's view, the applicability of *Griffin* at sentencing.

Finally, although the courts generally require strict adherence to the "no comment" prohibition, the harmless error rule greatly reduces the number of convictions overturned because of impermissible comments. Thus, even where a reviewing court finds that a defendant's Fifth Amendment rights were infringed by an impermissible comment, the conviction will stand if the evidence contains overwhelming evidence against the defendant. The reviewing court must ask the following question in order to determine whether the error was harmless: absent the prosecutor's reference to the defendant's silence, "is it clear beyond a reasonable doubt that the jury would have returned a verdict of guilty?"[23] If the answer is yes, then the error was harmless. If no, then the error was not harmless, and the conviction must be reversed.

Trial Hint: Because jurors may hold silence against a defendant (despite having been instructed not to do so), trial counsel must give serious consideration to whether the client should testify at trial. If the client has a bad prior record (which will cast doubts on his or her credibility), an exceptionally bad presentational style, or little credible evidence, the client probably should not take the stand. Otherwise, contrary to conventional wisdom, the client may be best advised to testify. The client should not, however, take the stand and raise the privilege as to particular questions, because in doing so, the client significantly increases the likelihood of conviction.[24]

c.   The "Hobson's Choice": Threat of Sanctions & Procedural Costs

One way to compel a person to speak is to make his silence costly: few persons would exercise their Fifth Amendment privileges if doing so caused

---

23.   United States v. Hasting, 461 U.S. 499, 510 (1983).

24.   Jeffrey T. Frederick, The Psychology of the American Jury 250–51 (1987). A poignant illustration of this last point can be found in the Patty Hearst case. *See supra*. Hearst was a member of a famously wealthy California family. Her grandfather, William Randolph Hearst, founded the Hearst newspaper dynasty and provided Orson Wells with the central figure for his movie Citizen Kane. Because of her family's wealth, Hearst was kidnapped and held for ransom by a radical political group known as the Symbionese Liberation Army (the "SLA"). During her eighteen months in captivity, she participated in the SLA's armed robbery of a San Francisco bank. After the SLA was apprehended, a grand jury indicted Hearst and SLA members for the robbery. Hearst's defense centered on her claim of duress—that she was afraid the SLA would injure or kill her if she refused to participate in the robbery. She testified in great detail at her trial about the events following her kidnapping, including physical and sexual abuse to which members of the SLA subjected her. Upon cross-examination, however, she refused to answer many of the prosecution's questions concerning a period of her captivity during which, according to the prosecution, she had become a willing member of the SLA. All in all, Hearst asserted her Fifth Amendment privilege forty-two times in front of the jury. The jury found her guilty.

them harm. On the other hand, the public interest sometimes requires people to provide information. As a result of these competing interests the Court decides on a case-by-case basis situations in which individuals are forced to choose between exercising their Fifth Amendment rights and losing something else of great value. This case-specific approach is best illustrated by a series of cases involving individuals given the "Hobson's choice" of answering questions or losing their jobs or other benefits. For example, in *Garrity v. New Jersey*,[25] officials conducting an investigation into police corruption asked questions of several police officers. The investigators warned the officers that they would be fired if they refused to answer. The officers answered the questions and were later convicted based on their incriminating statements. The Court overturned their convictions, holding that their statements had been impermissibly compelled by the Hobson's choice. On the other hand, lawyers are still put to that Hobson's choice, because although the Court has suggested that a lawyer may not be disbarred merely for refusing to answer questions by her state's licensing agency,[26] most jurisdictions have licensing rules requiring that lawyers respond to a lawful demand for information from an attorney disciplinary authority, and failure to do so can result in severe sanctions.[27]

More recently, in *Ohio Adult Parole Authority v. Woodard*,[28] the Court unanimously held that the Fifth Amendment is not violated by state procedures that give an inmate seeking clemency the option of voluntarily participating in an interview with parole authorities. Woodard pointed out that he faced a substantial risk of incrimination if he submitted to the clemency interview, because post conviction proceedings were still pending and because he could potentially incriminate himself with respect to other offenses. On the other hand, if he declined the interview, he likely would be denied clemency. As a result, he argued, the clemency interview "unconstitutionally conditions his assertion of the right to pursue clemency on his waiver of the right to remain silent." The Court responded to Woodard's claim as follows:

> . . . we do not think that respondent's testimony at a clemency interview would be "compelled" within the meaning of the Fifth Amendment. It is difficult to see how a voluntary interview could "compel" respondent to speak. He merely faces a choice quite similar to the sorts of choices that a criminal defendant must make in the course of criminal proceedings, none of which has ever been held to violate the Fifth Amendment.
>
> Long ago we held that a defendant who took the stand in his own defense could not claim the privilege against self-incrimination when the prosecution sought to cross-examine him. A defendant who takes

---

25. 385 U.S. 493 (1967).

26. Spevack v. Klein, 385 U.S. 511 (1967) (plurality opinion).

27. Perhaps in recognition of *Spevack*, Comment 2 to the Rule states that it is subject to the provisions of the Fifth Amendment.

28. 523 U.S. 272 (1998).

the stand in his own behalf may be impeached by proof of prior convictions without violation of the Fifth Amendment privilege. . . . In each of these situations there are undoubted pressures . . . pushing the criminal defendant to testify. But it has never been suggested that such pressures constitute "compulsion" for Fifth Amendment purposes.

Here, respondent has the same choice of providing information to the Authority—at the risk of damaging his case for clemency or for postconviction relief—or of remaining silent. But this pressure to speak in the hope of improving his chance of being granted clemency does not make the interview compelled.

Moving from parolees to actual prisoners, the Court has struggled to define compulsion in situations in which prison officials punish inmates (or deny them benefits) as a consequence of the inmates' refusal to incriminate themselves. A divided Court in *McKune v. Lile*[29] upheld an "incentive system" that accompanied the State of Kansas's Sexual Abuse Treatment Program (SATP) for incarcerated sex offenders, but the Court was unable to agree on a definition of compulsion. The program required inmates to complete and sign an "Admission of Responsibility," on the basis of evidence showing that such an admission enhances the effectiveness of treatment. Inmates who refused to sign the form were denied entrance to the program and were denied other benefits. Justice Kennedy, in a plurality opinion joined by Chief Justice Rehnquist and Justices Scalia and Thomas, disagreed. Kennedy began by contrasting the facts in *Garrity* and companion cases from Lile's situation. The *Garrity* line of cases, said Kennedy, "involved free citizens given the choice between invoking the Fifth Amendment privilege and sustaining their economic livelihood." On the other hand, Kennedy felt that compulsion was not so easily discerned in the prison context, "where inmates surrender upon incarceration their rights to pursue a livelihood and to contract freely with the State, as well as many other basic freedoms." In the prison context, Kennedy continued:

> Determining what constitutes unconstitutional compulsion involves a question of judgment: Courts must decide whether the consequences of an inmate's choice to remain silent are closer to the physical torture against which the Constitution clearly protects or the de minimis harms against which it does not. The *Sandin* framework [which recognizes as unconstitutional only those prison conditions that "constitute atypical and significant hardships on inmates in relation to the ordinary incidents of prison life"] provides a reasonable means of assessing whether the response of prison administrators to correctional and rehabilitative necessities are so out of the ordinary that one could sensibly say they rise to the level of unconstitutional compulsion.

Justice Kennedy went on to identify three factors that courts should use when examining claims of compulsion in the prison context. First, how great is the burden upon the prisoner's assertion of the privilege (presumably the "atypical hardship" test would come into play here), or, to put the

---

29. 536 U.S. 24 (2002).

question another way, how difficult is the choice that prison officials have imposed upon a prisoner? Second, what are the size and nature of the state's interest: does the interest justify the burden on the prisoner's assertion of the privilege, and does it suggest that the burden is "incidental" as opposed to maliciously motivated? Third and finally, does the burden follow automatically from the prisoner's assertion of the privilege, or is there a process that will ensue? Examining these factors in Lile's case, Kennedy concluded that compulsion was not present.

Justice O'Connor concurred in the judgment, agreeing that Lile's loss of privileges and transfer to maximum-security housing did not constitute compulsion. She did not join the plurality's opinion, however, because she disagreed with its reliance on the "atypical hardship" standard. The compulsion standard, she felt, is "broader" than the "atypical hardship" standard. According to O'Connor, the test for compulsion is simply this: "whether the pressure imposed in such [a] situation rises to a level where it is likely to compel a person to be a witness against himself." Justice Stevens, joined in dissent by Justices Souter, Ginsburg, and Breyer, found that the SATP was "inherently coercive": it required incriminating disclosures and it applied automatic sanctions to those who refused. Stevens argued that none of the Court's prior opinions "contains any suggestion that compulsion should have a different meaning in the prison context." In terms of measuring the level of pressure, Stevens said, "The coerciveness of the penalty in this case must be measured not by comparing the quality of life in a prison environment with that in a free society, but rather by the contrast between the favored and disfavored classes of prisoners."

In the context of criminal defendants and the procedural choices they face, the Court has sometimes held that such defendants cannot be forced to forfeit other constitutional rights to retain their privilege against self-incrimination. This rule arises when a criminal defendant moves to suppress evidence under the Fourth Amendment on the ground that it was obtained during an unconstitutional search. Frequently, such a defendant must testify at a pretrial suppression hearing in order to present his or her version of the search. Such testimony may incriminate the defendant, by placing the defendant at the scene or acknowledging ownership of weapons or illegal substances.[30] This is the defendant's Hobson's choice—either challenge the search under the Fourth Amendment and forego the privilege against self-incrimination, or forfeit the right to challenge the search and preserve the privilege at trial. In order to avoid this dilemma, the Court has ruled that such pretrial testimony generally is inadmissible at a criminal trial.[31]

Nonetheless, the Court has been willing to accept procedural structures that force defendants to forfeit other rights or opportunities to preserve their Fifth Amendment privileges. Most significant for our pur-

---

30. Recall that a defendant who moves to suppress evidence must have standing, a concept that sometimes requires an assertion of ownership or possession. *See* Rakas v. Illinois, 439 U.S. 128 (1978).

31. Simmons v. United States, 390 U.S. 377, 393–94 (1968).

poses is *McGautha v. California*[32] and its companion case, *Crampton v. Ohio*. Both cases involved statutes that consolidated into a single proceeding, before the same jury, the trial and sentencing phases of a death penalty case. By not bifurcating the two procedures, the statutes created a situation in which a defendant who chose to remain silent on the issue of guilt was denied an opportunity to testify at sentencing. The unitary procedure thus arguably created a compulsion to testify. In rejecting the defendants' Fifth Amendment claims in *McGautha* and *Crampton*, the Court viewed the decision whether to testify at a unitary trial as a purely strategic decision, a choice motivated by the need to respond to a strong prosecution case. The Court saw no difference between that choice and the choice always facing a defendant at the close of the prosecution's evidence: whether to testify and then face cross-examination that may help the prosecution. The Court relied in part on *Williams v. Florida*,[33] which made a similar point in the course of rejecting a Fifth Amendment challenge to state alibi disclosure rules:

> The defendant in a criminal trial is frequently forced to testify himself and to call other witnesses in an effort to reduce the risk of conviction. When he presents his witnesses, he must reveal their identity and submit them to cross-examination which in itself may prove incriminating or which may furnish the State with leads to incriminating rebuttal evidence. That the defendant faces such a dilemma demanding a choice between complete silence and presenting a defense has never been thought an invasion of the privilege against compelled self-incrimination.

In *Brooks v. Tennessee*,[34] by contrast, the Court struck down a Tennessee statute that permitted a defendant to testify only if he took the stand before calling any other defense witnesses. The asserted rationale for the rule was that a defendant who had an opportunity to see and hear the testimony of his witnesses before taking the stand would be tempted to mold his testimony to match that of the witnesses. The defendant argued that the statute imposed an undue penalty on his Fifth Amendment rights because his silence at the start of his case required him to forego the opportunity to testify later if defense witness testimony proved inadequate standing alone. The Court agreed, acknowledging first that a defendant's choice to take the stand "carries with it serious risks of impeachment and cross-examination; it may open the door to otherwise inadmissible evidence which is damaging to his case." The Court emphasized that the defendant should not have to face these risks where he may accomplish his defense goals through other witnesses. In most jurisdictions, the defendant may later choose to take the stand if his witnesses collapse under skillful cross-examination or fail to impress the jury. The statute at issue, however, "exacts a price for his silence by keeping him off the stand entirely unless he chooses to testify first. This, we think, casts a heavy burden on a

---

32. 402 U.S. 183 (1971).

33. 399 U.S. 78, 83–84 (1970).

34. 406 U.S. 605, 612 (1972).

defendant's otherwise unconditional right not to take the stand." The Court concluded that the state's purported interest in protecting the integrity of the truth-seeking process was not sufficient to outweigh Fifth Amendment concerns. Even an innocent defendant may prefer not to subject himself to impeachment and cross-examination at a time when the strength of his other evidence is not yet clear.

Not every procedural rule that imposes information costs constitutes compulsion. All Fifth Amendment analyses arguably come down to judgments about whether the need to promote the truth-finding functions of trial outweigh the concerns underlying the Fifth Amendment.[35] Sometimes truth-finding interests prevail because the Fifth Amendment concerns about compulsion are relatively minor. For example, in *Williams v. Florida*, the Court upheld a state rule that barred a defendant from presenting an alibi defense other than by his own testimony, unless he gave pretrial notice of the intent to offer the alibi, including the place where he claimed to have been and the names and addresses of his intended witnesses.[36] The Court reasoned that regardless of the potential testimonial or incriminating nature of the alibi defense, the alibi defense could not be considered compelled within the meaning of the Fifth Amendment because the defendant was under no obligation to rely on the alibi and nothing prevented him from abandoning the defense. Moreover, even in the absence of the rule, the alibi information would be revealed at trial and subject to government cross-examination. Thus, the alibi-notice statute merely accelerated the timing of the defendant's disclosure. The Court declared:

> The adversary system of trial is hardly an end in itself; it is not yet a poker game in which players enjoy an absolute right always to conceal their cards until played. We find ample room in that system, at least as far as "due process" is concerned, for the instant Florida rule, which is designed to enhance the search for truth in the criminal trial by insuring both the defendant and the State ample opportunity to investigate certain facts crucial to the determination of guilt or innocence.[37]

Florida's rule was substantially similar to Federal Rule of Criminal Procedure 12.1, which states as follows:

> Upon written demand of the attorney for the government stating the time, date, and place at which the alleged offense was committed, the defendant shall serve within ten days, or at such different time as the court may direct, upon the attorney for the government a written notice of the defendant's intention to offer a defense of alibi. Such notice by the defendant shall state the specific place or places at which

---

35. For other examples of cases involving a balancing of these interests, *see* Harris v. New York, 401 U.S. 222 (1971) (statements violative of the Miranda rule can be used for impeachment); United States v. Robinson, 485 U.S. 25 (1988) (government's comments on defendant's silence were a "fair response" to defense counsel's closing argument, in which he stated that the government had prevented defendant from telling his side of the story).

36. Williams v. Florida, 399 U.S. 78 (1970).

37. *See id.* at 82.

the defendant claims to have been at the time of the alleged offense and the names and addresses of the witnesses upon whom the defendant intends to rely to establish such alibi. . . .

Upon the failure of either party to comply with the requirements of this rule, the court may exclude the testimony of any undisclosed witness offered by such party as to the defendant's absence from or presence at, the scene of the alleged offense. This rule shall not limit the right of the defendant to testify.

Many states have "alibi-notice requirements" that impose upon the defendant the duty to give notice in advance of trial if the defendant intends to claim an alibi, and to give the prosecution information regarding the place where the defendant claims to have been along with the names and addresses of any alibi witnesses the defendant intends to call to testify. It should be noted that these rules are reciprocal: that is, they impose upon the prosecution the duty to notify the defendant of any witnesses it proposes to offer in rebuttal to the alibi defense.

PROBLEM 9–3

In the *Brunell* case in Chapter 1, assume that Brunell is called to the stand to testify in his divorce trial. Brunell's lawyer anticipates that one of the questions will be whether Brunell concealed income from Mrs. Brunell and the IRS. The lawyer advises him that his answers to these questions can be used in the criminal tax evasion case. The lawyer also advises that if he refuses to testify, the judge will draw an "adverse inference" from his refusal—in other words, the judge will conclude that Brunell's answer would be yes.

Question: Does the adverse inference pose a burden on Brunell's exercise of Fifth Amendment privileges? Is the burden so weighty as to violate the constitution? Why or why not?

2.   INCRIMINATION

The privilege can be asserted in "any proceeding, civil or criminal, administrative or judicial, investigatory or adjudicatory,"[38] so long as there is a "substantial and real" hazard that the disclosures sought could be incriminating—in other words, that they "could be used in a criminal prosecution or could lead to other evidence that might be so used" as a link in a chain of evidence.[39] In *Ohio v. Reiner*,[40] the Supreme Court affirmed

---

38.   Kastigar v. United States, 406 U.S. 441, 444 (1972).

39.   *Id.* at 445; *see also, e.g.*, Hoffman v. United States, 341 U.S. 479 (1951). The latter circumstance is frequently called the "link in a chain of evidence." The requirement of potential criminal liability means that a witness may not invoke the Fifth Amendment to avoid answering questions regarding a crime for which the statute of limitations has run. Brown v. Walker, 161 U.S. 591 (1896). Similarly, a witness may not refuse to answer if the witness has been immunized or pardoned for the crime.

40.   532 U.S. 17 (2001).

that the privilege applies even to a person who asserts his or her innocence, because "the truthful responses of an innocent witness, as well as those of a wrongdoer, may provide the government with incriminating evidence from the speaker's own mouth." On the other hand, the Court held in *United States v. Balsys* that the Fifth Amendment privilege does not apply where the "substantial and real hazard of incrimination" relates exclusively to criminal prosecution by a foreign sovereign.[41] But apart from this limitation, the test for incrimination is obviously very broad. As a result, a good working knowledge of Fifth Amendment law is important to lawyers representing clients in civil matters as well as criminal, because the "criminal case" language of the Fifth Amendment applies to the proceedings in which the testimony might eventually be *used*, and not to the proceedings at which the testimony is *compelled*.[42] The broad scope of the privilege means that it may be raised in civil and criminal discovery, in response to subpoenas requiring the production of documents, before grand juries, at trial, and during police interrogation.

For an example of the ease of satisfying the incrimination threshhold, consider the fact that a defendant who pleads guilty does *not* waive the privilege against self-incrimination at sentencing. The Supreme Court decided this issue in *Mitchell v. United States*.[43] The defendant in that case, Amanda Mitchell, had pleaded guilty to drug distribution charges. Her sentence would depend largely on the quantity of drugs with which she had been involved, but she and the prosecution did not agree in advance of sentencing as to that quantity. At her sentencing hearing, Ms. Mitchell vigorously cross-examined the prosecution's drug quantity evidence. She did not testify herself. The sentencing judge inferred from her failure to testify that she had been involved with a drug quantity sufficient to require the application of a 10–year mandatory minimum sentence. When defense counsel argued that the sentencing judge had used the defendant's silence against her, the judge agreed, explaining that such an adverse inference did not violate Mitchell's privilege against self-incrimination because she had waived her privilege when she pleaded guilty. The United States Court of Appeals for the Third Circuit affirmed, stating, "By voluntarily and knowingly pleading guilty to the offense Mitchell waived her Fifth Amendment privilege."

The Supreme Court reversed, stressing that significant risks of incrimination still remain for defendants who have pleaded guilty but who are as yet unsentenced. Writing for a 5–person majority, Justice Kennedy stated:

> . . . Where the sentence has not yet been imposed a defendant may have a legitimate fear of adverse consequences from further testimony.
> . . . [I]t appears that in this case, as is often true in the criminal justice system, the defendant was less concerned with the proof of her guilt or innocence than with the severity of her punishment. Petitioner faced

---

41. 524 U.S. 666 (1998).

42. Counselman v. Hitchcock, 142 U.S. 547 (1892).

43. 526 U.S. 314 (1999).

imprisonment from one year upwards to life, depending on the circumstances of the crime. To say that she had no right to remain silent but instead could be compelled to cooperate in the deprivation of her liberty would ignore the Fifth Amendment privilege at the precise stage where, from her point of view, it was most important.

We will return to the incrimination requirement later in this chapter, when we discuss the doctrine of immunity. Individuals who have been granted immunity are protected from the incriminating aspects of their testimony. As a result, they can be compelled to testify and cannot claim protection on the basis of the Fifth Amendment.

3.   TESTIMONY

Sometimes individuals are compelled to engage in physical acts such as giving blood samples or undergoing field sobriety tests. These do not implicate the privilege against self-incrimination because they are not considered testimonial. Because of this rule, many states have laws requiring drivers to submit to field sobriety tests. Drivers who refuse to acquiesce in the testing procedures lose their driving privileges. What of the driver who submits because of the threat of losing his driver's license, fails the test, and at trial contends that the test results should be suppressed because he was "compelled" to submit? The Court resolved this question in *South Dakota v. Neville*,[44] holding that the driver's compliance with the test was not compelled because he had the option of refusing and that, in any event, the results of the field sobriety tests did not implicate the Fifth Amendment because they were not testimonial.[45]

The distinction between testimonial and non-testimonial acts was highlighted in *Schmerber v. California*,[46] a case arising out of an automobile accident in Los Angeles. The accident caused injuries to the automobile driver, Armando Schmerber, who was hospitalized for treatment. Police officers investigating the accident suspected that Schmerber had been drinking and instructed a doctor to draw samples of his blood. Chemical analysis of the blood revealed the presence of an intoxication-producing quantity of alcohol, and prosecutors brought drunk-driving charges against him. At trial, the prosecutors offered into evidence a report of the blood analysis. Schmerber objected on several grounds, including the contention that the blood test had been compelled and therefore violated his privilege against self-incrimination. Writing for the majority, Justice William Brennan disagreed. The Court acknowledged that the testing had been compelled: there was no dispute about the fact that Schmerber had objected when the doctor drew the blood samples. However, the thing that had been compelled was a physical matter—blood—and not anything related to

---

44.   459 U.S. 553 (1983).

45.   Under some circumstances, however, field sobriety tests do call for testimonial responses. In those circumstances, the Fifth Amendment privilege against self-incrimination is implicated. *See* Pennsylvania v. Muniz, 496 U.S. 582 (1990).

46.   384 U.S. 757, 764 (1966).

Schmerber's "testimonial capacities." Examining a long line of cases in the Supreme Court and lower courts, the Court concluded that the privilege applies only to testimony, or "some communicative act or writing." It went on to explain that the Fifth Amendment "offers no protection against compulsions to submit to fingerprinting, photographing, or measurements, to write or speak for identification, to appear in court, to stand, to assume a stance, to walk, or make a particular gesture."

Schmerber stands for the proposition that the Fifth Amendment applies only to testimonial communications and does not protect an individual from the compelled production of physical evidence. In other cases the Court has declined to extend Fifth Amendment protection to "physical acts," including putting on a blouse for identification purposes,[47] speaking particular words in a lineup for identification purposes,[48] submitting samples of one's handwriting (these are known as "handwriting exemplars"),[49] submitting voice exemplars,[50] and submitting to "blood alcohol tests."[51] Similarly, using a person's physical characteristics to incriminate that person at trial does not violate the Fifth Amendment. For example, in an Alabama case, a robbery defendant was required to open his mouth and show his teeth during trial, after the victim testified that the robber had a "bigger gap than mine" in his front teeth. The defendant claimed that the procedure violated his privilege against self-incrimination—in effect, the state convicted him out of his own mouth. The Alabama appellate court rejected this argument, citing *Schmerber* and stating that it could "think of no set of circumstances under which the appearance of [the defendant's] teeth could qualify as testimonial rather than physical evidence."[52]

PROBLEM 9–4

In the *Brunell* case in Chapter 1, assume, as part of Terri Marvoal's agreement to cooperate, that the government asks her to secretly tape record a conversation with Brunell. Subsequently, the grand jury issues a subpoena to Brunell for a voice exemplar. As Brunell's attorney, you accompany him to the FBI office, where he is asked to read a typed statement into a tape recorder. You notice that the statement matches the one he allegedly made in a taped telephone conversation with Terri Marvoal.

Question: Should you advise Brunell to refuse to provide the voice exemplar? On what grounds? How will the prosecution respond and the court rule?

---

47. Holt v. United States, 218 U.S. 245 (1910).
48. United States v. Wade, 388 U.S. 218 (1967).
49. Gilbert v. California, 388 U.S. 263 (1967).
50. United States v. Dionisio, 410 U.S. 1 (1973).
51. South Dakota v. Neville, 459 U.S. 553 (1983).
52. Huff v. State, 452 So.2d 1352, 1353–54 (Ala.Crim.App.1984).

PROBLEM 9–5

You are deciding whether to prosecute a drunk driving case against Jonah Wilk. The arresting officer administered two field sobriety tests: one required Wilk to balance on one leg, which he was unable to do for more than a few seconds; the other required him to state the date of his sixth birthday. According to the officer, Wilk responded to the question about his birthday with the comment, "I don't remember."[53]

Question: Are the results of the balancing test admissible? Why or why not? What about Wilk's statement that he did not remember the date of his sixth birthday? Is there anything that distinguishes that response from the other test result? Does your decision whether to prosecute depend on your assessments of these questions about admissibility?

Note on Prosecutorial Ethics: Prosecutors are bound by special ethical restrictions beyond those of other lawyers. Because they exercise substantial discretion in deciding whether and whom to prosecute, ethical rules attempt to delineate the circumstances in which the exercise of that discretion is legitimate. Many of these rules permit a prosecutor to charge a person with a criminal offense only "when the prosecutor can support the charge with a valid statute and with facts available in the form of apparently admissible evidence."[54] The ABA Standards Relating to the Administration of Criminal Justice, Prosecution Function, expressly require that a charge be instituted only where there is "sufficient admissible evidence to support a conviction."[55] Moreover, prosecutors typically take an oath of office that includes a promise to uphold the constitution. Does this mean that prosecutors must take care not to use evidence that was obtained through a constitutional violation? Or does a "sporting theory" of justice permit the prosecution to try to get away with as much as possible?

According to a recent four-justice plurality opinion by Justice Thomas, there is one more threshold that must be crossed before one encounters the "core" Fifth Amendment right: the actual *use* of a compelled statement in a criminal case.[56] Justice Thomas explained that while a person may assert a Fifth Amendment *privilege* in non-criminal cases, that privilege is a prophylactic rule "designed to safeguard the core constitutional *right* protected by the Self–Incrimination Clause." One consequence of Thomas's distinction between a core constitutional right and its corollary privileges and rules is his insistence that only the core right is cognizable in § 1983

---

53.   This question is based on the facts in Pennsylvania v. Muniz, *supra*, in which the Court held that whether a suspect is exposed to the "cruel trilemma" determines whether a compelled revelation is physical or testimonial.

54.   CHARLES W. WOLFRAM, MODERN LEGAL ETHICS 763 (1986). *See, e.g.*, Standard 3–3.9(a), ABA Standards Relating to the Administration of Criminal Justice, Prosecution Function. Some codes provide only that there must be "probable cause" before instituting charges, remaining silent about the question of admissible evidence. *See, e.g.*, DR 7–103(A) of the Model Rules of Professional Conduct.

55.   *See* ABA Standard 3–3.9(a).

56.   Chavez v. Martinez, 538 U.S. 760 (2003) (Thomas, J.). The Chief Justice and Justices O'Connor and Scalia joined Justice Thomas's opinion on this point.

actions. In other words, according to Thomas, a government actor cannot be sued under § 1983 for a Fifth Amendment violation unless that actor caused a compelled statement to be used against a person in a criminal case. Three justices explicitly disagreed with Justice Thomas's core-versus-corollary position, as well as his ban on § 1983 remedies for violations of corollary privileges and rules.[57] The remaining two Justices appeared to accept Thomas's core-corollary distinction but not his absolute refusal to afford § 1983 remedies for violations of the corollary privileges and rules.

E.   The "Required Records" Exception to the Privilege

Recall from this text's earlier discussion of searches and seizures that special governmental needs sometimes exempt the government from traditional Fourth Amendment requirements. The same is true in the Fifth Amendment context: sometimes testimony the government seeks in order to fulfill an "administrative purpose" may be compelled despite the guarantees of the Fifth Amendment.[58] Under a doctrine known as the "required records" exception to the Fifth Amendment, the government may require certain records to be kept and reported. This doctrine has three articulated thresholds: first, the purpose of the record-keeping requirement must be regulatory; second, information requested within the required records must be of a kind that the party customarily maintains; and third, the records themselves must have a "public aspect [making] them analogous to public documents."[59]

A familiar example of the required records doctrine is the rule that a person must furnish identification after involvement in an automobile accident, even though that information is potentially incriminating. This is based on the premise that processing information about vehicle accidents is an important administrative function of local governments, even though that information will also be useful in a criminal prosecution. Courts have held that if the government articulates an important regulatory purpose, "[i]t is irrelevant that records kept for regulatory purposes may be useful to a criminal ... investigation."[60]

It is unclear whether the second of the three elements of the doctrine— that the records be of a type customarily kept—is always necessary. That factor is more likely merely supportive of the government's claim that its interest is regulatory, not criminal, and helpful in the "public aspects" balancing test. As is suggested by *Byers*, there may be instances where a regulatory interest is so strong that it justifies keeping records of activities that would not otherwise be recorded in the ordinary course of business.

---

57.   *See id.* Justice Kennedy concurred in part and dissented in part, joined on this point by Justices Stevens and Ginsburg. But Justice Kennedy (joined by Justice Stevens) agreed with Justice Thomas that *Miranda* violations are remediable only through an exclusionary remedy.

58.   Shapiro v. United States, 335 U.S. 1 (1948).

59.   Grosso v. United States, 390 U.S. 62 (1968).

60.   *See, e.g.*, In re Doe v. United States, 801 F.2d 1164, 1168 (9th Cir.1986).

Although the Court has not clearly defined when records have "public aspects," commentators, relying on *Byers* and on lower court interpretations of the required records doctrine, have generally concluded that the term is an invitation to "balance the public need on the one hand, and the individual claim to constitutional protections on the other."[61] Balancing must consider such factors as: (1) the significance of the government's regulatory interest, (2) the importance of the disclosure to making that interest effective, and (3) the significance of the disclosure on the individual. Presumably, an individual has little interest in withholding a document that truly has "public aspects,"[62] and that individual might be said to have waived any Fifth Amendment interests in such a document.[63]

The required records doctrine has its limits: a person may successfully assert the privilege against self-incrimination where the records requirement is directed not at the general public but at a "highly selective group inherently suspected of criminal activities," especially if it involves an "area permeated with criminal statutes."[64] Thus, a defendant may assert the privilege to avoid prosecution for failing to register a transfer of marijuana,[65] for failing to register and pay the occupational tax on gambling receipts,[66] and for failing to register a sawed-off shotgun.[67] A primary rationale for the limitation is that such records requirements are likely to be motivated by law enforcement, rather than administrative, concerns.

Applying this analysis to a case involving a hit-and-run driver, the Court concluded that a law requiring drivers involved in accidents to furnish information was so general as to be directed at the public at large. The Court continued:

> It is difficult to consider this group as either "highly selective" or "inherently suspect of criminal activities." Driving an automobile, unlike gambling, is a lawful activity. Moreover, it is not a criminal offense under [state] law to be a driver "involved in an accident." An accident may be the fault of others; it may occur without any driver having been at fault. No empirical data are suggested in support of the conclusion that there is a relevant correlation between being a driver and criminal prosecution of drivers. So far as any available information instructs us, most accidents occur without creating criminal liability even if one or both of the drivers are guilty of negligence as a matter of tort law.
>
> The disclosure of inherently illegal activity is inherently risky.... But disclosures with respect to automobile accidents simply do not

---

61. WAYNE R. LaFAVE AND JEROLD H. ISRAEL, CRIMINAL PROCEDURE 433 (2d ed. 1992) (quoting California v. Byers, 402 U.S. 424, 427 (1971)).

62. *See, e.g.,* United States v. Spano, 21 F.3d 226, 230 (8th Cir.1994).

63. United States v. Doe, 793 F.2d 69, 73 (2d Cir.1986).

64. *Byers*, 402 U.S. at 429 (quoting Albertson v. SACB, 382 U.S. 70, 79 (1965)).

65. Leary v. United States, 395 U.S. 6 (1969).

66. Marchetti v. United States, 390 U.S. 39 (1968).

67. Haynes v. United States, 390 U.S. 85 (1968).

entail ... substantial risk of self-incrimination.... Furthermore, the statutory purpose is noncriminal and self-reporting is indispensable to its fulfillment.[68]

Contrast this with federal tax laws applied to the business of "wagering." In a prosecution for failure to comply with these laws, the Court upheld the defendant's assertion of his Fifth Amendment privilege, reasoning that:

> ... Wagering and its ancillary activities are very widely prohibited under both federal and state law. Federal statutes impose criminal penalties upon the interstate transmission of wagering information; upon interstate and foreign travel or transportation in aid of racketeering enterprises, defined to include gambling; upon lotteries conducted through use of the mails or broadcasting; and upon the interstate transportation of wagering paraphernalia.
>
> State and local enactments are more comprehensive. The laws of every State, except Nevada, include broad prohibitions against gambling, wagering, and associated activities. Every State forbids, with essentially minor and carefully circumscribed exceptions, lotteries. Even Nevada, which permits many forms of gambling, retains criminal penalties upon lotteries and certain other wagering activities taxable under these statutes.
>
> Connecticut, in which petitioner allegedly conducted his activities, has adopted a variety of measures for the punishment of gambling and wagering. It punishes "[a]ny person, whether as principal, agent, or servant, who owns, possesses, keeps, manages, maintains or occupies" premises employed for purposes of wagering or pool selling. It imposes criminal penalties upon any person who possesses, keeps or maintains premises in which policy playing occurs, or lotteries are conducted, and upon any person who becomes the custodian of books, property, appliances, or apparatus employed for wagering. It provides additional penalties for those who conspire to organize or conduct unlawful wagering activities. Every aspect of petitioner's wagering activities thus subjected him to possible state or federal prosecution. By any standard, in Connecticut and throughout the United States, wagering is "an area permeated with criminal statutes," and those engaged in wagering are a group "inherently suspect of criminal activities."
>
> Information obtained as a consequence of the federal wagering tax laws is readily available to assist the efforts of state and federal authorities to enforce these penalties. Section 6107 of Title 26 requires the principal Internal Revenue offices to provide to prosecuting officers a listing of those who have paid the occupational tax. Section 6806 (c) obliges taxpayers either to post the revenue stamp "conspicuously" in their principal places of business, or to keep it on their persons, and to produce it on the demand of Treasury officers. Evidence of the possession of a federal wagering tax stamp, or of payment of the wagering

---

68. *Byers*, 402 U.S. at 431.

taxes, has often been admitted at trial in state and federal prosecutions for gambling offenses; such evidence has doubtless proved useful even more frequently to lead prosecuting authorities to other evidence upon which convictions have subsequently been obtained. Finally, we are obliged to notice that a former Commissioner of Internal Revenue has acknowledged that the Service "makes available" to law enforcement agencies the names and addresses of those who have paid the wagering taxes, and that it is in "full cooperation" with the efforts of the Attorney General of the United States to suppress organized gambling.

In these circumstances, it can scarcely be denied that the obligations to register and to pay the occupational tax created for petitioner "real and appreciable," and not merely "imaginary and insubstantial," hazards of self-incrimination. Petitioner was confronted by a comprehensive system of federal and state prohibitions against wagering activities; he was required, on pain of criminal prosecution, to provide information which he might reasonably suppose would be available to prosecuting authorities, and which would surely prove a significant link in a chain of evidence tending to establish his guilt.[69]

PROBLEM 9–6

In the *Brunell* case in Chapter 1, assume that you represent Brunell in the criminal tax fraud case. You advise him to make sure that he files all returns and pays all taxes for the years not involved in the investigation, because if he is convicted, the judge will consider that fact at sentencing. Brunell replies angrily that he will never file another income tax return, explaining that the "government just uses them against me." He asks you whether his Fifth Amendment privilege means that he does not have to create income tax returns.

Question: What is the answer to Brunell's question? How will you explain the law to Brunell? Articulate the required records doctrine in terms that the ordinary taxpayer would understand.

II.   The Compelled Production of Pre-Existing Documents

A.   The "Act of Production" Privilege Defined

Recall from the discussion above that incriminating testimony must be *compelled* before an individual can assert a Fifth Amendment privilege in order to avoid giving the testimony. What if the government compels a person not to testify but rather to hand over to the government documents that are already in existence—through, for example, a subpoena calling for a taxpayer to produce all tax records for certain years. The taxpayer may want to assert the privilege in order to avoid producing the incriminating

---

69.   *Marchetti*, 390 U.S. at 44–48.

documents, but the problem with the privilege assertion is that the documents were created *before* the subpoena was issued—in other words, before any government compulsion took place. Reviewing this situation, the Court announced bad news and good news for individuals. First (the bad news), it held that pre-existing documents cannot be the subject of a Fifth Amendment claim because their contents and creation were not compelled. Second (the good news), it held that the very act of producing those documents could be the subject of a privilege assertion because that act itself was compelled and might constitute incriminating testimony. Consider the following excerpt of the case in which the Court created these two rules and pay special attention to how the Court explained the potentially incriminating aspects to the act of producing documents. Notice also that there is a complicating factor in the case: the individuals involved had turned their documents over to attorneys and claimed that the attorneys should be able to assert their Fifth Amendment privilege on their behalf. Be sure to follow how the Court resolved this issue.

Fisher v. United States

425 U.S. 391 (1976).

■ WHITE, J. In these two [consolidated] cases we are called upon to decide whether a summons directing an attorney to produce documents delivered to him by his client in connection with the attorney-client relationship is enforceable over claims that the documents were constitutionally immune from summons in the hands of the client and retained that immunity in the hands of the attorney.

I

In each case, an Internal Revenue agent visited the taxpayer or taxpayers and interviewed them in connection with an investigation of possible civil or criminal liability under the federal income tax laws. Shortly after the interviews the taxpayers obtained from their respective accountants certain documents relating to the preparation by the accountants of their tax returns. Shortly after obtaining the documents the taxpayers transferred the documents to their lawyers . . . each of whom was retained to assist the taxpayer in connection with the investigation. Upon learning of the whereabouts of the documents, the Internal Revenue Service served summonses on the attorneys directing them to produce documents listed therein. . . . [T]he documents demanded were analyses by the accountant of the taxpayers' income and expenses which had been copied by the accountant from the taxpayers' canceled checks and deposit receipts. . . . In each case, the lawyer declined to comply with the summons directing production of the documents, and enforcement actions were commenced by the Government. . . . [T]he attorney[s] raised in defense of the enforcement action the taxpayer's . . . attorney-client privilege, and . . . claimed that enforcement would involve compulsory self-incrimination of the taxpayers in violation of their Fifth Amendment privilege. . . .

[I]n our view the documents were not privileged either in the hands of the lawyers or of their clients. . . .

II

[I]f the Fifth Amendment would have excused a Taxpayer from turning over the accountant's papers had he possessed them, the Attorney to whom they are delivered for the purpose of obtaining legal advice should also be immune from subpoena. . . . [But] it is not the taxpayer's Fifth Amendment privilege that would excuse the Attorney from production.

The relevant part of that Amendment provides: "No person . . . shall be Compelled in any criminal case to be a Witness against himself." The taxpayer's privilege under this Amendment is not violated by enforcement of the summonses involved in these cases because enforcement against a taxpayer's lawyer would not "compel" the taxpayer to do anything and certainly would not compel him to be a "witness" against himself. The Court has held repeatedly that the Fifth Amendment is limited to prohibiting the use of "physical or moral compulsion" exerted on the person asserting the privilege. . . .

The taxpayers' Fifth Amendment privilege is therefore not violated by enforcement of the summonses directed toward their attorneys. This is true whether or not the Amendment would have barred a subpoena directing the taxpayer to produce the documents while they were in his hands.

The fact that the attorneys are agents of the taxpayers does not change this result. . . . In *Hale v. Henkel*, 201 U.S. 43, 69–70 (1906), the Court said that the privilege "was never intended to permit (a person) to plead the fact that some third person might be incriminated by his testimony, even though he were the agent of such person. . . . [T]he Amendment is limited to a person who shall be compelled in any criminal case to be a witness against Himself." Agent or no, the lawyer is not the taxpayer. . . .

Nor is this one of those situations . . . where constructive possession is so clear or relinquishment of possession so temporary and insignificant as to leave the personal compulsion upon the taxpayer substantially intact. . . . [T]he documents sought were obtainable without personal compulsion on the accused. . . .

[P]etitioners argue . . . that if the summons was enforced, the taxpayers' Fifth Amendment privilege would be, but should not be, lost solely because they gave their documents to their lawyers in order to obtain legal advice. But this misconceives the nature of the constitutional privilege. The Amendment protects a person from being compelled to be a witness against himself. Here, the taxpayers retained any privilege they ever had not to be compelled to testify against themselves and not to be compelled themselves to produce private papers in their possession. This personal privilege was in no way decreased by the transfer. It is simply that by reason of the transfer of the documents to the attorneys, those papers may be subpoenaed without compulsion on the taxpayer. The protection of the Fifth Amendment is therefore not available. "A party is privileged from producing evidence but not from its production." . . .

III

Our above holding is that compelled production of documents from an attorney does not implicate whatever Fifth Amendment privilege the taxpayer might have enjoyed from being compelled to produce them himself. The taxpayers in these cases, however, have from the outset consistently urged that they should not be forced to expose otherwise protected documents to summons simply because they have sought legal advice and turned the papers over to their attorneys. The Government appears to agree unqualifiedly. The difficulty is that the taxpayers have erroneously relied on the Fifth Amendment without urging the attorney-client privilege in so many words. They have nevertheless invoked the relevant body of law and policies that govern the attorney-client privilege. In this posture of the case, we feel obliged to inquire whether the attorney-client privilege applies to documents in the hands of an attorney which would have been privileged in the hands of the client by reason of the Fifth Amendment.

Confidential disclosures by a client to an attorney made in order to obtain legal assistance are privileged. As a practical matter, if the client knows that damaging information could more readily be obtained from the attorney following disclosure than from himself in the absence of disclosure, the client would be reluctant to confide in his lawyer and it would be difficult to obtain fully informed legal advice. However, since the privilege has the effect of withholding relevant information from the fact-finder, it applies only where necessary to achieve its purpose. Accordingly it protects only those disclosures necessary to obtain informed legal advice which might not have been made absent the privilege. This Court and the lower courts have thus uniformly held that pre-existing documents which could have been obtained by court process from the client when he was in possession may also be obtained from the attorney by similar process following transfer by the client in order to obtain more informed legal advice. The purpose of the privilege requires no broader rule. . . . [I]f the documents are not obtainable by subpoena duces tecum or summons while in the exclusive possession of the client, [and] . . . [w]here the transfer is made for the purpose of obtaining legal advice, the purposes of the attorney-client privilege would be defeated unless the privilege is applicable. "It follows, then, that when the client himself would be privileged from production of the document . . . as exempt from self-incrimination, the attorney having possession of the document is not bound to produce."

Since each taxpayer transferred possession of the documents in question from himself to his attorney in order to obtain legal assistance in the tax investigations in question, the papers, if unobtainable by summons from the client, are unobtainable by summons directed to the attorney by reason of the attorney-client privilege. We accordingly proceed to the question whether the documents could have been obtained by summons addressed to the taxpayer while the documents were in his possession. The only bar to enforcement of such summons ... is the Fifth Amendment's privilege against self-incrimination.

IV

It is ... clear that the Fifth Amendment does not independently proscribe the compelled production of every sort of incriminating evidence but applies only when the accused is compelled to make a testimonial communication that is incriminating. . . .

A subpoena served on a taxpayer requiring him to produce ... workpapers in his possession without doubt involves substantial compulsion. But it does not compel oral testimony; nor would it ordinarily compel the taxpayer to restate, repeat, or affirm the truth of the contents of the documents sought. Therefore, the Fifth Amendment would not be violated by the fact alone that the papers on their face might incriminate the taxpayer, for the privilege protects a person only against being incriminated by his own compelled testimonial communications. . . . [A]s far as this record demonstrates, the preparation of all of the papers sought in these cases was wholly voluntary, and they cannot be said to contain compelled testimonial evidence. The taxpayer cannot avoid compliance with the subpoena merely by asserting that the item of evidence which he is required to produce contains incriminating writing. . . .

The act of producing evidence in response to a subpoena nevertheless has communicative aspects of its own, wholly aside from the contents of the papers produced. Compliance with the subpoena tacitly concedes the existence of the papers demanded and their possession or control by the taxpayer. It also would indicate the taxpayer's belief that the papers are those described in the subpoena. The elements of compulsion are clearly present, but the more difficult issues are whether the tacit averments of the taxpayer are both "testimonial" and "incriminating" for purposes of applying the Fifth Amendment. These questions perhaps do not lend themselves to categorical answers; their resolution may instead depend on the facts and circumstances of particular cases or classes thereof. In light of the records now before us, we are confident that however incriminating the contents of the accountant's workpapers might be, the act of producing them—the only thing which the taxpayer is compelled to do—would not itself involve testimonial self-incrimination.

It is doubtful that implicitly admitting the existence and possession of the papers rises to the level of testimony within the protection of the Fifth Amendment. The papers belong to the accountant, were prepared by him, and are the kind usually prepared by an accountant working on the tax returns of his client. Surely the Government is in no way relying on the "truth-telling" of the taxpayer to prove the existence of or his access to the documents. The existence and location of the papers are a foregone conclusion and the taxpayer adds little or nothing to the sum total of the Government's information by conceding that he in fact has the papers. . . .

When an accused is required to submit a handwriting exemplar he admits his ability to write and impliedly asserts that the exemplar is his writing. But in common experience, the first would be a near truism and the latter self-evident. In any event, although the exemplar may be incriminating to the accused and although he is compelled to furnish it, his Fifth Amendment privilege is not violated because nothing he has said or done is deemed to be sufficiently testimonial for purposes of the privilege. This Court has also time and again allowed subpoenas against the custodian of corporate documents or those belonging to other collective entities such as unions and partnerships and those of bankrupt businesses over claims that the documents will incriminate the custodian despite the fact that producing the documents tacitly admits their existence and their location in the hands of their possessor. The existence and possession or control of the subpoenaed documents being no more in issue here than in the above cases, the summons is equally enforceable.

Moreover, assuming that these aspects of producing the accountant's papers have some minimal testimonial significance, surely it is not illegal to seek accounting help in connection with one's tax returns or for the accountant to prepare workpapers and deliver them to the taxpayer. At this juncture, we are quite unprepared to hold that either the fact of existence of the papers or of their possession by the taxpayer poses any realistic threat of incrimination to the taxpayer.

As for the possibility that responding to the subpoena would authenticate the workpapers, production would express nothing more than the taxpayer's belief that the papers are those described in the subpoena. The taxpayer would be no more competent to authenticate the accountant's workpapers or reports by producing them than he would be to authenticate them if testifying orally. The taxpayer did not prepare the papers and could not vouch for their accuracy. The documents would not be admissible in evidence against the taxpayer without authenticating testimony. Without more, responding to the subpoena in the circumstances before us would not appear to represent a substantial threat of self-incrimination. . . .

Whether the Fifth Amendment would shield the taxpayer from producing his own tax records in his possession is a question not involved here; for the papers demanded here are not his "private papers." We do hold that compliance with a summons directing the taxpayer to produce the accountant's documents involved in these cases would involve no incriminating testimony within the protection of the Fifth Amendment.

NOTES AND QUESTIONS

1. *Fisher* established that only the person holding the privilege may assert it. We mentioned this standing-like limitation in Part I.B. of this chapter. However, an attorney may be able to withhold documents on the grounds of the attorney-client privilege, as the Court noted.

2. The holding in *Fisher* has given rise to several questions. First, after *Fisher*, does the Fifth Amendment extend a "zone of privacy" to the contents of pre-existing "private papers", as opposed to papers shared with accountants and attorneys? The Supreme Court has not yet definitively answered this question, but a concurrence by Justice O'Connor in a later case strongly indicates that private papers do not justify special treatment.[70] A federal trial court judge agreed with Justice O'Connor's concurrence in a case involving the subpoenaed diaries of Bob Packwood, former United States Senator from Oregon. A Senate committee had subpoenaed Packwood's diaries after he disclosed their existence in an effort to defend himself against accusations that he had made unwelcome sexual advances to aides and constituents. Packwood resisted the subpoena, relying on the "private papers" statement in *Fisher* and contending that the Supreme Court had "never expressly overruled the case with regard to personal papers such as diaries." The district court rejected Packwood's claim, observing that the Court had "largely repudiated" in *Fisher* the idea that the contents of pre-existing private papers were protected by the Fifth Amendment.[71] After losing in district court, Packwood filed an application in the United States Supreme Court seeking a stay of the district court's enforcement order. The Court denied certiorari.[72]

3.   A second question left by *Fisher* concerns the circumstances in which the existence, possession, and authentication of records would not be a "foregone conclusion" so that the subpoenaed party could claim a privilege from producing documents. Since *Fisher* was decided, the Court has provided substance to the "foregone conclusion" doctrine. Two important cases involved grand jury subpoenas, and in keeping with the rules of grand jury secrecy, each identified the subpoenaed party as "John Doe." In *United States v. Doe (Doe I)*,[73] a federal grand jury issued a subpoena directing the owner of several businesses to produce various business records, including lists of telephone calls made from company phones and bank account statements. The owner moved to quash the subpoena, claiming that the act of producing the records would incriminate him. Both the trial court and the Third Circuit Court of Appeals agreed that, under the circumstances, the production of documents, unlike in *Fisher*, had more than "minimal testimonial value." These documents incriminated Doe as to the fact that the documents existed, were in his possession, and were authentic. The Supreme Court affirmed. In *Doe v. United States (Doe II)*,[74] another John Doe was questioned by a grand jury about the existence and location of foreign bank account records. In response, he invoked his Fifth Amendment privilege. Attempting to complete its investigation through other avenues, the grand jury subpoenaed the banks themselves, but because of confidentiality laws they refused to release his account records without consent. The prosecutor then sought an order in federal district court

---

70.   United States v. Doe (Doe I), 465 U.S. 605, 618 (1984) (O'Connor, J., concurring).

71.   *See* Senate Select Committee on Ethics v. Packwood, 845 F.Supp. 17, 18, 22–23 (D.D.C.1994).

72.   Packwood v. Senate Select Committee on Ethics, 510 U.S. 1319 (1994).

73.   465 U.S. 605 (1984).

74.   487 U.S. 201 (1988).

compelling Doe to sign a "consent directive," which was crafted so that his signature did not constitute an acknowledgement that any of the accounts existed. The court ordered Doe to sign the form, but he refused to do so on Fifth Amendment grounds and was held in contempt. The Supreme Court upheld the lower courts' decision because executing the consent directive was not "testimonial" in the sense of communicating information:

> ... [I]n order to be testimonial, an accused's communication must itself, explicitly or implicitly, relate a factual assertion or disclose information. Only then is a person compelled to be a witness against himself. ...
>
> Given the consent directive's phraseology, [Doe's] compelled act of executing the form has no testimonial significance.... By signing the form, Doe makes no statement, explicit or implicit, regarding the existence of a foreign bank account or his control over any such account. Nor would his execution of the form admit the authenticity of any records produced by the bank. Not only does the directive express no view on the issue, but because petitioner did not prepare the document, any statement by Doe to the effect that it is authentic would not establish that the records are genuine. Authentication evidence would have to be provided by bank officials. ...
>
> In its testimonial significance, the execution of such a directive is analogous to the production of a handwriting sample or voice exemplar: it is a nontestimonial act. In neither case is the suspect's action compelled to obtain "any knowledge he might have." ...
>
> [I]f the Government obtains bank records after Doe signs the directive, the only factual statement made by anyone will be the bank's implicit declaration, by its act of production in response to the subpoena, that it believes the accounts to be petitioner's. The fact that the bank's customer has directed the disclosure of his records "would say nothing about the correctness of the bank's representations."

The authors of this text believe that the Court probably decided *Doe II* incorrectly. Consider the problem immediately below and decide whether you agree with us.

PROBLEM 9–7

Assume that Doe is eventually prosecuted and denies any connection to the bank accounts. During closing argument, the prosecutor makes the following statement in order to convince the jury that the accounts belonged to Doe: "At first, the bank would not release account information until its customer gave consent. Then, the defendant gave consent to release any records over which he had authority. Only after receiving that consent did the bank release the records. Ladies and gentlemen of the jury, isn't it reasonable to infer from this chain of events that the defendant was the account holder because he obviously had control over the records?"

Question: Does the fact that the bank refused to release the records without the defendant's consent indicate that the records relate to accounts held by Doe? If the Fifth Amendment applies to information that merely furnishes a "link in a chain of evidence," was Doe compelled to incriminate himself in violation of that right?[75]

PROBLEM 9–8

The *Brunell* case in Chapter 1 includes a grand jury subpoena to Brunell, which demands production of various documents, including "personal calendars or diaries containing notes, codes, or other indications of the income or expenditures of Arthur Graham Brunell."

Question: As Brunell's lawyer, should you advise him to resist the production of those documents? On what theory or theories? What are the chances of success on each theory?

PROBLEM 9–9

Doyle and Roberta Bayrd are sole proprietors of a used car dealership in Nashville, Tennessee. Because the dealership has never been incorporated, it does not file income tax returns. Instead, the Bayrds report the dealership's income on Schedule C of their annual individual income tax returns. In the course of a routine audit, the IRS discovered certain irregularities in the Bayrds' individual income tax returns for a four-year period. After notifying the Bayrds of its findings, the IRS referred the investigation to a grand jury. Meanwhile, the Bayrds hired an attorney, Randy Isman, to represent them in any and all matters arising out of the investigation, including litigation. The Bayrds provided Isman with documents pertinent to the investigation and Isman sent copies of the documents to Candace Frandi, an accountant whom he hired to assist him in representing the Bayrds. The documents consisted of records created by the Bayrds. While some of them were typed, others were handwritten by Doyle and Roberta.

The grand jury issued subpoenas to Isman and Frandi seeking business and financial records of the Bayrds' in their possession. Specifically, the subpoenas sought the following documents:

> [o]riginal records of Doyle Bayrd and Roberta Bayrd, and/or any business entity they have owned an interest in, which includes but is not limited to notes, letters, agreements, contracts, correspondence, schedules, workpapers, summaries, computer printouts, ledgers, journals, bank records (cancelled checks, statements, and deposits slips), loan applications, financial statements, contracts, recap sheets, car invoices, sales summaries, and other documents regarding financial transactions.

---

75. This question is based on Justice Stevens's dissent in Doe v. United States, 487 U.S. 201, 219 (1988).

Question: The Bayrds filed a motion to quash the subpoenas, arguing that compliance with them would violate their Fifth Amendment privilege against self-incrimination and their attorney-client privilege. As the judge evaluating their motion, how will you rule?

B. Outer Limits of the Act of Production Privilege

The act of production privilege applies theoretically to the production of *anything*—not just documents—if the act itself might be incriminating. It has even been asserted, as the case below demonstrates, when the compelled act is production of a person. As you read the famous *Bouknight* case, keep track of the Court's reasoning. Is the case properly viewed as a limitation on the act of production privilege, or is it a specialized application of the required records exception?

Baltimore City Dept. of Social Services v. Bouknight

493 U.S. 549 (1990).

■ O'CONNOR, J. In this action, we must decide whether a mother, the custodian of a child pursuant to a court order, may invoke the Fifth Amendment privilege against self-incrimination to resist an order of the juvenile court to produce the child. We hold that she may not.

I

Petitioner Maurice M. is an abused child. When he was three months old, he was hospitalized with a fractured left femur, and examination revealed several partially healed bone fractures and other indications of severe physical abuse. In the hospital, respondent Bouknight, Maurice's mother, was observed shaking Maurice, dropping him in his crib despite his . . . cast, and otherwise handling him in a manner inconsistent with his recovery and continued health. Hospital personnel notified the Baltimore City Department of Social Services (BCDSS) . . . of suspected child abuse.

In February 1987, BCDSS secured a court order removing Maurice from Bouknight's control and placing him in shelter care. Several months later, the shelter care order was inexplicably modified to return Maurice to Bouknight's custody temporarily. Following a hearing held shortly thereafter, the juvenile court declared Maurice to be a "child in need of assistance," thus asserting jurisdiction over Maurice and placing him under BCDSS' continuing oversight. BCDSS agreed that Bouknight could continue as custodian of the child, but only pursuant to extensive conditions set forth in a court-approved protective supervision order. The order required Bouknight to "cooperate with BCDSS," "continue in therapy," "participate in parental aid and training programs," and "refrain from physically punishing [Maurice]." The order's terms were "all subject to the further Order of the Court." Bouknight's attorney signed the order, and Bouknight in a separate form set forth her agreement to each term.

Eight months later, fearing for Maurice's safety, BCDSS returned to juvenile court. BCDSS caseworkers related that Bouknight would not cooperate with them and had in nearly every respect violated the terms of the protective order. BCDSS stated that Maurice's father had recently died in a shooting incident and that Bouknight, in light of the results of a psychological examination and her history of drug use, could not provide adequate care for the child. On April 20, 1988, the court granted BCDSS' petition to remove Maurice from Bouknight's control for placement in foster care. BCDSS officials also petitioned for judicial relief from Bouknight's failure to produce Maurice or reveal where he could be found. The petition recounted that on two recent visits by BCDSS officials to Bouknight's home, she had refused to reveal the location of the child or had indicated that the child was with an aunt whom she would not identify. The petition further asserted that inquiries of Bouknight's known relatives had revealed that none of them had recently seen Maurice and that BCDSS had prompted the police to issue a missing persons report and referred the case for investigation by the police homicide division. . . .

[T]he juvenile court, upon a hearing on the petition, cited Bouknight for violating the protective custody order and for failing to appear at the hearing. Bouknight had indicated to her attorney that she would appear with the child, but also expressed fear that if she appeared the State would "snatch the child." The court issued an order to show cause why Bouknight should not be held in civil contempt for failure to produce the child. Expressing concern that Maurice was endangered or perhaps dead, the court issued a bench warrant for Bouknight's appearance.

Maurice was not produced at subsequent hearings. At a hearing one week later, Bouknight claimed that Maurice was with a relative in Dallas. Investigation revealed that the relative had not seen Maurice. The next day, following another hearing at which Bouknight again declined to produce Maurice, the juvenile court found Bouknight in contempt for failure to produce the child as ordered. There was and has been no indication that she was unable to comply with the order. The court directed that Bouknight be imprisoned until she "purge[d] herself of contempt by either producing [Maurice] before the court or revealing to the court his exact whereabouts."

The juvenile court rejected Bouknight's subsequent claim that the contempt order violated the Fifth Amendment's guarantee against self-incrimination. . . . The Court of Appeals of Maryland vacated the juvenile court's judgment upholding the contempt order. The Court of Appeals found that the contempt order unconstitutionally compelled Bouknight to admit through the act of production "a measure of continuing control and dominion over Maurice's person" in circumstances in which "Bouknight has a reasonable apprehension that she will be prosecuted." . . . We granted certiorari and we now reverse.

II

The juvenile court concluded that Bouknight could comply with the order through the unadorned act of producing the child, and we thus address that aspect of the order. When the government demands that an item be produced, "the only thing compelled is the act of producing the [item]." The Fifth Amendment's protection may nonetheless be implicated because the act of complying with the government's demand testifies to the existence, possession, or authenticity of the things produced. But a person may not claim the Amendment's protections based upon the incrimination that may result from the contents or nature of the thing demanded. Bouknight therefore cannot claim the privilege based upon anything that examination of Maurice might reveal, nor can she assert the privilege upon the theory that compliance would assert that the child produced is in fact Maurice (a fact the State could readily establish, rendering any testimony regarding existence or authenticity insufficiently incriminating). Rather, Bouknight claims the benefit of the privilege because the act of production would amount to testimony regarding her control over, and possession of, Maurice. Although the State could readily introduce evidence of Bouknight's continuing control over the child—e.g., the custody order, testimony of relatives, and Bouknight's own statements to Maryland officials before invoking the privilege—her implicit communication of control over Maurice at the moment of production might aid the State in prosecuting Bouknight.

The possibility that a production order will compel testimonial assertions that may prove incriminating does not, in all contexts, justify invoking the privilege to resist production. Even assuming that this limited testimonial assertion is sufficiently incriminating and "sufficiently testimonial for purposes of the privilege," Bouknight may not invoke the privilege to resist the production order because she has assumed custodial duties related to production and because production is required as part of a noncriminal regulatory regime.

The Court has on several occasions recognized that the Fifth Amendment privilege may not be invoked to resist compliance with a regulatory regime constructed to effect the State's public purposes unrelated to the enforcement of its criminal laws. In *Shapiro v. United States*, 335 U.S. 1 (1948), the Court considered an application of the Emergency Price Control Act of 1942 and a regulation issued thereunder which required licensed businesses to maintain records and make them available for inspection by administrators. The Court indicated that no Fifth Amendment protection attached to production of the "required records," which the "defendant was required to keep, not for his private uses, but for the benefit of the public, and for public inspection." The Court's discussion of the constitutional implications of the scheme focused upon the relation between the Government's regulatory objectives and the Government's interest in gaining access to the records in Shapiro's possession:

> It may be assumed at the outset that there are limits which the Government cannot constitutionally exceed in requiring the keeping of records which may be inspected by an administrative agency and may be used in prosecuting statutory violations committed by the record-keeper himself. But no serious misgiving that those bounds have been overstepped would appear to be evoked when there is a sufficient

relation between the activity sought to be regulated and the public concern so that the Government can constitutionally regulate or forbid the basic activity concerned, and can constitutionally require the keeping of particular records, subject to inspection by the Administrator. . . .

The Court has since refined . . . limits to the government's authority to gain access to items or information vested with this public character. The Court has noted that "the requirements at issue in *Shapiro* were imposed in an essentially non-criminal and regulatory area of inquiry," and that *Shapiro's* reach is limited where requirements "are directed to a selective group inherently suspect of criminal activities." . . .

When a person assumes control over items that are the legitimate object of the government's noncriminal regulatory powers, the ability to invoke the privilege is reduced. "[W]here, by virtue of their character and the rules of law applicable to them, . . . books and papers are held subject to examination by the demanding authority, the custodian has no privilege to refuse production although their contents tend to criminate him. In assuming their custody he has accepted the incident obligation to permit inspection." . . .

In *Shapiro*, the Court interpreted this principle as extending well beyond the corporate context, and emphasized that Shapiro had assumed and retained control over documents in which the Government had a direct and particular regulatory interest. . . .

These principles readily apply to this case. Once Maurice was adjudicated a child in need of assistance, his care and safety became the particular object of the State's regulatory interests. Maryland first placed Maurice in shelter care, authorized placement in foster care, and then entrusted responsibility for Maurice's care to Bouknight. By accepting care of Maurice subject to the custodial order's conditions (including requirements that she cooperate with BCDSS, follow a prescribed training regime, and be subject to further court orders), Bouknight submitted to the routine operation of the regulatory system and agreed to hold Maurice in a manner consonant with the State's regulatory interests and subject to inspection by BCDSS. In assuming the obligations attending custody, Bouknight "has accepted the incident obligation to permit inspection." The State imposes and enforces that obligation as part of a broadly directed, noncriminal regulatory regime governing children cared for pursuant to custodial orders. . . .

Persons who care for children pursuant to a custody order, and who may be subject to a request for access to the child, are hardly a "selective group inherently suspect of criminal activities." The juvenile court may place a child within its jurisdiction with social service officials or "under supervision in his own home or in the custody or under the guardianship of a relative or other fit person, upon terms the court deems appropriate." Children may be placed, for example, in foster care, in homes of relatives, or in the care of state officials. Even when the court allows a parent to retain control of a child within the court's jurisdiction, that parent is not one singled out for criminal conduct, but rather has been deemed to be, without the State's assistance, simply "unable or unwilling to give proper care and attention to the child and his problems." The provision that authorized the juvenile court's efforts to gain production of Maurice reflects this broad applicability.... This provision "fairly may be said to be directed at ... parents, guardians, and custodians who accept placement of juveniles in custody."

Similarly, BCDSS' efforts to gain access to children, as well as judicial efforts to the same effect, do not focus almost exclusively on conduct which was criminal. Many orders will arise in circumstances entirely devoid of criminal conduct. Even when criminal conduct may exist, the court may properly request production and return of the child, and enforce that request through exercise of the contempt power, for reasons related entirely to the child's well-being and through measures unrelated to criminal law enforcement or investigation. This case provides an illustration: concern for the child's safety underlay the efforts to gain access to and then compel production of Maurice.

Finally, production in the vast majority of cases will embody no incriminating testimony, even if in particular cases the act of production may incriminate the custodian through an assertion of possession or the existence, or the identity, of the child. These orders to produce children cannot be characterized as efforts to gain some testimonial component of the act of production. The government demands production of the very public charge entrusted to a custodian, and makes the demand for compelling reasons unrelated to criminal law enforcement and as part of a broadly applied regulatory regime. In these circumstances, Bouknight cannot invoke the privilege to resist the order to produce Maurice.

We are not called upon to define the precise limitations that may exist upon the State's ability to use the testimonial aspects of Bouknight's act of production in subsequent criminal proceedings. But we note that imposition of such limitations is not foreclosed. The same custodial role that limited the ability to resist the production order may give rise to corresponding limitations upon the direct and indirect use of that testimony. The State's regulatory requirement in the usual case may neither compel incriminating testimony nor aid a criminal prosecution, but the Fifth Amendment protections are not thereby necessarily unavailable to the person who complies with the regulatory requirement after invoking the privilege and subsequently faces prosecution....

NOTES AND QUESTIONS

The Court in *Bouknight* indicated that the act-of-production privilege extends beyond the production of documentary evidence. This seems consistent with the *Fisher* and *Doe* line of cases, because the production of physical evidence may be as incriminating as the production of documents. As the Court noted, Jacqueline Bouknight would be incriminated by producing her child because her production would constitute an admission that the child was in her possession.

The Court's rationale for denying the mother's claimed act-of-production privilege rested on the fact that "she has assumed custodial duties related to production and because production is required as part of a noncriminal regulatory regime." Does the opinion mean that all parents, even with no prior interactions with a Social Services Department, are unable to assert the privilege against self-incrimination if ordered to produce their child? The Court had never before used this "custodian" characterization to override the privilege against self-incrimination except in cases where the claim was being made by an agent of a collective entity. In those cases, denial of protection was based on the rule that an entity, unlike a natural person, has no Fifth Amendment privilege against self-incrimination, and on the Court's determination that the act of production cannot be used against an individual who produces documents on behalf of the entity. How does the rule applied in *Bouknight* correspond with this reasoning?

Jacqueline Bouknight remained incarcerated for more than seven years after the Supreme Court's opinion. During that time, she refused to disclose Maurice's whereabouts. Finally, in October 1995, Maryland officials admitted that they could "no longer argue that keeping Bouknight in jail would help the court find Maurice."[76] The court freed Bouknight on October 31, 1995. After her release, her attorneys portrayed her "as a champion of civil disobedience, comparing her to the Rev. Martin Luther King Jr." State officials disagreed with this characterization, adding that they feared her son is dead.

PROBLEM 9–10

Congress passed the Health Security Act (the "Act"), which provides universal medical coverage for all Americans. The Act became effective on April 1 of last year. Part of the Act requires health care providers to charge their patients uniform prices for the same services and to keep records of each patient's charges. Another part of the Act requires the Federal Medical Advisory Board (the "Board") to pre-approve increases in prices. Pre-approval must be sought by filing an application with the Board explaining present prices, requested prices, and why an increase is necessary. Under the Act, it is a felony to make a false statement in the application. It is a misdemeanor to raise prices without receiving the Board's prior written approval and to charge different patients different prices for the same service. Although price records do not have to be filed with the Board, the Act permits the Board to engage in surprise inspections of records to ensure compliance.

The Act also amends the Internal Revenue Code in two ways. First, the Act requires each health care provider who raises prices without prior

---

76. Associated Press, *Judge Frees Defiant Mom Held 7 Years*, November 1, 1995.

approval of the Board to register with the Internal Revenue Service as a Price Independent Medical Health Organization ("PIMHO") and to report to the IRS the precise amount of any monies received from the higher prices. PIMHOs must pay income tax on such additional monies and are charged a higher tax rate on their entire income, including the income from Board-approved prices. Second, the Act provides that the willful failure to register and pay the additional tax constitutes a felony.

Dr. John Henry is Chair of the Otolaryngology (Ear, Nose, and Throat) Department at Thomastown University Hospital. As Chair, he is charged with ensuring that the Hospital complies with all federal regulations. While staff doctors, including Dr. Henry, treat patients under the Hospital's auspices, each staff doctor also is entitled to run a private practice on his or her own, and the doctor need not account to the Hospital for monies privately earned. Dr. Henry sometimes treats patients in his own practice. Pursuant to the Act, Dr. Henry asked the Hospital's attorney to prepare and file with the Board an application for increases in fees charged by the Hospital's Otolaryngology Unit. To assist the attorney's work, Dr. Henry turned over to the attorney several boxes of documents relevant to the application, as well as documents reflecting his own fee practices The attorney prepared the Hospital's application, which was granted on October 1, on which date the new prices took effect.

On December 10, the attorney received a subpoena to produce before a grand jury on December 17 the following:

> All records reviewed in preparing the application that you filed with the Medical Review Board for an increase in prices charged by the Thomastown University Hospital's Otolaryngology Unit, and all records of prices actually charged by all Hospital staff doctors for professional services rendered during the past three years, including records identifying precisely by name, address, and telephone number the identity of the clients charged, the services for which those clients paid, and the names of the doctors who provided the services and charged the fees.

Question: The day after he received the subpoena, the attorney retained you to advise him. What grounds, if any, might plausibly be raised in a motion to quash the subpoena? How will the prosecution respond? How should the court rule?

C. Review Problems

PROBLEM 9–11

Ruth Jones and Arthur Goldberg had been engaged to be married, but Ruth broke off the engagement. Arthur had difficulty accepting the break-up and continued to call Ruth, at times even harassing her. On March 28, Arthur called Ruth and begged her to come and see him at his parents' house, where he lived at the time. She reluctantly agreed. Later that day, Arthur's parents returned home from work to find this note on the kitchen table:

Mom, Dad, I love you and I'm so sorry for what has happened. I love you. Please forgive me. I will call you. If anyone calls for Ruth, say that we went to Newport Beach.

The Goldbergs thought little of the note until they noticed that Arthur's bedroom door was locked. When they unlocked the door, they discovered on the floor an object wrapped in a tarp and covered by a blanket. Mrs. Sanchez called the police, who found that the bundle contained Ruth's body. Her ankles, wrists and elbows were bound with telephone cord and a rope was doubled around her neck. At 6:30 p.m., Arthur knocked at his sister's door. He told her that someone had been killed.

The next day, Arthur surrendered to the police and was placed in custody. The court appointed a public defender for him, and during Arthur's first interview with the attorney, he recounted his memories of March 28th:

I was upset about Ruth and me, you know, so I probably had too much to drink, and, you know, snorted some cocaine to take the edge off, so I could talk to her. Then she came over and said she had to go somewhere so could I talk fast so she could go. Well, you know, it was her who left me, so I figured she could at least give me some of her precious time. She said she didn't owe me anything and we argued. Then the next thing I know is I'm sitting on the bedroom floor with a rope around my neck and I look up and see Ruth's eyes staring at me. I think she's dead, but I don't know why. I covered her with a blanket, and didn't know what to do. I went to my sister to get help, maybe she could help me with Ruth. And then, I don't remember anything else.

A week after his arrest, his parents cleaned out his bedroom. In a box under his bed they found the following note in Arthur's handwriting:

I don't want to hurt my girl but if she's not going to be mine, she won't be anyone else's either. Our love was meant to be 'til death do us part. Saturday could be the perfect opportunity to follow through with what may very well be necessary. I really do wish that I had a gun, it would be so much easier and less painful. Although if it needs to come to this, maybe pain should be felt?

1. strangle-stab

2. enter into 4–ply gray plastic bags

3. seal bags thoroughly

4. empty trunk and line w/blanket to place 4–ply into a cover with blanket. Check all oil, fluids, tires.

5. place two (5 gall.) gas containers in both corners of trunk

6. use credit card to fill gas tank and containers, purchase tire flat fix cans

7. Roy (cocaine)

8.   need two cocaine bullets to be able to snort and drive calmly and safely to Seattle

Arthur's parents delivered the two notes to a friend, who gave them to the public defender. The defender placed the papers in a sealed envelope and, without informing the prosecution, delivered them to the court. While preparing for trial, a prosecutor interviewed Arthur's brother-in-law, who revealed the existence of the notes. The prosecution immediately moved the trial court to unseal the papers and make them available to the state. The trial court did so, and the papers were admitted at Arthur's trial. Arthur was convicted of first degree murder and sentenced to life in prison. On appeal, he contends that the trial court erred in turning the papers over to the prosecution.

Question: Should the appellate court overturn Arthur's conviction?

Note on Defense Ethics: Our adversarial system delegates all evidence-gathering responsibilities to the parties. In order to encourage parties to investigate their positions thoroughly, they are relieved in most situations of any obligation to share the fruits of their investigation with the opposing side. While this rule has been modified in civil cases by measures that require reciprocal discovery,[77] it remains powerful in the criminal arena.[78] For example, a defense lawyer who uncovers a witness exonerating her client is not required to tell the prosecution. Generally, she may conceal that information until trial. Yet several jurisdictions require defense lawyers who come into possession of physical evidence pertaining to the crime to turn that evidence over to the prosecution, under an "officer of the court" rationale. While most of these cases involve discovery of fruits or instrumentalities of crime, some require defense lawyers to reveal other evidence as well.[79] There is a line, however, that the cases do not cross: defense lawyers cannot be required to reveal the source of the evidence, if that source is the client. To permit otherwise would be to sanction violations of the attorney-client privilege and put defense lawyers in an untenable ethical conflict.[80]

PROBLEM 9–12

Cynthia Dano was a high-ranking employee of Dynatex Corporation, which came under investigation for price-fixing. In an effort to determine

---

77. *See, e.g.*, Federal Rules of Civil Procedure 26 to 37 (governing discovery). Recent amendments to these rules require parties to disclose core information to their opponents, even if the opponent has not asked for the information. *See* F.R.Civ.P. 26(2).

78. The Federal Rules of Criminal Procedure limit discovery to narrowly-defined categories of information. *See* F.R.Cr.P. 16 and 26.2. Neither the prosecution nor the defense is generally permitted to serve interrogatories or take depositions. *See* F.R.Cr.P. 15.

79. Of course, defense lawyers may not destroy evidence, even if the jurisdiction does not require them to produce it voluntarily. For a discussion about lawyers and the destruction of evidence, *see* Note, *Legal Ethics and the Destruction of Evidence*, 88 Yale L.J. 1665 (1979).

80. *See* Morrell v. State, 575 P.2d 1200 (Alaska 1978); People v. Superior Court (Fairbank), 237 Cal.Rptr. 158 (1987).

whether Dynatex executives met with executives of competing firms (a fact that would be consistent with price-fixing), the grand jury subpoenaed a large variety of Dynatex records, including "diaries, appointment calendars, or schedules, maintained by corporate executives."

Dano kept an appointment calendar (which bore the Dynatex logo) to schedule business meetings, but she also used the calendar for personal matters. For example, she used the calendar to schedule social engagements, keep track of family birthdays, and record intimate thoughts and physical data. Dano made most of the calendar entries herself, although her secretary would write in it occasionally. Her secretary knew where to find the calendar in Dano's office, and the secretary consulted it frequently in order to establish meeting times for Dano and other Dynatex executives.

Dynatex refused to produce Dano's calendar, maintaining that it was a personal record of which the corporation lacked both possession and the authority to produce. In response, the grand jury moved to compel and also subpoenaed Dano for the document, who refused to produce it on the ground that it might incriminate her. The district court held an evidentiary hearing concerning the nature of the calendar and found it to be a corporate record. Dynatex appealed from the order compelling it to produce the calendar.

Question: Should Dynatex prevail on appeal? If so, should Dano be required to produce the calendar?

PROBLEM 9–13

Following a jury trial in a federal court in the District of Columbia, George Carter was convicted of armed robbery. The chief witness against him was one Gregory Edmonds, who testified that Carter had robbed him at gunpoint. Carter called his younger brother, Bruce, as his only witness. Carter proffered that Bruce would testify that he (Bruce) had spoken with Edmonds during a drug transaction that occurred after the robbery. During this transaction, according to the proffer, Edmonds had professed to be ignorant about the identity of the robber, had confessed to having been on drugs at the time of the robbery, and had sold drugs to Bruce. The proffer was necessary because Bruce indicated that he would assert his privilege against self-incrimination to the proposed line of questioning. Further, the prosecutor advised the court that if Bruce testified as the proffer indicated, he would be cross-examined about his own drug use, on the theory that his drug use was relevant to his ability to perceive and relate accurately his encounter with Edmonds.

Carter opposed Bruce's assertion of the privilege, arguing that the risk of prosecution as a result of his testimony was "fanciful." The judge contacted the Felony Division of the United States Attorney's Office and was told that prosecution of a simple drug possession charge solely on the basis of historical evidence would be unusual. Nevertheless, the judge ruled that there was a "legal possibility, although not a practical likelihood" that Bruce could be prosecuted if he revealed past drug use, and she sustained

Bruce's assertion of the privilege. Carter appealed his conviction on the ground, among others, that the trial judge should have compelled Bruce to testify.

Question: Should Carter's conviction be overturned?

III. Immunity

A. Types of Immunity

The privilege against self-incrimination protects individuals from disclosures that might subject them to criminal liability, so if the possibility of criminal liability is permanently removed, the privilege no longer applies. The possibility of criminal liability can be removed by prosecutors, who are authorized by the separation of powers doctrine to decide who to prosecute and who *not* to prosecute. The decision not to prosecute can be formalized in a grant of immunity from prosecution, because the United States Congress and state legislatures have enacted statutes that authorize prosecutors to grant immunity as a means of overriding assertions of the Fifth Amendment. Federal immunity statutes are found at 18 U.S.C. sections 6001–6005. Those statutes authorize immunity in judicial, administrative, and congressional proceedings. A grant of federal statutory immunity prohibits the use and derivative use of the testimony for which immunity was granted in state courts as well as federal.[81]

Most courts hold that they cannot, on their own initiative, immunize a witness. Rather, the immunization must follow a motion from the prosecution. Once immunized, a person's Fifth Amendment claim evaporates because there is no longer the possibility of incrimination, and he or she can lawfully be compelled to provide the requested information.

Immunity statutes come in two forms. The first creates what is known as "use and derivative use immunity," which prohibits the government from using, in a criminal case, a person's compelled testimony and any other compelled information, including information directly or indirectly derived from it.[82] This is the minimum scope of immunity required by the Fifth Amendment before an individual can be compelled to testify. The second kind of statute creates "transactional immunity," which prohibits the sovereign granting the immunity from prosecuting the person for offenses relating to the compelled testimony.[83] The difference between the two kinds of immunity is important: use and derivative use immunity does not protect the person from prosecution altogether, because the govern-

---

81. For those interested in the fine points of these distinctions and the interrelationship among statutory grants of immunity from one sovereign as affecting the immunity of another sovereign, *see* Adam H. Kurland, Successive Criminal Prosecutions: The Dual Sovereignty Exception to Double Jeopardy in State and Federal Courts (2001).

82. There is an exception, however, permitting prosecutions for perjury or false statement.

83. *See Kurland, Ol' Man River, supra* note 1.

ment may prosecute if it acquires evidence against the person from independent sources. Because of the greater protection afforded by transactional immunity, prosecutors rarely grant it.

The sole permissible use of immunized testimony against the immunized person is in a prosecution for perjury or false statement. One justification frequently given for this exception is that the Fifth Amendment does not give a person license to lie under oath. Perhaps a more thorough and accurate justification stems from the basic principle that the test for determining whether a person can properly claim the privilege against self-incrimination depends on "whether the claimant is confronted by substantial and real, and not merely trifling or imaginary, hazards of incrimination."[84] It can be argued that because an immunized person has control over whether to lie, he or she also has control over creating perjury liability. Therefore, an immunized person who tells the truth faces no more than a "trifling or imaginary" hazard of incrimination based upon perjury. On the other hand, impeachment use of immunized testimony does present a "substantial and real" hazard of incrimination, because the immunized person has little control over what questions the prosecutor will ask, so testimony resulting from a grant of immunity may not be used to impeach a defendant at trial.[85]

Testifying under a grant of immunity involves two potential dangers. First, the scope of immunity is limited to the subject matter spelled out in the immunity order. In the Brunell case, for example, if Terry Lynn Marvoal is immunized concerning testimony relating to "an investigation into tax fraud in the health food distribution business," she may be prosecuted on the basis of her testimony concerning an unrelated bankruptcy fraud. Thus, a defense attorney must closely monitor the immunized testimony to ensure that it remains within the scope of the immunity order.

Second, immunized testimony may potentially be used indirectly. For example, assume the government prosecutes Marvoal for tax fraud despite the grant of use and derivative use immunity. In order to vindicate her constitutional rights, she must determine whether the prosecution benefited from her testimony by obtaining, for example, information concerning the identity of witnesses or other sources of evidence. Monitoring such a post-immunity prosecution is so difficult that defendants have challenged use and derivative use immunity on the ground that it provides constitutionally inadequate protection. In *Kastigar v. United States*,[86] the Court attempted to resolve this problem by requiring prosecutors in such cases to prove that their evidence is untainted: "[O]nce a defendant demonstrates

---

84. United States v. Apfelbaum, 445 U.S. 115, 128 (1980). Once a person testifies under a grant of immunity, however, she cannot be required to repeat that testimony unless she is re-immunized. The reason is that if the details in the testimony differ, the person would face a "substantial and real" risk of a perjury prosecution. Pillsbury Co. v. Conboy, 459 U.S. 248 (1983).

85. New Jersey v. Portash, 440 U.S. 450, 459 (1979).

86. 406 U.S. 441 (1972).

that he has testified under a ... grant of immunity, to matters related to the [subsequent] prosecution, the [prosecuting] authorities have the burden of showing that their evidence is not tainted by establishing that they had an independent, legitimate source for the disputed evidence." This "imposes on the prosecution the affirmative duty to prove that the evidence it proposes to use is derived from a legitimate source wholly independent of the compelled testimony." According to the Court, this affords the same protection offered by the Fifth Amendment in that it assures that "compelled testimony can in no way lead to the infliction of criminal penalties."[87]

It can be difficult for prosecutors to prove that their evidence is untainted by immunized testimony. In the famous Iran–Contra investigation, for example, Oliver North testified before Congress pursuant to a grant of Congressional immunity. He later was successfully prosecuted, but his convictions were overturned on appeal even though prosecutors had taken extraordinary steps to seal off their criminal investigation from his Congressional testimony. The appellate court explained its decision by pointing out, among other things, that the testimony of witnesses at North's trial might have been subtly affected by North's earlier Congressional testimony, which had received extensive television exposure.[88]

PROBLEM 9–14

Recall that Problem 9–13 above involved a robbery defendant, Carter, who wished to procure the exculpatory testimony of his brother, Bruce. Suppose that after Bruce asserted his privilege against self-incrimination, Carter moved the trial court for an order immunizing Bruce, on the ground that Carter otherwise would be completely unable to put on his defense.

Question: Can the trial court order Bruce's immunity? What about issuing an order requiring the prosecution to immunize him? If the trial court refuses to do so, does not Carter effectively lose his Fifth, Sixth, and Fourteenth Amendment rights to a fair trial?

B. Immunity for an Act of Production

In *United States v. Hubbell*, a case growing out of Independent Counsel Kenneth Starr's investigation of President Clinton, the Supreme Court reaffirmed that individuals enjoy no direct privilege in pre-existing docu-

---

87. Kastigar imposed upon the prosecution a "heavy burden" of demonstrating the independent sources of its evidence. Many lower courts have interpreted this "heavy burden" language to mean only that the prosecution demonstrate the independence of its sources by a preponderance of the evidence. *See, e.g.*, United States v. Hampton, 775 F.2d 1479, 1485 (11th Cir.1985). In practice, the independent source rule means that it is very difficult for the prosecution to obtain an indictment from the same grand jury that heard the person's immunized testimony. *See, e.g.*, United States v. Zielezinski, 740 F.2d 727, 733 (9th Cir.1984); United States v. Hinton, 543 F.2d 1002, 1010 (2d Cir.), cert. denied, 429 U.S. 980 (1976).

88. *See* United States v. North, 920 F.2d 940, 941–42 (D.C.Cir.1990).

ments.[89] At the same time, the Court clarified the "foregone conclusion" doctrine and articulated broad protections under the act of production privilege for documents whose existence or whereabouts "the government is unable to describe with reasonable particularity."[90] The following excerpt from Justice Stevens' opinion is lengthy, but it will help you review the testimonial aspect of the privilege against self-incrimination. It will also help you understand the act of production privilege and how immunity can be granted to overcome that privilege.

United States v. Hubbell

530 U.S. 27 (2000).

■ STEVENS, J. This proceeding arises out of the second prosecution of respondent, Webster Hubbell, commenced by the Independent Counsel appointed in August 1994 to investigate possible violations of federal law relating to the Whitewater Development Corporation. The first prosecution was terminated pursuant to a plea bargain. In December 1994, respondent pleaded guilty to charges of mail fraud and tax evasion arising out of his billing practices as a member of an Arkansas law firm from 1989 to 1992, and was sentenced to 21 months in prison. In the plea agreement, respondent promised to provide the Independent Counsel with "full, complete, accurate, and truthful information" about matters relating to the Whitewater investigation.

The second prosecution resulted from the Independent Counsel's attempt to determine whether respondent had violated that promise. In October 1996, while respondent was incarcerated, the Independent Counsel served him with a subpoena duces tecum calling for the production of 11 categories of documents before a grand jury sitting in Little Rock, Arkansas.[91]

On November 19, he appeared before the grand jury and invoked his Fifth Amendment privilege against self-incrimination. In response to questioning by the prosecutor, respondent initially refused "to state whether there are documents within my possession, custody, or control responsive

---

89. United States v. Hubbell, 530 U.S. 27 (2000).

90. *Id.* at 30.

91. Authors' note: The categories of requested documents were broad. For example, among other things the subpoena asked for these two groups of documents: "[a]ny and all documents reflecting, referring, or relating to any direct or indirect sources of money or other things of value receive by or provided to Webster Hubbell, his wife, or children from January 1, 1993 to the present, including but not limited to billing memoranda, draft statements, bills, final statements, and/or bills for work performed or time billed from January 1, 1993 to the present," and "[a]ny and all documents reflecting, referring, or relating to Webster Hubbell's schedule of activities, including but not limited to any and all calendars, day-timers, time books, appointment books, diaries, records of reverse telephone toll calls, credit card calls, telephone message slips, logs, other telephone records, minutes, databases, electronic mail messages, travel records, itineraries, tickets for transportation of any kind, payments, bills, expense backup documentation, schedules, and/or any other document or database that would disclose Webster Hubbell's activities from January 1, 1993 to the present."

to the Subpoena." Thereafter, the prosecutor produced an order ... directing him to respond to the subpoena and granting him immunity "to the extent allowed by law." Respondent then produced 13,120 pages of documents and records and responded to a series of questions that established that those were all of the documents in his custody or control that were responsive to the commands in the subpoena, with the exception of a few documents he claimed were shielded by the attorney-client and attorney work-product privileges.

The contents of the documents produced by respondent provided the Independent Counsel with the information that led to this second prosecution. On April 30, 1998, a grand jury in the District of Columbia returned a 10–count indictment charging respondent with various tax-related crimes and mail and wire fraud. The District Court dismissed the indictment relying, in part, on the ground that the Independent Counsel's use of the subpoenaed documents violated [the grant of immunity] because all of the evidence he would offer against respondent at trial derived either directly or indirectly from the testimonial aspects of respondent's immunized act of producing those documents. Noting that the Independent Counsel had admitted that he was not investigating tax-related issues when he issued the subpoena, and that he had "learned about the unreported income and other crimes from studying the records' contents," the District Court characterized the subpoena as "the quintessential fishing expedition."

The Court of Appeals vacated the judgment and remanded for further proceedings. The majority concluded that the District Court had incorrectly relied on the fact that the Independent Counsel did not have prior knowledge of the contents of the subpoenaed documents. The question the District Court should have addressed was the extent of the Government's independent knowledge of the documents' existence and authenticity, and of respondent's possession or control of them. It explained: "On remand, the district court should hold a hearing in which it seeks to establish the extent and detail of the [G]overnment's knowledge of Hubbell's financial affairs (or of the paperwork documenting it) on the day the subpoena issued. It is only then that the court will be in a position to assess the testimonial value of Hubbell's response to the subpoena. Should the Independent Counsel prove capable of demonstrating with reasonable particularity a prior awareness that the exhaustive litany of documents sought in the subpoena existed and were in Hubbell's possession, then the wide distance evidently traveled from the subpoena to the substantive allegations contained in the indictment would be based upon legitimate intermediate steps. To the extent that the information conveyed through Hubbell's compelled act of production provides the necessary linkage, however, the indictment deriving therefrom is tainted."

On remand, the Independent Counsel acknowledged that he could not satisfy the "reasonable particularity" standard prescribed by the Court of Appeals and entered into a conditional plea agreement with respondent. ... [W]e granted the Independent Counsel's petition for a writ of certiorari in order to determine the precise scope of a grant of immunity with respect to the production of documents in response to a subpoena. We now affirm.

It is useful to preface our analysis of the constitutional issue with a restatement of certain propositions that are not in dispute. The term "privilege against self-incrimination" is not an entirely accurate description of a person's constitutional protection against being "compelled in any criminal case to be a witness against himself."

The word "witness" in the constitutional text limits the relevant category of compelled incriminating communications to those that are "testimonial" in character. As Justice Holmes observed, there is a significant difference between the use of compulsion to extort communications from a defendant and compelling a person to engage in conduct that may be incriminating. Thus, even though the act may provide incriminating evidence, a criminal suspect may be compelled to put on a shirt, to provide a blood sample or handwriting exemplar, or to make a recording of his voice. The act of exhibiting such physical characteristics is not the same as a sworn communication by a witness that relates either express or implied assertions of fact or belief. Similarly, the fact that incriminating evidence may be the byproduct of obedience to a regulatory requirement, such as filing an income tax return, maintaining required records, or reporting an accident, does not clothe such required conduct with the testimonial privilege.

More relevant to this case is the settled proposition that a person may be required to produce specific documents even though they contain incriminating assertions of fact or belief because the creation of those documents was not "compelled" within the meaning of the privilege. Our decision in Fisher v. United States dealt with summonses issued by the Internal Revenue Service (IRS) seeking working papers used in the preparation of tax returns. Because the papers had been voluntarily prepared prior to the issuance of the summonses, they could not be "said to contain compelled testimonial evidence, either of the taxpayers or of anyone else." Accordingly, the taxpayer could not "avoid compliance with the subpoena merely by asserting that the item of evidence which he is required to produce contains incriminating writing, whether his own or that of someone else." It is clear, therefore, that respondent Hubbell could not avoid compliance with the subpoena served on him merely because the demanded documents contained incriminating evidence, whether written by others or voluntarily prepared by himself.

On the other hand, we have also made it clear that the act of producing documents in response to a subpoena may have a compelled testimonial aspect. We have held that "the act of production" itself may implicitly communicate "statements of fact." By "producing documents in compliance with a subpoena, the witness would admit that the papers existed, were in his possession or control, and were authentic." Moreover, as was true in this case, when the custodian of documents responds to a subpoena, he may be compelled to take the witness stand and answer questions designed to determine whether he has produced everything demanded by the subpoena. The answers to those questions, as well as the act of production itself, may certainly communicate information about the existence, custody, and authenticity of the documents. Whether the constitutional privilege protects the answers to such questions, or protects the act of production itself, is a question that is distinct from the question whether the unprotected contents of the documents themselves are incriminating.

Finally, the phrase "in any criminal case" in the text of the Fifth Amendment might have been read to limit its coverage to compelled testimony that is used against the defendant in the trial itself. It has, however, long been settled that its protection encompasses compelled statements that lead to the discovery of incriminating evidence even though the statements themselves are not incriminating and are not introduced into evidence. Thus, a half-century ago we held that a trial judge had erroneously rejected a defendant's claim of privilege on the ground that his answer to the pending question would not itself constitute evidence of the charged offense. As we explained: "The privilege afforded not only extends to answers that would in themselves support a conviction under a federal criminal statute but likewise embraces those which would furnish a link in the chain of evidence needed to prosecute the claimant for a federal crime." Compelled testimony that communicates information that may "lead to incriminating evidence" is privileged even if the information itself is not inculpatory. It is the Fifth Amendment's protection against the prosecutor's use of incriminating information derived directly or indirectly from the compelled testimony of the respondent that is of primary relevance in this case. . . .

The "compelled testimony" that is relevant in this case is not to be found in the contents of the documents produced in response to the subpoena. It is, rather, the testimony inherent in the act of producing those documents. The disagreement between the parties focuses entirely on the significance of that testimonial aspect.

The Government correctly emphasizes that the testimonial aspect of a response to a subpoena duces tecum does nothing more than establish the existence, authenticity, and custody of items that are produced. We assume that the Government is also entirely correct in its submission that it would not have to advert to respondent's act of production in order to prove the existence, authenticity, or custody of any documents that it might offer in evidence at a criminal trial; indeed, the Government disclaims any need to introduce any of the documents produced by respondent into evidence in order to prove the charges against him. It follows, according to the Government, that it has no intention of making improper "use" of respondent's compelled testimony.

The question, however, is not whether the response to the subpoena may be introduced into evidence at his criminal trial. That would surely be a prohibited "use" of the immunized act of production. But the fact that the Government intends no such use of the act of production leaves open the separate question whether it has already made "derivative use" of the testimonial aspect of that act in obtaining the indictment against respondent and in preparing its case for trial. It clearly has.

It is apparent from the text of the subpoena itself that the prosecutor needed respondent's assistance both to identify potential sources of information and to produce those sources. Given the breadth of the description of the 11 categories of documents called for by the subpoena, the collection and production of the materials demanded was tantamount to answering a series of interrogatories asking a witness to disclose the existence and location of particular documents fitting certain broad descriptions. The assembly of literally hundreds of pages of material in response to a request for "any and all documents reflecting, referring, or relating to any direct or indirect sources of money or other things of value received by or provided to" an individual or members of his family during a 3–year period, is the functional equivalent of the preparation of an answer to either a detailed written interrogatory or a series of oral questions at a discovery deposition. Entirely apart from the contents of the 13,120 pages of materials that respondent produced in this case, it is undeniable that providing a catalog of existing documents fitting within any of the 11 broadly worded subpoena categories could provide a prosecutor with a "lead to incriminating evidence," or "a link in the chain of evidence needed to prosecute."

Indeed, the record makes it clear that that is what happened in this case. The documents were produced before a grand jury sitting in the Eastern District of Arkansas in aid of the Independent Counsel's attempt to determine whether respondent had violated a commitment in his first plea agreement. The use of those sources of information eventually led to the return of an indictment by a grand jury sitting in the District of Columbia for offenses that apparently are unrelated to that plea agreement. What the District Court characterized as a "fishing expedition" did produce a fish, but not the one that the Independent Counsel expected to hook. It is abundantly clear that the testimonial aspect of respondent's act of producing subpoenaed documents was the first step in a chain of evidence that led to this prosecution. The documents did not magically appear in the prosecutor's office like "manna from heaven." They arrived there only after respondent asserted his constitutional privilege, received a grant of immunity, and—under the compulsion of the District Court's order—took the mental and physical steps necessary to provide the prosecutor with an accurate inventory of the many sources of potentially incriminating evidence sought by the subpoena. It was only through respondent's truthful reply to the subpoena that the Government received the incriminating documents of which it made "substantial use . . . in the investigation that led to the indictment."

For these reasons, we cannot accept the Government's submission that respondent's immunity did not preclude its derivative use of the produced documents because its "possession of the documents [was] the fruit only of a simple physical act—the act of producing the documents." It was unquestionably necessary for respondent to make extensive use of "the contents of his own mind" in identifying the hundreds of documents responsive to the requests in the subpoena. The assembly of those documents was like telling an inquisitor the combination to a wall safe, not like being forced to surrender the key to a strongbox. The Government's anemic view of respondent's act of production as a mere physical act that is principally non-testimonial in character and can be entirely divorced from its "implicit" testimonial aspect so as to constitute a "legitimate, wholly independent source" ... for the documents produced simply fails to account for these realities.

In sum, we have no doubt that the constitutional privilege against self-incrimination protects the target of a grand jury investigation from being compelled to answer questions designed to elicit information about the existence of sources of potentially incriminating evidence. That constitutional privilege has the same application to the testimonial aspect of a response to a subpoena seeking discovery of those sources. Before the District Court, the Government arguably conceded that respondent's act of production in this case had a testimonial aspect that entitled him to respond to the subpoena by asserting his privilege against self-incrimination. On appeal and again before this Court, however, the Government has argued that the communicative aspect of respondent's act of producing ordinary business records is insufficiently "testimonial" to support a claim of privilege because the existence and possession of such records by any businessman is a "foregone conclusion" under our decision in *Fisher v. United States*. This argument both misreads *Fisher* and ignores our subsequent decision in [*Doe I*].

As noted [above], *Fisher* involved summonses seeking production of working papers prepared by the taxpayers' accountants that the IRS knew were in the possession of the taxpayers' attorneys. In rejecting the taxpayers' claim that these documents were protected by the Fifth Amendment privilege, we stated: "It is doubtful that implicitly admitting the existence and possession of the papers rises to the level of testimony within the protection of the Fifth Amendment. The papers belong to the accountant, were prepared by him, and are the kind usually prepared by an accountant working on the tax returns of his client. Surely the Government is in no way relying on the 'truthtelling' of the taxpayer to prove the existence of or his access to the documents.... The existence and location of the papers are a foregone conclusion and the taxpayer adds little or nothing to the sum total of the Government's information by conceding that he in fact has the papers."

Whatever the scope of this "foregone conclusion" rationale, the facts of this case plainly fall outside of it. While in *Fisher* the Government already knew that the documents were in the attorneys' possession and could independently confirm their existence and authenticity through the accountants who created them, here the Government has not shown that it had any prior knowledge of either the existence or the whereabouts of the 13,120 pages of documents ultimately produced by respondent. The Government cannot cure this deficiency through the overbroad argument that a businessman such as respondent will always possess general business and tax records that fall within the broad categories described in this subpoena. The *Doe* subpoenas also sought several broad categories of general business records, yet we upheld the District Court's finding that the act of producing those records would involve testimonial self-incrimination.

Given our conclusion that respondent's act of production had a testimonial aspect, at least with respect to the existence and location of the documents sought by the Government's subpoena, . . . the indictment against respondent must be dismissed.

————

PROBLEM 9–15

In what ways, if any, does *Hubbell* clarify or modify the rules articulated in *Fisher*? What is the significance of requesting "general business documents" rather than making a more specific request? What is the significance of the government's prior knowledge concerning the existence, location, or possession of the documents? Does the legal test vary based upon whether a subpoena reveals the suspect's possession of documents rather than their existence and location? How much help will use and derivative use immunity be to prosecutors wishing to charge those given such immunity with crimes? What remains of the "foregone conclusion" doctrine?

PROBLEM 9–16

Use your answers to the questions posed in Problem 9–15 to respond to the following hypotheticals. These hypotheticals are taken from an article by Professor Robert Mosteller[92] and were, in turn, suggested by the justices' questions during the *Hubbell* oral argument:

1A.   If the government has no idea whether the target of a subpoena to produce a gun has ever owned or possessed gun, can it serve the target with a subpoena requiring production of all guns in his or her possession, provide use immunity, and then use the gun or guns obtained in any way at trial?

1B.   Assume everyone knows that the target has a number of guns in his house. Without granting immunity, can the prosecutor, who is interested in a particular gun used in a specific crime, demand through a subpoena that the target produce all guns that are in his house because the target's possession of some guns is a well known fact and therefore arguably a "foregone conclusion"?

—————

92.   Robert P. Mosteller, *Cowboy Prosecutors and Subpoenas for Incriminating Evidence: The Consequences and Correction of Excess*, 58 WASH. & LEE L. REV. 487 (2002).

1C.   Instead of either of the above descriptions, the subpoena requires delivery of a precisely described .38 caliber Smith & Wesson revolver with ivory handles and a "K" carved into one of those handles.

2.   In a murder case, the prosecution has recovered the bullet that caused death, and it also knows that the defendant bought a gun of the same caliber because he purchased it in a state where all handguns are registered upon purchase. A subpoena demanding production of the gun is served on the defendant. Once the prosecution has control of the gun, it will perform forensic tests under the assumption that a bullet from that gun can be matched with the relatively intact and unmarred slug taken from the victim's body.

3.   The suspected murderer showed a distinctive and easily describable gun [a .38 caliber with the letter "K" carved on one of its ivory handles] to a witness and then fled to a cabin in some nearby woods where he was surrounded and captured. The prosecution thus knows that the gun still exists and that it must be somewhere in the cabin or in the adjacent woods, but the prosecution has been unable to find it. Because the gun's existence is a "foregone conclusion" as is possession during the chase, can the target be required by subpoena to produce the gun without a grant of immunity?

4.   A murder suspect is granted immunity and compelled to incriminate himself verbally. Under compulsion, he is asked to reveal the whereabouts of the murder weapon. The prosecution concedes that it would not have discovered the weapon where the suspect buried it. As a result of his information, police recover the knife, and scientific tests reveal the defendant's fingerprints and the victim's blood on the knife.

5.   A murder victim's body is found in the basement of a large apartment building, and an autopsy establishes stabbing as the cause of death. The prosecution serves a subpoena on every resident of the building requiring them to produce all knives and other forms of cutlery that are now, or in the preceding month have been, in their possession or control. An objection is made on Fifth Amendment grounds, and use immunity is granted. The residents of the building produce a quantity of knives. Upon testing, the victim's blood and a fingerprint are discovered on one knife.

6.   A murder suspect is known by his spouse to keep a diary in a specifically described green notebook with unique writing on the front. The suspect possessed the diary in his home within an hour (or a day or a week) of the time he was served with a subpoena describing the diary in precise detail and demanding its production. Does the production of the diary constitute testimonial communication?

C.   IMMUNITY NEGOTIATION EXERCISE

Read the article below about negotiating immunity in order to prepare for the immunity negotiation exercise that follows it.

Let's Make a Deal: Negotiating and Defending Immunity for "Targets and Subjects"

Peter H. White[93]

Successfully negotiating immunity for your client can feel like a terrific victory when the indictments are unsealed, and your client's name is not listed in the caption of the case. But just because your client has testified with the benefit of immunity does not mean that he or she is entirely out of danger. The threat of prosecution can still loom large even for the immunized witness.

Not long ago, I received a call from a lawyer (I will call him "Tom"), who was representing a publicly traded corporation. Several mid-level executives had been subpoenaed to testify before a federal grand jury. Tom's client then discovered that it had been the subject of a yearlong, nationwide, undercover operation. So far as he knew, only line personnel were directly implicated. The subpoenaed executives were not aware of any criminal violations. He asked me to represent one of the executives. I agreed to meet with her, and eventually I took on her representation.

The first issue to deal with was the imminent grand jury appearance. A phone call to the Assistant United States Attorney assigned to the case bought some time to consider our options. Once I explained that I was new to the case, did not yet know enough to advise my client, and wanted to cooperate in his investigation as much as possible, the prosecutor agreed to put the appearance off for a couple of weeks. This conversation also gave me an opportunity to begin to determine whether my new client faced potential criminal liability. After obtaining some very general information about the focus of the grand jury's inquiry—this is generally all one gets at the beginning—I asked the prosecutor what my client's status was in connection with this investigation. He responded that she (I will call her "Mary") was a "subject" of the grand jury probe. This was not comforting news. But my discomfort, and Mary's, was just beginning.

The Department of Justice (DOJ) has developed three categories to describe the status of a grand jury witness: witness, target, and subject.

Witnesses, Targets, and Subjects

A "witness" is one who has information relevant to the inquiry. *See* UNITED STATES DEPARTMENT OF JUSTICE CRIMINAL RESOURCE MANUAL § 9–11.151. This designation is applied to one who the prosecutor does not believe faces criminal liability. Unfortunately, the "witness" designation does not confer any substantive rights, nor is it necessarily permanent. And while it signals that the government is not currently considering indicting the witness, it also means the prosecutor does not believe that the witness has a Fifth Amendment privilege to refuse to testify. And any incriminating state-

---

93. Peter H. White, *Let's Make a Deal: Negotiating and Defending Immunity for "Targets and Subjects,"* 29 LITIGATION 44 (2002).

ments a witness makes can be used against the witness if the government later decides to indict.

A "target" is at the other end of the spectrum. A target "is a person [natural or corporate] as to whom the prosecutor or the grand jury has substantial evidence linking him or her to the commission of a crime and who, in the judgment of the prosecutor, is a putative defendant." The manual goes on to explain that an officer or employee is not automatically considered a "target" even if that individual's conduct contributed to the commission of the crime by the corporation. Conversely, not all organizations become targets when they employ, or employed, an individual who is a target.

A "subject" occupies that vast, vague space between witness and target and is defined by the manual as "a person whose conduct is within the scope of the grand jury investigation." Frequently, subjects become targets, and may eventually become defendants. And even for those who remain subjects, their involvement in the case may not end with their grand jury testimony. Depending on that testimony and the facts developed in the investigation, subjects can also become uncharged government witnesses at trial. Subjects of grand jury investigations can be the most challenging clients, as their representation often involves the most difficult strategic choices.

While easy to define, these categories are often difficult to apply. For example, is the teller who complies with the bank robber's demand for money a witness, a subject, or a target? The answer, unsatisfactory as it may seem, is, "It depends." Only a careful assessment of the facts can yield an answer.

The defense lawyer's advice to his client varies depending on the category into which the client falls. Suppose your client is the target of the investigation and is subpoenaed to the grand jury. The standard advice is to assert a Fifth Amendment right to refuse to testify. Notwithstanding the protective role the grand jury was initially intended to serve in our system, it has evolved into an investigative tool for the prosecution, a virtual extension of the U.S. Attorney's office. If a prosecutor is determined to secure an indictment in a colorable case, the grand jury will almost always comply.

Remember, the prosecutor is the only one who can address the grand jury; the defense attorney cannot. Thus, grand jury witnesses walk into the grand jury chambers alone. The only people in the room are the grand jurors, a court reporter, and the prosecutors. Unless you are convinced a target can talk his way out of an indictment in the face of unchecked cross-examination—while keeping in mind the obligation to avoid perjury and obstruction of justice—and do all of this without an attorney present, the target should assert his or her constitutional right to refuse to testify. There is little to gain and much to lose by voluntarily testifying.

Almost by definition, someone who is simply a witness was not involved in criminal activity. A pure witness, therefore, cannot refuse to testify before the grand jury barring invocation of some other privilege, and then only on a question-by-question basis. Still, even with a "witness," you need to be certain that the client will not face any liability by testifying. Again, bear in mind that the prosecutor's characterization of the client as a witness is not binding, confers no substantive rights, and is subject to change. While the lawyer has to be wary, those characterized as witnesses generally testify without incident.

Typically, the lawyer's advice to a subject is to assert the right not to testify without immunity. The reason is simple: The witness's status is too uncertain, and subjects easily and all too quickly can become targets as the investigation evolves. The key for the lawyer in this situation is determining whether the witness has criminal exposure. Typically, to do this, you first need to figure out if your client is telling the truth. Corroborating the story requires investigation. But conducting your own investigation can be difficult. Often, the only people who know whether your client was directly involved are the targets of the investigation. They are unlikely to speak with you. Sometimes, the prosecutor is willing to steer you in the direction you need, but not often.

The Joint Defense Agreement

Another possible source of information, at least in the corporate setting, is the general (or outside) counsel for the corporation, who often is the referring lawyer. Often an internal investigation will have been conducted once the company found out about the government's investigation. There will then be confidential and privileged interviews of people who had been and would become involved. In my case, this included both line personnel and mid-level executives like Mary. In order to let us know what he already had learned, Tom offered to allow me and my client to join a joint defense agreement with the corporation. If we would agree to respect the confidentiality and privilege that attached to his interviews and investigation, he agreed to give us access to some of the information he gathered. As with all joint defense agreements, this presented a delicate situation for Mary. At that point, our interests were directly aligned with those of Tom's client and with other individuals who had become parties to the agreement. We all wanted to avoid criminal charges being filed against the corporation, or Mary, or any one of its executives.

What would happen later, though, if Mary were asked to testify against her employer or other executives in exchange for immunity from prosecution or some favorable plea bargain? If she decided to do so, the common interest would disappear, and Mary would have to withdraw from the joint defense arrangement. Under most of these agreements, when someone withdraws, all privileged materials must be returned, and the withdrawing party cannot use the privileged information further. Disclosure of confidences in the context of a joint defense agreement does not constitute a waiver of attorney-client privilege. Courts have also been willing to enforce such agreements, even if they are oral and require the return and non-use of privileged information after a party withdraws from the joint defense group.

To advise Mary about testifying before the grand jury, we needed the information Tom had already gathered. We therefore decided to enter into the joint defense arrangement. We completed our investigation, including the information we were able to obtain from the prosecutor, the other attorneys in the joint defense group, and our client. At this point, we were ready to make a decision regarding Mary's grand jury appearance.

Theories of Criminal Liability

The prosecutor's goal was clear and explicit. He believed he had an overwhelmingly strong case against a number of line personnel, but he suspected that individuals at much higher levels of the company encouraged, or at least knowingly tolerated, the illegal activity uncovered by the federal investigation. Thus, I had grave concerns for Mary. Even though she never met the government's undercover agent, it only made sense that any prosecution of the organization's top management would implicate mid-level managers like Mary, who stood between the line personnel and upper management in the corporate chain-of-command and who would be the conduit for communications from senior executives to line personnel. I was troubled by the possibility that the government would find it appropriate to charge Mary as a conspirator or might attempt to prosecute executives like her on a "willful blindness" theory, which permits the convictions of corporate executives who willfully made themselves blind to the criminal acts regularly occurring in the sections of the business they controlled.

Given the various attenuated theories of criminal liability the government could devise, and the fact that I did not know all of the evidence available to the government, it was clear to me that Mary had a Fifth Amendment privilege, and I informed the prosecutor Mary would "take the Fifth" if called to testify. I politely told the prosecutor that the only way Mary would testify would be pursuant to a grant of immunity.

In theory, there are two forms an immunity agreement can take: "transactional" or "use" immunity. Under "transactional immunity," the government agrees not to prosecute the defendant for any criminal conduct within the scope of its present investigation. It leaves the door open only for prosecution of crimes the government was unaware of and which are not specified in the agreement. Contrary to popular belief, it is extremely rare for a witness to a federal criminal prosecution to receive transactional immunity. It typically is obtained only in the context of a plea agreement. In fact, other than Monica Lewinsky, I am not aware of any federal grand jury witness who has received transactional immunity in exchange for testimony without also agreeing to plead guilty to a federal offense.

The far more common and narrower form of immunity is "use immunity": Neither compelled testimony nor any leads derived from the testimony can thereafter be used against the witness in any criminal case. 18 U.S.C. § 6001. In theory, this allows the government to discover information relevant to its investigation without abrogating the Fifth Amendment rights of the witness. It also reserves to prosecutors the right to prosecute the witness if they obtain evidence of guilt through sources entirely independent of the immunized testimony. In practice, immunized witnesses are seldom prosecuted.

Our task was to convince the prosecutor to agree to a grant of use immunity. In practice, there are two means of securing use immunity in federal criminal prosecutions. The formal process is governed by § 6001. Under that statute, a witness who has asserted the Fifth Amendment is compelled to do so by an order signed by a United States District Judge sitting in the district in which the grand jury sits. Violation of this order can result in incarceration for contempt of court.

The other means is by letter from the United States Attorney's office investigating the case. This procedure relieves the prosecutor of the need to get an order from the court, and it allows more flexibility to define the terms of the immunized testimony. Unlike statutory immunity, though, the terms of letter immunity are not defined by statute. Instead, the scope of the immunity is determined by the terms of the contract, as reflected in the prosecutor's letter. While letter immunity may be expedient, the defense lawyer must be cautious not to secure less protection for his client than that to which the witness is entitled under the federal statute.

Let's Make a Deal

Because it is difficult to prosecute an immunized witness, the goal is to obtain immunity for the client. To do so, you must convince the prosecutor that although the witness might have some criminal exposure, he or she is not so culpable as to be prosecuted. This can be a tricky balancing act. One way is to make a "proffer" to the government of what your client will say if immunized and testifies. Most prosecutors will demand such a proffer and will refuse a grant of "blind" immunity. The goal of a proffer is to assure the government that the witness has information that is of value to it and to persuade it that the witness should not be targeted for prosecution. The willingness of the government to agree to immunity will depend in large part on how badly the prosecutors need your client's testimony.

Typically, government attorneys will not confer immunity on a subject based solely on a proffer from the defense lawyer as to what the client will say. They will want to sit down with the witness to determine credibility and culpability. The obvious danger here is that the government ultimately may decide not to confer immunity on that witness, yet it may learn information through the proffer that would assist it in prosecuting the witness later and will confine the witness to a particular version of the facts. This danger can be offset, in part, by a letter from the U.S. Attorney's office granting "proffer protection." These letters vary from office to office, but typically provide that no statements made by the witness during a proffer session can be used in the government's case-in-chief should the government later charge the witness with a crime. They also provide that leads derived from statements can be used against the proffering witness, and that statements made can be used for cross-examination in the event the witness is later indicted and tried. The risk of such impeachment is obvious.

Hence, the decision whether to make a proffer can be an agonizing one. The only reason to agree is if there is a realistic hope that it will lead to immunity for the witness. The risk of educating the government and locking the client into a story cannot be overlooked.

In Mary's case, after a brief proffer session, she was granted use immunity, and she testified in the grand jury. Now, the defense lawyer's job is to ensure that the witness testifies truthfully and fully, subject, of course, to any privileges.

Subsequent Grand Jury Subpoenas

To my surprise, Mary's involvement did not end there. The government later subpoenaed her to return to the grand jury for additional testimony. This development can be inconsequential or it can be highly significant and extremely troubling. The second subpoena simply may indicate that the government's investigation has revealed new areas of inquiry, or it can indicate that prosecutors are dissatisfied with the initial testimony and suspect that the witness is withholding relevant information.

Before I would allow Mary to testify again, I requested that the government provide a copy of her prior grand jury testimony. Rule 6(e)(2) of the Federal Rules of Criminal Procedure, which generally requires secrecy of grand jury proceedings, forbids court stenographers, grand jurors, and government lawyers from disclosing matters occurring before the grand jury. Courts are authorized under subsection 6(e)(3)(C) to make disclosures of grand jury material, but only after "a strong showing of particularized need." Rule 6, however, excludes grand jury witnesses from the list of persons forbidden from disclosing grand jury material. Grand jury witnesses, therefore, may reveal the contents of their own testimony without restriction. As such, the secrecy concerns underlying Rule 6(E) have much less force when grand jury witnesses request a copy of their own testimony.

In fact, many cases hold that grand jury witnesses have a presumptive right of access to their own testimony, particularly when they have been questioned on the same topic more than once. The Ninth Circuit in *Bursey v. United States*, 466 F.2d 1059 (9th Cir.1972) held that compelling a grand jury witness to answer questions to which he previously has responded presents "the hovering possibility that inconsistency in [the witness's] answers may expose him to prosecution for perjury."

Thus, the Ninth Circuit held that upon motion of a grand jury witness, the court should permit inspection of the prior recorded testimony, unless the prosecutor can demonstrate "particularized and substantial reasons why this should not be allowed in a particular case." But not all courts agree. Others have put the burden on the grand jury witness, who must satisfy the same "particularized need" standard as any other person seeking disclosure of grand jury material.

In Mary's case, the prosecutor agreed to give her access to the transcripts. Nevertheless, the prosecutor inquired again into areas Mary had covered previously. During the subsequent grand jury appearances, he openly accused Mary of "holding back" information to protect her employer and management colleagues. She answered these questions honestly, admitted her conflicting emotions regarding her testimony, but adamantly denied testifying falsely in any regard.

I was concerned that the government regretted its decision to immunize Mary and would attempt to develop a case against her. I was comforted, though, by the fact that it would be difficult, if not impossible, to develop sufficient evidence to indict her that was completely independent of her own testimony. My fears were realized when, after Mary had made several trips to the grand jury, I received a letter from the prosecutor, announcing that he had decided to seek an indictment of Mary for her role in managing others at the company who had allegedly engaged in criminal activity. I called the prosecutor and asked how he intended to prosecute a citizen who had been immunized and had testified before the grand jury, which was now to consider indicting her? The prosecutor's simplistic response was: She didn't directly incriminate herself or anyone else, and we won't be using her testimony against her. My response—that federal law supplies much greater protection for immunized witnesses than this—fell upon deaf ears. But this was just the beginning of our objection to and attack on the proposed indictment. We intended to seek review by the DOJ of the AUSA's decision to indict Mary. Although the U.S. Attorney's Manual does not confer substantive rights on a potential defendant, it does set policy for the Justice Department. According to the Manual, the Attorney General must approve the decision to indict an immunized witness:

> After a person has testified or provided information pursuant to a compulsion order—except in the case of act-of-production immunity—an attorney for the government shall not initiate or recommend prosecution of the person for an offense or offenses first disclosed in, or closely related to, such testimony or information without the express written authorization of the Attorney General.

This section of the U.S. Attorney's Manual goes on to require prosecutors to lay out how they will satisfy the standard the U.S. Supreme Court has set for charging an immunized witness:

> The request to prosecute should indicate the circumstances justifying prosecution and the method by which the government will be able to establish that the evidence it will use against the witness will meet the government's burden under *Kastigar v. United States*, 406 U.S. 441 (1972).

This gave us the grounds we needed to seek review of the AUSA's decision to seek an indictment of Mary.

I wrote to the AUSA, outlined these provisions, and asked whether he had complied with them. He unashamedly replied that he did not intend to on the theory that Mary testified pursuant to a letter immunity agreement that tracked the statutory language of 18 U.S.C. § 6001 et seq., and not pursuant to a "compulsion order" from the court. I argued that this was a distinction without a difference and reminded him of our conversation at the time the letter agreement was proffered by the United States: I had told him Mary would not sign unless she received the maximum protection allowed under the law. In response, the prosecutor had stated that his letter encompassed all of the protections afforded to a witness who testifies pursuant to a court order issued under 18 U.S.C. § 6001 et seq. In reliance on this express representation, we signed the immunity agreement, and Mary testified. The prosecutor was unmoved.

We then asked the Attorney General to review the decision to indict Mary. Realizing that the Attorney General would not read our submission personally, we wrote to the Assistant Attorney General for the Criminal Division, with copies to the Deputy Assistant Attorney General and the Director of the Office of Enforcement Operations, which is charged with oversight of witness immunity requests. I received a call from a DOJ official agreeing to review the matter. I then made a substantive attack on the problems the government would have in prosecuting Mary: the decision to prosecute Mary could not withstand judicial scrutiny, because in order to sustain an indictment, the government must meet the "heavy burden" of proving that its evidence and all of its strategic decisions are "derived from a legitimate source, wholly independent of the compelled testimony." *Kastigar*, 406 U.S. 441, 460–61. My goal was to convince DOJ officials it could not do so. See U.S. Attorney's Manual § 9–23. 400.

While the government labors under a "heavy burden" when it decides to bring charges against an immunized witness, the witness has virtually no burden beyond showing testimony was given under immunity. I stressed that the prosecutor must clearly show that had Mary never testified, the government would have built the same case against her as they now intend to bring and that that burden is almost "insurmountable." The government must negate the possibility that it was assisted in any fashion by the grand jury testimony of the immunized witness, whether in formulating its strategy or preparing its case.

There are many forbidden ways in which a prosecutor might try to use immunized testimony, only to end up invalidating an indictment. They include: using the testimony as "assistance in focusing the investigation, deciding to initiate prosecution, refusing to plea bargain, interpreting evidence, planning cross examination, and otherwise generally planning trial strategy," helping to motivate a witness, helping to motivate the prosecution, or, focusing the questioning of a witness.

The testimony of agents and prosecutors, that they did not use the immunized testimony, typically will not suffice, nor will good faith representations by members of the prosecution team that the testimony did not impact the subsequent investigation.

Courts have prescribed a variety of formal safeguards before the government can even consider a valid indictment of an immunized witness.

First, some cases suggest that the specific grand jury that heard testimony from the immunized witness cannot return an indictment against him, on the theory that grand jurors cannot be expected to put the immunized testimony completely out of their minds and return an indictment that did not, in some respect, use that testimony. The cases also suggest the prosecution team must be removed from the case before the immunized witness can be indicted. If the case against the witness is pursued, you should insist on the assignment of prosecutors and agents wholly unfamiliar with the testimony, and that the agents and attorneys who conducted the investigation be removed and walled off from those taking up the reins.

We also argued that the government had to produce a contemporaneous snapshot of the evidence against Mary as it existed before she testified. The DOJ acknowledges the importance of this safeguard. Section 726 of the Criminal Resource Manual instructs prosecutors to "prepare for the file a signed and dated memorandum summarizing the existing evidence against the witness and the date(s) and source(s) of such evidence" before the immunized witness testifies.

Given the breadth of the questioning in the grand jury, I argued it was inescapable that Mary's testimony contributed to the development of the government's theory of the case against her. If any part of her immunized testimony influenced the prosecution in any way, it would constitute an improper use of the testimony, which would mean that the government would not be able to satisfy its *Kastigar* burden. Additionally, although we were not informed of the identities of the witnesses the government planned to use to prove any charges against Mary, it was virtually certain that she had testified about many of them. Thus, I argued, it was unavoidable that the government's subsequent conversations with these witnesses were influenced by Mary's immunized testimony. In fact, in some cases, Mary's testimony was likely the impetus for the government contacting or re-interviewing these witnesses. In any event, if any of these individuals appeared on the government's witness list, or if the information they provided to the government played any role in the prosecution, that would constitute an improper use of Mary's immunized testimony.

The story had a happy ending: The DOJ acted responsibly, and Mary was not indicted. But the story shows that as critical as it is to obtain immunity for your client, the battle is only half won. You must be vigilant to ensure that the immunity is not lost either through governmental overzealousness or your client's own excesses in testimony.

The Exercise

Facts: William Persk was a commodities broker in Chicago. His business consisted of buying and selling currency futures and other commodities for his clients, and he derived income from this business by earning a commission on each transaction in which his clients engaged. He conducted his business under the name of Premium Investments ("Premium"), a sole proprietorship. On behalf of Premium, Persk rented office space, contracted with a brokerage house to clear Premium's commodities transactions, and hired a salesman named Frank Bauman. In addition, Persk managed clients' accounts, effectuated all commodities transactions, and handled Premium's voluminous paperwork. Persk had a history of questionable practices in the commodities industry.

It was Bauman's job to work the telephone, calling potential investors and encouraging them to place money in accounts with Premium. Bauman also handled telephone calls from existing clients. Persk taught Bauman how to handle these clients—how to soothe their anxieties and how to urge them to "re-load"—that is, to deposit more money in their Premium accounts. Bauman initially earned a straight salary, but he was so effective with Premium's clientele, especially after Perks trained him as a "re-loader," that Persk soon began giving him a portion of Premium's commission on each client transaction.

The commodities business is heavily regulated, but Premium habitually ignored the many regulations that applied to its business. Among other things, it failed to satisfy the Commodities Futures Trading Commission ("CFTC") reporting requirements to which commodities brokers are subject. In addition, Premium made misleading statements about the commodities market in its advertisements. One colorful Premium brochure, for example, used clever charts and graphs to extol the safety of the commodities market and to insinuate that its investors enjoyed "a virtually guaranteed annual return of at least fourteen percent." By this means of advertising and Bauman's extraordinary telephone skills, Premium developed a client base of inexperienced investors, many of whom were retirees seeking to place their retirement funds in safe, but lucrative, investments. Persk was delighted with Premium's success, and he frequently bragged to Bauman that he (Persk) could "bleed those old folks out of their last red cent." Through these practices, Premium made hundreds of thousands of dollars in commission profits.

For several years, Premium rode a wave of strong markets and experienced extraordinary success. Persk directed Bauman to play on these proven successes to convince clients to authorize Persk to buy and sell on their behalf at his own discretion—that is, Persk would make all their investment decisions. This authority benefited both Persk and Bauman tremendously, because Persk could "churn" client accounts, buying and selling frequently in order to generate more commission income. In order to increase commissions, Persk would sometimes buy and sell hundreds of commodities contracts in a single day for a particular customer. These transactions were reported to the customers in daily transaction reports and in monthly statements. Persk was proud of his ability to churn accounts and he promised Bauman that he would one day teach Bauman that skill.

So long as they had success in the commodities market, Premium's clients were satisfied with its services and did not question its practices. Once the market began to experience sharp declines, however, Premium's clients lost money. Despite Bauman's efforts to assuage their fears, clients complained to the CFTC about Premium. Churning of accounts was one of the things complained of, and one dissatisfied customer, Esther Hankin, provided the CFTC with copies of her monthly statements showing extraordinary numbers of transactions. During one month, Premium had completed over five hundred transactions in her account. The value of her account dropped by $7,607 during that month, while Premium had taken out of her account more than $10,000 in commissions. Mrs. Hankin was particularly distraught because she remembered that she called Premium after she received that statement. She specifically recalled speaking with Bauman and complaining about the number of transactions and the high commissions. According to Mrs. Hankin, Bauman replied, "I know about that, and that's a problem that I can't do anything about. But I can tell you that things are moving upward quickly, and you can recover your losses if you get smart and put your money to work in the market this month." Mrs. Hankin believed Bauman and invested another $10,000 in her Premium account before she ultimately closed it out and went to the CFTC.

The CFTC launched an investigation of Premium, Persk, and Bauman. Using its civil discovery authority, the CFTC subpoenaed all of Premium's records. In addition, it demanded that Persk and Bauman submit to depositions, and that they produce at their depositions "any and all documents in their possession or control having to do with Premium Investments, transactions in commodities of any kind, and/or Premium clients or persons solicited by Premium." At the same time, the CFTC informed lawyers for Persk and Bauman that it had alerted the United States Department of Justice about the matter and might recommend that a criminal prosecution be brought against the two men. Moreover, Persk and Bauman each retained a lawyer, who informed them that Premium's clients were likely to bring suit against Premium and against them individually, seeking damages and attorneys' fees. Finally, the Consumer Fraud Division of the State of Illinois Attorney General's Office also became involved and indicated that it might initiate civil and criminal actions against Premium and the two men for violations of state laws.

Assignment: Your instructor will assign you to represent one of two parties: the United States Department of Justice or Mr. Bauman. You will receive a packet of confidential information as the lawyer for that party. Your assignment is to represent that party in an out-of-class negotiation session concerning potential immunity for Mr. Bauman, and to draft, along with your opposing party, an immunity agreement. Your instructor may direct you to turn in that agreement. You may also be asked in class to explain your negotiating position and describe the factors that influenced your eventual decision.

As part of the exercise, you should be familiar with the following statutes (for purposes of this exercise, assume these are the only criminal statutes that apply):

- Under 7 U.S.C. section 6(b)(a)(A), it is a felony for any person to "cheat or defraud or attempt to cheat or defraud" another in connection with a commodities transaction. A violation of this provision subjects the violator to potential incarceration under the Federal Sentencing Guidelines, particularly if the aggregate amount of the loss to defrauded customers, or of the gain to the violator, exceeds $100,000.

● Under 18 U.S.C. section 1962(c), it is a felony for any person to conduct the affairs of an enterprise (such as Premium) through a "pattern of racketeering activity," which includes engaging in multiple, related acts of commodities fraud. A violation of this statute, known as the "Racketeer Influenced and Corrupt Organizations Act" [RICO], is accompanied by stiff penalties, including substantial incarceration.

You should also review the hints on negotiating in an earlier chapter. Finally, the immunity agreement in the *Brunell* file in Chapter 1 can serve as a model for your agreement.

IV. USING THE FIFTH AMENDMENT IN CIVIL CASES

From what you have read so far, you can discern that it is important for lawyers in civil cases to consider the incriminating aspects of depositions, interrogatories, and other parts of the civil process. Avoiding incrimination is often a paramount goal, even for the civil lawyer. Yet the costs of doing so are sometimes high. In the following article, Mark W. Williams explains the perils and costs of Fifth Amendment issues in civil cases.

Pleading the Fifth in Civil Cases

Mark W. Williams[94]

Jack Smith was the chief financial officer of Company, Inc. Along with Company and other officers and directors, Smith was recently sued in a class action case alleging violations of the securities laws. That wasn't the end of his troubles. The Securities and Exchange Commission also began proceedings against Smith. And there was more. The United States Attorney's office for Smith's district sent him a target letter. Does all this seem like piling on? Maybe, but, unfortunately, parallel civil, regulatory, and criminal proceedings are all too common these days. And it is not limited to securities cases. This can happen in environmental, banking, antitrust and forfeiture cases.

Such parallel proceedings also often create the following dilemma: Given a choice between the risk of a multi-million dollar judgment (plus administrative sanctions by a government agency) and the risk of going to jail, which would a person in Smith's position choose? Most would pay the judgment rather than spend a day in jail or have a criminal record.

---

94. Mark W. Williams, *Pleading the Fifth in Civil Cases*, 20 LITIGATION 31 (Spring 1994).

Despite this, people facing parallel proceedings still for some reason often testify at depositions, answer interrogatories, and produce documents.

Such conduct can be potentially incriminating and the answers may waive the Fifth Amendment right against self incrimination. By failing to invoke their privilege against self-incrimination in a timely way in civil cases, people can provide important evidence to prosecutors—thereby helping to build a criminal case against themselves. Worse, they can be convicted and go to jail.

How does this happen? Some litigants focus too much on the specter of a large civil judgment. Others ignore their lawyers or receive poor counsel. And the problem is difficult—a real Catch–22. A person ensnared in parallel proceedings faces hard choices: If he does invoke the privilege in a civil proceeding to protect himself in the criminal proceeding, he risks sanctions or adverse inferences being drawn against him in the civil case. If he does not assert the privilege in the civil case, he may waive it, thus hurting his criminal prospects, because the prosecution will have access to free discovery that it could not have gotten under the restrictive criminal discovery rules.

What is the answer? There are few hard and fast rules. Each case must be examined individually. Knowing the basics will, of course, help you make better decisions when the problem comes up. But the most important thing is to think, think, think before you act. . . .

Fifth Amendment issues are important at all points in litigation—even at the pleading and initial motions stage. Remember, the privilege is testimonial. A plaintiff who fears prosecution should not, if the issues in a civil case are similar to those in a possible criminal proceeding, verify a complaint; the act of verification makes the complaint the client's testimony and could result in a waiver. The complaint should be signed only by the lawyer.

For the same reason, a defendant should not verify an answer. Again, the lawyer should sign. Most courts hold that a lawyer's signing an answer in which admissions (or denials, which can have repercussions all their own) are made does not constitute a "testimonial" act of the client. . . .

It should almost go without saying that civil litigants facing parallel criminal proceedings should not sign affidavits in support of motions and should not use potentially incriminating documents in support of motions. Submitting an affidavit is a testimonial act; it may either contain incriminating statements or lead to a waiver. And, as described further below, the act of production of documents is "testimonial" in nature—with possibly serious consequences.

The thorniest stage of a civil or regulatory proceeding, at least when it comes to the Fifth Amendment, is discovery. Because of recent amendments to the federal discovery rules, a lawyer must determine his Fifth Amendment strategy early in a civil case. Federal Rule 26 now requires that civil litigants disclose the identities of relevant witnesses and produce relevant documents almost at the outset. The rule permits, as it always has, a claim of privilege. Fed. R. Civ. 26(a). But a decision on that point must be made sooner than ever.

A good starting point—and a way to avoid having to make a decision— is to try to get a stay of discovery. One of the first things you should do when retained by a civil litigant who fears prosecution is to file a motion seeking exactly that. Your argument will be that requiring a civil litigant to respond to discovery will unfairly intrude on his Fifth Amendment rights against self-incrimination (or will prevent him from offering a defense to the civil case). Remember that the scope of civil discovery is far broader than criminal discovery. Because plaintiffs' lawyers, regulators, and prosecutors often collaborate and exchange information, the lack of a stay may mean that the prosecutor will get discovery to which he would not be entitled in the criminal case itself.

Courts are not constitutionally required to stay civil proceedings, but such motions are granted. A stay lies within the discretion of the court and will be approached on a case-by-case basis. Judges look at a variety of factors in deciding such requests, including:

1. The interests of the plaintiff in proceeding expeditiously with the civil litigation and the prejudice to the plaintiff if delayed;

2. The private interests of, and burden on, the defendant;

3. The convenience to the court; and

4. The public interest. . . .

Let us review these criteria. First is the plaintiff's interest in speed. Plaintiffs obviously want the quickest results possible—especially when there are parallel criminal proceedings. If the criminal proceeding concludes first, and the defendant is jailed or heavily fined, a civil recovery may be speculative. In addition, the complex nature of parallel proceedings usually requires a battery of lawyers, experts, and other advisors. They cost money, and that too reduces the resources from which a plaintiff may recover a judgment. Delay in the civil proceeding may therefore be decidedly against the plaintiff's interests.

When such financial factors are not present, the prejudice to the plaintiff from a civil discovery stay ought to be minimal. In any event, the normal relative speed of criminal and civil proceedings means that stays should usually be acceptable. Under the Speedy Trial Act, most criminal proceedings must be concluded in a matter of months. Since civil litigation rarely concludes in less than one to two years, a delay of a few months rarely will impose serious prejudice on the plaintiff. This may not be true, however, if the criminal case has been determined "complex" by the court. If so, the deadlines of the Speedy Trial Act are waived, usually making it longer.

Next comes the defendant's point of view. The defendant's interests in a stay are equally obvious. The Catch–22 discussed earlier is ever present: Without a stay, the witness must invoke his privilege against self-incrimination in the civil case—an act that may be used against him in that proceeding at a later date. As also explained, the discovery taken in the civil and regulatory cases may provide much additional discovery to the prosecution in the criminal case.

The third criterion—judicial convenience—mostly concerns the problem of docket congestion. Courts want to keep civil cases moving; a stay of discovery slows a case down. In fact, however, the pendency of a criminal case many times will speed up the civil case by forcing a settlement. If a litigant pleads or is found guilty to charges arising out of the same transaction that is at the center of the civil case, the reasons for settlement may be obvious. At the other end of the spectrum, a decisive acquittal can also help a criminal defendant's position in a parallel civil case.

What about the public interest? This is often dependent on a particular judge's point of view. The public has an interest in having civil cases adjudicated. For the court system to be respected, victims of civil wrongdoing should be compensated sooner rather than later. The public also has an interest in regulatory agencies' ensuring that the laws are upheld for the benefit of all, not just plaintiffs in a lawsuit. But there is surely also a public interest in taking care that constitutional rights are upheld. Those who seek a discovery stay should therefore emphasize that all have a stake in seeing to it that a witness's Fifth Amendment privilege against self-incrimination is not compromised.

The timing of a motion to stay discovery is important. If no indictment has been returned, and your client simply fears he will be prosecuted, the chances of getting a stay are slight, even if the fear is obviously justified. The best chance for success exists after your client has been indicted, but before trial, plea agreement, or sentencing. If your client has gotten immunity, there is little chance of a stay, unless the immunity grant is narrow.

Do not make the mistake of thinking that a protective order in the civil case will help you in the criminal proceeding. An order sealing discovery under Rule 26(c) is not enforceable in a criminal case; it will not help you keep disclosed, incriminating information from the prosecution. The reason is that enforcement of a protective order in a criminal case would be tantamount to immunity granted by the court or perhaps by agreement of civil litigants. A court can issue an immunity order in a criminal case, of course, but it generally cannot do so on its own. The request for such an order comes from a United States Attorney, and immunity is usually granted in the form of an agreement between the government and the criminal target or defendant. . . .

If discovery is not stayed, it must be handled carefully, question by question. Not surprisingly, responding to deposition questions or to interrogatories are testimonial acts. A request for admission, if answered by a client, is also testimonial. Because the privilege is personal, a response to a request for admission by a lawyer should not, in theory, constitute a waiver, but don't take any chances. When discovery questions invite incriminating responses, the privilege generally should be invoked.

You cannot, however, invoke the privilege against self incrimination for every discovery question. Drawing this line is probably the hardest call you must make in the Fifth Amendment maze.

Certain questions are easy. Return for a minute to Jack Smith—the corporate executive being sued and prosecuted for securities violations. His deposition is noticed in the civil case. If asked his name, educational background, or the names of other employees, he should probably answer those questions; it is likely that such information would not furnish a link in the chain of evidence needed to prosecute Smith. Failure to respond to such basic questions could lead to sanctions under Federal Civil Rule 37. But be aware that, in some cases, such information could be incriminating—as it might if Smith had used several aliases. If you are unsure, always err on the side of caution and plead the privilege. Even a sanction is better than a jail sentence.

In making such determinations, courts will look at each question individually. If the issues in the case involve alleged false statements in a prospectus or statement filed with the SEC, Smith obviously should invoke his Fifth Amendment privilege against self incrimination to questions concerning the statements.

Unfortunately, gray areas and tough calls are more prevalent. Assume that an issue in the parallel proceedings concerns allegedly false accounting data in a report filed with the SEC. Assume also that part of Smith's initial defense is the traditional "I knew nothing about it." Later on, you discover that in similar positions at other companies, Smith was regularly involved in disclosure issues in SEC filings; allegations of similar improprieties were also raised at those companies, but nothing came of them. Now, such information may not be directly relevant to the issues in the civil case, but given the expansive reach of civil discovery, it may be discoverable. Smith should consider invoking his privilege against self-incrimination in response to any questions in any proceeding that will cover such facts. That evidence may well be usable in the criminal proceeding to show that Smith was more savvy about disclosure issues than he contends and might thus provide a connection in the chain of evidence needed to convict him.

The point is to think—and then think some more—well in advance of discovery about sensitive areas. You cannot anticipate every question that may be thrown at your client, but you need to try. Such an analysis, which should be made during your own investigation, will permit you to make better judgment calls—both on the spot in a deposition and in drafting responses to written discovery requests.

You must keep in mind the various entities in a case. Whether your client is an individual or sole proprietor, or instead is a corporation, union or partnership, is an important consideration. The individual or sole proprietor can invoke the privilege. The nonhuman entities cannot. If a person with criminal problems is asked to respond to a discovery request on behalf of an entity, or to act as a Rule 30(b)(6) designee for a deposition, or to testify as the custodian of documents at a records deposition, the entity should designate someone else. . . .

If the judge denies your motion to stay discovery and your client persists (wisely, given the risk of conviction and jail) in invoking the privilege, you can expect a motion for sanctions. Any of the sanctions mentioned in Rule 37 is possible; the most common sanction is to prevent the party asserting the privilege from offering evidence in support of claims or defenses related to the matters to which the privilege was asserted. In other words if you won't testify about an issue, you lose on it.

And there is another, sometimes more serious, risk: The Fifth Amendment does not prevent adverse inferences to be drawn and argued against parties in civil actions when they refuse to provide relevant evidence on the basis of the privilege against self incrimination. Your opponent in a civil or regulatory proceeding will push to introduce your client's invocation of the privilege in discovery—you can count on it. Not only is the inference valuable, but pointing out that someone has "taken the Fifth" will give him a tinge of criminality and evasion—especially with jurors.

Try to ward off this rhetorical, dramatic manipulation of the privilege with a motion in limine under Federal Rule of Evidence 403. Argue that the witness has already (probably) been sanctioned and cannot introduce evidence to support certain claims and defenses. Evidence that he relied on his constitutional right to assert the privilege is not needed, you should argue. And, anyway, its prejudicial effect outweighs its probative value. Also, and importantly, jurors may be confused; in fact, that may be exactly what your opponent wants to do. Jurors may not appreciate that the invocation of the privilege is a constitutional right, a right intended to protect the innocent and not just the guilty.

The Fifth Amendment in parallel civil proceedings is a briar patch. It can snare and tear you if you make a misstep. As a general proposition, your client should invoke the privilege in civil and regulatory proceedings when faced with questions that call for possibly incriminating responses. But do not outsmart yourself. Invoking the privilege when it is not necessary may bring unnecessary sanctions. The best you can do is to know the basics, investigate the case early, decide on a strategy, and constantly consult with criminal counsel. Above all, think, and then think twice more, before proceeding.

————

PROBLEM 9–17

Review the facts of Problem 9–2. Assume that during discovery in the divorce case, Cunningham requested copies of Brunell's tax returns for the past ten years, a list of all of his assets, and a statement of his annual income and expenditures. Responses to the discovery requests were due in 30 days. Brunell retained Danielle Stern to represent him in the divorce. Stern advised Brunell not to respond to the discovery requests and filed a motion in the divorce court to stay discovery. The divorce court denied the motion. On the day that the discovery responses were due, Stern prepared a statement that she attached to all of the discovery requests, which she then returned to Cunningham. The statement was signed by Brunell and related the following: "On advice of counsel, I decline to answer these requests on the grounds that they might incriminate me."

Cunningham moved to compel responses to the discovery requests and for sanctions, contending that Brunell's assertion of the Fifth Amendment privilege was groundless and improperly raised. The divorce court agreed and ordered Brunell to comply with the requests or risk contempt. Stern advised Brunell to continue to refuse to respond, and Brunell eventually was imprisoned for contempt. He filed an appeal from the divorce court's contempt order.

Question: You are the appeals court judge. Should the divorce court's order be reversed?

Note on Discovery Problems: Frequently, the client ensnared in both civil and criminal proceedings has a difficult choice: he can invoke the Fifth Amendment in the civil case, thereby incurring sanctions or adverse inferences that damage his position in that proceeding, or he can waive the privilege in the civil case, thereby exposing himself to liability in the criminal matter. What should the lawyer advise in these circumstances?

CHAPTER 10

EYEWITNESS IDENTIFICATION

- SCIENCE OF EYEWITNESS IDENTIFICATION
- PROTECTION AGAINST UNNECESSARY SUGGESTIVENESS
- RIGHT TO COUNSEL

I. THE SCIENCE BEHIND EYEWITNESS IDENTIFICATIONS: A GUIDE TO UNDERSTANDING LINEUPS AND PHOTOSPREADS

A. INTRODUCTION

Contrary to popular belief, eyewitness identification is notoriously unreliable. A jury may be profoundly impressed by a witness who says, "That's the man; I will never forget that face." But psychological research suggests that this trust in eyewitness testimony is misplaced.[1] The human brain and memory are little understood, and what scientists are learning casts doubt on our ability to perceive, store, and recall events accurately. The dangers of eyewitness error are magnified when police introduce what is called "suggestion" (in the form of subtle and even unconscious clues) when an eyewitness is asked to identify a suspect. In this chapter, we will explore constitutional rules that protect the integrity of eyewitness identification procedures to some extent.

B. IDENTIFICATION PROCEDURES

In the usual case, police rely on one of two initial identification procedures: lineups and photospreads. Records of one of these procedures, the lineup, appear in Chapter 1, in the Boson case file, and should be reviewed now. You will be given photospread records in a role-playing exercise later in this chapter.

1. LINEUPS AND SHOWUPS

In a lineup, a group of men (or of women, depending upon the gender of the wrongdoer) are placed in a line and the victim is asked whether he sees anyone whom he recognizes. The members of the line might be asked

---

1. This discussion is drawn primarily from three sources: BRIAN L. CUTLER & STEVEN D. PENROD, MISTAKEN IDENTIFICATION: THE EYEWITNESS, PSYCHOLOGY, AND THE LAW (1995); Note, *Did Your Eyes Deceive You? Expert Psychological Testimony on the Unreliability of Eyewitness Identifications*, 29 STAN. L. REV. 969 (1977); and ELIZABETH F. LOFTUS, EYEWITNESS TESTIMONY (1979). An effective summary of the literature on eyewitness identification is also found at Special Issue on Eyewitness Behavior, 4 L. & HUM. BEHAV. 237 (1980).

to speak certain words. If the victim identifies someone as the criminal actor, that identification may be used against the defendant at trial. But suppose that the person identified was much taller than anyone else in the line, or the only person with a beard, or the only one wearing a headband. Those are details that may suggest to the victim, "Pick this man." Where a lineup is not practicable because of time constraints, police may instead resort to a "showup," the presentation of a single person to the witness, who is then asked whether or not that person is the wrongdoer.

2. PHOTOSPREADS

A photospread may be done in two different ways. With the first approach, the victim is shown a group of perhaps six to eight photographs and asked whether he recognizes anyone. With the second approach, the victim may simply be asked to look through a "mug book" and pick out anyone whom the victim recognizes. Again, suggestion is possible if the photos are not all sufficiently similar to one another. For example, if the suspect's photo is the only color photograph or the only one with a mustache, that would be suggestive. A photographic identification also might be used at trial.[2]

C. Benefits of Counsel

The presence of a lawyer at a lineup or photospread might reduce the danger of misidentification, particularly if the lawyer can make recommendations for how to reduce suggestion. The lawyer can also observe subtleties of the proceeding, such as a wink by an officer or a change in his tone of voice in communicating with the victim. These observations might improve the lawyer's ability to cross-examine the suspect and the officers at trial about the reliability of the identification procedure. The need to prevent suggestion and to enable the defendant to attack the identification at trial have led to United States Supreme Court case law, to be discussed shortly, that seeks to reduce the dangers of suggestion (relying on the due process clauses) and, in some cases, to provide for the presence of a lawyer (relying on the Sixth Amendment right to counsel). That case law cannot be fully understood, however, without some brief understanding of what science has to tell us about the reliability of eyewitness identifications.

D. Current Science on Eyewitness Identification

1. GENERAL FINDINGS

Research on eyewitness identification has combined distinct fields of specializations within experimental psychology, including perception, mem-

---

2. At least one researcher has suggested, however, that too great a similarity improperly reduces the chances of a correct identification, at least for lineups. Thus, under the similarity theory, a perfect lineup or photospread would be one of all clones. The problem, of course, would be that the evil clone could not be identified other than by accident. This researcher suggests, therefore, that lineup members should be similar on characteristics mentioned in the witness's description but differ on other characteristics. *See* Cutler & Penrod, Mistaken, *supra* note 1, at 124.

ory, and social psychology. That research has revealed that perception is not the passive recording of an event like a tape recorder but is instead a constructive process by which people consciously and unconsciously attend selectively to only a minimal number of environmental stimuli. Over time, the representation of a stored event in memory undergoes change, with some details added or altered unconsciously to conform the original memory representation to new information about the event, while other details are forgotten. Moreover, subtle suggestions inherent in the manner in which information is retrieved from memory can distort the remembered image. Thus numerous studies have shown that even trained observers find it difficult to describe obvious characteristics like height, weight, and age. Perceptual inaccuracy is likely to be greater in an untrained layperson and will be magnified if the observer does not realize that a particular detail may be important later on.

People also tend to judge time by the amount of activity occurring, so that a flurry of activity leads them to believe that more time has passed than was true. Time is also perceived as passing more slowly when someone is in an anxiety-producing situation. Thus a victim may think he had much more time to observe his assailant than was true. For crimes that are brief, fast-moving events, the victim also will not likely have sufficient observation time to remember accurately what happened. Poor or rapidly changing lighting conditions or great distances, as well as distracting noises, may make correct perception even more difficult. Furthermore, perceptual abilities generally decrease under stress when the observer is in a fearful or anxiety-provoking situation.

Witnesses also have certain expectations about events that lead them unconsciously to reconstruct what has happened from what they assume must have happened. Additionally, once a figure has been classified, observers tend to conform their continuing perception to their idea of what that object should look like. A victim having made a composite picture of an attacker is therefore likely to minimize any perceived differences between that composite and a suspect resembling it. People are also generally poorer at identifying members of another race than their own. Personal needs and biases similarly affect the ability to perceive.

Several problems in encoding and storage in memory may also arise. People forget quickly so that the more time that passes between the crime and the identification, the less likely it is that the identification will be reliable. This problem is amplified by the tendency to fill gaps in memory, often making it difficult for a witness to distinguish what he originally saw from what he learned later. A witness's description of a suspect may thus mysteriously become more detailed over time. Witnesses will also simply add details to enable the entire mental picture to "make sense." The mere wording of a question can also affect memory processes.

Finally, memory retrieval suffers from being incomplete because of the difficulties most people have in articulating a thorough description. But more focused questions designed to get a more complete answer may simply lead witnesses to fill in gaps where their information is incomplete because they want to give a thorough story. As already noted, suggestion in the design and administration of identification procedures further affects retrieval processes.

2.   SPECIFIC FINDINGS

The research on eyewitness identification has identified as particularly important factors about the witness, factors about the perpetrator, the event, and postevent occurrences, and factors about the identification procedure itself:

a.   *Witness Factors*

Some characteristics of the witness, such as race, gender, various forms of intelligence, and personality, are poor predictors of identification accuracy. Other characteristics can be of some value. For example, it is known that the young and the elderly perform more poorly than average adults. Face recognition skills as measured by performance, not by an individual's own belief that he or she is good at recognizing faces, is also a promising accuracy predictor. Surprisingly, a witness who expects, during the crime, that he will have to perform at a later lineup has little effect on accuracy. Training in cross-racial identification also has little effect on accuracy.

The research leads to other surprising results regarding eyewitness testimony. Most interestingly, the accuracy, completeness, and congruence of a witness's prior descriptions of the perpetrator are only weakly related to the accuracy of the witness's current identification of the perpetrator. Moreover, a witness's good memory for peripheral details of a crime, such as the hand in which the robber held the weapon or the color of the victim's sweater, increases the witness's willingness positively to identify someone as the wrongdoer but also increases the inaccuracy of that identification! Furthermore, the consistency of a witness's testimony (concerning crime details, for example, or descriptions of persons) is unrelated to accuracy. The witness's confidence in his ability to identify the criminal is unrelated to accuracy, but his confidence in having made a correct identification is modestly related to accuracy. Yet juries routinely give this kind of confidence great weight.

b.   *Perpetrator, Event, and Postevent Factors*

Of stable perpetrator characteristics tested—gender, race, distinctiveness, and attractiveness—only facial distinctiveness is a good predictor of identification accuracy. Malleable characteristics, such as changes in facial characteristics (hair style, facial hair, the addition or removal of glasses) and disguises can substantially reduce accuracy.

Several factors about the crime environment—how much time the witness had to view the assailant ("exposure duration"), the presence of a weapon, and cross-race recognition—have clear effects on accuracy. The greater the exposure duration, the higher the likelihood of accuracy, although improvements likely become smaller as duration increases. When a weapon is present, victims tend to focus more time on the weapon, less on the perpetrator, so accuracy decreases. And witnesses tend to be more accurate in identifying those of their own race, less accurate with other races.

One key predictor of identification accuracy relates to the time between the event and the identification. The greater this period of time, known as the "retention interval," the greater the likelihood of misidentification. "Context reinstatement" is important too. That is, if an identification is done at the scene of the crime, accuracy improves. But where a suspect has been identified from mugshots, any later lineup identification is probably based at least in part on recognizing the suspect as having appeared in the mugshots, rather than on an independent recollection of the perpetrator.

c. Suggestive Procedure Factors

It probably will not surprise you to learn that biased instructions given by an officer administering a lineup—for example, instructions suggesting that the suspect is in fact in the lineup or that a particular individual is the wrongdoer—increase false identification rates substantially. Similarly, it is not surprising that false identifications are increased when the suspect stands out from others in the lineup, by wearing different clothes, for example, and that the quality and number of "foils"—other lineup members who resemble the perpetrator—help to reduce the false identification rate.

Other research results are less intuitively obvious. Here are two: first, the traditional method of simultaneous presentation—viewing all lineup members at the same time—carries no benefit in achieving correct identification when the true perpetrator is present but causes substantially more mistaken identifications when the true wrongdoer is not present in the array; and second, sequential presentation—showing one individual or one photo at a time—leads to much lower levels of false identifications.

These research results cause us to issue two pieces of advice to soon-to-be-practicing lawyers: first, keep up to date on research in order to plan your direct and cross-examinations and your closing arguments. Second, consider using identification experts at trial.[3] Such experts might be used to support a suppression motion arguing that a suggestive identification procedure has raised too great a danger of an inaccurate identification to permit its introduction at trial. Alternatively, if the evidence is admitted, the weight of the evidence may be attacked by explaining to the jury the weaknesses in eyewitness identifications, even non-suggestive ones. Recent

---

3. Courts are divided, however, over whether such testimony should be admissible. *Compare* United States v. Downing, 753 F.2d 1224 (3d Cir.1985) (holding that excluding expert testimony on the accuracy of eyewitness testimony is inconsistent with the liberal admissibility standard of Federal Rule of Evidence 702) *with* United States v. Poole, 794 F.2d 462 (9th Cir.1986) (upholding exclusion of eyewitness expert testimony because "effective cross-examination is adequate to reveal inconsistencies or deficiencies in the eyewitness testimony.").

research confirms that expert testimony helps jurors weigh properly those factors affecting identification accuracy. In fact, it helps more than voir dire, special jury instructions, or cross-examination.

E.   POLICE RESPONSES TO THE SCIENCE OF EYEWITNESS IDENTIFICATIONS

Some police departments are working to improve the accuracy of eyewitness identification procedures. These departments are adopting procedures that take into account the latest science on eyewitness identifications. (Ironically, the Supreme Court decisions that you will read about below do not necessarily reflect the best of what science now has to teach.) New Jersey police are among those experimenting with these new procedures, as journalist Mark Hansen explains:

Second Look at the Lineup

Mark Hansen[4]

In a typical police lineup, a witness to a crime is shown an array of possible suspects all at once and asked if he or she can identify the perpetrator. The process is usually conducted by someone who knows who the real suspect is. But not in New Jersey. There, a witness is shown a series of possible suspects one at a time. And the process, whenever possible, is administered to the witness by somebody who doesn't know who the real suspect is.

New Jersey's new lineup procedures took effect on Oct. 15 [2001]. They were precipitated by the growing number of innocent prisoners who have been exonerated through post-conviction DNA testing, according to John J. Farmer Jr., New Jersey attorney general. He outlined the changes in a memo last April to every law enforcement agency and county prosecutor in the state. A study of those cases, which now total nearly 100, shows that mistaken identification was the No. 1 cause of wrongful convictions, accounting for more innocent people being sent to prison than all other causes combined, experts say.

Kathryn Flicker, director of the state's division of criminal justice, says the adoption of the new guidelines doesn't mean there was anything wrong with the old way of doing lineups. "We're not saying the old way was bad," she says. "We just think there is a superior way to do it." Flicker also stresses the fact that the guidelines are only recommendations, not mandates. "They try to set forth a proper way of doing things, but they also try to recognize that not all police departments are created equal," she says. For instance, the rules allow the lineup to be administered by somebody who knows who the suspect is when someone who doesn't know is simply not available to do it.

---

4.   Mark Hansen, *Second Look at the Lineup*, ABA JOURNAL 20 (December 2001).

The new lineup procedures, which incorporate more than 20 years of psychological research into the causes of mistaken identification, include two big changes that have been shown to reduce the number of misidentifications witnesses make without adversely affecting the number of identifications they make correctly. One is sequential viewing, or showing the witness only one possible suspect at a time. The other is double-blind testing, which means simply that the person administering the lineup doesn't know who the real suspect is.

The reason for the changes is rather simple, says Iowa State University psychology professor Gary L. Wells, a pioneer in the field of eyewitness identification who helped New Jersey develop its new lineup procedures. Research demonstrates, Wells says, that a witness who is shown a group of possible suspects simultaneously has a tendency to compare each member of the lineup with one another and then pick out the one who looks most like the perpetrator relative to the others—even though that person may bear little or no resemblance to the actual perpetrator.

The problem with that approach, Wells adds, is that every lineup will contain somebody who looks more like the perpetrator than the others, even though it may not include the actual perpetrator. It's worth noting, he adds, that in most—if not all—of the DNA exoneration cases reported to date, the actual offender wasn't even part of the lineup from which the wrong person was selected.

If the lineup also happens to be conducted by someone who knows who the real suspect is, Wells points out, he or she may also inadvertently influence the outcome by saying or doing things that will tip off the witness. Examples include nodding approvingly when the witness picks out the "right" suspect or suggesting that the witness "take another look" at each of the suspects if he or she chooses the "wrong" person. "If the person giving the test knows what the desirable answer is, he or she is almost certainly going to leak that information to the witness," Wells says. "It's just human nature."

Wells says he's seen one case in which the detectives administering the lineup broke into applause after the witness picked out the "right" suspect. In another, a detective told a woman who had just picked an innocent man out of a lineup as her rapist, "Good. That's the guy we thought it was." Such positive reinforcement only serves to create a false sense of confidence in the mind of a witness who may become absolutely certain about—but totally mistaken in—his or her identification.

Someone who is shown a series of suspects one at a time, on the other hand, has to make a yes or no decision about one person before moving on to the next person. This forces the person to make the choice based solely on memory, not on relative comparisons between suspects. And having the procedure administered by somebody who doesn't know who the real suspect is helps ensure that the person conducting the lineup can't unintentionally influence the witness's decision one way or the other, Wells says.

New Jersey is the first state in the nation to implement the changes in police lineup procedures that Wells and other researchers have long recommended. He also points out that Farmer, the New Jersey attorney general, enjoys one big advantage over his colleagues elsewhere: He alone has the authority to implement a statewide change in police lineup procedures. Most of the country's 19,000 law enforcement agencies are under local control, Wells says, which has made widespread changes in police lineup procedures far more difficult to implement.

But Wells says there may be other reasons why the new lineup procedures have not been more widely implemented. One is a general lack of knowledge in law enforcement circles about what the research shows. Another is police tradition. And a third is the widespread fear among prosecutors that any acknowledgement of the need for change might undermine confidence in the convictions they have already gotten and open up new grounds for possible appeals.

Some prosecutors readily admit their skepticism. Clatsop County, Ore., District Attorney Joshua Marquis, a member of the National District Attorneys Associations' governing board, says he's a little suspicious of anyone who suggests that eyewitness identification evidence is inherently unreliable. Marquis, who has spent 20 years as a prosecutor, says he has heard of only one or two cases in his entire career in which an innocent person was exonerated after being erroneously picked out of a lineup. "It happens," he says. "There's no question about it. But does it happen so often we ought to scrap a process that has worked pretty well for such a long time? Certainly not." But Marquis says he is always open to ideas that could improve the system. "He may have some good ideas," he says of Wells' proposals. "I'd certainly be interested in hearing them."

Milwaukee County District Attorney E. Michael McCann says he's not very familiar with the research into eyewitness misidentification. And he doesn't understand how a sequential lineup could be considered an improvement over a simultaneous one. But McCann says he things the idea is worth exploring. "If the psychologists say there's a better way to do [lineups], then I say fine, let's do it their way," he says. Camden County, N.J., Prosecutor Lee A. Soloman, who implemented the new lineup procedures in his county nearly a year ago, says it's too early to tell whether the changes are working.

But in the New Jersey jurisdictions where the new guidelines have been in effect for several months, Flicker says, the results have been favorable. "We're getting a few less identifications, but the ones we are getting are of much better quality," she says.

Wells doesn't think New Jersey's new lineup procedures are perfect. But he says it's a good start. And now that New Jersey has taken the lead, other jurisdictions are sure to follow. The Brooklyn, N.Y., district attorney's office is already looking into the possibility of changing its lineup procedures, Wells says. So are officials in several states, including Hawaii, Iowa and New Mexico. "We've made more progress in the past 18 months than we made in the previous 18 years," Wells says. "And now that the message is getting out, I think other states will begin to emulate what New Jersey has done.''

––––––––

Now consider this question: if eyewitness identifications are so problematic, should there not be constitutional protections for defendants facing identifications conducted in a manner that may further magnify the danger of error? The answer to this question is ''yes,'' as we explain below.

Checklist 15: Eyewitness Identification Issues

1.   Right to Counsel

   a.   Is an identification procedure, such as a lineup, showup, or photospread involved?

   b.   If yes, is the procedure being held pre-or post-indictment, that is, have formal adversarial proceedings begun?

   c.   If yes, does any subsequent in-court identification have an independent basis from the tainted, uncounseled, out-of-court identification, based on these factors:

      (1)   prior opportunity to observe the alleged criminal act;

      (2)   the existence of any discrepancy between any pre-trial description and the defendant's actual description;

      (3)   any identification prior to the lineup of another person;

      (4)   the identification by picture of the defendant prior to any lineup;

      (5)   the failure to identify the defendant on a prior occasion; and

      (6)   the lapse of time between the alleged act and the lineup identification?

2.   Unnecessarily Suggestive Identification

   a.   Was there suggestion inherent in the lineup, for example, was the defendant the only person with a beard?

   b.   If there was suggestion, was it ''unnecessary'' suggestion?

   c.   If there was ''unnecessary'' suggestion, did it create a very substantial likelihood of misidentification, that is, did it call the reliability of the lineup into question based upon at least the following factors:

      (1)   the opportunity of the witness to view the criminal at the time of the crime;

      (2)   the witness's degree of attention;

      (3)   the accuracy of his prior description of the criminal;

      (4)   the level of certainty demonstrated at the confrontation; and

(5) the time between the crime and the confrontation (weighing against these factors the corrupting effect of the suggestion itself)?

d. If there was "unnecessary" suggestion, did it create a very substantial likelihood of irreparable misidentification (based on factors similar to those in "c" above), thus also calling into question the reliability of any in-court identification?

II. The Right to Counsel

A. Lineups

United States v. Wade

388 U.S. 218 (1967).

■ BRENNAN, J. The question here is whether courtroom identifications of an accused at trial are to be excluded from evidence because the accused was exhibited to the witnesses before trial at a post-indictment lineup conducted for identification purposes without notice to and in the absence of the accused's appointed counsel.

The federally insured bank in Eustace, Texas, was robbed on September 21, 1964. A man with a small strip of tape on each side of his face entered the bank, pointed a pistol at the female cashier and the vice president, the only persons in the bank at the time, and forced them to fill a pillowcase with the bank's money. The man then drove away with an accomplice who had been waiting in a stolen car outside the bank. On March 23, 1965, an indictment was returned against respondent, Wade, and two others for conspiring to rob the bank, and against Wade and the accomplice for the robbery itself. Wade was arrested on April 2, and counsel was appointed to represent him on April 26. Fifteen days later an FBI agent, without notice to Wade's lawyer, arranged to have the two bank employees observe a lineup made up of Wade and five or six other prisoners and conducted in a courtroom of the local county courthouse. Each person in the line wore strips of tape such as allegedly worn by the robber and upon direction each said something like "put the money in the bag," the words allegedly uttered by the robber. Both bank employees identified Wade in the lineup as the bank robber.

At trial the two employees, when asked on direct examination if the robber was in the courtroom, pointed to Wade. The prior lineup identification was then elicited from both employees on cross-examination. At the close of testimony, Wade's counsel moved for a judgment of acquittal or, alternatively, to strike the bank officials' courtroom identifications on the ground that conduct of the lineup, without notice to and in the absence of his appointed counsel, violated his Fifth Amendment privilege against self-incrimination and his Sixth Amendment right to the assistance of counsel.

The motion was denied, and Wade was convicted. The Court of Appeals for the Fifth Circuit reversed the conviction and ordered a new trial at which the in-court identification evidence was to be excluded, holding that, though the lineup did not violate Wade's Fifth Amendment rights, "the lineup, held as it was, in the absence of counsel, already chosen to represent appellant, was a violation of his Sixth Amendment rights...." We granted certiorari.... We reverse the judgment of the Court of Appeals and remand to that court with direction to enter a new judgment vacating the conviction and remanding the case to the District Court for further proceedings consistent with this opinion.

I

Neither the lineup itself nor anything shown by this record that Wade was required to do in the lineup violated his privilege against self-incrimination. We have only recently reaffirmed that the privilege "protects an accused only from being compelled to testify against himself, or otherwise provide the State with evidence of a testimonial or communicative nature ..." *Schmerber v. California*....

We have no doubt that compelling the accused merely to exhibit his person for observation by a prosecution witness prior to trial involves no compulsion of the accused to give evidence having testimonial significance. It is compulsion of the accused to exhibit his physical characteristics, not compulsion to disclose any knowledge he might have. ... Similarly, compelling Wade to speak within hearing distance of the witnesses, even to utter words purportedly uttered by the robber, was not compulsion to utter statements of a "testimonial" nature; he was required to use his voice as an identifying physical characteristic, not to speak his guilt. ...

II

The fact that the lineup involved no violation of Wade's privilege against self-incrimination does not, however, dispose of his contention that the courtroom identifications should have been excluded because the lineup was conducted without notice to and in the absence of his counsel. ... [I]t is urged that the assistance of counsel at the lineup was indispensable to protect Wade's most basic right as a criminal defendant—his right to a fair trial at which the witnesses against him might be meaningfully cross-examined.

The Framers of the Bill of Rights envisaged a broader role for counsel than under the practice then prevailing in England of merely advising his client in "matters of law," and eschewing any responsibility for "matters of fact." The constitutions in at least 11 of the 13 States expressly or impliedly abolished this distinction. "Though the colonial provisions about counsel were in accord on few things, they agreed on the necessity of abolishing the facts-law distinction; the colonists appreciated that if a defendant were forced to stand alone against the state, his case was foredoomed." This background is reflected in the scope given by our decisions to the Sixth Amendment's guarantee to an accused of the assistance of counsel for his defense. When the Bill of Rights was adopted, there were no organized police forces as we know them today. The accused confronted the prosecutor and the witnesses against him, and the evidence was marshalled, largely at the trial itself. In contrast, today's law enforcement machinery involves critical confrontations of the accused by the prosecution at pretrial proceedings where the results might well settle the accused's fate and reduce the trial itself to a mere formality. In recognition of these realities of modern criminal prosecution, our cases have construed the Sixth Amendment guarantee to apply to "critical" stages of the proceedings. The guarantee reads: "In all criminal prosecutions, the accused shall enjoy the right ... to have the Assistance of Counsel for his defence." The plain wording of this guarantee thus encompasses counsel's assistance whenever necessary to assure a meaningful "defence."

As early as *Powell v. Alabama,* we recognized that the period from arraignment to trial was "perhaps the most critical period of the proceedings ..." during which the accused "requires the guiding hand of counsel ..." if the guarantee is not to prove an empty right. ...

[T]he accused is guaranteed that he need not stand alone against the State at any stage of the prosecution, formal or informal, in court or out, where counsel's absence might derogate from the accused's right to a fair trial. The security of that right is as much the aim of the right to counsel as it is of the other guarantees of the Sixth Amendment—the right of the accused to a speedy and public trial by an impartial jury, his right to be informed of the nature and cause of the accusation, and his right to be confronted with the witnesses against him and to have compulsory process for obtaining witnesses in his favor. The presence of counsel at such critical confrontations, as at the trial itself, operates to assure that the accused's interests will be protected consistently with our adversary theory of criminal prosecution.

In sum, the principle of *Powell v. Alabama* and succeeding cases requires that we scrutinize any pretrial confrontation of the accused to determine whether the presence of his counsel is necessary to preserve the defendant's basic right to a fair trial as affected by his right meaningfully to cross-examine the witnesses against him and to have effective assistance of counsel at the trial itself. It calls upon us to analyze whether potential substantial prejudice to defendant's rights inheres in the particular confrontation and the ability of counsel to help avoid that prejudice.

III

The Government characterizes the lineup as a mere preparatory step in the gathering of the prosecution's evidence, not different—for Sixth Amendment purposes—from various other preparatory steps, such as systematized or scientific analyzing of the accused's fingerprints, blood sample, clothing, hair, and the like. We think there are differences which preclude such stages being characterized as critical stages at which the accused has the right to the presence of his counsel. Knowledge of the techniques of science and technology is sufficiently available, and the variables in techniques few enough, that the accused has the opportunity for a meaningful confrontation of the Government's case at trial through the ordinary processes of cross-examination of the Government's expert witnesses and the presentation of the evidence of his own experts. The denial of a right to have his counsel present at such analyses does not therefore violate the Sixth Amendment; they are not critical stages since there is minimal risk that his counsel's absence at such stages might derogate from his right to a fair trial.

IV

But the confrontation compelled by the State between the accused and the victim or witnesses to a crime to elicit identification evidence is peculiarly riddled with innumerable dangers and variable factors which might seriously, even crucially, derogate from a fair trial. The vagaries of eyewitness identification are well-known; the annals of criminal law are rife with instances of mistaken identification. Mr. Justice Frankfurter once said: "What is the worth of identification testimony even when uncontradicted? The identification of strangers is proverbially untrustworthy. The hazards of such testimony are established by a formidable number of instances in the records of English and American trials. These instances are recent—not due to the brutalities of ancient criminal procedure." THE CASE OF SACCO AND VANZETTI 30 (1927). A major factor contributing to the high incidence of miscarriage of justice from mistaken identification has been the degree of suggestion inherent in the manner in which the prosecution presents the suspect to witnesses for pretrial identification. A commentator has observed that "[t]he influence of improper suggestion upon identifying witnesses probably accounts for more miscarriages of justice than any other single factor—perhaps it is responsible for more such errors than all other factors combined." Wall, EYE-WITNESS IDENTIFICATION IN CRIMINAL CASES 26. Suggestion can be created intentionally or unintentionally in many subtle ways. And the dangers for the suspect are particularly grave when the witness's opportunity for observation was insubstantial, and thus his susceptibility to suggestion the greatest.

Moreover, "[i]t is a matter of common experience that, once a witness has picked out the accused at the line-up, he is not likely to go back on his word later on, so that in practice the issue of identity may (in the absence of other relevant evidence) for all practical purposes be determined there and then, before the trial."

The pretrial confrontation for purpose of identification may take the form of a lineup, also known as an "identification parade," or "showup," as in the present case, or presentation of the suspect alone to the witness. It is obvious that risks of suggestion attend either form of confrontation and increase the dangers inhering in eyewitness identification. But as is the case with secret interrogations, there is serious difficulty in depicting what transpires at lineups and other forms of identification confrontations. "Privacy results in secrecy and this in turn results in a gap in our knowledge as to what in fact goes on ..." *Miranda v. Arizona.* For the same reasons, the defense can seldom reconstruct the manner and mode of lineup identification for judge or jury at trial. Those participating in a lineup with the accused may often be police officers; in any event, the participants' names are rarely recorded or divulged at trial. The impediments to an objective observation are increased when the victim is the witness. Lineups are prevalent in rape and robbery prosecutions and present a particular hazard that a victim's understandable outrage may excite vengeful or spiteful motives. In any event, neither witnesses nor lineup participants are apt to be alert for conditions prejudicial to the suspect. And if they were, it would likely be of scant benefit to the suspect since neither witnesses nor lineup participants are likely to be schooled in the detection of suggestive influences. Improper influences may go undetected by a suspect, guilty or not, who experiences the emotional tension which we might expect in one being confronted with potential accusers. Even when he does observe abuse, if he has a criminal record he may be reluctant to take the stand and open up the admission of prior convictions. Moreover any protestations by the suspect of the fairness of the lineup made at trial are likely to be in vain; the jury's choice is between the accused's unsupported version and that of the police officers present. In short, the accused's inability effectively to reconstruct at trial any unfairness that occurred at the lineup may deprive him of his only opportunity meaningfully to attack the credibility of the witness's courtroom identification.

What facts have been disclosed in specific cases about the conduct of pretrial confrontations for identification illustrate both the potential for substantial prejudice to the accused at that stage and the need for its revelation at trial. A commentator provides some striking examples: "In a Canadian case ... the defendant had been picked out of a lineup of six men, of which he was the only Oriental. In other cases, a black-haired suspect was placed among a group of light-haired persons, tall suspects have been made to stand with short nonsuspects, and, in a case where the perpetrator of the crime was known to be a youth, a suspect under twenty was placed in a lineup with five other persons, all of whom were forty or over."

Similarly state reports, in the course of describing prior identifications admitted as evidence of guilt, reveal numerous instances of suggestive procedures, for example, that all in the lineup but the suspect were known to the identifying witness, that the other participants in a lineup were grossly dissimilar in appearance to the suspect, that only the suspect was required to wear distinctive clothing which the culprit allegedly wore, that the witness is told by the police that they have caught the culprit after which the defendant is brought before the witness alone or is viewed in jail, that the suspect is pointed out before or during a lineup, and that the participants in the lineup are asked to try on an article of clothing which fits only the suspect.

The potential for improper influence is illustrated by the circumstances, insofar as they appear, surrounding the prior identifications in the three cases we decide today. In the present case, the testimony of the identifying witnesses elicited on cross-examination revealed that those witnesses were taken to the courthouse and seated in the courtroom to await assembly of the lineup. The courtroom faced on a hallway observable to the witnesses through an open door. The cashier testified that she saw Wade "standing in the hall" within sight of an FBI agent. Five or six other prisoners later appeared in the hall. The vice president testified that he saw a person in the hall in the custody of the agent who "resembled the person that we identified as the one that had entered the bank."

The lineup in *Gilbert [v. California,* a companion case] was conducted in an auditorium in which some 100 witnesses to several alleged state and federal robberies charged to Gilbert made wholesale identifications of Gilbert as the robber in each other's presence, a procedure said to be fraught with dangers of suggestion. And the vice of suggestion created by the identification in *Stovall [v. Denno,* another companion case] was the presentation to the witness of the suspect alone handcuffed to police officers. It is hard to imagine a situation more clearly conveying the suggestion to the witness that the one presented is believed guilty by the police.

The few cases that have surfaced therefore reveal the existence of a process attended with hazards of serious unfairness to the criminal accused and strongly suggest the plight of the more numerous defendants who are unable to ferret out suggestive influences in the secrecy of the confrontation. We do not assume that these risks are the result of police procedures intentionally designed to prejudice an accused. Rather we assume they derive from the dangers inherent in eyewitness identification and the suggestibility inherent in the context of the pretrial identification. Williams & Hammelmann, in one of the most comprehensive studies of such forms of identification, said, "[T]he fact that the police themselves have, in a given case, little or no doubt that the man put up for identification has committed the offense, and that their chief pre-occupation is with the problem of getting sufficient proof, because he has not 'come clean,' involves a danger that this persuasion may communicate itself even in a doubtful case to the witness in some way . . ."

Insofar as the accused's conviction may rest on a courtroom identification in fact the fruit of a suspect pretrial identification which the accused is helpless to subject to effective scrutiny at trial, the accused is deprived of that right of cross-examination which is an essential safeguard to his right to confront the witnesses against him. And even though cross-examination is a precious safeguard to a fair trial, it cannot be viewed as an absolute assurance of accuracy and reliability. Thus in the present context, where so many variables and pitfalls exist, the first line of defense must be the prevention of unfairness and the lessening of the hazards of eyewitness identification at the lineup itself. The trial which might determine the accused's fate may well not be that in the courtroom but that at the pretrial confrontation, with the State aligned against the accused, the witness the sole jury, and the accused unprotected against the overreaching, intentional or unintentional, and with little or no effective appeal from the judgment there rendered by the witness—"that's the man."

Since it appears that there is grave potential for prejudice, intentional or not, in the pretrial lineup, which may not be capable of reconstruction at trial, and since presence of counsel itself can often avert prejudice and assure a meaningful confrontation at trial, there can be little doubt that for Wade the postindictment lineup was a critical stage of the prosecution at which he was "as much entitled to such aid [of counsel] . . . as at the trial itself." Thus both Wade and his counsel should have been notified of the impending lineup, and counsel's presence should have been a requisite to conduct of the lineup, absent an "intelligent waiver." No substantial countervailing policy considerations have been advanced against the requirement of the presence of counsel. Concern is expressed that the requirement will forestall prompt identifications and result in obstruction of the confrontations. As for the first, we note that in the two cases in which the right to counsel is today held to apply, counsel had already been appointed and no argument is made in either case that notice to counsel would have prejudicially delayed the confrontations. Moreover, we leave open the question whether the presence of substitute counsel might not suffice where notification and presence of the suspect's own counsel would result in prejudicial delay. And to refuse to recognize the right to counsel for fear that counsel will obstruct the course of justice is contrary to the basic assumptions upon which this Court has operated in Sixth Amendment cases. We rejected similar logic in *Miranda v. Arizona*, concerning presence of counsel during custodial interrogation:

> [A]n attorney is merely exercising the good professional judgment he has been taught. This is not cause for considering the attorney a menace to law enforcement. He is merely carrying out what he is sworn to do under his oath—to protect to the extent of his ability the rights of his client. In fulfilling this responsibility the attorney plays a vital role in the administration of criminal justice under our Constitution.

In our view counsel can hardly impede legitimate law enforcement; on the contrary, for the reasons expressed, law enforcement may be assisted by preventing the infiltration of taint in the prosecution's identification evidence. That result cannot help the guilty avoid conviction but can only help assure that the right man has been brought to justice.

Legislative or other regulations, such as those of local police departments, which eliminate the risks of abuse and unintentional suggestion at lineup proceedings and the impediments to meaningful confrontation at trial may also remove the basis for regarding the stage as "critical." But neither Congress nor the federal authorities have seen fit to provide a solution. What we hold today "in no way creates a constitutional straitjacket which will handicap sound efforts at reform, nor is it intended to have this effect." *Miranda v. Arizona.*

V

We come now to the question whether the denial of Wade's motion to strike the courtroom identification by the bank witnesses at trial because of the absence of his counsel at the lineup required, as the Court of Appeals held, the grant of a new trial at which such evidence is to be excluded. We do not think this disposition can be justified without first giving the Government the opportunity to establish by clear and convincing evidence that the in-court identifications were based upon observations of the suspect other than the lineup identification. Where, as here, the admissibility of evidence of the lineup identification itself is not involved, a per se rule of exclusion of courtroom identification would be unjustified. A rule limited solely to the exclusion of testimony concerning identification at the lineup itself, without regard to admissibility of the courtroom identification, would render the right to counsel an empty one. The lineup is most often used, as in the present case, to crystallize the witnesses' identification of the defendant for future reference. We have already noted that the lineup identification will have that effect. The State may then rest upon the witnesses' unequivocal courtroom identifications, and not mention the pretrial identification as part of the State's case at trial. Counsel is then in the predicament in which Wade's counsel found himself—realizing that possible unfairness at the lineup may be the sole means of attack upon the unequivocal courtroom identification, and having to probe in the dark in an attempt to discover and reveal unfairness, while bolstering the government witness's courtroom identification by bringing out and dwelling upon his prior identification. Since counsel's presence at the lineup would equip him to attack not only the lineup identification but the courtroom identification as well, limiting the impact of violation of the right to counsel to exclusion of evidence only of identification at the lineup itself disregards a critical element of that right.

We think it follows that the proper test to be applied in these situations is that quoted in *Wong Sun v. United States*: "[W]hether, granting establishment of the primary illegality, the evidence to which instant objection is made has been come at by exploitation of that illegality or instead by means sufficiently distinguishable to be purged of the primary taint." Application of this test in the present context requires consideration of various factors; for example, the prior opportunity to observe the alleged criminal act, the existence of any discrepancy between any pre-lineup description and the defendant's actual description, any identification prior to lineup of another person, the identification by picture of the defendant prior to the lineup, failure to identify the defendant on a prior occasion, and the lapse of time between the alleged act and the lineup identification. It is also relevant to consider those facts which, despite the absence of counsel, are disclosed concerning the conduct of the lineup. . . .

The judgment of the Court of Appeals is vacated and the case is remanded to that court with direction to enter a new judgment vacating the conviction and remanding the case to the District Court for further proceedings consistent with this opinion.

———

NOTES AND QUESTIONS

1. *Wade* established the rule that a defendant has a Sixth Amendment right to the presence of counsel at an in-person lineup (the rule does not, as we will see, extend to photospreads). If no counsel was provided at such a lineup, the lineup results are suppressed at trial.

2. Note that the rule now applies only to the "post-indictment" stage, that is, once adversarial criminal proceedings have begun, for example, by the filing of a criminal complaint. This is so even though the logic of *Wade* might suggest that the right to counsel should apply at any lineup, whether pre or post-indictment. As was established in *Kirby v. Illinois*,[5] however, the right to counsel does not apply before adversarial criminal proceedings have begun (that is, "post-indictment").[6] Consequently, if a robbery suspect is caught fleeing from the scene of a crime, and the victim is brought over to where the suspect is caught, counsel is not necessary if the victim then identifies the defendant at the location, for formal proceedings have not yet begun. Because most identifications occur before adversary proceedings have begun, the right to counsel rarely serves as a basis for suppressing lineup results.

What explains this odd rule? The general rule is that there is a Sixth Amendment right to counsel at every "critical stage" of the prosecution. *Wade* apparently found a lineup to be a "critical stage" because of the dangers of suggestion that might result in an identification that will determine the outcome at trial and because the "presence of counsel itself can often avert prejudice and assure a meaningful confrontation at trial." But in *Kirby* the Court seemed to retreat from this rationale:

> The initiation of judicial criminal proceedings is far from a mere formalism. It is the starting point of our whole system of adversary criminal justice. For it is only then that the government has committed itself to prosecute, and only then that the adverse positions of government and the defendant have solidified. It is then that a defendant finds himself faced with the prosecutorial forces of organized society, and immersed in the intricacies of substantive and procedural criminal law. It is this point, therefore, that marks the commencement of the

———

5. 406 U.S. 682 (1972).

6. The *Kirby* opinion was a plurality opinion written by Justice Stewart and joined by Chief Justice Burger and Justices Blackmun and Rehnquist. Justice Powell concurred only in the result. Justice Brennan filed a dissenting opinion, in which Justices Douglas and Marshall joined, and Justice White filed a separate dissenting opinion. Justice Brennan's dissent phrased the criticism of *Kirby* most strongly. That criticism in a nutshell was this: if *Wade* was designed to reduce the risks of abuse or unintentional suggestion at a lineup, then how is it relevant whether formal adversarial proceedings have begun? The same dangers exist, regardless of the stage of the prosecution.

"criminal prosecutions" to which alone the explicit guarantees of the Sixth Amendment are applicable.

In *Rothgery v. Gillespie County, Texas*, the Court recently considered just how early the Sixth Amendment right "attaches" in a criminal case. There, Rothgery was arrested without a warrant as a felon in possession of a firearm by officers relying on an erroneous record showing that Rothgery was a convicted felon. The police promptly brought Rothgery before a magistrate judge for an "article 15.17 hearing," which, under Texas law, combined the Fourth Amendment *Gerstein* probable cause hearing, the bail determination, and the advising an arrestee of the accusations against him functions. At that hearing, the magistrate judge reviewed an affidavit of probable cause submitted by the officer and, finding probable cause, set bail at $5000, on which Rothgery was readily released upon posting a surety bond. Rothgery's multiple oral and written requests for the appointment of counsel for him as an indigent went ignored, and he was rearrested after a grand jury indicted him on the felon in possession of a weapon charge, this time being unable to post the new higher bail of $15,000, remaining in jail for three weeks. Six months after the article 15.17 hearing, the court finally appointed a lawyer to represent Rothgery. That lawyer quickly gathered and presented to the prosecutor documents showing that Rothgery was not in fact a felon, finally resulting in the dismissal of the charges.

Rothgery brought a civil action under section 1983, title 42, of the United States Code, arguing that he spent unnecessary time in jail because Gillespie County's unwritten policy of denying appointed counsel to indigents out on bond until at least the entry of an information or indictment violated his Sixth Amendment right to counsel. The United States Court of Appeals affirmed the district court's grant of summary judgment in favor of the County, the appellate court concluding that, because prosecutors were unaware of Rothgery's arrest and appearance before the magistrate judge, and there was no evidence that the arresting officer had authority to commit the state to prosecute without the knowledge or involvement of the prosecutor, formal adversarial proceedings had not begun. The state had not, concluded that court, therefore firmly committed itself "to prosecute" Rothgery, so the Sixth Amendment right had not yet attached.

The United States Supreme Court vacated and remanded, holding that the right had indeed attached. The Court rejected the argument that prosecutorial awareness or involvement were relevant to the attachment question, for such a rule would be " 'wholly unworkable and impossible to administer,' "[7] bogging down the courts in prying inquiries into police-prosecutor communications and making the Sixth Amendment right turn on such random events as the day of arrest or the sophistication of the computer intake system. The Court summarized its reasoning thus:

> It is not that the Court of Appeals believed that any such regime would be desirable, but it thought originally that its rule was implied by this

---

7. 128 S.Ct. 2578, 2580 (quoting Escobedo v. Illinois, 378 U.S. 478, 496 (1964) (White, J., dissenting)).

Court's statement that the right attaches when the government has "committed itself to prosecute." *Kirby*, 406 U.S., at 689. The Court of Appeals reasoned that because "the decision not to prosecute is the quintessential function of a prosecutor" under Texas law, 491 F.3d, at 297 (internal quotation marks omitted), the State could not commit itself to prosecution until the prosecutor signaled that it had.

But what counts as a commitment to prosecute is an issue of federal law unaffected by allocations of power among state officials under a State's law, cf. *Moran*, 475 U. S., at 429, n. 3 ("[T]he type of circumstances that would give rise to the right would certainly have a federal definition"), and under the federal standard, an accusation filed with a judicial officer is sufficiently formal, and the government's commitment to prosecute it sufficiently concrete, when the accusation prompts arraignment and restrictions on the accused's liberty to facilitate the prosecution, see *Jackson*, 475 U.S., at 629, n. 3; *Brewer*, 430 15 U.S., at 399; *Kirby, supra*, at 689; see also n. 9, *supra*. From that point on, the defendant is "faced with the prosecutorial forces of organized society, and immersed in the intricacies of substantive and procedural criminal law" that define his capacity and control his actual ability to defend himself against a formal accusation that he is a criminal. *Kirby, supra*, at 689. By that point, it is too late to wonder whether he is "accused" within the meaning of the Sixth Amendment, and it makes no practical sense to deny it. See Grano, *Rhode Island* v. *Innis*: A Need to Reconsider the Constitutional Premises Underlying the Law of Confessions, 17 Am. Crim. L. Rev. 1, 31 (1979) ("[I]t would defy common sense to say that a criminal prosecution has not commenced against a defendant who, perhaps incarcerated and unable to afford judicially imposed bail, awaits preliminary examination on the authority of a charging document filed by the prosecutor, less typically by the police, and approved by a court of law" (internal quotation marks omitted)). All of this is equally true whether the machinery of prosecution was turned on by the local police or the state attorney general. In this case, for example, Rothgery alleges that after the initial appearance, he was "unable to find any employment for wages" because "all of the potential employers he contacted knew or learned of the criminal charge pending against him." Original Complaint in No. 1:04–CV–00456–LY (W.D. Tex., July 15, 2004), p. 5. One may assume that those potential employers would still have declined to make job offers if advised that the county prosecutor had not filed the complaint.[8]

The Court likewise rejected the County's alternative argument that an inquiry is necessary into whether the state in each individual case has committed itself to prosecute, the prosecutor's awareness of or involvement in the case being but one factor in this inquiry. The Court concluded that its precedent expressed " 'no doubt' that the right to counsel attache[s] at the initial appearance," for it is then "when the government has used the judicial machinery to signal a commitment to prosecute...." Although the

---

8. *Id.* at 2588–89.

state may rethink its commitment by not seeking an indictment or by *nolle prossing* (dropping the charges), absent a change of the state's position, "a defendant subject to accusation after initial appearance is headed for trial and needs to get a lawyer working, whether to attempt to avoid that trial or to be ready with a defense when the trial date arrives."[9]

The Court also explained that it was not deciding whether the officer's probable cause affidavit constituted a "complaint" under Texas law, indeed noting that reliance on a particular state's law in answering such federal constitutional questions was unacceptable, for the constitution's meaning cannot be allowed to "founder on the vagaries of the state criminal law, lest the attachment rule be rendered 'utterly vague and unpredictable.'"[10] "What counts," said the Court, is that under the particular circumstances before it the document "filed with the magistrate judge accused Rothgery of committing a particular crime and prompted the judicial officer to take legal action in response (here, to set the terms of bail and order the defendant locked up)."[11] Curiously, while ignoring Texas's law, the Court did deem it relevant to the Sixth Amendment issue, without explaining why, what the practices were in numerous states and other jurisdictions combined, pointedly noting that 43 states, the District of Columbia, and the federal government "take the first step toward appointing counsel 'before, at, or just after initial appearance.'"[12]

The Court emphasized, however, that it was holding only that the Sixth Amendment right in *Rothgery* had "attached," that is, that the time had arrived when the right to counsel kicks in. But that right assures the actual presence of counsel only at "critical stages" of the prosecution, and the Court stated squarely that it simply had not decided whether the article 15.17 hearing was a critical stage, nor had the Court decided whether the six month delay in the state's appointing counsel for Rothgery prejudiced his Sixth Amendment rights or inflicted any cognizable harm. (We will have more to say on "critical stages" after discussing *United States v. Ash* below). Justice Alito, in a concurring opinion joined by Chief Justice Roberts and Justice Scalia, vigorously stressed that he joined the majority opinion solely because of his understanding that it did not address the critical stage question. Justice Thomas dissented on the ground that the original meaning of the Sixth Amendment would not have attached the right at all at so early a stage of the case. Chief Justice Roberts, in a concurring opinion joined by Justice Scalia, declared that Thomas's dissent was "compelling" but that a sufficient case had not been made out to revisit clear precedent supporting the majority decision.

3. The *Wade* rule may result not merely in the suppression of the lineup but also of an in-court identification that is the fruit of the illegal lineup. In common sense terms, the question is whether the in-court identification is

---

9.   *Id.* at 2590.

10.   *Id.* at 2584 n. 9 (quoting Virginia v. Moore, 553 U.S. 164 (2008)).

11.   *Id.*

12.   *Id.* at 2580.

really the result of an independent recollection of what the wrongdoer looked like or is instead a recollection of his appearance at the tainted, uncounseled lineup procedure. In the words of the *Wade* Court, did the in-court identification have an "independent origin" from the uncounseled lineup? The factors to be considered in answering this question are listed in the next-to-the last paragraph of the reproduced portions of the *Wade* opinion above. The prosecutor has the burden of proving by clear and convincing evidence that, based upon these factors, the in-court identification is not tainted by the uncounseled out-of-court identification.

B. PHOTOSPREADS

In *United States v. Ash*,[13] the Court held that there was no Sixth Amendment right to counsel at a photospread, even if the procedure takes place after indictment. A photospread, held the Court, is not a "critical stage" of the prosecution. Apparently once again redefining *Wade*, the Court held that the purpose of a lawyer at an identification procedure is to act as a spokesperson or advisor, to help the accused cope with the intricacies of the law and the inequality inherent in trial-like confrontations. Because the accused is not present at a photospread, he cannot then receive advice and is not involved in a "trial like" confrontation. Nowhere in its opinion did the Court in *Ash* address the psychological research studies concerning suggestive identifications. The focus of *Wade* on preventing such suggestion, except perhaps in the most egregious of cases, seemed to be forgotten.

In *dicta* in *Rothgery v. Gillespie County Texas,* discussed above, the Court more recently offered this definition: "what makes a stage critical is what shows the need for counsel's presence."[14] This statement might suggest yet a third variation on the meaning of the term "critical stage": the first being *United States v. Wade's* focus on the potential for counsel's absence at a pretrial event prejudicing the trial outcome and eliminating the opportunity for meaningful confrontation of witnesses at trial; the second being *Ash's* focus on the need for a lawyer to serve as a spokesperson or advisor; and the third being *Rothgery's* focus on the simple "need for counsel's presence." But, immediately after mentioning this "need" test, the *Rothgery* Court dropped this footnote seemingly reaffirming the *Ash* approach:

> The cases have defined critical stages as proceedings between an individual and agents of the State (whether "formal or informal, in court or out," see *United States* v. *Wade*, 388 U.S. 218, 226 (1967)) that amount to "trial-like confrontations," at which counsel would help the accused "in coping with legal problems or . . . meeting his adversary," *United States* v. *Ash*, 413 U.S. 300, 312–313 (1973); see also *Massiah* v. *United States*, 377 U.S. 201 (1964).

---

13.   413 U.S. 300 (1973).

14.   Id. at 19.

Justice Alito, in his concurrence, joined by Chief Justice Roberts and Justice Scalia, stressed that the Sixth Amendment right is a *trial* right, for the word "defence" in that Amendment "means defense at trial, not defense in relation to other objectives that may be important to the accused."[15] For example, noted Alito, the Court, in his view, had rejected the argument that the assistance of counsel was needed at a *Gerstein* Fourth Amendment hearing, which focuses more on pretrial custody than on trial rights, and had rejected "the notion that the right to counsel entitles the defendant to a 'preindictment private investigator.' "[16] Alito conceded, however, that "certain pretrial events may so prejudice the outcome of the defendant's prosecution that, as a practical matter, the defendant must be represented at those events in order to enjoy genuinely effective assistance at trial." But Alito made some final comments both about what constitutes a critical stage and about how much time before a critical stage counsel must be appointed:

> Weaving together these strands of authority, I interpret the Sixth Amendment to require the appointment of counsel only after the defendant's prosecution has begun, and then only as necessary to guarantee the defendant effective assistance at trial. Cf. *McNeil*, 501 U.S., at 177–178 ("The purpose of the Sixth Amendment counsel guarantee—and hence the purpose of invoking it—is to protec[t] the unaided layman at critical confrontations with his expert adversary, the government, *after* the adverse positions of government and defendant have solidified with respect to a particular alleged crime" (emphasis and alteration in original; internal quotation marks omitted)). It follows that defendants in Texas will not necessarily be entitled to the assistance of counsel within some specified period after their magistrations. See *ante,* at 19 (opinion of the Court) (pointing out the "analytical mistake" of assuming "that attachment necessarily requires the occurrence or imminence of a critical stage"). Texas counties need only appoint counsel as far in advance of trial, and as far in advance of any pretrial "critical stage," as necessary to guarantee effective assistance at trial. Cf. *ibid.* ("[C]ounsel must be appointed within a reasonable time after attachment *to allow for adequate representation at any critical stage before trial, as well as at trial itself*" (emphasis added)).[17]

To Summarize: (1) The Sixth Amendment right to counsel "attaches" when "formal adversarial proceedings have begun," thus telling us when the right governs; (2) Once we know that the time for its applications has arrived, what it protects, however, is the presence of counsel at trial or at a pretrial "critical stage"; (3) even at a critical stage, however, a defendant may knowingly, intelligently, and voluntarily waive his Sixth Amendment right to counsel (as we discussed in the interrogations chapter); and, (4) as we will see in a later chapter, what is provided at trial and at a critical stage is merely the "effective assistance" of counsel, not the best counsel

---

15. *Id*. at 4 (Alito, J., concurring).

16. *Id*. at 4 (Alito, J., concurring) (citing United States v. Gouveia, 467 U.S. 180 (1984)).

17. *Id*. at 5–6 (Alito, J., concurring).

imaginable—indeed, a level of competence that, in the view of some commentators, is far below what professionalism requires. There is, however, also some ambiguity about the meaning of "formal adversarial proceedings," "critical stage," and "effective assistance" and some apparent disagreement about their meaning among the Justices.

Query:

(1) How should the lower courts decide the question whether the article 15.17 hearing in *Rothgery* was a "critical stage" upon remand? Do the majority opinion and Justice Alito's concurrence lead to different results? Do *Wade* and *Ash* help you in answering this question?

(2) If the police held a lineup during the six month period before Rothgery was appointed counsel, would the absence of counsel at that lineup violate Rothgery's Sixth Amendment right to counsel? Would your answer change if the police conducted a photospread instead of a lineup? A showup?

C. Role of Counsel at a Lineup or Photospread

A close reading of *Wade* suggests a passive role for defense counsel. Counsel may observe and, by his presence, may discourage police from introducing suggestion. But nothing in *Wade* suggests that there is a right of counsel to be heard on whether the identification procedure should be changed to be less suggestive. On the other hand, *Wade* clearly does not prohibit a lawyer from making suggestions to the police to improve the procedure, and in many jurisdictions, precisely to protect the value of the lineup as a powerful piece of evidence, the police will often follow many of a defense lawyer's reasonable suggestions. There is the danger, of course, that a lawyer who is too passive and does not even voice his objections may be deemed to have waived his client's right to object.[18] Moreover, to be effective, counsel must be well-versed in the relevant psychological literature.

Wade and its progeny significantly reduced the chance of an attorney's affecting the suggestiveness of an identification procedure, however, precisely because an attorney's presence is rarely required. There is no right to counsel at a photospread, nor is there a right to counsel at a pre-indictment lineup. The attorney's absence hamstrings him in challenging the pretrial identification at trial. He must rely on the untrained recollections of his client, who he may not want to put on the stand, and the biased recollections of the officers.

The data also suggest that many attorneys are less effective on cross-examination than they might otherwise be precisely because of their inadequate knowledge of the psychological research. Moreover, because eyewitness recollections of the event itself are often imprecise, a cross-examiner should seek concrete responses—for example, asking a witness to

---

18. *Compare* Gilligan, *Eyewitness Identification*, 58 Mil. L. Rev. 183, 201 (1972), with Panel Discussion, *The Role of a Defense Lawyer at a Lineup in Light of the* Wade, Gilbert, *and* Stovall *Decisions*, 4 Crim. L. Bull. 273, 290 (1968).

point out a distance in the courtroom and then measuring it, rather than asking the witness verbally to estimate her distance from her attacker.

III.   UNNECESSARY SUGGESTIVENESS

There is a second constitutional protection surrounding eyewitness identifications: the due process clause requires the suppression of any out-of-court identification that, based upon the totality of the circumstances, was so unnecessarily suggestive as to create a very substantial likelihood of misidentification.[19] If an out-of-court identification fails this test, any later in-court identification must also be suppressed if, based upon the totality of the circumstances, the out-of-court identification was so unnecessarily suggestive as to create a very substantial likelihood of irreparable misidentification. The two standards are thus very similar, except that the standard for suppressing the in-court identification adds the word "irreparable." The Court has never made clear how, if at all, the addition of the word "irreparable" changes the legal test.

A.   WHAT IS UNNECESSARY SUGGESTIVENESS?

First, there must be some kind of suggestion. Some examples of suggestion have already been discussed above—for example, if the suspect is a foot taller than everyone else in a lineup. Other typical types of suggestion to avoid are differences in race or gender; a statement by the police that the perpetrator is indeed in the lineup; or the presence of two witnesses at the lineup together so that the second witness sees who the first witness identifies. Some differences in appearance are, however, unavoidable, and, so long as "a reasonable effort to harmonize the lineup" is made, suggestion will likely not be found.

But it is not enough that there be suggestion. The suggestion must be "unnecessary." Thus in *Stovall v. Denno*,[20] a black male was handcuffed to one of five white police officers, all of whom entered the hospital room of a woman who was an eyewitness to the stabbing murder of her husband and a victim of a stabbing herself. The woman had just undergone potentially life-saving surgery. While there clearly was suggestion inherent in this procedure, the Court found the suggestion to be "necessary." No one knew how long the victim might live. There was thus a need for immediate action, and the victim was in no condition to visit the jail for a lineup. Under these emergency circumstances, the suggestive one-person showup

---

19.   Neil v. Biggers, 409 U.S. 188, 198 (1972) (where there is unnecessary suggestiveness, a subsequent in-court identification is inadmissible only if there is " 'a very substantial likelihood of irreparable misidentification,' and 'with the deletion of irreparable, [that test] . . . serves equally well as a standard for the admissibility of testimony concerning the out-of-court identification itself' ") (quoting in part Simmons v. United States 390 U.S. 377, 384 (1968)); *accord* Manson v. Brathwaite, 432 U.S. 98, 107, 109–14 (1977) (rejecting a per se rule and reaffirming the *Biggers* analysis).

20.   388 U.S. 293 (1967).

was the "only feasible procedure" and, therefore, the due process clause was not violated.

While the Court in *Stovall* treated "necessity" as "urgency," less dire circumstances may also justify suggestive procedures. For example, in *Simmons v. United States*,[21] the Court concluded that using photo arrays, instead of some other less suggestive identification procedure, one day after a gunpoint robbery, was necessary. The Court reasoned that:

> [a] serious felony had been committed. The perpetrators were still at large. The inconclusive clues which law enforcement officials possessed led to Andrews and Simmons. It was essential for the FBI agents swiftly to determine whether they were on the right track, so that they could properly deploy their forces in Chicago and, if necessary, alert officials in other cities.

The scope of the *Simmons* notion that suggestion may be necessary to determine whether the police are "on the right track" is uncertain. It is important to note, however, that the Court's discussion of necessity was directed to whether it was necessary to use the particular type of identification procedure—a photo array instead of a lineup. But the Court emphasized that each photo array, while not perfect, involved at least six photographs, with each witness being alone while viewing the photographs, and with no evidence that the FBI suggested which persons shown were under suspicion. The pressing need to conduct identifications by photo arrays did not in turn make it "necessary" that those photo arrays be conducted in a suggestive manner. Thus, the Court might have held that there was unnecessary suggestiveness if the police had been sloppy or careless in the manner in which they conducted the arrays, for example, by using only one or two photographs or declaring that "the perpetrators are probably in these photos."

Indeed, since *Simmons*, the Court has made it clear that the police are expected to make reasonable efforts to render lineups fair and that the technical difficulty of organizing fair lineups does not make the resulting suggestion "necessary." For example, in *Neil v. Biggers*,[22] the Court held that a showup was unnecessarily suggestive, despite the police finding no one at either the city jail or the juvenile home on the date of the identification procedure who fit a physical description comparable to the defendant's. The Court cited with approval the district court's opinion on this point: "In this case it appears to the Court that a lineup, which both sides admit is generally more reliable than a showup, could have been arranged. The fact that this was not done tended needlessly to decrease the fairness of the identification process to which petitioner was subjected."[23]

---

21. 390 U.S. 377 (1968).

22. 409 U.S. 188 (1972).

23. *Id.* at 199 n.6 (quoting lower court's opinion). *See also* Wayne LaFave & Jerold Israel, Criminal Procedure 462 (2d ed. 1985) (rejecting notion that "accidental" suggestion by the police renders the suggestion "necessary"); *cf.* Alpert and Smith, *Law Enforcement Defensibility of Law Enforcement Training*, 26 Crim. L. Bull. 452 (October 1990) (generally

B.   LIKELIHOOD OF MISIDENTIFICATION

Even unnecessarily suggestive pretrial identification procedures are admissible if the court is convinced that the witness had a reliable independent basis for the out-of-court identification. Thus a witness who observed a robber in bright light for twenty minutes and who gave an excellent detailed description of the robber to the police probably had a reliable independent basis for selecting the defendant from a visual lineup that was conducted one day after the crime, even though there was some unnecessary suggestion that he do so. Reliability is thus the "linchpin" of the analysis.

In *Manson v. Brathwaite*,[24] the Court articulated some of the factors to be considered in determining whether an unnecessarily suggestive identification was in fact reliable:

> the opportunity of the witness to view the criminal at the time of the crime, the witness' degree of attention, the accuracy of his prior description of the criminal, the level of certainty demonstrated at the confrontation, and the time between the crime and the confrontation. Against these factors must be weighed the corrupting effect of the suggestive identification itself.

> These same factors should be considered in determining the reliability of an in-court identification that is alleged to be the fruit of an unnecessarily suggestive out-of-court identification.

C.   REVIEW PROBLEMS

PROBLEM 10–1

Connie Hernandez was lying in her bed at 10:30 p.m. when she heard voices, speaking Spanish, in her living room. She ran into the living room and saw three men surrounding her husband. Two of the men had guns pointed at Ms. Hernandez' husband and one man had a knife. One of the gunman wore a beanie covering his hair and ears. The other gunman wore no hat or mask, and the man holding the knife wore a face mask. A bright living room light was on. When Ms. Hernandez' six-year-old child started crying, she asked for and received permission to go into the bedroom and comfort him. The gunman wearing the beanie accompanied her, and she said to her child in English, "Go out the window and ask the neighbors to call the police because there are three men here who want to hurt us. Go!" The assailant did not react. Ms. Hernandez returned to the living room to find her husband lying in a pool of blood and his wallet gone.

---

discussing the many ways in which the complexities of constitutionally-mandated procedures can be followed by the police, even if an expert must be retained to train the officers). Professor Taslitz has argued that this notion of police making reasonable efforts to render lineups fair requires them to retain properly trained experts. *See* Andrew E. Taslitz, *Does the Cold Nose Know? The Unscientific Myth of the Dog Scent Lineup*, 42 HASTINGS L.J. 15, 98–99 (1990).

24.   432 U.S. 98 (1977).

Defendant, Julio Marquez, was arrested based on the identification in a photo array by a neighbor who had seen the robbers leaving Ms. Hernandez' home. Marquez was placed in a lineup, two days after the robbery. Ms. Hernandez identified Marquez as the gunman wearing the beanie.

At a suppression hearing, Marquez testified that he did not speak any English and had trouble understanding the Spanish spoken by the interpreter. He claimed that he simply followed the example of the other participants. On cross-examination, a detective present at the lineup conceded that Marquez looked confused when receiving the first few commands and generally followed commands slowly, after the other lineup participants had complied. All had been told, however, not to move until the commands were spoken in both English and Spanish. Furthermore, in the detective's words, "All six participants were Hispanic males of medium height and slender build, but their facial features were distinctive."

Question: Should the motion to suppress be granted?

PROBLEM 10–2

George Green was on trial for sexually assaulting five-year-old Sandy Butterfield. Sandy has testified at trial that a man had put his "toy" in her. However, Sandy was asked seven times whether she was able to identify him and not once could she do so. An in-chambers conference was thereafter held during which the prosecution requested an in-court lineup. The request was granted. While the in-chambers conference was being held, Sandy had this conversation with her father:

[FATHER]: Did you see George here? Why didn't you tell them? Are you scared of him?

[SANDY]: Yes (starting to cry).

This conversation was revealed to the prosecutor after the in-chambers conference, and he promptly revealed the conversation to the trial judge and defense counsel. The lineup nevertheless proceeded over defense objection. The lineup consisted of seven men, including Sandy's father. Six men were arranged in a line in Sandy's presence. The seventh, Green, was added after Sandy left the courtroom. When Sandy was brought back into the room, the following conversation took place:

[COURT]: Now, I want you to just lead her up to the middle of the courtroom about ten or fifteen feet near those men and, young lady, you said a man put his toy in you, did you say that?

[SANDY]: Yes.

[COURT]: All we want you to do, and all we are asking you to do is to go up there and let us know who it is, if any of them. Can you point to the man?

[THE STATE]: Would you point to him, honey, point right to him.

Further evidence at trial revealed that Green had babysat for Sandy on two occasions about one year before the alleged incident, and Sandy described the incident as taking a "very long time." Green was convicted.

Question: Should the conviction be reversed on appeal?

PROBLEM 10–3

John Jackson was robbed at gunpoint while working at Sovern Bank. The robber wore no mask, and the bank was brightly lit. The robber approached John, who was behind the teller's cage, and said, "Give me all the money." While staring at the robber the whole time, John opened the cash register door and gave the money to the robber, who then fled.

John contacted the police and described the robber as a white male, with blond hair, about 5 feet, 11 inches tall, wearing blue jeans and black, low-top sneakers and a blue sweater.

About 10 minutes after the robbery, two police officers saw Jonathan Schultz walking down a street about five blocks from the bank. Jonathan was blond, about 5 feet, 9 inches tall, wearing faded blue jeans and black, low-top sneakers. He wore a white T-shirt. However, he also had what looked like a light blue shirt wrapped around his waist. The officers stopped him and told him they were taking him to Sovern Bank to be viewed as a suspect in a bank robbery.

When they arrived at the bank, Schultz was asked to remove the blue shirt wrapped around his waist and put the shirt on. He did so and, for the first time, the officers saw that his blue jeans were stained with red dye, which the officers knew had been placed in the stolen money in a dye-bomb set to explode shortly after the money was stolen.

John Jackson was asked, "Do you recognize this guy?" (No other suspects were present). John replied, "Yes, I'd know that face anywhere. He's the robber."

Question: Should the identification be suppressed? What about any subsequent in-court identification?

PROBLEM 10–4

A young white male came into Brenda Winton's grocery store at 3 p.m. He spent three minutes looking around the store and left. He returned twenty minutes later, bought a beer from Brenda Winton, made small talk with her about the weather for about five minutes, and then produced a gun and demanded all her money, which she gave to him.

Later that day, Ms. Winton viewed a photo array consisting of ten photographs. All the photos were of young, blond, white males, with slender features. A photo of defendant, Harold Buckingham, was in the array. However, Ms. Winton picked a different photo and said, "I'm sure that's the man." The photo was of George Manson.

At a lineup held the next day, however, a lineup that included both George Manson and Harold Buckingham, Ms. Winton identified Mr. Buckingham and said, "I'm 100% sure he's the man. I know that the guy I picked out yesterday is in the line, but I was wrong. They look so different in person." Defendant Buckingham was taller by four inches than anyone else in the line but otherwise everyone in the line of was similar build, coloring, and appearance.

Question: Should the identification be suppressed? What about any subsequent in-court identification?

PROBLEM 10–5

In the Boson case in Chapter 1, what arguments might you raise to suppress any pre-trial or trial identifications, and what are your chances of succeeding?

D. Suppression Hearing Role-Playing Exercise Assignment

Your instructor may assign you to a role-playing exercise having to do with an eyewitness identification. You will be given written materials to review, including secret instructions. Your preparation should include interviewing any witnesses, outlining direct and cross-examination of witnesses, and outlining a closing argument for the suppression motion. Defense counsel may be required to draft a written suppression motion.

Note on Prosecutorial Ethics: In preparing for the suppression hearing, keep in mind the dictates of Model Rule of Professional Conduct 3.8: "[a] prosecutor has the responsibility of a minister of justice and not simply that of an advocate. This responsibility carries with it specific obligations to see that the defendant is accorded procedural justice and that guilt is decided upon the basis of sufficient evidence." How, if at all, does this statement affect your preparation for, and conduct of, the suppression hearing? Remember too the rules governing "candor toward the tribunal" and "fairness to opposing party and counsel," and make sure that you conduct the hearing in accordance with those rules. Additionally, note that:

> A prosecutor should not discourage or obstruct communication between prospective witnesses and defense counsel. It is unprofessional conduct for the prosecutor to advise any person or cause any person to be advised to decline to give to the defense information which such person has the right to give.[25]

Note on Defense Ethics: Defense counsel should, of course, also remember the rules on candor toward the tribunal and fairness to opposing

---

25. ABA, Standards Relating to the Administration of Criminal Justice, Prosecution Function, Standard 3–3.1(c).

counsel. Note too that defense counsel, in an obligation similar to that imposed on the prosecution, should "not discourage or obstruct communication between prospective witnesses and the prosecutor," nor may defense counsel advise any person other than a client to refuse to give to the prosecutor information that such person has a right to give.[26] Additionally, defense counsel should not use means that "have no substantial purpose other than to embarrass, delay or burden a third person, or use methods of obtaining evidence that violate the legal rights of such person."[27] Finally, act on this admonition:

> Unless defense counsel is prepared to forgo impeachment of a witness by counsel's own testimony as to what the witness stated in an interview or to seek leave to withdraw from the case in order to present such impeaching testimony, defense counsel should avoid interviewing a prospective witness except in the presence of a third person.[28]

Is a similar obligation imposed on the prosecution?

IV.   DOG SCENT IDENTIFICATIONS

Not all lineups are done by human beings. Another form of lineup is the dog scent lineup. In a dog scent lineup, "a dog sniffs an object imbued with a scent known to be from a wrongdoer and then sniffs a line of either objects or people."[29] "If the dog 'alerts'—that is, barks at, sniffs and paws at, sits near, or mouths a suspect, or an object touched by a suspect, the 'alert,' in the form of an alleged match of the object's scent with that of the suspect, is admitted as substantive evidence that the person committed the crime."[30] Thousands of people have been subjected to dog scent lineups, and some have been sentenced to life imprisonment or even death.

The dog scent lineup is of interest because it once again points out the value of science to a criminal practitioner. Attached is an excerpt from an article by Professor Taslitz. The excerpt discusses the dangers of suggestion inherent in such a lineup and ways to minimize those dangers. Read the excerpt and then discuss the problem that follows it.

----

26.   ABA, Standards Relating to the Administration of Criminal Justice, Defense Function, Standard 4–4.3(c).

27.   *Id.*, Standard 4–4.3(a).

28.   *Id.*, Standard 4–4.3.

29.   Annotation, *Dog Scent Discrimination Lineups*, 63 A.L.R. 4th 143 (1988 & Supp. 1989). This annotation distinguishes between a "people lineup," in which the dog identifies the person in a line whose scent the dog determines matches that of an object, and an "inanimate object" lineup, in which a dog uses its scent to identify one object in a line of many objects and determines that it matches that of a particular person.

30.   *See, e.g.*, Sandy Bryson, SEARCH DOG TRAINING 302 (1988) (defining "alert"); United States v. McNiece, 558 F.Supp. 612, 613 (E.D.N.Y.1983) (lineup "alert" admitted as substantive evidence of identity).

Does the Cold Nose Know? The Unscientific Myth of the Dog Scent Lineup

Andrew E. Taslitz[31]

... Frederick Buytendijk has noted several canine behaviors, displayed even by well-trained police dogs, that must be kept in mind in designing a fair dog scent lineup. These behaviors include, among others: (1) a dog is more likely to select an object at the end of a row; (2) a dog will stop sniffing objects in a line—he will sniff no further—once he reaches an object that, to him, has a "special" smell; (3) a dog often will select an object with a "similar" but not identical smell to the object upon which the dog was scented—for example, odors from the same group, such as all tar smells, will be "matched"; (4) a dog often chooses an object because of visible characteristics instead of scent; and (5) a dog may choose the object that the trainer wants the dog to select, a desire that Buytendijk suggested might be conveyed to the dog by slight differences in the trainer's tone of voice but which, of course, also can be conveyed by other minimal cues. Although Buytendijk described his own experiments as yielding "very satisfactory results," he cautioned that the combination of these five (and other) behavioral tendencies establishes that lineup results "can never attain the degree of certainty that is necessary before condemning a human being."

Buytendijk recounts the following experiment to demonstrate the dangers inherent in dog scent lineups:

> In the police station there was a suspect. The officials wanted to find out whether a coat (a) which had been found somewhere belonged to this man, and the experiment was carried out in the following way. Six coats were placed in the passage, the coat (a) and five belonging to the office clerks. The dog was allowed to sniff at the suspected man, and it brought back coat (a). Such a test proves nothing. In any case that particular coat would have a different smell-complex from those of the five clerks. Let us imagine that smells are visible—then the dog, for example, would see five grey coats and one bright red one before it. The chances that the one that looked so prominent would be chosen are very great. Only when all the objects belong to the same odor-group and are also alike to the eye as far as size and shape are concerned, can there be a chance of trustworthy results.
>
> It is still more dangerous to let a dog choose a person out of a row of people on the score of the odor of an object offered to the dog. Even if the trainer knows nothing about the test, and has himself no suspicion of anybody, there still remains the possibility, by no means a slight one, that the dog may respond to the faintest movement of one of these persons.
>
> Since Buytendijk wrote these words, there has been little research to challenge his conclusions on the dangers of dog scent lineups. What

---

31. *See* Taslitz, *Cold Nose, supra* note 23, at 102–07.

has been challenged, however, is whether those dangers can, indeed, be controlled so that a fair dog scent lineup is possible.

de Bruin and Koster have designed techniques for conducting scent lineups that appear to address many of the concerns Buytendijk expressed. They suggest three different lineup methods, which are discussed seriatim below.

The first is a variation on the classic person lineup. All the persons participating in the lineup must stand behind a screen of horizontal slats so that the dog cannot see the lineup participants. This approach controls for minimal cues from those in the line. Fans are sometimes placed behind the screen to ensure that the scent reaches the dog's nostrils. All participants must come from the same environment and must not wear "strong smelling clothes." If the participants are not all from the same environment, they all wear similar clean overalls for two hours before the lineup.

Neither the dog nor the handler is present when the persons are placed in the line. Indeed, although the handler gives the dog the scent, the dog enters the lineup room without the handler, again eliminating minimal cues. If the dog finds a matching scent, the dog sits down at that lineup participant. The procedure is repeated twice, with the participants changing positions each time.

In de Bruin's tests, the suspect's position is selected either by the suspect or by lot; the better practice might be to increase the size of the line and never place the suspect at either end because of the dog's tendency to select items at the end of a line. Of course, if the screen keeps the dog from seeing where the line ends, this concern may be unwarranted.

An alternative procedure proposed by de Bruin involves the use of eighteen glass jars, each containing stainless steel tubes. The six participants wash their hands with the same odorless soap, then dry their hands with a clean piece of paper towel so that smells additional to human scent are equal for all. The participants hold three tubes in their hands for five minutes, and these tubes are returned to the jars. Next, a person other than the dog handler then puts the tubes on the floor of a special room, taking care not to touch them. Again, neither the dog nor the handler is present during this procedure. The handler gives the order "search," and the dog then sniffs the tubes and selects the one, if any, that matches the scent given to the dog earlier. The test is repeated twice with previously unused tubes used in each new experiment. A positive match is declared only if the dog makes a positive identification of the suspect's tube on each of the three tries. The handler is not present in the special room at the time that the lineup is actually performed. The position of the suspect is determined as with the person lineup described above, but since the dog can see the tubes, it might be wiser for the procedure to be modified by not placing the suspect's tube at the end of the line, perhaps compensating for the reduced variation by increasing the number of participants in the lineup.

This procedure has an advantage over the in-person lineup because the only scent on the tube is human body scent. The scents of clothing, shoes, and other sources are not present.

A variation on the tube method involves the use of cloths. A special sterilized cloth may be used to wipe an object found at a crime scene such as a gun. The cloth is placed in a glass jar for storage. Instead of holding tubes in their hands, lineup participants hold similar cloths; otherwise the tube lineup procedures are followed. The advantage of this method over the tube method is that the gun can be wiped of scent, the scent stored, and the gun then sent to a forensics laboratory.

In each of the above-described methods, the dogs used in the lineups were specially trained in dog scent lineups for at least eighteen months. A trainer-handler team is approved for work on actual cases only if the team has a success rate with known matches of ninety-five percent. In their training, the dogs used also must have proven that they are capable of "negative identification," that is, of not selecting anyone if there is no scent match in the lineup. As a consequence, the dogs are trained only to signal a match if an identical, and not merely a similar, scent is found within the line.

In addition, if at any time during the three lineups that include the suspect's scent the dog's identification appears to be "hesitant," de Bruin's technique calls for a series of five lineups that includes two negative identification tests (or two lineups in which the suspect does not partici-pate). A match is declared only if the dog identifies the suspect in each lineup in which the suspect's scent is present and identifies no one in each lineup in which the suspect's scent is absent. This procedure increases the likelihood that matches are derived from identical and not merely similar scents. A further improvement, however, would be to require the use of the five-lineup negative identification procedure in all cases, rather than allow-ing the decision to conduct negative identification lineups to depend on the handler's subjective judgment that the dog has made a "hesitant" identifi-cation.

Some variation on de Bruin's procedures seems well-suited to creating a fair dog scent lineup. Although he is working on a book that will address these matters, de Bruin has not yet published the details of his research and training methods. It is therefore impossible to know precisely how he trains his dogs or whether his research results are reliable. Once the results are available, however, their replication and the confirmation of their reliability by researchers in the United States may well suggest that fair lineup procedures are possible.

Although de Bruin's suggestions may go far towards creating a fairer scent lineup procedure, his suggestions are not perfect. Thus, he apparently does not account for and control variations in scent resulting from the accused's diet. It may, of course, turn out that dietary differences are unimportant but this must be experimentally verified. For example, if everyone but person "A" in a lineup eats the same garlic-free food while "A" eats garlic, yet in repeated lineups the dog always chooses non-garlic-eater "B" (who is the correct match) and in several negative identification trials that exclude "B" but include "A" the dog does not react at all, that should be strong evidence that the garlic does not affect the dog's reliability. Yet de Bruin reports no such experiments.

One other aspect of de Bruin's experiments requires particularly close examination. He maintains that his experiments have proven effective with scent stored for as long as three years. Indeed, he has begun a scent bank in which scent is taken from suspects arrested and stored or kept "on file." If a new crime is committed, a scent lineup can be done using the stored scents. The concept is very similar to fingerprinting all persons arrested and later using those prints in fingerprint comparisons.

If, as previously noted, human scent consists of vapors released from bacterial action, it is difficult to understand how a scent can be stored for so long without the bacteria dying. Brigadier de Bruin apparently theorizes that his special cloth, when stored in a glass container, can retain scent for very long periods and that his experiments prove this. If he is right, the bacterial action theory of human scent may need to be reexamined. Without further research, however, it is impossible to know whether he is right and thus whether, and under what circumstances, fair lineups are possible.

———

PROBLEM 10–6

Your client, Johnny Olssen, has been arrested on a rape charge. Three lineups were held. In one, there was a line of five blue shirts, four of which belonged to the husband of the secretary to the police chief. The fifth shirt, the victim's and the one identified by the dog as having a scent matching the defendant's (that is, the dog sniffed the defendant, then sniffed the shirts, and alerted at shirt number five), was the only shirt that had been worn by a female and the only shirt with blood on it. The second lineup involved five knives, only one of which—the knife found in the victim and later matched by the dog to the defendant—had blood on it. In the third lineup, the dog again sniffed the shirt worn by the victim during the rape and then sniffed a line consisting of four police officers and our client. Again, your client was identified. The lineups were conducted by a dog handler with some training in how to conduct dog scent lineups.

Question: What arguments would you raise at a motion to suppress these lineups? Does the case law that we have reviewed help you? What additional information might you try to solicit from the handler who conducted the lineup? As defense counsel, what might you ask the handler on cross-examination? Would you seek to call any witnesses of your own? Who, and why, and what would you ask them?

V.   Other Constitutional Issues

A.   Fifth Amendment

Remember that the Fifth Amendment declares that "[n]o person shall be compelled in any criminal case to be a witness against himself. . . ." Are you a witness against yourself if you are forced to appear in a lineup? The answer is no. The amendment "does not protect a suspect from being compelled by the State to provide real or physical evidence."[32] The reason for this is that the amendment extends solely to a suspect's being compelled to testify against himself or otherwise provide the State with evidence of a "testimonial or communicative nature." Placing yourself in a lineup is not of a testimonial or communicative nature because it does not compel you "to disclose any knowledge . . . [you] might have."[33]

Similarly, therefore, a suspect may be compelled to provide a blood sample, a handwriting exemplar, or a voice exemplar.

B. Fourth Amendment

Can you be picked up on the street on suspicion of a crime, taken down to a police station, and forced to stand in a lineup? Such an action is unquestionably a seizure within the meaning of the Fourth Amendment and, as discussed earlier in this text, is generally considered a full-blown arrest. Consequently, logic suggests that such action on suspicion, indeed on any level of belief in guilt short of probable cause, should be unconstitutional. Nevertheless, the Court has suggested that forced participation in a lineup on reasonable suspicion may be acceptable if the police first obtain judicial authorization.[34]

---

32. Pennsylvania v. Muniz, 496 U.S. 582, 589 (1990).

33. *Wade*, 388 U.S. at 222.

34. The suggestion came in Davis v. Mississippi, 394 U.S. 721 (1969), in which the Court held that officers acted improperly in rounding up and fingerprinting numerous black youths after a report of a rape victim who could offer little in the way of description of her attacker. Nevertheless, the Court left open the possibility that a court might authorize an identification procedure on something less than probable cause.

CHAPTER 11

THE RIGHT TO COUNSEL

- THE *STRICKLAND* TEST   • WORKLOAD ISSUES

I. INTRODUCTION

No book taking "a lawyering perspective" as a central theme would be complete without a chapter on the right to counsel. That right serves several important functions. First, counsel's presence can improve the likelihood of accurate factfinding. For example, coerced and therefore arguably unreliable confessions are less likely if a suspect is questioned in his lawyer's presence. Similarly, counsel can seek to correct suggestive lineup procedures. If the police ignore counsel's criticisms, he is better equipped to cross-examine officers about the flawed procedures at trial. Counsel can, at any hearing or trial, more effectively examine witnesses than can a defendant untrained in the law.

Second, counsel helps to improve the actual and perceived fairness of the procedures, for counsel's knowledge of the law and of fact-finding procedures enables him or her to ensure that the tribunal is as fully informed of the law and facts as the law permits. Counsel's pretrial role is essential in protecting an accused's fair trial rights, for as the Court in *Powell v. Alabama* declared: "[t]he most critical period of the proceedings ... [is] from the time of ... arraignment until the beginning of ... trial when consultation, thorough-going investigation and preparation [are] vitally important."[1]

Third, counsel's presence helps to equalize the contest between prosecution and the defense. Counsel's presence, as noted above, minimizes police abuses. But prosecution abuses, such as concealing exculpatory evidence, distorting evidence, and ignoring police officer perjury or sloppy police laboratory procedures, are also deterred, and, where not, are revealed to the court and the factfinder because of the presence of defense counsel.

Finally, the defendant accused of a crime is largely alone, a solitary individual who often may even be forsaken by family and friends. The lawyer serves as a friend, a guardian of the individual's claims of mistaken identification, self-defense, police abuses, overcharging of offenses, excessive sentencing, and the myriad other claims that only counsel can raise effectively.

---

1.   287 U.S. 45, 47 (1932).

II. Historical Underpinnings

The primary source of the right to counsel is the Sixth Amendment, which provides that "in all criminal prosecutions, the accused shall enjoy the right to have the assistance of counsel for his defense." Ever since the Supreme Court's decision in *Gideon v. Wainwright*,[2] the right to counsel has been incorporated against the states via the Fourteenth Amendment's due process clause. That clause, one should remember, incorporates against the states those rights in the Bill of Rights that are the essence of "fundamental fairness." The four reasons noted above convey the flavor of the argument that fundamental fairness requires the assistance of counsel at trial and during the pretrial investigatory and preparation stages. The right to assistance of counsel requires not only that a person be allowed to make use of counsel's advice, but also that the state provide counsel at its expense if the person is unable to bear the costs.

Recognition of this notion of fundamental fairness was slow in coming. The Court took a step in that direction in 1932 in *Powell*, holding that due process required state courts to appoint counsel for indigent defendants charged with capital offenses. Then, in 1938, in *Johnson v. Zerbst*,[3] the Court held that counsel must be appointed in federal non-capital criminal cases, although that right was not yet applicable to the states. In *Betts v. Brady*,[4] the Court held that due process rights do not obligate states to provide court-appointed counsel in all non-capital cases. Finally, in its landmark 1963 decision in *Gideon*, the Court overruled *Betts* and extended the right to counsel to all felonies prosecuted in the states and, in 1972, in *Argersinger v. Hamlin*,[5] to all misdemeanors in which the defendant receives a sentence of incarceration.

The Court has been adamant, however, that the right to counsel is not implicated unless the defendant receives a sentence of actual incarceration. In *Scott v. Illinois*,[6] it held that the right to a lawyer in misdemeanor cases does not apply where a jail sentence is merely a possibility. Instead, that right attaches only when the actual sentence results in confinement. Years after it decided *Scott*, the Court strongly reaffirmed the position it had taken in that case. In *Nichols v. United States*,[7] a defendant pleaded guilty to a federal drug offense, and the trial court increased his sentence by more than two years of extra incarceration time because of his previous misdemeanor drunk-driving conviction. The drunk-driving conviction had been uncounseled, but it had been constitutional at the time because it had not

---

2. 372 U.S. 335 (1963).

3. 304 U.S. 458 (1938).

4. 316 U.S. 455 (1942).

5. 407 U.S. 25 (1972).

6. 440 U.S. 367 (1979).

7. 511 U.S. 738 (1994).

resulted in incarceration. When it was used years later to "enhance" his sentence in the drug case, the defendant contended that the *Argersinger* rule had been violated. The Supreme Court disagreed, reasoning that the trial court's decision to enhance the sentence on the drug conviction did not alter the sentence on the drunk-driving conviction, which was the only one that was uncounseled. Moreover, the earlier drunk-driving conduct could have been considered at sentencing whether or not it had resulted in a conviction or sentence.

In every case in which the Sixth Amendment applies, it extends to every "critical stage" of the case, including post-indictment interrogations (see the *Massiah* doctrine discussed in Chapter 8), post-indictment lineups (see Chapter 10), arraignments, preliminary hearings, plea entries, trials, and sentencing hearings.[8] Defendants also are entitled to appointed counsel for their first appeal as of right,[9] but not to appointed counsel for discretionary appeals.[10] Similarly, there is no right to counsel in post conviction habeas proceedings,[11] even for death row inmates.[12]

Even where there is no general right to counsel, a case-by-case inquiry may reveal a violation of due process in denying counsel under particular circumstances. Thus the Court has found such a case-specific right in probation revocation proceedings, articulating the relevant considerations in *Gagnon v. Scarpelli*:[13]

> . . . Presumptively, it may be said that counsel should be provided in cases where, after being informed of his right to request counsel, the probationer or parolee makes such a request, based on a timely and colorable claim (i) that he has not committed the alleged violation of the conditions upon which he is at liberty; or (ii) that, even if the violation is a matter of public record or is uncontested, there are substantial reasons which justified or mitigated the violation and make revocation inappropriate, and that the reasons are complex or otherwise difficult to develop or present. In passing on a request for the appointment of counsel, the responsible agency also should consider, especially in doubtful cases, whether the probationer appears to be capable of speaking effectively for himself.

The extent to which the Court may be willing to engage in *Gagnon's* case-specific inquiry outside the probation revocation context is unclear.

---

8.   *See, e.g.*, Coramae Richey Mann, UNEQUAL JUSTICE: A QUESTION OF COLOR 174 (1993). For a more detailed discussion of the "critical stage" concept and on when the right to counsel attaches, *see* Chapter 10.

9.   Douglas v. California, 372 U.S. 353 (1963). Douglas seemed to rely as well on due process principles. *See* Dressler, *supra*, at 374.

10.   Ross v. Moffitt, 417 U.S. 600 (1974).

11.   Pennsylvania v. Finley, 481 U.S. 551 (1987).

12.   Murray v. Giarratano, 492 U.S. 1 (1989).

13.   411 U.S. 778 (1973).

III. Effective Assistance of Counsel

We addressed in Chapters 8 and 10 two specific places—the interrogation setting and lineups—in which the right to counsel may arise. In this section, we address a more general issue with which every lawyer must be concerned: the level of competence that a lawyer must exhibit before the right to counsel is satisfied. The right to counsel would be meaningless unless it gave criminal defendants a real opportunity to benefit from lawyers' special expertise. Consequently, defendants have not just a right to the assistance of counsel, but a right to the effective assistance of counsel.[14] If they have been denied the effective assistance of counsel, they may seek relief from their convictions or sentences on that ground. The remainder of this chapter will help you to discern the meaning of the right to effective assistance of counsel.

Checklist 16: Effective Assistance of Counsel

1. Was counsel's performance so deficient that it did not constitute the "assistance of counsel" guaranteed by the Sixth Amendment, considering all of the circumstances, including the following relevant, but not controlling, factors:

    a. whether counsel violated prevailing norms of practice or ethical canons;

    b. whether there were reasonable strategic justifications for counsel's actions, given counsel's experience, preparation time, the gravity of the charge, the complexity of possible defenses, and the accessibility of witnesses;

    c. whether counsel's performance is judged without the "distorting effects of hindsight" and in light of the usual strong presumption that counsel's conduct falls within the wide range of reasonable professional assistance?

2. If yes, did counsel's conduct prejudice the defendant—in other words, was there a "reasonable probability" (a probability sufficient to undermine confidence in the outcome) that, but for counsel's unprofessional errors, the result of the proceeding would have been different?

3. If yes, did the error deprive the defendant of a fair trial—one whose result is reliable?

A. The *Strickland* Test

The modern legal test for the effective assistance of counsel is articulated in *Strickland v. Washington*,[15] which rejected the old "farce or

---

14. *See, e.g.,* Evitts v. Lucey, 469 U.S. 387 (1985) (indigents' right to appointed counsel for first appeal as of right includes the right to the *effective* assistance of counsel).

15. 466 U.S. 668 (1984).

mockery of justice"[16] test that had previously prevailed in federal court. Because *Strickland* articulates the relevant test and well illustrates its application, a substantial excerpt from this leading case follows:

Strickland v. Washington

466 U.S. 668 (1984).

■ O'CONNOR, J. This case requires us to consider the proper standards for judging a criminal defendant's contention that the Constitution requires a conviction or death sentence to be set aside because counsel's assistance at the trial or sentencing was ineffective.

I

A

During a 10–day period in September 1976, respondent planned and committed three groups of crimes, which included three brutal stabbing murders, torture, kidnapping, severe assaults, attempted murders, attempted extortion, and theft. After his two accomplices were arrested, respondent surrendered to police and voluntarily gave a lengthy statement confessing to the third of the criminal episodes. The State of Florida indicted respondent for kidnapping and murder and appointed an experienced criminal lawyer to represent him.

Counsel actively pursued pretrial motions and discovery. He cut his efforts short, however, and he experienced a sense of hopelessness about the case, when he learned that, against his specific advice, respondent had also confessed to the first two murders. By the date set for trial, respondent was subject to indictment for three counts of first-degree murder and multiple counts of robbery, kidnapping for ransom, breaking and entering and assault, attempted murder, and conspiracy to commit robbery. Respondent waived his right to a jury trial, again acting against counsel's advice, and pleaded guilty to all charges, including the three capital murder charges.

In the plea colloquy, respondent told the trial judge that, although he had committed a string of burglaries, he had no significant prior criminal record and that at the time of his criminal spree he was under extreme stress caused by his inability to support his family. He also stated, however, that he accepted responsibility for the crimes. The trial judge told respondent that he had "a great deal of respect for people who are willing to step forward and admit their responsibility" but that he was making no statement at all about his likely sentencing decision.

Counsel advised respondent to invoke his right under Florida law to an advisory jury at his capital sentencing hearing. Respondent rejected the advice and waived the right. He chose instead to be sentenced by the trial judge without a jury recommendation.

---

16.   Diggs v. Welch, 148 F.2d 667 (D.C.Cir.1945).

In preparing for the sentencing hearing, counsel spoke with respondent about his background. He also spoke on the telephone with respondent's wife and mother, though he did not follow up on the one unsuccessful effort to meet with them. He did not otherwise seek out character witnesses for respondent. Nor did he request a psychiatric examination, since his conversations with his client gave no indication that respondent had psychological problems.

Counsel decided not to present and hence not to look further for evidence concerning respondent's character and emotional state. That decision reflected trial counsel's sense of hopelessness about overcoming the evidentiary effect of respondent's confessions to the gruesome crimes. It also reflected the judgment that it was advisable to rely on the plea colloquy for evidence about respondent's background and about his claim of emotional stress: the plea colloquy communicated sufficient information about these subjects, and by forgoing the opportunity to present new evidence on these subjects, counsel prevented the State from cross-examining respondent on his claim and from putting on psychiatric evidence of its own.

Counsel also excluded from the sentencing hearing other evidence he thought was potentially damaging. He successfully moved to exclude respondent's "rap sheet." Because he judged that a presentence report might prove more detrimental than helpful, as it would have included respondent's criminal history and thereby would have undermined the claim of no significant history of criminal activity, he did not request that one be prepared.

At the sentencing hearing, counsel's strategy was based primarily on the trial judge's remarks at the plea colloquy as well as on his reputation as a sentencing judge who thought it important for a convicted defendant to own up to his crime. Counsel argued that respondent's remorse and acceptance of responsibility justified sparing him from the death penalty. Counsel also argued that respondent had no history of criminal activity and that respondent committed the crimes under extreme mental or emotional disturbance, thus coming within the statutory list of mitigating circumstances. He further argued that respondent should be spared death because he had surrendered, confessed, and offered to testify against a codefendant and because respondent was fundamentally a good person who had briefly gone badly wrong in extremely stressful circumstances. The State put on evidence and witnesses largely for the purpose of describing the details of the crimes. Counsel did not cross-examine the medical experts who testified about the manner of death of respondent's victims.

The trial judge found several aggravating circumstances with respect to each of the three murders. He found that all three murders were especially heinous, atrocious, and cruel, all involving repeated stabbings. All three murders were committed in the course of at least one other dangerous and violent felony, and since all involved robbery, the murders were for pecuniary gain. All three murders were committed to avoid arrest for the accompanying crimes and to hinder law enforcement. In the course of one of the murders, respondent knowingly subjected numerous persons to a grave risk of death by deliberately stabbing and shooting the murder victim's sisters-in-law, who sustained severe—in one case, ultimately fatal—injuries.

With respect to mitigating circumstances, the trial judge made the same findings for all three capital murders. First, although there was no admitted evidence of prior convictions, respondent had stated that he had engaged in a course of stealing. In any case, even if respondent had no significant history of criminal activity, the aggravating circumstances "would still clearly far outweigh" that mitigating factor. Second, the judge found that, during all three crimes, respondent was not suffering from extreme mental or emotional disturbance and could appreciate the criminality of his acts. Third, none of the victims was a participant in, or consented to, respondent's conduct. Fourth, respondent's participation in the crimes was neither minor nor the result of duress or domination by an accomplice. Finally, respondent's age (26) could not be considered a factor in mitigation, especially when viewed in light of respondent's planning of the crimes and disposition of the proceeds of the various accompanying thefts.

In short, the trial judge found numerous aggravating circumstances and no (or a single comparatively insignificant) mitigating circumstance. With respect to each of the three convictions for capital murder, the trial judge concluded: "A careful consideration of all matters presented to the court impels the conclusion that there are insufficient mitigating circumstances ... to outweigh the aggravating circumstances." He therefore sentenced respondent to death on each of the three counts of murder and to prison terms for the other crimes. The Florida Supreme Court upheld the convictions and sentences on direct appeal.

B

Respondent subsequently sought collateral relief in state court on numerous grounds, among them that counsel had rendered ineffective assistance at the sentencing proceeding. Respondent challenged counsel's assistance in six respects. He asserted that counsel was ineffective because he failed to move for a continuance to prepare for sentencing, to request a psychiatric report, to investigate and present character witnesses, to seek a presentence investigation report, to present meaningful arguments to the sentencing judge, and to investigate the medical examiner's reports or cross-examine the medical experts. In support of the claim, respondent submitted 14 affidavits from friends, neighbors, and relatives stating that they would have testified if asked to do so. He also submitted one psychiatric report and one psychological report stating that respondent, though not under the influence of extreme mental or emotional disturbance, was "chronically frustrated and depressed because of his economic dilemma" at the time of his crimes.

The trial court denied relief without an evidentiary hearing, finding that the record evidence conclusively showed that the ineffectiveness claim was meritless. Four of the assertedly prejudicial errors required little discussion. First, there were no grounds to request a continuance, so there was no error in not requesting one when respondent pleaded guilty. Second, failure to request a presentence investigation was not a serious error because the trial judge had discretion not to grant such a request and because any presentence investigation would have resulted in admission of respondent's "rap sheet" and thus would have undermined his assertion of no significant history of criminal activity. Third, the argument and memorandum given to the sentencing judge were "admirable" in light of the overwhelming aggravating circumstances and absence of mitigating circumstances. Fourth, there was no error in failure to examine the medical examiner's reports or to cross-examine the medical witnesses testifying on the manner of death of respondent's victims, since respondent admitted that the victims died in the ways shown by the unchallenged medical evidence.

The trial court dealt at greater length with the two other bases for the ineffectiveness claim. The court pointed out that a psychiatric examination of respondent was conducted by state order soon after respondent's initial arraignment. That report states that there was no indication of major mental illness at the time of the crimes. Moreover, both the reports submitted in the collateral proceeding state that, although respondent was "chronically frustrated and depressed because of his economic dilemma," he was not under the influence of extreme mental or emotional disturbance. All three reports thus directly undermine the contention made at the sentencing hearing that respondent was suffering from extreme mental or emotional disturbance during his crime spree. Accordingly, counsel could reasonably decide not to seek psychiatric reports; indeed, by relying solely on the plea colloquy to support the emotional disturbance contention, counsel denied the State an opportunity to rebut his claim with psychiatric testimony. In any event, the aggravating circumstances were so overwhelming that no substantial prejudice resulted from the absence at sentencing of the psychiatric evidence offered in the collateral attack.

The court rejected the challenge to counsel's failure to develop and to present character evidence for much the same reasons. The affidavits submitted in the collateral proceeding showed nothing more than that certain persons would have testified that respondent was basically a good person who was worried about his family's financial problems. Respondent himself had already testified along those lines at the plea colloquy. Moreover, respondent's admission of a course of stealing rebutted many of the factual allegations in the affidavits. For those reasons, and because the sentencing judge had stated that the death sentence would be appropriate even if respondent had no significant prior criminal history, no substantial prejudice resulted from the absence at sentencing of the character evidence offered in the collateral attack.

Applying the standard for ineffectiveness claims articulated by the Florida Supreme Court, ... the trial court concluded that respondent had not shown that counsel's assistance reflected any substantial and serious deficiency measurably below that of competent counsel that was likely to have affected the outcome of the sentencing proceeding. The court specifically found: "[A]s a matter of law, the record affirmatively demonstrates beyond any doubt that even if [counsel] had done each of the ... things [that respondent alleged counsel had failed to do] at the time of sentencing, there is not even the remotest chance that the outcome would have been any different. The plain fact is that the aggravating circumstances proved in this case were completely overwhelming...."

The Florida Supreme Court affirmed the denial of relief. For essentially the reasons given by the trial court, the State Supreme Court concluded that respondent had failed to make out a prima facie case of either "substantial deficiency or possible prejudice" and, indeed, had "failed to such a degree that we believe, to the point of a moral certainty, that he is entitled to no relief...." Respondent's claims were "shown conclusively to be without merit so as to obviate the need for an evidentiary hearing." ...

D

We granted certiorari to consider the standards by which to judge a contention that the Constitution requires that a criminal judgment be overturned because of the actual ineffective assistance of counsel....

II

In a long line of cases that includes *Powell v. Alabama, Johnson v. Zerbst*, and *Gideon v. Wainwright*, this Court has recognized that the Sixth Amendment right to counsel exists, and is needed, in order to protect the fundamental right to a fair trial. The Constitution guarantees a fair trial through the Due Process Clauses, but it defines the basic elements of a fair trial largely through the several provisions of the Sixth Amendment, including the Counsel Clause: "In all criminal prosecutions, the accused shall enjoy the right to a speedy and public trial, by an impartial jury of the State and district wherein the crime shall have been committed, which district shall have been previously ascertained by law, and to be informed of the nature and cause of the accusation; to be confronted with the witnesses against him; to have compulsory process for obtaining witnesses in his favor, and to have the Assistance of Counsel for his defence." Thus, a fair trial is one in which evidence subject to adversarial testing is presented to an impartial tribunal for resolution of issues defined in advance of the proceeding. The right to counsel plays a crucial role in the adversarial system embodied in the Sixth Amendment, since access to counsel's skill and knowledge is necessary to accord defendants the "ample opportunity to meet the case of the prosecution" to which they are entitled.

Because of the vital importance of counsel's assistance, this Court has held that, with certain exceptions, a person accused of a federal or state crime has the right to have counsel appointed if retained counsel cannot be obtained. That a person who happens to be a lawyer is present at trial alongside the accused, however, is not enough to satisfy the constitutional command. The Sixth Amendment recognizes the right to the assistance of counsel because it envisions counsel's playing a role that is critical to the ability of the adversarial system to produce just results. An accused is entitled to be assisted by an attorney, whether retained or appointed, who plays the role necessary to ensure that the trial is fair.

For that reason, the Court has recognized that "the right to counsel is the right to the effective assistance of counsel." . . .

The Court has not elaborated on the meaning of the constitutional requirement of effective assistance in . . . cases . . . presenting claims of "actual ineffectiveness." In giving meaning to the requirement, however, we must take its purpose—to ensure a fair trial—as the guide. The benchmark for judging any claim of ineffectiveness must be whether counsel's conduct so undermined the proper functioning of the adversarial process that the trial cannot be relied on as having produced a just result.

The same principle applies to a capital sentencing proceeding such as that provided by Florida law. We need not consider the role of counsel in an ordinary sentencing, which may involve informal proceedings and standard-less discretion in the sentence, and hence may require a different approach to the definition of constitutionally effective assistance. A capital sentencing proceeding like the one involved in this case, however, is sufficiently like a trial in its adversarial format and in the existence of standards for decision that counsel's role in the proceeding is comparable to counsel's role at trial—to ensure that the adversarial testing process works to produce a just result under the standards governing decision. For purposes of describing counsel's duties, therefore, Florida's capital sentencing proceeding need not be distinguished from an ordinary trial.

III

A convicted defendant's claim that counsel's assistance was so defective as to require reversal of a conviction or death sentence has two components. First, the defendant must show that counsel's performance was deficient. This requires showing that counsel made errors so serious that counsel was not functioning as the "counsel" guaranteed the defendant by the Sixth Amendment. Second, the defendant must show that the deficient performance prejudiced the defense. This requires showing that counsel's errors were so serious as to deprive the defendant of a fair trial, a trial whose result is reliable. Unless a defendant makes both showings, it cannot be said that the conviction or death sentence resulted from a breakdown in the adversary process that renders the result unreliable.

A

As all the Federal Courts of Appeals have now held, the proper standard for attorney performance is that of reasonably effective assistance. . . . When a convicted defendant complains of the ineffectiveness of counsel's assistance, the defendant must show that counsel's representation fell below an objective standard of reasonableness.

More specific guidelines are not appropriate. The Sixth Amendment refers simply to "counsel," not specifying particular requirements of effective assistance. It relies instead on the legal profession's maintenance of standards sufficient to justify the law's presumption that counsel will fulfill the role in the adversary process that the Amendment envisions. The proper measure of attorney performance remains simply reasonableness under prevailing professional norms.

Representation of a criminal defendant entails certain basic duties. Counsel's function is to assist the defendant, and hence counsel owes the client a duty of loyalty, a duty to avoid conflicts of interest. From counsel's function as assistant to the defendant derive the overarching duty to advocate the defendant's cause and the more particular duties to consult with the defendant on important decisions and to keep the defendant informed of important developments in the course of the prosecution. Counsel also has a duty to bring to bear such skill and knowledge as will render the trial a reliable adversarial testing process.

These basic duties neither exhaustively define the obligations of counsel nor form a checklist for judicial evaluation of attorney performance. In any case presenting an ineffectiveness claim, the performance inquiry must be whether counsel's assistance was reasonable considering all the circumstances. Prevailing norms of practice as reflected in American Bar Association standards and the like, e.g., ABA Standards for Criminal Justice 4–1.1 to 4–8.6 (2d ed. 1980) ("The Defense Function"), are guides to determining what is reasonable, but they are only guides. ... [T]he purpose of the effective assistance guarantee of the Sixth Amendment is not to improve the quality of legal representation, although that is a goal of considerable importance to the legal system. The purpose is simply to ensure that criminal defendants receive a fair trial.

Judicial scrutiny of counsel's performance must be highly deferential. It is all too tempting for a defendant to second-guess counsel's assistance after conviction or adverse sentence, and it is all too easy for a court, examining counsel's defense after it has proved unsuccessful, to conclude that a particular act or omission of counsel was unreasonable. A fair assessment of attorney performance requires that every effort be made to eliminate the distorting effects of hindsight, to reconstruct the circumstances of counsel's challenged conduct, and to evaluate the conduct from counsel's perspective at the time. Because of the difficulties inherent in making the evaluation, a court must indulge a strong presumption that counsel's conduct falls within the wide range of reasonable professional assistance; that is, the defendant must overcome the presumption that, under the circumstances, the challenged action "might be considered sound trial strategy." There are countless ways to provide effective assistance in any given case. Even the best criminal defense attorneys would not defend a particular client in the same way. ...

Thus, a court deciding an actual ineffectiveness claim must judge the reasonableness of counsel's challenged conduct on the facts of the particular case, viewed as of the time of counsel's conduct. A convicted defendant making a claim of ineffective assistance must identify the acts or omissions of counsel that are alleged not to have been the result of reasonable professional judgment. The court must then determine whether, in light of all the circumstances, the identified acts or omissions were outside the wide range of professionally competent assistance. In making that determination, the court should keep in mind that counsel's function, as elaborated in prevailing professional norms, is to make the adversarial testing process work in the particular case. At the same time, the court should recognize that counsel is strongly presumed to have rendered adequate assistance and made all significant decisions in the exercise of reasonable professional judgment.

These standards require no special amplification in order to define counsel's duty to investigate, the duty at issue in this case. As the Court of Appeals concluded, strategic choices made after thorough investigation of law and facts relevant to plausible options are virtually unchallengeable; and strategic choices made after less than complete investigation are reasonable precisely to the extent that reasonable professional judgments support the limitations on investigation. In other words, counsel has a duty to make reasonable investigations or to make a reasonable decision that makes particular investigations unnecessary. In any ineffectiveness case, a particular decision not to investigate must be directly assessed for reasonableness in all the circumstances, applying a heavy measure of deference to counsel's judgments.

The reasonableness of counsel's actions may be determined or substantially influenced by the defendant's own statements or actions. Counsel's actions are usually based, quite properly, on informed strategic choices made by the defendant and on information supplied by the defendant. In particular, what investigation decisions are reasonable depends critically on such information. For example, when the facts that support a certain potential line of defense are generally known to counsel because of what the defendant has said, the need for further investigation may be considerably diminished or eliminated altogether. And when a defendant has given counsel reason to believe that pursuing certain investigations would be fruitless or even harmful, counsel's failure to pursue those investigations may not later be challenged as unreasonable. In short, inquiry into counsel's conversations with the defendant may be critical to a proper assessment of counsel's investigation decisions, just as it may be critical to a proper assessment of counsel's other litigation decisions.

B

An error by counsel, even if professionally unreasonable, does not warrant setting aside the judgment of a criminal proceeding if the error had no effect on the judgment. The purpose of the Sixth Amendment guarantee of counsel is to ensure that a defendant has the assistance necessary to justify reliance on the outcome of the proceeding. Accordingly, any deficiencies in counsel's performance must be prejudicial to the defense in order to constitute ineffective assistance under the Constitution.

In certain Sixth Amendment contexts, prejudice is presumed. Actual or constructive denial of the assistance of counsel altogether is legally presumed to result in prejudice. So are various kinds of state interference with counsel's assistance. Prejudice in these circumstances is so likely that case-by-case inquiry into prejudice is not worth the cost. Moreover, such circumstances involve impairments of the Sixth Amendment right that are easy to identify and, for that reason and because the prosecution is directly responsible, easy for the government to prevent.

One type of actual ineffectiveness claim warrants a similar, though more limited, presumption of prejudice.... [P]rejudice is presumed when counsel is burdened by an actual conflict of interest. In those circumstances, counsel breaches the duty of loyalty, perhaps the most basic of counsel's duties. Moreover, it is difficult to measure the precise effect on the defense of representation corrupted by conflicting interests. Given the obligation of counsel to avoid conflicts of interest and the ability of trial courts to make early inquiry in certain situations likely to give rise to conflicts, ... it is reasonable for the criminal justice system to maintain a fairly rigid rule of presumed prejudice for conflicts of interest. Even so, the rule is not quite the per se rule of prejudice that exists for the Sixth Amendment claims mentioned above. Prejudice is presumed only if the defendant demonstrates that counsel "actively represented conflicting interests" and that "an actual conflict of interest adversely affected his lawyer's performance."

Conflict of interest claims aside, actual ineffectiveness claims alleging a deficiency in attorney performance are subject to a general requirement that the defendant affirmatively prove prejudice. The government is not responsible for, and hence not able to prevent, attorney errors that will result in reversal of a conviction or sentence. ... Even if a defendant shows that particular errors of counsel were unreasonable, therefore, the defendant must show that they actually had an adverse effect on the defense.

It is not enough for the defendant to show that the errors had some conceivable effect on the outcome of the proceeding. Virtually every act or omission of counsel would meet that test, and not every error that conceivably could have influenced the outcome undermines the reliability of the result of the proceeding. ...

Accordingly, the ... defendant must show that there is a reasonable probability that, but for counsel's unprofessional errors, the result of the proceeding would have been different. A reasonable probability is a probability sufficient to undermine confidence in the outcome.

In making the determination whether the specified errors resulted in the required prejudice, a court should presume, absent challenge to the judgment on grounds of evidentiary insufficiency, that the judge or jury acted according to law. An assessment of the likelihood of a result more favorable to the defendant must exclude the possibility of arbitrariness, whimsy, caprice, "nullification," and the like. ... Thus, evidence about the actual process of decision, if not part of the record of the proceeding under review, and evidence about, for example, a particular judge's sentencing practices, should not be considered in the prejudice determination.

The governing legal standard plays a critical role in defining the question to be asked in assessing the prejudice from counsel's errors. When a defendant challenges a conviction, the question is whether there is a reasonable probability that, absent the errors, the factfinder would have had a reasonable doubt respecting guilt. When a defendant challenges a death sentence such as the one at issue in this case, the question is whether there is a reasonable probability that, absent the errors, the sentencing court—including an appellate court, to the extent it independently reweighs the evidence—would have concluded that the balance of aggravating and mitigating circumstances did not warrant death.

In making this determination, a court hearing an ineffectiveness claim must consider the totality of the evidence before the judge or jury. . . . Taking the unaffected findings as a given, and taking due account of the effect of the errors on the remaining findings, a court making the prejudice inquiry must ask if the defendant has met the burden of showing that the decision reached would reasonably likely have been different absent the errors. . . .

V

Having articulated general standards for judging ineffectiveness claims, we think it useful to apply those standards to the facts of this case in order to illustrate the meaning of the general principles. . . .

The facts as described above, make clear that the conduct of respondent's counsel at and before respondent's sentencing proceeding cannot be found unreasonable. They also make clear that, even assuming the challenged conduct of counsel was unreasonable, respondent suffered insufficient prejudice to warrant setting aside his death sentence.

With respect to the performance component, the record shows that respondent's counsel made a strategic choice to argue for the extreme emotional distress mitigating circumstance and to rely as fully as possible on respondent's acceptance of responsibility for his crimes. Although counsel understandably felt hopeless about respondent's prospects, nothing in the record indicates, . . . that counsel's sense of hopelessness distorted his professional judgment. Counsel's strategy choice was well within the range of professionally reasonable judgments, and the decision not to seek more character or psychological evidence than was already in hand was likewise reasonable.

The trial judge's views on the importance of owning up to one's crimes were well known to counsel. The aggravating circumstances were utterly overwhelming. Trial counsel could reasonably surmise from his conversations with respondent that character and psychological evidence would be of little help. Respondent had already been able to mention at the plea colloquy the substance of what there was to know about his financial and emotional troubles. Restricting testimony on respondent's character to what had come in at the plea colloquy ensured that contrary character and psychological evidence and respondent's criminal history, which counsel had successfully moved to exclude, would not come in. On these facts, there can be little question, even without application of the presumption of adequate performance, that trial counsel's defense, though unsuccessful, was the result of reasonable professional judgment.

With respect to the prejudice component, the lack of merit of respondent's claim is even more stark. The evidence that respondent says his trial counsel should have offered at the sentencing hearing would barely have altered the sentencing profile presented to the sentencing judge. . . . [A]t most this evidence shows that numerous people who knew respondent thought he was generally a good person and that a psychiatrist and a psychologist believed he was under considerable emotional stress that did not rise to the level of extreme disturbance. Given the overwhelming aggravating factors, there is no reasonable probability that the omitted evidence would have changed the conclusion that the aggravating circumstances outweighed the mitigating circumstances and, hence, the sentence imposed. Indeed, admission of the evidence respondent now offers might even have been harmful to his case: his "rap sheet" would probably have been admitted into evidence, and the psychological reports would have directly contradicted respondent's claim that the mitigating circumstance of extreme emotional disturbance applied to his case. . . .

Failure to make the required showing of either deficient performance or sufficient prejudice defeats the ineffectiveness claim. Here there is a double failure. More generally, respondent has made no showing that the justice of his sentence was rendered unreliable by a breakdown in the adversary process caused by deficiencies in counsel's assistance. Respondent's sentencing proceeding was not fundamentally unfair. . . .

QUESTIONS

1. Is the majority's ineffectiveness test clear? Specific? What more specific guidelines for effectiveness might you draft and how? Does the presumption of effectiveness impose too heavy a burden on the defense?

2. Does the Court's prejudice standard make any sense? Is the Court right that the only purpose of effective counsel is to reduce the chance of a false positive, that is, the risk of convicting the innocent?

3. Was the Court correct in finding its test passed here? What else might competent counsel have been expected to do in this case? Is the Court's standard too deferential to lawyer judgments?

In *Wiggins v. Smith*,[17] the Supreme Court determined that Wiggins successfully made out a claim of ineffectiveness under the *Strickland* test. According to the Court, Wiggins' lawyers in his murder trial had failed to investigate mitigating evidence that they might have presented to the jury in an effort to convince the jury to reject a death sentence. This failure to

---

17. 539 U.S. 510 (2003).

investigate fell below the standard of reasonable competence. Said the Court:

> Counsel's decision not to expand their [sic] investigation ... fell short of the professional standards that prevailed in Maryland in 1989. As [one of the defense lawyers] acknowledged, standard practice in Maryland in capital cases at the time of Wiggins' trial included the preparation of a social history report. Despite the fact that the Public Defender's office made funds available for the retention of a forensic social worker, counsel chose not to commission such a report. Counsel's conduct similarly fell short of the standards for capital defense work articulated by the American Bar Association (ABA)—standards to which we long have referred as "guides to determining what is reasonable."[18]

On the prejudice prong of the *Strickland* test, the Court determined that the mitigating evidence that Wiggins' lawyers had failed to investigate and discover "is powerful," that a reasonably competent attorney would have introduced it at sentencing, and that "had the jury been confronted with this considerable mitigating evidence, there is a reasonable probability that it would have returned with a different sentence."[19]

The Court found another occasion to reverse a capital sentence on *Strickland* grounds in *Rompilla v. Beard*.[20] There, Rompilla's attorneys failed to investigate the file of his prior conviction, which they knew the prosecution would use in arguing for the death penalty. No reasonable lawyer, according to the Court, would have neglected such an investigation. Moreover, Rompilla was prejudiced by the unreasonable investigation because the file would have revealed mitigating evidence about Rompilla's childhood and mental health. This evidence "might well have influenced the jury's appraisal" of Rompilla's culpability. Without it, his mitigation case was "a few naked pleas for mercy."

On the other hand, in *Schriro v. Landrigan*, the Court held that where a defendant instructs his attorney not to offer any mitigating evidence, he cannot later claim that the attorney's failure to investigate further constitutes ineffective assistance of counsel.[21] Landrigan had told his lawyer not to offer mitigating evidence at his capital sentencing hearing, and he also informed the judge at the hearing that there was no relevant mitigating evidence "as far as I'm concerned." Writing for a 5–justice majority, Justice Thomas agreed with the trial court in Landrigan's habeas action that the defendant would not have been able to demonstrate prejudice under *Strickland*. Justice Thomas distinguished *Rompilla* on the ground that the defendant in that case, unlike Landrigan, had not informed the court that he did not want mitigating evidence presented.[22] Justice Thomas also noted

---

18. *Id.* at 522.

19. *Id.* at 539.

20. 545 U.S. 374 (2005).

21. 550 U.S. 465, 475–76 (2007).

22. *Id.* at 478.

that there was no precedent for requiring Landrigan's waiver of mitigating evidence to be "knowing and intelligent."[23]

In dissent, Justice Stevens pointed out that, at the time of the sentencing hearing, counsel's failure to investigate had prevented Landrigan from knowing that he suffered "from a serious psychological condition that sheds important light on his earlier actions." According to Stevens and three justices who joined his dissent, this alone constituted prejudice. In addition, the dissenters contended that the Court's precedents—including two cases with which you are familiar, *Johnson v. Zerbst* and *Schneckloth v. Bustamonte*—require that a waiver as important as Landrigan's meet the "knowing and voluntary" standard.[24]

In *Knowles v. Mirzayance*,[25] the Court unanimously held, in a federal habeas proceeding, that a state court's determination that no sixth amendment violation had occurred when trial counsel withdrew his client's insanity defense was not contrary to, or an unreasonable application of, clearly established federal law—the relevant statutory habeas standard. There, Mirzayance had pled both not guilty and not guilty by reason of insanity. California law required bifurcated proceedings, first addressing substantive guilt under the usual standards, then a second proceeding addressing the insanity defense. Mirzayance's counsel, hoping to avoid a first-degree murder conviction and instead obtain a second-degree murder conviction, had presented medical testimony in the initial proceeding that his client was insane at the time of the crime, therefore incapable of the premeditation or deliberation necessary for first-degree murder. The jury convicted Mirzayance of first-degree.

His counsel had hoped at the subsequent insanity hearing to supplement the previous medical testimony with that of Mirzayance's parents, believing they would "provide an emotional account of Mirzayance's struggles with mental illness to supplement the medical evidence of insanity."[26] But, on the date of that hearing, Mirzayance's parents expressed a strong reluctance to testify, leaving counsel with the recognition that all he had left was to present to the same jury that had heard and rejected the medical testimony at the initial culpability stage the same testimony at the insanity defense stage. Given this reality, Mirzayance's counsel asked for and received permission to withdraw the insanity plea. Mirzayance was sentenced, and he subsequently challenged his conviction all the way through to federal habeas proceedings before the United States Supreme Court.

The Court concluded that counsel's performance had not been deficient, rejecting the argument that an attorney must present a defense whenever he has "nothing to lose." Explained the Court, "[j]udicial scrutiny of counsel's performance must be highly deferential," meaning counsel must be given a strong presumption of reasonable professional assistance, with the proper measure of such assistance being "prevailing professional

---

23. *Id.* at 478–79.

24. *Id.* at 482–87 (Stevens, J., dissenting).

25. 129 S.Ct. 1411 (2009).

26. *Id.* at 1415.

norms."[27] Professional norms do not require counsel to raise every available non-frivolous defense. Nor do they require counsel to have any tactical reason for recommending dropping a claim beyond reasonably appraising the claim's chances for success as dismal. These conclusions were strengthened, explained the Court, by the Magistrate judge's finding that counsel had made an informed decision after thorough investigation of all plausible legal and factual options—a factual finding that could only be reversed if "clearly erroneous." Furthermore, ineffective assistance of counsel claims require proof not only of deficient performance but also of prejudice, meaning a reasonable probability that a contrary decision would have altered the result or that the actual decision undermined confidence in the outcome. But the defense, said the Court, could not meet its burden of showing prejudice because it was highly improbable that a jury that had rejected medical testimony of insanity at a stage at which the prosecution bore the burden of proof would suddenly have accepted such testimony at the later stage of the proceedings, at which the defense bore the burden of proof.

As part of its reasoning, the Court also rejected the argument that trial counsel had an obligation to do all that he could to convince Mirazyance's parents to testify. Said the Court, "competence does not require an attorney to browbeat a reluctant witness into testifying, especially when the facts suggest that no amount of persuasion would have succeeded."[28]

Moreover, the Court said that it would reach the same conclusions under a de novo standard of review as under the "unreasonable application of clearly established federal law" standard of review provided in the federal habeas statute. Nevertheless, the Court did emphasize that the question under the habeas statute was not whether the reviewing court believed that state courts had incorrectly applied the *Strickland* standard but rather whether the state courts' determination " 'was unreasonable' a substantially higher threshold."[29]

B. The Presumption of Effectiveness

The *Strickland* test can be better understood by reviewing *United States v. Cronic*.[30] In reviewing this excerpt from Cronic, note the narrow circumstances in which the Court is willing to apply a presumption of ineffectiveness, rather than the usual presumption of competency:

United States v. Cronic
466 U.S. 648 (1984).

■ Stevens, J. Respondent and two associates were indicted on mail fraud charges involving the transfer of over $9,400,000 in checks between banks

---

27. *Id.* at 1420.

28. *Id.* at 1421.

29. *Id.* at 1420.

30. 466 U.S. 648 (1984).

in Tampa, Fla., and Norman, Okla., during a 4–month period in 1975. Shortly before the scheduled trial date, respondent's retained counsel withdrew. The court appointed a young lawyer with a real estate practice to represent respondent, but allowed him only 25 days for pretrial preparation, even though it had taken the Government over four and one-half years to investigate the case and it had reviewed thousands of documents during that investigation. The two codefendants agreed to testify for the Government; respondent was convicted on 11 of the 13 counts in the indictment and received a 25–year sentence.

The Court of Appeals reversed the conviction because it concluded that respondent did not "have the Assistance of Counsel for his defense" that is guaranteed by the Sixth Amendment to the Constitution. This conclusion was not supported by a determination that respondent's trial counsel had made any specified errors, that his actual performance had prejudiced the defense, or that he failed to exercise "the skill, judgment, and diligence of a reasonably competent defense attorney"; instead the conclusion rested on the premise that no such showing is necessary "when circumstances hamper a given lawyer's preparation of a defendant's case." The question presented by the Government's petition for certiorari is whether the Court of Appeals has correctly interpreted the Sixth Amendment.

I

The indictment alleged a "check kiting" scheme. At the direction of respondent, his codefendant Cummings opened a bank account in the name of Skyproof Manufacturing, Inc. (Skyproof), at a bank in Tampa, Fla., and codefendant Merritt opened two accounts, one in his own name and one in the name of Skyproof, at banks in Norman, Okla. Knowing that there were insufficient funds in either account, the defendants allegedly drew a series of checks and wire transfers on the Tampa account aggregating $4,841,073.95, all of which were deposited in Skyproof's Norman bank account during the period between June 23, 1975, and October 16, 1975; during approximately the same period they drew checks on Skyproof's Norman account for deposits in Tampa aggregating $4,600,881.39. The process of clearing the checks involved the use of the mails. By "kiting" insufficient funds checks between the banks in those two cities, defendants allegedly created false or inflated balances in the accounts. After outlining the overall scheme, Count I of the indictment alleged the mailing of two checks each for less than $1,000 early in May. Each of the additional 12 counts realleged the allegations in Count I except its reference to the two specific checks, and then added an allegation identifying other checks issued and mailed at later dates.

At trial the Government proved that Skyproof's checks were issued and deposited at the times and places, and in the amounts, described in the indictment. Having made plea bargains with defendants Cummings and Merritt, who had actually handled the issuance and delivery of the relevant written instruments, the Government proved through their testimony that respondent had conceived and directed the entire scheme, and that he had deliberately concealed his connection with Skyproof because of prior financial and tax problems.

After the District Court ruled that a prior conviction could be used to impeach his testimony, respondent decided not to testify. Counsel put on no defense. By cross-examination of Government witnesses, however, he established that Skyproof was not merely a sham, but actually was an operating company with a significant cash flow, though its revenues were not sufficient to justify as large a "float" as the record disclosed. Cross-examination also established the absence of written evidence that respondent had any control over Skyproof, or personally participated in the withdrawals or deposits.

The 4–day jury trial ended on July 17, 1980, and respondent was sentenced on August 28, 1980. His counsel perfected a timely appeal, which was docketed on September 11, 1980. Two months later respondent filed a motion to substitute a new attorney in the Court of Appeals, and also filed a motion in the District Court seeking to vacate his conviction on the ground that he had newly discovered evidence of perjury by officers of the Norman bank, and that the Government knew or should have known of that perjury. In that motion he also challenged the competence of his trial counsel. The District Court refused to entertain the motion while the appeal was pending. The Court of Appeals denied the motion to substitute the attorney designated by respondent, but did appoint still another attorney to handle the appeal. Later it allowed respondent's motion to supplement the record with material critical of trial counsel's performance.

The Court of Appeals reversed the conviction because it inferred that respondent's constitutional right to the effective assistance of counsel had been violated. That inference was based on its use of five criteria: "(1) [T]he time afforded for investigation and preparation; (2) the experience of counsel; (3) the gravity of the charge; (4) the complexity of possible defenses; and (5) the accessibility of witnesses to counsel." Under the test employed by the Court of Appeals, reversal is required even if the lawyer's actual performance was flawless. By utilizing this inferential approach, the Court of Appeals erred.

II

An accused's right to be represented by counsel is a fundamental component of our criminal justice system. Lawyers in criminal cases "are necessities, not luxuries." Their presence is essential because they are the means through which the other rights of the person on trial are secured. Without counsel, the right to a trial itself would be "of little avail." "Of all the rights that an accused person has, the right to be represented by counsel is by far the most pervasive for it affects his ability to assert any other rights he may have." . . .

The substance of the Constitution's guarantee of the effective assistance of counsel is illuminated by reference to its underlying purpose. "[T]ruth," Lord Eldon said, "is best discovered by powerful statements on both sides of the question." This dictum describes the unique strength of our system of criminal justice. "The very premise of our adversary system of criminal justice is that partisan advocacy on both sides of a case will best promote the ultimate objective that the guilty be convicted and the innocent go free." *Herring v. New York*, 422 U.S. 853 (1975). It is that "very premise" that underlies and gives meaning to the Sixth Amendment. It "is meant to assure fairness in the adversary criminal process." *United States v. Morrison*, 449 U.S. 361 (1981). Unless the accused receives the effective assistance of counsel, "a serious risk of injustice infects the trial itself."

Thus, the adversarial process protected by the Sixth Amendment requires that the accused have "counsel acting in the role of an advocate." *Anders v. California*, 386 U.S. 738 (1967). The right to the effective assistance of counsel is thus the right of the accused to require the prosecution's case to survive the crucible of meaningful adversarial testing. When a true adversarial criminal trial has been conducted—even if defense counsel may have made demonstrable errors—the kind of testing envisioned by the Sixth Amendment has occurred. But if the process loses its character as a confrontation between adversaries, the constitutional guarantee is violated. . . .

III

While the Court of Appeals purported to apply a standard of reasonable competence, it did not indicate that there had been an actual breakdown of the adversarial process during the trial of this case. Instead it concluded that the circumstances surrounding the representation of respondent mandated an inference that counsel was unable to discharge his duties.

In our evaluation of that conclusion, we begin by recognizing that the right to the effective assistance of counsel is recognized not for its own sake, but because of the effect it has on the ability of the accused to receive a fair trial. Absent some effect of challenged conduct on the reliability of the trial process, the Sixth Amendment guarantee is generally not implicated. Moreover, because we presume that the lawyer is competent to provide the guiding hand that the defendant needs, the burden rests on the accused to demonstrate a constitutional violation. There are, however, circumstances that are so likely to prejudice the accused that the cost of litigating their effect in a particular case is unjustified.

Most obvious, of course, is the complete denial of counsel. The presumption that counsel's assistance is essential requires us to conclude that a trial is unfair if the accused is denied counsel at a critical stage of his trial. Similarly, if counsel entirely fails to subject the prosecution's case to meaningful adversarial testing, then there has been a denial of Sixth Amendment rights that makes the adversary process itself presumptively unreliable. . . .

Circumstances of that magnitude may be present on some occasions when although counsel is available to assist the accused during trial, the likelihood that any lawyer, even a fully competent one, could provide effective assistance is so small that a presumption of prejudice is appropriate without inquiry into the actual conduct of the trial. *Powell v. Alabama*, 287 U.S. 45 (1932), was such a case.

The defendants had been indicted for a highly publicized capital offense. Six days before trial, the trial judge appointed "all the members of the bar" for purposes of arraignment. "Whether they would represent the defendants thereafter if no counsel appeared in their behalf, was a matter of speculation only, or, as the judge indicated, of mere anticipation on the part of the court." On the day of trial, a lawyer from Tennessee appeared on behalf of persons "interested" in the defendants, but stated that he had not had an opportunity to prepare the case or to familiarize himself with local procedure, and therefore was unwilling to represent the defendants on such short notice. The problem was resolved when the court decided that the Tennessee lawyer would represent the defendants, with whatever help the local bar could provide. "The defendants, young, ignorant, illiterate, surrounded by hostile sentiment, haled back and forth under guard of soldiers, charged with an atrocious crime regarded with especial horror in the community where they were to be tried, were thus put in peril of their lives within a few moments after counsel for the first time charged with any degree of responsibility began to represent them."

This Court held that "such designation of counsel as was attempted was either so indefinite or so close upon the trial as to amount to a denial of effective and substantial aid in that regard." The Court did not examine the actual performance of counsel at trial, but instead concluded that under these circumstances the likelihood that counsel could have performed "as an effective adversary was so remote as to have made the trial inherently unfair." *Powell* was thus a case in which the surrounding circumstances made it so unlikely that any lawyer could provide effective assistance that ineffectiveness was properly presumed without inquiry into actual performance at trial.

But every refusal to postpone a criminal trial will not give rise to such a presumption. In *Avery v. Alabama*, 308 U.S. 444 (1940), counsel was appointed in a capital case only three days before trial, and the trial court denied counsel's request for additional time to prepare. Nevertheless, the Court held that since evidence and witnesses were easily accessible to defense counsel, the circumstances did not make it unreasonable to expect that counsel could adequately prepare for trial during that period of time. Similarly, in *Chambers v. Maroney*, 399 U.S. 42 (1970), the Court refused "to fashion a per se rule requiring reversal of every conviction following tardy appointment of counsel." Thus, only when surrounding circumstances justify a presumption of ineffectiveness can a Sixth Amendment claim be sufficient without inquiry into counsel's actual performance at trial.

The Court of Appeals did not find that respondent was denied the presence of counsel at a critical stage of the prosecution. Nor did it find, based on the actual conduct of the trial, that there was a breakdown in the adversarial process that would justify a presumption that respondent's conviction was insufficiently reliable to satisfy the Constitution. The dispositive question in this case therefore is whether the circumstances surrounding respondent's representation—and in particular the five criteria identified by the Court of Appeals—justified such a presumption.

IV

The five factors listed in the Court of Appeals' opinion are relevant to an evaluation of a lawyer's effectiveness in a particular case, but neither separately nor in combination do they provide a basis for concluding that competent counsel was not able to provide this respondent with the guiding hand that the Constitution guarantees.

Respondent places special stress on the disparity between the duration of the Government's investigation and the period the District Court allowed to newly appointed counsel for trial preparation. The lawyer was appointed to represent respondent on June 12, 1980, and on June 19, filed a written motion for a continuance of the trial that was then scheduled to begin on June 30. Although counsel contended that he needed at least 30 days for preparation, the District Court reset the trial for July 14—thus allowing 25 additional days for preparation.

Neither the period of time that the Government spent investigating the case, nor the number of documents that its agents reviewed during that investigation, is necessarily relevant to the question whether a competent lawyer could prepare to defend the case in 25 days. The Government's task of finding and assembling admissible evidence that will carry its burden of proving guilt beyond a reasonable doubt is entirely different from the defendant's task in preparing to deny or rebut a criminal charge. Of course, in some cases the rebuttal may be equally burdensome and time consuming, but there is no necessary correlation between the two. In this case, the time devoted by the Government to the assembly, organization, and summarization of the thousands of written records evidencing the two streams of checks flowing between the banks in Florida and Oklahoma unquestionably simplified the work of defense counsel in identifying and understanding the basic character of the defendants' scheme. When a series of repetitious transactions fit into a single mold, the number of written exhibits that are needed to define the pattern may be unrelated to the time that is needed to understand it.

The significance of counsel's preparation time is further reduced by the nature of the charges against respondent. Most of the Government's case consisted merely of establishing the transactions between the two banks. A competent attorney would have no reason to question the authenticity, accuracy, or relevance of this evidence—there could be no dispute that these transactions actually occurred. As respondent appears to recognize, the only bona fide jury issue open to competent defense counsel on these facts was whether respondent acted with intent to defraud. When there is no reason to dispute the underlying historical facts, the period of 25 days to consider the question whether those facts justify an inference of criminal intent is not so short that it even arguably justifies a presumption that no lawyer could provide the respondent with the effective assistance of counsel required by the Constitution.

That conclusion is not undermined by the fact that respondent's lawyer was young, that his principal practice was in real estate, or that this was his first jury trial. Every experienced criminal defense attorney once tried his first criminal case. Moreover, a lawyer's experience with real estate transactions might be more useful in preparing to try a criminal case involving financial transactions than would prior experience in handling, for example, armed robbery prosecutions. The character of a particular lawyer's experience may shed light on an evaluation of his actual performance, but it does not justify a presumption of ineffectiveness in the absence of such an evaluation.

The three other criteria—the gravity of the charge, the complexity of the case, and the accessibility of witnesses—are all matters that may affect what a reasonably competent attorney could be expected to have done under the circumstances, but none identifies circumstances that in themselves make it unlikely that respondent received the effective assistance of counsel.

V

This case is not one in which the surrounding circumstances make it unlikely that the defendant could have received the effective assistance of counsel. The criteria used by the Court of Appeals do not demonstrate that counsel failed to function in any meaningful sense as the Government's adversary. Respondent can therefore make out a claim of ineffective assistance only by pointing to specific errors made by trial counsel. In this Court, respondent's present counsel argues that the record would support such an attack, but we leave that claim—as well as the other alleged trial errors raised by respondent which were not passed upon by the Court of Appeals—for the consideration of the Court of Appeals on remand. . . .

In *Florida v. Nixon*, the United States Supreme Court held that the Florida Supreme Court erred when it applied *Cronic* to a case in which a capital defender conceded his client's guilt in order to focus attention on sentencing issues.[31] The Court stated that unlike a guilty plea, a concession of guilt allows a defendant to retain the rights afforded by a criminal trial. Moreover, because the defendant retained and used those rights, the concession did not rank as a "fail[ure] to function in any meaningful sense as the government's adversary." Finally, the Court made it clear that a capital defendant's express consent is not required before defense counsel can concede guilt because "the gravity of the potential sentence in a capital trial and the proceeding's two-phase structure vitally affect counsel's strategic calculus." But consent may be required from a non-capital defen-

---

31.   543 U.S. 175 (2004).

dant: "such a concession in a run-of-the-mine trial might present a closer question."

NOTES AND QUESTIONS

1. The Court noted that *Strickland* requires proof that counsel's deficient performance rendered the trial unreliable or the proceeding fundamentally unfair, a standard that may not be met even where a reasonable probability of a different result has been shown. In *Lockhart v. Fretwell*,[32] the Court explained:

> [a]n analysis focussing solely on mere outcome determination, without attention to whether the result of the proceeding was fundamentally unfair or unreliable, is defective. To set a side a conviction or sentence solely because the outcome would have been different but for counsel's error may grant the defendant a windfall to which the law does not entitle him.

In *Lockhart*, defendant Fretwell was convicted of felony murder for a killing that took place during a robbery. He was sentenced to death based in part on the theory that the killing had been committed for pecuniary gain—an aggravating factor under the jurisdiction's capital sentencing laws. Fretwell contended that his Sixth Amendment right to effective assistance of counsel had been violated because his lawyer failed to object that the aggravating factor of pecuniary gain "duplicated" an element of the underlying felony—an objection that, at the time of the sentencing, might well have been successful. Several years after the sentencing hearing, however, the ban on duplicative aggravating factors was struck down. Thus, Fretwell's Sixth Amendment claim may have been good at the time he was sentenced, but it rested on an interpretation of the law that was later found to be incorrect. "Unreliability or unfairness," concluded the Court, "does not result if the ineffectiveness of counsel does not deprive the defendant of any substantive or procedural right to which the law entitles him."

Similarly, in *Nix v. Whiteside*,[33] the Court held there was no prejudice where counsel prevented the defendant from offering perjured testimony, even though there was a likelihood that the result would have been different had that testimony gotten before the jury. The Court stressed that the Sixth Amendment does not require counsel to assist defendants in presenting perjured testimony. In the words of the *Lockhart* decision, "unreliability or unfairness" does not result from a jury trial from which perjured testimony has been excluded.

In *Wright v. Van Patten,* the Court faced the question whether counsel's participation in a plea hearing by telephone, rather than in person, denied Van Patten his right to the effective assistance of counsel under the Sixth Amendment. More precisely, the Court faced the question whether in

---

32. 506 U.S. 364 (1993).

33. 475 U.S. 157 (1986).

a federal habeas proceeding a state appellate court's determination that Van Patten's right to counsel was not violated was contrary to, or an unreasonable application of, clearly established federal law—the relevant statutory habeas standard. In a *per curiam* opinion, the Court answered this latter question "no."

First the Court had to address whether, under *Cronic*, prejudice could be presumed. Remember that under *Cronic*, which the Court has described as a "narrow exception" to *Strickland*'s holding,[34] a Sixth Amendment violation can be found without inquiring into counsel's performance in the specific case and without requiring the defendant to show the effect that such performance likely had on the trial.[35] *Cronic*'s presumption applies "when . . . the likelihood that any lawyer, even a fully competent one, could provide effective assistance is so small that a presumption of prejudice is appropriate without inquiry into the actual conduct at the trial,"[36] or where "there [is] a breakdown in the adversarial process" stemming from counsel's complete failure to subject the prosecution's case to "meaningful adversarial testing."[37] Furthermore, one circumstance warranting the presumption—a circumstance that the defense argued to be relevant in *Van Patten*—was the "complete denial of counsel," meaning that "counsel [is] either totally absent, or prevented from assisting the accused during a critical stage of the proceeding."[38] But the Court rejected Van Patten's claim that prejudice should be presumed in the case before it, explaining its reasoning thus:

> No decision of this Court, however, squarely addresses the issue in this case, see Deppisch, supra, at 1040 (noting that this case "presents [a] novel . . . question"), or clearly establishes that Cronic should replace Strickland in this novel factual context. Our precedents do not clearly hold that counsel's participation by speaker phone should be treated as a "complete denial of counsel," on par with total absence. Even if we agree with Van Patten that a lawyer physically present will tend to perform better than one on the phone, it does not necessarily follow that mere telephone contact amounted to total absence or "prevented [counsel] from assisting the accused," so as to entail application of Cronic. The question is not whether counsel in those circumstances will perform less well than he otherwise would, but whether the circumstances are likely to result in such poor performance that an inquiry into its effects would not be worth the time. Cf. United States v. Gonzalez–Lopez, 548 U.S. __, __, 126 S.Ct. 2557, 2563, 165 L.Ed.2d 409 (2006) (Sixth Amendment ensures "effective (not mistake-free) representation" (emphasis in original)). Our cases provide no categorical answer to this question, and for that matter the several

34. Florida v. Nixon, 543 U.S. 175, 190 (2004).

35. *See* Bell v. Cone, 535 U.S. 685 (2002).

36. *Strickland*, 466 U.S. at 659–60.

37. *Id.* at 662; *see also Bell*, 535 U.S. at 696–97 (emphasizing that the attorney's failure to engage in adversary testing must be "complete.").

38. *Strickland*, 466 U.S. at 659 & n. 25.

proceedings in this case hardly point toward one. The Wisconsin Court of Appeals held counsel's performance by speaker phone to be constitutionally effective; neither the Magistrate Judge, the District Court, nor the Seventh Circuit disputed this conclusion; and the Seventh Circuit itself stated that "[u]nder Strickland, it seems clear Van Patten would have no viable claim." Deppisch, 434 F.3d, at 1042.

Because our cases give no clear answer to the question presented, let alone one in Van Patten's favor, "it cannot be said that the state court 'unreasonabl[y] appli[ed] clearly established Federal law.'" Musladin, 549 U.S., at ___, 127 S.Ct. 649, 654 (quoting 28 U.S.C. § 2254(d)(1)). Under the explicit terms of [section] 2254(d)(1), therefore, relief is unauthorized.[39]

The Court made clear, accordingly, that it found only that the habeas standard had not been violated. The Court left "consideration of the merits of telephone practice, however, . . . for another day," this case turning only "on the recognition that no clearly established law contrary to the state court's conclusion justifies collateral relief."[40]

2. What are the implications of the *Cronic* Court's opinion for claims by public defenders that overwork and underfunding by definition render their representation ineffective and furthermore require them to reject being assigned additional cases? Should a case specific inquiry really be necessary for complex cases with little preparation time? Does the Court's approach serve its goal of assuring the reliability of the verdict? Is the Court giving in to the practical pressures of having large caseloads and therefore compromising fairness? Stacking the deck in favor of the prosecution?

3. Are the five factors used by the Court adequate for a case-specific inquiry? What other factors or guidelines might help? Were the factors applied correctly by the Court here?

4. Remember that the Sixth Amendment provides that "in all criminal prosecutions, the accused shall enjoy the right . . . to have the Assistance of Counsel for his defense."[41] Additionally, the Sixth Amendment guarantees the right of the defendant "to be represented by an otherwise qualified attorney whom that defendant can afford to hire, or who is willing to represent the defendant even though he is with funds."[42] However, if a court rejects a criminal defendant's choice of trial counsel, does that rejection constitute a Sixth Amendment violation? Does the Sixth Amend-

---

39. Wright v. Van Patten, 552 U.S. 120, 126 (2008).

40. *Id.* It is useful to remember that, under the Sixth and Fourteenth Amendments, the defendant ordinarily also has a right to insist on proceeding without counsel if he knowingly, intelligently, and voluntarily waives that right. *See* Faretta v. California, 422 U.S. 806 (1975). However, the Court recently held that "the Constitution permits a State to limit that defendant's self-representation right by insisting upon representation by counsel at trial on the ground that the defendant lacks the mental capacity to conduct his trial defense unless represented." Indiana v. Edwards, 128 U.S. 2379, 2385–86 (2008).

41. U.S. CONSTITUTION, Amend. VI.

42. Caplin & Drysdale, Chartered v. United States, 491 U.S. 617, 624–25 (1989).

ment right to counsel in criminal prosecutions include the right to counsel of one's choice?

Yes, according to the Court's recent decision in *United States v. Cuauhtemoc Gonzalez–Lopez*.[43] There, Gonzalez–Lopez hired an attorney to represent him on a federal conspiracy to distribute (more than 100 kilograms of) marijuana drug charge. The court rejected his counsel of choice and the attorney's application for admission *pro hac vice*, as well as preventing counsel of choice from meeting or consulting with *Gonzalez–Lopez* on the ground that the attorney violated a state rule of professional responsibility regarding communication with represented parties. In *Gonzalez–Lopez*, the Court clarified the difference between the Constitutional guarantees of a fair trial through the Due Process Clauses and the basic elements of a fair trial, "largely through the several provisions of the Sixth Amendment, including the General Clause." Specifically, the Sixth Amendment right to counsel of choice "commands, not that a trial be fair, but that a particular guarantee of fairness be provided—to wit, that the accused be defended by the counsel he believes to be best:"

> [t]he right to select counsel of one's choice . . . has never been derived from the Sixth Amendment's purpose of ensuring a fair trial. It has regarded as the root meaning of the constitutional guarantee. . . . Where the right to be assisted by counsel of one's choice is wrongly denied, therefore, it is unnecessary to conduct an ineffectiveness or prejudice inquiry to establish a Sixth Amendment violation. Deprivation of the right is "complete" when the defendant is erroneously prevented from being represented by the lawyer he wants, regardless of the quality of the representation he received. To argue otherwise is to confuse the right to counsel of choice—which is the right to a particular lawyer regardless of comparative effectiveness—with the right to effective counsel—which imposes a baseline requirement of competence on whatever lawyer is chosen or appointed.

An erroneous governmental deprivation of the right to counsel of one's choice (conceded by the government here) constitutes a "structural defect," *i.e.*, one that affects "the framework within which the trial proceeds, and . . . [is] not simply an error in the trial process itself."[44] The Supreme Court had "little trouble" concluding that erroneous deprivation of the right to counsel of choice unquestionably qualifies as structural error which, unlike trial error, requires reversal of the accused's conviction without being subjected to a harmless error analysis:

> [d]ifferent attorneys will pursue different strategies with regard to investigation and discovery, development of the theory of the defense, selection of the jury, presentation of the witness examination and jury

---

43. 548 U.S. 140 (2006).

44. *Id.* at 141. "Trial error" is the other type of constitutional error and consists of miscues which occur "during presentation of the case to the jury . . . and their effect may be quantitatively assessed in the context of other evidence presented in order to determine whether [they were] harmless beyond a reasonable doubt." *Id.* at 148 (internal quotation marks omitted).

argument. And the choice of attorney will affect whether and on what terms the defendant cooperates with the prosecution, plea bargains, or decides instead to go to trial [if at all]. It is impossible to know what different choices the rejected counsel would have made, and then to quantify the impact of those different choices on the outcome of the proceedings.... Harmless-error analysis in such a context would be a speculative inquiry into what might have occurred in an alternate universe....

Justices Alito, Kennedy, Thomas, and the Chief Justice dissented. At a minimum, they would require that a defendant "make at least some showing that the trial court's erroneous ruling adversely affected the quality of assistance that the defendant received."

PROBLEM 11–1

Police responded to a report of a fire in a Chicago apartment building and discovered the dead bodies of three adults and a child. All four had died from stab wounds. John Apple, an acquaintance of the victims, and his half-brother, George Francis, were arrested. Francis, a twenty-eight-year-old African–American, fled when three white police officers approached him on the street to question him. The officers chased Francis over one-half mile through alleys, stairways, and streets until finally subduing him. They had received a tip from an anonymous informant, saying, "George Francis, street name, 'Pinky,' did it. I saw it all. He used a three-sided knife, the kind that makes sure wounds don't heal. He always bragged about owning that knife. He keeps it in his left boot. He always wears boots. I could see it all from my window." The police did not consider this sufficient to establish probable cause, but they certainly thought it justified further investigation. That was why they went to question Francis. Upon subduing him, the police patted him down but found no weapons. They did, however, retrace his steps, finding a blood-spattered three-sided knife in one of the alleys through which Francis had fled. Forensic tests later revealed the presence of both Francis's fingerprints and the blood of one of the victims.

Immediately after this arrest, the officers took Francis to the station-house for questioning. There, two detectives, Charles Parker and Rodney Quirk, questioned Francis. Mere minutes before the questioning of Francis began, these detectives had obtained a confession from Apple in which he admitted to the killings but fingered Francis as an accomplice. Later, at trial, however, Apple recanted and took full responsibility for the crime, exculpating Francis completely.

Francis was fully and properly *Mirandized*. He ultimately confessed, admitting to taking an active role in the killings. Here, however, is where the stories diverge.

Francis maintains that Detective Quirk struck Francis in the mouth in response to Francis's request for an attorney. Furthermore, he claims that during the interrogation Quirk used electroshock, stuck needles in Francis's buttocks, repeatedly squeezed his scrotum, and beat him with a bag filled with oranges (which do not leave bruises), all in an ultimately successful effort to coerce an untrue confession. Francis so testified at trial, but the two detectives testified that the alleged torture never took place. Francis admitted further at trial that he was at the victims' apartment on the night of the crime but claims that he left before the killings took place. Francis was convicted and sentenced to death. He has now retained you to handle postconviction relief on the grounds of the ineffective assistance of counsel.

During your first interview with Francis, he explained his basis for his claim. He believes that his trial counsel was ineffective for failing to conduct an adequate investigation. Specifically, counsel did not subpoena the disciplinary files of the detectives who interrogated Francis; did not seek expert testimony that would have indicated that the results of Francis's post-interrogation medical exams were consistent with his accounts of torture; did not consult with attorneys who represented other clients alleging police brutality in the same area; and did not subpoena personnel records in an effort to locate the paramedic who examined Francis and completed a report called a "bruise sheet." Francis also objects to his counsel's failing to file a motion to suppress the knife.

Your initial investigation has revealed that, according to a local citizens' watchdog group, there has been a pattern of police brutality over the last two years in the same area that is consistent with Francis's story of torture. However, neither of the detectives involved here were named by the watchdog group as involved in other cases. Additionally, you have located an expert who can testify that the kind of torture alleged by Francis is precisely the kind designed to leave no physical injuries. Furthermore, you have uncovered a report, released shortly after Francis's trial, by Chicago's Office of Police Standards concerning an internal investigation that revealed significant police brutality in the area during the last two years. Moreover, you have found an officer who will testify that he saw a Detective John Cage enter the interrogation room with Parker and Quirk, and Cage was named as an offender in the Police Standards report. Other officers deny, however, that Cage was there.

Your review of paramedic and physician reports revealed that Francis did complain at the time that he had been subjected to needle pricks and electronic probes, yet neither physical exam report corroborates these allegations, with one exception: The paramedic's "bruise sheet" contains a line pointing to a diagram of Francis's left buttock with the word "slight." But the paramedic did not testify at trial. The physician did testify at trial, reporting that he found no bruising or indication of tenderness on Francis's back, scrotum, or anus. The only mark on Francis's body that the physician noted was a slight pimple on his buttocks.

You have deposed trial counsel, Murphy Troland. He says that he did not talk to police to investigate Francis's brutality claims because "there were no specifics" and Francis did not then remember the names of the detectives involved in the interrogation. Trial counsel admits that he was contacted by attorneys representing Burton Wilson, a defendant in another case who alleged police abuse in that area. However, trial counsel did not seek more information because Wilson's case was distinguishable. Wilson had observable injuries seen by several eyewitnesses to his pre-and post-arrest condition, while Francis had neither observable marks nor witnesses. Troland did try to locate the paramedic who completed the bruise sheet, personally going to his home and later interviewing hospital personnel but to no avail. Troland also did not file a motion to suppress the knife, concluding Francis did not then have a possessory interest or reasonable expectation of privacy in the knife.

Question: Do you believe Francis has any significant chance of prevailing on a claim of ineffective assistance of counsel? Why? What further investigation, if any, should you undertake? What else, if anything, do you believe trial counsel should have done that he did not in fact do? Be ready to counsel Francis on the strength of his claim, or, alternatively, to engage in a brainstorming session with colleagues on this question.

C.   THE WORKLOAD PROBLEM

Remember the Court's assertion in *Cronic* that there may be occasions where "the likelihood that any lawyer, even a fully competent one, could provide effective assistance is so small that a presumption of prejudice is appropriate without inquiry into the actual conduct of the trial." Criminal caseloads for appointed counsel, including public defenders, have become so great in many cities as to raise a serious question whether such counsel can render effective assistance to any of their clients. Edward C. Monahan and James Clark address this difficult problem in the following article:

Coping With Excessive Workload

Edward C. Monahan and James Clark.[45]

What must a full-time public defender or appointed counsel do if the defender believes that she cannot competently handle any larger workload if assigned more cases or other work by a supervisor or if appointed to more cases by a judge? . . .

Work, Not Cases

Every person representing indigents accused or convicted of a crime eventually confronts the harsh reality of whether competent representation is provided given the number of clients, the demands of the cases, and the necessity of other work. The core of this perennial defender issue centers on the point at which a lawyer's workload exceeds ethical limits. It would

---

45.   Edward C. Monahan and James Clark, *Coping with Excessive Workload*, in ETHICAL PROBLEMS FACING THE CRIMINAL DEFENSE LAWYER: PRACTICAL ANSWERS TO TOUGH QUESTIONS 318 (ed. Rodney J. Uphoff 1995). Sadly, little has been done to address the workload problem identified by Monahan and Clark, even though the severity of that problem has been recognized for decades. *See, e.g.*, Richard Klein, *The Emperor* Gideon *Has No Clothes: The Empty Promise of the Constitutional Right to Effective Assistance of Counsel*, 13 HASTINGS L.Q. 625 (1986).

be naive to translate this issue into the question, "When does a lawyer's caseload exceed ethical limits?" The ethical lawyer has work beyond cases. To limit the question to caseloads is to ignore the full reality of legal representation of indigent criminal defendants at a professional level.

A defender's work includes more than her cases. She must consult with others about her cases, engage in review processes to assure quality of her cases, and handle other work, for example, brainstorming, case or peer review, mock presentations, post-case critiques, and performance evaluations. An ethical defender maintains and advances her knowledge by reading newly decided cases and newly enacted laws and rules, and by attending training sessions. She must support others in her office by doing case consultation for colleagues. Defenders must perform administrative and office duties. She must supervise support staff to ensure that their work is at the requisite standard.

Principles, Standards, Case Law, and Capacity for Work

To determine what a defender must do about excessive workload, it is necessary to answer three questions: (1) What ethical principles and benchmark standards must a lawyer meet? (2) How does a lawyer meet those principles and standards in criminal cases? (3) What influences a lawyer's capacity to perform assigned work effectively? A look at these three areas provides the basis for analysis and conclusions.

ABA Ethical Principles and ABA Standards

The ABA has pronounced substantial ethical commands in its . . . current Model Rules of Professional Conduct (1983), and has significant standards in its current Standards for Criminal Justice on the duties of lawyers in the representation of a criminal client, the standard of representation, and the limitations of workload. . . .

The ethical minimum is competent legal representation. . . . The ABA Model Rules affirmatively identified competence as the mandatory standard of professional duty to a client and embarked on a more deliberate definition of its dimensions. Model Rule 1.1, the first ethical rule, states, "[a] lawyer shall provide competent representation to a client." Model Rule 1.3 requires that a lawyer "act with reasonable diligence and promptness." Model Rule 1.4 mandates that a lawyer communicate promptly and effectively with her clients.

The national professional benchmark is quality legal representation. Both the ABA Standards for Criminal Justice, Providing Defense Services (3d ed. 1992) and The Defense Function (3d ed. 1993) set quality legal representation as the national benchmark for criminal defense lawyers. Standard 4–1.2, "The Function of Defense Counsel," declares that "[t]he basic duty defense counsel owes to the administration of justice and as an officer of the court is to . . . render effective, quality representation." Standard 5–1.1 echoes the principle that "[t]he objective in providing counsel should be to assure that quality legal representation is afforded . . ."

The Dimensions of Competence and Quality for Criminal Defense Lawyers

. . . The magnitude of the duties necessary for competent, quality representation of a criminal defendant is prodigious. The breadth of the responsibilities as defined in the Model Rules and the ABA Standards include the following eleven substantial areas.

Legal Knowledge and Skill. Model Rule 1.1 defines competence as requiring "the legal knowledge, skill, thoroughness and preparation reasonably necessary for representation." . . . [F]actors determining whether a lawyer has the necessary legal knowledge and skill include the relative complexity of the matter; the specialized nature of the matter; the general experience of the lawyer; the training and experience of the lawyer in the area; the preparation and study the lawyer can give the problem; and the ability to obtain the assistance of a lawyer who is knowledgeable and skilled in the area. . . .

Timeliness of Representation. Attorneys must act promptly to protect the rights of the accused, including informing the client of those rights, seeking pretrial release, obtaining mental health assistance, requesting a different venue, seeking a continuance, moving to suppress illegal evidence, asking for severance of counts or defendants, and requesting dismissal.

Thoroughness and Preparation. In explaining this dimension of competence, the Comment to Model Rule 1.1 sets out the following aspects included in this concept: (1) inquiry into the legal and factual elements of the problem; (2) analysis of the legal and factual elements of the problem; (3) adequate attention and preparation; (4) the attention and preparation necessary are partly determined by "what is at stake"; the greater the complexity or consequences, the greater the attention and preparation needed; and (5) use of methods and procedures which meet "the standards of competent practitioners." . . .

Ignorance of the "rules of procedure, constitutional law, the relationship between state and federal proceedings, and federal rules of evidence" caused the suspension of a lawyer handling a criminal case in federal court. *Matter of Dempsey*, 632 F. Supp. 908 (N.D. Cal. 1986).

Client Relationship and Interviewing. Attorneys are not technicians. Rather, a lawyer must seek to develop a relationship with the client. The relationship should be characterized by honesty, trust, and confidence. Axiomatically, a relationship of honesty, trust, and confidence necessarily involves a commitment of time. An initial interview of the accused should take place as soon as possible. Defense counsel must discuss the objectives of the lawyer's representation, explain the meaning of confidentiality, and "probe for all legally relevant information" known to the accused.

Communicating With the Accused. No relationship is successful without communication. The lawyer is required to communicate with the client, informing him about "developments in the case"; advising him about "the progress of preparing the defense"; explaining matters so that he can "make informed decisions regarding the representation"; and "promptly comply[ing] with reasonable requests for information from the client." . . .

A lawyer who failed to adequately communicate with his client was disciplined by the Nevada Supreme Court with the court observing, "[i]t cannot be overemphasized that communication with a client is, in many respects, at the center of all services. The failure to communicate creates the impression of a 'neglectful' attorney and leads to client discontent, even if the case is competently and expeditiously handled." *State Bar v. Schreiber*, 653 P.2d 151 (Nev. 1982).

Jonathan Casper, in his empirical study Criminal Courts: The Defendant's Perspective (1978), found that defendants represented by public defenders fared no worse than defendants represented by retained counsel in terms of sentences imposed. Nonetheless, the defendants had a significantly lower opinion of the service provided by their public defender. Casper found that defenders spend appreciably less time consulting with their clients. Casper, therefore, concluded that many clients' poor opinion of their public defender is caused by defenders' failure to spend time interviewing and consulting with their clients.

Advising the Accused. Once counsel obtains the facts, understands the applicable law, and interviews the client, she must advise the accused "with complete candor concerning all aspects of the case, including a candid estimate of the probable outcome." That candid assessment must include the risks, hazards, and prospects of the case. Moreover, the defender must advise in such a way that ensures that the client makes the decision. Also, the lawyer must caution the accused to avoid communication with witnesses, jurors, family, friends, or cellmates.

When a case warrants, a lawyer must explore alternative resolutions. Plea discussions with the prosecutor must be promptly communicated and explained to the accused.

Investigation. Prompt, thorough, focused investigation is essential to competent, quality representation. There must be an investigation into all facts relevant to the merits of the case and to possible penalties. The defender must look to all available sources, including the client, the police, and the prosecution. Lack of time or investigative staff does not excuse a defender's failure to conduct an adequate investigation. Many defenders labor in programs without adequate investigative staff. Defenders often do their own investigation. In such cases, interviews of witnesses should take place in the presence of another defender or a member of the defender's staff to allow effective impeachment. "The duty to investigate exists regardless of the accused's admissions or statements to defense counsel of facts constituting guilt or the accused's stated desire to plead guilty."

"Under no circumstances should defense counsel recommend to a defendant acceptance of a plea unless appropriate investigation and study of the case has been completed, including an analysis of controlling law and the evidence likely to be introduced at trial." . . .

The U.S. Supreme Court has not hesitated to find a constitutional violation when a lawyer failed to request discovery to learn about information actually or constructively possessed by the prosecutor. Such a discovery request would have revealed inculpatory evidence that would have necessitated a suppression motion. *Kimmelman v. Morrison*, 477 U.S. 365, 368–69, 385 (1986).

The less significant the charges, the more likely it is for a defender to ignore the duty to adequately investigate the case. The overworked defender often rationalizes waiver of the necessary investigation by claiming it is a logical causality of triage. Too often defenders efficiently lead clients to take the deal rather than delay disposition pending full investigation. The defender is able to live with herself because she's merely doing what the client wants or demands. Unfortunately for both the client and the defender, these rationalizations cheat the client.

A lawyer with three years experience joined the Wisconsin public defender staff and was assigned a complex homicide case the first day on the job. The case was tried and the client was convicted of second degree murder of her husband. The case was reversed because the new defender was ignorant of the defense of sudden heat of passion. The defender never educated his expert on that defense or the defense of insanity. The defender initially entered a plea of insanity and then withdrew it without discussion of the legal consequences with his client. The court in *State v. Felton*, 329 N.W.2d 161 (Wis. 1983), determined that the defender was ineffective for failing to inform himself of the law, to adequately advise his client on the defenses, and to adequately investigate the case through his expert and the state's expert as required under ABA Standard 4.1, 5.1(a), and 5.2. The novice defender recognized his probable incompetence to handle a case of this significance, and he "attempted to get experienced private counsel appointed, but his superiors encouraged him to undertake the defense. The administrators of the public defender's program provided him with the assistance of a more experienced attorney; but according to the trial attorney, he had only limited opportunity to consult with that attorney until just before the time of trial."

When an inexperienced lawyer is not competent to handle a serious criminal case, does not seek help from a competent lawyer, and does little investigation, research, or preparation, substantial ethical sanctions are appropriate. *See, e.g., Office of Disciplinary Counsel v. Henry*, 664 S.W.2d 62 (Tenn. 1983). . . .

Trial Court Representation. Much is required of the defender when the case proceeds to trial. Preparation must be conducted to select and challenge jurors effectively. Effective opening statements, cross-examinations, direct examination, and closings must be given, and appropriate jury instructions be offered. A competent defender must make and respond to prosecution objections promptly and effectively. No lawyer will be effective without an adequate understanding of the rules of evidence and the relevant case law interpreting those rules and any constitutional dimensions.

Sentencing. Defense counsel must be familiar with and consider all sentencing alternatives that would be appropriate in a given case. The lawyer must understand parole consequences and other practical or collateral consequences of a sentence and explain these to the client. The judge's sentencing practices must be discussed with the client. The lawyer is required to present any facts or legal grounds to the sentences to urge the most favorable disposition for the defendant.

Attorneys must be present at presentence investigation interviews conducted by probation and parole officers to ensure the convicted client is fully advised at this critical stage of the proceedings. Lawyers should verify information in the presentence report and supplement the report when this is in the interest of the defendant. Appropriate post-trial motions must be factually investigated, legally researched, and presented when in the convicted defendant's interest.

Appellate Representation. Trial defense counsel must explain to the convicted client the right to appeal, the consequences of an appeal, the grounds available for appellate review, and the advantages as well as disadvantages of an appeal. Defense counsel must take all steps necessary to ensure perfection of the appeal if the client chooses to challenge the conviction or sentence.

Appellate counsel must read or view the entire appellate record, consider all potential appellate guilt or penalty issues, do appropriate research, and present all pleadings in the interest of the client.

Maintaining Competence and Assuring Quality. Competence and quality require continuous learning. The Comment to Model Rule 1.1 explicitly recognizes a duty to maintain competence, and it provides mandatory and discretionary methods to achieve this maintenance: 1) "A lawyer should engage in continuing study and education," and 2) a lawyer should consider accessing "a system of peer review" in appropriate circumstances.

Although the Comment to Model Rule 1.1 devotes only a single paragraph to the obligation to maintain the requisite level of competence, this duty will increase in a professional environment that is constantly changing. As quality is increasingly defined by the customer, a defender cannot render quality representation without staying abreast of recent developments.

In the information revolution age, the necessity for continuous learning is inescapable. "The 'half-life' of knowledge in any given profession may now be as little as two to three years. The degree, in short, is today the beginning of the education of a professional." To avoid obsolescence the professional must constantly integrate new knowledge and learn new skills. Training for public defenders, as for all lawyers, is essential. Continual training "plays a significant role in supporting and driving a continuous improvement culture." Simply put, professionals who do not regularly enhance their competencies will not have the abilities to provide competent, quality representation for the criminal defendant.

Most states now mandate that lawyers annually participate in continuing legal education programs. Similarly, the ABA recognizes that lawyers representing indigent defendants need specialized training. Thus, ABA Standard 5–1.5, "Training and Professional Development," recommends that all plans or programs providing indigent defense services include "effective training, professional development and continuing education of all counsel and staff . . . [c]ontinuing education programs should be provided to enable all counsel and staff to attend such programs." . . .

These eleven performance areas add up to a substantial volume of duties. They require a demanding level of work for defenders. Too often they are not being performed by the overworked defender.

Capacity for Work

Persons' capacity for work vary. Some workers have the natural or trained strength to lift a certain weight, the capability to engineer certain results, or the ability to serve the needs of numerous clients. A defense lawyer's capacity for work is dependent on several factors, including available staff and resources; personal management skills; personally destructive consequences of excessive work; available work hours; and caseload standards. . . .

Assigning or Accepting Excessive Workloads
Legally and Ethically Prohibited

While neither the Model Code nor the Model Rules directly address defender workloads, both effectively prohibit a lawyer from accepting an amount of work that prevents competent representation. Model Rule 6.2, "Accepting Appointments," does not allow a lawyer to take a case if it would likely result in unreasonable financial burden or would likely cause a violation of any ethical rule. Model Rule 8.3, "Misconduct," identifies a violation of any other ethical rule as professional misconduct. A lawyer who represents another client when she already has more work than she can competently handle violates Model Rule 1.7(b), which commands that "[a] lawyer shall not represent a client if the representation of that client may be materially limited by the lawyer's responsibility to another client or to a third person, or by the lawyer's own interests. . . ." A lawyer who has so much work, so many cases, so many other clients that she is materially limited in her ability to effectively represent another client has an impermissible personal conflict of interest and cannot assume responsibility for an additional client.

These rules clearly establish that a lawyer cannot ethically accept another case or other work when she has so much work that accepting another case will preclude her from competently representing the new client or performing any of the other ethical requirements, for example, communicating fully and promptly with the client, fully and promptly interviewing the client, or investigating the case and adequately advising the client.

The ABA reiterated these ethical principles when formulating the standards for criminal defense work in The Defense Function. ABA Standard 4–1.3(e), "Workload," states: "[d]efense counsel should not carry a workload that, by reason of its excessive size, interferes with the rendering of quality representation, endangers the client's interest in the speedy disposition of charges, or may lead to the breach of professional obligations." It is significant that this standard speaks in terms of workload, not just caseload. This standard applies not only to the individual defense lawyer but also to defense organizations, appointed counsel and contract counsel.

The eleven areas of competent representation cannot be neglected by a defender because she is overworked. Nor can nonperformance in any of these areas be justified by too much work. Failure to keep caseload within manageable limits does not excuse failure to perform ethically. *See, e.g., Matter of Klipstine*, 775 P.2d 247 (N.M. 1989) ("While the members of this Court are well aware of the demands of sole practice, a failure to keep one's caseload within manageable proportions cannot and does not excuse the type of blatant neglect exhibited by Klipstine.").

Within this substantial context, the preeminent defender question—what to do about too much work—can be reliably answered. In theory, the answer is easy: A defender cannot take on more work than can be competently handled. In practice, however, it is difficult to apply this concept to legal work, which has subtle factual nuances entangled with complex and competing principles and standards and which is performed in the real world of power, funding, and politics. . . .

Forty years after the Supreme Court decided *Gideon v. Wainwright*, the American Bar Association's Standing Committee on Legal Aid and Indigent Defendants [SCLAID] held a series of public hearings to examine whether *Gideon's* promise of equal justice for the poor is being kept.[46] The testimony of diverse witnesses from all geographic parts of the U.S. supported "the disturbing conclusion that thousands of persons are processed through America's courts every year either with no lawyer at all or with a lawyer who does not have the time, resources, or in some cases the inclination to provide effective representation." The report outlines the nine main findings made by SCLAID:

1) Forty years after *Gideon v. Wainwright*, indigent defense in the United States remains in a state of crisis, resulting in a system that lacks fundamental fairness and places poor persons at constant risk of wrongful conviction.

2) Funding for indigent defense services is shamefully inadequate.

3) Lawyers who provide representation in indigent defense systems sometimes violate their professional duties by failing to furnish competent representation.

---

46. Standing Comm. on Legal Aid & Indigent Defendants, Am. Bar Ass'n, *Gideon's Broken Promise: America's Continuing Quest for Equal Justice* (2004).

4) Lawyers are not provided in numerous proceedings in which a right to counsel exists in accordance with the Constitution and/or state law. Too often, prosecutors seek to obtain waivers of counsel and guilty pleas from unrepresented accused persons, while judges accept and sometimes even encourage waivers of counsel that are not knowing, voluntary, intelligent, and on the record.

5) Judges and elected officials often exercise undue influence over indigent defense attorneys, threatening the professional independence of the defense function.

6) Indigent defense systems frequently lack basic oversight and accountability, impairing the provision of the uniform, quality services.

7) Efforts to reform indigent defense systems have been most successful when they involve multi-faceted approaches and representatives from a broad spectrum of interests.

8) The organized bar too often has failed to provide the requisite leadership in the indigent defense area.

9) Model approaches to providing quality indigent defense services exist in this country, but these models often are not adequately funded and cannot be replicated elsewhere absent sufficient financial support.

SCLAID also offered several recommendations that may help correct the failures of the indigent defense systems. Among other things, SCLAID suggested increased state and federal funding, decreased caseloads for indigent defense attorneys, and the creation of "oversight organizations that ensure the delivery of independent, uniform, quality indigent defense representation."

PROBLEM 11–2

If in the *Boson* problem in Chapter 1, Boson's attorney had not moved to suppress any or all of the noted items of evidence and Boson were convicted, would he succeed in overturning his conviction on the grounds of ineffective assistance of trial counsel?

INDEX

References are to Pages.

F

†